REVOLUTIONARY WAR BOUNTY LAND GRANTS

Awarded by State Governments

REVOLUTIONARY WAR BOUNTY LAND GRANTS

Awarded by State Governments

Lloyd DeWitt Bockstruck

GENEALOGICAL PUBLISHING Co., Inc

Published by Genealogical Publishing Co., Inc.
1001 N. Calvert St., Baltimore, Md. 21202
Second printing 1997
Third printing 1998
Library of Congress Catalogue Card Number 96-75099
International Standard Book Number 0-8063-1511-3
Made in the United States of America

Introduction

A land bounty is a grant of land from a government as a reward to repay citizens for the risks and hardships they endured in the service of their country, usually in a military related capacity.

By the time of the Revolutionary War, the practice of awarding bounty land as an inducement for enlisting in the military forces had been a long-standing practice in the British Empire in North America. Besides imperial bounty land grants, both colonial and municipal governments had routinely compensated participants in and victims of military conflicts with land. Land was a commodity in generous supply, and governments seized upon its availability for accomplishing their goals.

In their colonial tradition, the Revolutionary governments patterned their struggle for independence from Great Britain on the principle of bounty lands. They generally offered free lands in exchange for military service, but they strategically did so on the presumption that they would be victorious in their struggle. They would not actually award the lands until the war had been concluded and the British defeated. Such a policy not only imposed no financial constraints on the war effort but also insured a degree of support for the Revolutionary cause. The Revolutionary governments were cognizant that to the victor belonged the spoils and that defeat brought no reward. Bounty lands proved an effective technique for enrolling support for the war among the citizenry and preventing them from lapsing into the British fold when the tide of battle ebbed.

Those colonies with unseated lands used their advantage to enlist support for the cause with the offer of free lands. Unfortunately, some of the Original Thirteen enjoyed no such advantage. There was no bounty land policy in Delaware, New Jersey, New Hampshire, Rhode Island, or Vermont. Those states lacked enough vacant land to support such a policy. Bounty lands were a feature, however, in Connecticut, Georgia, Maryland, Massachusetts, New York, North Carolina, Pennsylvania, South Carolina, and Virginia. Administratively, these nine states selected reserves in their western domains for the location of bounty lands. Such a choice was seemingly quite logical. By placing veterans on the frontier, the states would be able to rely upon a military force which in turn would be able to protect the settlements from Indian incursions. These state governments also realized that they had to encourage the ex-soldiers to occupy their newly awarded bounty lands, so they granted exemptions from taxation ranging from a few years to life to those veterans who would locate on their respective bounty lands. Such a policy also had the effect of retarding the exodus of a state's population. Since most of the Indian nations had supported the British during the Revolutionary War, the Thirteen States were cautious in approaching their former enemies. Populating the frontier with citizens skilled in defense offered the best prospect in enticing other settlers to join them. Veterans were knowledgeable in the use of firearms and in military strategy. Knowing that they would be defended if the need arose was reassuring to many settlers. The state governments also realized that the revenue derived from the sale of vacant lands in the west was badly needed. The extension of settlements on the frontier would, in time, also increase the tax rolls and contribute to the reduction of their Revolutionary War debts. In the aftermath of the war, the states with transappalachian claims ceded some of those claims to the federal government, but not until they had the assurance of being able to fulfill their bounty land commitments.

Accordingly, the issue of bounty lands has far wider geographical implications than the area encompassed by the nine state governments which instituted the practice. Besides the original states of Connecticut, Georgia, Maryland, Massachusetts, New York, North Carolina, Pennsylvania, South Carolina, and Virginia, the future states of Indiana, Kentucky, Maine, Ohio, and Tennessee were directly affected by the bounty land system. While the administrative records were, with one exception, the purview of the former nine, the bounty land reserves involved the five transappalachian states. The states of Georgia, Maryland, New York, Pennsylvania, and South Carolina either had no claims to transappalachian territory or relinquished their claims to the national government. Accordingly, their reserves for bounty lands lay within their own western borders. In the cases of Georgia and New York, these reserves were to be situated on the definition of their western borders as they existed in 1783. The bounty land reserves in those two states today would be described as being centrally located. The Commonwealth of Massachusetts alloted its bounty lands in the District of Maine, which in 1820 achieved statehood status.

While most of the states awarded bounty lands for military service, there were two exceptions. Connecticut compensated its citizenry with lands in Ohio if their homes, outbuildings, and businesses were destroyed by the British. The Nutmeg State seemingly awarded no bounty land for military service *per se*. Georgia also issued lands to its civilian population who had remained loyal, or at the very least neutral, to the Revolutionary cause after the British restored royal control. There were no Revolutionary War bounty land grants within the current borders of the southern states of North Carolina and Virginia. The former issued its bounty lands in its western lands which became Tennessee. The latter selected reserves for its bounty lands in Indiana, Kentucky, and Ohio before ceding its claims to the federal government.

It is important to emphasize that the Continental Congress also made use of the policy of bounty lands. The index to those claims appears in the *Index to Revolutionary War Pension Applications in the National Archives* (Washington, D.C.: National Genealogical Society, 1976). The federal bounty land records are included in the National Archives micropublication, *Revolutionary War Pension and Bounty-Land Warrant Application Files, 1800–1900*, Series M804, 2,670 rolls. Abstracts of these files appear in the four-volume work of Virgil D. White, *Genealogical Abstracts of Revolutionary War Pension Files* (Waynesboro, Tenn.: The National Historical Publishing Company, 1990–1992). The federal government likewise selected a reserve in the Northwest Territory where bounty land warrants could be used to locate land. The U.S. Military Tract in Ohio encompassed portions or all of the counties of Coshochton, Delaware, Franklin, Guernsey, Holmes, Knox, Licking, Marion, Morrow, Muskingum, Noble, and Tuscarawas. These records appear in the micropublications *U.S. Revolutionary War Bounty-Land Warrants Used in the U.S. Military District of Ohio and Related Papers (Acts of 1788, 1803, 1806)*, Series M829, 16 rolls, and in *Register of Army Land Warrants Issued under the Act of 1788 for Service in the Revolutionary War: Military District of Ohio*, Series T1008, 1 roll. Since the federal land grants are readily accessible via these sources, they are not included in this work.

With the exception of the Commonwealth of Massachusetts, the other states permitted qualified veterans and/or their dependents to receive bounty lands from both the federal and the respective state governments. Accordingly, there may be relevant bounty land files for soldiers in the Continental Line at both the federal and state levels. While New York made some adjustments, double dipping was the norm in the other states.

Following the American victory at Yorktown in 1781, the various governments sought to implement their bounty land programs. The delay in establishing a governmental agency to fulfill the bounty land pledge holds dual benefits genealogically. Firstly, it increases the likelihood of the survival of a paper trail for proving Revolutionary War participation for many individuals who may not be mentioned in any other record. Secondly, because the benefits were still being processed as late as the 1870s in some jurisdictions, there may be a wealth of information pertaining to heirs in bounty land files. Not only do the records locate the veteran in time and place him in a given locality during the Revolutionary War, they also do so for him and/or his dependents in the years following independence when internal migrations within the nation complicate the identification of specific individuals in their various removals.

The appearance of an individual or family in the west after 1783 offers considerable challenge in learning the former domicile or in establishing filiation. A master index to the bounty land grants of the relevant state governments seemed to offer expeditious access to the records holding the potential solution to such a dilemma. While access to the federal records has long since been available in a master index, and while many localities have been treated individually by others works of varying quality, the absence of an overall index has impeded effective use of these significant state records.

It is a difficult task to create a master index to a body of records generated by so many different governments and pieces of legislation. Bringing uniformity to such an index is somewhat artifical. Typically, each entry contains the name of the claimant, who is usually the veteran, the state of service, the rank held, the date of the record, and the acreage. Any additional comments appear at the end of the entry.

Even though the bounty land policies of each state are outlined below, there were also special legislative acts for veterans who could not qualify under their state's statutory requirements. Accordingly, if a veteran fails to appear in the normal record series, the possibility of a special legislative act needs to be considered.

While most military ranks are familiar ones, it should be remembered that a subaltern was any commissioned officer below the rank of captain, including cornet, ensign, and lieutenant. An ensign was an army officer in the infantry ranking immediately below a lieutenant and was the equivalent of a cornet in the cavalry. It was not a naval rank in the Revolutionary era. A matross was a soldier in a train of artillery who assisted the gunner in loading, firing, and sponging the guns. A boatswain was a naval officer in charge of the hull and related equipment. A coxswain was a sailor who had charge of a ship's boat and its crew. A noncommissioned officer in the army included corporals and sergeants.

Finally, it is imperative to bear in mind that a great number of clerks prepared the records in the various jurisdictions, and uniformity of spelling is therefore lacking. Relevant entries may well be overlooked without a thorough examination of spelling variants. Both the accent of the claimant and the ear of the clerk must be taken into consideration in locating an entry arranged in alphabetical order. Finding one entry under the anticipated spelling should not preclude a further search for other possibilities. One of the common speech patterns is the substitution of the letter "r" for that of "n" as in Wilkerson for Wilkinson and Dickerson for Dickinson. "Ph" and "F" pose another difficulty as in Phelps and Felps. The letter "K" may conceal a variant of "C" as in Kerr and Carr. The letters "l" and "r" may be interchanged to yield seemingly totally different surnames as in Palmer, Parmer, and Palmour. The "g" and "j", as in Gosling and Josling, can also disguise entries. Such pronunciation variants as Graham for Grimes can cause the unskilled researcher to overlook relevant entries. Acuff may be phonetically rendered as Eccough. A silent initial letter, as in the unaspirated "H" in Harrell may very well produce entries under the next letter of the surname as in Arrell. A scribe's unfamiliarity with a non-British surname is perhaps best exemplified with the German surname of Geisensieder found spelled as Kycenceder in the Virginia bounty land files. Forenames can likewise be misleading. Augustine, for example, was pronounced Austin and appears under that spelling quite frequently. The abbreviation "Jos:" can represent not only Joseph but also Joshua, Josephus, and Josiah. "Rich:" is normally the abbreviation for Richard, but it could just as easily be for Richmond. Edmund and Edward are interchangeable, and Edwin can complicate the matter even more. "Abe" is the abbreviation for both Abraham and Absolam. "Zach:" can represent Zachery and Zacheriah. "Nath" may be either Nathan or Nathaniel. *Caveat lector.*

Connecticut

While the state of Connecticut did not award any bounty lands to its military personnel, it did convey title to its western lands to its citizens for Revolutionary War damages. British forces, having retaken New York City, operated out of the harbor on expeditions along the New England coast to destroy rebel stores and shipping. Under cover of darkness they could secretly arrive, inflict damage, and retreat before meeting any effective resistance. From the relative safety of their ships off shore, the British, assisted by Benedict Arnold, laid waste many of the towns in Connecticut. The nine towns so scorched during the war were Danbury in 1777, East Haven in 1779, Fairfield in 1779, Greenwich and Groton in 1781, New Haven in 1779, New London in 1781, Norwalk in 1779, and Ridgefield.

Connecticut set aside 500,000 acres of its lands in the west—the Western Reserve in the northeast corner of present Ohio on Lake Erie—as compensation to those residents of the nine towns who had lost their possessions and/or lives during the British forays. The acreage lay at the western end of the Western Reserve and embraced the counties of Huron and Erie, the township of Danbury in Ottawa County, and the township of Ruggles in Ashland County, Ohio. This area of the Western Reserve, therefore, became known as the Firelands.

While Connecticut initially granted tax abatements, it was not until 1791 that the legislature approved relief for losses amounting to £161,548.11.6 1/2. Approximately 1,870 applicants were approved. While businesses and churches were also destroyed in the British assaults, entries pertaining to them have been omitted from the text. By a Connecticut law of 1795, the deed for each sufferer's land was to be recorded in the town where he or she orginally lost property.

The Connecticut entries have been taken from *A Compilation of Laws, Treaties, Resolutions, and Ordinances, of the General and State Governments, Which Relate to Lands in the State of Ohio...* (Columbus, Ohio: Geo. Nashee, 1825) as well as from William W. Williams's *History of the Firelands, Comprising Huron and Erie Counties, Ohio, with Illustrations and Biographical Sketches of Some of the Prominent Men and Pioneers* (Evansville, Ind.: Unigraphic, Inc., 1973). Preference has been given to the former for the correct rendering of the orthography.

The Connecticut entries consist of the name of the warrantee, the state, the designation of sufferer rather than a rank, the town of residence, and the amount of the loss. The sum appearing for an individual from the town of Ridgefield reflects the balance after deductions were made for sums advanced by grants of the general assembly.

Georgia

Of all of the Revolutionary governments issuing bounty lands, Georgia's system was undoubtedly the most complex. Because the records of administering the process are piecemeal, it is almost certain that there are omissions in the Georgia entries. It is particularly important to note that Georgia was one of two states to issue lands to noncombattants or their heirs. A government seeking to extend benefits to its citizens had to design and implement a system not susceptible to fraud. Unfortunately, the situation in Georgia did not fare well.

Georgia was the youngest of the Thirteen Colonies. Its population was thinly distributed along the Savannah River and the Atlantic seaboard. For Georgia, a bounty land system which would entice residents of its more populous neighbors to the north to enlist in Georgia's forces was absolutely essential. A liberal bounty land policy seemed the most attractive solution in fielding an army and meeting the state's Continental quota. It also served to encourage settlement and augment the state's sparse population.

The area set aside for the location of the bounty lands in Georgia was in the south end of old Franklin County and the north end of old Washington County. Today the area is occupied by Oconee, Oglethorpe, and Green counties and lies between the Oconee and Appalachee rivers.

The various acts and resolutions of the legislature allocated bounty lands of acreage specified by classes and ranks. Such lands were to be exempt from taxation for a decade. One of the provisions of the Act of 25 February 1784 increased the respective amounts by fifteen per cent and eliminated the ten-year tax abatement. The first warrants issued for bounty land were dated 15 May 1785. Accordingly, if certificates for bounty land had been obtained prior to that date for the lesser amount, the warrants conformed to the greater amount. A private in the militia, for example, might have received a certificate entitling him to 250 acres. His warrant, however, would be issued for 287 1/2 acres.

The ranks and classes with the corresponding acreage for Georgia's Revolutionary War personnel and inhabitants were:

private in Georgia Line	230 acres
private in minute battalions	287 1/2 acres
private in militia	287 1/2 acres
refugee private in militia	287 1/2 acres
seaman in galleys	287 1/2 acres
citizen	287 1/2 acres
deserter from the British	287 1/2 acres
sergeant in minute battalions	345 acres
sergeant in militia	345 acres
sergeant in Georgia Line	345 acres
refugee sergeant in militia	345 acres
lieutenant in militia	460 acres

lieutenant in minute battalions	460 acres
lieutenant in Georgia Line	460 acres
refugee private in militia (also citizen)	575 acres
captain in militia	575 acres
captain in minute battalions	575 acres
refugee sergeant in militia (also citizen)	632 1/2 acres
captain in Georgia Line	690 acres
refugee lieutenant in militia	747 1/2 acres
major in militia	920 acres
major in minute battalions	920 acres
major in Georgia Line	920 acres
refugee captain in militia	977 1/2 acres
lieutenant colonel in Georgia Line	1035 acres
lieutenant colonel in militia	1035 acres
lieutenant colonel in minute battalions	1035 acres
colonel in militia	1150 acres
colonel in Georgia Line	1150 acres
refugee major in militia	1207 1/2 acres
brigadier general in militia	1955 acres

There were five classes of recipients who received bounty land grants in Georgia. The first included those who served in the Continental Army. Georgia was unique in that the bounty land acreage was actually greater for a man who served as a private in the militia than as a private in the Georgia Continental Line. There were four regiments of the Georgia Line attached to the Continental Army. While some have argued that this class of soldiers deserved the most but received the least, such a claim is distorted by a modern perspective which has elevated the Continental Line to a position it did not necessarily enjoy during the Revolutionary War. Even the Executive Council of Georgia dismissed the petitions of Continental Army veterans for additional refugee warrants on the basis that as Continental soldiers they had drawn their pay and performed their duties in a position of their own choosing.

From 3 June 1777 to 1 March 1778 Georgia had a second class of minutemen. These men and officers were in three Minute Battalions and were all non-residents of Georgia at the time of their enlistments.

Georgia's third class of bounty land recipients was the militia who sprang up to handle local emergencies and then disappeared.

The fourth class was that of refugees who were former Georgia residents who fled the state when the British reimposed royal authority and served in the militia regiments of neighboring South Carolina and North Carolina.

The fifth class was that of the citizen. The act of 20 August 1781 attempted to come to grips with the exodus of Georgia's population just ahead of the advancing British forces. Any resident who remained in Georgia until after the expulsion of the enemy in July 1782 had to produce a certificate from the commanding officer of his district to the legislature that he had steadfastly done his duty and was entitled to 250 acres. Moreover, the recipient could not have been convicted of plundering and distressing the country. In other words, he could not have been a Loyalist. There were approximately 3,000 warrants issued in this category of bounty lands, which was twice as large as all the other categories combined.

The sixth and smallest class involved deserters from the British.

It is important to be aware that many Georgia bounty land warrantees qualified in more than one class.

Applicants for bounty land pursued a five-step process. If they were citizens, they had to obtain their certificates from the commanding officer of the district in which they lived. If they were in the army or navy, they had to obtain a voucher from the commanding officer of their unit or battalion. They in turn presented the voucher to the Executive Council which sat as a land court for Franklin and Washington counties. If the Executive Council approved the voucher, the governor issued a numbered certificate in the name of the petitioner, giving his name; his classification of refugee, minuteman, or citizen; the acreage; and the name of the certifying officer found on the initial certificate. Although this certificate was issued in the name of the petitioner, it could actually be issued to anyone to whom the petitioner had assigned his rights. The Executive Council would then issue a numbered warrant directing the county surveyor to lay out the acreage stated in the bounty. The county surveyor, or his deputy, would then survey the land which the applicant had selected and make three plats. He would enter one in his own records and forward the other two to the Surveyor General. The Surveyor General would record and file one plat and attach the third copy to the warrant. The Surveyor General would transmit one copy of the plat and the executed warrant to the Secretary of State who would issue the grant after the filing fees had been paid. The designation of bounty would be entered in the grant book.

The petitioner could also locate his bounty land in one of the eight old counties of Georgia. In those counties the county land court rather than the governor and Executive Council handled the transaction. Of all the states with a bounty land program Georgia acted the most expeditiously to vest bounty lands in the possession of veterans or their heirs.

It is imperative to note that nothing but the governor's numbered certificate indicated the status of the recipient. Any other step in the paper trail could pertain to a soldier, a civilian, a transferee, or a purchaser of the right. More important is the caveat that around the year 1920 someone wrote the word "bounty" on many pages in the grant and survey books where the acreage suggested that it belonged, even though the date of the grant precluded such. It is estimated that no more than half of the numbered warrants signed by the governor survive. Half of the numbered warrants signed by the Executive Council's president also survive. The incomplete extant records defy any attempt to bring order out of chaos. Many of the vouchers signed by the commanding officers are interfiled in the Loose Headright and Bounty Documents File, Series 035, in the Georgia Department of Archives and History. It is important to bear in mind that these vouchers were signed—not by the state—just for having a man's application for bounty land considered.

On 22 February 1785 the General Assembly delegated to the land courts of the ten counties the duty of issuing warrants for bounty grants. The act stipulated that all applications had to be filed by 22 February 1786; otherwise, the bounty grant would not be allowed. The act further specified that a warrant issued by the president of the Executive Council or by a county land court would not expire if surveyed within two years from the date of issuance. Accordingly, true bounty land grants in Georgia cannot exist for warrants bearing a date after 22 February 1786.

There is still another factor contributing to the complex situation in Georgia. When the bounty land warrant process had expired, there were still vacant tracts in the Bounty Reserve. Such land was, therefore, opened for headright settlers. County land courts and surveyors, both of whom were far from meticulous, wrote on their warrants and plats "bounty reserve" as a description of where the land lay. It did not designate that the grant was for bounty, but it did contribute to widespread confusion and misinterpretation of the facts. One should bear in mind that there are hundreds of fraudulent surveys and grants on record in Georgia with the designation "bounty reserve." If the item in question is dated between 1790 and 1796, the suggestion of fraud is highly probable.

Lucian Lamar Knight in *Georgia's Roster of the Revolution* (Baltimore, Md.: Genealogical Publishing Company, 1967) further contributed to the difficult issue of what constituted a bounty land grant in Georgia. Holders of vouchers and numbered certificates used such legal instruments as a medium of exchange. They were treated as money or as stock certificates and could be sold or traded to other people. These people could then receive the grants themselves, and they may not have been entitled to bounty grants in any of the six classes. These purchasers in turn would present the vouchers and certificates singly and collectively to county land courts where they would receive new warrants in their own names, have surveys made, and subsequently have grants issued in their names. Knight mistakenly listed many of these grants which were in the amount of 230, 287, and 575 acres as going to Revolutionary soldiers when in fact the grantees were merely purchasers or assignees of the veterans.

While Georgia had ten counties with functioning land courts, the records of only one survive—Washington County. Its records have been transcribed by Mary Bondurant Warren and Jack Moreland Jones in *Washington County, GA Land Warrants, 1778–1787* (Athens, Ga.: Heritage Papers, 1992).

Revolutionary Soldiers' Receipts for Georgia Bounty Grants (Atlanta, Ga.: Foote and Davies Company, 1928) is a facsimile reproduction of a manuscript containing the names of more than a thousand refugees, citizens, soldiers of the Georgia Line, and officers and men of the Georgia State Galleys.

Marion Hemperley compiled a list of some 2,000 Revolutionary individuals who applied for bounty land based upon vouchers setting forth the Revolutionary War service of the applicant and the certificates issued by the governor after the service had been found valid. He also used other records found among the 200,000 documents so that there are a few entries included which seemingly have no bounty land connections. Hemperley's book, *Military Certificates of Georgia 1776–1800 on File in the Surveyor General Department* (Atlanta, Ga.: State Printing Office, 1983), also includes post-Revolutionary references to veterans of the Oconee War who qualified for bounty land.

The most inclusive collection of published Georgia Revolutionary War bounty land records is Nicole O'Kelley and Mary Bondurant Warren's *Georgia Revolutionary Bounty Land Records 1783–1785* (Athens, Ga.: Heritage Papers, 1992).

The Georgia entries in this book are an amalgamation of extracts made from the original records. Since many of the records did not bear a date, all of the data may not be reflective of the date shown.

Maine

Maine entered the Union as the twenty-third state in 1820. Prior to that time Maine was a district of Massachusetts. Maine was the only state in the Union which did not exist as a state during the Revolutionary War but which had a bounty land policy. Maine was also the only state which extended coverage to veterans of any state who had served in the Continental Line. Because a large number of soldiers living in Maine did not avail themselves of the Massachusetts law of 1801, the legislature of Maine resolved on 17 March 1835 that each noncommissioned officer and soldier of the Revolutionary Army who (1) had served a minimum of three years, (2) at the time of enlistment was an inhabitant of Massachusetts or Maine and was then a resident of Maine, and (3) had not received any bounty from Massachusetts, was to receive 200 acres in the Indian Purchase in the county of Penobscot or the county of Washington. Coverage was also extended to the widows of such officers and soldiers if the veteran at the time of his decease was an inhabitant of Maine. Each noncommissioned officer and soldier who was honorably discharged before the expiration of three years from the time of his entering the service in consequence of either wounds or bodily infirmity was also eligible. The widows of such veterans who died within three years from the time of entering the service were likewise eligible. Applicants had to prove their rights prior to 4 March 1838.

The resolve was modified by an additional resolve approved 8 February 1836 which provided that if the noncommissioned officer, soldier, or widow died after presenting his or her claim for bounty, the heirs of same would be entitled to the same lands as if the title had been perfected provided the heirs produced a certificate from the judge of probate of the county where the deceased resided certifying the number and names of such heirs and in what degrees. Two years later, on 23 March 1838, coverage was extended to each noncommissioned officer, soldier, or widow of any veteran who served in the line of any other state. The applicant, however, could not have received a grant in either land or money from any other state. While the majority of applicants had served in Massachusetts units during the Revolutionary War, a number of others had served from other New England states and the middle states of New Jersey, New York, and Pennsylvania. Probably the veteran who had lived the furthest from Maine during the Revolutionary War was James Brown, a native of Prince William County, Virginia, who had served in a Virginia unit. His application for a federal pension application had been denied. Such applicants had to have been a resident of Maine on 17 March 1835. The resolve also stipulated that soldiers who enlisted for less than three years but who actually served a minimum of three years were also eligible. The resolve was to remain valid for two years.

It was not until 20 March 1838 that Maine provided coverage for commissioned officers. The resolve stipulated that officers who had served a minimum of three years in the army, who were inhabitants of Massachusetts or Maine at the commencement of their service, who were then inhabitants of Maine, and who had not received any bounty in either land or money from the Commonwealth of Massachsuetts were eligible to receive 600 acres in Washington County. Officers discharged with less than three years of service because of wounds or bodily infirmity, and the widows of officers who died in the service, were also eligible for 600 acres. Claims had to be proved on or before 4 March 1840. Any claimant who had established his or her claim before the survey had been completed was entitled to the same 600 acres. Thirty-three commissioned officers or widows applied for the 600-acre tracts of land.

In addition to the resolves providing for bounty lands in Maine, there was also a resolve of 23 March 1838 which offered $50 in cash in lieu of land.

Charles J. House compiled the *Names of Soldiers of the American Revolution Who Applied for State Bounty under Resolves of March 17, 1835, March 24, 1836, and March 20, 1836, as Appears of Record in Land Office* (Augusta, Me.: Burleigh & Flynt, 1893). His work includes the names of recipients of bounties in both cash and land.

The Maine entries in this work have been taken from a microfilm copy of original Revolutionary War veterans' land records made in 1954 at the Department of Forestry in Augusta, Maine by the Genealogical Society of Utah.

Maryland

In November 1781 the General Assembly of Maryland appropriated all of the vacant lands west of Fort Cumberland as a bounty reserve for Maryland veterans. The area encompassed present Allegany and Garrett counties. Authorized by the legislature in April 1787, Francis Deakins finished a general plat of the area in lots of fifty acres each in November 1788. The limited supply of land available caused Maryland's bounty land grants to be rather modest. Officers received four lots for a total of 200 acres. Privates received one lot of 50 acres.

The list of Maryland's bounty land recipients has appeared in J. Thomas Scharf's *History of Western Maryland. Being a History of Frederick, Montgomery, Carroll, Washington, Allegany, and Garrett Counties from the Earliest Period to the Present Day* ... (Philadelphia, Pa.: Louis H. Everts, 1882), vol. I, pp. 145–161, and in Bettie Stirling Carothers's *Maryland Soldiers Entitled to Lands West of Fort Cumberland* (1973). John M. Brewer and Lewis Mayer in *The Laws and Rules of the Land Office of Maryland* (Baltimore, Md.: Kelly, Piett & Co., 1871), pp. 71–125, included the list of officers and soldiers entitled to bounty lands and a list of patented military lots. The most recent treatment of these records is Mary K. Meyer's *Westward of Fort Cumberland Military Lots Set Off for Maryland's Revolutionary Soldiers* (Finksburg, Md.: Pipe Creek Publications, 1994).

Massachusetts

Massachusetts did not have a policy providing bounty land to veterans during the Revolutionary War. It was not until 5 March 1801 that the Commonwealth of Massachusetts granted to each noncommissioned officer and soldier who had served three years and been honorably discharged 200 acres of land. Children or the widows of deceased veterans who died in service were also eligible for the same acreage. The expenses of laying out the said land was to be borne by the commonwealth. The allocation of the lands was to begin when the number of applicants was sufficient to take a quantity of land equal to one township of six miles square. The act provided for the option of $20 as an equivalent to the 200 acres to be paid out of the treasury by the selectmen of the town where the veteran or his heirs resided. The recipients could not convey the 200 acre tracts until they had made a settlement thereon and improved five acres thereof. If they failed to do so and tried to dispose of their bounty, the grant was null and void. Applications had to be made within three years from the passing of the resolve, and settlement and cultivation had to take place within six years. The land lay in that part of Massachusetts in the District of Maine, and the bounty grants bore the designation of "Mars Hill grants." Later legislative acts emanated from the state of Maine.

The Massachusetts entries in this index have been taken from the microfilm copy of the records described in the Maine section.

New York

New York instituted the policy of granting bounty lands on 20 March 1781, followed by subsequent acts. The tract chosen for bounty land was in the choice Finger Lakes region in central New York. It was called the Military Tract and included the present counties of Cayuga, Cortland, Onondaga, and Seneca and parts of Oswego, Schuyler, Tompkins, and Wayne. There were twenty-eight townships altogether. The whole tract contained over one and a half million acres. Each township contained 60,000 acres and bore the name of a classical literary hero, and each was subdivided into farm lots of 600 acres.

The state of New York purchased the land from the Onondaga Indian Nation and the Cayuga Nation in 1788 and 1789 respectively. Further purchases from the Oneida and Tuscaroras were also made. The Indians had supported the British during the Revolutionary War. Within three days after the final purchases from the Indians, New York held the balloting for distributing the land. The name of each veteran was written on a slip of paper and put into a box. The name of each lot was written on another slip of paper and placed in a separate box. As a slip was drawn from each box, they were matched as the veteran's land. The veterans then received patents to their land on the condition that the land be settled within seven years. They also had to pay surveying costs.

The formula for issuing New York bounty land grants was:

private	500 acres
noncommissioned officer	500 acres
surgeon's mate	1000 acres
subaltern	1000 acres
regimental surgeon	1500 acres
captain	1500 acres
chaplain	2000 acres
major	2000 acres
lieutenant colonel	2250 acres
colonel	2500 acres
brigadier general	4250 acres
major general	5500 acres

The New York entries have been taken from *The Balloting Book, and Other Documents Relating to Military Bounty Lands, in the State of New-York* (Albany, N.Y.: Packard & VanBenthuysen, 1825).

North Carolina

North Carolina resorted to bounty lands in order to raise her quota of Continental Line troops. Soldiers had to serve a minimum of two years in order to qualify for bounty. The formula for allocating bounty lands to North Carolina Continental Line veterans or their heirs was based on service from 1776 to 1783 or eighty-four months. The formula was:

private	640 acres
noncommissioned officer	1000 acres
subaltern (below rank of captain)	2560 acres
surgeon's mate	2560 acres
captain	3840 acres
surgeon	4600 acres
major	4800 acres
lieutenant colonel	5760 acres
lieutenant colonel commandant	7200 acres
chaplain	7200 acres
colonel	7200 acres
brigadier general	12,000 acres

The 1783 law prorated the acreage so that privates with two years' service got 225 acres and those with three years' service received 274 acres. Clearly, North Carolina was the most generous in the awards given to officers. In every case the service had to have been in the North Carolina Continental Line. No militia duty was allowed even if that duty was performed under Continental orders.

The North Carolina legislature passed an act in 1780 setting aside a tract in Tennessee bounded by the Holston River, the Powell River, and the Virginia state line for bounty land for officers and soldiers in the Continental Line. When North Carolina sought to implement its bounty land policy, however, significant settlement had already occurred in the area. Accordingly, a new location had to be selected. The new North Carolina bounty land reserve was located in that part of the country annexed to the state in 1776 which became Middle Tennessee south of the Kentucky border. This vast tract northeast of Nashville was reserved and laid out in 1783 for officers and soldiers of the North Carolina Continental Line. Initially the rectangular tract was 150 miles long and 50 miles wide. Eventually the supply of vacant lands in the reserve was exhausted, and the bounty warrants were then located elsewhere in Tennessee. No bounty land warrants were located within the present-day boundaries of North Carolina. Most of the North Carolina military land warrants bear the designation Davidson or Sumner County. Finding an entry to a military warrant in the index of the records of the North Carolina Land Office does not equate to military service for the individual. Land warrants were frequently sold, and some of them actually changed hands a half-dozen times.

North Carolina issued bounty land warrants from 1783 to 1841 in two series. The first included numbers 1 to 5312, issued from 1783 to 1797, which North Carolina agents located in the military district in Tennessee. The second series of warrants, numbered 1 to 1242, was issued from 1799 to 1841 by North Carolina, but Tennessee offficals located and granted the patents. A total of 6,554 Revolutionary War bounty land warrants were issued by North

Carolina. Both series are included in the Secretary of State's *Military Land Warrant Book,* which is the source used in this work. Each part is arranged in numerical order by warrant number. In addition to the name of the veteran, the acreage, the number of months of service in the Continental Line, the date of issue of the warrant, and the name of the individual to whom it was delivered also appear. In the second series the order of the acreage and the length of service is reversed.

In 1900 the North Carolina Society of the Daughters of the American Revolution issued their *Roster of Soldiers from North Carolina in the American Revolution* (reprinted by the Genealogical Publishing Company) which included on pages 233–312 a list of the North Carolina bounty land warrants. Unfortunately, this transcription was made from an incomplete and faulty register of the military bounty land warrants. Many of the names do not agree with the original. Moreover, the correct version contains no warrant numbered 236 but does duplicate warrant number 1171 so that all warrant numbers from 237 to 1170 are incorrectly given. They should instead be one number higher. Warrant numbers after 1171 are correct. The most serious flaw in this publication, however, is the omission of 1,579 warrants included in the *Military Land Warrant Book.* In other words, forty percent of the North Carolina entries are missing from the only published source heretofore available.

Illustrative of North Carolinans who benefited by both the federal and state bounty land programs was Simon Alderson who received North Carolina warrant no. 2071 in the amount of 1,000 acres for his eighty-four months of service in the North Carolina Continental Line. From the federal government he received bounty land warrant no. 11884.

If a soldier died before his warrant was issued, the register usually indicates that the warrant was issued to the heirs, but does not name them. If the heirs did not have the same surname, if their names are not known, and/or if the heirs sold the warrant, it is difficult to unravel the details. Shirley Hollis Rice's *The Hidden Revolutionary War Land Grants in the Tennessee Military Reservation* (Lawrenceburg, Tenn.: Family Tree Press, 1991) provides some much needed assistance. She records more than 3,000 North Carolina Revolutionary military warrants assigned and deeded to someone other than the veteran. Rice examined the deeds of the counties within the Military Reserve as well as a limited number of deed books in counties outside of the Reserve. Because of a courthouse fire in Jackson County, there are no entries for that county in her book. Some Revolutionary bounty land grants also appear in Goldene Fillers Burgner's *North Carolina Land Grants in Tennessee 1778–1791* (Easley, S.C.: Southern Historical Press, 1981).

Another tool to be used in linking the unknown names of heirs with the veteran involves the papers of the Glasgow Land Fraud. A group of a dozen men attempted to convey to themselves illegally millions of acres in Tennessee. The scandal involved several prominent politicans, and North Carolina Secretary of State James Glasgow was charged with complicity. The group gained control of approximately 2,000 bounty land warrants. Dr. A. B. Pruitt's

Glasgow Land Fraud Papers 1783–1800 North Carolina Revolutionary War Bounty Land in Tennessee (the author, 1988 and 1993) treats the complex crime and the incriminating records. The first volume is divided into four sections, and each has its own index.

One final caveat involves the provision by North Carolina for bounty lands in Tennessee to the guards and surveyors who laid out the Military Reserve. They were not Continental soldiers. A surveyor received 2,500 acres. Chain carriers, markers, and hunters received 640 acres. Guards received 320 acres. Fortunately, their warrants and patents do specify their service, so confusion ought to be minimal.

Pennsylvania

In Pennsylvania the term "donation lands" was used to designate bounty lands.

On 7 March 1780, the General Assembly of Pennsylvania, in an attempt to keep men in the fighting ranks as the hostilities dragged on, promised certain donations and quantities of land to soldiers in the Pennsylvania Continental Line who served to the end of the war. The lands were to be surveyed and divided off at the end of the war. On 12 March 1783 the General Assembly reserved a tract of land in western Pennsylvania for the sole purpose of implementing the resolve. The donation lands were bounded on the east by the Allegheny River, on the west by the Ohio border, and on the north by the New York border. The area comprised parts of the counties of Armstrong, Butler, Forest, Lawrence, Venango, and Warren; all of Crawford and Mercer; and that portion of Erie lying south of the triangle. Officers and men were allowed two years following the declaration of peace to make their applications. If they died during that time, their heirs, executors, or administrators had a third year to do so. Noncommissioned officers and privates were prohibited from selling their bounty lands until they had been surveyed and laid off. The General Assembly also exempted these lands from taxation during the lifetime of the veteran, unless the land was transferred or assigned.

The formula for allocating the Pennsylvania bounty lands was:

private	200 acres
corporal	200 acres
fife major	200 acres
drummer	200 acres
drum major	200 acres
quartermaster sergeant	250 acres
sergeant major	250 acres
sergeant	250 acres
regimental surgeon's mate	300 acres
ensign	300 acres
lieutenant	400 acres

captain	500 acres
major	600 acres
chaplain	600 acres
surgeon	600 acres
lieutenant colonel	800 acres
colonel	1000 acres
brigadier general	1500 acres
major general	2000 acres

The applicant had to bear the cost of the surveying, and these fees had to be paid before he could receive his bounty land draw.

After the boundary line between Pennsylvania and New York had been located in 1787, it was discovered that many of the bounty land lots fell within the Empire State. One hundred and twenty lots were wholly or partially involved. In most cases, patents had been issued for these lands. The General Assembly on 30 September 1791 addressed this unfortunate situation and allowed the veterans to choose other vacant lands in the reserve without the payment of any additional fees. The veterans were to give quit claims to the Commonwealth for compensation on account of any losses they might have suffered.

One unmarried officer who had been killed in service had his bounty claimed by a brother as heir-at-law, and the Pennsylvania Supreme Court deemed the claim to be valid. Accordingly, on 11 March 1808 the legislature passed an act that bounty lands could not be issued except to the widow or children of a deceased officer or soldier who died or was killed in service.

The last extension for filing applications expired 1 April 1810.

Claims to donation lands were published in the *Pennsylvania Archives*, Third Series, volumes III and VII. The former is *An Account of the Donation Lands of Pennsylvania* (Harrisburg, Pa.: Clarence M. Busch, 1894) and the latter is *Donation or Military Tracts of Land Granted the Soldiers of the Pennsylvania Line* (Harrisburg, Pa.: Clarence M. Busch, 1896).

In addition to compensating its soldiers and officers with bounty lands, Pennsylvania set aside another tract of 720,000 acres north of Pittsburgh known as the Depreciation Tract. It was intended as compensation for the depreciation in Continental currency which the veterans had received. Pennsylvania accepted the certificates of depreciation as payment for lands in the Depreciation Tract. These depreciation lands are not truly bounty lands and are excluded from this index.

The Pennsylvania entries have been taken from the microfilm copy of the Department of Internal Affairs Index Patent Donation Lands 1780–1800.

South Carolina

South Carolina in 1778 passed an act providing that 200 acres of land be reserved for and granted free of expense in fee simple to every soldier already enlisted or who subsequently enlisted in one of the six regiments in the South Carolina Continental Line. The soldier had to complete his term of service. If he died during the service, his heirs were to be entitled to the 200 acres.

An ordinance of 26 March 1784 directed the commissioners in the several districts to receive the entry of the respective officers and soldiers of the late South Carolina Continental Line, the officers on the staff, the three independent companies commanded by Captain Bowie and Captain Moore, and the officers of the state navy for the land to which they were entitled. They were to issue warrants of survey and to certify the plats. The Secretary of State prepared the grant, and the governor signed and passed the grant. All of the fees of the commissioners, the Secretary of State, the deputy surveyor, the Surveyor General and his secretary were to be paid by the state.

The South Carolina bounty lands were located on the frontier on the former Cherokee lands in the northwest corner of the state, between the Togolo and Keowee rivers, in present Anderson, Oconee, and Pickens counties. Besides this convenient tract of vacant land, any vacant land in the state could also be selected.

There are four manuscript volumes of bounty land grants in the South Carolina Department of Archives and History. On 19 January 1788, the Surveyor General submitted a report of the fees he had collected for the 477 plats for bounty land he had issued from July 1784. His fee for each plat was £0.12.2. The Secretary, Peter Freneaux, collected 10 shillings for each grant. An index to the bounty land grantees first appeared as "Historical Notes: Bounty Grants to Revolutionary Soldiers," *South Carolina Historical and Genealogical Magazine*, VII (1906): 173–78 and 217–24. Abstracts in a single alphabetical series appear in Tony Draine and John Skinner's *Revolutionary War Bounty Land Grants in South Carolina* (Columbia, S.C.: Congaree Publications, 1986). All of the these sources have been compared to obtain the best possible interpretation.

Virginia

The Commonwealth of Virginia was extremely generous in its bounty land program. Virginia was not only the largest of the Thirteen Colonies in area but also in population. The Old Dominion awarded bounty lands to soldiers and sailors or their heirs who served in either the State or Continental Line Revolutionary forces. Most of the bounty lands were located in the Military Districts in Kentucky and Ohio. No bounty lands were located within the present boundaries of either Virginia or West Virginia. The Virginia troops who served in the Illinois Regiment under George Rogers Clark are treated below in the section **Virginia—Indiana**.

The formula for awarding bounty lands to Virginia soldiers and sailors was:

sailor who served out his three year enlistment or served to the end of the war	100 acres

soldier who served out his three year enlistment or served to the end of the war	100 acres
noncommissioned officer who enlisted and served out his three year enlistment	200 acres
sailor who served throughout the war	400 acres
soldier who served throughout the war	400 acres
noncommissioned officer who served throughout the war	400 acres
subaltern—cornet	2000 to 2666 acres
subaltern—ensign	2000 to 2666 acres
subaltern—ieutenant	2000 to 2666 acres
surgeon's mate	2666 to 8000 acres
surgeon	2666 to 8000 acres
captain	3000 to 4666 acres
major	4000 to 5333 acres
lieutenant colonel	4500 to 6666 acres
colonel	5000 to 8888 acres
brigadier general	10,000 acres upwards
major general	15,000 to 17,500 acres

For any officer, sailor, or soldier who died or was killed in service, his heirs or legal representatives were entitled to receive the same quantity of land which a surviving veteran received.

There are far more Virginia entries than veterans because the references are to the certificates themselves. A veteran may have had multiple certificates for various reasons. In recording certificate numbers, the clerk sometimes re-used a number. When a veteran lost the original certificate, a new one with the same number had to be reissued. If the original certificate contained an error, it was necessary to issue a new one. The new certificate, known as an exchange warrant, most commonly existed when there was a mistake in the acreage or in the names of the heirs. Finally, multiple warrants could be obtained in smaller acreages as long as the total acreage equalled the allotment to which the veteran was entitled. The date in each entry is normally the date of the certificate; in its absence, the date is that of the warrant.

Virginia's first military district was south of the Green River in Kentucky. The area encompassed in it ran along a line from the head of the Green River to the Cumberland Mountains, to the North Carolina line, to the Tennessee River, to the Ohio River, and back to the Green River. Prior to 1797 no one except a soldier could enter a survey in the district. The Kentucky bounty land warrants appear in Samuel M. Wilson's *Catalogue of Revolutionary Soldiers and Sailors of the Commonwealth of Virginia to Whom Land Bounty Warrants Were Granted by Virginia for Military Services in the War for Independence* (Baltimore, Md.: Genealogical Publishing Company, 1977). Wilson arranged his book in quasi-alphabetical order by the initial letter of the surname. Each entry consists of the name of the veteran, his assignee or heir at law where appropriate, warrant number, acreage, rank, whether Continental or State Line or Navy, number of years of service, and date of warrant. It would appear that all of the bounty land grants in Kentucky had been made by 1798.

The second Virginia military district was in Ohio, bounded by the Ohio River on the south, the Scioto River on the east, and the Little Miami River on the west. It opened in 1790 when the Kentucky Reserve was used up. It contained 4,204,800 acres and included all or portions of the following Ohio counties: Adams, Brown, Champaign, Clark, Clermont, Clinton, Delaware, Fayette, Franklin, Greene, Hamilton, Hardin, Highland, Logan, Madison, Marion, Pickaway, Ross, Scioto, Union, and Warren. In his *Federal Land Series*, volume IV, parts 1 and 2, Clifford Neal Smith has treated *Grants in the Virginia Military District of Ohio* (Chicago, Ill.: American Library Association, 1982–86). He indicated that a third volume would be needed to complete the Virginia Military District records, but this has not yet been published.

Gaius M. Brumbaugh's *Revolutionary War Records in Virginia, Virginia Army and Navy Forces, with Bounty Land Warrants for Virginia, Military District of Ohio, and Virginia Military Script* (Baltimore, Md.: Genealogical Publishing Co., 1967) and Louis A. Burgess's three-volume set, *Virginia Soldiers of 1776 Compiled from Documents . . . in the Virginia Land Office* (Baltimore, Md.: Clearfield Company, Inc., 1994) contains much relevant data about Virginia's bounty lands. The latter is especially rich in genealogical data documenting proof of relationships from the bounty land files in the Archives Division of the Virginia State Library.

In 1852 the federal government allowed all claims to Virginia land warrants issued before that year to be exchanged for scrip. It was the last attempt to honor the 1781 Virginia act by which Virginia had ceded its western lands to the federal government on the condition that Virginia would be able to satisfy its promises of bounty lands. Margie G. Brown's *Genealogical Abstracts Revolutionary War Veterans Scrip Act 1852* (Decorah, Ia.: The Anundsen Publishing Co., 1990), abstracts the genealogical data of the 1,689 files created in response to the act. If the warrants were still in the possession of descendants, the files contain powers of attorney, wills, affidavits of heirship, proof of service, and correspondence from heirs. By 1852 the heirs of veterans were children, grandchildren, and even great-grandchildren.

While the Virginia entries in this index represent only the approved applications, there were numerous applications for bounty land which the Commonwealth of Virginia rejected. Frequently the applications were disallowed because the applicant failed to comply with the minimum period of service. In other cases, however, it would seem that there were simply no living witnesses who could attest to the service. Abstracts of the rejected bounty land files appear in William Lindsay Hopkins's *Virginia Revolutionary War Land Grant Claims 1783–1850 (Rejected)* (Richmond, Va.: the author, 1988).

Virginia—Indiana

On 2 January 1781, the General Assembly of Virginia adopted a resolution which provided that the officers and soldiers who served in the Illinois Regiment under Colonel George Rogers Clark be allowed a quantity of land not to exceed 150,000 acres, to be laid off in one tract, the length not to exceed twice the breadth in such a place on the north side of the Ohio River as the majority of the officers should choose. It was to be divided among the soldiers and officers in due proportions according to the laws of Virginia. The law applied not only to those who had marched into the area with Colonel Clark but also to those officers and soldiers who had since been incorporated into the Illinois Regiment. The General Assembly passed another act in 1783 to implement the resolution. Appointed as a board of commissioners to receive the claims were William Fleming, John Edwards, John Campbell, Walker Daniel, gentlemen; and George Rogers Clark, John Montgomery, Abraham Chaplin, John Bailey, Robert Todd, and William Clark, officers in the Illinois Regiment. The board of commissioners was to govern itself by the allowances made by law to the officers and soldiers of the Continental Army.

The land selected was on the north side of the Ohio River in Clark, Floyd, and Scott counties, Indiana. Primarily the grant was in Clark County.

Meeting at Louisville on 3 August 1784, the board refined the definition of eligibility for bounty. The board ruled that all officers and soldiers who marched and continued in service until the reduction of the British posts on the north side of the Ohio River and all who engaged and enlisted in the Illinois Regiment afterwards and who served during the war or for three years qualified for bounty land. Soldiers who enlisted in the regiment after 2 January 1781 for three years were not eligible. Officers of the regiment were entitled to a share of the land in proportion to the commissions they held on 2 January 1781 and not in consequence of any subsequent promotion. Officers commissioned after 2 January 1781 were not entitled at all. Those soldiers who enlisted to serve twelve months after their arrival at Kaskaskia for the protection and defense of the Illinois country and who did not re-enlist in the regiment were likewise disqualified. Officers who were commissioned under the act and resigned before the expiration of the twelve months were also ineligible. Those officers who continued during the year and then retired, not having a command, were eligible.

On 10 October 1787 the Board of Commissioners extended coverage to the officers and soldiers who were left at the falls on the Ohio River by order of Colonel Clark when the detachment was going against the Illinois Indians. The failure to locate the name of a soldier who served under George Rogers Clark in the Illinois or Clark Grant is due to the fact that the service was under Clark in his later campaigns against the Indians. Such service did not qualify for bounty in the Clark Grant.

The entries to the Clark Grant bounty land grantees are taken from William Haden English's *Conquest of the Country Northwest of the River Ohio,*

1778–1782 and Life of Gen. George Rogers Clark (Indianapolis, Ind.: The Bowen-Merrill Company, 1896). In his compilation English included the name of James Irby or James Irley with the rank of sergeant who received 216 acres. Because this name does not appear in any of the rosters of the soldiers under Clark, it is probable that he was an assignee of an unidentified veteran. His name has been omitted from this index.

Finally, I would like to express my thanks for all of the many kindnesses extended to me by fellow librarians, archivists, and genealogists who aided in obtaining copies of the records and in providing their particular expertise on obscure points. These include Michael Kalen Smith of the Dallas Public Library, Dallas, Texas; Judith P. Reid of the Library of Congress, Washington, D.C.; Joy Wade Moulton, C.G., of Columbus, Ohio; Brent H. Holcomb of Columbia, S.C.; Conley Edwards of the Archives of Virginia, Richmond, Virginia; and Ingrid Shields of the Georgia Archives, Atlanta, Georgia.

Addenda

Baily, Mountjoy. Md. Capt. 1825. 200 acres.

Chesley, Robert. Md. Capt. 1827. 200 acres to heirs.

Godman, Samuel. Md. Capt. 1856. 200 acres to heirs.

Goldsmith, Thomas. Md. ____. 1835. 200 acres to heirs James Mills, Thomas Mills, Elizabeth Mills, Sarah Campfield, and Harriet Goldsmith.

Hill, Richard. Md. ____. 1831. 50 acres to Lydia Brown and Ann Hill.

Howard, Benjamin. Md. ____. 1831. 50 acres.

Ireland, George. Md. Lt. 1828. 200 acres to heirs.

Jacob, John J. Md. ____. 1829. 200 acres.

Jones, Samuel. Md. Capt. 1827. 200 acres to daughter Lillias M. Jones.

Leonard, James. Md. Pvt. 1825. 50 acres.

Lord, Andrew. Md. Pvt. 1827. 50 acres to heirs or to his widow Amelia Lord.

Marshall, Benjamin. Md. ____. 1825. 50 acres.

Parran, Thomas. Md. Surgeon. 1827. 200 acres to heirs.

Truck, John. Md. Sgt. 1825. 50 acres.

Williams, Joseph. Md. ____. 1832. 50 acres.

Tillotson, Thomas. Md. Surgeon. 1831. 200 acres.

REVOLUTIONARY WAR BOUNTY LAND GRANTS

Awarded by State Governments

———, Brutus. [Negro] N.C. Private. 8 Aug. 1821. 640 acres.

———, Cubbit. [Negro]. N.C. Drummer. 8 Aug. 1821. 1000 acres.

———, Frederick. [Negro] N.C. Musician. 8 Aug. 1821. 640 acres.

———, Ned [Negro]. Conn. Sufferer. Fairfield. 7.4.0.

———. Pa. ———. 30 Mar. 1805. 200 acres to Michael Wann et al.

———, Roger [Negro]. Conn. Sufferer. Danbury. 0.6.8.

———, Shoram [Negro]. Conn. Sufferer. Groton. 6.9.0.

———, Syphax [Negro]. Conn. Sufferer. Norwalk. 0.7.0.

———. Tack and wife. [?Negro] Conn. Sufferers. New/East Haven. 17.11.11.

—iles, Anthony. N.C. Private. 15 Feb. 1797. 640 acres to heirs.

Aaron, William. Va. Private. 10 Jun. 1783. 100 acres.

Abacre, Pritte. N. Y. ———. ———. 500 acres.

Abanton, Isaac. Ga. Minute Man. 3 Apr. 1785. ———.

Abbett, Elijah. N.C. Private. 14 Jun. 1785. 640 acres to heirs.

Abbett, Jonathan. N.C. Private. 30 Sep. 1785. 640 acres.

Abbett, Robert. Va. Sergeant. 13 Jun. 1783. 200 acres.

Abbit, Ruben. Va. Private. 23 Jun. 1783. 200 acres.

Abbitt, John. N.C. Private. 9 Nov. 1784. 428 acres.

Abbitt, Woodington. N.C. Private. 10 Aug. 1785. 640 acres.

Abbot, Daniel. Conn. Sufferer. New/East Haven. 4.8.0.

Abbot, George. Md. Private. ———. 50 acres.

Abbot, Henry. Mass. Private. 12 Dec. 1828. 200 acres to heirs.

Abbot, John. Ga. Soldier. 15 Mar. 1784. 250 acres.

Abbot, John. Ga. Refugee. 17 May 1784. 250 acres to heirs.

Abbot, John. Me. Private. 5 Sep. 1835. 200 acres. North Berwick.

Abbot, John. Me. Private. 1 Oct. 1839. 200 acres to widow Rachel (McFredericks) Abbot. Bath.

Abbot, Nehemiah. Mass. Corporal. 9 Sep. 1834. 200 acres.

Abbott, Isaac. N.C. Private. 29 Sep. 1785. 640 acres.

Abbott, John. Conn. Sufferer. Ridgefield. 4.2.8.

Abbott, Lemuel. Conn. Sufferer. Ridgefield. 5.16.0.

Abbott, Seth. Conn. Sufferer. Norwalk. 55.7.3.

Abby, Samuel. N. Y. Sergeant. 13 Sep. 1790. 500 acres to heirs.

Abel, Elijah, Col. Conn. Sufferer. Fairfield. 719.14.4.

Abercrombie, Charles. Ga. ———. 17 May 1784. ———.

Aberrian, John. N.C. Private. 15 Jul. 1785. 640 acres to heirs.

Able, Cuthbert. Md. Sergeant. ———. 50 acres.

Able, John. N. Y. Private. 8 Jul. 1790. 600 acres.

Abner, Simon. Va. Private. 18 Apr. 1788. 200 acres.

Abney, William. Va. Private. 20 May 1823. 100 acres.

Abott, Alisha. N.C. Private. 14 Feb. 1796. 640 acres to heirs.

Abrams, Joseph. N.C. Private. 30 Sep. 1785. 640 acres to heirs.

Absalom, Edward. Va. Private. 25 Jul. 1835. 200 acres.

Absolam, Edmund. Va. Private. Aug. 1783. 200 acres.

Absolum, William. Md. Private. ———. 50 acres.

Abuck, John. N.C. ———. 8 Mar. 1785. 640 acres to heirs.

Accord, John. Ga. ———. 17 May 1784. ———.

Accrow, Silas. Me. ———. 9 Aug. 1836. 200 acres to widow Sarah (Boaz) Accrow.

Achison, Timothy. Pa. Private. 27 Nov. 1786. 200 acres.

Acinclash, Duncan. N.C. Private. 1 Sep. 1785. 640 acres to heirs.

Acinclash, Duncan. N.C. Private. 12 Sep. 1785. 640 acres to heirs.

Acker, Conradt. N. Y. Private. 8 Jul. 1790. 600 acres.

Ackerman, Daniel. N. Y. ———. 13 Sep. 1790. 500 acres to heirs.

Ackerman, Francis. Pa. Private. ———. 200 acres.

Ackerson, Benjamin. N.Y. ———. 13 Sep. 1790. 500 acres to heirs.

Ackinclash, John. N.C. Private. 30 Sep. 1785. 640 acres to heirs.

Ackler, John. N. Y. Private. 3 Jul. 1790. 600 acres.

Ackley, Joel. N. Y. Private. 6 Jul. 1790. 600 acres.

Ackley, John. N. Y. Private. 8 Jul. 1790. 600 acres.

Ackling, Francis. N. Y. Private. 6 Jul. 1790. 600 acres.

Acock, Moses. N.C. Private. 9 Nov. 1784. 640 acres to heir.

Acock, Robert. N.C. Private. 9 Nov. 1784. 228 acres to heir.

Acock, William. N.C. Private. 9 Nov. 1784. 640 acres to heir.

Acquard, Alexander. N.C. Private. 24 Oct. 1787. 274 acres.

Acre, Ambrose. Va. Private. 25 Dec. 1784. 100 acres.

Adair, William. Ga. Minute Man. 25 Feb. 1784. 250 acres.

Adaminson, Solomon. Ga. Refugee. 6 Aug. 1785. ———.

Adams, Adam. Ga. ———. ———. 287 1/2 acres.

Adams, Adam. Md. Private. ———. 50 acres.

Adams, Andrew. S.C. ———. 1 Aug. 1785. 200 acres.

Adams, Andrew. S.C. ———. 5 Nov. 1785. 200 acres.

Adams, Archibald. Ga. Soldier. 7 Jun. 1785. 230 acres.

Adams, Arthur. N.C. Private. 10 Dec. 1788. 274 acres.

Adams, Charles. N.C. Private. 17 Dec. 1785. 640 acres to heirs.

Adams, David. Ga. Minute Man. Sep. 1785. 250 acres.

Adams, Ellison E. Va. Private. 30 Jan. 1810. 100 acres.

Adams, Emanuel. N. Y. Private. 8 Jul. 1790. 500 acres.

Adams, Ezekiel. S.C. Soldier. 21 Jan. 1785. 200 acres.

Adams, George. Pa. Private. 18 Jul. 1787. 200 acres.

Adams, Hugh. Ga. Minute Man. 3 Sep. 1785. 287 1/2 acres.

Adams, Ignatius. Md. Private. ———. 50 acres.

Adams, Jacob. Ga. ———. 17 May 1784. ———.

Adams, Jacob. Md. Private. ———. 50 acres.

Adams, Jacob. Va. Private. 23 Jun. 1783. 200 acres.

Adams, James. Ga. ———. 17 May 1784. ———.

Adams, James. N. Y. Corporal. 3 Jul. 1790. 600 acres.

Adams, James. N. Y. Drummer. 8 Jul. 1790. 500 acres.

Adams, James. Va. Corporal. 23 Jun. 1783. 400 acres.

Adams, Jedediah. Me. ———. 11 May 1835. 200 acres to widow Rebecca Adams. Bowdoinham.

Adams, John. Ga. Soldier. 20 Apr. 1785. ———.

Adams, John. Md. Corporal. ———. 50 acres.

Adams, John. Md. Private. ———. 50 acres.

Adams, John. N.C. Sergeant. 3 Aug. 1820. 1000 acres to heirs.

Adams, John. Pa. Private. 7 Nov. 1804. 200 acres.

Adams, John. Pa. Private. 9 Oct. 1786. 200 acres.

Adams, John. Va. Private. 25 Nov. 1785. 200 acres.

Adams, John. Va. Private. 27 Mar. 1837. 100 acres.

Adams, Jonathan. Pa. Dragoon. 15 Feb. 1787. 200 acres.

Adams, Joseph. Conn. Sufferer. New/East Haven. 13.19.5.

Adams, Lanier. N.C. Private. 12 Dec. 1806. 640 acres to heirs.

Adams, Malone. Va. Private. 11 Jan. 1788. 100 acres.

Adams, Matthias. Ga. ———. 25 May 1784. 287 1/2 acres.

Adams, Nathan. Conn. Sufferer. Norwalk. 14.0.0.

Adams, Niper. N.C. Private. 21 Aug. 1820. 640 acres.

Adams, Peleg. N. Y. Private. 8 Jul. 1790. 500 acres.

Adams, Peter. Md. Colonel. ———. 200 acres.

Adams, Richard. Va. Private. 11 Jan. 1810. 100 acres.

Adams, Robert. Ga. ———. 17 May 1784. 575 acres to heirs.

Adams, Robert. Pa. ———. 17 Apr. 1796. 200 acres to George Wallace, assignee.

Adams, Robert. Pa. Ranger. 2 May 1787. 200 acres.

Adams, Robert. Pa. Private. ———. 200 acres.

Adams, Robert. Va. Private. 28 Mar. 1834. 200 acres.

Adams, Samuel. Me. Private. 1 May 1835. 200 acres. Bowdoin.

Adams, Samuel. Me. Surgeon. 15 Dec. 1838. 600 acres to widow Abigail Adams. Bath.

Adams, Solomon. Me. ———. 11 Jun. 1835. 200 acres to widow Hannah Adams. Farmington.

Adams, Thomas. Md. Private. ———. 50 acres.

Adams, Thomas. Va. Private. 1 Dec. 1783. 100 acres.

Adams, Thomas. Va. Private. 29 Nov. 1796. 100 acres.

Adams, William. Ga. ———. 30 Jul. 1784. 287 1/2 acres.

Adams, William. Md. Lieutenant. ———. 200 acres.

Adams, William. N. Y. Fifer. 8 Jul. 1790. 500 acres.

Adams, William. N.C. Private. 26 May 1784. 640 acres.

Adams, William. Pa. Surgeon. ———. 300 acres.

Adams, William. Pa. Surgeon. ———. 300 acres.

Adams, William. Va. Private. 30 Jan. 1810. 100 acres.

Adamson, Charles. Ga. ———. 28 Sep. 1784. 230 acres.

Adamson, Hugh. Ga. Minute Man. 14 Jul. 1785. ———.

Adcock, Edward. N.C. Private. 27 Aug. 1784. 640 acres.

Adcock, George. N.C. ———. 21 May 1784. 640 acres to heir.

Adcock, James. Ga. ———. 26 May 1784. 287 1/2 acres.

Adcock, John. N.C. Private. 20 Feb. 1784. 640 acres.

Adcock, Joshua. N.C. Private. 12 Feb. 1784. 274 acres.

Adcock, Thomas. Ga. ———. 17 May 1784. ———.

Adcock, Thomas. N.C. Private. 13 Dec. 1796. 640 acres to heirs.

Addington, John. Conn. Sufferer. Greenwich. 10.0.0.

Addison, John. S.C. ———. 3 Sep. 1792. 79 acres.

Addison, John. Va. Private. 23 Jan. 1834. 100 acres.

Addiston, Thomas. Me. Private. 5 Jun. 1835. 200 acres. Green.

Addlemon, John. N.C. Private. 20 Sep. 1784. 274 acres.

Addoms, Jonas. N. Y. Lieutenant. 8 Jul. 1790. 1200 acres.

Ademy, Henry. N. Y. Private. 8 Jul. 1790. 600 acres.

Aden, Jonathan. N.C. Private. 10 Sep. 1821. 640 acres to heirs.

Aderedge, Thomas. Ga. Refugee. Sep. 1785. ———.

Adkins, Alexander. Va. Private. 18 Nov. 1818. 100 acres.

Adkins, Bartlett. Va. Private. 7 Apr. 1784. 100 acres.

Adkins, David. Ga. Minute Man. 3 Sep. 1785. ———.

Adkins, David. N.C. Private. 23 Apr. 1784. 640 acres.

Adkins, Jesse. Ga. Minute Man. 3 Sep. 1785. ———.

Adkins, Solomon. Ga. Minute Man. 3 Sep. 1785. ———.

Adkins, William. Ga. ———. 1784. 250 acres. ———.

Adkinson, Thomas. Ga. ———. 22 May 1784. 287 1/2 acres.

Adley, Peter. Me. ———. 21 Jul. 1838. 200 acres. Hallowell.

Adley, Peter. Me. ———. 31 Jul. 1838. 200 acres. Hallowell.

Admons, John. N.C. Private. 30 Sep. 1785. 640 acres to heirs.

Agel, Benjamin. N.C. Private. 21 Aug. 1820. 228 acres.
Agnew, John. Va. Private. 5 Mar. 1819. 100 acres.
Ahorn, Philip. Pa. Private. ———. 200 acres.
Aiken, David. Va. Private. 8 Jan. 1812. 100 acres.
Aiken, David. Va. Sergeant. 8 Jan. 1812. 400 acres.
Aiken, George. Va. Sergeant. 20 Jan. 1785. 200 acres.
Aiken, John. Pa. ———. 27 May 1796. 200 acres to Jacob Miley, assignee.
Aiken, John. Pa. Matross. 19 Mar. 1787. 200 acres.
Ailstock, William. Va. Private. 12 Jul. 1783. 100 acres.
Aimes, Henry. Va. Colonel. 30 Dec. 1851. 8487 acres.
Aimes, Joseph. N.C. Private. 2 Aug. 1784. 640 acres to Thomas Aimes, heir.
Aimes, Thomas. N.C. Private. 2 Aug. 1784. 640 acres.
Airs, Francis. Va. Private. 15 Jun. 1807. 100 acres.
Airs, George. Mass. Matross. 15 Jan. 1834. 200 acres.
Airs, John. Mass. Private. 1 Mar. 1833. 200 acres.
Aitkin, Robert. Pa. Sergeant. 12 Feb. 1803. 250 acres to Martin Reiley, devisee.
Ajaton, John. N.C. Sergeant. 12 Mar. 1785. 1000 acres to heirs.
Akely, John. Pa. ———. 17 Feb. 1803. 200 acres.
Akely, John. Pa. ———. 14 May 1806. 200 acres.
Aken, Joel. Va. Private. 19 Apr. 1784. 100 acres.
Akerman, William. N. Y. Matross. 9 Jul. 1790. 600 acres.
Akers, Simon. Va. Private. 16 Feb. 1801. 100 acres.
Akinclas, Absalom. N.C. Private. 2 Feb. 1786. 274 acres.
Akins, Gideon. N.C. Non Commissioned Officer. 19 May 1784. 1000 acres.
Akins, James. N. Y. Matross. 9 Jul. 1790. 500 acres.
Akins, John. Ga. Minute Man. ———. 287 1/2 acres.
Akridge, William. Ga. Refugee. 22 Mar. 1785. 250 acres.
Albee, John E. Mass. Private. 19 Nov. 1832. 200 acres to heirs.
Albee, Jonathan. Me. Private. 8 Jun. 1835. 200 acres. Lexington.
Alberson, William. S.C. ———. 2 Jan. 1797. 200 acres to Mary Masfield, widow and heir.
Albert, Jacob. Pa. Private. ———. 200 acres.
Albertson, Caleb. N.C. Private. 6 Sep. 1821. 640 acres.
Alberty, Frederick. N.C. Ensign. 3 Dec. 1813. 731 acres.
Alberty, Frederick. N.C. Ensign. 23 Jan. 1818. 1098 acres.
Albright, Jacob. N. Y. Private. 3 Jul. 1790. 600 acres.
Albright, James. N.C. Private. 30 Sep. 1785. 640 acres to heirs.
Albright, John. N. Y. Corporal. 8 Jul. 1790. 600 acres.
Albright, John. Pa. Private. ———. 200 acres.
Albright, Simon. N.C. Private. 1 Dec. 1789. 640 acres to heirs.
Albritton, Henry. N.C. Private. 29 Sep. 1784. 640 acres.
Albrooks, Andrew. N.C. Private. 7 Dec. 1797. 640 acres.
Alden, Humphrey. Mass. Private. 27 Oct. 1835. 200 acres.
Alderson, John. Va. Private. 1 Apr. 1797. 200 acres.
Alderson, Simon. N.C. Sergeant. 26 Aug. 1785. 1000 acres.
Alderson, Simon. N.C. Captain. 29 Oct. 1821. 1097 acres to heirs.
Aldin, James. Va. Private. 16 Jan. 1786. 100 acres.
Aldin, Samuel. Va. Private. 16 Jan. 1786. 100 acres.
Aldred, Henry. Va. Private. 9 Aug. 1806. 100 acres.
Aldrich, Gustavus. Mass. ———. 8 Jul. 1832. 200 acres.
Aldridge, James. Ga. ———. 20 Feb. 1784. 250 acres.
Aldridge, John. Va. Private. 7 Apr. 1787. 100 acres.
Aldridge, Joseph. N.C. Private. 13 Nov. 1795. 274 acres.
Aldridge, Joseph. Pa. Private. 30 Jan. 1787. 200 acres.

Aldridge, Nathan. Md. Private. ———. 50 acres.
Aldridge, Richard. Va. Private. 6 Feb. 1787. 100 acres.
Aldridge, William. N.C. Private. 26 Apr. 1784. 228 acres.
Aldrige, James. Va. Private. 22 Dec. 1783. 100 acres.
Aleworth, James. Va. Private. 15 Jun. 1807. 100 acres.
Alexander, Adam. Ga. Surgeon. ———. 500 acres.
Alexander, Archibald. Va. Surgeon. 24 Jul. 1824. 2000 acres.
Alexander, Archibald. Va. Surgeon. 24 Jul. 1824. 2000 acres.
Alexander, Archibald. Va. Surgeon. 24 Jul. 1824. 2000 acres.
Alexander, Archibald. Va. Surgeon. 4 Aug. 1859. 1171 2/3 acres.
Alexander, Asa. Ga. Refugee. 18 Sep. 1784. 287 1/2 acres.
Alexander, Benjamin. N.C. Private. 1 Dec. 1797. 274 acres.
Alexander, Charles. N.C. Lieutenant. 27 Apr. 1784. 914 acres.
Alexander, Ellis. Va. Private. 18 Apr. 1783. 200 acres.
Alexander, Ezekiel. Ga. ———. 17 May 1784. ———.
Alexander, George Dent. Va. Surgeon. 9 Jun. 1784. 6000 acres.
Alexander, George Dent. Va. Surgeon. 6 Dec. 1834. 83 acres.
Alexander, George Dent. Va. Surgeon. 23 May 1835. 83 acres.
Alexander, George Dent. Va. Surgeon. 22 May 1841. 141 5/6 acres.
Alexander, George Dent. Va. Surgeon. 22 May 1841. 141 5/6 acres.
Alexander, George Dent. Va. Surgeon. 17 Sep. 1841. 201 1/3 acres.
Alexander, George Dent. Va. Surgeon. 17 Sep. 1841. 201 1/3 acres.
Alexander, Hugh. Ga. Lieutenant. 17 May 1784. ———.
Alexander, Isaac. N.C. Private. 6 Dec. 1797. 640 acres to heirs.
Alexander, James. Ga. Soldier. 15 Mar. 1784. 250 acres.
Alexander, James. Pa. ———. 27 Oct. ———. 200 acres.
Alexander, James. Va. Private. 3 Sep. 1784. 100 acres.
Alexander, James. Va. Corporal. 24 May 1786. 200 acres.
Alexander, John L. Ga. ———. 17 May 1784. ———.
Alexander, Joseph. N.C. Private. 2 Feb. 1786. 640 acres to heirs.
Alexander, Levi. N.C. Private. 28 Sep. 1785. 640 acres to widow.
Alexander, Morgan. Va. Colonel. 13 Jan. 1834. 6666 2/3 acres.
Alexander, Nathaniel. N.C. Sergeant. 30 Apr. 1784. 1000 acres.
Alexander, Robert. Ga. Minute Man. ———. ———.
Alexander, Ruebin. N.C. Private. 22 Dec. 1796. 640 acres to heirs.
Alexander, Samuel. Ga. Captain. 15 Mar. 1784. 500 acres.
Alexander, Thomas. N.C. Private. 22 Dec. 1796. 640 acres to heirs.
Alexander, Thomas. Pa. Matross. 19 May 1787. 200 acres.
Alexander, William. Ga. ———. 5 May 1785. ———.
Alexander, William. N.C. Lieutenant. 24 Oct. 1783. 2560 acres.
Alexander, William. N.C. ———. 21 Dec. 1787. 200 acres.
Alexander, William. N.C. ———. 21 Dec. 1787. 200 acres.
Alexander, William. N.C. ———. 21 Dec. 1787. 200 acres.
Alexander, William. N.C. ———. 21 Dec. 1787. 200 acres.
Alexander, William. N.C. ———. 21 Dec. 1787. 200 acres.
Alexander, William. Pa. Major. ———. 300 acres.
Alexander, William. Pa. Major. ———. 300 acres.
Alexander, William. Va. Private. 27 May 1783. 100 acres.
Alexon, Peter. N.C. Private. 29 Sep. 1784. 640 acres.
Alford, Jacob. Va. Private. 12 Jan. 1784. 100 acres.
Alford, James. Ga. ———. 17 May 1784. ———.
Alford, John. N.C. Private. 12 Sep. 1785. 640 acres to heirs.
Alford, John. Va. Private. 24 May 1784. 200 acres.
Alger, William B. Conn. Sufferer. Danbury. 19.7.4.

Alkead, Vernon. N.C. Private. 1 Sep. 1785. 640 acres to heirs.
Alkyser, George. N. Y. Corporal. 8 Jul. 1790. 600 acres.
Alld, William. Me. Private. 14 Jan. 1845. 200 acres to widow Hannah (Kent) Clark, widow of Joseph Clark. Hollis.
Allen, Abiah. Conn. Sufferer. New/East Haven. 13.13.7.
Allen, Amassy. N. Y. Private. 8 Jul. 1790. 500 acres.
Allen, Amos. Me. Private. 6 Jul. 1835. 200 acres. Dresden.
Allen, Benjamin. Conn. Sufferer. Fairfield. 5.3.3.
Allen, Charles. Ga. ———. 7 Jun. 1785. 287 1/2 acres.
Allen, Charles. N.C. Captain. 17 Oct. 1783. 1,695 acres.
Allen, Christopher. Conn. Sufferer. New/East Haven. 6.16.3.
Allen, Daniel. Me. ———. 27 Apr. 1835. 200 acres. Bowdoin.
Allen, Daniel. Me. Sergeant. 27 Apr. 1835. 200 acres. Winthrop.
Allen, Daniel. Va. Private. 20 Dec. 1784. 200 acres.
Allen, David. Va.-Ind. Private. 108 acres.
Allen, David. N.C. Private. 27 Mar. 1821. 640 acres to heirs.
Allen, David. Va. Lieutenant. 30 Nov. 1782. 2000 acres.
Allen, David. Va. Lieutenant. 30 Nov. 1782. 666 2/3 acres.
Allen, David. Va. Corporal. 3 Jun. 1784. 200 acres.
Allen, David. Va. Private. 21 May 1823. 100 acres.
Allen, David. Conn. Sufferer. Fairfield. 476.9.8.
Allen, Edward. S.C. Captain. 3 Mar. 1800. 222 acres.
Allen, Edward. S.C. Captain. 3 Mar. 1800. 200 acres.
Allen, Edward. Va. Lieutenant. 22 Nov. 1783. 2666 2/3 acres.
Allen, Edward. Va. Lieutenant. 16 Jan. 1834. 703 acres.
Allen, Emanuel. Md. Private. ———. 50 acres.
Allen, Francis. Va. Corporal. 3 Feb. 1784. 200 acres.
Allen, George. Mass. Sergeant. 2 Mar. 1833. 200 acres.
Allen, George. N. Y. Matross. 9 Jul. 1790. 600 acres.
Allen, George. Conn. Sufferer. Fairfield. 231.3.11.
Allen, Hezekiah Peter. Me. ———. 23 May 1835. 200 acres to Susannah Allen. Bowdoinham.
Allen, Isaac. Me. ———. 5 Jun. 1835. 200 acres. Minot.
Allen, Jacob. Me. ———. 18 Jun. 1835. 200 acres. Scarborough.
Allen, James. Ga. ———. 15 Mar. 1784. 250 acres.
Allen, James. Md. Private. ———. 50 acres.
Allen, James. N.C. ———. 3 Feb. 1785. 640 acres to heir.
Allen, Jeremiah. Mass. Private. 1 Dec. 1830. 200 acres.
Allen, Jesse. N.C. Private. 17 Dec. 1785. 228 acres.
Allen, John. Ga. ———. 30 Sep. 1784. ———.
Allen, John. Me. Private. 19 Aug. 1835. 200 acres to widow Eunice Allen. Thomaston.
Allen, John. Mass. Private. 13 Jan. 1834. 200 acres.
Allen, John. N. Y. Private. 7 Jul. 1790. 600 acres.
Allen, John. N.C. Captain. 15 Dec. 1783. 1600 acres.
Allen, John. N.C. Private. 10 Sep. 1821. 640 acres to heirs.
Allen, John. Pa. ———. 27 Aug. 1807. 200 acres to Susanna Allen, widow.
Allen, John. Va. Private. 22 Mar. 1784. 100 acres.
Allen, John. Va. Private. 2 Jul. 1784. 100 acres.
Allen, John. Va. Captain. 21 Dec. 1784. 1500 acres.
Allen, John. Va. Captain. 21 Dec. 1784. 2500 acres.
Allen, John. Va. Private. 16 Jul. 1819. 100 acres.
Allen, John. Va. Sergeant. 11 Mar. 1840. 200 acres.
Allen, John. Conn. Sufferer. Fairfield. 545.12.6.
Allen, John. Conn. Sufferer. New/East Haven. 15.17.6.
Allen, Joseph. Me. ———. 23 Jun. 1835. 200 acres. Gray.

Allen, Joseph. N.C. Private. 15 Dec. 1797. 640 acres to heirs.
Allen, Joseph. Va. Private. 17 Jun. 1783. 100 acres.
Allen, Moses. Va. Private. 9 Jul. 1783. 100 acres.
Allen, Moses (son of Rev. M.). Ga. ———. 1784. 500 acres.
Allen, Oliver. Conn. Sufferer. New/East Haven. 40.18.0.
Allen, Patrick. Ga. ———. 17 May 1784. ——— to heirs.
Allen, Philip. Conn. Sufferer. New London. 9.15.5 1/2.
Allen, Reuben. Va. Sergeant. 19 Jul. 1783. 466 2/3 acres.
Allen, Robert. Ga. ———. 27 May 1784. ———.
Allen, Samuel. N.C. Private. 27 Mar. 1821. 640 acres to heirs.
Allen, Samuel. Pa. Private. 6 Nov. 1786. 200 acres.
Allen, Thomas. Ga. ———. 17 May 1784. 287 1/2 acres.
Allen, Thomas. N.C. Sergeant. 2 Feb. 1784. 2560 acres to John Allen, administrator.
Allen, Thomas. N.C. Lieutenant. 13 Jun. 1785. 2560 acres to John Allen, heir.
Allen, Thomas. N.C. Private. 12 Sep. 1785. 640 acres to heirs.
Allen, Thomas. Va. Private. 28 Feb. 1783. 100 acres.
Allen, Thomas. Va. Boatswain. 28 Nov. 1783. 200 acres.
Allen, Thomas. Va. Sergeant. 26 Jul. 1785. 200 acres.
Allen, Thomas. Va. ———. 12 Nov. 1832. 2466 2/3 acres.
Allen, Thomas. Va. ———. 2 Aug. 1833. 493 1/3 acres.
Allen, Thomas. Va. ———. 2 Aug. 1833. 493 1/3 acres.
Allen, Thomas. Va. ———. 2 Aug. 1833. 493 1/3 acres.
Allen, Thomas. Va. ———. 2 Aug. 1833. 493 1/3 acres.
Allen, Thomas. Va. ———. 2 Aug. 1833. 493 1/3 acres.
Allen, Walter. N.C. Sergeant. 2 Feb. 1784. 912 acres.
Allen, William. Ga. Soldier. ———. ———.
Allen, William. Me. ———. 27 Apr. 1835. 200 acres. China.
Allen, William. Me. ———. 27 Apr. 1835. 200 acres to widow Jane Allen. China.
Allen, William. Md. Matross. ———. 50 acres.
Allen, William. N.C. Private. 28 Sep. 1785. 640 acres to heirs.
Allen, William. Va. Private. 15 Oct. 1810. 100 acres.
Allen, Wright. Me. ———. 8 Aug. 1834. 200 acres to widow Ruth Allen. Denmark.
Allentharpe, John. N.C. ———. 18 Jun. 1785. 640 acres to heirs.
Allery, Joseph. Va. Private. 31 Dec. 1851. 100 acres.
Allery, Joseph. Va. Private. 2 Apr. 1856. 100 acres.
Alley, Barnet. Md. Private. ———. 50 acres.
Alley, Ephraim. Me. ———. 16 May 1835. 200 acres. Boothbay.
Alligood, Henry. N.C. Private. 29 Sep. 1784. 640 acres to heirs.
Alligree, William. Va. Private. 13 Dec. 1788. 200 acres.
Alling, Ebenezer. Conn. Sufferer. New/East Haven. 16.0.6.
Alling, Hezekiah. Conn. Sufferer. New/ East Haven. 11.14.0.
Alling, Ichabod. N. Y. Matross. 9 Jul. 1790. 600 acres.
Alling, James. Conn. Sufferer. New/East Haven. 12.0.6.
Alling, John. N. Y. Matross. 9 Jul. 1790. 600 acres.
Alling, Joseph. Conn. Sufferer. New/East Haven. 4.7.0.
Alling, Lorrain. Conn. Sufferer. New/East Haven. 4.15.8.
Alling, Samuel. Conn. Sufferer. New/East Haven. 20.10.0.
Allinson, Henry. Ga. ———. 25 May 1784. 287 1/2 acres.
Allison, Andrew. N.C. Private. 25 Oct. 1783. 640 acres.
Allison, Henry. Ga. Lieutenant. ———. 450 acres.
Allison, James. Ga. Refugee. 15 Mar. 1784. 250 acres.
Allison, James. Pa. Private. 9 Mar. 1795. 200 acres to John Nicholson, assignee.

Allison, John. Va. Lieutenant Colonel. 2 Apr. 1834. 1013 2/3 acres.

Allison, John. Va. Lieutenant Colonel. 15 May 1838. 135 1/4 acres.

Allison, John. Va. Lieutenant Colonel. 15 May 1838. 405 3/4 acres.

Allison, Joseph. S.C. ———. 7 Sep 1795. 200 acres.

Allison, Richard. Pa. Surgeon's Mate. 5 Apr. 1787. 300 acres.

Allison, Robert. Pa. Lieutenant. 13 Aug.1787. 200 acres.

Allison, Robert. Pa. Private. 13 Aug. 1787. 200 acres.

Allison, Thomas. Md. Private. ———. 50 acres.

Allman, Joshua. N.C. Private. 30 Sep. 1785. 274 acres to heirs.

Allman, William. Va. Private. 4 Mar. 1813. 100 acres.

Allman, William. Va. Gunner. 12 Nov. 1832. 2566 2/3 acres.

Allwine, Barnet. Pa. Private. 10 Sep. 1789. 200 acres.

Ally, William. Conn. Sufferer. New/East Haven. 9.4.6.

Alman, William. Va. Gunner. 22 Nov. 1783. 200 acres.

Almand, John. Va. Sailor. 19 Dec. 1783. 100 acres.

Almond, John. Va. Private. 4 Mar. 1813. 100 acres.

Alport, John. N. Y. Private. 3 Jul. 1790. 600 acres.

Alsberry, Thomas. Va. Drummer. 16 Feb. 1801. 100 acres.

Alsobron, William John. N.C. Private. 2 Feb. 1786. 640 acres.

Alston, William. N.C. Lieutenant Colonel. 14 Dec. 1796. 1646 acres to heirs Jno. Jos. Alston, Wm Chy Aston, & Owen Davis Aston.

Altman, Garret. N.C. Private. 19 Jan. 1786. 640 acres.

Altop, Thomas. Va. Private. 27 Aug. 1783. 200 acres.

Alva, Robert. Va. Private. 22 Dec. 1783. 100 acres.

Alverson, James. Va. Private. 28 Mar. 1812. 100 acres.

Alvey, John. Md. Private. ———. 50 acres.

Alvey, Josias. Md. Private. ———. 50 acres.

Alvey, Thomas G. Md. Private. ———. 50 acres.

Alvey, Travers. Md. Private. ———. 50 acres.

Alvoid, G. Thomas, Sr. N. Y. Sergeant. 9 Jul. 1790. 500 acres.

Alvoid, G. Thomas, Jr. N. Y. Gunner. 9 Jul. 1790. 500 acres.

Alvord, Mary. Conn. Sufferer. Fairfield. 20.0.0.

Alvord, Mary. Conn. Sufferer. Fairfield. 8.0.0.

Amanda, Ambrose. Va. Gunner. 6 Dec. 1856. 2666 2/3 acres.

Amberson, James. Va. Private. 23 Jun. 1783. 200 acres.

Ambler, John. Ga. Minute Man. 3 Sep. 1785. ———.

Ambrose, David. N.C. Non Commissioned Officer. 19 May 1784. 1000 acres.

Ames, Elisha. Mass. Private. 13 Dec. 1831. 200 acres.

Ames, Samuel. Me. Musician. 7 May 1835. 200 acres. Norway.

Amey, John. N.C. Private. 9 Feb. 1796. 228 acres.

Amey, Lincoln. N.C. Private. 9 Feb. 1796. 228 acres.

Amick, Conrad. S.C. ———. 6 Aug. 1787. 200 acres.

Amis, John. N.C. Private. 10 Jun. 1808. 640 acres to heirs.

Amlane, Baptiste. N. Y. ———. ———. 500 acres.

Ammerman, Cornelius. N. Y. Corporal. 8 Jul. 1790. 500 acres.

Ammins, James. N.C. Private. 27 Mar. 1821. 640 acres.

Ammond, Peter. Va. Private. 5 Feb. 1785. 233 1/3 acres.

Ammons, Jesse. Ga. Minute Man. 3 Sep. 1785. ———.

Ammons, Robert. Ga. Minute Man. 29 Jul. 1874. 287 1/2 acres.

Ammons, William. Ga. Minute Man. 22 Mar. 1785. 250 acres.

Ammonson, Eli. Ga. ———. 17 May 1784. ———.

Ammorman, James. N. Y. ———. 13 Sep. 1790. 500 acres to heirs.

Amonile, Daniel. Va. Private. 27 Apr. 1784. 100 acres.

Amos, James. N.C. Private. 27 Jul. 1785. 640 acres.

Amos, John. Ga. ———. 17 May 1784. ———.

Anders, Henry. Va. Private. 21 Apr. 1784. 100 acres.

Anderson, Abraham. Pa. Private. 20 Sep. 1787. 200 acres.

Anderson, Adam. Va. Private. 20 Feb. 1784. 100 acres.

Anderson, Alexander. Ga. Private. 25 May 1784. 287 1/2 acres.

Anderson, Alexander. N. Y. Fifer. 8 Jul. 1790. 500 acres.

Anderson, Archibald. Md. Major. ———. 200 acres.

Anderson, Bailey. N.C. Private. 6 Dec. 1797. 640 acres to heirs.

Anderson, Baletha. N.C. Private. 2 Feb. 1786. 640 acres.

Anderson, Bartlett. Ga. Refugee. 24 May 1784. 287 1/2 acres.

Anderson, Charles. N.C. Private. 1 Sep. 1785. 640 acres to heirs.

Anderson, Charles. Va. Sergeant. 7 May 1783. 200 acres.

Anderson, Daniel. Md. Private. ———. 50 acres.

Anderson, Daniel. Va. Private. 20 Jun. 1783. 100 acres.

Anderson, David. S.C. Soldier. 21 Jan. 1785. 200 acres.

Anderson, David. Va. Private. 29 May 1819. 100 acres.

Anderson, Edmund. Ga. Soldier. ———. ———.

Anderson, Elijah. Ga. Refugee. 24 May 1784. 287 1/2 acres.

Anderson, Elisha. Ga. ———. 17 May 1784. ———.

Anderson, Ezekiel. Ga. ———. 17 May 1784. ———.

Anderson, George. Pa. Private. 1 Nov. 1786. 200 acres.

Anderson, Gideon. Ga. ———. 17 May 1784. ———.

Anderson, Henry. Ga. Minute Man. 24 May 1784. 287 1/2 acres.

Anderson, Henry. Va. Private. 23 Jun. 1783. 100 acres.

Anderson, Henry. Va. Drum Major. 31 Jan. 1784. 200 acres.

Anderson, Hugh. Ga. Minute Man. 3 Oct. 1783. ———.

Anderson, Isaac. N.C. Private. Nov. 1788. 183 acres.

Anderson, Isaac. Va. Private. 12 Mar. 1783. 100 acres.

Anderson, Isaac. Va. Private. 8 May 1783. 200 acres.

Anderson, Isaac. Conn. Sufferer. Greenwich. 44.10.0 1/2.

Anderson, James. Ga. Lieutenant. 26 May 1784. 460 acres.

Anderson, James. N.C. Private. 21 Apr. 1784. 640 acres to Willoughby Williams, heir.

Anderson, James. N.C. Drum Major. 15 Aug. 1823. 1000 acres.

Anderson, James. Va. Private. 19 Jun. 1783. 200 acres.

Anderson, James. Va. Private. 19 Jun. 1783. 100 acres.

Anderson, James. Va. Private. 20 Feb. 1784. 200 acres.

Anderson, John. Ga. Private. 14 Jul 1784. 287 1/2 acres.

Anderson, John. Md. Private. ———. 50 acres.

Anderson, John. Md. Private. ———. 50 acres.

Anderson, John. N. Y. Matross. 9 Jul. 1790. 500 acres.

Anderson, John. N.C. Private. 27 Aug. 1784. 640 acres.

Anderson, John. N.C. Private. 3 Feb. 1785. 640 acres to heirs.

Anderson, John. N.C. Private. 13 Jan. 1792. 640 acres to heirs.

Anderson, John. Va. Private. 20 Jun. 1783. 100 acres.

Anderson, John. Va. Sergeant. 6 Nov. 1783. 200 acres.

Anderson, John. Va. Captain. 2 Feb. 1784. 4666 2/3 acres.

Anderson, John. Va. Captain. 11 Sep. 1809. 555 acres.

Anderson, John Leonard. S.C. ———. 5 Jun. 1797. 200 acres.

Anderson, Jordan. Va. Private. 29 May 1819. 100 acres.

Anderson, Joseph. Ga. Refugee. ———. ———.

Anderson, Joseph. Va.-Ind. Private. 108 acres.

Anderson, Matthew. Va. Private. 13 May 1783. 100 acres.

Anderson, Michael. Md. Private. ———. 50 acres.

Anderson, Nathaniel. Va. Lieutenant. 12 Jan. 1784. 666 2/3 acres.

Anderson, Peter. Ga. Soldier. 4 Feb. 1785. ———.

Anderson, Philip. Ga. ———. 17 May 1784. ———.

Anderson, Richard. Ga. Soldier. 4 Oct. 1785. ———.

Anderson, Richard. Md. Captain. ———. 200 acres.

Anderson, Richard. Va. Private. 31 Oct. 1783. 100 acres.

Anderson, Richard C. Va. Lieutenant Colonel. 6 Dec. 1784. 6000 acres.

Anderson, Richard C. Va. Lieutenant Colonel. 14 Nov. 1794. 1000 acres.

Anderson, Richard C. Va. Lieutenant Colonel. 21 Nov. 1808. 833 1/3 acres.

Anderson, Robert. Va. Private. 28 May 1783. 100 acres.

Anderson, Samuel. Ga. ———. 17 May 1784. ———.

Anderson, Samuel. N. Y. Private. 8 Jul. 1790. 600 acres.

Anderson, Simmer. Ga. Minute Man. 3 Sep. 1785. ———.

Anderson, Thomas. N.C. Private. 29 Sep. 1784. 640 acres.

Anderson, Thomas. Pa. Private. ———. 200 acres.

Anderson, William. Ga. Soldier. 17 May 1784. 250 acres.

Anderson, William. Ga. Soldier. 17 May 1784. ———.

Anderson, William. N.C. Private. 20 Apr. 1784. 640 acres.

Anderson, William. N.C. Sergeant. 26 Nov. 1796. 425 acres.

Anderson, William. Va. Sergeant. 12 Jan. 1784. 200 acres.

Anderson, William. Va. Private. 31 Jan. 1784. 100 acres.

Anderson, William. Va. Private. 29 Mar. 1784. 200 acres.

Anderson, William. Va. Private. 1 Apr. 1784. 100 acres.

Anderson, William. Va. Private. 20 Feb. 1795. 100 acres.

Anderson, William. Va. Private. 3 Mar. 1808. 200 acres.

Anderson, Willis. N.C. Private. 9 Feb. 1796. 640 acres to heirs.

Anderton, Isaac. Va. Private. 2 Sep. 1783. 100 acres.

Anderton, John. Va. Private. 2 Sep. 1783. 100 acres.

Anderton, Ralph. Va. Private. 30 Jan. 1784. 100 acres.

Andress, William. Va. Private. 15 Jan. 1808. 261 acres.

Andrew, Abiel. N.C. Private. 1 Aug. 1821. 640 acres.

Andrew, John. Pa. Private. 21 Feb. 1787. 200 acres.

Andrews, Adam. Va. Private. 20 Feb. 1784. 100 acres.

Andrews, Alfred. N.C. Private. 6 Dec. 1796. 228 acres.

Andrews, Benjamin. Va. Sergeant. 29 Aug. 1783. 200 acres.

Andrews, Benjamin, Jr. Ga. Refugee. 30 Jul. 1784. 287 1/2 acres.

Andrews, Claibourne. Va. Private. 20 Jun. 1783. 100 acres.

Andrews, Eleany. Va. Seaman. 30 Jul. 1831. 100 acres.

Andrews, Ephraim. Va. Private. 3 Mar. 1808. 100 acres.

Andrews, Francis. Ga. Soldier. 19 Dec. 1785. 230 acres.

Andrews, Jesse. Va. Sergeant. 11 Aug. 1783. 200 acres.

Andrews, John. Ga. Refugee. 15 Jul. 1784. 287 1/2 acres.

Andrews, John. Me. ———. 3 Jul. 1835. 200 acres to widow Betsey Andrews.

Andrews, John. Md. Private. ———. 50 acres.

Andrews, John. N.C. Private. 22 Apr. 1785. 640 acres.

Andrews, John. Pa. ———. 7 Feb. 1804. 200 acres to William Whitman, assignee.

Andrews, Moses. Va. Private. 14 Jun. 1786. 200 acres.

Andrews, Richard. N.C. Lieutenant. 22 Oct. 1783. 2200 acres.

Andrews, Robert. Va. Chaplain. 17 May 1833. 1500 acres.

Andrews, Robert. Va. Chaplain. 17 May 1833. 1500 acres.

Andrews, Robert. Va. Chaplain. 17 May 1833. 1500 acres.

Andrews, Robert. Va. Chaplain. 17 May 1833. 1500 acres.

Andrews, Samuel. Ga. Citizen. 1 Aug. 1785. 287 1/2 acres.

Andrews, Samuel E. Me. ———. 7 Aug. 1838. 200 acres to widow Hannah (Elden) Andrews. Lovell.
Andrews, Thomas. N.C. Private. 12 Sep. 1785. 640 acres.
Andrews, Watson. N.C. Private. 8 Mar. 1796. 640 acres to heirs.
Andrews, William. Va. Sergeant. 12 Jan. 1784. 100 acres.
Andrews, William. Va. Sergeant. 15 Jun. 1807. 200 acres.
Andrews, William. Va. Seaman. 30 Jul. 1783. 100 acres.
Andrus, Abigail. Conn. Sufferer. New/East Haven. 2.8.6.
Andrus, Abraham. Conn. Sufferer. Fairfield. 430.6.0.
Andrus, Hannah. Conn. Sufferer. Danbury. 15.8.0.
Andrus, Jedediah. Conn. Sufferer. New/East Haven. 9.11.7.
Andrus, Phineas. Conn. Sufferer. New/East Haven. 18.17.6.
Andrus, Samuel. Conn. Sufferer. Danbury. 8.8.0.
Andrus, Sarah. Conn. Sufferer. Fairfield. 192.9.0.
Andsley, Abel. Ga. ———. 17 May 1784. ———.
Angel, Baker. Va. Sailor. 3 Dec. 1783. 100 acres.
Angel, James. Va. Drummer. 22 Jul. 1783. 100 acres.
Angel, James. Conn. Sufferer. New London. 169.2.2.
Angel, John. Va. Private. 2 May 1783. 200 acres.
Angel, Robert. Va. Private. 27 May 1783. 100 acres.
Angel, Thomas. N.C. Private. 22 Oct. 1783. 274 acres.
Angel, William. Va. Private. 31 Jul. 1783. 100 acres.
Angel, William. Va. Sailor. 8 Sep. 1783. 100 acres.
Angelly, Alexander. Ga. ———. 1784. 287 1/2 acres.
Anger, George. S.C. ———. 1 Apr. 1793. 192 acres.
Angle, Benjamin. N.C. Private. 2 Dec. 1785. 640 acres.
Anglin, Cornelius. N.C. Private. 12 Feb. 1784. 640 acres to heir.
Anglin, David. Ga. Soldier. 15 Mar. 1784. 250 acres.
Anglin, Henry. Ga. ———. 15 Mar. 1784. 250 acres.
Anglin, Isaac. Va. Private. 7 Nov. 1783. 100 acres.
Anglin, James. Va. Private. 15 Jun. 1807. 100 acres.
Anglin, John. Ga. Citizen. 6 Apr. 1785. 287 1/2 acres.
Anglin, Levi. Va. Private. 15 Jun. 1807. 200 acres.
Anglin, Micajah. Va. Private. 15 Jun. 1807. 100 acres.
Anglin, William. Ga. Soldier. 15 Mar. 1784. 250 acres.
Anguine, Anthony. Conn. Sufferer. Danbury. 3.6.0.
Anniball, Anthony. Conn. Sufferer. Fairfield. 155.5.2.
Annible, David. Conn. Sufferer. Fairfield. 43.18.10.
Ansgood, Thomas. N.C. Private. 28 Nov. 1795. 640 acres to heirs.
Ansley, Samuel. Ga. ———. 17 May 1784. ———.
Ansley, Thomas, Jr. Ga. Refugee. Sep. 1785. ———.
Ansley, Thomas, Sr. Ga. Refugee. Sep. 1785. ———.
Ansley, William. Ga. ———. 17 May 1784. ———.
Anspach, Peter. N. Y. Lieutenant. 9 Jul. 1790. 1200 acres.
Anthoney, James. N.C. Private. 24 May 1784. 640 acres.
Anthony, DeMarcelllan. Pa. Lieutenant. 20 May 1787. 200 acres.
Anthony, Francis. N. Y. ———. 13 Sep. 1790. 500 acres to heirs.
Anthony, John. N. Y. Private. 8 Jul. 1790. 600 acres.
Anthony, John. N.C. Private. 9 Feb. 1796. 640 acres to heirs.
Anthony, John. Va. Private. 7 May 1784. 200 acres.
Anthony, Joseph. Ga. ———. 17 May 1784. ———.
Anthony, Micajah. Ga. ———. 17 May 1784. ———.
Anthony, Nathan. Va. Private. 30 Jul. 1807. 100 acres.
Anthony, Peter. N. Y. Private. 8 Jul. 1790. 600 acres.

Antill, Edward. N. Y. Lieutenant Colonel. ———. 1000 acres.
Antill, Jacob. Va. Private. 13 Dec. 1786. 100 acres.
Antrim, John. Pa. Private. 28 Nov. 1786. 200 acres.
Aorson, Aaron. N. Y. Captain. 9 Jul. 1790. 1800 acres.
Apleton, John. N.C. Sergeant. 2 Feb. 1786. 1000 acres.
Apley, Jacob. N.C. Private. 2 Feb. 1795. 640 acres to heirs.
Apperson, Richard. Va. Captain. 15 Jan. 1807. 4666 2/3 acres.
Apperson, William. N.C. ———. 21 Apr. 1784. 228 acres.
Appleby, John. Md. Private. ———. 50 acres.
Appleby, Samuel. Va. Private. 30 May 1792. 200 acres.
Appleby, Thomas. Pa. Private. 28 Mar. 1809. 200 acres.
Applewhaite, John. Va. Surgeon. 7 Mar. 1834. 6000 acres.
Applewhaite, John. Va. Surgeon. 19 Aug. 1835. 5000 acres.
Applewhatie, John. Va. Surgeon. 19 Aug. 1835. 1000 acres.
Applewhite, Abraham. N.C. Private. 30 Sep. 1785. 640 acres to heirs.
Applewhite, Jesse. N.C. Private. 30 Sep. 1785. 640 acres to heirs.
Applewhite, John. N.C. Private. 30 Sep. 1785. 640 acres to heirs.
Appling, Daniel. Ga. Refugee. 23 Jul 1784. 287 1/2 acres.
Appling, John. Ga. Soldier. 23 Jul. 1784. 287 1/2 acres.
Arbor, Michael. N. Y. ———. ———. 500 acres.
Arbuckle, Matthew. Va. Captain. 19 Dec. 1799. 4000 acres.
Arbuckle, William. Va. Private. 29 Aug. 1807. 100 acres.
Archer, Benjamin. Va. Sergeant. 6 Apr. 1787. 100 acres.
Archer, Benjamin. Va. Sergeant. 16 Apr. 1812. 200 acres.
Archer, Dempsey. N.C. Private. 30 Sep. 1785. 640 acres to heirs.
Archer, Demsey. N.C. Private. 22 Oct. 1783. 640 acres to Baker Archer, heir.
Archer, Henry W. Pa. Captain. 28 Aug. 1787. 500 acres.
Archer, Isaac. Va. Private. 3 Apr. 1783. 200 acres.
Archer, Jeremiah. Va. Private. 28 Aug. 1786. 100 acres.
Archer, Jesse. N.C. Private. 22 Oct. 1783. 640 acres to Baker Archer, heir.
Archer, John. Va. Lieutenant. 8 Nov. 1832. 4000 acres.
Archer, Joseph. Va. Lieutenant. 13 Dec. 1782. 2666 2/3 acres.
Archer, Joseph. Va. Lieutenant. 19 Mar. 1834. 593 acres.
Archer, Peter Field. Va. Lieutenant. 13 Dec. 1782. 2666 2/3 acres.
Archer, Richard. Va. Subaltern. 24 Feb. 1784. 2666 2/3 acres.
Archer, Robert. Va. Private. 7 May 1784. 100 acres.
Archer, Stephen. Pa. Private. 29 Mar. 1803. 200 acres.
Arden, Jeffery. N.C. Private. 9 Feb. 1796. 228 acres.
Arlist, John. N.C. Private. 17 Dec. 1785. 274 acres.
Armistead, Adam. Va. Private. 28 Aug. 1784. 100 acres.
Armistead, Robert. Va. Private. 20 Feb. 1784. 100 acres.
Armistead, Thomas. Va. Captain. 28 Dec. 1782. 4000 acres.
Armistead, Thomas. Va. ———. 23 Feb. 1838. 538 3/4 acres.
Armistead, Thomas. Va. Captain. 21 Feb. 1838. 194 1/4 acres.
Armistead, Thomas. Va. ———. 18 Apr. 1845. 582 3/4 acres.
Armistead, Thomas. Va. Captain. 14 Dec. 1854. 582 3/4 acres.
Armistead, William. Va. Private 20 Nov. 1783. 100 acres.
Armistead, William. Va. Captain. 1 Nov. 1783. 4000 acres.
Armistead, William. Va. Paymaster. 1 Mar. 1851. 4000 acres.
Armond, John. Va. Private. 6 Nov. 1783. 100 acres.
Armond, Thomas. Va. Private. 16 Mar. 1822. 100 acres.
Armor, Andrew. Ga. ———. 17 May 1784. ———.
Armor, John. Ga. ———. 17 May 1784. ———.
Armour, Abigail. Conn. Sufferer. Greenwich. 6.0.0.

Armstong, William. N.C. Captain. 21 Oct. 1783. 3840 acres.
Armstrong, Abel. Va. Private. 27 Apr. 1784. 100 acres.
Armstrong, Adam. N. Y. Fifer. 8 Jul. 1790. 600 acres.
Armstrong, Adam. Va. Private. 31 Jan. 1784. 100 acres.
Armstrong, Adam. Va. Private. 23 Oct. 1784. 200 acres.
Armstrong, Ambrose. Va. Private. 23 Apr. 1784. 100 acres.
Armstrong, Ambrose. Va. Private. 12 Jan. 1842. 100 acres.
Armstrong, Andrew. N.C. Captain. 27 Nov. 1783. 1280 acres.
Armstrong, Archibald. N. Y. Drummer. 8 Jul. 1790. 600 acres.
Armstrong, Archibald. Va. Ensign. 16 Oct. 1798. 2666 2/3 acres.
Armstrong, Edward. Va. Lieutenant. 28 Jul. 1830. 2666 2/3 acres.
Armstrong, Edward. Va. Lieutenant. 28 Nov. 1868. 222 acres.
Armstrong, George. Md. Captain. ———. 200 acres.
Armstrong, James. Md. Chaplain. ———. 200 acres.
Armstrong, James. N.C. Colonel. 22 Oct. 1783. 7200 acres.
Armstrong, James. N.C. Lieutenant. 24 Nov. 1797. 2560 acres to heirs.
Armstrong, James. Pa. Captain. 7 Sep. 1787. 500 acres to Charles J. Delongelhamp, assignee.
Armstrong, James. Va. Private. 26 Mar. 1785. 100 acres.
Armstrong, James. Va. Private. 26 Mar. 1785. 200 acres.
Armstrong, James. Va. Sergeant. 11 Apr. 1786. 400 acres.
Armstrong, James. Va. Captain. 11 Aug. 1795. 4000 acres.
Armstrong, Jesse. Va. Private. 21 May 1784. 200 acres.
Armstrong, Jesse. Va. Matross. 29 Jul. 1834. 100 acres.
Armstrong, Jesse. Va. Matross. 7 Apr. 1835. 100 acres.
Armstrong, Joab. N.C. Private. 13 Dec. 1796. 640 acres to heirs.
Armstrong, John. Md. Private. ———. 50 acres.
Armstrong, John. Md. Private. ———. 50 acres.
Armstrong, John. N. Y. Private. 7 Jul. 1790. 600 acres.
Armstrong, John. N.C. Lieutenant Colonel. 16 Oct. 1783. 5760 acres.
Armstrong, John. Pa. ———. 31 Oct. 1786. 200 acres to Thomas Adams, assignee.
Armstrong, John. Pa. Lieutenant. ———. 200 acres.
Armstrong, John. Pa. Lieutenant. ———. 200 acres.
Armstrong, John. Va. Private. 20 Sep. 1783. 100 acres.
Armstrong, John. Va. Sergeant. 14 Dec. 1797. 200 acres.
Armstrong, John. Va. Private. 18 Apr. 1832. 100 acres.
Armstrong, John, Jr. Pa. Major. ———. 300 acres.
Armstrong, John, Jr. Pa. Major. ———. 300 acres.
Armstrong, Jonathan. N. Y. Private. 8 Jul. 1790. 600 acres.
Armstrong, Robert. Pa. Private. ———. 200 acres.
Armstrong, Thomas. N.C. Captain. 22 Oct. 1783. 3840 acres.
Armstrong, Tobias. Va. Private. 30 Jun. 1783. 200 acres.
Armstrong, William. Pa. Private. ———. 200 acres.
Armsworth, Thomas. N.C. Private. 12 Sep. 1785. 640 acres to heirs.
Arnando, Ambrose. Va. Gunner. 29 May 1788. 2666 2/3 acres.
Arnet, Samuel. S.C. ———. 3 Feb. 1794. 200 acres.
Arno, John. Me. Private. 30 May 1835. 200 acres to widow Meriam Arno. Leeds.
Arnold, Andrew. N.C. Private. 22 Mar. 1784. 640 acres.
Arnold, Arthur. N.C. Private. 1 Aug. 1821. 640 acres.
Arnold, Bewley. Conn. Sufferer. Norwalk. 12.8.0.
Arnold, Charles. Va. Private. 31 Dec. 1787. 100 acres.
Arnold, David. N.C. Private. 2 Dec. 1785. 274 acres.
Arnold, Edward. S.C. ———. 1 Dec. 1788. 180 acres.

Arnold, Elijah. Va. Private. 14 Feb. 1784. 100 acres.
Arnold, Jacob. Conn. Sufferer. Norwalk. 24.11.8.
Arnold, James. Va. Private. 26 Nov. 1783. 100 acres.
Arnold, John. Ga. Refugee. 20 Aug. 1785. ———.
Arnold, John. N.C. Private. 5 Sep. 1821. 640 acres.
Arnold, John. Pa. Sergeant. 15 Jan. 1789. 250 acres to Stephen Loudon, assignee.
Arnold, John. Va. Sergeant. 21 Aug. 1783. 200 acres.
Arnold, Lewis. Va. Private. 26 Nov. 1783. 100 acres.
Arnold, Lindsey. Va. Private. 17 Apr. 1784. 200 acres.
Arnold, Richard. Va. Fifer. 25 Apr. 1837. 100 acres.
Arnold, Robert. Me. Private. 27 Oct. 1835. 200 acres. Starks.
Arnold, Samuel. N.C. Private. 1 Dec. 1796. 640 acres to heirs.
Arnold, Samuel. Va. Sergeant. 21 Feb. 1784. 200 acres.
Arnold, Samuel. Va. Lieutenant. 9 Dec. 1807. 888 2/3 acres.
Arnold, Samuel. Va. Lieutenant. 9 Dec. 1807. 888 2/3 acres.
Arnold, Samuel. Va. Lieutenant. 9 Dec. 1807. 888 2/3 acres.
Arnold, Thomas. N.C. Private. 9 Dec. 1796. 640 acres to heirs.
Arnold, William. Ga. ———. 17 May 1784. ———.
Arnold, William. Va. Corporal. 9 Feb. 1784. 200 acres.
Arnold, William. Va. Private. 20 Jul. 1784. 100 acres.
Arrants, James. Md. Private. ———. 50 acres.
Arrell, David. Va. Captain. 26 Nov. 1785. 4000 acres.
Arriday, William. Ga. ———. 2 May 1785. ———.
Arrington, John. Ga. ———. 20 May 1785. ———.
Arrington, William. Va. Private. 25 Jun. 1783. 200 acres.
Arrowsmith, James. Va. Private. 22 Mar. 1839. 66 2/3 acres.
Arthur, Barnabus. Va. Lieutenant. 7 Nov. 1811. 1000 acres.
Arthur, Barnabus. Va. Lieutenant. 7 Nov. 1811. 1000 acres.
Arthur, Barnabus. Va. Lieutenant. 7 Nov. 1811. 666 2/3 acres.
Arthur, John. Pa. ———. 17 Feb. 1803. 200 acres.
Arthur, John Lawson. N.C. ———. 16 Dec. 1807. 428 acres.
Arthur, Stephen. N.C. Private. 31 Aug. 1795. 640 acres to heirs.
Arthur, Thomas. Md. Private. ———. 50 acres.
Arthur, William. N.C. ———. 10 Aug. 1785. 640 acres.
Artis John. S.C. ———. 4 Jul. 1785. 200 acres.
Artis, Isaac. Va. Private. 15 Jun. 1820. 100 acres.
Artwick, Lawrence. N. Y. Private. 8 Jul. 1790. 600 acres.
Arundel, Dohicky. Va. Captain. 29 Mar. 1837. 300 acres.
Arundel, Dohicky. Va. Captain. 29 Mar. 1837. 500 acres.
Arundel, Dohicky. Va. Captain. 29 Mar. 1837. 800 acres.
Arundel, Dohicky. Va. Captain. 29 Mar. 1837. 800 acres.
Arundel, Dohicky. Va. Captain. 29 Mar. 1837. 800 acres.
Arundel, Dohicky. Va. Captain. 29 Mar. 1837. 800 acres.
Arundel, Dohicky. Va. Captain. 10 Feb. 1838. 812 acres.
Arundel, Dohicky. Va. Captain. 10 Feb. 1838. 270 3/4 acres.
Arundel, Dohicky. Va. Captain. 24 Mar. 1848. 270 3/4 acres.
Arundle, Dohicky. Va. Captain. 11 May 1853. 500 acres.
Asbel, James. N.C. Private. 17 Feb. 1824. 640 acres.
Ash, Henry. N. Y. Matross. 9 Jul. 1790. 500 acres.
Ash, John. Va.-Ind. Private. 108 acres.
Ash, Stephen. N.C. Private. 30 Sep. 1785. 640 acres to heirs.
Ashbrook, Amos. N.C. Private. 8 Dec. 1802. 640 acres to heirs.
Ashburn, Lott. Va. Seaman. 9 Apr. 1835. 100 acres.
Ashburn, Luke. Va. Seaman. 28 Nov. 1783. 100 acres.

Ashbury, John. Md. Private. ———. 50 acres.
Ashbury, Jonathan. Ga. ———. 1784. 250 acres.
Ashby, Benjamin. Va. Lieutenant. 18 Dec. 1783. 2666 2/3 acres.
Ashby, David. Va. Private. 4 May 1833. 200 acres.
Ashby, James. S.C. Soldier. 4 Feb. 1799. 100 acres.
Ashby, James. Va. Sergeant. 4 May 1833. 200 acres.
Ashby, John. Va. Captain. 11 Aug. 1834. 400 acres.
Ashby, John. Va. Captain. 17 Dec. 1834. 400 acres.
Ashby, John. Va. Captain. 17 Dec. 1834. 400 acres.
Ashby, John. Va. Captain. 17 Dec. 1834. 400 acres.
Ashby, John. Va. Captain. 17 Dec. 1834. 50 acres.
Ashby, John. Va. Captain. 17 Dec. 1834. 50 acres.
Ashby, John. Va. Captain. 17 Dec. 1834. 400 acres.
Ashby, John. Va. Captain. 17 Dec. 1834. 400 acres.
Ashby, John. Va. Captain. 17 Dec. 1834. 150 acres.
Ashby, John. Va. Captain. 17 Dec. 1834. 50 acres.
Ashby, John. Va. Captain. 17 Dec. 1834. 342 6/7 acres.
Ashby, John. Va. Captain. 17 Dec. 1834. 171 3/7 acres.
Ashby, John. Va. Captain. 27 Feb. 1835. 228 4/7 acres.
Ashby, John. Va. Captain. 30 Apr. 1835. 400 acres.
Ashby, John. Va. Captain. 13 Apr. 1838. 108 1/5 acres.
Ashby, John. Va. Captain. 13 Apr. 1838. 108 1/5 acres.
Ashby, John. Va. Captain. 13 Apr. 1838. 108 1/5 acres.
Ashby, John. Va. Captain. 13 Apr. 1838. 108 1/5 acres.
Ashby, John. Va. Captain. 13 Apr. 1838. 108 1/5 acres.
Ashby, John. Va. Captain. 13 Apr. 1838. 108 1/5 acres.
Ashby, John. Va. Captain. 13 Apr. 1838. 108 1/5 acres.
Ashby, John. Va. Captain. 13 Apr. 1838. 108 1/5 acres.
Ashby, John. Va. Captain. 13 Apr. 1838. 108 1/5 acres.
Ashby, John. Va. Captain. 13 Apr. 1838. 108 1/5 acres.
Ashby, Stephen. Va. Captain. 3 Dec. 1783. 4000 acres.
Ashby, Thomas. Va. Private. 20 Jun. 1783. 100 acres.
Ashby, William. Va. Ensign. 18 Nov. 1830. 2666 2/3 acres.
Ashe, Charles. N.C. Private. 29 Sep. 1784. 640 acres.
Ashe, John Baptist. N.C. Lieutenant Colonel. 25 Mar. 1784. 4457 acres.
Ashe, Samuel. N.C. Captain. 21 Apr. 1784. 1500 acres.
Ashe, Samuel. N.C. Lieutenant. 21 Apr. 1784. 2560 acres.
Asher, Leroy. Va. Private. 23 Sep. 1784. 100 acres.
Asher, Warren. Va. Midshipman. 14 Jul. 1794. 2666 2/3 acres.
Asher, William. Va.-Ind. Private. 108 acres.
Ashley, James. Md. Private. ———. 50 acres.
Ashley, John. Ga. ———. 17 May 1784. ———.
Ashley, John. Pa. ———. 6 Mar. 1804. 200 acres.
Ashley, John. Pa. ———. 6 Mar. 1804. 200 acres.
Ashley, John. Pa. ———. 6 Mar. 1804. 200 acres.
Ashley, Thomas. Va. Private. 15 Jun. 1820. 100 acres.
Ashlock, Richard. Va. Private. 19 Nov. 1783. 100 acres.
Ashly, Abraham. Ga. ———. 15 Mar. 1784. 250 acres.
Ashly, John. Va. Corporal. 26 Feb. 1784. 200 acres.
Ashly, Thomas. N.C. Private. 5 Dec. 1796. 228 acres.
Ashmore, John. Ga. ———. 20 Feb. 1784. 250 acres.
Ashmore, John. Md. Private. ———. 50 acres.
Ashton, Benjamin. Pa. ———. ———. 200 acres.
Ashton, James. Pa. Private. 25 July 1787. 200 acres.

Ashton, Joseph. Pa. Lieutenant. ———. 200 acres.

Ashton, Joseph. Pa. Lieutenant. 9 Jan. 1787. 200 acres.

Ashworth, Adam. Ga. Minute Man. 22 Mar. 1785. 250 acres.

Ashworth, Arthur. Ga. Minute Man. 16 Sep. 1785. ———.

Ashworth, Benjamin. Ga. Refugee. 15 Mar. 1784. 250 acres.

Ask, Samuel. Conn. Sufferer. Greenwich. 11.18.2 1/2.

Askew, Coleman. N.C. Fifer. 9 Dec. 1797. 1000 acres to heirs.

Askew, James. Va. Private. 20 Jul. 1782. 100 acres.

Askew, Jesse. N.C. Private. 30 Sep. 1785. 640 acres to heirs.

Askew, Philip. N.C. Private. 12 Dec. 1797. 640 acres to heirs.

Askew, Scrug. N.C. Private. 12 Dec. 1797. 640 acres to heirs.

Askins, George. S.C. Soldier. 21 Jan. 1785. 200 acres.

Askins, John. N.C. Private. 30 Sep. 1785. 640 acres to heirs.

Aspenwal, John. Va. Private. 2 Oct. 1783. 100 acres.

Aspin, Thomas. Md. Private. ———. 50 acres.

Aspinwall, John. Va. Private. 31 Jan. 1784. 200 acres.

Aspley, John. N.C. Dragoon. 22 Feb. 1784. 640 acres.

Asque, Peregrine. Md. Matross. ———. 50 acres.

Asselin, Thomas. Va. Sergeant. 13 May 1783. 200 acres.

Asser, Charles. N.C. Sergeant. 7 Jan. 1786. 1000 acres to heirs.

Atayataghroughta, Lewis. N.Y. Lieutenant Colonel. 29 Jan. 1791. 2700 acres. [an Indian].

Atherton, Philip. Mass. Private. 24 Feb. 1834. 200 acres.

Atheson, David. Va. Private. 29 Jun. 1784 233 1/3 acres.

Athey, Benjamin. Va. Private. 29 Jun. 1784. 100 acres.

Athey, Thomas. Va. Private. 29 Jun. 1784. 100 acres.

Athey, Thomas. Va. Private. 29 Jun. 1784. 100 acres.

Atkenson, John. N.C. Private. 24 Oct. 1783. 228 acres.

Atkins, Benjamin. N.C. Private. 20 Dec. 1784. 308 acres.

Atkins, Elisha. Va. Private. 6 Jan. 1808. 100 acres.

Atkins, John. N.C. Private. 10 Dec. 1788. 640 acres to heirs.

Atkins, Lewis. Va. Private. 25 Jun. 1783. 233 1/3 acres.

Atkins, Moses. Va. Private. 6 Jan. 1808. 100 acres.

Atkins, Robert. N. Y. ———. 13 Sep. 1790. 500 acres to heirs.

Atkins, Thomas. N.C. Private. 4 Dec. 1783. 274 acres.

Atkinson, Charles. Ga. ———. 16 Jul. 1784. 287 1/2 acres.

Atkinson, James. N. Y. Corporal. 8 Jul. 1790. 500 acres.

Atkinson, John. N.C. Private. 9 Oct. 1820. 228 acres to heirs.

Atkinson, John. N.C. Private. 16 Aug. 1821. 640 acres.

Atkinson, John. Va. Private. 5 Jun. 1783. 100 acres.

Atkinson, Major. Va. Private. 5 Jun. 1783. 100 acres.

Atkinson, Michael. N.C. Private. 30 Mar. 1785. 640 acres to heirs.

Atkinson, Philip. N. Y. ———. 13 Sep. 1790. 500 acres to heirs.

Atkinson, Reuben. Va. Private. 30 May 1783. 100 acres.

Atkinson, Richard. N.C. Private. 4 Sep. 1820. 640 acres to heirs.

Atkinson, Thomas. Va. Corporal. 28 Apr. 1783. 400 acres.

Atkinson, William. Va. Private. 13 Sep. 1783. 200 acres.

Atterson, John. S.C. Soldier. 21 Jan. 1785. 200 acres.

Atwater, David. Conn. Sufferer. New/East Haven. 3.12.3.

Atwater, Eldad. Conn. Sufferer. New/East Haven. 52.0.7.

Atwater, Jeremiah. Conn. Sufferer. New/ East Haven. 227.11.3.

Atwater, Joel. Conn. Sufferer. New/East Haven. 1.0.0.

Atwater, Jonah. Conn. Sufferer. New/East Haven. 16.10.8.

Atwater, Timothy. Conn. Sufferer. New/ East Haven. 8.2.0.

Atway, Hardy. N.C. Private. 30 Sep. 1785. 640 acres to heirs.
Atwood, Isaac. Ga. ———. 17 May 1784. ———.
Aubany, Thomas. Va. Private. 31 Jul. 1783. 200 acres.
Auber, John. Md. Private. ———. 50 acres.
Auber, Peter. Va. Private. 30 Aug. 1783. 100 acres.
Aubery, Samuel. Va. Private. 20 Apr. 1785. 100 acres. [Avery]
Augur, Abraham. Conn. Sufferer. New/East Haven. 60.0.8.
Augur, Hezekiah. Conn. Sufferer. New/East Haven. 29.8.3.
Augustus, John. N.C. Private. 9 Feb. 1796. 640 acres to heirs.
Ausline, Presque. N. Y. ———. ——. 500 acres.
Ausmon, Jordan. N.C. Private. 31 Aug. 1795. 640 acres to heirs.
Austin, Abner. Conn. Sufferer. New/East Haven. 56.12.7.
Austin, Absalom. N.C. Private. 14 Aug. 1820. 640 acres to heirs.
Austin, Archibald. Conn. Sufferer. New/ East Haven. 71.13.8.
Austin, David. Conn. Sufferer. New/East Haven. 276.17.0.
Austin, David, Jr. Conn. Sufferer. New/ East Haven. 11.6.0.
Austin, Harris. Md. Private. ———. 50 acres.
Austin, Henry. Md. Private. ———. 50 acres.
Austin, Holmes. N. Y. Private. 8 Jul. 1790. 500 acres.
Austin, Jeremiah. N. Y. ———. 13 Sep. 1790. 500 acres to heirs.
Austin, John. Va. Private. 21 Jul. 1824. 100 acres.
Austin, John. Conn. Sufferer. New/East Haven. 10.6.0.
Austin, John W. Va. Sergeant Major. 1 Apr. 1783. 200 acres.
Austin, John Wilson. Va. Sergeant Major. 26 Apr. 1783. 400 acres.
Austin, Jonah. Me. ———. 20 Oct. 1835. 200 acres. Windham.
Austin, Mary. Conn. Sufferer. Greenwich. 3.3.7.
Austin, Richard. Ga. Captain. 8 Sep. 1784. 575 acres to heirs.
Austin, Samuel. Conn. Sufferer. New/East Haven. 69.13.0.
Austin, Stephen. Conn. Sufferer. New/East Haven. 12.12.6.
Austin, Thomas. N.C. Private. 8 Dec. 1796. 640 acres.
Austin, William. Va. Private. 19 Feb. 1808. 200 acres.
Autrey, James. N.C. Private. 12 Dec. 1796. 640 acres.
Autrey, John. Ga. ———. 25 Feb. 1784. 250 acres.
Autry, Alexander. Ga. Soldier. 25 Feb. 1784. ———.
Autry, Alexander, Jr. Ga. Captain. 15 Mar. 1784. 500 acres.
Autry, John. Ga. Refugee Captain. 25 Feb. 1784. ———.
Avent, James. Ga. ———. 17 May 1784. ———.
Avent, James. N.C. Private. 22 Oct. 1783. 228 acres.
Avent, Joseph. Ga. ———. 17 May 1784. ———.
Avent, Thomas. N.C. Private. 17 Dec. 1796. 640 acres to heirs.
Avera, Isaac. Ga. Refugee. 7 Apr. 1784. ———.
Averet, Arthur. Ga. ———. 1784. 150 acres.
Averet, Isaac. Ga. Refugee. 7 Apr. 1784. ———.
Averet, Thomas. Ga. ———. 17 May 1784. ———.
Averett, John. Ga. ———. 15 Mar. 1784. 250 acres.
Averill, Ezekiel. Me. Private. 12 Jun. 1835. 200 acres. Wiscasset.
Avery, Amos. Conn. Sufferer. Groton. 12.2.2.
Avery, Benjamin. Conn. Sufferer. Groton. 3.19.0.
Avery, Caleb. Conn. Sufferer. Groton. 7.0.6.
Avery, Ebenezer. Conn. Sufferer. Groton. 30.4.0.
Avery, Elisha. Conn. Sufferer. Groton. 10.14.5.
Avery, Elizabeth. Conn. Sufferer. Groton. 2.6.0.
Avery, Estrige. N.C. Private. 7 Jan. 1786. 640 acres to heirs.
Avery, George. Conn. Sufferer. Groton. 8.8.2.

Avery, Hannah. Conn. Sufferer. Groton. 15.6.6.

Avery, James. N.C. Private. 29 Sep. 1784. 640 acres.

Avery, James. N.C. Private. 3 Feb. 1795. 228 acres.

Avery, Latham. Conn. Sufferer. Groton. 103.5.6.

Avery, Lydia. Conn. Sufferer. Groton. 157.12.1.

Avery, Mary. Conn. Sufferer. Norwalk. 11.2.6.

Avery, Nicholas. N. Y. Private. 8 Jul. 1790. 600 acres.

Avery, Peter. Conn. Sufferer. Groton. 4.13.0.

Avery, Phebe. Conn. Sufferer. Groton. 2.2.0.

Avery, Prudence. Conn. Sufferer. Groton. 270.14.8.

Avery, Rufus. Conn. Sufferer. Groton. 132.18.4.

Avery, Thankful. Conn. Sufferer. Groton. 263.16.8.

Avery, Thomas. N.C. Private. 4 May 1785. 640 acres to heirs.

Avery, Thomas. N.C. Private. 11 Jul. 1785. 640 acres.

Avery, William Haly. Va. Captain. 15 Jul. 1818. 100 acres.

Avery, William Haly. Va. Captain. 15 Jul. 1818. 800 acres.

Avery, William Haly. Va. Captain. 15 Jul. 1818. 200 acres.

Avery, William Haly. Va. Captain. 15 Jul. 1818. 80 acres.

Avery, William Haly. Va. Captain. 15 Jul. 1818. 80 acres.

Avery, William Haly. Va. Captain. 15 Jul. 1818. 80 acres.

Avery, William Haly. Va. Captain. 15 Jul. 1818. 80 acres.

Avery, William Haly. Va. Captain. 15 Jul. 1818. 80 acres.

Avery, William Haly. Va. Captain. 15 Jul. 1818. 320 acres.

Avery, William Haly. Va. Captain. 15 Jul. 1818. 320 acres.

Avery, William Haly. Va. Captain. 15 Jul. 1818. 320 acres.

Avery, William Haly. Va. Captain. 15 Jul. 1818. 320 acres.

Avery, William Haly. Va. Captain. 15 Jul. 1818. 320 acres.

Avery, William Haly. Va. Captain. 18 Oct. 1851. 1227 2/3 acres.

Awtrey, Jacob. Ga. Refugee. 15 Mar. 1784. 250 acres.

Axtell, Henry. Mass. Private. 20 May 1836. 200 acres.

Aycock, Richard. Ga. Soldier. 15 Mar. 1784. 250 acres.

Aycock, William. Ga. ———. 1784. 287 1/2 acres.

Ayhern, William. Md. Private. ———. 50 acres.

Aylett, William. Va. Colonel. 21 Oct. 1808. 1333 acres.

Aylett, William. Va. Colonel. 21 Oct. 1808. 1333 acres.

Aylett, William. Va. Colonel. 21 Oct. 1808. 1333 acres.

Aylett, William. Va. Colonel. 21 Oct. 1808. 1333 acres.

Aylett, William. Va. Colonel. 21 Oct. 1808. 1333 acres.

Aylett, William. Va. Colonel. 21 Oct. 1808. 1187 1/2 acres.

Aylett, William. Va. Colonel. 23 Apr. 1839. 395 5/8 acres.

Aylett, William. Va. Colonel. 28 Jul. 1855. 395 5/6 acres.

Aylett, William. Va. Colonel. 25 Sep. 1852. 395 5/6 acres.

Aylett, William. Va. Colonel. 6 Dec. 1852. 131 5/6 acres.

Aylett, William. Va. Colonel. 6 Dec. 1852. 1055 4/6 acres.

Aymand, John. N. Y. ———. ———. 500 acres.

Ayot, Pierre. N. Y. ———. ———. 333 1/3 acres.

Ayres, Abraham. Ga. ———. 17 May 1784. ——— to heirs.

Ayres, Abraham. Ga. Refugee. 20 Feb. 1784. 500 acres.

Ayres, Daniel. Ga. Lieutenant. 6 Dec. 1784. ———.

Ayres, Frederick. Md. Private. ———. 50 acres.

Ayres, Henry. Va. Sergeant. 15 Jul. 1818. 200 acres.

Ayres, James. Ga. Soldier. 5 Sep. 1785. ———.

Ayres, Thomas. Ga. ———. 15 Mar. 1784. 250 acres.

Ayres, Thomas. Ga. ———. 17 Feb. 1784. 250 acres.

Ayres, Thomas. Md. Private. ———. 50 acres.
Ayres, William. Ga. Captain. 13 Sep. 1784. 287 1/2 acres.
Ayres, William. Ga. ———. 17 Feb. 1784. 250 acres.
Babb, John. N.C. Private. 11 Feb. 1796. 640 acres.
Babb, Joseph. N.C. Private. 17 Dec. 1796. 640 acres to heirs.
Babb, Peter. Me. Private. 29 Jun. 1836. 200 acres. Buxton.
Babbet, Reuben. N. Y. ———. 13 Sep. 1790. 500 acres to heirs.
Babbit, John. N. Y. Fifer. 8 Jul. 1790. 600 acres.
Babcock, Stephen. Conn. Sufferer. New London. 34.9.1 1/2.
Baber, Edward. Va. Private. 3 May 1823. 100 acres.
Baber, Edward. Va. Private. 3 Dec. 1833. 100 acres.
Baber, James. Md. Private. ———. 50 acres.
Babtiste, Jean. Va. Private. 30 Jan. 1784. 200 acres.
Baccote, Peter. N.C. Captain. 27 Oct. 1783. 3840 acres.
Bachelor, George. N.C. Private. 25 Jun. 1785. 640 acres to heir.
Bachus, George. N. Y. Private. 8 Jul. 1790. 600 acres.
Backus, George. Va. Lieutenant. 16 Nov. 1824. 1333 1/3 acres.
Backus, George. Va. Lieutenant. 16 Nov. 1824. 1333 1/3 acres.
Backus, Joseph. N.C. Private. 27 Nov. 1819. 274 acres.
Baclannen, Henry. N. Y. ———. 13 Sep. 1790. 500 acres to heirs.
Bacon, Burwell. Va. Corporal. 24 Apr. 1783. 200 acres.
Bacon, Burwell. Va. Corporal. 13 Feb. 1858. 200 acres.
Bacon, John. Ga. Refugee. 8 Jun. 1784. 250 acres.
Bacon, Jonathan. Ga. Refugee. 10 May 1784. ———.
Bacon, Ludwell. Va. Private. 20 Apr. 1784. 100 acres.
Bacon, Reubin. Ga. ———. ———. 287 1/2 acres.
Bacon, Robert. Va. Private. 23 Jun. 1783. 200 acres.
Bacon, Thomas. Ga. Refugee. 4 Apr. 1785. ———.
Bacon, William. N. Y. Bombardier. 9 Jul. 1790. 600 acres.
Baconham, John. N.C. Private. 30 Sep. 1785. 640 acres to heirs.
Baddel, Moses. N. Y. ———. 1 Mar. 1791. 500 acres to heirs.
Badlam, Sylvanus. Mass. Quarter Master Sergeant. 6 Jul. 1832. 200 acres.
Badsley, John. N.C. Sergeant. 30 Sep. 1785. 1000 acres to heirs.
Baduly, William. Ga. ———. 15 Mar. 1784. 250 acres.
Badwell, Zachariah. N.C. Corporal. 30 Sep. 1785. 1000 acres to heirs.
Bagby, George. Ga. ———. 16 Jul. 1784. 287 1/2 acres.
Baggott, Allen. N.C. Private. 5 Sep. 1821. 640 acres.
Baggs, John. Ga. Private. 6 Apr. 1785. 287 1/2 acres.
Bagley, Isaac. N.C. Private. 11 May 1785. 640 acres to heirs.
Bagley, Josiah. N. Y. Lieutenant. 9 Jul. 1790. 1200 acres.
Bagley, Mathias. N.C. Private. 8 Dec. 1795. 640 acres to heirs.
Bagnall, John. N.C. Private. 8 Aug. 1821. 640 acres.
Bagnall, Low. Va. Private. 3 Feb. 1791. 200 acres.
Bagues, Jacques. Md. Lieutenant. ———. 200 acres.
Bagwell, Frederick. N.C. Private. 9 Sep. 1785. 640 acres to heirs.
Bagwell, Josiah. Va. Private. 15 Jun. 1791. 200 acres.
Bagwell, Thomas. Va. Sergeant. 30 Dec. 1808. 200 acres.
Bailey, Anselm. Va. Private. 3 Dec. 1783. 100 acres.
Bailey, Anselm. Va. Private. 18 Sep. 1875. 100 acres.
Bailey, Anselm. Va. Private. 2 Jan. 1811. 100 acres.
Bailey, Azariah. Ga. ———. 17 May 1784. ———.
Bailey, Benjamin. Mass. Private. 30 Dec. 1832. 200 acres to heirs.
Bailey, Benjamin. N.C. Captain. 20 Apr. 1784. 3840 acres.
Bailey, Charles. N.C. Private. 8 May 1784. 640 acres.

Bailey, David. Va.-Ind. Private. 108 acres.
Bailey, Druland. Ga. Minute Man. 3 Sep. 1785. ———.
Bailey, Ebenezer. N. Y. Private. 8 Jul. 1790. 500 acres.
Bailey, Edmond. Ga. Minute Man. 3 Sep. 1785. ———.
Bailey, Edward. Va. Sergeant. 28 Aug. 1783. 200 acres.
Bailey, Ephraim. Mass. Private. 26 Feb. 1833. 200 acres to assignee Samuel Cook.
Bailey, Ethelred. N.C. Private. 7 Jan. 1786. 640 acres to heirs.
Bailey, Ezekiel. Conn. Sufferer. Groton. 2.19.5.
Bailey, Hudson. Me. ———. Jul. 1835. 200 acres to widow Sarah Bailey. Portland.
Bailey, Isham. Ga. Minute Man. ———. ———.
Bailey, Ishmael. Va. Private. 25 Jan. 1812. 100 acres.
Bailey, Isme. Va. Sergeant. 30 Dec. 1808. 200 acres.
Bailey, James. Ga. ———. 17 May 1784. ———.
Bailey, James. Md. Private. ———. 50 acres.
Bailey, James. Mass. Sergeant. 30 Dec. 1831. 200 acres to heirs.
Bailey, James. Va. Private. 11 Nov. 1784. 100 acres.
Bailey, James. Va. Private. 18 Mar. 1784. 100 acres.
Bailey, James. Va. Corporal. 17 Dec. 1784. 400 acres.
Bailey, James. Conn. Sufferer. Groton. 2.10.0.
Bailey, Jesse. Va. Sailor. 17 Aug. 1784. 100 acres.
Bailey, John. Ga. Minute Man. 3 Sep. 1785. ———.
Bailey, John. Va.-Ind. Captain. Mar. 1784. 3234 acres.
Bailey, John. Me. ———. 1 May 1835. 200 acres to widow Abigail Bailey. Vassalboro.
Bailey, John. Mass. Drummer. 24 Sep. 1830. 200 acres.
Bailey, John. N.C. Private. 25 Oct. 1783. 640 acres.
Bailey, John. Va. Captain. 3 Mar. 1784. 4000 acres.
Bailey, Joseph. N. Y. Private. 3 Jul. 1790. 600 acres.
Bailey, Joseph. N.C. ———. 14 Jun. 1785. 640 acres to heirs.
Bailey, Joseph. N.C. Sergeant. 20 Oct. 1787. 570 acres.
Bailey, Joseph. S.C. ———. 2 Jul. 1787. 200 acres.
Bailey, Laban. Va. Quartermaster. 26 Feb. 1831. 1333 1/3 acres.
Bailey, Laban. Va. Quartermaster. 26 Feb. 1831. 1333 1/3 acres.
Bailey, Lewis. N.C. Private. 2 Aug. 1784. 228 acres.
Bailey, Mason. N.C. Private. 19 Jan. 1786. 640 acres.
Bailey, Michael. Va. Private. 30 Apr. 1783. 200 acres.
Bailey, Morris. N.C. Private. 19 Jan. 1786. 640 acres.
Bailey, Nathan. Conn. Sufferer. New London. 20.3.10 1/2.
Bailey, Peter. Ga. Minute Man. 3 Sep. 1785. ———.
Bailey, Philip. Md. Private. ———. 50 acres.
Bailey, Prince. Me. Private. 5 Sep. 1835. 200 acres. Leeds.
Bailey, Robert. Ga. Refugee. 3 Apr. 1785. ———.
Bailey, Robert. N.C. ———. 8 Mar. 1785. 640 acres to heirs.
Bailey, Samuel. Mass. Sergeant. 12 Dec. 1834. 200 acres.
Bailey, Samule. Me. ———. 20 Jul. 1835. 200 acres to widow Elenor Bailey. Lincoln.
Bailey, Simon. Va. Private. 9 Dec. 1796. 200 acres.
Bailey, Southey. Va. Private. 18 Sep. 1807. 60 acres.
Bailey, Southey. Va. ———. 28 Mar. 1837. 100 acres.
Bailey, Southey. Va. Seaman. 29 Jul. 1834. 100 acres.
Bailey, Southy. Va. Private. 8 Dec. 1783. 200 acres.
Bailey, Thomas. Md. Private. ———. 50 acres.
Bailey, Thomas. Va. Private. 21 Nov. 1783. 100 acres.
Bailey, William. Ga. Refugee Lieutenant. 15 Mar. 1784. 250 acres.

Bailey, William. Ga. Lieutenant. 15 Mar. 1784. 350 acres.
Bailey, William. N.C. Private. 17 Dec. 1785. 640 acres to heirs.
Bailey, William. Va. Private. 7 Aug. 1783. 200 acres.
Bailey, William. Va. Private. 10 Feb. 1784. 100 acres.
Bailey, William. Va. Private. 26 Apr. 1784. 100 acres.
Bailey, William. Va. Private. 9 Dec. 1796. 100 acres.
Bailey, William. Va. Private. 2 Dec. 1837. 100 acres.
Bailey, William. Va. Private. 16 Jun. 1854. 100 acres.
Bailey, William Henry. N.C. Private. 1 Aug. 1792. 640 acres to heirs.
Bailey, William Henry. N.C. Private. 1 Dec. 1796. 360 acres to heirs.
Bailey, Zadock. Va. Private. 8 Nov. 1784. 200 acres.
Bailey, Zadock. Va. Private. 30 Dec. 1808. 60 acres.
Baily, Pierce. Va. ———. 13 Sep. 1785. 200 acres.
Baine, Reuben. Ga. Minute Man. 14 Jul. 1785. ———.
Baird, Absalom. Pa. Surgeon. 12 Oct. 1786. 300 acres.
Baird, Absalom. Pa. Surgeon. 12 Oct. 1786. 300 acres.
Baird, Joseph. N.C. Private. 8 Dec. 1795. 640 acres to heirs.
Bakehorn, Jacob. N. Y. Private. 8 Jul. 1790. 500 acres.
Baker, Aaron. N.C. Private. 30 Sep. 1785. 640 acres to heirs.
Baker, Amos. N.C. ———. 8 Mar. 1785. 640 acres to heirs.
Baker, Artemas. Ga. Refugee. 15 Mar. 1784. 250 acres.
Baker, Caleb. S.C. ———. 4 Dec. 1786. 200 acres.
Baker, Chester. Ga. ———. 17 May 1784. 230 acres.
Baker, Christian. N. Y. Private. 8 Jul. 1790. 600 acres.
Baker, Ebenezer. Conn. Sufferer. Fairfield. 21.18.0.
Baker, Elias. N.C. Private. 1 Sep. 1785. 640 acres to heirs.
Baker, Ephraim. Ga. ———. 17 May 1784. ———.
Baker, Henry. Md. Lieutenant. ———. 200 acres.
Baker, Isaac. Ga. Minute Man. 3 Sep. 1785. ———.
Baker, James. Pa. Private. 27 Sep. 1787. 200 acres to William Banquet, assignee.
Baker, James. Va. Drummer. 26 Apr. 1783. 200 acres.
Baker, James. Va. Ensign. 16 Sep. 1850. 2666 2/3 acres.
Baker, James. Va. Ensign. 12 Sep. 1851. 1333 1/3 acres.
Baker, James. Va. Ensign. 12 Sep. 1851. 1333 1/3 acres.
Baker, Jesse. S.C. Captain. 15 Jul. 1784. 300 acres.
Baker, Joel. Md. Private. ———. 50 acres.
Baker, John. Ga. Colonel. 14 Apr. 1784. ———.
Baker, John. Md. Private. ———. 50 acres.
Baker, John. N. Y. Private. 8 Jul. 1790. 600 acres.
Baker, John. N.C. Captain. 29 Apr. 1784. 1462 acres.
Baker, John. N.C. Captain. 16 Aug. 1821. 3840 acres.
Baker, John. N.C. Private. 13 Jan. 1823. 273 acres.
Baker, John. Pa. Private. 13 Oct. 1786. 200 acres to Benjamin Say, assignee.
Baker, John. Pa. Private. 21 Dec. 1786. 200 acres.
Baker, John. Va. Private. 15 Jun. 1807. 100 acres.
Baker, John. Va. Lieutenant. 26 Feb. 1834. 1333 1/3 acres.
Baker, John. Va. Lieutenant. 26 Feb. 1834. 666 2/3 acres.
Baker, John. Va. Lieutenant. 26 Feb. 1834. 666 2/3 acres.
Baker, Jonathan. N.C. Private. 30 Sep. 1785. 640 acres to heirs.
Baker, Joseph. N.C. Private. 26 May 1784. 640 acres.
Baker, Lemon. N.C. Private. 30 Sep. 1785. 640 acres to heirs.
Baker, Nathaniel. Ga. Refugee. 28 Apr. 1784. ———.
Baker, Norris. N.C. Private. 10 Jan. 1794. 640 acres.
Baker, Peter. N.C. Private. 30 Sep. 1785. 640 acres to heirs.

Baker, Pierce. N. Y. Private. 8 Jul. 1790. 600 acres.

Baker, Richard. Va. Private. 18 Apr. 1785. 200 acres.

Baker, Richard Bohun. S.C. Captain. 21 Jan. 1785. 300 acres.

Baker, Silas, Jr. Me. Private. 6 May 1835. 200 acres. Freeman.

Baker, Thomas. Ga. Refugee. 15 Jul 1784. 287 1/2 acres.

Baker, Thomas. Md. Private. ———. 50 acres.

Baker, Thomas. Va. Private. 30 Jun. 1783. 100 acres.

Baker, Whitmarsh. Ga. Refugee. 20 Feb. 1784. 250 acres.

Baker, William. Ga. Minute Man. 22 Mar. 1785. 250 acres.

Baker, William. N.C. Private. 30 Sep. 1785. 640 acres to heirs.

Baker, William. N.C. Private. 4 Aug. 1821. 640 acres.

Baker, William. N.C. Private. 13 Jan. 1823. 274 acres to heirs.

Baker, William. Pa. ———. 6 Oct. 1786. 200 acres to Moses Bartram, assignee.

Baker, William Jeans. Ga. Refugee. 15 Mar. 1784. 250 acres.

Baker, William, Sr. Ga. Refugee. 26 May 1784. 250 acres.

Baker, William, Sr. Ga. Major. 15 Mar. 1784. 250 acres to heirs.

Balantine, William. N. Y. Private. 8 Jul. 1790. 600 acres.

Baldridge, Daniel. N.C. Private. 6 Dec. 1797. 640 acres.

Baldridge, Thomas. N.C. Private. 6 Dec. 1797. 640 acres to heirs.

Baldwin, Abraham. Ga. ———. 17 May 1784. ———.

Baldwin, Benjamin. Va. Sergeant. 23 Jun. 1812. 100 acres.

Baldwin, Benjamin. Va. Sergeant. 23 Jun. 1812. 100 acres.

Baldwin, Caleb. Conn. Sufferer. Danbury. 2.0.0. 3/4.

Baldwin, Cornelius. Va. Surgeon. 4 Apr. 1783. 6000 acres.

Baldwin, Cornelius. Va. Surgeon. 16 May 1807. 500 acres.

Baldwin, David. Ga. ———. 25 May 1784. 575 acres to heirs.

Baldwin, David, Jr. Ga. ———. ———. 287 1/2 acres.

Baldwin, David, Sr. Ga. Captain. 15 May 1784. 575 acres to heirs.

Baldwin, Dudley. Conn. Sufferer. Fairfield. 7.13.0.

Baldwin, Henry. Md. Lieutenant. ———. 200 acres.

Baldwin, Henry. N.C. Private. 17 Dec. 1785. 640 acres to heirs.

Baldwin, James. Va. Private. 18 Dec. 1783. 100 acres.

Baldwin, John. Mass. ———. 22 Jul. 1833. 200 acres.

Baldwin, John. Va. Captain. 16 Apr. 1812. 2000 acres.

Baldwin, John. Va. Captain. 16 Apr. 1812. 2000 acres.

Baldwin, Mordecai. Ga. Lieutenant. 25 May 1784. 460 acres.

Baldwin, William. Ga. ———. 17 May 1784. ———.

Baldwin, William. Ga. ———. 25 Feb. 1784. ———.

Baldy, Branson. Va. Seaman. 26 May 1831. 100 acres.

Bale, Henry. N.C. Private. 12 Dec. 1797. 274 acres.

Balentine, James. N.C. Sergeant. 8 Aug. 1821. 1000 acres.

Baley, Simon. Va. Private. 19 Dec. 1783. 100 acres.

Balford, John. N.C. Private. 30 Sep. 1785. 640 acres to heirs.

Balip, James. Md. Private. ———. 50 acres.

Balis, Elias. N. Y. Private. 8 Jul. 1790. 600 acres.

Ball, Aaron. Va. Private. 19 Aug. 1783. 100 acres.

Ball, Burgess. Va. Lieutenant Colonel Commandant. 18 Dec. 1809. 648 acres.

Ball, Burgess. Va. Lieutenant Colonel Commandant. 20 Jun. 1783. 7777 2/3 acres.

Ball, Daniel. Va. Subaltern. 2 Feb. 1784. 2666 2/3 acres.

Ball, Elias. N.C. ———. 8 Mar. 1785. 640 acres to heirs.

Ball, James. Va. Private. 1 Jun. 1785. 100 acres.

Ball, James. Va. Lieutenant. 16 Apr. 1833. 1411 1/3 acres.

Ball, James. Va. Lieutenant. 28 Aug. 1835. 533 1/3 acres.

Ball, James. Va. Lieutenant. 28 Aug. 1835. 88 1/3 acres.

Ball, James. Va. Lieutenant. 28 Aug. 1835. 533 1/3 acres.

Ball, James. Va. Lieutenant. 10 Oct. 1835. 178 acres.

Ball, James. Va. Lieutenant. 10 Oct. 1836. 133 1/3 acres.

Ball, James. Va. Lieutenant. 10 Oct. 1836. 289 acres.

Ball, James. Va. Lieutenant. 10 Oct. 1836. 123 acres.

Ball, James. Va. Lieutenant. 10 Oct. 1836. 82 acres.

Ball, James. Va. Lieutenant. 10 Oct. 1836. 41 acres.

Ball, James. Va. Lieutenant. 7 Oct. 1837. 44 1/2 acres.

Ball, James. Va. Lieutenant. 7 Oct. 1837. 44 1/2 acres.

Ball, James. Va. Lieutenant. 7 Oct. 1837. 44 1/2 acres.

Ball, James. Va. Lieutenant. 16 May 1838. 41 acres.

Ball, James. Va. Lieutenant. 16 May 1838. 41 acres.

Ball, James. Va. Lieutenant. 16 May 1838. 41 acres.

Ball, James. Va. Lieutenant. 8 May 1839. 88 8/9 acres.

Ball, John. Ga. Private. ———. 9 Apr. 1784. ———.

Ball, John. Me. ———. 12 Sep. 1835. 200 acres to widow Rachel Ball.

Ball, John. Mass. Private. 18 Oct. 1833. 200 acres.

Ball, John. N. Y. Lieutenant. 16 Apr. 1794. 1200 acres.

Ball, Joseph. N. Y. ———. 13 Sep. 1790. 500 acres to heirs.

Ball, Sampson. Ga. Refugee. 19 May 1784. ———.

Ball, Stephen. Conn. Sufferer. New/East Haven. 36.0.6.

Ball, Toby. Va. Private. 14 Feb. 1834. 100 acres.

Ball, William. Ga. Refugee. 15 Mar. 1784. 250 acres.

Ball, William. Va. Private. 24 Dec. 1784. 200 acres.

Ballance, Henry. Va. Sergeant. 21 Oct. 1783. 200 acres.

Ballance, Willis. Va. Corporal. 21 Oct. 1781. 200 acres.

Ballard, Benjamin. N.C. Private. 26 Nov. 1796. 228 acres.

Ballard, Benoni. N. Y. Private. 8 Jul. 1790. 600 acres.

Ballard, Bland. Va. Sergeant. 19 Mar. 1834. 400 acres.

Ballard, Bland. Va. Private. 14 Feb. 1834. 200 acres.

Ballard, Burwell. N.C. Private. 7 Jan. 1786. 640 acres to heirs.

Ballard, Drewry. N.C. Private. 30 Sep. 1785. 640 acres to heirs.

Ballard, Dudley. Va. Private. 29 Mar. 1787. 100 acres.

Ballard, James. N.C. Private. 23 Apr. 1785. 640 acres to heirs.

Ballard, James. Va. Corporal. 17 Oct. 1834. 400 acres.

Ballard, John. N.C. Private. 11 Nov. 1814. 640 acres to heirs.

Ballard, Jonathan. Me. Private. 7 May 1835. 200 acres to widow Betty Ballard. Temple.

Ballard, Joshua. N.C. Private. 30 Sep. 1785. 640 acres to heirs.

Ballard, Kedar. N.C. Captain. 3 Feb. 1785. 3840 acres.

Ballard, Peter. N.C. Private. 12 Sep. 1785. 640 acres to heirs.

Ballard, Philip. Va. Private. 23 Feb. 1831. 100 acres.

Ballard, Reuben. Ga. ———. 17 May 1784. ———.

Ballard, Robert. Va. Lieutenant Colonel. 1 Jul. 1784. 6000 acres.

Ballard, Uriah. Me. ———. 30 Apr. 1838. 200 acres. Fryburg.

Ballard, Wakor. N.C. Private. 30 Sep. 1785. 640 acres to heirs.

Ballard, William. Va. Lieutenant. 6 Mar. 1783. 2666 2/3 acres.

Ballard, William. Va. Pilot. 22 Nov. 1783. 2666 2/3 acres.

Ballatine, Maltire. N.C. Private. 8 Jun. 1792. 640 acres.

Ballender, Jethro. N.C. Corporal. 30 Sep. 1785. 1000 acres to heirs.

Ballenger, John. Va. Private. 25 Jun. 1783. 100 acres.

Ballentine, Alexander. N.C. Sergeant. 15 Nov. 1793. 1000 acres.

Ballinger, William. Va. Sergeant. 12 Dec. 1788. 200 acres.

Ballow, Charles. Va. Sergeant. 27 Jul. 1783. 200 acres.
Balmain, Alexander. Va. Brigade Chaplain. 31 Mar. 1783. 6666 2/3 acres.
Balmain, Alexander. Va. Brigade Chaplain. 16 May 1783. 833 acres.
Balmer, John. N.C. Private. 23 Apr. 1785. 640 acres to heirs.
Balsely, John. Pa. Private. 6 Aug. 1787. 200 acres.
Balson, John. N.C. Private. 30 Sep. 1785. 640 acres to heirs.
Balthazer, Ignatius. Pa. Private. 6 Nov. 1786. 200 acres.
Baltimore, Jacob. Pa. ———. 7 Apr. 1807. 200 acres.
Baltrip, John. N.C. Private. 28 Sep. 1785. 640 acres to heirs.
Baltzell, Charles. Md. Captain. ———. 200 acres.
Bamus, Lambert. Pa. Corporal. ———. 200 acres.
Bancker, James. N. Y. Matross. 9 Jul. 1790. 600 acres.
Bancroft, James. Mass. Sergeant. 11 Apr. 1833. 200 acres to heirs.
Bandey, John. N.C. Private. 24 Nov. 1796. 640 acres to heirs.
Banks, Benjamin. N. Y. Private. 7 Jul. 1790. 600 acres.
Banks, Charity. Conn. Sufferer. Greenwich. 8.4.6.
Banks, Gershom. Conn. Sufferer. Fairfield. 14.15.0.
Banks, James. Va. Sailing Master. 5 Aug. 1783. 2666 2/3 acres.
Banks, Jeremiah. N.C. Private. 30 Sep. 1785. 640 acres to heirs.
Banks, John. Conn. Sufferer. Fairfield. 22.12.2.
Banks, Joseph. Pa. Private. 30 Sep. 1787. 200 acres to Robert Ralson assignee.
Banks, Josiah. Va. Private. 1 Aug. 1835. 100 acres.
Banks, Nehemiah. Conn. Sufferer. Fairfield. 4.15.0.
Banks, Obediah. Conn. Sufferer. Greenwich. 41.17.8.
Banks, Reuben. Ga. Soldier. 22 Jul. 1784. 287 1/2 acres.
Banks, Richard. N.C. Private. 13 Dec. 1796. 640 acres to heirs.
Banks, Samuel. Conn. Sufferer. Greenwich. 2.5.1 1/2.
Banks, Stephen. N.C. Private. 6 Dec. 1797. 640 acres to heirs.
Banks, William. Va. Sailor. 5 Aug. 1783. 100 acres.
Bankson, John. Pa. Captain. ———. 500 acres.
Bankston, Daniel. Ga. ———. 1784. 287 1/2 acres.
Bankston, Elijah. Ga. ———. 25 May 1784. 287 1/2 acres.
Bankston, Jacob. Ga. ———. 17 May 1784. 250 acres.
Bankston, James. Ga. Citizen. 3 May 1785. 287 1/2 acres.
Bankston, John. Ga. ———. 15 Mar. 1784. 250 acres.
Bankston, Laurence. Ga. ———. 17 May 1784. ———.
Bankston, Peter. Ga. ———. 17 May 1784. ———.
Bankwood, William. Pa. Sergeant. 4 Oct. 1786. 250 acres.
Bannon, Jeremiah. Pa. Private. 28 Feb. 1794. 200 acres.
Banns, William. N.C. Private. 30 Sep. 1785. 640 acres to heirs.
Banny, James. Md. Private. ———. 50 acres.
Bantham, John. Md. Private. ———. 50 acres.
Bany, Lyon. N.C. Private. 17 Feb. 1824. 640 acres.
Bapticle, Jean. Va. Private. 1 Mar. 1784. 100 acres.
Barbee, Daniel. Va. Sergeant. 19 Jun. 1784. 200 acres.
Barbee, Elijah. Va. Private. 11 Feb. 1784. 200 acres.
Barbee, Francis. Va. Corporal. 26 Jun. 1783. 200 acres.
Barbee, John. Va. Corporal. 26 Jun. 1783. 200 acres.
Barbee, John. Va. Sergeant. 21 Jun. 1784. 200 acres.
Barbee, Joshua. Va. Sergeant. 21 Jun. 1784. 200 acres.
Barbee, Thomas. Va. Captain. 31 Mar. 1783. 4000 acres.
Barbee, Thomas. Va. Captain. 8 Feb. 1808. 1111 acres.
Barbee, William. Va. Private. 19 Jun. 1784. 200 [100] acres.
Barber, Chester. Ga. Soldier. 10 Nov. 1783. 200 acres.

Barber, Edward. Ga. ———. 2 May 1785. 287 1/2 acres.
Barber, George. Ga. Lieutenant. 15 Mar. 1784. 250 acres.
Barber, George. Ga. Lieutenant. 15 Mar. 1784. 350 acres. [there are two Georges]
Barber, James. N.C. Private. 17 Dec. 1785. 640 acres to heirs.
Barber, Joshua. N.C. Private. 28 Sep. 1785. 274 acres to heirs.
Barber, Lewis. Ga. ———. 17 May 1784. ———.
Barber, Nicholas. N.C. Private. 30 Sep. 1785. 640 acres to heirs.
Barber, Thomas. Md. Matross. ———. 50 acres.
Barber, William. Ga. ———. 25 May 1784. 287 1/2 acres.
Barber, William. N.C. Private. 17 Dec. 1785. 640 acres.
Barber, William. N.C. Lieutenant. 1 Aug. 1821. 2560 acres.
Barbour, James. Va. Lieutenant. 25 Jun. 1783. 2666 2/3 acres.
Barclay, Henry. Ga. ———. 20 May 1785. ———.
Barclay, Jacob. Va. Private. 13 Mar. 1850. 100 acres.
Barclay, John. Ga. ———. 3 Apr. 1787. 400 acres.
Barclay, John. Pa. Lieutenant. 16 Jul. 1788. 200 acres.
Barclay, Thomas. Md. Private. ———. 50 acres.
Barcot, John. N.C. Private. 12 May 1784. 365 acres.
Bard, John. Ga. Soldier. ———. 24 Dec. 178-. ———.
Barden, Robert. N. Y. ———. 13 Sep. 1790. 500 acres to heirs.
Bardin, Gilbert. Ga. ———. 22 Jul. 1784. 287 1/2 acres.
Barefield, Richard. Ga. ———. 30 Sep. 1784. ———.
Barefield, Solomon. Ga. Soldier. 3 Oct. 1785. 230 acres.
Bareth, John. Va. Private. 22 Sep. 1804. 200 acres.
Barfield, James. N.C. Private. 2 Apr. 1784. 342 acres.
Barfield, Marmaduke. N.C. Private. 16 Feb. 1784. 640 acres to Richard Barfield, heir.
Barge, Baltzer. Pa. Private. 25 Jul. 1787. 200 acres.
Barge, Robert. N.C. Private. 24 Nov. 1796. 640 acres.
Bargess, Israel. Pa. Band Sergeant. 19 Dec. 1786. 200 acres to Samuel Benezet, assignee.
Barginer, John. N.C. Private. 21 Oct. 1783. 228 acres.
Barham, Moody. Va. Private. 31 Oct. 1783. 100 acres.
Barick, Samuel. N. Y. ———. 13 Sep. 1790. 500 acres to heirs.
Baris, John. N.C. Private. 8 Dec. 1796. 274 acres.
Baris, Simon. N.C. Private. 21 Apr. 1784. 640 acres.
Baris, Willis. N.C. Private. 25 Nov. 1796. 640 acres.
Barkelow, Richard. Ga. Refugee. 26 Apr. 1784. 287 1/2 acres to heirs.
Barker, Barnabus. Mass. ———. 8 Jul. 1833. 200 acres.
Barker, Charles. Va. Private. 20 Apr. 1784. 100 acres.
Barker, Daniel. Me. Private. 26 May 1835. 200 acres to widow Rachel Barker. Bethel.
Barker, Drury. Ga. ———. 17 May 1784. ———.
Barker, Edward. Va. Private. 22 Apr. 1784. 100 acres.
Barker, James. Me. ———. 23 Aug. 1836. 200 acres. Westbrook.
Barker, John. Va. Private. 26 Jun. 1784. 100 acres.
Barker, Joseph. N.C. Private. 1 Dec. 1797. 640 acres to heir John Barker.
Barker, Levi. N.C. Private. 28 May 1784. 640 acres.
Barker, Lewis. Ga. ———. 17 May 1784. ———.
Barker, Lucy. Conn. Sufferer. New/East Haven. 1.12.9.
Barker, Samuel. N.C. Private. 12 Sep. 1785. 640 acres to heirs.
Barker, Stephen. N. Y. Corporal. 8 Jul. 1790. 600 acres.
Barker, William. S.C. ———. 6 Feb. 1797. 86 acres to James Timms, administrator, in trust for the heirs.
Barker, William. S.C. ———. 6 Feb. 1797. 46 acres to James Timms, administrator, in trust for the heirs.

Barker, William. S.C. ———. 6 Feb. 1797. 62 acres to James Timms, administrator, in trust for the heirs.

Barker, William. Va. Sergeant. 17 Sep. 1850. 50 acres.

Barker, William. Va. Private. 9 Nov. 1831. 100 acres.

Barker, William. Va. Sergeant. 30 Oct. 1856. 50 acres.

Barkley, William. N.C. Private. 30 Sep. 1785. 640 acres to heirs.

Barksdale, Allen. Ga. ———. 14 Sep. 1784. 287 1/2 acres.

Barksdale, Daniel. Ga. ———. 17 May 1784. ———.

Barksdale, Daniel. Va. Private. 3 Jan. 1785. 100 acres.

Barksdale, Dickey. Ga. ———. 17 May 1784. ———.

Barksdale, Jeffrey. Ga. ———. 17 May 1784. ———.

Barksdale, John. Va. Subaltern. 25 Jun. 1784. 2666 2/3 acres.

Barksdale, Thomas. Ga. ———. 15 Mar. 1784. 250 acres.

Barkshire, Richard. Ga. ———. 1784. 287 1/2 acres.

Barler, William. N.C. Private. 17 Jul. 1820. 640 acres to heirs.

Barley, Nathaniel. Md. Private. ———. 50 acres.

Barleymore, Benjamin. Ga. ———. 17 May 1784. 575 acres.

Barlow, Christopher. N.C. Private. 8 Aug. 1821. 640 acres.

Barlow, David. Conn. Sufferer. Fairfield. 374.14.0.

Barlow, George. N.C. Private. 9 Sep. 1785. 640 acres to heirs.

Barlow, Robert. N.C. Private. 29 Sep. 1784. 640 acres to John Walker, heir.

Barlow, Thomas. Pa. Private. 22 Jun. 1797. 200 acres to Daniel Vanosten, assignee.

Barlow, Thomas. Va. Private. 21 Nov. 1783. 100 acres.

Barna, John. Conn. Sufferer. New London. 84.6.7 1/4.

Barnard, Claybourn. Ga. ———. 20 Feb. 1784. 250 acres.

Barnard, Germond. Ga. ———. 17 May 1784. ———.

Barnard, Jesse. Ga. ———. 20 Feb. 1784. 250 acres.

Barnard, Joel. Ga. Refugee. 20 Feb. 1784. 250 acres.

Barnard, William. Ga. Refugee. 17 Feb. 1784. 250 acres.

Barnecastle, Richard. N.C. Private. 11 Jan. 1822. 182 acres to heirs.

Barnes, Abraham. N. Y. Gunner. 9 Jul. 1790. 600 acres.

Barnes, Abraham. Conn. Sufferer. New/East Haven. 3.10.0.

Barnes, Andrew. Ga. Soldier. 5 May 1785. ———.

Barnes, Armistead. Va. Private. 9 Sep. 1812. 100 acres.

Barnes, Charles. N.C. Private. 8 Dec. 1796. 640 acres to heirs.

Barnes, Hezekiah. N.C. Corporal. 8 Mar. 1785. 357 acres.

Barnes, James. Mass. Private. 2 Mar. 1833. 200 acres to heirs.

Barnes, James. N.C. Private. 12 Dec. 1785. 274 acres.

Barnes, James. Va. Private. 10 Dec. 1783. 200 acres.

Barnes, James, Jr. N.C. Private. 17 Dec. 1796. 640 acres to heirs.

Barnes, John. N.C. Private. 23 Apr. 1784. 640 acres.

Barnes, John. Va. Private. 10 Jun. 1783. 100 acres.

Barnes, John. Va. Private. 14 Jan. 1785. 100 acres.

Barnes, John. Va. Private. 1 Mar. 1785. 200 acres.

Barnes, Samuel. Mass. Corporal. 13 Dec. 1831. 200 acres to heirs Samuel Russel Barnes, William Barnes, Catharine Barnes, Sena Smith wife of one Smith a hatter of Southburg, Conn., Mary Delia Baldwin wife of Merrett Baldwin, and Susan Smith wife of Nathan M. Smith.

Barnes, Samuel. Conn. Sufferer. New/East Haven. 13.16.8.

Barnes, Solomon. N. Y. Corporal. 9 Jul. 1790. 600 acres.

Barnes, Thomas, Sr. N.C. Private. 29 Apr. 1784. 640 acres to Burrell Barnes, his heir.

Barnes, William. Ga. Soldier. Jan. 1785. 287 1/2 acres.

Barnes, William. N.C. Private. 29 Sep. 1784. 640 acres to heir.

Barnes, William. N.C. Private. 17 Feb. 1824. 640 acres.

Barnes, William. Va. Private. 14 Apr. 1783. 100 acres.
Barnes, William. Va. Private. 17 Dec. 1784. 100 acres.
Barnet, George. Pa. Private. 3 Apr. 1805. 200 acres.
Barnet, Jesse. S.C. ———. 2 Dec. 1793. 100 acres to Lance Barnet, heir at law.
Barnet, Jesse. S.C. ———. 6 Jan. 1794. 100 acres to Lance Barnet, heir at law.
Barnet, Lance. S.C. ———. 6 Jan. 1794. 100 acres.
Barnet, Lance. S.C. ———. 18 Dec. 1793. 100 acres.
Barnet, Robert. Va.-Ind. Private. 108 acres.
Barnet, Robert. Md. Private. ———. 50 acres.
Barnett, Ambrose. Va. Private. 21 Aug. 1783. 100 acres.
Barnett, Daniel. Ga. Refugee. 15 Mar. 1784. 250 acres.
Barnett, Daniel. Va. Private. 19 Aug. 1822. 200 acres.
Barnett, James. Va. Lieutenant. 16 Sep. 1808 & 15 Apr. 1809. 1000 acres.
Barnett, James. Va. Lieutenant. 16 Sep. 1808 & 15 Apr. 1809. 1000 acres.
Barnett, James. Va. Lieutenant. 16 Sep. 1808 & 15 Apr. 1809. 1000 acres.
Barnett, James. Va. Lieutenant. 16 Sep. 1808 & 15 Apr. 1809. 444 acres.
Barnett, Jesse. Md. Fifer. ———. 50 acres.
Barnett, Joel. Ga. Refugee. 1784. 250 acres.
Barnett, John. Ga. ———. 17 May 1784. ———.
Barnett, John. Ga. Refugee. 15 Mar. 1784. 250 acres.
Barnett, John. Md. Private. ———. 50 acres.
Barnett, John. S.C. ———. 2 Jan. 1792. 123 acres.
Barnett, John. S.C. ———. 2 Oct. 1786. 200 acres.
Barnett, John. Va. Private. 23 Jun. 1783. 200 acres.
Barnett, Joshua. Ga. ———. 30 Sep. 1784. ———.
Barnett, Mial. Ga. Refugee. 22 Sep. 1784. 575 acres.
Barnett, Michael. Ga. Refugee. 15 Mar. 1784. 250 acres.
Barnett, Michael. Va. Private. 12 Apr. 1784. 100 acres.
Barnett, Millington. Va. ———. 15 Apr. 1853. 200 acres.
Barnett, Nathan. Ga. Refugee. 15 Mar. 1784. 250 acres.
Barnett, Nathaniel. Ga. Soldier. 15 Mar. 1784. 250 acres.
Barnett, Peter. N.C. Private. 7 Jan. 1786. 640 acres to heirs.
Barnett, Philip. Ga. Soldier. 19 Jul. 1784. 287 1/2 acres.
Barnett, Sion. N.C. Private. 27 Aug. 1784. 320 acres.
Barnett, William. Ga. Refugee. 22 Sep. 1784. 287 1/2 acres.
Barney, Barnabas. Pa. ———. 9 Mar. 1795. 250 acres to John Nicholson, assignee.
Barney, Hanover. Conn. Sufferer. New/East Haven. 11.11.10.
Barney, Joseph. Mass. Private. 25 Feb. 1833. 200 acres to heirs.
Barney, Moses. Md. Private. ———. 50 acres.
Barney, Nathaniel. Mass. Private. 26 Jan. 1833. 200 acres to heirs.
Barney, Thomas. Pa. Corporal. 10 Aug. 1787. 200 acres.
Barnhanhart, David. N. Y. Private. 8 Jul. 1790. 500 acres.
Barnhard, George, Jr. Ga. ———. 15 Mar. 1784. 250 acres.
Barnhart, Daniel. Pa. Private. ———. 200 acres.
Barnhart, John. N. Y. Private. 7 Jul. 1790. 600 acres.
Barns, Andrew. Va. Private. 29 Apr. 1835. 200 acres.
Barns, Frederick. Va. Private. 11 Jun. 1833. 100 acres.
Barns, George. Va. Private. 15 Aug. 1834. 100 acres.
Barns, Henry. N. Y. Private. 8 Jul. 1790. 500 acres.
Barns, Hezekiah. N.C. Corporal. 24 Nov. 1797. 357 acres.
Barns, James. Va. Private. 12 Aug. 1785. 100 acres.
Barns, James. Conn. Sufferer. Greenwich. 51.9.10 1/4.
Barns, John. Va. Lieutenant. 28 Mar. 1834. 2666 2/3 acres.
Barns, Nehemiah. Md. Private. ———. 50 acres.

Barns, Robert. Va. Private. 31 Mar. 1783. 100 acres.
Barnum, Abijah. Conn. Sufferer. Danbury. 7.4.0.
Barnum, Comfort. Conn. Sufferer. Danbury. 2.0.0.
Barnum, Eliphalet. Conn. Sufferer. Danbury. 42.6.8.
Barnum, Ephraim. Conn. Sufferer. Danbury. 3.10.0.
Barnum, John. Conn. Sufferer. Danbury. 5.17.0.
Barnum, Mary. Conn. Sufferer. Danbury. 22.12.0.
Barnum, Matthew. Conn. Sufferer. Danbury. 2.10.8.
Barnum, Thaddeus. Conn. Sufferer. Danbury. 17.9.5.
Barr, Jacob. S.C. ———. 4 Jul. 1785. 200 acres.
Barr, Jacob. S.C. ———. 4 Sep. 1786. 200 acres.
Barr, John. N. Y. Ensign. 9 Jul. 1790. 1150 acres.
Barr, John. Pa. Private. 10 Aug. 1787. 200 acres.
Barr, John. S.C. ———. 4 Sep. 1786. 200 acres to Jacob Barr, heir at law.
Barr, John. Va. Private. 26 Oct. 1803. 200 acres.
Barr, John. Conn. Sufferer. New London. 71.11.4.
Barr, Silas. N.C. Private. 7 Dec. 1797. 640 acres to heirs.
Barr, Silas. N.C. Private. 14 Dec. 1797. 640 acres to heirs.
Barr, Thomas. Pa. ———. 200 acres to Martha Barr, widow.
Barr, Thomas. Pa. Private. 30 Aug. 1787. 200 acres to widow Martha Barr.
Barr, William. Va. Private. 23 Jun. 1783. 200 acres.
Barrager, John. N. Y. Matross. 9 Jul. 1790. 600 acres.
Barrager, Walter. N. Y. Private. 8 Jul. 1790. 500 acres.
Barrall, Jacob. Pa. Private. 22 Nov. 1798. 200 acres.
Barras, Christian. Pa. Private. ———. 200 acres.
Barrer, Reubin. Ga. Soldier. 7 Jan. 1785. ———.
Barres, Moses. N.C. Private. 10 Dec. 1788. 640 acres to heirs.
Barret, Beetley. Va. Private. 6 Jun. 1807. 100 acres.
Barret, James. N. Y. Lieutenant. 9 Jul. 1790. 1000 acres.
Barret, Joshua. Md. Sergeant. ———. 50 acres.
Barret, William. Va. Captain. 25 May 1809. 444 acres.
Barrett, Abel. Conn. Sufferer. New/East Haven. 27.12.6
Barrett, Chiswell. Va. Captain. 17 Jul. 1783. 4000 acres.
Barrett, James. N. Y. ———. 13 Sep. 1790. 500 acres to heirs.
Barrett, John. Md. Private. ———. 50 acres.
Barrett, John. N. Y. ———. 13 Sep. 1790. 500 acres to heirs.
Barrett, Jonathan. Mass. Private. 20 Feb. 1834. 200 acres.
Barrett, Jonathan. Va. Lieutenant. 18 Apr. 1832. 4000 acres.
Barrett, Nathaniel. Me. ———. 15 Jun. 1835. 200 acres. Fairfield.
Barrett, Peter. N. Y. Private. 7 Jul. 1790. 600 acres.
Barrett, Solomon. Md. Private. ———. 50 acres.
Barrett, Thomas. Ga. ———. 26 May 1784. 287 1/2 acres.
Barrett, Walter. N. Y. ———. 13 Sep. 1790. 500 acres to heirs.
Barrett, William. N. Y. Corporal. 6 Jul. 1790. 500 acres.
Barrett, William. N.C. ———. 21 Apr. 1784. 3840 acres to Thomas Barritt, Jr., heir.
Barrett, William. Va. Captain. 17 Jul. 1783. 4000 acres.
Barrington, Frederick. N.C. Private. 14 Dec. 1797. 640 acres to heirs.
Barrom, Fielding. Va. Sergeant. 1 Feb. 1785. 400 acres.
Barron, Fielding. Va. Private. 19 Jun. 1783. 100 acres.
Barron, James. Md. Private. ———. 50 acres.
Barron, James. Va. Commodore. 2 Jun. 1783. 7888 2/3 acrs.
Barron, James. Va. Brigadier General. 4 Apr. 1831. 1087 1/3 acres.
Barron, James. Va. Brigadier General. 4 Apr. 1831. 1087 1/3 acres.

Barron, James. Va. Brigadier General. 4 Apr. 1831. 2175 1/3 acres.
Barron, James. Va. Midshipman. 21 Dec. 1833. 2666 2/3 acres.
Barron, James. Va. Commodore. 4 Nov. 1857. 6077 5/6 acres.
Barron, Richard. Va. Captain. 3 Jun. 1783. 5333 1/3 acres.
Barron, Richard. Va. Captain. 3 Nov. 1831. 1111 1/9 acres.
Barron, Samuel. Ga. ———. 17 May 1784. ——— to heirs.
Barron, Samuel. Va. Lieutenant. 14 Jan. 1832. 2000 acres.
Barron, Samuel. Va. Lieutenant. 14 Jan. 1832. 2000 acres.
Barron, Samuel. Va. Captain. 17 Sep. 1850. 1333 1/3 acres.
Barron, William. Ga. ———. 17 May 1784. ———.
Barron, William. Va. Lieutenant. 7 Aug. 1783. 4000 acres.
Barrott, John. N.C. Private. 30 Sep. 1785. 640 acres to heirs.
Barrow, James. Md. Private. ———. 50 acres.
Barrow, James. N.C. Drummer. 13 Dec. 1787. 357 acres.
Barrow, John. N.C. Private. 3 Dec. 1801. 228 acres.
Barrow, Reuben. Ga. Soldier. 3 Feb. 1785. 287 1/2 acres.
Barrows, Peter. Me. Private. 29 Jun. 1844. 200 acres to widow Elizabeth (Hunting) Barrows. Camden.
Barry, James. Pa. Private. 21 Oct. 1786. 200 acres.
Barry, John. Ga. ———. 17 May 1784. 230 acres.
Barry, John. Pa. Sergeant. ———. 250 acres.
Barry, Simon. Va. Private. 10 Dec. 1785. 100 acres.
Barstow, Benjamin. Me. ———. 28 Sep. 1835. 200 acres to widow Susannah Barstow. Nobleboro.
Bartee, Samuel. Va. Carpenter's Mate. 11 Apr. 1838. 2666 2/3 acres.
Barter, John. N.C. Private. 30 Sep. 1785. 640 acres.
Bartholomew, Benjamin. Pa. Captain. ———. 500 acres.
Bartholomew, John. N. Y. Private. 8 Jul. 1790. 600 acres.
Bartholomew, John. N.C. Private. 12 Mar. 1785. 228 acres.
Bartle, George. Pa. Private. 31 Aug. 1787. 200 acres.
Bartlett, Benjamin. Va. Private. 18 Jul. 1796. 100 acres.
Bartlett, John. Mass. Sergeant. 19 Nov. 1832. 200 acres to heirs.
Bartlett, John. Va. Private. 12 Apr. 1783. 200 acres.
Bartlett, John. Va. Sergeant. 3 Jul. 1784. 400 acres.
Bartlett, Jonathan. Mass. Sergeant. 10 Feb. 1830. 200 acres to heirs.
Bartlett, Joseph. Me. Private. 20 May 1835. 200 acres to widow Hannah Bartlett. Whitefield.
Bartlett, Lemuel. N. Y. Private. 8 Jul. 1790. 600 acres.
Bartlett, Philip. Va. Surgeon. 31 Dec. 1851. 6000 acres.
Bartlett, William. Mass. Private. 20 Feb. 1834. 200 acres to widow Lois Bartlett.
Bartley, Alexander. Va. Private. 20 Aug. 1784. 100 acres.
Bartley, John. Ga. ———. 20 Aug. 1785. ———.
Bartley, Joshua. Va. Corporal. 5 Jun. 1784. 200 acres.
Bartley, William. Va. Private. 19 Aug. 1783. 100 acres.
Bartlie, John. N.C. Private. 26 Aug. 1785. 640 acres to heirs.
Bartoe, Jonas. N. Y. Private. 8 Jul. 1790. 500 acres.
Bartoe, Morris. N. Y. Private. 8 Jul. 1790. 600 acres.
Barton, Ebenezer. Me. ———. 10 Oct. 1835. 200 acres. Windham.
Barton, Ephraim. N.C. Private. 13 Sep. 1820. 640 acres.
Barton, Henry. Va. Private. 5 Nov. 1790. 100 acres.
Barton, James. Va. Private. 10 Feb. 1784. 100 acres.
Barton, John. Me. Private. 3 Jul. 1835. 200 acres to widow Abigail Barton. Lisbon.
Barton, Joseph. Md. Private. ———. 50 acres.
Barton, Robert. N.Y. ———. 13 Sep. 1790. 500 acres to heirs.
Barton, Sylvannus. N.C. Private. 15 Feb. 1797. 320 acres.

Barton, William. Ga. ———. 6 Feb. 1784. 500 acres.
Barton, Willoughby. Ga. Sergeant. 26 May 1784. 287 1/2 acres.
Bartow, Silas. Conn. Sufferer. Norwalk. 48.12.6.
Bartram, Ebenezer. Conn. Sufferer. Fairfield. 144.10.3.
Bartram, Job. Conn. Sufferer. Fairfield. 962.17.5.
Bartran, Job. Conn. Sufferer. Fairfield. 13.10.0.
Basdel, Jacob. N.C. Private. 28 Sep. 1785. 640 acres.
Basey, Jeremiah. Va. Corporal. 11 Oct. 1826. 400 acres.
Basey, William. Va. Sergeant. 16 Feb. 1787. 400 acres.
Basey, William. Va. Private. 16 Feb. 1787. 100 acres.
Basford, James. Pa. Dragoon. 29 Jan. 1787. 200 acres.
Basil, Daniel. Md. Fifer. ———. 50 acres.
Basil, Owen. Ga. ———. 20 Aug. 1785. ———.
Baskerville, John. Va. Sergeant. 24 Feb. 1812. 200 acres.
Baskerville, John. Va. Sergeant. 2 Jun. 1857. 200 acres.
Baskerville, Samuel. Va. Lieutenant. 23 May 1783. 1500 acres.
Baskerville, Samuel. Va. Lieutenant. 23 May 1783. 1610 2/3 acres.
Baskerville, Samuel. Va. Lieutenant. 7 Apr. 1808. 333 1/3 acres.
Bason, Daniel. N. Y. Private. 8 Jul. 1790. 600 acres.
Bason, Michael. N. Y. ———. 14 Jun. 1790. 500 acres.
Bass, Britain. N.C. Private. 17 Dec. 1785. 640 acres to heirs.
Bass, Drewry. N.C. Private. 10 May 1784. 243 acres.
Bass, Esau. N.C. Private. 2 Feb. 1785. 274 acres.
Bass, Ezdras. N.C. Private. 17 Feb. 1824. 640 acres.
Bass, Henry. N. Y. Private. 8 Jul. 1790. 600 acres.
Bass, Jonathan. N.C. Private. 19 Jan. 1786. 640 acres.
Bass, Moses. N.C. Private. 17 Dec. 1785. 640 acres.
Bass, Samuel. Mass. Private. 11 Jul. 1837. 200 acres to assignee Samuel Cook.
Bass, Thomas. Va. Private. 23 Feb. 1831. 100 acres.
Basset, Richard. Md. Private. ———. 50 acres.
Basset, Sarah. Conn. Sufferer. Danbury. 0.18.8.
Basset, William. N. Y. ———. 13 Sep. 1790. 500 acres to heirs.
Bassett, George. Ga. Soldier. 13 Sep. 1784. 287 1/2 acres.
Bassett, James. Va. Private. 20 Sep. 1806. 100 acres.
Bassett, James. Va. Private. 20 Sep. 1806. 200 acres.
Basye, Benjamin. Va. Private. 8 May 1830. 100 acres.
Basye, Benjamin. Va. Private. 27 Dec. 1841. 100 acres.
Basye, Benjmain. Va. Private. 8 May 1830. 100 acres.
Basye, Jesse. Va. Private. 8 May 1830. 100 acres.
Batchelder, Henry. Va. Private. 4 Jan. 1834. 100 acres.
Batchelor, Peter. Va. Private. 19 Feb. 1784. 200 acres.
Batchelor, Peter. Va. Sergeant. 19 Feb. 1784. 200 acres.
Batchley, Joshua. Md. Private. ———. 50 acres.
Bateman, George. Md. Private. ———. 50 acres.
Bateman, John. N. Y. Lieutenant. 13 Sep. 1790. 1000 acres.
Bateman, John. N. Y. Lieutenant. ———. 1000 acres.
Bateman, Nathan. Md. Private. ———. 50 acres.
Bateman, Navey. N.C. Private. 2 Feb. 1786. 640 acres to heirs.
Bates, Caspar. Pa. Private. 7 Feb. 1787. 200 acres to Richard Leedom, assignee.
Bates, Conradt. N. Y. Private. 8 Jul. 1790. 500 acres.
Bates, David. N. Y. ———. 30 Oct. 1802. 1000 acres.
Bates, David. Pa. Sergeant. 29 Jan. 1803. 250 acres to Patrick Cample, assignee.
Bates, Edward. N.C. Private. 14 Sep. 1820. 274 acres.

Bates, George. Pa. ———. 27 Jan. 1824. 200 acres to Adam Reigart, executor in trust.
Bates, John. Ga. ———. 28 Feb. 1784. 250 acres.
Bates, John. Va. Private. 24 Sep. 1783. 200 acres.
Bates, John. Va. Private. 22 Aug. 1786. 200 acres.
Bates, Lebbens. Mass. Corporal. 19 Mar. 1834. 200 acres.
Bates, Luke. N.C. Private. 25 Mar. 1784. 640 acres.
Bates, Matthias. N.C. Private. 12 Dec. 1785. 640 acres.
Bates, Samuel. Me. ———. 7 May 1835. 200 acres to widow Susanna Bates. Fairfield.
Bates, Simeon. N.C. Private. 22 Apr. 1785. 228 acres.
Bates, Thomas. Va. Private. 27 Dec. 1796. 200 acres.
Bates, Thomas. Va. Private. 22 Apr. 1820. 200 acres.
Batman, William. N.C. Sergeant. 22 Dec. 1796. 1000 acres to heirs.
Batson, Thomas. Va. Sailor. 30 Jun. 1834. 100 acres.
Batten, Thomas. Va.-Ind. Private. 108 acres. [Benton].
Batten, William. Md. Private. ———. 50 acres.
Battersby, Robert. N. Y. Private. 8 Jul. 1790. 500 acres.
Batterson, George. Conn. Sufferer. Fairfield. 55.13.3.
Batterson, William. Conn. Sufferer. Fairfield. 16.3.0.
Batterton, Samuel. Va. Private. 12 Apr. 1784. 100 acres.
Battles, Shadrach. Va. Private. 11 Jun. 1821. 100 acres.
Batton, Hugh. Md. Private. ———. 50 acres.
Batton, John. Md. Private. ———. 50 acres.
Batts, Sampson. N.C. Private. 28 Sep. 1785. 640 acres to heirs.
Batty, William. Ga. ———. 20 Feb. 1784. 250 acres.
Baty, Hugh. N.C. Corporal. 14 Apr. 1800. 1000 acres.
Baudifield, Silas. N.C. Private. 23 Nov. 1797. 640 acres to heirs.
Baughan, Aris. Va. Private. 27 Mar. 1783. 100 acres.
Baughan, William. Va. Private. 31 Jan. 1784. 100 acres.
Baughman, George. Pa. Private. 17 Jun. 1786. 200 acres to Samuel Benizet, assignee.
Bauman, Sebastian. N. Y. Major. 7 Jul. 1790. 2400 acres.
Baumgartner, Henry. Va. Private. 15 Apr. 1793. 200 acres.
Baumgartner, Leonard. Va. Private. 23 May 1835. 200 acres.
Bauswell, William. Va. Private. 18 Apr. 1823. 100 acre.
Bawcat, William. Va. Forage Master. 12 Apr. 1796. 400 acres.
Bawcut, William. Va. Forage Master. 4 Nov. 1859. 1800 acres.
Bawcut, William. Va. Forage Master. 4 Nov. 1859. 1800 acres.
Bawcut, William. Va. Forage Master. 4 Nov. 1859. 1000 acres.
Bawcut, William. Va. Forage Master. 4 Nov. 1859. 500 acres.
Bawcut, William. Va. Forage Master. 4 Nov. 1859. 150 acres.
Bawcut, William. Va. Forage Master. 4 Nov. 1859. 150 acres.
Baxley, Joseph. N.C. Private. 26 May 1784. 640 acres.
Baxter, Alexander. Pa. Private. 21 Oct. 1786. 200 acres.
Baxter, Andrew. Ga. Private. ———. 287 1/2 acres.
Baxter, James. Va.-Ind. Private. 108 acres.
Baxter, James. Pa Private. 9 Mar. 1795. 200 acres to John Nicholson, assignee.
Baxter, James. Pa. Private. 25 Nov. 1786. 200 acres.
Baxter, John. Md. Private. ———. 50 acres.
Baxter, Samuel. N.C. Sergeant. 27 Oct. 1783. 1000 acres.
Baxter, Thomas. Md. Private. ———. 50 acres.
Baxter, Thomas. N.C. Private. 30 Sep. 1785. 640 acres.
Bay, Andrew. N.C. Sergeant Major. 8 May 1784. 357 acres.
Bayard, Stephen. Pa. Lieutenant Colonel. 15 Dec. 1786. 500 acres.
Bayard, Stephen. Pa. Lieutenant Colonel. 15 Dec. 1786. 250 acres.

Bayes, Joseph, Jr. Ga. ———. 17 May 1784. ———.
Bayles, Jesse. Va. Private. 12 Nov. 1787. 100 acres.
Bayles, Noah. Va. Private. 6 Oct. 1783. 100 acres.
Bayley, James. Md. Drummer. ———. 50 acres.
Bayley, James. Pa. Private. 16 Nov. 1786. 200 acres.
Bayley, James. Va. Sergeant. 24 Feb. 1784. 200 acres.
Bayley, John. Md. Private. ———. 50 acres.
Bayley, Robert. Va. Private. 18 Apr. 1832. 100 acres.
Bayley, Sacker. Va. Private. 16 Dec. 1833. 200 acres.
Bayley, Southey. Va. ———. 10 Mar. 1840. 100 acres.
Baylie, Peter. Va. Sailor. 3 Dec. 1783. 100 acres.
Baylis, Henry. Va. Subaltern. 16 Jun. 1784. 2666 2/3 acres.
Baylis, William. Ga. ———. 24 May 1784. 287 1/2 acres to heirs.
Baylis, William. Va. Private. 11 Aug. 1783. 100 acres.
Baylis, William. Va. Subaltern. 16 Jun. 1784. 2666 2/3 acres.
Baylor, George. Va. Colonel. 25 Jan. 1783. 6666 2/3 acres.
Baylor, George. Va. Colonel. 29 Jan. 1784. 2222 acres.
Baylor, John. Va. Lieutenant. 10 Aug. 1835. 106 1/3 acres.
Baylor, John. Va. Lieutenant. 10 Aug. 1835. 533 1/3 acres.
Baylor, John. Va. Lieutenant. 10 Aug. 1835. 427 acres.
Baylor, John. Va. Lieutenant. 10 Aug. 1835. 533 1/3 acres.
Baylor, John. Va. Lieutenant. 10 Aug. 1835. 533 1/3 acres.
Baylor, John. Va. Lieutenant. 23 Sep. 1837. 381 acres.
Baylor, John. Va. Lieutenant. 10 Jan. 1843. 76 1/7 acres.
Baylor, John. Va. Lieutenant. 10 Jan. 1843. 76 1/7 acres.
Baylor, John. Va. Lieutenant. 29 Oct. 1836. 400 acres.
Baylor, John. Va. Lieutenant. 12 Jul. 1841. 66 2/3 acres.
Baylor, John. Va. Lieutenant. 1 Dec. 1841. 66 2/3 acres.
Baylor, Walker. Va. Captain. 23 May 1783. 2000 acres.
Baylor, Walker. Va. Captain. 23 May 1783. 2000 acres.
Baylor, Walker. Va. Captain. 19 May 1823. 500 acres.
Bayne, John. N.C. Private. 24 Dec. 1796. 274 acres.
Baynham, John. Va. Lieutenant. 18 Mar. 1784. 2666 2/3 acres.
Bays, Joseph. Ga. ———. 17 May 1784. ———.
Bayse, Jesse. Va. Private. 8 May 1830. 100 acres.
Bayse, Richard. Va. Private. 23 Jul. 1824. 100 acres.
Baytop, John. Va. Captain. 13 Aug. 1783. 4000 acres.
Baytop, John. Va. Lieutenant. 13 Aug. 1783. 2666 2/3 acres.
Baytop, Thomas. Va. Captain. 19 May 1784. 4000 acres.
Bazemore, Robert. N.C. Private. 30 Sep. 1785. 640 acres to heirs.
Bazilille, John. Pa. Private. ———. 200 acres.
Bazzmore, Michael. N.C. Private. 30 Sep. 1785. 640 acres to heirs.
Beach, Amos. N. Y. Private. 8 Jul. 1790. 600 acres.
Beach, Benjamin. Va. Master's Mate. 20 May 1834. 2666 2/3 acres.
Beach, Ignatious. N.C. Private. 2 Feb. 1786. 640 acres to heirs.
Beach, John. Md. Drummer. ———. 50 acres.
Beach, Peter. Ga. ———. 5 Aug. 1785. ———.
Beach, Robert. N.C. Private. 2 Feb. 1786. 640 acres to heirs.
Beach, Samuel. Mass. ———. 22 Jul. 1833. 200 acres.
Beacon, Thompson. N. Y. Sergeant. 8 Jul. 1790. 600 acres.
Beal, Archibald. Ga. Adjutant. 6 Feb. 1784. 500 acres.
Beal, Isaac. Va. Major. 19 May 1823. 1000 acres.
Beal, Isaac. Va. Major. 19 May 1823. 1000 acres.
Beal, Isaac. Va. Major. 19 May 1823. 2000 acres.

Beal, Isaac. Va. Major. 19 May 1823. 1333 1/3 acres.
Beal, Jeremiah. Ga. Refugee. 22 Mar. 1789. To son James Beal, ward of Zephaniah Beal, father of said Jeremiah.
Beal, John. N.C. Private. 21 Aug. 1820. 640 acres.
Beal, Nathaniel. Ga. ———. 6 Feb. 1784. 250 acres.
Beal, William. S.C. ———. 2 Oct. 1786. 200 acres.
Beal, William. Va. Sergeant. 7 Nov. 1783. 400 acres.
Beal, Zephaniah. Ga. ———. 6 Feb. 1784. 250 acres.
Beale, Robert. Va. Captain. 26 Mar. 1783. 4666 2/3 acres.
Beale, Robert. Va. Captain. 27 Sep. 1808. 555 acres.
Beall, Garratt. Ga. Private. 10 Dec. 1784. 250 acres.
Beall, George. Ga. Soldier. 4 Feb. 1785. ———.
Beall, Henry. Ga. Minute Man. 1785. 500 acres.
Beall, Hezekiah. Ga. ———. 17 May 1784. ———.
Beall, John. Ga. Soldier. 4 Feb. 1785. ———.
Beall, Lloyd. Md. Captain. ———. 200 acres.
Beall, Nathaniel. Ga. Private. 10 Dec. 1784. 250 acres.
Beall, Nathaniel. Va. Private. 4 Apr. 1810. 100 acres.
Beall, Nathaniel. Va. Private. 4 Apr. 1810. 200 acres.
Beall, Robert. Va. Captain. 6 Aug. 1808. 1055 1/2 acres.
Beall, Samuel B. Md. Lieutenant. ———. 200 acres.
Beall, William Dent. Md. Major. ———. 200 acres.
Bealle, Robert. Va. Captain. 17 Jun. 1783. 4000 acres.
Beals, Isaac. Mass. Quartermaster Gunner/Sergeant. 23 Oct. 1834. 200 acres to widow Sarah Pierce.
Beals, Joshua. Mass. Private. 18 Oct. 1833. 200 acres.
Beam, Frederick. Pa. Private. 9 Oct. 1786. 200 acres.
Beaman, Francis. N.C. Private. 10 Aug. 1785. 640 acres to heirs.
Beaman, Jeremiah. N.C. Private. 1 Jul. 1820. 640 acres to heirs.
Bean, Edmund. N.C. Private. 2 Feb. 1786. 640 acres to heirs.
Bean, Henry. Pa. Private. ———. 200 acres.
Bean, Jesse. N.C. Private. 2 Feb. 1786. 640 acres to heirs.
Bean, John. Md. Private. ———. 50 acres.
Bean, Leonard. Md. Corporal. ———. 50 acres.
Bean, Reubin. Ga. Minute Man. 3 Oct. 1783. ———.
Bean, Richard. N.C. Private. 17 Dec. 1796. 274 acres.
Bean, Robert. N.C. Private. 2 Feb. 1786. 640 acres.
Bean, William. N.C. Private. 2 Feb. 1786. 640 acres to heirs.
Bear, Edward. N. Y. Matross. 6 Jul. 1790. 600 acres.
Bear, Thomas. Md. Private. ———. 50 acres.
Beard, Edmund. Ga. ———. 17 May 1784. ———.
Beard, George. Ga. Refugee. Nov. 1784. ———.
Beard, James. N.C. Private. 30 Sep. 1785. 640 acres to heirs.
Beard, John. Ga. Private. 20 Feb. 1784. 250 acres.
Beard, Lewis. N.C. Private. 17 Dec. 1785. 640 acres to heirs.
Beard, Peter. Ga. Minute Man. 3 Sep. 1785. ———.
Bears, David. N. Y. ———. 13 Sep. 1790. 500 acres to heirs.
Beasely, Burwell. Ga. ———. 15 Mar. 1784. 250 acres.
Beasely, Richard. Ga. ———. 15 Mar. 1784. 250 acres.
Beasley, Ephraim. Va. Private. 22 Jan. 1812. 200 acres.
Beasley, Hardy. N.C. Private. 15 Feb. 1797. 320 acres.
Beasley, James. Ga. ———. 15 Mar. 1784. 250 acres.
Beasley, John. N.C. Fifer. 17 Dec. 1785. 357 acres.
Beasley, John. N.C. Corporal. 24 Aug. 1819. 428 acres.
Beasley, Joseph. Ga. ———. 28 Feb. 1784. 250 acres.

Beasley, Larkin. Va. Private. 12 Nov. 1787. 100 acres.
Beasley, Peter. S.C. ———. 6 Oct. 1794. 200 acres to James Timms, administrator.
Beasley, Richard. Va. Private. 9 Jun. 1783. 100 acres.
Beasley, Samuel. N.C. Private. 2 Sep. 1820. 274 acres.
Beasley, Smith. Va. Private. 14 Feb. 1834. 200 acres.
Beasley, William. Ga. ———. 15 Mar. 1784. 250 acres.
Beasly, William. Pa. Private. ———. 200 acres.
Beatley, James. Va. Private. 12 Dec. 1783. 200 acres.
Beatley, Ralph. Va. Sailor. 30 Jun. 1784. 100 acres.
Beatley, William. Va. Sailor. 30 Jun. 1784. 100 acres.
Beatty, Erarias. Pa. Lieutenant. 12 Oct. 1786. 200 acres.
Beatty, Ercurius. Pa. Lieutenant. 12 Oct. 1786. 200 acres.
Beatty, John. Pa. Private. 17 Oct. 1786. 200 acres.
Beatty, Reading. Pa. Surgeon. 13 Oct. 1786. 300 acres.
Beatty, Reading. Pa. Surgeon. 13 Oct. 1786. 300 acres.
Beatty, Samuel. Ga. Minute Man. 17 May 1784. ———.
Beatty, Thomas. Ga. Soldier. 5 May 1785. ———.
Beatty, Thomas. Md. Lieutenant. ———. 200 acres.
Beatty, William. Ga. ———. 17 May 1784. ———.
Beatty, William. Md. Captain. ———. 200 acres.
Beatty, William. Pa. Matross. 30 July 1787. 200 acres.
Beaty, Charles. Pa. Private. 8 Mar. 1809. 200 acres to heirs.
Beaty, Charles. Pa. Lieutenant. 8 Mar. 1809. 200 acres to heirs.
Beaufort, Casper. Pa. Private. 24 Sep. 1787. 200 acres.
Beaumont, Joseph. N.C. Sergeant. 16 Aug. 1821. 1000 acres.
Beaver, Edward. N. Y. Matross. 9 Jul. 1790. 600 acres.
Beaver, John. N.C. Sergeant. 22 Apr. 1785. 1000 acres.
Beaver, Samuel. Va. Corporal. 4 Jun. 1783. 200 acres.
Beaver, William. Va. Drummer. 20 Aug. 1783. 100 acres.
Beavers, Benjamin. Va. Sergeant. 30 Aug. 1783. 200 acres.
Beazley, Cornelius. Va. Private. 1 Sep. 1794. 100 acres.
Bebee, Joseph. Conn. Sufferer. Danbury. 12.10.8.
Becam, Robert. Va. Private. 18 Jun. 1783. 200 acres.
Becannon, Samuel. N. Y. Private. 8 Jul. 1790. 500 acres.
Becchus, Jacob. N. Y. Private. 7 Jul. 1790. 600 acres.
Beck, Alexander. Md. Private. ———. 50 acres.
Beck, George. N.C. Sergeant. 22 Apr. 1785. 1000 acres to heirs.
Beck, John. Va. Lieutenant. 17 Jun. 1783. 2666 2/3 acres.
Beck, John. Va. Lieutenant. 31 Dec. 1806. 444 2/3 acres.
Beck, Simon. Ga. ———. 17 May 1784. ———.
Beckenham, William. N.C. Private. 4 May 1785. 640 acres to heirs.
Becker, Henry. N. Y. Sergeant. 13 Sep. 1790. 500 acres to heirs.
Becket, George. Va. Seaman. 9 Dec. 1833. 100 acres.
Beckett, Humphrey. Md. Sergeant. ———. 50 acres.
Beckett, Humphrey. Va. Private. 27 Apr. 1801. 100 acres.
Beckham, Abner. Ga. Refugee. 17 May 1784. ———.
Beckham, Allen. Ga. ———. 23 Jul. 1784. 287 1/2 acres.
Beckham, Archibald. N.C. Private. 7 Jan. 1786. 640 acres to heirs.
Beckham, James. Va. Private. 2 May 1785. 100 acres.
Beckham, John. Ga. ———. 17 May 1784. ———.
Beckham, Laban. Ga. Citizen. 5 Apr. 1785. 287 1/2 acres.
Beckham, Samuel. Ga. ———. 15 Mar. 1784. 250 acres.
Beckham, Sherwood. Ga. ———. 30 Sep. 1784. ———.

Beckham, Simon. Ga. ———. 28 Feb. 1784. 250 acres.
Beckham, Solomon. Ga. ———. 15 Mar. 1784. 250 acres.
Beckham, William. Va. Private. 1 Jul. 1784. 100 acres.
Beckler, Daniel. Me. Private. 8 May 1835. 200 acres to widow Elizabeth Beckler. Greenwood.
Beckley, William. Va.-Ind. Private. 108 acres.
Beckley, William. Va. Private. 9 Apr. 1835. 100 acres.
Beckman, James. Ga. ———. 5 Aug. 1785. ———.
Beckman, John. N. Y. Sergeant. 8 Jul. 1790. 600 acres.
Beckman, Robert. Ga. ———. 5 Aug. 1785. ———.
Becknall, James. Va. Private. 10 Mar. 1784. 100 acres.
Becknall, Thomas. Va. Private. 10 Mar. 1784. 100 acres.
Becks, Christopher. Va. Private. 20 Jun. 1783. 100 acres.
Becks, William. N.C. Ensign. 28 May 1784. 1096 acres.
Beddoe, Laurence. Va. Private. 15 Jun. 1812. 100 acres.
Beden, Elijah. Ga. Minute Man. 3 Sep. 1785. ———.
Bedford, Antoine. N. Y. ———. ———. 500 acres.
Bedford, James. Va. Sergeant. 4 Mar. 1784. 400 acres.
Bedinger, Daniel. Va. Private. 3 Apr. 1783. 100 acres.
Bedinger, Daniel. Va. Lieutenant. 23 Dec. 1783. 2666 2/3 acres.
Bedinger, Daniel. Va. Lieutenant. 5 Feb. 1810. 592 1/4 acres.
Bedinger, Daniel. Va. Lieutenant. 17 Jan. 1839. 418 14/27 acres.
Bedinger, Daniel. Va. Lieutenant. 17 Jan. 1839. 418 14/27 acres.
Bedinger, Henry. Va. Captain. 1 Apr. 1784. 666 2/3 acres.
Bedinger, Henry. Va. Captain. 3 Apr. 1783. 4000 acres.
Bedinger, Henry. Va. Captain. 28 Oct. 1793. 1333 1/3 acres.
Bedinger, Philip. N. Y. Corporal. 8 Jul. 1790. 600 acres.
Bedingfield, Charles. Ga. ———. ———. 250 acres.
Bedingfield, Nathaniel. Ga. ———. 22 Jul. 1784. 287 1/2 acres.
Bedle, David. Pa. Private. 6 Nov. 1788. 200 acres.
Bedner, Christopher [or Christian]. N. Y. ———. 13 Sep. 1790. 500 acres to heirs.
Bedo, John. N.C. Private. 22 Dec. 1796. 274 acres.
Bedworth, William. Pa. Private. 25 Apr. 1787. 200 acres.
Bedworth, William. Va. Private. 15 Oct. 1783. 200 acres.
Beebe, Elizabeth. Conn. Sufferer. New London. 16.6.0.
Beebe, Hannah. Conn. Sufferer. New London. 6.18.9.
Beebe, Jonah. Conn. Sufferer. New London. 236.2.6.
Beebe, Lydia. Conn. Sufferer. New London. 24.5.0.
Beebe, Stephen. Mass. Private. 20 May 1836. 200 acres.
Beebe, Walter. Conn. Sufferer. New London. 9.8.9.
Beebee, Boanerges. N. Y. Private. 8 Jul. 1790. 600 acres.
Beech, Elias. Conn. Sufferer. New/East Haven. 3.10.0.
Beecher, David. Conn. Sufferer. New/East Haven. 19.5.0.
Beecher, Isaac. Conn. Sufferer. New/East Haven. 3.15.9.
Beecher, John. Conn. Sufferer. New/East Haven. 25.17.0.
Beecher, John, Jr. Conn. Sufferer. New/ East Haven. 23.9.10.
Beecher, Titus. Conn. Sufferer. New/East Haven. 5.8.0.
Beeckhorn, Jeremiah. N.Y. ———. 13 Sep. 1790. 500 acres to heirs.
Beeckman, Terrick. N. Y. Lieutenant. 9 Jul. 1790. 1200 acres.
Beedle, John. N. Y. Private. 8 Jul. 1790. 600 acres.
Beek, George. N.C. Private. 23 Nov. 1797. 640 acres to heirs.
Beekman, Barnard. S.C. Colonel. 21 Jan. 1785. 500 acres.
Beekman, Samuel. S.C. Lieutenant. 21 Jan. 1785. 200 acres.

Beel, Henry. Mass. Corporal. 28 Feb. 1832. 200 acres.

Beeman, Moses. Pa. ———. 7 Oct. 1802. 200 acres.

Been, John. Va. Sailor. 19 Dec. 1783. 100 acres.

Beeney, Joseph. N.C. Private. 17 Feb. 1824. 640 acres.

Beer, Percy. Conn. Sufferer. New London. 6.17.2.

Beers, David. Conn. Sufferer. Fairfield. 164.4.6.

Beers, James. Va. Private. Dec. 1783. 200 acres.

Beers, Joseph. Conn. Sufferer. Fairfield. 90.17.0.

Beers, Nathan. Conn. Sufferer. Norwalk. 195.1.0.

Beers, Nathan. Conn. Sufferer. New/East Haven. 13.0.0.

Beers, Reuben. Conn. Sufferer. Fairfield. 510.4.2.

Beers, Samuel. Conn. Sufferer. Fairfield. 96.8.5.

Beery, Peter. Pa. Corporal. ———. 200 acres.

Beeson, Edward. Va. Ensign. 1 Jul. 1819. 2666 2/3 acres.

Beeson, Mercer. Va. Private. 16 Feb. 1819. 200 acres.

Beetam, Jacob. Pa. Private. 11 May 1787. 200 acres.

Beets, Benjamin, Jr. Conn. Sufferer. Norwalk. 3.10.0.

Begeant, William. Va. Private. 4 Aug. 1834. 200 acres.

Begelston, Isaiah. N.C. Private. 30 Sep. 1785. 640 acres to heirs.

Begent, John. Va. Private. 21 Aug. 1809. 100 acres.

Beggett, Jesse. N.C. Private. 23 Apr. 1785. 640 acres to heirs.

Beggs, Moore. Pa. Sergeant. 17 Aug. 1789. 250 acres.

Begley, John. S.C. Sergeant. 21 Jan. 1785. 200 acres.

Begworth, Stephen. N.C. Private. 30 Sep. 1785. 640 acres to heirs.

Beham, James. Va. Private. 23 Jun. 1783. 200 acres.

Belanger, Julian. N. Y. ———. ———. 500 acres.

Belch, James. N.C. Private. 30 Sep. 1785. 640 acres to heirs.

Belcher, Benjamin. Md. Private. ———. 50 acres.

Belcher, Elisha. Conn. Sufferer. Greenwich. 39.1.0.

Belcher, George. Va. Private. 12 Nov. 1783. 100 acres.

Belcher, Robert. Va. Private. 5 Nov. 1783. 100 aces.

Belden, John. Conn. Sufferer. Norwalk. 303.14.6.

Belden, Samuel. Conn. Sufferer. New London. 1,771.15.6.

Belfast, George. Md. Private. ———. 50 acres.

Belfield, John. Va. Major. 1 Nov. 1783. 5333 1/3 acres.

Belfield, John. Va. Major. 22 Nov. 1798. 888 5/6 acres.

Belfield, John. Va. Major. 6 Nov. 1807. 370 acres.

Belknap, William. N. Y. Lieutenant. 6 Jul. 1790. 1200 acres.

Bell, Abigail. Conn. Sufferer. New London. 6.11.9.

Bell, Benjamin. N.C. Private. 17 Feb. 1804. 640 acres to heirs.

Bell, Daniel. Mass. Private. 14 Mar. 1839. 200 acres.

Bell, George. N.C. Private. 15 Nov. 1793. 640 acres to heirs.

Bell, Henry. Ga. ———. ———. 287 1/2 acres.

Bell, Henry. Va. Lieutenant. 21 Jan. 1784. 2666 2/3 acres.

Bell, Henry. Va. Lieutenant. 15 Feb. 1809. 666 acres.

Bell, Hugh. Ga. Soldier. 16 Mar. 1784. 200 acres.

Bell, James. Ga. ———. 17 May 1784. ———.

Bell, James. Va. Sergeant. 16 Sep. 1783. 200 acres.

Bell, James. Va. Sergeant. 1 Jun. 1805. 200 acres.

Bell, Joab. N.C. Private. 8 Sep. 1823. 640 acres to his heirs.

Bell, John. Ga. Soldier. 17 May 1784. ———.

Bell, John. N. Y. Corporal. 13 Sep. 1790. 500 acres to heirs.

Bell, John. Pa. Private. ———. 200 acres.

Bell, John. Va. Lieutenant. 20 Dec. 1784. 1666 2/3 acres.

Bell, John. Va. Lieutenant. 20 Dec. 1784. 1000 acres.
Bell, Matthew. N. Y. Private. 7 Jul. 1790. 600 acres.
Bell, Ning. Va. Private. 22 Jul. 1783. 100 acres.
Bell, Robert. Ga. Refugee. 5 Nov. 1784. ———.
Bell, Robert. N.C. Lieutenant. 16 Oct. 1783. 2560 acres.
Bell, Ruebin D. N.C. Private. 5 Dec. 1797. 274 acres.
Bell, Samuel. Va.-Ind. Private. 108 acres.
Bell, Samuel. Va. Captain. 22 Jul. 1824. 1000 acres.
Bell, Samuel. Va. Captain. 22 Jul. 1824. 1000 acres.
Bell, Samuel. Va. Captain. 28 Sep. 1832. 666 2/3 acres.
Bell, Samuel. Va. Captain. 19 Oct. 1860. 1769 2/3 acres.
Bell, Thomas. Va. Captain. 8 Apr. 1783. 4000 acres.
Bell, Thomas. Va. Private. 1 Mar. 1784. 100 acres.
Bell, Thomas. Va. Sergeant. 21 Dec. 1833. 400 acres.
Bell, William. Va.-Ind. Private. 108 acres.
Bell, William. N.C. Private. 8 Dec. 1796. 640 acres.
Bell, William. Va. Private. 1 Apr. 1784. 100 acres.
Bell, William. Va. Private. 7 Sep. 1784. 100 acres.
Bellamy, Richard. Ga. ———. 17 May 1784. 250 acres.
Bellanger, Noel. N. Y. ———. ———. 500 acres.
Bellows, Elihu. Mass. Private. 11 Jul. 1837. 200 acres to assignee Samuel Cook.
Bellwood, Samuel. N.C. Private. 30 Sep. 1785. 640 acres to heirs.
Belmy, Silas. N. Y. ———. 13 Sep. 1790. 500 acres to heirs.
Belote, Noah. Va. Sergeant. 19 Mar. 1831. 66 2/3 acres.
Belote, Noah. Va. ———. 5 Jun. 1834. 66 2/3 acres.
Belote, Noah. Va. ———. 14 Mar. 1837. 66 2/3 acres.
Belote, William. Va. Private. 14 Feb. 1834. 200 acres.
Belsh, Philip. N.C. Private. 7 Dec. 1797. 640 acres to heirs.
Belsire, Thomas. N.C. Private. 22 Dec. 1803. 640 acres.
Belt, John Sprigg. Md. Captain. ———. 200 acres.
Belvin, George. Va. Private. 29 Oct. 1783. 100 acres.
Belvin, John. Va. Private. 25 Apr. 1832. 100 acres.
Belvin, Lewis. Va. Private. 29 Oct. 1783. 100 acres.
Belvin, Robert. Va. Matross. 11 May 1790. 200 acres.
Belvin, Robert. Va. Private. 25 Apr. 1832. 100 acres.
Belvin, Thomas. Va. Private. 25 Apr. 1832. 100 acres.
Belvin, William. Va. Sergeant. 29 Apr. 1783. 400 acres.
Belvin, William. Va. Private. 25 Apr. 1832. 100 acres.
Bement, Joel. N.C. Sergeant. 7 Mar. 1785. 357 acres.
Bemis, Daniel. Mass. Private. 18 Oct. 1833. 200 acres.
Bemis, Jesse. Mass. Sergeant. 17 Feb. 1834. 200 acres.
Bemis, John. Mass. Private. 14 May 1833. 200 acres.
Bemis, Thaddeus. Me. Private. 28 Feb. 1837. 200 acres. Fryburg.
Benbrook, Ezekiel. Ga. ———. 17 May 1784. ———.
Bencham, Hodges. N.C. Private. 17 Dec. 1785. 640 acres to heirs.
Bender, John. Ga. Soldier. 1784. 287 1/2 acres.
Bendes, Aaron. N.C. Private. 7 Dec. 1797. 640 acres to heirs.
Benedict, Abijah. Conn. Sufferer. Danbury. 5.1.4.
Benedict, Abraham. Conn. Sufferer. Norwalk. 73.3.1.
Benedict, Ambrose. N. Y. Private. 8 Jul. 1790. 600 acres.
Benedict, Ebenezer. Conn. Sufferer. Danbury. 5.16.10.
Benedict, Ebenezer, Jr. Conn. Sufferer. Danbury. 4.14.4.
Benedict, Enoch. Conn. Sufferer. Norwalk. 84.1.8.
Benedict, George. Pa. Private. ———. 200 acres.

Benedict, Isaac. Conn. Sufferer. Danbury. 4.4.6.

Benedict, Jesse. Conn. Sufferer. Norwalk. 114.7.6.

Benedict, Jesse. Conn. Sufferer. Ridgefield. 11.10.2.

Benedict, John. Conn. Sufferer. Norwalk. 172.12.8.

Benedict, Jonah. Conn. Sufferer. Danbury. 206.6.4 1/2.

Benedict, Jonas. Conn. Sufferer. Danbury. 1.10.8.

Benedict, Joseph. Conn. Sufferer. Danbury. 7.15.8.

Benedict, Joseph, Jr. Conn. Sufferer. Danbury. 7.18.0.

Benedict, Joshua. Conn. Sufferer. Danbury. 12.18.8.

Benedict, Lemuel. Conn. Sufferer. Danbury. 2.10.4.

Benedict, Mary. Conn. Sufferer. Norwalk. 40.0.0.

Benedict, Matthew. Conn. Sufferer. Danbury. 176.16.5.

Benedict, Matthew, Jr. Conn. Sufferer. Danbury. 218.7.4.

Benedict, Nathaniel. Conn. Sufferer. Norwalk. 359.13.3.

Benedict, Nathaniel. Conn. Sufferer. Danbury. 4.10.8.

Benedict, Nathaniel, 2d. Conn. Sufferer. Norwalk. 152.1.3.

Benedict, Oliver. Conn. Sufferer. Danbury. 4.14.4.

Benedict, Robert. Conn. Sufferer. Danbury. 2.9.4.

Benedict, Samuel. Conn. Sufferer. Danbury. 4.5.6.

Benedict, Samuel, Jr. Conn. Sufferer. Danbury. 7.16.8.

Benedict, Sarah. Conn. Sufferer. Danbury. 40.12.10.

Benedict, Thaddeus. Conn. Sufferer. Danbury. 349.7.4.

Benedict, Thomas. Conn. Sufferer. Norwalk. 779.1.10.

Benedict, Thomas. Conn. Sufferer. Danbury. 13.10.0.

Benedict, Thomas. Conn. Sufferer. Danbury. 1.11.6.

Benedict, Thomas H. Conn. Sufferer. Danbury. 8.15.9.

Benedict, Thomas, Jr. Conn. Sufferer. Danbury. 10.1.4.

Benedict, Timothy. Conn. Sufferer. Danbury. 2.5.6 1/2.

Benedict, Timothy. Conn. Sufferer. Ridgefield. 6.18.6.

Benedict, Zadock. Conn. Sufferer. Danbury. 67.13.4.

Benfield, Richard. Ga. ———. 15 Mar. 1784. 250 acres.

Benford, Isaac. N.C. Private. 30 Sep. 1785. 640 acres to heirs.

Benham, Lemuel. Conn. Sufferer. New/East Haven. 12.19.7.

Benham, Thomas. Conn. Sufferer. New/East Haven. 10.10.0.

Benheir, Peter. Conn. Sufferer. New/East Haven. 70.14.9.

Benion, John. N.C. Private. 20 Apr. 1784. 640 acres.

Benitcou, Eleanor. Conn. Sufferer. New/East Haven. 33.9.2.

Benjamin, Daniel. Mass. ———. 11 Sep. 1834. 200 acres to widow Jane Hutchinson.

Benjamin, John. Me. ———. 17 Nov. 1835. 200 acres to widow Betsy Ducker. Freedom.

Benjamin, Jonathan. N.Y. ———. 13 Sep. 1790. 500 acres to heirs.

Benjamin, Roger. Mass. ———. 22 Jul. 1833. 200 acres.

Benjamin, Samuel. N. Y. Private. 8 Jul. 1790. 600 acres.

Benn, James. S.C. ———. 2 Sep. 1793. 200 acres.

Benn, William. S.C. ———. 2 Sep. 1793. 200 acres.

Bennell, William, Sr. N.C. Private. 9 Sep. 1785. 640 acres to heirs.

Benner, Christopher. Me. Private. 26 Oct. 1835. 200 acres. Dennysville.

Bennet, Arthur. S.C. ———. 4 Sep. 1786. 200 acres.

Bennet, Charles. N. Y. Private. 7 Jul. 1790. 600 acres.

Bennet, Ebenezer, Jr. Conn. Sufferer. Norwalk. 14.2.8.

Bennet, Henry. N. Y. Private. 8 Jul. 1790. 500 acres.

Bennet, Henry. N.C. Private. 30 Sep. 1785. 640 acres to heirs.

Bennet, James. Pa. Sergeant. 9 Oct. 1786. 250 acres.

Bennet, John. Md. Private. ———. 50 acres.

Bennet, John. Md. Private. ———. 50 acres.
Bennet, Peter. N.C. Private. 12 Dec. 1796. 228 acres.
Bennet, Thomas. N.C. Private. 19 Nov. 1796. 228 acres.
Bennet, William. Va. Private. 19 Dec. 1783. 100 acres.
Bennet, William. Va. Master. 24 Mar. 1831. 2666 2/3 acres.
Bennet, William. Va. Master. 8 Nov. 1831. 533 1/3 acres.
Bennet, William. Va. Master. 8 Nov. 1831. 533 1/3 acres.
Bennet, William. Va. Master. 8 Nov. 1831. 533 1/3 acres.
Bennet, William. Va. Master. 8 Nov. 1831. 533 1/3 acres.
Bennet, William. Va. Master. 8 Nov. 1831. 533 1/3 acres.
Bennett, Andrew. Me. ———. 25 Jul. 1836. 200 acres. Gray.
Bennett, Artax. Va. Private. 21 Apr. 1784. 100 acres.
Bennett, Artax. Va. Gunner. 25 Sep. 1788. 2666 2/3 acres.
Bennett, Benjamin. N.C. Private. 4 Aug. 1821. 640 acres.
Bennett, Caleb P. Va. Lieutenant. 8 Nov. 1832. 2666 2/3 acres.
Bennett, Deliverance. Mass. Private. 15 Jan. 1834. 200 acres.
Bennett, Elias. Conn. Sufferer. Fairfield. 19.15.5.
Bennett, Frederick. Md. Fifer. ———. 50 acres.
Bennett, Jacob. N. Y. Private. 8 Jul. 1790. 600 acres.
Bennett, Jacob. N.C. Private. 12 Dec. 1785. 640 acres to heirs.
Bennett, James. N.C. Private. 27 Nov. 1819. 640 acres to heirs.
Bennett, James. N.C. Private. 9 Jun. 1820. 640 acres to heirs.
Bennett, James. Conn. Sufferer. Fairfield. 26.3.0.
Bennett, Jeremiah. N. Y. Private. 8 Jul. 1790. 600 acres.
Bennett, John. Ga. Soldier. 2 Jan. 1786. ———.
Bennett, John. Va. Private. 10 Jun. 1819. 100 acres.
Bennett, Joseph. N. Y. Corporal. 9 Jul. 1790. 600 acres.
Bennett, Joseph. Conn. Sufferer. Fairfield. 56.0.7.
Bennett, Moses. N.C. Private. 22 Apr. 1785. 304 acres.
Bennett, Nathan. Conn. Sufferer. Fairfield. 15.2.0.
Bennett, Richard. Ga. Soldier. 2 Jan. 1786. ———.
Bennett, Richard. Va. Private. 2 Feb. 1820. 100 acres.
Bennett, Richard. Va. Private. 15 Jun. 1820. 200 acres.
Bennett, Solomon. N.C. Private. 30 Sep. 1785. 640 acres to heirs.
Bennett, Thomas. Va. Private. 30 Dec. 1808. 261 acres.
Bennett, Thomas. Conn. Sufferer. Fairfield. 3.2.3.
Bennett, Timothy. N. Y. Sergeant. 8 Jul. 1790. 600 acres.
Bennett, William. Ga. Soldier. 2 Jan. 1786. ———.
Bennett, William. N.C. Private. 20 Jan. 1785. 640 acres to heirs.
Bennett, William. Va. Private. 13 Apr. 1833. 200 acres.
Benningfield, Henry. Va. Artificer. 5 Mar. 1784. 100 acres.
Bennit, Nehemiah. N.C. Private. 20 Jan. 1785. 640 acres to heirs.
Bennitt, John. Ga. ———. 25 May 1784. 230 acres to heirs.
Benny, John. Md. Private. ———. 50 acres.
Benson, Bailey. N.C. Private. 2 Apr. 1784. 640 acres to Sarah Benson, heiress.
Benson, George. Va. Private. 15 Jan. 1808. 100 acres.
Benson, Henry. Ga. ———. 2 Jan. 1786. ———.
Benson, John. Ga. ———. 2 Jan. 1786. ———.
Benson, John. N.C. Private. 12 Sep. 1785. 640 acres to heirs.
Benson, Perry. Md. Captain. ———. 200 acres.
Benson, William. N. Y. ———. 13 Sep. 1790. 500 acres to heirs.
Benstead, Alexander. Pa. Lieutenant. 1 Feb. 1787. 200 acres.
Benstead, Alexander. Pa. Lieutenant. 1 Feb. 1786. 200 acres.
Bentford, James. N.C. Private. 30 Sep. 1785. 640 acres to heirs.

Benticou, Timothy, Jr. Conn. Sufferer. New/East Haven. 13.8.0.
Bentley, Balaam. Ga. ———. 17 May 1784. ———.
Bentley, Henry. Pa. Private. ———. 200 acres.
Bentley, Isaac. N.C. Private. 1 Sep. 1785. 640 acres to heirs.
Bentley, James. Ga. ———. 17 May 1784. ———.
Bentley, James. Va.-Ind. Private. 108 acres.
Bentley, Jeremiah. Va. Private. 23 Oct. 1783. 100 acres.
Bentley, Jesse. Ga. ———. 25 Feb. 1784. 250 acres.
Bentley, John. Ga. ———. 25 Feb. 1784. 250 acres.
Bentley, John. Va.-Ind. Private. 108 acres.
Bentley, John. N.C. Private. 11 Jul. 1785. 640 acres.
Bentley, John. Pa. Private. 27 Oct. 1786. 200 acres.
Bentley, William. Ga. Soldier. 17 May 1784. ———.
Bentley, William. Va. Captain. 14 Dec. 1782. 4000 acres.
Bentley, William. Va. Captain. 10 Jun. 1783. 666 2/3 acres.
Bentley, William. Va. Captain. 14 Aug. 1807. 555 acres.
Bently, William. N. Y. ———. 13 Sep. 1790. 500 acres heirs.
Benton, Alexander. N.C. Private. 13 Dec. 1796. 640 acres.
Benton, David. N.C. Private. 21 Apr. 1784. 274 acres.
Benton, Edom. N.C. Private. 21 Aug. 1820. 640 acres.
Benton, Jesse. N.C. Sergeant. 22 Dec. 1796. 357 acres.
Benton, Jesse. N.C. Private. 4 Aug. 1821. 640 acres.
Benton, Kedar. N.C. Private. 30 Sep. 1785. 228 acres.
Benton, Robert. Ga. ———. 17 May 1784. ———.
Benton, Solomon. N.C. Private. 30 Sep. 1785. 640 acres to heirs.
Benton, William. N.C. Private. 30 Sep. 1785. 640 acres to heirs.
Beranrd, William. Va. Lieutenant. 10 Jun. 1783. 2666 2/3 acres.
Berdeen, Timothy. Mass. Private. 16 Jun. 1830. 200 acres.
Berjarong, Gilliam. N. Y. ———. ———. 500 acres.
Berjarong, Joseph. N. Y. ———. ———. 500 acres.
Berkley, William. Va. Private. 20 Jun. 1783. 100 acres.
Berklow, Richard. Ga. ———. 17 May 1784. ———.
Berlin, Isaac. Pa. Private. 23 Oct. 1786. 200 acres.
Bernard, Peter. Va. Captain. 19 Mar. 1834. 250 acres.
Bernard, Peter. Va. Captain. 2 Jan. 1835. 250 acres.
Bernard, Peter. Va. Captain. 13 Feb. 1835. 250 acres.
Bernard, Peter. Va. Captain. 14 Apr. 1835. 500 acres.
Bernard, Peter. Va. Captain. 14 Apr. 1835. 250 acres.
Bernard, Peter. Va. Captain. 10 Aug. 1835. 4000 acres.
Bernard, Peter. Va. Captain. 5 Aug. 1837. 400 acres.
Bernard, Peter. Va. Captain. 5 Aug. 1837. 400 acres.
Bernard, Peter. Va. Captain. 5 Aug. 1837. 400 acres.
Bernard, Peter. Va. Captain. 5 Aug. 1837. 400 acres.
Bernard, Peter. Va. Captain. 5 Aug. 1837. 400 acres.
Bernard, Peter. Va. Captain. 5 Sep. 1837. 250 acres.
Bernard, Peter. Va. Captain. 5 Sep. 1837. 500 acres.
Bernard, Peter. Va. Captain. 1 Jun. 1838. 320 acres.
Bernard, Peter. Va. Captain. 1 Jun. 1838. 80 acres.
Bernard, Thomas. Va. Corporal. 10 Jun. 1783. 200 acres.
Berrien, John. Ga. Captain. Aug. 1783. 600 acres.
Berrien, John. Ga. Major. 23 Apr. 1784. 200 acres.
Berriman [or Banneman], John. Md. Private. ———. 50 acres.
Berro, John. Va. Private. 4 Jul. 1783. 200 acres.
Berry, Amos. N.C. Private. 9 Sep. 1820. 640 acres to heirs.
Berry, Bartholomew. Pa. Private. 30 Jul. 1787. 200 acres.

Berry, Caleb. N.C. Private. 24 Nov. 1796. 274 acres.
Berry, Caleb. N.C. Private. 22 Dec. 1796. 274 acres.
Berry, Charles. N. Y. ———. 13 Sep. 1790. 500 acres to heirs.
Berry, David. Va. Private. 15 Nov. 1784. 100 acres.
Berry, Edward. Md. Matross. ———. 50 acres.
Berry, Francis. N.C. Private. 28 Sep. 1785. 640 acres.
Berry, George. Me. Private. 15 Sep. 1835. 200 acres. Green.
Berry, George. Va. Captain. 27 Oct. 1783. 4000 acres.
Berry, Gideon. Ga. ———. 17 May 1784. ———.
Berry, Isaac. Ga. Minute Man. 3 Sep. 1785. ———.
Berry, James. Md. Matross. ———. 50 acres.
Berry, James. Pa. Private. 18 May 1787. 200 acres.
Berry, James. Va. Private. 17 Mar. 1784. 100 acres.
Berry, John. Ga. ———. 17 May 1784. ———.
Berry, John. N.C. Sergeant. 4 Dec. 1783. 1000 acres.
Berry, John. N.C. Private. 30 Sep. 1785. 640 acres to heirs.
Berry, John. Va. Private. 23 Jun. 1783. 200 acres.
Berry, John. Va. Private. 30 Dec. 1784. 100 acres.
Berry, Michael. Pa. Private. 21 Nov. 1786. 200 acres.
Berry, Nathaniel. Me. ———. 19 Sep. 1835. 200 acres to his guardian Rufus Gay. Gardiner.
Berry, Nathaniel. Va. Private. 19 Mar. 1783. 100 acres.
Berry, Pelatiah. Me. Private. 16 Sep. 1835. 200 acres to widow Louisa Berry. Gray.
Berry, Richard. Ga. ———. 30 Jul. 1784. 287 1/2 acres.
Berry, Robert. N.C. ———. 30 Apr. 1784. 640 acres to James Berry, heir.
Berry, Roger. Ga. Minute Man. 3 Sep. 1785. ———.
Berry, Samuel. Me. Lieutenant. 19 Nov. 1842. 200 acres to widow Ruth Berry. Auburn.
Berry, Solomon. N.C. Sergeant. 4 Dec. 1783. 1000 acres.
Berry, Thomas. Va. Private. 30 Dec. 1784. 100 acres.
Berry, Timothy. Me. ———. 5 Oct. 1835. 200 acres. Cornish.
Berry, William. Ga. ———. 26 May 1784. 230 acres.
Berry, William. Va. Ensign. 3 Dec. 1812. 2666 2/3 acres.
Berry, William. Va. Quartermaster Sergeant. 10 Dec. 1832. 200 acres.
Berry, William. Va. Quartermaster Sergeant. 4 Feb. 1834. 200 acres.
Berry, Zacheriah. Md. Private. ———. 50 acres.
Berryhill, Alexander. ———. Ga. 17 May 1784. ———.
Berryhill, Andrew. Ga. Refugee. 17 May 1784. ———.
Berryhill, Samuel. Ga. Refugee. 17 May 1784. ———.
Berryman, Philip. Va. Private. 31 Oct. 1856. 100 acres.
Bertie, John. N.C. Corporal. 2 Aug. 1784. 1000 acres.
Berwick, James. Va. Lieutenant. 9 Dec. 1784. 2666 2/3 acres.
Berwick, John. N. Y. ———. 13 Aug. 1794. 600 acres.
Berwick, White. S.C. ———. 4 Jul. 1791. 200 acres.
Besall, Elisha. N.C. ———. 10 Aug. 1785. 274 acres.
Beson, Peter. Ga. ———. 17 May 1784. ———.
Bess, Right. N.C. Private. 1 Aug. 1821. 640 acres.
Bessey, Silas. Conn. Sufferer. Norwalk. 12.16.3.
Best, James. Va. Private. 16 Mar. 1822. 100 acres.
Best, John. N.C. Private. 2 Feb. 1786. 640 acres to heirs.
Best, John. Va. Lieutenant. 9 Mar. 1831. 666 2/3 acres.
Best, John. Va. Lieutenant. 9 Mar. 1831. 666 2/3 acres.
Best, John. Va. Lieutenant. 9 Mar. 1831. 666 2/3 acres.
Best, John. Va. Lieutenant. 9 Mar. 1831. 666 2/3 acres.
Best, Thomas. N.C. Private. 8 Dec. 1796. 640 acres.

Best, Tucker. Va. Sergeant. 28 Jun. 1783. 200 acres.
Bethell, Valentine. Va. Private. 12 Jul. 1787. 200 acres.
Bethey, Elisha. Va.-Ind. Private. 108 acres.
Betsell, Isaac. Ga. ———. 17 May 1784. ———.
Betsell, John. Ga. ———. 30 Sep. 1784. ———.
Bett, Jonathan. N.C. Private. 28 Sep. 1785. 640 acres to heirs.
Betts, Benjamn. Conn. Sufferer. Norwalk. 2.11.11.
Betts, Charles. Pa. Private. 25 Mar. 1789. 200 acres to John Kline, assignee.
Betts, James. N. Y. Corporal. 8 Jul. 1790. 500 acres.
Betts, James. Conn. Sufferer. Norwalk. 17.2.0.
Betts, John. N.C. Private. 23 Apr. 1785. 640 acres to heirs.
Betts, John. Conn. Sufferer. Norwalk. 303.16.0.
Betts, Peter. Conn. Sufferer. Norwalk. 180.6.10 1/2.
Betts, Thaddeus. Conn. Sufferer. Norwalk. 254.9.3.
Betts, Thaddeus. Conn. Sufferer. Norwalk. 18.8.6.
Betts, Thomas. Conn. Sufferer. Norwalk. 167.16.7 1/2.
Betts, Thomas, Jr. Conn. Sufferer. Norwalk. 13.14.0.
Bevan, John. Va. Private. 30 Jan. 1813. 100 acres.
Bevans, Welder. Pa. Lieutenant. 16 Jan. 1787. 200 acres.
Bevans, Welder. Pa. Lieutenant. 16 Jan. 1787. 200 acres.
Bevens, Benjamin. N. Y. Private. 7 Jul. 1790. 600 acres.
Beverley, Charles. Va. Private. 10 Nov. 1796. 100 acres. [free mulatto].
Bevers, James. N.C. Private. 12 Mar. 1785. 640 acres to heirs.
Bevers, William. N.C. Private. 12 Mar. 1785. 640 acres to heirs.
Bevier, D. Philip. N. Y. Captain. 7 Jul. 1790. 1800 acres.
Bevil, James. Ga. ———. 26 May 1784. 575 acres.
Bevil, Paul. Ga. Refugee. 26 May 1784. 575 acres.
Bevil, Robert. Ga. ———. 20 Feb. 1784. 500 acres.
Beyer, Godfrey. N. Y. Sergeant. 8 Jul. 1790. 600 acres.
Bezely, John. N.C. Private. 14 Feb. 1796. 640 acres to heirs.
Bhurrer, Michael. S.C. ———. 2 Oct. 1786. 195 acres.
Biass, James. Md. Private. ———. 50 acres.
Bibbey, Solomon. N.C. Private. 25 Oct. 1783. 274 acres.
Bibble, David, Sr. N.C. Sergeant. 22 Dec. 1796. 1000 acres to heirs.
Bibee, Samuel. Va. Private. 21 Dec. 1799. 200 acres.
Bibley, Edmund. N.C. Private. 8 Dec. 1795. 640 acres to heirs.
Bicker, Henry. Pa. Captain. 27 Sep. 1787. 500 acres.
Biddle, Absolam. Ga. Citizen. 5 Apr. 1785. 575 acres.
Biddle, John. Pa. ———. ———. 200 acres.
Biddle, John. Pa. Private. 4 Nov. 1786. 200 acres.
Biddle, Richard. Md. Private. ———. 50 acres.
Biddlebizer, Lewis. N.C. Private. 16 Aug. 1821. 640 acres.
Bidgood, Philip. Va. Private. 8 Mar. 1784. 200 acres.
Bidgood, Philip. Va. Private. 2 May 1810. 200 acres.
Bierly, Jacob. Va. Private. 9 May 1785. 100 acres.
Bigbie, William. Va. Private. 20 Aug. 1783. 200 acres.
Bigby, David. N.C. Private. 22 Dec. 1796. 640 acres to heirs.
Biggar, James. Va.-Ind. Private. 108 acres.
Bigger, William. Va. Sergeant. 25 May 1837. 400 acres.
Biggs, Benjamin. Va. Captain. 31 Mar. 1783. 2000 acres.
Biggs, Benjamin. Va. Captain. 31 Mar. 1783. 2000 acres.
Biggs, Benjamin. Va. Captain. 31 Oct. 1793. 666 2/3 acres.
Biggs, John. Md. Private. ———. 50 acres.
Biggs, John. Va. Private. 22 Aug. 1783. 200 acres.

Biggs, Nathaniel. N.C. Private. 30 Sep. 1785. 640 acres to heirs.
Biggs, Richard. Pa. Private. 21 Jul. 1789. 200 acres.
Biggs, Robert. N.C. Private. 8 Dec. 1795. 640 acres.
Biggs, Silas. N.C. Private. 30 Sep. 1785. 640 acres to heirs.
Bigley, Lewis. Va. Private. 1 Apr. 1783. 100 acres.
Bignall, Thomas. Pa. ———. 19 Oct. 1786. 250 acres.
Bigsby, James. N.C. Private. 24 Dec. 1796. 640 acres.
Bigsby, John. Conn. Sufferer. Norwalk. 7.0.6.
Bigwood, James. Md. Private. ———. 50 acres.
Bilberry, Nathaniel. N.C. Private. 22 Feb. 1792. 228 acres.
Bilderback, Charles. Va.-Ind. Private. 108 acres.
Bill, Elijah. N.Y. Lieutenant. 8 Jul. 1790. 1000 acres.
Bill, John. Va. Private. 20 Jun. 1783. 100 acres.
Bill, Thomas. Conn. Sufferer. New/East Haven. 9.16.4.
Billego, John. N.C. Private. 19 Jan. 1786. 640 acres to heirs.
Billers, Charles. N.C. Private. 22 Dec. 1796. 274 acres.
Billings, Stephen. Conn. Sufferer. Groton. 74.6.7.
Billips, Thomas. N.C. Private. 30 Sep. 1785. 640 acres to heirs.
Billop, Henry. Md. Private. ———. 50 acres.
Billops, John. N.C. Private. 22 Oct. 1783. 274 acres.
Billows, John. Pa. Matross. 18 Dec. 1786. 200 acres.
Bills, Thomas. N. Y. Corporal. 9 Jul. 1790. 600 acres.
Billups, Thomas. N.C. Drummer. 26 Nov. 1796. 425 acres.
Bindon, Joseph. N. Y. ———. ———. 500 acres.
Bingham, Hugh. Va. Boatswain. 1 Dec. 1840. 1777 7/9 acres.
Bingham, Hugh. Va. Boatswain. 1 Dec. 1840. 888 8/9 acres.
Bingham, James. N. Y. ———. 13 Sep. 1790. 500 acres to heirs.
Bingley, Hannah. Conn. Sufferer. New/East Haven. 10.5.6.
Binnell, William, Jr. N.C. Private. 9 Sep. 1785. 640 acres to heirs.
Binns, William. Va. Private. 11 Dec. 1783. 200 acres.
Binson, William. Va. Private. 24 Feb. 1784. 100 acres.
Birch, Charles. Ga. ———. 17 May 1784. ———.
Birchard, Benjamin. Conn. Sufferer. Ridgefield. 0.12.0.
Birchard, Jesse. Conn. Sufferer. Norwalk. 7.12.0.
Birchard, John. Conn. Sufferer. Norwalk. 35.9.10.
Birchard, Joseph. Conn. Sufferer. Danbury. 1.12.10.
Bird, Andrew. Pa. Private. 21 Sep. 1787. 200 acres.
Bird, Benjamin. N.C. Private. 5 Sep. 1821. 640 acres.
Bird, Francis. N.C. Private. 30 Nov. 1785. 640 acres to heirs.
Bird, Francis. N.C. Private. 13 Sep. 1820. 640 acres.
Bird, Hardy. N.C. ———. 20 Sep. 1784. 640 acres to Joseph Hail, heir.
Bird, Isaac. Va. Private. 14 Jan. 1824. 200 acres.
Bird, John. Ga. Private. ———. 287 1/2 acres.
Bird, Joshua. Va. Private. 16 Dec. 1784. 100 acres.
Bird, Levin. Va. Pilot. 26 Feb. 1831. 2666 2/3 acres.
Bird, Michael. Ga. Private. ———. 287 1/2 acres.
Bird, Moses. N.C. Private. 29 Sep. 1784. 274 acres.
Bird, Reuben. Va. Private. 21 Jan. 1784. 200 acres.
Bird, Richard. Md. Captain. ———. 200 acres.
Bird, Richard. Va. Private. 31 Jul. 1784. 100 acres.
Bird, Samuel. Conn. Sufferer. New/East Haven. 42.2.5.
Bird, Thomas. Md. Private. ———. 50 acres.
Bird, Thomas. Va. Private. 9 Dec. 1783. 100 acres.
Bird, Thomas. Va. Sergeant. 5 Feb. 1785. 400 acres.

Biron, Henry. Va. Private. 31 Dec. 1851. 100 acres.
Biron, Henry. Va. Private. 2 Apr. 1856. 100 acres.
Bisbee, Elisha. Me. Private. 9 Dec. 1836. 200 acres to widow Chloe Stetson. Hartford.
Biscoe, James. Va. Boatswain. 21 Nov. 1783. 200 acres.
Biscoe, James. Va. ———. 17 Feb. 1838. 1233 1/3 acres.
Biscoe, James. Va. ———. 17 Feb. 1838. 1233 1/3 acres.
Bishaw, John. Va. Private. 16 Sep. 1783. 100 acres.
Bishop, Daniel. Conn. Sufferer. New/East Haven. 79.5.6.
Bishop, Gabriel. N. Y. Gunner. 9 Jul. 1790. 500 acres.
Bishop, Isaac. Conn. Sufferer. New/East Haven. 37.0.7.
Bishop, Israel. Conn. Sufferer. New/East Haven. 31.16.9.
Bishop, James. Ga. ———. 15 Mar. 1784. 250 acres.
Bishop, John. N. Y. ———. ———. 200 acres.
Bishop, Joseph. Va. Private. 30 Sep. 1783. 100 acres.
Bishop, Joseph. Conn. Sufferer. New/East Haven. 8.4.0.
Bishop, Joshua. Ga. ———. 17 May 1784. 250 acres.
Bishop, Joshua. N. Y. Matross. 3 Jul. 1790. 600 acres.
Bishop, Levi. N. Y. Matross. 9 Jul. 1790. 600 acres.
Bishop, Nathaniel. N. Y. Matross. 9 Jul. 1790. 600 acres.
Bishop, Samuel. Ga. ———. 3 Oct. 1785. 287 1/2 acres.
Bishop, Samuel. Conn. Sufferer. New/East Haven. 13.13.3.
Bishop, Stephen. Ga. Lieutenant. 15 Mar. 1784. 250 acres.
Bishop, Stephen. Va. Private. 20 Dec. 1820. 100 acres.
Bishop, Thomas. Md. Private. ———. 50 acres.
Bishop, Thomas. Va. Private. 19 Mar. 1784. 100 acres.
Bishop, William. Ga. Soldier. 20 Feb. 1784. 200 acres.
Biswell, John. Va. Corporal. 6 Nov. 1783. 400 acres.
Bitten, Adam. Pa. Captain. 11 June 1787. 500 acres to Debora Bitten et al.
Bivins, Abner. Mass. Sergeant. 18 Jul. 1832. 200 acres.
Bizzell, Enus. N.C. ———. 22 Oct. 1783. 640 acres to David Bizzell, heir.
Blaar, Jacob. N. Y. ———. 13 Sep. 1790. 500 acres to heirs.
Black, Anthony. N.C. Private. 30 Nov. 1785. 640 acres to heirs.
Black, Archibald. N. Y. ———. 13 Sep. 1790. 500 acres to heirs.
Black, David. N. Y. Private. 8 Jul. 1790. 500 acres.
Black, Edward. Ga. ———. 14 Sep. 1784. 287 1/2 acres.
Black, George. Va. Private. 20 Jun. 1783. 100 acres.
Black, Henry. Ga. ———. 15 Mar. 1784. 250 acres.
Black, James. Ga. Soldier. 2 Jan. 1786. ———.
Black, John. Ga. ———. 26 May 1784. 287 1/2 acres.
Black, John. N. Y. Private. 8 Jul. 1790. 600 acres.
Black, John. N.C. Private. 9 Nov. 1784. 640 acres.
Black, John. N.C. ———. 12 Mar. 1785. 640 acres to heirs.
Black, Josiah. Me. ———. 5 Aug. 1836. 200 acres. Limington.
Black, Martin. N.C. Private. 24 Nov. 1796. 274 acres.
Black, Matthew. Va. Private. 29 Jan. 1788. 100 acres.
Black, Peter. N.C. Private. 7 Jan. 1786. 640 acres to heirs.
Black, William. Ga. ———. 15 Mar. 1784. 250 acres.
Black, William. Pa. Private. 25 Jul. 1787. 200 acres.
Blackburn, Christopher. Va. Lieutenant. 3 Feb. 1834. 2666 2/3 acres.
Blackburn, Christopher. Va. Lieutenant. 19 Dec. 1835. 2133 1/3 acres.
Blackburn, Christopher. Va. Lieutenant. 19 Dec. 1835. 533 1/3 acres.
Blackburn, Julius. Va. Sergeant. 1 Dec. 1785. 200 acres.
Blackford, Samuel. Va.-Ind. Private. 108 acres.

Blackhall, William Ball. Pa. Lieutenant. 28 Aug. 1787. 200 acres.
Blackham, George. Md. Private. ———. 50 acres.
Blackhill, William Ball. Pa. Lieutenant. 28 Aug. 1787. 200 acres.
Blackleach, Thomas. N.C. Sergeant. 4 Aug. 1821. 1000 acres.
Blackley, Ebenezer. N.C. Private. 6 Sep. 1821. 640 acres.
Blackman, A. Randall. N.C. Private. 30 Sep. 1785. 640 acres to heirs.
Blackmore, Aaron. N.C. Private. 17 Dec. 1785. 640 acres.
Blackmore, George. S.C. Soldier. 21 Jan. 1785. 200 acres.
Blackmore, George. Va. Lieutenant. 7 Oct. 1783. 2666 2/3 acres.
Blackmore, Thomas. Va. Private. 11 Aug. 1785. 200 acres.
Blacksille, Thomas. Ga. Refugee. 28 Feb. 1784. 500 acres.
Blackson, Pridax. Va. Private. 7 Oct. 1783. 200 acres.
Blackson, Sovereighn. N.C. Private. 30 Mar. 1784. 274 acres.
Blackston, Henry. N.C. Fifer. 9 Feb. 1796. 1000 acres.
Blackstone, Peter. N.C. Private. 15 Feb. 1797. 320 acres.
Blackwell, Daniel. S.C. ———. 4 Jul. 1785. 200 acres.
Blackwell, Daniel, Jr. S.C. ———. 1 Aug. 1785. 200 acres to Zacheriah Blackwell, heir at law.
Blackwell, James. N.C. Private. 20 Jan. 1785. 640 acres to heirs.
Blackwell, James. N.C. Sergeant. 21 Feb. 1821. 357 acres.
Blackwell, John. Va. Captain. 16 May 1783. 4666 2/3 acres.
Blackwell, John. Va. Captain. 6 Feb. 1808. 500 acres.
Blackwell, Joseph. Va. Captain. 14 Apr. 1783. 4000 acres.
Blackwell, Joseph. Va. Captain. 9 Aug. 1806. 1333 1/3 acres.
Blackwell, Joseph. Va. Lieutenant. 16 Sep. 1850. 724 8/9 acres.
Blackwell, Joseph. Va. Lieutenant. 16 Sep. 1850. 362 4/9 acres.
Blackwell, Joseph. Va. Lieutenant. 16 Sep. 1850. 310 2/3 acres,
Blackwell, Joseph. Va. Lieutenant. 16 Sep. 1850. 310 2/3 acres.
Blackwell, Joseph. Va. Lieutenant. 16 Sep. 1850. 310 2/3 acres.
Blackwell, Joseph. Va. Lieutenant. 16 Sep. 1850. 310 2/3 acres.
Blackwell, Joseph. Va. Lieutenant. 16 Sep. 1850. 310 2/3 acres.
Blackwell, Joseph. Va. Lieutenant. 16 Sep. 1850. 310 2/3 acres.
Blackwell, Joseph. Va. Lieutenant. 16 Sep. 1850. 155 1/3 acres.
Blackwell, Joseph. Va. Lieutenant. 16 Sep. 1850. 155 1/3 acres.
Blackwell, Joseph. Va. Brigade Quartermaster. 31 Dec. 1851. 888 2/3 acres.
Blackwell, Joseph. Va. Brigade Quartermaster. 31 Dec. 1851. 888 2/3 acres.
Blackwell, Joseph. Va. Brigade Quartermaster. 31 Dec. 1851. 508 acres.
Blackwell, Joseph. Va. Brigade Quartermaster. 31 Dec. 1851. 508 acres.
Blackwell, Joseph. Va. Brigade Quartermaster. 31 Dec. 1851. 508 acres.
Blackwell, Joseph. Va. Brigade Quartermaster. 31 Dec. 1851. 508 acres.
Blackwell, Joseph. Va. Brigade Quartermaster. 31 Dec. 1851. 508 acres.
Blackwell, Joseph. Va. Brigade Quartermaster. 31 Dec. 1851. 508 acres.
Blackwell, Joseph. Va. Brigade Quartermaster. 31 Dec. 1851. 254 acres.
Blackwell, Joseph. Va. Brigade Quartermaster. 31 Dec. 1851. 254 acres.
Blackwell, Samuel. Va. Captain. 14 Oct. 1783. 4000 acres.
Blackwell, Thomas. Va. Captain. 30 Sep. 1783. 4000 acres.
Blackwell, Thomas. Va. Captain. 9 Aug. 1806. 1333 1/3 acres.
Blackwell, William. Va. Captain. 22 Apr. 1831. 4000 acres.
Blackwell, Zacheriah, Jr. S.C. ———. 1 Aug. 1785. 200 acres.
Blackwood, Archibald. Pa. Sergeant. 26 Oct. 1786. 250 acres.
Blackwood, John. Pa. Private. 30 Sep. 1787. 200 acres.
Blackwood, Samuel. N.C. Private. 17 Dec. 1796. 640 acres to heirs.
Blackwood, Samuel. Pa. Sergeant. 9 Jun. 1787. 250 acres.
Blades, John. Md. Private. ———. 50 acres.

Blainer, John. N.C. Private. 26 May 1784. 640 acres.
Blair, Daniel. Va. Private. 16 Jul. 1783. 200 acres.
Blair, James. Me. ———. 22 Aug. 1835. 200 acres. Woolwich.
Blair, John. Md. Private. ———. 50 acres.
Blair, John. Md. Private. ———. 50 acres.
Blair, John. Pa. Private. 13 May 1789. 200 acres.
Blair, John. Va. Captain Lieutenant. 12 Dec. 1782. 4000 acres.
Blair, John. Va. Captain. 26 Mar. 1798. 4000 acres.
Blair, John. Va. Captain. 26 Apr. 1838. 1222 acres.
Blair, John. Va. Captain. 10 Jul. 1838. 244 acres.
Blair, John. Va. Captain. 10 Jul. 1838. 978 acres.
Blair, Robert. Va. Private. 20 Jun. 1783. 100 acres.
Blair, Samuel. Ga. ———. 17 May 1784. ———.
Blair, Samuel. Pa. Chaplain. 29 Aug. 1787. 300 acres.
Blair, Samuel. Pa. Chaplain. 29 Aug. 1787. 300 acres.
Blair, Samuel. Va. Private. 9 May 1785. 100 acres.
Blair, Samuel. Va. Sergeant. 15 Dec. 1808. 400 acres.
Blair, Thomas. N.C. Private. 6 Dec. 1797. 274 acres.
Blair, Wade. S.C. Soldier. 21 Jan. 1785. 200 acres.
Blair, William. Ga. ———. 17 May 1784. ——— to heirs.
Blair, William. N.C. Private. 17 Dec. 1796. 640 acres to heirs.
Blaisdell, Jonathan. Me. ———. 25 Apr. 1835. 200 acres to widow Elizabeth Coffin. Brunswick.
Blaize, Joseph. Md. Private. ———. 50 acres.
Blake, Benjamin. Ga. ———. 17 May 1784. ———.
Blake, Benjamin. Ga. ———. 17 May 1784. ———.
Blake, Benjamin. Me. ———. 8 Mar. 1836. 200 acres. Brownfield.
Blake, Charles. Va. Private. 13 Jun. 1783. 100 acres.
Blake, Christopher. N.C. Private. 21 Dec. 1803. 640 acres.
Blake, Edward. Pa. Sergeant. 24 Jan. 1795. 250 acres.
Blake, Jacob. Md. Private. ———. 50 acres.
Blake, James. N. Y. ———. 18 Nov. 1800. 500 acres.
Blake, James. N. Y. ———. ———. 333 1/3 acres.
Blake, James. Va. Private. 9 Nov. 1811. 100 acres.
Blake, Jason. Mass. Sergeant. 14 Jan. 1833. 200 acres.
Blake, John. Me. ———. 26 Jun. 1835. 200 acres to widow Deborah Blake. Gorham.
Blake, John. Me. Lieutenant. 10 May 1838. 600 acres. Brewer.
Blake, John. N. Y. ———. ———. 500 acres.
Blake, Joseph. Me. ———. 26 Jun. 1835. 200 acres. Gorham.
Blake, Thomas. Mass. Quartermaster Sergeant. 18 Oct. 1833. 200 acres.
Blake, William. Ga. ———. 17 May 1784. ———.
Blake, William. Mass. Private. 20 Feb. 1833. 200 acres to heirs.
Blake, William. N.C. Sergeant. 25 Jun. 1785. 1000 acres to heir.
Blake, William. Pa. Private. 2 Jul. 1789. 200 acres.
Blake, William. Conn. Sufferer. Greenwich. 3.1.3.
Blakeley, Archibald. Conn. Sufferer. New/East Haven. 11.5.11.
Blakeley, Pero. Me. Private. 22 May 1835. 200 acres to widow Dina Blakeley. China.
Blakeley, Tilley. Conn. Sufferer. New/East Haven. 13.7.2.
Blakely, Churchill. Ga. ———. 17 May 1784. ———.
Blakely, John. N. Y. Lieutenant. 13 Sep. 1790. 1000 acres.
Blakely, John. Pa. Private. 10 Sep. 1789. 200 acres.
Blakey, Benjamin. Ga. ———. 24 May 1784. 345 acres.
Blakey, John. Va. Private. 2 May 1783. 100 acres.
Blakey, John. Va. Corporal. 19 Mar. 1783. 200 acres.

Blalock, Zacheriah. Va. Private. 9 Jul. 1783. 100 acres.

Blamer, John. N.C. Private. 30 Sep. 1785. 640 acres to heirs.

Blammer, John. N.C. Private. 10 Dec. 1788. 640 acres to heirs.

Blanchard, Ephraim. N. Y. Private. 8 Jul. 1790. 600 acres.

Blanchard, James. N.C. Private. 14 Dec. 1797. 640 acres to heirs.

Blanchard, John. N.C. Private. 25 Nov. 1789. 640 acres to heirs.

Blanchard, Peter. N. Y. ———. ———. 500 acres.

Blanchard, Reuben. Ga. ———. 17 May 1784. ———.

Blanchard, William. Ga. ———. 17 May 1784. ———.

Bland, Christopher. Va. Drummer. 9 Jun. 1813. 100 acres.

Bland, James. Va. Private. 25 Feb. 1783. 100 acres.

Bland, James. Va. Private. 11 Jun. 1784. 200 acres.

Bland, Jesse. Va. Private. 16 Feb. 1801. 100 acres.

Bland, John. Va. Private. 16 Apr. 1784. 100 acres.

Bland, John. Va. Private. 27 Feb. 1840. 100 acres.

Bland, Theoderick. Va. Colonel. 31 Dec. 1782. 6666 2/3 acres.

Blandin, Elisha. Mass. Matross. 22 Jul. 1833. 200 acres.

Blaney, Samuel. Mass. Corporal. 18 Oct. 1833. 200 acres.

Blank, Cornelius. N. Y. Sergeant. 7 Jul. 1790. 600 acres.

Blankenship, Daniel. Va. Private. 10 Nov. 1784. 200 acres.

Blankenship, Henry. Va.-Ind. Private. 108 acres.

Blankenship, Henry. Va. Private. 20 May 1834. 200 acres.

Blankenship, Womack. Va. Corporal. 18 Apr. 1783. 200 acres.

Blanks, Nicholas. N.C. Private. 13 Sep. 1820. 640 acres.

Blansett, Frederick. N.C. Private. 27 Jul. 1785. 274 acres.

Blansett, Thomas. N.C. Corporal. 27 Jul. 1785. 1000 acres to heir.

Blansford, Richard. Md. Private. ———. 50 acres.

Blanshet, Robert. N.C. Private. 30 Sep. 1785. 640 acres to heirs.

Blanton, Christopher. Ga. ———. 17 May 1784. ———.

Blayer, William. Ga. ———. 6 Feb. 1784. 250 acres.

Blaze, Christian. N.Y. ———. 13 Sep. 1790. 500 acres to heirs.

Blaze, John. Pa. Private. 28 Sep. 1787. 200 acres to Elizabeth Blaze, widow.

Bledsoe, Aaron. N.C. Private. 29 Sep. 1784. 640 acres to Jacob Bledsoe, heir.

Bledsoe, George. Ga. Soldier. 20 Dec. 1785. 460 acres.

Bledsoe, Isaiah. N.C. Private. 9 Feb. 1796. 640 acres.

Bledsoe, Miller. Va. Private. 18 Aug. 1784. 100 acres.

Bleecker, Leonard. N. Y. Captain. 7 Jul. 1790. 1800 acres.

Blenefield, James. S.C. 4 Jul. 1785. 200 acres.

Blewer, George. Pa. Lieutenant. 3 Sep. 1787. 200 acres to Joseph Blewer, administrator.

Blewer, George. Pa. Private. 3 Sep. 1787. 200 acres to Joseph Blewer, administrator.

Blewer, James. Md. Private. ———. 50 acres.

Blewford, William. Va. Private. 8 Jun. 1784. 100 acres.

Bliss, Theodore. N. Y. Captain. 9 Jul. 1790. 1800 acres.

Blithen, Increase. Me. Private. 12 May 1835. 200 acres. Philips.

Blome, John. Pa. Private. 14 Feb. 1789. 200 acres.

Blondon, John Peter. Pa. Private. 26 Dec. 1786. 200 acres.

Bloodgood, Isaac. N.C. Private. 2 Feb. 1786. 274 acres.

Bloodsworth, Samuel. Ga. ———. 15 Mar. 1784. 250 acres.

Bloom, Albert. N. Y. Private. 8 Jul. 1790. 500 acres.

Blossom, Peter. N.Y. ———. 16 Apr. 1794. 500 acres to heirs.

Blount, Benjamin. N.C. Private. 19 May 1784. 640 acres.

Blount, Benjamin Hodges. N.C. Private. 21 Apr. 1784. 640 acres.

Blount, Emanuel. N.C. Private. 5 Sep. 1821. 640 acres.

Blount, Frederick. N.C. Private. 20 Apr. 1784. 640 acres.
Blount, Isaac. Ga. ———. 25 May 1784. 690 acres to heirs.
Blount, Jacob. Ga. Surgeon's Mate on a galley. 1784. 690 acres to Oliver Lewis, administrator.
Blount, John. N.C. Private. 2 Sep. 1820. 640 acres.
Blount, Jonathan. Mass. Sergeant. 10 Sep. 1832. 200 acres to heirs.
Blount, Reading. N.C. Major. 27 Oct. 1783. 4800 acres.
Blount, Stephen. Ga. ———. 26 Oct. 1784. 575 acres.
Blount, Thomas. N.C. Lieutenant. 27 Oct. 1783. 853 acres.
Blount, Thomas. N.C. Private. 21 Apr. 1784. 274 acres.
Blow, Benjamin. N.C. Private. 10 Aug. 1785. 640 acres to heirs.
Blowers, Ephraim. N. Y. Private. 7 Jul. 1790. 500 acres.
Bloxom, Arthur. Va. Private. 29 Dec. 1785. 200 acres.
Bloxom, Charles Stuart. Va. Private. 15 Jun. 1807. 100 acres.
Bloxom, Ezekiel. Va. Private. 15 Jun. 1807. 100 acres.
Bloxom, George. Va. Seaman. 30 Jul. 1831. 100 acres.
Bloxom, John. Va. Private. 15 Jun. 1807. 100 acres.
Bloxom, Levi. Va. Private. 15 Jun. 1807. 100 acres.
Bloxom, Scarborough. Va. Midshipman. 9 Dec. 1830. 2666 2/3 acres.
Bloxom, Stephen. Va. Seaman. 30 Jul. 1831. 100 acres.
Bloxom, Thomas. Va. Private. 15 Jun. 1807. 100 acres.
Bloxom, Woodman. Va. Private. 15 Jun. 1807. 100 acres.
Blue, Christian. N.Y. ———. 13 Sep. 1790. 500 acres to heirs.
Blundan, William. N. Y. ———. ———. 420 acres.
Blundel, Samuel. Va. Private. 30 Jun. 1807. 100 acres.
Blundell, Francis. Pa. Sergeant. 12 Oct. 1786. 250 acres.
Blundon, Seth. Va. Midshipman. 10 Dec. 1783. 2666 2/3 acres.
Blundon, Swann. Va. Sailor. 9 Dec. 1783. 100 acres.
Blundon, William. Va. Sailor. 9 Dec. 1783. 100 acres.
Blurton, Edward. N.C. Private. 17 Feb. 1824. 640 acres.
Blurton, Henry. N.C. Sergeant. 5 Sep. 1821. 1000 acres.
Blys, William. Va. Private. 3 Feb. 1784. 100 acres.
Blythe, Joseph. N.C. Surgeon. 24 Oct. 1783. 4800 acres.
Blythe, Sylvanus. N.C. Private. 6 Dec. 1797. 640 acres to heirs.
Boadley, Andrew. N. Y. Private. 8 Jul. 1790. 500 acres.
Boan, Joseph. Va. Private. 30 Jun. 1784. 100 acres.
Boazman, Jacob. Ga. ———. 25 May 1784. 287 1/2 acres.
Bobbet, Jacob. Ga. ———. 17 May 1784. ———.
Bobley, William. N.C. Private. 5 Dec. 1796. 228 acres.
Bobough, Lewis. Ga. ———. 13 Sep. 1784. 287 1/2 acres.
Bochard, Peter. Md. Private. ———. 50 acres.
Bockner, Michael. N.C. Private. 17 Dec. 1785. 640 acres.
Boder, Nicholas. N.C. Private. 6 Dec. 1797. 640 acres to heirs.
Bodimes, George. Ga. Private. 6 Apr. 1784. ———.
Bodin, Alexander. N.C. Private. 6 Dec. 1797. 640 acres to heirs.
Bodine, John. Va. Sergeant. 1 Apr. 1784. 200 acres.
Bodle, Abraham. Pa. ———. 10 Dec. 1802. 200 acres.
Bodwin, Henry. Pa. Dragoon. 5 Mar. 1787. 200 acres.
Body, Robert. Md. Fifer. ———. 50 acres.
Bogart, Tunis. N.C. Private. 2 Sep. 1820. 640 acres.
Bogert, Cornelius. Va. Private 20 Jun. 1783. 100 acres.
Bogert, Isaac. N. Y. Lieutenant. 9 Jul. 1790. 1200 acres.
Bogg, John. N. Y. Private. 3 Jul. 1790. 600 acres.
Bogg, John. N. Y. Private. 8 Jul. 1790. 600 acres.

Boggs, Ezekiel. N.C. Private. 20 Sep. 1784. 274 acres.

Boggs, Jeremiah. Ga. ———. 17 May 1784. ———.

Boggs, John. Ga. ———. 17 May 1784. ———.

Boggs, John. N.C. Private. 26 May 1784. 274 acres.

Boggs, Joseph. Ga. ———. 28 Feb. 1784. 250 acres.

Boggs, Thomas. Pa. Sergeant. 25 Oct. 1786. 250 acres.

Bogle, Archibald. N.C. Sergeant. 21 Aug. 1820. 1000 acres.

Bogue, Mark. N.C. Private. 10 Aug. 1785. 640 acres to heirs.

Bohan, Dennis. Pa. Private. 26 Sep. 1787. 200 acres to heirs.

Bohannan, Ambrose. Va. Captain Lieutenant. 11 Sep. 1807. 500 acres.

Bohannan, Ambrose. Va. Captain Lieutenant. 31 Mar. 1783. 4666 2/3 acres.

Bohannan, Henry. Va. Private. 18 Jul. 1783. 100 acres.

Bohannan, Henry. Va. Private. 31 Oct. 1856. 100 acres.

Bohannan, Henry. Va. Private. 12 Jan. 1858. 100 acres.

Bohannan, Joseph. Va. Drummer. 5 Dec. 1809. 100 acres.

Boice, James. N. Y. Private. 7 Jul. 1790. 500 acres.

Boice, Jesse. N.C. Private. 22 Feb. 1785. 228 acres.

Boies, John. Me. Private. 1 Apr. 1839. 200 acres to widow Mary (Parker) Boies. Skowhegan.

Boileau, Amable. N. Y. ———. ———. 500 acres.

Boileau, Peter. N. Y. ———. ———. 500 acres.

Boileau, Pierre. N. Y. Lieutenant. ———. 100 acres.

Boils, David. Va. Private. 20 Aug. 1783. 200 acres.

Boise, Louis. N. Y. ———. ———. 500 acres.

Boise, Peter. N. Y. Private. 8 Jul. 1790. 600 acres.

Boise, Peter. N. Y. ———. 20 Nov. 1806. 200 acres.

Boivan, Charles. N. Y. ———. ———. 500 acres.

Bolboth, John. Ga. ———. 17 May 1784. ——— to heir Hannah Bolboth.

Boldin, Wood. Va. Lieutenant. 1 Oct. 1810. 2666 2/3 acres.

Boles, Francis. Ga. Minute Man. 16 Sep. 1785. ———.

Boley, Presley. Va. Corporal. 29 Jun. 1785. 400 acres.

Boley, Presley. Va. Private. 9 Dec. 1820. 200 acres.

Bolin, Andrew. N.C. Private. 28 Oct. 1783. 640 acres to heir.

Boling, Baxter. N.C. Private. 14 Sep. 1821. 640 acres.

Boling, Robert. Ga. ———. 17 May 1784. ———.

Bolling, Jesse. Va. Private. 23 Jun. 1783. 100 acres.

Bolling, John. Va. Private. 25 Feb. 1823. 100 acres.

Bolling, Joseph. Va. Private. 22 May 1784. 100 acres.

Bolling, Robert. Va. Lieutenant. 23 Jan. 1817. 500 acres.

Bolling, Robert. Va. Lieutenant. 23 Jan. 1817. 333 1/3 acres.

Bolling, Robert. Va. Lieutenant. 23 Jan. 1817. 100 acres.

Bolling, Robert. Va. Lieutenant. 23 Jan. 1817. 100 acres.

Bolling, Robert. Va. Lieutenant. 23 Jan. 1817. 100 acres.

Bolling, Robert. Va. Lieutenant. 23 Jan. 1817. 100 acres.

Bolling, Robert. Va. Lieutenant. 23 Jan. 1817. 100 acres.

Bolling, Robert. Va. Lieutenant. 23 Jan. 1817. 500 acres.

Bolling, Robert. Va. Lieutenant. 23 Jan. 1817. 333 1/3 acres.

Bolling, Robert. Va. Lieutenant. 23 Jan. 1817. 100 acres.

Bolling, Robert. Va. Lieutenant. 23 Jan. 1817. 100 acres.

Bolling, Robert. Va. Lieutenant. 23 Jan. 1817. 100 acres.

Bolling, Robert. Va. Lieutenant. 23 Jan. 1817. 100 acres.

Bolling, Robert. Va. Lieutenant. 23 Jan. 1817. 100 acres.

Bolling, Robert. Va. Lieutenant. 19 Aug. 1837. 444 1/3 acres.

Bolling, Robert. Va. Lieutenant. 19 Aug. 1837. 444 1/3 acres.

Bolling, Robert. Va. Lieutenant. 19 Aug. 1837. 444 1/3 acres.
Bolling, Robert. Va. Lieutenant. 4 Jun. 1856. 700 acres.
Bolling, Robert. Va. Lieutenant. 22 Apr. 1853. 333 1/3 acres.
Bolling, Robert. Va. Lieutenant. 22 Apr. 1853. 111 acres.
Bollington, John. Va. Private. 2 Apr. 1784. 100 acres.
Bolton, Bolling. Va. Sergeant. 9 Dec. 1783. 200 acres.
Bolton, Francis. Ga. Minute Man. 29 Jan. 1795. ———.
Bolton, George. N. Y. Private. 8 Jul. 1790. 600 acres.
Bolton, Hannah. Conn. Sufferer. New London. 32.1.10 1/2.
Bolton, Matthew. N. Y. Private. 6 Jul. 1790. 600 acres.
Bolton, Philip. Mass. ———. 30 May 1834. 200 acres to widow Bethiah Bolton.
Bolton, Ralph. Ga. ———. 4 Oct. 1785. ———.
Bolton, Richard. Ga. ———. 4 Oct. 1785. ———.
Bolton, Thomas. N.C. Private. 8 Dec. 1796. 640 acres.
Bolton, William. Md. Private. ———. 50 acres.
Bond, Charles. N.C. Private. 22 Dec. 1796. 640 acres.
Bond, Elisha. N.C. Private. 18 Oct. 1783. 274 acres.
Bond, George. Ga. ———. 17 May 1784. ———.
Bond, George. Va. Private. 9 Dec. 1783. 100 acres.
Bond, James. N.C. Private. 19 May 1784. 640 acres.
Bond, James. N.C. Private. 29 Sep. 1784. 396 acres.
Bond, John. Va. Private. 30 Jun. 1786. 100 acres.
Bond, John. Va. Private. 28 Mar. 1834. 100 acres.
Bond, Jonas. Me. ———. 27 Apr. 1835. 200 acres. Lisbon.
Bond, Joseph. Mass. Private. 9 Mar. 1832. 200 acres.
Bond, Joseph. Va. Private. 17 May 1822. 200 acres.
Bond, Richard. N.C. Private. 6 Sep. 1821. 640 acres.
Bond, Thomas. N.C. Private. 10 Dec. 1788. 640 acres to heirs.
Bond, William. N.C. Private. 29 Sep. 1784. 640 acres to heirs.
Bond, Zacheriah. N.C. Private. 22 Dec. 1796. 228 acres.
Bonham, Malachi. Md. Lieutenant. ———. 200 acres.
Bonham, Moses. Pa. Private. ———. 200 acres to his widow.
Bonker, William. N. Y. ———. 13 Sep. 1790. 500 acres to heirs.
Bonnell, John. Ga. ———. 15 Mar. 1784. 250 acres.
Bonnell, John. N. Y. Gunner. 8 Jul. 1790. 600 acres.
Bonner, Richard. Va. Sergeant. 1 Sep. 1783. 200 acres.
Bonner, Robert. Ga. ———. 23 Jul. 1784. 287 1/2 acres.
Bonner, Ruth. Ga. ———. 17 May 1784. ———.
Bonner, William. Ga. ———. 15 Mar. 1784. 287 acres to heirs.
Bonner, William. N.C. Corporal. 15 Feb. 1797. 1000 acres to heirs.
Bonnewell, Thomas. Va. Master. 1 May 1832. 444 4/9 acres.
Bonnewell, Thomas. Va. Master. 1 May 1832. 444 4/9 acres.
Bonnewell, Thomas. Va. Master. 1 May 1832. 444 4/9 acres.
Bonney, Gideon. N.C. Corporal. 27 Nov. 1819. 428 acres.
Bonniface, William. Va. Sergeant. 2 Dec. 1809. 400 acres.
Bonnowell, Thomas. Va. ———. 18 Jul. 1832. 148 acres.
Bonnowell, Thomas. Va. ———. 18 Jul. 1832. 148 acres.
Bonticou, Timothy P. Conn. Sufferer. New/ East Haven. 4.4.0.
Bontique, Timothy. Conn. Sufferer. New/ East Haven. 23.7.5.
Bonwell, Thomas. Va. Master. 24 Aug. 1835. 296 1/6 acres.
Bonwell, Thomas. Va. Master. 24 Aug. 1835. 445 acres.
Bonwell, Thomas. Va. Master. 24 Aug. 1835. 148 acres.
Bonwell, Thomas. Va. Master. 25 May 1840. 148 1/3 acres.

Bonwell, Thomas. Va. Master. 2 Apr. 1845. 21 7/21 acres.
Bonwell, Thomas. Va. Master. 2 Apr. 1845. 121 acres.
Bonwell, Thomas. Va. Master. 2 Apr. 1845. 98 8/9 acres.
Bonwell, Thomas. Va. Master. 2 Apr. 1845. 49 4/9 acres.
Boody, John. Md. Private. ———. 50 acres.
Book, George. Ga. ———. 4 May 1785. ———.
Booke, Joseph. Pa. Private. 26 Dec. 1786. 200 acres.
Booker, Gideon. Ga. Captain. 20 Sep. 1783. 600 acres.
Booker, Isaiah. Me. ———. 22 Apr. 1835. 200 acres to widow Sarah Booker. Bowdoinham.
Booker, Lewis. Va. Captain Lieutenant. 31 Jan. 1784. 4000 acres.
Booker, Lewis. Va. Captain Lieutenant. 31 Jan. 1784. 666 2/3 acres.
Booker, Lewis. Va. Captain Lieutenant. 30 Oct. 1807. 555 acres.
Booker, Richard. Va. Captain. 7 Oct. 1833. 2000 acres.
Booker, Richard. Va. ———. 23 Jan. 1834. 2000 acres.
Booker, Richeson. Va. Sergeant. 29 May 1783. 200 acres.
Booker, Samuel. Va. Captain. 24 Dec. 1782. 4000 acres.
Booker, Samuel. Va. Captain. 9 Dec. 1807. 1222 acres.
Boom, John. N. Y. Private. 7 Jul. 1790. 500 acres.
Boomer, William. N.C. Private. 3 Aug. 1820. 274 acres to heirs.
Boon, David. N.C. Private. 30 Sep. 1785. 640 acres to heirs.
Boon, Elisha. N.C. Private. 30 Sep. 1785. 640 acres to heirs.
Boon, Hawkins. Pa. Captain. 9 Oct. 1789. 500 acres.
Boon, Jacob. N.C. Private. 30 Sep. 1785. 640 acres to heirs.
Boon, James. N.C. Private. 20 Jan. 1785. 640 acres to heirs.
Boon, John. N.C. Private. 16 Aug. 1821. 640 acres.
Boon, John. Pa. Private. ———. 200 acres.
Boon, Joseph. N.C. Private. 24 Nov. 1797. 228 acres.
Boon, Peter. Pa. Private. 16 Jan. 1796. 200 acres to Joseph Jeffries, assignee.
Boon, Peter. Pa. Matross. 8 Mar. 1787. 200 acres to Stephen Loudon, assignee.
Boon, Samuel. Pa. ———. 2 Nov. 1786. 200 acres to Philip Boehm, assignee.
Boon, Willis. N.C. Private. 26 Dec. 1800. 228 acres.
Boone, Joshua. N.C. Private. 10 Aug. 1785. 640 acres to heirs.
Boone, Moses. Pa. Private. 21 Sep. 1787. 200 acres.
Boone, Richard. Md. Private. ———. 50 acres.
Booth, Abner. Conn. Sufferer. Norwalk. 40.1.6.
Booth, Abraham. Ga. ———. 14 Jul. 1784. 287 1/2 acres.
Booth, Absalom. Ga. ———. ———. 250 acres.
Booth, George. S.C. ———. 3 Mar. 1788. 200 acres.
Booth, George. Va. Corporal. 7 Jan. 1791. 200 acres.
Booth, George. Va. Corporal. 12 Jan. 1843. 200 acres.
Booth, James. Va. Private. 2 May 1783. 200 acres.
Booth, Jesse. N.C. Private. 30 Sep. 1785. 640 acres to heirs.
Booth, John. N.C. Private. 4 Aug. 1821. 640 acres.
Booth, John. S.C. ———. 3 Mar. 1788. 200 acres.
Booth, Matthew. S.C. ———. 3 Mar. 1788 200 acres.
Booth, Michael. Va. Sergeant. 10 Feb. 1817. 400 acres.
Booth, Michael. Va. Sergeant. 28 Feb. 1841. 400 acres.
Booth, Michael. Va. Sergeant. 7 Nov. 1853. 400 acres.
Booth, William. Ga. ———. 20 Aug. 1785. ———.
Booth, William. Va. Warrant Officer. 30 Jun. 1784. 200 acres.
Booth, William. Va. ———. 20 Aug. 1835. 2466 2/3 acres.
Boothe, Abner. N.C. Private. 22 Dec. 1796. 312 acres.
Boothe, James. Va. Private. 9 Nov. 1818. 100 acres.
Boothy, William. Me. Private. 1 Aug. 1836.

200 acres to widow Elizabeth Boothy. Limerick.

Bootle, Thomas. N.C. Private. 22 Dec. 1796. 274 acres.

Boram, William. Ga. ———. 17 May 1784. ———.

Boreman, David. P. Private. 21 Apr. 1787. 200 acres.

Boren, Jacob. N.C. Sergeant. 21 Jan. 1818. 1000 acres to heirs.

Borland, Baxter. N.C. Private. 4 Aug. 1821. 640 acres.

Borne, Jesse. Va. Private. 1 Jun. 1805. 100 acres.

Borough, Joel. N.C. Sergeant. 22 Apr. 1785. 1000 acres.

Borough, Wiley. N.C. Private. 9 Nov. 1784. 457 acres.

Borr, James. N.C. Private. 17 Dec. 1796. 640 acres to heirs.

Bose, John. Va. Private. 8 Dec. 1787. 200 acres.

Bosman, Ralph. S.C. ———. 7 May 1792. 200 acres.

Boss, Nicholas. N.C. Private. 9 Feb. 1796. 640 acres.

Bostain, Andrew. N.C. Private. 18 Jun. 1785. 228 acres.

Bostick, Chesley. Ga. ———. 29 Jan. 1784. 250 acres.

Bostick, Littlebury. Ga. ———. 24 Jan. 1784. 500 acres.

Bostick, Nathan. Ga. Refugee. 25 May 1784. 287 1/2 acres.

Bostile, Philip. Pa. Sergeant. ———. 250 acres to widow.

Boston, Adam. Va. Private. 12 Apr. 1783. 200 acres.

Boston, Elijah. Va. Private. 30 Mar. 1833. 50 acres.

Boston, Elijah. Va. Private. 30 Mar. 1833. 50 acres.

Boston, Elijah. Va. Private. 30 Mar. 1833. 50 acres.

Boston, Elijah. Va. Private. 30 Mar. 1833. 50 acres.

Boston, Jacob. N.C. Private. 18 Jun. 1785. 228 acres.

Boston, Thomas. Me. Private. 4 Aug. 1835. 200 acres. Kennebunkport.

Boston, Travis. Va.-Ind. Private. 108 acres.

Boston, William. Va.-Ind. Private. 108 acres.

Bostwick, John. Pa. Private. ———. 200 acres.

Boswalt, Jacob. Pa. Private. ———. 200 acres.

Boswell, Jesse. Md. Corporal. ———. 50 acres.

Boswell, Machen. Va. Captain. Jan. 1783. 4000 acres.

Boswell, Samuel. Md. Private. ———. 50 acres.

Boswell, William. N.C. Sergeant. 27 Jun. 1788. 1000 acres.

Boswith, James. N. Y. Drum Major. 8 Jul. 1790. 600 acres.

Bosworth, Obadiah. Ga. Citizen. 6 Apr. 1785. 287 1/2 acres.

Botkin, Charles. Va. Private. 27 Mar. 1784. 100 acres.

Bott, David. Conn. Sufferer. Norwalk. 5.19.9.

Bottle, Robert. S.C. Soldier. 21 Jan. 1785. 200 acres.

Botts, Archibald. Va. Sergeant. 20 Jun. 1783. 200 acres.

Botts, Joseph. Md. Private. ———. 50 acres.

Botts, Leonard. Va. Corporal. 15 Dec. 1784. 400 acres.

Boude, S. B. Pa. Lieutenant. 1 Mar. 1809. 200 acres.

Boude, Samuel B. Pa. Lieutenant. 17 Feb. 1809. 200 acres to heirs.

Boude, Thomas. Pa. Captain. ———. 500 acres.

Boudy, John. Md. Private. ———. 50 acres.

Bough, Benjamin. Md. Private. ———. 50 acres.

Bough, George. Md. Private. ———. 50 acres.

Boughter, Martin. Pa. Private. 25 Jun. 1789. 200 acres to heirs.

Boughton, Benjamin. Conn. Sufferer. Danbury. 2.2.8.

Boughton, Catharine. Conn. Sufferer. Norwalk. 23.11.0.

Boughton, William. Va. Private. 3 Mar. 1809. 100 acres.

Boulton, Jonathan. N.Y. ———. 13 Sep. 1790. 500 acres to heirs.

Boulware, Obadiah. Va. Private. 28 Apr. 1783. 100 acres.

Boulware, Samuel. Va. Private. 1 Sep. 1786. 100 acres.

Bourks, Isham. Ga. ———. 15 Mar. 1784. 250 acres.
Bourn, Francis. Va. Drummer. 14 May 1783. 100 acres.
Bourn, John. Mass. Sergeant. 2 Sep. 1834. 200 acres.
Bourn, John. Va. Sergeant. 20 Dec. 1783. 200 acres.
Bourn, John. Va. Private. 15 Oct. 1787. 100 acres.
Boush, Charles. Va. Lieutenant. 26 Apr. 1784. 2666 2/3 acres.
Boush, Charles S. Va. Lieutenant. 5 Aug. 1831. 1333 1/3 acres.
Boush, Dennis. Va. Private. 20 Jun. 1783. 100 acres.
Boush, Goodrich. Va. Captain. 1 Mar. 1791. 5333 1/3 acres.
Boush, Goodrich. Va. Captain. 1 Nov. 1860. 381 1/2 acres.
Boush, Goodrich. Va. Captain. 1 Nov. 1860. 381 1/2 acres.
Boush, Robert. Va. Subaltern. 18 Jun. 1784. 1666 2/3 acres.
Boush, Robert. Va. Subaltern. 18 Jun. 1784. 700 acres.
Boush, Robert. Va. Subaltern. 18 Jun. 1784. 300 acres.
Boush, Robert. Va. Subaltern. 4 Apr. 1861. 300 acres.
Boush, Robert. Va. Paymaster. 1 Mar. 1851. 4000 acres.
Boush, Robert. Va. Paymaster. 4 Feb. 1853. 1333 1/3 acres.
Boush, Robert. Va. Paymaster. 4 Feb. 1853. 1333 1/3 acres.
Boush, Robert. Va. Paymaster. 4 Feb. 1853. 1333 1/3 acres.
Bouve, Jonathan. Mass. Matross. 12 Sep. 1834. 200 acres to widow Lydia Bouve.
Bouvet, Louis. N. Y. ———. ———. 500 acres.
Bouy, William. N. Y. Private. 6 Jul. 1790. 600 acres.
Bowden, Hampton. N.C. Private. 19 Jan. 1786. 640 acres.
Bowden, Jesse. Va. Private. 6 Jan. 1808. 100 acres.
Bowden, John. Va. Private. 6 Jan. 1808. 100 acres.
Bowden, Joseph. Pa. Private. 24 Nov. 1788. 200 acres.
Bowden, Thomas. Va. Private. 6 Jan. 1808. 100 acres.
Bowden, Thomas. Va. Sergeant. 27 Sep. 1808. 100 acres.
Bowden, William. Va. Private. 13 Jan. 1813. 100 acres.
Bowdire, Lewis. Va. Private. 30 Jun. 1784. 100 acres.
Bowe, George. Md. Private. ———. 50 acres.
Bowen, Abram. Md. Private. ———. 50 acres.
Bowen, Ebenezer. Va.-Ind. Private. 108 acres.
Bowen, Ephraim. Ga. ———. 15 Mar. 1784. 250 acres.
Bowen, Henry. Va. Sergeant. 23 Jun. 1783. 200 acres.
Bowen, Henry. Va. Sergeant. 16 Apr. 1784. 200 acres.
Bowen, James. Md. Private. ———. 50 acres.
Bowen, James. N.C. Private. 11 Aug. 1820. 274 acres to heirs.
Bowen, James. Va. Private. 21 Apr. 1784. 100 acres.
Bowen, Joel. Ga. ———. 26 May 1784. 287 1/2 acres.
Bowen, John. Va. Lieutenant. 24 Jan. 1783. 2666 2/3 acres.
Bowen, John. Va. Lieutenant. 23 Jun. 1808. 555 acres.
Bowen, John. Va. Private. 14 Mar. 1840. 100 acres.
Bowen, Michael. Mass. Fifer. 17 Jan. 1833. 200 acres to heirs.
Bowen, Oliver. Ga. Commodore. 27 Jan. 1784. 1000 acres.
Bowen, Prentice. N. Y. Lieutenant. 6 Jul. 1790. 1200 acres.
Bowen, Rees. Va. Ensign. 24 Feb. 1820. 200 acres.
Bowen, Rees. Va. Ensign. 24 Feb. 1820. 200 acres.
Bowen, Rees. Va. Ensign. 24 Feb. 1820. 200 acres.
Bowen, Rees. Va. Ensign. 24 Feb. 1820. 200 acres.
Bowen, Rees. Va. Ensign. 24 Feb. 1820. 200 acres.
Bowen, Rees. Va. Ensign. 24 Feb. 1820. 200 acres.
Bowen, Rees. Va. Ensign. 24 Feb. 1820. 200 acres.
Bowen, Rees. Va. Ensign. 24 Feb. 1820. 200 acres.

Bowen, Rees. Va. Ensign. 24 Feb. 1820. 200 acres.

Bowen, Rees. Va. Ensign. 24 Feb. 1820. 200 acres.

Bowen, Rees. Va. Ensign. 24 Feb. 1820. 200 acres.

Bowen, Rees. Va. Ensign. 24 Feb. 1820. 200 acres.

Bowen, Rees. Va. Ensign. 24 Feb. 1820. 200 acres.

Bowen, Richard. Ga. Minute Man. 17 May 1784. ———.

Bowen, Robert. Md. Fifer. ———. 50 acres.

Bowen, Silas. Ga. Soldier. ———. ———.

Bowen, Stephen. N.C. Sergeant. 25 Oct. 1783. 428 acres.

Bowen, Thomas. S.C. ———. 4 Sep. 1786. 200 acres.

Bowen, Thomas B. Pa. Captain. 31 May 1787. 500 acres.

Bower, Henry. Va. Lieutenant. 1 Jun. 1805. 444 2/3 acres.

Bower, Jacob. Pa. Captain. ———. 500 acres.

Bower, Robert. Va. Sergeant. 17 Apr. 1784. 200 acres.

Bowers, Benjamin. Ga. ———. 17 May 1784. ———.

Bowers, George. Md. Private. ———. 50 acres.

Bowers, George. Va. Private. 15 Oct. 1788. 100 acres.

Bowers, George. Va. Private. 11 Dec. 1833. 200 acres.

Bowers, Giles. N.C. Private. 3 Mar. 1784. 640 acres.

Bowers, Jacob. Va. Private. 11 Feb. 1784. 100 acres.

Bowers, James. Va. Sergeant. 11 Dec. 1833. 400 acres.

Bowers, John. N.C. Private. 22 Oct. 1783. 228 acres.

Bowers, Josiah. Mass. Matross. 24 Apr. 1832. 200 acres.

Bowers, Morris. Va. Private. 14 Aug. 1785. 200 acres.

Bowers, Morris. Va. Private. 11 Dec. 1833. 200 acres.

Bowers, Philemon. Va. Private. 11 Dec. 1833. 200 acres.

Bowers, Philip. Va. Private. 11 Aug. 1783. 100 acres.

Bowers, Thomas. Va. Private. 11 Dec. 1833. 200 acres.

Bowers, William. Ga. ———. 17 May 1784. ———.

Bowers, William. N.C. Private. 2 Sep. 1820. 640 acres.

Bowhay, Thomas. Conn. Sufferer. New London. 49.17.1.

Bowie, James. Ga. ———. 28 Feb. 1784. 250 acres.

Bowie, John. S.C. Captain. 16 Jul. 1784. 300 acres.

Bowie, Reason. Ga. ———. 28 Feb. 1784. 250 acres.

Bowin, Ephaditus. N.C. Private. 6 Dec. 1797. 640 acres to heirs.

Bowler, James. N.C. Private. 9 Sep. 1785. 640 acres to heirs.

Bowler, Peter. Md. Private. ———. 50 acres.

Bowler, Thomas. Md. Matross. ———. 50 acres.

Bowles, Martin. Md. Private. ———. 50 acres.

Bowles, Peter. Va. Private. 16 Mar. 1819. 100 acres.

Bowles, Ralph H. Me. Lieutenant. 30 May 1838. 600 acres to widow Hannah Bowles. Brooklyn, N.Y.

Bowles, Thomas. Va. Sergeant. 19 Feb. 1784. 200 acres.

Bowles, William. Md. Private. ———. 50 acres.

Bowles, Zacheriah. Va. Private. 12 Jul. 1784 [1783]. 100 acres.

Bowling, James. S.C. ———. 7 May 1787. 200 acres.

Bowling, Robert. Ga. Soldier. 4 Mar. 1784. ———.

Bowling, Thomas. Ga. Soldier. 15 Apr. 1785. ———.

Bowling, Thornberry. Va. Private. 10 Sep. 1783. 100 acres.

Bowling, William. N.C. Private. 4 Aug. 1821. 640 acres.

Bowman, Abraham. Va. Colonel. 23 Jul. 1816. 3795 2/3 acres.

Bowman, Abraham. Va. Colonel. 23 Jul. 1816. 1896 acres.

Bowman, Abraham. Va. Colonel. 23 Jul. 1816. 1300 acres.

Bowman, Abraham. Va. Colonel. 23 Jul. 1816. 600 acres.

Bowman, Charles. N.C. Sergeant. 7 Jan. 1786. 1000 acres to heirs.
Bowman, Isaac. Va.-Ind. Lieutenant. 2156 acres.
Bowman, James. Va. Private. 30 Jan. 1784. 200 acres.
Bowman, John. N.C. Private. 9 Apr. 1788. 640 acres to heirs.
Bowman, John. Va. Private. 24 Feb. 1784. 100 acres.
Bowman, John. Va. Private. 10 Mar. 1784. 100 acres.
Bowman, Joseph. Va.-Ind. Major. 4312 acres.
Bowman, Joseph. Va. Major. 13 Dec. 1830. 5333 1/3 acres.
Bowman, Luke. N. Y. Private. 8 Jul. 1790. 500 acres.
Bowman, Mackness. Va. Private. 16 Aug. 1783. 100 acres.
Bowman, Robert. N.C. Private. 30 Sep. 1785. 640 acres to heirs.
Bowne, Thomas. Va. Captain. 16 Dec. 1782. 4000 acres.
Bowne, Thomas. Va. Captain. 3 Dec. 1795. 666 2/3 acres.
Bowry, Giles. Va. Private. 12 Feb. 1785. 100 acres.
Bowser, James. Va. Private. 20 May 1783. 200 acres.
Bowser, James. Va. Private. 26 Feb. & 20 Mar 1834. 200 acres.
Bowser, Thomas. Md. Private. ———. 50 acres.
Bowsman, Morris. N.C. Private. 9 Dec. 1797. 640 acres.
Bowyer, Henry. Va. Lieutenant. 22 Aug. 1783. 2666 2/3 acres.
Bowyer, Michael. Va. Captain. 16 Jun. 1784. 4000 acres.
Bowyer, Michael. Va. Captain. 26 Jan. 1809. 416 1/2 acres.
Bowyer, Michael. Va. Captain. 26 Jan. 1809. 416 1/2 acres.
Bowyer, Thomas. Va. Captain. 27 May 1783. 4000 acres.
Bowyer, Thomas. Va. Captain. 1 Jun. 1805. 666 2/3 acres.
Boy, Henry. Va. Private. 31 Aug. 1786. 100 acres.
Boyatt, James. N.C. Private. 21 Aug. 1820. 640 acres to heirs.
Boyce, Arthur. N.C. Sergeant. 12 Mar. 1785. 1000 acres to heirs.
Boyce, Jesse. N.C. Private. 29 Apr. 1784. 236 acres.
Boyce, John. N.C. Private. 18 Oct. 1808. 640 acres to heirs.
Boyce, Joseph. Pa. Private. 10 Mar. 1795. 200 acres to Clement Biddle, assignee.
Boyce, Seth. N.C. Private. 29 Sep. 1784. 640 acres to heirs.
Boyce, William. Va. Lieutenant. 5 Jun. 1784. 2666 2/3 acres.
Boyce, William. Va. Lieutenant. 3 Jul. 1807. 389 acres.
Boyce, William. Va. Lieutenant. 3 Jul. 1807. 389 acres.
Boyd, Abraham. Pa. Private. 23 Aug. 1787. 200 acres.
Boyd, Adam. N.C. Chaplain. 25 Oct. 1783. 7200 acres.
Boyd, Alexander. Pa. Private. 30 Sep. 1787. 200 acres.
Boyd, Andrew. S.C. Soldier. 3 Aug. 1801. 18 acres.
Boyd, Benjamin. Md. Private. ———. 50 acres.
Boyd, Edward. Ga. Refugee. 6 Feb. 1784. 250 acres.
Boyd, Francis. Va. Private. 9 Oct. 1783. 100 acres.
Boyd, James. Va. Private. 20 Dec. 1783. 100 acres.
Boyd, John. Ga. ———. 16 Jul. 1784. 287 1/2 acres.
Boyd, John. N.C. Sergeant. 9 Nov. 1784. 476 acres.
Boyd, John. N.C. Private. 10 Oct. 1811. 640 acres to heirs.
Boyd, John. Pa. Private. 15 Dec. 1788. 200 acres.
Boyd, John. Pa. Colonel. 4 Oct. 1786. 500 acres.
Boyd, John. S.C. ———. 3 Feb. 1800. 11 acres to Andrew Boyd, heir.
Boyd, John. S.C. ———. 3 Feb. 1800. 22 1/2 acres to Andrew Boyd, heir.
Boyd, John. S.C. ———. 3 Feb. 1800. 23 acres to Andrew Boyd, heir.
Boyd, John. S.C. ———. 3 Jan. 1800. 2 1/2 acres to Andrew Boyd, heir.
Boyd, John. S.C. ———. 3 Feb. 1800. 73 acres to Andrew Boyd, heir.
Boyd, John. Va. Private. 5 Apr. 1784. 100 acres.
Boyd, Nicodemus. Ga. ———. 17 May 1784. ———.

Boyd, Patrick. Va. Private. 25 Jan. 1809. 100 acres.
Boyd, Robert. Ga. ———. 20 Feb. 1784. 250 acres.
Boyd, Thomas. Md. Lieutenant. ———. 200 acres.
Boyd, Thomas. N.C. Private. 24 Dec. 1785. 228 acres.
Boyd, Thomas. Pa. Lieutenant. 16 Feb. 1809. 200 acres to heirs.
Boyd, Thomas. Pa. Ensign. 16 Feb. 1809. 200 acres to John Boyd, devisee.
Boyd, Thomas. Pa. Private. ———. 200 acres.
Boyd, Thomas. Pa. Private. 13 Mar. 1789. 200 acres to Peter B. Audibert, assignee.
Boyd, William. N. Y. Private. 8 Jul. 1790. 600 acres.
Boyd, William. N.C. Private. 10 Oct. 1811. 640 acres to heirs.
Boyd, William. Pa. Ensign. 16 Feb. 1809. 300 acres to heirs.
Boyden, Amos. Mass. Private. 5 Feb. 1833. 200 acres.
Boyea, P. John. N. Y. Private. 8 Jul. 1790. 600 acres.
Boyer, Michael. Md. Captain. ———. 200 acres.
Boyer, Peter. Pa. ———. 23 Feb. 1787. 200 acres.
Boyer, Peter. Pa. Captain. ———. 500 acres.
Boyer, Thomas. N.C. Private. 2 Feb. 1786. 640 acres.
Boykin, Francis. Ga. ———. 30 Jan. 1784. 250 acres.
Boykin, Francis. Va. Major. 9 Jan. 1809. 2666 1/2 acres.
Boykin, Francis. Va. Major. 9 Jan. 1809. 2666 1/2 acres.
Boykin, Jesse. Ga. ———. 17 May 1784. ———.
Boykin, Thomas. N.C. Private. 10 Aug. 1785. 640 acres to heirs.
Boykin, Tobias. Ga. ———. 30 Jan. 1784. 250 acres.
Boyle, Abraham. Pa. ———. 12 Mar. 1806. 200 acres to George Moore, assignee.
Boyle, Charles. Va. Private. 12 Jul. 1783. 100 acres.
Boyle, James. Md. Private. ———. 50 acres.
Boyle, Neal. Pa. Private. ———. 200 acres.
Boyle, Walter. Va. Sailor. 24 Dec. 1789. 100 acres.
Boyles, Daniel. Md. Private. ———. 50 acres.
Boyles, James. N. Y. Private. 8 Jul. 1790. 600 acres.
Boyles, Job. N. Y. Drummer. 13 Sep. 1790. 500 acres to heirs.
Boyles, John. Va.-Ind. Private. 108 acres.
Boylin, John. N.C. Private. 12 Dec. 1796. 640 acres to heirs.
Boyling, Matthew. Va. Drummer. 26 Aug. 1783. 200 acres.
Boyls, Henry. N.C. Private. 17 Dec. 1796. 274 acres.
Bozar, Thomas. N.C. Private. 7 Sep. 1820. 640 acres.
Bozeman, Jesse. N.C. Private. 30 Sep. 1785. 640 acres to heirs.
Bozman, Gabriel. N.C. Private. 5 Sep. 1821. 640 acres.
Bozwell, Robert. Va. Private. 30 Apr. 1783. 200 acres.
Bozwell, Robert. Va. Private. 9 Dec. 1783. 100 acres.
Bozzell, George. Va. Private. 27 May 1793. 200 acres.
Bqwen, Sebrit. Pa. Sergeant. 20 Sep. 1787. 250 acres.
Brabble, James. N.C. Private. 29 Sep. 1784. 640 acres to John Brabble, heir.
Braboy, Jacob. N.C. Private. 29 Sep. 1784. 228 acres.
Brabston, William. Va. Private. 4 Dec. 1783. 200 acres.
Brack, Benjamin. Ga. ———. 17 May 1784. ———.
Brack, Eleazer. Ga. ———. 17 May 1784. ———.
Bracken, Joseph. N.C. Private. 17 Dec. 1785. 640 acres to heirs.
Brackett, Cornelius. N. Y. Matross. 9 Jul. 1790. 600 acres.
Brackins, John. N.C. Private. 17 Dec. 1785. 274 acres.
Braddock, David. Ga. ———. Apr. 1784. 200 acres.
Braddock, John. Ga. ———. Apr. 1784. 600 acres.
Braden, James. Pa. ———. 6 Apr. 1832. 200 acres.

Bradford, Charles. Va. Lieutenant. 5 Oct. 1789. 2666 2/3 acres.
Bradford, Henry. Ga. ———. 17 May 1784. ———.
Bradford, Henry. Va. Sergeant. 19 Dec. 1783. 200 acres.
Bradford, James. N. Y. Lieutenant. 9 Jul. 1790. 1200 acres.
Bradford, Nathaniel. Ga. ———. 17 May 1784. ———.
Bradford, Osia. Ga. ———. 17 May 1784. ———.
Bradford, Samuel K. Va. Captain Lieutenant. 16 Apr. 1783. 4000 acres.
Bradley, Abraham. Ga. ———. 27 Sep. 1784. 287 1/2 acres.
Bradley, Abraham. Conn. Sufferer. New/East Haven. 101.6.8.
Bradley, Abraham, Jr. Conn. Sufferer. New/East Haven. 6.9.6.
Bradley, Azariah. Conn. Sufferer. New/East Haven. 19.0.2.
Bradley, Christopher. Va. Subaltern. 19 Oct. 1784. 2666 2/3 acres.
Bradley, Edward. Pa. Sergeant. 26 Mar. 1787. 250 acres.
Bradley, Francis, 3d. Conn. Sufferer. Fairfield. 2.10.6.
Bradley, George. Md. Corporal. ———. 50 acres.
Bradley, George. N.C. Captain. 27 Nov. 1783. 3840 acres.
Bradley, Gurdon. Conn. Sufferer. New/East Haven. 66.0.10.
Bradley, Hugh. Pa. Sergeant. 24 Sep. 1786. 250 acres to heirs.
Bradley, Increase. Conn. Sufferer. Fairfield. 180.0.0.
Bradley, James. N.C. Private. 27 Apr. 1784. 274 acres.
Bradley, James. N.C. Captain. 29 Apr. 1784. 1280 acres.
Bradley, James. Pa. Private. 10 Sep. 1789. 200 acres.
Bradley, James. S.C. Soldier. 15 Oct. 1784. 200 acres.
Bradley, James. Va. Captain. 2 Mar. 1784. 4000 acres.
Bradley, James. Conn. Sufferer. New/East Haven. 48.8.10.
Bradley, John. N.C. Private. 12 Sep. 1785. 640 acres to heirs.
Bradley, John. Va. Sergeant. 25 Aug. 1783. 400 acres.
Bradley, John, Jr. Conn. Sufferer. New/East Haven. 31.6.2.
Bradley, Jonas. Ga. ———. 17 May 1784. ———.
Bradley, Joseph. Conn. Sufferer. New/East Haven. 403.9.2.
Bradley, Joshua. Ga. ———. 27 Sep. 1784. 287 1/2 acres.
Bradley, Michael. Ga. ———. 19 Mar. 1784. 200 acres to son Abraham Bradley, a minor.
Bradley, Nimrod. N.C. Private. 13 Dec. 1796. 640 acres to heirs.
Bradley, Philip B. Conn. Sufferer. Ridgefield. 20.9.0.
Bradley, Phineas, Jr. Conn. Sufferer. New/East Haven. 19.13.6.
Bradley, Richard. Ga. Private on a galley. 1784. 200 acres.
Bradley, Richard. Ga. Refugee. 27 Mar. 1784. ———.
Bradley, Richard. N.C. Private. 20 Jan. 1785. 274 acres.
Bradley, Richard. N.C. Paymaster. 5 Sep. 1821. 2560 acres.
Bradley, Robert. N.C. Private. 23 Apr. 1784. 640 acres.
Bradley, Robert. Pa. Sergeant. 7 Aug. 1787. 250 acres.
Bradley, Samuel. N.C. Private. 16 Aug. 1821. 640 acres.
Bradley, Stephen. Conn. Sufferer. New/East Haven. 4.3.3.
Bradley, William. N.C. Private. 28 Sep. 1785. 640 acres to heirs.
Bradley, William. Va. Sergeant. 12 Nov. 1783. 200 acres.
Bradley, William, Sr. Ga. Lieutenant. 25 Feb. 1784. ———.
Bradley, Zion. N.C. Private. 8 Mar. 1796. 228 acres.
Bradner, Andrew. N. Y. Private. 8 Jul. 1790. 600 acres.
Bradner, Thomas C. N.Y. ———. 13 Sep. 1790. 500 acres to heirs.
Bradshaw, David. Ga. Refugee. 6 Aug. 1785. ———.
Bradshaw, John. Ga. ———. ———. 250 acres.
Bradshaw, John. N.C. Private. 20 Jan. 1785. 640 acres to heirs.
Bradshaw, Peter. Ga. Minute Man. 22 Mar. 1785. 250 acres.

Bradshaw, Robert. Va. Corporal. 13 Feb. 1784. 200 acres.
Bradwell, Nathaniel. S.C. Lieutenant. 21 Jan. 1785. 200 acres.
Brady, Christopher. Va. Lieutenant. 16 Dec. 1831. 2666 2/3 acres.
Brady, Christopher. Va. Lieutenant. 25 Jun. 1856. 569 acres.
Brady, John. Md. Sergeant. ———. 50 acres.
Brady, John. Md. Matross. ———. 50 acres.
Brady, John. Pa. Captain. 30 May 1804. 500 acres to heirs.
Brady, Joseph. Va. Corporal. 17 Mar. 1787. 200 acres.
Brady, Luke. Va. Private. 22 Aug. 1783. 200 acres.
Brady, Michael. Pa. Private. 16 Oct. 1786. 200 acres.
Brady, Michael. Va. Corporal. 7 Oct. 1783. 466 2/3 acres.
Brady, Samuel. Pa. Captain. 20 Mar. 1787. 500 acres.
Brady, Thomas. Md. Private. ———. 50 acres.
Brady, Thomas. Va. Private. 31 Dec. 1851. 100 acres.
Brady, Thomas. Va. Private. 2 Apr. 1856. 100 acres.
Brady, William. Md. Private. ———. 50 acres.
Brady, William. Va. Captain. 16 Dec. 1831. 4000 acres.
Brady, William. Va. Captain. 25 Jun. 1856. 853 acres.
Brady, William, Jr. Ga. Minute Man. 20 Sep. 1784. 287 1/2 acres.
Brady, William, Sr. Ga. ———. 17 May 1784. ———.
Bragdon, John. Me. ———. 3 Aug. 1835. 200 acres. Kennebunk.
Bragg, Benjamin. Va. Private. 4 Oct. 1784. 200 acres.
Bragg, Henry. Mass. ———. 7 Sep. 1829. 200 acres to assignee Richard Billings.
Bragg, Joah. Me. Private. 24 Aug. 1835. 200 acres to widow Lydia Bragg. Vassalborough.
Bragg, Joel. Va. Private. 3 Mar. 1784. 100 acres.
Bragg, William. Va. Corporal. 19 Mar 1783. 200 acres.
Braidfoote, John. Va. Chaplain. 18 Jun. 1832. 6000 acres.
Braint, William. Va. Private. 3 Feb. 1784. 200 acres.
Braithwait, William. Md. Private. ———. 50 acres.
Braken, Matthew. N.C. Private. 30 Sep. 1785. 640 acres to heirs.
Brakenridge, Alexander. Va. Captain. 22 May 1783. 4000 acres.
Bramble, Andrew. Md. Private. ———. 50 acres.
Bramble, David. Md. Private. ———. 50 acres.
Bramble, Levin. Md. Private. ———. 50 acres.
Bramfield, Peter. N.C. Private. 5 Dec. 1796. 228 acres.
Branam, John. Va. Private. 20 Aug. 1783. 200 acres.
Branam, Thomas. Va. Sergeant. 12 Aug. 1783. 466 2/3 acres.
Branch, Arthur. N.C. Private. 10 Aug. 1785. 640 acres to heirs.
Branch, Job. N.C. Private. 9 Nov. 1784. 350 acres.
Brancil, Isaac. N. Y. ———. 13 Sep. 1790. 450 acres to heirs.
Brand, Gabriel. Md. Private. ———. 50 acres.
Brand, John. Va.-Ind. Sergeant. 216 acres.
Brandom, Lewis. Va. Sergeant. 7 Feb. 1784. 200 acres.
Brandon, John. Ga. ———. 17 May 1784. 287 1/2 acres.
Brandon, Peter. Va. Private. 23 Jun. 1783. 200 acres.
Brandon, William. N.C. Private. 17 Feb. 1824. 640 acres.
Brandt, Christian. N. Y. Private. 8 Jul. 1790. 600 acres.
Braner, Joseph. N.C. Private. 29 Sep. 1785. 640 acres.
Braner, Michael. N.C. Private. 30 Sep. 1785. 640 acres to heirs.
Branham, Eben. Va. Sergeant. 29 May 1783. 200 acres.
Branham, John. Va. Corporal. 6 May 1784. 400 acres.
Branham, William. Va. Private. 27 Aug. 1784. 200 acres.
Branhan, Samuel. Ga. Minute Man. 17 May 1784. 287 1/2 acres.

Braninger, George. Pa. Private. 27 Sep. 1787. 200 acres.
Brann, Andrew. Va. Private. 1 Dec. 1783. 200 acres.
Brann, Joseph. Va. Private. 17 Aug. 1787. 200 acres.
Brannan, James. Md. Private. ———. 50 acres.
Brannan, Laurence. Md. Sergeant. ———. 50 acres.
Brannon, Christopher. N.C. Sergeant. 4 Aug. 1821. 1000 acres.
Brannon, James. N.C. Corporal. 9 Nov. 1784. 1000 acres.
Brannon, Michael. Pa. ———. 6 Dec. 1804. 200 acres.
Brannon, Richard. Pa. Private. 20 Sep. 1787. 200 acres.
Brannon, Thomas. Ga. ———. 15 Mar. 1784. 250 acres.
Brannon, Thomas. N.C. Private. 25 Oct. 1783. 274 acres.
Brannor, Michael. N.C. Private. 22 Mar. 1785. 274 acres.
Bransford, William. Va. Private. 20 Aug. 1783. 200 acres.
Bransom, Benjamin. Va. Sergeant. 28 Feb. 1784. 200 acres.
Bransom, John. Va. Fifer. 11 May 1792. 200 acres.
Branson, John. Md. Private. ———. 50 acres.
Brantley, Benjamin. Ga. ———. 17 May 1784. ———.
Brantley, Henry. N.C. Private. 8 Aug. 1821. 640 acres.
Brantley, Jeremiah. Ga. Sergeant. 1784. 345 acres.
Brantley, Jeremiah. N.C. Private. 26 Aug. 1785. 640 acres to heirs.
Brantley, John. N.C. Private. 24 Dec. 1796. 228 acres.
Brantley, Lewis. Ga. Refugee. Sep. 1785. 287 1/2 acres.
Brantley, Marmaduke. N.C. Private. 30 Sep. 1785. 640 acres to heirs.
Brantley, Philip. Ga. ———. 17 May 1784. ———.
Brantley, Thomas. Ga. ———. 250 acres. 17 May 1784.
Brantly, Britain. Va. Private. 10 Jun. 1826. 100 acres.
Branton, Britian. N.C. ———. 8 Mar. 1785. 640 acres to heirs.
Branton, Levi. N.C. Private. 11 Aug. 1820. 640 acres to heir Uriah Branton.
Branton, Levy. N.C. Private. 13 Dec. 1796. 640 acres.
Brantum, Timothy. Va. Private. 21 Jan. 1834. 100 acres.
Brashear, Richard. Va.-Ind. Captain. Mar. 1784. 3234 acres.
Brasheer, Richard. Va. Captain. 3 Mar. 1784. 4000 acres.
Braswell, Allen. Ga. Refugee. 15 Apr. 1785. 500 acres.
Braswell, Baker. N.C. Private. 19 Jan. 1786. 640 acres to heirs
Braswell, Byrd. N.C. Private. 24 May 1784. 228 acres.
Braswell, David. N.C. Private. 30 Sep. 1785. 640 acres to heirs.
Braswell, Ferdinand. Ga. ———. 25 May 1784. 287 1/2 acres.
Braswell, Frederick. Ga. ———. 25 May 1784. 287 1/2 acres.
Braswell, George. Ga. Minute Man. 1785. 500 acres.
Braswell, James. Ga. Minute Man. 15 Apr. 1785. 500 acres.
Braswell, James, Jr. Ga. ———. ———. 287 1/2 acres.
Braswell, John. Ga. ———. 25 May 1784. 287 1/2 acres.
Braswell, Joseph. Ga. Minute Man. ———. 500 acres.
Braswell, Sampson. Ga. ———. 13 Sep. 1784. 287 1/2 acres.
Braswell, Samuel, Jr. Ga. ———. 14 Sep. 1784. 287 1/2 acres.
Braswell, William. Ga. Private. 10 Dec. 1784. 250 acres.
Bratcher, Ephraim. N.C. Private. 12 Oct. 1795. 640 acres to heirs.
Bratcher, Isaac. N.C. Private. 10 Sep. 1821. 640 acres to heirs.
Bratcher, John. Ga. Citizen. 28 Apr. 1785. ———.
Bratcher, John. N.C. Private. 28 Jul. 1784. 640 acres to heir.
Braughton, William. Va. Sergeant. 20 Feb. 1784. 400 acres.
Brawn, Frederick. Ga. Soldier. 13 Sep. 1784. 287 1/2 acres.
Braxton, Moses. N.C. Private. 30 Sep. 1785. 640 acres to heirs.
Bray, Cornelius. N.C. Private. 4 Dec. 1783. 320 acres.

Bray, Jacob. N.C. Private. 24 Nov. 1796. 640 acres to heirs.
Bray, James. Va. Private. 2 Sep. 1786. 100 acres.
Bray, John. Va. Private. 30 Nov. 1784. 100 acres.
Bray, Thomas. N. Y. Corporal. 13 Sep. 1790. 500 acres to heirs.
Brayboy, John. N.C. Private. 9 Feb. 1796. 640 acres.
Braydon, Aaron. Me. ———. 2 Feb. 1844. 200 acres. Cornith.
Brayson, Robert. Va. Private. 18 Jul. 1783. 200 acres.
Brayson, Robert. Va. Private. 24 Nov. 1783. 33 1/3 acres.
Brazel, John. N.C. Musician. 26 Oct. 1801. 1000 acres.
Brazen, William. Va. Private. 23 Jun. 1783. 200 acres.
Breaden, John. N. Y. Corporal. 8 Jul. 1790. 600 acres.
Breadlove, William B. Va. Private. 30 Apr. 1783. 200 acres.
Bready, John. Va. Private. 23 Jun. 1783. 200 acres.
Bready, Lewis. N. Y. Private. 8 Jul. 1790. 500 acres.
Brean, John. Va. Private. 23 Jun. 1783. 200 acres.
Breckenridge, Robert. Va. Lieutenant. 22 Aug. 1783. 3110 2/3 acres.
Breece, Thomas. N.C. Private. 26 Dec. 1792. 365 acres.
Breech, George. Va. Private. 4 Apr. 1798. 100 acres.
Breedlove, Benjamin. Ga. ———. 25 May 1784. 1000 acres.
Breedlove, Spencer. N.C. Private. 30 Mar. 1785. 640 acres to heirs.
Breemer, Anthony. N. Y. Fifer. 9 Jul. 1790. 600 acres.
Brees, Thomas. N.C. Private. 9 Sep. 1820. 274 acres to heirs.
Bremar, Francis. S.C. Muster Master. 21 Jan. 1785. 50 acres.
Bremar, Francis. S.C. Muster Master. 2 May 1785. 100 acres.
Bremar, Francis. S.C. ———. 5 Sep. 1785. 75 acres.
Bremer, Lewis. Pa. Private. 8 Feb. 1787. 200 acres.
Brent, George. Va. Lieutenant. 4 Mar. 1833. 1177 1/3 acres.
Brent, George. Va. Lieutenant. 4 Apr. 1833. 888 2/3 acres.
Brent, John. Md. Fifer. ———. 50 acres.
Brent, John. Va. Private. 19 Jun. 1783. 100 acres.
Brent, John. Va. Private. 7 Jun. 1791. 200 acres.
Brent, John. Va. Captain. 26 Feb. 1834. 1000 acres.
Brent, John. Va. Captain. 28 Aug. 1835. 1500 acres.
Brent, John. Va. Captain. 28 Aug. 1835. 1500 acres.
Brent, John. Va. Captain. 29 Jul. 1837. 750 acres.
Brent, John. Va. Captain. 29 Jul. 1837. 750 acres.
Brent, John. Va. ———. 26 Sep. 1837. 1500 acres.
Brent, John. Va. Major. 12 Mar. 1840. 1333 2/3 acres.
Brent, William. Va. Colonel. 31 May 1783. 6666 2/3 acres.
Brent, William. Va. Colonel. 30 Mar. 1850. 1047 3/4 acres.
Brent, William. Va. Colonel. 28 Jun. 1854. 349 1/4 acres.
Brentall, William. Conn. Sufferer. New/East Haven. 16.14.2.
Brentnal, Willard. Conn. Sufferer. New/East Haven. 36.2.0.
Brentnall, Buckminster. Conn. Sufferer. New/East Haven. 51.7.10.
Bressie, Thomas. Va. Captain. 24 Jul. 1830. 4666 2/3 acres.
Bressie, William. Va. Captain. 16 Apr. 1833. 4000 acres.
Bresson, Alexis. Va. Private. 31 Dec. 1851. 100 acres.
Bresson, Alexis. Va. Private. 2 Apr. 1856. 100 acres.
Brett, John. Va. Private. 11 Sep. 1783. 200 acres.
Brevard, Alexander. N.C. Captain. 29 Apr. 1784. 3840 acres.
Brevard, Joel. N.C. Captain. 2 Dec. 1825. 3840 acres to heirs.
Brevard, John. N.C. Lieutenant. 1 Aug. 1821. 2560 acres.
Brevard, Joseph. N.C. Lieutenant. 29 Apr. 1784. 2560 acres.
Brevett, John. Md. Lieutenant. ———. 200 acres.

Brewer, Benjamin. N.C. Private. 2 Feb. 1786. 640 acres to heirs.
Brewer, Benjamin. N.C. Private. 19 Dec. 1812. 640 acres to heirs.
Brewer, Daniel. Pa. Dragoon. 5 Mar. 1787. 200 acres.
Brewer, Erasmus. Ga. ———. 17 May 1784. 250 acres.
Brewer, George. Ga. ———. 17 May 1784. 250 acres.
Brewer, Henry. N.C. Private. 24 Oct. 1783. 360 acres.
Brewer, Henry. Va. Drummer. 21 May 1783. 100 acres.
Brewer, John. Ga. ———. 17 May 1784. ———.
Brewer, John. Md. Private. ———. 50 acres.
Brewer, Morris. Ga. Private. 22 Mar. 1785. 250 acres.
Brewer, Reas. N.C. Private. 24 Dec. 1796. 320 acres.
Brewer, Robert. N.C. Private. 4 Aug. 1821. 640 acres.
Brewer, William. Ga. Refugee. 17 May 1784. ———.
Brewington, Benjamin. N.C. Private. 20 Jan. 1785. 640 acres to heirs.
Brewster, Caleb. N. Y. Lieutenant. 17 Aug. 1790. 1200 acres.
Brewster, James. N. Y. Lieutenant. 8 Jul. 1790. 1200 acres.
Brian, Henry. Va. Carpenter. 29 Dec. 1796. 100 acres.
Brian, Henry. Va. Carpenter. 22 Sep. 1860. 2566 2/3 acres.
Brian, John. Md. Private. ———. 50 acres.
Brian, William. Va. Private. 27 Oct. 1787. 200 acres.
Briant, James. Va. Private. 17 Jul. 1784. 100 acres.
Briant, Thomas. Va. Lieutenant. 14 Mar. 1834. 2666 2/3 acres.
Brice, Jacob. Md. Captain. ———. 200 acres.
Brice, John. Pa. Captain. 10 Sep. 1787. 500 acres.
Brickle, Mathias. N.C. Sergeant Major. 6 Sep. 1821. 1000 acres.
Brickle, Nathaniel Richard. N.C. Private 8 Mar. 1796. 640 acres to heirs.
Brickle, Thomas. N.C. Captain. 6 Jan. 1784. 10,970 acres.
Bricknell, Matthew. N.C. Sergeant. 8 Aug. 1821. 1000 acres.
Bridgeman, Franklin. Va. Private. 27 May 1783. 100 acres.
Bridgeman, Hezekiah. Va. Private. 6 Oct. 1783. 100 acres.
Bridgeman, Joseph. Va. Drummer. 27 Jun. 1783. 200 acres.
Bridgeman, Thomas. Va. Private. 19 Aug. 1783. 200 acres.
Bridger, James. N.C. Private. 19 Jan. 1786. 640 acres.
Bridges, Benjamin. N.C. Private. 11 May 1784. 274 acres.
Bridges, Daniel. Me. Private. 1 Jul. 1836. 200 acres. York.
Bridges, Edward. S.C. ———. 3 Sep. 1792. 196 acres.
Bridges, John. Va. Dragoon. 19 Dec. 1789. 200 acres.
Bridges, Ransom. Va. Private. 25 Jan. 1808. 200 acres.
Bridget, James. Va. Private. 4 Nov. 1809. 200 acres.
Bridget, William. N.C. Private. 21 Aug. 1820. 640 acres.
Bridgewater, Levi. Va. Private. 5 Mar. 1785. 100 acres.
Bridglen, Jonathan. Conn. Sufferer. New/East Haven. 8.15.0.
Bridgman, Boswell. Va. Private. 1 May 1784. 200 acres.
Brierly, William. N.C. Private. 29 Sep. 1784. 640 acres to heir.
Briggs, Jesse. Me. ———. 18 May 1835. 200 acres to widow Naomi Briggs. Paris.
Briggs, Jonathan. N. Y. Private. 8 Jul. 1790. 600 acres.
Briggs, Samuel. Ga. Refugee. 17 May 1784. ———.
Brigham, Joel. Mass. ———. 8 May 1829. 200 acres to heirs.
Bright, Charles. N.C. Non Commissioned Officer. 19 May 1784. 1000 acres.
Bright, Francis. Va. Captain. 18 Apr. 1832. 2666 2/3 acres.
Bright, Francis. Va. Captain. 18 Apr. 1832. 533 1/3 acres.
Bright, Francis. Va. Captain. 18 Apr. 1832. 533 1/3 acres.
Bright, Francis. Va. Captain. 18 Apr. 1832. 533 1/3 acres.

Bright, Francis. Va. Captain. 18 Apr. 1832. 533 1/3 acres.
Bright, Francis. Va. Captain. 18 Apr. 1832. 533 1/3 acres.
Bright, Francis. Va. Captain. 6 Aug. 1868. 1381 acres.
Bright, James. N. Y. Sergeant. 9 Jul. 1790. 600 acres.
Bright, Job. N.C. Corporal. 24 Aug. 1819. 428 acres.
Bright, Job. N.C. Corporal. 23 Dec. 1819. 572 acres to heirs.
Bright, William. Md. Private. ———. 50 acres.
Brightwell, Anderson. Va. Private. 19 Aug. 1822. 200 acres.
Brightwell, Jesse. Va. Private. 22 Apr. 1833. 200 acres.
Brightwell, William. Va. Private. 21 May 1823. 100 acres.
Brightwell, William. Va. Private. 21 May 1823. 100 acres.
Brigs, Nathan. N.C. Private. 6 Dec. 1796. 640 acres to heirs.
Briley, John. Md. Private. ———. 50 acres.
Brimmer, Isaac. Va. Private. 18 Apr. 1783. 100 acres.
Brimmit, John. Ga. Soldier. 5 Dec. 1785. 230 acres.
Brindly, Francis. N. Y. Lieutenant. 13 Sep. 1790. 1200 acres.
Brinkley, Isaiah. N.C. Private. 30 Sep. 1785. 640 acres to heirs.
Brinkley, Michael. N.C. Private. 15 Aug. 1820. 185 acres to heirs.
Brinkley, William. N.C. Captain. 4 Jan. 1819. 1097 acres to heirs.
Briscoe, John. Va. Private. 20 Nov. 1783. 100 acres.
Briscoe, Reubin. Va. Captain. 26 Apr. 1800. 1000 acres.
Briscoe, Reubin. Va. Captain. 26 Apr. 1800. 1000 acres.
Briscoe, Reubin. Va. Captain. 26 Apr. 1800. 1000 acres.
Briscoe, Reubin. Va. Captain. 26 Apr. 1800. 1000 acres.
Briscoe, Reubin. Va. Captain. 11 Dec. 1807. 533 1/3 acres.
Briscoe, Reubin. Va. Captain. 11 Dec. 1807. 800 acres.
Briscoe, Robert. Ga. ———. ———. 287 1/2 acres.
Brisner, Charles. N.C. Private. 9 Feb. 1796. 640 acres.
Brison, Samuel. Pa. Lieutenant. 22 Jun. 1797. 200 acres to Daniel Vanosten, assignee.
Bristler, James. N.C. Private. 29 Nov. 1783. 228 acres.
Bristoe, Charles. N.C. Sergeant. 14 Feb. 1796. 1000 acres to heirs.
Bristoe, Saunders. Va. Private. 17 Jul. 1783. 100 acres.
Bristow, Philemon. N.C. Private. 19 May 1784. 228 acres.
Britain, Hardy. N.C. Private. 30 Sep. 1785. 640 acres to heirs.
Britain, James. N.C. Private. 21 May 1784. 274 acres.
Britain, John. Va. Sailing Master. 4 Aug. 1783. 2666 2/3 acres.
Britain, John. Va. Sergeant. 6 Apr. 1784. 200 acres.
Britain, Joseph. Md. Lieutentant. ———. 200 acres.
Britain, Philip. N.C. Musician. 16 Feb. 1802. 428 acres.
Britain, Phillip. N.C. Private. 21 May 1784. 274 acres.
Brite, Willis. N.C. Private. 31 Jul. 1820. 274 acres.
Britewell, John. Va. Private. 15 Mar. 1823. 200 acres.
Britewell, Leonard. Va. Private. 15 Mar. 1823. 200 acres.
Britnall, James. N.C. Private. 29 Apr. 1784. 274 acres.
Britnom, John. Va. Private. 14 Feb. 1834. 100 acres.
Britt, Arthur. N.C. Private. 17 Dec. 1785. 640 acres to heirs.
Britt, Charles. Ga. Minute Man. 17 May 1784. ———.
Britt, James. N. Y. Private. 24 Aug. 1790. 500 acres.
Britt, John. Va. Private. 19 Jun. 1783. 100 acres.
Britt, Richard. S.C. ———. 7 May 1787. 200 acres.
Britt, Robert. Md. Private. ———. 50 acres.
Britt, Sherrard. N.C. Private. 12 Sep. 1785. 640 acres to heirs.
Britt, Thomas. S.C. ———. 7 May 1787. 200 acres.

Brittain, Henry. Ga. Sergeant. 26 May 1784. 345 acres.
Brittain, Samuel. Va. Private. 4 Jun. 1789. 200 acres.
Brittenham, Solomon. Md. Private. ———. 50 acres.
Brittle, Benjamin. N.C. Private. 23 Apr. 1785. 640 acres to heirs.
Brittle, Thomas. Va. Private. 6 Dec. 1785. 200 acres.
Britton, Henry. Ga. ———. 26 May 1784. 287 1/2 acres.
Britton, John. Md. Private. ———. 50 acres.
Britton, John. Va. Private. 23 Jun. 1783. 200 acres.
Britton, Jonathan. Me. ———. 3 Apr. 1835. 200 acres. Otsifield.
Britton, Joseph. Va. Lieutenant. 14 Jun. 1820. 2666 2/3 acres.
Britton, William. Mass. Private. 12 Sep. 1832. 200 acres.
Brizner, Henry. N.C. ———. 28 Oct. 1783. 640 acres to heir.
Broach, Charles. Va. Private. 29 Nov. 1833. 100 acres.
Broach, Charles. Va. ———. 10 Jul. 1833. 100 acres.
Broadbent, Richard. N.C. Private. 29 Sep. 1784. 640 acres to heirs.
Broadbrooks, Joseph. Conn. Sufferer. Danbury. 4.0.0.
Broaddus, William. Va. Subaltern. 18 Feb. 1784. 1666 2/3 acres.
Broaddus, William. Va. Subaltern. 18 Feb. 1784. 1000 acres.
Broaddus, William. Va. Subaltern. 24 Aug. 1860. 1666 2/3 acres.
Broadfield, Charles. Va. Private. 3 Dec. 1783. 100 acres.
Broadfield, Charles. Va. Private. 22 Jan. 1834. 100 acres.
Broadhead, Daniel. Pa. Colonel. 27 Feb. 1794. 500 acres.
Broadstreet, James. N.C. Private. 3 Feb. 1785. 640 acres.
Broadus, Edward. Va. Private. 4 Jan. 1785. 100 acres.
Broadus, James. Va. Ensign. 14 Feb. 1784. 2666 2/3 acres.
Broadus, Richard. Va. Private. 24 Dec. 1784. 100 acres.
Broadus, Robert. Va. Private. 7 May 1783. 100 acres.
Broadwater, Caleb. Va. Private. 30 Dec. 1808. 100 acres.
Broadwater, Covington. Va. Midshipman. 5 Apr. 1831. 2666 2/3 acres.
Broadwater, James. Va. Quartermaster. 26 Feb. 1831. 889 acres.
Broadwater, James. Va. Quartermaster. 26 Feb. 1831. 889 acres.
Broadwater, James. Va. Quartermaster. 26 Feb. 1831. 889 acres.
Broadwater, John. Va. Gunner. 26 Feb. 1831. 2666 2/3 acres.
Broadwell, David. N.C. Private. 6 Sep. 1821. 640 acres.
Brock, Elias. Va. Private. 19 Dec. 1783. 100 acres.
Brock, Henry. Va. Quartermaster Sergeant. 22 May 1827. 200 acres.
Brock, James. N.C. Private. 9 Feb. 1796. 640 acres.
Brock, John. N.C. Private. 21 Aug. 1820. 84 acres.
Brock, Nathaniel. N. Y. ———. 13 Sep. 1790. 500 acres to heirs.
Brock, Zedekiah. N.C. Private. 8 Dec. 1795. 640 acres to heirs.
Brockway, Russell. N. Y. Private. 8 Jul. 1790. 500 acres.
Brodhead, Daniel. Pa. Colonel. 9 Feb. 1786. 500 acres.
Brodhead, Daniel. Pa. Captain. 9 Oct. 1786. 500 acres.
Brodie, Lodowick. Va. Surgeon. Feb. 1783. 6000 acres.
Brodrick, David. N.C. Private. 7 Dec. 1796. 640 acres.
Brogdon, Hardy. N.C. Private. 25 Nov. 1796. 640 acres to heirs.
Bromfield, William. Va. Private. 14 Jan. 1786. 100 acres.
Bromley, Philip. Va. Seaman. 21 Mar. 1840. 100 acres.
Bromley, William. Va. Seaman. 21 Mar. 1840. 100 acres.
Bromly, John. N. Y. Corporal. 13 Sep. 1790. 500 acres to heirs.
Brook, James. Va. Private. 7 Mar. 1786. 200 acres.
Brookbank, John. Md. Private. ———. 50 acres.
Brooke, Edmund. Va. Lieutenant. 19 Feb. 1784. 2666 2/3 acres.
Brooke, Francis. Va. Lieutenant. 21 Jan. 1784. 2666 2/3 acres.

Brooke, Francis T. Va. Deputy Quartermaster. 22 Apr. 1838. 1000 acres.
Brooke, Francis T. Va. Deputy Quartermaster. 22 Apr. 1838. 1666 2/3 acres.
Brooke, Francis T. Va. Deputy Quartermaster. 30 Nov. 1860. 2666 2/3 acres.
Brooke, George. Va. Colonel. 26 Feb. 1834. 6666 2/3 acres.
Brooke, John. Va. Lieutenant. 21 Jan. 1784. 2666 2/3 acres.
Brooke, John T. Va. Brigade Major. 28 Mar. 1834. 2666 2/3 acres.
Brooke, John T. Va. Brigade Major. 30 Jun. 1860. 444 1/3 acres.
Brooke, John T. Va. Brigade Major. 30 Jun. 1860. 444 1/3 acres.
Brooke, John T. Va. Brigade Major. 30 Jun. 1860. 444 1/3 acres.
Brooke, John T. Va. Brigade Major. 30 Jun. 1860. 1333 1/3 acres.
Brooke, Reuben. Va. Private. 13 Nov. 1810. 100 acres.
Brooke, Walter. Va. Commodore. 19 Apr. 1831. 3333 1/3 acres.
Brooke, Walter. Va. Commodore. 18 Nov. 1867. 5000 acres.
Brooker, Walter. N. Y. Private. 3 Jul. 1790. 600 acres.
Brookes, David. Va. Private. 8 Dec. 1796. 100 acres.
Brookes, James. Va. Private. 19 Feb. 1784. 100 acres.
Brookes, John. Va. Private. 21 Dec. 1796. 200 acres.
Brookes, John. Va. Private. 3 Jul. 1784. 200 acres.
Brookes, Thomas. N.C. Sergeant. 2 Sep. 1820. 360 acres.
Brookes, William. Md. Private. ———. 50 acres.
Brookhouse, Rudolph. Pa. Private. 14 Feb. 1787. 200 acres.
Brooking, Samuel. Va. Corporal. 19 Feb. 1784. 200 acres.
Brooks, Asa. N.C. Corporal. 1 Sep. 1785. 1000 acres to heirs.
Brooks, Benjamin. Md. Major. ———. 200 acres.
Brooks, Benjamin. Va. Private. 23 Jun. 1783. 200 acres.
Brooks, Charles. Va. Private. 23 Jun. 1783. 200 acres.
Brooks, David. N.C. Private. 30 Sep. 1785. 640 acres to heirs.
Brooks, George. N.C. Sergeant. 25 Nov. 1783. 1000 acres to Cornet William Brooks, heir.
Brooks, George. Va. Private. 27 May 1783. 100 acres.
Brooks, Giles. N.C. Private. 19 Jan. 1786. 640 acres.
Brooks, Jacob. Ga. ———. 27 Sep. 1784. 287 1/2 acres.
Brooks, James. Ga. ———. 20 Feb. 1784. 250 acres.
Brooks, Jesse. Ga. ———. 17 May 1784. ———.
Brooks, Joab. Ga. ———. 27 Sep. 1784. 287 1/2 acres.
Brooks, John. Ga. ———. 17 May 1784. 250 acres.
Brooks, John. N.C. Private. 18 Dec. 1793. 228 acres.
Brooks, John. Va. Private. 1 May 1783. 200 acres.
Brooks, Joseph. Pa. Private. 18 Jan. 1787. 200 acres to Margaret Brooks, widow.
Brooks, Juriah. Ga. ———. 17 Jul. 1784. 300 acres.
Brooks, Lemuel. Conn. Sufferer. Norwalk. 287.15.4.
Brooks, Nathaniel. Va. Private. 17 Mar. 1783. 100 acres.
Brooks, Robert. N.C. Private. 30 Sep. 1785. 428 acres to heirs.
Brooks, Roger. Ga. ———. 18 Sep. 1784. 287 1/2 acres.
Brooks, Roger. S.C. ———. 3 Sep. 1787. 200 acres.
Brooks, Samuel. Me. ———. 13 Sep. 1835. 200 acres to widow Lucy Brooks. Porter.
Brooks, Samuel. N. Y. Gunner. 8 Jul. 1790. 500 acres.
Brooks, Samuel. N.C. Private. 2 Feb. 1786. 274 acres.
Brooks, Thomas. N. Y. Private. 8 Jul. 1790. 500 acres.
Brooks, Thomas. Va. Private. 9 Dec. 1783. 100 acres.
Brooks, Walter. Va. Commodore. 21 Jun. 1783. 6666 2/3 acres.
Brooks, William. Pa. Sergeant. 9 Oct. 1786. 250 acres.
Brooks, William. Va. Sergeant. 9 Apr. 1838. 266 2/3 acres.
Brooks, William. Va. Sergeant. 9 Apr. 1838. 133 1/3 acres.

Brooks, William. Conn. Sufferer. New London. 65.11.6 1/2.
Broom, John. Va. Sergeant. 30 Aug. 1783. 200 acres.
Broom, Leonard. Pa. Sergeant. 15 Aug. 1787. 250 acres.
Broom, Mason. N.C. Private. 28 Jul. 1784. 274 acres.
Broom, Thomas. Ga. Refugee. 26 May 1784. 287 1/2 acres.
Broome, Thomas. Md. Private. ———. 50 acres.
Brooner, Adam. S.C. ———. 7 May 1787. 143 acres.
Brossard, Celerin. Ga. Major. 20 Aug. 1784. ———.
Brothers, Matthew. Pa. Private. 24 Apr. 1787. 200 acres.
Brough, George. S.C. Soldier. 16 Jul. 1784. 200 acres.
Brough, James. S.C. Soldier. 16 Jul. 1784. 200 acres.
Brough, William. Va. Sailor. 5 Jun. 1783. 100 acres.
Broughton, Atkins. Conn. Sufferer. New/East Haven. 8.1.0.
Broughton, Bartholomew. N. Y. Private. 6 Jul. 1790. 600 acres.
Browder, Frederick. Va. Private. 15 Jun. 1786. 300 [100] acres.
Browder, Harrison. Va. Private. 15 Jun. 1786. 300 [100] acres.
Browder, Isham. Va. Private. 7 Mar. 1786. 100 acres.
Browder, Samuel. Va. Private. 15 Jun. 1786. 300 [100] acres.
Browener, John. N.C. Sergeant. 30 Sep. 1785. 1000 acres to heirs.
Brower, Garret. N. Y. Lieutenant. 13 Sep. 1790. 1200 acres.
Brown, Absolum. Va. Private. 20 Jun. 1783. 100 acres.
Brown, Allen. Ga. Refugee. 26 May 1784. 287 1/2 acres.
Brown, Amos. Me. ———. 16 Oct. 1835. 200 acres to widow Hannah Brown. Limington.
Brown, Andrew. Ga. Refugee. 25 May 1784. 287 1/2 acres.
Brown, Andrew. Me. Private. 30 Apr. 1835. 200 acres. Litchfield.
Brown, Andrew. Mass. Private. 18 Oct. 1833. 200 acres.
Brown, Andrew. S.C. ———. 4 Sep. 1786. 200 acres.
Brown, Aries. Va. Corporal. 20 May 1784. 200 acres.
Brown, Basil. Md. Private. ———. 50 acres.
Brown, Bazaleel. Conn. Sufferer. Greenwich. 67.15.8.
Brown, Bedford. Ga. ———. 6 Aug. 1787. 920 acres.
Brown, Benjamin. Ga. ———. 22 May 1784. 287 1/2 acres.
Brown, Benjamin. N.C. Private. 14 May 1784. 640 acres to Lewis Brown.
Brown, Benjamin. N.C. Private. 30 Sep. 1785. 640 acres to heirs.
Brown, Benjamin. S.C. Captain. 21 Jan. 1785. 300 acres.
Brown, Benjamin. Conn. Sufferer. New/East Haven. 30.1.1.
Brown, Berryman. Va. Sailor. 7 Jun. 1783. 100 acres.
Brown, Charles. Ga. ———. 18 Sep. 1784. 287 1/2 acres.
Brown, Charles. S.C. Lieutenant. 21 Jan. 1785. 200 acres.
Brown, Clement. N.C. ———. 30 Apr. 1784. 640 acres to John Brown, heir.
Brown, Collin. N.C. Corporal. 4 Aug. 1821. 1000 acres.
Brown, Collins. N.C. Private. 21 Aug. 1820. 640 acres.
Brown, David. Me. Private. 21 Oct. 1835. 200 acres. Boothbay.
Brown, David. N.C. Private. 29 Sep. 1784. 640 acres to heir.
Brown, David. N.C. Private. 1 Dec. 1796. 640 acres to heirs.
Brown, David. Va. Surgeon. 1 Mar. 1851. 6000 acres.
Brown, David. Conn. Sufferer. New/East Haven. 5.16.0.
Brown, David Evan. N.C. Private. 23 Mar. 1813. 228 acres.
Brown, Dennis. S.C. ———. 6 Aug. 1787. 200 acres.
Brown, Duncan. N.C. Private. 25 Nov. 1795. 228 acres.
Brown, Duncan. Va. Private. 18 Mar. 1784. 100 acres.
Brown, Edmund. Va. Private. 1 Mar. 1821. 100 acres.
Brown, Eleazer. Conn. Sufferer. New/East Haven. 8.12.3.

Brown, Elias. N. Y. Fife Major. 8 Jul. 1790. 500 acres.
Brown, Emanuel. N.C. Private. 21 Dec. 1803. 640 acres.
Brown, Enoch. Me. ———. 12 Sep. 1835. 200 acres. Sebec.
Brown, Ephraim. Ga. ———. 17 May 1784. ———.
Brown, F. Charles. N. Y. Private. 8 Jul. 1790. 600 acres.
Brown, Francis. Ga. Private. 28 Sep. 1784. 230 acres.
Brown, Francis. Va. Steward. 18 Jun. 1835. 100 acres.
Brown, Francis. Va. ———. 20 May 1839. 855 5/9 acres.
Brown, Francis. Va. ———. 16 Dec. 1839. 855 5/9 acres.
Brown, Francis. Va. ———. 20 May 1839. 855 5/9 acres.
Brown, Francis. Va. ———. 16 Dec. 1839. 855 5/9 acres.
Brown, Francis. Va. Steward. 20 Jul. 1853. 285 2/9 acres.
Brown, Francis. Va. ———. 20 Jul. 1853. 285 2/9 acres.
Brown, Francis. Va. ———. 20 Jul. 1853. 142 5/9 acres.
Brown, Francis. Va. Steward. 9 Aug. 1853. 142 5/9 acres.
Brown, Francis. Va. Steward. 31 May 1842. 570 1/3 acres.
Brown, Francis. Va. Steward. 31 May 1842. 570 1/3 acres.
Brown, Francis. Va. Steward. 31 May 1842. 570 1/3 acres.
Brown, Francis. Conn. Sufferer. New/East Haven. 12.16.9.
Brown, Frederick. Ga. ———. 18 Sep. 1784. 287 1/2 acres.
Brown, Frederick. N.C. Private. 26 Aug. 1785. 640 acres to heirs.
Brown, George. Md. Private. ———. 50 acres.
Brown, George. Md. Private. ———. 50 acres.
Brown, George. Va. Sergeant. 19 Mar. 1783. 200 acres.
Brown, George. Va. Private. 25 Oct. 1783. 100 acres.
Brown, George. Va. Midshipman. 2 Jun. 1835. 1333 1/3 acres.
Brown, George. Va. Midshipman. 2 Jun. 1835. 1333 1/3 acres.
Brown, Hannah. Conn. Sufferer. Norwalk. 6.3.6.
Brown, Henry. N.C. Private. 21 Aug. 1820. 640 acres.
Brown, Henry. Va. Sergeant. 19 Mar. 1783. 200 acres.
Brown, Henry. Va. Private. 4 Nov. 1783. 100 acres.
Brown, Herbert. Ga. Private. 22 Mar. 1785. 250 acres.
Brown, Isaac. N.C. Private. 10 Dec. 1788. 640 acres to heirs.
Brown, Isaac. Va. Sergeant. 20 Jun. 1783. 100 acres.
Brown, Jacob. Me. Ensign. 30 Jan. 1839. 600 acres to widow Judith Brown. Windham.
Brown, Jacob. Mass. Sergeant. 17 Sep. 1833. 200 acres.
Brown, Jacob. Va. Lieutenant. 23 May 1784. 3110 2/3 acres.
Brown, James. Ga. Minute Man. 6 May 1785. 287 1/2 acres.
Brown, James. Va.-Ind. Sergeant. 216 acres.
Brown, James. Me. ———. 27 Apr. 1835. 200 acres to widow Asenath Brown.
Brown, James. Me. Private. 25 Jun. 1838. 200 acres. Parsonsfield.
Brown, James. Md. Private. ———. 50 acres.
Brown, James. Md. Private. ———. 50 acres.
Brown, James. N.Y. ———. 13 Sep. 1790. 500 acres to heirs.
Brown, James. N.C. Private. 9 Nov . 1784. 640 acres to heir.
Brown, James. N.C. Private. 9 Nov. 1784. 274 acres.
Brown, James. Pa. Private. 16 Jul. 1787. 200 acres.
Brown, James. Va. Private. 25 Oct. 1783. 100 acres.
Brown, James. Va. Private. 21 Feb. 1784. 100 acres.
Brown, James. Conn. Sufferer. Greenwich. 15.5.5 1/2.
Brown, James, Jr. Mass. Private. 20 May 1836. 200 acres.
Brown, Jedediah. Conn. Sufferer. Norwalk. 162.7.0.
Brown, Jennings. N.C. Private. 22 Apr. 1785. 228 acres.

Brown, Jeremiah. Md. Private. ———. 50 acres.
Brown, Jeremiah. Conn. Sufferer. New London. 124.9.5 1/2.
Brown, Jesse. N.C. Fifer. 9 Sep. 1785. 1000 acres to heirs.
Brown, Jesse. Conn. Sufferer. Norwalk. 44.0.0.
Brown, John. Ga. ———. 25 Feb. 1784. 250 acres.
Brown, John. Ga. Soldier. 17 May 1784. 200 acres.
Brown, John. Md. Private. ———. 50 acres.
Brown, John. Md. Sergeant. ———. 50 acres.
Brown, John. Md. Corporal. ———. 50 acres.
Brown, John. Md. Private. ———. 50 acres.
Brown, John. N. Y. Private. 8 Jul. 1790. 600 acres.
Brown, John. N. Y. Matross. 3 Jul. 1790. 600 acres.
Brown, John. N. Y. Matross. 6 Jul. 1790. 600 acres.
Brown, John. N. Y. ———. 13 Sep. 1790. 500 acres to heirs.
Brown, John. N.C. Captain. 5 May 1784. 317 acres.
Brown, John. N.C. Private. 26 Aug. 1785. 640 acres to heirs.
Brown, John. Pa. Private. 9 Mar. 1793. 200 acres to John Nicholson, assignee.
Brown, John. Pa. Private. ———. 200 acres.
Brown, John. Pa. Private. 30 Jul. 1787. 200 acres.
Brown, John. Pa. Private. 27 Oct. 1786. 200 acres.
Brown, John. Pa. Private. 5 Mar. 1787. 200 acres.
Brown, John. Va. Private. 25 Apr. 1783. 200 acres.
Brown, John. Va. Private. 21 Aug. 1783. 200 acres.
Brown, John. Va. Seaman. 28 Nov. 1783. 100 acres.
Brown, John. Va. Sergeant. 8 Dec 1783. 200 acres.
Brown, John. Va. Private. 19 Feb. 1784. 200 acres.
Brown, John. Va. Private. 20 Feb 1784. 100 acres.
Brown, John. Va. Private. 23 Jun. 1784. 100 acres.
Brown, John. Va. Sergeant. 2 Feb. 1787. 200 acres.
Brown, John. Va. Private. 26 Oct. 1798. 100 acres.
Brown, John. Va. Private. 5 Feb. 1808. 200 acres.
Brown, John. Conn. Sufferer. Groton. 29.5.8.
Brown, John L. Va. Corporal. 12 Apr. 1783. 200 acres.
Brown, John, Jr. N. Y. Matross. 6 Jul. 1790. 600 acres.
Brown, Jonas. N. Y. Sergeant. 13 Sep. 1790. 600 acres to heirs.
Brown, Jonathan. Va. Private. 31 Oct. 1783. 100 acres.
Brown, Joseph. N. Y. Private. 8 Jul. 1790. 600 acres.
Brown, Joseph. N.C. Private. 27 Jun. 1788. 640 acres.
Brown, Joseph. N.C. Private. 22 Dec. 1796. 274 acres.
Brown, Joseph. Pa. Surgeon. 19 Oct. 1786. 300 acres.
Brown, Joseph. Pa. Surgeon. 19 Oct. 1786. 300 acres.
Brown, Joshua. Md. Private. ———. 50 acres.
Brown, Low. Va. Private. 15 Aug. 1834. 100 acres.
Brown, Mary. Conn. Sufferer. Norwalk. 9.18.0.
Brown, Micjah. N.C. Private. 8 Sep. 1823. 640 acres to his heirs.
Brown, Moses. N.C. Private. 21 Nov. 1800. 640 acres.
Brown, Nathan. N.C. Private. 5 Dec. 1797. 274 acres.
Brown, Nehemiah. Conn. Sufferer. Greenwich. 94.16.2.
Brown, Nicholas. N. Y. Private. 8 Jul. 1790. 500 acres.
Brown, Paten. Va. Private. 23 Nov. 1814. 100 acres.
Brown, Peter. Mass. Private. 19 Nov. 1832. 200 acres.
Brown, Peter. N.C. Private. 8 Aug. 1821. 640 acres.
Brown, Peter. Conn. Sufferer. Greenwich. 5.5.0.
Brown, Phebe. Conn. Sufferer. New/East Haven. 7.0.0.

Brown, Reubin. Va. Private. 23 May 1800. 200 acres.
Brown, Richard. N. Y. Fifer. 6 Jul. 1790. 600 acres.
Brown, Robert. Ga. ———. 18 Jul. 1784. 450 acres.
Brown, Robert. N.C. Private. 30 Nov. 1811. 274 acres to heirs.
Brown, Robert. Va. Trumpeter. 2 Jun. 1783. 100 acres.
Brown, Robert. Va. Private. 15 Oct. 1783. 100 acres.
Brown, Robert. Va. Private. 8 Dec. 1783. 100 acres.
Brown, Robert. Va. Lieutenant. 13 Apr. 1784. 2666 2/3 acres.
Brown, Robert. Va. Lieutenant. 15 Apr. 1853. 2666 2/3 acres.
Brown, Robert. Va. Private. 4 Sep. 1784. 100 acres.
Brown, Robert. Va. Private. 21 May 1794. 100 acres.
Brown, Robert. Va. Private. 24 Dec. 1827. 200 acres.
Brown, Roger. Conn. Sufferer. Greenwich. 147.13.10 3/4.
Brown, Russell. Ga. ———. 17 May 1784. ———.
Brown, Samuel. Ga. ———. 17 May 1784. ———.
Brown, Samuel. Mass. Private. 19 Nov. 1832. 200 acres.
Brown, Samuel. N.C. Private. 17 Feb. 1824. 640 acres.
Brown, Samuel. Va. Private. 24 Sep. 1783. 200 acres.
Brown, Samuel. Conn. Sufferer. Danbury. 1.3.10.
Brown, Samuel. Conn. Sufferer. New London. 493.7.8.
Brown, Sarah. Conn. Sufferer. New/East Haven. 12.11.6.
Brown, Stephen. Conn. Sufferer. New/East Haven. 19.2.0.
Brown, Sylvanus. Pa. Fifer. ———. 200 acres.
Brown, Thomas. Ga. ———. 15 Mar. 1784. 250 acres.
Brown, Thomas. Md. Corporal. ———. 50 acres.
Brown, Thomas. Md. Sergeant. ———. 50 acres.
Brown, Thomas. Md. Matross. ———. 50 acres.
Brown, Thomas. N.C. Private. 19 May 1784. 640 acres.
Brown, Thomas. N.C. Private. 4 Sep. 1817. 640 acres.
Brown, Thomas. Pa. Private. 10 Mar. 1795. 200 acres to Clement Biddle, assignee.
Brown, Thomas. Pa. Private. 5 Apr. 1787. 200 acres.
Brown, Thomas. Va. Drum Major. 3 Apr. 1783. 400 acres.
Brown, Thomas. Va. Private. 21 Apr. 1784. 100 acres.
Brown, Thomas, Jr. Ga. ———. 17 May 1784. ———.
Brown, William. Ga. ———. ———. 287 1/2 acres.
Brown, William. Md. Major. ———. 200 acres.
Brown, William. Md. Private. ———. 50 acres.
Brown, William. N.C. Private. 19 May 1784. 640 acres.
Brown, William. N.C. Private. 27 Nov. 1789. 274 acres.
Brown, William. N.C. Private. 24 Nov. 1797. 228 acres.
Brown, William. Pa. Fifer. 26 Sep. 1787. 200 acres.
Brown, William. Pa. Private. 27 Oct. 1786. 200 acres.
Brown, William. S.C. ———. 2 Oct. 1786. 150 acres.
Brown, William. S.C. ———. 1 Jun. 1795. 200 acres.
Brown, William. Va. Private. 2 May 1783. 100 acres.
Brown, William. Va. Regimental Surgeon. 28 May 1783. 6000 acres.
Brown, William. Va. Midshipman. 23 Jul. 1833. 2666 2/3 acres.
Brown, William. Va. Major. 1 Jan. 1840. 2667 acres.
Brown, William. Va. Major. 1 Jan. 1840. 888 1/3 acres.
Brown, William. Va. Major. 1 Jan. 1840. 889 acres.
Brown, William. Va. Major. 1 Jan. 1840. 889 acres.
Brown, Windsor. Va. Captain. 25 Mar. 1783. 4666 2/3 acres.
Brown, Windsor. Va. Captain. 11 May 1838. 395 acres.
Brown, Windsor. Va. Captain. 16 Nov. 1839. 131 2/3 acres.

Brown, Windsor. Va. Captain. 16 Nov. 1839. 263 1/4 acres.
Brownen, Hubert. Ga. ———. 19 Dec. 1785. 287 1/2 acres.
Brownen, Oliver. Ga. ———. 17 May 1784. 1150 acres.
Brownen, Samuel. N.C. Private. 17 Dec. 1785. 640 acres.
Brownen, William. N.C. Private. 17 Dec. 1785. 640 acres.
Browner, Charles. Ga. Soldier. 13 Sep. 1784. 287 1/2 acres.
Browner, John. N.C. Private. 2 Feb. 1786. 274 acres.
Browner, John. Va. Private. 5 May 1784. 200 acres.
Brownfield, Robert. N.C. Surgeon. 30 Apr. 1784. 1000 acres.
Brownguary, Casper. N.C. Private. 30 Sep. 1785. 640 acres to heirs.
Brownin, David. N.C. Private. 9 Dec. 1796. 640 acres.
Browning, Enos. Va. Private. 4 Mar. 1840. 100 acres.
Browning, George. N.C. Sergeant. 20 Apr. 1784. 1000 acres.
Browning, Isaac. Va. Captain. 11 Feb. 1848. 888 8/9 acres.
Browning, Isaac. Va. Lieutenant. 25 Jan. 1805. 2666 2/3 acres.
Browning, Isaac. Va. Captain. 11 Feb. 1848. 444 4/9 acres.
Browning, William. Va. Private. 20 Nov. 1787. 100 acres.
Brownlay, Robert. N.C. Corporal. 21 Aug. 1820. 1000 acres.
Brownlee, Alexander. Va. Ensign. 2 Nov. 1824. 2666 2/3 acres.
Brownlee, John. Va. Private. 18 Nov. 1818. 100 acres.
Brownlee, John. Va. Surgeon's Mate. 13 Dec. 1786. 1000 acres.
Brownlee, John. Va. Surgeon's Mate. 13 Dec. 1786. 500 acres.
Brownlee, John. Va. Surgeon's Mate. 13 Dec. 1786. 1666 2/3 acres.
Brownlee, John. Va. Surgeon's Mate. 18 May 1858. 1333 1/3 acres.
Brownlee, Thomas. Va. Private. 5 Apr. 1784. 100 acres.
Brownlee, William. Va. Captain Lieutenant. 30 May 1783. 4000 acres.
Brownsburry, Lewis. Pa. Private. 27 Nov. 1786. 200 acres to John Donnell, assignee.
Brownson, Nathan. Ga. Deputy Purveyor. 28 Feb. 1784. 1000 acres.
Brubank, Thomas. Mass. Matross. 16 Dec. 1834. 200 acres to widow Elizabeth Burbank.
Bruce, Charles. Ga. ———. 17 May 1784. ———.
Bruce, George. N.C. Private. 26 Nov. 1795. 640 acres to heirs.
Bruce, George. Va. Corporal. 31 May 1783. 200 acres.
Bruce, Giles. N.C. Private. 7 Jan. 1786. 228 acres.
Bruce, John. Ga. Soldier. 4 Oct. 1785. 230 acres to heirs.
Bruce, John. N.C. Private. 20 Dec. 1796. 640 acres to heirs.
Bruce, John. Va. Sergeant. 23 Jun. 1783. 200 acres.
Bruce, Josiah. Ga. ———. 4 Oct. 1785. ———.
Bruce, William. Md. Captain. ———. 200 acres.
Bruce, William. Va. Sergeant. 20 Apr. 1784. 200 acres.
Bruff, James. Md. Captain. ———. 200 acres.
Bruff, William. Md. Private. ———. 50 acres.
Bruin, Peter Bryan. Va. Major. 20 Dec. 1783. 5333 1/3 acres.
Brukins, Thomas. N.C. Private. 18 May 1784. 640 acres to heir.
Brumagem, Patrick. Va. Private. 3 Apr. 1783. 200 acres.
Brumall, Laurau. Conn. Sufferer. Greenwich. 4.0.0.
Brumingham, William. Va. Private. 23 Jun. 1783. 200 acres.
Brumley, Robert. Va. Private. 26 Jun. 1783. 100 acres.
Brumley, Simeon. N. Y. Private. 8 Jul. 1790. 600 acres.
Brumley, William. N. Y. Private. 8 Jul. 1790. 600 acres.
Brumley, William. N.C. Private. 17 Dec. 1785. 640 acres.
Brundage, Charles. Conn. Sufferer. Greenwich. 3.19.4.
Brundage, James. Conn. Sufferer. Greenwich. 30.1.4.

Brundage, William. Conn. Sufferer. Greenwich. 49.10.11.

Brunson, David. Ga. ———. 17 Feb. 1784. 250 acres.

Brunson, Ebenezer. Ga. ———. 29 Jan. 1784. 575 acres to heirs.

Brunson, John. Ga. Refugee. 17 May 1784. 287 1/2 acres.

Brunson, William. Ga. Refugee. 29 Jan. 1784. 287 1/2 acres.

Brunston, Jacob. S.C. ———. 4 Jul. 1785. 200 acres.

Brunt, John. N.C. Private. 17 Dec. 1785. 640 acres to heirs.

Brunt, Samuel. N.C. Private. 18 Dec. 1802. 640 acres to heirs.

Brush, Deborah. Conn. Sufferer. Greenwich. 31.5.1.

Brush, Eliakim. N. Y. Private. 8 Jul. 1790. 600 acres.

Brush, James. Va. Sergeant. 17 Oct. 1782. 200 acres.

Brush, James. Conn. Sufferer. Greenwich. 0.0.0.

Brush, Samuel. Conn. Sufferer. Greenwich. 13.13.8.

Brush, Selah. N. Y. Sergeant. 8 Jul. 1790. 500 acres.

Brusley, Charles. Va. Private. 20 Jun. 1785. 200 acres.

Brute, Thomas. Va. Private. 23 Jun. 1783. 200 acres.

Bruton, John. Ga. Refugee. 14 May 1784. ———.

Bruton, John. N.C. Private. 29 Sep. 1784. 640 acres to Elenor Taylor, heiress.

Brutton, Arthur. N. Y. Private. 7 Jul. 1790. 600 acres.

Bruyn, S. Jacobus. N.Y. Lieutenant Colonel. 7 Jul. 1790. 2700 acres.

Bryan, Benjamin. N.C. Ensign. 23 Jun. 182-. 2560 acres to heir Lucy C. Massenb——.

Bryan, Charles. Pa. ———. 2 May 1787. 250 acres.

Bryan, Dempsey. N.C. Non Commissioned Officer. 19 May 1784. 1000 acres.

Bryan, Edward. Pa. Matross. 17 Nov. 1786. 200 acres to Richard Leedom, assignee.

Bryan, Gilbert. Conn. Sufferer. Fairfield. 19.17.0.

Bryan, James. Ga. Refugee. 13 Sep. 1784. 287 1/2 acres.

Bryan, James. Ga. ———. 3 Jan. 1784. 250 acres.

Bryan, James. Md. Private. ———. 50 acres.

Bryan, John. N.C. Sergeant. 25 Oct. 1783. 430 acres.

Bryan, John. N.C. Private. 30 Sep. 1785. 640 acres to heirs.

Bryan, John. N.C. Private. 1 May 1826. 640 acres to heirs.

Bryan, John. Pa. ———. 20 Feb. 1787. 200 acres to Stephen Loudon, assignee.

Bryan, Mills. N.C. Private. 30 Sep. 1785. 640 acres to heirs.

Bryan, Reubin. Ga. ———. 4 May 1785. ———.

Bryan, Richard. N.C. Private. 6 Dec. 1797. 640 acres to heirs.

Bryan, Thomas. N. Y. ———. 13 Sep. 1790. 500 acres to heirs.

Bryan, William. Pa. Private. 10 Aug. 1787. 200 acres.

Bryant, Ambrose. N.C. ———. 25 Nov. 1783. 640 acres to James Bryant, heir.

Bryant, Anderson. Va. Private. 6 Aug. 1835. 200 acres.

Bryant, Benjamin. Ga. ———. 27 Sep. 1784. 287 1/2 acres.

Bryant, Daniel. Me. Private. 10 Jul. 1835. 200 acres. Saco.

Bryant, Henry. Ga. ———. 17 May 1784. ———.

Bryant, James. Va.-Ind. Private. 108 acres.

Bryant, John. Ga. Lieutenant. 25 May 1784. 626 acres.

Bryant, John. Pa. Private. 20 Nov. 1788. 200 acres.

Bryant, John. Va. Private. 16 Dec. 1783. 100 acres.

Bryant, John. Va. Sergeant. 21 Mar. 1823. 200 acres.

Bryant, Obed. N.C. Private. 12 Sep. 1785. 640 acres to heirs.

Bryant, Randol. N.C. Private. 4 Aug. 1821. 640 acres.

Bryant, Sarah. Conn. Sufferer. Fairfield. 17.10.0.

Bryant, Thomas. N.C. Fifer. 27 Nov. 1783. 595 acres.

Bryant, Thomas. Va. Private. 9 Jun. 1785. 100 acres.

Bryant, William. Ga. ———. 25 May 1784. 287 1/2 acres.

Bryant, William. N.C. Private. 12 Mar. 1785. 640 acres to heirs.
Bryant, William. N.C. Private. 30 Sep. 1785. 640 acres.
Bryant, William. Va. Private. 21 Feb. 1784. 100 acres.
Bryant, William. Va. Private. 19 Apr. 1784. 100 acres.
Bryant, William. Va. Private. 18 Oct. 1808. 260 acres.
Bryant, William, Jr. Ga. ———. 20 Feb. 1784. 250 acres.
Bryar, William. N.C. Private. 29 Apr. 1784. 274 acres.
Bryen, John. Va. Private. 27 Jan. 1808. 200 acres.
Bryley, Charles. N.C. Private. 9 Dec. 1809. 640 acres to heirs.
Bryner, William. N.C. Private. 30 Sep. 1785. 640 acres to heirs.
Bryson, Samuel. Pa. ———. ———. 200 acres.
Bryson, Samuel. Pa. Lieutenant. 20 Sep. 1787. 200 acres.
Buchanan. John. Va. Lieutenant. 27 Mar. 1787. 2666 2/3 acres.
Buchanan, Benjamin. S.C. ———. 2 Oct. 1786. 44 acres.
Buchanan, Benjamin. S.C. ———. 7 Aug. 1786. 100 acres.
Buchanan, James. Ga. Citizen. 5 Apr. 1785. 287 1/2 acres.
Buchanan, John. Ga. Citizen. 5 Apr. 1785. 287 1/2 acres.
Buchanan, John. Md. Drummer. ———. 50 acres.
Buchanan, John. Va. Lieutenant. 3 Nov. 1868. 666 26/27 acres.
Buchanan, John. Va. Lieutenant. 3 Nov. 1868. 666 26/27acres.
Buchanan, Joseph. Ga. Citizen. 5 Apr. 1785. 287 1/2 acres.
Buchanan, Robert. S.C. ———. 21 Jan. 1785. 200 acres.
Buchanan, William. Ga. ———. ———. 287 1/2 acres.
Buchannan, James. S.C. ———. 7 Aug. 1786. 200 acres.
Buchannan, John. S.C. Captain. 15 Oct. 1784. 300 acres.
Buchannon, James, Sr. S.C. ———. 21 Jan. 1785. 200 acres.
Buck, Abraham. N.C. Private. 30 Sep. 1785. 640 acres to heirs.
Buck, George. Md. Private. ———. 50 acres.
Buck, Isaac. Mass. Matross. 6 Nov. 1832. 200 acres.
Buck, John. Va. Private. 21 Aug. 1783. 100 acres.
Buck, Moses. Me. Private. 21 Jul. 1835. 200 acres to widow Hannah Buck. Sumner.
Buck, William. Mass. Private. 1 Mar. 1833. 200 acres.
Buck, William. Mass. Sergeant. 9 Jul. 1834. 200 acres.
Buck, William. N.C. Private. 1 Sep. 1785. 640 acres to heirs.
Buckannon, James. S.C. ———. 2 Oct. 1786. 200 acres.
Buckannon, Robert. S.C. ———. 21 Jan. 1785. 200 acres.
Buckhalter, Jacob. Ga. ———. 24 May 1784. 287 1/2 acres.
Buckhalter, Jeremiah. Ga. ———. 5 Apr. 1785. 287 1/2 acres.
Buckhalter, John. Ga. ———. 24 May 1784. 287 1/2 acres.
Buckhalter, Joshua. Ga. ———. 24 May 1784. 287 1/2 acres.
Buckhalter, Micajah. Ga. ———. 17 May 1784. 250 acres.
Buckhalter, William. Ga. ———. 17 May 1784. ———.
Buckhannon, Benjamin. N.C. Private. 30 Sep. 1785. 640 acres to heirs.
Buckhout, John. N. Y. Private. 13 Sep. 1790. 600 acres.
Buckhoutt, William. N.Y. ———. 13 Sep. 1790. 500 acres to heirs.
Buckle, Thomas. N.C. Drummer. 30 Sep. 1785. 1000 acres to heirs.
Buckleay, John. N.C. Private. 15 Feb. 1797. 640 acres to heirs.
Buckley, Abraham. Va. Private. 20 Jun. 1783. 100 acres.
Buckley, Daniel. Md. Private. ———. 50 acres.
Buckley, John. Md. Private. ———. 50 acres.
Buckley, Joshua. Va. Private. 20 Jun. 1783. 200 acres.
Buckley, Michael. Va. Private. 27 Jun. 1783. 233 1/3 acres.
Buckley, Peter. Conn. Sufferer. New/East Haven. 2.11.0.

Buckley, Thomas. Md. Sergeant. ———. 50 acres.
Buckliss, Charles. Md. Private. ———. 50 acres.
Buckner, Mordecai. Va. Colonel. 7 May 1838. 4444 2/3 acres.
Buckner, Mordecai. Va. Colonel. 7 May 1838. 1311 acres.
Buckner, Mordecai. Va. Colonel. 7 May 1838. 911 acres.
Buckner, Mordecai. Va. Colonel. 19 Jan. 1839. 1111 acres.
Buckner, Mordecai. Va. Colonel. 19 Jan. 1839. 1111 acres.
Buckner, Mordecai. Va. Colonel. 19 Jan. 1839. 1111 acres.
Buckner, Mordecai. Va. Colonel. 19 Jan. 1839. 1111 acres.
Buckner, Thomas. Va. Captain. 23 Feb. 1783. 4666 2/3 acres.
Buckner, William. Va. Master Navigating Officer. 24 Jun. 1833. 2666 2/3 acres.
Budd, John Shivers. S.C. Captain. 21 Jan. 1785. 300 acres.
Budd, Major. Va. Private. 14 Feb. 1834. 100 acres.
Budd, Samuel. N.C. Captain. 29 Apr. 1784. 3840 acres.
Budd, Thomas. Va. Seaman. 9 Aug. 1834. 100 acres.
Buddington, Edward. Conn. Sufferer. Fairfield. 81.0.0.
Buddington, Nehemiah. Conn. Sufferer. Fairfield. 15.1.7.
Buddington, Nehemiah. Conn. Sufferer. Fairfield. 0.10.0 to be added.
Buddington, Walter. Conn. Sufferer. Fairfield. 20.19.8.
Buddington, William. Conn. Sufferer. Fairfield. 37.7.9.
Buding, Conrad. Va. Private. 14 Mar. 1840. 100 acres.
Buffenton, Samuel. N.C. Corporal. 30 Sep. 1785. 1000 acres to heirs.
Buffington, David. Va. Private. 21 Apr. 1784. 200 acres.
Buford, Abraham. Va. Colonel. 29 May 1783. 6666 2/3 acres.
Buford, Abraham. Va. Colonel. 1 Jun. 1805. 1111 acres.
Buford, Abraham. Va. Colonel. 29 Aug. 1807. 833 acres.
Buford, John. Va. Private. 31 May 1785. 200 acres.
Bugarrow, John. N. Y. Private. 8 Jul. 1790. 600 acres.
Buges, George. N.C. Private. 17 Dec. 1785. 274 acres.
Bugg, Edmund. Ga. Refugee. 22 Mar. 1784. ———.
Bugg, Elizabeth. Ga. ———. 17 May 1784. ———.
Bugg, Jacob. Ga. ———. 17 May 1784. ———.
Bugg, Jeremiah. Ga. Refugee. 3 Apr. 1784. ———.
Bugg, John. Ga. ———. 23 Nov. 1784. 287 1/2 acres.
Bugg, John, Jr. Ga. ———. 17 May 1784. ———.
Bugg, Nicholas. Ga. ———. 17 May 1784. ———.
Bugg, Samuel. Ga. Citizen. 3 Apr. 1784. ———.
Bugg, Sherwood. Ga. Refugee Captain. 5 Apr. 1784. ———.
Bugg, William. Ga. ———. 17 May 1784. ———.
Bugg, William. N.C. Private. 20 Apr. 1784. 228 acres.
Bulger, Daniel. Md. Private. ———. 50 acres.
Bulger, Edward. Va.-Ind. Private. 108 acres.
Bulkley, Abigail and Jonathan Bulkley. Conn. Sufferers. Fairfield. 54.17.3.
Bulkley, Andrew. Conn. Sufferer. Fairfield. 33.10.11.
Bulkley, Ann. Conn. Sufferer. New London. 493.14.11 1/4.
Bulkley, Ebenezer. Conn. Sufferer. Fairfield. 0.7.2.
Bulkley, James. Conn. Sufferer. Fairfield. 0.15.5.
Bulkley, Jonah. Conn. Sufferer. Fairfield. 0.6.0.
Bulkley, Josiah. Conn. Sufferer. Fairfield. 10.0.0.
Bulkley, Moses. Conn. Sufferer. Fairfield. 50.0.0.
Bulkley, Nathan. Conn. Sufferer. Fairfield. 11.14.0.
Bulkley, Olive. Conn. Sufferer. Fairfield. 30.5.3.
Bulkley, Peter and Jos: Sturgess. Conn. Sufferers. Fairfield. 91.0.0.
Bull, Michael. N.C. Private. 5 Aug. 1820. 640 acres to heirs.

Bull, William. N. Y. Captain. 9 Jul. 1790. 1800 acres.
Bullen, Luke. Va. Corporal. 12 Sep. 1783. 400 acres.
Buller, James. N.C. Private. 23 Feb. 1820. 640 acres to heirs.
Bullet, Thomas. Va. Colonel. 16 Jul. 1832. 740 2/3 acres.
Bullet, Thomas. Va. Colonel. 28 Jul. 1831. 555 1/2 acres.
Bullet, Thomas. Va. Colonel. 28 Jul. 1831. 555 1/2 acres.
Bullet, Thomas. Va. Colonel. 28 Jul. 1831. 1481 1/3 acres.
Bullet, Thomas. Va. ———. 16 Aug. 1832. 370 2/3 acres.
Bullet, Thomas. Va. ———. 16 Aug. 1832. 1852 1/3 acres.
Bullet, Thomas. Va. ———. 18 Oct. 1833. 555 1/2 acres.
Bullet, Thomas. Va. ———. 5 Nov. 1835. 555 acres.
Bullet, Thomas. Va. Colonel. 2 Dec. 1846. 555 acres.
Bullet, Thomas. Va. Colonel. 12 Feb. 1838. 133 acres.
Bullet, Thomas. Va. ———. 20 Feb. 1838. 267 acres.
Bullet, Thomas. Va. ———. 20 Feb. 1838. 267 acres.
Bullet, Thomas. Va. ———. 27 Feb. 1838. 133 acres.
Bullet, Thomas. Va. ———. 9 Mar. 1838. 133 acres.
Bullet, Thomas. Va. ———. 4 Sep. 1838. 267 acres.
Bullet, Thomas. Va. ———. 20 Jul. 1838. 200 3/4 acres.
Bullet, Thomas. Va. ———. 20 Jul. 1838. 200 3/4 acres.
Bullet, Thomas. Va. ———. 20 Jul. 1838. 200 3/4 acres.
Bullet, Thomas. Va. ———. 20 Jul. 1838. 200 3/4 acres.
Bullet, Thomas. Va. ———. 16 Apr. 1839. 133 3/4 acres.
Bulley, John. Va. Seaman. 5 Aug. 1783. 100 acres.
Bullifant, Charles. Va. Private. 5 Mar. 1833. 100 acres.
Bullifant, Francis. Va. Private. 5 Mar. 1833. 100 acres.
Bullifant, James. Va. Private. 20 Jun. 1810. 100 acres.
Bullifant, James. Va. Private. 24 Mar. 1831. 100 acres.
Bullin, Michael. N.C. Private. 23 Apr. 1784. 640 acres.
Bullin, William. N. Y. ———. 13 Sep. 1790. 500 acres to heirs.
Bullman, John. Ga. Soldier. 5 Sep. 1785. ———.
Bulloch, Hawkins. Ga. ———. 17 May 1784. ———.
Bulloch, Hawkins. Ga. ———. 17 May 1784. ———.
Bulloch, Nathaniel. Ga. ———. 17 May 1784. ———.
Bulloch, Nathaniel. Ga. ———. 17 May 1784. ———.
Bullock, Balaam. N.C. Private. 22 Feb. 1784. 640 acres to Drury Bullock, heir.
Bullock, Daniel. N.C. Sergeant. 29 Apr. 1784. 1000 acres.
Bullock, Daniel. N.C. Lieutenant. 17 Feb. 1824. 2560 acres.
Bullock, James. N.C. Private. 17 Dec. 1785. 640 acres to heirs.
Bullock, Jeremiah. N.C. Lieutenant. 27 Oct. 1835. 914 acres to heir George Bullock.
Bullock, John. N.C. Private. 22 Feb. 1784. 223 acres.
Bullock, John. N.C. Private. 22 Feb. 1784. 640 acres to Drury Bullock, heir.
Bullock, Joshua. N.C. Lieutenant. 10 Sep. 1827. 888 acres to heir Richard Bullock.
Bullock, Lemuel. N.C. ———. 8 Mar. 1796. 1000 acres to heirs.
Bullock, Moses. N.C. ———. 22 Feb. 1784. 640 acres to heir.
Bullock, Rice. Va. Subaltern. 19 Jun. 1784. 2000 acres.
Bullock, Rice. Va. Subaltern. 19 Jun. 1784. 666 2/3 acres.
Bullock, Thomas. N.C. Sergeant. 10 May 1802. 428 acres.
Bullock, Thomas. N.C. Sergeant. 4 Aug. 1821. 1000 acres.
Bully, Edward. Va. Boatswain. 13 Jan. 1838. 411 acres.
Bully, Edward. Va. Boatswain. 13 Jan. 1838. 411 acres.
Bully, Edward. Va. Boatswain. 13 Jan. 1838. 411 acres.
Bully, Edward. Va. Boatswain. 13 Jan. 1838. 206 acres.

Bully, Edward. Va. Boatswain. 13 Jan. 1838. 41 acres.

Bully, Edward. Va. Boatswain. 13 Jan. 1838. 206 acres.

Bully, Edward. Va. Boatswain. 13 Jan. 1838. 41 acres.

Bully, Edward. Va. Boatswain. 13 Jan. 1838. 246 2/3 acres.

Bully, Edward. Va. Boatswain. 13 Jan. 1838. 246 2/3 acres.

Bully, Edward. Va. Boatswain. 13 Jan. 1838. 246 2/3 acres.

Bully, Edward. Va. Boatswain. 19 Dec. 1783. 200 acres.

Bully, Edward. Va. Boatswain. 28 Aug. 1835. 2466 2/3 acres.

Bully, Edward. Va. Boatswain. 18 Jul. 1838. 2555 2/3 acres.

Bully, John. Va. Boatswain. 2 Feb. 1832. 888 7/9 acres.

Bully, John. Va. Boatswain. 2 Feb. 1832. 888 7/9 acres.

Bully, John. Va. Boatswain. 2 Feb. 1832. 888 7/9 acres.

Bultenstone, Philip. Pa. Private. 28 Feb. 1794. 200 acres to Jacob Wilhelm, assignee.

Bulworth, James. N.C. Private. 30 Sep. 1785. 640 acres to heirs.

Bumback, Peter. Va. Private. 8 Apr. 1785. 200 acres.

Bumberdee, John. N.C. Private. 9 Feb. 1796. 640 acres.

Bumgardner, George. Md. Private. ———. 50 acres.

Bump, Jonathan. Mass. Private. 1 Mar. 1833. 200 acres.

Bumpus, Shubal. Me. Private. 5 Sep. 1835. 200 acres. Montville.

Bunberry, William. Va. Lieutenant. 20 Nov. 1798. 2666 2/3 acres.

Bunce, John. Mass. Private. 13 Dec. 1831. 200 acres to heirs.

Bunch, John. N.C. Private. 9 Dec. 1797. 640 acres to heirs.

Bunch, John. S.C. ———. 2 Oct. 1786. 200 acres.

Bunch, Winslow. Va. Private. 16 Sep. 1785. 100 acres.

Bunch, Winston. Va. Private. 23 Aug. 1782. 100 acres.

Buncombe, Edward. N.C. Colonel. 28 May 1784. 7200 acres to Thomas Buncombe, heir.

Bundge, Michael. N. Y. Sergeant. 8 Jul. 1790. 600 acres.

Bundy, Francis. Va. Private. 12 Jan. 1784. 200 acres.

Bundy, James. N.C. Private. 20 Mar. 1785. 274 acres.

Bundy, James. N.C. Private. 23 Dec. 1819. 91 acres to heirs.

Bunker, Roger. Ga. – ———. 4 Oct. 1785. ———.

Bunn, Daniel. Va. Private. 22 Aug. 1783. 200 acres.

Bunner, Jacob. Pa. Captain. 29 Sep. 1787. 500 acres.

Bunnington, Dempsey. N.C. Private. 30 Sep. 1785. 274 acres.

Bunnington, William. N.C. Private. 30 Sep. 1785. 640 acres.

Buns, John. Va. Private. 30 Dec. 1783. 100 acres.

Bunt, Lodowick. N. Y. Private. 8 Jul. 1790. 600 acres.

Buntin, James. N.C. Private. 30 Sep. 1785. 640 acres to heirs.

Bunting, Holloway. Va. Private. 15 Jan. 1808. 100 acres.

Bunting, Richard. Va. Private. 15 Jun. 1807. 100 acres.

Bunting, Sacker. Va. Private. 7 May 1785. 100 acres.

Bunting, Sacker. Va. Private. 15 Jan. 1808. 200 acres.

Bunting, Smith. Va. Private. 15 Jun. 1807. 100 acres.

Bunting, Solomon. Va. Private. 14 Feb. 1834. 200 acres.

Bunting, Thomas. N. Y. Sergeant. 8 Jul. 1790. 500 acres.

Bunting, William B. Va. Ensign. 15 Jun. 1807. 2666 2/3 acres.

Bunting, William B. Va. Lieutenant. 30 May 1839. 814 acres.

Burbage, John. S.C. ———. 4 Sep. 1786. 200 acres.

Burbage, Jonathan. S.C. ———. 2 Oct. 1786. 200 acres.

Burbage, William. S.C. ———. 4 Sep. 1786. 200 acres.

Burbank, Eleazer. Me. Musician. 27 Apr. 1835. 200 acres. Belgrade.

Burch, Benjamin. Md. Corporal. ———. 50 acres.

Burch, Benjamin. Md. Sergeant. ———. 50 acres.

Burch, Charles. Ga. Refugee. 6 Feb. 1784. 500 acres.
Burch, Edward. Ga. ———. 6 Feb. 1784. 500 acres.
Burch, Isaiah. N. Y. Private. 8 Jul. 1790. 600 acres.
Burch, John. N. Y. Sergeant. 8 Jul. 1790. 600 acres.
Burch, John. N.C. Private. 20 Apr. 1784. 640 acres to Willilam Burch, heir.
Burch, Joseph. Md. Private. ———. 50 acres.
Burch, Philip. N. Y. Private. 8 Jul. 1790. 600 acres.
Burch, Samuel. Va. Private. 27 Jun. 1783. 100 acres.
Burch, Thomas. Md. Private. ———. 50 acres.
Burch, William. N.C. Corporal. 20 Apr. 1784. 1000 acres.
Burch, Zacheriah. Md. Private. ———. 50 acres.
Burchell, John. Pa. Dragoon. 4 Sep. 1789. 200 acres to Stephen Louden, assignee.
Burcolow, William. Ga. ———. 27 Sep. 1784. 287 1/2 acres.
Burden, Jacob. N.C. Private. 30 Sep. 1785. 640 acres to heirs.
Burden, Thomas. N.C. Private. 9 Feb. 1796. 640 acres.
Burdey, Peter. Ga. Soldier. 20 Aug. 1784. ———.
Burdick, Henry. N. Y. Corporal. 8 Jul. 1790. 500 acres.
Burdick, Levin. Va. Private. 18 Apr. 1832. 100 acres.
Burdict, Elisha. N. Y. Private. 8 Jul. 1790. 600 acres.
Burdine, Francis. N. Y. Private. 8 Jul. 1790. 600 acres.
Burdoin, John. Va. Private. 2 Apr. 1784. 200 acres.
Burdon, Archibald. N.C. Private. 2 Feb. 1786. 640 acres.
Burdox, Ezekiel. N.C. Private. 30 Sep. 1785. 640 acres to heirs.
Burdyshaw, Peter. Ga. ———. 1784. 287 1/2 acres.
Burelay, John. Pa. Lieutenant. 16 Jul. 1788. 200 acres.
Burfoot, Thomas. Va. Lieutenant. 17 Jul. 1783. 2666 2/3 acres.
Burford, John. Ga. ———. 17 May 1784. ———.
Burford, William. Ga. ———. 17 May 1784. ———.
Burfott, William. Va. Private. 24 Mar. 1784. 100 acres.
Burge, William. Va. Sergeant. 5 Mar. 1788. 400 acres.
Burge, Wooden. Va. Private. 21 Jun. 1810. 100 acres.
Burges, John. N. Y. Matross. 9 Jul. 1790. 600 acres.
Burges, John. N.C. Private. 16 Aug. 1821. 640 acres.
Burgess, Absalom. N.C. Sergeant. 21 May 1784. 1000 acres.
Burgess, Basil. Md. Lieutenant. ———. 200 acres.
Burgess, David. Me. ———. 11 May 1835. 200 acres to widow Sylvia Burgess. Fairfield.
Burgess, Dawson. Va. Sergeant. 24 Feb. 1784. 200 acres.
Burgess, Drury. N.C Private. 27 Jul. 1785. 274 acres.
Burgess, Isaac. N.C. Private. 25 Nov. 1796. 640 acres to heirs.
Burgess, John. Va. Private. 22 Feb. 1812. 200 acres.
Burgess, Joseph. Ga. Private. 10 Dec. 1784. 250 acres.
Burgess, Joseph. Md. Captain. ———. 200 acres.
Burgess, Joseph. N.C. Private. 2 Sep. 1820. 640 acres.
Burgess, Joshua. Md. Lieutenant. ———. 200 acres.
Burgess, Josiah. Md. Private. ———. 50 acres.
Burgess, Michael. N. Y. Private. 6 Jul. 1790. 600 acres.
Burgess, Philip. N.C. Private. 23 Apr. 1784. 640 acres.
Burgess, William. Md. Private. ———. 50 acres.
Burgess, William. Va. Second Lieutenant. 15 Jan. 1841. 666 2/3 acres.
Burgess, William. Va. Second Lieutenant. 15 Jan. 1841. 666 2/3 acres.
Burgess, William. Va. Second Lieutenant. 15 Jan. 1841. 133 1/3 acres.
Burgess, William. Va. Second Lieutenant. 15 Jan. 1841. 133 1/3 acres.
Burgess, William. Va. Second Lieutenant. 15 Jan. 1841. 133 1/3 acres.

Burgess, William. Va. Second Lieutenant. 15 Jan. 1841. 400 acres.
Burgess, William. Va. Second Lieutenant. 2 Dec. 1841. 133 1/3 acres.
Burgess, William. Va. Second Lieutenant. 2 Dec. 1841. 133 1/3 acres.
Burgiss, Peter. N.C. Private. 12 Dec. 1797. 640 acres.
Burgstiner, Daniel. Ga. ———. 6 Feb. 1784. 500 acres.
Burk, Charles. N.C. Private. 27 Jul. 1785. 640 acres.
Burk, Edmund. N. Y. ———. 13 Sep. 1790. 500 acres to heirs.
Burk, Jacob. N.C. Private. 9 Nov. 1784. 640 acres to heirs.
Burk, James. Ga. Private. 25 May 1784. 287 1/2 acres to widow Mary Burk.
Burk, James. Md. Private. ———. 50 acres.
Burk, James. Va. Gunner. 22 Nov. 1783. 100 acres.
Burk, James. Va. Gunner. 30 Mar. 1831. 2566 2/3 acres.
Burk, John. Va. Fifer. 22 Aug. 1783. 200 acres.
Burk, John. Va. ———. 30 Mar. 1831. 2666 2/3 acres.
Burk, Levy. Md. Private. ———. 50 acres.
Burk, Matthew. Va. Private. 1 Jun. 1785. 100 acres.
Burk, Meredith. N.C. Private. 20 Jan. 1785. 640 acres to heirs.
Burk, Nicholas. Va.-Ind. Private. 108 acres.
Burk, Nicholas. Va. Private. 17 Jul. 1784. 100 acres.
Burk, Samuel. Va. Sergeant. 30 Jun. 1784. 200 acres.
Burk, Theophilus. Ga. ———. 17 May 1784. ———.
Burk, Thomas. Va. Private. 10 Jul. 1782. 100 acres.
Burk, William. N.C. Private. 7 Jan. 1786. 228 acres.
Burk, William. Va. Private. 20 Aug. 1783. 200 acres.
Burk, William. Va. Private. 31 Aug. 1859. 200 acres.
Burk, William. Va. Private. 22 Feb. 1783. 28 acres.
Burkdoff, John. N. Y. Private. 7 Jul. 1790. 600 acres.
Burke, Edmund. Pa. Captain. ———. 500 acres.
Burke, Francis. N.C. Private. 24 Dec. 1785. 640 acres to heirs.
Burke, James. N.C. ———. 28 Oct. 1783. 640 acres to John Burke.
Burke, John. N. Y. Private. 8 Jul. 1790. 500 acres.
Burke, John. Va. Private. 5 Mar. 1784. 100 acres.
Burke, William. Ga. ———. 30 Sep. 1784. ———.
Burke, William. Va. Private. 24 May 1784. 200 acres.
Burket, Samuel. Va. Private. 30 May 1837. 200 acres.
Burket, Thomas. S.C. ———. 4 Jul. 1791. 200 acres.
Burks, Charles. Ga. ———. 17 May 1784. 287 1/2 acres.
Burks, David. Ga. ———. 5 May 1785. ———.
Burks, Edward. Ga. ———. 20 Feb. 1784. 250 acres.
Burks, Jacob John. Ga. ———. 17 May 1784. ———.
Burks, John. Ga. Captain. 29 Jul. 1784. 287 1/2 acres.
Burks, Joseph. Ga. Minute Man. 29 Jul. 1784. 287 1/2 acres.
Burks, Rowland. Ga. ———. 19 Jul. 1784. 287 1/2 acres.
Burks, Silas. Ga. Minute Man. 3 Sep. 1785. ———.
Burlamon, Benjamin. Ga. Refugee. 3 Apr. 1784. ———.
Burling, Levi. N. Y. ———. 13 Sep. 1790. 500 acres to heirs.
Burnel, Israel. Conn. Sufferer. New/East Haven. 9.16.6.
Burnes, Ezekiel. Md. Private. ———. 50 acres.
Burnes, Harvey. Md. Private. ———. 50 acres.
Burnes, James. N.C. Private. 7 Dec. 1796. 274 acres.
Burnes, Jeremiah. Va. Private. 21 May 1781. 200 acres.
Burnes, John. Md. Private. ———. 50 acres.
Burnes, John. Md. Private. ———. 50 acres.
Burnes, John. N.C. Private. 21 Apr. 1784. 640 acres to Wiilliam Burnes, heir.
Burnes, Laurence. Pa. Private. 14 Oct. 1786. 200 acres.

Burnes, Luke. Md. Private. ———. 50 acres.
Burnes, William. Pa. Sergeant. 5 Jul. 1786. 250 acres.
Burnet, John. N. Y. Lieutenant. 17 Aug. 1790. 1200 acres.
Burnet, William. N.C. Private. 19 May 1784. 640 acres.
Burnett, Charles. N.C. Private. 2 Sep. 1820. 640 acres.
Burnett, David. N.C. Private. 8 Aug. 1821. 640 acres.
Burnett, Ebenezer. N. Y. Private. 8 Jul. 1790. 600 acres.
Burnett, George. Pa. Fife Major. 6 Apr. 1787. 200 acres.
Burnett, John. Ga. Refugee Captain. 25 May 1784. 287 1/2 acres.
Burnett, John. N. Y. Private. 8 Jul. 1790. 500 acres.
Burnett, John. Va. Private. 31 Oct. 1783. 200 acres.
Burnett, Joshua. Ga. Refugee. 17 May 1784. ———.
Burnett, Millington. Va. Corporal. 26 Jun. 1786. 200 acres.
Burnett, Robert. N. Y. Lieutenant. 7 Jul. 1790. 1200 acres.
Burnett, William. Va. Private. 28 Apr. 1783. 200 acres.
Burney, David. Ga. ———. 2 Aug. 1785. 287 1/2 acres.
Burney, John. Ga. ———. ———. 250 acres.
Burney, John. Ga. ———. 17 May 1784. ———.
Burney, John, Jr. Ga. Private. 17 May 1784. ————.
Burney, Nicholas. Pa. Private. ———. 200 acres.
Burney, Randal. Ga. ———. 17 May 1784. ———.
Burnfield, Moses. N.C. Private. 12 Sep. 1785. 640 acres to heirs.
Burnham, Isaac. N.C. Private. 24 May 1784. 640 acres.
Burnham, William. N. Y. Private. 3 Jul. 1790. 600 acres.
Burnley, Garland. Va. Captain. 26 Feb. 1834. 4000 acres.
Burnley, James. Va. Private. 13 Mar. 1822. 100 acres.
Burnley, Reuben. Va. Private. 29 Dec. 1796. 200 acres.
Burnley, Samuel. Ga. Refugee. 26 May 1784. ———.
Burns, Alexander. Pa. Private. ———. 200 acres.
Burns, Andrew. Ga. ———. 17 May 1784. ———.
Burns, Barnabas. N.C. Private. 29 Sep. 1784. 640 acres to heirs.
Burns, Carberry. Pa. Private. 1 Jun. 1787. 200 acres.
Burns, Hugh. Md. Private. ———. 50 acres.
Burns, Isum. N.C. Private. 12 Sep. 1785. 640 acres to heirs.
Burns, James. Pa. Matross. 30 July 1787. 200 acres.
Burns, James, Jr. Pa. ———. 16 Nov. 1786. 200 acres to Francis Murray, assignee.
Burns, John. Ga. ———. 250 acres. ———.
Burns, John. Pa. Drummer. 13 Oct. 1786. 200 acres to heirs.
Burns, John. Pa. ———. 19 Dec. 1808. 200 acres.
Burns, John. Va. Private. 26 Mar. 1784. 100 acres.
Burns, Levi. Pa. Private. 20 Aug. 1787. 200 acres.
Burns, Michael. Md. Private. ———. 50 acres.
Burns, Michal. Pa. Private. 9 Mar. 1795. 200 acres to John Nicholson, assignee.
Burns, Nathan. Conn. Sufferer. Fairfield. 1.17.6.
Burns, Thomas. Pa. Sergeant. 1 Sep. 1789. 250 acres.
Burns, Thomas. S.C. ———. 2 Jan. 1792. 200 acres.
Burns, Thomas. Va. Private. 8 Mar. 1785. 200 acres.
Burns, Timothy. Pa. Private. 18 Nov. 1803. 200 acres.
Burnside, James. Pa. Private. 14 Sep. 1808. 200 acres.
Burnside, John. N.Y. Lieutenant. 13 Sep. 1790. 1000 acres to heirs.
Burnsides, David. N.C. Sergeant. 25 Oct. 1783. 360 acres.
Burnsides, David. N.C. Private. 14 Dec. 1796. 640 acres to heirs.
Burnsides, John, Jr. Ga. Citizen. 26 Apr. 1784. ———.

Burnsides, John, Sr. Ga. Refugee. 30 Sep. 1784. ———.
Burnum, Isaac. N.C. Private. 20 Sep. 1784. 640 acres.
Burr, Abigail. Conn. Sufferer. Fairfield. 58.17.9.
Burr, Abigail, Jr. Conn. Sufferer. Fairfield. 50.2.6.
Burr, Amelia. Conn. Sufferer. Fairfield. 10.0.0.
Burr, Charles. Conn. Sufferer. Fairfield. 24.16.0.
Burr, Daniel. Me. Private. 30 Jul. 1835. 200 acres to widow Susannah Burr. Mercer.
Burr, David. Conn. Sufferer. Fairfield. 388.2.9.
Burr, David. Conn. Sufferer. Fairfield. 10.5.4.
Burr, Ephraim, Jr. Conn. Sufferer. Fairfield. 95.17.10.
Burr, Ephraim, Jr. Conn. Sufferer. Fairfield. 4.18.11.
Burr, George. Conn. Sufferer. Fairfield. 15.16.10.
Burr, Gershom. Conn. Sufferer. Fairfield. 300.10.4
Burr, Isaac. Conn. Sufferer. Fairfield. 23.5.0.
Burr, Luce. Conn. Sufferer. Fairfield. 4.13.0.
Burr, Nathan. Conn. Sufferer. Fairfield. 4.9.0.
Burr, Nathaniel. Conn. Sufferer. Fairfield. 22.18.0.
Burr, Peter. Conn. Sufferer. Fairfield. 282.9.1.
Burr, Pinckney. Conn. Sufferer. Fairfield. 14.0.0.
Burr, Priscilla. Conn. Sufferer. Fairfield. 282.8.6.
Burr, Ruth. Conn. Sufferer. Fairfield. 3.19.6.
Burr, Samuel. Conn. Sufferer. Fairfield. 481.3.10.
Burr, Samuel, 3d. Conn. Sufferer. Fairfield. 14.14.0.
Burr, Samuel, Jr. Conn. Sufferer. Fairfield. 2.14.6.
Burr, Thaddeus. Conn. Sufferer. Fairfield. 1,373.18.1.
Burr, Wakeman. Conn. Sufferer. Fairfield. 363.14.9.
Burrage, Charles. Va. Private. 13 Apr. 1784. 100 acres.
Burrage, John. Pa. Private. 25 Oct. 1787. 200 acres.
Burrall, Nathan. Conn. Sufferer. Norwalk. 2.17.4.
Burrall, Samuel. Conn. Sufferer. Norwalk. 30.18.6.
Burrall, Thomas. Conn. Sufferer. New/East Haven. 17.2.11.
Burrance, Henry. N. Y. ———. 13 Sep. 1790. 500 acres to heirs.
Burrance, Richard. Pa. Private. 21 Sep. 1787. 200 acres.
Burrance, Robert. N. Y. Private. 8 Jul. 1790. 600 acres.
Burress, Absolum. N.C. Private. 30 Sep. 1785. 640 acres to heirs.
Burress, Elisha. Ga. ———. 5 May 1785. 287 1/2 acres.
Burress, Hezekiah. Ga. ———. ———. 287 1/2 acres.
Burress, Matthew. Ga. ———. ———. 287 1/2 acres.
Burrill, Humphrey. Me. Matross. 13 May 1835. 200 acres. Milburn.
Burris, Frederick. Va. Private. 1 Apr. 1783. 100 acres.
Burris, John. Va. Private. 4 Jun. 1835. 100 acres.
Burris, William. Ga. ———. 7 Jun. 1785. 287 1/2 acres.
Burrn, Andrew. N.C. Private. 30 Sep. 1785. 640 acres to heirs.
Burros, Thomas. N. Y. Private. 8 Jul. 1790. 600 acres.
Burroughs, Samuel. N. Y. Matross. 9 Jul. 1790. 600 acres.
Burrows, Amos. Mass. Private. 8 Feb. 1830. 200 acres to his heir Anne Caldwell.
Burrows, John. N.C. Private. 5 Sep. 1821. 640 acres.
Burrows, Jonathan. Me. ———. 6 Oct. 1838. 200 acres to Elizabeth (Witherel) Burrows. Lebanon.
Burrows, Samuel. N.C. Private. 5 Sep. 1821. 640 acres.
Burshaw, John. N.C. Private. 9 Feb. 1796. 640 acres.
Burt, Moody. Ga. ———. 29 Jan. 1784. 250 acres.
Burtham, Perry. Md. Private. ———. 50 acres.

Burton, Andrew. N.C. Private. 22 Apr. 1785. 228 acres.
Burton, Benjamin. Va. Private. 15 Jun. 1807. 100 acres.
Burton, Hutchens. Va. Lieutenant. 17 May 1783. 2666 2/3 acres.
Burton, Isaac. Md. Matross. ———. 50 acres.
Burton, Jacob. N.C. Private. 22 Apr. 1785. 228 acres.
Burton, James. Va. Private. 28 May 1783. 100 acres.
Burton, James. Va. Lieutenant. 3 Apr. 1812. 2666 2/3 acres.
Burton, James. Va. Captain. 17 Mar. 1834. 2055 1/3 acres.
Burton, James. Va. Captain. 13 Nov. 1834. 352 acres.
Burton, John. Ga. Soldier. 3 Jan. 1785. 287 1/2 acres.
Burton, John. N.C. Adjutant. 23 Oct. 1783. 1168 acres.
Burton, Julius. N.C. Private. 10 Dec. 1788. 640 acres to heirs.
Burton, Richard. Ga. Soldier. 29 Jan. 1784. 200 acres.
Burton, Richard. Va. Private. 10 May 1784. 100 acres.
Burton, Samuel. N.C. Private. 8 May 1784. 228 acres.
Burton, Sibley. Mass. Sergeant. 22 Jul. 1833. 200 acres.
Burton, Thomas. Ga. Refugee. 16 Jul. 1784. 287 1/2 acres.
Burton, William. S.C. ———. 4 Sep. 1786. 100 acres.
Burton, William. Va. Private. 31 Jan. 1784. 100 acres.
Burwell, Nathaniel. Va. Captain. 13 Jun. 1783. 4666 2/3 acres.
Burwell, Nathaniel. Va. Captain. 3 Oct. 1807. 722 acres.
Busby, Benjamin. Pa. Private. 28 Oct. 1786. 200 acres to Mary Busby, widow.
Busby, James. Va. Private. 9 May 1786. 100 acres.
Busby, James. Va. Corporal. 26 Feb. 1822. 300 acres.
Busby, John. Va. Private. 9 May 1786. 100 acres.
Buser, Caleb. Ga. Refugee. 6 Aug. 1785. ———.
Buser, John. Ga. Refugee. 6 Aug. 1785. ———.
Bush, Aaron. N.C. Private. 19 Jan. 1786. 640 acres.
Bush, Chaney. N.C. Private. 21 Aug. 1820. 640 acres.
Bush, Conradt. N. Y. Matross. 9 Jul. 1790. 600 acres.
Bush, David. Conn. Sufferer. Greenwich. 159.5.11.
Bush, George. Pa. Captain. ———. 500 acres.
Bush, Isaac. Conn. Sufferer. Greenwich. 4.10.0.
Bush, James. Ga. ———. 17 May 1784. ———.
Bush, James. Va. Private. 23 May 1800. 200 acres.
Bush, John. N.C. Lieutenant. 25 Oct. 1783. 914 acres.
Bush, John. Pa. Captain. 9 Jan. 1787. 500 acres.
Bush, John. S.C. Lieutenant. 4 Jul. 1786. 200 acres to heirs.
Bush, John. Conn. Sufferer. Greenwich. 10.10.9.
Bush, Thomas. Ga. ———. 5 Sep. 1785. 287 1/2 acres.
Bush, William. Ga. ———. 5 Sep. 1785. 287 1/2 acres.
Bush, William. Va.-Ind. Private. 108 acres.
Bush, William. N,C. Lieuteant. 23 Oct. 1783. 2560 acres.
Bush, William. Conn. Sufferer. Greenwich. 41.6.9. 1/4.
Bushell, John. Va. Private. 22 Nov. 1783. 100 acres.
Bushell, Peter. Md. Private. ———. 50 acres.
Bushey, Peter. N. Y. Matross. 9 Jul. 1790. 500 acres.
Bushop, Colden. N.C. Private. 30 Sep. 1785. 640 acres to heirs.
Bushop, Solomon. Va. Private. 22 Nov. 1783. 100 acres.
Bushop, William. N.C. Private. 30 Sep. 1785. 640 acres to heirs.
Buss, John. Mass. Corporal. 16 Sep. 1834. 200 acres.
Bussell, Charles. Va. Corporal. 26 Nov. 1783. 200 acres.
Bussell, Isaac. Me. Private. 4 Aug. 1835. 200 acres. Columbia.
Bussell, Vincent. Va. Private. 12 Aug. 1785. 100 acres.

Bussell, William. Va. Private. 6 Jun. 1783. 100 acres.
Bussey, Hezekiah. Ga. ———. 25 Feb. 1784. 250 acres.
Bussey, Thomas. Ga. ———. 17 May 1784. ———.
Busson, Jonathan. Ga. ———. ———. 287 1/2 acres.
Bustenton, John. N.C. Private. 9 Feb. 1796. 640 acres.
Butcher, John. Md. Private. ———. 50 acres.
Butcher, John. N.C. Private. 15 Feb. 1797. 365 acres.
Butcher, John. Pa. Private. 6 Sep. 1787. 200 acres.
Buteau, Charles. Va. Private. 31 Dec. 1851. 100 acres.
Buteau, Charles. Va. Private. 2 Apr. 1856. 100 acres.
Buteau, Joseph. Va. Private. 31 Dec. 1851. 100 acres.
Buteau, Joseph. Va. Private. 2 Apr. 1856. 100 acres.
Buteau, Michael. Va. Private. 31 Dec. 1851. 100 acres.
Buteau, Michael. Va. Private. 2 Apr. 1856. 100 acres.
Buteau, Pierre. Va. Private. 2 Apr. 1856. 100 acres.
Buteau, Pierre. Va. Private. 31 Dec. 1851. 100 acres.
Butler, Charles. N.C. Private. 13 Dec. 1783. 228 acres.
Butler, Charys. N.C. Private. 7 Sep. 1820. 228 acres.
Butler, Daniel. Ga. ———. 17 Sep. 1784. 287 1/2 acres.
Butler, Daniel. Ga. ———. 17 May 1784. 575 acres.
Butler, Edward. Ga. ———. 17 May 1784. ———.
Butler, Edward. N.C. Sergeant. 22 Apr. 1785. 1000 acres.
Butler, Edward. Pa. Lieutenant. 19 Dec. 1786. 200 acres.
Butler, Edward. Pa. Lieutenant. ———. 200 acres.
Butler, Edward. Va. Sailor. 19 Dec 1783. 200 acres.
Butler, Ford. Ga. Refugee. 15 Mar. 1784. 250 acres.
Butler, Francis. Ga. ———. ———. 287 1/2 acres.
Butler, Isaac. N.C. Private. 22 Oct. 1783. 228 acres.
Butler, James. Pa. ———. 25 Jan. 1804. 200 acres.
Butler, John. Ga. Minute Man. 22 Mar. 1785. 250 acres.
Butler, John. Me. Private. 18 Jul. 1835. 200 acres to widow Dolly Butler. Saco.
Butler, John. N.C. Private. 22 Oct. 1783. 228 acres.
Butler, John. N.C. Private. 9 Dec. 1805. 640 acres.
Butler, John. Pa. Private. 19 Sep. 1787. 200 acres.
Butler, John. Pa. Private. 27 Aug. 1787. 200 acres.
Butler, John. Pa. Private. 6 Oct. 1808. 200 acres.
Butler, John. Va. Sergeant Major. 28 Apr. 1783. 400 acres.
Butler, John. Va. Sergeant Major. 10 Nov. 1846. 400 acres.
Butler, John. Va. Sergeant Major. 11 Nov. 1846. 200 acres.
Butler, John. Va. Sergeant Major. 11 Nov. 1846. 100 acres.
Butler, John. Va. Sergeant Major. 11 Nov. 1846. 100 acres.
Butler, Joseph. Va. Private. 2 May 1783. 200 acres.
Butler, Lawrence. Va. Captain. 26 Mar. 1783. 4000 acres.
Butler, Lawrence. Va. Captain. 17 Jul. 1807. 666 2/3 acres.
Butler, Nathan. N.C. Private. 2 Feb. 1786. 640 acres.
Butler, Patrick. Pa. ———. 9 Mar. 1795. 200 acres to John Nicholson, assignee.
Butler, Percival. Pa. Lieutenant. 19 Oct. 1786. 200 acres.
Butler, Percival. Pa. Lieutenant. 19 Oct. 1786. 200 acres.
Butler, Peter. Mass. Corporal. 16 Sep. 1833. 200 acres.
Butler, Phineas. Me. ———. 19 Aug. 1835. 200 acres. Thomaston.
Butler, Richard. Md. Private. ———. 50 acres.
Butler, Richard. Pa. Colonel. 2 Oct. 1786. 500 acres.
Butler, Richard. Pa. Captain. 2 Oct. 1786. 500 acres.
Butler, Robert. Ga. Minute Man. 1784. 287 1/2 acres.

Butler, Samuel. S.C. ———. 2 Jul. 1792. 200 acres.
Butler, Samuel. Va. Lieutenant. 3 Feb. 1784. 2666 2/3 acres.
Butler, Susannah. Conn. Sufferer. Norwalk. 6.10.0.
Butler, Thomas. Pa. Captain. 25 Sep. 1787. 500 acres.
Butler, Thomas. Va. Pilot. 22 May 1832. 2666 2/3 acres.
Butler, Walter. Conn. Sufferer. Greenwich. 2.0.0.
Butler, William. Ga. ———. 25 Jul. 1784. 287 1/2 acres.
Butler, William. Pa. ———. 18 Feb. 1803. 200 acres.
Butler, William. Pa. Lieutenant Colonel. ———. 500 acres.
Butler, William. Pa. Lieutenant Colonel. 10 Nov. 1786. 500 acres.
Butler, William. Pa. Private. 16 Aug. 1787. 200 acres to Thomas Gallagher, assignee.
Butler, William. Va. Private. 7 Oct. 1784. 100 acres.
Butler, William. Va. Private. 23 Jan. 1788. 100 acres.
Butt, Barruch. Md. Private. ———. 50 acres.
Butt, Edward. Md. Private. ———. 50 acres.
Butt, Simon. Va. Corporal. 1 Mar. 1851. 160 acres.
Butt, Simon. Va. Corporal. 1 Mar. 1851. 40 acres.
Butt, Thomas. Md. Private. ———. 50 acres.
Butt, Zacheriah. Md. Private. ———. 50 acres.
Butt, Zacheriah. Va. Private. 21 Apr. 1784. 100 acres.
Buttery, Thomas. Md. Private. ———. 50 acres.
Buttery, William. Va. Private. 18 Sep. 1797. 100 acres.
Buttery, Zachery. Ga. ———. 28 Jul. 1784. 230 acres.
Buttinstone, Philip. Pa. Dragoon. 6 Mar. 1787. 200 acres.
Button, Harman. Va. Private. 5 Jun. 1783. 100 acres.
Button, Levy. Md. Private. ———. 50 acres.
Butts, Archibald. N.C. Drummer. 6 Jan. 1784. 1000 acres.
Butts, Job. N.C. Corporal. 4 Aug. 1821. 1000 acres.
Butts, Malachi. Ga. ———. 17 May 1784. ———.
Butts, Peter. N.C. Private. 9 Feb. 1796. 640 acres.
Butts, Silas. Conn. Sufferer. Greenwich. 217.4.1.
Butts, Thomas. Pa. Private. ———. 200 acres.
Butts, William. N.C. Private. 30 Apr. 1784. 640 acres to Nancy Butts, heiress.
Butts, William. Va. Private. 29 Jul. 1834. 100 acres.
Butty, Thomas. Va. Sailor. 22 Nov. 1783. 100 acres.
Buxton, Abijah. Md. Private. ———. 50 acres.
Buxton, John. Ga. ———. 24 May 1784. 287 1/2 acres.
Buxton, John. Pa. Private. 9 Dec. 1786. 200 acres.
Buxton, Samuel. Ga. ———. 24 May 1784. 287 1/2 acres.
Buyford, Henry. N. Y. Private. 8 Jul. 1790. 600 acres.
Byan, George. Va. Private. 9 Dec. 1783. 100 acres.
Bybby, Edward. Va. Sailor. 8 Nov. 1784. 100 acres.
Byerly, Frederick. Pa. Private. ———. 200 acres.
Bymer, George. Pa. Private. 6 Dec. 1786. 200 acres.
Bynum, Drewry. N.C. Sergeant. 9 Feb. 1784. 1000 acres.
Byram, William. Ga. ———. 30 Sep. 1784. ———.
Byrd, John. Va. Private. 12 Mar. 1783. 100 acres.
Byrd, Moses. N.C. Musician. 8 Aug. 1821. 1000 acres.
Byrd, Otway. Va. Lieutenant Colonel. 18 Jun. 1784. 6000 acres.
Byrn, Charles. Md. Private. ———. 50 acres.
Byrne, David. Conn. Sufferer. New London. 336.4.7.
Byrnes, James. Pa. Private. 20 Oct. 1786. 200 acres.
Byrnes, John. Va. Private. 8 Dec. 1832. 200 acres.

Byrns, Thomas. Va. Private. 30 Dec. 1784. 100 acres.
Byron, Laurence. N.C. Private. 24 Oct. 1783. 228 acres.
Byrum, Lawrence. N.C. Private. 15 Jan. 1821. 228 acres.
Cabbage, Conrad. Va. Private. 18 Dec. 1818. 100 acres.
Cabbell, Samuel. Va. Lieutenant Colonel. 14 Jun. 1783. 1000 acres.
Cabbell, Samuel. Va. Lieutenant Colonel. 30 Sep. 1782. 6000 acres.
Cabbell, Samuel. Va. Lieutenant Colonel. 20 Oct. 1807. 833 1/3 acres.
Cable, George. Conn. Sufferer. Fairfield. 400.0.0.
Caddenhead, James. Ga. ———. 17 May 1784. ———.
Cade, Drury. Ga. Captain. 15 Mar. 1784. 250 acres.
Cadey, Palmer. N. Y. Lieutenant. 7 Jul. 1790. 1200 acres.
Caesar, Jesse. Mass. Private. 17 Jan. 1833. 200 acres to heirs.
Caffield, Benjamin. N.C. Adjutant. 5 Sep. 1821. 2560 acres.
Cahall, John. N. Y. Matross. 9 Jul. 1790. 500 acres.
Cahill, John. Pa. Private. 20 Sep. 1787. 200 acres.
Cahill, Timothy. Md. Private. ———. 50 acres.
Cahoe, Thomas, Jr. Md. Fifer. ———. 50 acres.
Cahoe, Thomas, Sr. Md. Private. ———. 50 acres.
Cahoon, Jonathan. N.C. Fifer. Nov. 1788. 1000 acres to heirs.
Cahoon, Jonathan. N.C. Private. 3 Aug. 1821. 640 acres to heirs.
Cahoon, Joseph. N.C. Private. 30 Sep. 1785. 640 acres.
Cail, Amos. N.C. Private. 22 Apr. 1809. 640 acres to heirs.
Cail, Rice. N.C. Private. 10 Oct. 1820. 640 acres to heirs.
Cail, William. N.C. Private. 27 Nov. 1789. 640 acres.
Caile, David. Md. Private. ———. 50 acres.
Cain, Abel. N.Y. ———. 13 Sep. 1790. 500 acres to heirs.
Cain, Edward. Md. Private. ———. 50 acres.
Cain, Hugh. Md. Private. ———. 50 acres.
Cain, John. Ga. ———. 15 Mar. 1784. 250 acres.
Cain, Matthias. Va. Private. 18 Apr. 1788. 200 acres.
Cake, Philip. N.C. Private. 23 Apr. 1784. 640 acres.
Calaghan, John. N.Y. ———. 13 Sep. 1790. 500 acres to heirs.
Calderwood, James. Va. Captain. 6 Jun. 1797. 4000 acres.
Caldwater, John. Va. Private. 17 Jul. 1784. 200 acres.
Caldwell, Ann. Conn. Sufferer. Fairfield. 8.8.0.
Caldwell, George. Ga. Refugee. 13 Jul. 1784. ———.
Caldwell, James. Ga. ———. 26 May 1784. 287 1/2 acres.
Caldwell, James. Pa. Private. 9 Oct. 1786. 200 acres.
Caldwell, James. S.C. ———. 5 Mar. 1787. 200 acres.
Caldwell, John. N.C. Private. 28 May 1784. 389 acres.
Caldwell, John. S.C. ———. 3 Sep. 1787. 23 acres.
Caldwell, John. S.C. ———. 3 Sep. 1787. 147 acres.
Caldwell, John. S.C. ———. 3 Sep. 1787. 30 acres.
Caldwell, Lemuel. N.C. Private. 7 Jan. 1786. 640 acres to heirs.
Caldwell, Matthew. N. Y. Private. 8 Jul. 1790. 600 acres.
Caldwell, Philip. N. Y. Private. 8 Jul. 1790. 600 acres.
Caldwell, Thomas. Pa. Private. 6 Apr. 1794. 200 acres.
Caldwell, William. N.C. Private. 7 Jan. 1786. 640 acres to heirs.
Caldwell, William. S.C. Captain. 7 Apr. 1788. 300 acres.
Cale, Abner. N.C. Private. 24 Dec. 1785. 640 acres to heirs.
Calendar, Thomas. N.C. Captain. 14 May 1784. 3840 acres.
Calf, Robert. N.C. Musician. 6 Sep. 1821. 1000 acres.
Calfrey, Charles. Va. Private. 10 Jun. 1783. 100 acres.
Calhoon, William. Pa. Lieutenant. 29 Dec. 1794. 200 acres to Ann Calhoon, devisee.

Calhoun, George. Pa. ———. 11 Apr. 1809. 500 acres to Thomas Grant, executor.

Calhoun, William. Pa. Lieutenant. 29 Dec. 1794. 200 acres to Anne Calhoun, widow.

Calis, John. Ga. ———. 7 Jun. 1785. 287 1/2 acres.

Calk, James, Jr. Ga. Minute Man. 17 May 1784. ———.

Calk, James, Sr. Ga. Minute Man. 17 May 1784. ———.

Calk, William. Ga. ———. 17 May 1784. ———.

Call, John. Mass. Sergeant. 9 Jul. 1834. 200 acres.

Call, Richard. Ga. Citizen. 5 Dec. 1785. 287 1/2 acres.

Call, Richard. Va. Major. 21 Jan. 1784. 5333 1/3 acres.

Call, Richard. Va. Major. 31 Dec. 1800. 888 2/3 acres.

Call, Richard. Va. Major. 17 Jul. 1807. 370 acres.

Callaham, Major. Va. Private. 21 Feb. 1784. 100 acres.

Callahan, Daniel. Pa. Private. 16 Oct. 1786. 200 acres.

Callahan, John. N.C. Private. 18 May 1784. 640 acres.

Callahan, John. Pa. Private. 30 Jul. 1787. 200 acres.

Callahan, John. Pa. Private. 19 Sep. 1787. 200 acres.

Callahan, Michael. Md. Private. ———. 50 acres.

Callahan, Patrick. Pa. ———. 6 Nov. 1786. 200 acres to Stephen Loudon, assignee.

Callahan, Robert. Md. Private. ———. 50 acres.

Callahan, Samuel. Md. Private. ———. 50 acres.

Calleham, Cornelius. N.C. Private. 21 Apr. 1784. 274 acres.

Calleham, Robert. N.C. Private. 21 Apr. 1784. 640 acres to heirs.

Callender, Eleazer. Va. Captain. 25 Jan. 1783. 5000 [5333 1/3] acres.

Callender, Samuel. Va. Private. 28 Feb. 1797. 100 acres.

Callender, William. Mass. Bombardiner. 28 May 1833. 200 acres to assignee Abner Coburn.

Callis, William O. Va. Captain. 24 Jul. 1824. 4000 acres.

Callis, William O. Va. Captain. 14 Aug. 1868. 771 acres.

Calloway, Job. Ga. ———. 17 May 1784. ———.

Calloway, Joseph. Ga. ———. 17 May 1784. ———.

Calloway, Joshua. Ga. ———. 17 May 1784. ———.

Callum, Frederick. N.C. Private. 2 Dec. 1819. 640 acres to heirs.

Cally, John. Ga. Soldier. 3 Oct. 1785. 230 acres.

Calmes, Marquis. Va. Captain. 11 Apr. 1783. 4000 acres.

Calvert, John. Va. Captain. 30 Dec. 1851. 5333 1/3 acres.

Calvert, Jonathan. Va. Surgeon's Mate. 21 May 1832. 2666 2/3 acres.

Calvert, Jonathan. Va. Surgeon's Mate. 2 Feb. 1833. 533 1/3 acres.

Calvert, Jonathan. Va. Surgeon's Mate. 2 Feb. 1833. 400 acres.

Calvert, Jonathan. Va. Surgeon's Mate. 2 Feb. 1833. 400 acres.

Calvert, Joseph. Va. Lieutenant. 3 Mar. 1784. 2666 2/3 acres.

Calvert, Reuben. Va. Private. 14 Jun. 1820. 100 acres.

Calvin, John. N.C. Private. 13 Nov. 1795. 640 acres to heirs.

Calvit, Joseph. Va.-Ind. Lieutenant. 2156 acres. [Calvert].

Calvit, Joseph. Va. Lieutenant. 14 Mar. 1868. 2666 2/3 acres.

Camble, Dennis. Va. Private. 22 Aug. 1783. 233 1/3 acres.

Cambridge, Nanda. Conn. Sufferer. New/East Haven. 14.11.4.

Cambry, James. N. Y. Private. 8 Jul. 1790. 600 acres.

Camburn, John. Va. Private. 25 Apr. 1783. 200 acres.

Cameron, Abel. N.C. Private. 9 Feb. 1796. 84 acres.

Cameron, Alexander. N.C. Private. 10 Dec. 1788. 491 acres.

Cameron, Alexander. N.C. Private. Jan. 1795. 320 acres.

Cameron, Angus. Va.-Ind. Private. 108 acres.

Cameron, Charles. Va. Lieutenant. 28 Feb. 1833. 2666 2/3 acres.

Cameron, Daniel. N.C. Private. 24 Nov. 1796. 640 acres to heir Allen Cameron.

Cameron, Francis. N.C. Private. 6 Dec. 1797. 640 acres to heirs.

Cameron, Hugh. Va. Private. 4 Jun. 1813. 100 acres.

Cameron, John. N.C. Private. 26 Aug. 1785. 640 acres to heirs.

Cameron, Sampson. N.C. Private. 9 Feb. 1796. 640 acres to heirs.

Camfield, Aaron. Va. Captain. 30 Dec. 1851. 5092 2/3 acres.

Cammack, George. Ga. ———. 17 May 1784. ———.

Cammell, Henry. N.C. Private. 7 Jan. 1786. 640 acres to heirs.

Camp, Abraham. Conn. Sufferer. Norwalk. 142.13.3 to his heirs.

Camp, Casper. Pa. Dragoon. 19 Feb. 1789. 200 acres.

Camp, Edmond. Ga. Soldier. 24 Dec. 178-. ———.

Camp, Enos. Conn. Sufferer. Danbury. 3.19.4.

Camp, James. Va. Private. 19 Feb. 1784. 100 acres.

Camp, James. Va. Private. 6 Feb. 1786. 100 acres.

Camp, Joseph. Ga. ———. 17 May 1784. ———.

Camp, Marshall. Va. Private. 8 Jul. 1785. 200 acres.

Camp, Matthias. Pa. Private. 23 Oct. 1786. 200 acres.

Camp, Reuben. Va.-Ind. Private. 108 acres.

Camp, Richard. Conn. Sufferer. Norwalk. 241.19.0.

Camp, Samuel. Ga. Soldier. 3 Oct. 1785. 230 acres.

Camp, Samuel. Conn. Sufferer. Ridgefield. 38.17.10.

Camp, Thomas. Va. Corporal. 20 Mar. 1784. 400 acres.

Camp, William. Ga. Refugee. 6 Sep. 1785. 287 1/2 acres.

Camp, William. Va. ———. 22 Nov. 1783. 2666 2/3 acres.

Campain, James. N.C. Lieutenant. 27 Nov. 1783. 2560 acres.

Campbell, Alexander. Ga. Minute Man. ———. 287 1/2 acres.

Campbell, Andrew. N. Y. Corporal. 8 Jul. 1790. 500 acres.

Campbell, Angus. N.C. Private. 15 Feb. 1797. 274 acres.

Campbell, Archibald. Pa. ———. 24 Feb. 1809. 200 acres to heirs.

Campbell, Archibald. Pa. Lieutenant. 24 Feb. 1809. 200 acres to heirs.

Campbell, Archibald. Va. Private. 19 Jun. 1783. 200 acres.

Campbell, Archibald. Va. Lieutenant. 24 Oct. 1783. 2666 2/3 acres.

Campbell, Burdice. N. Y. Private. 8 Jul. 1790. 500 acres.

Campbell, Daniel. N.C. Private. 22 Apr. 1785. 640 acres.

Campbell, Daniel. Pa. Private. ———. 200 acres.

Campbell, Daniel, Jr. N.C. Private. 18 Jun. 1785. 640 acres to heirs.

Campbell, David. N.C. ———. 29 Dec. 1821. 320 acres.

Campbell, David. Va. Sergeant. 22 Aug. 1785. 200 acres.

Campbell, Dennis. Va. Private. 21 Apr. 1784. 200 acres.

Campbell, Drury. Ga. Lieutenant. 17 May 1784. ———.

Campbell, Duncan. N..Y. Private. 2 Sep. 1790. 600 acres.

Campbell, Duncan. N. Y. Lieutenant. ———. 1000 acres.

Campbell, George. Pa. Matross. 27 Mar. 1786. 200 acres to Patrick Harvey, administrator.

Campbell, George. Va. Sergeant. 9 Apr. 1835. 200 acres.

Campbell, Gilbert. Ga. Minute Man. 17 May 1784. ———.

Campbell, James. Mass. Private. 13 Dec. 1832. 200 acres to heirs.

Campbell, James. N.C. Captain. 6 Dec. 1783. 2057 acres.

Campbell, James. N.C. Private. 29 Sep. 1784. 640 acres to Mary Campbell, heiress.

Campbell, James. N.C. Captain. 20 Dec. 1812. 1783 acres.

Campbell, James. Pa. Lieutenant. 24 Aug. 1787. 200 acres to Thomas Hale, assignee.

Campbell, James. Pa. Private. 24 Aug. 1787. 200 acres.

Campbell, James. S.C. ———. 4 Jan. 1790. 200 acres.

Campbell, James. Va. Private. 3 Feb. 1812. 100 acres.
Campbell, Jeremiah. Pa. Private. 15 Nov. 1786. 200 acres.
Campbell, John. Ga. Soldier. 4 Nov. 1783. 200 acres.
Campbell, John. Va.-Ind. Private. 108 acres.
Campbell, John. Md. Private. ———. 50 acres.
Campbell, John. N. Y. Private. 3 Jul. 1790. 600 acres.
Campbell, John. N. Y. Lieutenant. 7 Jul. 1790. 1000 acres.
Campbell, John. N.C. Private. 21 Oct. 1783. 2560 acres.
Campbell, John. N.C. Private. 16 Aug. 1821. 640 acres.
Campbell, John. Pa. ———. 9 Mar. 1795. 200 acres.
Campbell, John. S.C. Soldier. 21 Jan. 1785. 200 acres.
Campbell, John. Va. Private. 21 Jan. 1786. 100 acres.
Campbell, John. Va. Private. 1 Dec. 1784. 100 acres.
Campbell, Joseph. Va. Private. 3 Feb. 1812. 100 acres.
Campbell, Kenneth. N. Y. Private. 8 Jul. 1790. 600 acres.
Campbell, Laughlin. N.C. Sergeant. 23 Apr. 1784. 1000 acres.
Campbell, Nicholas. Md. Private. ———. 50 acres.
Campbell, Patrick. N.C. Sergeant. 22 Oct. 1783. 428 acres.
Campbell, Peter. Ga. ———. 30 Sep. 1784. ———.
Campbell, Richard. Va. Lieutenant Colonel. 21 Oct. 1784 [1783]. 6000 acres.
Campbell, Richard. Va. Lieutenant Colonel. 6 Apr. 1838. 557 1/3 acres.
Campbell, Richard. Va. Lieutenant Colonel. 6 Apr. 1838. 557 1/3 acres.
Campbell, Richard. Va. Lieutenant Colonel. 4 Jun. 1840. 92 8/9 acres.
Campbell, Richard. Va. Lieutenant Colonel. 4 Jun. 1840. 185 7/9 acres.
Campbell, Richard. Va. Lieutenant Colonel. 1 Aug. 1840. 139 1/3 acres.
Campbell, Richard. Va. Lieutenant Colonel. 20 Feb. 1844. 69 2/3 acres.
Campbell, Richard. Va. Lieutenant Colonel. 11 May 1846. 69 2/3 acres.
Campbell, Richard. Va. Lieutenant Colonel. 19 Feb. 1855. 92 8/9 acres.
Campbell, Robert. Md. Matross. ———. 50 acres.
Campbell, Robert. Md. Private. ———. 50 acres.
Campbell, Robert. Pa. Captain. 14 Oct. 1786. 500 acres to Alexander Fullerton, assignee.
Campbell, Robert. Pa. Private. 10 Feb. 1801. 200 acres to William Duncan, assignee.
Campbell, Robert. Pa. Private. ———. 200 acres.
Campbell, Samuel. Va. Lieutenant. 3 Sep. 1782. 2666 2/3 acres.
Campbell, Solomon. N.C. Private. 30 Apr. 1784. 640 acres to Dempsey Campbell, heir.
Campbell, Solomon. N.C. Private. 13 Sep. 1820. 640 acres.
Campbell, Thomas. N.C. Private. 21 May 1784. 274 acres.
Campbell, Thomas. Pa. Captain. ———. 500 acres.
Campbell, Thomas. Pa. ———. 3 Apr. 1809. 200 acres in trust. [He may not be a veteran]
Campbell, Thomas. Pa. Dragoon. 26 Sep. 1787. 200 acres.
Campbell, Thomas. Pa. Private. 7 May 1817. 200 acres.
Campbell, Thomas. Pa. ———. 7 May 1812. 200 acres.
Campbell, Thomas. S.C. ———. 2 Oct. 1786. 200 acres.
Campbell, Thomas. Va. Private. 27 Sep. 1786. 100 acres.
Campbell, William. Ga. Minute Man. 25 Feb. 1784. 250 acres.
Campbell, William. N.C. Private. 23 Apr. 1784. 640 acres.
Campbell, William. N.C. Private. 4 May 1784. 640 acres.
Campbell, William. N.C. Corporal. 21 Aug. 1820. 1000 acres.
Campbell, William. N.C. Corporal. 12 Sep. 1820. 1000 acres to heirs.
Campbell, William. Pa. Fifer. 16 Oct. 1786. 200 acres.
Campbell, William. Va. Captain. 15 Oct. 1782. 4000 acres.
Campbell, William. Va. General. 23 Dec. 1783. 5000 acres.

Campbell, William. Va. Private. 26 Mar. 1784. 100 acres.
Campbell, William. Va. Brigadier General. 24 Mar. 1834. 13,056 acres.
Campbell, William. Va. Captain. 19 Nov. 1833. 1333 1/3 acres.
Campbell, William. Va. Brigadier General. 5 Dec. 1860. 970 acres.
Campble, Andrew. N.C. Private. 22 Dec. 1796. 640 acres.
Campen, John. N.C. Private. 19 May 1784. 640 acres.
Camper, Moses. Va.-Ind. Private. 108 acres.
Camper, Tilman. Va.-Ind. Private. 108 acres.
Camper, Tilman. Va. Private. 15 Aug. 1834. 200 acres.
Campfield, Timothy. N. Y. Private. 8 Jul. 1790. 600 acres.
Camphen, John. Md. Private. ———. 50 acres.
Campher, Thomas. Md. Private. ———. 50 acres.
Camron, Hugh. Va. Private. 17 May 1784. 100 acres.
Canaday, David. Va. Seaman. 10 Apr. 1835. 100 acres.
Canaday, John. Va. Seaman. 19 Nov. 1833. 100 acres.
Canary, William. Va. Private. 12 Dec. 1783. 100 acres.
Canddy, David. N.C. Private. 8 Dec. 1795. 640 acres to heirs.
Candee, Zacheriah. Conn. Sufferer. New/East Haven. 7.19.2.
Candler, Henry. Ga. ———. 17 Feb. 1784. 250 acres.
Candler, Henry. Ga. ———. 20 Feb. 1784. 250 acres.
Candler, Joseph. N.C. Private. 28 Sep. 1785. 640 acres.
Candler, William, Jr. Ga. ———. 25 Feb. 1784. 250 acres.
Candler, William, Sr. Ga. Colonel. 20 Feb. 1784. 1000 acres.
Candy, John. N.C. Private. 9 Sep. 1820. 640 acres to heirs.
Candy, Samuel. Conn. Sufferer. New/East Haven. 51.4.6.
Cane, William. N.C. Private. 9 Sep. 1785. 640 acres to heirs.
Canfield, Dennis. N. Y. Private. 8 Jul. 1790. 600 acres.
Canfield, James. N. Y. Private. 8 Jul. 1790. 600 acres.
Canley, Asa. Va. Private. 26 Jun. 1783. 200 acres.
Cann, Augustine. Md. Private. ———. 50 acres.
Cann, John. N. Y. Sergeant. 9 Jul. 1790. 600 acres.
Cann, William. Md. Private. ———. 50 acres.
Cannady, James. N.C. Private. 9 Sep. 1785. 640 acres to heirs.
Cannady, Thomas. Md. Private. ———. 50 acres.
Cannafax, Edward. Va. Private. 11 Aug. 1783. 100 acres.
Cannon, Benjamin. N.C. Musician. 21 Aug. 1820. 1000 acres.
Cannon, Edward. N.C. Private. 12 Oct. 1795. 640 acres to heirs.
Cannon, Jesse. Va. Lieutenant. 16 Mar. 1832. 4000 acres.
Cannon, John. Ga. ———. 17 May 1784. ———.
Cannon, John. Md. Private. ———. 50 acres.
Cannon, John. N.Y. ———. 13 Sep. 1790. 500 acres to heirs.
Cannon, John. N.C. Private. 21 Aug. 1820. 640 acres.
Cannon, John. Va. Lieutenant. 17 Jun. 1833. 888 2/3 acres.
Cannon, John. Va. Lieutenant. 17 Jun. 1833. 888 2/3 acres.
Cannon, John. Va. Lieutenant. 17 Jun. 1833. 888 2/3 acres.
Cannon, John. Conn. Sufferer. Norwalk. 1933.8.2 3/4.
Cannon, Lewis. N.C. Lieutenant. 20 Sep. 1784. 1584 acres.
Cannon, Luke. Va. Lieutenant. 30 May 1783. 2666 2/3 acres.
Cannon, Luke. Va. Lieutenant. 8 Feb. 1808. 148 acres.
Cannon, Luke. Va. Midshipman. 15 Mar. 1832. 2666 2/3 acres.
Cannon, Roger. Ga. ———. 17 May 1784. ———.
Cannon, Sampson. N.C. Private. 2 Feb. 1786. 274 acres.
Cannon, Sterling. Pa. Private. ———. 200 acres.
Cannon, Thomas. Ga. Minute Man. ———. 287 1/2 acres.

Cannon, Thomas. N. Y. Sergeant. 8 Jul. 1790. 600 acres.
Cannon, Thomas. N.C. Private. 12 Sep. 1785. 640 acres to heirs.
Canore, Andrew. Va. Private. 17 Jul. 1784. 200 acres.
Cantrell, John. N.C. Private. 8 Dec. 1795. 640 acres.
Cantrell, Simon. N.C. Private. 24 Nov. 1796. 640 acres to heirs.
Canty, Zacheriah. Ga. ———. 17 May 1784. ———.
Capehart, John. N.C. Private. 30 Sep. 1785. 640 acres to heirs.
Caper, Robert. N.C. Sergeant. 10 May 1784. 1000 acres.
Capps, Dempsey. N.C. Private. 24 Dec. 1785. 274 acres.
Capps, James. N.C. Corporal. 9 Sep. 1785. 1000 acres to heirs.
Capps, William. N.C. Private. 3 Mar. 1784. 640 acres
Capps, William. N.C. Private. 21 Nov. 1795. 274 acres.
Capps, William. N.C. Private. 15 Feb. 1797. 274 acres balance. He was of Johnston County.
Capton, John. N.C. Private. 30 Sep. 1785. 640 acres to heirs.
Capts, Obadiah. Va. Private. 15 Apr. 1784. 100 acres.
Car, Solomon. N.C. Private. 29 Sep. 1784. 274 acres.
Carba, Edward. N.C. Sergeant. 24 Nov. 1802. 1000 acres to heirs.
Carberry, Henry. Pa. Captain. 18 Feb. 1803. 500 acres.
Carberry, Peter. Md. Private. ———. 50 acres.
Card, Joseph. N.C. Private. 29 Sep. 1784. 640 acres to heirs.
Carden, Cornelius. Ga. ———. 15 Mar. 1784. 250 acres.
Cardiff, Miles. Va. Private. 23 Jun. 1785. 100 acres.
Cardiff, Thomas. Md. Private. ———. 50 acres.
Cardwell, John. Va. Private. 6 Feb. 1784. 100 acres.
Cardwell, William. Va. Private. 6 Feb. 1786. 100 acres.
Cardwell, William. Va. Sergeant. 21 Dec. 1833. 400 acres.
Cardwell, William. Va. Private. 12 Dec. 1833. 200 acres.
Care, Teunis. N. Y. Matross. 9 Jul. 1790. 600 acres.
Carew, John. Conn. Sufferer. New/East Haven. 8.14.0.
Carey, Andrew H. N.C. Sergeant. 29 Jun. 1815. 1000 acres to heirs.
Carey, Arthur. Pa. Private. 1 Nov. 1786. 200 acres to Adam Kerr, assignee.
Carey, James. N. Y. Drummer. 9 Jul. 1790. 600 acres.
Carey, John. N.C. Private. 17 Feb. 1824. 640 acres.
Carey, Owen. Md. Corporal. ———. 50 acres.
Carl, John. Me. ———. 6 Jul. 1835. 200 acres to widow Lois Carl. Unity.
Carler, Samuel. N.C. Private. 31 Aug. 1795. 640 acres to heirs.
Carleton, John. Pa. Private. 19 Oct. 1786. 200 acres.
Carleton, Patrick. Ga. Minute Man. 17 May 1784. ———.
Carley, Joseph. N. Y. Private. 8 Jul. 1790. 500 acres.
Carlile, Basil. Va. Private. 22 Feb. 1799. 200 acres.
Carlile, Edward. N.C. Private. 22 Dec. 1796. 274 acres.
Carlile, John. Md. Captain. ———. 200 acres.
Carlock, George. N.C. Private. 1 Dec. 1789. 182 acres.
Carlton, John. N.C. Private. 17 Dec. 1785. 640 acres to heirs.
Carlton, Lewis. Va. Private. 14 Jun. 1784. 100 acres.
Carlton, William. Va. Private. 30 Jun. 1783. 100 acres.
Carlyle, Benjamin. Ga. ———. 19 Dec. 1785. 287 1/2 acres.
Carlyle, John. Ga. ———. 15 Mar. 1784. 287 1/2 acres.
Carmack, James. N.C. Private. 30 Sep. 1785. 640 acres.
Carmack, Oliver. N.C. Private. 20 Dec. 1796. 640 acres to heirs.
Carman, Joseph. N. Y. Private. 8 Jul. 1790. 500 acres.
Carman, Willett. N. Y. Private. 8 Jul. 1790. 500 acres.
Carmical, Dugald. N.C. Private. 1 Dec. 1796. 640 acres to heirs.

Carmichael, Robert. N.C. Private. 23 Dec. 1799. 640 acres.

Carmile, Calothile. Md. Private. ———. 50 acres.

Carnady, James. N.C. Private. 17 Sep. 1808. 640 acres to heirs.

Carnaham, Robert. Pa. Captain. ———. 500 acres.

Carnaham, William. Pa. Private. 26 Sep. 1787. 200 acres.

Carnahan, Dennis. N.C. Private. 24 Dec. 1796. 228 acres.

Carnahan, John. Va. Private. 9 Dec. 1783. 100 acres.

Carnal, William. Va. Private. 31 Jul. 1783. 200 acres.

Carnant, Jacob. Md. Private. ———. 50 acres.

Carnart, John. Ga. ———. 15 Mar. 1784. 250 acres.

Carne, John. S.C. Deputy Apothecary. 2 Jun. 1789. 125 acres.

Carne, John. S.C. Deputy Apothecary. 2 Jun. 1789. 175 acres.

Carner, Isum. N.C. Private. 9 Nov. 1784. 640 acres to heir.

Carnes, Daniel. Va. Private. 28 Apr. 1783. 200 acres.

Carnes, Joshua. Va. Private. 16 Mar. 1785. 200 acres.

Carnes, Patrick. Va. Captain. 7 Jan. 1784. 4000 acres.

Carnes, Robert. Md. Private. ———. 50 acres.

Carney, Andrew. N.C. Private. 9 Feb. 1796. 640 acres to heirs.

Carney, Anthony. Va. Sergeant. 7 Oct. 1784. 400 acres.

Carney, George. Md. Private. ———. 50 acres.

Carney, James. Va. Captain. 8 Feb. 1848. 600 acres.

Carney, James. Va. Captain. 8 Feb. 1848. 3400 acres.

Carney, James. Va. Captain. 12 Sep. 1848. 2000 acres.

Carney, James. Va. Captain. 12 Sep. 1848. 1400 acres.

Carney, Martin. Va.-Ind. Lieutenant. 2156 acres.

Carney, Martin. Va. Lieutenant. 14 Jun. 1783. 2666 2/3 acres.

Carney, Matthew. Ga. Private. 28 Sep. 1784. 230 acres.

Carney, Onsby. Ga. Soldier. 14 Sep. 1784. 287 1/2 acres.

Carney, Patrick. N.C. Private. 9 Dec. 1797. 640 acres.

Carney, Patrick. Va. Private. 25 Aug. 1783. 200 acres.

Carney, Richard. Va. Lieutenant. 14 Mar. 1833. 2666 2/3 acres.

Carney, Thomas. Md. Private. ———. 50 acres.

Carnine, Jeremiah. Va. Private. 31 Jan. 1786. 200 acres.

Carnish, Samuel. N.C. Private. 18 Dec. 1797. 274 acres.

Carns, Arthur. Md. Corporal. ———. 50 acres.

Carns, Benjamin. Md. Private. ———. 50 acres.

Carns, Isham. N.C. Private. 5 Sep. 1821. 640 acres.

Carns, William. Pa. Private. 2 Apr. 1787. 200 acres.

Carothers, James. Pa. Private. 18 Dec. 1802. 200 acres to heirs.

Carothers, Robert. Pa. Private. 7 May 1795. 200 acres.

Carothers, Thomas. Pa. Private. 5 Oct. 1786. 200 acres.

Caroway, Jacob. Ga. ———. 17 May 1784. ———.

Carpenter, Benjamin. N.C. Sergeant. 14 Jul. 1820. 428 acres.

Carpenter, Christopher. Va. Private. 23 Jun. 1783. 200 acres.

Carpenter, Duncan. N.C. Private. 6 Dec. 1797. 228 acres.

Carpenter, George. Va. Private. 14 Jun. 1784. 100 acres.

Carpenter, James. N.C. Private. 6 Sep. 1821. 640 acres to heirs.

Carpenter, Job. N.C. Private. 2 Feb. 1786. 640 acres.

Carpenter, John. Va. Sergeant. 27 Jul. 1783. 200 acres.

Carpenter, John. Va. Private. 12 Jun. 1787. 200 acres.

Carpenter, Jonathan. N.C. Lieutenant. 17 Feb. 1824. 1097 acres to heir William Carpenter.

Carpenter, Nehemiah. N. Y. Ensign. 7 Jul. 1790. 1150 acres.

Carpenter, Solomon. N.C. Ensign. 5 Sep. 1820. 2560 acres to heir Benjamin Carpenter.

Carpenter, William. N.C. Private. 17 Dec. 1785. 185 acres.
Carpenter, William Green. N.C. Private. 11 May 1785. 640 acres to heirs.
Carr, Abner. N.C. Sergeant. 2 Feb. 1786. 428 acres.
Carr, Henry. Ga. Lieutenant. 22 Apr. 1784. 600 acres acres.
Carr, Henry. Ga. Refugee. 22 Apr. 1784. 287 1/2 acres.
Carr, Hezekiah. Md. Drummer. ———. 50 acres.
Carr, Isaiah. N.C. Private. 9 Dec. 1797. 640 acres.
Carr, John. Md. Private. ———. 50 acres.
Carr, John, Jr. Va. Private. 24 May 1813. 100 acres.
Carr, John, Sr. Va. Private. 24 May 1813. 100 acres.
Carr, Joseph. Va. Sergeant. 11 Oct. 1784. 400 acres.
Carr, Matthew. Pa. ———. 4 May 1789. 200 acres to Alexander Power, assignee.
Carr, Michael. Md. Private. ———. 50 acres to administrator.
Carr, Patrick. Ga. Major. 25 May. 1784. 1035 acres.
Carr, Samuel. Va. Captain. 6 Dec. 1790. 4666 2/3 acres.
Carr, Samuel. Va. Captain. 19 Jan. 1855. 1704 acres.
Carr, Stephen. Md. Private. ———. 50 acres.
Carr, Thomas. Ga. ———. 5 Apr. 1785. 287 1/2 acres.
Carr, Thomas. Va. Private. 8 Aug. 1811. 66 2/3 acres.
Carr, Thomas. Va. Private. 8 Aug. 1811. 66 2/3 acres.
Carr, Thomas. Va. Private. 8 Aug. 1811. 66 2/3 acres.
Carr, William. N.C. Sergeant. 7 Jan. 1786. 1000 acres to heirs.
Carr, William. Va. Private. 19 Jun. 1783. 100 acres.
Carr, William. Va. Private. 16 Jan. 1784. 200 acres.
Carr, William. Va. Private. 21 Jan. 1787. 100 acres.
Carrell, Benjamin. N.C. Private. 22 Jul. 1814. 640 acres to heirs.
Carrell, Daniel. N.C. Private. 12 Mar. 1785. 228 acres.
Carrell, George. Va. ———. 29 Sep. 1836. 2666 2/3 acres.
Carrell, Harvel. N.C. Private. 12 Mar. 1785. 640 acres to heirs.
Carrell, John. Va. Sergeant. 9 Oct. 1783. 200 acres.
Carrell, John. Va. Lieutenant. 11 Dec. 1810. 500 acres.
Carrell, John. Va. Lieutenant. 11 Dec. 1810. 500 acres.
Carrell, John. Va. Lieutenant. 11 Dec. 1810. 500 acres.
Carrell, John. Va. Lieutenant. 11 Dec. 1810. 500 acres.
Carrell, John. Va. Lieutenant. 11 Dec. 1810. 666 2/3 acres.
Carrell, William. N.C. Private. 23 Apr. 1785. 640 acres to heirs.
Carreway, Thomas. N.C. Private. 25 Jun. 1785. 640 acres.
Carrick, James. Va. Private. 18 Mar. 1784. 100 acres.
Carrick, Patrick. Va. Private. 1 Apr. 1783. 100 acres.
Carrick, Patrick. Va. Private. 25 Jun. 1783. 200 acres.
Carrick, Zacheriah. N.C. Fifer. 22 Dec. 1796. 1000 acres to heirs.
Carrier, John. N.C. Private. 30 Sep. 1785. 640 acres to heirs.
Carrigan, Abel. N.C. Private. 14 Dec. 1796. ——— acres.
Carrigon, John. N.C. Private. 14 Dec. 1796. 274 acres.
Carringer, Martin. Pa. Private. 28 Aug. 1784. 200 acres to William Turnbull, assignee.
Carrington, Clement. Va. Ensign. 12 Jan. 1784. 2666 2/3 acres.
Carrington, Edward. Va. Lieutenant Colonel. 25 Sep. 1783. 7000 acres.
Carrington, Edward. Va. Lieutenant Colonel. 2 Oct. 1807. 833 1/3 acres.
Carrington, George. Va. Lieutenant. 31 Oct. 1783. 2666 2/3 acres.
Carrington, James. N.C. Private. 14 Dec. 1796. 640 acres.
Carrington, John. N.C. Private. 14 Dec. 1796. 640 acres.
Carrington, Mark. N.C. Private. 14 Dec. 1796. 274 acres.
Carrington, Mayo. Va. Captain. 29 Nov. 1782. 4000 acres.

Carrington, Mayo. Va. Captain. 10 May 1783. 666 2/3 acres.
Carrington, Mayo. Va. Captain. 2 Oct. 1807. 555 acres.
Carrington, William. N.C. Private. 9 Feb. 1796. 228 acres.
Carrol, Edward. Va. Sergeant. 17 Apr. 1783. 400 acres.
Carrol, Joseph. Va. Private. 19 Jun. 1783. 100 acres.
Carrol, Joseph. Va. Private. 4 Aug. 1783. 100 acres.
Carroll, Berry. Va. Private. 8 Sep. 1783. 200 acres.
Carroll, Bryan. Md. Private. ———. 50 acres.
Carroll, Douglass. N.C. Fifer. 22 Oct. 1783. 4289 acres.
Carroll, Hardy. N.C. Private. 15 Feb. 1797. 228 acres.
Carroll, John. Md. Private. ———. 50 acres.
Carroll, John. Md. Private. ———. 50 acres.
Carroll, Thomas. Va. Private. 1 May 1783. 200 acres.
Carroll, William. Ga. ———. 17 May 1784. 287 1/2 acres.
Carrom, James. N.C. Private. 30 Sep. 1785. 640 acres to heirs.
Carron, Samuel. N.C. Drummer. 9 Dec. 1797. 1000 acres to heirs.
Carry, John. N.C. Private. 21 Jul. 1821. 640 acres to heirs.
Carry, Samuel. N.C. Private. 2 Feb. 1786. 274 acres.
Carry, William. N.C. Private. 31 Aug. 1795. 640 acres to heirs.
Carsey, Stephen, Jr. Ga. Refugee. 15 Mar. 1784. 250 acres.
Carson, Adam. Ga. Minute Man. 24 May 1784. 287 1/2 acres.
Carson, David. Ga. Refugee. 24 May 1784. 287 1/2 acres.
Carson, James. N. Y. Private. 8 Jul. 1790. 600 acres.
Carson, James. Va. Lieutenant. 16 Nov. 1824. 2666 2/3 acres.
Carson, John. Ga. Minute Man. 25 May 1784. 287 1/2 acres.
Carson, John. Md. Lieutenant. ———. 200 acres.
Carson, John. Md. Sergeant. ———. 50 acres.
Carson, John. N.C. Private. 30 Sep. 1785. 640 acres to heirs.
Carson, John. Va. Lieutenant. 30 Mar. 1837. 533 1/3 acres.
Carson, John. Va. Lieutenant. 30 Mar. 1837. 533 1/3 acres.
Carson, John. Va. Lieutenant. 9 Mar. 1843. 533 1/3 acres.
Carson, John. Va. Lieutenant. 16 Dec. 1844. 533 1/3 acres.
Carson, John. Va. Lieutenant. 9 Mar. 1841. 533 1/3 acres.
Carson, John. Va. Lieutenant. 9 Mar. 1841. 533 1/3 acres.
Carson, John. Va. Lieutenant. 13 Mar. 1854. 533 1/3 acres.
Carson, Joseph. Ga. Minute Man. 24 May 1784. 287 1/2 acres.
Carson, Samuel. Ga. ———. 15 Mar. 1784. 250 acres.
Carson, Samuel. Ga. ———. 28 Feb. 1784. 250 acres.
Carson, Samuel. Pa. Private. 17 Feb. 1796. 200 acres.
Carson, Simon. N.C. Private. 30 Sep. 1785. 640 acres to heirs.
Carson, Thomas. N.C. Private. 14 Dec. 1796. 274 acres.
Carson, Thomas. Pa. ———. ———. 200 acres.
Carson, Thomas, Jr. Ga. Refugee. 26 May 1784. 287 1/2 acres.
Carson, Thomas, Sr. Ga. Minute Man. 24 May 1784. 287 1/2 acres.
Carson, Walter. Conn. Sufferer. Fairfield. 27.0.7.
Carss, John. Va. Private. 15 Jun. 1807. 100 acres.
Carter, Abraham. N.C. Private. 23 Nov. 1790. 640 acres to heirs.
Carter, Armistead. Va. Private. 1783. 100 acres.
Carter, Benjamin. N.C. Captain. 27 Apr. 1784. 3840 acres.
Carter, Benjamin. S.C. ———. 7 Jul. 1787. 133 acres.
Carter, Benjamin. S.C. ———. 7 Jul. 1787. 16 acres.
Carter, Benjamin. S.C. ———. 7 Jul. 1787. 51 acres.
Carter, Charles. Va. Private. 9 Jun. 1783. 100 acres.
Carter, Charles. Va. Private. 16 Feb. 1795. 100 acres.

Carter, Charles. Va. Private. 5 Feb. 1808. 200 acres.
Carter, Dale. Va. Private. 16 Dec. 1784. 100 acres.
Carter, Daniel. Conn. Sufferer. Greenwich. 4.10.0.
Carter, David. Ga. ———. 24 May 1784. 287 1/2 acres.
Carter, David. N.C. Private. 22 Apr. 1785. 640 acres.
Carter, David. N.C. Corporal. 19 Aug. 1820. 360 acres to heirs.
Carter, George. N.C. Private. 7 Jan. 1786. 640 acres to heirs.
Carter, George. S.C. ———. 7 Jan. 1793. 32 acres to James Timms, administrator.
Carter, George. S.C. ———. 7 Jan. 1793. 89 acres to James Timms, administrator.
Carter, George. Va. Private. 17 Nov. 1784. 100 acres.
Carter, Giles. N.C. Private. 14 May 1784. 274 acres.
Carter, Giles. N.C. Private. 28 Aug. 1820. 366 acres to heirs.
Carter, Henry. Ga. Minute Man. 17 May 1784. ———.
Carter, Henry. N.C. Private. 12 Sep. 1785. 640 acres to heirs.
Carter, Henry. Va. Private. 5 Jun. 1783. 100 acres.
Carter, Hepworth. Ga. ———. 21 Jan. 1784. 1000 acres.
Carter, Hubbard. Me. Ensign. 25 Jun. 1838. 200 acres to widow Abigal (Cross) Andrews. Lovell.
Carter, Hubbard. N.C. Private. 28 Aug. 1820. 640 acres.
Carter, Hulsey. Va. Private. 19 Feb. 1818. 100 acres.
Carter, Humphrey. N.C. Private. 21 May 1784. 640 acres to John Carter, heir.
Carter, Isaac. N.C. Private. 28 May 1784. 274 acres.
Carter, Isaac. N.C. Private. 14 Dec. 1796. 640 acres.
Carter, Jacob. N.C. Private. 23 Nov. 1797. 274 acres.
Carter, James. Ga. Captain. 22 Jul. 1784. 287 1/2 acres to heirs.
Carter, James. Ga. ———. 22 Jul. 1784. 287 1/2 acres.
Carter, James. N.C. Private. 28 Aug. 1820. 274 acres.
Carter, James. S.C. ———. 7 Jul. 1788. 200 acres.
Carter, James. Va. Private. 30 Apr. 1783. 200 acres.
Carter, James M. Va. Private. 8 Nov. 1784. 100 acres.
Carter, John. Ga. ———. 25 May 1784. 287 1/2 acres.
Carter, John. Md. Private. ———. 50 acres.
Carter, John. N.C. Private. 19 May 1784. 640 acres.
Carter, John. N.C. Private. 23 Nov. 1790. 228 acres.
Carter, John. N.C. Private. 24 Nov. 1802. 640 acres.
Carter, John. N.C. Private. 27 Nov. 1819. 640 acres to heirs.
Carter, John. Va. Private. 30 May 1783. 100 acres.
Carter, John. Va. Sailor. 29 Aug. 1783. 100 acres.
Carter, John. Va. Sergeant. 9 Jun. 1783. 200 acres.
Carter, John. Va. Sergeant. 6 Apr. 1784. 200 acres.
Carter, John C. Va. Captain. 8 Apr. 1783. 4666 2/3 acres.
Carter, John C. Va. Captain. 20 May 1808. 555 acres.
Carter, John, Jr. N.C. Private. 5 Aug. 1813. 640 acres.
Carter, John, Sr. N.C. Private. 5 Aug. 1813. 640 acres.
Carter, Joseph. N.C. Private. 10 Dec. 1788. 640 acres to heirs.
Carter, Joseph. Va. Private. 13 May 1783. 100 acres.
Carter, Josiah. Ga. ———. 17 May 1784. ———.
Carter, Justinian. Md. Private. ———. 50 acres.
Carter, Luke. Md. Private. ———. 50 acres.
Carter, Moses. N.C. Private. 15 Feb. 1797. 228 acres.
Carter, Nicholas. Va. Private. 23 Jun. 1783. 200 acres.
Carter, Obadiah. Va. Sergeant. 6 Aug. 1784. 200 acres.
Carter, Obediah. Va. Private. 9 Nov. 1818. 100 acres.
Carter, Patrick. Ga. Minute Man. 17 May 1784. ———.

Carter, Philip. N. Y. Private. 8 Jul. 1790. 600 acres.
Carter, Richard. Ga. ———. 17 May 1784. ———.
Carter, Richard. Va. Private. 23 Jun. 1783. 200 acres.
Carter, Robert. N.C. Private. 29 Apr. 1784. 228 acres.
Carter, Robert. Va. Sergeant. 1783. 200 acres.
Carter, Robert. Va. Private. 6 Feb. 1784. 200 acres.
Carter, Samuel. Md. Sergeant. ———. 50 acres.
Carter, Samuel. N.C. Private. 1 Oct. 1792. 228 acres.
Carter, Samuel. Va. Corporal. 28 Feb. 1837. 200 acres.
Carter, Simon. N.C. Private. 9 Feb. 1796. 640 acres.
Carter, Thomas. Va. Surgeon. 6 Aug. 1783. 6000 acres.
Carter, Thomas. Va. Private. 30 Jun. 1784. 100 acres.
Carter, William. Md. Private. ———. 50 acres.
Carter, William. N.C. Private. 24 Nov. 1802. 640 acres to heirs.
Carter, William. Va. Private. 1 Jul. 1783. 100 acres.
Carter, William. Va. Private. 7 May 1784. 100 ares.
Carter, William. Va. Surgeon. 29 Apr. 1807. 1416 2/3 acres.
Carter, William. Conn. Sufferer. Fairfield. 16.0.0.
Carter, William, Sr. Va. Surgeon. 7 Feb. 1784. 6000 acres.
Carthagone, Emanuel. Md. Private. ———. 50 acres.
Cartin, Thomas. N.Y. ———. ———. 500 acres to heirs.
Cartledge, Edmund. Ga. ———. 30 Jul. 1784. 287 1/2 acres.
Cartledge, James. Ga. Minute Man. 28 Feb. 1784. 250 acres.
Cartledge, Samuel. Ga. ———. 17 May 1784. ———.
Carto, William. Md. Private. ———. 50 acres.
Cartrite, Timothy. N.C. Private. 28 Nov. 1795. 640 acres to heirs.
Cartwright, Jesse. Va. Private. 7 Apr. 1784. 100 acres.
Cartwright, Joseph. N.C. Private. 12 May 1784. 640 acres.
Cartwright, Justinian. Va. Sergeant. 18 Nov. 1783. 466 2/3 acres.
Cartwright, Robert. N.C. Private. 12 May 1784. 640 acres.
Cartwright, Thomas. N.C. Private. 12 May 1784. 640 acres.
Carty, John. Pa. ———. 30 Oct. 1787. 200 acres to John McLean.
Caruthers, John. Pa. Lieutenant. ———. 200 acres.
Caruthers, John. Pa. Lieutenant. 11 Nov. 1786. 200 acres.
Carver, Henry. Va. Private. 25 Feb. 1797. 200 acres.
Carver, Lawrence. Va. Private. 28 Apr. 1783. 200 acres.
Carwell, Peter. Md. Sergeant. ———. 50 acres.
Cary, Andrew. N.C. Private. 9 Feb. 1796. 640 acres to heirs.
Cary, James. Va. Private. 9 May 1783. 100 acre.
Cary, James. Va. Sergeant. 12 Jul. 1784. 200 acres.
Cary, John. Md. Lieutenant. ———. 200 acres.
Cary, Luther. Me. Fifer. 1 Jul. 1838. 200 acres. Turner.
Cary, Robert. Ga. Soldier. ———. 4 Feb. 1785. ———.
Cary, Samuel. Va. Lieutenant. 19 Jun. 1783. 2666 2/3 acres.
Casady, James. Va. Sergeant. 2 Feb. 1785. 466 2/3 acres.
Case, John. Va. Private. 15 Jun. 1807. 200 acres.
Case, Joseph. N.C. Private. 5 May 1784. 274 acres.
Case, William. Va. Private. 25 Oct. 1783. 100 acres.
Case, William. Va. Private. 4 Dec. 1783. 200 acres.
Case, William. Va. Private. 15 Jun. 1807. 200 acres.
Casell, William. Va. Private. 20 Jun. 1783. 100 acres.
Casety, James. N. Y. ———. ———. 333 1/3 acres.
Casey, Archibald. Va. Private. 3 Jun. 1783. 200 acres.
Casey, Benjamin. Va. Captain. 3 Jun. 1783. 4000 acres.

Casey, James. Md. Private. ———. 50 acres.
Casey, James. N. Y. Matross. 9 Jul. 1790. 600 acres.
Casey, James. Va. Private. 12 Feb. 1785. 100 acres.
Casey, John. N. Y. Corporal. 13 Sep. 1790. 500 acres.
Casey, John. Va. Private. 18 Sep. 1784. 200 acres.
Casey, Morris. Pa. Private. 12 Oct. 1786. 200 acres.
Casey, Peter. Md. Private. ———. 50 acres.
Casey, Robert. N. Y. Sergeant. 8 Jul. 1790. 600 acres.
Casey, Robert. Va. Private. 21 Jun. 1783. 100 acres.
Casey, William. Md. Private. ———. 50 acres.
Casey, William. Va. Private. 22 Jan. 1834. 100 acres.
Cash, John. Me. ———. 21 Sep. 1835. 200 acres. Raymond.
Cash, John. N.C. Private. 22 Apr. 1785. 640 acres.
Cash, Warren. Va. Private. 21 Feb. 1783. 100 acres.
Casner, Michael. Md. Private. ———. 50 acres.
Cason, Cannon. N.C. Private. 3 Aug. 1820. 640 acres to heirs.
Cason, Hillery. N.C. Corporal. 3 Aug. 1820. 1000 acres to heirs.
Cason, James. Va. Private. 30 Sep. 1783. 100 acres.
Cason, John. Va. Sergeant. 30 Sep. 1783. 200 acres.
Cason, William. N.C. Private. 20 Apr. 1784. 640 acres.
Cason, William. Va. Private. 30 Sep. 1783. 100 acres.
Cass, Oliver. N.C. Private. 24 Dec. 1796. 228 acres.
Cassaday, Barney. Md. Private. ———. 50 acres.
Cassady, Peter. N. Y. Private. 6 Jul. 1790. 600 acres.
Cassady, William. Pa. Matross. 19 Apr. 1787. 200 acres.
Cassedy, Edward. N. Y. Private. 8 Jul. 1790. 600 acres.
Cassels, John. Ga. ———. 15 Mar. 1784. 250 acres.
Cassidy, Michael. Va. Private. 9 Dec. 1783. 100 acres.
Castander, Metrue. N.C. Private. 30 Sep. 1785. 640 acres to heirs.
Casteel, Samuel. Pa. ———. 17 Mar. 1803. 200 acres.
Casteele, William. N.C. Private. 24 Dec. 1785. 640 acres to heirs.
Castello, James. S.C. ———. 4 May 1789. 200 acres.
Castelman, Christian. N. Y. Private. 8 Jul. 1790. 600 acres.
Caster, Josiah. Ga. ———. 17 May 1784. ———.
Castillo, Edward. Ga. Minute Man. 17 May 1784. ———.
Castillo, Michael. Ga. Minute Man. 17 May 1784. ———.
Castle, Richard. N.C. Private. 31 Dec. 1824. 458 acres to heirs.
Castleberry, Henry. Ga. ———. 17 Jun. 1784. 287 1/2 acres.
Castleberry, Jacob. Ga. ———. 17 May 1784. ———.
Castleberry, John, Sr. Ga. ———. 26 May 1784. 287 1/2 acres.
Castleberry, Peter. Ga. ———. ———. 287 1/2 acres.
Castleberry, Richard. Ga. ———. 17 May 1784. ———.
Castles, Thomas. N.C. Private. 18 Jun. 1785. 274 acres.
Castles, Thomas. N.C. Private. 23 Nov. 1797. 274 acres.
Castor, Philip. Pa. Private. 4 May 1795. 200 acres to Alexander Power, assignee.
Caswell, Alexander. Ga. ———. 17 May 1784. ———.
Caswell, Michael. Va. Private. 22 Oct. 1787. 100 acres.
Caswell, Thomas. N.C. Captain. 22 Oct. 1783. 1280 acres.
Caswell, Thomas. N.C. Corporal. 3 Aug. 1820. 428 acres to heirs.
Casy, John. Va. Private. 8 Nov. 1784. 200 acres.
Catchings, Benjamin. Ga. Citizen. 24 Feb. 1784. 297 1/2 acres.
Catchings, Joseph. Ga. ———. 24 Feb. 1784. 250 acres.
Catchings, Meredith. Ga. Soldier. 22 May 1784. 287 1/2 acres.
Catchings, Seymore. Ga. ———. 24 Feb. 1784. 250 acres.

Catchsides, Abram. Md. Private. ———. 50 acres.
Caterat, Stephen. Ga. Minute Man. 17 May 1784. ———.
Cates, Aaron. Ga. ———. 17 May 1784. ———.
Cates, Matthias. N.C. Private. 22 Dec. 1796. 640 acres.
Cates, Zacheriah. N.C. Private. 9 Nov. 1784. 640 acres.
Catlett, George. Va. Lieutenant. 20 Jan. 1834. 2666 2/3 acres.
Catlett, George. Va. Lieutenant. 25 Apr. 1838. 1333 1/3 acres.
Catlett, George. Va. Lieutenant. 29 Jun. 1839. 666 2/3 acres.
Catlett, George. Va. Lieutenant. 25 Jan. 1853. 666 2/3 acres.
Catlett, George. Va. Lieutenant. 29 Jun. 1839. 666 2/3 acres.
Catlett, Thomas. Va. Captain. 17 Jun. 1783. 4000 acres.
Catlett, Thomas. Va. Captain. 11 May 1838. 699 acres.
Catlett, Thomas. Va. Captain. 15 Jul. 1854. 583 acres.
Catlin, John. Conn. Sufferer. New/East Haven. 8.7.0.
Catlin, Nathan. Conn. Sufferer. New/East Haven. 8.16.6.
Cato, Sterling. Ga. ———. 17 May 1784. ———.
Cato, William. Ga. Refugee. 1 Jul. 1784. ———.
Cato, William. Md. Private. ———. 50 acres.
Caton, James. N.C. Private. 29 Sep. 1784. 640 acres to heir.
Cator, John. N.C. Private. 28 Sep. 1785. 640 acres to heirs.
Cator, William. N. Y. Private. 8 Jul. 1790. 600 acres.
Catton, Thomas. N.C. Private. 17 Dec. 1785. 640 acres to heirs.
Causey, James. Va. Seaman. 2 Sep. 1783. 100 acres.
Cave, James. Va. Private. 6 Dec. 1783. 100 acres.
Cavenaugh, John. Pa. Corporal. 6 Jul. 1787. 200 acres.
Cavenaugh, Patrick. Md. Private. ———. 50 acres.
Cavender, James. Va. Private. 2 May 1783. 200 acres.
Cavender, Joseph. Va. Sergeant. 18 Aug. 1783. 400 acres.
Cavender, Moses. N. Y. Private. 8 Jul. 1790. 600 acres.
Cavenear, Garret. Va. Private. 23 Jun. 1783. 200 acres.
Cavenough, Barnabas. Pa. Private. 22 May 1787. 200 acres.
Caves, John. Md. Private. ———. 50 acres.
Cavuner, Timothy. N.C. Private. 30 Sep. 1785. 640 acres.
Cawley, Caleb. Ga. Minute Man. 22 Mar. 1785. 250 acres.
Cawley, Catlett. Ga. Minute Man. 2 Mar. 1784. ———.
Cawley, John. Ga. ———. 5 May 1785. ———.
Cawley, Richard. Ga. Minute Man. 22 Mar. 1785. 250 acres.
Cawthon, Christopher. Va. Sergeant. 8 May 1783. 200 acres.
Cawthon, William. Va. Private. 12 Jul. 1784 [1783]. 100 acres.
Cawthorn, Joseph. Ga. ———. ———. 287 1/2 acres to heirs.
Cayeaux, Joseph. N. Y. ———. ———. 500 acres.
Cayeaux, Peter. N. Y. ———. ———. 500 acres.
Cayner, Matthew. Va. Private. 2 Sep. 1783. 100 acres.
Cazeau, Francis. N. Y. ———. ———. 333 1/3 acres.
Cecil, Barton. Md. Private. ———. 50 acres.
Cecile, Joseph. Va. Private. 31 Dec. 1851. 100 acres.
Cecile, Joseph. Va. Private. 2 Apr. 1856. 100 acres.
Cee, Hack. N.C. Private. 15 Jul. 1785. 640 acres to heir.
Cersey, Henry. N.C. Private. 27 Nov. 1789. 182 acres.
Cersey, Jacob. N.C. Private. 27 Nov. 1789. 182 acres.
Chadbourn, Silas. Me. Lieutenant. 8 May 1838. 600 acres to widow Lucy Edwards. Gorham.
Chadwick, Benjamin. N.C. Private. 21 Apr. 1784. 640 acres.
Chaffery, Nimrod. N.C. Private. 24 Dec. 1796. 228 acres.

Chaffin, Comfort. Mass. Private. 28 May 1833. 200 acres.
Chaffin, Isham. Va. Private. 20 Feb. 1845. 100 acres.
Chaffin, John. Va. Private. 1 Aug. 1783. 200 acres.
Chafin, Solomon. Va. Private. 30 Jun. 1784. 100 acres.
Chalk, William. N.C. Private. 2 Nov. 1795. 640 acres.
Chalk, William. N.C. Sergeant. 2 Dec. 1818. 452 acres to heirs.
Chalmers, John. Ga. ———. 15 Mar. 1784. 250 acres.
Chals, Joseph. Conn. Sufferer. New London. 75.11.6.
Chamberlain, Charles. N.C. Private. 8 Jun. 1792. 640 acres.
Chamberlain, Silas. Me. ———. 25 May 1835. 200 acres to widow Susanna Chamberlain. Minot.
Chamberlane, George. Va. Lieutenant. 5 Jun. 1783. 4000 acres.
Chamberlayne, Byrd. Va. Lieutenant. 28 Feb. 1831. 4000 acres.
Chamberlayne, Edward P. Va. Lieutenant. 29 Mar. 1834. 4000 acres.
Chamberlayne, Edward P. Va. Lieutenant. 28 Jun. 1835. 800 acres.
Chamberlayne, Edward P. Va. Lieutenant. 28 Jun. 1835. 800 acres.
Chamberlayne, Edward P. Va. Lieutenant. 13 Jul. 1835. 800 acres.
Chamberlayne, Edward P. Va. Lieutenant. 20 Aug. 1835. 800 acres.
Chamberlayne, Edward P. Va. Lieutenant. 24 Nov. 1835. 800 acres.
Chamberlayne, Philip. Va. Lieutenant. 8 Mar. 1831. 4000 acres.
Chamberlin, Henry. N.C. Private. 30 Sep. 1785. 640 acres to heirs.
Chambers, Alexander. Va. Private. 17 Jun. 1783. 100 acres.
Chambers, Andrew. Pa. Private. 24 Jul. 1789. 200 acres.
Chambers, David. Va. Private. 24 Jun. 1783. 100 acres.
Chambers, Edward. Md. Private. ———. 50 acres.
Chambers, Hancock. Va. Seaman. 24 Mar. 1831. 100 acres.
Chambers, James. Md. Private. ———. 50 acres.
Chambers, James. N.C. Private. 5 Sep. 1821. 640 acres.
Chambers, James. Pa. Private. 8 Jan. 1803. 200 acres.
Chambers, James. Pa. Colonel. 17 Aug. 1787. 500 acres.
Chambers, James. Pa. Colonel. 17 Aug. 1787. 500 acres to Matthew McConnell, assignee.
Chambers, James. Va. Private. 1 Jun. 1785. 100 acres.
Chambers, James. Va. Private. 12 Apr. 1786. 200 acres.
Chambers, James. Va. Private. 10 Oct. 1821. 100 acres.
Chambers, John. Ga. ———. 15 Mar. 1784. 287 1/2 acres.
Chambers, John. Pa. Private. 26 Oct. 1786. 200 acres to Matthew McConnell, assignee.
Chambers, John. Pa. ———. 16 May 1809. 200 acres to heirs William Berkley et al.
Chambers, Joseph. Conn. Sufferer. Greenwich. 9.0.0.
Chambers, Leonard. N. Y. Private. 7 Jul. 1790. 500 acres.
Chambers, Robert. Va. Sergeant. 24 Jun. 1784. 200 acres.
Chambers, Thomas. Pa. Ensign. 15 Dec. 1786. 300 acres.
Chambers, William. Pa. Private. 25 Nov. 1786. 200 acres to Stephen Loudon, assignee.
Chambless, Christopher. Ga. Refugee. 20 Feb. 1784. 250 acres.
Chambless, Joel. N.C. Private. 7 Dec. 1797. 228 acres.
Chambless, Littleton. Ga. Soldier. 20 Feb. 1784. 250 acres.
Chambless, Peter. S.C. ———. 2 May 1785. 200 acres.
Champ, William. Va. Private. 4 Mar. 1815. 100 acres.
Champe, John. Va. Sergeant Major. 9 Nov. 1832. 400 acres.
Champion, Thomas. N.C. Private. 4 Sep. 1820. 228 acres to heirs.
Champlin, Isaac. Conn. Sufferer. New London. 142.3.2.
Champlin, John. Conn. Sufferer. New London. 104.8.5.
Champlin, Joseph. Conn. Sufferer. New London. 72.11.9.

Champlin, Lodwick. Conn. Sufferer. New London. 11.9.10.

Champney, Nathan. Mass. Quartermaster Sergeant. 1 Feb. 1833. 200 acres to heirs.

Chance, Jacob. Va. Private. 27 Dec. 1832. 100 acres.

Chance, Philemon. N.C. Private. 28 Jul. 1784. 274 acres.

Chance, Shadrack. Va. Seaman. 8 Jun. 1833. 100 acres.

Chance, Shadrack. Va. Quartermaster. 10 Apr. 1833. 2566 2/3 acres.

Chance, Stephen. N.C. Private. 17 Mar. 1784. 365 acres.

Chandler, Abedego. Ga. Minute Man. 17 May 1784. ———.

Chandler, Jesse. Va. Private. 3 Jan. 1786. 200 acres.

Chandler, John. Ga. ———. 17 May 1784. 287 1/2 acres.

Chandler, John. Conn. Sufferer. New/East Haven. 108.5.0.

Chandler, Mordecai. Ga. Minute Man. 17 May 1784. ———.

Chandler, Moses. Me. ———. 7 Aug. 1838. 200 acres to widow Mary Chandler.

Chandler, Moses. Mass. Private. 22 Nov. 1831. 200 acres to heirs.

Chandler, Thomas. Va. Lieutenant. 28 Feb. 1785. 1466 2/3 acres.

Chandler, Thomas. Va. Lieutenant. 28 Feb. 1785. 1200 acres.

Chandler, Thomas. Va. Captain. 19 Apr. 1831. 1333 1/3 acres.

Chandler, Thomas. Va. Private. 13 Nov. 1810. 100 acres.

Chandonet, Francis. N. Y. Lieutenant. ———. 1000 acres.

Chaney, Emanuel. Ga. Refugee. 25 May 1784. 575 acres.

Chaney, Greenberry. Ga. Refugee. 25 May 1784. 287 1/2 acres.

Chapellon, Peter. N. Y. ———. ———. 500 acres.

Chapin, Benjamin. Va. Surgeon. 21 Jan. 1792. 6000 acres.

Chapin, Benjamin. Va. Surgeon. 22 Aug. 1785. 1580 acres.

Chapin, Isaac. Mass. Private. 9 Jul. 1834. 200 acres.

Chapin, John. Va. Private. 30 Jun. 1783. 100 acres.

Chapin, Leonard. N. Y. Matross. 9 Jul. 1790. 600 acres.

Chapin, Paul. Mass. ———. 22 Jul. 1833. 200 acres.

Chaplain, Abraham. Va. Captain. 20 Dec. 1793. 1333 1/3 acres.

Chaplain, Joseph. Ga. ———. 17 May 1784. ———.

Chaplin, Abraham. Va. Lieutenant. 3 Mar. 1784. 2666 2/3 acres.

Chaplin, Hugh. Md. Matross. ———. 50 acres.

Chapline, Abraham. Va.-Ind. Lieutenant. Mar. 1784. 2156 acres.

Chapman, Abigail. Conn. Sufferer. Fairfield. 2.11.0.

Chapman, Benjamin. Ga. Refugee. 6 Aug. 1785. ———.

Chapman, Deborah. Ga. ———. 17 May 1784. ———.

Chapman, George. Pa. Sergeant. 9 Mar. 1795. 250 acres to John Nicholson, assignee.

Chapman, Hart. Ga. ———. 17 May 1784. ———.

Chapman, Henry. Md. Lieutenant. ———. 200 acres.

Chapman, Jeremiah. Conn. Sufferer. Greenwich. 3.12.11.

Chapman, John. Ga. Sergeant. 17 May 1784. ———.

Chapman, John. Va. Captain. 11 Jun. 1783. 4000 acres.

Chapman, John. Va. Captain. 11 Jul. 1783. 4000 acres.

Chapman, John. Va. Sergeant. 19 Nov. 1783. 200 acres.

Chapman, Nathaniel. Me. ———. 13 Jun. 1835. 200 acres to widow Sally Chapman. Starks.

Chapman, Nathaniel. Va. Private. 11 Oct. 1826. 100 acres.

Chapman, Reuben. Va. Captain. 12 Dec. 1832. 4000 acres.

Chapman, Reuben. Va. ———. 13 Sep. 1833. 444 4/9 acres.

Chapman, Reuben. Va. ———. 13 Sep. 1833. 2222 2/9 acres.

Chapman, Reuben. Va. ———. 13 Sep. 1833. 888 8/9 acres.

Chapman, Reuben. Va. ———. 8 May 1834. 444 4/9 acres.

Chapman, Richard. Conn. Sufferer. New London. 73.1.6 1/2.

Chapman, Robert. S.C. Soldier. 5 Nov. 1787. 200 acres.
Chapman, Samuel. N.C. Captain. 18 May 1784. 3291 acres.
Chapman, Thomas. Md. Private. ———. 50 acres.
Chapman, Thomas. Va. Private. 20 Jun. 1783. 100 acres.
Chapman, Thompson. N.C. Private. 7 Jan. 1786. 640 acres to heirs.
Chapman, William. Va.-Ind. Private. 108 acres.
Chapman, William. Md. Private. ———. 50 acres.
Chapman, William. S.C. ———. 1 Oct. 1787. 200 acres.
Chapman, William. Va. Private. 17 Oct. 1825. 200 acres.
Chapman, William, Jr. Ga. Refugee. 15 Mar. 1784. 250 acres.
Chapman, William, Sr. Ga. Refugee. 10 Dec. 1784. 250 acres.
Chappel, Benjamin. N. Y. Private. ———. 600 acres.
Chappel, Benjamin, Jr. N. Y. Private. 8 Jul. 1790. 500 acres.
Chappell, Benjamin. Va. Private. 11 Dec. 1811. 100 acres.
Chappell, Edward. N.C. Private. 30 Sep. 1785. 640 acres to heirs.
Chappell, John. Ga. ———. 17 May 1784. ———.
Chappell, Samuel. N.C. Private. 21 May 1784. 274 acres.
Chappell, Samuel. N.C. Private. 7 Jan. 1786. 640 acres.
Chapple, Samuel. Md. Private. ———. 50 acres.
Chappoik, Simon. Md. Private. ———. 50 acres.
Chard, James. Md. Private. ———. 50 acres.
Charity, Charles. Va. Private. 22 Aug. 1783. 200 acres.
Charles, Christian. N. Y. Private. 8 Jul. 1790. 600 acres.
Charles, James. Pa. Private. 11 Sep. 1787. 200 acres to Abram Smith, assignee.
Charles, Samuel. Va. Sergeant. 31 Oct. 1783. 200 acres.
Charles, Thomas. N.C. Private. 11 Feb. 1796. 640 acres to heirs.
Charles, William. Va. Private. 31 May 1783. 100 acres.
Charlescraft, James. N.C. Private. 8 Mar. 1785. 228 acres.
Charlesworth, M. John. N. Y. Sergeant. 8 Jul. 1790. 600 acres.
Charleton, George. N.C. Private. 17 Feb. 1824. 640 acres.
Charlong, Peter. N. Y. ———. ———. 500 acres.
Charlton, George. Va. Private. 9 Dec. 1802. 200 acres.
Charlton, William. N.C. Private. 13 Dec. 1783. 274 acres.
Charlton, William. N.C. Private. 29 Sep. 1785. 640 acres.
Charlton, William. N.C. Lieutenant. 3 Feb. 1795. 2560 acres to heirs.
Charney, David. N.C. Private. 26 Sep. 1821. 185 acres.
Charter, Anthony. N.C. Private. 23 Apr. 1785. 640 acres to heirs.
Charter, John. Ga. ———. 17 May 1784. ———.
Chartier, Anthony. N. Y. ———. ———. 500 acres.
Chartier, John. N. Y. ———. ———. 500 acres.
Chartier, Joseph. N. Y. ———. ———. 500 acres.
Chartier, Joseph, Jr. N. Y. ———. ———. 500 acres.
Chartier, Peter. N. Y. ———. ———. 500 acres.
Chartier, Theodore. N. Y. ———. ———. 500 acres.
Chase, David. Mass. Private. 20 Feb. 1833. 200 acres to heirs.
Chase, Ezekiel. Me. ———. 6 Jul. 1835. 200 acres. Sebec.
Chase, Jeremiah. Mass. ———. 20 Mar. 1832. 200 acres to heirs.
Chase, John. N. Y. ———. 8 Oct. 1792. 600 acres.
Chase, Reuben. Mass. Private. 3 Mar. 1831. 200 acres.
Chase, Robert. N. Y. Private. 8 Jul. 1790. 600 acres.
Chaseley, Peter. N.Y. ———. 13 Sep. 1790. 500 acres to heirs.
Chasy, Stephen. N.Y. ———. 13 Sep. 1790. 500 acres to heirs.
Chatfield, David. N.Y. ———. 13 Sep. 1790. 500 acres to heirs.
Chatfield, Samuel. N.Y. ———. 13 Sep. 1790. 500 acres to heirs.

Chatham, John. Va. Private. 4 Sep. 1783. 200 acres.
Chatland, William. Md. Private. ———. 50 acres.
Chatterton, Samuel. Conn. Sufferer. New/ East Haven. 33.13.8.
Chauncey, Charles. Conn. Sufferer. New/ East Haven. 47.15.8.
Chavers, James. Va. Private. 8 Dec. 1784. 100 acres.
Chavers, John. S.C. ———. 21 Jan. 1785. 200 acres.
Chavers, John. Va. Private. 22 Mar. 1783. 100 acres.
Chavers, Robert W. Va. Private. 4 Nov. 1784. 100 acres.
Chaves, John. Va. Private. 16 Feb. 1819. 200 acres.
Chaves, Samuel. Va. Private. 16 Sep. 1785. 100 acres.
Chavious, James. Va. Private. 18 Feb. 1784. 100 acres.
Chavis, William. N.C. Private. 6 Dec. 1797. 640 acres to heirs.
Chavous, Drury. N.C. Private. 6 Sep. 1821. 640 acres.
Cheason, Joshua. N.C. Private. 22 Mar. 1785. 274 acres.
Cheek, James. N.C. Sergeant. 9 Dec. 1797. 1000 acres.
Cheek, John. N.C. Private. 9 Dec. 1797. 640 acres to heirs.
Cheek, William. N.C. Private. 10 Dec. 1788. 640 acres to heirs.
Cheesborough, John. N.C. Paymaster. 5 Sep. 1821. 2560 acres.
Cheeseman, Thomas. Va. Surgeon. 8 May 1838. 4500 acres.
Cheeseman, Thomas. Va. Surgeon. 8 May 1838. 1500 acres.
Chenault, John. Va. Private. 12 Mar. 1785. 100 acres.
Chenowith, Richard. Va.-Ind. Private. 108 acres.
Chermmy, Robert. N.C. Private. 20 Feb. 1784. 640 acres.
Cherrix, Arthur. Va. Private. 15 Jun. 1807. 200 acres.
Cherry, Alexander. N.C. Private. 17 Dec. 1785. 640 acres to heirs.
Cherry, Clemigal. N.C. Private. 29 Oct. 1821. 640 acres to heirs.
Cherry, Daniel. N.C. Private. 2 Jan. 1810. 640 acres to heirs.
Cherry, Job. N.C. Private. 12 Sep. 1785. 640 acres to heirs.
Cherry, John. N. Y. Fifer. 6 Jul. 1790. 600 acres.
Cherry, John. N.C. Private. 2 Aug. 1784. 640 acres to Jesse Cherry, heir.
Cherry, Jonathan. N.C. Private. 30 Sep. 1785. 640 acres to heirs.
Cherry, William. Va. Captain. 26 Nov. 1783. 1000 acres.
Cherry, William. Va. Captain. 26 Nov. 1783. 3000 acres.
Cherry, William. Va. Captain. 17 Mar. 1832. 520 acres.
Cherry, William. Va. Captain. 17 Mar. 1832. 480 acres.
Cherry, William. Va. ———. 28 Dec. 1833. 333 1/3 acres.
Cherry, William. Va. ———. 28 Dec. 1833. 666 2/3 acres.
Cheseldon, Edward. Pa. Private. 8 Sep. 1789. 200 acres.
Cheser, Bennet. Md. Private. ———. 50 acres.
Cheserounds, John. Va. Private. 6 Mar. 1784. 100 acres.
Cheshire, Hardy. N.C. Drum Major. 1 Aug. 1821. 1000 acres.
Cheshire, John. Md. Sergeant. ———. 50 acres.
Cheshire, John. Va. Private. 15 Jan. 1808. 261 acres.
Cheshire, John. Va. Lieutenant. 3 May 1838. 2000 acres.
Cheshire, John. Va. Lieutenant. 3 May 1838. 1000 acres.
Cheshire, John. Va. Lieutenant. 3 May 1838. 1000 acres.
Cheshire, John. Va. Lieutenant. 28 Jun. 1848. 1000 acres.
Cheshire, John. Va. Lieutenant. 28 Jun. 1848. 1000 acres.
Chesire, Henry. N.C. ———. 16 Dec. 1807. 428 acres to heirs.
Chesney, Benjamin. Va. Private. 16 Dec. 1812. 200 acres.
Chesney, Thomas. Pa. ———. 4 May 1795. 200 acres to Alexander Power, assignee.
Chesnut, William or Benjamin. Md. Private. ———. 50 acres.
Chesser, John. Ga. Minute Man. 22 Mar. 1785. 250 acres.

Chester, Benjamin. Conn. Sufferer. Groton. 442.3.0.
Chester, Benjamin, as executor. Conn. Sufferer. Groton. 300.15.0.
Chester, Charles. Conn. Sufferer. Groton. 6.19.0.
Chester, Daniel. Conn. Sufferer. Groton. 9.15.6.
Chester, David. N.C. Sergeant. 19 Nov. 1802. 1000 acres.
Chester, Eldridge. Conn. Sufferer. Groton. 6.11.0.
Chester, Jason. Conn. Sufferer. Groton. 20.18.0.
Chester, Jedediah. Conn. Sufferer. Groton. 21.13.2.
Chester, John. N.C. Private. 20 Jan. 1785. 640 acres to heir.
Chester, Samuel. Conn. Sufferer. Groton. 10.6.6.
Chester, Simeon. Conn. Sufferer. Groton. 8.15.0.
Chester, Thomas. Conn. Sufferer. Groton. 0.15.5.
Chestnut, Joseph. N.C. Private. 30 Sep. 1785. 640 acres to heirs.
Chestnut, Robert. Pa. Private. ———. 200 acres.
Chetier, Pierre. Va. Private. 31 Dec. 1851. 100 acres.
Chetier, Pierre. Va. Private. 2 Apr. 1856. 100 acres.
Chevalier, Anthony. Va. Private. 30 Aug. 1783. 100 acres.
Chevalier, Charles Francis. Ga. 17 May 1784. ———.
Chevalier, John. N. Y. Private. 8 Jul. 1790. 600 acres.
Chevalier, Joseph. N. Y. ———. ———. 500 acres.
Chevallier, Francis. Va. Private. 31 Dec. 1851. 100 acres.
Chevallier, Francis. Va. Private. 2 Apr. 1856. 100 acres.
Chevaus, Jeremiah. Ga. Refugee. 15 Mar. 1784. 250 acres.
Chever, John. Md. Lieutenant. ———. 200 acres.
Chevis, William. Va. Gunner. 8 May 1868. 2666 2/3 acres.
Chevis, William. Va. Gunner. 3 Sep. 1868. 2666 2/3 acres.
Chew, Robert B. Va. Lieutenant. 19 Mar. 1838. 2666 2/3 acres.
Chewning, Christopher. Va. Private. 21 Jun. 1786. 100 acres.
Chewnings, Thomas. Va. Private. 3 Feb. 1784. 100 acres.
Chilaer, Christopher. N. Y. Private. 2 Sep. 1790. 600 acres.
Chilcott, Thomas. Pa. Sergeant. 12 Jan. 1787. 250 acres.
Child, Francis. N.C. Captain. 20 Oct. 1783. 3840 acres.
Child, Jonas. Me. Private. 18 Aug. 1835. 200 acres to widow Anna Child. Hallowell.
Child, Smith. N.C Private. 14 Feb. 1796. 365 acres.
Childers, David. Ga. Soldier. 23 Mar. 1784. 200 acres.
Childers, John. Ga. ———. 5 Apr. 1784. 287 1/2 acres.
Childers, John. N.C. Private. 8 Dec. 1795. 640 acres.
Childers, Robert. N.C. Private. 7 Jan. 1786. 640 acres to heirs.
Childers, Thomas. Ga. Soldier. 23 Mar. 1784. 200 acres.
Childress, Alexander. Va. Private. 20 Jan. 1785. 100 acres.
Childress, Henry. Va. Private. 22 Dec. 1783. 100 acres.
Childress, Meredith. Va. Private. 23 Mar. 1784. 100 acres.
Childress, Meredith. Va. Private. 22 Jan. 1788. 100 acres.
Childress, Mosby. Va. Private. 8 Sep. 1783. 100 acres.
Childrey, Thomas. Ga. ———. 28 Feb. 1784. 250 acres.
Childrey, William. Ga. ———. 1784. 287 1/2 acres.
Childs, George. Md. Corporal. ———. 50 acres.
Childs, James. Ga. ———. 17 May 1784. ———.
Childs, John. Ga. ———. 17 May 1784. ———.
Childs, Jonas. Me. ———. 18 Aug. 1835. 200 acres to widow Anna Childs. Hallowell.
Chilton, Andrew. Va. Private. 29 May 1819. 100 acres.
Chilton, John. Va. Captain. 9 Nov. 1782. 400 acres.
Chilton, John. Va. Captain. 18 Mar. 1834. 716 acres.

Chilton, Newman. Va. Corporal. 13 Jul. 1783. 200 acres.
Chilton, Stephen. Va. Private. 29 Mar. 1838. 100 acres.
Chinn, Edward. N. Y. Lieutenant. ———. 1000 acres.
Chinn, Samuel. Md. Private. ———. 50 acres.
Chinworth, John. Va. Private. 23 Jun. 1783. 100 acres.
Chiram, James. Va. Private. 21 Feb. 1784. 100 acres.
Chisham, James. Va. Private. 7 Jun. 1785. 100 acres.
Chisholm, Benjamin. Ga. Refugee. 24 May 1784. 287 1/2 acres.
Chisholm, George. Va. Private. 27 Jun. 1783. 233 1/3 acres.
Chisholm, John. Ga. Sergeant. 22 Jul. 1784. 230 acres.
Chisholm, Thomas. Ga. Refugee. 26 May 1784. 287 1/2 acres.
Chissum, Ignatius. N.C. Private. 8 Dec. 1795. 274 acres.
Chissum, James. N.C. Private. 8 Dec. 1795. 640 acres.
Chitham, Aquilla. Md. Sergeant. ———. 50 acres.
Chittenden, Jared. N. Y. Sergeant. 9 Jul. 1790. 600 acres.
Choheren, Dennis. Va.-Ind. Private. 108 acres.
Chowning, William. Va. Surgeon's Mate. 4 Aug. 1834. 2000 acres.
Chowning, William. Va. Surgeon's Mate. 4 Aug. 1834. 2000 acres.
Chrisler, Elias. Pa. Sergeant. 13 Feb. 1787. 250 acres.
Christee, James. Va. Private. 9 Apr. 1783. 200 acres.
Christey, John. N.Y. Corporal. ———. 500 acres to heirs.
Christian, Anthony. N.Y. ———. 13 Sep. 1790. 500 acres to heirs.
Christian, Benjamin. N.Y. ———. 13 Sep. 1790. 500 acres to heirs.
Christian, James. N.C. Private. 21 Oct. 1783. 640 acres.
Christian, James. N.C. Private. 22 Oct. 1783. 640 acres.
Christian, James. Va. Corporal. 3 Sep. 1784. 400 acres.
Christian, John. N. Y. Private. 8 Jul. 1790. 600 acres.
Christian, Joseph. Va. Lieutenant. 28 Mar. 1834. 2666 2/3 acres.
Christian, Michael. N. Yk. Matross. 9 Jul. 1790. 500 acres.
Christian, Nicholas. Va. Steward. 27 Jul. 1784. 200 acres.
Christian, Nicholas. Va. Steward. 28 Jun. 1860. 2466 2/3 acres.
Christian, Peter. N.Y. ———. 13 Sep. 1790. 500 acres to heirs. N.B. He may have been alive.
Christian, Raleigh C. Va. Private. 21 May 1823. 200 acres.
Christian, Walter, Sr. Va. Private. 2 Mar. 1833. 100 acres.
Christian, William. Va. Lieutenant. 12 Oct. 1824. 1333 1/3 acres.
Christian, William. Va. Lieutenant. 12 Oct. 1824. 666 2/3 acres.
Christian, William. Va. Lieutenant. 12 Oct. 1824. 666 2/3 acres.
Christian, William. Va. Lieutenant. 9 Dec. 1830. 2000 acres.
Christian, William. Va. Lieutenant. 9 Dec. 1830. 2000 acres.
Christie, Archibald. Ga. Refugee Private. 1 Jun. 1784. 250 acres.
Christie, David. N.C. Sergeant. 21 Oct. 1783. 1000 acres.
Christie, James. Va. Private. 14 Dec. 1833. 200 acres,
Christie, John. N. Y. Matross. 9 Jul. 1790. 600 acres.
Christie, John. N.C. Fife Major. 21 Oct. 1783. 358 acres.
Christie, John. Pa. Captain. 25 Oct. 1786. 500 acres.
Christie, Thomas. Va. Surgeon. 25 Oct. 1783. 7000 acres.
Christie, Thomas. Va. Surgeon. 11 Apr. 1812. 625 acres.
Christmas, John. N.C. Private. 21 Oct. 1783. 640 acres.
Christmas, Nathaniel. Ga. ———. 2 Aug. 1785. 862 1/2 acres.
Christmas, Robert. Ga. Soldier. 19 Dec. 1785. 230 acres.
Christopher, Andrias. N. Y. Private. 3 Jul. 1790. 600 acres.
Christopher, Elizabeth. Conn. Sufferer. New London. 49.4.6.
Christopher, Simon. N.C. Private. 25 Jul. 1821. 640 acres.

Chronicle, William. N.C. Captain. 23 Nov. 1820. 3840 acres to heirs.
Chryselius, Adolph. Pa. Sergeant. ———. 250 acres.
Chrystie, James. Pa. Captain. 23 Apr. 1845. 500 acres to Jonathan McMillan.
Chubb, Jonathan. Md. Private. ———. 50 acres.
Chudwick, Thomas. Mass. Private. 13 Jan. 1831. 200 acres.
Chumney, John. N.C. Sergeant. 21 May 1784. 428 acres.
Chuning, Chatwin. Va. Sailor. 19 Aug. 1793. 100 acres.
Chuning, George. Va. Sailor. 19 Aug. 1793. 100 acres.
Chunn, Sylvester. Va. Private. 21 Jun. 1784. 100 acres.
Church, Caleb. Conn. Sufferer. Danbury. 3.19.4.
Church, Christopher. N.C. Private. 17 Dec. 1785. 640 acres to heirs.
Church, Daniel. Conn. Sufferer. Danbury. 40.8.10.
Church, Horse N. Conn. Sufferer. Greenwich. 25.2.10.
Church, John. Va. Private. 2 Aug. 1783. 200 acres.
Church, Rebecca. Conn. Sufferer. New London. 52.11.10.
Church, Thomas. Pa. Major. ———. 300 acres.
Church, Thomas. Pa. Major. 25 Oct. 1786. 300 acres.
Church, William. N.C. Private. 29 Sep. 1784. 228 acres.
Churchell, Samuel. N.C. Non Commissioned Officer. 9 Nov. 1784. 1000 acres.
Churchill, Jabesh. Me. ———. 3 Sep. 1835. 200 acres. Buckfield.
Churchman, Charles. N.C. Private. 9 Dec. 1797. 640 acres to heirs.
Churn, John. N.C. Private. 2 Sep. 1820. 640 acres.
Chute, Josiah. Me. Sergeant. 27 Feb. 1836. 200 acres to widow Mary Chute. Windham.
Citizen, Morris. Md. Private. ———. 50 acres.
Civill, William. Md. Private. ———. 50 acres.
Clagg, David. N.C. Private. 3 May 1792. 274 acres.
Clagget, Hezekiah. Ga. ———. 16 Jul. 1784. 250 acres.
Claggett, Horatio. Md. Captain. ———. 200 acres.
Claggett, John. Md. Private. ———. 50 acres.
Claiborne, Buller. Va. Captain. 14 Feb. 1807. 5333 1/3 acres.
Claiborne, Richard. Va. Lieutenant. 31 Jan. 1784. 2666 2/3 acres.
Claibourne, Richard. Va. Lieutenant. 30 May 1799. 444 1/3 acres.
Claibourne, Richard. Va. Lieutenant. 18 Jun. 1799. 444 1/3 acres.
Clancey, John. Md. Corporal. ———. 50 acres.
Claney, Daniel. Md. Private. ———. 50 acres.
Claney, Edward. Md. Fifer. ———. 50 acres.
Claney, Michael. Md. Fifer. ———. 50 acres.
Claney, Michael, Sr. Md. Sergeant. ———. 50 acres.
Clapp, Eliakin. Mass. Private. 16 Sep. 1833. 200 acres.
Clapp, John, Jr. Conn. Sufferer. Greenwich. 129.2.3.
Clapp, Thomas. Conn. Sufferer. Greenwich. 333.17.7.
Clappard, John. S.C. ———. 2 May 1785. 200 acres.
Clapper, Valentine. Md. Private. ———. 50 acres.
Clark, Abner. N.C. Private. 7 Dec. 1797. 640 acres to heirs.
Clark, Abraham. N.C. ———. 8 Mar. 1785. 640 acres to heirs.
Clark, Andrew. Va.-Ind. Private. 108 acres.
Clark, Benjamin. Ga. Refugee. 25 May 1784. 287 1/2 acres.
Clark, Charles. Ga. ———. 17 May 1784. ———.
Clark, Christopher. Ga. ———. 17 May 1784. ———.
Clark, David. N. Y. Sergeant. 8 Jul. 1790. 600 acres.
Clark, David. Va. Private. 23 Jun. 1783. 200 acres.
Clark, Ebenezer. Mass. Private. 29 Jan. 1832. 200 acres to heirs.
Clark, Edmund. Va. Sergeant. 29 Jun. 1784. 200 acres.

Clark, Elijah. Ga. Lieutenant Colonel. 2 Feb. 1784. 700 acres.
Clark, George. Ga. ———. 28 Jul. 1784. 200 acres.
Clark, George. Va.-Ind. Private. 108 acres.
Clark, George. N. Y. Matross. 9 Jul. 1790. 600 acres.
Clark, George. Pa. Private. 2 Jul. 1812. 200 acres to heirs.
Clark, George Rogers. Va.-Ind. Brigadier General. Jan. 1784. 8049 acres.
Clark, Gibson. Ga. ———. 17 May 1784. ———.
Clark, Gideon. S.C. Soldier. 21 Jan. 1785. 200 acres.
Clark, Isaac. N.C. Private. 19 May 1784. 640 acres.
Clark, Isaac. N.C. Private. 29 Sep. 1784. 640 acres to heir.
Clark, Jacob. N.C. Private. 10 Jul. 1820. 336 acres to heirs.
Clark, Jacob. N.C. Private. 29 Jul. 1820. 640 acres to heirs.
Clark, James. Ga. Citizen. 22 Mar. 1785. 250 acres.
Clark, James. Mass. Drummer. 2 Mar. 1833. 200 acres.
Clark, James. N.Y. ———. 13 Sep. 1790. 500 acres to heirs.
Clark, James. N.C. Private. 13 Dec. 1783. 274 acres.
Clark, James. N.C. ———. 18 Jun. 1785. 640 acres to William Clark, heir.
Clark, James. N.C. Corporal. 26 Aug. 1785. 428 acres.
Clark, James. Pa. ———. ———. 200 acres to Richard Leedom, assignee.
Clark, James. Va. Sergeant. 30 May 1783. 200 acres.
Clark, James. Conn. Sufferer. Danbury. 524.3.4.
Clark, John. Md. Gunner. ———. 50 acres.
Clark, John. N. Y. Sergeant. 8 Jul. 1790. 600 acres.
Clark, John. N. Y. Bombardier. 6 Jul. 1790. 600 acres.
Clark, John. N. Y. Matross. 6 Jul. 1790. 600 acres.
Clark, John. N.C. Private. 9 Nov. 1784. 226 acres.
Clark, John. N.C. Private. 15 Dec. 1797. 640 acres to heirs.
Clark, John. Pa. Sergeant. 1 Jun. 1782. 250 acres.
Clark, John. Pa. Private. 9 Oct. 1786. 200 acres.
Clark, John. Pa. Captain. 20 Sep. 1787. 500 acres.
Clark, John. S.C. Soldier. 21 Jan. 1785. 200 acres.
Clark, John. Va. Captain. 8 Apr. 1783. 4000 acres.
Clark, John. Va. Private. 7 Jun. 1784. 100 acres.
Clark, John. Va. Private. 19 Feb. 1785. 100 acres.
Clark, John. Va. Sergeant. 19 Aug. 1822. 200 acres.
Clark, John. Va. Sergeant. 19 Aug. 1822. 200 acres.
Clark, John & sons. Conn. Sufferers. New London. 135.6.5.
Clark, John, Jr. Ga. Minute Man. 25 May 1784. 287 1/2 acres.
Clark, John, Sr. Ga. Captain. 15 Mar. 1784. 500 acres.
Clark, Johnston. Ga. ———. 17 May 1784. ———.
Clark, Jonathan. Va. Lieutenant Colonel. 10 Mar. 1783. 7000 acres.
Clark, Joseph. Mass. Private. 4 Jun. 1829. 200 acres.
Clark, Josiah. N.C. Private. 1 Sep. 1785. 640 acres to heirs.
Clark, Lewis. Ga. Refugee. 15 Mar. 1784. 250 acres.
Clark, Michael. Md. Private. ———. 50 acres.
Clark, Moses. Ga. Minute Man. 14 Sep. 1784. 287 1/2 acres.
Clark, Moses. Va. Private. 13 Oct. 1783. 200 acres.
Clark, Neil. N.C. Private. 8 Nov. 1784. 640 acres to heirs.
Clark, Osborn. N.C. Private. 30 Nov. 1785. 640 acres.
Clark, Patrick. N.C. Private. 7 Dec. 1797. 640 acres to heirs.
Clark, Phineas. Mass. ———. 22 Jul. 1833. 200 acres.
Clark, Richard. Va.-Ind. Lieutenant. Mar. 1784. 2156 acres.
Clark, Robert. Pa. Private. 10 May 1787. 200 acres.
Clark, Robert. Pa. Private. 11 Nov. 1788. 200 acres.

Clark, Russell. Conn. Sufferer. New/East Haven. 1.18.10.
Clark, Sampson. Va. Private. 8 Feb. 1809. 100 acres.
Clark, Samuel. Md. Private. ———. 50 acres.
Clark, Samuel. Conn. Sufferer. New/East Haven. 7.14.9.
Clark, Seth. Mass. Private. 18 Oct. 1833. 200 acres.
Clark, Thomas. Md. Private. ———. 50 acres.
Clark, Thomas. N.C. Colonel. 27 Oct. 1783. 7200 acres.
Clark, Thomas. Va. Private. 19 Nov. 1783. 200 acres.
Clark, Walter. N.C. Private. 7 Dec. 1796. 640 acres to heirs.
Clark, William. Ga. ———. 16 Jul. 1784. 200 acres.
Clark, William. Va.-Ind. Lieutenant. Mar. 1784. 2156 acres.
Clark, William. Mass. Private. 18 Oct. 1833. 200 acres.
Clark, William. Pa. Ranger. 23 Mar. 1789. 200 acres.
Clark, William. Pa. Ranger. ———. 200 acres.
Clark, William. Pa. Private. 9 Feb. 1808. 200 acres.
Clark, William. Pa. Private. 30 Mar. 1787. 200 acres.
Clark, William. Va. Private. 22 May 1783. 100 acres.
Clark, William. Va. Private. 21 Jan. 1784. 100 acres.
Clark, Williams. N.C. Sergeant. 14 Jun. 1785. 357 acres.
Clark, Zachariah. Md. Fifer. ———. 50 acres.
Clarke, Abner. N.C. Private. 2 Dec. 1796. 228 acres.
Clarke, Benjamin. N.C. Private. 22 Dec. 1796. 640 acres to heirs.
Clarke, Edmund. Va. Lieutenant. 2 Feb. 1784. 2666 2/3 acres.
Clarke, Edward. Va. Private. 13 Mar. 1783. 1000 acres.
Clarke, George. Md. Private. ———. 50 acres.
Clarke, George. Va. Private. 14 Feb. 1834. 100 acres.
Clarke, George R. Va. Brigadier General. 26 Jan. 1784. 10,000 acres.
Clarke, Henry. Va. Sergeant. 16 Jun. 1784. 200 acres.
Clarke, James. Md. Matross. ———. 50 acres.
Clarke, James. Va. Private. 18 Mar. 1784. 100 acres.
Clarke, John. Md. Private. ———. 50 acres.
Clarke, John. Va. Private. 18 Apr. 1823. 100 acres.
Clarke, John. Va. Lieutenant. 14 Jun. 1831. 1777 2/3 acres.
Clarke, John. Va. Lieutenant. 14 Jun. 1831. 888 2/3 acres.
Clarke, John. Va. Cornet. 3 Dec. 1832. 2666 2/3 acres.
Clarke, Jonathan. Va. Lieutenant Colonel. 6 Jun. 1807. 666 2/3 acres.
Clarke, Richard. Md. Private. ———. 50 acres.
Clarke, Richard. Va. Lieutenant. 3 Mar. 1784. 2666 2/3 acres.
Clarke, Robert. Va. Private. 23 Dec. 1784. 100 acres.
Clarke, Robert. Va. Private. 21 Mar. 1785. 266 2/3 acres.
Clarke, Tally. Va. Private. 26 Feb. 1834. 200 acres.
Clarke, Thomas. Md. Private. ———. 50 acres.
Clarke, Thomas. N.C. Lieutenant. 22 Oct. 1783. 2560 acres.
Clarke, Thomas. S.C. ———. 1 Jun. 1789. 200 acres.
Clarke, Thomas. Va. Sergeant. 23 Jul. 1824. 400 acres.
Clarke, William. Va. Lieutenant. 3 Mar. 1784. 2666 2/3 acres.
Clary, William. Md. Private. ———. 50 acres.
Clausby, Nathan. Va. Private. 2 Jan. 1813. 100 acres.
Clause, Jacob. Pa. Private. 5 Dec. 1788. 200 acres.
Clause, John. Conn. Sufferer. New/East Haven. 3.0.0.
Clautiere, Charles. N. Y. ———. ———. 500 acres.
Clavenger, Edwin. Va. Private. 20 Jun. 1783. 100 acres.
Clawser, Michael. Pa. Private. 30 Sep. 1787. 200 acres.
Clay, Abia [?]. Ga. ———. 17 May 1784. ———.

Clay, George. Pa. Private. 19 Sep. 1787. 200 acres.
Clay, Jeremiah. N.C. Sergeant. 2 Dec. 1785. 1000 acres to heirs.
Clay, John. N.C. Private. 17 Dec. 1785. 640 acres to heirs.
Clay, Matthew. Va. Lieutenant. 13 Dec. 1782. 2666 2/3 acres.
Clay, Matthew. Va. Lieutenant. 22 Oct. 1807. 814 acres.
Clay, Thomas. Va. Captain. 23 Jan. 1784. 4000 acres.
Claybrook, Anderson. Va. Private. 12 Apr. 1811. 200 acres.
Claypoole, Abraham. Pa. Captain. 12 Oct. 1786. 500 acres.
Clayton, Henry. Va. Private. 14 Jun. 1784. 100 acres.
Clayton, Joseph. Va. ———. 8 Jul. 1783. 200 acres.
Clayton, Miles. N.C. Private. 8 Dec. 1795. 640 acres to heirs.
Clayton, Phillip. Va. Lieutenant. 10 Jun. 1783. 2666 2/3 acres.
Clayton, Phillip. Va. Lieutenant. 24 Nov. 1794. 444 1/2 acres.
Clearwater, Martin. N. Y. Private. 8 Jul. 1790. 600 acres.
Cleaveland, Benjamin. Mass. Matross. 6 Jul. 1832. 200 acres to heirs.
Cleaveland, Josiah. Mass. Private. 18 Jul. 1832. 200 acres.
Cleaver, Benjamin. Md. Private. ———. 50 acres.
Cleaves, William. Me. ———. 18 Jun. 1835. 200 acres. Cumberland.
Cleeland, Adam. Pa. Private. 25 Aug. 1787. 200 acres.
Cleggle, Joseph. N. Y. Matross. 9 Jul. 1790. 500 acres.
Cleghorn, Shubal. N.C. Private. 7 Dec. 1796. 640 acres to heirs.
Cleiverius, Benjamin. Va. Captain Lieutenant. 5 Feb. 1784. 4000 acres.
Clemens, John. Pa. Private. 8 Sep. 1787. 200 acres.
Clemens, John. Va. Private. 6 May 1784. 200 acres.
Clement, Barnard. Va. Quartermaster Sergeant. 18 Nov. 1818. 200 acres.
Clement, Edward W. Va. Private. 14 Dec. 1785. 100 acres.
Clement, Nicholas. N. Y. Private. 8 Jul. 1790. 600 acres.
Clements, Bennet H. Md. Private. ———. 50 acres.
Clements, Bernard. Va. Private. 19 Mar. 1834. 100 acres.
Clements, Charles. Md. Private. ———. 50 acres.
Clements, Charles. Va. Private. 6 Apr. 1838. 100 acres.
Clements, Henry. Md. Lieutenant. ———. 200 acres.
Clements, James. Md. Private. ———. 50 acres.
Clements, John. Ga. ———. 6 Feb. 1784. 500 acres.
Clements, John. N.C. Private. 30 Jun. 1803. 640 acres.
Clements, Mace. Va. Regimental Surgeon. 4 Jun. 1783. 7000 acres.
Clements, Samuel. Ga. ———. 17 May 1784. ———.
Clements, Thomas B. Md. Private. ———. 50 acres.
Clements, William. Ga. ———. 17 May 1784. ———.
Clements, William. Md. Private. ———. 50 acres.
Clemm, John. Ga. Minute Man. 25 May 1784. 287 1/2 acres.
Clemments, William. Md. Private. ———. 50 acres.
Clemmons, Isaac. Ga. ———. 26 May 1784. 287 1/2 acres to heirs.
Clemmons, Thomas. S.C. ———. 4 Dec. 1786. 200 acres to John Clemmons, heir.
Clemons, Curtis. N.C. Private. 29 Sep. 1784. 274 acres.
Clendenin, Adam. Pa. Private. 9 Mar. 1795. 200 acres to John Nicholson, assignee.
Clendenin, Samuel. Pa. Private. 12 Sep. 1808. 200 acres to William Cochran, assignee.
Clendennin, Samuel. Pa. ———. 7 Sep. 1808. 200 acres.
Clendennon, John. N.C. Lieutenant. 6 May 1784. 2560 acres.
Clendeny, George. Va. Sailor. 27 Jul. 1783. 100 acres.
Cleon [?], Jacob. N.C. Sergeant. 26 May 1784. 358 acres.
Clerk, Hezekiah. Va. Private. 19 Jan. 1785. 100 acres.
Clerk, William. N.C. Sergeant. 22 Apr. 1785. 1000 acres.

Clermont, Joseph. Va. Private. 3 Nov. 1838. 200 acres.
Clermont, Joseph. Va. Private. 27 Mar. 1855. 200 acres.
Clermont, Lewis. Va. Private. 27 Mar. 1855. 200 acres.
Clermont, Louis. Va. Private. 3 Nov. 1838. 200 acres.
Cleveland, Benjamin. Ga. ———. 17 May 1784. ———.
Cleveland, John. Va. Private. 20 Apr. 1784. 100 acres.
Cleveland, Larkin. Ga. ———. 17 May 1784. ———.
Cleverdence, John. Md. Private. ———. 50 acres.
Clift, Joseph. N. Y. Private. 8 Jul. 1790. 500 acres.
Clift, William. Va. Private. 21 Aug. 1783. 200 acres.
Clifton, Abraham. N.C. Private. 22 Apr. 1785. 640 acres to heirs.
Clifton, Daniel. N.C. Private. 20 Sep. 1784. 640 acres.
Clifton, Joshua. Va. Private. 27 Jun. 1783. 233 1/3 acres.
Clifton, Peter. N.C. Private. 30 Sep. 1785. 640 acres to heirs.
Clifton, Richard. N.C. Private. 29 Sep. 1784. 640 acres to Sarah Hays, heiress.
Clifton, Thomas. Va.-Ind. Private. 108 acres.
Clifton, William. N.C. Sergeant. 25 Jul. 1821. 1000 acres.
Cline, Jacob. N. Y. Private. 8 Jul. 1790. 500 acres.
Cline, Jacob. N.Y. ———. 13 Sep. 1790. 500 acres to heirs.
Clinton, Alexander. N. Y. Lieutenant. 7 Jul. 1790. 1200 acres.
Clinton, Anna. Conn. Sufferer. New/East Haven. 4.8.0.
Clinton, George. N. Y. Brigadier General. 9 Jul. 1790. 5100 acres.
Clinton, James. N. Y. Brigadier General. 3 Jul. 1790. 4200 acres.
Clinton, John. N.C. Private. 7 Jan. 1784. 228 acres.
Clinton, Joseph. N. Y. Private. 3 Jul. 1790. 600 acres.
Clinton, Levi. Conn. Sufferer. New/East Haven. 6.8.0.
Clinton, Matthew. Pa. Private. 23 Aug. 1787. 200 acres.
Clinton, Thomas. Md. Fifer. ———. 50 acres.
Clod, Robert. Va. Corporal. 28 May 1783. 200 acres.
Clonsey, George. N.C. Private. 7 Dec. 1797. 640 acres to heirs.
Close, Abraham. Conn. Sufferer. Greenwich. 17.0.0.
Close, Deborah. Conn. Sufferer. Greenwich. 12.7.11.
Close, George. N.C. Private. 5 Sep. 1821. 640 acres.
Close, Hannah. Conn. Sufferer. Greenwich. 38.15.11.
Close, Odel. Conn. Sufferer. Greenwich. 257.10.3.
Close, Odel (administrator). Conn. Sufferer. Greenwich. 49.3.10.
Close, Odel, Jr. Conn. Sufferer. Greenwich. 15.7.11.
Close,Joseph. Conn. Sufferer. Greenwich. 144.15.2.
Closer, Christopher. N. Y. Sergeant. 7 Jul. 1790. 600 acres.
Cloud, Ezekiel. Ga. ———. 15 Mar. 1784. 250 acres.
Cloud, Jeremiah, Jr. Ga. Refugee. 15 Mar. 1784. 250 acres.
Cloud, Jeremiah, Sr. Ga. Citizen. 15 Mar. 1784. 250 acres.
Cloud, John. Ga. Soldier. 25 Feb. 1784. 500 acres.
Cloud, Nenough. Ga. Refugee Citizen. 7 Apr. 1784. ———.
Cloudas, George. Ga. ———. 19 Jul. 1784. 287 1/2 acres.
Clough, Benjamin. N. Y. Private. 8 Jul. 1790. 600 acres.
Clough, John. Va. Sergeant. 24 Jun. 1784. 400 acres.
Clower, William. N.C. ———. 18 Jun. 1785. 640 acres.
Clowers, John. Ga. ———. 15 Mar. 1784. 250 acres.
Clowers, Peter. Ga. Private. 10 Dec. 1784. 250 acres.
Cloyd, William. Va. Private. 23 Jun. 1783. 200 acres.
Clozier, Matthias. Pa. Private. 9 Oct. 1786. 200 acres.
Clyer, James. N.C. Private. 10 Dec. 1788. 640 acres to heirs.
Coalston, James. N.C. Private. 29 Apr. 1784. 274 acres.

Coates, Aaron. Ga. ———. 17 May 1784. ———.

Coates, Benjamin. N.C. Private. 30 Sep. 1785. 365 acres.

Coates, George. Va. Private. 5 Mar. 1784. 100 acres.

Coates, Henry. Ga. ———. 17 May 1784. ———.

Coates, John. Ga. ———. 25 Feb. 1784. 287 1/2 acres.

Coates, John. Pa. Private. 13 Sep. 1787. 200 acres to William Powers, assignee.

Coates, Lesley. Ga. ———. 25 Feb. 1784. 250 acres.

Coates, Nathaniel. Ga. ———. 25 Feb. 1784. 250 acres.

Coats, John. N.C. Private. 5 Dec. 1797. 640 acres to heirs.

Coats, Samuel. Va. Seaman. 24 Oct. 1786. 100 acres.

Cobb, Anthony. N.C. Private. 7 Jan. 1786. 640 acres to heirs.

Cobb, Ezekiel. Ga. ———. 17 May 1784. 250 acres.

Cobb, James, Sr. Ga. ———. 17 May 1784. ———.

Cobb, John. Ga. ———. 30 Sep. 1784. ———.

Cobb, Joseph. Ga. ———. ———. 250 acres.

Cobb, Kindall. Md. Private. ———. 50 acres.

Cobb, Melatiah. Mass. ———. 2 Apr. 1813. 200 acres.

Cobb, Peter. N.C. Private. 12 Sep. 1785. 640 acres to heirs.

Cobb, Rowland. Me. ———. 23 Apr. 1835. 200 acres. Union.

Cobb, Shadrack. N.C. Private. 15 Jul. 1785. 640 acres to heir.

Cobb, William. N.C. Private. 30 Sep. 1785. 640 acres to heirs.

Cobb, Zebulon. N.C. Private. 30 Sep. 1785. 640 acres to heirs.

Cobbert, John. Va. Private. 2 Jul. 1784. 100 acres.

Cobbs, Samuel. Va. Lieutenant. 29 Aug. 1807. 942 acres.

Cobbs, Samuel. Va. Lieutenant. 29 Aug. 1807. 2688 acres.

Cobbs, Stratton. Va. Private. 15 Jun. 1807. 100 acres.

Cobea, John. Pa. ———. 18 Dec. 1802. 500 acres to Mary Donovan, administratrix.

Cochran, Edward. Pa. Private. 25 Oct. 1786. 200 acres to William M. Power, assignee.

Cochran, George. Pa. Sergeant. 30 Jul. 1787. 250 acres.

Cochran, James. Md. Private. ———. 50 acres.

Cochran, John. Me. Private. 30 Sep. 1835. 200 acres to widow Agnes Cochran. Edgecomb.

Cochran, John. Md. Private. ———. 50 acres.

Cochran, John. N.Y. Director of the Hospital & Physician General. 10 Aug. 1792. 5100 acres.

Cochran, Robert. N.Y. Lieutenant Colonel. 7 Jul. 1790. 2700 acres.

Cochran, Simon. Va. Sergeant. 31 Dec. 1806. 200 acres.

Cock, Caleb. Ga. Refugee. 4 Mar. 1784. ———.

Cockar, John. N.C. Private. 30 Sep. 1785. 640 acres to heirs.

Cockburn, John. N.C. Private. 2 Feb. 1786. 640 acres to heirs.

Cocke, Colin. Va. Captain. 20 Aug. 1783. 4666 2/3 acres.

Cocke, Colin. Va. Captain. 3 Jul. 1807. 250 acres.

Cocke, Colin. Va. Captain. 3 Jul. 1807. 250 acres.

Cocke, John Catesby. Va. Marine Captain. 18 Jun. 1835. 5333 1/3 acres.

Cocke, John Catesby. Va. Marine Captain. 10 Jun. 1836. 1066 2/3 acres.

Cocke, John Catesby. Va. Marine Captain. 10 Jun. 1836. 1066 2/3 acres.

Cocke, John Catesby. Va. Marine Captain. 10 Jun. 1836. 356 acres.

Cocke, John Catesby. Va. Marine Captain. 10 Jun. 1836. 1066 acres.

Cocke, John Catesby. Va. Marine Captain. 10 Jun. 1836. 710 acres.

Cocke, John Catesby. Va. Marine Captain. 10 Jun. 1836. 356 acres.

Cocke, John Catesby. Va. Marine Captain. 10 Jun. 1836. 710 acres.

Cocke, Nathaniel. Va. Lieutenant Colonel. 13 Feb. 1834. 6000 acres.

Cocke, Pleasant. Va. Captain. 28 Jun. 1784. 4000 acres.

Cocke, William. Va. Sergeant. 19 May 1797. 200 acres.
Cockendall, Elijah. Md. Corporal. ———. 50 acres.
Cockerel, William. S.C. ———. 2 Jul. 1792. 100 acres.
Cockerel, William. S.C. ———. 2 Jul. 1792. 90 acres.
Cockey, Peter. Md. Ensign. ———. 200 acres.
Cockle, John. Mass. ———. 13 Jan. 1830. 200 acres to heir Polly Watts who assigned it to Abner Coburn.
Cockley, John. N. Y. Private. 2 Sep. 1790. 600 acres.
Cockram, Daniel. Va. Private. 10 Jun. 1811. 100 acres.
Cockram, John. N.C. Private. 4 May 1784. 228 acres.
Cockran, James. Ga. Refugee. 5 Jun. 1784. 250 acres.
Cockran, Samuel. Va. Sergeant. 19 Nov. 1783. 200 acres.
Cockran, William. Va. Sergeant. 28 Nov. 1783. 200 acres.
Cockrel, Presley. Va. Sergeant. 3 Feb. 1784. 100 acres.
Cockrell, Littleton. Va. Sailor. 30 Jun. 1784. 100 acres.
Cockrell, Peter. Va. Corporal. 29 Nov. 1796. 200 acres.
Cockrell, William. Va. Private. 22 Mar. 1839. 200 acres.
Cockrem, Thomas. N. Y. Sergeant. 9 Jul. 1790. 600 acres.
Cockrill, John. Va. Sergeant. 22 Jul. 1824. 200 acres.
Cocks, Aaron. N.C. Private. 30 Sep. 1785. 640 acres to heirs.
Cocks, Joseph. Conn. Sufferer. New London. 1.5.3.
Cocks, Robert. N.C. Sergeant. 15 Dec. 1818. 1000 acres to heir James Cocks.
Cocks, William. Ga. Soldier. 5 May 1785. ———.
Cod, Philip. Pa. ———. 21 Oct. 1805. 200 acres to Henry and Jane Dickson.
Code, William. N. Y. Private. 8 Jul. 1790. 500 acres.
Codwise, Christopher. N.Y. Lieutenant. 7 Jul. 1790. 1200 acres.
Coe, Ichabod. N. Y. ———. 12 Sep. 1803. 500 acres.
Coe, Jonathan. Conn. Sufferer. Greenwich. 40.10.5.
Coe, Reuben. Conn. Sufferer. Greenwich. 33.16.4.
Coe, William. Md. Private. ———. 50 acres.
Cofer, George. Va. Corporal. 19 Mar. 1783. 200 acres.
Cofer, William. Va.-Ind. Private. 108 acres.
Coffee, John. Pa. Private. 9 Mar. 1795. 200 acres to John Nicholson, assignee.
Coffee, Peter. Ga. ———. 30 Sep. 1784. ———.
Coffer, Reubin. Va. Private. 21 May 1823. 100 acres.
Coffey, Ozbourn. Va. Private. 26 May 1809. 100 acres.
Coffield, Benjamin. N.C. Lieutenant. 6 Jan. 1784. 1607 acres.
Coffield, Owen. Md. Private. ———. 50 acres.
Coffin, Arthur. Md. Private. ———. 50 acres.
Coffin, George. Mass. Private. 2 Sep. 1834. 200 acres.
Coffin, John. Va. Private. 15 Jun. 1792. 100 acres.
Coffin, Lemuel. Va. Private. 15 Jun. 1792. 100 acres.
Coffin, Nicholas. Me. Private. 4 Sep. 1839. 200 acres. Lincoln.
Coffle, William. Va. Private. 29 Jun. 1784. 200 acres.
Cogay, John. Va. Private. 12 Jul. 1783. 100 acres.
Cogden, John. N. Y. Private. 7 Jul. 1790. 500 acres.
Coggin, Herbert. Va. Private. 28 Apr. 1783. 200 acres.
Coggleshouds, Isaac. N. Y. Private. 8 Jul. 1790. 500 acres.
Coghill, Reuben. Va. Private. 22 Jun. 1810. 100 acres.
Cogwell, Frederick. Va. Private. 27 Oct. 1783. 100 acres.
Cohen, Jacob. Va. Captain. 13 Mar. 1838. 4000 acres.
Cohorn, Cornelius. Ga. ———. ———. 17 May 1784.
Coins, Dominick. Md. Private. ———. 50 acres.
Coit, Joseph. Conn. Sufferer. New London. 1,298.18.5.

Coit, Joshua. Conn. Sufferer. New London. 40.0.0.

Coit, Nathaniel, Jr. Conn. Sufferer. New London. 15.15.10.

Coit, Samuel. Conn. Sufferer. New London. 19.8.6.

Coit, Thomas. Conn. Sufferer. New London. 23.13.4.

Coit, William. Conn. Sufferer. New London. 44.17.10.

Coke, John. Conn. Sufferer. Fairfield. 0.9.2.

Coker, Henry. N.C. Private. 4 Aug. 1821. 640 acres.

Colants, John. N.C. Private. 26 May 1784. 640 acres.

Colben, Obed. N.C. Private. 19 Jan. 1786. 640 acres.

Colbert, Elisha. Va. Private. 22 Jun. 1789. 100 acres.

Colbert, John. Va. Private. 3 Jun. 1783. 200 acres.

Colbert, John. Va. Private. 7 Aug. 1859. 200 acres.

Colbert, Lawrence. N.C. Private. 19 Jan. 1786. 640 acres.

Colbert, Susannah. Ga. ———. 17 May 1784. ———.

Colbey, John. N.C. Private. 8 Dec. 1796. 640 acres.

Colbreath, William. N. Y. Lieutenant. 7 Jul. 1790. 1200 acres.

Colbrough, Daniel. Me. Corporal. 13 Oct. 1835. 200 acres to widow Elizabeth Colbrough. Hartford. Surname also spelled Coolbroth.

Colby, Sylvanus. Mass. Private. 1 Mar. 1833. 200 acres to heirs.

Colden, James. Va. Private. 1 Apr. 1783. 100 acres.

Colden, James. Va. Private. 28 Apr. 1783. 200 acres.

Colden, Philip. N.C. Sergeant. 19 Jan. 1786. 428 acres.

Coldwater. Philip. Pa. Private. 20 Feb. 1787. 200 acres.

Cole, Abimelech. N.C. Private. 28 Oct. 1783. 640 acres to heir.

Cole, Abraham. Va. Captain. 26 Jun. 1833. 4000 acres.

Cole, Alexander. N.C. Private. 20 Oct. 1792. 640 acres to heirs.

Cole, Barnet. Me. ———. 3 Apr. 1835. 200 acres. Windsor.

Cole, Benjamin. Md. Private. ———. 50 acres.

Cole, Benjamin. N.Y. Private. 13 Sep. 1790. 500 acres to heirs.

Cole, Burwell. N.C. Private. 30 Sep. 1785. 640 acres to heirs.

Cole, David. N. Y. Private. 8 Jul. 1790. 500 acres.

Cole, Edward. N.C. Private. 20 Sep. 1784. 640 acres.

Cole, George. N.C. Private. 26 Apr. 1784. 274 acres.

Cole, Hamlin. Va. Sergeant. 31 May 1783. 200 acres.

Cole, Henry. N.Y. ———. ———. 500 acres to his heirs.

Cole, Henry. N.C. Drummer. 22 Apr. 1785. 1000 acres.

Cole, James. Ga. Citizen. 20 Dec. 1785. 287 1/2 acres.

Cole, Jesse. N.C. Private. 20 Sep. 1784. 640 acres.

Cole, John. Me. ———. 7 Jul. 1835. 200 acres to widow Polly Cole. Albion.

Cole, John. Md. Private. ———. 50 acres.

Cole, John. Md. Private. ———. 50 acres.

Cole, John. N. Y. Excellency's Guards. 6 Jul. 1790. 600 acres.

Cole, John. N.C. Private. 1 Sep. 1785. 640 acres to heirs.

Cole, John. N.C. Private. 7 Dec. 1797. 640 acres to heirs.

Cole, John. Va. Sergeant. 19 Jun. 1783. 200 acres.

Cole, John. Va. Captain. 28 May 1803. 3000 acres.

Cole, John. Va. Captain. 28 May 1803. 1000 acres.

Cole, John, Jr. Ga. ———. 15 Mar. 1784. 287 1/2 acres.

Cole, John, Sr. Ga. Citizen. 15 Mar. 1784. 287 1/2 acres.

Cole, Josiah. Ga. ———. 30 Sep. 1784. ———.

Cole, Martin. N.C. Sergeant. 22 Oct. 1783. 1000 acres.

Cole, Martin. N.C. Private. 8 Aug. 1821. 640 acres.

Cole, Melchiah. N.C. Private. 9 Dec. 1797. 640 acres to heirs.

Cole, Michael. Md Private. ———. 50 acres.

Cole, Philip. N. Y. ———. 16 May 1808. 200 acres to legal representatives Tobias

Cole, Mary Scott, Daniel Wakeman, Martha Wakeman, and Sarah Wakeman.

Cole, Richard. Va. Private. 2 Jun. 1835. 100 acres.

Cole, Robert. N.C. Private. 7 Sep. 1820. 640 acres.

Cole, Samuel. Me. ———. 28 Apr. 1835. 200 acres. Lewiston.

Cole, Samuel. Va. Private. 19 Jun. 1783. 100 acres.

Cole, Teunis. N. Y. Private. 8 Jul. 1790. 600 acres.

Cole, Thomas. N.C. Private. 20 Feb. 1784. 365 acres.

Cole, Thomas. Va. Private. 2 May 1783. 100 acres.

Cole, William. Ga. Citizen. 5 Apr. 1785. Ga. 287 1/2 acres.

Cole, William. N.C. Private. 26 Apr. 1784. 274 acres.

Cole, William. N.C. Non Commissioned Officer. 18 May 1784. 1000 acres.

Cole, William. Va. Private. 12 Apr. 1783. 200 acres.

Cole, William. Va. Private. 13 Dec. 1786. 100 acres.

Cole, William Temple. N.C. Captain. 25 Oct. 1783. 1500 acres.

Colechester, John. N.C. Private. 30 Sep. 1785. 640 acres to heirs.

Colefax, Jonathan. Conn. Sufferer. New London. 15.11.3.

Colegate, Aseph. Md. Private. ———. 50 acres.

Coleman, Benjamin. N.C. Captian. 27 Oct. 1783. 3840 acres.

Coleman, Caleb. Ga. ———. 17 May 1784. 1000 acres.

Coleman, Charles. N.C. Quartermaster Sergeant. 16 Aug. 1821. 1000 acres.

Coleman, Daniel. Ga. ———. 24 Feb. 1784. 250 acres.

Coleman, George. Ga. ———. 17 May 1784. ———.

Coleman, Harris. Ga. Refugee. 24 Feb. 1784. 250 acres.

Coleman, Isham. Md. Private. ———. 50 acres.

Coleman, Israel. N. Y. Corporal. 9 Jul. 1790. 600 acres.

Coleman, Jacob. S.C. ———. 5 Oct. 1789. 200 acres.

Coleman, Jacob. Va. Lieutenant. 31 Mar. 1783. 1300 acres.

Coleman, Jacob. Va. Lieutenant. 31 Mar. 1783. 1366 2/3 acres.

Coleman, Jacob. Va. Lieutenant. 5 Jun. 1807. 444 2/3 acres.

Coleman, James. Ga. Refugee. 15 Mar. 1784. 250 acres.

Coleman, James. Va. Sergeant. 29 Jul. 1783. 400 acres.

Coleman, James. Va. Private. 28 Apr. 1785. 100 acres.

Coleman, John. Ga. ———. 15 Mar. 1784. 250 acres.

Coleman, John. Va. Ensign. 16 Dec. 1783. 2666 2/3 acres.

Coleman, Joseph. Va. Sergeant. 23 Feb. 1784. 100 acres.

Coleman, Richard. Va. Captain. 12 Jan. 1784. 400 acres.

Coleman, Richard. Va. Private. 8 Apr. 1789. 100 acres.

Coleman, Samuel. Va. Lieutenant. 24 Feb. 1783. 2666 2/3 acres.

Coleman, Samuel. Va. Private. 30 Apr. 1791. 100 acres.

Coleman, Samuel. Va. Lieutenant. 22 Mar. 1796. 444 1/2 acres.

Coleman, Samuel. Va. Lieutenant. 16 May 1807. 370 acres.

Coleman, Thomas. Ga. ———. 2 Aug. 1785. 287 1/2 acres.

Coleman, Thomas. Va. Sergeant. 3 Mar. 1784. 200 acres.

Coleman, Thomas. Va. Private. 9 Mar. 1784. 100 acres.

Coleman, Whitehead. Va. Captain. 26 Jun. 1783. 4000 acres.

Coleman, Whitehead. Va. Captain. 17 Oct. 1799. 666 2/3 acres.

Coleman, Whitehead. Va. Captain. 11 Sep. 1807. 388 2/3 acres.

Coleman, Wyatt. Va. Lieutenant. 9 Feb. 1784. 3110 2/3 acres.

Coles, Alexander. N.C. Corporal. 14 Jul. 1820. 360 acres to heirs.

Coleston, Henry. N.C. Private. 23 Oct. 1783. 274 acres.

Colf, Robert. N.C. Private. 21 Apr. 1784. 274 acres.

Colford, Mathew. N.Y. Fifer. 13 Sep. 1790. 500 acres to heirs.

Colgan, Barnabas. Pa. ———. 1 Apr. 1796. 200 acres to Timothy Buell, administrator.

Colgin, William. Va. Private. 12 Nov. 1787. 100 acres.
Colgrve, Arthur. N.C. Lieutenant. 8 Mar. 1785. 640 acres.
Colin, John. Md. Sergeant. ———. 50 acres.
Collard, James. Md. Fifer. ———. 50 acres.
Collens, John. N.C. Private. 21 May 1784. 274 acres.
Coller, Isaac. Conn. Sufferer. Danbury. 4.14.0.
Coller, James. Pa. Private. 17 Mar. 1787. 200 acres.
Collet, John. N.C. Private. 14 Feb. 1796. 640 acres to heirs.
Colley, Absolam. N.C. Private. 28 Sep. 1785. 640 acres.
Colley, Asa. Va. Private. 25 Aug. 1836. 300 acres.
Colley, Charles. Va. Private. 9 Oct. 1798. 100 acres.
Collier, Charles. Va. Captain. 25 Jan. 1812. 4000 acres.
Collier, James. Va. Sergeant. 3 Aug. 1798. 200 acres.
Collier, James. Va. Private. 19 Jun. 1813. 200 acres.
Collier, John. Va. Private. 9 Jun. 1813. 100 acres.
Collier, John. Va. Private. 12 Dec. 1833. 100 acres.
Collier, Joseph. Pa. Lieutenant. 2 Oct. 1786. 200 acres.
Collier, Joseph. Pa. Lieutenant. 2 Oct. 1786. 200 acres.
Collier, Richard. N. Y. Matross. 9 Jul. 1790. 600 acres.
Collier, Thomas. Va. Lieutenant. 16 Jun. 1813. 222 acres.
Collier, Thomas. Va. Lieutenant. 16 Jun. 1813. 222 acres.
Collier, Thomas. Va. Lieutenant. 16 Jun. 1813. 222 acres.
Collier, Thomas. Va. Lieutenant. 16 Jun. 1813. 222 acres.
Collier, Thomas. Va. Lieutenant. 16 Jun. 1813. 222 acres.
Collier, Thomas. Va. Lieutenant. 16 Jun. 1813. 222 acres.
Collier, Thomas. Va. Lieutenant. 16 Jun. 1813. 223 1/3 acres.
Collier, Thomas. Va. Lieutenant. 16 Jun. 1813. 1333 1/3 acres.
Collier, Thomas. Va. Private. 9 Jun. 1813. 100 acres.
Collier, Thomas. Va. Sergeant. 9 Jun. 1813. 200 acres.
Collier, William. Ga. ———. 17 May 1784. ———.
Collier, William. Md. Private. ———. 50 acres.
Collier, Wyatt. Va. Sergeant. 19 Feb. 1798. 200 acres.
Collin, James. Va. Private. 31 Jul. 1784. 100 acres.
Collingsworth, Edmund. Va. Private. 15 Feb. 1783. 100 acres.
Collingsworth, John. Va. Private. 15 Feb. 1783. 144 acres.
Collins, Adam. Va. Private. 12 May 1784. 100 acres.
Collins, Amos. Conn. Sufferer. Danbury. 4.17.6.
Collins, Benjamin. Me. Private. 28 Mar. 1835. 200 acres. St. Albans.
Collins, Benjamin. N.C. Private. 3 Feb. 1785. 289 acres.
Collins, Britain. N.C. Private. 7 Jan. 1786. 640 acres to heirs.
Collins, Burwell. N.C. Private. 2 Aug. 1784. 640 acres to heir.
Collins, Charles. Ga. ———. 17 May 1784. ———.
Collins, Charles. N.C. Private. 26 Apr. 1784. 640 acres to William Collins, heir.
Collins, Cornelius. Ga. Lieutenant. 22 Sep. 1783. 400 acres.
Collins, Dilleard. N.C. Private. 2 Aug. 1784. 640 acres to heir.
Collins, George. Md. Private. ———. 50 acres.
Collins, George. N.C. Private. 30 Sep. 1785. 640 acres to heirs.
Collins, George. Va. Private. 19 Jun. 1783. 100 acres.
Collins, George. Va. Private. 26 May 1875. 100 acres.
Collins, Jacob. Md. Private. ———. 50 acres.
Collins, James. Md. Sergeant. ———. 50 acres.
Collins, James. N. Y. Private. 8 Jul. 1790. 600 acres.
Collins, James. Va. Seaman. 27 Nov. 1832. 100 acres.
Collins, John. Ga. ———. 17 May 1784. 690 acres.

Collins, John. Ga. Minute Man. Jul. 1784. 287 1/2 acres.
Collins, John. Md. Private. ———. 50 acres.
Collins, John. Md. Private. ———. 50 acres.
Collins, John. N.C. Sergeant. 26 Apr. 1784. 428 acres.
Collins, John. N.C. Private. 6 Dec. 1796. 640 acres.
Collins, John. N.C. Private. 27 Nov. 1819. 640 acres to heirs.
Collins, John. Pa. Private. 16 Oct. 1786. 200 acres.
Collins, John. Pa. Private. 10 Aug. 1787. 200 acres.
Collins, John. Va. Private. 16 Jun. 1783. 200 acres.
Collins, John. Va. Private. 4 May 1784. 200 acres.
Collins, Joseph. Ga. ———. 15 Mar. 1784. 250 acres.
Collins, Joseph. N. Y. Private. 8 Jul. 1790. 500 acres.
Collins, Joseph. N.C. Private. 29 Sep. 1784. 274 acres.
Collins, Joseph. N.C. Drummer. 28 Nov. 1795. 428 acres.
Collins, Joseph. Conn. Sufferer. New London. 41.0.8 3/4.
Collins, Josiah. N.C. Private. 30 Sep. 1785. 640 acres to heirs.
Collins, Lemuel. Me. Private. 8 May 1835. 200 acres. Industry.
Collins, Mason. Va. Private. 14 Jun. 1783. 100 acres.
Collins, Mason. Va. Private. 26 May 1875. 100 acres.
Collins, Matthew. N.C. Private. 10 Mar. 1788. 640 acres.
Collins, Moses. Ga. ———. ———. 287 1/2 acres.
Collins, Oliver. Mass. Matross. 1 Feb. 1833. 200 acres.
Collins, Peter. Va. Private. 15 Oct. 1783. 200 acres.
Collins, Richard. Va. Private. 19 Jun. 1784. 100 acrs.
Collins, Sampson. N.C. Private. 17 Dec. 1785. 274 acres.
Collins, Samuel. N.C. Private. 12 Sep. 1785. 640 acres to heirs.
Collins, Solomon. Ga. ———. 1784. 287 1/2 acres.
Collins, Stephen. Ga. Soldier. 17 May 1784. 230 acres.
Collins, Stephen. Va. Seaman. 27 Nov. 1832. 100 acres.
Collins, Thomas. N.C. Private. 24 Nov. 1796. 640 acres to heirs.
Collins, Thomas. Va. Sergeant. 11 Mar. 1785. 200 acres.
Collins, Thomas. Va. Private. 31 Jan. 1787. 200 acres.
Collins, William. N.C. Private. 21 Apr. 1784. 640 acres.
Collins, William. Pa. ———. 19 Feb. 1787. 200 acres to Ralph Philips, assignee.
Collins, William. Va. Private. 23 Mar. 1814. 200 acres.
Collis, William. Md. Sergeant. ———. 50 acres.
Collison, William. N.C. Private. 30 Sep. 1785. 640 acres to heirs.
Colly, James. N.C. Private. 8 Dec. 1808. 274 acres.
Coloney, Southey. Va. Private. 14 Feb. 1834. 200 acres.
Coloney, Timothy. Va. Private. 14 Feb. 1834. 200 acres.
Colony, George. Va. Private. 27 Nov. 1832. 100 acres.
Colony, William. Va. Private. 5 Apr. 1833. 200 acres.
Colquehon, James. Va. Private. 4 Apr. 1783. 100 acres.
Colquett, Ransome. Va. Private. 21 May 1823. 100 acres.
Colson, James. N.C. Private. 15 Feb. 1797. 274 acres.
Colson, William. Ga. ———. 26 May 1784. 287 1/2 acres.
Colston, Seth. N.C. Sergeant. 13 Dec. 1796. 428 acres.
Coltain, Abraham. N.C. Private. 30 Nov. 1785. 640 acres to heirs.
Colter, Alexander. N.C. Private. 9 Dec. 1797. 640 acres to heirs.
Colter, Andrew. Pa. Private. ———. 200 acres.
Colter, James. Pa. Private. 8 Sep. 1787. 200 acres.
Colter, John. Pa. Private. 12 Jan. 1787. 200 acres.
Colter, John. Pa. Private. 19 Oct. 1786. 200 acres to Alexander Power, assignee.

Colter, William. S.C. ———. 4 Jul. 1785. 200 acres.
Coltman, Robert. Pa. Captain. 28 Feb. 1794. 500 acres.
Colvin, Daniel. Va. Private. 14 Aug. 1834. 100 acres.
Colvin, James. Va. Private. 5 Apr. 1784. 100 acres.
Colvin, Jeremiah. Va. Sergeant. 26 Nov. 1783. 200 acres.
Colvin, Mason. Va. Private. 14 Aug. 1834. 100 acres.
Colvin, Mason. Va. Private. 21 Jun. 1837. 100 acres.
Combs, John. Ga. ———. ———. 250 acres.
Comer, Jacob. N.C. Private. 14 Dec. 1796. 274 acres.
Comer, James. N.C. Sergeant. 22 Oct. 1783. 428 acres.
Comer, Thomas. Va. Private. 13 Jan. 1813. 100 acres.
Comidine, Nicholas. N. Y. Private. 8 Jul. 1790. 600 acres.
Compton, Augustine. Va. Private. 26 Nov. 1783. 100 acres.
Compton, Edward. Md. Lieutenant. ———. 200 acres.
Compton, Ignatius. Md. Private. ———. 50 acres.
Compton, John. Md. Matross. ———. 50 acres.
Compton, Thomas. Md. Private. ———. 50 acres.
Comstock, Andrew. Conn. Sufferer. Danbury. 5.4.8.
Comstock, Daniel. Conn. Sufferer. Danbury. 9.6.8.
Comstock, David. Conn. Sufferer. Norwalk. 313.18.0.
Comstock, Lydia. Conn. Sufferer. Norwalk. 9.6.0.
Comstock, Samuel, Capt. Conn. Sufferer. Norwalk. 2.0.0.
Comstock, William. Conn. Sufferer. New London. 3.16.0.
Conally, William. Va. Private. 23 Jun. 1783. 200 acres.
Conant, Daniel. Mass. Private. 5 Oct. 1833. 200 acres to widow Milly Wallace.
Conant, John. Va. Private. 4 Dec. 1783. 200 acres.
Conard, James. Va. Private. 1 Jun. 1785. 100 acres.
Concklin, Sylvanus. N. Y. Lieutenant. 13 Sep. 1790. 1000 acres to heirs.
Condon, David. N.Y. ———. 13 Sep. 1790. 500 acres to heirs.
Condon, John. N.C. Private. 4 Aug. 1821. 640 acres.
Condron, Thomas. Md. Corporal. ———. 50 acres.
Condy, Roger. N.C. Private. 9 Dec. 1797. 274 acres.
Cone, Elijah. Me. ———. 20 Aug. 1838. 200 acres to widow Judith (Perry) Cone. Lovell.
Cone, James. Ga. ———. 15 Jul. 1784. 500 acres.
Cone, John. Ga. ———. Jul. 1784. 287 1/2 acres.
Cone, Joseph. N. Y. Lieutenant. ———. 666 2/3 acres.
Cone, Samuel. Me. Private. 24 Sep. 1838. 200 acres. Hampden.
Cone, William. N.C. Private. 11 Sep. 1820. 640 acres to heirs.
Cone, William, Jr. Ga. ———. 28 Feb. 1784. 250 acres.
Congur, Stephen. N.C. Sergeant Major. 28 Dec. 1792. 357 acres.
Conine, Philip. N. Y. Lieutenant. 7 Jul. 1790. 1200 acres.
Conklin, Esther. Conn. Sufferer. Groton. 39.1.6.
Conklin, Jacob. Conn. Sufferer. Greenwich. 63.1.3.
Conklin, Joseph. N. Y. Private. 8 Jul. 1790. 600 acres.
Conklin, Newell. Conn. Sufferer. Greenwich. 2.19.3.
Conley, Timothy. Va. Private. 3 Jul. 1784. 200 acres.
Conly, John. N.C. Private. 4 Aug. 1821. 640 acres.
Conn, David. N.C. Private. 16 Aug. 1821. 640 acres.
Conn, Jonathan. Me. ———. 3 Oct. 1835. 200 acres. Bethel.
Connell, Daniel. Ga. ———. 17 May 1784. ———.
Connell, Jesse. Ga. ———. 17 May 1784. ———.
Connell, Thomas. Ga. ———. 14 Jul. 1784. 287 1/2 acres.
Connell, Torrence. Pa. Sergeant. 13 Oct. 1786. 250 acres.

Connelly, Hugh. Md. Private. ———. 50 acres.
Connelly, James. Ga. ———. 26 Jul. 1784. 230 acres.
Connelly, James. Pa. Private. 13 Oct. 1786. 200 acres.
Connelly, John. Md. Private. ———. 50 acres.
Connelly, John. Md. Private. ———. 50 acres.
Connelly, Patrick. Ga. ———. 30 Sep. 1784. ———.
Connelly, Patrick. Pa. Private. 10 Mar. 1795. 200 acres to Clement Biddle, assignee.
Connelly, Timothy. Md. Sergeant. ———. 50 acres.
Connelly, William. Ga. ———. 17 May 1784. 230 acres.
Conner, Benjamin. N.C. Private. 22 Feb. 1785. 640 acres to heirs. Wetherington,
Conner, Charles. N.C. Private. 4 Aug. 1821. 640 acres.
Conner, Daniel. Ga. ———. ———. 500 acres.
Conner, Daniel. Mass. Corporal. 20 Feb. 1833. 200 acres to heirs.
Conner, Davey. N.C. Private. 26 May 1784. 640 acres.
Conner, David. Md. Private. ———. 50 acres.
Conner, Douglas. Va. Private. 6 Mar. 1834. 100 acres.
Conner, Edward. Va. Cornet. 25 Mar. 1785. 2666 2/3 acres.
Conner, Jacob. N.C. Private. 23 Jun. 1820. 640 acres to heirs.
Conner, James. Md. Private. ———. 50 acres.
Conner, James. Va. Sergeant. 29 Jun. 1784. 200 acres.
Conner, John. Ga. Soldier. 15 Mar. 1784. 250 acres.
Conner, John. Mass. Private. 1 May 1832. 200 acres.
Conner, John. N. Y. Matross. 9 Jul. 1790. 600 acres.
Conner, John. N.C. Private. 9 Nov. 1784. 274 acres.
Conner, John. N.C. Private. 14 Dec. 1797. 274 acres.
Conner, John. N.C. Private. 23 Jun. 1820. 640 acres to heirs.
Conner, John. Pa. Private. 9 Aug. 1787. 200 acres to Charlotte King, widow.
Conner, John. Va. Sergeant. 14 Dec. 1782. 200 acres.
Conner, John. Va. Sergeant. 6 May 1783. 400 acres.
Conner, John. Va. Private. 12 Aug. 1834. 200 acres.
Conner, John. Va. Private. 2 Sep. 1847. 100 acres.
Conner, John. Va. Private. 2 Sep. 1847. 100 acres.
Conner, Matthew. Pa. Private. 9 Mar. 1789. 200 acres.
Conner, Michael. Md. Matross. ———. 50 acres.
Conner, Patrick. Md. Private. ———. 50 acres.
Conner, Terence. Va. Private. 11 Aug. 1785. 200 acres.
Conner, Timothy. N. Y. Private. 13 Sep. 1790. 500 acres.
Conner, Wiliam. Md. Private. ———. 50 acres.
Conner, William. N.C. Private. 8 Dec. 1796. 640 acres to heirs.
Conner, William. N.C. Musician. 4 Aug. 1821. 1000 acres.
Conner, William. Pa. Artillery. 18 May 1789. 200 acres.
Conner, William. Va. Private. 6 Mar. 1834. 100 acres.
Conner, William J. Va. Private. 9 Feb. 1808. 100 acres.
Connery, Jonathan. Conn. Sufferer. Greenwich. 63.0.0.
Connite, Conrad. N. Y. Private. 8 Jul. 1790. 600 acres.
Connolly, Michael. N. Y. Lieutenant. 3 Jul. 1790. 1200 acres.
Connor, Charles. Pa. Private. 6 Jul. 1788. 200 acres.
Connor, Christopher. N.C. Private. 22 Apr. 1785. 640 acres to heirs.
Connor, John. Pa. Private. 30 July 1787. 200 acres.
Connor, John. Va. Private. 8 Dec. 1783. 100 acres.
Connor, Patrick. Pa. Private. 14 Oct. 1786. 200 acres.
Connor, Phillip. Va. Sergeant. 23 Apr. 1783. 200 acres.
Connor, William. Va. Ensign. 10 Oct. 1812. 500 acres.

Connor, William. Va. Ensign. 10 Oct. 1812. 500 acres.

Connor, William. Va. Ensign. 10 Oct. 1812. 500 acres.

Connor, William. Va. Ensign. 10 Oct. 1812. 666 2/3 acres.

Conolly, Philip. Va. Private. 9 May 1785. 100 acres.

Conore, Andrew. Va.-Ind. Private. 108 acres.

Conrad, Charles. Pa. Private. ———. 200 aces.

Conrad, Jacob. Va. Private. 23 Jun. 1783. 200 acres.

Conroy, James. Pa. Private. 20 Nov. 1788. 200 acres.

Consalver, Charles. Va. Private. 13 Aug. 1784. 100 acres.

Consolver, John. Va. Private. 2 Dec. 1782. 200 acre.

Constantine, Cornelius. S.C. ———. 3 Mar. 1788. 200 acres to William Constantine, heir at law.

Constantine, Nicholas. N. Y. ———. ———. 500 acres.

Consule, Harman. Va.-Ind. Private. 108 acres.

Conway, Francis. Va. Captain. 9 Mar. 1838. 1666 2/3 acres.

Conway, Francis. Va. Captain. 9 Mar. 1838. 1666 2/3 acres.

Conway, Francis. Va. Captain. 9 Mar. 1838. 666 2/3 acres.

Conway, Henry. Va. Captain. 14 Feb. 1807. 1000 acres.

Conway, Henry. Va. Captain. 14 Feb. 1807. 1000 acres.

Conway, Henry. Va. Captain. 14 Feb. 1807. 1000 acres.

Conway, Henry. Va. Captain. 14 Feb. 1807. 1000 acres.

Conway, Henry. Va. Captain. 14 Feb. 1807. 666 2/3 acres.

Conway, James. Va. Lieutenant. 9 Mar. 1838. 1252 1/4 acres.

Conway, James. Va. Lieutenant. 9 Mar. 1838. 1252 1/4 acres.

Conway, James. Va. Lieutenant. 9 Mar. 1838. 417 acres.

Conway, James. Va. Lieutenant. 9 Mar. 1838. 417 acres.

Conway, James. Va. Lieutenant. 30 Dec. 1854. 250 acres.

Conway, James. Va. Lieutenant. 30 Dec. 1854. 1002 1/4 acres.

Conway, John. N.C. Private. 3 Jun. 1820. 640 acres.

Conway, Joseph. Va. Lieutenant. 22 Aug. 1783. 3110 2/3 acres.

Conway, Robert. Va. Lieutenant. 6 May 1834. 2666 2/3 acres.

Conway, Samuel. Va. Corporal. 19 Feb. 1784. 200 acres.

Conway, Thomas. Ga. ———. 26 Jul. 1784. 230 acres.

Conyers, John. Ga. Captain. 1784. 500 acres.

Conyers, John, Jr. Ga. Refugee. 1784. 250 acres.

Conyers, William. Ga. Refugee. 17 Feb. 1784. 250 acres to heir Margaret Conyers.

Cook, Abraham. Me. Private. 20 Dec. 1838. 200 acres to widow Sarah Cook.

Cook, Andrew. Pa. Private. 16 Oct. 1786. 200 acres to Anne Cook, executrix.

Cook, Benjamin. Ga. ———. 17 May 1784. ———.

Cook, Benjamin. Va. Private. 20 Jun. 1786. 100 acres.

Cook, David. Conn. Sufferer. New/East Haven. 29.13.0.

Cook, Dawson. Va. Midshipman. 13 May 1794. 2666 2/3 acres.

Cook, Dawson. Va. ———. 19 Jul. 1830. 2666 2/3 acres.

Cook, Frederick. N.C. Private. 30 Nov. 1785. 640 acres.

Cook, George. Ga. Minute Man. ———. 17 May 1784. 287 1/2 acres to heir Lucy Cook.

Cook, George. N. Y. Private. 8 Jul. 1790. 600 acres.

Cook, George. N.C. Lieuenant. 21 Oct. 1783. 2560 acres to Pettit Cook, heir.

Cook, George. N.C. Corporal. 30 Sep. 1785. 1000 acres to heirs.

Cook, George. Conn. Sufferer. New/East Haven. 45.10.7.

Cook, Isaac. Ga. ———. 15 Mar. 1784. 250 acres.

Cook, Isaac. N.C. Private. 30 Sep. 1785. 640 acres.

Cook, Isham. Ga. Captain. 26 May 1784. 690 acres to heirs.

Cook, James. Va. Private. 18 Apr. 1801. 100 acres.

Cook, John. N. Y. Private. 8 Jul. 1790. 600 acres.
Cook, John. N.Y. ———. 13 Sep. 1790. 500 acres to heirs.
Cook, John. N.C. Private. 16 Aug. 1821. 640 acres.
Cook, John. N.C. Corporal. 6 Sep. 1821. 1000 acres. Of Stevenson's company.
Cook, John, Sr. Ga. ———. 27 Sep. 1784. 287 1/2 acres.
Cook, Joseph. N.C. Private. 16 Aug. 1821. 640 acres.
Cook, Joseph. Va. Private. 20 Dec. 1783. 200 acres.
Cook, Joseph P. Conn. Sufferer. Danbury. 53.6.8.
Cook, Joshua. Ga. ———. 25 May 1784. 287 1/2 acres.
Cook, Levi. Ga. Citizen. 6 Sep. 1785. 287 1/2 acres.
Cook, Nicholas. N. Y. Fifer. 7 Jul. 1790. 600 acres.
Cook, Noah. Mass. Private. 18 Oct. 1833. 200 acres.
Cook, Philip. Pa. ———. 18 Oct. 1786. 200 acres to William Smith, assignee.
Cook, Rains. Ga. ———. 17 May 1784. 230 acres.
Cook, Richard D. N.C. Captain. 6 Sep. 1821. 3840 acres.
Cook, Roger. Va. Private. 4 Oct. 1799. 100 acres.
Cook, Samuel. Mass. Private. 11 Jul. 1837. 200 acres to assignee Samuel Cook.
Cook, Samuel. N. Y. Surgeon. 7 Jul. 1790. 1900 acres.
Cook, Samuel. Conn. Sufferer. New/East Haven. 19.7.9.
Cook, Sanders. N.C. Private. 12 May 1784. 640 acres.
Cook, Stephen. N.C. Private. 7 Sep. 1820. 640 acres.
Cook, Thomas. N.C. Sergeant. 16 Aug. 1821. 1000 acres.
Cook, William. Ga. Citizen. 6 Apr. 1785. 287 1/2 acres.
Cook, William. Md. Private. ———. 50 acres.
Cook, William. Va. Sergeant. 23 Sep. 1783. 200 acres.
Cook, William. Va. Private. 2 Dec. 1784. 100 acres.
Cook, William. Va. Gunner. 24 Oct. 1787. 2666 2/3 acres.
Cook, William. Va. Gunner. 31 Oct. 1868. 2666 2/3 acres.
Cook, William. Va. Private. 28 Jun. 1784. 200 acres.
Cook, Zacheriah. Va. Private. 11 Apr. 1786. 100 acres.
Cooke, Isaiah. N.C. Private. 30 Sep. 1785. 640 acres.
Cooke, John. Va. Private. 21 May 1823. 100 acres.
Cooke, William. Va. Sergeant. 26 Mar. 1784. 400 acres.
Cookes, Michael. Va. Private. 9 Dec. 1783. 100 acres.
Cookley, Robert. Pa. Dragoon. ———. 200 acres.
Cooksey, Hezekiah. N.C. Private. 17 Dec. 1796. 640 acres to heirs.
Cooksey, Thomas. N.C. Private. 17 Dec. 1796. 640 acres to heirs.
Cool, John. Me. Private. 26 May 1835. 200 acres. Waterville.
Cooley, Daniel. Conn. Sufferer. Ridgefield. 1.18.8.
Cooley, Gabriel. N.C. Private. 21 Apr. 1800. 640 acres to heirs.
Cooley, Hezekiah. Conn. Sufferer. Fairfield. 3.6.0.
Cooley, James. Va. Private. 13 Jun. 1783. 100 acres.
Cooley, Jeffery. N.C. Private. 23 Nov. 1797. 274 acres.
Cooley, Joseph. Md. Private. ———. 50 acres.
Cooley, Robert. Md. Private. ———. 50 acres.
Cooley, Samuel. N.C. Surgeon. 6 Jan. 1784. 1428 acres.
Coolidge, Silas. Me. ———. 14 Nov. 1836. 200 acres to widow Elizabeth Coolidge. Trenton.
Cooly, James. Pa. Private. 11 May 1787. 200 acres.
Coom, Jacob. N. Y. Private. 8 Jul. 1790. 600 acres.
Coombes, Francis. Va. Private. 2 Dec. 1782. 200 acres.
Coombs, Joseph. Me. ———. 17 Apr. 1835. 200 acres to heirs Lucy Coombs and Thankful Green.
Coombs, Peter. N. Y. Private. 8 Jul. 1790. 600 acres.
Coombs, Samuel C. Me. Private. 25 Aug.

1836. 200 acres to widow Rachel Coombs.

Coomy [or Kumy], John. Md. Private. ———. 50 acres.

Coon, Andrew. Va. Private. 11 Apr. 1799. 200 acres.

Coon, Anthony. Va. Private. 5 Apr. 1784. 100 acres.

Coon, Israel. Va. Corporal. 12 May 1819. 400 acres.

Coon, Israel. Va. Corporal. 22 Feb. 1861. 400 acres.

Coon, William. N.Y. ———. ———. 500 acres to heirs.

Cooney, James. Pa. Private. 9 Sep. 1789. 200 acres.

Cooney, John. Pa. Private. 8 Feb. 1787. 200 acres.

Coons, Frederick. Va. Private. 5 Jun. 1783. 100 acres.

Cooper, Anthony. Ga. Minute Man. 3 Oct. 1783. 287 1/2 acres.

Cooper, Apollos. Va. Lieutenant. 14 Mar. 1840. 629 1/3 acres.

Cooper, Apollos. Va. Lieutenant. 21 Nov. 1787. 2666 2/3 acres.

Cooper, Benjamin A. Va. Lieutenant. 1 Mar. 1851. 2666 2/3 acres.

Cooper, Charles. Md. Private. ———. 50 acres.

Cooper, Charles. Pa. ———. 9 Mar. 1795. 200 acres to John Nicholson, assignee.

Cooper, Charles. Va. Private. 26 Nov. 1784. 100 acres.

Cooper, David. Ga. Minute Man. 14 Jul. 1785. ———.

Cooper, Ephraim. Va. Sergeant. 5 Aug. 1783. 400 acres.

Cooper, Ezekiel. S.C. ———. 7 May 1784. 150 acres.

Cooper, Henry. N.C. Private. 27 Dec. 1792. 440 acres.

Cooper, Hillary. Va. Private. 9 Dec. 1784. 100 acres.

Cooper, Isaac. N. Y. Bombardier. 9 Jul. 1790. 600 acres.

Cooper, Jacob. Ga. Citizen. 19 Dec. 1785. 287 1/2 acres.

Cooper, James. N.C. Private. 6 Dec. 1797. 640 acres to heirs.

Cooper, James. Va. Private. 4 Nov. 1819. 100 acres.

Cooper, James. Va. Private. 29 Jun. 1842. 100 acres.

Cooper, Jeremiah. N.C. Private. 17 Jul. 1813. 640 acres to heirs.

Cooper, Jesse. Ga. Soldier. 4 Feb. 1785. ———.

Cooper, John. Ga. ———. 17 May 1784. ———.

Cooper, John. Md. Private. ———. 50 acres.

Cooper, John. N. Y. Private. 8 Jul. 1790. 500 acres.

Cooper, John. N. Y. Private. 8 Jul. 1790. 600 acres.

Cooper, John. N.Y. ———. 13 Sep. 1790. 500 acres to heirs.

Cooper, John. N.C. Corporal. 21 Nov. 1805. 1000 acres to heirs.

Cooper, John. N.C. Private. 30 May 1820. 640 acres to heirs.

Cooper, Josiah. N.C. Private. 17 Jul. 1813. 640 acres to heirs.

Cooper, Leonard. Va. Captain. 18 Oct. 1784. 1000 acres.

Cooper, Leonard. Va. Captain. 18 Oct. 1784. 1000 acres.

Cooper, Leonard. Va. Captain. 18 Oct. 1784. 1000 acres.

Cooper, Leonard. Va. Captain. 18 Oct. 1784. 1000 acres.

Cooper, Leonard. Va. Captain. 18 Oct. 1784. 666 2/3 acres.

Cooper, Leonard. Va. Captain. 13 Dec. 1796. 4666 2/3 acres.

Cooper, Nathan. N.C. Private. 1 Sep. 1785. 640 acres to heirs.

Cooper, Nathaniel. N.C. Private. 29 Sep. 1784. 228 acres.

Cooper, Nathaniel. N.C. Private. 14 Jul. 1820. 640 acres to heirs.

Cooper, Reuben. Va. Sergeant. 26 Nov. 1784. 200 acres.

Cooper, Richard. Va. Private. 18 Jul. 1783. 233 1/3 acres.

Cooper, Samuel. N.C. Private. 3 Feb. 1785. 274 acres.

Cooper, Simon. Va. Private. 16 Feb. 1801. 100 acres.

Cooper, Solomon. N.C. Private. 12 Sep. 1785. 640 acres to heirs.

Cooper, Solomon. N.C. Lieutenant. 5 Sep. 1821. 2560 acres.

Cooper, Spencer. Va. Corporal. 9 Aug. 1783. 400 acres.

Cooper, Sterling. Va. Private. 26 May 1831. 50 acres.

Cooper, Sterling. Va. Private. 26 May 1831. 50 acres.
Cooper, Thomas. Md. Private. ———. 50 acres.
Cooper, Thomas. Va. Private. 16 Apr. 1787. 100 acres.
Cooper, William. N.C. Private. 14 Dec. 1797. 640 acres to heirs.
Cooper, William. N.C. Private. 23 Feb. 1820. 228 acres.
Cooper, William. N.C. Lieutenant. 21 Jul. 1821. 2560 acres to heirs.
Cooper, William. Pa. ———. 10 Mar. 1796. 300 acres.
Cooper, William. Pa. Ensign. 7 Mar. 1807. 300 acres.
Cooper, William. S.C. ———. 4 Dec. 1786. 200 acres.
Cooper, William. Va. Private. 30 Jun. 1783. 200 acres.
Cooper, William, Jr. S.C. ———. 4 Dec. 1786. 200 acres.
Coops, Francis. N.C. Private. 29 Nov. 1810. 274 acres.
Coots, James. N.C. Lieutenant. 27 Nov. 1783. 853 acres.
Coots, William. Va. Sergeant. 3 May 1798. 400 acres.
Cope, Henry. Ga. Sergeant. 25 May 1784. 345 acres.
Cope, Thomas. Va. Private. 20 Dec. 1784. 100 acres.
Copeland, Joab. N.C. Private. 26 May 1784. 640 acres.
Copeland, Job. N.C. Private. 27 Nov. 1817. 640 acres to heirs.
Copeland, John. N.C. Sergeant. 18 Aug. 1784. 1000 acres.
Copeland, Joseph. N.C. Private. 30 Apr. 1784. 640 acres to heirs.
Copeland, Kedar. N.C. Private. 14 Oct. 1783. 640 acres.
Copeland, Richard. N.C. Private. 22 Oct. 1783. 228 acres.
Copeland, Ripley. N.C. Private. 21 Oct. 1783. 274 acres.
Copeland, Stephen. S.C. ———. 1 Dec. 1788. 200 acres to Mary Graves, heiress.
Copeland, William. N. Y. ———. 8 Oct. 1792. 600 acres.
Copes, Beverly. Va. Midshipman. 26 Feb. 1831. 533 acres.
Copes, Beverly. Va. Midshipman. 26 Feb. 1831. 533 acres.
Copes, Beverly. Va. Midshipman. 26 Feb. 1831. 533 acres.
Copes, Beverly. Va. Midshipman. 26 Feb. 1831. 533 acres.
Copes, Beverly. Va. Midshipman. 26 Feb. 1831. 533 acres.
Copes, Charles. Va. Private. 17 Jun. 183-. 200 acres.
Copes, Southy. Va. Sergeant. 15 Jun. 1807. 200 acres.
Copes, William. N.C. Private. 7 Jan. 1813. 640 acres to heirs.
Copin, John. Va. Sergeant. 20 Sep. 1806. 200 acres.
Copin, Samuel. Va. Private. 8 Feb. 1812. 200 acres.
Copland, Cornelius. Va.-Ind. Private. 108 acres.
Copland, William. Va. Corporal. 30 Aug. 1783. 200 acres.
Coplar, Barnabas. Pa. Private. 29 Sep. 1787. 200 acres.
Coppage, James. N.C. Private. 16 Dec. 1797. 640 acres to heirs.
Coppernol, Adam. N. Y. ———. 6 Apr. 1795. 600 acres.
Coppinger, Higgins. Va. Private. 7 Aug. 1783. 200 acres.
Copple, Nicholas. Pa. Sergeant. 13 Oct. 1786. 250 acres.
Coram, John. N.C. Private. 17 Dec. 1785. 640 acres to heirs.
Coram, Robert. S.C. Lieutenant. 2 May 1785. 300 acres.
Coran, William. Va. Private. 31 Jul. 1783. 233 1/3 acres.
Corban, Arthur. N.C. Private. 17 Dec. 1785. 274 acres.
Corbell, Peter. Va. Corporal. 8 Sep. 1783. 200 acres.
Corben, Richard. N.C. Private. 9 Feb. 1796. 640 acres to heirs.
Corbert, Richard. N.C. Private. 20 Jan. 1785. 640 acres to heirs.
Corbett, John. N.C. Private. 22 Apr. 1785. 640 acres to heirs.
Corbett, John. Va. Private. 15 Oct. 1783. 200 acres.
Corbin, Arthur. N.C. Private. 17 Dec. 1785. 274 acres.
Corbin, Francis. N.C. Private. 29 Sep. 1784. 640 acres to heir.

Corbin, Isaiah. Va. Private. 6 Dec. 1808. 100 acres.
Corbin, James. N.C. Private. 29 Sep. 1784. 640 acres to heir.
Corbin, Philip. Conn. Sufferer. Danbury. 10.4.5.
Corbin, William. Ga. Soldier. 5 Mar. 1784. 200 acres.
Corbin, William. N.C. Private. 15 Feb. 1797. 640 acres to heirs.
Corbin, William. Va. Master at Arms. 26 Feb. 1831. 1333 1/3 acres.
Corbin, William. Va. Master at Arms. 26 Feb. 1831. 1333 1/3 acres.
Corbin, William. Va. Master at Arms. 27 Sep. 1831. 666 2/3 acres.
Corbin, William. Va. Master at Arms. 27 Sep. 1831. 666 2/3 acres.
Corbin, William. Va. Master at Arms. 27 Sep. 1831. 666 2/3 acres.
Corbin, William. Va. Master at Arms. 27 Sep. 1831. 666 2/3 acres.
Corbitt, James. N.C. Corporal. 21 Jul. 1814. 428 acres.
Corbitt, James. N.C. Corporal. 26 Dec. 1814. 572 acres to heirs.
Cordell, John. Va. Chaplain. 20 May 1836. 6000 acres.
Corder, James. Va. Corporal. 2 May 1783. 400 acres.
Cordle, Richard. N.C. Private. 8 Aug. 1821. 640 acres.
Cordones, John. Va. Private. 23 Jun. 1783. 200 acres.
Corey, Philip. Mass. Ensign. 10 Sep. 1832. 200 acres.
Cork, William. Md. Private. ———. 50 acres.
Corker, Thomas. Ga. ———. 2 May 1785. 200 acres.
Corne, Thomas. N.C. Private. 9 Sep. 1785. 640 acres to heirs.
Cornelies, Elijah. N.C. Private. 30 Sep. 1785. 640 acres to heirs.
Cornelius, Isaac. N.C. Fifer. 9 Sep. 1785. 1000 acres to heirs.
Cornelius, Isaac. N.C. Private. 6 Sep. 1821. 640 acres.
Cornelius, Josiah. Va. Private. 11 Dec. 1783. 100 acres.
Cornelius, William. N.C. Matross. 17 Feb. 1824. 640 acres.
Cornelius, William. Va. Gunner. 18 Aug. 1835. 2533 1/3 acres.
Cornelius, William. Va. Gunner. 28 Nov. 1783. 200 acres.
Cornelius, William. Va. Sailor. 1 Nov. 1786. 100 acres.
Cornelius, William. Va. Gunner. 19 Jan. 1837. 2566 2/3 acres.
Cornelus, John. N. Y. Private. 7 Jul. 1790. 600 acres.
Cornick, Robert. Md. Private. ———. 50 acres.
Cornish, Gabriel. Mass. Private. 18 Feb. 1833. 200 acres.
Cornish, John. Me. ———. 30 Apr. 1835. 200 acres. Brunswick.
Cornish, John. Md. Private. ———. 50 acres.
Cornish, William. N.C. Private. 7 Sep. 1820. 640 acres.
Cornwall, Caleb. N. Y. Private. 3 Jul. 1790. 600 acres.
Cornwall, David. N. Y. Matross. 9 Jul. 1790. 600 acres.
Cornwall, Francis. N.C. Private. 15 Feb. 1797. 274 acres.
Cornwall, William. Md. Sergeant. ———. 50 acres.
Cornwall, William. N. Y. Matross. 9 Jul. 1790. 500 acres.
Corr, Michael. Md. Sergeant. ———. 50 acres.
Corrigill, John. N. Y. Private. 8 Jul. 1790. 500 acres.
Corroll, John. Va. Private. 26 Apr. 1783. 200 acres.
Corry, Shadrack. N.C. Private. 29 Nov. 1809. 274 acres.
Corsey, David. Ga. ———. 20 Feb. 1784. 250 acres.
Corsey, William. Ga. ———. 28 Feb. 1784. 250 acres.
Corter, John. N. Y. Private. 8 Jul. 1790. 600 acres.
Corwin, Gershom. N. Y. ———. ———. 450 acres.
Corwin, Silas. N.Y. ———. 13 Sep. 1790. 500 acres to heirs.
Cosby, Nelson. Va. Sergeant. 16 Nov. 1795. 200 acres.
Cosby, Sydner. Va. Sergeant. 22 Mar. 1784. 400 acres.
Cosby, Thomas. Va. Private. 2 Jul. 1784. 100 acres.
Cosby, William. Va. Sergeant. 5 Dec. 1787. 400 acres.

Cosgrove, Edward. Md. Private. ———. 50 acres.
Cosgrove, John. N.Y. ———. 13 Sep. 1790. 500 acres to heirs.
Cosgrove, Thomas. Pa. Private. 27 Aug. 1787. 200 acres to William Powers, assignee.
Coshall, Thomas. N. Y. Matross. 3 Jul. 1790. 600 acres.
Cosse, Richard. N.C. Private. 24 Dec. 1796. 228 acres.
Cosse, William. Va. Private. 20 Jun. 1783. 100 acres.
Cossey, Joseph. N.C. Private. 9 Nov. 1784. 640 acres.
Costen, Henry. N.C. Private. 23 Dec. 1792. 640 acres.
Coster, John. Conn. Sufferer. New London. 14.9.0.
Cotanch, John. N.C. Private. 2 Feb. 1786. 640 acres to heirs.
Cotanch, Peter. N.C. Private. 2 Feb. 1786. 640 acres to heirs.
Cotelle, Philip. N. Y. Matross. 9 Jul. 1790. 600 acres.
Coteree, Richard. N. Y. Private. 8 Jul. 1790. 600 acres.
Cotes, Matthew. N.C. Private. 26 May 1784. 274 acres.
Cotgrove, James. N.C. Private. 9 Dec. 1797. 640 acres.
Cothorn, Josiah. Ga. Refugee. 15 Mar. 1784. 250 acres to heirs.
Cothorn, William. Ga. Refugee. 15 Mar. 1784. 500 acres.
Cotten, Chambers. N.C. Private. 14 Feb. 1796. 640 acres.
Cotten, Ephraim. N.C. Private. 23 Apr. 1785. 640 acres to heirs.
Cotteral, Richard. Va. Private. 20 May 1829. 200 acres.
Cottle, John. N.C. Private. 5 Sep. 1821. 640 acres.
Cottle, William. Va. Private. 29 Jun. 1784. 200 acres.
Cotton, Charles. N.C. Private. 9 Dec. 1797. 640 acres.
Cotton, Edward. Pa. Matross. ———. 200 acres.
Cotton, Elijah. N.C. Private. 20 Dec. 1784. 274 acres.
Cotton, Henry. Pa. Private. 22 Oct. 1786. 200 acres.
Cottorel, William. Va. Midshipman. 15 Aug. 1783. 2666 2/3 acres.
Couch, George. Me. ———. 11 Aug. 1835. 200 acres to widow Ann Norton. Readfield.
Couch, John. Me. ———. 10 Apr. 1835. 200 acres to widow Jane Couch. Hallowell.
Couch, John. Conn. Sufferer. Danbury. 5.10.8.
Couch, Simeon, 3d. Conn. Sufferer. Fairfield. 227.9.3.
Couch, Thomas and Simon Couch. Conn. Sufferers. Fairfield. 10.0.0.
Couflin, James. N.C. Sergeant. 7 Dec. 1796. 1000 acres.
Couflin, McMark. N.C. Corporal. 7 Dec. 1796. 1000 acres.
Cougleton, William. Md. Private. ———. 50 acres.
Couling, John. N.C. Private. 7 Dec. 1797. 640 acres to heirs.
Coulter, Levi. N.C. Private. 19 May 1784. 640 acres.
Coulter, Samuel. Va. Sergeant. 11 Oct. 1826. 400 acres.
Coumbs, John. N.C. Private. 30 Sep. 1785. 640 acres to heirs.
Counch, John W. N.C. Sergeant. 22 Dec. 1796. 1000 acres to heirs.
Council, Arthur. N.C. Captain. 2 Aug. 1784. 3840 acres to heirs.
Couns, Henry. N.C. Private. 14 Dec. 1797. 365 acres.
Countryman, Jacob. N. Y. Private. 8 Jul. 1790. 600 acres.
Counts, Adam. N. Y. Corporal. 8 Jul. 1790. 600 acres.
Coursey, Hampton. Md. Private. ———. 50 acres.
Coursey, William. Md. Private. ———. 50 acres.
Courtney, Cornelius. Pa. ———. 11 Jan. 1803. 200 acres to Hannah Henry, devisee.
Courtney, Francis. N. Y. Sergeant. 8 Jul. 1790. 600 acres.
Courtney, Philip. Va. Ensign. 15 Mar. 1806. 2666 2/3 acres.
Courtney, Samuel. Va. Private. 26 Jun. 1783. 233 1/3 acres.
Courtney, Thomas. Va. Private. 26 Apr. 1783. 200 acres.

Courtney, Thomas. Va. Private. 14 Feb. 1861. 200 acres.
Courtney, William. Pa. Private. 25 Oct. 1786. 200 acres.
Courts, John. Md. Private. ———. 50 acres.
Cousins, William. Ga. Soldier. 2 Jan. 1786. ———.
Coutch, James. S.C. ———. 7 May 1787. 200 acres.
Covenan, Benjamin. N.C. Private. 28 Sep. 1785. 640 acres.
Coventon, William. N.C. Subaltern. 13 Jun. 1785. 2560 acres to heir.
Coventry, John. N.Y. Mate in General Hospital. 31 May 1794. 1800 acres.
Coverley, Thomas. Va. Lieutenant. 22 Jul. 1783. 2000 acres.
Coverley, Thomas. Va. Lieutenant. 22 Jul. 1783. 1110 2/3 acres.
Coverley, Thomas. Va. Lieutenant. 11 Aug. 1807. 370 acres.
Covey, Drury. Va. Sergeant. 6 Apr. 1787. 100 acres.
Covil, Ephraim. Mass. Sergeant. 18 May 1831. 200 acres to heirs.
Covington, Francis. Ga. ———. 17 May 1784. ———.
Cowan, Edward. Ga. Lieutenant. 5 Sep. 1783. 400 acres.
Cowan, Edward. Ga. Captain. 17 May 1784. ———.
Cowan, Edward. N.C. Private. 7 Dec. 1797. 640 acres to heirs.
Cowan, John. Va.-Ind. Private. 108 acres.
Cowan, Robert. N.C. Sergeant. 29 Nov. 1809. 428 acres.
Coward, Absalom. N.C. Private. 30 Sep. 1785. 640 acres to heirs.
Cowden, Robert. Ga. ———. 17 May 1784. ———.
Cowdrey, Benjamin. N. Y. Corporal. 8 Jul. 1790. 600 acres.
Cowell, Butler. N.C. Ensign. 21 Jul. 1820. 2560 acres to heirs.
Cowen, Joseph. N.C. Private. 10 Dec. 1788. 228 acres.
Cowens, James. N.C. Private. 30 Sep. 1785. 640 acres to heirs.
Cowens, William. Ga. Refugee. 15 Mar. 1784. 250 acres.
Cowgill, John. Va. Private. 20 Feb. 1784. 100 acres.
Cowhawk, James. Pa. Private. 12 Jan. 1796. 200 acres to Joseph Jeffries, assignee.
Cowhawk, James. Pa. Private. ———. 200 acres.
Cowherd, Francis. Va. Captain. 11 Mar. 1783. 4000 acres.
Cowherd, Francis. Va. Captain. 26 Feb. 1784. 666 2/3 acres.
Cowherd, Francis. Va. Captain. 25 May 1808. 722 acres.
Cowherd, Francis. Va. Captain. 25 May 1808. 722 acres.
Cowherd, James. Va. Sergeant. 7 Aug. 1783. 200 acres.
Cowherd, James. Va. Sergeant. 11 Aug. 1834. 200 acres.
Cowin, John. N.C. Sergeant. 6 Dec. 1797. 1000 acres to heirs.
Cowley, Caleb. Ga. Minute Man. 1784. ———.
Cowley, Richard. Ga. Minuet Man. 1784. ———.
Cowne, Augustine. Va. Lieutenant. 6 Mar. 1783. 2666 2/3 acres.
Cowne, Robert. Va. Captain Lieutenant. 6 Mar. 1783. 4000 acres.
Cowper, Edward. Va. Pilot. 23 Mar. 1838. 1777 7/9 acres.
Cowper, Edward. Va. Pilot. 23 Mar. 1838. 888 8/9 acres.
Cowper, John. Va. Captain. 25 Mar. 1838. 1777 7/9 acres.
Cowper, John. Va. Captain. 25 Mar. 1838. 3555 5/9 acres.
Cox, Benjamin. Ga. Minute Man. ———. 287 1/2 acres.
Cox, Caleb. Ga. ———. 17 May 1784. ———.
Cox, Charles. N. Y. Private. 3 Jul. 1790. 600 acres.
Cox, Charles. N.C. Private. 2 Feb. 1786. 640 acres.
Cox, Edward. N.C. Private. 29 Sep. 1784. 640 acres to John Cox, heir.
Cox, Edward. N.C. Private. 24 Nov. 1797. 640 acres to heirs.
Cox, Edward. N.C. Musician. 16 Aug. 1821. 1000 acres.
Cox, George. N.C. Private. 15 Feb. 1797. 640 acres to heirs.
Cox, Jesse. N.C. Private. 24 Nov. 1797. 274 acres.

Cox, John. Ga. ———. 26 May 1784. 287 1/2 acres.
Cox, John. Md. Private. ———. 50 acres.
Cox, John. N. Y. Private. 8 Jul. 1790. 600 acres.
Cox, John. N.Y. ———. 13 Sep. 1790. 500 acres to heirs.
Cox, John. Va. Private. 14 Oct. 1820. 100 acres.
Cox, John. Va. Carpenter. 15 Aug. 1834. 100 acres.
Cox, John. Va. Captain. 26 Mar. 1838. 3833 1/3 acres.
Cox, John. Va. Captain. 26 Mar. 1838. 1916 1/3 acres.
Cox, John. Va. Carpenter. 29 Jul. 1839. 1925 acres.
Cox, John. Va. Carpenter. 17 Sep. 1840. 641 2/3 acres.
Cox, John. Va. Carpenter. 12 Nov. 1840. 641 2/3 acres.
Cox, Joseph. N.C. Private. 18 Dec. 1804. 640 acres to heirs.
Cox, Joseph. Pa. Lieutenant. 17 Jan. 1789. 200 acres.
Cox, Joshua. Md. Private. ———. 50 acres.
Cox, Presley. Va. Private. 4 Nov. 1783. 100 acres.
Cox, Radford. Va. Corporal. 26 May 1783. 200 acres.
Cox, Richard. Va.-Ind. Private. 108 acres.
Cox, Robert. N. Y. Private. 8 Jul. 1790. 500 acres.
Cox, Samuel. Va. Private. 24 Feb. 1784. 100 acres.
Cox, Symon. N. Y. Private. 3 Jul. 1790. 600 acres.
Cox, Thomas. N.C. Private. 29 Sep. 1784. 274 acres.
Cox, Thomas. N.C. Private. 3 Feb. 1785. 640 acres.
Cox, William. Md. Private. ———. 50 acres.
Cox, William. N.C. Private. 10 Aug. 1785. 228 acres.
Cox, William. N.C. Private. 15 Mar. 1813. 640 acres to heirs.
Cox, William. Va. Sergeant. 12 Jul. 1783. 200 acres.
Cox, William. Va. Private. 25 Aug. 1783. 200 acres.
Coxe, John. Pa. Private. 11 Sep. 1787. 200 acres.
Coxe, Joseph. Pa. Lieutenant. 17 Jan. 1789. 200 acres.
Coxor, William. Va. Fifer. 23 Jun. 1783. 200 acres.
Coyle, Mark. Pa. Private. 16 Feb. 1803. 200 acres.
Coyle, Michael. Md. Private. ———. 50 acres.
Cozart, David. N.C. Private. 21 Apr. 1784. 274 acres.
Cozens, Matthew. N. Y. Private. 8 Jul. 1790. 600 acres.
Cozer, Jacob. Va.-Ind. Private. 108 acres. [Coger].
Cozer, Peter. Va.-Ind. Private. 108 acres. [Coger].
Crab, Hillery. N.C. Private. 23 Apr. 1785. 640 acres to heirs.
Crabb, Abijah. N. Y. Matross. 6 Jul. 1790. 600 acres.
Crabb, Benjamin. N.C. Private. 12 Dec. 1785. 274 acres.
Crabb, Samuel. Ga. ———. 17 May 1784. ———.
Craben, Charles. N.C. Private. 8 Aug. 1821. 640 acres.
Crabtree, Campbell. N.C. Private. 17 Dec. 1796. 320 acres.
Crabtree, John. N.C. Private. 18 May 1784. 640 acres.
Craddock, Henry. Va. Sergeant. 19 Mar. 1783. 200 acres.
Craddock, John. N.C. Captain. 20 Apr. 1784. 3840 acres.
Craddock, Robert. Va. Lieutenant. 19 Mar. 1783. 2666 2/3 acres.
Craddock, Robert. Va. Captain. 8 Feb. 1808. 555 acres.
Craddock, Shadrack. N.C. Private. 24 Dec. 1796. 228 acres.
Crady, David. Md. Fifer. ———. 50 acres.
Crafford, Charles. Va. Private. 23 Jun. 1783. 200 acres.
Craft, James. N.C. Private. 5 Sep. 1821. 228 acres to heirs.
Craft, Nathaniel. N. Y. Private. 8 Jul. 1790. 600 acres.
Craft, Stephen. N.C. Private. 5 Sep. 1821. 228 acres to heirs.
Crafton, Richard. Va. Private. 29 Jun. 1810. 100 acres.
Crafts, Henry. N. Y. Matross. 9 Jul. 1790. 500 acres.

Cragan, Dennis. Md. Private. ———. 50 acres.
Craicke, Archibald. N.C. Private. 8 Nov. 1784. 640 acres to heir.
Craig, George. N.C. Private. 21 Aug. 1820. 640 acres.
Craig, Gerard. Pa. Private. 12 Sep. 1787. 200 acres.
Craig, Gerard. Pa. Private. 12 Sep. 1787. 200 acres.
Craig, Gerrard. N.C. Private. 5 Sep. 1821. 640 acres.
Craig, Isaac. Pa. Major. 28 Feb. 1794. 300 acres.
Craig, Isaac. Pa. Major. 28 Aug. 1787. 300 acres.
Craig, Isaac. Pa. Major. 28 Aug. 1787. 300 acres.
Craig, James. Md. Surgeon General. ———. 200 acres.
Craig, James. N.C. Private. 17 Dec. 1785. 640 acres to heirs.
Craig, James. Va. Captain. 5 Dec. 1783. 4000 acres.
Craig, James. Va. Captain. 12 Jul. 1810. 1166 acres.
Craig, John. Md. Private. ———. 50 acres.
Craig, John. Md. Private. ———. 50 acres.
Craig, John. N.Y. ———. 13 Sep. 1790. 500 acres to heirs.
Craig, John. N.Y. ———. 13 Sep. 1790. 500 acres to heirs.
Craig, John. Pa. Captain. ———. 500 acres.
Craig, John. Va. Private. 29 Oct. 1784. 100 acres.
Craig, Matthew. Pa. Private. 28 Nov. 1786. 200 acres.
Craig, Samuel. Pa. Captain. ———. 500 acres.
Craig, Thomas. Md. Sergeant. ———. 50 acres.
Craig, Thomas. Pa. Colonel. 16 Jan. 1787. 500 acres to John Nicholson, assignee.
Craig, Thomas. Pa. Colonel. 16 Jan. 1787. 500 acres.
Craig, Thomas. Va. Private. 23 Jun. 1783. 200 acres.
Craige, John. N.C. Private. 30 Sep. 1785. 640 acres to heirs.
Craigge, Archibald. N.C. Private. 20 Apr. 1784. 640 acres to heir.
Craigs, George. Md. Private. ———. 50 acres.
Craik, James. Va. Surgeon. 5 Aug. 1831. 3000 acres.
Craik, James. Va. Surgeon. 5 Aug. 1831. 1000 acres.
Craik, James. Va. Surgeon. 5 Aug. 1831. 1000 acres.
Craik, James. Va. Surgeon. 5 Aug. 1831. 1000 acres.
Craile, William. Md. Private. ———. 50 acres.
Crain, James. Va. Surgeon. 23 Nov. 1868. 1838 2/3 acres.
Crain, Lewis. Ga. Soldier. 13 Sep. 1784. 287 1/2 acres.
Crain, Spencer. Ga. ———. 27 Sep. 1784. ———.
Crain, Thomas. N.C. Private. 30 Sep. 1785. 640 acres to heirs.
Craine, Henry. Md. Private. ———. 50 acres.
Craine, James. Va. Captain. 21 Jun. 1808. 1500 acres.
Cralle, Rodham K. Va. Private. 2 May 1785. 100 acres.
Cramer, Andrew. Pa. Dragoon. 24 Oct. 1786. 200 acres.
Cramer, Jacob. Pa. ———. 200 acres. 12 July 1787 to James Moore, assignee.
Cramer, Jacob. Pa. ———. ———. 200 acres.
Cramer, Jacob. Pa. Lieutenant. 12 Jul. 1787. 200 acres.
Cramer, Jesse. Pa. ———. ———. 200 acres.
Crampshier, D. John. N. Y. Paymaster. 24 Aug. 1790. 1500 acres.
Crandle, Godfrey. N. Y. Private. 8 Jul. 1790. 600 acres.
Crane, Abijah. Me. Private. 12 May 1835. 200 acres. Fayette.
Crane, Joshua. Mass. Private. 20 Dec. 1833. 200 acres to widow Mary Fisher.
Crank, John. N.C. Private. 14 Dec. 1797. 228 acres.
Crantz, Mark. N. Y. Private. 8 Jul. 1790. 600 acres.
Crary, James. Conn. Sufferer. Danbury. 4.14.8.
Crasbie, Jesse. Md. Private. ———. 50 acres.
Crasbury, James. Md. Private. ———. 50 acres.
Craslin, Samuel. S.C. Soldier. 21 Jan. 1785. 200 acres.

Cratton, William. Va. Private. 5 Jun. 1783. 200 acres.
Cratty, Andrew. Pa. Private. 31 Oct. 1786. 200 acres.
Craven, James. N.C. Lieutenant. 28 Sep. 1785. 1242 acres.
Craven, Peter. N.C. Private. 14 Dec. 1796. 274 acres.
Crawford, Anderson. Ga. ———. 17 Feb. 1784. 250 acres.
Crawford, Andrew. Ga. ———. 17 Feb. 1784. 250 acres.
Crawford, Andrew. Pa. Private. ———. 200 acres.
Crawford, Charles. Ga. ———. 1784. 250 acres.
Crawford, David. Ga. Soldier. 10 Jun. 1784. 230 acres to heir John Crawford of Albemarle Co., Va.
Crawford, David. Va. Private. 25 Jun. 1783. 100 acres.
Crawford, Edward. Pa. Lieutenant. 21 Aug.1787. 200 acres.
Crawford, Edward. Pa. Lieutenant. 21 Aug. 1787. 200 acres.
Crawford, Jacob. Md. Lieutenant. ———. 200 acres.
Crawford, James. Ga. ———. 17 May 1784. ———.
Crawford, James. Md. Private. ———. 50 acres.
Crawford, John. Ga. ———. 20 Feb. 1784. 250 acres.
Crawford, John. Ga. Refugee. 15 Sep. 1784. 287 1/2 acres.
Crawford, John. N.C. Private. 23 Apr. 1785. 640 acres to heirs.
Crawford, John. Pa. Lieutenant. 13 Nov. 1784. 200 acres.
Crawford, John. Pa. Lieutenant. 13 Nov. 1786. 200 acres.
Crawford, John. Va. Lieutenant. 9 Apr. 1783. 2666 2/3 acres.
Crawford, John. Va. Sergeant. 20 Jun. 1783. 200 acres.
Crawford, John. Va. Private. 23 Jun. 1783. 100 acres.
Crawford, John. Va. Lieutenant. 20 Feb. 1784. 444 acres.
Crawford, John. Va. Lieutenant. 17 Apr. 1807. 444 2/3 acres.
Crawford, Malachi. N.C. Private. 30 Sep. 1785. 640 acres.
Crawford, Nathan. Ga. ———. 25 May 1784. 287 1/2 acres.
Crawford, Nehemiah. Va. Private. 27 May 1793. 100 acres.
Crawford, Patrick. Pa. Private. ———. 200 acres.
Crawford, Peter. Ga. ———. 3 Oct. 1785. 690 acres.
Crawford, Robert. Va. Private. 23 Jun. 1783. 200 acres.
Crawford, Samuel. Ga. ———. ———. 287 1/2 acres.
Crawford, Samuel. N. Y. ———. 16 Sep. 1802. 500 acres.
Crawford, Samuel. Pa. Private. 25 Feb. 1797. 200 acres to Robert Porterfield, assignee.
Crawford, Strother. Ga. ———. 26 May 1784. 230 acres.
Crawford, Thomas. Va. Private. 29 Jun. 1835. 100 acres.
Crawford, William. Pa. Captain. 4 Oct. 1786. 500 acres.
Crawford, William. Va. Colonel. 17 Jun. 1783. 6666 2/3 acres.
Crawford, William. Va. Colonel. 18 Dec. 1838. 2037 acres.
Crawford, William. Va. Colonel. 26 Aug. 1843. 2037 acres.
Crawley, David. N.C. Sergeant. 17 Feb. 1824. 1000 acres.
Crawley, James. Va. Private. 4 Aug. 1783. 100 acres.
Crawley, Samuel. Va. ———. 7 Feb. 1834. 500 acres.
Crawley, Samuel. Va. Captain. 1 Aug. 1832. 1000 acres.
Crawley, Samuel. Va. ———. 17 Aug. 1832. 500 acres.
Crawley, Samuel. Va. Captain. 27 May 1831. 2000 acres.
Crawley, William. N.C. ———. 14 Jun. 1785. 640 acres to heir.
Crawson, Samuel. N. Y. Private. 7 Jul. 1790. 600 acres.
Craze, Noah. Va.-Ind. Private. 108 acres.
Creamer, William. Va. Private. 21 Feb. 1784. 100 acres.
Creaton, John. Pa. Private. ———. 200 acres.
Crediford, Abner. Me. ———. 31 Jul. 1835. 200 acres to widow Ruth Crediford.

Creech, Richard. Me. Private. 5 Jun. 1835. 200 acres to widow Elizabeth Creech. Leeds.

Creed, Thomas. Va. Sergeant. 19 Sep. 1791. 466 2/3 acres.

Creef, Willoughby. N.C. Private. 2 Dec. 1785. 640 acres to heirs.

Creekman, Matthew. N.C. Private. 21 Dec. 1803. 640 acres.

Creekman, William. Va. Private. 1 Apr. 1783. 100 acres.

Creekmur, William. Va. Private. 3 Feb. 1812. 100 acres.

Creeley, Peter. N. Y. Matross. 9 Jul. 1790. 600 acres.

Creighton, Daniel. Va. Private. 5 Mar. 1833. 100 acres.

Crekenboom, John. N. Y. Private. 8 Jul. 1790. 600 acres.

Cremer, George. Pa. Private. 18 Jul. 1787. 200 acres to Caspar Snyder, assignee.

Crenshaw, Charles. Ga. ———. 17 May 1784. ———.

Crenshaw, Nathaniel. Va. Private. 6 Apr. 1838. 200 acres.

Cresey, Benjamin. Me. ———. 15 Aug. 1836. 200 acres. Falmouth.

Creswell, Samuel. Ga. Surgeon. 17 May 1784. ———.

Crether, Jermeiah. N.C. Private. 31 Mar. 1810. 640 acres to heirs.

Creveston, Jacob. Pa. Private. 7 Oct. 1802. 200 acres.

Crew, John. Va. Lieutenant. 30 Dec. 1851. 2000 acres.

Crew, John. Va. Lieutenant. 30 Dec. 1851. 2000 acres.

Crew, John. Va. Lieutenant. 21 Sep. 1855. 2000 acres.

Crews, Edward. Va. Private. 29 Jun. 1784. 100 acres.

Crews, Joseph. Va. Private. 29 Oct. 1785. 200 acres.

Criag, William. Va. Private. 23 Jun. 1783. 200 acres.

Cribbs [alias Crips], John. Pa. Private. 3 Aug. 1787. 200 acres.

Cribbs, Thomas. Ga. ———. 20 Feb. 1784. 250 acres.

Cridor, Jacob. N.C. Noncommisioned Officer. 12 Dec. 1785. 1000 acres.

Crippin, William. Va. Private. 15 Jun. 1807. 100 acres.

Crispus, James. Ga. ———. 17 May 1784. ———.

Crissip, James. Ga. Citizen. 6 Apr. 1785. 287 1/2 acres.

Cristian, William. N.C. Private. 9 Feb. 1796. 640 acres to heirs.

Cristie, William. Va. Surgeon. 18 Dec. 1833. 6000 acres.

Criswell, David. Ga. ———. 6 Dec. 1785. 287 1/2 acres.

Critchett, John. Conn. Sufferer. New London. 6.6.5 1/2.

Crittenden, John. Ga. ———. 24 Feb. 1784. 250 acres.

Crittenden, John. Va. Lieutenant. 21 Jun. 1783. 2666 2/3 acres.

Crittenden, John. Va. Lieutenant. 28 Jul. 1810. 148 acres.

Crittenden, William. Va. Private. 19 Nov. 1783. 100 acres.

Crocker, John. Conn. Sufferer. New London. 34.13.2.

Crocket, Samuel. Ga. ———. 22 Jul. 1784. 287 1/2 acres.

Crockett, Anthony. Va. Lieutenant. 9 Aug. 1834. 2666 2/3 acres.

Crockett, Joseph. Va. Lieutenant Colonel. 7 Mar. 1783. 6666 2/3 acres.

Crockett, Joseph. Va. Major. 28 Dec. 1809. 2443 2/3 acres.

Crockett, Samuel. Me. ———. 22 Jun. 1835. 200 acres. Cape Elizabeth.

Crockley, Allen. N.C. Private. 19 Jan. 1786. 640 acres.

Croft, Jesse Thorney. Pa. Private. 200 acres. 10 Sep. 1789.

Crogham, William. Va. Major. 13 Sep. 1808. 740 acres.

Croghan, William. Va. Major. 29 Nov. 1782. 5333 2/3 acres.

Croghan, William. Va. Major. 21 Nov. 1783. 888 2/3 acres.

Croghan, William. Va. ———. 18 Nov. 1783. 6420 acres.

Croker, Abraham. N.C. Private. 19 Jan. 1786. 274 acres.

Croker, William. Ga. Private. 17 May 1784. 230 acres.

Croker, William. Va. Drum Major. 3 May 1783. 400 acres.

Cromleer, Charles. Va. Private. 28 Apr. 1783. 200 acres.

Cromley, Anthony. Ga. ———. 17 May 1784. ———.

Cromlin, Francis. N.C. Private. 13 Dec. 1796. 320 acres.

Cromwell, Rolen. N.C. Private. 2 Feb. 1786. 274 acres.

Cron, Williferd. N.C. Private. 24 Dec. 1796. 228 acres.

Cronburger, Christopher. Ga. Refugee. 1784. 250 acres [to widow Barbara Cronburger.

Cronck, Garret. N. Y. Private. 13 Sep. 1790. 600 acres.

Cronck, John. N. Y. Private. 7 Jul. 1790. 600 acres.

Cronin, Patrick. N. Y. Ensign. 9 Jul. 1790. 1150 acres.

Cronister, James. N.C. Private. 25 Nov. 1808. 640 acres.

Cronister, William. N.C. Private. 2 Aug. 1784. 640 acres.

Cronk, Garret. Va. Private. 2 Feb. 1819. 100 acres.

Crook, Henry. Md. Private. ———. 50 acres.

Crook, Henry. Va. Private. 8 Aug. 1800. 100 acres.

Crook, Hillery. N.C. Private. 30 Sep. 1785. 640 acres to heirs.

Crook, Joseph. Va. Sergeant. 5 May 1785. 200 acres.

Crook, William. Ga. Minute Man. 26 May 1784. 287 1/2 acres.

Crook, William. N.C. Corporal. 30 Sep. 1785. 1000 acres to heirs.

Crooker, Thomas. N.C. Private. 2 Feb. 1786. 274 acres.

Cropper, James. Va. Private. 7 May 1785. 200 acres.

Cropper, James. Va. Private. 30 Dec. 1808. 60 acres.

Cropper, John. Va. Lieutenant Colonel Commandant. 21 Jun. 1783. 6666 2/3 acres.

Cropper, John. Va. Lieutenant Colonel Commandant. 18 Nov. 1807. 2222 acres.

Cropper, John. Va. Carpenter. 26 Feb. 1831. 2666 2/3 acres.

Crosby, Charles. Me. ———. 27 Jun. 1839. 200 acres to widow Mary Crosby. Garland.

Crosby, Jesse. Va. Private. 12 Jun. 1819. 200 acres.

Crosby, John. Md. Private. ———. 50 acres.

Crosby, Simon. Mass. Private. 4 Mar. 1840. 200 acres to heirs.

Crosby, William. Ga. Minute Man. 17 May 1784. ———.

Crosby, William. N.C. Private. 19 May 1784. 640 acres.

Crosby, William. Va. Private. 29 Dec. 1784. 100 acres.

Crosley, William. Va.-Ind. Private. 108 acres.

Cross, Anthony. N.C. Private. 9 Sep. 1785. 640 acres to heirs.

Cross, Caleb. N.C. Private. 6 Dec. 1797. 640 acres to heirs.

Cross, Danel. Pa. Private. 4 Jan. 1786. 200 acres to Jesse Hunt, assignee.

Cross, Frederick. N.C. Private. 30 Sep. 1785. 640 acres to heirs.

Cross, Joel. N.C. Private. 30 Sep. 1785. 640 acres to heirs.

Cross, John. Va. Private. 21 Dec. 1784. 200 acres.

Cross, Joseph. Md. Lieutenant. ———. 200 acres.

Cross, Martin. N.C. Drum Major. 30 Apr. 1784. 607 acres.

Cross, Patrick. Pa. Private. 19 Sep. 1787. 200 acres.

Cross, Randall. N.C. Private. 30 Sep. 1785. 640 acres to heirs.

Cross, Richard. Va. Private. 28 Sep. 1786. 100 acres.

Cross, Samuel. Va. Sergeant. 27 May 1783. 200 acres.

Cross, Silus. N.C. Private. 30 Sep. 1785. 640 acres to heirs.

Crossen, Gustavus. Va. Private. 28 Dec. 1787. 100 acres.

Crossey, Anthony. N.C. Private. 9 Feb. 1796. 640 acres to heirs.

Crossin, John. Pa. Private. 3 Nov. 1788. 200 acres.

Crossley, George. S.C. ———. 5 Feb. 1787. 200 acres.

Crossley, Jesse. Pa. Private. 19 Feb. 1797. 200 acres.

Crossley, Jesse. Pa. Lieutenant. 19 Feb. 1787. 200 acres.

Crossman, John. Conn. Sufferer. Fairfield. 5.12.2.

Crosson, Hanson. Va. Private. 25 Apr. 1785. 100 acres.

Crosstick, Edward. Va. Private. 10 Jun. 1783. 100 acres.

Crotty, Thomas. Pa. Private. 26 Sep. 1787. 200 acres.

Crouch, Charles. Md. Sergeant. ———. 50 acres.

Crouch, Joseph. Md. Private. ———. 50 acres.

Crouch, Robert. Md. Private. ———. 50 acres.

Crouch, Robert. Va. Trumpeter. 11 Jun. 1819. 200 acres.

Crouch, William. Va. Private. 15 Jan. 1808. 100 acres.

Crouse, Elbert. N. Y. Private. 8 Jul. 1790. 600 acres.

Crow, Adam. Md. Private. ———. 50 acres.

Crow, Christian. Pa. ———. 1 Jul. 1789. 200 acres to John Nicholson, assignee.

Crow, George. Pa. Private. 27 Mar. 1824. 200 acres.

Crow, Isham. Va. Private. 9 Nov. 1868. 100 acres.

Crow, Thomas. S.C. ———. 29 Jun. 1793. 200 acres.

Crow, William. N.C. Private. 3 Feb. 1785. 640 acres.

Crow, William. N.C. Private. 15 Feb. 1797. 228 acres.

Crow, William. S.C. ———. 29 Jun. 1793. 200 acres to Thomas Crown, heir at law.

Crowan, Henry. Pa. Private. 5 Mar. 1787. 200 acres.

Crowder, Matthew. Va. Private. 15 Dec. 1796. 100 acres.

Crowder, Robert. Va. Seaman. 28 Nov. 1783. 100 acres.

Crowfeet, Matthew. Conn. Sufferer. Danbury. 3.15.4.

Crowfeet, Rebecca. Conn. Sufferer. Danbury. 1.11.4.

Crowfeet, Seth. Conn. Sufferer. Danbury. 3.11.8.

Crowley, Charles. S.C. Captain. 21 Jan. 1785. 450 acres.

Crowley, Darby. Md. Private. ———. 50 acres.

Crowley, David. Pa. Private. 18 Oct. 1786. 200 acres.

Crowley, David. Va. Private. 16 Jun. 1783. 100 acres.

Crowley, James. Conn. Sufferer. Norwalk. 3.14.7.

Crowley, Thomas. Pa. Private. 3 Jan. 1787. 200 acres.

Croxall, Charles. Md. Captain. ———. 200 acres.

Croxford, John. Me. ———. 20 Apr. 1835. 200 acres to widow Wilmot Croxford. Newburgh.

Croxton, Carter. Va. Sergeant. 4 Jan. 1784. 200 acres.

Croxton, John. Va. Private. 27 Aug. 1784. 100 acres.

Croxton, John. Va. Private. 24 Mar. 1840. 100 acres.

Croxton, Richard. Va. Private. 4 Aug. 1784. 100 acres.

Crozier, Arthur. N.C. Private. 9 Feb. 1796. 640 acres to heirs.

Crozier, James. Md. Private. ———. 50 acres.

Crozier, John. Md. Sergeant. ———. 50 acres.

Crudders, William. Ga. Minute Man. 17 May 1784. ———.

Cruddy, William. Ga. Minute Man. 19 Jul. 1784. 287 1/2 acres.

Cruder, Jacob. N.C. Noncommissioned Officer. 17 Dec. 1785. 428 acres.

Cruidson, Benjamin. Va. Private. 7 Dec. 1785. 200 acres.

Cruise, Thomas. Ga. ———. 17 May 1784. ———.

Cruise, William. N.C. Private. 20 May 1784. 640 acres.

Crule, John. Va. Lieutenant. 19 Mar. 1783. 2666 2/3 acres.

Crumb, Christopher. N. Y. Private. 7 Jul. 1790. 500 acres.

Crumby, Charles. Ga. Citizen. 5 Sep. 1785. 287 1/2 acres.

Crumley, Anthony. Ga. ———. ———. 250 acres.

Crumm, Richard. N. Y. Matross. 9 Jul. 1790. 600 acres.

Crummy, Andrew. Md. Private. ———. 50 acres.

Crump, Abner. Va. Captain. 1 May 1783. 4000 acres.

Crump, Abraham. N.C. Private. 28 Sep. 1785. 228 acres.

Crump, Benjamin. Va. Sergeant. 30 Apr. 1783. 400 acres.

Crump, Jesse. Va. Sergeant. 26 May 1783. 200 acres.

Crump, John. Va. Private. 14 Oct. 1811. 100 acres.
Crump, Richard. Va. Captain. 20 Jan. 1834. 3000 acres.
Crump, Richard. Va. Captain. 20 Jan. 1834. 1000 acres.
Crump, Richard. Va. Captain. 16 Sep. 1850. 4000 acres.
Crump, Thomas. Va. Private. 4 Apr. 1783. 100 acre.
Crump, Willian. Va.-Ind. Sergeant. 216 acres.
Crunden, Ralph Edward. Va. Surgeon's Mate. 16 Dec. 1834. 4000 acres.
Cruse, Johnson. N.C. Private. 10 Aug. 1785. 640 acres to heir.
Cruswell, Samuel. Va. Private. 23 Jun. 1783. 200 acres.
Crutcher, Anthony. N.C. Lieutenant. 27 Nov. 1783. 2560 acres.
Crutchfield, John. Ga. ———. 250 acres. ———.
Crutchfield, John. Va. Private. 24 Feb. 1826. 100 acres.
Crutchfield, Stapleton. Va. Private. 12 Jun. 1783. 100 acres.
Crute, John. Va. Lieutenant. 30 Apr. 1808. 407 acres.
Cruthers, James. N.C. Private. 26 Apr. 1784. 274 acres.
Cruthers, Thomas. N.C. Private. 27 Apr. 1784. 274 acres.
Cruze, Redman. Va. Private. 10 Dec. 1783. 100 acres.
Cucksey, William. Ga. Minute Man. 28 Apr. 1785. ———.
Cuffman, John. N.Y. ———. 13 Sep. 1790. 500 acres to heirs.
Culbertson, James. Va. Captain. 6 Nov. 1783. 4000 acres.
Culbertson, James. Va. Captain. 18 Dec. 1800. 666 2/3 acres.
Culbreath, Archibald. N.C. Private. 10 Dec. 1788. 640 acres to heirs.
Culbreath, James. Ga. Refugee. 20 Feb. 1784. 250 acres.
Culbreath, John. Ga. Soldier. 20 Feb. 1784. 250 acres.
Culbreath, Peter. Ga. ———. 17 May 1784. ———.
Culbreth, Daniel, Jr. N.C. Private. 9 Feb. 1796. 640 acres.
Culbreth, Daniel, Sr. N.C. Private. 9 Feb. 1796. 640 acres.
Cull, Hugh. Pa. ———. 26 Mar. 1807. 200 acres.
Cull, Hugh. Pa. Private. 9 Mar. 1795. 200 acres to John Nicholson, assignee.
Cullamine, Joseph. Md. Private. ———. 50 acres.
Cullars, Henry. Ga. Minute Man. 16 Dec. 1784. 287 1/2 acres.
Cullickan, John. Va. Private. 20 Jun. 1785. 200 acres.
Cullifor, James. N.C. Private. 13 Dec. 1796. 640 acres to heirs.
Cullinver [?], Sampson. N.C. Private. 30 Sep. 1785. 274 acres.
Cullum, Israel. N.C. Private. 30 Mar. 1785. 640 acres.
Culpeper, Joseph. S.C. ———. 6 Sep. 1790. 200 acres.
Culpepper, Joseph. Ga. Refugee. ———. 575 acres.
Culpepper, Malachi. Ga. ———. 17 May 1784. ———.
Culver, James. Conn. Sufferer. New London. 8.9.1.
Culver, Joannah. Conn. Sufferer. New London. 10.15.0.
Culver, Stephen. Conn. Sufferer. New London. 3.16.0.
Cumberford, Isaac. Va. Private. 30 Nov. 1785. 100 acres.
Cumbo, Daniel. Va. Private. 20 Jun. 1783. 100 acres.
Cumming, Benjamin. N.C. Private. 9 Sep. 1820. 640 acres to heirs.
Cummings, Edward. Pa. Private. ———. 200 acres.
Cummings, John. Pa. Lieutenant. 30 Sep. 1787. 200 acres.
Cummings, Matthew. Va. Sergeant. 25 Jan. 1822. 200 acres.
Cummings, Matthew. Va. Sergeant. 25 Jan. 1822. 200 acres.
Cummings, Samuel. Mass. Private. 10 Sep. 1834. 200 acres.
Cummings, Thomas F. Me. Lieutenant. 18 Feb. 1839. 600 acres to widow Mary Cummings. Castine.
Cummins, Alexander. Va. Captain. 25 Apr. 1797. 4000 acres.
Cummins, Cornelius. N. Y. Private. 7 Jul. 1790. 600 acres.
Cummins, Ebenezer. N. Y. Private. 8 Jul. 1790. 600 acres.

Cummins, Edmund. N.C. Private. 26 May 1784. 640 acres.
Cummins, George. N.C. Sergeant. 11 Jan. 1822. 377 acres to heirs.
Cummins, George. Va. Private. 9 Feb. 1785. 100 acres.
Cummins, John. N.C. Private. 15 Nov. 1793. 640 acres to heirs.
Cummins, John. Pa. Lieutenant. 30 Sep. 1787. 200 acres.
Cummins, John. Pa. ———. 7 Mar. 1807. 200 acres.
Cummins, Shardrack. N.C. Private. 19 May 1784. 640 acres.
Cummins, William. Md. Private. ———. 50 acres.
Cumpton, Matthias. N. Y. Matross. 9 Jul. 1790. 600 acres.
Cunias, John. Pa. Private. 12 Jul. 1787. 200 acres.
Cunningham, Alexander. Pa. Private. 5 Dec. 1786. 200 acres.
Cunningham, Archibald. N. Y. Private. 8 Jul. 1790. 600 acres.
Cunningham, Barney. N.C. Private. 7 Dec. 1796. 640 acres.
Cunningham, Cornelius. Conn. Sufferer. New/East Haven. 20.11.0.
Cunningham, Cornelius. Conn. Sufferer. New London. 62.14.7 1/4.
Cunningham, David. Pa. Private. 30 Mar. 1787. 200 acres to Jonathan Hoge, assignee.
Cunningham, Henry. N. Y. Lieutenant. 9 Jul. 1790. 1200 acres.
Cunningham, James. N.C. Private. 27 Jul. 1785. 640 acres.
Cunningham, James. Va. Private. 23 Jun. 1783. 200 acres.
Cunningham, James. Va. Lieutenant. 23 Dec. 1841. 1000 acres.
Cunningham, James. Va. Lieutenant. 23 Dec. 1841. 3000 acres.
Cunningham, James. Conn. Sufferer. Greenwich. 12.0.0.
Cunningham, James, Jr. Ga. ———. 1784. 287 1/2 acres.
Cunningham, James, Sr. Ga. ———. 1784. 287 1/2 acres.
Cunningham, John. Ga. Colonel. 28 Feb. 1784. 900 acres.
Cunningham, John. N. Y. Bombardier. 9 Jul. 1790. 600 acres.
Cunningham, John. N.C. Private. 6 Sep. 1821. 640 acres.
Cunningham, Lewis. Md. Private. ———. 50 acres.
Cunningham, Matthew. Pa. ———. 25 Oct. 1786. 200 acres.
Cunningham, Nathaniel. Va. Sergeant. 11 Aug. 1783. 200 acres.
Cunningham, Patrick. Ga. ———. 25 May 1784. 287 1/2 acres.
Cunningham, Peter. Md. Private. ———. 50 acres.
Cunningham, Robert. Pa. ———. ———. 200 acres.
Cunningham, Samuel. Me. Private. 15 Jun. 1835. 200 acres to widow Sarah Cunningham. Newcastle.
Cunningham, William. Ga. Soldier. 7 Jun. 1785. 230 acres to heirs.
Cunningham, William. Va. Major. 10 Jun. 1783. 5333 1/3 acres.
Cunningham, William. Va. Major. 17 Apr. 1809. 500 acres.
Cunningham, William. Va. Major. 17 Apr. 1809. 200 acres.
Cunningham, William. Va. Major. 17 Apr. 1809. 200 acres.
Cunningham, William. Va. Major. 17 Apr. 1809. 150 acres.
Cunningham, William. Va. Major. 17 Apr. 1809. 100 acres.
Cunningham, William. Va. Major. 17 Apr. 1809. 100 acres.
Cunningham, William. Va. Major. 17 Apr. 1809. 100 acres.
Cunningham, William. Va. Major. 17 Apr. 1809. 100 acres.
Cunningham, William. Va. Major. 17 Apr. 1809. 100 acres.
Cunningham, William. Va. Major. 17 Arp. 1809. 100 acres.
Cunningham, William. Va. Major. 17 Apr. 1809. 124 acres.
Cunningham, William. Va. Major. 17 Apr. 1809. 500 acres.
Cunningham, William. Va. Major. 17 Apr. 1809. 1000 acres.
Cunningham, William. Va. Major. 17 Apr. 1809. 424 acres.
Cunningham, William. Va. Lieutenant. 19 Jan. 1831. 800 acres.
Cunningham, William. Va. Lieutenant. 19 Jan. 1831. 800 acres.

Cunningham, William. Va. Lieutenant. 19 Jan. 1831. 800 acres.
Cunningham, William. Va. Lieutenant. 19 Jan. 1831. 800 acres.
Cunningham, William. Va. Lieutenant. 19 Jan. 1831. 800 acres.
Cup, Michael. Ga. Minute Man. 26 Jul. 1784. 287 1/2 acres.
Curbon, James. N.C. Private. 22 Dec. 1796. 274 acres.
Curbon, James. N.C. Private. 29 Jul. 1820. 366 acres to heirs.
Curbon, William. N.C. Private. 22 Dec. 1796. 274 acres.
Curbon, William. N.C. Private. 29 Jul. 1820. 366 acres to heirs.
Cureton, Boling. Ga. ———. 15 Mar. 1784. 250 acres.
Cureton, Richard. Ga. ———. 15 Mar. 1784. 250 acres.
Cureton, Thomas. Ga. ———. 17 May 1784. ———.
Cureton, William, Jr. Ga. Minute Man. 17 May 1784. ———.
Cureton, William, Sr. Ga. ———. 17 May 1784. ———.
Curl, John. Md. Private. ———. 50 acres.
Curl, Richard. Va. Private. 22 Aug. 1783. 200 acres.
Curle, Henry. Ga. Minute Man. 19 Jul. 1784. 287 1/2 acres.
Curle, Jacob. Va. Private. 26 Feb. 1834. 200 acres.
Curle, John. Ga. Minute Man. 17 May 1784. ———.
Curle, John. Va. Private. 26 Feb. 1834. 100 acres.
Curlee, John. N.C. Private. 10 Aug. 1785. 640 acres.
Curlee, Thomas. N.C. Private. 10 Aug. 1785. 640 acres.
Curley, Barney. Pa. Private. 30 Jan. 1787. 200 acres.
Curling, Sampson. N.C. Private. 1 Dec. 1797. 640 acres to heirs.
Curling, Willis. N.C. Private. 1 Dec. 1797. 640 acres to heirs.
Currell, George. Va. Midshipman. 29 Aug. 1835. 2666 2/3 acres.
Currell, Jacob. Va. Sailor. 1 Nov. 1786. 100 acres.
Currell, James. Va. Midshipman. 29 Oct. 1789. 1333 1/3 acres.
Currell, James. Va. Midshipman. 16 Nov. 1843. 1333 1/3 acres.
Currell, James. Va. Midshipman. 29 Oct. 1789. 1333 1/3 acres.
Currell, James. Va. Midshipman. 16 Nov. 1843. 1333 1/3 acres.
Currell, John. S.C. Soldier. 21 Jan. 1795. 200 acres.
Currell, Nicholas. Va. Lieutenant. 3 Sep. 1783. 2666 2/3 acres.
Currell, Nicholas. Va. Lieutenant. 26 Dec. 1797. 2666 2/3 acres.
Curren, Elisha. N.C. Private. 23 Apr. 1784. 640 acres to heir.
Curren, Elisha. N.C. Private. 27 Mar. 1821. 640 acres to heirs.
Curren, Hugh. N.C. Private. 23 Apr. 1784. 640 acres to heir.
Curren, Hugh. N.C. Private. 27 Mar. 1821. 640 acres to heirs.
Curren, James. Md. Private. ———. 50 acres.
Currins, James. Ga. ———. 17 May 1784. ———.
Curritt, John. Md. Private. ———. 50 acres.
Curry, Alexander. Ga. ———. 17 May 1784. ———.
Curry, Carey. Ga. Minute Man. 17 May 1784. ———.
Curry, Jacob. Ga. Minute Man. ———. 287 1/2 acres.
Curry, James. Va.-Ind. Private. 108 acres.
Curry, James. Va. Captain. 16 Apr. 1783. 4000 acres.
Curry, James. Va. Captain. 25 Nov. 1808. 333 1/3 acres.
Curry, John. N.C. Private. 11 Jul. 1785. 640 acres.
Curry, John. N.C. Private. 18 Jan. 1792. 640 acres.
Curry, Nicholas. Ga. Refugee. 17 May 1784. ———.
Curry, Peter. Ga. Private. 1784. 287 1/2 acres.
Curry, Robert. Ga. Citizen. 19 Dec. 1785. 287 1/2 acres.
Curry, Thompson. N.C. Private. 24 Dec. 1796. 428 acres.
Curry, Thompson. N.C. Noncomissioned officer. 9 Mar. 1801. 357 acres.
Curry, Thomson. N.C. Private. 13 Dec. 1787. 357 acres.

Curry, William. Ga. ———. 17 May 1784. ———.
Curtice, Henry. Va. Sailor. 30 Jun. 1784. 100 acres.
Curtis, Bartholomew. N.C. Private. 30 Sep. 1785. 185 acres.
Curtis, Benjamin. Conn. Sufferer. Danbury. 4.7.4.
Curtis, Bowlin. Va. Private. 2 Sep. 1847. 100 acres.
Curtis, James. Va. Private. 12 Apr. 1784. 100 acres.
Curtis, James. Va. Midshipman. 29 Dec. 1851. 2666 2/3 acres.
Curtis, John. Ga. Citizen. 6 Apr. 1785. 287 1/2 acres.
Curtis, John. Va. Private. 10 Nov. 1791. 200 acres.
Curtis, Jonathan. Mass. Sergeant. 7 Dec. 1831. 200 acres to his heirs.
Curtis, Joshua. N.C. Ensign. 30 Sep. 1785. 741 acres.
Curtis, Michael. Md. Private. ———. 50 acres.
Curtis, Rice. Va.-Ind. Private. 108 acres.
Curtis, Thomas. N.C. Private. 22 Apr. 1785. 274 acres.
Curtiss, Nehemiah. Mass. Sergeant. 20 Feb. 1833. 200 acres.
Curtz, Francis. Pa. Private. 16 Nov. 1786. 200 acres to John Donnelly, assignee.
Curtz, Low. Pa. Private. ———. 200 acres.
Curvin, Edward. N. Y. Private. 8 Jul. 1790. 500 acres.
Curvin, Samuel. N. Y. Private. 8 Jul. 1790. 600 acres.
Cushman, Andrew. Me. Private. 4 May 1835. 200 acres. Leeds.
Cusick, Christopher. Md. Private. ———. 50 acres.
Cusick, John. Pa. Private. 8 June 1787. 200 acres to Micahel Andrews, assignee.
Custard, George. Va. Private. 19 Jan. 1785. 100 acres.
Custard, John. Va. Private. 19 Jan. 1785. 100 acres.
Custavus, Micajah. Ga. ———. 17 May 1784. ———.
Custis, John. N.C. Lieutenant. 5 Sep. 1821. 2560 acres.
Custis, Thomas. Va. Lieutenant. 29 Aug. 1807. 2666 2/3 acres.
Cuthbert, Alexander Daniel. Ga. Captain. 24 Sep. 1783. 600 acres.
Cuthbert, Seth John. Ga. ———. 30 Sep. 1784. ———.
Cuthbert, William. Va. Corporal. 28 Feb. 1784. 200 acres.
Cutler, Esther. Conn. Sufferer. New London. 7.0.0.
Cutler, George. Ga. ———. 17 May 1784. ———.
Cutler, Henry. N. Y. Matross. 9 Jul. 1790. 600 acres.
Cutler, Mary. Conn. Sufferer. Fairfield. 48.18.1.
Cutler, William. Md. Private. ———. 50 acres.
Cutler, William. Mass. Private. 18 Oct. 1833. 200 acres.
Cutright, Peter. Va. Private. 9 May 1785. 100 acres.
Cutter, William. Mass. Private. 19 Sep. 1832. 200 acres to heirs.
Cutts, Shadrack. Va. Private. 30 Apr. 1783. 200 acres.
Cutts, William. Va. Private. 30 Apr. 1783. 200 acres.
Cyle, Robert. N.C. Private. 9 Feb. 1796. 640 acres.
Cyphart, Matthias. Md. Private. ———. 50 acres.
Cyphus, Peter. Conn. Sufferer. Greenwich. 22.13.0.
Cyprell, John. N.C. Sergeant. 21 Oct. 1783. 358 acres.
Cypress, Andrew. Va. Private. 27 Jun. 1783. 233 1/3 acres.
Cypress, Bartholomew. Va. Private. 1 Aug. 1783. 200 acres.
D'Ellient, Andrew. S.C. Major. 21 Jan. 1785. 400 acres.
D'Oyley, Daniel. S.C. Lieutenant. 21 Jan. 1785. 200 acres.
Dabney, Austin. Ga. Refugee. 15 Mar. 1784. 250 acres.
Dabney, Charles. Va. Lieutenant Colonel. 27 Nov. 1782. 6666 2/3 acres.
Dabney, Charles. Va. Lieutenant Colonel Commandant. 2 Apr. 1834. 1533 5/6 acres.
Dabney, Cornelius. Va. Lieutenant. 29 Dec. 1851 3395 acres.
Dade, Francis. Va. Captain. 29 Jan. 1784. 4000 acres.
Dadrick, Jacob. N.C. Private. 17 Sep. 1785. 640 acres to heirs.

Daffin, James. Md. Corporal. ———. 50 acres.
Daffin, John. N.C. Private. 30 Sep. 1785. 640 acres to heirs.
Dager, Peter. Va. Sergeant. 29 Dec. 1808. 200 acres.
Daget, James. N.C. Private. 15 Jul. 1785. 640 acres to heir.
Daggett, Henry. Conn. Sufferer. New/East Haven. 37.14.4.
Daggett, Jacob. Conn. Sufferer. New/East Haven. 50.9.7.
Daggett, Naphtali, Dr. Conn. Sufferer. New/East Haven. 32.11.0.
Dagnell, Stephen. Va. Sergeant. 2 Jun. 1783. 200 acres.
Dailey, Benjamin. Conn. Sufferer. Danbury. 1.14.6.
Dailey, Charles. N.C. Private. 17 Dec. 1785. 274 acres.
Dailey, James. Va. Drummer. 8 Aug. 1783. 200 acres.
Dailey, Jeremiah. N.C. Private. 21 Aug. 1820. 228 acres.
Dailey, John. N.C. Sergeant. 17 Dec. 1796. 1000 acres to heirs.
Dailey, John. Pa. ———. 2 Nov. 1807. 200 acres to Mary Poteel, devisee.
Dailey, John. Pa. Private. 29 Mar. 1805. 200 acres to James Dailey in trust.
Dailey, John. Va. Private. 1 Jun. 1785. 200 acres.
Dailey, John. Va. Private. 13 Feb. 1861. 200 acres.
Dailey, Joseph. Pa. Lieutenant. 28 Feb. 1797. 250 acres to Francis Murray, assignee.
Dailey, Zadock. Va. Sergeant. 10 Jul. 1851. 100 acres.
Dailey, Zadock. Va. Sergeant. 10 Jul. 1851. 100 acres.
Dailey, Zadock. Va. Sergeant. 18 Sep. 1850. 200 acres.
Daily, Robert. N. Y. Matross. 9 Jul. 1790. 500 acres.
Dain, John. Me. ———. 22 Apr. 1835. 200 acres. Lisbon.
Daingerfield, William. Va. Sergeant. 8 Dec. 1784. 400 acres.
Daisy, John. Me. ———. 29 Sep. 1835. 200 acres to widow Mehitable Daisy. Poland.
Dale, Richard. Va. Lieutenant. 26 May 1832. 1000 acres.
Dale, Richard. Va. Lieutenant. 26 May 1832. 1000 acres.
Dale, Richard. Va. Lieutenant. 26 May 1832. 1000 acres.
Dale, Richard. Va. Lieutenant. 26 May 1832. 1000 acres.
Daley, Joshua. N.C. Captain. 6 Jan. 1794. 2840 acres to heirs.
Daley, Thomas. Md. Private. ———. 50 acres.
Dallis, Robert. Va. Private. 15 Jun. 1783. 100 acres.
Dally, Benjamin. Ga. Private. 25 May. 1784. 287 1/2 acres.
Dally, George. Va. Private. 24 Dec. 1784. 200 acres.
Dalton, Matthew. Ga. ———. 17 May 1784. ———.
Dalton, Thomas. Ga. ———. 17 May 1784. ———.
Dalton, Thomas V. Va. Lieutenant. 31 Jan. 1834. 2666 3/4 acres.
Dalton, V. T. Va. ———. 1 Jul. 1836. 2666 2/3 acres.
Dalton, Valentine Thomas. Va.-Ind. Lieutenant. 2156 acres.
Dalzen, Joseph. N. Y. Captain. ———. 1000 acres.
Damaster, Edward. Va. Corporal. 21 Dec. 1799. 400 acres.
Dameron, Jacob. Va. Private. 15 Jun. 1807. 100 acres.
Damerson, Thomas. Va. Private. 9 Apr. 1835. 100 acres.
Dampier, Daniel. Ga. Sergeant. 7 Mar. 1784. ———.
Dan, Jeffrey. N.C. Private. 2 Dec. 1785. 640 acres to heirs.
Dan, Malicha. N.C. Private. 2 Dec. 1785. 640 acres to heirs.
Danby, Solomon. N.C. Fifer. 30 Sep. 1785. 1000 acres to heirs.
Dance, Etheldred. N.C. Ensign. 11 Apr. 1823. 914 acres to heir James W. Dance.
Dancer, John. Va. Private. 23 May 1800. 200 acres.
Dandridge, Alexander Spotswood. Va. Captain. 10 Jun. 1783. 1000 acres.
Dandridge, Alexander Spotswood. Va. Captain. 10 Jun. 1783. 1000 acres.
Dandridge, Alexander Spotswood. Va. Captain. 10 Jun. 1783. 1000 acres.

Dandridge, Alexander Spotswood. Va. Captain. 10 Jun. 1783. 1000 acres.
Dandridge, John. Va. Captain. 14 Dec. 1782. 4000 acres.
Dandridge, John. Va. Captain. 19 Aug. 1794. 666 2/3 acres.
Dandridge, Robert. Va. Lieutenant. 3 Jun. 1783. 2666 2/3 acres.
Danelly, John. Va. Private. 12 Jun. 1783. 100 acres.
Danford, Prince. N. Y. Private. 8 Jul. 1790. 600 acres.
Daniel. George. Va. Sailor. 3 May 1784. 100 acres.
Daniel, Benjamin. Ga. Private. 7 Apr. 1784. ———.
Daniel, Benjamin. N.C. Private. 30 Sep. 1785. 640 acres to heirs.
Daniel, Charles. Ga. 5 Feb. 1787. 200 acres. ———.
Daniel, Christopher. Va. Private. 27 Aug. 1789. 100 acres.
Daniel, Christopher. Va. Private. 28 Nov. 1822. 100 acres.
Daniel, Davis. N. Y. Private. 17 Aug. 1790. 600 acres.
Daniel, Ephraim. N.C. Private. 30 Sep. 1785. 640 acres to heirs.
Daniel, Eustace. Ga. ———. 17 May 1784. ———.
Daniel, Jacob. Va. Private. 7 Aug. 1813. 200 acres.
Daniel, John. Ga. ———. 17 May 1784. ———.
Daniel, John. N.C. Private. 22 Dec. 1796. 640 acres.
Daniel, John. Va. Corporal. 26 Jun. 1783. 200 acres.
Daniel, John. Va. Private. 13 Nov. 1810. 100 acres.
Daniel, Joseph. N.C. Musician. 27 Nov. 1819. 1000 acres to heirs.
Daniel, Thomas. Ga. ———. 7 Jun. 1785. 287 1/2 acres.
Daniel, Thomas. N.C. Sergeant. 7 Jan. 1786. 1000 acres to heirs.
Daniel, Thomas. Va. Sailor. 3 May 1784. 100 acres.
Daniel, William. Ga. Refugee. 15 Mar. 1784. 250 acres.
Daniels, Henry. N. Y. Private. 8 Jul. 1790. 600 acres.
Danielson, Isaac. N. Y. Private. 8 Jul. 1790. 500 acres.
Dannelly, Daniel. Ga. Lieutenant. 15 Mar. 1784. ——— acres.
Dannelly, Francis. Ga. ———. 17 May 1784. ———.
Dannelly, James. Ga. Captain. 23 Mar. 1784. ———.
Dannelly, James. Ga. Minute Man. 1 Apr. 1784. ———.
Dannelly, James. Ga. Citizen. 7 Apr. 1784. ———.
Dannelly, James. Ga. Refugee. 5 Apr. 1784. ———.
Dannelly, John. Ga. ———. 17 May 1784. ———.
Danniley, Francis. N.C. Private. 6 Dec. 1797. 640 acres to heirs.
Darbey, Patrick. N.C. Private. 30 Sep. 1785. 640 acres.
Darby, Abraham. Ga. Minute Man. 3 Sep. 1785. ———.
Darby, Ayres. Va. Seaman. 18 Jun. 1834. 100 acres.
Darby, Charles. N. Y. Fifer. 8 Jul. 1790. 500 acres.
Darby, Darmon. Va. Pilot. 12 Jun. 1784. 100 acres.
Darby, Darmon. Va. Pilot. 31 Dec. 1851. 2566 2/3 acres.
Darby, Darmon. Va. Pilot. 6 Apr. 1853. 1925 acres.
Darby, Dramon. Va. Pilot. 6 Apr. 1853. 641 2/3 acres.
Darby, John. Ga. Minute Man. 6 Feb. 1784. 250 acres.
Darby, John. N.C. Private. 4 Aug. 1821. 640 acres.
Darby, Nathaniel. Va. Lieutenant. 28 Jun. 1783. 3110 2/3 acres.
Darby, Nathaniel. Va. Lieutenant. 8 Jun. 1809. 370 acres.
Darby, Severn. Va. Private. 15 Jun. 1807. 100 acres.
Darcey, Benjamin. Ga. ———. 17 May 1784. ———.
Darcey, James. Ga. Refugee. 4 Mar. 1784. ———.
Darcey, Joel. Ga. Refugee. 4 Mar. 1784. 575 acres.
Darcey, William. Ga. ———. 17 May 1784. ———.
Darden, George, Jr. Refugee. 17 May 1784. ———.
Darden, George, Sr. Refugee. 17 May 1784. ———.

Darden, Jacob. Ga. Soldier. 3 Oct. 1785. 230 acres.
Darden, John. N.C. Private. 3 Feb. 1785. 640 acres.
Darden, Joseph. N.C. Private. 22 Dec. 1796. 640 acres to heirs.
Darden, Noah. N.C. Sergeant. 9 Dec. 1797. 1000 acres.
Dardin, John. Ga. ———. 17 May 1784. ———.
Daring, Henry. Va. Ensign. Nov. 1790. 2666 2/3 acres.
Daring, Henry. Va. Ensign. 27 Feb. 1838. 2666 2/3 acres.
Dark, William. Va. Lieutenant Colonel Commandant. 5 Mar. 1790. 1111 1/2 acres.
Darke, William. Va. Lieutenant Colonel Commandant. 13 Jun. 1783. 6666 2/3 acres.
Darke, William. Va. Colonel. 22 Dec. 1809. 833 acres.
Darling, Abraham. Ga. Refugee. Sep. 1785. ———.
Darling, Ephraim. N. Y. Private. 8 Jul. 1790. 600 acres.
Darling, Moses. N. Y. Private. 6 Jul. 1790. 500 acres.
Darling, Noble. Ga. Minute Man. 3 Sep. 1785. ———.
Darnal, Henry. N.C. ———. 2 Dec. 1800. 2515 acres to heirs.
Darnald, Augustine. N.C. Private. 29 Sep. 1785. 640 acres to heirs.
Darnald, Henry. N.C. Captain. 29 Sep. 1784. 1325 acres to heir.
Darnald, William. N.C. Private. 30 Sep. 1785. 640 acres.
Darnold, Aaron. Va. Drummer. 30 Sep. 1783. 100 acres.
Darragh, John. Pa. Private. 18 Jul. 1787. 200 acres.
Darrington, Robert. Ga. ———. 17 May 1784. ———.
Darrow, Daniel. Conn. Sufferer. Greenwich. 19.4.4.
Darrow, James. Ga. ———. 17 May 1784. ———.
Darrow, James. Conn. Sufferer. New London. 2.3.7.
Darrow, John. Conn. Sufferer. Norwalk. 192.19.0.
Darrow, Jonathan. Conn. Sufferer. Fairfield. 254.5.2.
Darrow, Nathan. Conn. Sufferer. Groton. 9.1.1.
Darrow, Nicholas. Conn. Sufferer. New London. 9.12.2.
Darrow, Peter. Conn. Sufferer. New London. 10.0.0.
Darrow, Thomas. Conn. Sufferer. Norwalk. 17.5.2.
Darumple, Robert. Pa. Private. 6 Jul. 1789. 200 acres.
Darvill, William. Va. Lieutenant. 23 Jun. 1788. 2666 2/3 acres.
Dasher, Christian. Ga. Refugee. 1784. 575 acres to son Christian Dasher.
Dasher, Christopher. N.C. Private. 30 Sep. 1785. 640 acres to heirs.
Dasher, John Martin. Ga. Refugee. 17 Jul. 1784. 575 acres.
Dashper, John. Va. Private. 23 Oct. 1789. 100 acres.
Dauchey, John. Conn. Sufferer. Ridgefield. 11.4.0.
Dauchey, Philip. Conn. Sufferer. Ridgefield. 3.8.4.
Dauge, Peter. N.C. Private. 1 Jun. 1792. 274 acres.
Dauge, Peter. N.C. Lieutenant Colonel. 28 Dec. 1792. 2057 acres.
Daugherty, George. N.C. Major. 16 Oct. 1783. 4800 acres.
Daugherty, James. Va. Lieutenant. 26 Mar. 1831. 2666 2/3 acres.
Daugherty, James. Va. ———. 3 Dec. 1832. 1333 1/3 acres.
Daugherty, Patrick. Va. Private. 3 Apr. 1783. 200 acres.
Daugherty, Samuel. N.C. ———. 13 Jun. 1785. 228 acres.
Daughtery, Dempsey. N.C. Private. 26 Sep. 1821. 640 acres to heirs.
Daughtrey, John. N.C. Private. 2 Apr. 1784. 640 acres.
Daughtry, Jacob. N.C. Private. 13 Dec. 1796. 228 acres.
Daughtry, Lewis. N.C. Private. 20 Jan. 1785. 640 acres to heirs.
Daulton, Moses. Va. Sergeant. 13 Sep. 1783. 200 acres.
Davenport, Abraham. Va. Sergeant. 22 Feb. 1817. 200 acres.
Davenport, Adrien. Va. Private. 19 Feb. 1818. 100 acres.
Davenport, Ashael. N.C. Private. 26 Aug. 1785. 640 acres to heirs.

Davenport, Claiborne. Va. Private. 2 Oct. 1783. 100 acres.
Davenport, Joel. Va. Private. 3 Feb. 1784. 100 acres.
Davenport, Joseph. Va. Private. 10 Nov. 1784. 100 acres.
Davenport, Joseph. Va. Sergeant Major. 22 Nov. 1833. 200 acres.
Davenport, Moses. Va. Private. 10 Nov. 1784. 100 acres.
Davenport, Opie. Va. Lieutenant. 5 Feb. 1784. 2666 2/3 acres.
Davenport, Reuben. Va. Private. 24 Jan. 1817. 100 acres.
Davenport, Sarah. Conn. Sufferer. New/ East Haven. 1.2.0.
Davenport, Stephen. Ga. Soldier. 10 Sep. 1783. 200 acres.
Davenport, Thomas. Ga. Lieutenant. 2 Apr. 1784. 460 acres.
Davenport, Thomas. Ga. Surgeon. 17 May 1784. 920 acres to heirs. Died 1780 in captivity.
Davenport, William. Ga. ———. 22 Jul. 1784. 500 acres.
Davenport, William. Va. Captain. 3 Dec. 1785. 4000 acres.
Daverson, Peter. Ga. ———. 5 Dec. 1785. ———.
Daves, Spillsby. Va. Sergeant. 31 Jul. 1783. 400 acres.
Daves, Syrus. N.C. Private. 29 Sep. 1784. 228 acres.
Davey, James. N.C. Private. 17 Feb. 1824. 640 acres.
Daveys, John. S.C. Soldier. 18 Jul. 1784. 200 acres.
Davice, Arthur. Va. Private. 11 Jan. 1786. 200 acres.
Davice, Richard. N.C. Private. 20 Oct. 1783. 274 acres.
Davice, Richard. Va. Sergeant. 27 May 1783. 200 acres.
Davice, William. N.C. Private. 27 Nov. 1783. 274 acres.
David, Peter. S.C. ———. 4 Mar. 1793. 100 acres.
David, Peter. S.C. ———. 4 Mar. 1793. 100 acres.
David, William. Ga. Refugee. 20 Apr. 1784. ———.
Davidson, Alexander. Me. Private. 29 Jun. 1835. 200 acres. Edgecomb.
Davidson, Alexander. Pa. Private. 9 Oct. 1786. 200 acres.
Davidson, David. Pa. Sergeant. 26 Jun. 1787. 250 acres.
Davidson, Emanuel. N.C. Private. 12 Dec. 1796. 640 acres to heirs.
Davidson, George. N.C. Lieutenant Colonel. 25 Oct. 1783. 5760 acres to William Davidson, heir.
Davidson, James. Md. Private. ———. 50 acres.
Davidson, James. Md. Private. ———. 50 acres.
Davidson, James. N.C. Private. 9 Apr. 1788. 640 acres.
Davidson, James. N.C. Private. 10 Dec. 1788. 640 acres to heirs.
Davidson, James. Pa. Surgeon. ———. 300 acres.
Davidson, James. Pa. Surgeon. 11 Apr. 1787. 300 acres.
Davidson, John. Ga. Soldier. 5 Aug. 1785. ———.
Davidson, John. Md. Major. ———. 200 acres.
Davidson, John. N. Y. Private. 8 Jul. 1790. 600 acres.
Davidson, John. N.C. Private. 14 Dec. 1796. 640 acres.
Davidson, Joseph. N.C. Private. 6 Apr. 1806. 228 acres.
Davidson, Robert. Ga. Soldier. 5 Aug. 1785. ———.
Davidson, Thomas. N.C. Private. 20 Oct. 1787. 640 acres.
Davidson, William. Va. Private. 27 Mar. 1837. 100 acres.
Davidson, William. Va. ———. 10 Jul. 1838. 100 acres.
Davie, Samuel. N.C. Drummer. 20 Sep. 1784. 357 acres.
Davies, Asael. Va.-Ind. Private. 108 acres.
Davies, Edward. Ga. Refugee Captain. 30 Jul. 1784. 575 acres.
Davies, James. Ga. ———. 15 Mar. 1784. 250 acres.
Davies, Joel. Ga. Refugee. 15 Mar. 1784. 250 acres.
Davies, John. Ga. Minute Man. 20 Feb. 1784. 250 acres.
Davies, Joseph. Va. Surgeon. 29 Nov. 1782. 6000 acres.
Davies, Samuel. N. Y. Private. 8 Jul. 1790. 600 acres.

Davies, William. Va. Colonel. 11 Feb. 1784. 7777 2/3 acres.
Davies, William. Va. Colonel. 22 Nov. 1838. 1053 acres.
Davies, William. Va. Colonel. 22 Nov. 1838. 351 acres.
Davis, Aaron. N.C. Private. 16 Aug. 1821. 640 acres.
Davis, Absalom. Ga. Refugee. 28 Feb. 1784. 250 acres.
Davis, Achiles. N.C. Private. 29 Sep. 1784. 640 acres to Augustin Davis, heir.
Davis, Alexander. Ga. Minute Man. 14 Feb. 1785. ———.
Davis, Allen. Me. ———. 30 Jun. 1835. 200 acres. Minot.
Davis, Aquilla. Va. Private. 21 Dec. 1784. 200 acres.
Davis, Archibald. N.C. Private. 9 Nov. 1784. 274 acres.
Davis, Asa. N.C. Private. 30 Nov. 1804. 640 acres.
Davis, Bartley. N.C. ———. 20 Dec. 1784. 640 acres to heirs.
Davis, Benjamin. Ga. Refugee. 24 May 1784. 287 1/2 acres.
Davis, Benjamin. Me. ———. 28 Mar. 1836. 200 acres. Belfast.
Davis, Benjamin. N.C. Private. 11 May 1784. 376 acres.
Davis, Benjamin. N.C. Private. 12 Dec. 1796. 640 acres to heirs.
Davis, Blanford. Ga. Refugee. 14 May 1784. ———.
Davis, Burrell. N.C. Private. 6 Sep. 1821. 640 acres.
Davis, Chapman. N. Y. Private. 8 Jul. 1790. 500 acres.
Davis, Charles. Ga. Sergeant. 17 May 17840. 230 acres to heirs.
Davis, Charles. Md. Private. ———. 50 acres.
Davis, Charles. Va. Private. 21 Feb. 1840. 80 acres.
Davis, Charles. Va. Private. 21 Feb. 1840. 20 acres.
Davis, Chesley. Ga. Refugee. 28 Feb. 1784. 250 acres.
Davis, Clementius. Ga. ———. 17 May 1784. ———.
Davis, David. Ga. Soldier. 29 Jul. 1784. 587 1/2 acres.
Davis, David. N. Y. Fifer. 8 Jul. 1790. 500 acres.
Davis, David. N.C. Private. 8 Dec. 1795. 640 acres to heirs.
Davis, David. Pa. Private. 30 Mar. 1805. 200 acres.
Davis, Ebenezer B. Mass. Private. 15 Jan. 1834. 200 acres.
Davis, Elias. Ga. Refugee. Sep. 1785. ———.
Davis, Elijah. Me. ———. 7 Aug. 1835. 200 acres to widow Phebe Whitney. Bridgeton.
Davis, Elisha. N.C. Private. 12 May 1784. 365 acres.
Davis, Ezra. Me. ———. 22 Jun. 1835. 200 acres to widow Abigail Davis. Ellsworth.
Davis, Frederick. N.C. Private. 8 Dec. 1796. 365 acres.
Davis, George. Ga. Minute Man. 3 Sep. 1785. ———.
Davis, George. N.C. Private. 9 Nov. 1784. 228 acres.
Davis, Gideon. Ga. ———. 28 Feb. 1784. 250 acres.
Davis, Granville. N.C. Private. 10 Aug. 1785. 640 acres.
Davis, Hardy. Ga. Soldier. 16 Dec. 1784. ———.
Davis, Harman. S.C. Captain. 21 Jan. 1785. 300 acres.
Davis, Henry. Ga. Soldier. 16 Dec. 1784. 287 1/2 acres.
Davis, Henry. N. Y. Fifer. 9 Jul. 1790. 600 acres.
Davis, Henry. N.C. Private. 10 Dec. 1788. 640 acres to heirs.
Davis, Henry. Va. Private. 22 Oct. 1787. 100 acres.
Davis, Hugh. N.C. Private. 22 Dec. 1796. 640 acres.
Davis, Hugh. Va. Sergeant. 24 May 1813. 200 acres.
Davis, Isaac. Conn. Sufferer. Greenwich. 15.16.0.
Davis, Isaac. Conn. Sufferer. Danbury. 1.12.8.
Davis, Ishmael. Va. Private. 15 Jun. 1807. 100 acres.
Davis, Issac. Ga. Minute Man. 30 Jul. 1784. 287 1/2 acres.
Davis, Jacob. Ga. Minute Man. 1784. 287 1/2 acres.
Davis, Jacob. N.Y. ———. ———. 500 acres to heirs.

Davis, Jacob. Va. Private. 31 Jul. 1810. 100 acres.
Davis, Jacob. Va. Private. 20 Aug. 1810. 100 acres.
Davis, James. Ga. ———. 17 May 1784. ———.
Davis, James. Va.-Ind. Lieutenant. 2156 acres.
Davis, James. N.C. Private. 1 Sep. 1785. 640 acres to heirs.
Davis, James. N.C. Private. 8 Sep. 1804. 640 acres.
Davis, James. Va. Private. 13 May 1783. 100 acres.
Davis, James. Va. Private. 19 Dec. 1783. 100 acres.
Davis, James. Va. Private. 17 Apr. 1784. 100 acres.
Davis, James. Va. Captain. 19 Aug. 1822. 4000 acres.
Davis, James. Va. Captain. 29 Mar. 1838. 666 2/3 acres.
Davis, Jeduthan. Va. Sailor. 24 Oct. 1786. 100 acres.
Davis, Jenkins. Ga. Colonel. 8 Jan. 1784. 1050 acres.
Davis, Jeremiah. Va. Private. 15 Feb. 1798. 200 acres.
Davis, Jeremiah. Va. Private. 30 Mar. 1846. 200 acres.
Davis, Jesee. Va. Captain. 4 Jan. 1804. 1000 acres.
Davis, Jesse. N.C. Private. 30 Sep. 1785. 640 acres to heirs.
Davis, Jesse. Va. Captain. 4 Jan. 1804. 1000 acres.
Davis, Jesse. Va. Captain. 4 Jan. 1804. 1000 acres.
Davis, Jesse. Va. Captain. 4 Jan. 1804. 1000 acres.
Davis, Joel. N.C. Private. 7 Dec. 1797. 640 acres to heirs.
Davis, John. Ga. ———. 25 May 1784. 287 1/2 acres to heirs.
Davis, John. Me. ———. 6 May 1836. 200 acres to widow Eliza Davis. Cutler.
Davis, John. Me. Musician. 11 Apr. 1835. 200 acres. Warterville.
Davis, John. Me. ———. 20 Aug. 1835. 200 acres to widow Eunice Davis. Thomaston.
Davis, John. Md. Private. ———. 50 acres.
Davis, John. Md. Private. ———. 50 acres.
Davis, John. Md. Private. ———. 50 acres.
Davis, John. Md. Private. ———. 50 acres.
Davis, John. N. Y. Private. 8 Jul. 1790. 500 acres.
Davis, John. N. Y. Major. 9 Jul. 1790. 2400 acres.
Davis, John. N.C. Captain. 10 Nov. 1783. 3840 acres.
Davis, John. N.C. Private. 3 Mar. 1784. 640 acres.
Davis, John. N.C. Sergeant. 26 Aug. 1785. 1000 acres to heirs.
Davis, John. N.C. Private. 17 Dec. 1796. 640 acres to heirs.
Davis, John. N.C. Ensign. 25 Aug. 1820. 2560 acres to heirs.
Davis, John. Pa. ———. 11 Dec. 1794. 200 acres to Mary Davis, widow.
Davis, John. Pa. Matross. 8 Jan. 1787. 200 acres.
Davis, John. Pa. Private. 29 Sep. 1787. 200 acres to Howell Reading, assignee.
Davis, John. Pa. Captain. 17 Nov. 1786. 500 acres.
Davis, John. Pa. Private. 11 Dec. 1794. 200 acres to widow Mary Davis.
Davis, John. Va. Sergeant. 10 Feb. 1783. 200 acres.
Davis, John. Va. Private. 14 Apr. 1783. 200 acres.
Davis, John. Va. Private. 30 Jun. 1783. 100 acres.
Davis, John. Va. Private. 19 Aug. 1783. 100 acres.
Davis, John. Va. Sergeant. 3 Aug. 1784. 200 acres.
Davis, John. Va. Private. 17 Jun. 1784. 200 acres.
Davis, John. Va. Seaman. 30 Dec. 1784. 100 acres.
Davis, John. Va. Private. 15 Feb. 1833. 100 acres.
Davis, John. Conn. Sufferer. Fairfield. 62.14.11.
Davis, John R. Va. Lieutenant. 4 May 1838. 3111 acres.
Davis, John R. Va. Lieutenant. 4 May 1838. 1555 acres.
Davis, John R. Va. Lieutenant. 20 Feb. 1850. 1089 acres.

Davis, John R. Va. Lieutenant. 20 Feb. 1850. 777 3/4 acres.
Davis, John R. Va. Lieutenant. 22 Oct. 1852. 777 3/4 acres.
Davis, John R. Va. Lieutenant. 14 Jul. 1859. 77 2/3 acres.
Davis, John R. Va. Lieutenant. 14 May 1859. 129 1/3 acres.
Davis, John R. Va. Lieutenant. 14 May 1859. 129 1/3 acres.
Davis, John R. Va. Lieutenant. 14 May 1859. 129 1/3 acres.
Davis, John R. Va. Lieutenant. 4 Aug. 1859. 25 acres.
Davis, John R. Va. Lieutenant. 4 Aug. 1859. 25 acres.
Davis, John R. Va. Lieutenant. 23 Sep. 1859. 311 acres.
Davis, John R. Va. Lieutenant. 23 Sep. 1859. 52 3/4 acres.
Davis, John R. Va. Lieutenant. 28 Nov. 1859. 311 acres.
Davis, John R. Va. Lieutenant. 28 Nov. 1859. 52 3/4 acres.
Davis, John R. Va. Lieutenant. 14 May 1859. 129 1/3 acres.
Davis, John R. Va. Lieutenant. 29 Jul. 1859. 50 acres.
Davis, John, Sr. Ga. ———. 26 May 1784. 287 1/2 acres.
Davis, Jonathan. N.C. Private. 2 Feb. 1786. 640 acres to heirs.
Davis, Joseph. N.C. Private. 22 Apr. 1785. 320 acres.
Davis, Joseph. Va. Private. 26 Apr. 1783. 200 acres.
Davis, Joseph. Va. Private. 31 May 1784. 200 acres.
Davis, Joshua. Me. ———. 7 Jul. 1835. 200 acres. Canton.
Davis, Joshua. N. Y. Private. 8 Jul. 1790. 600 acres.
Davis, Joshua. N.C. Private. 11 May 1785. 640 acres to heir.
Davis, Josiah. N.C. Quartermaster. 6 Sep. 1821. 1000 acres.
Davis, Josiah. N.C. Private. 11 Jan. 1822. 228 acres to heirs.
Davis, Leonard. N.C. Private. 24 May 1784. 640 acres to heir.
Davis, Leonard. N.C. Private. 9 Feb. 1796. 640 acres to heirs.
Davis, Lewis. Ga. ———. 28 Feb. 1784. 250 acres.
Davis, Lewis C. Va. Private. 25 Apr. 1783. 200 acres.
Davis, Llewellen. Pa. Lieutenant. 20 Oct. 1786. 200 acres.
Davis, Llewellian. Pa. Lieutenant. 20 Oct. 1786. 200 acres.
Davis, Meredith. Ga. Sergeant. 17 May 1784. 345 acres.
Davis, Micajah. N.C. Private. 29 Sep. 1784. 274 acres.
Davis, Moses. Ga. ———. 17 May 1784. ———.
Davis, Moses. N.C. Private. 2 Feb. 1786. 640 acres to heirs.
Davis, Moses. N.C. Private. 15 Nov. 1793. 640 acres to heirs.
Davis, Myrick. Ga. Refugee. 15 Mar. 1784. 250 acres to widow Sarah Davis.
Davis, Nicholas. Va. Private. 1 Jul. 1784. 100 acres.
Davis, Patrick. N. Y. Private. 8 Jul. 1790. 600 acres.
Davis, Peter. Md. Drummer. ———. 50 acres.
Davis, Peter. Mass. Private. 12 Sep. 1832. 200 acres.
Davis, Peter. N. Y. ———. 8 Jul. 1790. 600 acres.
Davis, Philip. Me. Private. 13 May 1835. 200 acres. Fayette.
Davis, Presley. Va. Sergeant. 18 Nov. 1818. 200 acres.
Davis, Ralph. N.C. Private. 13 Dec. 1796. 457 acres.
Davis, Rezin. Md. Captain. ———. 200 acres.
Davis, Richard. N. Y. Sergeant. 8 Jul. 1790. 600 acres.
Davis, Richard. N. Y. Matross. 9 Jul. 1790. 600 acres.
Davis, Richard. Va. Private. 12 Mar. 1798. 200 acres.
Davis, Richard. Va. Private. 21 Mar. 1807. 100 acres.
Davis, Robert. Ga. ———. 1 May 1785. ———.
Davis, Robert. Ga. ———. 1 May 1785. ———. [a second man]
Davis, Robert. Va.-Ind. Private. 108 acres.
Davis, Robert. Md. Private. ———. 50 acres.
Davis, Robert. S.C. ———. 2 Mar. 1789. 200 acres.

Davis, Robert. Va. Private. 15 Jun. 1807. 100 acres.
Davis, Samuel. Ga. ———. 15 Mar. 1784. 250 acres.
Davis, Samuel. Md. Sergeant. ———. 50 acres.
Davis, Samuel. N.C. Drummer. 9 Nov. 1784. 357 acres.
Davis, Samuel. N.C. Private. 7 Dec. 1797. 228 acres.
Davis, Samuel. Pa. Private. 10 Nov. 1786. 200 acres.
Davis, Samuel. Va. Private. 14 Oct. 1783. 100 acres.
Davis, Samuel. Va. Private. 29 May 1784. 200 acres.
Davis, Sarah. Conn. Sufferer. New London. 8.0.0.
Davis, Sherwood. Ga. Minute Man. 3 Apr. 1785. ———.
Davis, Solomon. Ga. Minute Man. 25 May 1784. 287 1/2 acres.
Davis, Stephen. Conn. Sufferer. Greenwich. 112.14.6.
Davis, Syrus. N.C. Noncommissioned Officer. 23 Nov. 1790. 762 acres.
Davis, Thomas. Ga. Minute Man. 26 May 1784. 287 1/2 acres.
Davis, Thomas. Md. Private. ———. 50 acres.
Davis, Thomas. N.C. Sergeant. 28 May 1784. 642 acres.
Davis, Thomas. S.C. ———. 2 Dec. 1793. 100 acres.
Davis, Thomas. S.C. ———. 2 Dec. 1793. 100 acres.
Davis, Thomas. Va. Corporal. 20 Jun. 1785. 400 acres.
Davis, Thomas. Va. Ensign. 16 Apr. 1831. 2666 2/3 acres.
Davis, Thomas. Va. Private. 28 Mar. 1834. 100 acres.
Davis, Thomas. Conn. Sufferer. Greenwich. 8.5.0.
Davis, Thomas. Conn. Sufferer. New/East Haven. 21.1.3 3/4.
Davis, Thompson. Va. Private. 22 Mar. 1786. 200 acres.
Davis, Vachal. Ga. Refugee. 17 May 1784. ———.
Davis, Van. Va. Private. 14 Aug. 1834. 200 acres.
Davis, Ward. Ga. Minute Man. 22 Mar. 1785. 250 acres.
Davis, Wiley. Ga. Refugee. 28 Feb. 1784. 250 acres.
Davis, William. Ga. ———. 1784. 287 1/2 acres. ———.
Davis, William. Me. Private. 12 May 1835. 200 acres. Whitfield.
Davis, William. Me. ———. 1 May 1835. 200 acres. Eddington.
Davis, William. Me. Private. 11 Aug. 1838. 200 acres to widow Jane Davis. Sidney.
Davis, William. Md. Matross. ———. 50 acres.
Davis, William. N.C. Lieutenant Colonel. 25 Oct. 1783. 2468 acres.
Davis, William. N.C. Private. 22 Apr. 1785. 640 acres to heirs.
Davis, William. Pa. Private. 30 Jul. 1787. 200 acres.
Davis, William. Pa. Private. 27 Aug. 1787. 200 acres.
Davis, William. S.C. Soldier. 21 Jan. 1785. 200 acres.
Davis, William. Va. Private. 26 Apr. 1783. 200 acres.
Davis, William. Va. Sergeant. 2 Aug. 1783. 200 acres.
Davis, William. Va. Private. 31 Jan. 1784. 200 acres.
Davis, William. Va. Corporal. 18 Oct. 1785. 400 acres.
Davis, William. Va. Private. 27 Mar. 1787. 100 acres.
Davis, William. Va. Private. 18 Apr. 1801. 100 acres.
Davis, William. Va. Private. 2 Dec. 1833. 100 acres.
Davis, Willis. N.C. Private. 5 Sep. 1821. 640 acres.
Davis, Zacheriah. N.C. Private. 17 Dec. 1785. 640 acres to heirs.
Davison, Ambrose. Va. Private. 22 May 1784. 100 acres.
Davison, Amos. N.C. Private. 30 Sep. 1785. 640 acres to heirs.
Davison, Benjamin. N.C. Private. 30 Sep. 1785. 274 acres.
Davison, David. Va. Private. 30 Jun. 1784. 200 acres.
Davison, Joseph. Ga. ———. 17 May 1784. ———.
Davison, Joseph. Va. Private. 1 Mar. 1784. 100 acres.
Davison, Joshua. Va. Private. 22 May 1784. 200 acres.

Davison, Josiah. Va. Private. 4 Jan. 1789. 100 acres.
Davison, Thomas. Ga. Soldier. 8 May 1785. ———.
Davison, William. Ga. Soldier. 9 Feb. 1784. ———.
Davison, William. Va. Private. 4 Apr. 1783. 200 acres.
Dawkens, Charles. Md. Sergeant. ———. 50 acres.
Dawley, David. N.C. Corporal. 19 Dec. 1801. 428 acres.
Daws, John. Va. Private. 3 Dec. 1911. 100 acres.
Daws, William. N.C. Private. 30 Sep. 1785. 640 acres to heirs.
Dawson, Benjamin. Ga. ———. 17 May 1784. ———.
Dawson, Benjamin. Va. Private. 30 Jan. 1805. 100 acres.
Dawson, Britton. Ga. ———. 17 May 1784. ———.
Dawson, Daniel. N. Y. Private. 8 Jul. 1790. 600 acres.
Dawson, David. Ga. ———. 17 May 1784. ———.
Dawson, Francis. Va. Sergeant. 25 Nov. 1783. 400 acres.
Dawson, George. Ga. ———. 17 May 1784. ———.
Dawson, Henry. N.C. Captain. 17 Feb. 1824. 3840 acres.
Dawson, Henry. Va. Lieutenant. 31 Mar. 1783. 1300 acres.
Dawson, Henry. Va. Lieutenant. 31 Mar. 1783. 1366 2/3 acres.
Dawson, Henry. Va. Lieutenant. 21 Feb. 1810. 444 acres.
Dawson, Isaac. N.C. Private. 10 Aug. 1785. 274 acres.
Dawson, James. Ga. ———. 17 May 1784. ———.
Dawson, James. Va.-Ind. Private. 108 acres.
Dawson, James. Md. Private. ———. 50 acres.
Dawson, James. Va. Private. 20 Sep. 1784. 200 acres.
Dawson, John. Pa. Ranger. 11 Sep. 1787. 200 acres.
Dawson, Levi. N.C. Lieutenant Colonel. 9 Nov. 1784. 2125 acres.
Dawson, Martin. Ga. ———. 17 May 1784. 230 acres to heirs.
Dawson, Matthew. N.C. Private. 24 Dec. 1785. 640 acres.
Dawson, Thomas. Va. Private. 5 Jul. 1783. 100 acres.
Dawson, Thomas B. Va. Seaman. 15 Jun. 1833. 100 acres.
Dawson, Thomas B. Va. Midshipman. 29 Aug. 1835. 2566 2/3 acres.
Dawson, Thomas B. Va. Midshipman. 26 Oct. 1839. 148 4/7 acres.
Dawson, Thomas B. Va. Midshipman. 26 Oct. 1839. 118 14/27 acres.
Dawson, Thomas B. Va. Midshipman. 26 Oct. 1839. 266 2/3 acres.
Dawson, Thomas B. Va. Midshipman. 17 Dec. 1839. 266 2/3 acres.
Dawson, Thomas B. Va. Midshipman. 17 Dec. 1839. 133 1/3 acres.
Dawson, Thomas B. Va. Midshipman. 17 Dec. 1839. 266 2/3 acres.
Dawson, Thomas B. Va. Midshipman. 6 May 1841. 266 2/3 acres.
Dawson, Thomas B. Va. Midshipman. 23 Jan. 1843. 59 1/3 acres.
Dawson, Thomas B. Va. Midshipman. 23 Jan. 1843. 178 acres.
Dawson, Thomas B. Va. Midshipman. 23 Jan. 1843. 29 2/3 acres.
Dawson, Thomas B. Va. Midshipman. 12 Aug. 1845. 133 1/3 acres.
Dawson, Thomas B. Va. Midshipman. 7 Jan. 1846. 178 acres.
Dawson, Thomas B. Va. Midshipman. 7 Jan. 1846. 108 2/3 acres.
Dawson, Thomas B. Va. Midshipman. 7 Jan. 1846. 54 1/3 acres.
Dawson, Thomas B. Va. Midshipman. 7 Jan. 1846. 133 1/3 acres.
Dawson, Thomas B. Va. Midshipman. 7 Jan. 1846. 88 88/89 acres.
Dawson, Thomas B. Va. Midshipman. 7 Jan. 1846. 88 88/89 acres.
Dawson, Thomas B. Va. Midshipman. 7 Jan. 1846. 33 8/9 acres.
Dawson, William. Ga. Soldier. 17 May 1784. 230 acres to heirs.
Dawson, William. Md. Private. ———. 50 acres.
Dawson, William. Pa. Sergeant. 20 Nov. 1787. 250 acres.
Day, Amary. Ga. Soldier. 6 Sep. 1785. 230 acres.
Day, Ambrose. Va. Private. 2 Apr. 1834. 100 acres.

Day, David. Mass. Sergeant. 2 Mar. 1833. 200 acres.

Day, Francis. Ga. ———. 17 May 1784. ———.

Day, George. Va. Sailor. 10 Dec. 1783. 100 acres.

Day, Henry. Ga. Refugee. 17 May 1784. ———.

Day, Henson. Ga. Soldier. 1 Aug. 1785. 230 acres.

Day, John. N. Y. Gunner. 9 Jul. 1790. 500 acres.

Day, John. N.C. Private. 11 Jan. 1822. 640 acres to heirs.

Day, John. Pa. Private. 29 Aug. 1787. 200 acres to George Bycroft, assignee.

Day, John. Va. Private. 6 Feb. 1784. 200 acres.

Day, Joseph. Ga. Captain. 6 Apr. 1784. 600 acres.

Day, Matthew. Ga. Soldier. 1 Aug. 1785. 230 acres.

Day, Moses. Pa. Private. 8 May 1787. 200 acres.

Day, Peter. N.C. Private. 9 Dec. 1797. 640 acres.

Day, Robert, Jr. Ga. Refugee. 30 Sep. 1784. 287 1/2 acres.

Day, Robert, Sr. Ga. Refugee. 13 Sep. 1784. 287 1/2 acres.

Day, Stephen. Ga. ———. 20 Feb. 1784. 250 acres.

Day, Thomas. Va. Sailor. 12 Apr. 1785. 100 acres.

Day, Westbrook. Va. Private. 21 Dec. 1786. 100 acres.

Day, William. Md. Private. ———. 50 acres.

Day, William. Va. Private. 23 Nov. 1784. 100 acres.

Dayton, Bennet. N. Y. Private. 24 Aug. 1790. 600 acres.

Dayton, Frederick. N. Y. Gunner. 9 Jul. 1790. 500 acres.

Dayton, Samuel. N.Y. ———. 13 Sep. 1790. 500 acres to heirs.

Dayton, Samuel, Jr. N.Y. ———. 13 Sep. 1790. 500 acres to heirs.

De'Ell, William. N.C. Private. 17 Feb. 1824. 640 acres.

Deacon, William. N.C. Private. 11 Jul. 1785. 182 acres.

Deakins, John. Md. Private. ———. 50 acres.

Deakins, William. Ga. Soldier. 20 Jul. 1785. ———.

Deakins, William. Md. Private. ———. 50 acres.

Deakon, Pearce. Md. Private. ———. 50 acres.

Deal, Andrew. Pa. Private. 25 July 1787. 200 acres to Henry Thull, assignee.

Deal, Edward. N.C. Private. 16 Feb. 1784. 640 acres.

Deal, Isaac. N.C. Private. 17 Dec. 1796. 640 acres.

Deal, James. N.C. Dragoon. 29 Apr. 1784. 274 acres.

Deal, John. N.C. Private. 28 May 1784. 380 acres.

Deal, John. N.C. Private. 6 Dec. 1796. 640 acres. He was of Perquimans County.

Deal, Lewis. N.C. Private. 30 Sep. 1785. 640 acres to heirs.

Deal, Reuben. N.C. Private. 13 Sep. 1820. 640 acres.

Deal, Thomas. Ga. Soldier. 6 Apr. 1785. 230 acres.

Deal, William. N.C. Private. 29 Nov. 1810. 640 acres to heirs.

Deale, Joseph. Md. Private. ———. 50 acres.

Dealer, George. N.C. Private. 2 Feb. 1786. 274 acres.

Deall, George. Mass. Private. 1 Nov. 1830. 200 acres.

Dean, Abner. S.C. ———. 1 Jul. 1793. 80 acres.

Dean, Abner. S.C. ———. 1 Jul. 1793. 120 acres.

Dean, Abram. N.C. Private. 15 Jul. 1785. 640 acres to heirs.

Dean, Absalom. S.C. ———. 1 Jul. 1793. 55 acres.

Dean, Absalom. S.C. ———. 29 June 1795. 145 acres.

Dean, Ashbel. N. Y. Matross. 9 Jul. 1790. 500 acres.

Dean, Benjamin. N. Y. Gunner. 9 Jul. 1790. 500 acres.

Dean, Benjamin. N.C. Private. 22 Dec. 1796. 640 acres to heirs.

Dean, Charles. Ga. ———. 17 May 1784. ———.

Dean, Cornelius. N.C. Private. 17 Dec. 1796. 274 acres.

Dean, Edmond. Me. ———. 11 May 1835. 200 acres. Paris.

Dean, Henry. Ga. Soldier. 2 Jan. 1786. ———.
Dean, Isaac. N. Y. Private. 8 Jul. 1790. 500 acres.
Dean, James. N. Y. Private. 8 Jul. 1790. 500 acres.
Dean, John. Ga. ———. 17 May 1784. 287 1/2 acres.
Dean, John. N. Y. Matross. 9 Jul. 1790. 600 acres.
Dean, John. N.C. Private. 30 Nov. 1808. 640 acres to heir at law William Dean.
Dean, John. S.C. ———. 1 Jul. 1793. 50 acres.
Dean, John. S.C. ———. 1 Jul. 1793. 150 acres.
Dean, John. Va. Private. 17 Apr. 1783. 200 acres.
Dean, John. Va. Sergeant. 27 Jun. 1783. 200 acres.
Dean, Jones. Va. Private. 30 Aug. 1797. 100 acres.
Dean, Joseph. Va. Private. 20 Jun. 1783. 100 acres.
Dean, Joshua. Va. Private. 16 Jul. 1783. 100 acres.
Dean, Joshua. Va. Private. 15 Nov. 1856. 100 acres.
Dean, Michel. Va. Private. 20 Jun. 1783. 100 acres.
Dean, Moses. N. Y. ———. 10 Jun. 1807. 250 acres.
Dean, Nathaniel. Ga. ———. 17 May 1784. ———.
Dean, Philip. N.C. Private. 11 Dec. 1804. 640 acres.
Dean, Robert. N.C. Private. 26 May 1784. 640 acres.
Dean, Samuel. Ga. Lighthorseman. Jun. 1783. ———.
Dean, Samuel. N. Y. Private. 6 Jul. 1790. 600 acres.
Dean, Sterling. N.C. Private. 11 Dec. 1804. 640 acres.
Dean, Thomas. Ga. ———. 17 May 1784. ———.
Dean, Thomas. S.C. ———. 2 Mar. 1795. 200 acres.
Dean, William. Ga. ———. 25 May 1784. 287 1/2 acres.
Dean, William. Ga. ———. 26 May 1784. 230 acres.
Dean, William. Pa. Private. ———. 200 acres.
Deane, Charles. Md. Private. ———. 50 acres.
Deane, Elijah. Md. Private. ———. 50 acres.
Deane, John. Md. Major. ———. 200 acres.
Deane, John. Md. Private. ———. 50 acres.
Deane, John. Va. Private. 23 May 1783. 100 acres.
Deane, Peter. Va. Private. 18 Jan. 1821. 100 acres.
Dear, Benjamin. Va. Private. 14 Jun. 1784. 100 acres.
Dearborn, Simeon. Me. Private. 15 Sep. 1838. 200 acres. Monmouth.
Dearden, George, Sr. Ga. Refugee. 20 Apr. 1784. ———.
Dearman, Malcom. N.C. Private. 12 Dec. 1796. 274 acres.
Deason, John. Ga. Minute Man. 2 May 1784. ———.
Deaster, Abraham. Ga. Refugee. Sep. 1785. ———.
Death, Randolph. Pa. Sergeant. 24 Aug. 1787. 250 acres.
Death, William. Va. Sergeant Major. 20 Jun. 1783. 200 acres.
Deaver, Aquilla. Md. Private. ———. 50 acres.
Deaver, William. Md. Private. ———. 50 acres.
Deavor, Thomas. Md. Private. ———. 50 acres.
DeBenneville, Daniel. Va. Surgeon. 1 Jun. 1795. 6000 acres.
DeBois, Lewis. N. Y. Private. 8 Jul. 1790. 600 acres.
Debosk, Peter. Ga. Captain. ———. 575 acres.
Debourd, James. Va. Private. 24 Nov. 1796. 100 acres.
Deboyce, Nicholas. N.C. Private. 13 Dec. 1796. 640 acres.
Decker, Christopher. N. Y. Private. 8 Jul. 1790. 600 acres.
Decker, John. N.Y. ———. 13 Sep. 1790. 500 acres to heirs.
Decker, Martin. N. Y. Private. 8 Jul. 1790. 600 acres.
Decker, Michael. N. Y. Private. 8 Jul. 1790. 500 acres.
Decker, Nicholas. Va. Private. 19 Jan. 1785. 100 acres.

Decker, Samuel. Va. Private. 22 May 1784. 100 acres.
Deckert, Peter. Pa. ———. 14 Mar. 1798. 500 acres to Jacob Bower, administrator, for the heirs.
Declandiness, Mathias. Ga. Sergeant. 23 Sep. 1784. ———.
DeClark, Abraham. N. Y. Private. 8 Jul. 1790. 600 acres.
Decloux, Alexis. N. Y. ———. ———. 500 acres.
Dedman, Robert. Va. Sergeant. 9 Dec. 1784. 200 acres.
Dedman, Samuel. Va. Sergeant. 5 Aug. 1784. 200 acres.
Deen, Absalom. S.C. ———. 1 Jul. 1793. 145 acres.
Deen, Charles. S.C. ———. 1 Jul. 1793. 200 acres.
Deen, Sterling. N.C. Private. 10 Aug. 1785. 640 acres.
Deenwell, Samuel. Conn. Sufferer. New/East Haven. 34.2.0.
Deffendorf, Henry. N. Y. Lieutenant. 9 Jul. 1790. 1200 acres.
Defnell, David. N.C. Private. 15 Sep. 1784. 487 acres.
Defnell, William. N.C. Private. 15 Sep. 1784. 640 acres to heirs.
Deford, John. Md. Private. ———. 50 acres.
Deford, Joseph. Md. Private. ———. 50 acres.
Deforest, Elihu. Conn. Sufferer. Ridgefield. 2.0.0.
Deforest, Rebecca. Conn. Sufferer. Norwalk. 7.15.8.
DeFreest, Abraham. N.Y. ———. 18 Mar. 1791. 500 acres to heirs.
Degazoon, Peter. Md. Private. ———. 50 acres.
Degraffenreidt, Tscharner. Va. Sergeant. 4 Nov. 1809. 400 acres.
DeGrote, John. N. Y. Drummer. 9 Jul. 1790. 600 acres.
Dehart, Abram. Pa. Sergeant. 20 Nov. ——. 300 acres.
Dehay, J. B. Va. Priavte. 31 Dec. 1851. 100 acres.
Dehay, J. B. Va. Private. 2 Apr. 1856. 100 acres.
Deiner, Jacob. Va. Sergeant. 26 Aug. 1783. 200 acres.
DeJarnette, Robert. Ga. ———. 17 May 1784. ———.
DeKay, Charles. Va. Sailing Master. 20 Oct. 1855. 3097 1/3 acres.
DeKlauman, Christian Charles. Va. Major. 4 Jun. 1784. 1000 acres.
DeKlauman, Christian Charles. Va. Major. 4 Jun. 1784. 1000 acres.
DeKlauman, Christian Charles. Va. Major. 4 Jun. 1784. 1000 acres.
DeKlauman, Chrsitian Charles. Va. Major. 4 Jan. 1784. 1000 acres.
Delameter, John. N. Y. Sergeant. 8 Jul. 1790. 600 acres.
Delanaway, John. Md. Private. ———. 50 acres.
Delaney, Abraham Johnson. N.C. Private. 8 Mar. 1796. 640 acres to heirs.
Delaney, Anthony. Va. Corporal. 5 Jun. 1784. 200 acres.
Delaney, Daniel. Ga. ———. 15 Mar. 1784. 250 acres.
Delaney, James. Ga. Private. 24 May 1784. 287 1/2 acres.
Delaney, Michael. N.C. Private. 16 Mar. 1795. 640 acres to heirs.
Delano, Jabez. Me. ———. 20 Jun. 1835. 200 acres. Livermore.
Delano, Jeptha. Mass. Sergeant. 19 Mar. 1835. 200 acres.
Delano, Jonathan. Me. Private. 16 May 1836. 200 acres to widow Ruth Delano. Woolwich.
Delano, Philip. Mass. Private. 19 Mar. 1835. 200 acres.
Delano, Seth. Me. Private. 12 May 1835. 200 acres. Phillips.
Delany, John. N.C. Private. 30 Nov. 1785. 640 acres.
Delany, William. Pa. Private. 10 Jul. 1787. 200 acres.
Delap, Thomas. Pa. Private. 14 Oct. 1786. 200 acres.
Delaplaigne, Emanuel Peter. Ga. Captain. 5 Sep. 1783. 600 acres.
Delaplane, James. Va. Lieutenant. 5 Jul. 1783. 2666 2/3 acres.
Delastatious, Joseph. Va. Private. 14 Feb. 1834. 100 acres.
Delastatious, Peter. Va. Sergeant. 14 Feb. 1834. 200 acres.
Delastatious, William. Va. Private. 14 Feb. 1834. 100 acres.

Delastatius, John. Va. Private. 30 Dec. 1808. 261 acres.

Delastatius, Severn. Va. Sergeant. 15 May 1838. 400 acres.

Delastatius, Severn. Va. Sergeant. 10 Jul. 1838. 200 acres.

Delastatius, Severn. Va. Sergeant. 10 Jul. 1838. 200 acres.

Deleonser, Abraham. Ga. Minute Man. 3 Sep. 1785. ———.

Delezeene, Joseph. N.Y. Captain. 8 Jul. 1790. 1000 acres.

Delisle, John. N. Y. ———. ———. 500 acres.

Delk, David. Ga. Soldier. 2 Jan 1785. 287 1/2 acres.

Dell, Joseph. Va. Private. 3 Feb. 1784. 100 acres.

Delmore, Joseph. N.C. Private. 30 Sep. 1785. 274 acres.

Deloach, Thomas. N.C. Private. 5 Dec. 1796. 228 acres.

Deloge, Joseph. Va. Private. 2 Apr. 1856. 100 acres.

Delong, Francis. N.C. Musician. 3 Aug. 1820. 1000 acres to heirs.

Deloze, Joseph. Va. Private. 31 Dec. 1851. 100 acres.

Delozer, Asa. Va. Private. 13 Dec. 1783. 200 acres.

Delozier, Richard D. Va. Sergeant. 31 Mar. 1786. 200 acres.

Delph, Daniel. Va. Private. 14 Jun. 1784. 100 acres.

Delvin, Francis. N.Y. ———. ———. 500 acres to heirs.

DeMarcellin, Anthony. Pa. Lieutenant. 28 May 1787. 200 acres.

Demaster, James. Va. Private. 21 Dec. 1799. 200 acres.

Demler, Henry. N. Y. Lieutenant. 9 Jul. 1790. 1200 acres.

Demmon, Amos. Mass. Private. 20 Sep. 1834. 200 acres to heirs.

Demomcee [?], Timothy. N.C. Lieutenant. 24 Dec. 1785. 1000 acres.

DemonBreun, Timothy. Va. Lieutenant. 13 Dec. 1791. 2666 2/3 acres.

Demoss, John. Va. Private. 5 Apr. 1784. 200 acres.

DeMott, Peter. N.Y. ———. 13 Sep. 1790. 500 acres to heirs.

Demott, William. N. Y. Fifer. 9 Jul. 1790. 600 acres.

Demovill, Samuel. Va. Seaman. 26 Jun. 1784. 100 acres.

Dempsey, Charles. Pa. Private. 15 Mar. 1787. 200 acres.

Dempsey, Luke. Md. Private. ———. 50 acres.

Dempsey, Sampson. Pa. Private. ———. 200 acres.

Dempsey, Squire. N.C. Private. 11 Nov. 1814. 640 acres to heirs.

Demsey, John. Va. Private. 20 Jun. 1783. 100 acres.

Denby, Jonathan. Va. Private. 14 Feb. 1784. 100 acres.

Denby, William. Ga. ———. 17 May 1784. ———.

Dener, Jacob. Va. Sergeant. 22 Aug. 1783. 400 acres.

Denham, Charles. Ga. ———. 17 May 1784. ———.

Denholm, Archibald. Va. Captain. 19 May 1783. 4000 acres.

Denison, Rhoda. Conn. Sufferer. New/East Haven. 10.6.0.

Denkins, Theophilus. N.C. Private. 23 Nov. 1797. 640 acres to heirs.

Denmark, John. Pa. Private. 25 Nov. 1786. 200 acres.

Dennestow, Eleven. N.C. Private. 17 Dec. 1796. 640 acres to heirs.

Denney, Abraham. N.C. Private. 20 Feb. 1784. 365 acres.

Denney, David. N.C. Private. 20 Feb. 1784. 274 acres.

Denney, David. N.C. Private. 29 Sep. 1784. 274 acres.

Dennis, Abner. N.C. Private. 17 Dec. 1785. 640 acres to heirs.

Dennis, Abraham. Ga. ———. 17 May 1784. ———.

Dennis, Ezekiah. N.C. Private. 20 Jan. 1785. 640 acres.

Dennis, Henry. Va. Private. 30 Aug. 1783. 233 1/3 acres.

Dennis, Isaac. Ga. ———. 17 May 1784. ———.

Dennis, Jacob. Ga. ———. 30 Jul. 1784. 287 1/2 acres.

Dennis, John. N. Y. Matross. 9 Jul. 1790. 600 acres.

Dennis, John, Jr. Ga. ———. 17 May 1784. ———.

Dennis, Michael. Pa. Private. 10 Aug. 1787. 200 acres.

Dennis, Myndert. N. Y. Private. 8 Jul. 1790. 600 acres.
Dennis, Philip. Pa. Private. ———. 200 acres.
Dennis, Richard. Ga. Soldier. 5 Dec. 1785. ———.
Dennis, Richmond. Ga. ———. 28 Feb. 1784. 250 acres.
Dennis, Robert. Ga. Soldier. 15 Jul. 1785. ———.
Dennis, Robert. N.C. Private. 15 Feb. 1797. 640 acres to heirs.
Dennis, William. N.C. Captain. 27 Jan. 1800. 1097 acres.
Dennis, William. N.C. Private. 9 Dec. 1809. 228 acres.
Dennis, William. N.C. Private. 2 Sep. 1820. 640 acres.
Dennis, William. N.C. Private. 15 Sep. 1820. 640 acres to heirs.
Dennis, William. Va. Private. 31 Dec. 1785. 200 acres.
Dennis, William. Va. Private. 24 Jul. 1830. 100 acres.
Dennison, Daniel. Ga. ———. 17 May 1784. ———.
Dennison, Elijah. Ga. Sergeant. 24 Apr. 1784. ———.
Dennison, John, Sr. Ga. Soldier. 10 Jul. 1785. 287 1/2 acres.
Dennison, Joseph. Va. Private. 23 Jun. 1783. 200 acres.
Dennison, Patrick. Md. Private. ———. 50 acres.
Dennison, Thomas. N. Y. Private. 8 Jul. 1790. 500 acres.
Dennison, William. Ga. Soldier. 10 Jul. 1785. ———.
Denniston, Daniel. N. Y. Lieutenant. 7 Jul. 1790. 1200 acres.
Denniston, George. N. Y. Lieutenant. 7 Jul. 1790. 1200 acres.
Denniston, James. Pa. Private. 24 Feb. 1789. 200 acres.
Denny, Ebenezer. Pa. Lieutenant. ———. 200 acres.
Denny, Ebenezer. Pa. Lieutenant. ———. 200 acres.
Denny, Henry. Va. Sergeant. 4 Dec. 1783. 466 2/3 acres.
Denny, John. N. Y. ———. 4 Apr. 1805. 200 acres to trustees Joseph C. Yates and Peter R. Ludlow.
Denny, Peter. N. Y. Private. 8 Jul. 1790. 600 acres.
Denny, Robert. Md. Lieutenant. ———. 200 acres.
Denny, Samuel. Md. Private. ———. 50 acres.
Denny, Samuel. Va. Captain. 4 Feb. 1784. 4000 acres.
Dension, James. Md. Private. ———. 50 acres.
Denson, John. Md. Private. ———. 50 acres.
Denson, John. Md. Drummer. ———. 50 acres.
Denson, William. N.C. Private. 12 Mar. 1785. 640 acres to heirs.
Dent, John. Md. Private. ———. 50 acres.
Dent, John. Va. Lieutenant. 2 Aug. 1785. 2000 acres.
Dent, John. Va. Lieutenant. 2 Aug. 1785. 666 2/3 acres.
Dentham, John. Ga. Minute Man. 22 Mar. 1785. 250 acres.
Denton, Humphrey. Conn. Sufferer. Greenwich. 73.19.10.
Denton, John. Va. Private. 21 Nov. 1783. 100 acres.
Denton, Reuben. S.C. Soldier. 15 Oct. 1784. 200 acres.
Denton, Thomas. Va. Sergeant. 27 Nov. 1790. 400 acres.
Denton, William. Pa. Private. 14 Jan. 1789. 200 acres.
Denwood, Levin. Md. Surgeon. ———. 200 acres.
Depeau, Henry. N. Y. Private. 8 Jul. 1790. 600 acres.
Depriest, John. Va. Sergeant. 3 Jun. 1783. 200 acres.
Depriest, Robert. Va. Drummer. 31 Jul. 1783. 100 acres.
Depuy, John. N.Y. ———. 13 Sep. 1790. 500 acres to his heirs.
Derbe, Richard. Ga. ———. 17 May 1784. ———.
Dermot, Richard. N. Y. Private. 8 Jul. 1790. 600 acres.
DeRoche, Abraham. Ga. ———. 5 Mar. 1784. 250 acres.
DeRotter, George. N.Y. ———. ———. 500 acres to heirs.
Derr, John. Pa. ———. 19 Sep. 1787. 200 acres.

Desaissure, Lewis. S.C. Lieutenant. 2 May 1785. 200 acres to Henry William Desaissur.

Desbrow, Abigail. Conn. Sufferer. Fairfield. 9.11.8.

Desbrow, Caleb. Conn. Sufferer. Fairfield. 18.0.6.

Desbrow, Caleb. Conn. Sufferer. Fairfield. 8.16.4.

Desbrow, Jabez. Conn. Sufferer. Fairfield. 5.9.6.

Desbrow, Jason. Conn. Sufferer. Fairfield. 16.2.4.

Desbrow, John. Conn. Sufferer. Fairfield. 15.14.0.

Desbrow, Wait. Conn. Sufferer. Danbury. 9.11.0.

Desdevans, Maurice. N. Y. Captain. ———. 1000 acres.

Deseern, Francis. N.C. Private. 10 Jan. 1794. 640 acres.

Desern, Frederick. N.C. Private. 20 Apr. 1784. 274 acres.

Deshazo, William. Va. Private. 21 Oct. 1784. 100 acres.

Deshon & Co. Conn. Sufferer. New London. 556.10.0.

Deshon, Henry. Conn. Sufferer. New London. 900.0.2.

Deshon, John. Conn. Sufferer. New London. 1,177.6.2

Deshon, Joseph. Conn. Sufferer. New London. 100.1.0.

Deshon, Richard. Conn. Sufferer. New London. 266.19.8.

Desmond, John. Pa. Private. 29 Sep. 1787. 200 acres to Thomas Carpenter, assignee.

Desperate, Henry. Pa. Private. 15 Dec. 1786. 200 acres.

DeStaatsman, Jean. N.Y. ———. ———. 500 acres to heirs.

Deter, Michael. Pa. Private. 5 May 1787. 200 acres.

DeValtz, Peter. N. Y. Private. 7 Jul. 1790. 600 acres.

Devaney, Nehemiah. N.C. Private. 15 Feb. 1797. 228 acres.

Devaney, Sterling. N.C. Private. 15 Feb. 1797. 640 acres to heirs.

Deveaux, Butoc. Md. Private. ———. 50 acres.

Deveaux, Peter. Ga. Captain. 1784. 750 acres.

Develin, James. S.C. ———. 4 Jun. 1787. 200 acres.

Devenport, Thomas. N.C. Private. 2 Feb. 1786. 274 acres.

Deveny, John. Pa. Private. 15 Jun. 1789. 200 acres.

Dever, Patrick. Pa. Matross. 12 Jan. 1787. 200 acres.

Devere, James. Va. Private. 23 Jun. 1783. 200 acres.

Devereaux, Charles. Ga. ———. 17 May 1784. ———.

Devereux, James. Md. Sergeant. ———. 50 acres.

Devier, John. Va. Private. 18 Nov. 1783. 100 acres.

Devine, William. Md. Private. ———. 50 acres.

Devit, George. Md. Private. ———. 50 acres.

Devitt, James. Pa. ———. 13 Oct. 1786. 200 acres to John Adams.

Devoe, Jeremiah. N. Y. ———. 13 Sep. 1790. 600 acres.

Devonshire, Joshua. N.C. Private. 19 Jan. 1786. 640 acres.

Devor, Jeremiah. Va. Private. 2 Feb. 1819. 100 acres.

Devrance, H. John. N. Y. Private. 8 Jul. 1790. 600 acres.

Dew, Leonard. N.C. Private. 9 Dec. 1797. 640 acres.

Dewees, Samuel. Pa. Private. ———. 200 acres to Richard Leedom.

Dewet, Jesse. N.C. Private. 30 Sep. 1785. 640 acres to heirs.

Dewey, John. Mass. Private. 22 Oct. 1830. 200 acres to asignee Josiah King.

Dewit, Henry. Va.-Ind. Sergeant. 216 acres.

DeWit, Henry. Va. Private. 26 Mar. 1784. 100 acres.

DeWitt, Aaron. N.Y. ———. 13 Sep. 1790. 500 acres to heirs.

DeWitt, John. N. Y. Matross. 6 Jul. 1790. 600 acres.

Dewitt, Peter. Va. Private. 30 Nov. 1784. 100 acres.

Dewny, Elisha. N.Y. ———. 13 Sep. 1790. 500 acres to heirs.

Deymont, Hanjost. N. Y. Private. 8 Jul. 1790. 600 acres.

Diamond, John. Ga. ———. 17 May 1784. ———.

Diamond, William. Ga. ———. 17 May 1784. ———.

Diamond, William. N. Y. Private. 8 Jul. 1790. 600 acres.

Dibble, Elisha. Conn. Sufferer. Danbury. 4.6.8.

Dibble, Ezra, Jr. Conn. Sufferer. Danbury. 17.7.11.

Dice, George. Md. Private. ———. 50 acres.

Dick, Alexander. Va. Major. 31 Dec. 1782. 5333 1/3 acres.

Dick, Alexander. Va. Major. 26 Feb. 1834. 344 acres.

Dick, Alexander. Va. Major. 26 Feb. 1834. 344 acres.

Dick, Alexander. Va. Major. 26 Feb. 1834. 344 acres.

Dick, Alexander. Va. Major. 22 Jan. 1841. 150 2/3 acres.

Dick, Alexander. Va. Major. 19 Feb. 1858. 150 2/3 acres.

Dick, Alexander. Va. Major. 22 Jan. 1841. 150 2/3 acres.

Dick, Alexander. Va. Major. 22 Jan. 1841. 150 2/3 acres.

Dicke, William. Ga. ———. 17 May 1784. ———.

Dickens, Edmund. N.C. Private. 6 Dec. 1797. 640 acres to heirs.

Dickens, Peter. N.Y. ———. 13 Sep. 1790. 500 acres to heirs.

Dickens, William. N. Y. Private. 8 Jul. 1790. 600 acres.

Dickenson, Griffith, Sr. Va. Corporal. 9 Feb. 1833. 200 acres.

Dickenson, Hannah. Conn. Sufferer. Norwalk. 23.19.7.

Dickenson, John. Va. Private. 8 Jul. 1841. 100 acres.

Dickenson, Moses. Conn. Sufferer. Norwalk. 259.16.10 to heirs.

Dickenson, Nathaniel. Conn. Sufferer. New London. 15.1.0.

Dickerman, Isaac. Conn. Sufferer. New/ East Haven. 32.4.0.

Dickerson, Abraham. N. Y. Sergeant. 8 Jul. 1790. 600 acres.

Dickerson, David. N. Y. Corporal. 8 Jul. 1790. 600 acres.

Dickerson, Edmund. Va. Major. 27 Mar. 1783. 5333 1/3 acres.

Dickerson, Edmund. Va. Major. 6 Apr. 1838. 1522 acres.

Dickerson, Henry. N.C. Private. 10 Dec. 1788. 640 acres to heirs.

Dickerson, John. N.C. Captain. 27 Mar. 1821. 1371 acres to heirs. He was of Granville County.

Dickerson, Nathaniel. N.C. Lieutenant. 21 Oct. 1783. 949 acres.

Dickerson, Robert. Va. Private. 23 May 1836. 200 acres.

Dickes, Henry. Va. Sailor. 24 Dec. 1788. 100 acres.

Dickeson, Edward. Va. Private. 15 Jun. 1807. 100 acres.

Dickey, Alexander. Va. Private. 18 Nov. 1783. 233 1/3 acres.

Dickey, Eleazer. Me. Private. 15 May 1835. 200 acres. Monroe.

Dickey, Jacob. N.C. Private. 22 Apr. 1785. 640 acres to heirs.

Dickey, James. Pa. Corporal. 14 Nov. 1786. 200 acres.

Dickie, William. Va. Private. 15 May 1783. 100 acres.

Dickin, James. Va. Private. 18 Nov. 1818. 100 acres.

Dickinson, Deborah. Conn. Sufferer. Norwalk. 17.2.6.

Dickinson, Henry. N.C. Private. 2 Feb. 1786. 274 acres.

Dickison, Thomas. Md. Private. ———. 50 acres.

Dicks, Andrew. Ga. Refugee. 15 Mar. 1784. 250 acres.

Dicks, David. Ga. Refugee. 15 Mar. 1784. 250 acres to Andrew Dicks, administrator, for the heirs.

Dicks, George. Pa. Private. 19 Dec. 1786. 200 acres.

Dicks, George. Va. Private. 9 Jan. 1786. 200 acres.

Dicks, Jacob. Pa. Private. 9 Apr. 1799. 200 acres.

Dicks, Jacob. Pa. Private. ———. 200 acres.

Dickson, Benjamin. N.C. Private. 1 Dec. 1789. 182 acres.

Dickson, David. Ga. Captain. 17 May 1784. ———.

Dickson, Hugh. Ga. Sergeant. 17 May 1784. ———.

Dickson, James. Va. Private. 29 Aug. 1783. 200 acres.

Dickson, John. Pa. Sergeant. ———. 250 acres.

Dickson, Joseph. N.C. Private. 2 Dec. 1819. 640 acres.
Dickson, Nathan. Ga. Soldier. 4 Jan. 1785. ———.
Dickson, Nathaniel. Ga. Private. 13 Mar. 1784. ———.
Diddy, Jeremiah. Pa. Private. 11 Feb. 1785. 200 acres to Stephen Loudon, assignee.
Didlake, James. Va. Sergeant. 13 Aug. 1787. 200 acres.
Didlick, William. Va. Private. 12 Dec. 1833. 200 acres.
Die, John. Va. Private. 23 Jun. 1784. 100 acres.
Digges, Cole. Va. Lieutenant. 19 Dec. 1807. 2666 2/3 acres.
Digges, Dudley. Va. Lieutenant. 31 Dec. 1782. 2666 2/3 acres.
Digges, Edward. Va. ———. 11 Apr. 1838. 250 acres.
Digges, Edward. Va. Captain. 4 Feb. 1834. 250 acres.
Digges, Edward. Va. Captain. 4 Feb. 1834. 250 acres.
Digges, Edward. Va. Captain. 4 Feb. 1834. 250 acres.
Digges, Edward. Va. Captain. 4 Feb. 1834. 250 acres.
Digges, Edward. Va. Captain. 3 Jun. 1840. 250 acres.
Digges, Edward. Va. Captain. 28 Jul. 1849. 166 2/3 acres.
Digges, Edward. Va. Captain. 28 Jul. 1849. 83 1/3 acres.
Digges, Edward. Va. Captain. 11 Apr. 1851. 500 acres.
Digges, Edward. Va. Captain. 10 May 1851. 250 acres.
Digges, Edward. Va. Captain. 4 Apr. 1854. 62 1/2 acres.
Digges, Edward. Va. Captain. 17 Apr. 1855. 125 acres.
Digges, Edward. Va. Captain. 20 May 1856. 62 1/2 acres.
Digges, Edward. Va. Captain. 7 Apr. 1838. 250 acres.
Digges, Edward. Va. Captain. 7 Apr. 1838. 250 acres.
Digges, Edward. Va. Captain. 7 Apr. 1838. 250 acres.
Digges, Edward. Va. Captain. 7 Apr. 1838. 250 acres.
Diggs, Anthony. N.C. Private. 28 Jul. 1784. 1097 acres.
Dignam, Thomas. N.C. Private. 13 Jan. 1823. 640 acres.
Dihouse, Edward. Va. Private. 22 May 1783. 200 acres.
Dihouse, Edward. Va. Private. 3 Mar. 1784. 100 acres.
Dikous, Edmund. N.C. Corporal. 31 Jan. 1800. 1000 acres.
Dill, George. N.C. Private. 30 Sep. 1785. 640 acres to heirs.
Dill, James. Pa. Private. ———. 200 acres.
Dill, Nicholas. N. Y. Gunner. 9 Jul. 1790. 600 acres.
Dillan, Benjamin. N.C. Lieutenant. Jan. 1795. 2560 acres.
Dillar, John. N.C. Private. 10 Dec. 1788. 640 acres to heirs.
Dillard, James. Va. Captain. 5 Dec. 1809. 1000 acres.
Dillard, James. Va. Captain. 5 Dec. 1809. 1000 acres.
Dillard, James. Va. Captain. 5 Dec. 1809. 1000 acres.
Dillard, John. N.C. Sergeant. 7 May 1784. 357 acres.
Dillard, Osborn. N.C. Private. 5 May 1784. 228 acres.
Dillard, Peter. N.C. Private. 12 Sep. 1785. 640 acres to heirs.
Dillard, Sampson. N.C. Private. 14 Dec. 1787. 640 acres.
Dillard, William. N.C. Private. 5 May 1784. 228 acres.
Dillebow, Andrew. N.C. Private. 24 Nov. 1796. 640 acres to heirs.
Dilleway, George. N.C. Private. 19 Jan. 1786. 274 acres.
Dillon, Benjamin. N.C. Lieutenant. 2 Feb. 1786. 2560 acres.
Dillon, Jesse. Va. Corporal. Jan. 1783. 200 acres.
Dillon, Joshua. N.C. Private. 9 Feb. 1796. 228 acres.
Dillon, Thomas. N.C. Sergeant. 22 Dec. 1796. 1000 acres to heirs.
Dillyard, John. Va. Drummer. 7 Aug. 1783. 200 acres.
Dilman, William. Pa. Private. 11 Jan. 1787. 200 acres.
Dimery, Jehu. N.C. Private. 25 Nov. 1795. 640 acres to heirs.
Dimmitt, William. N.C. Private. 22 Apr. 1785. 640 acres to heirs.

Dimon, Ann. Conn. Sufferer. Fairfield. 317.18.4.
Dimon, William. Conn. Sufferer. Fairfield. 625.8.1.
Dimond, Moses. N.Y. ———. 13 Sep. 1790. 500 acres to heirs.
Dimpsey, Thomas. Pa. Private. 5 Apr. 1787. 200 acres.
Dimsey, Timothy. Pa. Private. ———. 200 acres.
Dines, Isaac. N.C. Private. 30 Sep. 1785. 274 acres.
Dingley, Levi. Me. Private. 25 Aug. 1838. 200 acres. Harpswell.
Dingman, Abraham. N. Y. Private. 8 Jul. 1790. 500 acres.
Dingman, Adam. N.Y. ———. 13 Sep. 1790. 500 acres to heirs.
Dingman, Gerardus. N. Y. Private. 8 Jul. 1790. 600 acres.
Dinkins, Gilbert. Ga. ———. 17 May 1784. ———.
Dinkins, John. Ga. Minute Man. 3 Sep. 1785. ———.
Dinkins, Sabray. Ga. Minute Man. 22 Mar. 1785. 250 acres.
Dione, Germain. N. Y. Lieutenant. ———. 1000 acres.
Disern, Francis. N.C. Private. 29 Sep. 1784. 640 acres.
Disharoon, Thomas. Md. Private. ———. 50 acres.
Dishman, James. Va. Private. 13 Nov. 1810. 200 acres.
Dishman, James. Va. Private. 21 Jan. 1784. 100 acres.
Dishman, John. Va. Private. 13 Nov. 1810. 100 acres.
Dishman, William. Va. Private. 13 Nov. 1810. 100 acres.
Diskell, Nathaniel. N. Y. Corporal. 9 Jul. 1790. 600 acres.
Diskin, Daniel. Va. Private. 16 Apr. 1787. 100 acres.
Dismukes, George. N.C. Private. 5 Sep. 1821. 228 acres.
Dison, Thomas. N.C. Private. 29 Sep. 1784. 640 acres.
Diver, Robert. Va. Private. 24 Aug. 1788. 100 acres.
Diver, William. Va. Sergeant. 24 Aug. 1785. 200 acres.
Divine, Ellis. Va. Private. 17 Mar. 1832. 100 acres.
Divine, James. Md. Private. ———. 50 acres.
Dix, Benjamin. Ga. Minute Man. 3 Sep. 1785. ———.
Dix, David. Ga. Refugee. 6 Aug. 1785. ———.
Dix, Peter. Ga. Minute Man. 3 Sep. 1785. ———.
Dix, Randolph. Ga. Refugee. 6 Aug. 1785. ———.
Dix, Thomas. Va. Captain Lieutenant. 27 Feb. 1783. 4000 acres.
Dix, Thomas. Va. Captain Lieutenant. 27 Sep. 1796. 666 2/3 acres.
Dix, Thomas. Va. Captain Lieutenant. 30 Oct. 1807. 555 acres.
Dix, William. Me. Sergeant. 16 Feb. 1836. 200 acres to widow Abigail Dix. Newburg.
Dix, William. Va. Sergeant. 20 May 1823. 200 acres.
Dixen, John Liddle. Ga. ———. 19 Dec. 1785. 600 acres.
Dixon, Anthony Tucker. Va. Surgeon. 16 Dec. 1783. 1000 acres.
Dixon, Anthony Tucker. Va. Surgeon. 16 Dec. 1783. 5000 acres.
Dixon, Anthony Tucker. Va. Surgeon. 1 Feb. 1809. 2000 acres.
Dixon, Charles. N.C. Lieutenant. 21 Oct. 1783. 2560 acres.
Dixon, David. Ga. ———. 17 May 1784. ———.
Dixon, Edward. Ga. ———. 30 Sep. 1784. ———.
Dixon, Edward. Va. Private. 12 Mar. 1785. 100 acres.
Dixon, George. Md. Private. ———. 50 acres.
Dixon, George. N.C. Musician. 16 Aug. 1821. 1000 acres.
Dixon, Henry. Md. Private. ———. 50 acres.
Dixon, Henry. N.C. Lieutenant Colonel. 21 Oct. 1783. 5760 acres to Charles Dixon, executor, in trust for the legatees.
Dixon, Henry. N.C. Private. 11 May 1785. 640 acres to heirs.
Dixon, Jacob. Pa. Private. 12 Jan. 1787. 200 acres.
Dixon, James. Pa. Sergeant. 6 Nov. 1786. 250 acres.
Dixon, James. Va. Drummer. 9 Dec. 1783. 100 acres.

Dixon, James. Va. Drummer. 26 Feb. 1861. 100 acres.
Dixon, Jeremiah. N.C. Private. 19 Dec. 1809. 274 acres.
Dixon, Joel. N.C. Private. 11 May 1785. 640 acres.
Dixon, John. Ga. ———. 17 May 1784. ———.
Dixon, John. Md. Private. ———. 50 acres.
Dixon, John. N.C. Private. 11 May 1785. 640 acres to heirs.
Dixon, John. N.C. Sergeant. 15 Nov. 1793. 1000 acres to heirs.
Dixon, John. Pa. Private. 12 Jan. 1787. 200 acres.
Dixon, John. Va. Private. 14 Feb. 1834. 100 acres.
Dixon, Joseph. Va. Private. 27 Jul. 1784. 200 acres.
Dixon, Michael. Ga. Captain. 17 May 1784. ———.
Dixon, Patrick. Pa. Private. ———. 200 acres.
Dixon, Richard. Md. Private. ———. 50 acres.
Dixon, Robert. Ga. ———. 17 May 1784. ———.
Dixon, Sanky. Pa. Lieutenant. 27 Feb. 1787. 200 acres.
Dixon, Sanky. Pa. Private. 27 Feb. 1787. 200 acres.
Dixon, Thomas. N. Y. Matross. 7 Jul. 1790. 600 acres.
Dixon, Thomas. Va. Private. 21 Dec. 1798. 200 acres.
Dixon, Tillmon. N.C. Captain. 21 Oct. 1783. 3840 acres.
Dixon, Walter. N.C. Private. 22 Dec. 1796. 640 acres to heirs.
Dixon, Wenne. N.C. Lieutenant. 21 Oct. 1783. 2560 acres.
Dixon, William. Ga. Sergeant. 17 May 1784. ———.
Dixon, William. Md. Private. ———. 50 acres.
Dixon, William. Md. Bombadier. ———. 50 acres.
Dixon, William. N.C. Private. 12 Dec. 1796. 640 acres to heirs.
Dixon, William. Pa. Private. 11 Sep. 1789. 200 acres.
Dixon, William. Pa. Private. 27 Aug. 1787. 200 acres.
Dixon, William. Va. Private. 16 Aug. 1834. 100 acres.
Doak, William. Conn. Sufferer. New/East Haven. 15.9.6.
Doane, Amos. Me. ———. 7 Jul. 1835. 200 acres. Hampden.
Dobbins, Charles. Va. Private. 14 Aug. 1783. 200 acres.
Dobbins, Hugh. N.C. Lieutenant. 17 Feb. 1824. 2560 acres.
Dobbins, William. N.C. Private. 26 May 1784. 640 acres.
Dobbins, William. N.C. Corporal. 21 Aug. 1820. 1000 acres.
Dobbs, Kedar. Va. Private. 22 Jan. 1812. 200 acres.
Dobbs, Nathaniel. Va. Private. 20 Oct. 1796. 200 acres.
Dobey, John. Ga. Soldier. 1 May 1785. ———.
Dobey, Nathaniel. N.C. Private. 21 Oct. 1783. 228 acres.
Dobey, William. Ga. ———. 1 May 1785. ———.
Dobson, Elias. N.C. Private. 30 Sep. 1785. 640 acres to heirs.
Dobson, Henry. Md. Captain. ———. 200 acres.
Dobson, John. Md. Private. ———. 50 acres.
Dobson, John. N. Y. Private. 8 Jul. 1790. 600 acres.
Dobson, Robert. Va. Sailing Master. 4 Aug. 1783. 2666 2/3 acres.
Dobson, Thomas. Pa. Private. 10 Aug. 1787. 200 acres.
Dobson, William. Pa. Private. ———. ———.
Doby, Robert. Va. Sailor. 25 Mar. 1800. 100 acres.
Docan, John. N.C. Private. 17 Feb. 1824. 640 acres.
Docherty, John. Va. Private. 23 Jun. 1783. 200 acres.
Dodd, David. N.C. Private. 29 Apr. 1784. 274 acres.
Dodd, David. N.C. Sergeant. 24 Dec. 1796. 1000 acres.
Dodd, Edmund. N.C. Private. 18 Dec. 1797. 365 acres.
Dodd, Jesse. N.C. Private. 22 Dec. 1796. 274 acres.
Dodd, John. Va. Private. 14 Jun. 1820. 100 acres.

Dodd, Sampson. N.C. Private. 9 Dec. 1797. 640 acres to heirs.
Dodd, Thomas. N.C. Private. 25 Nov. 1795. 640 acres to heirs.
Dodd, William. Va. Private. 21 Jun. 1783. 100 acres.
Dodds, George. Ga. Soldier. 4 Oct. 1785. ———.
Dodge, Henry. N. Y. Lieutenant. 9 Jul. 1790. 1200 acres.
Dodge, Mary. Conn. Sufferer. Groton. 14.6.0.
Dodge, Nicholas. Me. Private. 7 Sep. 1838. 200 acres to widow Elizabeth Dodge. Burnham.
Dodge, Richard. N. Y. Fifer. 8 Jul. 1790. 600 acres.
Dodge, Samuel. Mass. Private. 26 Sep. 1833. 200 acres to his widow Esther Dodge.
Dodge, Samuel. N. Y. Ensign. 9 Jul. 1790. 1150 acres.
Dodge, Samuel. N. Y. Lieutenant. 9 Jul. 1790. 1200 acres.
Dodridge, Jacob. Pa. Private. ———. 200 acres.
Dodrill, James. N.C. Noncommissioned Officer. 16 Dec. 1807. 1000 acres to heirs.
Dodson, Beletha. N.C. Private. 9 Feb. 1796. 640 acres to heirs.
Dodson, Charles. N.C. Private. 21 Oct. 1783. 640 acres.
Dodson, Charles. N.C. Private. 22 Dec. 1796. 274 acres.
Dodson, Charles. N.C. Private. 24 Dec. 1796. 640 acres.
Dodson, John. N.C. Private. 22 Apr. 1785. 274 acres.
Dodson, Thomas. Pa. Private. 30 Dec. 1788. 200 acres.
Dodson, Walter. Ga. Soldier. 5 Aug. 1785. ———.
Dodson, William, Jr. Ga. Soldier. 5 Aug. 1785. ———.
Dodson, William, Sr. Ga. Soldier. 5 Aug. 1785. ———.
Doe, William. Va. Private. 18 Aug. 1835. 100 acres.
Doer, John. Ga. Soldier. 20 Aug. 1785. ———.
Dogan, Henry. Va. Private. 22 Dec. 1783. 100 acres.
Dogan, Timothy. Va. Private. 9 Dec. 1795. 200 acres.
Dogget, Benjamin. Va. Private. 27 Nov. 1832. 100 acres.
Dogget, Clement. Va. Sailor. 30 Jun. 1784. 100 acres.
Dogget, George. Va. Carpenter. 7 Apr. 183-. 1333 acres.
Dogget, George. Va. Carpenter. 7 Apr. 183-. 1333 acres.
Dogget, George. Va. Carpenter. 3 Apr. 1849. 1333 1/3 acres.
Dogget, Richard. Va. Captain. 16 Aug. 1832. 4000 acres.
Doherty, Dennis. N.C. Private. 9 Feb. 1796. 228 acres.
Doherty, Frederick. Va.-Ind. Private. 108 acres.
Doherty, John. Va. Private. 6 Jan. 1834. 200 acres.
Doherty, Neal. Va.-Ind. Private. 108 acres.
Dohorty, Barnaby. Md. Private. ———. 50 acres.
Dolack, John. Ga. ———. 15 Mar. 1784. 250 acres.
Doland, John. Va. Private. 5 Feb. 1785. 200 acres.
Dolby, William. Va. Sergeant. 21 Apr. 1791. 200 acres.
Dole, Amos. Me. Sergeant. 2 Nov. 1836. 200 acres to widow Matilda Dole. Orrington.
Doll, Robert. Va. Private. 3 Dec. 1783. 200 acres.
Dollar, Anson. Ga. Refugee. 20 Sep. 1784. 287 1/2 acres.
Dollar, John. Ga. Lieutenant. 19 Mar. 1784. 400 acres.
Dollar, William. Va. Private. 20 Jun. 1783. 100 acres.
Dollins, William. Va. Private. 28 Jun. 1783. 200 acres.
Dolly, Benjamin. Ga. Refugee. 22 Dec. 1783. ———.
Dolphin, John. N.C. Private. 9 Dec. 1797. 274 acres.
Dolton, Frederick. N. Y. Private. 8 Jul. 1790. 600 acres.
Dolton, George. Pa. Sergeant. 6 Jan. 1787. 250 acres to John Dolton, administrator.
Dolton, John. N. Y. Sergeant. 6 Jul. 1790. 600 acres.
Dolvin, Richard. Md. Private. ———. 50 acres.

Dominick, Beryer. Md. Private. ———. 50 acres.
Dominick, Edward. Md. Private. ———. 50 acres.
Donaghan, John. Md. Private. ———. 50 acres.
Donald, Absolam. Ga. Minute Man. 3 Apr. 1785. ———.
Donaldson, Jesse. N.C. Private. 16 Feb. 1784. 640 acres.
Donaldson, Spencer. N.C. Drummer. 28 May 1784. 428 acres.
Donaldson, William. Va. Private. 17 Jul. 1795. 100 acres.
Doney, James. Pa. Private. 10 Feb. 1812. 200 acres to James Gordon in right of.
Donnakin, Daniel. Va. Private. 18 Dec. 1783. 100 acres.
Donnally, Hugh. N.C. Private. 30 May 1820. 640 acres to heirs.
Donnally, William. Pa. Private. 28 Sep.1787. 200 acres.
Donnavan, John. N. Y. Private. 3 Jul. 1790. 600 acres.
Donnell, John. Pa. ———. ———. 200 acres to Felix McLaughlin, assignee.
Donnelly, James. Ga. ———. 15 Mar. 1784. 250 acres.
Donnelly, John. N.C. Private. 20 Sep. 1821. 640 acres.
Donnom, Benjamin. S.C. ———. 4 Mar. 1783. 92 acres.
Donnom, William. S.C. Captain. 21 Jan. 1785. 300 acres to heirs.
Donoho, Thomas. N.C. Major. 24 Oct. 1783. 4800 acres.
Donohoe, Joseph. Md. Private. ———. 50 acres.
Donohoo, John. Pa. Private. 9 Mar. 1795. 200 acres.
Donovan, John. Md. Private. ———. 50 acres.
Donovan, Matthew. Va. Major. 22 Aug. 1835. 5333 1/3 acres.
Donovan, Matthew. Va. Major. 9 Apr. 1838. 530 acres.
Donovan, Matthew. Va. Major. 9 Apr. 1838. 500 acres.
Donovan, Matthew. Va. Major. 9 Apr. 1838. 530 acres.
Donovan, Richard. Md. Lieutenant. ———. 200 acres.
Donovan, Timothy. Md. Matross. ———. 50 acres.
Donovan, Timothy. Pa. Private. ———. 200 acres.
Donovan, Timothy. Pa. Private. 13 Nov. 1786. 200 acres to Anna Mears, widow.
Dooley, George. Ga. Captain. 15 Mar. 1784. 500 acres.
Dooley, Hull. Ga. Navy Lieutenant. 6 Feb. 1784. ———.
Dooley, Jacob. Va. Private. 23 Jul. 1824. 100 acres.
Dooley, John Mitchell. Ga. ———. 17 May 1784. ———.
Dooley, Thomas. Ga. Soldier. 17 May 1784. ——— acres to heir brother George Dooley.
Doolittle, Amos. Conn. Sufferer. New/East Haven. 11.6.6 1/2.
Doolittle, Ichabod. Conn. Sufferer. Ridgefield. 5.15.4.
Doolittle, Isaac. Conn. Sufferer. New/East Haven. 26.17.0.
Dooly, John. Ga. Colonel. ———. 500 acres to sons Thomas Dooly and John Dooly.
Dooly, William. Ga. ———. 1784. 250 acres.
Doran, James. Pa. Private. 28 Nov. 1786. 200 acres.
Doran, James. Va. Corporal. 12 Apr. 1793. 200 acres.
Doran, Patrick. Va.-Ind. Private. 108 acres.
Doran, Patrick. Md. Sergeant. ———. 50 acres.
Doran, Terence. Va. Private. 17 Apr. 1784. 100 acres.
Doreshee, Anthony. N. Y. Private. 8 Jul. 1790. 600 acres.
Dorland, Abraham. Pa. ———. 21 Apr. 1787. 200 acres to Balinda Dorland, widow.
Dorland, Benjamin. N.C. Private. 20 Sep. 1821. 640 acres.
Dorman, West. N.C. Private. 19 Jan. 1786. 640 acres.
Dorn, John. N. Y. Private. 8 Jul. 1790. 600 acres.
Dorsett, ——— Widow. Conn. Sufferer. New London. 2.0.0.
Dorsey, Matthew. Pa. ———. 9 Dec. 1786. 200 acres to John McDonnel, assignee.
Dorsey, Richard. Md. Major. ———. 200 acres.
Dorsey, Richard. Va. Captain. 15 Nov. 1822. 2000 acres.

Dorsey, Richard. Va. Captain. 15 Nov. 1822. 2000 acres.

Dortch, William. Md. Private. ———. 50 acres.

Dorton, Benjamin. N.C. Private. 28 Nov. 1795. 228 acres to heirs.

Dorton, Thomas. Ga. ———. 17 May 1784. ———.

Dosier, James. N.C. Private. 10 Dec. 1788. 640 acres to heirs.

Doss, Joel. Ga. Refugee. 17 May 1784. ———.

Dosson, Ellick. N.C. Corporal. 6 Dec. 1797. 1000 acres to heirs.

Dotey, Isaac. N.C. Sergeant. 8 Dec. 1796. 1000 acres.

Dotey, James. N.C. Private. 7 Jan. 1786. 640 acres to heirs.

Doty, Isaac. N. Y. Gunner. 9 Jul. 1790. 600 acres.

Doty, Samuel. Pa. Lieutenant. 5 Oct. 1786. 200 acres.

Doty, Samuel. Pa. Lieutenant. 5 Oct. 1786. 200 acres.

Doubleday, Benjamin. Mass. ———. 24 Jan. 1832. 200 acres to daughters Mary Doubleday and Deborah Potter.

Dougan, Henry. Pa. Sergeant Ranger. 12 Jan. 1787. 250 acres.

Douge, Griffith. N.C. Sergeant. 6 Jan. 1784. 1000 acres.

Douge, James. N.C. Sergeant. 21 May 1784. 1000 acres.

Douge, James. N.C. Private. 29 Sep. 1784. 640 acres to heir.

Douge, Joab. N.C. Private. 6 Jan. 1784. 274 acres.

Douge, Joab. N.C. Drummer. 19 Jul. 1821. 726 acres to heirs.

Douge, Richard. N.C. Private. 6 Jan. 1784. 640 acres.

Douge, Richard. N.C. Sergeant. 21 Apr. 1784. 1000 acres.

Douge, Zacheriah. N.C. Private. 29 Sep. 1784. 274 acres.

Dougherty, Edmund. Md. Sergeant. ———. 50 acres.

Dougherty, Edward. Pa. Private. 24 Aug. 1787. 200 acres to John Cummins, administrator.

Dougherty, George. Pa. Private. 12 Jan. 1787. 200 acres.

Dougherty, Henry. Pa. ———. 9 Jun. 1806. 200 acres.

Dougherty, Henry. Pa. ———. 30 Jun. 1806. 200 acres.

Dougherty, James. Pa. Private. 2 Nov. 1808. 200 acres.

Dougherty, James. Pa. Private. 12 Sep. 1789. 200 acres.

Dougherty, Matthew. Pa. Private. 11 Nov.1786. 200 acres.

Dougherty, William. N. Y. Private. 17 Aug. 1790. 500 acres.

Dougherty, William. Pa. Private. 28 Oct. 1786. 200 acres to Alexander McDowell, assignee.

Dougherty, William F. N. Y. Major. 8 Jul. 1790. 600 acres.

Doughlas, Benjamin. N.C. Private. 30 Sep. 1785. 640 acres to heirs.

Doughlass, Martin. N.C. Sergeant. 30 Sep. 1785. 1000 acres to heirs.

Doughterty, James. Pa. Private. ———. 200 acres.

Doughty, Hull. Ga. Lieutenant of a galley. 1784. 400 acres to J. Hull, administrator.

Doughty, Ichabod. Me. ———. 30 Apr. 1835. 200 acres. Brunswick.

Doughty, Ichabod. Me. ———. 30 Apr. 1835. 200 acres. Brunsick.

Doughty, John. N. Y. Captain. 7 Jul. 1790. 1800 acres.

Douglas, James. Md. Private. ———. 50 acres.

Douglas, Malcolm. N.C. Private. 9 Dec. 1797. 428 acres.

Douglas, Robert. N.C. Sergeant. 21 Apr. 1784. 2560 acres.

Douglass, Alexander. Ga. Minute Man. 17 May 1784. ———.

Douglass, Ebenezer. Conn. Sufferer. New London. 17.9.4.

Douglass, George. Ga. ———. 1 Oct. 1784. 287 1/2 acres.

Douglass, George. N. Y. Sergeant. 8 Jul. 1790. 600 acres.

Douglass, James. Ga. ———. 17 May 1784. ———.

Douglass, James. N. Y. Private. 8 Jul. 1790. 600 acres.

Douglass, James. N.C. Private. 15 Nov. 1793. 640 acres to heirs.

Douglass, John. Ga. ———. 25 May 1784. 287 1/2 acres.

Douglass, John. N.C. Private. 20 Apr. 1784. 640 acres.

Douglass, John. Va. Private. 8 Aug. 1835. 100 acres.
Douglass, Jonathan. Conn. Sufferer. New London. 1,446.14.7.
Douglass, Nathan. Conn. Sufferer. New London. 941.11.9.
Douglass, Richard. Conn. Sufferer. New London. 262.18.6.
Douglass, Robert. Conn. Sufferer. New London. 200.0.0.
Douglass, Spere. Conn. Sufferer. New London. 8.15.7.
Douglass, Thomas. Pa. Captain. 15 May 1850. 500 acres.
Douglass, Thomas. S.C. ———. 3 Sep. 1787. 200 acres.
Douglass, William. Ga. ———. 1784. 287 1/2 acres.
Douglass, William. N.C. Corporal. 21 Oct. 1783. 1000 acres.
Douglass, William. N.C. Quartermaster. 5 Sep. 1821. 1000 acres.
Douley, William. Md. Private. ———. 50 acres.
Doust, John. Pa. Private. 12 Apr. 1787. 200 acres.
Dove, John. Md. Sergeant. ———. 50 acres.
Dove, Josiah. N.C. Private. 28 Sep. 1785. 274 acres.
Dove, Thomas. Va. Private. 7 Apr. 1808. 100 acres.
Dove, William. N.C. Private. 17 Dec. 1785. 274 acres.
Dover, Andrew. Pa. Lieutenant. 3 Jan. 1787. 200 acres.
Dover, Andrew. Pa. Lieutenant. ———. 200 acres.
Dover, Richard. Ga. ———. 17 May 1784. ———.
Dow, Alexander. N. Y. Lieutenant. 13 Sep. 1790. 1200 acres.
Dow, Alexander. Pa. Lieutenant. ———. 200 acres.
Dow, Alexander. Pa. Lieutenant. 11 Oct. 1786. 200 acres.
Dow, Joseph. Me. ———. 6 Jun. 1835. 200 acres to widow Lucy Dow. Standish.
Dow, Volkert. N. Y. Private. 8 Jul. 1790. 600 acres.
Dowall, James. N.C. Private. 24 Oct. 1783. 274 acres.
Dowd, John. N.C. Private. 19 May 1784. 640 acres.
Dowday, George. N.C. Private. 23 Nov. 1797. 640 acres to heirs.
Dowden, James. Md. Private. ———. 50 acres.
Dowden, John. Va. Private. 21 Jun. 1808. 100 acres.
Dowden, Samuel. N.C. Private. 29 Sep. 1784. 640 acres to Anthony Dowden, heir.
Dowden, Thomas. Va. Private. 21 Jun. 1808. 100 acres.
Dowdle, William. Md. Private. ———. 50 acres.
Dowdy, Bolin. N.C. Private. 30 Sep. 1785. 640 acres to heirs.
Dowdy, Claiborne. Va. Private. 5 Aug. 1784. 100 acres.
Dowdy, Richard. Ga. Soldier. 28 Feb. 1784. 250 acres.
Dowell, George. Ga. ———. 17 May 1784. ———.
Dowell, James. N.C. Private. 21 Apr. 1784. 411 acres.
Dowell, William. Va. Private. 18 Jun. 1783. 100 acres.
Dowell, William. Va. Sergeant. 27 Oct. 1783. 100 acres.
Dowell, William. Va. Private. 6 Mar. 1834. 100 acres.
Dowlan, Michael. Md. Private. ———. 50 acres.
Dowlar, George. N. Y. Sergeant. 8 Jul. 1790. 500 acres.
Dowling, Andrew. N. Y. Matross. 9 Jul. 1790. 500 acres.
Dowling, Dennis. N.C. Private. 4 Aug. 1821. 640 acres.
Dowling, Lambert. Pa. Private. 28 Dec. 1786. 200 acres.
Downes, William. Md. Private. ———. 50 acres.
Downey, Alexander. Md. Private. ———. 50 acres.
Downey, John. Md. Private. ———. 50 acres.
Downey, John. Pa. Private. 20 Sep. 1787. 200 acres.
Downey, John. Va. Sergeant. 21 Jul. 1783. 200 acres.
Downey, Michael. Va. Private. 18 Feb. 1784. 100 acres.

Downey, Patrick. Pa. Private. 12 Dec. 1786. 200 acres.

Downham, Richard. N.C. Private. 2 Aug. 1784. 274 acres.

Downham, Speakman. N.C. Private. 2 Aug. 1784. 274 acres.

Downing, Francis. Va. Private. 27 Apr. 1811. 100 acres.

Downing, George. N.C. Private. 9 Nov. 1784. 274 acres.

Downing, John. Mass. Matross. 1 Feb. 1833. 200 acres to heirs.

Downs, Ambrose, Jr. Ga. Refugee. 17 May 1784. ———.

Downs, Ambrose, Sr. Ga. Refugee. 17 May 1784. ———.

Downs, George. Ga. Refugee. 17 May 1784. ———.

Downs, John. N.C. Sergeant. 24 Jul. 1820. 1000 acres to heirs.

Downs, John. Va. Private. Aug. 1782. 100 acres.

Downs, Jonathan. Ga. ———. 17 May 1784. ———.

Downs, Patrick. N.Y. ———. ———. 500 acres to his heirs.

Downs, Richard. Md. Private. ———. 50 acres.

Downs, William. Ga. Refugee. 28 Feb. 1784. 500 acres.

Downton, George. Va. Private. 17 Nov. 1784. 100 acres.

Downton, William. Va. Gunner's Mate. 27 Jul. 1783. 200 acres.

Downton, William. Va. Gunner's Mate. 25 Jun. 1844. 1644 4/9 acres.

Downton, William. Va. Gunner's Mate. 25 Jun. 1844. 822 2/9 acres.

Downton, William. Va. Gunner's Mate. 1 Jan. 1856. 822 2/9 acres.

Dowse, Gideon. Ga. Refugee. 5 Sep. 1785. ———.

Dowther, John. Pa. ———. 11 May 1796. 200 acres.

Doxey, Jeremiah. N.C. Private. 9 Feb. 1796. 228 acres.

Doyle, Charles. Pa. ———. ———. 200 acres to widow.

Doyle, James. Md. Private. ———. 50 acres.

Doyle, John. Pa. Captain. 10 Nov. 1786. 500 acres.

Doyle, John. Va. Private. 23 Feb. 1784. 200 acres.

Doyle, Morris. Pa. Private. 19 Nov. 1788. 200 acres.

Doyle, Robert. Va. Private. 22 Aug. 1783. 200 acres.

Doyle, Samuel. Pa. Ranger. 6 Apr. 1787. 200 acres.

Doyle, Thomas. Md. Private. ———. 50 acres.

Doyle, Thomas. Pa. Lieutenant. ———. 200 acres.

Doyle, Thomas [or Francis]. Pa. Lieutenant. 5 Apr. 1787. 200 acres.

Doyles, John. Va. Sailor. 21 Feb. 1784. 100 acres.

Drake, Andrew. Va. Private. 20 Jun. 1783. 100 acres.

Drake, Cornelius. N.C. Sergeant. 6 Jan. 1784. 571 acres.

Drake, Joshua. N. Y. Lieutenant. 9 Jul. 1790. 1000 acres.

Drake, Michael. Va. Private. 17 Oct. 1783. 200 acres.

Drake, Thomas. Va. Lieutenant. 2 Nov. 1787. 2666 2/3 acres.

Drake, William. N. Y. Matross. 9 Jul. 1790. 600 acres.

Drake, William. Va. Orderly Sergeant. 18 Dec. 1827. 200 acres.

Draper, George. Va. Regimental Surgeon. 24 Jun. 1783. 2000 acres.

Draper, George. Va. Regimental Surgeon. 24 Jun. 1783. 2000 acres.

Draper, George. Va. Regimental Surgeon. 24 Jun. 1783. 2000 acres.

Draper, Robert. Va. Private. 31 Jan. 1785. 100 acres.

Draper, Roger. N.C. Private. 31 Mar. 1810. 640 acres to heirs.

Drawohon, John. N.C. Private. 30 Sep. 1785. 640 acres to heirs.

Drayton, Stephen. S.C. Quartermaster General. ———. 500 acres.

Dreece, John. N.C. Private. 18 Dec. 1802. 640 acres.

Dresser, Jonathan. Me. ———. 1 May 1835. 200 acres. 200 acres to widow Elizabeth Dresser. Denmark.

Dresser, Richard. Me. ———. 25 May 1835. 200 acres. Hollis.

Dreury, James. Va. Private. 29 Nov. 1833. 200 acres.

Drew, John. N.C. Private. 10 Dec. 1788. 640 acres to heirs.

Drew, John. Va. Lieutenant. 23 Dec. 1783. 1000 acres.
Drew, John. Va. Lieutenant. 23 Dec. 1783. 1666 2/3 acres.
Drew, Thomas H. Va. Captain. 14 Dec. 1782. 4000 acres.
Drew, Thomas Haines. Va. Captain. 29 Nov. 1782. 4000 acres.
Drew, William. N.C. Private. 21 Aug. 1820. 640 acres.
Drewery, Henry. N.C. Private. 2 Feb. 1786. 228 acres.
Drewry, John. N.C. Private. 14 May 1784. 640 acres.
Drian, James. Md. Private. ———. 50 acres.
Driggs, Deveraux. S.C. Soldier. 21 Jan. 1785. 200 acres.
Drine, James. N.C. Private. 14 Feb. 1796. 640 acres to heirs.
Dring, Thomas. N.C. Private. 30 Sep. 1785. 640 acres to heirs.
Driskell, David. N.C. Private. 26 May 1784. 274 acres.
Driskill, Dennis. Va. Private. 1 Mar. 1784. 100 acres.
Driskill, Jeremiah. Md. Private. ———. 50 acres.
Driver, Charles. N.C. Private. 25 Apr. 1785. 640 acres to Giles Driver, Jr., heir.
Driver, Edward. Va. Sergeant. 30 Jun. 1783. 200 acres.
Driver, Francis. Va. Sergeant. 21 Feb. 1783. 200 acres.
Driver, Henry. Ga. Minute Man. 24 May 1784. 287 1/2 acres.
Dromenas, Demana. N.C. Drummer. 30 Sep. 1785. 1000 acres to heirs.
Drossett, Samuel. Va. Private. 13 Sep. 1788. 200 acres.
Drown, Stephen. Me. ———. 3 Aug. 1835. 200 acres. Kennebunkport.
Drudge, Thomas. Md. Private. ———. 50 acres.
Drummon, Joseph. N.C. Private. 19 Jan. 1786. 640 acres to heirs.
Drummond, Alexander. Va. Private. 5 Feb. 1785. 200 acres.
Drummond, David. N.Y. ———. 13 Sep. 1790. 500 acres to heirs.
Drummond, David. Va. Private. 15 Jun. 1807. 100 acres.
Drummond, James. Va. Lieutenant. 20 Mar. 1807. 2666 2/3 acres.
Drummond, James. Va. Lieutenant. 17 Sep. 1851. 172 2/3 acres.
Drummond, James. Va. Lieutenant. 17 Sep. 1851. 173 2/3 acres.
Drummond, James. Va. Lieutenant. 17 Sep. 1851. 173 2/3 acres.
Drummond, James. Va. Lieutenant. 17 Sep. 1851. 28 2/3 acres.
Drummond, James. Va. Lieutenant. 29 Apr. 1854. 173 2/3 acres.
Drummond, James. Va. Lieutenant. 29 Apr. 1854. 116 acres.
Drummond, James. Va. Lieutenant. 29 Apr. 1854. 86 2/3 acres.
Drummond, James. Va. Lieutenant. 3 May 1855. 86 1/3 acres.
Drummond, John. Va. Drum Major. 2 Aug. 1783. 466 2/3 acres.
Drummond, Joshua. Va. Private. 24 Feb. 1784. 100 acres.
Drummond, Nathan. Conn. Sufferer. New/East Haven. 6.2.9.
Drummond, William. Va. Sergeant. 15 Jul. 1818. 200 acres.
Drury, Benjamin. Va. Private. 29 Apr. 1783. 200 acres.
Drury, Morgan. N.C. Private. 14 May 1784. 640 acres.
Drury, Samuel. Va. Private. 19 Jun. 1783. 100 acres.
Dubar, John. N. Y. ———. ———. 500 acres.
Dubois, John. N. Y. Private. 8 Jul. 1790. 600 acres.
Dubois, Lewis. N. Y. ———. 22 Oct. 1805. 2500 acres.
Duboise, Issac. Ga. ———. 17 May 1784. ———.
Ducacom, James. N.C. Private. 30 Sep. 1785. 640 acres to heirs.
Duckworth, Jacob. Ga. ———. 19 Nov. 1784. 287 1/2 acres.
Duckworth, Jeremiah. Ga. Soldier. 20 Feb. 1784. 250 acres.
DuCoin, John. Ga. Captain. 24 Sep. 1783. 600 acres.
Duders, Jacob. Md. Private. ———. 50 acres.
Dudley, Armistead. Va.-Ind. Private. 108 acres.
Dudley, Banks. Va. Sergeant. 11 Nov. 1814. 200 acres.

Dudley, Banks. Va. Lieutenant. 12 Nov. 1838. 822 2/9 acres.
Dudley, Banks. Va. Lieutenant. 12 Nov. 1838. 548 4/27 acres.
Dudley, Banks. Va. Lieutenant. 12 Nov. 1838. 548 4/27 acres.
Dudley, Banks. Va. Lieutenant. 12 Nov. 1838. 548 4/27 acres.
Dudley, Banks. Va. Lieutenant. 18 Feb. 1842. 822 2/9 acres.
Dudley, Bennet. N.C. Private. 7 Jan. 1786. 640 acres to heirs.
Dudley, George. N.C. Corporal. 24 Dec. 1818. 1000 acres.
Dudley, Henry. Va. Captain. 27 Nov. 1782. 4000 acres.
Dudley, Henry. Va. Captain. 17 Apr. 1838. 1000 acres.
Dudley, John. Va. Captain. 17 Apr. 1838. 333 1/3 acres.
Dudley, John. Va. Captain. 15 Nov. 1838. 333 1/3 acres.
Dudley, John. Va. Captain. 11 Dec. 1838. 500 acres.
Dudley, John. Va. Captain. 11 Dec. 1838. 166 1/3 acres.
Dudley, John. Va. Captain. 1 Feb. 1839. 500 acres.
Dudley, John. Va. Captain. 1 Feb. 1839. 166 2/3 acres.
Dudley, John. Va. Captain. 26 Mar. 1840. 111 1/9 acres.
Dudley, John. Va. Captain. 26 Mar. 1840. 222 2/9 acres.
Dudley, John. Va. Seaman. 25 Aug. 1835. 100 acres.
Dudley, John. Va. Lieutenant. 27 Feb. 1851. 2000 acres.
Dudley, John. Va. Lieutenant. 27 Feb. 1851. 2000 acres.
Dudley, John. Va. Captain. 7 Feb. 1847. 333 1/3 acres.
Dudley, John. Va. Captain. 6 Jun. 1857. 166 2/3 acres.
Dudley, Matthias. N.C. Private. 7 Jan. 1786. 640 acres to heirs.
Dudley, Nathan. Me. ———. 30 Jun. 1835. 200 acres. Hebron.
Dudley, Robert. Va. Lieutenant. 24 Jun. 1783. 2666 2/3 acres.
Dudley, Robert. Va. Private. 31 Oct. 1792. 100 acres.
Dudley, Robert. Va. Lieutenant. 18 Mar. 1834. 490 acres.
Dudley, Robert. Va. Lieutenant. 18 Mar. 1834. 490 acres.
Dudley, Robert. Va. Lieutenant. 18 Mar. 1834. 490 acres.
Dudley, Robert. Va. Lieutenant. 18 Mar. 1834. 490 acres.
Dudley, Robert. Va. Lieutenant. 18 Mar. 1834. 490 acres.
Dudley, Robert. Va. Lieutenant. 18 Mar. 1834. 490 acres.
Dudley, Robert. Va. Lieutenant. 18 Mar. 1834. 490 acres.
Dudley, Thomas. N.C. Lieutenant. 23 Oct. 1783. 2560 acres.
Due, James. Md. Private. ———. 50 acres.
Duel, Henry. Va. Private. 12 Apr. 1783. 200 acres.
Duester, Abraham. N.C. Private. 30 Sep. 1785. 640 acres to heirs.
Duester, James. N.C. Private. 30 Sep. 1785. 640 acres to heirs.
Duff, Edward. Va. Surgeon. 16 May 1783. 6000 acres.
Duff, John. Va.-Ind. Private. 108 acres.
Duffel, Peter. N.C. Private. 29 Apr. 1784. 640 acres.
Duffell, Thomas. N.C. Private. 25 Mar. 1784. 411 acres.
Duffey, James. Pa. Sergeant. 5 Apr. 1787. 250 acres.
Duffey, James. Va. Private. 17 May 1783. 100 acres.
Duffey, James. Va. Private. 23 Jun. 1783. 200 acres.
Duffey, John. Ga. Minute Man. 19 Jul. 1784. 287 1/2 acres.
Duffey, Peter. N.C. Private. 29 Apr. 1784. 640 acres.
Duffield, Anthony. S.C. ———. 4 Jul. 1785. 200 acres.
Duffry, James. Pa. Private. 4 Oct. 1786. 200 acres.
Duffy, Francis. Md. Sergeant. ———. 50 acres.
Duffy, Michael. Md. Private. ———. 50 acres.
Duffy, Terrence. Md. Private. ———. 50 acres.
Duffy, Thomas. Md. Private. ———. 50 acres.
Dufons, Michael. N. Y. ———. ———. 500 acres.
Dufrans, Joseph. N. Y. ———. ———. 500 acres.

Dugald, John. N.C. Private. 30 Sep. 1785. 640 acres to heirs.
Dugan, Abram. Md. Private. ———. 50 acres.
Dugan, Francis. N.C. Private. 20 Mar. 1785. 274 acres.
Dugan, James. N. Y. ———. ———. 500 acres.
Dugan, Robert. Pa. Private. 24 Aug. 1787. 200 acres to John Cummins, administrator.
Dugan, Thomas. Ga. Captain. 23 Nov. 1784. 575 acres.
Dugan, William. N. Y. ———. ———. 500 acres.
Dugar, Robert. Va. Sergeant. 6 Mar. 1783. 200 acres.
Dugar, Robert. Va. Private. 5 Sep. 1811. 100 acres.
Duggan, James. N. Y. ———. 6 Apr. 1795. 500 acres.
Duggan, John. N.C. Private. 30 Sep. 1785. 640 acres to heirs.
Duggan, William. N. Y. ———. 6 Apr. 1795. 500 acres.
Duggin, Jesse. N.C. Private. 2 Aug. 1784. 640 acres to William Duggin.
Duggin, Thomas. N.C. ———. 2 Aug. 1784. 640 acres to William Duggin, heir.
Duggins, William. Mass. Private. 15 Jan. 1834. 200 acres.
Duggs, William. N.C. Private. 7 Jan. 1786. 640 acres to heirs.
Dugmore, John. Va. Private. 15 Sep. 1783. 100 acres
Duhague, John. Md. Private. ———. 50 acres.
Duhamel, John B. Pa. Private. ———. 200 acres.
Duhart, John. Ga. Refugee. 20 Feb. 1784. 250 acres.
Duke, Buckner. Ga. ———. 17 May 1784. 250 acres.
Duke, Clevears. Va. Private. 7 Sep. 1822. 200 acres.
Duke, Gran. N.C. Private. 30 Sep. 1785. 640 acres to heirs.
Duke, Harmon. N.C. Non Comissioned Officer. 10 Aug. 1785. 439 acres.
Duke, Henry. Ga. Captain. 26 Oct. 1784. 287 1/2 acres to heirs.
Duke, Henry. Va. Private. 1 Feb. 1820. 100 acres.
Duke, James. Ga. Minute Man. 17 May 1784. ——— acres to heirs.
Duke, John Taylor, Sr. Ga. Minute Man. 26 May 1784. 287 1/2 acres.
Duke, Sherrod. N.C. Private. 28 Sep. 1785. 640 acres to heirs.
Duke, Taylor. Ga. ———. 14 Sep. 1784. 287 1/2 acres.
Duke, William. Ga. Lieutenant. 5 Sep. 1785. 287 1/2 acres.
Duke, William. N.C. Sergeant. 27 May 1784. 357 acres.
Dukemore, Marine. N.C. Private. 17 Feb. 1824. 640 acres.
Dukes, Arthur. N.C. Private. 12 Sep. 1785. 640 acres to heirs.
Dukes, Elisha. N.C. Corporal. 28 Sep. 1785. 1000 acres.
Dukes, John. N.C. Private. 22 Apr. 1785. 640 acres to heirs.
Dulany, Thomas. Va. Private. 19 Jun. 1783. 100 acres.
Dull, William. Pa. ———. 31 Mar. 1804. 200 acres.
Dumaplin, Elijah. Ga. Minute Man. 22 Mar. 1785. 250 acres.
Dumas, Elijah. Ga. Minute Man. 22 Mar. 1785. 250 acres.
Dumas, Peter. N. Y. Gunner. 9 Jul. 1790. 500 acres.
Dumont, Mons. Conn. Sufferer. New London. 263.10.8.
Dunagan, John. N.C. Private. 2 Apr. 1784. 640 acres.
Dunar, Anthony. N.C. Private. 6 Dec. 1797. 640 acres to heirs.
Dunar, Francis. Md. Private. ———. 50 acres.
Dunaway, John. Ga. ———. 26 May 1784. 287 1/2 acres.
Dunaway, William. Ga. ———. 17 May 1784. 250 acres.
Dunbar, Dan. N.C. Corporal. 25 Nov. 1783. 688 acres.
Dunbar, David. Me. ———. 11 Jun. 1838. 200 acres. Penobscot.
Dunbar, Hamilton. Va. Sergeant. 23 Dec. 1784. 200 acres.
Dunbar, Hamilton. Va. Sergeant. 28 Aug. 1800. 200 acres
Dunbar, Isaac. N.C. Private. 7 Jan. 1786. 640 acres to heirs.
Dunbar, James. Ga. ———. 17 May 1784. ———.

Dunbar, John. N.C. Private. 31 Aug. 1795. 640 acres to heirs.
Dunbar, Thomas. S.C. ———. 4 Jul. 1785. 200 acres.
Dunbar, William. N. Y. Private. 8 Jul. 1790. 500 acres.
Dunbar, William. N. Y. Private. 8 Jul. 1790. 600 acres.
Dunbare, James. Va. Sergeant. 23 Jun. 1783. 200 acres.
Dunby, Richard. Md. Private. ———. 50 acres.
Dunca, Joseph. N. Y. ———. ———. 500 acres.
Duncan, Alexander. N.C. Private. 9 Dec. 1797. 274 acres.
Duncan, Charles. Va. Private. 1 Aug. 1783. 100 acres.
Duncan, David. Ga. Lieutenant. 17 Jan. 1784. 460 acres.
Duncan, Elijah. N.C. Private. 23 Oct. 1783. 274 acres.
Duncan, George. N.C. Private. 3 Feb. 1785. 228 acres.
Duncan, James. Ga. Lieutenant. 17 Jan. 1785. 460 acres.
Duncan, James. N. Y. Private. 8 Jul. 1790. 600 acres.
Duncan, James. Pa. Captain. ———. 500 acres.
Duncan, Jesse. N.C. Private. 20 Apr. 1784. 274 acres.
Duncan, John. Va. Private. 19 Mar. 1783. 100 acres.
Duncan, Joseph. Ga. Captain. 17 May 1784. ——— acres to heirs.
Duncan, Matthew. Ga. ———. 17 Feb. 1784. 250 acres.
Duncan, Peter. N.C. Sergeant. 1 Aug. 1821. 1000 acres.
Duncan, Robert. N.C. Paymaster. 5 Sep. 1821. 2560 acres.
Duncan, Samuel. Ga. ———. 17 May 1784. ———.
Duncan, Thomas. Ga. Private. ———. 250 acres.
Duncan, Thomas. N. Y. Private. 8 Jul. 1790. 500 acres.
Duncan, William. Ga. Minute Man. ———. 287 1/2 acres.
Dunckle, Peter. Pa. Private. 9 Mar. 1809. 200 acres to William Falwell, assignee.
Duncos, Joseph. N. Y. ———. ———. 500 acres.
Dundalow, Henry. N.C. Corporal. 12 Dec. 1806. 428 acres to heirs.
Dundele, Hugh. N.C. Private. 30 Sep. 1785. 640 acres to heirs.
Dundelow, Benjamin. N.C. Private. 30 Sep. 1785. 640 acres to heirs.
Duneth, John. Va. Private. 3 Jun. 1783. 200 acres.
Dunford, William. Ga. ———. 17 May 1784. ———.
Dunford, William. Va. Master. 31 Dec. 1851. 1777 2/3 acres.
Dunford, William. Va. Master. 31 Dec. 1851. 888 2/3 acres.
Dunford, William. Va. Master. 1 Dec. 1853. 888 8/9 acres.
Dunford, William. Va. Master. 25 Jan. 1854. 444 4/9 acres.
Dunford, William. Va. Master. 25 Jan. 1854. 444 4/9 acres.
Dungan, John. Ga. ———. 5 Dec. 1785. ———.
Dungan, Thomas. Pa. Lieutenant. ———. 200 acres.
Dungan, Thomas. Pa. ———. 21 Oct. 1786. 200 acres.
Dungie, James. Va. Private. 19 Nov. 1783. 100 acres.
Dunham, Israel. N.Y. ———. ———. 500 acres to heirs.
Dunham, Jeremiah. Mass. Private. 6 Jul. 1831. 200 acres.
Dunham, Moses. Me. ———. 18 Jul. 1835. 200 acres. Hartford.
Dunivan, John. Pa. Private. 10 Nov. 1786. 200 acres.
Dunivan, John. Pa. Private. ———. 200 acres.
Dunivans, James. Pa. Private. 28 Dec. 1786. 200 acres.
Dunkin, Robert. Md. Private. ———. 50 acres.
Dunkin, William. N.C. Private. 12 Mar. 1785. 228 acres.
Dunkinson, John. N.C. Private. 30 Sep. 1785. 640 acres to heirs.
Dunlap, Andrew. N. Y. Sergeant. 13 Sep. 1790. 600 acres.
Dunlap, Francis F. Va. Chaplain. 10 Feb. 1838. 875 acres.
Dunlap, Francis F. Va. Chaplain. 10 Feb. 1838. 875 acres.
Dunlap, Francis F. Va. Chaplain. 10 Feb. 1838. 875 acres.

Dunlap, Francis F. Va. Chaplain. 10 Feb. 1838. 875 acres.
Dunlap, Francis Farnklin. Va. Chaplain. 26 Aug. 1836. 1500 acres.
Dunlap, Francis Franklin. Va. Chaplain. 26 Aug. 1836. 1500 acres.
Dunlap, Francis Franklin. Va. Chaplain. 26 Aug. 1836. 1500 acres.
Dunlap, Francis Franklin. Va. Chaplain. 26 Aug. 1836. 1500 acres.
Dunlap, Francis Franklin. Va. Chaplain. 22 Aug. 1839. 1666 2/3 acres.
Dunlap, Francis Franklin. Va. Chaplain. 22 Aug. 1839. 833 1/3 acres.
Dunlap, Francis Franklin. Va. Chaplain. 22 Aug. 1839. 1250 acres.
Dunlap, Francis Franklin. Va. Chaplain. 22 Aug. 1839. 416 2/3 acres.
Dunlap, Francis Franklin. Va. Chaplain. 22 Aug. 1839. 833 1/3 acres.
Dunlap, Francis Franklin. Va. Chaplain. 21 Nov. 1839. 416 2/3 acres.
Dunlap, Francis Franklin. Va. Chaplain. 21 Nov. 1839. 1250 acres.
Dunlap, Francis Franklin. Va. Chaplain. 21 Nov. 1839. 833 1/3 acres.
Dunlap, Francis Franklin. Va. Chaplain. 20 Oct. 1852. 833 1/3 acres.
Dunlap, Francis Franklin. Va. Chaplain. 20 Oct. 1852. 833 1/3 acres.
Dunlap, George. Mass. Private. 16 Sep. 1833. 200 acres.
Dunlap, James. N.Y. ———. 13 Sep. 1790. 500 acres to heirs.
Dunlap, Joseph. Va. Private. 19 Feb. 1808. 100 acres.
Dunlap, Robert. Ga. Deserter from British. 25 May 1784. 230 acres.
Dunlap, Robert. S.C. ———. 2 Oct. 1786. 200 acres.
Dunlap, Thomas. N.C. Private. 7 Dec. 1796. 640 acres to heirs.
Dunlop, John. Va. Private. 2 Dec. 1784. 200 acres.
Dunlop, Samuel. Va. Private. 5 Aug. 1826. 100 acres.
Dunn, Abner. Pa. Private. ———. 200 acres.
Dunn, Abner M. Pa. Private. 9 Feb. 1787. 200 acres.
Dunn, Alexander. N. Y. Quartermaster Sergeant. 6 Jul. 1790. 600 acres.
Dunn, Christopher. Me. Private. 11 May 1835. 200 acres. Belgrade.
Dunn, Isaac B. Pa. Captain. 9 Feb. 1787. 500 acres.
Dunn, James. Va. Private. 20 Sep. 1783. 200 acres.
Dunn, James. Va. Private. 11 Oct. 1784. 100 acres.
Dunn, James. Va. Private. 5 Aug. 1813. 200 acres.
Dunn, John. Pa. Private. ———. 200 acres.
Dunn, John. Va. Private. 1 May 1783. 200 acres.
Dunn, John. Va. Private. 9 Aug. 1783. 100 acres.
Dunn, John. Conn. Sufferer. Greenwich. 15.10.0.
Dunn, Joshua. Va. Private. 7 Oct. 1783. 100 acres.
Dunn, Josiah. Ga. Colonel. 20 May 1784. ———.
Dunn, Nehemiah. Ga. Refugee. 25 May 1784. 287 1/2 acres.
Dunn, Nicholas. N.C. Private. 3 Dec. 1797. 640 acres.
Dunn, Patrick. Va. Private. 23 May 1785. 100 acres.
Dunn, Peter. Va. Captain. 4 Apr. 1797. 4000 acres.
Dunn, Peter. Va. Captain. 24 Apr. 1841. 704 acres.
Dunn, Peter. Va. Captain. 24 Apr. 1841. 351 2/3 acres.
Dunn, Peter. Va. Captain. 17 Apr. 1855. 309 1/2 acres.
Dunn, Peter. Va. Captain. 17 Apr. 1855. 61 2/3 acres.
Dunn, Richard. Va. Private. 1 Apr. 1783. 100 acres.
Dunn, Thomas. N.C. Private. 10 Aug. 1785. 640 acres to heirs.
Dunn, Thomas. Va. Private. 19 Aug. 1822. 200 acres.
Dunn, Thomas. Va. First Sergeant. 4 Mar. 1831. 200 acres.
Dunnavant, Abraham. Va. Private. 10 May 1784. 100 acres.
Dunnick, Peter. N.C. Private. 23 Apr. 1784. 640 acres.
Dunning, Dennis. Md. Drummer. ———. 50 acres.
Dunning, Elizabeth. Conn. Sufferer. Norwalk. 7.1.4.
Dunning, James. N.C. Private. 7 Jan. 1786. 274 acres.

Dunning, James. N.C. Sergeant. 9 Dec. 1796. 357 acres.
Dunning, Jeremiah. Conn. Sufferer. Danbury. 2.2.0.
Dunning, Michael. N. Y. Captain. 13 Sep. 1790. 1800 acres.
Dunning, Richard. Conn. Sufferer. Norwalk. 25.10.6.
Dunnington [or Derrington], William. Md. Private. ———. 50 acres.
Dunnington, Francis. Md. Private. ———. 50 acres.
Dunnock, David. N.C. Sergeant. 27 Nov. 1789. 360 acres.
Dunnom, Benjamin. S.C. ———. 4 Mar. 1783. 108 acres.
Dunscomb, Edward. New York. Captain. 8 Jul. 1790. 1800 acres.
Dunscomb, Samuel. Pa. Private. 17 Sep. 1795. 200 acres.
Dunsmore, James. Ga. Minute Man. Feb. 1785. 287 1/2 acres.
Dunstan, Warner. Va. Private. 30 Mar. 1784. 100 acres.
Dunston, Alman. Va. Private. 10 May 1784. 100 acres.
Dunston, Peter. Md. Private. ———. 50 acres.
Dunton, Samuel. Mass. ———. 22 Jul. 1833. 200 acres.
Dunton, Stephen. Va. Private. 24 Apr. 1783. 200 acres.
Dupee, William. Va. Corporal. 5 Jan. 1784. 200 acres.
Dupelle, Anthony. N. Y. ———. ———. 500 acres.
Duplossier, Henry. N. Y. ———. ———. 500 acres.
Dupont, Jesse. N.C. Private. 30 Sep. 1785. 640 acres to heirs.
Dupont, Joseph. N.C. Private. 30 Sep. 1785. 640 acres to heirs.
Dupre, John Baptist. N. Y. ———. ———. 500 acres.
Dupreast, James. N.C. Private. 28 Sep. 1785. 640 acres to heirs.
Dupree, James. N.C. Private. 16 Aug. 1821. 640 acres.
Dupree, Mial. N.C. Private. 14 Feb. 1796. 640 acres to heirs.
Durban, Luke. Ga. ———. 17 May 1784. ———.
Durden, Mills. N.C. Private. 10 Dec. 1788. 640 acres to heirs.
Durfey, Timothy. Conn. Sufferer. New London. 20.14.0.
Durgan, Patrick. Md. Private. ———. 50 acres.
Durham, James. Va. Private. 10 Oct. 1783. 100 acres.
Durham, John. N.C. ———. 12 Dec. 1806. 1000 acres to heirs.
Durham, Nathaniel. N.C. Private. 25 Oct. 1783. 600 acres.
Durham, Samuel. Ga. ———. 17 May 1784. ———.
Durham, Stephen. N. Y. Private. 7 Jul. 1790. 500 acres.
Durham, Zacheriah. N.C. Private. 30 Sep. 1785. 640 acres to heirs.
Durning, James. N.C. Sergeant. 14 May 1784. 428 acres.
Duron, William. Me. Private. 21 Jan. 1838. 200 acres to widow Ruth Duron. Boothbay.
Duroy, Timothy. N.C. Private. 15 Feb. 1797. 320 acres.
Durrett, James. Va. Private. 14 Oct. 1818. 200 acres.
Dusenbury, John. N. Y. ———. 31 Mar. 1808. 500 acres.
Dutcher, Barnard. N. Y. Private. 8 Jul. 1790. 500 acres.
Dutill, John. Pa. Private. ———. 200 acres.
Dutton, Thomas. Md. Private. ———. 50 acres.
Dutton, Thomas. Md. Private. ———. 50 acres to administrator.
DuVal, Daniel. Va. Captain. 13 Feb. 1784. 4000 acres.
Duvall, Edward. Md. Lieutenant. ———. 200 acres.
Duvall, Isaac. Md. Lieutenant. ———. 200 acres.
Duvall, Richard. Md. Private. ———. 50 acres.
Duvist, Francis. Md. Private. ———. 50 acres.
Dwight, Hamlin. Conn. Sufferer. New/East Haven. 2.19.0.
Dwight, Samuel. Conn. Sufferer. New/East Haven. 9.6.6.
Dwight, Timothy. Conn. Sufferer. New/ East Haven. 10.13.6.
Dyas, John Thomas. Ga. ———. 26 May 1784. 287 1/2 acres.

Dyche, Matthias. Md. Private. ———. 50 acres.
Dyckman, Richard. N. Y. Matross. 9 Jul. 1790. 500 acres.
Dye, Hopkins. N.C. Private. 27 Nov. 1789. 274 acres.
Dye, Hopkins. N.C. Private. 18 Dec. 1793. 274 acres.
Dye, Jonathan. Va. Lieutenant. 24 Nov. 1783. 2666 2/3 acres.
Dyer, Benjamin. Me. Private. 19 Sep. 1835. 200 acres to widow Hannah Dyer. Lisbon.
Dyer, Bickford. Me. Private. 11 Aug. 1835. 200 acres to widow Dolly Dyer. Baldwin.
Dyer, Edward. Md. Captain. ———. 200 acres.
Dyer, Ephraim. Me. ———. 15 Dec. 1835. 200 acres to widow Hannay Dyer. Sullivan.
Dyer, Francis. Va. Private. 16 Aug. 1784. 100 acres.
Dyer, George. Md. Private. ———. 50 acres.
Dyer, Henry. Ga. Minute Man. 17 May 1784. 287 1/2 acres to heirs.
Dyer, Isaac. Me. ———. 12 Sep. 1838. 200 acres. Limington.
Dyer, James. Md. Private. ———. 50 acres.
Dyer, James. Md. Private. ———. 50 acres.
Dyer, John. Md. Private. ———. 50 acres.
Dyer, Samuel. Va. Private. 19 Jun. 1783. 100 acres.
Dyer, Thomas. Mass. Private. 2 Mar. 1833. 200 acres.
Dyer, Walter. Md. Lieutenant. ———. 200 acres.
Dykes, Robert. Va. Seaman. 2 Sep. 1783. 100 acres.
Dysart, Cornelius. Ga. ———. 17 May 1784. ———.
Dyson, Thomas A. Md. Lieutenant. ——. 200 acres.
Eacols, Edward. Ga. ———. 15 Mar. 1784. 250 acres.
Eadens, Samuel. Va. Captain. 27 Mar. 1783. 4000 acres.
Eades, John. Ga. ———. 15 Mar. 1784. 250 acres.
Eades, Joseph. N. Y. Private. 7 Jul. 1790. 600 acres.
Eades, Mary. Ga. ———. 17 May 1784. ———.
Eads, John. Ga. ———. 15 Mar. 1784. 250 acres.
Eady, John. Ga. ———. 15 Mar. 1784. 250 acres.
Eager, Robert. Va. Private. 24 Dec. 1807. 200 acres.
Eagin, John. Pa. Private. 25 Aug. 1787. 200 acres.
Eagins, Joshua. N. Y. Private. 17 Aug. 1790. 500 acres.
Eagle, William. Va. Private. 11 Apr. 1787. 100 acres.
Eakin, Samuel. Va. Sergeant. 9 Dec. 1783. 200 acres.
Earl, Daniel. N. Y. ———. ———. 500 acres.
Earl, Daniel, Jr. N. Y. ———. ———. 500 acres.
Earl, James. N.C. Private. 9 Nov. 1784. 640 acres to heir.
Earl, Jonas. N. Y. ———. ———. 500 acres.
Earl, Nathaniel. N. Y. Lieutenant. ———. 1000 acres.
Earl, Robert. N. Y. ———. ———. 500 acres.
Earl, Watson. N. Y. ———. ———. 500 acres.
Earle, Samuel. S.C. Lieutenant. 21 Jan. 1785. 200 acres.
Earlywine, Daniel. Va. Private. 23 Jun. 1783. 200 acres.
Earnest, Jacob. Ga. ———. 1784. 287 1/2 acres.
Earnest, William. Ga. Refugee. 15 Mar. 1784. 250 acres.
Earp, Edward. N.C. Private. 2 Dec. 1796. 228 acres.
Earpe, John. N.C. Private. 22 Dec. 1796. 228 acres.
Easler, David. N.C. Private. 16 Aug. 1821. 640 acres.
Easman, Benjamin. N.C. Private. 15 Dec. 1783. 274 acres.
Eason, Jacob. N.C. Private. 27 Dec. 1786. 228 acres.
Eason, Thomas. N.C. Private. 29 Sep. 1784. 640 acres to Joseph Eason, heir.
Eason, Thomas. N.C. Private. Nov. 1788. 640 acres to heirs.
Eason, Thomas. N.C. Private. 1 Jan. 1794. 640 acres to heirs.

Easop, Samuel. Pa. Private. 5 Oct. 1786. 200 acres.

East, Sampson. N.C. Private. 9 Feb. 1796. 640 acres to heirs.

East, Southy. Va. Seaman. 27 May 1832. 100 acres.

Easten, Moses. N.C. Private. 26 Aug. 1785. 640 acres to heirs.

Easten, William. Va. Sergeant. 27 Jun. 1783. 200 acres.

Easter, James. Ga. ———. 30 Jul. 1784. 287 1/2 acres.

Eastes, Elisha. Va. Private. 20 May 1823. 100 acres.

Eastin, Phiip. Va. Lieutenant. 5 Apr. 1783. 3110 2/3 acres.

Eastin, Richard. Va. Lieutenant. 5 Apr. 1783. 2666 2/3 acres.

Eastis, Samuel. N.C. Private. 9 Nov. 1784. 640 acres to heir.

Eastman, Jacob. Me. Private. 11 Apr. 1838. 200 acres. Bangor.

Eastman, Jacob. Me. ———. 14 Nov. 1835. 200 acres. Parsonfield.

Eastman, Zacheriah. Me. ———. 19 Oct. 1835. 200 acres. Scarborough.

Easton, Henry. N. Y. Private. 8 Jul. 1790. 600 acres.

Eastus, Moses. N.C. Private. 19 Jul. 1820. 640 acres to heir Burrus Eastus.

Eastward, John. N.C. Private. 21 Aug. 1820. 640 acres.

Eastwood, Dempsey. Va. Corporal. 26 Jan. 1833. 400 acres.

Eastwood, Demsy. Va. Private. 28 Jun. 1783. 100 acres.

Eastwood, John. Ga. ———. 17 May 1784. ———.

Eastwood, John. N.C. Private. 30 Sep. 1785. 640 acres to heirs.

Eaton, Abiather. Mass. ———. 24 Jul. 1829. 200 acres to assignee William Eaton.

Eaton, Henry. Pa. Sergeant. ———. 250 acres.

Eaton, Isaac. Ga. ———. 17 May 1784. ———.

Eaton, Joseph. Va. Private. 14 Oct. 1783. 100 acres.

Eaton, Micajah. Va. Private. 10 Mar. 1784. 100 acres.

Eaton, Peter. Ga. Soldier. 20 Aug. 1785. ———.

Eaton, Pinkerton. N.C. Major. 29 Nov. 1783. 4800 acres to John Eaton, administrator.

Eaton, Uriah. Mass. Sergeant. 4 Nov. 1831. 200 acres.

Eaton, William. Me. Sergeant. 16 Jul. 1835. 200 acres. Wells.

Eaton, William. Va. Private. 12 Apr. 1784. 100 acres.

Eaves, Nathaniel. Ga. Soldier. Private. ———.

Ebb, William. Va. Private. 20 Dec. 1784. 100 acres.

Ebbs, Emanuel. Md. Private. ———. 50 acres.

Ebbs, John. Va. Private. 28 Oct. 1785. 200 acres.

Eberhart, Philip. Pa. Sergeant. 1 Jun. 1787. 250 acres.

Eberman, Christian. Pa. Private. 18 May 1787. 200 acres to widow.

Ebert, John. Pa. Ranger. 24 Jul. 1787. 200 acres.

Ebling, John. Pa. Private. 23 Mar. 1787. 200 acres.

Ebner, Caspar. Pa. Private. 16 Oct. 1786. 200 acres.

Eborn, John. N.C. Captain. 22 Oct. 1783. 1645 acres.

Eburn, Thomas. N.C. Lieutenant. 16 Aug. 1821. 2560 acres.

Eccart, Robert. N.C. Fife Major. 30 Apr. 1784. 297 acres.

Eccleston, Jarvis. Md. Private. ———. 50 acres.

Eccleston, John. Md. Major. ———. 200 acres.

Echols, Abner. N.C. Private. 17 Dec. 1785. 640 acres.

Echolts, John. Pa. Private. 2 Feb. 1787. 200 acres.

Echoltz, John. Pa. ———. 13 Apr. 1804. 200 acres to John Ashley, assignee.

Eckhart, Michael. Va. Private. 17 Mar. 1798. 100 acres.

Eckols, William. N.C. Sergeant. 29 Sep. 1784. 738 acres.

Ecloes, William. N.C. Sergeant. 28 May 1784. 1000 acres.

Ecols, Ephraim. Ga. Soldier. 17 May 1784. 230 acres to heirs.

Ecum, Ethelred. N.C. Private. 15 Jul. 1785. 640 acres to heirs.

Eddins, Samuel. Va. Captain. 3 Sep. 1796. 666 2/3 acres.
Eddins, Samuel. Va. Captain. 17 Nov. 1796. 666 2/3 acres.
Eddy, James. Md. Private. ———. 50 acres.
Edens, John. N.C. Private. 30 Sep. 1785. 640 acres to heirs.
Edes, James. Md. Private. ———. 50 acres.
Edgar, David. Pa. Private. 30 Oct. 1786. 200 acres.
Edge, John. Va. Private. 26 Jan. 1784. 100 acres.
Edge, Joseph. N.C. Private. 12 Oct. 1795. 640 acres to heirs.
Edge, Marmaduke. N.C. Private. 12 Oct. 1795. 640 acres to heirs.
Edge, Thomas. N.C. Private. 22 Dec. 1796. 640 acres.
Edgerly, Edward. Md. Captain. ———. 200 acres.
Edgerly, John. N. Y. Corporal. 8 Jul. 1790. 500 acres.
Edgerton, Edward. Pa. Ranger. ———. 200 acres.
Edleman, Francis. N.C. Private. 27 Nov. 1789. 274 acres.
Edminston, David. S.C. ———. 1 Aug. 1785. 200 acres.
Edminston, Samuel. Pa. Surgeon. 4 Aug. 1807. 300 acres.
Edmiston, Samuel. Md. Lieutenant. ———. 200 acres.
Edmiston, Samuel. N.C. Private. 14 Dec. 1797. 640 acres to heirs.
Edmiston, Samuel. Pa. Surgeon. 3 Aug. 1807. 300 acres.
Edmonds, Daniel. Va. Private. 29 Mar. 1784. 200 acres.
Edmonds, Daniel. Va. Private. 26 Jan. 1833. 200 acres.
Edmonds, Elias. Va. Lieutenant Colonel. 4 May 1783. 6000 acres.
Edmonds, Elias. Va. Lieutenant Colonel. 2 May 1834. 6000 acres.
Edmonds, Joshua. Ga. Minute Man. 14 Feb. 1785. ———.
Edmondson, Edmond. Va. Corporal. 18 Oct. 1808. 200 acres.
Edmondson, William. Va. Sergeant. 23 Jun. 1783. 200 acres.
Edmunds, Abel. N.C. Private. 9 Nov. 1784. 274 acres.
Edmunds, Absalom. Ga. ———. 1784. 250 acres.
Edmunds, David. S.C. Soldier. 21 Jan. 1785. 200 acres.
Edmunds, John. Ga. ———. 17 Dec. 1784. ———.
Edmunds, Nichols. N.C. Captain. 5 Sep. 1821. 3840 acres.
Edmunds, Sarah. Conn. Sufferer. New London. 20.2.6.
Edmunds, Thomas. Va. Captain. 7 Dec. 1782. 4000 acres.
Edmunds, Thomas. Va. Captain. 22 Jan. 1808. 500 acres.
Edmundson, Benjamin. Va. Lieutenant. 6 Mar. 1783. 2666 2/3 acres.
Edmundson, Richard. Va. Sergeant. 24 Nov. 1782. 200 acres.
Edwards, Benjamin. N.C. Private. 17 Feb. 1824. 640 acres.
Edwards, Benjamin. Va. Private. 1 May 1783. 200 acres.
Edwards, Charles. Pa. Dragoon. 16 Feb. 1787. 200 acres.
Edwards, Charles. Va. Private. 4 Dec. 1795. 200 acres.
Edwards, David. N.Y. ———. 13 Sep. 1790. 500 acres to heirs.
Edwards, David. N.C. Private. 12 Dec. 1785. 573 acres.
Edwards, Edward. Va. Private. 15 Dec. 1783. 200 acres.
Edwards, Ellis. Va. Sailor. 30 Jun. 1784. 100 acres.
Edwards, Enoch. Va. Seaman. 22 Nov. 1783. 100 acres.
Edwards, Etheridge. N.C. Private. 31 Aug. 1795. 640 acres to heirs.
Edwards, Evan. Pa. Major. 5 Jul. 1787. 300 acres.
Edwards, Evan. Pa. Major. 5 Jul. 1787. 300 acres.
Edwards, George. Va. Sailor. 5 Mar. 1788. 100 acres.
Edwards, Heathesat. Md. Private. ———. 50 acres.
Edwards, James. Ga. Soldier. 28 Apr. 1785. ———.
Edwards, James. Va. Private. 19 Mar. 1784. 100 acres.
Edwards, Jesse. N.C. Private. 12 Dec. 1785. 640 acres.
Edwards, John. Ga. Refugee. 25 May 1784. 575 acres.

Edwards, John. Md. Private. ———. 50 acres.
Edwards, John. Md. Sergeant. ———. 50 acres.
Edwards, John. N.C. Private. 2 Sep. 1820. 640 acres.
Edwards, John. N.C. Private. 13 Sep. 1820. 640 acres.
Edwards, John. N.C. Corporal. 5 Sep. 1821. 1000 acres.
Edwards, John. Va. Private. 9 Jul. 1783. 200 acres.
Edwards, John. Va. Private. 15 Aug. 1783. 100 acres.
Edwards, Jonathan. Ga. ———. ———. 287 1/2 acres.
Edwards, Jonathan, Rev. Conn. Sufferer. New/East Haven. 57.15.4.
Edwards, Joseph. Ga. ———. ———. 287 1/2 acres.
Edwards, Lemuel. N.C. Private. 17 Feb. 1824. 640 acres.
Edwards, Leroy. Va. Captain. 2 Aug. 1783. 4000 acres.
Edwards, Leroy. Va. Captain. 14 Jun. 1784. 666 2/3 acres.
Edwards, Leroy. Va. Captain. 22 Jan. 1808. 250 acres.
Edwards, Leroy. Va. Captain. 22 Jan. 1808. 250 acres.
Edwards, Nathaniel. Me. Corporal. 20 May 1836. 200 acres. Parsonsfield.
Edwards, Peter. Ga. ———. 15 Mar. 1784. 250 acres.
Edwards, Pumfret. N.C. Private. 15 Jan. 1821. 228 acres.
Edwards, Ralph. Ga. Soldier. 7 Jun. 1785. 230 acres.
Edwards, Richard. Va. Private. 2 Jun. 1783. 100 acres.
Edwards, Robert. N.C. Sergeant. 20 Sep. 1784. 1000 acres.
Edwards, Robert. N.C. Private. Jan. 1795. 320 acres.
Edwards, Rodham. Va. Sailor. 10 Dec. 1783. 100 acres.
Edwards, Spencer. Va. Private. 26 Jan. 1785. 100 acres.
Edwards, Thomas. Me. Lieutenant. 4 Jan. 1839. 600 acres to widow Mary Edwards. Portland.
Edwards, Thomas. Md. Sergeant. ———. 50 acres.
Edwards, Thomas. Va. Private. 15 May 1783. 100 acres.
Edwards, William. Ga. ———. 17 May 1784. ———.
Edwards, William. Va. Sailor. 3 Dec. 1783. 100 acres.
Edwell, Samuel. N.C. Private. 17 Dec. 1785. 640 acres to heirs.
Egars, John. N.C. Private. 28 Jul. 1820. 274 acres to heir William Egars [Agurs].
Egberts, Jacob Visscher. N.Y. Hospital Mate. ———. 1800 acres.
Eggen, Elijah. N.Y. ———. 13 Sep. 1790. 500 acres to heirs.
Eggleston, Joseph. Va. Major. 17 Jul. 1783. 5333 1/3 acres.
Eggleston, William. Va. Lieutenant. 2 Feb. 1784. 2666 2/3 acres.
Eggs, Samuel. N. Y. Private. 8 Jul. 1790. 500 acres.
Egner, Matthias. N.C. Private. 19 May 1784. 640 acres.
Ehinger, Daniel. Pa. Private. 28 Aug. 1787. 200 acres.
Eicholtz, John. Pa. Private. ———. 200 acres.
Eigle, John. Ga. Refugee. 2 Feb. 1784. ———.
Eimbeck, George. Ga. Barrack Master. 16 Mar. 1784. 600 acres.
Elam, Alexander. Va. Private. 14 Apr. 1838. 100 acres.
Elam, Lodowick. Va. Private. 3 Oct. 1783. 100 acres.
Elam, Martin. Ga. ———. 17 May 1784. ———.
Elbert. John L. Md. Surgeon. ———. 200 acres.
Elbert, Samuel. Ga. Colonel. 5 Jan. 1784. 1000 acres.
Elbert, Samuel. Ga. Brigadier General. 26 Mar. 1784. 700 acres.
Elder, Ephraim. Va. Private. 18 Aug. 1783. 200 acres.
Eldredge, Daniel. Me. Private. 11 May 1835. 200 acres to widow Phebe Eldredge. Turner.
Eldridge, Charles, Jr. Conn. Sufferer. Groton. 775.6.7.
Eldridge, Christopher. Va. Private. 25 May 1785. 100 acres.
Eldridge, Daniel. Conn. Sufferer. Groton. 4.14.0.

Eldridge, Daniel, Sgt. Conn. Sufferer. Groton. 1.1.9.
Eldridge, Levi. N.C. Private. 28 Oct. 1783. 640 acres to heir.
Elinwood, Samuel. Mass. Private. 15 Jan. 1834. 200 acres.
Elkinburgh, Peter. N. Y. Private. 8 Jul. 1790. 500 acres.
Elkins, Johnston. S.C. ———. 4 Mar. 1793. 200 acres to Thomas Seal, Jr., assignee.
Elkins, Joseph. N.C. Private. 9 Apr. 1788. 640 acres to heirs.
Elkins, Joseph. N.C. Corporal. 6 Jan. 1825. 360 acres to heirs.
Elkins, William. Md. Private. ———. 50 acres.
Elks, Williams. N.C. Private. 5 Sep. 1821. 640 acres.
Eller, John. N.C. Private. 17 Sep. 1785. 640 acres to heirs.
Eller, Joseph. N.C. Private. 20 Sep. 1784. 640 acres to heirs.
Elleron, Evert. Conn. Sufferer. Norwalk. 13.10.0.
Elleson, Andrew. N.C. Private. 22 Dec. 1796. 274 acres.
Ellicott, Edward. Md. Private. ———. 50 acres.
Ellicott, John. Md. Private. ———. 50 acres.
Ellicott, Joseph. Md. Private. ———. 50 acres.
Ellicott, Thomas. Md. Private. ———. 50 acres.
Elliot, Abigail. Conn. Sufferer. New London. 496.13.10.
Elliot, Andrew, Rev. Conn. Sufferer. Fairfield. 549.11.6.
Elliot, Clark. Conn. Sufferer. New London. 296.11.3
Elliot, John. Conn. Sufferer. Danbury. 2.5.4.
Elliot, John, Sr. N.C. Sergeant. 25 Jun. 1785. 642 acres.
Elliott, Alexander. Va. Midshipman. 30 May 1788. 2666 2/3 acres.
Elliott, Archibald. N. Y. Private. 6 Jul. 1790. 600 acres.
Elliott, Archibald. Va. Private. 14 Dec. 1797. 100 acres.
Elliott, Archibald. Va. Corporal. 15 Dec. 1808. 300 acres.
Elliott, Barnard. S.C. Captain. 21 Jan. 1785. 300 acres.
Elliott, Benjamin. S.C. ———. 2 Oct. 1786. 200 acres.
Elliott, Daniel. Ga. Soldier. 19 Mar. 1784. 200 acres to heirs.
Elliott, Francis. Mass. Private. 13 Feb. 1833. 200 acres.
Elliott, Francis. N. Y. Private. 8 Jul. 1790. 600 acres.
Elliott, George. Va. Captain. 7 Apr. 1836. 152 2/3 acres.
Elliott, George. Va. Captain. 7 Apr. 1836. 37 1/4 acres.
Elliott, George. Va. Captain. 30 May 1788. 4000 acres.
Elliott, George. Va. Captain. 21 Jan. 1834. 1333 1/3 acres.
Elliott, George. Va. Captain. 7 Aug. 1835. 190 3/7 acres.
Elliott, George. Va. Captain. 7 Aug. 1835. 190 3/7 acres.
Elliott, George. Va. Captain. 7 Aug. 1835. 190 3/7 acres.
Elliott, George. Va. Captain. 7 Aug. 1835. 190 3/7 acres.
Elliott, George. Va. Captain. 20 Nov. 1835. 190 3/7 acres.
Elliott, Henry. Ga. Refugee. 19 Jul. 1784. 575 acres.
Elliott, Henry. N. Y. Private. 24 Aug. 1790. 500 acres.
Elliott, Jabesh. N.C. ———. 29 Sep. 1784. 640 acres.
Elliott, Jadithan. Va. Carpenter. 13 Apr. 1784. 100 acres.
Elliott, Jadithan. Va. Carpenter. 8 Jan. 1852. 1283 acres.
Elliott, Jadithan. Va. Carpenter. 8 Jan. 1852. 641 1/2 acres.
Elliott, Jadithan. Va. Carpenter. 8 Jan. 1852. 428 1/2 acres.
Elliott, Jadithan. Va. Carpenter. 8 Jan. 1852. 213 1/2 acres.
Elliott, James. N.C. Private. 20 Feb. 1784. 274 acres.
Elliott, James. Va. Private. 23 Feb. 1784. 200 acres.
Elliott, Jeremiah. Va. Private. 2 May 1783. 200 acres.
Elliott, John. Ga. Refugee. 24 May 178-. 287 1/2 acres.
Elliott, John. N. Y. Surgeon's Mate. 7 Jul. 1790. 1300 acres.

Elliott, John. N.C. Private. 12 Feb. 1784. 365 acres.

Elliott, John. N.C. Private. 24 Dec. 1785. 277 acres.

Elliott, John. Va. Private. 14 Feb. 1834. 100 acres.

Elliott, Joseph. N.C. Private. 30 Sep. 1785. 640 acres to heirs.

Elliott, Joseph. S.C. ———. 21 Jan. 1785. 300 acres to Abraham Ladson, executor.

Elliott, Nicholas. Md. Private. ———. 50 acres.

Elliott, Robert. Va. Lieutenant. 14 Dec. 1805. 2666 2/3 acres.

Elliott, Robert. Va. Lieutenant. 11 Sep. 1807. 259 acres.

Elliott, Samuel. Va. Private. 4 Jan. 1806. 100 acres.

Elliott, Teackle. Va. Private. 14 Feb. 1834. 100 acres.

Elliott, Thomas. Md. Private. ———. 50 acres.

Elliott, Thomas. N.C. Private. 2 Feb. 1786. 640 acres to heirs.

Elliott, Thomas. Va. Colonel. 16 Jun. 1784. 6666 2/3 acres.

Elliott, Thomas. Va. Private. 15 Jun. 1807. 100 acres.

Elliott, William. S.C. ———. 1 Feb. 1790. 200 acres.

Elliott, William. Va. Corporal. 21 Nov. 1783. 200 acres.

Elliott, William. Va. Private. 14 Feb. 1834. 100 acres.

Elliott, William. Va. Private. 13 Apr. 1853. 100 acres.

Elliott, William, Jr. Ga. ———. 19 Jul. 1784. 287 1/2 acres.

Elliott, William, Sr. Ga. ———. 19 Jul. 1784. 287 1/2 acres.

Elliott, Wyatt. Va. Sergeant. 10 Jun. 1783. 200 acres.

Ellis, Atkins. Me. ———. 16 Apr. 1835. 200 acres to widow Elizabeth Ellis. St. Albans.

Ellis, Charles. N.C. Private. 15 Feb. 1797. 274 acres.

Ellis, Daniel. Va. Private. 27 Feb. 1797. 100 acres.

Ellis, Edward. S.C. ———. 2 May 1791. 200 acres.

Ellis, George. Ga. Soldier. 2 Jan. 1786. ———.

Ellis, Isham. S.C. ———. 7 Oct. 1793. 200 acres.

Ellis, Jacob. N.Y. ———. 13 Sep. 1790. 500 acres to heirs.

Ellis, James. Va. Drummer. 6 Feb. 1784. 100 acres.

Ellis, John. Ga. ———. 19 Dec. 1785. 287 1/2 acres.

Ellis, John. N. Y. Sergeant. 8 Jul. 1790. 500 acres.

Ellis, John. N.C. Private. 19 May 1784. 640 acres.

Ellis, John. N.C. Private. 23 Aug. 1820. 228 acres.

Ellis, John. Va. Sergeant. 20 Feb. 1784. 200 acres.

Ellis, Matthew. Va. Private. 2 Apr. 1788. 100 acres.

Ellis, Michael. Md. Fifer. ———. 50 acres.

Ellis, Reuben. Pa. Gunner. 19 Oct. 1786. 200 acres to widow.

Ellis, Reuben. S.C. ———. 1 Apr. 1793. 200 acres.

Ellis, Richard. Md. ———. ———. 50 acres to administrator.

Ellis, Robert. Ga. Soldier. 17 May 1784. 230 acres.

Ellis, Robert. N.C. Private. 26 Aug. 1785. 274 acres.

Ellis, Robert. Pa. Private. 29 Sep. 1787. 200 acres to Eunice Ellis, widow.

Ellis, Samuel. Me. ———. 17 Jun. 1835. 200 acres to widow Mary Ellis. East Machias.

Ellis, Stephen. Ga. ———. 27 Sep. 1784. ———.

Ellis, Thomas. Md. Private. ———. 50 acres.

Ellis, William. Ga. Refugee. 16 Jul. 1784. 287 1/2 acres.

Ellis, William. Md. Private. ———. 50 acres.

Ellis, William. Pa. Private. 6 Apr. 1794. 200 acres to Sarah Ross, widow.

Ellis, William. Pa. Private. ———. 200 acres to Sarah Ross.

Ellis, William. Va. Private. 19 Feb. 1784. 100 acres.

Ellison, Ackess. N.C. Private. 27 Jul. 1785. 640 acres.

Ellison, David. Va. Private. 30 Nov. 1833. 100 acres.

Ellison, Henry. Ga. ———. 17 May 1784. ———.

Ellison, James. Ga. ———. 1784. 250 acres.
Ellison, John. N. Y. Corporal. 8 Jul. 1790. 600 acres.
Ellison, John. Pa. Sergeant. 19 Sep. 1787. 250 acres.
Ellison, Richard. Md. Private. ———. 50 acres.
Ellison, Robert. N. Y. Private. 8 Jul. 1790. 600 acres.
Ellison, Thomas. Md. Private. ———. 50 acres.
Ellrod, Conrad. Ga. Minute Man. 22 Mar. 1785. 250 acres.
Ellum, Charles. N.C. Private. 24 Oct. 1820. 228 acres.
Elmore, Daniel. N.C. Private. 20 Jan. 1785. 640 acres to heirs.
Elmore, Daniel. Va. Private. 7 May 1783. 100 acres.
Elmore, George. Va. Private. 21 Jul. 1783. 100 acres.
Elmore, John. Va. Sergeant. 11 Feb. 1784. 200 acres.
Elmore, Morgan. N.C. Private. 19 Jan. 1786. 640 acres.
Elmore, William. Va. Sergeant. 7 May 1783. 200 acres.
Elmoure, George. N.C. Private. 30 Apr. 1784. 274 acres.
Elms, George. Md. Fife Major. ———. 50 acres.
Elms, James. Va.-Ind. Private. 108 acres.
Elms, James. Va. Private. 17 Jul. 1784. 100 acres.
Elms, James. Va. Private. 31 Oct. 1791. 100 acres.
Elms, John. Va.-Ind. Private. 108 acres.
Elms, William. Va.-Ind. Sergeant. 216 acres.
Elms, William. Va. Sergeant. 29 Oct. 1791. 200 acres.
Elridge, John. Ga. Soldier. 5 Aug. 1785. ———.
Elridge, Thomas. Ga. Soldier. 5 Aug. 1785. ———.
Elrod, Joseph. Pa. ———. 10 Jan. 1849. 200 acres.
Elsworth, Peter. N.Y. Captain Lieutenant. 7 Jul. 1790. 1200 acres.
Elvin, John. Ga. Soldier. 2 May 1785. ———.
Elwell, Thomas. Va. Corporal. 7 Mar. 1786. 400 acres.
Ely, Eli. N.C. Captain. 5 Sep. 1821. 3840 acres.
Elzey, Edward. Va. Private. 26 May 1783. 200 acres.
Elzey, Thomas. Va. Private. 24 Mar. 1783. 100 acres.
Emanuel, Amos. Ga. Refugee. 17 May 1784. 500 acres.
Emanuel, Asa. Ga. Refugee. 6 Feb. 1784. 500 acres.
Emanuel, David. Ga. Captain. 17 May 1784. ———.
Emanuel, Henry. Va. Private. 26 Aug. 1783. 200 acres.
Emanuel, Levi. Ga. Sergeant. 20 Feb. 1784. 500 acres.
Embickim, William. Ga. ———. 26 May 1784. 287 1/2 acres.
Embry, Jesse. Ga. ———. 1784. 287 1/2 acres.
Embry, John. N.C. Private. 21 Aug. 1820. 274 acres.
Emerson, Henry. Va. Sergeant. 4 Feb. 1784. 200 acres.
Emerson, Samuel. N.C. Private. 25 Feb. 1800. 640 acres.
Emery, Abraham. S.C. ———. 7 May 1792. 200 acres.
Emery, Jesse. Me. Private. 18 May 1838. 200 acres to widow Ruth Emery. Newry.
Emery, John. Me. ———. 27 Apr. 1835. 200 acres. Bloomfield.
Emery, Nathaniel. Me. ———. 22 Apr. 1835. 200 acres to widow Patience Emory. Anson.
Emery, Samuel. Me. Private. 28 Apr. 1835. 200 acres. Ripley.
Emes, Worsley. Pa. Captain. ———. 500 acres.
Emmerson, John. Va. Lieutenant. 14 Jun. 1820. 1333 1/3 acres.
Emmerson, John. Va. Lieutenant. 14 Jun. 1820. 1333 1/3 acres.
Emmerson, John. Va. Lieutenant. 6 May 1834. 166 acres.
Emmery, John. N.C. ———. 25 Nov. 1783. 640 acres to heirs.
Emmery, Stephen. N.C. Private. 9 Nov. 1784. 640 acres to Zachariah Williams, heir.
Emmet, James. N.C. Major. 6 Dec. 1783. 1600 acres.

Emmett, James. Ga. ———. 17 May 1784. ———.

Emmins, William. Va. Sergeant. 2 Jun. 1783. 200 acres.

Emmons, John. Va. Private. 28 Feb. 1785. 200 acres.

Emmons, John. Va. Private. 4 Aug. 1834. 300 acres.

Emmons, Peter. Va. Private. 5 Feb. 1820. 200 acres.

Empson, John. N.C. Private. 9 Feb. 1796. 640 acres to heirs.

Emry, Thomas. Va. Private. 15 Apr. 1783. 200 acres.

Endless, Thomas. N.C. Musician. 16 Aug. 1821. 1000 acres.

Engel, Windle. Va. Private. 2 Nov. 1789. 200 acres.

Engle, William. Va. Private. 20 Dec. 1813. 100 acres.

Engledo, Thomas. Pa. Private. 10 Mar. 1795. 200 acres to Christopher Biddle, assignee.

English, Charles. Va. Private. 1 Apr. 1783. 100 acres.

English, Charles. Va. Private. 28 Jun. 1783. 200 acres.

English, James. Pa. Private. 8 Feb. 1787. 200 acres.

English, John. N.Y. ———. 13 Sep. 1790. 500 acres to heirs.

English, John. N.C. Private. 14 May 1784. 640 acres.

English, John. S.C. ———. 2 Oct. 1786. 194 acres.

English, John. Va. Private. 23 Jun. 1783. 200 acres.

English, Joseph. N.C. Private. 29 Sep. 1784. 640 acres to heir.

English, Joshua. N.C. Private. 30 Sep. 1785. 640 acres to heirs.

English, Samuel. N. Y. Lieutenant. 7 Jul. 1790. 1200 acres.

English, William. Ga. ———. 17 May 1784. ———.

Enloe, John. N.C. Captain. 22 Oct. 1783. 1280 acres to Suckey Enloe, legatee.

Ennis, David. N.Y. ———. 13 Sep. 1790. 500 acres to heirs.

Ennis, Enoch. Md. Private. ———. 50 acres.

Ennis, Francis. Pa. Private. 9 Oct. 1787. 200 acres.

Ennis, Henry. N. Y. Private. 3 Jul. 1790. 600 acres.

Ennis, John. Md. Private. ———. 50 acres.

Ennis, Leonard. Md. Private. ———. 50 acres.

Ennis, Richard. Pa. ———. 21 Mar. 1803. 200 acres to Mary Ennis, widow.

Ent, William. Pa. Private. 31 Oct. 1786. 200 acres.

Entrican, William. Ga. ———. 15 Jul. 1784. 287 1/2 acres.

Entrot, Henry. Mass. Private. 1 Feb. 1833. 200 acres.

Epperson, Richard. Va. Midhsipman. 18 Sep. 1850. 1000 acres.

Epperson, Richard. Va. Midshipman. 18 Sep. 1850. 1000 acres.

Epperson, Richard. Va. Midshipman. 18 Sep. 1850. 666 2/3 acres.

Epperson, Richard. Va. Midshipman. 3 Nov. 1852. 666 2/3 acres.

Epperson, Samuel. Va. Private. 4 Jun. 1785. 200 acres.

Eppes, Francis. Va. Lieutenant Colonel. 28 May 1803. 1000 acres.

Eppes, Francis. Va. Lieutenant Colonel. 28 May 1803. 1000 acres.

Eppes, Francis. Va. Lieutenant Colonel. 28 May 1803. 1000 acres.

Eppes, Francis. Va. Lieutenant Colonel. 28 May 1803. 1000 acres.

Eppes, Francis. Va. Lieutenant Colonel. 28 May 1803. 1000 acres.

Eppes, Francis. Va. Lieutenant Colonel. 28 May 1803. 1000 acres.

Eppes, Francis. Va. Lieutenant Colonel. 1 May 1840. 200 acres.

Eppes, Francis. Va. Lieutenant Colonel. 1 May 1840. 1472 2/9 acres.

Eppes, Francis. Va. Lieutenant Colonel. 1 May 1840. 536 1/9 acres.

Eppes, Francis. Va. Lieutenant Colonel. 9 Jan. 1843. 736 1/9 acres.

Eppes, Francis. Va. Lieutenant Colonel. 9 Jan. 1843. 736 1/9 acres

Eppes, John. N.C. Private. 5 Sep. 1792. 274 acres.

Eppes, Richard. Va. Sergeant. 14 Oct. 1783. 200 acres.

Eppes, William. Va. Captain Lieutenant. 1 Aug. 1783. 4000 acres.

Eppes, Wyatt. Va. Private. 4 Mar. 1784. 100 acres.

Epps, William. N.C. Private. 21 Nov. 1795. 274 acres.
Epps, William. Va. Captain Lieutenant. 29 May 1783. 4000 acres.
Epton, Benjmain. N. Y. Private. 6 Jul. 1790. 600 acres.
Equidowney, Peter. Md. Private. ———. 50 acres.
Erb, Lawrence. Pa. Lieutenant. 9 Jul. 1787. 200 acres.
Erb, Lawrence. Pa. Lieutenant of Rangers. 17 Apr. 1787. 200 acres.
Ermine, Thomas. Va. Private. 11 Mar. 1786. 100 acres.
Erskine, Alexander. Me. Private. 31 Oct. 1835. 200 acres to widow Mary Erskine. Bristol.
Erskine, Charles. Va. Lieutenant. 17 Feb. 1784. 2666 2/3 acres.
Ervin, Edward. Md. Private. ———. 50 acres.
Ervine, Edward. Md. Private. ———. 50 acres.
Ervine, James. Md. Private. ———. 50 acres.
Erwin, James. N. Y. Private. 7 Jul. 1790. 500 acres.
Erwin, John. N. Y. Private. 8 Jul. 1790. 600 acres.
Erwin, John. N.Y. Drum Major. 13 Sep. 1790. 500 acres to heirs.
Erwin, John. N.C. Private. 16 Aug. 1821. 640 acres.
Eskridge, Edwin. Va. Midshipman. 13 Jan. 1786. 2666 2/3 acres.
Eskridge, George. Va. Lieutenant. 18 Jan. 1838. 2666 2/3 acres.
Eskridge, George. Va. Lieutenant. 24 Mar. 1838. 2000 2/3 acres.
Eskridge, George. Va. Lieutenant. 24 Mar. 1838. 666 acres.
Eskridge, George. Va. Lieutenant. 10 Oct. 1844. 666 2/3 acres.
Eskridge, George. Va. Lieutenant. 10 Oct. 1844. 666 2/3 acres.
Eskridge, George. Va. Lieutenant. 10 Oct. 1844. 666 2/3 acres.
Eskridge, George. Va. Lieutenant. 18 Aug. 1852. 666 2/3 acres.
Eskridge, George. Va. Lieutenant. 18 Aug. 1852. 666 2/3 acres.
Eskridge, George. Va. Sergeant. 28 Oct. 1784. 200 acres.
Eskridge, Samuel. Va. Midshipman. 18 Feb. 1786. 2666 2/3 acres.
Eskridge, William. Va. Lieutenant. 3 Jan. 1783. 1000 acres.
Eskridge, William. Va. Lieutenant. 3 Jan. 1783. 2110 2/3 acres.
Eskridge, William. Va. Lieutenant. 15 Jun. 1807. 512 acres.
Eslick, James. N.C. Private. 5 Sep. 1821. 640 acres to heirs.
Esom, Bartholomew. Md. Corporal. ———. 50 acres.
Esom, John. S.C. Soldier. 21 Jan. 1785. 200 acres.
Espey, Thomas. Ga. Captain. 28 Feb. 1784. 500 acres to heirs.
Espey, William. Ga. Refugee. 28 Feb. 1784. 250 acres to heirs.
Essins, Thomas. N.C. Private. 8 Nov. 1784. 640 acres to heir.
Ester, William. N.C. Private. 30 Sep. 1785. 640 acres to heirs.
Estes, Elisha. Va. Sergeant. 16 Jun. 1783. 200 acres.
Estis, George. Va. Private. 28 Jan. 1786. 100 acres.
Estis, Rowland. Va. Private. 28 Jan. 1786. 100 acres.
Estridge, Thomas. N.C. Private. 26 Apr. 1784. 640 acres.
Estridge, Thomas. N.C. Private. 9 Nov. 1784. 640 acres.
Ethel, Benjamin. Va. Private. 20 Apr. 1785. 100 acres.
Etheredge, William. N.C. Private. 30 Sep. 1785. 640 acres to heirs.
Etheridge, Daniel. N.C. Corporal. 24 Dec. 1785. 1000 acres to heirs.
Etheridge, Isaac. N.C. Private. 12 Dec. 1797. 640 acres to heirs.
Etheridge, John. Md. ———. ———. 50 acres.
Etherige, John. N.C. Private. 19 May 1784. 640 acres.
Etherington, John. Va. Private. 21 Oct. 1785. 100 acres.
Etter, John. Va. Private. 18 Jan. 1786. 200 acres.
Ettinger, William. Pa. Private. 27 Oct. 1787. 200 acres.
Eubank, John. Va. Private. 28 Feb. 1837. 100 acres.
Eubank, John. Va. Corporal. 20 Apr. 1785. 200 acres.

Eubank, Royal. Va. Private. 19 Jun. 1783. 100 acres.
Eubank, Thomas. Va. Private. 25 Apr. 1838. 100 acres.
Eustace, John. Va. Captain. 19 Dec. 1783. 4000 acres.
Eustace, John. Va. Lieutenant. 26 Feb. 1784. 2666 2/3 acres.
Eustace, John Sky. Ga. Major. 17 May 1784. 920 acres.
Evance, John. N.Y. ———. 13 Sep. 1790. 500 acres to heirs.
Evance, William. N.Y. ———. 13 Sep. 1790. 500 acres to heirs. N.B. He appears to have deserted.
Evans, Anthony. Pa. Fife Major. 22 May 1787. 200 acres.
Evans, Archibald. Ga. Soldier. 2 May 1785. ———.
Evans, Benjamin. Ga. Sergeant. 17 May 1784. ———.
Evans, Benjamin. Md. ———. ———. 50 acres.
Evans, Benjamin. S.C. ———. 6 Jun. 1791. 95 acres.
Evans, Benjamin. S.C. ———. 7 May 1792. 200 acres.
Evans, Charles. Va.-Ind. Private. 108 acres.
Evans, Charles. Va. Private. 5 Jun. 1783. 100 acres.
Evans, Daniel. Ga. Soldier. 25 May 1784. 287 1/2 acres.
Evans, David. Ga. Private. 13 Sep. 1784. 287 1/2 acres.
Evans, Edward. Md. Private. ———. 50 acres.
Evans, Edward. Md. Sergeant. ———. 50 acres.
Evans, Elijah. Md. Captain. ———. 200 acres.
Evans, Euel. Md. Private. ———. 50 acres.
Evans, George. Va. Surgeon. 19 Dec. 1783. 6000 acres.
Evans, Harding. Ga. ———. 17 May 1784. ———.
Evans, Henry. Md. Private. ———. 50 acres.
Evans, Henry. Va. Private. 14 Feb. 1784. 100 acres.
Evans, James. Ga. ———. 30 Sep. 1784. ———.
Evans, James. Md. Private. ———. 50 acres.
Evans, Jeremiah. N.C. Private. 30 Sep. 1785. 640 acres to heirs.
Evans, Jesse. Va. Fifer. 15 Jun. 1807. 100 acres.
Evans, Jesse. Va. Captain. 15 Jan. 1834. 4000 acres.
Evans, John. Ga. Private. 10 Dec. 1784. 250 acres.
Evans, John. Md. Matross. ———. 50 acres.
Evans, John. N.C. Private. 29 Aug. 1820. 640 acres.
Evans, John. Pa. ———. 8 Nov. 1803. 200 acres.
Evans, John. Pa. Private. 21 Mar. 1806. 200 acres to Thomas Collins, assignee.
Evans, John. Va. Private. 2 Aug. 1783. 100 acres.
Evans, John. Va. Private. 11 Dec. 1783. 200 acres.
Evans, John. Va. Private. 23 Mar. 1796. 200 acres.
Evans, John. Va. Corporal. 20 May 1808. 200 acres.
Evans, John Gibson. Ga. ———. 17 May 1784. ———.
Evans, Joseph. N. Y. Private. 7 Jul. 1790. 600 acres.
Evans, Joseph. N.C. Private. 17 Dec. 1785. 640 acres to heirs.
Evans, Joseph. Va. Sergeant. 9 Dec 1790. 200 acres.
Evans, Peregrine. Md. Sergeant. ———. 50 acres.
Evans, Peter. Va. Private. 5 Sep. 1807. 100 acres.
Evans, Philip. N.C. Private. 30 Sep. 1785. 640 acres to heirs.
Evans, Philip. Va. Private. 21 Jul. 1783. 100 acres.
Evans, Philip. Va. Private. 23 May 1834. 100 acres.
Evans, Philip. Va. Carpenter. 7 Nov. 1787. 2666 2/3 acres.
Evans, Richard. N.C. Private. 29 Sep. 1784. 640 acres.
Evans, Richard. N.C. Private. 13 Nov. 1795. 640 acres to heirs.
Evans, Samuel. Md. Corporal. ———. 50 acres.
Evans, Stephen. Ga. Refugee. 17 May 1784. 287 1/2 acres.
Evans, Stephen. Va. Corporal. 12 Dec. 1785. 400 acres.

Evans, Thomas. Md. Private. ———. 50 acres.
Evans, Thomas. Md. Private. ———. 50 acres.
Evans, Thomas. N.C. Captain. 20 Apr. 1784. 3840 acres.
Evans, Thomas. N.C. Private. 9 Sep. 1820. 640 acres to heirs.
Evans, Thomas. Va. Private. 25 Apr. 1783. 200 acres.
Evans, Thomas. Va. Private. 17 Aug. 1784. 100 acres.
Evans, Thomas. Va. Private. 15 Jun. 1807. 100 acres.
Evans, William. Ga. Refugee. 15 Apr. 1785. 500 acres.
Evans, William. Ga. ———. 24 May 1784. 287 1/2 acres.
Evans, William. Md. Private. ———. 50 acres.
Evans, William. N.C. Private. 30 Sep. 1785. 640 acres to heirs.
Evans, William. Va. Lieutenant. 1 Apr. 1783. 1000 acres.
Evans, William. Va. Lieutenant. 1 Apr. 1783. 1666 2/3 acres.
Evans, William. Va. Private. 27 Apr. 1785. 200 acres.
Evans, William. Va. Lieutenant. 13 Sep 1808. 407 acres.
Everedge, Abner. N.C. Private. 14 Jun. 1785. 640 acres.
Everett, Henry. Va. Private. 5 Dec. 1833. 100 acres.
Everett, John. N.C. Private. 7 Dec. 1797. 640 acres to heirs.
Everett, Matthew. N.C. Private. 6 Sep. 1821. 640 acres to heirs.
Everett, Thomas. N.C. Private. 2 Feb. 1786. 640 acres to heirs.
Everett, William. Va. Private. 5 Dec. 1833. 100 acres.
Everhart, Andrew. Va. Private. 29 Apr. 1785. 200 acres.
Everhart, Lawrence. Va. Sergeant. 4 Nov. 1784. 200 acres.
Everly, George. Pa. Private. ———. 200 acres.
Everly, Michael. Pa. Lieutenant. 27 Mar. 1787. 200 acres.
Everly, Michael. Pa. Lieutenant. 7 Mar. 1787. 200 acres.
Eversley, John. Conn. Sufferer. Norwalk. 11.1.2.
Eversley, John & Daniel Eversley. Conn. Sufferer. Norwalk. 154.9.6 1/2.
Eversley, Sarah. Conn. Sufferer. Norwalk. 26.13.5.
Everton, Edward. N.C. Private. 2 Feb. 1785. 640 acres to heirs.
Everton, Zephaniah. Me. ———. 25 Oct. 1836. 200 acres. Thomaston.
Every, Thomas. Pa. Private. 21 Oct. 1787. 200 acres.
Eves, Nathaniel. Ga. ———. 22 Sep. 1784. 230 acres.
Evitt, William. Pa. Private. ———. 200 acres to widow.
Eweleth, John. Mass. Private. 18 Oct. 1833. 200 acres.
Ewell, Charles. Va. Captain. 13 May 1783. 4000 acres.
Ewell, Nathan. N.C. Private. 3 Feb. 1785. 228 acres.
Ewell, Stephen. N.C. Sergeant. 28 Jul. 1784. 523 acres.
Ewell, Thomas. Va. Captain. 4 Jul. 1783. 4000 acres.
Ewell, William. N.C. Sergeant. 22 Jan. 1784. 404 acres.
Ewell, William. N.C. Lieutenant. 16 Aug. 1821. 2560 acres.
Ewen, John. Me. ———. 25 Apr. 1835. 200 acres. Brunswick.
Ewens, Thomas. N.C. Private. 27 May 1784. 640 acres.
Ewing, Alexander. Va. Lieutenant. 3 Sep. 1782. 2666 2/3 acres.
Ewing, David. Pa. Private. 21 Sep. 1787. 200 acres.
Ewing, Edward. Va. Private. 17 Dec. 1785. 100 acres.
Ewing, James. Md. Captain. ———. 200 acres.
Exum, Philip. N.C. Private. 4 May 1785. 640 acres to heirs.
Eyen, Frederick. Md. ———. ———. 50 acres.
Eyers, William. Conn. Sufferer. New/East Haven. 5.6.0.
Factor, John. N. Y. Fifer. 6 Jul. 1790. 600 acres.
Faddes, Andrew. N.C. Private. 20 Sep. 1784. 640 acres.
Faddes, James. N.C. Private. 26 Apr. 1784. 640 acres to John Faddes, heir.
Faddles, James. N.C. Private. 6 Sep. 1821. 640 acres.

Fadlock, Drewry. N.C. Private. 2 Feb. 1786. 640 acres.
Faent, George. Va. Private. 5 Feb. 1785. 100 acres.
Faent, Philip. Va. Private. 5 Feb. 1785. 200 acres.
Fagan, Garret. Pa. Private. 23 Nov. 1787. 200 acres.
Faigan, George. N.C. Private. 26 Aug. 1785. 640 acres to heirs.
Fail, Thomas. N.C. Private. 17 Feb. 1824. 640 acres.
Fail, William. S.C. ———. 7 Jan. 1789. 200 acres to William Fair, heir.
Fain, Melcher. N.C. Private. 10 Dec. 1788. 640 acres.
Fair, James. Va. Sergeant. 26 Apr. 1783. 200 acres.
Fairbank, John. Md. ———. ———. 50 acres.
Fairbanks, John. Mass. Private. 25 Nov. 1831. 200 acres to heirs.
Fairbrother, Francis. Md. Private. ———. 50 acres.
Fairburn, William. Md. Private. ———. 50 acres.
Fairchild, Martha. Conn. Sufferer. Fairfield. 44.8.2.
Fairchild, Oliver. Conn. Sufferer. Greenwich. 8.10.8.
Fairchild, Robert. Conn. Sufferer. New/East Haven. 14.12.0.
Fairchild, Samuel. Conn. Sufferer. Norwalk. 131.3.11.
Faircloth, John. N.C. Private. 13 Dec. 1796. 640 acres to heirs.
Faircloth, John. N.C. Sergeant. 28 Jul. 1804. 1000 acres to heirs.
Faircloth, William. N.C. Lieutenant. 5 Dec. 1796. 731 acres.
Faircloth, William. N.C. Private. 14 Dec. 1797. 640 acres.
Fairfax, Dorman. N.C. Private. 7 Dec. 1797. 640 acres to heirs.
Fairfax, Frederick. N.C. Sergeant. 28 Sep. 1785. 1000 acres.
Fairfax, Harrington. N.C. Private. 7 Dec. 1797. 640 acres to heirs.
Fairfax, William. N.C. Private. 28 Sep. 1785. 640 acres to heirs.
Fairfield, John. Me. ———. 20 Jan. 1836. 200 acres to widow Hannah Fairfield. Kennebunkport.
Fairfield, William. Me. Private. 3 Jul. 1835. 200 acres to widow Mary Fairfield. Kennebunkport.
Fairlie, James. N. Y. Lieutenant. 6 Jul. 1790. 1200 acres.
Faison, James. N.C. Private. 25 Nov. 1796. 274 acres.
Faithful, William. N.C. Private. 19 May 1784. 640 acres.
Falconer, James. N.C. Sergeant. 29 Mar. 1805. 428 acres.
Falconer, Uriah. Pa. Private. 28 Sep. 1787. 200 acres to John Sanderson, assignee.
Falkner, Francis. N.C. Private. 22 Dec. 1796. 640 acres.
Falkner, Ralph. Va. Major. 23 Jan. 1808. 2666 2/3 acres.
Falkner, Ralph. Va. Major. 23 Jan. 1808. 2666 2/3 acres.
Fall, Henry. Va. Private. 30 Jul. 1783. 100 acres.
Fall, Samuel. Mass. Private. 11 Jul. 1837. 200 acres to assignee Samuel Cook.
Falvey, Patrick. Va. Private. 29 Apr. 1783. 200 acres.
Fame, John. Pa. Private. 12 Oct. 1786. 200 acres.
Fancher, Isaac. Va. Private. 23 Jun. 1832. 100 acres.
Fanner, William. Ga. ———. 19 Jul. 1784. 287 1/2 acres.
Fanning, Thomas. Md. Matross. ———. 50 acres.
Farara, Emanuel. Md. Private. ———. 50 acres.
Farden, Joseph. N.C. Private. 30 Sep. 1785. 640 acres to heirs.
Fardo, Absolom. Md. Private. ———. 50 acres.
Farguson, Charles. Ga. ———. 17 May 1784. ———.
Farguson, William. Va. Private. 13 Mar. 1784. 100 acres.
Farinholtz, David. Va. Private. 8 Sep. 1783. 100 acres.
Faris, Isaac. Va.-Ind. Private. 108 acres.
Faris, Martin. Va. Private. 2 Jun. 1835. 100 acres.
Faris, William. Va. Private. 15 Aug. 1783. 100 acres.
Farish, Robert. Ga. Lieutenant. ———. 460 acres.
Farish, Robert. Va. Surgeon's Mate. 29 Jul. 1835. 4000 acres.

Farish, Robert. Va. Surgeon's Mate. 20 Aug. 1836. 1000 acres.

Farish, Robert. Va. Surgeon's Mate. 18 Aug. 1836. 1000 acres.

Farish, Robert. Va. Surgeon's Mate. 18 Aug. 1836. 800 acres.

Farish, Robert. Va. Surgeon's Mate. 18 Aug. 18356. 1000 acres.

Farish, Robert. Va. Surgeon's Mate. 23 Sep. 1837. 100 acres.

Farish, Robert. Va. Surgeon's Mate. 18 Feb. 1843. 100 acres.

Farley, Jonathan. Mass Private. 30 Dec. 1831. 200 acres.

Farling, Robert. Ga. Soldier. 20 May 1785. ———.

Farmer, Asael. Ga. Refugee. 29 Jan. 1784. 250 acres.

Farmer, Jesse. Va. Private. 12 Jan. 1784. 100 acres.

Farmer, John. N.C. Private. 30 Sep. 1785. 640 acres to heirs.

Farmer, John. Va. Private. 13 Nov. 1784. 200 acres.

Farmer, Lodowick. Va. Private. 25 Mar. 1784. 100 acres.

Farmer, Peter. N.C. Sergeant. 24 Dec. 1785. 1000 acres to heirs.

Farmer, Samuel. Md. Lieutenant. ———. 200 acres.

Farmer, Thomas. N.C. Private. 30 Sep. 1785. 640 acres to heirs.

Farmer, William. N.C. Private. 6 Jan. 1784. 228 acres.

Farmer, William. S.C. ———. 4 Dec. 1786. 200 acres.

Farnham, Jonathan. Me. Private. 21 Oct. 1835. 200 acres to widow Dorcas Farnham. Boothbay.

Farnsworth, Edmund. Mass. ———. 21 May 1830. 200 acres.

Farr, George. N.C. Private. 1 Dec. 1789. 182 acres.

Farr, Jacob. Ga. ———. 17 May 1784. ———.

Farraby, Richard. Md. Private. ———. 50 acres.

Farrar, Field. S. C. Captain. 15 Oct. 1784. 300 acres.

Farrar, Thomas. S.C. Lieutenant. 15 Oct. 1784. 200 acres.

Farrel, Edmund. Va. Private. 2 Apr. 1810. 100 acres.

Farrel, James. Md. Private. ———. 50 acres.

Farrel, Robert. Md. Private. ———. 50 acres.

Farrel, Thomas. Va. Private. 2 Apr. 1810. 100 acres.

Farrel, Walter. Md. Private. ———. 50 acres.

Farrel, Zephaniah. Va. Private. 20 Oct. 1796. 200 acres.

Farrell, Isaac. Va. Private. 23 Jul. 1824. 200 acres.

Farrell, John. Ga. Soldier. 24 — 1785. ———.

Farrell, John. Md. Private. ———. 50 acres.

Farrell, John. Va. Drummer. 19 Jun. 1783. 200 acres.

Farrell, John. Va. Drummer. 19 Jun. 1783. 100 acres.

Farrell, Peter. Md. Corporal. ———. 50 acres.

Farrell, William. Ga. Lieutenant. 21 Jul. 1784. 287 1/2 acres.

Farrell, William. Md. Drummer. ———. 50 acres.

Farrell, William. Pa. Matross. ———. 200 acres.

Farrington, Abner. Me. Private. 6 Jun. 1835. 200 acres. Warren.

Farrington, James. N. Y. Matross. 9 Jul. 1790. 600 acres.

Farrow, Robert. Va. Private. 1 May 1783. 200 acres.

Farrow, Thomas. N.C. Private. 26 May 1784. 640 acres.

Farrow, William. N.C. Private. 28 May 1784. 228 acres.

Fatheree, Benjamin. S.C. ———. 2 Oct. 1786. 200 acres.

Fathom, Edward. Va. Private. 8 Dec. 1783. 200 acres.

Faulkner, Peter. Va. Sergeant. 21 May 1823. 400 acres.

Faulkner, Ralph. Va. Lieutenant Colonel. 30 Dec. 1840. 1555 7/9 acres.

Faulkner, Ralph. Va. Lieutenant Colonel. 30 Dec. 1840. 777 2/9 acres.

Faulks, James. N.C. Private. 26 May 1784. 640 acres.

Faulks, John. N.C. Private. 19 May 1784. 640 acres.

Faulks, Joseph. N.C. Private. 27 Oct. 1783. 640 acres.

Faunce, Jonas. Ga. ———. 5 Feb. 1787. 575 acres.
Faunt, William. N.C. Private. 21 Apr. 1784. 640 acres.
Fauntleroy, Griffin. Va. Captain. 26 Jun. 1784. 4000 acres.
Fauntleroy, Henry. Va. Captain. 22 Nov. 1783. 4000 acres.
Fauntleroy, Moore. Va. Major. 11 May 1790. 100 acres.
Fautz, Valentine. Va. Private. 20 Jun. 1783. 100 acres.
Favours, John. Ga. ———. 25 Feb. 1784. 250 acres.
Fawn, William. N.C. Captain. 25 Oct. 1783. 3840 acres.
Fayrer, William. Pa. Private. 24 Nov. 178-. 200 acres.
Fayssoux, Peter. S.C. Surgeon General. 21 Jan. 1785. 500 acres.
Feagan, John. Va. Private. 26 Apr. 1783. 200 acres.
Feagan, William. N. Y. ———. 21 Aug. 1800. 500 acres.
Feagle, Micahel. Va. Private. 31 Jan. 1785. 100 acres.
Fear, Edmund. Va.-Ind. Private. 108 acres.
Fear, Edward. Va. Private. 26 Jul. 1786. 100 acres.
Fear, Hamner. Va. Private. 31 Oct. 1783. 100 acres.
Fear, Jacob. Va. Private. 4 Dec. 1783. 200 acres.
Fearl, Ansol. N.C. Corporal. 17 Feb. 1824. 640 acres.
Fearless, Elisha. N.C. Private. 17 Feb. 1824. 640 acres.
Fears, Absalom. Ga. ———. 17 May 1784. ———.
Fears, Thomas. Va. Private. 12 Apr. 1783. 200 acres.
Feary, Jacob. Pa. Private. 5 Jul. 1786. 200 acres.
Feast, James. S.C. Soldier. 15 Oct. 1784. 200 acres.
Featherly, John. N. Y. Private. 8 Jul. 1790. 600 acres.
Featherly, Thomas. N. Y. Private. 8 Jul. 1790. 600 acres.
Febiger, Christain. Va. Colonel. 24 Jan. 1784. 7777 2/3 acres.
Febiger, Christain. Va. Colonel. 28 Jul. 1810. 1570 acres.
Feckel, Benjamin. Md. Lieutenant. ———. 200 acres.
Federson, John. Me. ———. 17 Mar. 1836. 200 acres. Parsonsfield.
Feegan, William. Pa. ———. ———. 200 acres to widow.
Feely, Timothy. Va. Lieutenant. 29 Jul. 1788. 2666 2/3 acres.
Feggins, James. Va. Private. 4 Dec. 1783. 200 acres.
Fellason [or Fenlayson], George. Md. Private. ———. 50 acres.
Felty, Henry. Pa. Private. 19 Nov. 1786. 200 acres.
Femalle, Alexander. N. Y. ———. ———. 500 acres.
Fenck, David. Pa. ———. 6 Apr. 1794. 200 acres to Francis Kirkpatrick, assignee.
Fenderson, Pelatiah. Me. ———. 16 Jun. 1835. 200 acres. Scarboro.
Fenn, John. Ga. Refugee. 6 Feb. 1784. 250 acres.
Fenn, Thomas. Va. Captain Lieutenant. 13 Feb. 1783. 4000 acres.
Fenn, Thomas. Va. Captain Lieutenant. 5 Feb. 1798. 666 2/3 acres.
Fenn, Travis. Ga. ———. 17 May 1784. ———.
Fenn, William. Ga. Refugee. 19 Jul. 1784. 287 1/2 acres.
Fenn, Zacharias. Ga. Citizen. 5 Jan. 1784. 250 acres.
Fenn, Zacheriah. Ga. ———. 6 Feb. 1784. 250 acres.
Fennel, Edward. Md. ———. ———. 50 acres.
Fennel, John. Md. Sergeant. ———. 50 acres.
Fennell, Hardy. N.C. Private. 15 Dec. 1797. 640 acres to heirs.
Fennell, Patrick. Pa. Private. 6 Apr. 1786. 200 acres.
Fennell, Stephen. Md. Private. ———. 50 acres.
Fenner, Richard. N.C. Lieutenant. 6 Jan. 1784. 2560 acres.
Fenno, Ephraim. N. Y. Lieutenant. 9 Jul. 1790. 1200 acres.
Fennon, Simon. Pa. Private. 24 Nov. 1788. 200 acres.
Fenton, Amos. N.Y. Private. 13 Sep. 1790. 500 acres to heirs.

Fenton, Caleb. N.C. ———. 29 Apr. 1784. 640 acres to Mary Parr[,] Elizabeth [Fenton] & Sarah Fenton, coheiresses.
Fenton, Caleb. N.C. Private. 3 Dec. 1797. 640 acres to heirs.
Fenton, James. Ga. Soldier. 20 Aug. 1785. ———.
Fenton, Joshua. N.C. Private. 16 Aug. 1821. 640 acres.
Fenton, Jotham. N. Y. Matross. 9 Jul. 1790. 600 acres.
Fenton, Thomas. N.C. Private. 3 Dec. 1797. 640 acres to heirs.
Fenwick, Nathaniel. N.C. Private. 14 Feb. 1796. 640 acres.
Fenwick, Richard. Md. Private. ———. 50 acres.
Ferdon, John. N. Y. Private. 3 Jul. 1790. 600 acres.
Ferebee, Joseph. N.C. Captain. 26 Apr. 1784. 1371 acres.
Ferebee, William. N.C. Captain. 26 Apr. 1784. 3062 acres.
Ferges, James. N.C. Surgeon. 29 Apr. 1784. 4800 acres.
Ferguson, Artemas Elliott. S.C. ———. 4 Dec. 1786. 7 acres.
Ferguson, Artemas Elliott. S.C. ———. 4 Jun. 1787. 15 1/2 acres.
Ferguson, Charles. Ga. ———. 28 Feb. 1784. 250 acres.
Ferguson, Henry. N.C. Private. 22 Dec. 1796. 640 acres.
Ferguson, Isham. N.C. Private. 22 Dec. 1796. 640 acres.
Ferguson, James. N. Y. Private. 8 Jul. 1790. 500 acres.
Ferguson, John. Ga. ———. ———. 287 1/2 acres.
Ferguson, John. Md. Private. ———. 50 acres.
Ferguson, John. Va. Private. 6 Mar. 1784. 100 acres.
Ferguson, John. Va. Fifer. 29 Aug. 1784. 100 acres.
Ferguson, Joseph. Pa. ———. 28 Feb. 1794. 200 acres to Walter Stewart.
Ferguson, Joseph. Pa. Private. ———. 200 acres to widow.
Ferguson, Peter. N.C. Private. 29 Apr. 1784. 228 acres.
Ferguson, Robert. Va. Surgeon's Mate. 20 Aug. 1784. 2666 2/3 acres.
Ferguson, Robert. Va. Private. 3 Jan. 1834. 200 acres.
Ferguson, Robert. Va. Surgeon's Mate. 31 Dec. 1851. 1333 1/3 acres.
Ferguson, Robert. Va. Surgeon's Mate. 24 Mar. 1853. 666 2/3 acres.
Ferguson, Robert. Va. Surgeon's Mate. 24 Mar. 1853. 666 2/3 acres.
Ferguson, William. Pa. ———. 10 Mar. 1787. 200 acres to Clement Biddle, assignee.
Ferguson, William. Pa. Captain. ———. 500 acres.
Fernan, Andrew. Md. Private. ———. 50 acres.
Ferrall, Dennis. Va. Private. 31 Dec. 1807. 100 acres.
Ferrell, Clemen. N.C. Private. 26 May 1784. 640 acres.
Ferrell, Edward. N.C. ———. 28 May 1784. 640 acres to William Ferrell, heir.
Ferrell, Enoch. N.C. Private. 17 Oct. 1783. 366 acres.
Ferrell, Henry. N.C. Private. 17 Dec. 1785. 640 acres to heirs.
Ferrell, Jacob. N.C. Private. 23 Apr. 1785. 640 acres to heirs.
Ferrell, James. N.C. Private. 21 Oct. 1783. 274 acres.
Ferrell, James Lamb. N.C. Lieutenant. 2 Dec. 1785. 2560 acres.
Ferrell, John. N.C. Private. 21 May 1784. 274 acres.
Ferrell, John. N.C. Private. 17 Dec. 1785. 640 acres to heirs.
Ferrell, Michael. Pa. Private. ———. 200 acres.
Ferrell, Thomas. N.C. Private. 16 Aug. 1821. 640 acres to heir Veazey Ferrell.
Ferrell, William. N.C. Lieutenant. 2 Dec. 1785. 2560 acres.
Ferril, James. N.C. Private. 23 Nov. 1797. 274 acres.
Ferrill, James. Ga. ———. 17 May 1784. ———.
Ferrill, William. Ga. Lieutenant Colonel. 24 May 1784. 977 1/2 acres.
Ferrington, Jacob. Ga. ———. 17 May 1784. ———.
Ferriole, Alexander. N. Y. Lieutenant. ———. 1000 acres.
Ferriole, Joseph. N. Y. ———. ———. 500 acres.

Ferris, Jabez. Conn. Sufferer. Greenwich. 28.5.7.
Ferris, James. Conn. Sufferer. Greenwich. 42.13.3.
Ferris, Joseph. Conn. Sufferer. Greenwich. 11.0.0.
Ferris, Joseph. Conn. Sufferer. Greenwich. 7.0.0.
Ferris, Josiah. Conn. Sufferer. Greenwich. 20.3.4.
Ferris, Moses. Conn. Sufferer. Greenwich. 6.0.0.
Ferris, Park. Conn. Sufferer. Greenwich. 6.10.0.
Ferris, Peter. N. Y. Matross. 9 Jul. 1790. 600 acres.
Ferris, Sylvanus. Conn. Sufferer. Greenwich. 42.14.4.
Ferris, Timothy. Conn. Sufferer. Greenwich. 16.10.0.
Ferroll, Patrick. Pa. Private. 31 Oct. 1787. 200 acres to David Walker, assignee.
Ferrot, John. Va. Private. 21 May 1784. 100 acres.
Ferry, Beverley. Va. Private. 8 Sep. 1813. 100 acres.
Fessenden, Benjamin. Mass. ———. 2 Mar. 1813. 200 acres.
Fetner, Henry. N.C. Corporal. 30 Sep. 1785. 1000 acres to heirs.
Few, Alexander. N.C. Private. 12 Oct. 1795. 640 acres to heirs.
Few, Benjamin. Ga. Colonel. 2 May 1785. 287 1/2 acres.
Few, Ignatius. Ga. ———. 11 Mar. 1784. 287 1/2 acres.
Few, William. Ga. Lieutenant Colonel. 28 Feb. 1784. 1050 acres.
Few, William, Sr. Ga. ———. 28 Feb. 1784. 250 acres.
Fick, David. Pa. Lieutenant. 26 Sep. 1787. 200 acres.
Fick, David. Pa. Lieutenant. 26 Sep. 1787. 200 acres.
Fickett, Nathaniel. Me. Private. 20 Mar. 1840. 200 acres to widow Abigail (Gammon) Fickett. Cape Elizabeth.
Fickett, Vinson. Me. Private. 19 Sep. 1835. 200 acres. Lewiston.
Ficklin, Charles. Va. Private. 20 May 1785. 100 acres.
Field, Benjamin. Va. Captain. 13 Aug. 1832. 4000 acres.
Field, Daniel. Me. ———. 3 Jun. 1835. 200 acres to widow Rachel Field. Greenwood.
Field, Henry. Va. Lieutenant. 28 Apr. 1804. 2666 2/3 acres.
Field, Henry. Va. Lieutenant. 15 May 1838. 744 acres.
Field, Reuben. Va. Captain. 1 Apr. 1783. 4000 acres.
Field, Reuben. Va. Captain. 15 Jun. 1812. 1139 acres.
Field, Stephen. Va. Lieutenant. 25 Jul. 1834. 2666 2/3 acres.
Field, Stephen. Va. Lieutenant. 19 Jul. 1838. 2666 2/3 acres.
Field, Theoplilus. Va. Lieutenant. 24 Mar. 1838. 4000 acres.
Field, William. Va. Private 30 Jun. 1783. 100 acres.
Fielder, George. Va. Private. 10 Jun. 1785. 100 acres.
Fielding, Benjamin. Ga. ———. 1784. ——— acres to heirs.
Fielding, Edwin. Va. Private. 9 Dec. 1796. 100 acres.
Fielding, Eppa. Va. Private. 19 Apr. 1799. 200 acres.
Fielding, James. Conn. Sufferer. Danbury. 3.0.8.
Fields, Abraham. S.C. ———. 2 Oct. 1786. 200 acres.
Fields, George. Md. Sergeant. ———. 50 acres.
Fields, James. S.C. Captain. 21 Jan. 1785. 300 acres.
Fields, John. Va. Steward. 26 Feb. 1831. 1333 1/3 acres.
Fields, John. Va. Steward. 26 Feb. 1831. 1333 1/3 acres.
Fields, Lewis. N.C. Private. 9 Feb. 1796. 640 acres to heirs.
Fields, Philip. N.Y. ———. 13 Sep. 1790. 500 acres to heirs.
Fields, Timothy. N.C. Private. 7 Jan. 1786. 274 acres.
Fields, Timothy. N.C. Private. 17 Jul. 1820. 640 acres to heirs.
Fields, Uriah. Conn. Sufferer. Greenwich. 212.15.1.
Fields, William. Ga. ———. 19 Jul. 1784. 287 1/2 acres.
Fields, William. Va. Private. 13 Dec. 1850. 100 acres.

Fields, Zacheriah. N.C. Private. 6 Dec. 1797. 274 acres.
Fierer, Charles. Va. Captain. 9 Dec. 1793. 2000 acres.
Fierer, Charles. Va. Captain. 9 Dec. 1793. 2000 acres.
Figg, Thomas. Va. Private. 15 Oct. 1784. 200 [100] acres.
Fike, James. N.C. Private. 8 Dec. 1795. 640 acres to heir Malachi Fike.
Fikes, James. N.C. Sergeant. 30 Aug. 1820. 1000 acres to heirs.
Filberry, George. Va. Private. 7 May 1785. 200 acres.
Filbert, Anthony. N. Y. ———. ———. 500 acres.
Filby, George. Va. Private. 15 Jan. 1808. 60 acres.
Filcher, Nathan. Ga. ———. 19 Dec. 1785. 287 1/2 acres.
Filer, Thomas. N. Y. ———. ———. 200 acres to his legal representatives Zephaniah Filer, Thomas Filer, Philip Filer, Alpheus Filer, Hester the wife of John Damon, Phebe Filer, and Jane the wife of Thomas Osborn.
Fillco, John. Conn. Sufferer. Norwalk. 1.15.2.
Fillebrown, John. Mass. Gunner. 18 Oct. 1833. 200 acres.
Fillebrown, Thomas. Me. ———. 27 Apr. 1835. 200 acres. Winthrop.
Fillet, Avery. N.C. Private. 8 Dec. 1796. 640 acres.
Fillgon, William. N.C. Private. 30 Sep. 1785. 640 acres to heirs.
Filling, Richard. N.C. Private. 9 Dec. 1797. 365 acres.
Fillips, Joseph. N.C. Private. 17 Feb. 1824. 640 acres.
Filmont, Doras. Md. Private. ———. 50 acres.
Filpot, Edward. S.C. ——. 4 Apr. 1796. 200 acres to James Filpot.
Filsby, Richard. N.C. Private. 13 Jan. 1823. 274 acres.
Filson, Samuel. Md. Sergeant. ———. 50 acres.
Finch, Charles. Ga. ———. 17 May 1784. ———.
Finch, Daniel. Conn. Sufferer. Norwalk. 119.14.7.
Finch, Ezra. Conn. Sufferer. Greenwich. 86.0.0.
Finch, Jacob. Conn. Sufferer. Danbury. 2.16.8.
Finch, Jacob. Conn. Sufferer. New London. 130.8.10.
Finch, James. Pa. Private. 9 Mar. 1795. 200 acres to John Nicholson, assignee.
Finch, James. Va. Private. 26 Apr. 1783. 200 acres.
Finch, John. Pa. Private. 25 Oct. 1786. 200 acres.
Finch, Jonathan. Conn. Sufferer. Greenwich. 0.0.0.
Finch, Nathauel. Conn. Sufferer. Greenwich. 27.16.3.
Finch, Timothy. Conn. Sufferer. Greenwich. 60.8.5.
Fincham, Edward. Md. Private. ———. 50 acres.
Finchwell, Joseph. Ga. ———. 25 May 1784. 287 1/2 acres.
Findley, Archibald. Va. Private. 20 Jun. 1783. 100 acres.
Findley, Ebenezer. Va. Captain. 25 Mar. 1840. 888 8/9 acres.
Findley, Ebenezer. Va. Captain. 25 Mar. 1840. 444 4/9 acres.
Findley, Ebenezer. Va. Captain. 25 Mar. 1840. 296 8/27 acres.
Findley, Ebenezer. Va. Captain. 25 Mar. 1840. 148 4/27 acres.
Findley, Ebenezer. Va. Captain. 25 Mar. 1840. 296 8/29 acres.
Findley, Ebenezer. Va. Captain. 25 Mar. 1840. 148 4/27 acres.
Findley, Ebenezer. Va. Captain. 16 Jul. 1840. 148 4/27 acres.
Findley, Ebenezer. Va. Captain. 16 Jul. 1840. 74 2/27 acres.
Findley, Ebenezer. Va. Captain. 15 Aug. 1840. 888 8/9 acres.
Findley, Ebenezer. Va. Captain. 15 Aug. 1840. 444 4/9 acres.
Findley, Ebenezer. Va. Captain. 25 Aug. 1840. 888 8/9 acres.
Findley, Ebenezer. Va. Captain. 25 Aug. 1840. 444 4/9 acres.
Findley, Ebenezer. Va. Captain. 14 Oct. 1840. 888 8/9 acres.
Findley, Ebenezer. Va. Captain. 14 Oct. 1840. 444 4/9 acres.
Findley, Ebenezer. Va. Captain. 3 Nov. 1842. 55 1/2 acres.
Findley, Ebenezer. Va. Captain. 3 Nov. 1842. 111 acres.

Findley, Ebenezer. Va. Captain. 3 Nov. 1842. 55 1/2 acres.

Findley, Samuel. Va. Major. 31 Jul. 1783. 6222 acres.

Findley, Samuel. Va. Major. 3 Aug. 1807. 1258 acres.

Fink, Adam. Pa. Private. 26 Sep. 1787. 200 acres.

Fink, Andrew. N. Y. Captain. 9 Jul. 1790. 1800 acres.

Finlay, George. Md. Sergeant. ———. 50 acres.

Finley, Abraham. N.C. Private. 30 Sep. 1785. 640 acres to heirs.

Finley, Andrew. Pa. Private. 3 May 1813. 200 acres.

Finley, Andrew. Pa. ———. 3 May 1813. 200 acres.

Finley, Boaz. N.C. Private. 9 Dec. 1797. 274 acres.

Finley, Charles. Ga. ———. 19 Dec. 1785. 287 1/2 acres.

Finley, Ebenezer. Md. Captain. ———. 200 acres.

Finley, James. Ga. ———. 17 May 1784. ———.

Finley, John. Ga. ———. 17 May 1784. ———.

Finley, John. Pa. Captain. ———. 500 acres.

Finley, John H. Pa. Lieutenant. ———. 200 acres to John Beatty, assignee.

Finley, John H. Pa. Lieutenant. 8 May 1787. 200 acres to John Beatty, assignee.

Finley, Joseph. Pa. Captain. 2 Jun. 1789. 500 acres.

Finley, Matthew. Ga. ———. 17 May 1784. ———.

Finley, Robert. Pa. Private. ———. 200 acres.

Finley, Samuel. Va.-Ind. Private. 108 acres.

Finley, William. Ga. Soldier. 20 Aug. 1785. ———.

Finn, James. Va.-Ind. Private. 108 acres.

Finn, Philip. Va. Private. 19 Jan. 1785. 100 acres.

Finnegan, Patrick. Va. Private. 23 Jun. 1783. 200 acres.

Finnell, Reuben. Va. Private. 18 Nov. 1783. 100 acres.

Finner, Hobert. N.C. Captain. 27 Nov. 1783. 3840 acres.

Finner, William. N.C. Major. 27 Nov. 1783. 2057 acres to Hobert Finner, heir.

Finney, James. S.C. ———. 2 Oct. 1788. 133 acres.

Finney, John. S.Ca. ———. 7 May 1787. 110 acres.

Finney, John. Va. Private. 23 Jun. 1783. 200 acres.

Finney, John. Va. Private. 30 Dec. 1808. 100 acres.

Finney, Michael. S.C. ———. 7 May 1787. 200 acres.

Finney, Samuel. N.C. Private. 26 May 1784. 640 acres.

Finney, Solomon. Conn. Sufferer. Greenwich. 17.6.0.

Finney, Thomas. N.C. Lieutenant. 22 Oct. 1783. 2560 acres.

Finney, Thomas. N.C. ———. 10 Aug. 1785. 274 acres.

Finney, Walter. Pa. Captain. 5 Apr. 1787. 500 acres.

Finnie, William. Va. Deputy Quartermaster General. 10 Nov. 1784. 2000 acres.

Finnie, William. Va. Deputy Quartermaster General. 10 Nov. 1784. 2000 acres.

Finnie, William. Va. Deputy Quartermaster General. 10 Nov. 1784. 666 2/3 acres.

Finny, Reuben. Va. Private. 3 Dec. 1785. 200 acres.

Finson, Peter. S.C. Soldier. 21 Jan. 1785. 200 acres.

Firth, Robert. Md. Sergeant. ———. 50 acres.

Fisby, John. N.C. Private. 3 Mar. 1801. 640 acres to heirs.

Fish, Adam. Me. Lieutenant. 4 Mar. 1840. 600 acres to widow Jane Fish whose sole heir was Harvey Hall. Bristol.

Fish, Nicholas. N. Y. Major. 3 Jul. 1790. 2400 acres.

Fishback, Jacob. Va. Private. 26 Oct. 1791. 200 acres.

Fishback, Jacob. Va. Private. 6 Jan. 1834. 200 acres.

Fishbourn, Benjamin. Pa. Captain. 28 Aug. 1787. 500 acres.

Fisher. John. Va. Ensign. 26 Jan. 1832. 555 5/9 acres.

Fisher, Bartholomew. Va. Private. 15 Jun. 1807. 100 acres.

Fisher, Ebenezer. Me. Brewer. 9 Oct. 1838. 200 acres to widow Sarah Fisher.

Fisher, Elijah. Me. Private. 18 May 1835. 200 acres. Livermore.
Fisher, George. Pa. Private. 6 Oct. 1786. 200 acres.
Fisher, Henry. Md. Private. ———. 50 acres.
Fisher, Henry. Md. Private. ———. 50 acres.
Fisher, Henry. Pa. Private. ———. 200 acres.
Fisher, Isaac. Va. Private. 19 Dec. 1799. 100 acres.
Fisher, Isaac. Va. Seaman. 29 Jul. 1834. 100 acres.
Fisher, Jacob. Me. ———. 3 Aug. 1835. 200 acres. Kennebunk.
Fisher, James. N.C. Private. 19 Dec. 1801. 274 acres.
Fisher, James. Pa. Private. 31 Aug. 1787. 200 acres.
Fisher, Joel. N.C. Private. 30 Sep. 1785. 640 acres to heirs.
Fisher, John. N.C. Private. 9 Dec. 1797. 274 acres.
Fisher, John. Va. Private. 26 May 1783. 100 acres.
Fisher, John. Va. Private. 15 Jun. 1807. 100 acres.
Fisher, John. Va. Ensign. 26 Jan. 1832. 333 1/3 acres.
Fisher, John. Va. Ensign. 26 Jan. 1832. 444 4/9 acres.
Fisher, John. Va. Ensign. 26 Jan. 1832. 266 2/3 acres.
Fisher, John. Va. Ensign. 26 Jan. 1832. 266 2/3 acres.
Fisher, John. Va. Ensign. 26 Jan. 1832. 266 2/3 acres.
Fisher, John. Va. Ensign. 26 Jan. 1832. 266 2/3 acres.
Fisher, John. Va. Ensign. 26 Jan. 1832. 266 2/3 acres.
Fisher, John. Va. Ensign. 17 Sep. 1851. 142 acres.
Fisher, John. Va. Ensign. 17 Sep. 1851. 106 2/3 acres.
Fisher, John. Va. Ensign. 17 Sep. 1851. 85 4/10 acres.
Fisher, John. Va. Ensign. 17 Sep. 1851. 176 2/3 acres.
Fisher, John. Va. Ensign. 17 Sep. 1851. 85 4/10 acres.
Fisher, John. Va. Ensign. 17 Sep. 1851. 85 4/10 acres.
Fisher, John. Va. Ensign. 4 Apr. 1856. 85 4/10 acres.
Fisher, John. Va. Ensign. 4 Apr. 1856. 85 4/10 acres.
Fisher, John A. Pa. Private. 24 Jan. 1787. 200 acres to John P. Fisher, executor.
Fisher, Joseph. Md. Sergeant. ———. 50 acres.
Fisher, Philip. Md. Private. ———. 50 acres.
Fisher, Thomas. Va. Private. 20 Aug. 1783. 200 acres.
Fisher, William. Md. Private. ———. 50 acres.
Fisher, William. Va. Private. 25 May 1785. 200 acres.
Fisk, George. N.C. Private. 14 Dec. 1797. 640 acres to heirs.
Fist, John. N.C. Private. 10 Dec. 1788. 640 acres to heiress Nancy McCallup.
Fist, Samuel. N.C. Private. 20 Sep. 1784. 640 acres.
Fitch, Dan. Conn. Sufferer. Norwalk. 3.0.0.
Fitch, Daniel. Conn. Sufferer. Norwalk. 259.9.1 to his heirs.
Fitch, Ebenezer. Conn. Sufferer. Norwalk. 2.10.0.
Fitch, Elijah. Conn. Sufferer. Norwalk. 10.5.2.
Fitch, Hannah. Conn. Sufferer. Norwalk. 141.2.7 to her heirs.
Fitch, Haynes. Conn. Sufferer. Norwalk. 42.1.3.
Fitch, Haynes. Conn. Sufferer. Norwalk. 47.10.0.
Fitch, Jabez. Conn. Sufferer. Greenwich. 41.3.1.
Fitch, James. Conn. Sufferer. Norwalk. 219.9.5.
Fitch, James, Jr. Conn. Sufferer. Norwalk. 319.16.6 1/4.
Fitch, James, Jr. Conn. Sufferer. Norwalk. 23.12.0.
Fitch, Jonathan. Conn. Sufferer. Norwalk. 195.0.0 to his heirs.
Fitch, Jonathan. Conn. Sufferer. New/East Haven. 170.3.4.
Fitch, Lydia. Conn. Sufferer. Norwalk. 19.19.10.
Fitch, Rebecca. Conn. Sufferer. Norwalk. 63.3.0.
Fitch, Susannah. Conn. Sufferer. Norwalk. 24.0.0.

Fitch, Thomas. Conn. Sufferer. Norwalk. 387.14.5 1/4.
Fitch, Thomas. Conn. Sufferer. Norwalk. 415.3.0 to his heirs.
Fitchjarrell, Joab. N.C. Private. 2 Feb. 1786. 640 acres.
Fites, John. Pa. Private. 3 Oct. 1786. 200 acres.
Fitzgerald, Benjamin. Md. Sergeant. ———. 50 acres.
Fitzgerald, Charles. Ga. ———. 17 May 1784. ———.
Fitzgerald, Charles. Md. Private. ———. 50 acres.
Fitzgerald, James. Va. Private. 12 Jul. 1783. 100 acres.
Fitzgerald, James. Va. Private. 18 Nov. 1783. 200 acres.
Fitzgerald, John. Va. Captain. 29 Jan. 1784. 4666 2/3 acres.
Fitzgerald, John. Va. Major. 2 Apr. 1784. 5333 1/3 acres.
Fitzgerald, Nicholas. Md. Private. ———. 50 acres.
Fitzgerald, Thomas. N. Y. Private. 8 Jul. 1790. 600 acres.
Fitzgerald, Thomas. S.C. Lieutenant. 21 Jan. 1785. 300 acres.
Fitzgerald, William. Md. Private. ———. 50 acres.
Fitzgibbons, David. Pa. Private. 5 Sep. 1787. 200 acres.
Fitzherbert, Theophilus. N.C. Private. 15 Feb. 1797. 274 acres.
Fitzhugh, Peregrine. Md. Captain. ———. 200 acres.
Fitzhugh, Peregrine. Va. Lieutenant. 5 Oct. 1784. 2666 2/3 acres.
Fitzhugh, Peregrine. Va. Captain. 19 Sep. 1785. 1333 1/3 acres.
Fitzhugh, William. Md. Captain. ———. 200 acres.
Fitzhugh, William. Va. Lieutenant. 9 Feb. 1784. 2666 2/3 acres.
Fitzhugh, William Beverley. Va. Private. 20 Jan. 1785. 100 acres.
Fitzjerald, James. Md. Private. ———. 50 acres.
Fitzjerald, Jeremiah. Md. Private. ———. 50 acres.
Fitzjerald, John, Jr. Md. Matross. ———. 50 acres.
Fitzpatarick, Jacob. S.C. ———. 6 Sep. 1790. 200 acres.
Fitzpatrick, Benjamin. Ga. Soldier. 6 Apr. 1785. 230 acres.
Fitzpatrick, James. Va. Private. 29 Nov. 1784. 200 acres.
Fitzpatrick, John. Va. Private. 8 May 1838. 2666 2/3 acres.
Fitzpatrick, John. Va. Ensign. 29 Apr. 1840. 666 2/3 acres.
Fitzpatrick, John. Va. Ensign. 29 Apr. 1840. 666 2/3 acres.
Fitzpatrick, John. Va. Ensign. 29 Apr. 1840. 666 2/3 acres.
Fitzpatrick, John. Va. Ensign. 29 Apr. 1840. 666 2/3 acres.
Fitzpatrick, John. Va. Ensign. 29 Apr. 1840. 666 2/3 acres.
Fitzpatrick, Peter. Pa. Private. ———. 200 acres.
Fitzpatrick, Philip. Md. Private. ———. 50 acres.
Fitzpatrick, Solomon. Va. Sergeant. 20 Feb. 1784. 400 acres.
Fitzsimmons, James. Pa. Private. ———. 200 acres.
Fitzsimmons, Nicholas. Va. Private. 7 Oct. 1783. 100 acres.
Fitzsimmons, Thomas. Va. Private. 22 Apr. 1820. 200 acres.
Fitzsimmons, Thomas. Va. Private. 21 Dec. 1833. 200 acres.
Flack, James. Md. Sergeant. ———. 50 acres.
Flageler, Elizabeth. N. Y. ———. 20 Nov. 1806. 200 acres.
Flagg, Henry Collins. S.C. Surgeon. 15 Oct. 1784. 450 acres.
Flagg, Jonathan. Mass. ———. 22 Jul. 1833. 200 acres.
Flagg, Samuel A. Maine. Drummer. 1 Jun. 1835. 200 acres. Nobleboro.
Flagley, John. N.Y. ———. 13 Sep. 1790. 500 acres to heirs.
Flanagan, Dennis. Md. Matross. ———. 50 acres.
Flanaghan, Dominick. Va.-Ind. Private. 108 acres.
Flandegame, James. Ga. ———. 5 Sep. 1785. 460 acres.
Flanders, John. Mass. Corporal. 15 Nov. 1832. 200 acres.
Flanegan, George. N.C. Private. 7 Jan. 1786. 640 acres to heirs.
Flanigan, Timothy. Pa. Private. 17 Jan. 1787. 200 acres.

Flatford, Robert. Va. Sergeant. 1 Sep. 1783. 400 acres.
Flaugherty, James. Va. Sergeant. 20 Jun. 1783. 200 acres.
Flax, John. Va. Private. 2 May 1783. 200 acres.
Fleary, John. N.C. Private. 5 Dec. 1796. 640 acres.
Fleck, John. S.C. Soldier. 21 Jan. 1785. 200 acres.
Fleece, John. Va. Corporal 27 May 1831. 200 acres.
Fleet, Henry. Va. Midshipman. 28 Nov. 1783. 2666 2/3 acres.
Fleet, John. Va. Lieutenant. 29 Apr. 1783. 2600 2/3 acres.
Fleet, Mary. Conn. Sufferer. Norwalk. 15.10.0.
Fleetwood, Isaac. Va. Seaman. 28 Nov. 1783. 100 acres.
Flemin, Samuel. N.C. Private. 30 Sep. 1785. 640 acres to heirs.
Fleming, Bernard. Va. Private. 24 Apr. 1784. 100 acres.
Fleming, Charles. Va. Lieutenant Colonel. 31 Oct. 1783. 6000 acres.
Fleming, George. N. Y. Captain. 6 & 9 Jul. 1790. 1800 acres.
Fleming, James. Ga. Major. 17 May 1784. ———.
Fleming, John. Va. Sergeant. 12 Sep. 1783. 200 acres.
Fleming, John. Va. Major. 15 Mar. 1784. 5333 1/3 acres.
Fleming, John. Va. Private. 22 Nov. 1784. 200 acres.
Fleming, John. Va. Major. 30 May 1838. 285 1/2 acres.
Fleming, John. Va. Major. 30 May 1838. 856 1/2 acres.
Fleming, Joseph. N.C. Private. 23 Apr. 1784. 640 acres.
Fleming, Ludwell Carter. Va. Private. 10 May 1784. 100 acres.
Fleming, Michael. N. Y. Sergeant. 8 Jul. 1790. 600 acres.
Fleming, Robert. Ga. ———. 17 May 1784. ———.
Fleming, Samuel. Ga. ———. 25 May 1784. 287 1/2 acres.
Fleming, Thomas. Va. Colonel. 15 Mar. 1784. 6666 2/3 acres.
Fleming, William. Ga. Soldier. 17 Feb. 1784. 250 acres.
Fleming, William. Va. Corporal. 22 Aug. 1783. 400 acres.
Fleming, William. Va. Private. 9 Feb. 1813. 100 acres.
Flemister, Lewis. Va. Private. 18 Aug. 1783. 233 1/3 acres.
Flemming, Thomas. Md. Sergeant. ———. 50 acres.
Flemming, Thomas. N.C. Private. 15 Nov. 1793. 640 acres to heirs.
Flemming, William. N.C. Private. 8 Aug. 1821. 640 acres.
Flemmings, Thomas. N.C. Private. 22 Apr. 1785. 640 acres to heirs.
Flennikin, James. Ga. Private. 1784. 287 1/2 acres.
Flesher, Henry. Va. Sergeant. 25 Jan. 1809. 200 acres.
Fletcher, David. N. Y. Matross. 9 Jul. 1790. 500 acres.
Fletcher, James. N. Y. Private. 8 Jul. 1790. 600 acres.
Fletcher, James. Va. Private. 14 Jun. 1820. 200 acres.
Fletcher, Jeremiah. N.C. Private. 30 Sep. 1785. 640 acres to heirs.
Fletcher, John. Me. ———. 30 Apr. 1835. 200 acres to widow Elizabeth Fletcher. Sumner.
Fletcher, John. N. Y. Matross. 9 Jul. 1790. 500 acres.
Fletcher, Joseph. N.C. Private. 7 Jan. 1786. 640 acres to heirs.
Fletcher, Joshua. N.C. Private. 10 Aug. 1785. 640 acres to heirs.
Fletcher, Robert. N.C. ———. 14 Jun. 1785. 640 acres to heirs.
Fletcher, Samuel. N.Y. ———. 13 Sep. 1790. 500 acres to heirs.
Fletcher, Simon. Pa. Quartermaster Sergeant. ———. 250 acres.
Fletcher, Stephen. Va. Private. 20 Aug. 1783. 200 acres.
Fletcher, Thomas. N.C. Sergeant. 26 Apr. 1784. 580 acres.
Fletcher, Thomas. Va. Private. 18 Apr. 1783. 200 acres.
Fletcher, William. N.C. Sergeant. 21 May 1784. 1000 acres.
Flether, John. Va. Private. 23 Jul. 1824. 100 acres.
Flewry, Henry. N.C. Sergeant. 14 Dec. 1787. 1000 acres.

Flick, Martin. N. Y. Private. 8 Jul. 1790. 500 acres.
Flin, Thomas. Va. Private. 31 Jan. 1784. 100 acres.
Fling, Edward. Va. Private. 11 Jun. 1788. 200 acres.
Fling, James. Va. Private. 23 Apr. 1783. 100 acres.
Fling, Michael. N.C. Private. 9 Sep. 1785. 640 acres to heirs.
Flinn, Andrew. N.Y. ———. 13 Sep. 1790. 500 acres to heirs.
Flinn, John. N.C. Private. 7 Dec. 1797. 640 acres to heirs.
Flinn, Nicholas. N.C. Private. 14 Dec. 1796. 640 acres to heirs.
Flinn, Osburn. Va. Sergeant. 5 Feb. 1785. 400 acres.
Flinn, Robert. N.C. Private. 14 Dec. 1796. 640 acres.
Flinn, Thomas. N.C. Private. 29 Apr. 1784. 640 acres to Elizabeth Flinn & Laughlin Flinn, coheirs.
Flinn, William. N.C. Private. 21 Aug. 1820. 640 acres.
Flinon, Frederick. Md. Private. ———. 50 acres.
Flint, Benjamin. Mass. Private. 11 Mar. 1830. 200 acres to heirs.
Flint, John. Va. Carpenter. 9 Dec. 1783. 100 acres.
Flint, Tapley. Ga. ———. 14 Jul. 1784. 300 acres.
Flinthorn, John. N.C. Private. 9 Dec. 1797. 640 acres to heirs.
Flinthorn, Robert. N.C. Private. 9 Dec. 1797. 640 acres to heirs.
Flippen, Robert. Va. Private. 4 Aug. 1783. 100 acres.
Flippo, Joseph. Va. Private. 24 Dec. 1798. 100 acres.
Flitcher, Joseph. Pa. Private. 28 Nov. 1786. 200 acres.
Flogget, William. Va.-Ind. Private. 108 acres. [Frogget].
Flood, Alexander. Mass. Matross. 12 Dec. 1832. 200 acres to son Alexander Flood.
Flood, Alexander. N.C. Private. 29 Apr. 1784. 304 acres.
Flood, Benjamin. N.C. Private. 6 Jan. 1784. 640 acres.
Flood, Edward. N.C. Private. 9 Dec. 1797. 640 acres to heirs.
Flood, Elisha. N.C. ———. 10 Aug. 1785. 640 acres to heirs.
Flood, Frederick. N.C. Private. 26 May 1784. 640 acres.
Flood, Henry. Me. ———. 18 Jul. 1835. 200 acres to widow Jemima Flood.
Flood, James. Md. ———. ———. 50 acres.
Flood, Joseph. N.C. Private. 28 Sep. 1785. 640 acres.
Flood, Timothy. Pa. Private. ———. 200 acres.
Flood, William. N.C. Private. 8 Dec. 1796. 274 acres.
Flood, Zacheriah. N.C. Private. 28 Sep. 1785. 640 acres.
Flora, Jacob. Md. Private. ———. 50 acres.
Florey, William. Va. Private. 16 Oct. 1806. 100 acres.
Flourney, Jacob. Va. Private. 31 May 1783. 100 acres.
Flourney, Samuel. Va. Sergeant. 15 Aug. 1783. 200 acres.
Flournoy, Robert. Ga. ———. 17 May 1784. 287 1/2 acres.
Flower, Benjamin. Pa. Colonel. 20 Aug. 1787. 500 acres to Martha Flower, widow.
Flower, Philip. Pa. ———. 6 Apr. 1796. 200 acres to Margaret Flower, widow.
Flower, Philip. Pa. Private. ———. 200 acres to widow Mary Flower.
Flower, Thomas. Pa. ———. 9 Oct. 1786. 200 acres.
Flowers, Benjamin. Pa. Colonel. 28 Aug. 1787. 500 acres to heirs.
Flowers, Charles. N.C. Private. 12 Sep. 1785. 640 acres to heirs.
Flowers, Edmund. Md. ———. ———. 50 acres.
Flowers, Edward. Md. Private. ———. 50 acres.
Flowers, John. Va. Sergeant. 21 Feb. 1784. 200 acres.
Flowers, Robert. Ga. ———. 5 Sep. 1785. ———.
Flowers, William. Ga. Minute Man. 17 May 1784. ———.
Flowers, William. N.C. Private. 17 Dec. 1796. 274 acres.
Flowron, Lazarus. N.C. Private. 21 May 1784. 274 acres.

Flowron, Richard. N.C. Private. 21 May 1784. 274 acres.
Floyd, Augustine. N.C. Private. 30 Sep. 1785. 640 acres to heirs.
Floyd, Charles. N.C. Private. 12 Mar. 1785. 640 acres to heirs.
Floyd, Francis. N.C. ———. 10 Aug. 1785. 640 acres to heirs.
Floyd, Frederick. Pa. Private. 14 Feb. 1787. 200 acres.
Floyd, Henry. Va.-Ind. Lieutenant. 2156 acres.
Floyd, Isham. Va.-Ind. Private. 108 acres.
Floyd, John. N.C. Private. 23 Apr. 1785. 640 acres to heirs.
Floyd, Perman. Ga. Minute Man. ———. 287 1/2 acres.
Floyd, Thomas. Va. Private. 19 Jun. 1783. 100 acres.
Floyd, William. Va. Private. 4 Dec. 1783. 200 acres.
Fluallen, Jonas. N.C. Private. 19 Jan. 1786. 640 acres.
Fluart, Massey. Md. ———. ———. 50 acres.
Fluhart, Stephen. Md. Sergeant. ———. 50 acres.
Fluker, John. Ga. ———. 17 May 1784. ———.
Fluker, Owen. Ga. ———. 17 May 1784. ———.
Fluker, William. Ga. ———. 17 May 1784. ———.
Flury, William. N.C. Sergeant. 23 Jun. 1820. 640 acres to heirs.
Flusher, James, Jr. N.C. Private. 9 Sep. 1785. 640 acres to heirs.
Flusher, James, Sr. N.C. Private. 9 Sep. 1785. 640 acres to heirs.
Fly, Charles. N.C. Private. 17 Feb. 1824. 640 acres.
Fly, Jeremiah. Ga. ———. 17 May 1784. ———.
Flyharty, Stephen. N.Y. ———. 13 Sep. 1790. 500 acres to heirs.
Flyng, John. Ga. Soldier. 17 May 1784. ———.
Flynn, James. Ga. Refugee. 26 May 1784. 287 1/2 acres.
Flynn, John. Ga. Refugee. 26 May 1784. 287 1/2 acres.
Flynt, John. Va. Carpenter. 13 Nov. 1832. 2566 2/3 acres.
Fogelsong, Henry. Pa. ———. 19 Sep. 1787. 200 acres.
Fogetree, James. N.C. Private. 24 Oct. 1783. 274 acres.
Fogett, William. Va. Private. 30 Apr. 1783. 200 acres.
Folar, John. N.C. Private. 8 Dec. 1795. 640 acres to heirs.
Folds, George, Sr. Ga. ———. 26 May 1784. 287 1/2 acres.
Foley, Enoch. Va. Private. 7 Dec. 1785. 100 acres.
Folger, Robert. Md. Private. ———. 50 acres.
Foliard, John. N. Y. Private. 8 Jul. 1790. 600 acres.
Folk, Christopher. N.C. Private. 29 Sep. 1784. 640 acres to heirs.
Folks, James. N.C. Private. 21 Aug. 1820. 640 acres.
Folkson, Charles. Ga. Soldier. 9 Feb. 1782. ———.
Folling, John. Md. Private. ———. 50 acres.
Folliott, Benjamin. Md. Private. ———. 50 acres.
Folliott, Joseph. Md. Private. ———. 50 acres.
Folwell, William. Pa. ———. 9 Mar. 1809. 200 acres.
Fonday, John, Jr. N. Y. Ensign. 9 Jul. 1790. 1150 acres.
Fondy, Douw. N. Y. Ensign. 9 Jul. 1790. 1150 acres.
Fones, John. N.C. Private. 30 Sep. 1785. 640 acres to heirs.
Fones, William. N.C. Private. 23 Apr. 1784. 640 acres to Thomas Fones, heir.
Font, Matthew. Pa. Private. ———. 200 acres.
Fontaine, James. Ga. ———. 17 May 1784. ———.
Fontaine, William. Va. Lieutenant Colonel. 20 Nov. 1835. 1200 acres.
Fontaine, William. Va. Lieutenant Colonel. 20 Nov. 1835. 1300 acres.
Fontaine, William. Va. Lieutenant Colonel. 20 Nov. 1835. 1200 acres.
Fontaine, William. Va. Lieutenant Colonel. 9 Dec. 1796. 1200 acres.
Fontaine, William. Va. Lieutenant Colonel. 24 Feb. 1834. 6000 acres.
Fontaine, William. Va. Lieutenant Colonel. 23 Jun. 1855. 2116 acres.

Fontaine, William. Va. Lieutenant Colonel. 11 Nov. 1835. 1200 acres.

Fonvielle, Isaac. N.C. Corporal. 4 Feb. 1820. 1000 acres to heir David Fonvielle.

Fooks, John. N.C. Private. 13 Jan. 1823. 228 acres.

Foor, C. John. N. Y. Private. 8 Jul. 1790. 600 acres.

Foot, Isaac. N. Y. Corporal. 9 Jul. 1790. 600 acres.

Forbes, James. N. Y. Sergeant. 9 Jul. 1790. 600 acres.

Forbes, Jehiel. Conn. Sufferer. New/East Haven. 173.13.1.

Forbes, Levi. Conn. Sufferer. New/East Haven. 5.17.6.

Forbis, Joshua. N.C. Sergeant. 26 Apr. 1784. 428 acres.

Forbis, Patrick. S.C. ———. 5 Mar. 1787. 200 acres.

Forbis, William. S.C. ———. 5 Mar. 1787. 200 acres.

Forbush, Alexander. N. Y. Private. 3 Jul. 1790. 600 acres.

Forbush, Robert. N.C. Private. 2 Dec. 1801. 640 acres to heirs.

Force, David. N. Y. Private. 8 Jul. 1790. 600 acres.

Force, Timothy. N. Y. Sergeant. 6 Jul. 1790. 600 acres.

Ford, Alexander. Pa. Dragoon. 30 Jul. 1789. 200 acres.

Ford, Benjamin. Ga. Citizen. 19 Dec. 1785. 287 1/2 acres.

Ford, Benjamin. Md. Lieutenant Colonel. ———. 200 acres.

Ford, Chilion. N. Y. Lieutenant. 9 Jul. 1790. 1200 acres.

Ford, Elias. N.C. ———. 6 Dec. 1800. 428 acres.

Ford, Elijah. Va. Private. 9 Dec. 1796. 100 acres.

Ford, Ezra. Conn. Sufferer. New/East Haven. 16.17.0.

Ford, George. Md. Private. ———. 50 acres.

Ford, Hezekiah. Md. Lieutenant. ———. 200 acres.

Ford, Hezekiah. N.C. Chaplain. 11 Oct. 1821. 7200 acres to heirs.

Ford, James. Ga. Citizen. 19 Dec. 1785. 287 1/2 acres.

Ford, John. N.C. Lieutenant. 10 Nov. 1783. 2560 acres.

Ford, John, Jr. Ga. Refugee. 28 Jul. 1784. 287 1/2 acres.

Ford, Joshua. Ga. ———. 17 May 1784. ———.

Ford, Miles. Me. Private. 15 May 1835. 200 acres to widow Susannah Ford. Clinton.

Ford, Owen. Ga. ———. 17 May 1784. 250 acres.

Ford, Robert. Md. Sergeant. ———. 50 acres.

Ford, Simon. N.C. Private. 22 Apr. 1785. 228 acres.

Ford, Thomas. Ga. ———. 15 Mar. 1784. 250 acres.

Ford, William. Ga. Refugee. 17 May 1784. ———.

Ford, William. N.C. Private. 4 Aug. 1821. 640 acres.

Fordene, Francis. N.C. Sergeant. 5 May 1784. 428 acres.

Forehand, Darby. Va. Private. 21 Mar. 1784. 100 acres.

Forehand, Harris. N.C. Private. 6 Dec. 1797. 228 acres.

Forehand, John. Va. Private. 3 May 1784. 100 acres.

Foreman, Caleb. N.C. Lieutenant. 17 Feb. 1824. 640 acres.

Foreman, William. Md. Sergeant. ———. 50 acres.

Forest, Andrew. N.C. Private. 9 Dec. 1797. 640 acres.

Forgue, Francis. Conn. Sufferer. Fairfield. 151.16.0.

Fornes, John. N.C. Private. 21 Apr. 1784. 640 acres to Thomas Fornes, heir.

Fornes, Jonathan. N.C. Private. 21 Apr. 1784. 640 acres to Thomas Fornes, heir.

Forrest, George. Va. Private. 2 May 1783. 100 acres.

Forrest, Matthew. N.C. Private. 30 Sep. 1785. 640 acres to heirs.

Forrest, Thomas. Pa. Private. 15 Jan. 1789. 200 acres to Stephen Loudon, assignee.

Forrest, Uriah. Md. Lieutenant Colonel. ———. 200 acres.

Forrest, William. Va. Seaman. 11 Apr. 1838. 100 acres.

Forrest, Zachariah. Va. Sergeant. 7 Feb. 1784. 200 acres.

Forrester, John. Va. Private. 18 Nov. 1818. 100 acres.
Forrister, Thomas. N.C. Private. 28 Aug. 1820. 640 acres.
Forrister, William. N.C. Private. 20 Apr. 1784. 1000 acres to heirs.
Forster, Arthur. Ga. ———. 17 May 1784. ———.
Forster, George. Pa. Private. 9 Mar. 1795. 200 acres to John Nicholson in right of the widow.
Forster, James. Md. Private. ———. 50 acres.
Forster, Mark. Md. Private. ———. 50 acres.
Forster, Moses. Md. Private. ———. 50 acres.
Forster, William. Ga. ———. 17 May 1784. ———.
Forsyth, Abraham. Va. Private. 10 Oct. 1821. 200 acres.
Forsyth, Robert. Va. Captain. 11 Aug. 1795. 4000 acres.
Forsyth, Robert. Va. Major. 7 Dec. 1831. 1333 1/3 acres.
Forsyth, Robert. Va. Major. 6 Dec. 1860. 4000 acres.
Fort, Arthur. Ga. ———. 17 May 1784. ———.
Fortune, Garnder. Va. Private. 2 Apr. 1783. 100 acres.
Fortune, Jacob. Ga. ———. 26 May 1784. 287 1/2 acres.
Fortune, Nathan. Va. Private. 22 Aug. 1783. 200 acres.
Fosbrook, John. Pa. ———. ———. 200 acres to David Thomas, assignee.
Fosdale, Stafford. Md. Private. ———. 50 acres.
Fosdick, Ann & sons. Conn. Sufferer. New London. 1,045.10.11.
Foss, Zachariah. Me. ———. 5 Jun. 1835. 200 acres. Scarborough.
Fosset, John. Md. Private. ———. 50 acres.
Fossett, Edward. N.C. Private. 1 Aug. 1821. 640 acres.
Fossett, Robert. N.C. Private. 2 Jan. 1784. 274 acres.
Fossett, Robert. Pa. Private. 13 Nov. 1787. 200 acres.
Fossil, Christopher. Va. Private. 22 Dec. 1785. 200 acres.
Foster, Burwell. N.C. Private. 30 Sep. 1785. 640 acres to heirs.
Foster, Cosby. Va. Private. 17 Mar. 1784. 200 acres.
Foster, Edward. Va. Corporal. 19 Feb. 1785. 200 acres.
Foster, Francis. Ga. Refugee. 4 Aug. 1784. ———.
Foster, George. Pa. Private. 9 Mar. 1795. 200 acres to widow.
Foster, George. Va. Private. 15 Oct. 1783. 200 acres.
Foster, James. Va. Captain. 25 Feb. 1784. 4000 acres.
Foster, John. Ga. ———. 17 May 1784. ———.
Foster, John. N. Y. Matross. 8 Jul. 1790. 600 acres.
Foster, John. Va. Sergeant. 15 Jul. 1783. 200 acres.
Foster, John. Va. Private. 20 Nov. 1783. 100 acres.
Foster, John. Va. Subaltern. 24 Feb. 1784. 2666 2/3 acres.
Foster, John. Va. Private. 15 Apr. 1784. 100 acres.
Foster, Jonah. Conn. Sufferer. Ridgefield. 10.3.10.
Foster, Joshua. Va. Private. 17 Feb. 1809. 100 acres.
Foster, Nathan. Conn. Sufferer. Ridgefield. 0.10.8.
Foster, Peter. Va. Sergeant. 29 Jul. 1783. 200 acres.
Foster, Peter. Va. Sailor. 15 Dec. 1783. 100 acres.
Foster, Peter. Va. Lieutenant. 15 May 1832. 2666 2/3 acres.
Foster, Peter. Va. Carpenter's Mate. 24 Jul. 1835. 2666 2/3 acres.
Foster, Peter. Va. Lieutenant. 7 Apr. 1838. 372 1/3 acres.
Foster, Peter. Va. Carpenter's Mate. 22 Mar. 1837. 2666 2/3 acres.
Foster, Pinckney. Ga. Citizen. 19 Dec. 1785. 287 1/2 acres.
Foster, Richard. Va. Lieutenant. 8 Jan. 1810. 2666 2/3 acres.
Foster, Richard. Va. Lieutenant. 22 May 1783. 2666 2/3 acres.
Foster, Rigby. Md. Private. ———. 50 acres.
Foster, Simpson. Va. Ensign. 15 Nov. 1806. 2666 2/3 acres.

Foster, Thomas. N.C. Private. 3 Feb. 1795. 640 acres to heirs.
Foster, Thomas. Via. Private. 20 Jan. 1786. 100 acres.
Foster, William. Ga. Refugee. 15 Mar. 1784. 250 acres.
Foster, William. Va.-Ind. Private. 108 acres.
Foster, William. N.C. Private. 9 Feb. 1796. 640 acres to heirs.
Foster, William. N.C. Private. 24 Oct. 1820. 640 acres.
Foster, William. Va. Private. 14 Oct. 1783. 200 acres.
Foster, William. Va. Private. 29 Nov. 1783. 200 acres.
Foster, William. Va. Private. 13 Oct. 1796. 100 acres.
Fothergill, Hugh. N. Y. Private. 8 Jul. 1790. 500 acres.
Fountain, Peter. Md. Private. ———. 50 acres.
Fountain, William. Md. ———. ———. 50 acres.
Foushee, William. Va. Surgeon. 28 Mar. 1834. 6000 acres.
Foust, Michael. Pa. Private. ———. 200 acres.
Fowke, John. Va. Lieutenant. 5 Mar. 1804. 2666 2/3 acres.
Fowler, Abraham. N.C. Private. 15 Feb. 1797. 640 acres.
Fowler, Anderson. Va. Private. 3 Feb. 1784. 100 acres.
Fowler, Beal. Pa. Sergeant. 7 Sep. 1787. 250 acres.
Fowler, Daniel. N.C. Private. 2 Jan. 1801. 274 acres.
Fowler, Francis. N.C. Private. 30 Sep. 1785. 640 acres to heirs.
Fowler, John. Pa. Private. 29 Aug. 1787. 200 acres to George Bycroft, administrator.
Fowler, John. Va. Private. 13 Sep. 1785. 100 acres.
Fowler, John. Va. Private. 22 Jan. 1834. 100 acres.
Fowler, Jonathan. Md. Private. ———. 50 acres.
Fowler, Joseph. Md. Private. ———. 50 acres.
Fowler, Joseph. Va. Private. 23 Jun. 1783. 200 acres.
Fowler, Joseph. Va. Private. 2 Mar. 1786. 100 acres.
Fowler, Joshua. N.C. Private. 30 Sep. 1785. 640 acres.
Fowler, Matthew. Me. Private. 7 May 1835. 200 acres. Unity.
Fowler, Nathan. Ga. ———. 25 May 1784. 287 1/2 acres.
Fowler, Patrick. Pa. Private. 12 Sep. 1789. 200 acres.
Fowler, Robert Martin. Va. Private. 10 Nov. 1784. 100 acres.
Fowler, Theodosius. N. Y. Captain. 9 Jul. 1790. 1800 acres.
Fowler, William. N.C. Private. 28 Aug. 1820. 640 acres.
Fowler, William. Va. Captain. 24 Feb. 1783. 4000 acres.
Fowles, James. N.Y. ———. 13 Sep. 1790. 500 acres to heirs.
Fox, Adam. Va. Private. 24 Jul. 1835. 100 acres.
Fox, Francis. N.C. Private. 30 Mar. 1784. 274 acres.
Fox, Joel. Mass. Private. 15 Jan. 1834. 200 acres.
Fox, John. Va. Private. 6 May 1786. 100 acres.
Fox, Lewis. Va. Private. 25 Mar. 1783. 100 acres.
Fox, Nathaniel. Va. Captain. 31 May 1783. 4000 acres.
Fox, Nathaniel. Va. Captain. 29 Oct. 1783. 666 1/3 acres.
Fox, Nathaniel. Va. Captain. 27 Jan. 1808. 500 acres.
Fox, Nathaniel. Va. Lieutenant. 9 Jan. 1810. 2666 2/3 acres.
Fox, Thomas. Va. Captain. 19 May 1783. 4000 acres.
Fox, Thomas. Va. Captain. 1 Aug. 1799. 666 2/3 acres.
Fox, Thomas. Va. Captain. 11 Sep. 1807. 222 acres.
Fox, William. N.C. Private. 30 Sep. 1785. 640 acres.
Fox, William. N.C. Sergeant. 8 Aug. 1821. 1000 acres.
Fox, William. Pa. Private. 16 Mar. 1787. 200 acres.
Foxall, David. Md. Private. ———. 50 acres.
Foxall, Thomas. Md. Private. ———. 50 acres.
Foy, Edmond. N.Y. Sergeant. 13 Sep. 1790. 500 acres to heirs.

Foy, Mathias. Pa. Private. 6 Nov. 1786. 200 acres to John Connell.
Foy, Patrick. N.C. Corporal. 2 Aug. 1784. 1000 acres.
Fradford, Thomas. Va. Private. 11 Nov. 1814. 100 acres.
Frails, Charles. Va. Private. 1 Aug. 1789. 100 acres.
France, Abraham. Ga. Refugee. 25 May 1784. 575 acres.
France, Conradt. N. Y. Private. 8 Jul. 1790. 600 acres.
France, John. N.Y. ———. 13 Sep. 1790. 500 acres to heirs.
France, Lewis. Va. Private. 20 Jun. 1783. 100 acres.
France, Peter. N.Y. ———. 13 Sep. 1790. 500 acres to heirs.
France, Peter. Va. Private. 20 Jun. 1783. 100 acres.
Francis, Alexander. Md. Private. ———. 50 acres.
Francis, Charles. Ga. Soldier. 5 Dec. 1785. ———.
Francis, Christopher. Va. Private. 18 Oct. 1784. 100 acres.
Francis, Frederick. Ga. Refugee. 17 May 1784. ———.
Francis, George. Pa. Sergeant. ———. 250 acres.
Francis, Richard. Pa. Private. 14 Feb. 1787. 200 acres.
Francis, William. Pa. Private. 23 Oct. 1786. 200 acres.
Francisco, Peter. Va. Private. 25 Dec. 1795. 100 acres.
Francisco, Thomas. N.C. Private. 21 Aug. 1820. 640 acres.
Francks, John. N.C. Private. 23 Apr. 1784. 640 acres.
Franeway, John. Md. Private. ———. 50 acres.
Frank, Jacob. N.Y. ———. 13 Sep. 1790. 500 acres to heirs.
Frank, Peter. Pa. Private. 5 Dec. 1805. 200 acres to heirs.
Frank, Thomas. Me. ———. 15 Oct. 1835. 200 acres to widow Hannah Frank. Gray.
Franklin, Ambrose. N.C. Private. 18 Dec. 1802. 228 acres to heirs.
Franklin, Ambrose. N.C. ———. 9 Dec. 1805. 412 acres to heirs.
Franklin, Charles. N.C. Private. 18 Dec. 1802. 228 acres to heirs.
Franklin, Charles. N.C. ———. 9 Dec. 1805. 412 acres to heirs.
Franklin, Esham. S.C. ———. 2 Jul. 1792. 128 acres.
Franklin, George. Ga. ———. 17 May 1784. ———.
Franklin, Henry. Va. Private. 22 May 1784. 100 acres.
Franklin, Isham. S.C. ———. 3 Jun. 1793. 53 1/2 acres.
Franklin, James. Va. Private. 27 Jan. 1783. 100 acres.
Franklin, James. Va. Captain. 13 Dec. 1832. 3750 acres.
Franklin, James. Va. ———. 14 Dec. 1832. 250 acres.
Franklin, John. Md. Private. ———. 50 acres.
Franklin, John. Va. Private. 9 Jun. 1785. 200 acres.
Franklin, Joseph. Va. Corporal. 3 Dec. 1783. 200 acres.
Franklin, Joshua. Conn. Sufferer. Greenwich. 26.16.1.
Franklin, William. Ga. ———. 17 May 1784. ———.
Franklin, William R. Md. Private. ———. 50 acres.
Franklin, William, Jr. Ga. ———. 23 Sep. 1784. ———.
Franks, Andrew. N.C. Private. 6 Dec. 1796. 640 acres to heirs.
Franks, David. N. Y. Major. ———. 1000 acres.
Franks, David L. Pa. Major. 2 Jun. 1787. 300 acres.
Franks, David S. Pa. Major. ———. 300 acres.
Franks, Jacob. Ga. ———. 17 May 1784. ———.
Franks, John. N. Y. Paymaster with rank of Captain. 9 Jul. 1790. 1500 acres.
Franks, Joseph. Ga. ———. 17 May 1784. ———.
Franks, Michael. N. Y. Private. 8 Jul. 1790. 600 acres.
Franquer, John. Pa. Private. ———. 200 acres.
Franry, James. Pa. Dragoon. 25 Jul. 1787. 200 acres.
Fraser, Alexander. S.C. ———. 7 May 1792. 65 acres.

Fraser, Alexander. S.C. ———. 4 Feb. 1788. 135 acres.
Fraser, John. Ga. Lieutenant. 21 Apr. 1784. 400 acres to heirs.
Fraser, Malachi. Ga. ———. 1784. 287 1/2 acres.
Fraser, Roderick. Va. Sergeant. 26 Feb. 1784. 200 acres.
Fraser, Simon. Ga. Refugee. 21 Apr 1784. 250 acres.
Frasur, Jeremiah. N.C. Private. 30 Sep. 1785. 640 acres to heirs.
Frawney, John. Md. Private. ———. 50 acres.
Fraysher, Hugh. N.C. Sergeant. 30 Sep. 1785. 1000 acres to heirs.
Frazer, Alexander. Ga. ———. 17 May 1784. ———.
Frazer, Alexander. Va. Sergeant. 23 Jun. 1783. 400 acres.
Frazer, Andrew. Ga. Refugee. 1 Oct. 1784. 287 1/2 acres.
Frazer, Benjamin. Pa. Private. ———. 200 acres.
Frazer, Dyar. Ga. ———. 17 May 1784. ———.
Frazer, Falvey. Va. Lieutenant. 29 Mar. 1784. 2666 2/3 acres.
Frazer, Jeremiah. N.Y. ———. 18 Mar. 1791. 500 acres to heirs.
Frazer, William. Va. Captain Lieutenant. 16 Dec. 1795. 4000 acres.
Frazier, James. Va. Sergeant. 10 Jun. 1784. 400 acres.
Frazier, John. N.C. Private. 30 Mar. 1785. 640 acres.
Frazier, Samuel. Md. ———. ———. 50 acres.
Frazier, Simon. N. Y. ———. ———. 500 acres.
Frazier, Simon. N.C. Private. 15 Jul. 1785. 274 acres.
Frederick, John. N. Y. Private. 8 Jul. 1790. 600 acres.
Frederick, Thomas. Ga. ———. 17 May 1784. ———.
Freeborn, George. Pa. Matross. 22 Jan. 1787. 200 acres.
Freeland, Isaac. Va. Private. 9 Nov. 1784. 100 acres.
Freeland, Jacob. N.C. Private. 30 Sep. 1785. 640 acres to heirs.
Freeman, Abel. N.C. Private. 14 Dec. 1796. 640 acres.
Freeman, Anderson. Va. Sergeant Major. 22 Mar. 1784. 200 acres.
Freeman, Andrew. Mass. Private. 7 Oct. 1833. 200 acres.
Freeman, Coldrop. Va. Private. 22 Dec. 1785. 200 acres.
Freeman, Constant. N. Y. Captain. ———. 1000 acres.
Freeman, Daniel. N.C. Private. 6 Aug. 1800. 228 acres.
Freeman, David. N.C. Private. 11 Jul. 1785. 640 acres to heirs.
Freeman, Francis. Md. Private. ———. 50 acres.
Freeman, Henry. S.C. ———. 2 Oct. 1786. 200 acres to Lucy Freeman.
Freeman, Hezekiah. Va. Private. 13 Feb. 1784. 100 acres.
Freeman, Holman. Ga. Adjutant. 15 Mar. 1784. 250 acres.
Freeman, Isaac. N.C. Private. 9 Dec. 1797. 640 acres to heirs.
Freeman, James. Ga. Refugee. 15 Mar. 1784. 250 acres.
Freeman, Jeremiah. Pa. Captain. 4 Oct. 1786. 500 acres to John Young, assignee.
Freeman, John. Ga. Refugee. 15 Mar. 1784. 250 acres.
Freeman, John. Ga. Quartermaster. 15 Mar. 1784. 250 acres.
Freeman, John. Va. Private. 22 Jan. 1788. 200 acres.
Freeman, John. Va. Private. 12 Mar. 1840. 66 2/3 acres.
Freeman, John. Va. Private. 12 Mar. 1840. 33 1/3 acres.
Freeman, Nathan. N.C. Private. 21 Oct. 1783. 640 acres to Daniel Freeman, heir.
Freeman, Obadiah. N. Y. Private. 7 Jul. 1790. 600 acres.
Freeman, Richard. Md. Private. ———. 50 acres.
Freeman, Richard. N.C. Private. 29 Sep. 1784. 640 acres to heir.
Freeman, Samuel. N.C. Private. 4 Mar. 1800. 640 acres.
Freeman, Stephen. Va. Private. 12 Mar. 1840. 100 acres.
Freeman, William. Ga. Refugee. 15 Mar. 1784. 250 acres.
Freeman, William. Va.-Ind. Private. 108 acres.

Freeman, William. N.C. Private. 30 Sep. 1785. 640 acres to heirs.
Freeman, William. Pa. Private. 17 Apr. 1787. 200 acres.
Freeman, William. Va. Private. 19 Dec. 1812. 100 acres.
Freemoutt, Robert. Md. ———. ———. 50 acres.
Freenbush, Matthew. N. Y. Private. 8 Jul. 1790. 600 acres.
Freethy, Joseph. Me. ———. 5 Sep. 1835. 200 acres. Sedgwick.
Freeze, John. Me. ———. 17 Nov. 1835. 200 acres to widow Sarah Card. Bowdoin.
Freligh, Joseph. N. Y. Lieutenant. 7 Jul. 1790. 1000 acres.
French, Abner. N. Y. Captain. 9 Jul. 1790. 1800 acres.
French, Asa. Mass. Private. 18 Oct. 1833. 200 acres.
French, Christian. Pa. ———. ———. 250 acres.
French, Jacob. Me. Private. 30 May 1839. 200 acres to widow Mary French. Jay.
French, James. Ga. Private. 10 Dec. 1784. 250 acres.
French, Jeremiah. Md. Private. ———. 50 acres.
French, Peter. Md. Corporal. ———. 50 acres.
French, Richard. Va. Private. 21 Jan. 1784. 100 acres.
French, Thomas. Va. Private. 19 Jun. 1783. 200 acres.
French, William. Md. ———. ———. 50 acres.
Fresh, Stephen. Md. Private. ———. 50 acres.
Freshwater, Benjamin. Md. ———. ———. 50 acres.
Fretwell, Leonard. Ga. ———. 17 May 1784. ———.
Fretwell, Richard. Ga. ———. 17 May 1784. ———.
Fretwell, Thomas. Ga. ———. 17 May 1784. ———.
Friday, John. Ga. Soldier. 4 Oct. 1785. ———.
Friel, John. Ga. Minute Man. 28 Feb. 1784. 250 acres.
Friel, Lewis. Ga. ———. 26 May 1784. 287 1/2 acres.
Friend, Nathaniel. Mass. Private. 19 Mar. 1834. 200 acres.
Frierson, John. S.C. ———. 1 Aug. 1785. 200 acres.
Frigonier, Conrad. Ga. Private. 17 May 1784. ———.
Frisbie, Abel. Conn. Sufferer. New/East Haven. 25.15.0.
Friskett, George. Va. Private. 8 Aug. 1786. 200 acres.
Frison, Peter. N. Y. ———. ———. 500 acres.
Fritts, George. Va. Drummer. 14 Jun. 1786. 100 acres.
Frizzle, Daniel. N.C. Private. 7 Dec. 1797. 228 acres.
Fromaget, Roman. Va. Private. 27 Jun. 1783. 200 acres.
Froman, Elijah. Va. Private. 31 Dec. 1782. 100 acres.
Froman, Temple. Va. Private. 15 Jul. 1818. 100 acres.
Frond, James. Va. Private. 21 Sep. 1787. 100 acres.
Frost, Daniel. N.C. Private. 9 Dec. 1797. 640 acres.
Frost, Elliot. Me. ———. 18 May 1835. 200 acres. Eliot.
Frost, Jacob. S.C. ———. 5 May 1788. 200 acres.
Frost, Nathaniel. Me. ———. 25 Apr. 1835. 200 acres to widow Sarah Frost. Eliot.
Frost, Samuel. Me. ———. 4 May 1835. 200 acres to widow Patience Billington. Wayne.
Frost, Stephen. Va.-Ind. Private. 108 acres.
Frost, Stephen. Me. ———. 10 Dec. 1838. 200 acres to widow Sarah Frost. Berwick.
Frost, William. N.C. Private. 17 Dec. 1785. 640 acres.
Frumley, Thomas. Md. Private. ———. 50 acres.
Fruz, Martin. Pa. Private. ———. 200 acres.
Fry, Joseph. Va. Private. 3 Mar. 1784. 100 acres.
Fryar, Josiah. N.C. Private. 13 Sep. 1784. 640 acres to William Fryar, heir.
Fryar, William. N.C. Private. 13 Sep. 1784. 228 acres.
Fryday, Conradt. N. Y. Private. 8 Jul. 1790. 600 acres.

Frye, Nathaniel. Me. Lieutenant. 26 Feb. 1839. 600 acres to widow Dolly Frye. Fryeburg.

Frye, Philip. S.C. ———. 6 Feb. 1791. 200 acres.

Fryer, Charles. N. Y. Matross. 9 Jul. 1790. 600 acres.

Fryer, Humphrey. Ga. ———. 17 May 1784. ———.

Fryer, Richard. Va. Private. 22 Nov. 1784. 100 acres.

Frymier, John. N.Y. Drummer. 13 Sep. 1790. 500 acres to heirs.

Fuglar, William. Va. Private. 7 Nov. 1783. 200 acres.

Fulford, John. Md. Private. ———. 50 acres.

Fulham, Charles. Md. Corporal. ———. 50 acres.

Fulham, John. Md. Private. ———. 50 acres.

Fulkerson, William. Va. Private. 25 Oct. 1820. 100 acres.

Fulks, Garret. N.C. Private. 30 Sep. 1785. 640 acres to heirs.

Fuller, Andrew. Me. ———. 6 Jun. 1835. 200 acres to widow Hannah Fuller.

Fuller, Isaac. Ga. Refugee. 17 Feb. 1784. 250 acres.

Fuller, John. Ga. ———. 30 Jul. 1784. 287 1/2 acres.

Fuller, John. N.C. Private. 26 May 1784. 640 acres.

Fuller, John. N.C. Private. 7 Jan. 1786. 640 acres to heirs.

Fuller, John, Sr. Ga. ———. 17 May 1784. ———.

Fuller, Joseph. Va. Private. 21 Mar. 1807. 200 acres.

Fuller, Joshua. Ga. ———. 30 Sep. 1784. ———.

Fuller, Peter. N. Y. Matross. 9 Jul. 1790. 600 acres.

Fuller, Stephen. Ga. Refugee. 17 May 1784. ———.

Fuller, Stephen. Mass. Private. 9 Jul. 1834. 200 acres.

Fuller, William. N.C. Private. 7 Jan. 1786. 640 acres to heirs.

Fullerton, Humphrey. Va. Surgeon. 31 Dec. 1800. 3000 acres.

Fullerton, Humphrey. Va. Surgeon. 31 Dec. 1800. 500 acres.

Fullerton, Humphrey. Va. Surgeon. 31 Dec. 1800. 500 acres.

Fullerton, Humphrey. Va. Surgeon. 31 Dec. 1800. 500 acres.

Fullerton, Humphrey. Va. Surgeon. 31 Dec. 1800. 500 acres.

Fullerton, Humphrey. Va. Surgeon. 31 Dec. 1800. 500 acres.

Fullerton, Humphrey. Va. Surgeon. 31 Dec. 1800. 250 acres.

Fullerton, Humphrey. Va. Surgeon. 31 Dec. 1800. 250 acres.

Fullerton, Robert. Pa. Lieutenant. ———. 200 acres.

Fullilove, John. Ga. ———. 17 May 1784. ———.

Fullin, William. Va. Private. 14 Jan. 1786. 100 acres.

Fullington, Micajah. N.C. Private. 27 Jul. 1785. 228 acres.

Fullom, Peter. Va. Private. 19 Mar. 1784. 100 acres.

Fulmer, George. Me. ———. 25 Jun. 1838. 200 acres to widow Nancy Fulmer.

Fulmer, George. N. Y. Private. 8 Jul. 1790. 600 acres.

Fulsom, Benjamin. Ga. Captain. 17 May 1784. —— acres to heirs.

Fulsom, John. Ga. Refugee. 17 May 1784. ———.

Fulsom, Lawrence. Ga. Minute Man. 22 Mar. 1785. 250 acres.

Fulton, John. Ga. Refugee. 29 Jan. 1785. ———.

Fulton, John. N. Y. Private. 6 Jul. 1790. 600 acres.

Fulton, Samuel, Jr. Ga. Minute Man. 17 May 1784. ———.

Fulton, Samuel, Sr. Ga. Captain. ———. ———.

Fund, Nicholas. N. Y. ———. ———. 500 acres.

Funk, Henry. Va.-Ind. Private. 108 acres.

Funner, John M. Md. Private. ———. 50 acres.

Funno, Anthony. N.Y. ———. 13 Sep. 1790. 500 acres to heirs.

Fuqua, Joseph. Va. Private. 5 Mar. 1784. 100 acres.

Fuqua, Prater. Ga. ———. 17 May 1784. ———.

Fuqua, Thomas. Ga. ———. 17 May 1784. ———.

Furbee, David. N.C. Private. 30 Sep. 1785. 640 acres to heirs.
Furbush, William. Va. Sergeant. 25 Nov. 1783. 200 acres.
Furgason, Larkin. Va. Private. 29 Mar. 1784. 100 acres.
Furguson, John. N.C. Private. 21 Aug. 1820. 640 acres.
Furguson, Robert. Va. Private. 9 Nov. 1790. 200 acres.
Furlow, James. Ga. ———. 17 May 1784. ———.
Furlow, William. Ga. ———. 30 Sep. 1784. 287 1/2 acres.
Furman, Gabriel. N. Y. Private. 8 Jul. 1790. 500 acres.
Furman, John. N. Y. Lieutenant. 9 Jul. 1790. 1200 acres.
Furnace, Abraham. Pa. Private. 21 Oct. 1786. 200 acres to Lucinda Bishop, widow.
Furney, Peter. N.C. Private. 9 Sep. 1785. 640 acres to heirs.
Furriner, Edward. Md. Private. ———. 50 acres.
Fushman, John. N.C. Private. 30 Sep. 1785. 640 acres to heirs.
Fussell, Ezra. Ga. Refugee. 17 May 1784. ———.
Fussell, Samuel. N.C. Private. 12 Dec. 1796. 640 acres to heirs.
Fussell, Thomas. Ga. Refugee. 17 May 1784. ———.
Futon, Solomon. N.C. Private. 6 Dec. 1796. 640 acres to heirs.
Gable, Henry. Pa. Private. 12 Mar. 1806. 200 acres.
Gable, Peter. Pa. Private. 30 Jan. 1787. 200 acres.
Gable, Stephen. Pa. Private Ranger. 11 May 1787. 200 acres.
Gabriel, James. Va. Private. 1 Aug. 1789. 100 acres.
Gabriel, Peter. Pa. Sergeant. ———. 250 acres.
Gadd, Thomas. Md. Private. ———. 50 acres.
Gaddis, Henry. Va. Private. 23 Jul. 1824. 100 acres.
Gaddis, William. Va. Private. 23 Jul. 1824. 100 acres.
Gadsden, Thomas. S.C. Captain. 15 Oct. 1784. 300 acres.
Gafford, William. N.C. Private. 7 Jan. 1786. 640 acres to heirs.
Gage, John. N. Y. Sergeant. 8 Jul. 1790. 600 acres.
Gagney, Lewis. Va. Private. 17 Jul. 1784. 200 acres.
Gagnia, Lewis. Va.-Ind. Private. 108 acres.
Gagnia, Lewis. Va. Private. 14 Jul. 1835. 200 acres.
Gagnia, Lewis. Va. Private. 2 May 1856. 100 acres.
Gagnia, Pierre. Va. Private. 14 Jul. 1835. 100 acres.
Gagnia, Pierre. Va. Private. 2 May 1856. 100 acres.
Gahagan, John. Va. Private. 27 Apr. 1785. 200 acres.
Gainer, Hugh. Md. Private. ———. 50 acres.
Gainer, Peter. Pa. Private. ———. 200 acres.
Gainer, Samuel. N.C. Private. 27 Nov. 1783. 640 acres.
Gainer, Stephen. N.C. Private. 14 Sep. 1820. 274 acres.
Gaines, Absalom. Ga. Minute Man. ————. 287 1/2 acres.
Gaines, Ambrose. Ga. Minute Man. 14 Feb. 1785. ———.
Gaines, Anthony. N.C. Private. 22 Oct. 1783. 640 acres.
Gaines, Bailey. Ga. Minute Man. 22 Mar. 1785. 250 acres.
Gaines, Thomas. Va. Private [Corporal]. 19 Feb. 1784. 100 [200] acres.
Gaines, Thomas. Va. Private. 16 Nov. 1820. 100 acres.
Gaines, William Fleming. Va. Captain Lieutenant. 28 Apr. 1783. 4000 acres.
Gaines, William Fleming. Va. Captain Lieutenant. 11 Sep. 1807. 555 acres.
Gainey, Stephen. N.C. ———. 9 Nov. 1784. 640 acres to heir.
Gains, John. Va. Private. 7 Nov. 1783. 100 acres.
Gains, Richard. N.C. Private. 28 Oct. 1783. 640 acres to heir.
Gaither, Henry. Md. Major. ———. 200 acres.
Gaither, Henry. Pa. Private. 28 Nov. 1786. 200 acres.
Gaitskill, William. Me. ———. 1 Sep. 1835. 200 acres to widow Dorcas Gaitskill. Sidney.

Galaspy, Thomas. Va. Private. 23 Jun. 1784. 100 acres.
Galbraith, Alexander. Pa. Private. ———. 200 acres.
Galbraith, James. Pa. Private. ———. 200 acres.
Galbraith, Josiah. Pa. Private. 12 Jan. 1787. 200 acres.
Galbreath, Robert. Va. Sergeant. 1 Sep. 1783. 200 acres.
Galdon, William. Ga. ———. 5 Dec. 1785. ———.
Gale, Daniel. N.C. Corporal. 22 Apr. 185. 1000 acres to heirs.
Gale, Edmund. Mass. ———. 18 Apr. 1828. 200 acres to assignee Ebenezer Seccomb.
Gale, Edward. Md. Captain. ———. 200 acres.
Gale, George C. N.C. Private. 9 Feb. 1796. 640 acres to heirs.
Gale, John. Md. Captain. ———. 200 acres.
Galford, Thomas. Va. Sergeant. 29 Jan. 1808. 200 acres.
Gall, Jack. N. Y. Private. 8 Jul. 1790. 600 acres.
Gallagher, Daniel. Pa. Private. 2 Nov. 1786. 200 acres.
Gallagher, James. Pa. Private. 2 Dec. 1786. 200 acres.
Gallagher, John. Pa. Private. 24 Apr. 1787. 200 acres.
Gallaher, Hugh. Pa. Sergeant. 24 Aug. 1787. 250 acres.
Gallahue, Charles. Va. Captain. 23 Dec. 1785. 4000 ares.
Gallaspy, George. Va. Private. 3 Nov. 1784. 100 acres.
Gallaway, John. N.C. Sergeant. 23 Apr. 1785. 1000 acres to heirs.
Gallaway, Robert. N.C. Private. 22 Dec. 1796. 640 acres.
Galley, Peter. Pa. Private. 13 Oct. 1786. 200 acres.
Galley, William. Va. Private. 26 Jun. 1784. 200 acres.
Galliday, Joseph. Va. Corporal. 7 Mar. 1786. 400 acres.
Gallop, Isaac. N.C. Private. 2 Dec. 1785. 320 acres.
Galloway, John. Va. Lieutenant. 15 May 1809. 2666 2/3 acres.
Galloway, Marshall. Md. Private. ———. 50 acres.
Galloway, Richard. N.C. Private. 28 Sep. 1785. 640 acres to heirs.
Galloway, Terry. Va. Private. 10 Jun. 1783. 100 acres.
Gallup, Andrew. Conn. Sufferer. Groton. 14.8.0.
Gallup, Robert. Conn. Sufferer. Groton. 11.6.6.
Galphin, George. Ga. ———. 6 Apr. 1785. 287 1/2 acres.
Galphin, John. Ga. ———. 25 May 1784. 287 1/2 acres.
Galphin, Thomas. Ga. ———. 25 May 1784. 287 1/2 acres.
Galt, John Minson. Va. Surgeon. 29 Nov. 1783. 6000 acres.
Galt, Patrick. Va. Surgeon. 3 Dec. 1782. 6000 acres.
Galt, Patrick. Va. Surgeon. 26 May 1838. 990 8/9 acres.
Galt, Patrick. Va. Surgeon. 26 May 1838. 495 3/9 acres.
Galt, Patrick. Va. Surgeon. 26 May 1838. 123 8/9 acres.
Galt, Patrick. Va. Surgeon. 26 May 1838. 61 8/9 acres.
Galtby, Thomas. Pa. Private. 25 Aug. 1787. 200 acres.
Galvin, John. Pa. Private. 19 Jan. ——. 200 acres.
Gamble, Abraham. Md. Private. ———. 50 acres.
Gamble, Edmund. N.C. Subaltern. 21 Apr. 1784. 1158 acres.
Gamble, James. Pa. Lieutenant. ———. 200 acres.
Gamble, James. Pa. Lieutenant. 15 Nov. 1785. 200 acres.
Gamble, Robert. Va. Captain. 4 Aug. 1783. 4000 acres.
Gamble, Robert. Va. Captain. 16 Feb. 1796 [1797]. 666 2/3 acres.
Gamble, Robert. Va. Captain. 14 Sep 1807. 250 acres.
Gamble, Sergeant. S.C. Soldier. 21 Jan. 1785. 200 acres.
Gambling, James. N.C. Private. 12 May 1784. 350 acres.
Gambol, John. Ga. Refugee. 20 Feb. 1784. 500 acres.
Gamboll, John. S.C. Soldier. 21 Jan. 1785. 200 acres.

Games, Jacob. Md. Private. ———. 50 acres.
Gamewell, William. N.C. Private. 8 Jun. 1792. 640 acres.
Gammel, Alexander. N.C. Private. 7 Dec. 1797. 640 acres to heirs.
Gammel, Robert. N.C. Private. 9 Dec. 1797. 640 acres to heirs.
Gammells, Nathan. Va. Sergeant. 31 May 1783. 200 acres.
Gammon, Joshua. Me. Private. 16 Aug. 1839. 200 acres. Cape Elizabeth.
Gammon, Moses. Me. ———. 7 May 1835. 200 acres. Oxford.
Gammond, Christopher. S.C. Soldier. 2 May 1785. 200 acres.
Ganet, Enoch. Md. Private. ———. 50 acres.
Gannie, Michael. N. Y. ———. ———. 500 acres.
Ganno, John. N. Y. Chaplain. 9 Jul. 1790. 2000 acres.
Gannon, Thomas. N.C. Private. 30 Sep. 1785. 274 acres.
Gansevoort, Peter. N. Yk. Colonel. 7 Jul. 1790. 3000 acres.
Garbett, George. Ga. ———. 27 Sep. 1784. 287 1/2 acres.
Garbins, Henry. Va. Private. 5 Apr. 1784. 100 acres.
Garcena, Abraham. Md. Private. ———. 50 acres.
Garden, Alexander. Va. Lieutenant. 9 Nov. 1832. 2666 2/3 acres.
Gardiner, Benoni. N. Y. Matross. 9 Jul. 1790. 600 acres.
Gardner, Andries. N. Y. Private. 7 Jul. 1790. 500 acres.
Gardner, Caswell. Va. Sergeant. 26 Mar. 1787. 200 acres.
Gardner, David. Conn. Sufferer. New London. 11.0.0.
Gardner, Demsey. N.C. Private. 20 Feb. 1784. 274 acres.
Gardner, Elijah. Me. ———. 4 May 1835. 200 acres. Dennysville.
Gardner, George. N.C. Private. 29 Sep. 1784. 640 acres to heir.
Gardner, George. Va. Corporal. 30 Apr. 1783. 400 acres.
Gardner, Gilbert. N. Y. Private. 8 Jul. 1790. 600 acres.
Gardner, James. N.C. Private. 10 Aug. 1785. 640 acres to heirs.
Gardner, Jesse. N. Y. Private. 8 Jul. 1790. 600 acres.
Gardner, John. Me. Mariner. 24 Aug. 1835. 200 acres. Oxford.
Gardner, John. Va. Sergeant. 13 Sep. 1783. 200 acres.
Gardner, Lewis. Ga. ———. 28 Feb. 1784. 250 acres.
Gardner, Mary. Conn. Sufferer. New London. 123.16.0.
Gardner, Nathan. N.C. Private. 30 Sep. 1785. 640 acres to heirs.
Gardner, Samuel. N. Y. Private. 7 Jul. 1790. 600 acres.
Gardner, Thomas. Ga. ———. 17 May 1784. ———.
Gardner, Thomas. Mass. Corporal. 30 Dec. 1831. 200 acres.
Gardner, Thomas. N. Y. Matross. 9 Jul. 1790. 600 acres.
Gardner, Thomas. Va. Sergeant. 18 Dec. 1784. 200 acres.
Gardner, Thomas. Conn. Sufferer. New London. 22.2.0.
Gardner, William. Ga. ———. 17 May 1784. ———.
Gardnor, John. N.C. Private. 10 Dec. 1788. 640 acres to heirs.
Garger [Geiger], Henry. Pa. ———. Private. 200 acres.
Garland, Edward. Va. Captain. 7 Jun. 1818. 1000 acres.
Garland, Edward. Va. Captain. 7 Jun. 1818. 1000 acres.
Garland, Edward. Va. Captain. 7 Jun. 1818. 1000 acres.
Garland, Edward. Va. Captain. 7 Jun. 1818. 1000 acres.
Garland, Elisha. N.C. Private. 24 Dec. 1796. 228 acres.
Garland, George. N. Y. Matross. 9 Jul. 1790. 600 acres.
Garland, Humphrey. N.C. Private. 17 Feb. 1824. 640 acres.
Garland, Huymphrey. N.C. Private. 14 May 1784. 228 acres.
Garland, James. Va. Private. 26 Dec. 1796. 100 acres.
Garland, John. N.C. Private. 24 Dec. 1796. 228 acrers.
Garland, Peter. Va. Captain. 8 May 1783. 4000 acres.
Garland, Peter. Va. Captain. 20 Nov. 1809. 1222 acres.

Garland, William. S.C. ———. 2 Dec. 1793. 65 acres.
Garland, William. S.C. ———. 2 Dec. 1793. 50 acres.
Garland, William. S.C. ———. 2 Dec. 1793. 25 acres.
Garland, William. S.C. ———. 2 Dec. 1793. 60 acres.
Garlington, Christoher. S.C. ———. 7 Aug. 1786. 200 acres.
Garlon, Benjamin. Va. Sailor. 25 Oct. 1786. 100 acres.
Garner, Gregory. N.C. Drummer. 9 Dec. 1796. 1000 acres.
Garner, James. Va. Drum Major. 20 Nov. 1821. 200 acres.
Garner, John. Va. Private. 18 Sep. 1783. 200 acres.
Garner, John. Va. Private. 26 Feb. 1784. 100 acres.
Garner, Joseph. Va. Sergeant. 21 Nov. 1799. 200 acres.
Garner, Presly. Va. Seaman. 26 Sep. 1783. 100 acres.
Garner, Samuel. S.C. ———. 7 May 1792. 200 acres.
Garner, Thomas. N.C. Private. 9 Feb. 1796. 640 acres to heirs.
Garner, William. Va. Private. 18 Sep. 1783. 200 acres.
Garner, William. Va. Private. 17 Nov. 1784. 100 acres.
Garner, William. Va. Private. 20 Feb. 1833. 100 acres.
Garner, William. Va. Private. 10 Jan. 1834. 100 acres.
Garner, William. Conn. Sufferer. Norwalk. 11.4.3.
Garnes, Gabriel. N.C. Private. 17 Feb. 1824. 640 acres.
Garnes, Jeffrey. N.C. ———. 29 Apr. 1784. 640 acres to Anthony Garnes, heir.
Garnet, Andrew. Md. Fifer. ———. 50 acres.
Garnett, Anthony. Va. Private. 7 Dec. 1784. 100 acres.
Garnett, Benjamin. Md. Lieutenant. ———. 200 acres.
Garnett, Benjamin. Va. Lieutenant. 26 Feb. 1810. 2666 2/3 acres.
Garnett, Ely. Ga. Refugee. 6 Feb. 1784. 250 acres.
Garnett, Henry. Va. Captain. 12 Dec. 1833 [1832]. 4000 acres.
Garnett, Henry. Va. Captain. 9 Sep. 1833. 400 acres.
Garnett, Henry. Va. Captain. 9 Sep. 1833. 2000 acres.
Garnett, Henry Va. Captain. 9 Sep. 1833. 400 acres.
Garnett, Henry. Va. Captain. 9 Sep. 1833. 400 acres.
Garnett, Henry. Va. Captain. 9 Sep. 1833. 400 acres.
Garnett, Henry. Va. Captain. 9 Sep. 1833. 400 acres.
Garnett, John. N. Y. Matross. 9 Jul. 1790. 600 acres.
Garorn, John. Ga. Soldier. 5 Dec. 1785. 230 acres.
Garrell, John. N.C. Sergeant. 21 May 1784. 440 acres.
Garret, Abraham. S.C. ———. 2 Oct. 1786. 200 acres.
Garret, Anthony. N.C. Private. 10 Jan. 1794. 640 acres.
Garret, Daniel. N.C. Private. 8 Dec. 1796. 274 acres.
Garret, James. N.Y. ———. 13 Sep. 1790. 500 acres to heirs.
Garret, Robert. Pa. Drummer. 30 Nov. 1786. 200 acres to Samuel Benezet, assignee.
Garret, William. N.C. Private. 30 Mar. 1785. 640 acres to heirs.
Garrett, Henry. Va. Private. 15 Jun. 1807. 100 acres.
Garrett, James. N.C. Private. 11 Nov. 1814. 640 acres to heirs.
Garrett, Jesse. N.C. Private. 30 Sep. 1785. 640 acres to heirs.
Garrett, John. Ga. ———. 12 Jun. 1784. 278 1/2 acres.
Garrett, John. Va. Private. 1 Jun. 1785. 100 acres.
Garrett, Mark. Va. Sergeant. 29 Apr. 1783. 200 acres.
Garrick, Black. N.C. Musician. 8 Aug. 1821. 1000 acres.
Garris, Bedford. N.C. Private. 9 Nov. 1784. 640 acres.
Garris, Sykes. N.C. Private. 19 May 1784. 640 acres.
Garrish, Edward. Md. Private. ———. 50 acres.

Garrisham, James. Pa. Private. 15 Aug. 1787. 200 acres to James Martin, assignee.

Garrison, Abraham. N. Y. Private. 8 Jul. 1790. 600 acres.

Garrison, Isaac. Pa. Drummer. 21 Oct. 1786. 200 acres.

Garrison, John. N. Y. Private. 8 Jul. 1790. 600 acres.

Garrison, Peter. N. Y. Matross. 9 Jul. 1790. 600 acres.

Garrison, Stephen. N.C. Private. 21 Apr. 1784. 640 acres.

Garrison, Thomas. N. Y. Matross. 9 Jul. 1790. 600 acres.

Garrison, William. N.C. Private. 7 Jan. 1786. 640 acres to heirs.

Garriss, Stephen. N.C. Private. 17 Dec. 1785. 640 acres to heirs.

Garrithy, Richard. Pa. Private. 30 July 1787. 200 acres.

Garrot, Robert. Va.-Ind. Private. 108 acres.

Garrot, Thomas. N.C. Sergeant. 24 Nov. 1796. 489 acres.

Garrott, John. Va. Private. 1 Jun. 1812. 100 acres.

Garth, James. Md. Private. ———. 50 acres.

Gartsel, John. Mass. Corporal. 6 Jul. 1832. 200 acres.

Garvey, Bartholomew. Pa. Matross. 28 Aug. 1787. 200 acres to William Turnbull, assignee.

Garvey, Job. Va. Private. 19 Aug. 1819. 100 acres.

Garvey, John. Pa. Private. ———. 200 acres.

Garvey, Matthew. N.C. Private. 24 Nov. 1796. 640 acres to heirs.

Garvey, Thomas. N.C. Private. 20 Oct. 1792. 640 acres.

Garvin, Benjmain. Va. Private. 6 Nov. 1787. 100 acres.

Garvin, Henry. Pa. Private. 3 Feb. 1789. 200 acres.

Garvin, Joseph. Ga. ———. 17 May 1784. ———.

Garvin, Thomas. Pa. Dragoon. ———. 200 acres.

Garvis, Nicholas. N.C. Private. 7 Jan. 1786. 640 acres to heirs.

Gary, John. Va. Sergeant. 31 Dec. 1782. 200 acres.

Gary, John. Va. Sergeant. 20 Aug. 1783. 200 acres.

Gasaway, John. Va. Private. 20 Jun. 1783. 100 acres.

Gaskey, Richard. Va. Private. 25 Apr. 1783. 200 acres.

Gaskins, Jesse. Va. Private. 25 Feb. 1797. 200 acres.

Gaskins, Job. Va. Private. 23 Dec. 1839. 50 acres.

Gaskins, Job. Va. Private. 23 Dec. 1839. 50 acres.

Gaskins, Thomas. Va.-Ind. Private. 108 acres.

Gaskins, Thomas. Va. Lieutenant Colonel. 6 Jun. 1783. 6000 acres.

Gaskins, Thomas. Va. Lieutenant Colonel. 26 Feb. 1784. 1000 acres.

Gaskins, Thomas. Va. Lieutenant Colonel. 19 Aug. 1808. 229 acres.

Gaskins, Thomas. Va. Lieutenant Colonel. 19 Aug. 1808. 229 acres.

Gaskins, Thomas. Va. Lieutenant Colonel. 19 Aug. 1808. 229 acres.

Gaskins, Thomas. Va. Lieutenant Colonel. 19 Aug. 1808. 229 acres.

Gaskins, Thomas. Va. Lieutenant Colonel. 19 Aug. 1808. 229 acres.

Gaskins, Thomas. Va. Lieutenant Colonel. 19 Aug. 1808. 229 acres.

Gaskins, Thomas. Va. Lieutenant Colonel. 19 Aug. 1808. 229 acres.

Gaskins, Thomas. Va. Lieutenant Colonel. 19 Aug. 1808. 229 acres.

Gaskins, Thomas. Va. Lieutenant Colonel. 9 Apr. 1835. 200 acres.

Gaskins, William. N.C. Corporal. 28 Aug. 1820. 1000 acres.

Gasner, John. Va. Private. 5 Feb. 1785. 200 acres.

Gasper, Peter. N. Y. Sergeant. 8 Jul. 1790. 600 acres.

Gassaway, Henry. Md. Lieutenant. ———. 200 acres.

Gassaway, James. Va. Private. 20 Jun. 1783. 100 acres.

Gassaway, John. Md. Captain. ———. 200 acres.

Gassaway, Nicholas. Md. Lieutenant. ———. 200 acres.

Gaster, John. Ga. Minute Man. 16 Mar. 1785. ———.

Gaston, Alexander. Ga. Lieutenant. 17 May 1784. —— acres to heirs.

Gaston, David. Ga. Sergeant. 17 May 1784. ———.

Gaston, John. S.C. ———. 3 Jan. 1791. 200 acres.

Gaston, Robert. S.C. ———. 4 Jul. 1785. 200 acres.

Gatchell, Zacheriah. Me. ———. 17 Jul. 1835. 200 acres to widow Mary Goodale. Wells.

Gateley, Isaac. N.C. Private. 28 May 1784. 640 acres.

Gater, Benjamin. Md. Private. ———. 50 acres.

Gates, Christian. S.C. ———. 4 Dec. 1786. 200 acres.

Gates, Horatio. Va. Major General. 30 May 1783. 2000 acres.

Gates, Horatio. Va. Major General. 30 May 1783. 2000 acres.

Gates, Horatio. Va. Major General. 30 May 1783. 2000 acres.

Gates, Horatio. Va. Major General. 30 May 1783. 2000 acres.

Gates, Horatio. Va. Major General. 30 May 1783. 2000 acres.

Gates, Horatio. Va. Major General. 30 May 1783. 2000 acres.

Gates, Horatio. Va. Major General. 30 May 1783. 1500 acres.

Gates, Horatio. Va. Major General. 30 May 1783. 15,000 acres.

Gates, Horatio. Va. Major General. 30 May 1783. 2500 acres.

Gates, John. Va. Private. 21 May 1783. 100 acres.

Gates, Jonas. Mass. Sergeant. 1 Feb. 1834. 200 acres.

Gates, Samuel. Ga. ———. 17 May 1784. ———.

Gates, William. Md. Drummer. ———. 50 acres.

Gather, John. Md. Private. ———. 50 acres.

Gatting, Sylvester. Md. Private. ———. 50 acres.

Gauld, John. N.Y. ———. 13 Sep. 1790. 500 acres to heirs.

Gauley, John. N. Y. ———. ———. 500 acres.

Gaulor, Daniel. N.C. Private. 30 Sep. 1785. 640 acres to heirs.

Gaultney, John. Ga. ———. 17 May 1784. ———.

Gaultney, John. N.C. Private. 28 Sep. 1785. 640 acres.

Gay, Allen. Ga. Private. Sep. 1785. 250 acres.

Gay, Dennis. Ga. Soldier. 5 Sep. 1785. ———.

Gay, Isham. N.C. Private. 22 Dec. 1796. 228 acres.

Gay, James. N.C. Fifer. 22 Dec. 1796. 1000 acres to heirs.

Gay, John. Mass. Private. 22 Jul. 1829. 200 acres.

Gay, Jonathan. N.C. Private. 28 Sep. 1785. 274 acres.

Gay, Joshua. Ga. Private. 10 Dec. 1784. 250 acres.

Gay, Samuel. Va. Regimental Surgeon. 17 Mar. 1832. 6000 acres.

Gay, Samuel. Va. Regimental Surgeon. 8 Jan. 1834. 2000 acres.

Gay, Samuel. Va. Regimental Surgeon. 8 Jan. 1834. 2000 acres.

Gay, Samuel. Va. Regimental Surgeon. 8 Jan. 1834. 1500 acres.

Gay, Samuel. Va. Regimental Surgeon. 8 Jan. 1834. 500 acres.

Gay, Solomon. N.C. Private. 3 Dec. 1813. 640 acres to heirs.

Gay, Solomon. N.C. Private. 20 Sep. 1821. 640 acres to heirs.

Gay, William. Ga. Citizen. 22 Mar. 1785. 250 acres.

Gay, William. N.C. ———. 8 Mar. 1785. 640 acres to heirs.

Gay, William. N.C. Private. 5 Dec. 1797. 274 acres to heirs.

Gaylor, Gasper. Va.-Ind. Private. 108 acres.

Gaylord, Aaron. N.C. Private. 28 Sep. 1785. 640 acres.

Gaylord, Elizabeth. Conn. Sufferer. Norwalk. 5.8.0.

Gayne, John. N. Y. ———. ———. 500 acres.

Gazbly, George. Pa. Private. 23 Nov. 1786. 200 acres.

Gearreell, John. Va. Private. 26 Dec. 1795. 100 acres.

Geary, Jonathan. Mass. ———. 11 Jul. 1837. 200 acres.

Geary, Peter. Pa. Private. 17 Oct. 1786. 200 acres.

Geau, James. Ga. Soldier. 20 Dec. 1785. 230 acres.

Geddy, Thomas. N.C. Private. 7 Mar. 1785. 640 acres.
Gee, David. N. Y. Private. 8 Jul. 1790. 500 acres.
Gee, Ezekiel. N. Y. Private. 6 Jul. 1790. 500 acres.
Gee, Howell. N.C. Lieutenant. 5 Sep. 1821. 2560 acres.
Gee, James. N.C. Captain. 21 Oct. 1783. 3840 acres to heir John Gee.
Gee, John. Ga. ———. 5 Sep. 1785. 287 1/2 acres.
Gee, John. Md. Private. ———. 50 acres.
Gee, John. N. Y. Private. 8 Jul. 1790. 600 acres.
Gee, Joseph. Ga. ———. 17 May 1784. ———.
Gee, Moses. N. Y. Private. 8 Jul. 1790. 600 acres.
Gee, Richard. Md. Private. ———. 50 acres.
Gee, Richard. N.C. Sergeant. 14 Dec. 1796. 428 acres.
Gee, Thomas. N.Y. Quartermaster Sergeant. 8 Jul. 1790. 600 acres.
Gee, William. N.C. Private. 21 Oct. 1783. 228 acres.
Geeen, James. Va. Midshipman. 25 Apr. 1837. 666 2/3 acres.
Geers, Benjamin. N. Y. Private. 8 Jul. 1790. 600 acres.
Geeson, Matthew. N. Y. Matross. 9 Jul. 1790. 500 acres.
Gehon, Peter. Pa. Private. ———. 200 acres.
Geisensieder, Martin. Va. Private. 23 Jun. 1848. 100 acres.
Geisensieder, Martin. Va. Private. 23 Jun. 1848. 100 acres.
Gelhampton, Robert. Md. Private. ———. 50 acres.
Gellen, Caspar. Virginia. Private. 1 May 1783. 200 acres.
Gent, Charles. Ga. Refugee. 15 Mar. 1784. 250 acres.
Gent, William. Ga. Refugee. 15 Mar. 1784. 250 acres.
Gentry, James. Va. Corporal. 8 May 1783. 200 acres.
Gentry, William. Va. Private. 26 Jun. 1783. 100 acres.
Geohagan, Anthony. Md. Drummer. ———. 50 acres.
George, Benjamin. Va. Sailor. 1 Aug. 1786. 100 acres.
George, Bennet. Md. Private. ———. 50 acres.
George, Britain. N.C. Private. 29 Nov. 1783. 640 acres.
George, David. Ga. Minute Man. 3 Sep. 1785. ———.
George, Demsey. Ga. Minute Man. 3 Apr. 1785. ———.
George, Duke. Va. Sailor. 1 Dec. 1789. 100 acres.
George, Edward. S.C. ———. 4 Mar. 1789. 200 acres.
George, Henry. Ga. Soldier. 7 Jun. 1785. 230 acres to heirs.
George, Isaac. Ga. Minute Man. 3 Sep. 1785. ———.
George, Jacob. S.C. ———. 5 May 1788. 200 acres.
George, James Mayo. Va. Private. 1 Jun. 1805. 100 acres.
George, James Mayo. Va. Private. 27 Jun. 1783. 100 acres.
George, Jesse. Va. Lieutenant. 1 Aug. 1834. 4000 acres.
George, John. Ga. Minute Man. 3 Apr. 1785. ———.
George, John. Pa. Private. 29 Aug. 1787. 200 acres.
George, John. Va. Private. 30 Jun. 1784. 100 acres.
George, John. Va. Private. 11 Mar. 1858. 100 acres.
George, Reubin. Va. Private. 24 Mar. 1831. 100 acres.
George, Robert. Va.-Ind. Captain. Apr. 1784. 3234 acres.
George, Robert. N.Y. ———. 13 Sep. 1790. 500 acres to heirs.
George, Robert. Va. Captain. 29 Apr. 1784. 4000 acres.
George, Samson. N.C. Private. 30 Sep. 1785. 640 acres.
George, Silas. Ga. Minute Man. 3 Sep. 1785. ———.
George, Solomon. Ga. Minute Man. 3 Apr. 1785. ———.
George, Southey. Md. Private. ———. 50 acres.
George, Thomas. Me. ———. 30 Apr. 1838. 200 acres. Newport.
George, Thomas. N.C. Private. 30 Sep. 1785. 640 acres to heirs.

George, Travis. Va. Private. 26 Jun. 1783. 200 acres.
George, William. Ga. ———. 17 May 1784. ———.
George, William. Md. Private. ———. 50 acres.
George, William. Va. Captain. 28 Nov. 1783. 4000 acres.
Gerard, Charles. N.C. Lieutenant. 22 Oct. 1783. 2560 acres.
Gerault, John. Va.-Ind. Lieutenant. Mar. 1784. 2156 acres.
German, Benjamin. N.C. Private. 18 Aug. 1784. 365 acres.
German, Lawrence. Pa. Private. ———. 200 acres.
Germany, John. Ga. ———. 6 Feb. 1784. 287 1/2 acres.
Germany, John, Jr. Ga. ———. 6 Feb. 1784. 250 acres.
Germany, Samuel. Ga. ———. 5 Mar. 1784. 250 acres.
Germany, William. Ga. ———. 6 Feb. 1784. 250 acres.
Germany, William, Jr. Ga. ———. 28 Feb. 1784. 250 acres.
Germany, William, Sr. Ga. ———. 28 Feb. 1784. 250 acres.
Gerrard, Jacob. N.C. Private. 26 May 1784. 640 acres.
Gerraull, John. Va. Captain. 3 Mar. 1784. 4000 acres.
Gerrell, William. N.C. Private. 17 Feb. 1824. 640 acres.
Gerrit, Samuel. N.Y. ———. ———. 500 acres to heirs.
Gerry, James. N.C. Private. 9 Dec. 1797. 274 acres.
Gerry, Samuel. Md. Private. ———. 50 acres.
Gervis, John. N.C. Private. 26 May 1784. 640 acres.
Gester, John. Va. Captain. 7 May 1785. 100 acres.
Gestwhite, Henry. Pa. Private. 11 Jul. 1787. 200 acres.
Getting, George. Pa. Private. 29 Sep. 1787. 200 acres.
Gibb, John. Ga. ———. 19 Dec. 1785. 287 1/2 acres.
Gibb, William. Pa. Sergeant. 8 May 1787. 250 acres.
Gibbons [or Gibson], James. Pa. Captain. 28 Sep. 1787. 500 acres.
Gibbons, David. Pa. Private. 28 Aug. 1787. 200 acres to William Turnbull, assignee.
Gibbons, Isaac. Pa. Private. 20 Aug. 1787. 200 acres.
Gibbons, James. Pa. Captain. 17 Aug. 1787. 500 acres.
Gibbons, James. Pa. Private. 5 Apr. 1787. 200 acres.
Gibbons, John. N. Y. Private. 3 Jul. 1790. 600 acres.
Gibbons, Patrick. N.C. Private. 7 Dec. 1797. 640 acres to heirs.
Gibbs, Churchill. Va. Lieutenant. 25 May 1784. 2666 2/3 acres.
Gibbs, Churchill. Va. Lieutenant. 30 May 1818. 440 70/100 acres.
Gibbs, George. Conn. Sufferer. New London. 21.7.0.
Gibbs, Harrod. Va. Lieutenant. 24 Dec. 1813. 2666 2/3 acres.
Gibbs, Henry. Conn. Sufferer. New/East Haven. 4.8.0.
Gibbs, James. Va. Seaman. 18 Apr. 1835. 100 acres.
Gibbs, Joel. N.C. Private. 23 Oct. 1783. 640 acres to Rabon Gibbs, heir.
Gibbs, Joel. N.C. Musician. 23 Aug. 1821. 360 acres to heirs.
Gibbs, John. Va. Private. 22 Jan. 1834. 100 acres.
Gibbs, Joseph. Va. Private. 29 Apr. 1785. 200 acres.
Gibbs, Richard. Ga. Soldier. ———. 287 1/2 acres.
Gibbs, William. Ga. Soldier. 19 Dec. 1783. 200 acres.
Gibbs, William. Va. Private. 20 Jun. 1783. 100 acres.
Gible, Philip. Pa. Private. 16 Oct. 1786. 200 acres.
Gibson, Aaron. Va. Sergeant. 5 Mar. 1784. 200 acres.
Gibson, Charles. N.C. Private. 9 Feb. 1796. 640 acres to heirs.
Gibson, Colen. N.C. ———. 24 Dec. 1796. 1000 acres.
Gibson, Elisha. N.C. Private. 22 Dec. 1796. 640 acres.
Gibson, Fuller. N.C. Private. 22 Apr. 1785. 228 acres.
Gibson, George. Va. Colonel. 26 Apr. 1785. 6666 2/3 acres.
Gibson, George. Va. Colonel. 28 Jul. 1830. 2222 acres.

Gibson, Jacob. Va. Private. 24 Feb. 1784. 100 acres.
Gibson, James. Va. Gunner. 30 Mar. 1831. 2666 2/3 acres.
Gibson, Joel. N.C. Private. 17 Dec. 1785. 640 acres to heirs.
Gibson, John. Ga. Soldier. 20 Feb. 1784. 250 acres.
Gibson, John. Md. Private. ———. 50 acres.
Gibson, John. N.C. Private. 1 Sep. 1785. 640 acres to heirs.
Gibson, John. Va. Colonel. 31 Mar. 1783. 1000 acres.
Gibson, John. Va. Colonel. 31 Mar. 1783. 1000 acers.
Gibson, John. Va. Colonel. 31 Mar. 1783. 1000 acres.
Gibson, John. Va. Colonel. 31 Mar. 1783. 3666 2/3 acres.
Gibson, John. Va. Sailing Master. 2 Jun. 1783. 2666 2/3 acres.
Gibson, John. Va. Lieutenant Colonel. 7 Apr. 1808. 1000 acres.
Gibson, John. Va. Gunner. 23 Jul. 1832. 2666 2/3 acres.
Gibson, John, Jr. Va. Ensign. 27 Oct. 1783. 2666 2/3 acres.
Gibson, Jonathan. Md. Captain. ———. 200 acres.
Gibson, Jonathan. N.C. Private. 9 Dec. 1797. 640 acres.
Gibson, Robert. Va. Corporal. 10 Jun. 1783. 200 acres.
Gibson, Roger. Conn. Sufferer. New London. 884.18.6 1/2.
Gibson, Thomas. Ga. ———. 17 May 1784. ———.
Gibson, Thomas. N.C. Ensign. 15 May 1820. 2560 acres to heirs.
Gibson, William. N.C. Private. 26 Apr. 1784. 640 acres.
Giddens, William. Ga. Refugee. ———. 287 1/2 acres.
Gidean, Rcihard. N.C. Fifer. 30 Sep. 1785. 1000 acres to heirs.
Gideon, Jacob. Va. Bugleman. 26 Oct. 1820. 100 acres.
Gidions, Francis. Ga. Captain. 28 Jul. 1784. 287 1/2 acres.
Gidions, William. Ga. ———. 15 Jan. 1784. 287 1/2 acres.
Gies, Nicholas. Pa. Private. 19 Jan. 1787. 200 acres.
Gifford, James. N.C. Sergeant. 2 Dec. 1785. 428 acres.
Gigo, Francis. N. Y. ———. ———. 500 acres.
Gilbank, John. S.C. ———. 21 Jan. 1785. 300 acres to Ephraim Mitchell, administrator, for the heirs.
Gilbert, Abraham. N.C. Private. 13 Dec. 1796. 640 acres to heirs.
Gilbert, Amos. Conn. Sufferer. New/East Haven. 13.7.0.
Gilbert, Benjamin. Md. Private. ———. 50 acres.
Gilbert, Benjamin. N. Y. Lieutenant. 6 Jul. 1790. 1000 acres.
Gilbert, Caleb. Conn. Sufferer. New/East Haven. 48.18.8 1/2.
Gilbert, David. Conn. Sufferer. New/East Haven. 8.2.6.
Gilbert, James. Ga. Private. 10 Dec. 1784. 250 acres.
Gilbert, James. N.C. Private. 29 Sep. 1784. 640 acres to heir.
Gilbert, James. Conn. Sufferer. New/East Haven. 12.2.0.
Gilbert, Joel. Conn. Sufferer. New/East Haven. 2.9.0.
Gilbert, John. N. Y. Corporal. 8 Jul. 1790. 500 acres.
Gilbert, John. N.C. Private. 2 Dec. 1785. 640 acres.
Gilbert, Joseph. Va. Private. 27 Jul. 1783. 200 acres.
Gilbert, Lydia. Conn. Sufferer. Ridgefield. 34.10.6.
Gilbert, Samuel. N. Y. Private. 8 Jul. 1790. 600 acres.
Gilbert, Seth. N. Y. Private. 8 Jul. 1790. 600 acres.
Gilbert, Stephen. Pa. Private. 26 Apr. 1787. 200 acres.
Gilbert, Thomas. Ga. ———. 17 May 1784. ———.
Gilbert, Timothy. Conn. Sufferer. New/East Haven. 3.10.3 1/2.
Gilbert, William. Ga. Private. 10 Dec. 1784. 250 acres.
Gilbert, William. N. Y. Private. 8 Jul. 1790. 600 acres.
Gilbert, William. N.C. Private. 30 Sep. 1785. 640 acres to heirs.
Gilbrown, Rene. N. Y. ———. ———. 500 acres.

Gilby, Henry. Md. Private. ———. 50 acres.
Gilby, Thomas. Pa. Private. ———. 200 acres.
Gilchrist, George. Va. Major. 9 Jun. 1783. 5333 1/3 acres.
Gilchrist, George. Va. Major. 26 Mar. 1798. 888 5/6 acres.
Gilchrist, George. Va. Major. 23 Jun. 1808. 666 2/3 acres.
Gilchrist, James. Pa. Lieutenant. 13 Aug. 1787. 200 acres.
Gilchrist, James. Pa. Lieutenant. 13 Aug. 1786. 200 acres.
Gilchrist, John. N.Y. ———. 13 Sep. 1790. 500 acres to heirs.
Gilchrist, William. N. Y. Private. 8 Jul. 1790. 600 acres.
Gilder, Henry. S.C. ———. 5 Apr. 1790. 200 acres.
Gildersleive, Finch. N. Y. Lieutenant. 9 Jul. 1790. 1200 acres.
Giles, Arthur. Ga. Private. 26 May 1784. 287 1/2 acres.
Giles, Erasmus. Va. Captain. 4 Jul. 1783. 4666 2/3 acres.
Giles, Erasmus. Va. Captain. 9 Nov. 1796. 666 2/3 acres.
Giles, George. Ga. ———. 4 Oct. 1785. ———.
Giles, James. Va. Private. 20 Jun. 1783. 100 acres.
Giles, John. Ga. ———. 22 Sep. 1784. 287 1/2 acres.
Giles, John. Md. Private. ———. 50 acres.
Giles, John. N.C. Sergeant. 21 Oct. 1783. 358 acres.
Giles, John. Va. Ensign. 13 Dec. 1782. 2666 2/3 acres.
Giles, Robert. Ga. ———. 17 May 1784. 250 acres.
Giles, Samuel. Ga. Refugee. 15 Mar. 1784. 250 acres.
Giles, Thomas. S.C. Major. 4 Jul. 1785. 400 acres.
Giles, William. Ga. Minute Man. 24 May 1784. 287 1/2 acres.
Gilham, Ezekiel. Ga. ———. 17 May 1784. ———.
Gilham, Thomas. Md. Private. ———. 50 acres.
Gilkey, Samuel. N.C. Private. 9 Feb. 1796. 640 acres to heirs.
Gill, Alexander. N.C. Private. 26 May 1784. 640 acres.
Gill, John. N.C. Private. 19 May 1784. 640 acres.
Gill, John. Pa. Private. ———. 200 acres.
Gill, Jonathan. Md. Matross. ———. 50 acres.
Gill, Samuel. Va. Captain. 30 Apr. 1784. 4000 acres.
Gill, William. Pa. Matross. 2 Feb. 1787. 200 acres.
Gillam, Deveruex. N.C. Private. 7 Dec. 1797. 640 acres to heirs.
Gillas, Arthur. Pa. Matross. 30 Jan. 1787. 200 acres.
Gillaspee, William. N. Y. Sergeant. 6 Jul. 1790. 600 acres.
Gillaspy, James. N.Y. ———. 13 Sep. 1790. 500 acres to heirs.
Gillaspy, Joseph. N. Y. Fifer. 9 Jul. 1790. 600 acres.
Gilleham, Clem. Va. Private. 23 Jun. 1783. 200 acres.
Gilleland, Alexander. N.C. Private. 30 Aug. 1820. 640 acres to heirs.
Gillespie, Robert. N. Y. ———. 16 Aug. 1807. 200 acres to representatives James Gillespie, Samuel Gillespie, William Gillespie, John Gillespie, Barbara Gillespie, Matthew Gillespie, Jane Gillespie, Polly Gillespie, Ann Gillespie, Olive Gillespie, Burr Gillespie, and James Gillespie, Jr.
Gillespie, Robert. N.C. Sergeant. 6 Dec. 1783. 793 acres.
Gillet, Aaron. S.C. Surgeon. 4 Jul. 1785. 440 acres.
Gillet, Elijah. Ga. ———. 17 May 1784. ———.
Gillett, Aaron. S.C. Surgeon. 4 Jul. 1785. 92 acres.
Gilliam, Anselm. Va. Private. 27 Feb. 1797. 100 acres.
Gilliam, Harris. Va. Private. 27 Feb. 1797. 100 acres.
Gilliam, John. Va. Lieutenant. 30 Jun. 1791. 2666 2/3 acres.
Gilliam, Joshua. S.C. ———. 5 Feb. 1787. 200 acres.
Gilliham, William. S.C. ———. 2 Jan. 1792. 200 acres.
Gillihan, James. N.C. Private. 4 Aug. 1821. 640 acres.

Gilliland, Hugh. Ga. Refugee. 15 Jul. 1784. 287 1/2 acres.
Gilliland, Thomas. Ga. ———. 17 May 1784. 250 acres.
Gilliland, William. Ga. Refugee. 1784. 250 acres.
Gilliner, John. Ga. ———. 17 May 1784. ———.
Gilling, Daniel. Pa. Private. 23 Jun. 1787. 200 acres.
Gillion, Joshua. Ga. Soldier. 4 Feb. 1785. ———.
Gillison, John. Va. Captain. 16 May 1783. 4000 acres.
Gillison, John. Va. Captain. 1 Jun. 1805. 666 2/3 acres.
Gillison, John. Va. Captain. 29 Aug. 1807. 555 acres.
Gillison, Peter. Ga. Soldier. 4 Feb. 1785. ———.
Gillispie, David. N.C. Private. 22 Oct. 1783. 274 acres.
Gillispie, William. Md. Private. ———. 50 acres.
Gillispy, William. Va. Private. 9 May 1785. 100 acres.
Gillmore, William. N. Y. Private. 8 Jul. 1790. 600 acres.
Gillon, Alexander. S.C. Commodore. 21 Jan. 1785. 400 acres.
Gillon, Alexander. S.C. Commodore. 21 Jan. 1785. 450 acres.
Gillon, Hugh. Va. Captain. 23 Apr. 1784. 200 acres.
Gillon, Thomas. Md. Private. ———. 50 acres.
Gills, Samuel. Conn. Sufferer. New/East Haven. 58.4.3.
Gillum, Howell. N.C. Sergeant. 7 Jan. 1784. 1000 acres to John Gillum, heir.
Gilmart, Francis. N. Y. Lieutenant. ———. 1000 acres.
Gilmore, Elander. Ga. Soldier. 5 Dec. 1785. 230 acres.
Gilmore, George. Va.-Ind. Private. 108 acres.
Gilmore, James. S.C. ———. 3 Sep. 1782. 180 acres.
Gilmore, James. Va. Lieutenant. 6 Dec. 1806. 2666 2/3 acres.
Gilmore, John. Pa. Matross. 9 Dec. 1786. 200 acres to Dorothy Gilmore, widow.
Gilmore, Robert. Va. Private. 20 Apr. 1784. 100 acres.
Gilpatrick, Joseph. Me. Private. 6 Aug. 1835. 200 acres. Kennebunk.
Gilston, David. N.C. Sergeant. 24 Oct. 1783. 1000 acres to Samuel Gilston.
Gilston, David. N.C. Private. 9 Feb. 1796. 640 acres.
Gilston, David. N.C. Corporal. 9 Dec. 1797. 1000 acres.
Gilston, James. N.C. Private. 9 Feb. 1796. 228 acres.
Gimbo, William. Va. Sergeant. 2 Dec. 1783. 100 acres.
Ginalien, Abraham. N.C. Private. 19 Jan. 1786. 640 acres.
Ginew, William. N.C. Private. 17 Feb. 1824. 640 acres.
Ginn, David. N.C. Private. 30 Sep. 1785. 640 acres.
Ginn, Henry. N.C. Private. 30 Sep. 1785. 640 acres to heirs.
Ginnings, Thomas. N.C. Private. 21 May 1784. 365 acres.
Ginnins, Thomas. N.C. Private. 17 Dec. 1785. 640 acres.
Ginnis, George. N.C. Private. 26 May 1784. 640 acres.
Ginoman, Henry. Va. Private. 20 Jun. 1783. 100 acres.
Gipson, Robert. N.Y. ———. 13 Sep. 1790. 500 acres to heirs.
Girardeau, John. Ga. Refugee. 11 Feb. 1785. ———.
Girardeau, William. Ga. Refugee. 8 Mar. 1784. ———.
Girdler, Charles. Md. Private. ———. 50 acres.
Gist, John. Md. Captain. ———. 200 acres.
Gist, John. Va. Captain. 1 Apr. 1820. 4000 acres.
Gist, Jonathan. Ga. ———. 13 Sep. 1784. 287 1/2 acres.
Gist, Mordecai. Md. Brigadier General. ———. 200 acres.
Gist, Nathaniel. Va. Colonel. 24 Feb. 1783. 6666 2/3 acres.
Gist, Nathaniel. Va. Colonel. 15 Jan. 1812. 847 1/3 acres.
Gist, Robert. N.C. Private. 29 Sep. 1784. 640 acres.
Gist, Thomas. Va. Private. 7 Dec. 1786. 100 acres.
Givin, John. Va. Drummer. 31 Dec. 1806. 100 acres.

Givin, Thomas. Va. Private. 31 Dec. 1806. 100 acres.
Gladdin, John. Pa. Private. 24 Nov. 1788. 200 acres.
Gladding, John. Va. Private. 20 Nov. 1809. 261 acres.
Gladers, George. N.C. Private. 9 Feb. 1796. 640 acres to heirs.
Glamkin, John. Ga. ———. 25 May 1784. 287 1/2 acres.
Glancer [or Gleener] John. Pa. ———. 10 Mar. 1795. 200 acres to Clement Biddle, assignee.
Glandon, Major. N.C. Sergeant. 14 Oct. 1783. 1000 acres.
Glascock, Thomas. Va. Lieutenant. 17 Apr. 1784. 2666 2/3 acres.
Glascow, William. Md. Private. ———. 50 acres.
Glasgow, Walter. Md. Private. ———. 50 acres.
Glasmire, Jacob. Pa. Private. 3 Nov. 1786. 200 acres.
Glason, Patrick. Va. Private. 11 Dec. 1783. 200 acres.
Glaspy, John. Ga. ———. 17 May 1784. ———.
Glass, Hugh. Va. Private. 20 Jun. 1783. 100 acres.
Glass, Isaac. Va. Private. 19 Jun. 1783. 200 acres.
Glass, Isaac. Va. Private. 19 Jun. 1783. 100 acres.
Glass, Joel. Ga. Soldier. 25 Feb. 1784. 250 acres.
Glass, John. Ga. Soldier. 25 Feb. 1784. 250 acres.
Glass, John. Me. ———. 27 Apr. 1835. 200 acres. Gardiner.
Glass, Joseph. Ga. ———. ———. 287 1/2 acres.
Glass, Joshua. Ga. ———. 25 Feb. 1784. 250 acres.
Glass, Michael. Va.-Ind. Private. 108 acres.
Glasscock, Robert. Va. Private. 22 Jan. 1788. 100 acres.
Glasscock, Thomas. Ga. Lieutenant. 25 May 1784. 400 acres.
Glasscock, William. Ga. ———. 17 May 1784. ———.
Glaughan, Daniel. N.C. Private. 17 Feb. 1824. 640 acres.
Glaughan, Jeremiah. N.C. Sergeant. 23 Feb. 1820. 1000 acres to heirs.
Glaze, Jonathan. N.C. Corporal. 14 May 1784. 1000 acres to Samuel Glaze.
Gleeson, Thomas. Md. Matross. ———. 50 acres.
Glen, Robert. N. Y. Corporal. 8 Jul. 1790. 600 acres.
Glen, Samuel. Va. Private. 11 Mar. 1800. 200 acres.
Glenn, Bernard. Va. Lieutenant. 5 Aug. 1789. 2666 2/3 acres.
Glenn, Bernard. Va. Captain. 24 Mar. 1838. 190 1/2 acres.
Glenn, Bernard. Va. Captain. 24 Mar. 1838. 190 1/2 acres.
Glenn, Bernard. Va. Captain. 24 Mar. 1838. 190 1/2 acres.
Glenn, Bernard. Va. Captain. 24 Mar. 1838. 190 1/2 acres.
Glenn, Bernard. Va. Captain. 24 Mar. 1838. 190 1/2 acres.
Glenn, Bernard. Va. Captain. 24 Mar. 1838. 190 1/2 acres.
Glenn, Bernard. Va. Captain. 24 Mar. 1838. 190 1/2 acres.
Glenn, David. Ga. ———. 17 May 1784. ———.
Glenn, David. Va.-Ind. Private. 108 acres.
Glenn, Duke. Ga. ———. 17 May 1784. ———.
Glenn, Thompson. N.C. Private. 14 Dec. 1797. 320 acres.
Glenn, Tobias. N.C. Musician. 17 Feb. 1824. 1000 acres.
Glenn, William. Va. Captain. 31 Dec. 1806. 200 acres.
Glenny, William. N. Y. Lieutenat. 13 Sep. 1790. 1000 acres.
Glentworth, James. Pa. ———. 11 Oct. 1787. 200 acres.
Glentworth, James. Pa. Private. 11 Oct. 1786. 200 acres.
Glidden, Arnold. Me. ———. 25 Apr. 1835. 200 acres. Chester.
Glory, William. Md. Private. ———. 50 acres.
Gloucester, James. Va. Private. 25 Jun. 1783. 200 acres.
Gloughn, William. N.C. Private. 30 Sep. 1785. 640 acres to heirs.
Glover, Benjamin. N.C. Private. 17 Dec. 1796. 640 acres.
Glover, David. N.C. Private. 24 Dec. 1796. 640 acres.

Glover, Hardy. Ga. ———. 17 May 1784. —— acres to heirs.
Glover, James. N.C. Private. 28 Sep. 1785. 228 acres to heirs.
Glover, John. N.C. Private. 12 Mar. 1785. 228 acres.
Glover, Jones. N.C. Private. 14 Dec. 1796. 228 acres.
Glover, Samuel. N.C. Sergeant. 13 Jan. 1792. 1000 acres to heirs.
Glover, Stephen. Ga. Lieutenant. 17 May 1784. —— acres.
Glover, Thomas. Md. Private. ———. 50 acres.
Glover, Thomas. N. Y. Private. 8 Jul. 1790. 600 acres.
Glover, Thomas. Pa. Matross. 23 Jan. 1787. 200 acres.
Glozar, Nicholas. S.C. ———. 4 Jul. 1784. 200 acres.
Goatley, John. Va. Private. 31 Jul. 1784. 233 1/3 acres.
Godby, George. Va. Private. 9 Nov. 1811. 100 acres.
Godby, William. Ga. Refugee. 30 Sep. 1784. ———.
Goddard, Ebenezer. Conn. Sufferer. New London. 7.0.0.
Goddard, John. Md. Private. ———. 50 acres.
Godfrey, Ann. Conn. Sufferer. Fairfield. 3.18.0.
Godfrey, Anthony. N.C. Corporal. 22 Apr. 1785. 1000 acres to hiers.
Godfrey, Anthony. N.C. Private. 18 Jun. 1785. 274 acres.
Godfrey, Clement. N.C. Private. 27 Jun. 1788. 274 acres.
Godfrey, Francis. Va.-Ind. Private. 108 acres.
Godfrey, Francis. N.C. Private. 29 Nov. 1810. 640 acres to heirs.
Godfrey, Nathan. Conn. Sufferer. Fairfield. 309.12.2.
Godfry, William. N.C. Private. 29 Sep. 1784. 274 acres.
Godin, Peter. Va. Private. 31 Dec. 1851. 100 acres.
Godin, Peter. Va. Private. 2 Apr. 1856. 100 acres.
Godman, William. Va. Captain. 26 Mar. 1811. 4000 acres.
Godreau, Gabriel. N. Y. ———. ———. 500 acres.
Godsby, Carey. Ga. Refugee. 26 May 1784. 287 1/2 acres.
Godwin, Abraham. N. Y. Fife Major. 8 Jul. 1790. 600 acres.
Godwin, Henry. N. Y. Captain. 6 Jul. 1790. 1800 acres.
Godwin, John. N.C. Sergeant. 9 Dec. 1796. 1000 acres.
Godwin, Joseph. Va. Lieutenant. 13 Feb. 1838. 4000 acres.
Godwin, William. N. Y. Private. 8 Jul. 1790. 600 acres.
Goff, Abel. Mass. Fifer. 6 Jul. 1832. 200 acres.
Goff, Abraham. Va. Private. 2 Jan. 1810. 100 acres.
Goff, Adam. Va. Sergeant. 29 Dec. 1784. 200 acres.
Goff, Adam. Va. Sergeant. 23 Jan. 1810. 200 acres.
Goff, Charles. Md. Private. ———. 50 acres.
Goff, Philip. Va. Musician. 30 Jul. 1783. 200 acres.
Goff, Philip. Va. Musician. 22 Feb. 1861. 200 acres.
Goff, Samuel. Va. Private. 27 May 1783. 200 acres.
Goff, Thomas. N.C. Private. 5 Sep. 1821. 640 acres.
Goff, William. Me. ———. 12 Apr. 1835. 200 acres to widow Anna Tucker. Sumner.
Goff, Zacheriah. Va. Private. 2 Jan. 1810. 100 acres.
Goffigan, Laban. Va. Lieutenant. 31 Dec. 1851. 2666 2/3 acres.
Goffigan, Laban. Va. Lieutenant. 31 Dec. 1851. 1333 1/3 acres.
Goffigan, Peter. Va. Pilot. 22 May 1832. 1333 1/3 acres.
Goffigan, Peter. Va. Pilot. 22 May 1832. 1333 1/3 acres.
Goggin, John. Va. Lieutenant. 24 Mar. 1834. 2666 2/3 acres.
Goggin, John. Va. Lieutenant. 29 Dec. 1851. 727 acres.
Gogum, John. N.C. Private. 9 Feb. 1796. 640 acres to heirs.
Gold, Abel. Conn. Sufferer. Fairfield. 113.16.9.
Gold, Abel, Jr. Conn. Sufferer. Fairfield. 3.17.6.

Gold, David. N.C. Private. 30 Sep. 1785. 640 acres to heirs.
Gold, Elizabeth. Conn. Sufferer. Fairfield. 246.16.0.
Gold, James. Va. Private. 1 Jun. 1785. 100 acres.
Gold, John. Pa. Private. 28 Mar. 1789. 200 acres.
Gold, Joseph. Conn. Sufferer. Fairfield. 17.0.0 to his heirs.
Gold, Levi. Pa. Dragoon. ———. 200 acres.
Gold, Michael. Va. Private. 17 Nov. 1783. 233 1/3 acres.
Golden, Jesse. Va. Private. 10 May 1785. 100 acres.
Golden, Palmer. Ga. Refugee. 21 Apr. 1784. 250 acres.
Golden, Peter. Ga. Refugee. 21 Apr. 1785. 250 acres.
Golden, William. Ga. Refugee. 21 Apr. 1784. 250 acres.
Golding, John. Ga. ———. 17 May 1784. ———.
Golding, William. Pa. Drummer. ———. 200 acres.
Goldman, Daniel. Va. Private. 18 Apr. 1783. 200 acres.
Goldsborough, Charles. Md. Private. ———. 50 acres.
Goldsborough, Henry. Md. Private. ———. 50 acres.
Goldsborough, Jonathan. Ga. ———. 15 Mar. 1784. 250 acres.
Goldsborough, Mark. Md. ————. ———. 50 acres.
Goldsborough, William. Md. Lieutenant. ———. 200 acres.
Goldsburry, William. N.C. ———. 18 Jun. 1785. 640 acres.
Goldsby, Edward Thomas. Va. Private. 9 Jul. 1813. 100 acres.
Goldsmith, Jesse. N.C. Private. 23 Nov. 1790. 640 acres to heirs.
Goldsmith, Sarah. Conn. Sufferer. New/East Haven. 53.1.0.
Goldwin, William. Ga. ———. 5 Dec. 1785. 287 1/2 acres.
Goldwire, James. Ga. Refugee. 17 May 1784. —— acres to heirs.
Gole, Stephen. N.C. Private. 7 Jan. 1786. 640 acres to heirs.
Golson, John. Ga. ———. 17 May 1784. ———.
Golson, William. Va. Sergeant. 20 May 1784. 400 acres.
Gonter, John. Pa. Private. 5 Jul. 1805. 200 acres.
Good, John. N.C. Private. 15 Feb. 1797. 228 acres.
Goodale, Benjamin. N. Y. Private. 8 Jul. 1790. 600 acres.
Goodale, Nathan. Mass. Fifer. 1 Feb. 1833. 200 acres to heirs.
Goodale, Zacheriah. Me. ———. 17 Jul. 1835. 200 acres to widow Mary Goodale. Wells.
Goodall, James. N. Y. Private. 8 Jul. 1790. 600 acres.
Goodall, John. Va. Sergeant. 28 Jun. 1783. 200 acres.
Goodall, Pleasant. Ga. Refugee. 17 May 1784. ———.
Goodcourage, John. N. Y. Private. 7 Jul. 1790. 600 acres.
Goode, Edmund. Va. Private. 19 Dec. 1807. 100 acres.
Gooden, Christopher. N.C. Captain. 19 May 1784. 3840 acres to heir.
Goodenow, Ephraim. Mass. ———. 22 Jul. 1833. 200 acres.
Goodfaith, Mary. Conn. Sufferer. New London. 15.0.0.
Goodin, Benjamin. Va. Private. 5 Apr. 1791. 200 acres.
Gooding, William. N.C. Private. 30 Sep. 1785. 640 acres to heirs.
Goodman, Samuel. N.C. Corporal. 18 Nov. 1820. 357 acres.
Goodman, Samuel. N.C. Corporal. 26 Sep. 1821. 357 acres.
Goodman, Thomas. Va. Private. 8 Nov. 1791. 200 acres.
Goodman, William. N.C. Captain. 10 Nov. 1783. 3840 acres to Jacob Goodman, heir.
Goodman, William. N.C. ———. 29 Apr. 1784. 640 acres to Chole Goodman, heiress.
Goodnass, Richard. N.C. Private. 12 Sep. 1785. 640 acres to heirs.
Goodrich, John. Va. Captain. 12 Jan. 1810. 500 acres.
Goodrich, John. Va. Captain. 12 Jan. 1810. 500 acres.
Goodrich, John. Va. Captain. 12 Jan. 1810. 500 acres.

Goodrich, John. Va. Captain. 12 Jan. 1810. 500 acres.
Goodrich, John. Va. Captain. 12 Jan. 1810. 500 acres.
Goodrich, John. Va. Captain. 12 Jan. 1810. 500 acres.
Goodrich, John. Va. Captain. 12 Jan. 1810. 500 acres.
Goodrich, John. Va. Captain. 12 Jan. 1810. 500 acres.
Goodrich, John. Conn. Sufferer. New/East Haven. 140.17.4.
Goodridge, Daniel. Mass. ———. 28 Feb. 1832. 200 acres.
Goodrum, John. Va. Private. 21 Dec. 1831. 100 acres.
Goodrum, Thomas. N.C. Private. 10 Dec. 1788. 640 acres to heirs.
Goodrum, Thomas. Va. Corporal. 21 Nov. 1783. 200 acres.
Goodsell, Daniel. Conn. Sufferer. New/East Haven. 12.6.0.
Goodsell, John. Conn. Sufferer. New/East Haven. 8.13.0.
Goodson, Enos. N.C. Private. 28 Sep. 1785. 640 acres.
Goodson, James. N.C. Private. 23 Apr. 1785. 640 acres to heirs.
Goodson, William. Ga. ———. 17 May 1784. ———.
Goodson, William. N.C. Private. 5 Dec. 1796. 640 acres.
Goodwin, Amos. Va. Private. 19 Mar. 1834. 200 acres.
Goodwin, Dinwiddie. Va. Sublatern. 17 Nov. 1784. 2666 2/3 acres.
Goodwin, George. N. Y. Private. 8 Jul. 1790. 600 acres.
Goodwin, James. Md. Private. ———. 50 acres.
Goodwin, John. S.C. Captain. 15 Oct. 1784. 300 acres.
Goodwin, Joseph. N.Y. ———. 18 Mar. 1791. 500 acres to heirs.
Goodwin, Peter. N.C. Private. 22 Apr. 1785. 640 acres.
Goodwin, Samuel. Conn. Sufferer. New/ East Haven. 14.1.0.
Goodwin, Tobias. N.C. Private. 30 Nov. 1785. 640 acres to heirs.
Goodwin, Uriah. S.C. Captain. 16 Jul. 1784. 300 acres.
Goodwin, William. Va.-Ind. Private. 108 acres.
Goodwin, William. N.C. Private. 30 Sep. 1785. 640 acres to heirs.
Goody, Lambert. Md. Private. ———. 50 acres.
Goolsby, Isaiah. Ga. ———. 22 Jul. 1784. 287 1/2 acres.
Gooseley, George. Va. Captain. 21 Mar. 1831. 1333 1/3 acres.
Gooseley, George. Va. Captain. 21 Mar. 1831. 1333 1/3 acres.
Gooseley, George. Va. Captain. 21 Mar. 1831. 1333 1/3 acres.
Gooseley, George. Va. Captain. 6 Apr. 1831. 1333 1/3 acres.
Goostry, Rubin. Md. Private. ———. 50 acres.
Goran, Henry. Va. Private. 23 Aug. 1784. 200 acres.
Gordon, Albin. Va. Sergeant. 15 Feb. 1783. 200 acres.
Gordon, Alexander. Ga. ———. 17 May 1784. ———.
Gordon, Ambrose. Ga. ———. 17 May 1784. ———.
Gordon, Ambrose. Va. Lieutenant. 21 Jan. 1784. 2666 2/3 acres.
Gordon, Archibald. Va. Private. 24 Oct. 1822. 200 acres.
Gordon, Arthur. Va. Lieutenant. 10 Mar. 1784. 2666 2/3 acres.
Gordon, Benjamin. Ga. ———. 17 May 1784. ———.
Gordon, Benjamin. Me. ———. 12 May 1835. 200 acres. Waldo.
Gordon, Caleb. Me. ———. 6 Apr. 1835. 200 acres to widow Miriam Gordon. Augusta.
Gordon, Chapman. Ga. ———. 17 May 1784. ———.
Gordon, Charles. Ga. Colonel. 17 May 1784. ———.
Gordon, Churchill. Va. Midshipman. 23 Jul. 1835. 2666 2/3 acres.
Gordon, Cornelius. Ga. ———. ———. 287 1/2 acres.
Gordon, George. Ga. ———. 17 May 1784. ———.
Gordon, Haston. N.C. Private. 7 Jan. 1786. 640 acres to heirs.
Gordon, Jesse. Ga. Minute Man. 22 Jul. 1784. 287 1/2 acres.
Gordon, John. Md. Private. ———. 50 acres.

Gordon, John. Md. Private. ———. 50 acres.
Gordon, John. Md. Private. ———. 50 acres.
Gordon, John. Pa. Private. 23 Apr. 1787. 200 acres to John McCrary, assignee.
Gordon, John. Va. Private. 17 Jul. 1786. 100 acres.
Gordon, John. Conn. Sufferer. New London. 1.16.3.
Gordon, Joseph. Me. ———. 9 Feb. 1839. 200 acres. Belfast.
Gordon, Joseph. Md. Private. ———. 50 acres.
Gordon, Nathaniel. S.C. Soldier. 21 Jan. 1785. 200 acres.
Gordon, Nathaniel. S.C. ———. 2 Oct. 1786. 200 acres.
Gordon, Peter. Pa. Private. 4 Aug. 1787. 200 acres.
Gordon, Robert. Pa. Private. 20 Sep. 1787. 200 acres.
Gordon, Ruth. Conn. Sufferer. New/East Haven. 7.10.0.
Gordon, Thomas. Ga. ———. 17 May 1784. ———.
Gordon, Thomas. Va. Private. 21 Jun. 1810. 100 acres.
Gordon, Thomas. Va. Lieutenant. 16 Aug. 1836. 2000 acres.
Gordon, Thomas. Va. Lieutenant. 16 Aug. 1836. 666 2/3 acres.
Gordon, Thomas. Va. Lieutenant. 30 Mar. 1839. 500 acres.
Gordon, Thomas. Va. Lieutenant. 16 Jun. 1840. 500 acres.
Gordon, Thomas. Va. Lieutenant. 16 Jun. 1840. 500 acres.
Gordon, Thomas. Va. Lieutenant. 16 Jun. 1840. 500 acres.
Gordon, William. Me. Corporal. 1 Aug. 1835. 200 acres to widow Bethiah Chamberlain. Minot.
Gordon, William. Pa. ———. 9 Dec. 1803. 200 acres to Catherine Blake, widow.
Gore, Jacob. Va. Sergeant. 6 Apr. 1786. 400 acres.
Gore, James. S.C. ———. 4 Jul. 1785. 200 acres.
Gore, Jonathan. N.C. Private. 3 Dec. 1796. 274 acres.
Gore, Thomas. Ga. Minute Man. 16 Nov. 1784. 287 1/2 acres.
Gorges, Job. N.C. Private. 17 Feb. 1824. 274 acres.
Gorget, John Francis. S.C. ———. 21 Jan. 1785. 300 acres to Ephraim Mitchell, administrator.
Gorham, Daniel. Conn. Sufferer. Fairfield. 20.2.0.
Gorham, Hezekiah. Conn. Sufferer. New/East Haven. 21.5.7.
Gorham, John. Ga. Refugee. 26 May 1784. 287 1/2 acres.
Gorham, Joseph. Mass. Private. 18 Oct. 1833. 200 acres.
Gorham, Joseph. N. Y. Corporal. 9 Jul. 1790. 600 acres.
Gorham, Samuel. Conn. Sufferer. New/East Haven. 9.8.3.
Gorham, Shubael. Conn. Sufferer. Fairfield. 4.15.0.
Gorham, Stephen. Conn. Sufferer. New/East Haven. 27.14.11.
Gorham, Timothy. Conn. Sufferer. New/East Haven. 10.19.6.
Gorley, Ayres. Ga. ———. 17 May 1784. ———.
Gorman, John. Md. Private. ———. 50 acres.
Gorman, Richard. N.Y. ———. 13 Sep. 1790. 500 acres to heirs.
Gortner, Michael. Pa. Private. 12 Jun. 1787. 200 acres.
Gosham, John. Ga. ———. 26 May 1784. 287 1/2 acres.
Goslin, Ambrose. N.C. Private. 9 Dec. 1805. 640 acres to heirs.
Goslin, John. Pa. Private. 6 Jul. 1805. 200 acres to William Teagarden, assignee.
Gosline, Clement. N. Y. Captain. ———. 1000 acres.
Gosline, Lewis. N. Y. Ensign. ———. 1000 acres.
Gossage, Thomas. Md. Private. ———. 50 acres.
Gosset, John. Va. Private. 23 Jun. 1783. 200 acres.
Gossett, Jacob. Ga. ———. 12 Jun. 1784. 287 1/2 acres.
Gossling, George. S.C. ———. 3 Jul. 1786. 200 acres.
Gostnill, George. Pa. ———. 21 Oct. 1786. 250 acres to Eleanor Gostnill, widow.
Gothrop, John. N.C. Private. 9 Nov. 1784. 640 acres.

Gott, Collier. N.C. Private. 24 Nov. 1796. 274 acres to heirs.
Gotter, Martin. Conn. Sufferer. New/East Haven. 19.6.7 to heirs.
Gouch, John. N.C. Private. 11 Feb. 1796. 640 acres.
Gouch, William. N.C. Private. 19 May 1784. 640 acres.
Gouge, John. N.C. Private. 20 Apr. 1784. 640 acres.
Gough, William. N.C. Noncommissioned Officer. Aug. 1787. 1000 acres.
Gould, David. Va. Surgeon. 19 Mar. 1834. 2000 acres.
Gould, David. Va. Surgeon. 19 Mar. 1834. 2000 acres.
Gould, David. Va. Surgeon. 28 Aug. 1835. 2000 acres.
Gould, David. Va. Surgeon. 15 Jan. 1839. 4000 acres.
Gould, David. Va. Surgeon. 15 Jan. 1839. 333 1/3 acres.
Gould, David. Va. Surgeon. 28 Nov. 1839. 166 2/3 acres.
Gould, David. Va. Surgeon. 28 Nov. 1839. 166 2/3 acres.
Gould, David. Va. Surgeon. 28 Nov. 1839. 166 2/3 acres.
Gould, David. Va. Surgeon. 28 Nov. 1839. 166 2/3 acres.
Gould, David. Va. Surgeon. 28 May 1840. 1000 acres.
Gould, James. Md. Lieutenant. ———. 200 acres.
Gould, Jemima. Conn. Sufferer. Fairfield. 6.2.0.
Gould, John. Pa. Private. 28 Dec. 1786. 200 acres.
Gould, William. Md. Private. ———. 50 acres.
Goulden, Reuben. S.C. ———. 3 Mar. 1788. 200 acres.
Goulding, Jesse. Va. Private. 23 Oct. 1783. 100 acres.
Gove, John. Me. Fifer. 2 Jan. 1836. 200 acres to widow Lois Gove. Limington.
Goven, John. N.C. Corporal. 14 Sep. 1820. 1000 acres.
Gowan, Francis. Pa. Private. 22 Nov. 1787. 200 acres to Joseph Johnston, assignee.
Gowan, Hugh. Pa. Sergeant. 4 Oct. 1786. 250 acres.
Gowden, William. Va. Private. 22 Mar. 1784. 100 acres.
Gower, John. Pa. Corporal. 25 Oct. 1786. 200 acres.
Gower, Russell. N.C. Private. 9 Feb. 1796. 228 acres.
Gowin, David. N.C. Sergeant. 30 Sep. 1785. 1000 acres to heirs.
Gowin, Sherod. Va. Private. 17 Nov. 1783. 100 acres.
Gowing, Raverly. Va. Private. 26 Mar. 1808. 100 acres.
Gowran, Bryan. Va. Private. 23 Jun. 1783. 200 acres.
Grace, Aaron. Pa. Dragoon. 13 Nov. 1786. 200 acres to George Wescott, administrator.
Grace, George. Pa. Private. 11 Oct. 1786. 200 acres.
Grace, James. N.C. Private. 9 Sep. 1785. 640 acres to heirs.
Grace, Jesse. Md. Drummer. ———. 50 acres.
Grace, John. Pa. Private. 30 Nov. 1786. 200 acres.
Grace, Richard. Md. Lieutenant. ———. 200 acres.
Gracer, James. N. Y. Private. 3 Jul. 1790. 600 acres.
Grady, Jonathan. Va. Private. 22 Dec. 1785. 100 acres.
Grady, Jonathan. Va. Sergeant. 28 Nov. 1834. 200 acres.
Grady, Ruebin. N.C. Private. 10 Jan. 1794. 640 acres to heirs.
Grafton, John. Va. Private. 4 Aug. 1783. 100 acres.
Gragg, Thomas. Ga. Refugee. 7 Apr. 1784. ———.
Graham, Arthur. Va. Sergeant. 16 Apr. 1783. 400 acres.
Graham, Arthur. Va. Private. 9 Dec. 1783. 100 acres.
Graham, Charles. N. Y. Captain. 6 Jul. 1790. 1800 acres.
Graham, James. Ga. ———. 6 Jun. 1785. 287 1/2 acres.
Graham, John. Md. Fifer. ———. 50 acres.
Graham, John. N. Y. Major. 9 Jul. 1790. 2400 acres.
Graham, John. Pa. Private. ———. 200 acres.
Graham, Martin. N.C. Private. 15 Feb. 1797. 274 acres.
Graham, Moses. N.Y. ———. 13 Sep. 1790. 500 acres to heirs.

Graham, Peter. N.C. Private. 17 Dec. 1785. 640 acres to heirs.
Graham, Philip. Md. Private. ———. 50 acres.
Graham, Stephen. Va. Surgeon's Mate. 7 Oct. 1833. 4000 acres.
Graham, Walter. Va. Captain Lieutenant. 15 May 1783. 4000 acres.
Graham, William. Ga. Private. 19 Jul. 1784. 287 1/2 acres.
Graham, William. Va. Private. 3 Jun. 1831. 100 acres.
Graham, Williamson. Va. Private. 23 Feb. 1784. 100 acres.
Grahame, Moses. Md. Private. ———. 50 acres.
Grainger, Caleb. N.C. Captain. 29 Apr. 1814. 1097 acres to heirs.
Gramsell, Harry. Va. Private. 8 Sep. 1813. 100 acres.
Gramsell, John. Va. Private. 8 Sep. 1813. 100 acres.
Granberry, John. N.C. Lieutenant. 22 Oct. 1783. 792 acres.
Grandall, John. N.C. Private. 10 Aug. 1785. 640 acres to heirs.
Grandison, Simeon. Mass. Private. 12 Oct. 1835. 200 acres.
Granger, John. N. Y. Private. 8 Jul. 1790. 600 acres.
Granger, William. Va. Private. 26 Apr. 1783. 200 acres.
Grant, Andrew. Ga. ———. 6 Feb. 1784. 250 acres.
Grant, Daniel. Va. Private. 9 Jul. 1783. 100 acres.
Grant, Daniel. Va. Gunner's Mate. 4 Nov. 1783. 100 acres.
Grant, Daniel. Va. Gunner's Mate. 8 Mar. 1854. 641 2/3 acres.
Grant, Daniel. Va. Gunner's Mate. 8 Mar. 1854. 80 5/24 acres.
Grant, Daniel. Va. Gunner's Mate. 8 Mar. 1854. 1283 1/3 acres.
Grant, Daniel. Va. Gunner's Mate. 1 Aug. 1854. 561 acres.
Grant, Daniel. Va. Gunner's Mate. 21 Aug. 1854. 1283 1/3 acres.
Grant, David. N.C. Private. 5 Sep. 1792. 274 acres.
Grant, Elijah. N.C. Private. 4 Jan. 1819. 640 acres.
Grant, Elisha. Me. ———. 5 Nov. 1835. 200 acres to widow Lydia Hilton. Wiscasset.
Grant, Elisha. N.C. Private. 13 Sep. 1784. 640 acres.
Grant, Ephraim. N.C. Private. 20 Jan. 1785. 640 acres to heirs.
Grant, Gilbert. N.C. Private. 30 Sep. 1785. 640 acres to heirs.
Grant, Joel. N.C. Private. 30 Sep. 1785. 640 acres to heirs.
Grant, John. Ga. Captain. 25 May 1784. 575 acres.
Grant, John. N.C. Private. 20 Jan. 1785. 640 acres to heir.
Grant, John. Va. Private. 20 Oct. 1783. 100 acres.
Grant, Lewis. N.C. Private. 26 Aug. 1785. 640 acres to heirs.
Grant, Peter. Ga. Refugee. 6 Feb. 1784. 500 acres.
Grant, Thomas. Pa. ———. 14 Feb. 1809. 500 acres.
Grant, Thomas. Va. Midshipman. 9 Aug. 1834. 2000 acres.
Grant, Thomas. Va. Midshipman. 9 Aug. 1834. 666 2/3 acres.
Grant, William. Ga. ———. 1784. 250 acres.
Grant, William. Md. Private. ———. 50 acres.
Grant, William. N.C. Private. 2 Sep. 1820. 640 acres,
Grant, William. Va. Private. 12 Sep. 1783. 100 acres.
Grantson, George. N.C. Private. 30 Sep. 1785. 640 acres to heirs.
Grass, Frederick. Va. Private. 6 Nov. 1787. 100 acres.
Grass, Frederick. Va. Private. 28 Jan. 1833. 100 acres.
Gratton, John. Va. Lieutenant. 4 Aug. 1783. 2666 2/3 acres.
Grave, David. N.C. Private. 18 Dec. 1797. 640 acres.
Graves, Asa. Mass. Sergeant Major. 18 Jul. 1832. 200 acres to heirs.
Graves, Ebenezer. Mass. Private. 20 May 1836. 200 acres.
Graves, Francis. N.C. Lieutenant. 29 Nov. 1783. 2560 acres.
Graves, Francis. Va. Private. 5 Feb. 1784. 100 acres.
Graves, Isaac. Md. Private. ———. 50 acres.

Graves, James. Ga. Refugee. 17 May 1784. ———.
Graves, Jeremiah. Va. Private. 30 Dec. 1784. 100 acres.
Graves, John. Ga. ———. 17 May 1784. ———.
Graves, John. Va. Private. 28 May 1784. 200 acres.
Graves, John. Va. Major. 6 Oct. 1810. 5333 1/3 acres.
Graves, Joseph. N.C. Private. 12 Sep. 1785. 640 acres to heirs.
Graves, Joshua. N.C. Private. 30 Sep. 1785. 640 acres to heirs.
Graves, Moses. Md. Private. ———. 50 acres.
Graves, Ralph. Va. Cornet. 5 Jan. 1830. 2666 2/3 acres.
Graves, Richard. Ga. ———. 25 May 1784. 250 acres.
Graves, Robert, Jr. Ga. ———. 17 May 1784. ———.
Graves, Robert, Sr. Ga. ———. 14 Sep. 1784. 287 1/2 acres.
Graves, Thomas. Ga. ———. 25 May 1784. 250 acres.
Graves, William. Ga. ———. 17 May 1784. ———.
Graves, William. Va. Cornet. 8 Feb. 1783. 2666 2/3 acres.
Graves, William. Va. Private. 9 May 1783. 100 acres.
Graves, William. Va. Artificer. 21 Feb. 1784. 100 acres.
Graves, William. Va. Artificer. 12 Jan. 1842. 100 acres.
Graves, William. Va. Private. 1 Oct. 1784. 200 acres.
Graves, William. Va. Lieutenant. 31 Dec. 1851. 1333 1/3 acres.
Graves, William. Va. Lieutenant. 31 Dec. 1851. 1333 1/3 acres.
Graves, William. Va. Lieutenant. 31 Dec. 1851. 1333 1/3 acres.
Graves, William. Va. Brigade Quartermaster. 29 Dec. 1851. 5333 1/3 acres.
Gravett, Obadiah. Ga. Private. 3 Oct. 1785. ———.
Gravey, James. Md. Private. ———. 50 acres.
Gray, Alexander. Pa. Private. 23 Nov. 1786. 200 acres.
Gray, Alexander. Pa. Private. 1 Aug. 1787. 200 acres.
Gray, Andrew. N.C. Private. 19 Jan. 1786. 640 acres.
Gray, Archibald. N.C. Sergeant. 23 Apr. 1784. 1000 acres.
Gray, Benjamin. Md. Sergeant. ———. 50 acres.
Gray, Benjamin. N.Y. ———. 13 Sep. 1790. 500 acres to heirs.
Gray, Benjamin. Va. Private. 20 Jun. 1783. 100 acres.
Gray, Daniel. Va. Private. 6 Nov. 1783. 200 acres.
Gray, Daniel. Va. Private. 27 Mar./28 Dec. 1840. 100 acres.
Gray, David. Va. Sergeant. 9 Dec. 1783. 200 acres.
Gray, Dennis. Ga. ———. 5 Sep. 1785. ———.
Gray, Francis. Va. Lieutenant. 27 Oct. 1783. 2666 2/3 acres.
Gray, Francis. Va. Private. 29 Aug. 1807. 100 acres.
Gray, George. Va.-Ind. Private. 108 acres.
Gray, George. N.C. Private. 8 Mar. 1785. 228 acres.
Gray, George. N.C. Captain. 13 Jun. 1785. 3840 acres to heirs.
Gray, George. N.C. Private. 22 May 1820. 228 acres.
Gray, George. Va. Captain. 31 Mar. 1783. 4000 acres.
Gray, George. Va. Private. 19 Dec. 1783. 100 acres.
Gray, Harvey. Md. Private. ———. 50 acres.
Gray, Henry. N.C. Corporal. 30 Sep. 1785. 1000 acres to heirs.
Gray, Henry. N.C. Sergeant. 13 Jan. 1792. 1000 acres.
Gray, Jacob. Ga. ———. 1784. 250 acres.
Gray, Jacob. Md. Sergeant. ———. 50 acres.
Gray, James. Ga. Minute Man. 30 Sep. 1784. ———.
Gray, James. Md. Private. ———. 50 acres.
Gray, James. N.C. Sergeant. 21 Oct. 1783. 429 acres.
Gray, James. Va. Sergeant. 11 Sep. 1783. 400 acres.
Gray, James. Va. Captain. 25 Feb. 1784. 4000 acres.
Gray, James. Va. Lieutenant. 28 Mar. 1834. 4677 acres.

Gray, James. Va. Lieutenant. 30 Jun. 1841. 266 4/9 acres.
Gray, James. Va. Lieutenant. 30 Jun. 1841. 133 2/9 acres.
Gray, James. Va. Captain. 4 Mar. 1850. 1673 2/3 acres.
Gray, James Woolford. Md. Captain. ———. 200 acres.
Gray, John. Ga. ———. 5 Sep. 1785. ———.
Gray, John. N.C. Captain. 12 Dec. 1785. 3840 acres to heirs Joseph Gray and James Gray.
Gray, John. Va. Private. 29 May 1784. 200 acres.
Gray, Joseph. N.C. Private. 8 Mar. 1785. 228 acres.
Gray, Joseph. N.C. Private. 22 May 1820. 640 acres to heirs.
Gray, Joseph. Va. Private. 12 Aug. 1834. 200 acres.
Gray, Mary. Conn. Sufferer. Ridgefield. 1.6.8.
Gray, Matthias. Ga. ———. 15 Mar. 1784. 250 acres.
Gray, Nathan. Pa. Private. 19 Sep. 1787. 200 acres.
Gray, Peter. N.C. Private. 30 Sep. 1785. 640 acres to heirs.
Gray, Peter. S.C. Captain. 21 Jan. 1785. 300 acres.
Gray, Richard. Ga. Soldier. 2 Jan. 1786. ———.
Gray, Richard. Md. Private. ———. 50 acres.
Gray, Robert. Ga. ———. 13 Sep. 1784. 287 1/2 acres.
Gray, Robert. Va. Private. 5 Mar. 1784. 100 acres.
Gray, Samuel. Md. Private. ———. 50 acres.
Gray, Samuel. N.C. Private. 28 May 1784. 640 acres.
Gray, Silas. N. Y. Captain. 6 Jul. 1790. 1800 acres.
Gray, Silas. N.C. Private. 28 May 1784. 640 acres.
Gray, Solomon. Conn. Sufferer. Fairfield. 1.3.6.
Gray, Thomas. Ga. ———. 17 May 1784. ———.
Gray, Thomas. Md. Private. ———. 50 acres.
Gray, Thomas. N. Y. Corporal. 8 Jul. 1790. 600 acres.
Gray, Thomas. Va. Private. 15 Jun. 1807. 100 acres.
Gray, Vincent [or Wilson]. Md. Private. ———. 50 acres.
Gray, William. Ga. ———. 5 Sep. 1785. 575 acres.
Gray, William. Mass. Private. 15 Jan. 1833. 200 acres to heirs.
Gray, William. N.C. Private. 3 Mar. 1784. 274 acres.
Gray, William. N.C. Private. 28 May 1784. 640 acres.
Gray, William. Pa. Sergeant. 8 Dec. 1794. 250 acres to Philip Kissler, assignee.
Gray, William. Pa. Captain. 25 Feb. 1943. 500 acres.
Gray, William. Va. Private. 31 Mar. 1783. 2666 2/3 acres.
Gray, Wilson. Va. Private. 27 May 1783. 100 acres.
Graybill, Henry. Ga. ———. 17 May 1784. ———.
Grayham, John. N.C. Private. 18 May 1784. 640 acres.
Grayham, William. Mass. Corporal. 1 May 1832. 200 acres.
Grayson, John. S.C. Lieutenant. 2 May 1785. 200 acres.
Grayson, William. Va. Colonel. 23 Jun. 1783. 6666 2/3 acres.
Grayson, William. Va. Colonel. 12 Sep. 1809. 926 acres.
Gready, Thomas. N. Y. Private. 8 Jul. 1790. 600 acres.
Grear, Charles. Va. Surgeon. 9 Dec. 1830. 6000 acres.
Grear, John. Pa. ———. 19 Mar. 1808. 200 acres.
Greasel, Elam. Ga. ———. 17 May 1784. ———.
Greasel, George. Ga. Soldier. 17 May 1784. ———.
Greathouse, Jacob. Ga. ———. 30 Jul. 1784. 287 1/2 acres.
Greathouse, William. Va.-Ind. Private. 108 acres.
Green, Abraham. N.C. Private. 30 Sep. 1785. 640 acres to heirs.
Green, Amos. Md. Private. ———. 50 acres.
Green, Benjamin. Ga. Refugee. 6 Feb. 1784. 500 acres.

Green, Berryman. Va. Captain. 18 Oct. 1808. 4000 acres.
Green, Charles. Va. Private. 14 Jun. 1820. 100 acres.
Green, Charles. Conn. Sufferer. Greenwich. 197.12.4.
Green, Clement. Va. Private. 26 May 1798. 100 acres.
Green, Cleophas. Mass. Private. 21 Feb. 1835. 200 acres.
Green, Dempsey. N.C. Private. 30 Sep. 1785. 640 acres to heirs.
Green, Frederick. Ga. ———. 17 May 1784. ———.
Green, Gabriel. Va. Lieutenant. 30 Oct. 1783. 2666 2/3 acres.
Green, Henry. Ga. Private. 22 Mar. 1785. 250 acres.
Green, Henry. Md. Private. ———. 50 acres.
Green, Isaac. Ga. ———. 15 Mar. 1784. 287 1/2 acres.
Green, Isaac. Md. Private. ———. 50 acres.
Green, James. Ga. Private. 10 Dec. 1784. 250 acres.
Green, James. Ga. ———. 15 Mar. 1784. 250 acres.
Green, James. Pa. Private. ———. 200 acres.
Green, James. Va. Seaman. 9 Apr. 1835. 100 acres.
Green, James. Va. Midshipman. 25 Apr. 1837. 1834 acres.
Green, James. Va. Midshipman. 25 Apr. 1837. 166 acres.
Green, James. Va. Midshipman. 16 Mar. 1847. 166 acres.
Green, James West. N.C. Surgeon. 22 Jan. 1784. 4800 acres.
Green, Jesse. Va. Private. 31 May 1783. 100 acres.
Green, Jesse. Va. Private. 22 Apr. 1861. 100 acres.
Green, John. Ga. Soldier. 4 Feb. 1785. 287 1/2.
Green, John. Ga. Private. 10 Dec. 1784. 250 acres.
Green, John. Ga. ———. 24 Feb. 1784. 250 acres.
Green, John. Va.-Ind. Private. 108 acres.
Green, John. Me. ———. 15 Sep. 1835. 200 acres to widow Elizabeth Green. Scarborough.
Green, John. Md. Private. ———. 50 acres.
Green, John. Md. Private. ———. 50 acres.
Green, John. N. Y. Private. 8 Jul. 1790. 600 acres.
Green, John. N.C. Private. 27 Nov. 1819. 640 acres to heirs.
Green, John. Pa. Private. 18 Oct. 1786. 200 acres.
Green, John. Pa. Corporal. 12 Oct. 1787. 200 acres to Stephen Loudon, assignee.
Green, John. Va. Colonel. Dec. 1782. 7777 2/3 acres.
Green, John. Va. Lieutenant. Dec. 1782. 2666 2/3 acres.
Green, John. Va. Private. 20 Jun. 1783. 100 acres.
Green, John. Va. Private. 20 Aug. 1783. 200 acres.
Green, John. Va. Sergeant. 20 Dec. 1794. 400 acres.
Green, John. Va. Colonel. 1 Jun. 1805. 1111 acres.
Green, John. Va. Colonel. 11 Sep. 1807. 185 acres.
Green, John. Va. Lieutenant. 19 Jan. 1855. 570 acres.
Green, John G. N.C. Private. 17 Dec. 1796. 228 acres.
Green, Jonathan. Me. Private. 14 May 1835. 200 acres to widow Rebecca Green. Jackson.
Green, Joseph. Md. Private. ———. 50 acres.
Green, Joseph. N.C. Captain. 13 Jan. 1823. 1645 acres to heirs.
Green, Joshua. Ga. Soldier. 4 Feb. 1785. ———.
Green, Josiah. N.C. Private. 5 Sep. 1821. 640 acres.
Green, Lydia. Conn. Sufferer. New London. 12.16.0.
Green, McKeen. Ga. Refugee. 29 Jan. 1784. 250 acres.
Green, Moses. Va. Private. 31 Jul. 1784. 100 acres.
Green, Nathan. Mass. Sergeant. 20 May 1836. 200 acres.
Green, Peter. N. Y. Private. 8 Jul. 1790. 600 acres.
Green, Robert. Va. Lieutenant. 12 Apr. 1783. 2666 2/3 acres.

Green, Robert. Va. Private. 9 Jul. 1813. 100 acres.
Green, Robert. Va. Lieutenant. 25 Oct. 1822. 888 8/9 acres.
Green, Samuel. Md. Private. ———. 50 acres.
Green, Samuel. N. Y. Drummer. 6 Jul. 1790. 600 acres.
Green, Samuel. N.C. Private. 30 Sep. 1785. 640 acres to heirs.
Green, Samuel. N.C. Private. 4 Mar. 1792. 228 acres.
Green, Samuel. Conn. Sufferer. New/East Haven. 54.4.6.
Green, Samuel B. Va. Ensign. 24 Sep. 1784. 2666 2/3 acres.
Green, Sulivan. Ga. ———. 6 Feb. 1784. 250 acres.
Green, Thomas. Ga. ———. 25 Feb. 1784. 250 acres.
Green, Thomas. Va. Private. 16 Jun. 1784. 100 acres.
Green, Thomas, Jr. Ga. ———. 17 May 1784. ———.
Green, Timothy. Mass. Private. 27 Dec. 1831. 200 acres to heirs.
Green, Timothy. N. Y. Private. 7 Jul. 1790. 600 acres.
Green, Vernon. Ga. ———. 17 May 1784. ———.
Green, William. Ga. ———. 17 May 1784. ———.
Green, William. N.C. Private. 31 Jan. 1784. 640 acres.
Green, William. Va. Private. 1 Aug. 1782. 200 acres.
Green, William. Va. Private. 25 Nov. 1783. 100 acres.
Green, William. Va. Gunner. 18 Apr. 1788. 1400 acres.
Green, William. Va. ———. 16 Apr. 1835. 1400 acres.
Green, William. Va. Gunner. 18 Apr. 1788. 1266 2/3 acres.
Green, William. Va. ———. 16 Apr. 1835. 1266 2/3 acres.
Green, William. Va. Captain. 24 Jul. 1824. 5333 1/3 acres.
Green, William G. N.C. Lieutenant. 21 Jul. 1821. 2560 acres to heirs.
Green, William, Sr Ga. ———. 25 May 1784. 287 1/2 acres.
Greenage, William. Md. Private. ———. 50 acres.
Greenawalt, Abraham. Pa. ———. 14 Jan. 1807. 200 acres.
Greene, Nathaniel. N.C. Major General. 13 Apr. 1782. 25,000 acres.
Greene, Randall. N.C. Private. 1 Sep. 1785. 640 acres to heirs.
Greene, Solomon. Md. Private. ———. 50 acres.
Greene, Thomas. N.C. Private. 23 Apr. 1785. 640 acres to heirs.
Greenland, James. Pa. Private. 8 Sep. 1789. 200 acres.
Greenleaf, Enoch. Me. Private. 12 Jun. 1835. 200 acres. Westport.
Greenslate, Mary. Conn. Sufferer. Danbury. 9.12.0.
Greenway, George. Va. Lieutenant. 27 Jun. 1813. 1000 acres.
Greenway, George. Va. Lieutenant. 27 Jun. 1813. 1000 acres.
Greenway, George. Va. Lieutenant. 27 Jun. 1813. 666 2/3 acres.
Greenway, George. Va. Lieutenant. 23 Feb. 1861. 410 acres.
Greenway, John. N.C. Private. 7 Jan. 1786. 640 acres to heirs.
Greenwood, James. Md. Drummer. ———. 50 acres.
Greer, Charles. Va. Surgeon. 29 May 1783. 2000 acres.
Greer, Charles. Va. Surgeon. 29 May 1783. 1000 acres.
Greer, Charles. Va. Surgeon. 29 May 1783. 1000 acres.
Greer, Charles. Va. Surgeon. 29 May 1783. 2000 acres.
Greer, Henry. Pa. Lieutenant. 27 Oct. 1786. 200 acres.
Greer, Henry. Pa. Lieutenant. 17 Oct. 1786. 200 acres to Griffith Evans, assignee.
Greer, James. Pa. Major. ———. 300 acres.
Greer, James. Pa. Major. ———. 300 acres.
Greer, John. Pa. Private. 17 Apr. 1787. 200 acres to Stephen Loudon.
Greer, Robert. N.C. Lieutenant. 20 Sep. 1784. 1005 acres.
Greer, Smart. Md. Private. ———. 50 acres.
Greerson, John. Ga. 17 Jul. 1784. 287 1/2 acres.
Greeson, John. Ga. ———. 28 Feb. 1784. 250 acres.

Gregg, David. N. Y. Corporal. 8 Jul. 1790. 500 acres.
Gregg, James. N. Y. Captain. 3 Jul. 1790. 1800 acres.
Gregg, John. Conn. Sufferer. Greenwich. 213.8.7.
Gregle, Charles. N.C. Private. 9 Dec. 1797. 640 acres.
Gregory, Abraham. Conn. Sufferer. Norwalk. 50.9.8.
Gregory, Charles. Va. Sergeant. 1 Sep. 1783. 200 acres.
Gregory, Daniel. Conn. Sufferer. Norwalk. 18.18.8.
Gregory, Ebenezer. Conn. Sufferer. Norwalk. 57.2.9.
Gregory, Elnathan. Conn. Sufferer. Danbury. 31.6.1 1/4.
Gregory, Hannah. Conn. Sufferer. Norwalk. 13.3.4.
Gregory, Henry. Ga. ———. 17 May 1784. ———.
Gregory, Hosea. N.C. Private. 22 Feb. 1784. 274 acres.
Gregory, Isaac. N.C. Private. 7 Dec. 1783. 640 acres.
Gregory, Isaac. N.C. Private. 29 Sep. 1784. 640 acres.
Gregory, James. N.C. Private. 29 Oct. 1821. 640 acres to heirs.
Gregory, John. Md. Private. ———. 50 acres.
Gregory, John. Pa. Sergeant. ———. 250 acres.
Gregory, John. Va. Lieutenant. 21 Jul. 1792. 2666 2/3 acres.
Gregory, John. Va. Captain. 30 Jan. 1834. 4000 acres.
Gregory, John. Va. Captain. 9 Dec. 1833. 4000 acres.
Gregory, John. Va. Lieutenant. 26 Feb. 1834. 555 2/3 acres.
Gregory, John. Conn. Sufferer. Danbury. 4.0.1.
Gregory, John, Jr. Conn. Sufferer. Norwalk. 221.11.0.
Gregory, Joseph. Conn. Sufferer. Danbury. 8.8.10.
Gregory, Matthew. Conn. Sufferer. Danbury. 12.7.9 1/2.
Gregory, Naphthalim. Va. Private. 15 Dec. 1808. 100 acres.
Gregory, Nathaniel. Conn. Sufferer. Danbury. 18.17.3 1/2.
Gregory, Obediah. Va. Sergeant. 11 Feb. 1784. 200 acres.
Gregory, Rachel. Conn. Sufferer. Danbury. 4.7.7.
Gregory, Robert. N.C. Private. 23 Feb. 1820. 640 acres to heirs.
Gregory, Samuel. Conn. Sufferer. Danbury. 61.15.10.
Gregory, Spillsby. Va. Sergeant. Aug. 1834. 400 acres.
Gregory, Thomas. N.C. Private. 24 Aug. 1819. 640 acres.
Gregory, William. N.C. Sergeant. 26 Sep. 1821. 414 acres.
Gregory, William. Pa. Private. 5 Feb. 1806. 200 acres to heirs.
Gregory, William. Va. Captain. 29 Sep. 1833. 1333 1/3 acres.
Gregory, William. Va. Private. 29 Jul. 1783. 100 acres.
Gregory, William. Va. Private. 1 Sep. 1783. 100 acres.
Gregory, William. Va. Captain. 4 Mar. 1833. 1333 1/3 acres.
Gregory, William. Va. Captain. 26 Feb. 1834. 833 1/3 acres.
Gregory, William. Va. Captain. 24 Aug. 1836. 2000 acres.
Gregory, William. Va. Captain. 24 Aug. 1836. 2000 acres.
Gregory, William. Va. Captain. 7 May 1839. 574 acres.
Gregory, William. Va. Captain. 7 May 1839. 574 acres.
Gregory, William, Jr. Va. Lieutenant. 30 Mar. 1812. 2666 2/3 acres.
Gregory, Willis. N.C. Private. 27 Jun. 1788. 640 acres to heirs.
Grenard, Paul. Md. Private. ———. 50 acres.
Grenough, William. Conn. Sufferer. New/East Haven. 27.14.6.
Gresham, Archibald. Ga. ———. 17 May 1784. ———.
Gresham, John. Va. Private. 9 Jun. 1783. 100 acres.
Gresham, Oliver. N.C. Private. 22 Dec. 1796. 228 acres.
Gresham, Richard. Ga. ———. 17 May 1784. ———.
Grey, James. Ga. ———. ———. 287 1/2 acres.
Grey, Sabrit. Va. Private. 12 Jan. 1788. 100 acres.

Grey, William. Va. Private. 14 Oct. 1783. 100 acres.
Grice, Theophilus. N.C. Private. 31 Aug. 1795. 640 acres to heirs.
Gridler, James. Pa. ———. 20 Aug. 1807. 200 acres.
Gridley, Daniel. Pa. Private. 10 Sep. 1787. 200 acres.
Grier, Aaron. Ga. ———. 15 Sep. 1784. 287 1/2 acres.
Grier, Gilbert. Ga. ———. 17 May 1784. ———.
Grier, John. Ga. ———. 1 May 1786. 287 1/2 acres.
Grier, Robert. Ga. Lieutenant. 2 Feb. 1784. 400 acres.
Grier, Robert. Ga. ———. 17 May 1784. ———.
Grier, Thomas, Jr. Ga. ———. 20 Feb. 1784. 250 acres.
Grier, Thomas, Sr. Ga. ———. 17 Feb. 1784. 250 acres.
Grier, William. Ga. ———. 20 Feb. 1784. 250 acres.
Griffe, Hugh. Va. Private. 16 Dec. 1809. 100 acres.
Griffen, John. N.C. Private. 7 Dec. 1797. 640 acres to heirs.
Griffen, Joseph. N.C. Private. 10 Dec. 1788. 640 acres to heirs.
Griffen, Joshua. N. Y. Private. 8 Jul. 1790. 600 acres.
Griffin, Benjamin. Ga. ———. 5 Jun. 1787. 287 1/2 acres.
Griffin, Benjamin. N. Y. Private. 8 Jul. 1790. 500 acres.
Griffin, Corbin. Va. Surgeon. 17 Sep. 1850. 6000 acres.
Griffin, Daniel. N.C. Sergeant. 2 Dec. 1785. 1000 acres to heirs.
Griffin, Edmund. N.C. Sergeant. 2 Dec. 1785. 452 acres.
Griffin, Edward. N.C. Private. 12 Sep. 1785. 640 acres to heirs.
Griffin, Elizabeth. Conn. Sufferer. New London. 5.0.0.
Griffin, Ezekiel. N.C. Private. 5 Sep. 1821. 640 acres.
Griffin, Gideon. S.C. ———. 2 Oct. 1786. 200 acres.
Griffin, Isaac. N.C. Private. 30 Sep. 1785. 640 acres to heirs.
Griffin, Isaac. N.C. Private. 15 Feb. 1797. 274 acres.
Griffin, Jacob. N.C. Private. 1 Sep. 1785. 640 acres to heirs.
Griffin, James. N.C. Private. 13 Aug. 1784. 274 acres.
Griffin, James. Va. Private. 20 Jun. 1785. 200 acres.
Griffin, John. N.C. Private. 8 Mar. 1796. 640 acres to heirs.
Griffin, Joshua. N.C. Private. 30 Sep. 1785. 640 acres to heirs.
Griffin, Josiah. N.C. Private. 30 Sep. 1785. 640 acres.
Griffin, Lemon. N.C. Private. 29 Sep. 1785. 640 acres.
Griffin, Lewis, Sr. S.C. Soldier. 1 Aug. 1785. 150 acres to Lewis Griffin, his son.
Griffin, Mark. Md. Private. ———. 50 acres.
Griffin, Martin. N.C. Private. 2 Feb. 1786. 640 acres to heirs.
Griffin, Matthew. Ga. Citizen. 24 Dec. 1783. 250 acres.
Griffin, Michael. Ga. ———. 17 May 1784. ———.
Griffin, Morgan. S.C. ———. 6 Nov. 1786. 200 acres.
Griffin, Nathan. Md. Private. ———. 50 acres.
Griffin, Peter. Va. Private. 26 May 1784. 200 acres.
Griffin, Randolph. Ga. ———. 15 Mar. 1784. 250 acres.
Griffin, Reuben. Va. Private. 30 Jun. 1783. 100 acres.
Griffin, Robert. N.C. Private. 16 Aug. 1821. 640 acres.
Griffin, Robert. Va. Private. 4 Sep. 1783. 100 acres.
Griffin, Robert. Va. Sergeant. 19 Aug. 1841. 100 acres.
Griffin, Robert. Va. Sergeant. 30 Jun. 1856. 100 acres.
Griffin, Samuel. Ga. Minute Man. 22 Mar. 1785. 250 acres.
Griffin, Samuel. N.C. Private. 26 Aug. 1785. 640 acres to heirs.
Griffin, Samuel. Va. Colonel. 17 Sep. 1850. 4444 2/3 acres.
Griffin, Samuel. Va. Colonel. 17 Sep. 1850. 2222 acres.
Griffin, Thomas. Conn. Sufferer. Groton. 3.8.0.

Griffin, Thomas, Jr. Va. Private. 15 Dec. 1783. 100 acres.
Griffin, Thompson. Va. Private. 27 Nov. 1783. 100 acres.
Griffin, William. Md. Fifer. ———. 50 acres.
Griffin, William. N.C. Private. 4 Dec. 1783. 640 acres.
Griffin, William. Conn. Sufferer. Danbury. 3.14.8.
Griffis, Allen. N.C. Private. 17 Feb. 1824. 640 acres.
Griffis, John. N.C. Private. 15 Feb. 1797. 640 acres.
Griffis, Reuben. Va. Corporal. 14 May 1832. 200 acres.
Griffis, Samuel. N.C. Sergeant. 9 Sep. 1785. 1000 acres to heirs.
Griffith, Amos. Md. Private. ———. 50 acres.
Griffith, Benjamin. Pa. Lieutenant. 27 Jan. 1787. 200 acres to Mary Griffith, widow.
Griffith, Benjamin. Pa. Lieutenant. 27 Jan. 1787. 200 acres to Margaret Griffith, widow.
Griffith, David. Pa. Private. 17 Apr. 1799. 200 acres to Thomas Griffith, devisee.
Griffith, David. Va. Brigade Chaplain. 17 Apr. 1783. 6666 2/3 acres.
Griffith, David. Va. Surgeon. 19 Apr. 1783. 6000 acres.
Griffith, David. Va. Corporal. 11 Mar. 1788. 400 acres.
Griffith, Edward. N.C. Sergeant. 4 Sep. 1820. 1000 acres to heirs.
Griffith, Isaac. N.C. ———. 22 Nov. 1808. 428 acres.
Griffith, John. Me. ———. 19 Jun. 1844. 200 acres to widow Mary Griffith. Livermore.
Griffith, John. Pa. Private. 24 Oct. 1786. 200 acres.
Griffith, Joseph. Va. Private. 19 Jun. 1833. 100 acres.
Griffith, Levi. Pa. ———. ———. 200 acres.
Griffith, Levi. Pa. Private. ———. 200 acres.
Griffith, Levi. Pa. Private. 25 Feb. 1943. 200 acres.
Griffith, Michael. Va. Private. 8 Apr. 1784. 200 acres.
Griffith, Peter. Va. Private. 14 Feb. 1834. 100 acres.
Griffith, Philemon. Va. Captain. 3 Nov. 1831. 2000 acres.
Griffith, Philemon. Va. Captain. 3 Nov. 1831. 2000 acres.
Griffiths, David. Pa. Private. 23 Jan. 1787. 200 acres.
Griffiths, Henry. N.C. Private. 30 Sep. 1785. 640 acres to heirs.
Griffiths, Thomas. N. Y. Matross. 3 Jul. 1790. 600 acres.
Griffy, William. Pa. Private. 7 Mar. 1806. 200 acres. 7 Mar. 1806. Alias Guffy.
Grig, George. Va. Private. 27 Jun. 1783. 233 1/3 acres.
Grigg, Abner. Va. Private. 11 Sep. 1783. 100 acres.
Grigg, Lewis. Va. Private. 11 Sep. 1783. 100 acres.
Grigg, Matthew. Va. Private. 15 Apr. 1800. 100 acres.
Grigg, Thomas. Ga. ———. 15 Mar. 1784. 250 acres.
Grigg, Thomas. N. Y. Private. 8 Jul. 1790. 600 acres.
Griggs, Anne. Conn. Sufferer. Greenwich. 43.12.1.
Griggs, Charles. N.C. Private. 21 May 1784. 274 acres.
Griggs, Philip. Va. Private. 8 Jun. 1839. 100 acres.
Grigsby, Archibald. Ga. Minute Man. 16 Mar. 1785. ———.
Grigsby, James. Ga. ———. 17 May 1784. ———.
Grigsby, Moses. Va. Private. 30 Oct. 1784. 100 acres.
Grill, Thomas. N. Y. Private. 8 Jul. 1790. 600 acres.
Grimes, Andrew. N.C. Private. 30 Sep. 1785. 640 acres to heirs.
Grimes, Benjamin. N.C. Private. 27 Jul. 1785. 274 acres.
Grimes, James. Pa. Ranger. 2 Jul. 1787. 200 acres.
Grimes, John. Va.-Ind. Private. 108 acres.
Grimes, John. Pa. Private. 10 Sep. 1787. 200 acres.
Grimes, Simon. N.C. Private. 30 Sep. 1785. 640 acres.
Grimes, William. Md. Matross. ———. 50 acres.

Grimes, William. N.C. Private. 8 Nov. 1784. 640 acres to heir.
Grimes, William. Va. Captain. 24 Aug. 1797. 4000 acres.
Grimes, William. Va. Major. 30 Jan. 1810. 1333 1/3 acres.
Grimes, William. Va. Private. 29 Nov. 1833. 100 acres.
Grimison, Samuel. Pa. Private. 16 Oct. 1786. 200 acre.
Grimke, John Faucheraud. S.C. Lieutenant Colonel. 16 Jul. 1784. 450 acres.
Grimmage, John. N.C. Private. 26 May 1784. 640 acres.
Grimsey, Richard. Ga. Private. 10 Dec. 1784. 250 acres.
Grimsley, Adam. Ga. Private. ———. 250 acres.
Grimsley, Elijah. Ga. Sergeant. 24 May 1784. 345 acres.
Grimsley, James. Va. Private. 13 Oct. 1783. 100 acres.
Grimsley, John. Ga. ———. 17 May 1784. ———.
Grimsley, Joseph. Ga. Citizen. 22 Mar. 1785. 250 acres.
Grimsley, William. N. Y. Private. 8 Jul. 1790. 600 acres.
Grinage, John. N.C. Private. 13 Sep. 1820. 640 acres.
Grinder, John. N.C. Sergeant. 20 Sep. 1784. 1000 acres.
Griner, Philip. Ga. Refugee. 17 May 1784. 575 acres.
Grinnage, John. N.C. Private. 15 Sep. 1820. 640 acres to heirs.
Grinstead, James. Va. Private. 9 Jun. 1783. 100 acres.
Grinstead, James. Va. Private. 31 Jan. 1832. 100 acres.
Grinter, John. Va. Sergeant. 14 May 1784. 200 acres.
Grisham, Major. N.C. Private. 13 Jan. 1823. 640 acres.
Grisham, Major. S.C. ———. 7 Aug. 1786. 50 acres.
Grisham, Major. S.C. ———. 4 Sep. 1786. 50 acres.
Grisham, Major. S.C. ———. 2 Oct. 1786. 100 acres.
Grissel, Joel. Va. Sergeant. 5 Dec. 1783. 200 acres.
Grissell, John. Va. Private. 25 Aug. 1783. 100 acres.
Grissitt, Thomas. Va. Private. 9 Mar. 1784. 100 acres.
Grissom, Robert. N.C. Fifer. 14 Dec. 1796. 1000 acres to heirs.
Grisurt, Thomas. N.C. Private. 4 Aug. 1821. 640 acres.
Griswold, Matthew. Conn. Sufferer. New London. 10.0.0.
Griswold, Samuel. Conn. Sufferer. New/ East Haven. 21.11.0.
Grite, William. N. Y. Private. 8 Jul. 1790. 600 acres.
Gritman, James. Ga. ———. 17 May 1784. ———.
Grizzell, John. Ga. Minute Man. 22 Mar. 1785. 250 acres.
Grogan, Jacob. N.C. Private. 30 Sep. 1785. 274 acres.
Grogan, James. N.C. Private. 30 Sep. 1785. 640 acres.
Grogan, John. N. Y. Private. 8 Jul. 1790. 600 acres.
Grogan, John. N.C. Fifer. 29 Sep. 1785. 1000 acres.
Gromith, Jacob. Md. Lieutenant. ———. 200 acres.
Groom, Charles. Md. Matross. ———. 50 acres.
Grooms, Gilbert. S.C. Soldier. 21 Jan. 1785. 200 acres.
Grooms, Levi. Va. Lieutenant. 20 Jul. 1833. 2666 2/3 acres.
Grosh, Michael. Md. Private. ———. 50 acres.
Gross, Alexander. Pa. Private. 19 Feb. 1789. 200 acres.
Gross, John. N.Y. ———. 18 Mar. 1791. 500 acres to his heirs.
Gross, Peter. N. Y. Matross. 9 Jul. 1790. 600 acres.
Grote, William. N. Y. Private. 8 Jul. 1790. 600 acres.
Grout, Mathias. Pa. Private. 4 Aug. 1787. 200 acres to Joshua Russell, assignee.
Grouter, Jesse. S.C. Soldier. 21 Jan. 1785. 200 acres.
Grove, Anthony. Va. Private. 20 Jun. 1783. 100 acres.
Grover, Benjamin. Mass. Private. 2 Apr. 1830. 200 acres.
Groves, Solomon. N.C. Private. 12 Sep. 1785. 640 acres to heirs.
Groves, Thomas. Va. Drummer. 28 Jun. 1783. 200 acres.

Groves, William. Md. Private. ———. 50 acres.
Groves, William. N.C. Private. 9 Sep. 1785. 640 acres to heirs.
Groves, William. N.C. Captain. 5 Sep. 1821. 3840 acres.
Groves, William. S.C. ———. 7 May 1787. 200 acres.
Grubbs, Benjamin. Ga. ———. 20 Feb. 1784. 250 acres.
Grubbs, Demsey. Ga. Minute Man. 3 Sep. 1785. ———.
Grubbs, Francis. Ga. ———. 15 Mar. 1784. 250 acres.
Grubbs, Hensley. Va. Private. 31 Jan. 1784. 200 acres.
Grubbs, Thomas. Va. Private. 29 Dec. 1796. 100 acres.
Gruber, Philip, Sr. S.C. ———. 3 Jul. 1786. 144 acres.
Grummond, Samuel. Conn. Sufferer. Norwalk. 30.8.6.
Grummond, Thomas. Conn. Sufferer. Norwalk. 205.11.4.
Grundy, Obediah. N.C. Private. 17 Feb. 1824. 640 acres.
Grymes, Benjamin. Va. Captain. 26 Jan. 1803. 1000 acres.
Grymes, Benjamin. Va. Captain. 26 Jan. 1803. 1000 acres.
Grymes, Benjamin. Va. Captain. 26 Jan. 1830. 1000 acres.
Grymes, Benjamin. Va. Captain. 26 Jan. 1830. 1000 acres.
Grymes, George. Va. Sergeant. 19 Aug. 1783. 200 acres.
Grymes, William. Va. Corporal. 12 Jul. 1783. 200 acres.
Grymes, William. Va. Captain. 14 Dec. 1784. 4000 acres.
Guan, Peter. N.C. Private. 7 Dec. 1796. 640 acres.
Guard, John. N.C. Private. 9 Sep. 1820. 640 acres to heirs.
Gudgeon, William. Md. Private. ———. 50 acres.
Gue, John. Va. Private. 30 Dec. 1823. 100 acres.
Guest, Albion. Pa. Private. 20 Nov. 1788. 200 acres.
Guest, Henry. Pa. Private. ———. 200 acres.
Guffy, John. N.C. Private. 14 Dec. 1797. 640 acres to heirs.
Guilder, Daniel. Va. Private. 22 Aug. 1787. 100 acres.
Guillam, John. Pa. Matross. 31 Oct. 1786. 200 acres.
Guille, John. Va. Private. 24 Jun. 1783. 100 acres.
Guilliams, William. Va. Private. 13 Dec. 1783. 200 acres.
Guin, Andrew. Pa. Private. 9 Mar. 1795. 200 acres to John Nicholson, assignee.
Guin, David. N.C. Private. 15 Jul. 1785. 640 acres to heirs.
Guin, Samuel. N.C. Private. 2 Dec. 1785. 640 acres.
Guin, William. N.C. Private. 10 Dec. 1788. 274 acres.
Guinn, Daniel. N.C. Private. 30 Sep. 1785. 640 acres.
Guinn, Thomas. N.C. Private. 28 May 1784. 365 acres.
Guist, Thomas. N.C. Private. 30 Sep. 1785. 640 acres to heirs.
Guize, Philip. Ga. ———. 17 May 1784. ———.
Gulderslieve, Daniel. N.Y. Sergeant. 13 Sep. 1790. 500 acres to heirs.
Gulley, Richard. Va. Private. 22 May 1787. 100 acres.
Gum, Daniel. N.C. Private. 7 Dec. 1797. 640 acres to heirs.
Gumbs, Isaac. N.C. Private. 9 Dec. 1805. 640 acres to heirs.
Gunby, John. Md. Colonel. ———. 200 acres.
Guner, James. Va. Private. 5 Mar. 1785. 100 acres.
Gunn, Abraham. N.C. Private. 30 Sep. 1785. 640 acres to heirs.
Gunn, Alexander. N.C. Non Commissioned Officer. 29 Apr. 1784. 1000 acres.
Gunn, Hardy. N.C. Private. 30 Sep. 1785. 640 acres to heirs.
Gunn, James. N.C. Private. 16 Aug. 1821. 640 acres.
Gunn, James. Va. Captain. 17 Jul. 1793. 4666 2/3 acres.
Gunn, James. Va. Captain. 23 Sep. 1808. 777 acres.
Gunn, John. N.C. Drummer. 29 Apr. 1784. 1000 acres.
Gunn, Joseph. Conn. Sufferer. Danbury. 4.8.8.
Gunnel, John. Va. Private. 17 Dec. 1784. 200 acres.

Gunnell, Joseph. Va. Private. 28 Apr. 1783. 200 acres.
Gunnell, William. Va. Private. 20 Oct. 1784. 200 acres.
Gunnels, Daniel. Ga. ———. 17 May 1784. ———.
Gunnels, Joseph. Ga. ———. 15 Mar. 1784. 250 acres.
Gunnels, Nicholas. Ga. Minute Man. 22 Jul. 1784. 287 1/2 acres.
Gunter, Charles Va. Private. 16 Dec. 1783. 100 acres.
Gunter, Henry. S.C. Soldier. 2 May 1785. 200 acres.
Gunter, Henry. S.C. ———. 7 May 1786. 150 acres.
Gunter, Joel. N.C. Private. 12 Mar. 1785. 274 acres.
Gunter, Lazarus. Ga. ———. 17 May 1784.
Gunter, Samuel. N.C. Private. 13 Dec. 1796. 205 acres.
Gunyon, John. Va. Private. 30 Sep. 1812. 100 acres.
Gurganus, Jeremiah. N.C. Private. 28 Sep. 1785. 640 acres.
Gurley, Ayers. N.C. ———. 13 Jun. 1785. 640 acres to heirs.
Gurley, James. N.C. Corporal. 22 Apr. 1785. 1000 acres to heirs.
Gurley, Joseph. N.C. Private. 17 Mar. 1784. 640 acres.
Gurley, Simon. N.C. Private. 1 Sep. 1800. 640 acres to heirs.
Gurtley, William. N. Y. Matross. 7 Jul. 1790. 600 acres.
Guth, G. John. N. Y. Private. 8 Jul. 1790. 600 acres.
Guthery, George. Va. Lieutenant. 18 Oct. 1783. 2666 2/3 acres.
Guthery, George. Va. Lieutenant. 12 Nov. 1801. 444 1/3 acres.
Guthrey, John. Va. Private. 23 Jun. 1783. 200 acres.
Guthrie, Archibald. Pa. Private. 25 Apr. 1787. 200 acres to heirs.
Guthrie, James. Va. Sergeant. 31 May 1783. 200 acres.
Guthrie, John. Va. Fifer. 20 Feb. 1783. 100 acres.
Guthrie, John. Va. Private. 31 May 1783. 100 acres.
Guthrie, Lewis. Va. Private. 9 Jun. 1813. 100 acres.
Guthrie, Patience. Conn. Sufferer. Danbury. 3.19.8.
Guthrie, William. Va.-Ind. Private. 108 acres.
Guttery, Henry. N.C. Private. 9 Nov. 1784. 640 acres to heir.
Guttrick, Christian. N.Y. ———. 13 Sep. 1790. 500 acres to heirs.
Guttridge, Matthew. N.C. Private. 20 Dec. 1796. 228 acres.
Guttrige, Lewis. N.C. Private. 20 Dec. 1796. 640 acres to heirs.
Guy, John. Ga. Soldier. 5 Sep. 1785. ———.
Guy, Thomas. Ga. ———. 5 Dec. 1785. ———.
Guyon, Isaac. N. Y. Lieutenant. 7 Jul. 1790. 1200 acres.
Gwaltiney, John. Ga. ———. 20 Feb. 1784. 250 acres.
Gwin, James. N.C. Private. 22 Dec. 1796. 640 acres.
Gwin, John. Va. Drummer. 31 Dec. 1806. 100 acres.
Gwin, Thomas. Va. Private. 31 Dec. 1806. 100 acres.
Gwin, William. Va.-Ind. Private. 108 acres.
Gwin, Willis. Va. Private. 17 Jul. 1786. 200 acres.
Gwinn, Jacob. N.C. Private. 22 Apr. 1785. 640 acres to heirs.
Gwinn, Jacob. Va. Private. 27 Sep. 1788. 200 acres.
Gwynn, John. Md. Sergeant. ———. 50 acres.
Habbett, Anthony. N.C. Private. 30 Sep. 1785. 640 acres to heirs.
Habbit, Ezekiel. N.C. Drummer. 25 Aug. 1813. 1000 acres to heirs.
Habersham, John. Ga. Major. 5 Jan. 1784. 800 acres.
Habersham, Joseph. Ga. ———. 17 May 1784. ———.
Haburn, William. N. Y. Sergeant. 8 Jul. 1790. 600 acres.
Hackel, Frederick. S.C. ———. 4 Sep. 1786. 200 acres.
Hacker, John. Va.-Ind. Private. 108 acres.
Hacker, John. Va. Private. 16 Jul. 1784. 100 acres.
Hacket, Nicholas. Pa. Private. 6 Mar. 1787. 200 acres.
Hackett, James. Va. Private. 27 Jun. 1783. 200 acres.

Hackett, John. Md. Private. ———. 50 acres.
Hackett, John. Va. Private. 25 Jun. 1783. 233 1/3 acres.
Hackley, James. Va. Lieutenant. 30 Jul. 1835. 889 acres.
Hackley, James. Va. Lieutenant. 31 Jan. 1839. 888 acres.
Hackley, James. Va. Lieutenant. 12 Dec. 1844. 888 8/9 acres.
Hackley, John. Va. Lieutenant. 15 Apr. 1783. 2666 2/3 acres.
Hackley, John. Va. Lieutenant. 2 Oct. 1807. 444 2/3 acres.
Hackley, Michael. N.C. Private. 7 Dec. 1797. 640 acres to heirs.
Hackner, Daniel. N.C. Private. 7 Jan. 1786. 640 acres to heirs.
Hackney, William. N. Y. Matross. 9 Jul. 1790. 600 acres.
Hackney, William. Va. Private. 26 Jun. 1784. 100 acres.
Hacksaw, James. N.C. Private. 30 Sep. 1785. 640 acres to heirs.
Hackworth, William. Va. Corporal. 21 Sep. 1784. 200 acres.
Hackworth, William. Va. Corporal. 3 Jul. 1854. 200 acres.
Hadder, Nehemiah. Md. Private. ———. 50 acres.
Hadding, James. Ga. ———. 5 Aug. 1785. ———.
Hadding, William. Ga. ———. 20 Feb. 1784. 250 acres.
Haddock, Admerel. N.C. Private. 29 Sep. 1784. 228 acres.
Haddock, Andrew. N.C. Sergeant. 25 Nov. 1783. 429 acres.
Haddock, Andrew. N.C. Sergeant. 28 May 1784. 1000 acres.
Haddock, Solomon. N.C. Private. 5 Dec. 1796. 220 acres.
Haddock, William. N.C. Private. 17 Dec. 1785. 640 acres to heirs.
Haddow, Isaac. S.C. Soldier. 5 Jun. 1786. 200 acres to Sarah Haddow, widow.
Haden, George. Md. Corporal. ———. 50 acres.
Haden, John. Md. Private. 50 acres.
Hadley, Joshua. N.C. Captain. 21 Oct. 1783. 3840 acres.
Hadly, Isaac. Va. Private. 24 Apr. 1783. 200 acres.
Hadner, John. Va. Private. 1 Jul. 1783. 100 acres.
Hadnot, West. N.C. Sergeant. 24 Dec. 1785. 1000 acres.
Hadsock, Josiah. N.C. Private. 30 Sep. 1785. 640 acres to heirs.
Hadsock, Peter. N.C. Private. 19 Feb. 1784. 640 acres.
Hadson, Joel. N.C. Private. 30 Sep. 1785. 640 acres to heirs.
Hafford, Thomas. Ga. ———. ———. 250 acres.
Hafner, Jacob. N.C. Private. 6 Sep. 1821. 640 acres.
Hagan, Francis. Va. Private. 16 Jun. 1784. 100 acres.
Hagan, James. Md. Corporal. ———. 50 acres.
Hagan, James. S.C. ———. 2 Oct. 1786. 200 acres.
Hagan, Leonard. Md. Private. ———. 50 acres.
Hagan, Michael. Va. Private. 21 Jul. 1792. 200 acres.
Hagan, Raphael. Md. Private. ———. 50 acres.
Hagan, Walter. Md. Private. ———. 50 acres.
Hagans, Edward. Ga. ———. 15 Mar. 1784. 250 acres.
Hagans, James. Minute Man. Ga. 16 Sep. 1785. 250 acres.
Hagar, Abraham. Mass. Private. 18 Oct. 1833. 200 acres.
Hagard, Baker. Va. Private. 19 Mar. 1784. 200 acres.
Hagarthy, George. Md. Sergeant. ———. 50 acres.
Hagen, Barney. Va. Sergeant. 5 Apr. 1784. 400 acres.
Hagens, James. N.C. Private. 19 May 1784. 640 acres.
Hagerly, Nicholas. Va. Corporal. 23 Jun. 1783. 400 acres.
Hagerty, John. Va. Private. 7 Dec. 1785. 100 acres.
Hagerty, Patrick. Va. Sergeant. 11 Jul. 1783. 400 acres.
Haggerty, Dennis. Pa. Private. 2 Apr. 1787. 200 acres.
Haggerty, Enos. N.Y. ———. 13 Sep. 1790. 500 acres to heirs.
Hagin, John. Va. Private. 20 Nov. 1784. 100 acres.

Haging, Dennis. N.C. Private. 5 Dec. 1797. 365 acres.
Hague, Christain. Pa. Private. 9 Mar. 1795. 200 acres to John Nicholson, assignee.
Hagwood, James. N.C. Private. 23 Apr. 1785. 640 acres to heirs.
Hail, Bradley. Ga. ———. 17 May 1784. ———.
Hail, Edward. Ga. Minute Man. 13 Sep. 1784. 287 1/2 acres.
Hail, Edward. N.C. Private. 10 Aug. 1785. 640 acres to heirs.
Hail, Edward Gortney. Ga. ———. 17 May 1784. ———.
Hail, George. Ga. ———. 30 Sep. 1784. ———.
Hail, James. Ga. ———. 15 Mar. 1784. 250 acres.
Hail, Leonard. Va. Private. 30 Apr. 1783. 200 acres.
Hail, Samuel. N.C. Private. 2 Jan. 1810. 640 acres to heirs.
Hail, William. Ga. ———. 15 Mar. 1784. 250 acres.
Haild, Caleb. Va. Private. 26 Mar. 1784. 100 acres.
Hailey, Robert. N.C. Private. 30 Sep. 1785. 274 acres to heirs.
Hain, John. Pa. Ranger. 8 Dec. 1798. 200 acres.
Haines, Peter. Va. Private. 20 Jun. 1783. 100 acres.
Haines, Phillip. N.C. Private. 22 Arp. 1785. 640 acres.
Hainey, Michael. Va. Private. 23 Jun. 1783. 200 acres.
Hains, John. N. Y. Private. 8 Jul. 1790. 600 acres.
Hains, William. N.C. Private. 9 Apr. 1788. 640 acres.
Hair, David. N.C. Private. 2 Feb. 1786. 640 acres to heirs.
Hair, James. N.C. Private. 15 Jul. 1785. 640 acres to heir.
Hair, John. N.C. Private. 15 Jul. 1785. 640 acres to heir.
Hair, John. N.C. Private. 13 Dec. 1796. 640 acres.
Hair, Matthew. S.C. Soldier. 21 Jan. 1785. 200 acres.
Hair, Thomas. N.C. Private. 9 Feb. 1796. 640 acres to heirs.
Hair, William. N.C. Private. 15 Jul. 1785. 640 acres to heir.
Hait, Sarah. Conn. Sufferer. Greenwich. 3.18.0.
Halbert, William. Va. Private. 23 Feb. 1784. 233 1/3 acres.
Halcolm, William. N.C. ———. 13 Jun. 1785. 1000 acres to heirs.
Halcom, Phillip. N.C. Private. 28 Oct. 1783. 185 acres.
Halcomb, John. Va. Captain. 14 Jun. 1783. 4000 acres.
Haldrop, Thomas. Va. Private. 31 Jan. 1784. 100 acres.
Haldrop, Thomas. Va. Fifer. 31 Jan. 1784. 100 acres.
Hale, Betsey. Conn. Sufferer. Norwalk. 22.9.11.
Hale, Delany. N.C. Private. 19 Dec. 1808. 640 acres to heirs.
Hale, Israel. Me. ———. 22 Jul. 1835. 200 acres. Waterford.
Hale, Jackson. N.C. Private. 22 Dec. 1803. 640 acres to heirs.
Hale, John. Pa. Private. 26 Oct. 1786. 200 acres.
Hale, Mordecai. N. Y. Surgeon's Mate. 9 Jul. 1790. 1300 acres.
Hale, Thomas. S.C. Soldier. 2 May 1785. 200 acres.
Haley, Calib. Md. Private. ———. 50 acres.
Haley, Daniel. Va. Private. 31 Jan. 1784. 200 acres.
Haley, Daniel. Va. Private. 22 May 1784. 100 acres.
Haley, Daniel. Va. Private. 26 Jan. 1833. 200 acres.
Haley, George. Va. Private. 19 Apr. 1784. 200 acres.
Haley, John. Va. Private. 2 Dec. 1837. 133 1/3 acres.
Haley, Joseph. N.C. Private. 15 Dec. 1797. 640 acres to heirs.
Haley, Morris. Pa. ———. 22 Dec. 1786. 200 acres to Ralph Phillips, assignee.
Haley, Peter. Va. Private. 8 Dec. 1783. 100 acres.
Haley, Peter. Va. Sailor. 3 Aug. 1784. 100 acres.
Haley, Samuel. Va. ———. 12 Apr. 1834. 533 1/8 acres.
Haley, Samuel. Va. ———. 12 Apr. 1834. 533 1/8 acres.
Haley, Samuel. Va. ———. 30 Aug. 1834. 1066 acres.

Haley, Samuel. Va. ———. 27 Jul. 1836. 533 1/8 acres.
Haley, Thomas. Va. Private. 23 Jun. 1783. 200 acres.
Haley, William. Va. Private. 14 Aug. 1783. 200 acres.
Haley, William. Va. Private. 11 Nov. 1783. 233 1/3 acres.
Haley, William. Va. Private. 19 Apr. 1784. 100 acres.
Halfacer, Conrod. N.C. Private. 8 Dec. 1795. 640 acres to heirs.
Halfpenny, Isaac. Va. Private. 23 Jun. 1783. 200 acres.
Halfpenny, John. Va. Private. 20 Jun. 1783. 200 acres.
Halks, James. Va. Private. 10 Jan. 1786. 100 acres.
Hall, ———. S.C. ———. 4 Sep. 1786. 200 acres to Silvia Hall.
Hall, Aaron. Mass. Private. 18 Oct. 1833. 200 acres.
Hall, Abiah. Conn. Sufferer. New/East Haven. 3.19.9.
Hall, Benjamin. Ga. Private. 10 Dec. 1784. 250 acres.
Hall, Charles. Me. ———. 8 Sep. 1835. 200 acres. Standish.
Hall, Clement. N.C. Captain. 20 Apr. 1784. 3840 acres.
Hall, Daniel. Md. Private. ———. 50 acres.
Hall, David. N.C. Private. 21 Apr. 1784. 274 acres.
Hall, David. N.C. Sergeant. 7 Dec. 1796. 428 acres.
Hall, Edward. Ga. ———. 17 May 1784. ———.
Hall, Edward. Md. Captain. ———. 200 acres.
Hall, Edward. Va. Private. 25 Jan. 1812. 100 acres.
Hall, Ephraim. Va. Seaman. 7 Mar. 1834. 100 acres.
Hall, Futrell. N.C. Private. 9 Feb. 1796. 274 acres to heirs.
Hall, George. Ga. ———. 17 May 1784. ———.
Hall, George. Va. Sailor. 3 Jul. 1786. 100 acres.
Hall, Isaac. N.C. Private. 12 Dec. 1796. 274 acres.
Hall, James. Ga. Minute Man. 17 May 1784. ———.
Hall, James. N. Y. Private. 8 Jul. 1790. 500 acres.
Hall, James. N.C. Private. 30 Sep. 1785. 640 acres to heirs.
Hall, James. N.C. Captain. 16 Aug. 1821. 3840 acres.
Hall, Jesse. Ga. ———. 1784. 287 1/2 acres.
Hall, Job. Mass. Private. 1 Mar. 1833. 200 acres.
Hall, John. Me. ———. 3 Aug. 1835. 200 acres to widow Judith Shackley.
Hall, John. Md. Private. ———. 50 acres.
Hall, John. Md. Private. ———. 50 acres.
Hall, John. Md. Corporal. ———. 50 acres.
Hall, John. N. Y. Private. 8 Jul. 1790. 500 acres.
Hall, John. S.C. Adjutant & Quarter Master General. 7 Nov. 1785. 300 acres to Mary Ann Hall, widow and heir.
Hall, John. Va. Private. 9 Dec. 1782. 100 acres.
Hall, John. Va. Sergeant. 30 Jan. 1784. 533 1/3 acres.
Hall, John. Va. Corporal. 3 May 1784. 200 acres.
Hall, John. Va. Seaman. 7 Mar. 1834. 100 acres.
Hall, Joseph. Md. Private. ———. 50 acres.
Hall, Joseph. Pa. Drum Major. 8 Jun. 1785. 200 acres.
Hall, Josiah C. Md. Colonel. ———. 200 acres.
Hall, Levi. Me. ———. 9 Jun. 1835. 200 acres. Bangor.
Hall, Luther. Me. ———. 30 Apr. 1835. 200 acres to widow Elizabeth Hall. Brunswick.
Hall, Lyman. Ga. ———. 17 May 1784. ———.
Hall, Nathan. N.C. Drummer. 12 Mar. 1785. 1000 acres to heirs.
Hall, Oliver. Mass. Fifer. 30 Nov. 1832. 200 acres to heirs.
Hall, Reuben. S.C. ———. 2 Oct. 1786. 93 acres.
Hall, Reuben. S.C. ———. 2 Oct. 1786. 100 acres.
Hall, Richard. Md. Private. ———. 50 acres.
Hall, Robert. Va. Master. 28 Sep. 1787. 2666 2/3 acres.

Hall, Robert. Va. Master. 22 Feb. 1834. 2666 2/3 acres.
Hall, Thomas. Ga. Soldier. 5 May 1785. ———.
Hall, Thomas. N.C. Lieutenant. 28 May 1784. 640 acres to John Hall, heir.
Hall, Thomas. Va. Sergeant. 20 Jun. 1783. 200 acres.
Hall, William. Ga. ———. 17 May 1784. ———.
Hall, William. Va. Private. 23 Aug. 1782. 100 acres.
Hall, William. Va. Sergeant. 11 Feb. 1797. 200 acres.
Hall, William. Va. Private. 11 Jul. 1835. 100 acres.
Hallack, Jonathan. N.Y. ———. 13 Sep. 1790. 500 acres to heirs.
Hallam, Edward. Conn. Sufferer. New London. 10.16.0.
Hallam, Edward & George Hallam. Conn. Sufferers. New London. 215.0.0.
Hallam, Edward & John Hallam. Conn. Sufferers. New London. 310.9.8.
Hallam, John. Conn. Sufferers. New London. 417.10.0.
Hallam, John & Benjamin Harriss. Conn. Sufferers. New London. 300.0.0.
Hallcock, David. Conn. Sufferer. Greenwich. 0.15.0.
Hallen, William. Md. Bombadier. ———. 50 acres.
Halleron, James. Md. Private. ———. 50 acres.
Hallett, Jonah. N. Y. Lieutenant. 13 Sep. 1790. 1200 acres.
Hallett, Jonathan. N. Y. Captain. 7 Jul. 1790. 1800 acres.
Halley, Isham. S.C. ———. 4 Sep. 1786. 140 acres.
Halliman, Mark. Ga. ———. 250 acres. ———.
Halling, Solomon. N.C. Surgeon. 25 Mar. 1791. 2067 acres.
Halloby, Thomas. Va. Sergeant. 3 Apr. 1783. 400 acres.
Hallook, Joseph. N. Y. Matross. 9 Jul. 1790. 500 acres.
Hallowell, Samuel. N.C. Lieutenant. 16 Aug. 1821. 2560 acres.
Hallowell, William. Me. ———. 11 May 1835. 200 acres to widow Mary Hallowell. Windsor.
Hallum, Thomas. S.C. ———. 5 Mar. 1787. 200 acres.
Halsey, Abraham. N. Y. Private. 8 Jul. 1790. 600 acres.
Halsey, Thomas. N. Y. Corporal. 8 Jul. 1790. 600 acres.
Halstead, John. N. Y. ———. ———. 333 1/3 acres.
Halstead, Joseph. N. Y. Sergeant. 9 Jul. 1790. 600 acres.
Haltzapple, Zacheriah. N. Y. Private. 8 Jul. 1790. 600 acres.
Halwell, Luther. Ga. ———. 26 Feb. 1784. 500 acres.
Ham, John. Me. Private. 9 Jun. 1838. 200 acres. Monmouth.
Ham, John. N.C. Private. 22 Dec. 1796. 640 acres.
Ham, William. Ga. ———. 17 May 1784. ———.
Ham, William. Va. Seaman. 5 Aug. 1783. 100 acres.
Hambleton, Hanes. N.C. Surgeon. 26 Apr. 1784. 4800 acres to Thomas Hambleton.
Hambleton, James. Ga. Minute Man. 22 Mar. 1785. 250 acres.
Hambleton, James. N.C. Private. 30 Sep. 1785. 640 acres to heirs.
Hambleton, John. N.C. Private. 15 Jun. 1785. 640 acres to heirs.
Hamblett, Gideon. Va. Private. 22 Jul. 1834. 100 acres.
Hambrick, David. Va. Corporal. 24 Feb. 1784. 200 acres.
Hamilton, Cumberland. Pa. Private. 29 Jul. 1789. 200 acres.
Hamilton, Edward. Md. Lieutenant. ———. 200 acres.
Hamilton, George. Md. Captain. ———. 200 acres.
Hamilton, George. Md. Private. ———. 50 acres.
Hamilton, Henry. Pa. Private. 19 Jun. 1787. 200 acres.
Hamilton, James. Pa. Major. 9 Apr. 1796. 300 acres.
Hamilton, James. Pa. Major. 15 Jun. 1807. 300 acres.
Hamilton, James. Va. Lieutenant. 30 May 1783. 2666 2/3 acres.
Hamilton, James. Va. Lieutenant. 19 Sep. 1867. 814 22/27 acres.
Hamilton, James, Jr. S.C. Soldier. 16 Jul. 1784. 200 acres.

Hamilton, James, Sr. S.C. Soldier. 16 Jul. 1784. 200 acres.
Hamilton, Jeremiah. Ga. ———. 17 May 1784. ———.
Hamilton, John. Md. Lieutenant. ———. 200 acres.
Hamilton, John. Md. Private. ———. 50 acres.
Hamilton, John. Pa. Sergeant. 10 Aug. 1787. 250 acres.
Hamilton, John. S.C. Adjutant & Lieutenant. 21 Jan. 1785. 300 acres.
Hamilton, John. S.C. Soldier. 15 Oct. 1784. 200 acres.
Hamilton, John. Va. Private. 5 Apr. 1784. 100 acres.
Hamilton, John. Va. Lieutenant. 6 Jan. 1786. 2666 2/3 acres.
Hamilton, John. Va. Private. 16 Nov. 1791. 100 acres.
Hamilton, John. Va. Lieutenant. 19 Aug. 1832. 1333 1/3 acres.
Hamilton, John A. Md. Captain. ———. 200 acres.
Hamilton, Jonathan. Me. ———. 8 Aug. 1836. 200 acres. Sanford.
Hamilton, Mark. N.C. Private. 14 Dec. 1796. 640 acres.
Hamilton, Richard. Me. Soldier. 30 Jul. 1835. 200 acres to widow Mary Hamilton. Linneus.
Hamilton, Robert. Pa. ———. 26 Mar. 1813. 200 acres.
Hamilton, Robert. Va. Sergeant. 28 Aug. 1786. 400 acres.
Hamilton, Samuel. Md. Private. ———. 50 acres.
Hamilton, Thomas. Ga. Refugee. 17 Feb. 1784. 250 acres.
Hamilton, Thomas. Pa. Private. ———. 200 acres.
Hamilton, Thomas. Pa. Private. 4 Dec. 1806. 200 acres.
Hamilton, Thomas. Va. Captain. 4 Mar. 1788. 4000 acres.
Hamilton, William. Ga. ———. 24 May 1784. 287 1/2 acres.
Hamilton, William. Me. Private. 27 Oct. 1835. 200 acres. North Yarmouth.
Hamilton, William. Md. Drummer. ———. 50 acres.
Hamlett, William P. Va. Private. 19 Mar. 1832. 200 acres.
Hamlin, Africa. Me. ———. 21 Oct. 1835. 200 acres to widow Susanna Hamlin.
Hamlin, John. Va. Quartermaster Sergeant. 20 May 1808. 200 acres.
Hamlin, Richard. Ga. ———. 15 Mar. 1784. 250 acres.
Hamm, Rubin. N.C. Private. 26 Nov. 1796. 640 acres to heirs.
Hamm, William. N.C. Private. 1 Sep. 1785. 640 acres to heirs.
Hammenger, James. S.C. Soldier. 21 Jan. 1785. 200 acres.
Hammet, James. Va.-Ind. Private. 108 acres.
Hammett, James. Ga. ———. 17 May 1784. ———.
Hammett, John. N.C. Private. 30 Sep. 1785. 640 acres to heirs.
Hammett, Robert. Ga. ———. 17 May 1784. 287 1/2 acres.
Hammett, Sitha. Ga. ———. 17 May 1784. ———.
Hammett, William. Ga. ———. 15 Mar. 1784. 250 acres.
Hammock, Benedict. Ga. ———. 17 May 1785. ———.
Hammock, John. Ga. ———. 25 May 1784. 287 1/2 acres.
Hammock, Robert. Ga. ———. 17 May 1784. ———.
Hammock, Samuel. N.C. Private. 30 Sep. 1785. 640 acres to heirs.
Hammon, James. N.C. Private. 30 Sep. 1785. 640 acres to heirs.
Hammond, Abner. Ga. ———. 17 May 1784. ———.
Hammond, Abraham. Ga. ———. 17 May 1784. ———.
Hammond, Charles. Ga. Refugee. 17 May 1784. ———.
Hammond, David. Pa. Lieutenant. 4 Oct. 1786. 200 acres.
Hammond, David. Pa. Lieutenant. 4 Oct. 1786. 200 acres.
Hammond, Ed. Md. Private. ———. 50 acres.
Hammond, Edmund. N.C. Private. 23 Apr. 1785. 640 acres to heirs.
Hammond, George. Ga. Refugee. 17 May 1784. ———.
Hammond, Isaac. N.C. Private. 11 Jan. 1822. 640 acres.
Hammond, James. Md. Corporal. ———. 50 acres.

Hammond, John. Va. Private. 24 Feb. 1784. 100 acres.
Hammond, John B. N.C. Sergeant. 29 Apr. 1784. 640 acres.
Hammond, Lewis. N.C. Private. 7 Jan. 1786. 640 acres to heirs.
Hammond, Paulipus. Me. Private. 20 May 1835. 200 acres. Peru.
Hammond, Philip. Va. Private. 16 Feb. 1801. 100 acres.
Hammond, Thomas. Md. Private. ———. 50 acres.
Hammond, Thomas. Pa. Private. 11 Sep. 1789. 200 acres.
Hammond, William. Md. Private. ———. 50 acres.
Hammonds, Festor. N.C. Private. 30 Sep. 1785. 640 acres to heirs.
Hammonds, Ralph. N.C. Private. 30 Sep. 1785. 640 acres to heirs.
Hammons, Abraham. N.C. Private. 28 Sep. 1785. 640 acres.
Hammons, Isaac. N.C. Private. 21 Aug. 1820. 640 acres.
Hammons, Judah. N.C. Private. 18 Dec. 1801. 640 acres to heirs.
Hammons, Matthias. N.C. Private. 2 Dec. 1785. 640 acres.
Hammons, Willis. N.C. Private. 30 Sep. 1785. 640 acres to heirs.
Hammontree, John. Va. Sailor. 30 Jun. 1784. 100 acres.
Hamphill, Samuel. Ga. ———. 17 May 1784. ———.
Hamphill, William. Ga. ———. 17 May 1784. ———.
Hampton, Adam. N.C. Private. 9 Feb. 1796. 228 acres.
Hampton, George. N.C. Private. 30 Sep. 1785. 274 acres.
Hampton, John. Ga. Refugee. 15 Mar. 1784. 250 acres.
Hampton, John. Pa. ———. ———. 200 acres.
Hampton, John. Va. Private. 10 Dec. 1784. 200 acres.
Hampton, Thomas. Va. Private. 10 Oct. 1783. 100 acres.
Hampton, Wade. Ga. ———. 17 May 1784. ———.
Hampton, William. Va. Private. 1 Apr. 1783. 100 acres.
Hampton, Zacheriah. N.C. Private. 16 Aug. 1821. 640 acres to heirs.
Hamston, William. Md. Private. ———. 50 acres.
Hamtramck, F. John. N. Y. Captain. 6 Jul. 1790. 1800 acres.
Hamtramk, John F. N. Y. Captain. ———. 1000 acres.
Hance, Job. N.C. Private. 14 Dec. 1796. 640 acres to heirs.
Hancock, Ann. Conn. Sufferer. New London. 140.3.6.
Hancock, Bennett. Va. Private. 6 Feb. 1784. 200 acres.
Hancock, George. Ga. Captain. 13 Sep. 1783. 690 acres.
Hancock, Henry. N.C. Private. 6 Dec. 1797. 640 acres to heirs.
Hancock, Hiram. Pa. Sergeant. 6 Sep. 1787. 250 acres to Debora Hancock, widow.
Hancock, Isaac. N.C. Sergeant. 9 Nov. 1784. 1000 acres.
Hancock, John. Ga. ———. 17 May 1784. ———.
Hancock, John. Md. Private. ———. 50 acres.
Hancock, Nehemiah. N.C. Private. 2 Jun. 1813. 640 acres to heirs.
Hancock, Randal. N.C. Private. 15 Jul. 1785. 640 acres to heirs.
Hancock, Stephen. Md. Private. ———. 50 acres.
Hancock, Thomas. Pa. Matross. 18 Jan. 1787. 200 acres.
Hancock, Thomas. Conn. Sufferer. New London. 148.7.5.
Hancock, William. Ga. Soldier. 15 Apr. 1785. ———.
Hancock, William. Me. ———. 5 May 1835. 200 acres. Buxton.
Hancocke, Henry. Va. Private. 21 Nov. 1783. 100 acres.
Hand, Edward. Pa. Brigadier General. 13 Oct. 1786. 500 acres to Dorothy Brien 13 May 1846.
Hand, Edward. Pa. Brigadier General. 13 Oct. 1786. 500 acres.
Hand, Edward. Pa. Brigadier General. 12 Oct. 1786. 500 acres.
Handcock, Isaac. N.C. Sergeant. 20 Apr. 1784. 1000 acres.
Handford, David. Conn. Sufferer. Norwalk. 41.13.9 to his heirs.
Handley, George. Ga. Captain. 8 Sep. 1783. 600 acres.

Handley, John. S.C. Soldier. 21 Jan. 1785. 200 acres.
Handshaw, Thomas. Ga. Soldier. 24 Sep. 1785. 230 acres.
Handy, George. Md. Captain. ———. 200 acres.
Handy, George. Va. Captain. 4 Oct. 1808. 2666 2/3 acres.
Handy, George. Va. Captain. 4 Oct. 1808. 1333 1/3 acres.
Haney, Barney. Md. Private. ———. 50 acres.
Haney, Holland. Va. Lieutenant. 22 Mar. 1784. 2666 2/3 acres.
Haney, John. Md. Private. ———. 50 acres.
Haney, William. Md. ———. ———. 50 acres.
Hanford, Daniel. Conn. Sufferer. Norwalk. 303.16.4.
Hanford, Daniel. Conn. Sufferer. Norwalk. 20.0.0.
Hanford, Hannah. Conn. Sufferer. Norwalk. 60.3.1.
Hanford, Hezekiah. Conn. Sufferer. Norwalk. 268.13.8.
Hanford, Hezekiah. Conn. Sufferer. Norwalk. 59.10.0.
Hanford, Jedediah. Conn. Sufferer. Norwalk. 39.1.11.
Hanford, Phineas, Capt. Conn. Sufferer. Norwalk. 43.14.0.
Hanford, Phineas, Jr. Conn. Sufferer. Norwalk. 25.19.2.
Hankins, Joseph. Va. Private. 7 Apr. 1784. 100 acres.
Hankins, Thomas. Va. Private. 21 Sep. 1798. 200 acres.
Hanley, James. N. Y. Private. 6 Jul. 1790. 500 acres.
Hanley, James. N.C. Private. 9 Feb. 1796. 228 acres.
Hanley, John, Sr. Ga. ———. 17 May 1784. ———.
Hanly, Michael. Pa. Private. 18 May 1785. 200 acres.
Hanmer, Francis. N. Y. Lieutenant. 7 Jul. 1790. 1200 acres.
Hanmore, Moses. N. Y. Matross. 9 Jul. 1790. 500 acres.
Hanna, John. Va. Private. 24 Feb. 1813. 100 acres.
Hannah, Archibald. Pa. Private. 14 Nov. 1786. 200 acres.
Hannah, John. Pa. Sergeant. 1 Jun. 1787. 250 acres.
Hannah, Robert. Va. Private. 11 Nov. 1783. 100 acres.
Hannah, Thomas. Ga. Refugee. 13 Sep. 1784. 575 acres.
Hannah, William. S.C.. Soldier. 21 Jan. 1785. 200 acres.
Hannam, John. Va. Private. 31 Jul. 1784. 100 acres.
Hannan, John. Md. Private. ———. 50 acres.
Hanners, Henry. N.C. Private. 23 Feb. 1820. 640 acres to heirs.
Hanners, Joseph. N.C. Private. 17 Dec. 1785. 640 acres to heirs.
Hannon, William. Pa. Ranger. 28 Jul. 1787. 200 acres.
Hannus, Henry. N.C. Private. 21 May 1784. 274 acres.
Hans, William. Me. Private. 16 Nov. 1836. 200 acres to widow Thankful Hans. Portland.
Hanscom, Nathaniel. Me. Private. 18 Jun. 1835. 200 acres to widow Lucy Hanscom.
Hanscomb, Gideon. Me. ———. 3 Aug. 1835. 200 acres to widow Mehitable Hanscomb.
Hanscomb, Reuben. Me. Marine. 17 Oct. 1835. 200 acres to widow Alice Hanscom. North Berwick.
Hansel, Charles. N.C. Private. 30 Sep. 1785. 640 acres to heirs.
Hansen, Nicholas. N.Y. ———. 13 Sep. 1790. 500 acres to heirs.
Hansford, Cary. Va. Surgeon's Mate. 4 Dec. 1837. 4000 acres.
Hansford, William. Va. Private. 23 Jun. 1783. 200 acres.
Hanson, Christian. Conn. Sufferer. New/East Haven. 21.5.6.
Hanson, Dirck. N. Y. Captain. 17 Aug. 1790. 1800 acres.
Hanson, Isaac. Md. Lieutenant. ———. 200 acres.
Hanson, John. Va. Private. 24 Aug. 1786. 100 acres.
Hanson, Samuel. Ga. ———. 17 May 1784. ———.
Hanson, Samuel. Md. Lieutenant. ———. 200 acres.
Hanson, Thomas. Va. Private. 13 May 1784. 100 acres.

Hanson, William. Md. Lieutenant. ———. 200 acres.
Hanton, Patrick. Pa. Private. 11 Sep. 1789. 200 acres.
Happer, Moses. Va. Private. 16 Feb. 1784. 100 acres.
Harcum, Lot. Va. Midshipman. 2 Jan. 1788. 2666 2/3 acres.
Harcum, Lot. Va. Midshipman. 17 Oct. 1856. 2666 2/3 acres.
Harcum, Rodham. Va. Midshipman. 10 Dec. 1783. 2666 2/3 acres.
Hardaway, Joseph. Va. Private. 20 May 1783. 200 acres.
Hardcastle, Timothy. N.C. Private. 24 Nov. 1796. 640 acres to heirs.
Harden, John. N.C. Private. 22 Oct. 1783. 228 acres.
Hardenbergh, Abraham. N. Y. Lieutenant. 7 Jul. 1790. 1200 acres.
Hardenburgh, L. John. N. Y. Lieutenant. 7 Jul. 1790. 1200 acres.
Hardenson, Samuel. N.C. Private. 30 Sep. 1785. 640 acres to heirs.
Hardgroves, James. N.C. Private. 7 Jan. 1786. 640 acres to heirs.
Hardick, Richard. N.C. Private. 19 May 1784. 640 acres.
Hardiman, John. Va. Sergeant. 19 Jul. 1808. 400 acres.
Hardin, Enos. Va. Private. 2 Jun. 1783. 100 acres.
Hardin, Francis. Va.-Ind. Private. 108 acres.
Harding, Abraham. N.C. Private. 21 Jul. 1821. 640 acres to heirs.
Harding, Frederick. Conn. Sufferer. New/ East Haven. 12.4.0.
Harding, Joshua. Mass. Sergeant. 19 Nov. 1833. 200 acres.
Harding, Oliver. N. Y. Matross. 9 Jul. 1790. 500 acres.
Harding, Robert. Ga. ———. 2 Jan. 1786. ———.
Harding, Robert. Md. Private. ———. 50 acres.
Harding, William. Ga. ———. 2 Jan. 1786. ———.
Hardison, Hardy. N.C. Private. 8 Dec. 1796. 640 acres to heirs.
Hardisty, Obadiah. Pa. Private. 30 Jan. 1805. 200 acres.
Hardman, Henry. Md. Major. ———. 200 acres.
Hardman, John. Md. Lieutenant. ———. 200 acres.
Hardon, Robert. N.C. Private. 1 Dec. 1789. 182 acres.
Hardy, Benjamin. N. Y. Matross. 9 Jul. 1790. 600 acres.
Hardy, Elias. Md. Private. ———. 50 acres.
Hardy, Ephraim. Ga. Soldier. 20 Aug. 1785. ———.
Hardy, Isaac. N.C. Lieutenant. 10 Dec. 1817. 1097 acres to heirs.
Hardy, James. Ga. Soldier. 5 Aug. 1785. ———.
Hardy, John. Ga. Captain of a galley. 27 Jan. 1784. 600 acres.
Hardy, John. Ga. Soldier. 5 Aug. 1785. ———.
Hardy, John. N.C. Private. 26 Aug. 1785. 640 acres to heirs.
Hardy, John. N.C. Sergeant. 8 Aug. 1821. 360 acres.
Hardy, John. Va. Private. 12 Mar. 1785. 100 acres.
Hardy, John. Va. Private. 14 Jun. 1784. 200 acres.
Hardy, Joseph. N.C. Private. 17 Feb. 1824. 640 acres.
Hardy, Nehemiah. N.C. Private. 18 Dec. 1797. 640 acres.
Hardy, Rhodius. Va. Private. 2 May 1783. 200 acres.
Hardy, Robert. Ga. Soldier. 20 Aug. 1785. ———.
Hardy, Thomas. N.C. Private. 10 Aug. 1820. 228 acres to heir David Hardy.
Hardyman, John. Va. Lieutenant. Feb. 1783. 2666 2/3 acres.
Hardyman, John. Va. Lieutenant. 31 May 1854. 2666 2/3 acres.
Hardyman, John. Va. Sergeant. 15 May 1783. 200 acres.
Hardyman, John. Va. Captain. 6 Dec. 1852. 5333 1/3 acres.
Hare, James. Md. Private. ———. 50 acres.
Hare, John. Md. Private. ———. 50 acres.
Hare, John Laurance. N.C. Lieutenant. 22 Oct. 1783. 914 acres.
Hare, Michael. Pa. Ranger. ———. [200 acres].
Harebuck, Michael. Ga. ———. 15 Mar. 1784. 250 acres.

Harebuck, Nicholas. Ga. ———. 15 Mar. 1784. 250 acres.
Haregroves, William. N.C. Sergeant. 20 Oct. 1787. 1000 acres to heirs.
Harget, Frederick. N.C. Captain. 25 Oct. 1783. 1508 acres.
Hargis, Abraham. N.C. Private. 12 Feb. 1784. 228 acres.
Hargrove, Dempsey. N.C. Private. 6 Dec. 1797. 640 acres to heirs.
Hargrove, John. N.C. Private. 25 Nov. 1783. 274 acres.
Hargrove, William. N.C. Lieutenant. 25 Nov. 1783. 2560 acres.
Hargus, John. Va. Ensign. 23 Mar. 1812. 800 acres.
Hargus, John. Va. Ensign. 23 Mar. 1812. 800 acres.
Hargus, John. Va. Ensign. 23 Mar. 1812. 1066 2/3 acres.
Haring, Jacob. N. Y. Private. 8 Jul. 1790. 600 acres.
Harker, William, Jr. N.C. Private. 9 Feb. 1796. 640 acres to heirs.
Harker, William, Sr. N.C. Private. 9 Feb. 1796. 640 acres to heirs.
Harkins, Thomas. Ga. ———. 17 May 1784. ———.
Harksheimer, John. Va. Private. 22 May 1827. 100 acres.
Harlan, George. Va. Private. 6 Apr. 1787. 100 acres.
Harland, Silas. Va.-Ind. Private. 108 acres.
Harleston, Isaac. S.C. Major. 16 Jul. 1784. 400 acres.
Harley, Henry. Md. Private. ———. 50 acres.
Harley, James. Ga. Soldier. 20 Aug. 1785. ———.
Harley, William. N.C. Corporal. 6 Sep. 1821. 1000 acres.
Harling, Cornelius. Md. Matross. ———. 50 acres.
Harlow, Josiah. Me. Private. 21 Nov. 1835. 200 acres to widow Olive Harlow. Monroe.
Harman, Conrad. Pa. Private. 28 Sep. 1787. 200 acres.
Harman, Ezekiel. Va. Private 15 Jun. 1807. 100 acres.
Harman, George. Va. Private. 15 Jun. 1807. 200 acres.
Harman, John. Va. Private. 15 Jun. 1807. 100 acres.
Harman, Lazarus. Md. Private. ———. 50 acres.
Harman, Levin. Va. Private. 15 Jun. 1807. 100 acres.
Harman, Peter. N.C. Private. 9 Dec. 1797. 365 acres.
Harman, Stephen. Va. Private. 18 Apr. 1832. 100 acres.
Harman, Tire. Va. Private. 18 Apr. 1832. 100 acres.
Harman, Zorobabel. Va. Private. 30 Dec. 1808. 100 acres.
Harmer, Josiah. Pa. Lieutenant Colonel. 16 Nov. 1786. 500 acres.
Harmer, Josiah. Pa. Lieutenant Colonel. 16 Nov. 1785. 250 acres.
Harmon, Abner. Me. Sergeant Major. 12 Jan. 1836. 200 acres. Buxton.
Harmon, John. N.C. Private. 22 Apr. 1785. 640 acres.
Harmon, Josiah. Me. Musician. 23 Jun. 1835. 200 acres. Thorndike.
Harmon, Samuel. Me. Private. 6 May 1835. 200 acres. Dixmont.
Harmon, Thomas. Me. Private. 9 Sep. 1836. 200 acres to widow Mary Harmon. Buxton.
Harmon, William. Me. ———. 29 Jun. 1835. 200 acres. Standish.
Harnett, Ephraim. N.C. Private. 30 Sep. 1785. 640 acres to heirs.
Harney, Silby. N.C. Lieutenant Colonel Commandant. 22 Oct. 1783. 7200 acres.
Harper, David. Va. Sergeant. 30 Sep. 1784. 200 acres.
Harper, Frederick. N.C. Private. 20 Jan. 1785. 640 acres to heirs.
Harper, Frederick. N.C. Private. 30 Sep. 1785. 640 acres to heirs.
Harper, George. Ga. ———. 17 May 1784. 250 acres.
Harper, Henry. Ga. ———. 17 May 1784. ———.
Harper, Henry. Pa. Private. 9 Oct. 1786. 200 acres.
Harper, James. N. Y. Private. 6 Jul. 1790. 600 acres.
Harper, James. S.C. ———. 3 Mar. 1788. 200 acres.
Harper, James. Va. Lieutenant. 10 Apr. 1783. 2666 2/3 acres.
Harper, James. Va. Brigade Quartermaster. 27 Oct. 1852. 3555 1/3 acres.

Harper, James. Va. Brigade Quartermaster. 27 Oct. 1852. 1777 2/3 acres.
Harper, James. Va. Brigade Quartermaster. 2 Feb. 1854. 1333 1/3 acres.
Harper, James. Va. Brigade Quartermaster. 2 Feb. 1854. 1333 1/3 acres.
Harper, James. Va. Brigade Quartermaster. 2 Feb. 1854. 1333 1/3 acres.
Harper, James. Va. Brigade Quartermaster. 8 Mar. 1854. 190 10/21 acres.
Harper, James. Va. Brigade Quartermaster. 8 Mar. 1854. 190 10/21 acres.
Harper, James. Va. Brigade Quartermaster. 8 Mar. 1854. 190 10/21 acres.
Harper, James. Va. Brigade Quartermaster. 8 Mar. 1854. 190 10/21 acres.
Harper, James. Va. Brigade Quartermaster. 8 Mar. 1854. 190 10/21 acres.
Harper, James. Va. Brigade Quartermaster. 8 Mar. 1854. 380 10/21 acres.
Harper, James. Va. Brigade Quartermaster. 31 Jul. 1854. 190 10/21 acres.
Harper, James. Va. Brigade Quartermaster. 22 Aug. 1854. 1777 2/3 acres.
Harper, James. Va. Brigade Quartermaster. 28 Oct. 1852. 3555 1/3 acres.
Harper, James. Va. Brigade Quartermater. 28 Oct. 1852. 3555 1/3 acres.
Harper, John. Ga. ———. 26 May 1784. 287 1/2 acres.
Harper, John. N. Y. ———. 16 Nov. 1806. 600 acres.
Harper, John. Pa. Lieutenant. 30 Sep. 1787. 200 acres.
Harper, John. Pa. Private. 30 Sep. 1787. 200 acres.
Harper, John. S.C. ———. 3 Aug. 1801. 50 acres to Robert Harper, administrator, in trust.
Harper, John. S.C. ———. 3 Aug. 1801. 36 acres to Robert Harper, administrator, in trust.
Harper, John. S.C. ———. 3 Aug. 1801. 77 acres to Robert Harper, administrator, in trust.
Harper, John. S.C. ———. 3 Aug. 1801. 37 acres to Robert Harper, administrator, in trust.
Harper, John. Va. Corporal. 2 Jun. 1783. 200 acres.
Harper, Joseph. Ga. Sergeant. 17 May 1784. ———.
Harper, Joseph. Md. Private. ———. 50 acres.
Harper, Nathan. Md. Private. ———. 50 acres.
Harper, Reading. N.C. Private. 9 Dec. 1797. 640 acres to heirs.
Harper, Richard. Md. Private. ———. 50 acres.
Harper, Richard. Md. Private. ———. 50 acres.
Harper, Robert. Ga. Captain. 15 Mar. 1784. 250 acres.
Harper, Robert. Ga. Lieutenant. 15 Mar. 1784. 250 acres.
Harper, Robert. N.C. Private. 6 Sep. 1821. 640 acres.
Harper, Samuel. Ga. Captain. 15 Mar. 1784. 500 acres.
Harper, Samuel. Md. Private. ———. 50 acres.
Harper, Thomas. Pa. ———. 200 acres.
Harper, William. Ga. ———. 17 May 1784. 250 acres.
Harper, William. Md. Private. ———. 50 acres.
Harper, William. Md. Private. ———. 50 acres.
Harper, William. N. Y. ———. 8 Jul. 1790. 500 acres.
Harpham, Robert. Md. Sergeant. ———. 50 acres.
Harpool, Henry. Pa. Private. 19 Sep. 1787. 200 acres.
Harrard, James. N.C. Private. 20 May 1811. 274 acres.
Harrell, Benjamin. N.C. Private. 5 Dec. 1796. 640 acres.
Harrell, Holland. N.C. Private. 9 Nov. 1784. 640 acres to John Harrell.
Harrell, Holland. N.C. ———. 9 Nov. 1784. 640 acres to John Harrell.
Harrell, James. N.C. Private. 12 Sep. 1785. 640 acres to heirs.
Harrell, James. Va. Private. 16 Mar. 1784. 200 acres.
Harrell, John. Md. Private. ———. 50 acres.
Harrell, Peter. N.C. Sergeant. 29 Sep. 1784. 535 acres.
Harrell, Thomas. N.C. Private. 7 Jan. 1786. 640 acres to heirs.
Harress, Abraham. N.C. Private. 30 Sep. 1785. 640 acres to heirs.
Harress, Hardy. N.C. Private. 30 Sep. 1785. 640 acres to heirs.

Harrick, William. N.Y. ———. 13 Sep. 1790. 500 acres to heirs.
Harrill, John. N.C. Private. 29 Jul. 1820. 228 acres to heirs.
Harriman, Simon. Me. ———. 15 Mar. 1843. 200 acres to widow Elizabeth Harriman.
Harrin, Michael. N.Y. ———. 13 Sep. 1790. 500 acres to heirs.
Harrington, Charles. Ga. ———. 17 May 1784. ———.
Harrington, Elisha. Mass. Fife Major. 22 Jul. 1833. 200 acres.
Harrington, Isaac. Pa. Private. 12 Apr. 1785. 200 acres.
Harrington, Jacob. Pa. Private. ———. 200 acres.
Harrington, John. Ga. ———. 17 May 1784. ———.
Harrington, Levin. Md. Private. ———. 50 acres.
Harrington, Peter. N.C. Private. 20 Sep. 1821. 640 acres.
Harrington, Richard. Md. Private. ———. 50 acres.
Harrington, Richard. N.C. Private. 30 Sep. 1785. 640 acres to heirs.
Harrington, Thomas. Ga. ———. 17 May 1784. ———.
Harrington, Thomas. Pa. Private. 21 Oct. 1786. 200 acres.
Harriott, Israel. N. Y. Sergeant. 9 Jul. 1790. 600 acres.
Harris, Abner. N.C. Private. 23 May 1821. 640 acres to heirs.
Harris, Arthur. Md. Lieutenant. ———. 200 acres.
Harris, Augustine. Ga. ———. 2 May 1785. 287 1/2 acres.
Harris, Benjamin. Ga. ———. 15 Mar. 1784. 250 acres.
Harris, Benjamin. Conn. Sufferer. New London. 19.9.5.
Harris, Benton. Md. Private. ———. 50 acres.
Harris, Bridgett. Conn. Sufferer. New London. 24.19.0.
Harris, Buckner. Ga. Refguee. 15 Mar. 1784. 250 acres.
Harris, Cato. N.Y. ———. 13 Sep. 1790. 500 acres to heirs.
Harris, Charles. Va. Private. 21 Mar. 1812. 100 acres.
Harris, Clabern. N.C. Private. 19 May 1784. 640 acres.
Harris, Daniel. Conn. Sufferer. New London. 5.6.0.
Harris, David. Ga. Refugee. 24 Feb. 1784. 250 acres.
Harris, David. Ga. Captain. 20 Feb. 1784. 500 acres.
Harris, David. Va. Private. 5 Jun. 1786. 100 acres.
Harris, Drury. S.C. ———. 6 Jan. 1794. 200 acres.
Harris, Edward. N.C. Private. 29 Sep. 1784. 640 acres to heir.
Harris, Edward. Va. Drum Major. 4 Jul. 1783. 400 acres.
Harris, Eliphalet. Conn. Sufferer. New London. 20.12.5.
Harris, Elisha. N.C. Private. 30 Sep. 1785. 640 acres to heirs.
Harris, Ezekiel. Ga. ———. 17 May 1784. ———.
Harris, George. Ga. Private. 1784. 287 1/2 acres.
Harris, George. N.C. Private. 30 Sep. 1785. 640 acres.
Harris, George. Pa. Matross. 29 Jan. 1787. 200 acres.
Harris, Goldman. N.C. Private. 9 Nov. 1784. 228 acres.
Harris, Grace. Conn. Sufferer. New London. 29.0.0.
Harris, Henry. Md. Private. ———. 50 acres.
Harris, Henry. N. Y. Private. 8 Jul. 1790. 600 acres.
Harris, Henry. N. Y. Matross. 9 Jul. 1790. 500 acres.
Harris, Henry. N.C. Private. 9 Nov. 1784. 274 acres.
Harris, Henry. Va. Private. 3 May 1832. 100 acres.
Harris, James. Ga. ———. 17 May 1784. ———.
Harris, James. Va.-Ind. Private. 108 acres.
Harris, James. Md. Private. ———. 50 acres.
Harris, James. N. Y. Matross. 9 Jul. 1790. 500 acres.
Harris, James. N.C. Private. 2 Aug. 1784. 228 acres.
Harris, James. Va. Private. 19 Feb. 1784. 100 acres.

Harris, James. Va. Private. 27 Jul. 1784. 200 acres.
Harris, Jesse. N.C. Private. 7 Jan. 1807. 640 acres to heirs.
Harris, Jesse. N.C. Private. 23 May 1821. 640 acres to heirs.
Harris, Job. N.C. Private. 30 Sep. 1785. 640 acres to heirs.
Harris, Joel. Ga. ———. 25 Feb. 1784. 250 acres.
Harris, John. Ga. ———. 17 May 1784. 287 1/2 acres to heirs.
Harris, John. Ga. Soldier. 19 Dec. 1785. 230 acres.
Harris, John. Md. Private. ———. 50 acres.
Harris, John. Md. Private. ———. 50 acres.
Harris, John. N.C. Private. 22 Oct. 1783. 640 acres.
Harris, John. N.C. Private. 12 Mar. 1785. 228 acres.
Harris, John. N.C. Private. 30 Sep. 1785. 640 acres to heirs.
Harris, John. Pa. ———. 6 Apr. 1794. 200 acres to Daniel Steever, assignee.
Harris, John. Pa. Private. 13 Oct. 1785. 200 acres.
Harris, John. Pa. Matross. ———. 200 acres.
Harris, John. Pa. Private. 27 Dec. 1786. 200 acres.
Harris, John. Va. Lieutenant. 21 Jan. 1784. 2666 2/3 acres.
Harris, John. Va. Captain. 2 Mar. 1784. 5333 1/3 acres.
Harris, John. Va. Private. 24 Nov. 1790. 100 acres.
Harris, John. Va. Private. 21 Feb. 1792. 100 acres.
Harris, John. Va. Captain. 30 Jun. 1804. 4000 acres.
Harris, John. Va. Captain. 4 Apr. 1838. 1333 1/3 acres.
Harris, John. Va. Captain. 22 May 1868. 2222 21/100 acres.
Harris, John. Va. Captain. 28 Jul. 1868. 471 acres.
Harris, John Maline. Va.-Ind. Private. 108 acres.
Harris, John, 1st. Conn. Sufferer. New London. 0.11.1.
Harris, John, 2d. Conn. Sufferer. New London. 33.1.4.
Harris, Jordon. Va. Lieutenant. 3 Feb. 1784. 2666 2/3 acres.
Harris, Joseph, Jr. Conn. Sufferer. New London. 5.15.0.
Harris, Josias. Md. Private. ———. 50 acres.
Harris, Laird. Ga. ———. 20 Dec. 1785. 287 1/2 acres.
Harris, Laird. Ga. Soldier. 19 Dec. 1785. 230 acres to heirs.
Harris, Lydia. Conn. Sufferer. New London. 60.3.11.
Harris, Matthew. Ga. Soldier. 20 Dec. 1785. 230 acres.
Harris, Nathan. Ga. ———. 15 Mar. 1784. 250 acres.
Harris, Nathan. Ga. ———. 17 May 1784. ———.
Harris, Nathan. N.C. Private. 15 Jul. 1785. 640 acres to heirs.
Harris, Nathaniel. N.C. Private. 4 Apr. 1821. 228 acres.
Harris, Peter. Ga. ———. 17 May 1784. ———.
Harris, Peter. N.C. Drummer. 22 Apr. 1785. 1000 acres.
Harris, Peter. S.C. ———. 6 Oct. 1794. 170 acres.
Harris, Peter. S.C. ———. 6 Oct. 1794. 17 acres.
Harris, Peter. S.C. ———. 6 Oct. 1794. 13 acres.
Harris, Rees. Ga. ———. 20 Feb. 1784. 250 acres. [alias Morris].
Harris, Richard. Ga. ———. 17 May 1784. ———.
Harris, Richard. Va. Sergeant. 5 Jan. 1788. 200 acres.
Harris, Richard. Va. Private. 30 Jul. 1835. 100 acres.
Harris, Richard. Va. ———. 3 Nov. 1838. 100 acres.
Harris, Robert. Ga. Private. 10 Dec. 1784. 250 acres.
Harris, Robert. Pa. Surgeon's Mate. 7 Sep. 1787. 300 acres to Robert Clark, guardian of his heirs.
Harris, Robert. Va. Private. 16 Feb. 1784. 100 acres.
Harris, Ruth. Conn. Sufferer. New London. 63.0.0.
Harris, Sampson. Ga. ———. 25 Feb. 1784. 250 acres.

Harris, Sampson. Ga. ———. 17 May 1784. ———.
Harris, Samuel. Ga. Refugee. 17 Jan. 1785. 287 1/2 acres.
Harris, Samuel. N.C. Private. 28 Sep. 1785. 228 acres to heirs.
Harris, Samuel. Va. Surgeon. 25 Mar. 1840. 2000 acres.
Harris, Samuel. Va. Surgeon. 25 Mar. 1840. 2000 acres.
Harris, Samuel. Va. Surgeon. 25 Mar. 1840. 1500 acres.
Harris, Samuel. Va. Surgeon. 25 Mar. 1840. 500 acres.
Harris, Samuel, Jr. Va.-Ind. Private. 108 acres.
Harris, Samuel, Sr. Va.-Ind. Private. 108 acres.
Harris, Sarah. Conn. Sufferer. New London. 177.7.5.
Harris, Sherrod. N.C. Private. 23 Nov. 1797. 228 acres.
Harris, Sherwood H. N.C. Private. 22 Apr. 1785. 228 acres.
Harris, Simon. Va. Surgeon. 16 Mar. 1840. 3000 acres.
Harris, Simon. Va. Surgeon. 16 Mar. 1840. 1500 acres.
Harris, Simon. Va. Surgeon. 16 Mar. 1840. 1500 acres.
Harris, Simon. Va. Surgeon. 28 Oct. 1854. 3000 acres.
Harris, Simon. Va. Surgeon. 28 Oct. 1854. 1800 acres.
Harris, Simon. Va. Surgeon. 28 Oct. 1854. 600 acres.
Harris, Simon. Via. Surgeon. 28 Oct. 1854. 600 acres.
Harris, Stephen. N.C. Private. 16 Aug. 1821. 640 acres. Served in Danrnal's company.
Harris, Stephen. N.C. Private. 16 Aug. 1821. 640 acres. Served in Stedman's company.
Harris, Thomas. Md. Private. ———. 50 acres.
Harris, Thomas. N.C. Major. 9 Nov. 1784. 1000 acres.
Harris, Thomas. N.C. Major. 9 Nov. 1784. 1000 acres.
Harris, Thomas. N.C. Major. 9 Nov. 1784. 1000 acres.
Harris, Thomas. N.C. Major. 9 Nov. 1784. 1000 acres.
Harris, Thomas. N.C. Private. 3 Feb. 1785. 213 acres.
Harris, Thomas. Va. Private. 30 Jan. 1784. 100 acres.
Harris, Thomas. Va. Private. 21 Jun. 1808. 100 acres.
Harris, Thompson. N.C. Private. 20 Sep. 1784. 640 acres to heirs.
Harris, Tyre Glen. Ga. Soldier. 17 May 1784. ———.
Harris, Walter. Va. Private. 11 Aug. 1783. 100 acres.
Harris, Walter. Conn. Sufferer. New London. 17.15.10.
Harris, Walton. Ga. ———. 17 May 1784. ———.
Harris, William. Md. Private. ———. 50 acres.
Harris, William. Md. Private. ———. 50 acres.
Harris, William. Md. Private. ———. 50 acres.
Harris, William. N. Y. Sergeant. 8 Jul. 1790. 500 acres.
Harris, William. N.C. Private. 9 Sep. 1785. 640 acres to heirs.
Harris, William. Pa. Private. 13 Oct. ——. 200 acres to Michael Ferrick.
Harris, William. Va. Drum Major. 21 Jul. 1783. 400 acres.
Harris, William. Va. Private. 14 Nov. 1821. 100 acres.
Harrison, Alexander. Va. Private. 9 Jan. 1833. 200 acres.
Harrison, Alexander. Va. Private. 9 Jan. 1833. 200 acres.
Harrison, Andrew. Va. Private. 9 Aug. 1806. 100 acres.
Harrison, Augustine. N.C. Private. 30 Sep. 1785. 640 acres to heirs.
Harrison, Battle. Va. Lieutenant. 28 Nov. 1796. 2666 2/3 acres.
Harrison, Benjamin. Va. Captain. 20 Apr. 1812. 4000 acres.
Harrison, Benjamin, Jr. Va. Deputy Quartermaster General. 6 Apr. 1833. 6666 2/3 acres.
Harrison, Charles. N.C. Private. 30 Sep. 1785. 640 acres.
Harrison, Charles. Va. Colonel. 23 Jan. 1784. 6666 2/3 acres.
Harrison, Charles. Va. Colonel. 12 Jan. 1808. 2036 acres.

Harrison, Cuthbert. Va. Captain. 26 Nov. 1824. 2000 acres.
Harrison, Cuthbert. Va. Captain. 26 Nov. 1824. 2000 acres,
Harrison, Cuthbert. Va. Captain. 16 Aug. 1868. 1077 acres.
Harrison, Cuthbert. Va. Captain. 11 Sep. 1875. 1077 acres.
Harrison, Daniel. N.C. Private. 24 Aug. 1819. 274 acres.
Harrison, Demsey. N.C. Private. 21 Apr. 1784. 383 acres.
Harrison, Edward. Ga. ———. 17 May 1784. ———.
Harrison, Edward. N.C. Private. 30 Sep. 1785. 640 acres to heirs.
Harrison, Elisha. Md. Surgeon's Mate. ———. 200 acres.
Harrison, George. N.C. Private. 5 Sep. 1821. 640 acres.
Harrison, Gilbert. N.C. Private. 2 Feb. 1786. 640 acres to heirs.
Harrison, Henry. N.C. Private. 30 Sep. 1785. 640 acres to heirs.
Harrison, James. N.C. Private. 7 Mar. 1785. 640 acres to Francis Harrison, heir.
Harrison, James. N.C. Private. 15 Jul. 1785. 640 acres to heirs.
Harrison, James. N.C. Private. 17 Dec. 1785. 640 acres to heir Francis Harrison. He was of Bertie Co.
Harrison, James. N.C. Sergeant. 3 Mar. 1801. 1000 acres to heirs.
Harrison, James. Va. Lieutenant. 26 Mar. 1784. 2666 2/3 acres.
Harrison, James. Va. Private. 10 Oct. 1806. 100 acres.
Harrison, Jesse. N.C. Private. 12 May 1784. 274 acres.
Harrison, John. N.C. Private. 30 Sep. 1785. 640 acres to heirs.
Harrison, John. N.C. Private. 23 Jun. 1823. 640 acres.
Harrison, John. S.C. ———. 21 Jan. 1785. 200 acres.
Harrison, John. Va. Lieutenant. 31 Mar. 1783. 1333 1/3 acres.
Harrison, John. Va. Lieutenant. 31 Mar. 1783. 1333 1/3 acres.
Harrison, John. Va. Private. 5 Jun. 1784. 100 acres.
Harrison, John. Va. Private. 30 Dec. 1784. 100 acres.
Harrison, John. Va. Lieutenant. 11 Mar. 1800. 444 1/2 acres.
Harrison, John. Va. Lieutenant. 22 Jun. 1820. 204 acres.
Harrison, John. Va. Lieutenant. 22 Jun. 1820. 203 acres.
Harrison, John. Va. Private. 9 Nov. 1831. 100 acres.
Harrison, John Oxley. N.C. ———. 10 Aug. 1785. 640 acres to heirs.
Harrison, John Peyton. Va. Captain. 10 Mar. 1783. 4000 acres.
Harrison, Jonathan. N.C. Sergeant. 9 Sep. 1785. 1000 acres to heirs.
Harrison, Joseph. N.C. Private. 18 Dec. 1802. 640 acres.
Harrison, Joseph. Va. Sergeant. 10 Jul. 1783. 200 acres.
Harrison, Joseph. Va. Surgeon's Mate. 2 Jun. 1838. 1333 1/3 acres.
Harrison, Joseph. Va. Surgeon's Mate. 2 Jun. 1838. 1333 1/3 acres.
Harrison, Joseph. Va. Surgeon's Mate. 2 Jun. 1838. 1333 1/3 acres.
Harrison, Laurence. Va. Lieutenant. 28 Nov. 1796. 3111 acres.
Harrison, Lovell. Va. Sergeant. 10 Oct. 1806. 200 acres.
Harrison, Philip. N.Y. ———. 13 Sep. 1790. 500 acres to heirs.
Harrison, Philip. Va. Sergeant. 15 Oct. 1792. 400 acres.
Harrison, Richard. Ga. ———. 17 May 1784. ———.
Harrison, Richard. Va.-Ind. Lieutenant. Apr. 1784. 2156 acres.
Harrison, Richard. Va. Lieutenant. 29 Apr. 1784. 2666 2/3 acres.
Harrison, Richard. Va. Private. 30 Jun. 1784. 100 acres.
Harrison, Richard. Va. Captain Lieutenant. 11 Apr. 1838. 1333 1/3 acres.
Harrison, Robert. N.C. Private. 30 Sep. 1785. 640 acres to heirs.
Harrison, Robert. Va. Private. 17 Jul. 1788. 200 acres.
Harrison, Robert Hanson. Va. Lieutenant Colonel. 11 May 1838. 1339 acres.
Harrison, Robert Hanson. Va. Lieutenant Colonel. 11 May 1838. 669 acres.
Harrison, Robert Hanson. Va. Lieutenant Colonel. 31 May 1838. 669 1/2 acres.
Harrison, Robert Hanson. Va. Lieutenant Colonel. 31 May 1838. 669 1/2 acres.

Harrison, Robert Hanson. Va. Lieutenant Colonel. 9 Feb. 1814. 250 acres.
Harrison, Robert Hanson. Va. Lieutenant Colonel. 9 Feb. 1814. 250 acres.
Harrison, Robert Hanson. Va. Lieutenant Colonel. 9 Feb. 1814. 250 acres.
Harrison, Robert Hanson. Va. Lieutenant Colonel. 9 Feb. 1814. 250 acres.
Harrison, Robert Hanson. Va. Lieutenant Colonel. 9 Feb. 1814. 250 acres.
Harrison, Robert Hanson. Va. Lieutenant Colonel. 9 Feb. 1814. 250 acres.
Harrison, Robert Hanson. Va. Lieutenant Colonel. 9 Feb. 1814. 250 acres.
Harrison, Robert Hanson. Va. Lieutenant Colonel. 9 Feb. 1814. 250 acres.
Harrison, Robert Hanson. Va. Lieutenant Colonel. 9 Feb. 1814. 250 acres.
Harrison, Robert Hanson. Va. Lieutenant Colonel. 9 Feb. 1814. 250 acres.
Harrison, Robert Hanson. Va. Lieutenant Colonel. 9 Feb. 1814. 250 acres.
Harrison, Robert Hanson. Va. Lieutenant Colonel. 9 Feb. 1814. 250 acres.
Harrison, Robert Hanson. Va. Lieutenant Colonel. 9 Feb. 1814. 250 acres.
Harrison, Robert Hanson. Va. Lieutenant Colonel. 9 Feb. 1814. 250 acres.
Harrison, Robert Hanson. Va. Lieutenant Colonel. 9 Feb. 1814. 250 acres.
Harrison, Robert Hanson. Va. Lieutenant Colonel. 9 Feb. 1814. 250 acres.
Harrison, Robert Hanson. Va. Lieutenant Colonel. 9 Feb. 1814. 250 acres.
Harrison, Robert Hanson. Va. Lieutenant Colonel. 9 Feb. 1814. 250 acres.
Harrison, Samuel. Md. Private. ———. 50 acres.
Harrison, Simmons. N.C. Private. 24 Nov. 1796. 640 acres to heirs.
Harrison, Stephen. N.C. Private. 26 Aug. 1785. 640 acres to heirs.
Harrison, Thomas. Md. Sergeant. ———. 50 acres.
Harrison, Thomas. Md. Private. ———. 50 acres.
Harrison, Thomas. N.C. Private. 13 Dec. 1783. 274 acres.
Harrison, Valentine. Va. Captain. 18 Aug. 1783. 4000 acres.
Harrison, Walter. Ga. Soldier. 5 Sep. 1785. ———.
Harrison, William. Md. Private. ———. 50 acres.
Harrison, William. N.C. Lieutenant. 3 Dec. 1796. 1097 acres.
Harrison, William. N.C. Private. 24 Jul. 1820. 640 acres to heirs.
Harrison, William. Va. Drummer. 21 Oct. 1783. 100 acres.
Harrison, William Butler. Va. Cornet. 19 Sep. 1783. 2666 2/3 acres.
Harriss, John. Va. Private. 9 Oct. 1783. 100 acres.
Harriss, Nathaniel. Conn. Sufferer. New London. 3.5.0.
Harriss, Richard. N.C. ———. 8 Mar. 1785. 640 acres to heirs.
Harriss, Thomas. N.C. Major. 23 Oct. 1783. 2057 acres.
Harriss, William. Va. Private. 22 Oct. 1783. 100 acres.
Harrod, Howell. N.C. Sergeant. 22 Apr. 1785. 1000 acres to heirs.
Harrod, Robert. Ga. Soldier. 20 Aug. 1785. ———.
Harrod, William. Va.-Ind. Captain. 3234 acres.
Harrold, James. Pa. Private. 2 Oct. 1786. 200 acres to widow.
Harrold, John. Va. Sergeant. 23 Jul. 1824. 200 acres.
Harrup, Arthur. Va. Sergeant. 9 Dec. 1783. 400 acres.
Hart, Adam. N.C. Private. 27 Oct. 1783. 640 acres.
Hart, Anthony. N.C. Lieutenant. 14 May 1784. 2194 acres.
Hart, Benjamin. Ga. ———. 27 Sep. 1784. 287 1/2 acres.
Hart, Ebenezer. Mass. Corporal. 20 Feb. 1833. 200 acres.
Hart, George. Ga. Private. 2 Feb. 1784. 250 acres.
Hart, George. Pa. Private. 26 Aug. 1789. 200 acres to Richard Howell, assignee.
Hart, Hardy. N.C. Private. 30 Sep. 1785. 640 acres to heirs.
Hart, Henry. N.C. Private. 22 Dec. 1796. 640 acres.
Hart, James. Va. Private. 15 May 1783. 100 acres.
Hart, John. Ga. Refugee. 15 Mar. 1784. 250 acres.
Hart, John. N.C. Private. 29 Sep. 1784. 640 acres to heirs.
Hart, John. N.C. Private. 16 Aug. 1821. 640 acres.

Hart, John. S.C. Captain. 2 May 1785. 300 acres.
Hart, John. Va. Private. 30 Dec. 1808. 261 acres.
Hart, John. Va. Private. 13 Dec. 1832. 100 acres.
Hart, Joseph. N.C. Private. 7 Jan. 1786. 640 acres to heirs.
Hart, Martin. Pa. Private. 26 Oct. 1786. 200 acres.
Hart, Morgan. N.C. Corporal. 22 Dec. 1796. 1000 acres to heirs.
Hart, Nicholas. Pa. Private. 18 Oct. 1786. 200 acres to Rachel Hart, widow.
Hart, Richard. Ga. Soldier. 1 May 1785. ———.
Hart, Robert. Va. Drum Major. 25 Aug. 1783. 400 acres.
Hart, Robert. Va. Drum Major. 26 Aug. 1783. 200 acres.
Hart, Samuel. Ga. ———. 17 May 1784. ———.
Hart, Samuel. N.C. Private. 9 Apr. 1788. 274 acres.
Hart, Samuel. N.C. Private. 17 Feb. 1824. 640 acres.
Hart, Thomas. Md. Private. ———. 50 acres.
Hart, Thomas. N. Y. Private. 8 Jul. 1790. 500 acres.
Hart, Thomas. N.C. Private. 27 Apr. 1784. 640 acres to Peggy Hart, heiress.
Hart, Thomas. Va. Private. 30 Aug. 1784. 100 acres.
Hart, William. N. Y. Matross. 9 Jul. 1790. 600 acres.
Hart, William. Va. Private. 19 Jun. 1783. 100 acres.
Hartdwick, Christian. N.Y. ———. 21 Aug. 1800. 500 acres.
Harter, Adam. N. Y. Private. 8 Jul. 1790. 600 acres.
Hartfield, James. N.C. Private. 5 Dec. 1796. 274 acres.
Hartford, James. Ga. Soldier. 5 Sep. 1785. ———.
Hartford, John. Ga. Soldier. 5 Sep. 1785. ———.
Hartford, William. Va. Sergeant. 20 Jun. 1783. 200 acres.
Harthman, James. Ga. ———. ———. 287 1/2 acres.
Harthman, Thomas. Ga. ———. ———. 287 1/2 acres.
Hartle, John. Conn. Sufferer. New London. 44.19.4.
Hartley, Henry. Ga. ———. 1784. 287 1/2 acres.
Hartley, John. N.C. Private. 30 Mar. 1785. 640 acres to Thomas Hartley, heir.
Hartley, John. N.C. ———. 12 Dec. 1785. 640 acres to heirs.
Hartley, Joseph. N.C. Private. 27 Nov. 1783. 383 acres.
Hartman, Christian. Pa. Private. 15 Jun. 1804. 200 acres.
Hartman, Conrad. Pa. Private. 3 Nov. 1786. 200 acres.
Hartman, George. Pa. Private. 29 Mar. 1803. 200 acres.
Hartman, Michael. Md. Private. ———. 50 acres.
Hartman, William. Md. Private. ———. 50 acres.
Hartsfield, Andrew. N.C. Private. 22 Dec. 1796. 640 acres to heirs.
Hartsfield, David. N.C. Private. 22 Dec. 1796. 640 acres to heirs.
Hartsfield, Jacob. N.C. Private. 6 Dec. 1797. 274 acres.
Hartsfield, John. Ga. ———. 17 May 1784. ———.
Hartshorn John. Ga. Citizen. 5 Apr. 1785. 287 1/2 acres.
Hartshorn, John. Md. Lieutenant. ———. 200 acres.
Hartwick, John. N. Y. Drum Major. 9 Jul. 1790. 600 acres.
Harty, Frederick. Md. Private. ———. 50 acres.
Harvell, Edward. Ga. ———. 17 May 1784. ———.
Harvell, James. Ga. ———. 17 May 1784. ———.
Harvell, Joseph. Ga. Refugee. 17 May 1784. 287 1/2 acres.
Harvell, Samuel. Ga. ———. 1784. 287 1/2 acres.
Harvest, John Adams. Me. ———. 21 Jul. 1835. 200 acres to widow Anna Harvest. Waldo.
Harvey, Absalom. N.C. Private. 17 Feb. 1824. 640 acres.
Harvey, Blassingham. Ga. ———. 17 May 1784. ———.
Harvey, Charles. Ga. ———. 15 Jul. 1784. 287 1/2 acres.

Harvey, Charles. Md. Sergeant. ———. 50 acres.
Harvey, Daniel. Md. Matross. ———. 50 acres.
Harvey, Edward. Va. Private. 25 Apr. 1785. 100 acres.
Harvey, Elisha. N. Y. Lieutenant. 9 Jul. 1790. 1200 acres.
Harvey, Evan. Ga. ———. 19 Dec. 1785. 1150 acres.
Harvey, Evin. Ga. ———. 20 Feb. 1784. 250 acres.
Harvey, George. Pa. ———. 14 Jan. 1796. 200 acres to Daniel Richards, executor.
Harvey, James. Ga. Refugee. 20 Feb. 1784. 250 acres.
Harvey, James Hill. Ga. ———. 17 May 1784. ———.
Harvey, Joel. Ga. Refugee. ———. 17 May 1784. ———.
Harvey, John. Ga. Refugee. 22 Mar. 1785. 287 1/2 acres.
Harvey, John. Mass. Private. 6 Jul. 1832. 200 acres.
Harvey, John. N.C. Private. 31 Mar. 1820. 274 acres.
Harvey, Joshua. Md. ———. ———. 50 acres.
Harvey, Joshua. N.C. Private. 21 May 1784. 640 acres.
Harvey, Littleberry. Ga. Refugee. 28 Jul. 1784. 287 1/2 acres.
Harvey, Mary. Conn. Sufferer. Norwalk. 14.11.0.
Harvey, Michael. Ga. ———. 17 May 1784. ———.
Harvey, Norman. Va. Private. 1 Oct. 1796. 100 acres.
Harvey, Norment. Va. Private. 25 Mar. 1831. 100 acres.
Harvey, Richard. Ga. ———. 17 May 1784. ——— acres to heirs.
Harvey, Richard. Va. Private. 31 Aug. 1784. 100 acres.
Harvey, Thomas. Ga. ———. 6 Apr. 1785. 287 1/2 acres.
Harvey, William. Me. ———. 26 Sep. 1835. 200 acres. South Berwick.
Harvey, William. N. Y. Private. 8 Jul. 1790. 600 acres.
Harvey, Zachary. Ga. ———. ———. 575 acres.
Harvey, Zadock. Md. Private. ———. 50 acres.
Harwell, John. S.C. ———. 6 Oct. 1794. 200 acres.
Harwell, Richard. Ga. ———. 17 May 1784. ———.
Harwood, Littlebury. Va. Sergeant. 19 May 1783. 200 acres.
Harwood, Thomas. N. Y. Matross. 3 Jul. 1790. 600 acres.
Harwood, Thomas. N.C. Private. 30 Sep. 1785. 640 acres to heirs.
Hasbrouck, George. N. Y. Private. 6 Jul. 1790. 600 acres.
Hasel, Jesse. N.C. Private. 7 Dec. 1797. 640 acres to heirs.
Haseland, William. S.C. Soldier. 7 Jan. 1799. 200 acres.
Haskell, John. Me. ———. 11 Jul. 1837. 200 acres to widow Mary Haskell. Knox.
Haskell, Philip. Mass. Private. 22 Jul. 1833. 200 acres.
Hasker, Thomas. N.C. Private. 5 Dec. 1796. 228 acres.
Haslet, Samuel. Pa. Private. 1 Sep. 1789. 200 acres.
Haslip, Charles. N.C. Private. 20 Sep. 1821. 640 acres.
Haslip, John B. Md. Private. ———. 50 acres.
Haslip, Richard B. Md. Private. ———. 50 acres.
Hassle, Stephen. N.C. Private. 17 Feb. 1824. 640 acres.
Hastin, Carter. N.C. Private. 9 Feb. 1796. 640 acres to heirs.
Hastin, Oliver. N.C. Private. 30 Sep. 1785. 640 acres to heirs.
Hastings, Thomas. Va. Seaman. 9 Dec. 1833. 100 acres.
Hastings, Willis. N.C. Private. 30 Sep. 1785. 640 acres.
Haston, Daniel. N.C. Private. 29 Sep. 1785. 640 acres.
Hasty, Clem. Va. Private. 15 Aug. 1787. 100 acres.
Hasty, John. Va. Private. 21 May 1784. 100 acres.
Haswell, Robert. N.C. Private. 18 Dec. 1797. 640 acres.
Hatch, Simeon. Me. Private. 29 Jun. 1835. 200 acres to widow Jemima Hatch. Dresden.
Hatcher, Archibald. Ga. Captain of a

galley. 27 Jan. 1784. 600 acres to John Hardy, executor.

Hatcher, Archibald. Ga. ———. 6 Feb. 1784. 250 acres.

Hatcher, David. N.C. Private. 12 Mar. 1785. 640 acres to heirs.

Hatcher, Henry. Ga. Refugee. 17 May 1784. ———.

Hatcher, Jeremiah. Ga. Refugee. 17 May 1784. ———.

Hatcher, John. Ga. Refugee. 15 Mar. 1784. 250 acres.

Hatcher, Josiah. Ga. ———. 6 Feb. 1784. 500 acres.

Hatcher, Robert. Ga. Refugee. 16 Jul. 1784. 287 1/2 acres.

Hatcher, Valentine. Ga. ———. 6 Feb. 1784. 250 acres.

Hatcher, Valentine. Ga. ———. 17 May 1784. ———.

Hatcher, William. Ga. Refugee. 26 May 1784. 287 1/2 acres.

Hatcher, William. Va. Corporal. 8 Jun. 1784. 400 acres.

Hatcher, William. Va. Corporal. 22 Oct. 1787. 400 acres.

Hatdorffer, Michael. Va. Private. 18 Dec. 1818. 200 acres.

Hatewood, Richard. Ga. Minute Man. 22 Mar. 1785. 250 acres.

Hath, Peter. Ga. Minute Man. 14 Feb. 1785. ———.

Hathaway, John. N.C. Private. 6 Sep. 1821. 640 acres to heirs.

Hathcock, Amos. N.C. Private. 30 Sep. 1785. 640 acres to heirs.

Hathcock, Frederick. N.C. Private. 2 Feb. 1786. 228 acres.

Hathcock, Holladay. N.C. Private. 23 Apr. 1785. 640 acres to heirs.

Hathcock, John. N.C. Private. 30 Sep. 1785. 640 acres to heirs.

Hatkerston, Robert. Md. Lieutenant. ———. 200 acres.

Hatten, Christopher. Va.-Ind. Private. 108 acres.

Hattin, Basdel. Ga. Soldier. 5 Sep. 1785. 230 acres.

Hatton, David. Md. Private. ———. 50 acres.

Hatton, Samuel. Va. Private. 29 Dec. 1784. 100 acres.

Hatton, William. Va. Private. 20 Aug. 1783. 200 acres.

Hatwell, Luther. Ga. Refugee. ———. 500 acres.

Haughton, Levi. N.C. Private. 7 Dec. 1796. 640 acres to heirs. He was of Tyrrell County.

Haughton, Thomas. Ga. ———. 17 May 1784. 250 acres.

Hause, Cornelius. N. Y. Matross. 6 Jul. 1790. 600 acres.

Hause, Ludwig. Pa. ———. 25 Aug. 1787. 250 acres to Elizabeth Hause, widow.

Havalash, Michael. N. Y. Private. 3 Jul. 1790. 600 acres.

Havens, Jonathan. Conn. Sufferer. Groton. 11.9.0.

Havens, Joseph. N. Y. Sergeant. 7 Jul. 1790. 600 acres.

Havens, Peter. N. Y. Private. 8 Jul. 1790. 600 acres.

Havens, William. N. Y. Private. 8 Jul. 1790. 600 acres.

Haverman, Hugh. Pa. Sergeant. 12 Jan. 1787. 250 acres.

Haviland, Ebenezer. N. Y. Surgeon. 7 Jul. & 13 Sep. 1790. 1500 acres to his heirs.

Hawes, Samuel. Va. Lieutenant Colonel. 13 Jun. 1783. 7000 acres.

Hawes, Samuel. Va. Lieutenant. 29 Aug. 1809. 833 1/3 acres.

Hawk, Andrew. Ga. ———. 17 May 1784. ———.

Hawke, Michael. Md. Corporal. ———. 50 acres.

Hawkey, Henry. N. Y. Private. 8 Jul. 1790. 500 acres.

Hawkins James. Va. Private. 21 Nov. 1783. 100 acres.

Hawkins, Barlett. Va. Private. 6 Sep. 1796. 200 acres.

Hawkins, Benjamin. Va. Private. 27 Aug. 1784. 200 acres.

Hawkins, Benjamin. Va. Private. 30 Dec. 1784. 100 acres.

Hawkins, Cesar. Ga. Minute Man. 17 May 1784. 287 1/2 acres to heirs.

Hawkins, Francis. Pa. Private. ———. 200 acres to widow.

Hawkins, Hardy. N.C. Private. 2 Apr. 1784. 274 acres.

Hawkins, Henry. Md. Lieutenant. ———. 200 acres.

Hawkins, Isaac. N.Y. ———. 13 Sep. 1790. 500 acres to heirs.

Hawkins, James. Ga. Soldier. 17 May 1784 acres to heirs.
Hawkins, James. N.C. Private. 2 Apr. 1784. 640 acres.
Hawkins, James. S.C. ———. 7 Jan. 1793. 125 acres to James Timms, administrator.
Hawkins, James. S.C. ———. 7 Jan. 1793. 23 3/4 acres to James Timms, administrator.
Hawkins, James. S.C. ———. 4 Jun. 1798. 2 3/4 acres to James Timms, administrator.
Hawkins, James. S.C. ———. 4 Jun. 1798. 10 acres to James Timms, administrator.
Hawkins, James. S.C. ———. 4 Jun. 1798. 11 acres to James Timms, administrator.
Hawkins, James. S.C. ———. 45 Oct. 1800. 22 acres to James Timms, administrator.
Hawkins, John. Ga. Minute Man. 26 May 1784. 287 1/2 acres.
Hawkins, John. Pa. Sergeant. 13 Feb. 1787. 250 acres to Francis Murray, assignee.
Hawkins, John. Va. Lieutenant. 26 Jun. 1784. 2666 2/3 acres.
Hawkins, John. Va. Captain. 26 Apr. 1785. 1333 1/3 acres.
Hawkins, Joseph. Va. Sergeant. 20 Jan. 1809. 200 acres.
Hawkins, Matthew. Ga. ———. 17 May 1784. ———.
Hawkins, Moses. Va. Captain. 17 Jul. 1784. 4000 acres.
Hawkins, Moses. Va. Captain. 18 Dec. 1833. 666 2/3 acres.
Hawkins, Nicholas. Ga. Soldier. 29 July. 1784. 287 1/2 acres.
Hawkins, Noel. Ga. Minute Man. 3 Sep. 1785. ———.
Hawkins, Samuel. Ga. ———. 17 May 1784. ———.
Hawkins, Thomas. Ga. Refugee. 15 Apr. 1785. 500 acres.
Hawkins, Zopher. N. Y. Private. 8 Jul. 1790. 500 acres.
Hawks, John. N.C. Private. 29 Sep. 1814. 640 acres to heirs.
Hawley, Benjamin. N.C. ———. 9 Nov. 1784. 640 acres to Jacob Hawley.
Hawley, Caleb. N.C. Private. 30 Nov. 1785. 640 acres.
Hawley, Joseph. N.C. Private. 29 Sep. 1784. 640 acres to heir.
Hawley, Rawleigh. Va. Private. 6 Oct. 1783. 200 acres.
Hawley, William. N.C. Private. 17 Sep. 1785. 640 acres to heirs.
Haws, Joseph. Me. Private. 29 Jan. 1836. 200 acres. Minot.
Hawson, Thomas. Md. Private. ———. 50 acres.
Hawstory, Henry. N.C. Private. 3 Dec. 1797. 640 acres to heirs.
Hawthorn, John. Ga. Refugee. 6 Apr. 1784. 250 acres.
Hawthorn, John. N.C. Private. 15 Feb. 1797. 274 acres.
Hawthorn, Stephen. Ga. Refugee. 15 Oct. 1784. ———.
Hawthorn, William. N.C. Private. 13 Dec. 1796. 640 acres to heirs.
Hay, Abraham. N.C. Private. 16 Feb. 1784. 640 acres to heirs.
Hay, Isaac. N.C. Private. 17 Mar. 1784. 365 acres.
Hay, Joseph. Va. Hospital Surgeon. 27 Nov. 1792. 6000 acres.
Hay, Mourning. Va. Private. 6 Mar. 1784. 100 acres.
Hay, Samuel. N.C. Private. 17 Sep. 1785. 640 acres to heirs.
Hay, Samuel. Pa. Lieutenant Colonel. 16 Nov. 1785. 500 acres.
Hay, Samuel. Pa. Lieutenant Colonel. ———. 250 acres.
Hay, Udny. N. Y. Lieutenant Colonel. ———. 1000 acres.
Hay, William. Ga. ———. 19 Jul. 1784. 600 acres.
Hayar, Robert. N.C. Private. 30 Sep. 1785. 640 acres to heirs.
Hayatt, Alvan. N. Y. Matross. 9 Jul. 1790. 600 acres.
Haycock, John. N. Y. Private. 8 Jul. 1790. 600 acres.
Haycraft, Mark. N.C. Private. 28 May 1784. 640 acres.
Hayden, Jeremiah. Va. Private. 29 Aug. 1835. 200 acres.
Hayden, Ziba. Mass. Sergeant. 5 Aug. 1833. 200 acres.
Hayes, Andrew. Ga. ———. 17 May 1784. ———.
Hayes, Arthur. Ga. Lieutenant. 8 Sep. 1783. 400 acres.
Hayes, Gabriel. Va. Sergeant. 9 Dec. 1783. 200 acres.

Hayes, Isaac. Conn. Sufferer. Fairfield. 86.17.8.

Hayes, Isaac. Conn. Sufferer. Fairfield. 28.0.7.

Hayes, John. Va. Private. 30 Sep. 1783. 200 acres.

Hayes, John. Va. Major. 4 Jun. 1798. 888 2/3 acres.

Hayes, Jonathan. Conn. Sufferer. Danbury. 11.10.0.

Hayes, Mary. Conn. Sufferer. Ridgefield. 3.16.0.

Hayes, Richard. Md. Private. ———. 50 acres.

Hayes, Thomas. Va.-Ind. Private. 108 acres.

Hayes, Thomas. Va. Lieutenant. 22 Jul. 1783. 2666 2/3 acres.

Hayes, Thomas. Conn. Sufferer. Norwalk. 18.0.0.

Hayes, Vachel. Md. Drummer. ———. 50 acres.

Haygood, William. N.C. Private. 8 Aug. 1821. 640 acres.

Haylewood, Richard. Ga. Minute Man. 16 Mar. 1784. ———.

Haynes, Ephraim. Me. ———. 7 Feb. 1837. 200 acres. Eden.

Haynes, Griffith. Va. Private. 23 Mar. 1784. 200 acres.

Haynes, John. Ga. ———. 17 May 1784. ———.

Haynes, John. Md. Private. ———. 50 acres.

Haynes, John. N.C. Private. 11 May 1785. 228 acres.

Haynes, Simeon. Me. Private. 12 Feb. 1839. 200 acres. Swanville.

Haynes, Thomas. Ga. ———. 17 May 1784. ———.

Haynes, Thomas. N. Y. Private. 8 Jul. 1790. 600 acres.

Haynes, William. N.C. Private. 7 Jan. 1786. 320 acres.

Haynes, William. N.C. Private. 29 Apr. 1800. 640 acres to heirs.

Haynes, William. Va. Private. 20 Aug. 1783. 200 acres.

Haynes, William. Va. Private. 19 Apr. 1784. 100 acres.

Haynie, Ezekiel. Md. Surgeon. ———. 200 acres.

Haynie, William. Va. Private. 24 Nov. 1784. 100 acres.

Hayrne, John. S.C. Soldier. 2 May 1785. 200 acres.

Hays, Abraham. Conn. Sufferer. Greenwich. 23.19.10.

Hays, Archibald. Pa. Private. 4 Nov. 1786. 200 acres.

Hays, Daniel. Va. Private. 27 Dec. 1796. 100 acres.

Hays, Ezekiel. Conn. Sufferer. New/East Haven. 72.17.6.

Hays, Hannah. Conn. Sufferer. Greenwich. 1.13.3.

Hays, Isaac. N.C. Private. 17 Dec. 1785. 640 acres to heirs.

Hays, James. Ga. Soldier. ———. 287 1/2 acres.

Hays, James. N.C. Lieutenant. 14 Dec. 1796. 1097 acres.

Hays, James. N.C. Lieutenant. 6 Sep. 1821. 2560 acres to heirs.

Hays, James. S.C. ———. 5 Sep. 1791. 170 acres.

Hays, John. N.C. Private. 27 Aug. 1784. 640 acres.

Hays, John. N.C. Private. 29 Sep. 1784. 274 acres.

Hays, John. Va. Major. 27 Mar. 1783. 5333 1/3 acres.

Hays, John. Va. Sergeant. 19 Jan. 1785. 200 acres.

Hays, John. Va. Major. 23 Jan. 1808. 592 acres.

Hays, John M. Va. Private. 31 Jul. 1784. 100 acres.

Hays, Joseph. Va. Private. 28 Apr. 1783. 200 acres.

Hays, Robert. N.C. Lieutenant. 6 Dec. 1783. 2560 acres.

Hays, Southey. N.C. Private. 1 Jan. 1794. 640 acres to heirs.

Hays, Theophilus. N.C. Private. 10 Nov. 1783. 411 acres.

Hays, Thomas. N.Y. ———. 13 Sep. 1790. 500 acres to heirs.

Hays, William. Pa. Private. 3 Oct. 1806. 200 acres to Mary McCulla et al., executors.

Hays, William. Va. Private. 31 Dec. 1785. 200 acres.

Hayse, John. S.C. ———. 2 Dec. 1793. 100 acres.

Hayse, John. S.C. ———. 2 Dec. 1793. 100 acres.

Hayse, Thomas. N.C. Private. 20 Sep. 1784. 274 acres.
Hayse, William. N.C. Sergeant. 22 Apr. 1785. 1000 acres.
Hayt, Asa. Conn. Sufferer. Norwalk. 381.17.0.
Hayt, Gold. Conn. Sufferer. Norwalk. 195.8.0.
Hayt, James. Conn. Sufferer. Norwalk. 26.2.0 to his heirs.
Hayt, John. Conn. Sufferer. Norwalk. 72.5.2.
Hayt, Nathan. Conn. Sufferer. Norwalk. 180.4.6.
Hayt, Timothy. Conn. Sufferer. Norwalk. 6.0.0.
Haywood, William. N. Y. ———. ———. 500 acres.
Hazberry, William. N.C. Private. 14 Feb. 1796. 640 acres.
Hazelhurst, John. Pa. Private. 29 Nov. 1786. 200 acres to Samuel Benezet, assignee.
Hazen, Moses. N. Y. General. ———. 1000 acres.
Hazle, Henry. S.C. ———. 7 May 1787. 200 acres.
Hazle, Thomas. N.C. Private. 13 Sep. 1820. 640 acres.
Hazleton, Isaac. Pa. ———. 13 Nov. 1786. 200 acres to Catharine Hazleton, widow.
Hazlewood, Richard. Va. Private. 14 Nov. 1783. 100 acres.
Hazlewood, William. Va. Sergeant. 21 Nov. 1783. 400 acres.
Hazzard, William. S.C. Lieutenant. 2 May 1785. 200 acres.
Head, Benjamin. Va. Private. 3 Mar. 1784. 100 acres.
Head, John. Md. Matross. ———. 50 acres.
Head, John. Md. Drummer. ———. 50 acres.
Head, Luke. N.C. Corporal. 30 Sep. 1785. 1000 acres to heirs.
Head, William. Ga. ———. 17 May 1784. ———.
Headen, Anthony. Va. Private. 19 Jun. 1783. 200 acres.
Headley, James. Pa. Corporal. ———. 200 acres.
Headly, Bishop. N.Y. ———. 13 Sep. 1790. 500 acres to heirs.
Heaken, William. Va. Private. 1 Apr. 1783. 100 acres.
Heald, Olive. Me. ———. 22 Apr. 1835. 200 acres. Madison.
Heald, Oliver. Me. ———. 22 Apr. 1835. 200 acres. Madison.
Healey, James. Va. Sergeant. 19 Feb. 1784. 200 acres.
Healey, Samuel. Va. Lieutenant. 2 Apr. 1834. 533 1/8 acres.
Healey, Samuel. Va. Lieutenant. 6 Jul. 1840. 444 4/9 acres.
Healey, Samuel. Va. Lieutenant. 6 Jul. 1840. 888 8/9 acres.
Heally, William. Va. Private. 3 Apr. 1783. 100 acres.
Healy, Martin. Va. Captain. 17 Jun. 1784. 4000 acres.
Heard, Bernard. Ga. Refugee. 15 Mar. 1784. 250 acres.
Heard, Charles. Ga. ———. 30 Sep. 1784. ———.
Heard, Charles. S.C. ———. 3 Nov. 1788. 130 acres.
Heard, George. Ga. ———. 17 May 1784. ———.
Heard, James. Va. Captain. 19 Sep. 1799. 2000 acres.
Heard, James. Va. Captain. 29 Sep. 1799. 2000 acres.
Heard, James. Va. Captain. 5 Feb. 1819. 666 2/3 acres.
Heard, John. Ga. ———. 15 Mar. 1784. 250 acres.
Heard, John, Jr. Ga. ———. 17 May 1784. ———.
Heard, John, Sr. Ga. ———. 17 May 1784. ———.
Heard, Joseph. Ga. Refugee. 15 Mar. 1784. 500 acres.
Heard, Richard. Ga. Captain. 15 Mar. 1784. 250 acres.
Heard, Richard. Ga. ———. 15 Mar. 1784. 500 acres.
Heard, Stephen. Ga. Refugee. 15 Mar. 1784. 250 acres.
Heard, Thomas. Ga. ———. 17 May 1784. ———.
Heard, William. Ga. ———. 15 Mar. 1784. 250 acres.
Hearing, Samuel. Ga. ———. 19 Dec. 1785. 575 acres.
Hearn, Daniel. Va. Sergeant. 29 Oct. 1783. 200 acres.

Hearn, Daniel. Va. Sergeant. 20 Jun. 1854. 200 acres.
Hearn, George. N.C. Private. 7 Jan. 1786. 640 acres to heirs.
Hearn, Nathaniel. Va. Private. 27 Feb. 1797. 100 acres.
Hearn, Samuel. Ga. Private. 26 May 1784. 500 acres.
Hearn, Thomas. Ga. Private. 26 May 1784. 500 acres.
Hearn, William. Ga. Soldier. 15 Jul. 1785. ———.
Hearn, William. Ga. Refugee. 4 May 1784. ———.
Hearns, John. Ga. Soldier. 5 Sep. 1785. ———.
Hearon, Matthew. N.C. Private. 28 May 1784. 640 acres.
Heart, Lazerous. N.C. Private. 30 Sep. 1785. 640 acres to heirs.
Hearthhorn, Thomas. Ga. ———. 17 Sep. 1784. 287 1/2 acres.
Hearthhorn, William. Ga. ———. 17 Sep. 1784. 287 1/2 acres.
Heath, Charles. Md. Private. ———. 50 acres.
Heath, Ethel. Ga. ———. 17 May 1784. ———.
Heath, Francis. Ga. Minute Man. 2 May 1785. ———.
Heath, Joseph. Va. Private. 15 Jun. 1807. 100 acres.
Heath, Thomas. Ga. Private. 22 Mar. 1785. 250 acres.
Heath, William. Me. ———. 9 Oct. 1844. 200 acres to widow Hannah Heath. Mount Desert.
Heatley, Henry. Ga. Soldier. 30 Sep. 1784. ———.
Heatley, Robert. Ga. Minute Man. 24 May 1784. 287 1/2 acres.
Heaton, James. Md. ———. ———. 50 acres.
Heator, George. N. Y. Matross. 9 Jul. 1790. 500 acres.
Hebard, Samuel. N. Y. Matross. 9 Jul. 1790. 500 acres.
Hebb, William. Va. Private. 14 Jan. 1824. 100 acres.
Hebburn, William. Va. ———. 29 Aug. 1837. 100 acres.
Hebburn, William. Va. Private. 22 Jun. 1835. 100 acres.
Hebron, John. Va. Private. 15 Apr. 1783. 200 acres.
Heckerson, John. Ga. Soldier. ———. ———.
Hector, Lewis. N.C. Private. 30 Sep. 1785. 640 acres.
Hedge, William. Md. Private. ———. 50 acres.
Hedgebeth, Moses. Va. Private. 5 Dec. 1833. 100 acres.
Hedgepeth, Moses. N.C. Private. 7 Dec. 1797. 640 acres to heirs.
Hedgepeth, Stephen. N.C. Private. 5 Dec. 1796. 640 acres.
Hedgpeth, Marmaduke. N.C. Private. 6 Aug. 1785. 274 acres.
Hedspeth, John. N.C. Private. 22 Apr. 1785. 640 acres.
Heel, Joseph. N.C. Private. 1 Sep. 1785. 640 acres to heirs.
Hefferling, John. Va. Private. 31 May 1787. 200 acres.
Hefferman, Thomas. Pa. Sergeant. 20 Sep.1787. 250 acres.
Height, Christian. Pa. Private. ———. 200 acres.
Heiner, Daniel. Pa. Private. 14 Oct. 1786. 200 acres to Eleanor Heiner, administratrix.
Heirs, Henry. Va. Private. 22 Sep. 1784. 100 acres.
Heldereth, Eliseath. N.Y. ———. 13 Sep. 1790. 500 acres to heirs.
Helderman, Nicholas. N.C. Private. 21 Nov. 1809. 640 acres.
Helen, Bernard. N.C. Private. 9 Sep. 1785. 640 acres to heirs.
Hellen, William. Md. Bombadier. ———. 50 acres.
Hellenberger, Henry. Ga. ———. 30 Sep. 1784. ———.
Helm, Leonard. Va.-Ind. Captain. 3234 acres.
Helm, Leonard. Va. Private. 29 Apr. 1785. 200 acres.
Helm, Thomas. Va. Captain. 28 Jan. 1834. 4000 acres.
Helm, Thomas. Va. Captain. 25 Jul. 1834. 749 2/3 acres.
Helm, Thomas. Va. ———. 5 Jun. 1835. 55 1/2 acres.
Helm, Thomas. Va. Captain. 20 Apr. 1841. 355 acres.

Helm, Thomas. Va. Captain. 10 Nov. 1848. 177 1/2 acres.
Helm, Thomas. Va. Captain. 10 Nov. 1848. 177 1/2 acres.
Helm, William. Va. Captain. Aug. 1834. 444 4/9 acres.
Helm, William. Va. Captain. Aug. 1834. 444 4/9 acres.
Helm, William. Va. Captain. Aug. 1834. 444 4/9 acres.
Helm, William. Va. Captain. Aug. 1834. 444 4/9 acres.
Helm, William. Va. Captain. Aug. 1834. 444 4/9 acres.
Helm, William. Va. Captain. 21 Feb. 1835. 444 4/9 acres.
Helm, William. Va. Captain. 10 Jul. 1835. 444 4/9 acres.
Helm, William. Va. Captain. 10 Jul. 1835. 444 4/9 acres.
Helm, William. Va. Captain. 9 May 1846. 444 4/9 acres.
Helmer, John. N. Y. Corporal. 8 Jul. 1790. 600 acres.
Helms, Leonard. Va. Captain. 21 Jan. 1834. 4000 acres.
Helphinstine, Peter. Va. Major. 26 Mar. 1803. 670 acres.
Helphinstine, Peter. Va. Major. 26 Mar. 1803. 447 acres.
Helphinstine, Peter. Va. Major. 26 Mar. 1803. 447 acres.
Helphinstine, Peter. Va. Major. 26 Mar. 1803. 447 acres.
Helphinstine, Peter. Va. Major. 26 Mar. 1803. 1341 acres.
Helphinstine, Peter. Va. Major. 26 Mar. 1803. 1981 1/3 acres.
Helphinstine, Peter. Va. Major. 13 Feb. 1861 1702 acres.
Helps, Ludwig. Pa. Private. 28 Sep. 1787. 200 acres.
Hemby, Dennis. Ga. Refugee. 14 Sep. 1784. 287 1/2 acres.
Hemmingway, Jared. Conn. Sufferer. New/ East Haven. 5.4.6.
Hemphill, Joseph. Md. ———. ———. 50 acres.
Hempleman, Adam. Pa. Private. ———. 200 acres.
Hempstead, John et al. Conn. Sufferers. New London. 30.18.0.
Hempstead, Joshua. Conn. Sufferer. New London. 62.15.3.
Hempstead, Nathaniel. Conn. Sufferer. New London. 7.1.10.
Hempstead, Stephen. Conn. Sufferer. New London. 70.6.1.
Hender, Frederick. N. Y. Private. 8 Jul. 1790. 600 acres.
Henderson, Abraham. N.C. Private. 30 Sep. 1785. 640 acres to heirs.
Henderson, Alexander. Pa. Private. 12 Feb. 1805. 200 acres.
Henderson, Andrew. N.C. Private. 8 Dec. 1796. 640 acres to heir James Henderson.
Henderson, Andrew. Pa. Private. 21 Dec. 1786. 200 acres.
Henderson, Andrew. Pa. Lieutenant. 21 Dec. 1786. 200 acres.
Henderson, Archibald. N. C. Drummer. 23 Oct. 1783. 773 acres.
Henderson, Bennett. Ga. ———. 19 Jul. 1784. 1000 acres.
Henderson, David. Md. ———. ———. 50 acres.
Henderson, David. Va. Midshipman. 30 Oct. 1783. 2666 2/3 acres.
Henderson, Elisha. N.Y. ———. 13 Sep. 1790. 500 acres to heirs.
Henderson, Gustavius. Pa. Surgeon. 14 Oct. 1786. 300 acres to John Henderson, administrator.
Henderson, Henry. Pa. Private. 6 Oct. 1786. 200 acres.
Henderson, James. N.C. Private. 10 Dec. 1788. 640 acres to heirs.
Henderson, John. Va. Private. 17 Feb. 1785. 100 acres.
Henderson, Joseph. Ga. ———. 17 May 1784. ———.
Henderson, Robert. N.C. Private & Sergeant. 28 Jul. 1784. 307 acres.
Henderson, Sampson. Va. Private. 26 May 1786. 100 acres.
Henderson, Samuel. Ga. ———. 17 May 1784. ———.
Henderson, Samuel. N. Y. Private. 8 Jul. 1790. 600 acres.
Henderson, Samuel. Pa. ———. 8 Jan. 1803. 200 acres to heirs.
Henderson, Simon. N.C. Private. 5 Dec. 1796. 640 acres.
Henderson, William. Ga. ———. 25 May 1784. 460 acres.
Henderson, William. Pa. Captain. 30 Jan. 1787. 500 acres.

Henderson, William. S.C. Colonel. 15 Oct. 1784. 500 acres.

Henderson, William. S.C. ———. 4 Apr. 1785. 200 acres.

Henderson, William. S.C. ———. 1 Aug. 1785. 200 acres.

Henderson, William. S.C. ———. 2 Jul. 1787. 200 acres.

Henderson, William. Va. Captain. 29 Dec. 1851. 666 2/3 acres.

Henderson, William. Va. Captain. 29 Dec. 1851. 333 1/3 acres.

Henderson, William. Va. Captain. 16 Apr. 1852. 333 1/3 acres.

Henderson, William. Va. Captain. 16 Apr. 1852. 333 1/3 acres.

Henderson, William. Va. Captain. 16 Apr. 1852. 333 1/3 acres.

Henderson, William. Va. Captain. 16 Apr. 1852. 333 1/3 acres.

Henderson, William. Va. Captain. 16 Apr. 1852. 333 1/3 acres.

Henderson, William. Va. Captain. 16 Apr. 1832. 333 1/3 acres.

Henderson, William. Va. Captain. 16 Apr. 1852. 833 1/3 acres.

Henderson, William. Va. Captain. 15 Dec. 1852. 500 acres.

Henderson, William. Va. Captain. 21 Feb. 1853. 833 1/3 acres.

Henderson, Zachariah. Ga. Lieutenant. 15 Mar. 1784. 250 acres.

Hendley, Charles. Va. Private. 29 Mar. 1833. 100 acres.

Hendly, William. N.C. Private. 1 Sep. 1785. 640 acres to heirs.

Hendrake, Moses. Va. Private. 5 Mar. 1784. 100 acres.

Hendren, Ephraim. Va. Private. 17 Apr. 1783. 200 acres.

Hendren, Robert. Va. Private. 23 May 1785. 100 acres.

Hendren, William. Va. Sergeant. 10 Apr. 1784. 400 acres.

Hendrick, Benjamin. Va. Private. 2 Jul. 1787. 100 acres.

Hendrick, Nathan. Conn. Sufferer. Norwalk. 19.8.3.

Hendrick, Peter. Conn. Sufferer. Fairfield. 399.6.9.

Hendricks, Albert. N.C. Private. 24 Dec. 1796. 640 acres.

Hendricks, Elijah. Va. Sergeant. 14 Jul. 1782. 200 acres.

Hendricks, James. Va. Lieutenant Colonel. 13 Feb. 1834. 6000 acres.

Hendricks, Thomas. N.C. Private. 27 Jun. 1788. 640 acres.

Hendrickson, Cornelius. N. Y. Private. 8 Jul. 1790. 600 acres.

Hendrickson, James. Md. Matross. ———. 50 acres.

Henesey, John. N. Y. Private. 8 Jul. 1790. 600 acres.

Henesey, William. Va. Private. 26 Jun. 1797. 100 acres.

Henis John. Va. Private. 23 Feb. 1784. 100 acres.

Henley, Henry. Pa. ———. 5 Oct. 1786. 200 acres to Alexander Power, assignee.

Henley, Henry. Pa. Lieutenant. 1 Oct. 1786. 200 acres to Alexander Power, assignee.

Henley, John. Ga. Soldier. 20 Aug. 1785. ———.

Henly, David. N.Y. ———. 13 Sep. 1790. 500 acres to heirs.

Henly, Hugh. Pa. Private. 3 Nov. 1786. 200 acres.

Henly, John. Pa. Private. 9 Mar. 1795. 200 acres to John Nicholson, assignee.

Henly, Marmaduke. Pa. Private. 4 Mar. 1785. 200 acres.

Hennage, George. Va. Private. 13 Dec. 1784. 100 acres.

Henning, George. Va. Private. 25 Feb. 1807. 100 acres.

Hennisee, Edward. Md. Private. ———. 50 acres.

Henries, Elizabeth. Conn. Sufferer. Danbury. 18.9.8.

Henry, Christopher. Va. Private. 5 May 1783. 200 acres.

Henry, David. Va.-Ind. Private. 108 acres.

Henry, David. Pa. ———. 26 Feb. 1808. 200 acres.

Henry, George. Pa. Private. 4 Aug. 1787. 200 acres.

Henry, Hugh. Va.-Ind. Private. 108 acres.

Henry, Isaac. Va.-Ind. Private. 108 acres.

Henry, Isham. N.C. Private. 30 Sep. 1785. 640 acres to heirs.

Henry, James. Va. Private. 19 Dec. 1783. 100 acres.

Henry, James, Jr. Ga. Citizen. 19 Dec. 1785. 287 1/2 acres.

Henry, John. Va.-Ind. Private. 108 acres.

Henry, John. N.C. Private. 28 May 1784. 640 acres.

Henry, John. Pa. Private. 20 Nov. 1787. 200 acres to Richard Leedom, assignee.
Henry, Jonathan. N.C. Private. 17 Dec. 1785. 640 acres to heirs.
Henry, Joseph. Va. Private. 2 Dec. 1783. 100 acres.
Henry, Michael. N.Y. ———. 13 Sep. 1790. 500 acres to heirs.
Henry, Micjah. N.C. Private. 15 Feb. 1797. 320 acres.
Henry, Philip. Pa. Private. 5 Oct. 1786. 200 acres.
Henshaw, Josiah. Mass. Corporal. 6 Nov. 1834. 200 acres.
Henshaw, William. Va. Private. 6 Nov. 1783. 200 acres.
Hensley, Thomas, Jr. Ga. Private. ———. 250 acres.
Hensley, William. Va. Private. 26 — 1784. 100 acres.
Henson, James. Ga. Soldier. 15 Jul. 1785. ———.
Henson, Samuel. Ga. Refugee. 7 Apr. 1784. ———.
Henson, Shadrack. Va. Private. 29 Sep. 1810. 200 acres.
Henson, Shadrack. Va. Private. 17 Dec. 1785. 200 acres.
Henthorn, Philip. Va. Private. 23 Jun. 1783. 200 acres.
Hentz, Frederick. Va. Private. 30 Jan. 1807. 100 acres.
Herbert, Argyle. Va. Lieutenant. 18 Mar. 1834. 4000 acres.
Herbert, Pascow. Va. Lieutenant. 14 Jul. 1794. 2666 2/3 acres.
Herbert, Pascow. Va. ———. 27 Jun. 1838. 1333 1/3 acres.
Herbert, Pascow. Va. ———. 14 Jan. 1839. 1000 acres.
Herbert, Pascow. Va. ———. 14 Jan. 1839. 333 acres.
Herbert, Stewart. Pa. Lieutenant. 11 Oct. 1786. 200 acres.
Herbert, Stewart. Pa. Lieutenant. 9 Oct. 1786. 200 acres.
Herbert, Thomas. Va. Captain. 5 Jul. 1784. 4000 acres.
Herbert, Thomas. Va. Captain. 19 Mar. 1834. 1333 1/3 acres.
Herbert, Thomas. Va. Captain. 19 Mar. 1834. 148 4/27 acres.
Herbert, Thomas. Va. Captain. 19 Mar. 1834. 148 4/27 acres.
Herbert, Thomas. Va. Captain. 19 Mar. 1834. 148 4/27 acres.
Herbert, Thomas. Va. Captain. 19 Mar. 1834. 74 2/27 acres.
Herbert, Thomas. Va. Captain. 19 Mar. 1834. 444 4/9 acres.
Herbert, Thomas. Va. Captain. 19 Mar. 1834. 74 2/27 acres.
Herbert, Thomas. Va. Captain. 19 Mar. 1834. 74 2/27 acres.
Herbert, Thomas. Va. Captain. 19 Mar. 1834. 111 1/9 acres.
Herbert, Thomas. Va. Captain. 19 Mar. 1834. 111 1/9 acres.
Herbert, William. N.C. Sergeant. 27 Nov. 1816. 1000 acres to heirs.
Herbert, William. Va. Private. 23 Jun. 1783. 200 acres.
Herbold, Adam. Pa. ———. 31 Mar. 1803. 200 acres.
Herd, Charles. S.C. ———. 2 Jun. 1788. 70 acres.
Herd, George. Ga. Refugee. 15 Mar. 1784. 250 acres.
Hern, Drury. N.C. Private. 21 Oct. 1783. 228 acres.
Hern, Ephraim. Va. Private. 23 Mar. 1796. 200 acres.
Hern, John. N.C. Private. 9 Dec. 1808. 640 acres to heirs.
Herndon, Drury. N.C. Private. 15 Dec. 1797. 640 acres.
Herndon, Edward. Va. Sergeant. 17 Dec. 1808. 200 acres.
Herndon, Edward. Va. Captain. 1 Aug. 1834. 4000 acres.
Herndon, George. Ga. ———. 17 May 1784. ———.
Herndon, George. N.C. Private. 14 Dec. 1796. 640 acres to heirs.
Herndon, Joseph. Ga. ———. 17 May 1784. ———.
Herndon, Roger. N.C. Private. 9 Feb. 1796. 640 acres to heirs.
Heron, Henry. N.C. Private. 14 Feb. 1796. 640 acres.
Heron, Howell. N.C. Private. 17 Feb. 1824. 640 acres.
Heron, Patrick. Pa. Private. 20 Mar. 1787. 200 acres to Mary Heron, administratrix.
Herrall, John. N.C. Sergeant. 3 Dec. 1796. 1000 acres to heirs.

Herrick, Stephen. Conn. Sufferer. New/East Haven. 15.0.0.
Herrin, Job. N.C. Private. 6 Dec. 1797. 640 acres to heirs.
Herring, Benjamin. N. Y. Ensign. 6 Jul. 1790. 1150 acres.
Herring, Burwell. N.C. Private. 10 Dec. 1788. 640 acres to heirs.
Herring, Henry. N.C. Private. 5 Dec. 1796. 640 acres.
Herring, Jacob. N.C. Private. 23 Apr. 1785. 640 acres to heirs.
Herrington, Drury. N.C. Private. 30 Sep. 1785. 640 acres to heirs.
Herrington, Isaac. N.C. Private. 24 Nov. 1796. 274 acres.
Herrington, Samuel. N.C. Private. 12 Dec. 1796. 640 acres to heirs.
Herrington, William. Md. Private. ———. 50 acres.
Herrington, William. N.C. Private. 24 Nov. 1796. 274 acres.
Herritage, John. N.C. Captain. 22 Oct. 1783. 1280 acres.
Herron, Armwell. N.C.. Captain. 20 Sep. 1821. 3840 acres.
Hertford, William. Ga. Soldier. 26 Apr. 1785. ———.
Hester, David. N.C. Private. 10 Aug. 1785. 640 acres to heir.
Hester, John. N.C. Private. 10 Aug. 1785. 640 acres to heir.
Hesum, John. N. Y. Private. 8 Jul. 1790. 600 acres.
Heswell, Thomas. Ga. ———. 17 May 1784. ———.
Heth, Andrew. Va. Lieutenant. 30 Jan. 1834. 2666 2/3 acres.
Heth, Andrew. Va. ———. 19 Dec. 1835. 1778 1/3 acres.
Heth, Henry. Va. Captain. 20 Oct. 1783. 4000 acres.
Heth, John. Va. Lieutenant. 10 Jun. 1783. 1000 acres.
Heth, John. Va. Lieutenant. 10 Jun. 1783. 1666 acre.
Heth, John. Va. Lieutenant. 3 Aug. 1807. 370 acres.
Heth, William. Va. Colonel. 10 Dec. 1783. 1000 acres.
Heth, William. Va. Colonel. 10 Dec. 1783. 6777 acres.
Heth, William. Va. Colonel. 8 Dec. 1809. 926 acres.
Heusted, Abraham. Conn. Sufferer. Greenwich. 0.0.0.
Heusted, Benjamin. Conn. Sufferer. Greenwich. 6.0.0.
Heusted, Moses, Jr. Conn. Sufferer. Greenwich. 2.0.3.
Heusted, Nat. Conn. Sufferer. Greenwich. 41.7.5.
Heusted, Peter. Conn. Sufferer. Greenwich. 86.8.11.
Hewell, Thomas. Va. Private. 2 Sep. 1783. 200 acres.
Hewet, Caleb. Pa. Sergeant. 20 Sep. 1787. 250 acres.
Hewett, James. Md. Private. ———. 50 acres.
Hewings, Thomas. N.C. Private. 4 Aug. 1821. 640 acres.
Hewit, Ebenezer. N.C. Private. 29 Nov. 1792. 640 acres.
Hewit, William. Ga. ———. ———. 250 acres.
Hewitt, Asa. Mass. Fifer. 19 Nov. 1832. 200 acres to heirs.
Hews, Sarah. Conn. Sufferer. Fairfield. 15.9.6.
Hext, William. S.C. Captain. 21 Jan. 1785. 300 acres.
Heyren, Frederick. S.C. ———. 3 Sep. 1787. 200 acres.
Heyward, John Hall [?Hill]. Va. Private. 28 May 1783. 200 acres.
Hezard, Moses. N.C. Private. 21 Apr. 1784. 640 acres to heirs.
Hibbard, Jonathan, Jr. Conn. Sufferer. Greenwich. 31.9.7.
Hickell, Abijah. Md. ———. ———. 50 acres.
Hickens, John. Md. Private. ———. 50 acres.
Hickenson, William. Md. Private. ———. 50 acres.
Hickerison, Chester. N.C. Private. 30 Sep. 1785. 640 acres to heirs.
Hickey, Charles. Md. Private. ———. 50 acres.
Hickingbottom, Burrows. Ga. ———. 17 May 1784. ———.
Hickingbottom, Joseph. Ga. ———. 17 May 1784. ———.
Hickman, Charles. N.C. Private. 12 Sep. 1785. 640 acres to heirs.
Hickman, Corbin. N.C. Private. 7 Jan. 1786. 640 acres to heirs.

Hickman, Edward. N.C. Private. 3 Dec. 1796. 274 acres.
Hickman, Elijah. Va. Private. 15 Jan. 1808. 100 acres.
Hickman, Ezekiel. Va. Private. 15 Jan. 1808. 100 acres.
Hickman, Jacob. Ga. ———. 17 May 1784. ———.
Hickman, John. N.C. Private. 3 Dec. 1796. 274 acres.
Hicks, Benjamin. N. Y. Captain. 9 Jul. 1790. 1800 acres.
Hicks, Edmund Bugg. Ga. ———. 26 May 1784. 287 1/2 acres.
Hicks, Gersham. Pa. Private. ———. 200 acres.
Hicks, Hansel. N.C. Private. 29 Sep. 1784. 274 acres.
Hicks, Harris. N.C. Private. 22 Dec. 1796. 640 acres to heirs.
Hicks, Henry. N.C. Private. 6 May 1784. 640 acres.
Hicks, Henry. N.C. Private. 28 May 1784. 640 acres to Andrew Haddock.
Hicks, Isaac. Ga. Major. ———. 920 acres.
Hicks, Isaac. N.C. Private. 14 Dec. 1796. 228 acres.
Hicks, Jacob. N. Y. Sergeant. 8 Jul. 1790. 600 acres.
Hicks, Jacob. N. Y. Sergeant. 9 Jul. 1790. 600 acres.
Hicks, Jacob. N.C. Private. 22 Apr. 1785. 228 acres.
Hicks, John. Ga. Refugee. 17 Feb. 1784. 250 acres.
Hicks, John. N.C. Private. 30 Sep. 1785. 640 acres to heirs.
Hicks, John. Conn. Sufferer. Groton. 7.8.0.
Hicks, Micajah. N.C. Private. 14 Dec. 1797. 228 acres to heirs.
Hicks, Micajah. N.C. Private. 9 Sep. 1835. 640 acres.
Hicks, Mordecai. Va. Private. 14 Aug. 1834. 100 acres.
Hicks, Nathaniel, Jr. Ga. ———. 17 May 1784. ———.
Hicks, Nathaniel, Sr. Ga. ———. 15 Mar. 1784. 250 acres.
Hicks, Robert. N.C. Private. 27 Nov. 1783. 228 acres.
Hicks, Samuel. Ga. ———. 17 May 1784. ———.
Hicks, Samuel. Me. ———. 21 Nov. 1835. 200 acres to widow Clarissa Hicks. Portland.
Hicks, Theophilus. N.C. Private. 7 Dec. 1797. 640 acres.
Hicks, Thomas. N.C. Musician. 16 Aug. 1821. 1000 acres.
Hicks, Tuebell. N.C. Sergeant. 30 Mar. 1785. 1000 acres to heirs.
Hicks, William. Md. Private. ———. 50 acres.
Hicks, William. N.C. Private. 30 Sep. 1785. 640 acres to heirs.
Hicks, William. Va. Private. 20 Jun. 1783. 100 acres.
Hicks, William. Va. Private. 9 Jun. 1783. 100 acres.
Hicks, Zebulon. N.C. Private. 23 Nov. 1797. 228 acres.
Hickson, James. Va. Private. 20 Dec. 1803. 200 acres.
Hickson, James. Va. Private. 25 Mar. 1857. 200 acres.
Hicock, Benjamin. Conn. Sufferer. Danbury. 9.14.4.
Hicock, Daniel. Conn. Sufferer. Danbury. 6.4.3.
Hicock, Nathan. Conn. Sufferer. Norwalk. 2.5.3.
Hicock, Silas. Conn. Sufferer. Norwalk. 3.12.6.
Hide, Samuel. N.C. Private. 17 Feb. 1824. 640 acres.
Hiden, William. Va. Private. 29 Apr. 1807. 100 acres.
Hifferlin, John. Va. Private. 16 Dec. 1784. 100 acres.
Higby, Samuel. N. Y. Private. 8 Jul. 1790. 500 acres.
Higden, John. Va. Sailor. 6 Jun. 1783. 100 acres.
Higden, Ridgnal. Va. Seaman. 30 Dec. 1839. 75 acres.
Higder, Charles. Va. Sailor. 27 Sep. 1786. 100 acres.
Higdon, John. Va. Seaman. 15 Jun. 1858. 100 acres.
Higdon, John. Va. Corporal. 21 Jan. 1799. 200 acres.
Higgens, John. Md. Private. ———. 50 acres.
Higginbotham, William. Va. Sergeant. 9 Mar. 1793. 400 acres.

Higginbotham, William. Va. Sergeant. 28 Feb. 1810. 55 acres.

Higginbotham, William. Va. Lieutenant. 5 Nov. 1811. 500 acres.

Higginbotham, William. Va. Lieutenant. 5 Nov. 1811. 500 acres.

Higginbotham, William. Va. Lieutenant. 5 Nov. 1811. 500 acres.

Higginbotham, William. Va. Lieutenant. 5 Nov. 1811. 500 acres.

Higginbotham, William. Va. Lieutenant. 5 Nov. 1811. 666 2/3 acres.

Higgins, Absalom. N.C. Private. 9 Dec. 1805. 640 acres to heirs.

Higgins, Barney. Va.-Ind. Private. 108 acres.

Higgins, James. Pa. Private. 9 Dec. 1786. 200 acres to John Donnelly, assignee.

Higgins, James. Va. Lieutenant. 3 Jul. 1821. 1333 1/3 acres.

Higgins, James. Va. Lieutenant. 3 Jul. 1821. 1333 1/3 acres.

Higgins, John. Va. Private. 4 Oct. 1783. 100 acres.

Higgins, Nathaniel. N. Y. Sergeant. 9 Jul. 1790. 600 acres.

Higgins, Nehemiah. Conn. Sufferer. New/East Haven. 2.8.11.

Higgins, Nicholas. Ga. Minute Man. 22 Mar. 1785. 250 acres.

Higgins, Peter. N.C. Private. 4 Sep. 1820. 640 acres to heirs.

Higgins, Peter. Va. Lieutenant. 5 Jun. 1783. 2666 2/3 acres.

Higgins, Robert. Va. Captain. 30 Aug. 1783. 4000 acres.

Higgins, Thomas. N.Y. ———. 13 Sep. 1790. 500 acres to heirs.

Higgins, Thomas. N.C. Private. 13 Sep. 1820. 640 acres.

Higgins, Valentine. N.C. Private. 6 Dec. 1797. 640 acres to heirs.

Higgins, William. Conn. Sufferer. New London. 4.11.0.

Higgs, Henry. Md. Matross. ———. 50 acres.

Higgs, Lazarus. Md. Private. ———. 50 acres.

Highdon, Joseph. Va. Corporal. 28 Mar. 1799. 400 acres.

Highland, Robert. Va. Drummer. 25 Aug. 1783. 200 acres.

Highland, William. Va. Private. 17 Apr. 1783. 200 acres.

Hight, George. Va. Private. 30 Jun. 1784. 100 acres.

Hightower, William. Ga. ———. 17 May 1784. ———.

Hilbert, John. N.C. Private. 21 Aug. 1820. 640 acres.

Hilbert, John. Va. Trumpeter. 14 Sep. 1799. 200 acres.

Hilher, Henry. Pa. Private. ———. 200 acres.

Hill, Abner. Ga. ———. 17 May 1784. ———.

Hill, Abraham. Ga. ———. 17 May 1784. ———.

Hill, Abraham. Ga. ———. 15 Mar. 1784. 250 acres.

Hill, Abraham. Va. Private. 8 Dec. 1784 [1785]. 100 acres.

Hill, Adam. Pa. Private. 28 Nov. 1786. 200 acres.

Hill, Amos. Va. Private. 18 Apr. 1783. 200 acres.

Hill, Archibald. Ga. ———. 22 Sep. 1784. 287 1/2 acres.

Hill, Baylor. Va. Captain. 20 Jan. 1783. 4000 acres.

Hill, Baylor. Va. Captain. 14 Sep. 1797. 666 2/3 acres.

Hill, Benjamin. N.C. Private. 9 Dec. 1797. 640 acres to heirs.

Hill, Caleb. Va. Private. 21 Jun. 1792. 100 acres.

Hill, Charles. Md. Private. ———. 50 acres.

Hill, Christopher. Ga. ———. 15 Mar. 1784. 250 acres.

Hill, Daniel. Mass. Private. 18 Oct. 1833. 200 acres.

Hill, David. Me. Sergeant. 23 Aug. 1839. 200 acres to widow Parnel Hill. Waterborough.

Hill, E. Edmond. N. Y. Matross. 9 Jul. 1790. 500 acres.

Hill, Edward. Ga. ——— 17 May 1784. ———.

Hill, Elijah. Conn. Sufferer. New/East Haven. 16.11.6.

Hill, George. Md. ———. ———. 50 acres.

Hill, George. N.C. Private. 16 Aug. 1821. 640 acres.

Hill, George. Va. Private. 25 Feb. 1797. 200 acres.

Hill, Gideon. Va. Private. 6 Feb 1784. 100 acres.
Hill, Hardy. N.C. Sergeant. 9 Feb. 1796. 1000 acres to heirs.
Hill, Henry. N. Y. Drummer. 7 Jul. 1790. 600 acres.
Hill, Henry. Va. Private. 18 Nov. 1783. 100 acres.
Hill, Isaac. Ga. ———. 17 May 1784. ———.
Hill, Isaac. Md. Drummer. ———. 50 acres.
Hill, Isaac. N.C. Private. 22 Apr. 1785. 228 acres.
Hill, Jacob. Ga. ———. 15 Mar. 1784. 250 acres.
Hill, Jacob. Pa. Private. 29 Dec. 1786. 200 acres.
Hill, Jacob. Pa. Private. 26 Sep. 1787. 200 acres.
Hill, James. Ga. Refugee. 15 Mar. 1784. 500 acres.
Hill, James. Md. Private. ———. 50 acres.
Hill, James. N.C. Private. 30 Sep. 1785. 640 acres to heirs.
Hill, James. Va. Sergeant. 2 May 1783. 200 acres.
Hill, James. Va. Sailor. 13 Apr. 1784. 100 acres.
Hill, James. Va. Sailor. 15 Apr. 1853. 100 acres.
Hill, James. Va. Private. 12 Sep. 1785. 100 acres.
Hill, James. Va. Private. 5 May 1832. 200 acres.
Hill, John. Ga. Captain. 24 May 1784. 287 1/2 acres.
Hill, John. N.C. Lieutenant. 20 Apr. 1784. 2560 acres.
Hill, John. N.C. Private. 9 Nov. 1784. 365 acres.
Hill, John. Pa. Private. 17 Apr. 1785. 200 acres.
Hill, John. S.C. ———. 4 Jul. 1785. 196 acres.
Hill, John. Va. Private. 4 Apr. 1783. 100 acres.
Hill, John. Va. Private. 24 Jan. 1789. 200 acres.
Hill, Joseph. Ga. ———. 17 May 1784. ———.
Hill, Joseph. N.C. Private. 2 Feb. 1786. 640 acres to heirs.
Hill, Joshua. Ga. Refugee. 17 May 1784. 250 acres.
Hill, Joshua. N.Y. ———. 13 Sep. 1790. 500 acres to heirs.
Hill, Moses. Ga. ———. 17 May 1784. ———.
Hill, Nicholas. N. Y. Sergeant. 7 Jul. 1790. 600 acres.
Hill, Noah. Mass. Private. 8 Oct. 1834. 200 acres.
Hill, Obadiah. N. Y. Matross. 9 Jul. 1790. 500 acres.
Hill, Peter. Ga. Soldier. 4 Feb. 1785. ———.
Hill, Philip. Md. Lieutenant. ———. 200 acres.
Hill, Richard. Ga. ———. 19 Jul. 1784. 287 1/2 acres.
Hill, Richard. Va. Lieutenant. 18 Sep. 1850. 889 acres.
Hill, Richard. Va. Lieutenant. 18 Sep. 1850. 444 1/2 acres.
Hill, Richard. Va. Lieutenant. 18 Sep. 1850. 222 1/3 acres.
Hill, Richard. Va. Lieutenant. 18 Sep. 1850. 777 1/3 acres.
Hill, Richard. Va. Lieutenant. 16 Oct. 1851. 222 acres.
Hill, Richard. Va. Lieutenant. 16 Oct. 1851. 111 acres.
Hill, Robertson. N.C. Private. 30 Sep. 1785. 640 acres to heirs.
Hill, Spencer. Va. Private. 23 May 1785. 100 acres.
Hill, Thomas. Me. ———. 16 Jul. 1835. 200 acres to widow Ruth (Allen) Stubbs. Cumberland.
Hill, Thomas. Md. Private. ———. 50 acres.
Hill, Thomas. N. Y. Private. 8 Jul. 1790. 500 acres.
Hill, Thomas. N.C. Corporal. 30 May 1820. 357 acres to heirs.
Hill, Thomas. N.C. Private. 16 Aug. 1821. 640 acres.
Hill, Thomas. Va. Major. 27 Dec. 1782. 5333 1/3 acres.
Hill, Thomas. Va. Private. 22 Aug. 1783. 200 acres.
Hill, Thomas. Va. Major. 16 Sep. 1808. 361 1/2 acres.
Hill, Thomas. Va. Major. 16 Sep. 1808. 361 1/2 acres.

Hill, Thomas. Va. Major. 16 Sep. 1808. 181 acres.
Hill, Thomas. Va. Major. 16 Sep. 1808. 181 acres.
Hill, Thomas. Va. Major. 16 Sep. 1808. 181 acres.
Hill, Thomas. Va. Major. 16 Sep. 1808. 181 acres.
Hill, Thomas. Va. Major. 16 Sep. 1808. 181 acres.
Hill, William. Ga. Refugee. 15 Mar. 1784. 250 acres.
Hill, William. Md. Private. ———. 50 acres.
Hill, William. N.C. Private. 5 Sep. 1821. 640 acres.
Hillard, James. Ga. ———. 17 May 1784. ———.
Hillard, James. N.C. Private. 4 Aug. 1821. 640 acres.
Hillary, Christopher. Ga. Lieutenant. 8 Sep. 1783. 460 acres.
Hillary, John. Md. Private. ———. 50 acres.
Hillery, Rignel. Md. Lieutenant. ———. 200 acres.
Hilliard, Joseph. Va. Private. 22 Aug. 1783. 200 acres.
Hillier, John. Via. Private. 4 Nov. 1784. 100 acres.
Hillman, William. Md. Private. ———. 50 acres.
Hillyea, David. Pa. Sergeant. 5 Apr. 1787. 250 acres.
Hilton, Moral. Me. Private. 25 Aug. 1835. 200 acres. Wiscasset.
Hilton, Roger. N.C. Private. 17 Dec. 1785. 640 acres to heirs.
Hilton, William. Me. ———. 22 Apr. 1835. 200 acres. Solon.
Hilton, William. N.C. Lieutenant. 16 Oct. 1783. 2560 acres to Daniel Hilton, heir at law.
Hilty, Conrad. N. Y. Matross. 9 Jul. 1790. 600 acres.
Hiltz, Frederick. N. Y. ———. 6 Apr. 1808. 200 acres to trustee Nathan Smith.
Himebright, John. Pa. Private. 4 Jun. 1789. 200 acres.
Hinckley, Joshua. N. Y. Matross. 9 Jul. 1790. 600 acres.
Hinckley, Philip. Mass. Corporal. 3 Mar. 1831. 200 acres.
Hinckley, Seth. Me. Fifer. 22 May 1844. 200 acres to widow Gennett Mayo, late widow of Joseph Mayo. Fairfield.
Hinckley, Seth. Mass. Fife Major. 3 Mar. 1831. 200 acres to heirs.
Hindley, Jacob. Ga. ———. 30 Sep. 1784. 287 1/2 acres.
Hinds, Benjamin. Me. Private. 27 May 1835. 200 acres to widow Anna Hinds. Madison.
Hinds, John. Va. Fifer. 23 Jun. 1783. 200 acres.
Hinds, John. Va. Private. 18 Jan. 1822. 100 acres.
Hinds, Thomas. Va. Private. 4 Jan. 1812. 100 acres.
Hine, Richard. Me. ———. 8 Apr. 1835. 200 acres to widow Abiah Hine. Hartford.
Hiner, Nicholas. Md. Private. ———. 50 acres.
Hines, Andrew. N.C. Private. 30 Sep. 1785. 640 acres to heirs.
Hines, George. Va. Sergeant. 26 Jun. 1783. 200 acres.
Hines, Hardy. N.C. Private. 23 Apr. 1785. 640 acres to heirs.
Hines, Hardy. N.C. Private. 4 Aug. 1821. 640 acres.
Hines, Henry. Md. Private. ———. 50 acres.
Hines, Isaac. Md. Private. ———. 50 acres.
Hines, Jacob. Md. Private. ———. 50 acres.
Hines, James. Va. Corporal. 13 Jun. 1783. 200 acres.
Hines, James. Va. Private. 22 Nov. 1783. — acres.
Hiney, Jacob. Pa. Matross. ———. 200 acres.
Hinley, Henry. Va. Sergeant. 27 Jul. 1784. 200 acres.
Hinman, Baily. Va. Private. 14 Feb. 1834. 200 acres.
Hinman, Elijah. Va. Private. 15 Jun. 1807. 100 acres.
Hinman, Ralph. Va. Private. 14 Feb. 1834. 100 acres.
Hinmon, Bundeck. Va. Private. 19 Nov. 1833. 100 acres.
Hinnis, Benberry. N.C. Private. 30 Sep. 1785. 640 acres to heirs.

Hinson, Benjamin. N.C. Private. 17 Dec. 1812. 640 acres to heirs.
Hinson, Jesse. S.C. ———. 2 Oct. 1786. 200 acres.
Hinson, John. Ga. Soldier 5 Dec. 1785. 230 acres.
Hinson, William. N.C. Private. 18 Dec. 1817. 640 acres to heirs.
Hinson, William. S.C. ———. 2 Oct. 1786. 200 acres.
Hinson, William, Sr. S.C. ———. 4 Sep. 1786. 200 acres.
Hinton, Hardy. Ga. ———. 15 Mar. 1784. 250 acres.
Hinton, Job. Ga. ———. 15 Mar. 1784. 250 acres.
Hinton, John. N.C. Private. 30 Sep. 1785. 640 acres to heirs.
Hinton, Joseph. N.C. Musician. 2 Sep. 1820. 1000 acres.
Hinton, Lewis. Va. Seaman. 19 Mar. 1835. 100 acres.
Hinton, Spencer. Va. Seaman. 9 Aug. 183-. 100 acres.
Hinton, William. Va. Sailor. 27 Jul. 1783. 100 acres.
Hipkenstall, James. Va. Private. 20 Oct. 1784. 200 acres.
Hislip, Kindle. N.C. Private. 23 Apr. 1784. 640 acres.
Hitchcock, Brampton. N. Y. Matross. 9 Jul. 1790. 500 acres.
Hitchcock, Jane. Conn. Sufferer. Norwalk. 19.8.6.
Hitchcock, John. N.C. Private. 7 Jan. 1786. 640 acres to heirs.
Hitchcock, Mindwell. Conn. Sufferer. Greenwich. 18.17.10.
Hitchcock, Peter. Conn. Sufferer. Norwalk. 11.13.6.
Hitchcock, Samuel. N. Y. Private. 8 Jul. 1790. 600 acres.
Hitchcock, Thomas. Conn. Sufferer. Greenwich. 33.2.0.
Hitcherick, Philip. Pa. Private. 10 Mar. 1795. 200 acres to Clement Biddle, assignee.
Hite, Abraham. Va. Captain. 7 Apr. 1783. 2000 acres.
Hite, Abraham. Va. Colonel. 7 Apr. 1783. 2000 acres.
Hite, Abraham. Va. Captain. 4 Nov. 1808. 611 acres.
Hite, George. Va. Subaltern. 24 Feb. 1784. 2666 2/3 acres.
Hite, Isaac. Va. Lieutenant. 5 Jun. 1784. 2666 2/3 acres.
Hite, Joseph. Va. Ensign. 22 Dec. 1809. 2666 2/3 acres.
Hite, Julius. Va. Corporal. 5 May 1784. 400 acres.
Hitherly, Thomas. Va. Private. 23 Jan. 1810. 100 acres.
Hitson, John. N.C. Private. 30 Sep. 1785. 640 acres to heirs.
Hix, Daniel. Va. Private. 21 Dec. 1833. 100 acres.
Hix, David. Va. Lieutenant. 11 Oct. 1826. 2666 2/3 acres.
Hix, Edward. Va. Private. 9 Aug. 1783. 100 acres.
Hix, James. N.C. Private. 7 Dec. 1797. 228 acres.
Hix, James. Va. Private. 30 Jun. 1784. 100 acres.
Hix, William. Va. Private. 27 May 1783. 100 acres.
Hoaksly, James. N. Y. Drummer. 8 Jul. 1790. 600 acres.
Hoback, Philip. Pa. Private. 20 Mar. 1789. 200 acres.
Hobart, Justin. Conn. Sufferer. Fairfield. 15.10.9.
Hobbs, Frederick. Va. Private. 26 Jun. 1783. 2333 1/3 acres.
Hobbs, Isaac. N.C. Private. 30 Sep. 1785. 640 acres to heirs.
Hobbs, Joel. N.C. Private. 30 Sep. 1785. 640 acres to heirs.
Hobbs, Jonathan. Ga. ———. 17 May 1784. ———.
Hobbs, Josiah. Me. Musician. 4 Jun. 1835. 200 acres. Falmouth.
Hobbs, Moses. N.C. Private. 30 Sep. 1785. 640 acres to heirs.
Hobbs, Thomas. Va. Private. 17 Apr. 1783. 200 acres.
Hobby, John. Conn. Sufferer. Greenwich. 146.4.9.
Hobby, Joseph, Jr. Conn. Sufferer. Greenwich. 25.16.5.
Hobby, Mills. Conn. Sufferer. Greenwich. 6.0.0.
Hobby, Thomas. Conn. Sufferer. Greenwich. 69.19.3.
Hobby, Thomas, Jr. Conn. Sufferer. Greenwich. 18.13.4.

Hobday, Francis. Va. Seaman. 9 Nov. 1868. 200 acres.
Hobday, William. Va. Private. 20 Sep. 1783. 100 acres.
Hobson, Briggs. Ga. ———. 17 May 1784. ———.
Hobson, John. Ga. ———. 17 May 1784. ———.
Hobson, Nicholas. Va. Captain. 16 Sep. 1808. 1000 acres.
Hobson, Nicholas. Va. Captain. 16 Sep. 1808. 1000 acres.
Hobson, Nicholas. Va. Captain. 16 Sep. 1808. 1000 acres.
Hobson, Nicholas. Va. Captain. 16 Sep. 1808. 1000 acres.
Hochamer, Phillip. N.C. Private. 27 Jul. 1785. 640 acres.
Hockaday, John. Va. Captain. 23 Jul. 1808. 1000 acres.
Hockaday, John. Va. Captain. 23 Jul. 1808. 1000 acres.
Hockaday, John. Va. Captain. 23 Jul. 1808. 1000 acres.
Hockaday, John. Va. Captain. 23 Jul. 1808. 1000 acres.
Hockaday, Philip. Va. Lieutenant. 18 Mar. 1840. 703 2/3 acres.
Hockaday, Philip. Va. Lieutenant. 24 Nov. 1783. 2666 2/3 acres.
Hockaday, William. N.C. Private. 23 Aug. 1820. 640 acres to heirs Betsey (Hockaday) Jones and Warrick Hockaday.
Hockley, Richard. Pa. Private. 26 Sep. 1787. 200 acres.
Hodgdon, Jeremiah. Me. Private. 2 Aug. 1836. 200 acres to widow Thankful Hodgdon. Hebron.
Hodge, Abraham. N. Y. Private. 8 Jul. 1790. 600 acres.
Hodge, James. N. Y. Private. 8 Jul. 1790. 600 acres.
Hodge, James. Va. Sergeant. 31 Jul. 1783. 200 acres.
Hodge, John. Ga. Refugee. 1784. 250 acres.
Hodge, Robert. Ga. Refugee. 28 Feb. 1784. 500 acres.
Hodge, Roger. Ga. Refugee. Mar. 1785. ———.
Hodge, Thomas. Ga. Soldier. 6 Apr. 1785. 230 acres.
Hodge, Willoughby. Ga. Refugee. 28 Feb. 1784. 250 acres.
Hodges, Benjamin. N.C. Sergeant. 28 May 1784. 1000 acres.
Hodges, Hardy. N.C. Fifer. 7 Mar. 1785. 1000 acres to heir.
Hodges, James. N.C. Private. 22 Mar. 1804. 640 acres to heirs.
Hodges, John. N.C. Lieutenant. 25 Jul. 1784. 792 acres.
Hodges, Joseph. N.C. Private. 5 Sep. 1821. 640 acres.
Hodges, William. N.C. Private. 9 Feb. 1796. 640 acres to heirs.
Hodges, Williamson. Va. Private. 28 Jun. 1783. 233 1/3 acres.
Hodgings, Samuel. Va. Private. 22 Dec. 1783. 200 acres.
Hodgins, Joseph. Va. Private. 29 Apr. 1783. 200 acres.
Hodgton, Alvery. N.C. Lieutenant & Adjutant. 17 Feb. 1824. 2506 acres.
Hodibuck, Conrad. Md. Private. ———. 50 acres.
Hodsdon, Samuel. Me. Private. 19 Aug. 1836. 200 acres to widow Ann Hodsdon. South Berwick.
Hodsdon, Stephen. Me. ———. 23 Apr. 1835. 200 acres. Rumford.
Hoffler, William. Va. Captain. 5 Feb. 1783. 4000 acres.
Hoffler, William. Va. Captain. 17 Sep. 1783. 563 acres.
Hoffman, Christian. Pa. Private. 12 Jun. 1787. 200 acres.
Hoffman, Cornelius. Pa. ———. 18 Feb. 1803. 200 acres.
Hoffman, Reuben. Va. Private. 19 Mar. 1783. 100 acres.
Hofman, Charles. Pa. Private. ———. 200 acres to widow.
Hogan, David. N.C. Private. 9 Dec. 1796. 640 acres to heirs.
Hogan, David. Va. Private. 28 Jul. 1830. 200 acres.
Hogan, James. N.C. Brigadier General. 27 Nov. 1783. 12,000 acres to Samuel Hogan, heir.
Hogan, John. N. Y. Private. 8 Jul. 1790. 600 acres.
Hogan, John. Va. Private. 28 Jul. 1830. 200 acres.
Hogan, John C. N.C. Private. 17 Dec. 1796. 228 acres.

Hogan, Peter. Pa. Private. ———. 200 acres.
Hogan, Peter. Va. Private. 28 Jul. 1830. 200 acres.
Hogan, Roger. N.C. Private. 15 Feb. 1797. 274 acres.
Hogan, Thomas. Va. Sergeant. 13 Jan. 1834. 400 acres.
Hogan, William. Va. Private. 19 Mar. 1832. 200 acres.
Hogans, Rawley. N.C. Private. 7 Dec. 1797. 640 acres to heirs.
Hogarth, John. Ga. Soldier. 6 Apr. 1785. 230 acres.
Hogg Eleanore. Conn. Sufferer. New/East Haven. 1.17.0.
Hogg, Jacob. Ga. ———. 17 May 1784. 250 acres.
Hogg, James. Ga. Minute Man. 24 May 1784. 287 1/2 acres.
Hogg, John. Ga. ———. ———. 287 1/2 acres
Hogg, Samuel. Ga. Minute Man. 24 May 1784. 287 1/2 acres.
Hogg, Samuel. Va. Captain. 14 Dec. 1782. 4000 acres.
Hogg, Samuel. Va. Captain. 17 Jul. 1829. 1000 acres.
Hogg, Samuel. Va. Captain. 13 Nov. 1837. 500 acres.
Hogg, Samuel. Va. Captain. 8 Sep. 1838. 500 acres.
Hogg, Stephen. Ga. ———. 17 May 1784. ———.
Hogg, Thomas. N.C. Major. 10 Nov. 1783. 4800 acres.
Hogg, William. Ga. ———. 15 Mar. 1784. 250 acres.
Hogg, William. N.C. Sergeant. Nov. 1788. 1000 acres to heirs.
Hoggard, Daniel. Va. Private. 6 Sep. 1784. 100 acres.
Hoggard, William. N.C. Private. 15 Jul. 1785. 228 acres.
Hoggins, Robert. Ga. ———. ———. 287 1/2 acres.
Hogins, Isham. Va. Sergeant. 22 Dec. 1783. 200 acres.
Hogland, Evert. Va. Corporal. 24 Oct. 1783. 200 acres.
Hogshire, Robert. Va. Private. 15 Jun. 1807. 100 acres.
Hogskiss, Samuel. S.C. Soldier. 21 Jan. 1785. 200 acres.
Hoit, John M. Me. Private. 22 Oct. 1835. 200 acres to widow Catherine Hoit. Standish.
Holbrook, Eddy. Va. Private. 5 Aug. 1784. 100 acres.
Holbrook, Jesse. Va. Private. 5 Aug. 1784. 100 acres.
Holbrook, John. N.C. ———. 11 Jul. 1785. 640 acres to heirs.
Holden, Daniel. Me. ———. 22 Sep. 1835. 200 acres. Sweden.
Holden, Daniel. Mass. ———. 24 Jul. 1829. 200 acres to assignee William Eaton.
Holden, Isaac. N.C. Private. 2 Feb. 1786. 274 acres.
Holden, James. N.C. Corporal. 5 Sep. 1821. 1000 acres.
Holden, Richard. Mass. Private. 24 Apr. 1834. 200 acres to widow Abigail Holden.
Holden, Samuel. Me. Orderly Sergeant. 9 Jun. 1838. 600 acres. Sweden.
Holder, John. Md. Private. ———. 50 acres.
Holderby, William. Va. Sergeant. 28 Oct. 1785. 400 acres.
Holding, Willis. N.C. Private. 11 Jan. 1822. 640 acres to heir Samuel Holding.
Holdman, Daniel. Md. Private. ———. 50 acres.
Holdman, Mordecai. N.C. Private. 22 Apr. 1785. 640 acres.
Hole, James. N. Y. Private. 13 Sep. 1790. 500 acres.
Holestead, Tolley. N.C. Private. 21 May 1784. 274 acres.
Holesworth, Elizabeth. Conn. Sufferer. New London. 46.8.0.
Holison, John. Ga. Soldier. 5 Dec. 1785. 230 acres.
Hollan, Thomas. N.C. Private. 15 Feb. 1797. 274 acres.
Holland, Cary. Va. Private. 11 Oct. 1826. 200 acres.
Holland, Charles. N.C. Private. 2 Feb. 1786. 640 acres to heirs.
Holland, Dominico. S.C. Soldier. 21 Jan. 1785. 200 acres.
Holland, Drury. Va. Private. 28 Feb. 1784. 100 acres.
Holland, Edward. Md. Drummer. ———. 50 acres.

Holland, George. Va. Lieutenant. 2 Feb. 1784. 500 acres.
Holland, George. Va. Lieutenant. 2 Feb. 1784. 2166 2/3 acres.
Holland, H. John. N. Y. Matross. 9 Jul. 1790. 500 acres.
Holland, John. S.C. Soldier. 21 Jan. 1785. 200 acres.
Holland, Joseph. Va. Private. 5 Dec. 1833. 100 acres.
Holland, Josiah. N.C. Private. 29 Apr. 1784. 640 acres to Joseph Holland, heir.
Holland, Park. Me. ———. 22 Apr. 1835. 200 acres. Orono.
Holland, Park. Me. Ensign & Adjutant. 16 Apr. 1838. 600 acres. Orono.
Holland, Peter. Ga. Minute Man. 14 Feb. 1785. ———.
Holland, Reason. N.C. Private. 25 Oct. 1783. 274 acres.
Holland, Reason. N.C. Private. 17 Feb. 1824. Balance of 366 acres.
Holland, Thomas. Ga. Minute Man. 22 Mar. 1785. 250 acres.
Holland, William. N.C. Private. 29 Apr. 1784. 640 acres to Joseph Holland, heir.
Holland, Willis. Va. Private. 5 Dec. 1833. 100 acres.
Hollem, William. S.C. ———. 2 Oct. 1786. 173 acres.
Hollem, William, Jr. S.C. ———. 2 Oct. 1786. 200 acres.
Hollenbeck, Jacob. N. Y. Private. 8 Jul. 1790. 600 acres.
Hollenbeck, John. N.C. Private. 17 Feb. 1824. 640 acres.
Holley, Benjamin. S.C. ———. 1 Aug. 1791. 200 acres.
Holley, Caleb. N.C. Private. 20 Jan. 1785. 640 acres to heirs.
Holley, Henry. N.C. Private. 22 Apr. 1785. 228 acres.
Holley, John, Jr. N.C. Private. 16 Mar. 1795. 640 acres to heirs.
Holley, Samuel. N. Y. Private. 7 Jul. 1790. 500 acres.
Holliday, Ambrose. Ga. Refugee. 28 Feb. 1784. 250 acres.
Holliday, Ayres. Ga. ———. 17 May 1784. ———.
Holliday, Isaac. Md. Private. ———. 50 acres.
Holliday, James. Va. Private. 22 Dec. 1783. 100 acres.
Holliday, John. Ga. ———. 17 May 1784. ———.
Holliday, John. Md. Private. ———. 50 acres.
Holliday, John. Pa. ———. 5 Apr. 1809. 200 acres to heirs.
Holliday, John. Pa. ———. 5 Apr. 1809. 200 acres to heirs.
Holliday, John, Sr. Md. Private. ———. 50 acres.
Holliday, Joseph. Va. Lieutenant. 31 Mar. 1838. 1722 1/3 acres.
Holliday, Joseph. Va. Lieutenant. 31 Mar. 1838. 1722 1/3 acres.
Holliday, Ruth. Conn. Sufferer. Groton. 43.11.3.
Holliday, Thomas. Ga. Refugee. 30 Sep. 1784. ———.
Holliday, William. Ga. Lieutenant. ———. 250 acres.
Holliman, Absalom. Ga. Refugee. ———. 250 acres.
Holliman, Kinchin. N.C. Private. 20 Oct. 1787. 228 acres.
Holliman, Mark, Sr. Ga. ———. 28 Feb. 1784. 287 1/2 acres.
Holliman, Richard. Ga. ———. 17 May 1784. ———.
Holliman, Samuel. Ga. ———. 17 May 1784. ———.
Hollinger, Absalom. Ga. ———. 17 May 1784. ———.
Hollinger, Titus. Ga. ———. 17 May 1784. 287 1/2.
Hollinger, William. Ga. ———. 17 May 1784. ———.
Hollingsworth, Thomas. N.C. Private. 7 Jan. 1786. 640 acres to heirs.
Hollis, Pompey. Md. Private. ———. 50 acres.
Hollis, Stephen. Me. Private. 10 May 1836. 200 acres to widow Abigail Hollis. New Sharon.
Hollomon, Aaron. N.C. Private. 30 Sep. 1785. 640 acres to heirs.
Holloway, Barnes. Ga. ———. 22 Sep. 1784. ———.
Holloway, Charles. Va. Private. 29 Mar. 1838. 200 acres.
Holloway, George. Va. Private. 23 Jul. 1784. 200 acres.
Holloway, James. Va. Second Lieutenant. 10 Feb. 1831. 444 acres.

Holloway, James. Va. Second Lieutenant. 10 Feb. 1831. 444 acres.

Holloway, James. Va. Second Lieutenant. 10 Feb. 1831. 444 acres.

Holloway, James. Va. Second Lieutenant. 10 Feb. 1831. 444 acres.

Holloway, James. Va. Second Lieutenant. 10 Feb. 1831. 444 acres.

Holloway, James. Va. Second Lieutenant. 10 Feb. 1831. 444 acres.

Holloway, James. Va. Second Lieutenant. 10 Feb. 1831. 444 acres.

Holloway, James. Va. Second Lieutenant. 28 Feb. 1833. 81 acres.

Holloway, John. N.C. Private. 30 Sep. 1785. 640 acres to heirs.

Holloway, John. Va. Private. 20 May 1823. 200 acres.

Holloway, Martin. Va. Private. 1 Aug. 1799. 100 acres.

Holloway, William. Va. Private. 2 Aug. 1799. 100 acres.

Hollowday, Thomas. Va. Sergeant. 19 Jan. 1785. 200 acres.

Hollows, James. S.C. ———. 7 Jan. 1793. 200 acres.

Holly, Benjamin. N.Y. ———. 13 Sep. 1790. 500 acres to heirs.

Holly, Benjamin. N.C. Private. 10 Feb. 1796. 640 acres.

Holly, Jacob. N.C. Private. 19 Jul. 1808. 640 acres.

Holly, Josiah. Conn. Sufferer. New/East Haven. 52.17.3.

Holly, Nathaniel. N.C. Private. 30 Sep. 1785. 640 acres to heirs.

Hollyday, Henry. Va. Drummer. 14 Nov. 1791. 200 acres.

Hollyday, William. Va. Fifer. 14 Nov. 1791. 100 acres.

Holman, Christian. Va. Major. 13 Dec. 1783. 5333 1/3 acres.

Holman, David. Ga. ———. 17 May 1784. ———.

Holman, George. Pa. Private. 23 Nov. 1787. 200 acres to Stephen Loudon, assignee.

Holman, Mark. Ga. ———. 17 May 1784. ———.

Holman, Tandy. Va. Private. 27 Sep. 1788. 200 acres.

Holmes. Thomas. N. Y. Private. 6 Jul. 1790. 600 acres.

Holmes, Abner. Mass. Private. 18 Oct. 1833. 200 acres.

Holmes, Bartlett. Va. Private. 29 May 1788. 200 acres.

Holmes, Benjamin. Ga. ———. 17 May 1784. ———.

Holmes, Benjamin. Va. Captain. 17 Sep. 1782. 4000 acres.

Holmes, Daniel. N.C. Private. 5 Dec. 1796. 228 acres.

Holmes, David. Va. Surgeon. 31 Mar. 1783. 3000 acres.

Holmes, David. Va. Surgeon. 31 Mar. 1783. 3000 acres.

Holmes, Ebenezer. Conn. Sufferer. Greenwich. 9.6.8.

Holmes, Hardy. N.C. Lieutenant. 25 Oct. 1783. 2560 acres.

Holmes, Isaac. Va. Lieutenant. 9 Sep. 1783. 2666 2/3 acres.

Holmes, Isaac. Conn. Sufferer. Greenwich. 63.10.10.

Holmes, Isaac, Jr. Conn. Sufferer. Greenwich. 95.16.11.

Holmes, Jabez. Conn. Sufferer. Greenwich. 0.5.0.

Holmes, James. Ga. ———. 17 May 1784. ———.

Holmes, James. Va. Private. 4 Nov. 1819. 100 acres.

Holmes, James. Va. Private. 18 Apr. 1835. 100 acres.

Holmes, John. Ga. ———. 15 Mar. 1784. 500 acres.

Holmes, John. Md. Private. ———. 50 acres.

Holmes, John. N. Y. Private. 8 Jul. 1790. 600 acres.

Holmes, Lewis. Va. Private. 27 Aug. 1783. 100 acres.

Holmes, Reuben. Conn. Sufferer. Greenwich. 32.10.2.

Holmes, Robert. Ga. ———. 17 May 1784. ———.

Holmes, Shadrach. N.C. Private. 29 Apr. 1784. 228 acres.

Holmes, William. Conn. Sufferer. New/East Haven. 43.7.0.

Holms, James. Va.-Ind. Private. 108 acres.

Holstead, Samuel. N.C. Private. 29 Sep. 1784. 640 acres to Jesse Holstead, heir.

Holston, John. Md. Private. ———. 50 acres.

Holt, Abigail. Conn. Sufferer. New London. 18.11.2.
Holt, Beverly. Ga. Private. 9 Jan. 1786. ———.
Holt, Claiborne. Va. Private. 20 May 1829. 100 acres.
Holt, Daniel. Conn. Sufferer. New London. 32.2.6.
Holt, Ebenezer. Conn. Sufferer. New London. 15.5.1.
Holt, Evan. Pa. Private. ———. 200 acres.
Holt, Henry. Va. Midshipman. 17 Mar. 1832. 2666 2/3 acres.
Holt, James. Va. Lieutenant. 27 Sep. 1783. 2666 2/3 acres.
Holt, James. Va. Lieutenant. 5 Feb. 1808. 333 1/3 acres.
Holt, James. Conn. Sufferer. New London. 21.18.6.
Holt, John Hunter. Va. Captain. 3 Dec. 1782. 4000 acres.
Holt, Jonathan. Conn. Sufferer. New London. 35.13.0.
Holt, Joseph. Va. Lieutenant. 20 Apr. 1838. 2666 2/3 acres.
Holt, Joseph. Conn. Sufferer. New London. 2.13.0.
Holt, Leonard. Md. Private. ———. 50 acres.
Holt, Michael. Va. Captain. 14 Mar. 1834. 4000 acres.
Holt, Michael. Va. Captain. 26 Nov. 1860. 666 2/3 acres.
Holt, Reuben. Ga. Soldier. 9 Jan. 1786. ——— to heirs.
Holt, Samuel. Va. Private. 16 May 1789. 100 acres.
Holt, Samuel. Va. Private. 9 Jun. 1857. 100 acres.
Holt, Samuel. Va. Private. 28 Jan. 1809. 100 acres.
Holt, Stephen. Conn. Sufferer. New London. 229.5.2.
Holt, Thomas. N.C. Private. 17 Feb. 1824. 640 acres.
Holt, Thomas. Va. Captain. 22 May 1783. 4000 acres.
Holt, Thomas. Va. Captain. 19 Aug. 1794. 666 2/3 acres.
Holt, Thomas. Va. Captain. 17 Apr. 1821. 333 1/3 acres.
Holt, Thomas. Conn. Sufferer. New London. 4.18.7.
Holt, William. Me. Fifer. 8 Jun. 1836. 200 acres to widow Esther Holt. Fryeburg.
Holt, William. Va. Lieutenant. 10 Feb. 1817. 2666 2/3 acres.
Holton, Francis. Ga. Private. 24 May 1784. 287 1/2 acres.
Holton, George. Md. Sergeant. ———. 50 acres.
Holton, James. N.C. Private. 12 Sep. 1785. 640 acres to heirs.
Holzendorf, William. Ga. Refugee. 15 Mar. 1784. 250 acres.
Homes, Andrew. N.C. Private. 30 Sep. 1785. 640 acres to heirs.
Homes, James. Md. Private. ———. 50 acres.
Homes, Shadrack. N.C. Private. 16 Aug. 1821. 640 acres.
Honaker, Henry. Va.-Ind. Private. 108 acres.
Honaker, Peter. Va.-Ind. Private. 108 acres.
Honey, Elias. Va. Private. 12 Dec. 1783. 200 acres.
Honeycut, Daniel. N.C. Private. 6 Dec. 1797. 640 acres to heirs.
Honeycut, John. N.C. Private. 6 Dec. 1797. 640 acres to heirs.
Honeyman, William. Pa. Lieutenant. 2 Feb. 1787. 200 acres.
Honeywell, John. N. Y. Private. 6 Jul. 1790. 600 acres.
Honeywell, Stephen. Conn. Sufferer. New/East Haven. 1.19.6.
Honyman, William. Pa. Lieutenant. 2 Feb. 1785. 200 acres.
Hood [or Wood], John. Md. Private. ———. 50 acres.
Hood, Archibald. N.C. Private. 22 Dec. 1796. 640 acres.
Hood, Charles. N.C. Private. 25 Apr. 1784. 274 acres.
Hood, George. Va. Private. 13 May 1830. 200 acres.
Hood, John. Md. Private. ———. 50 acres.
Hood, John. N.C. Private. Nov. 1788. 183 acres.
Hood, John. Va. Private. 23 Jun. 1783. 100 acres.
Hood, Richard. Conn. Sufferer. New/East Haven. 36.15.0.
Hood, Thomas. Va. Sergeant Major. 18 Oct. 1783. 400 acres.
Hood, William. N.C. Private. 21 May 1784. 274 acres.

Hood, William. N.C. Private. 23 Feb. 1820. 640 acres.
Hood, William. Va. Private. 9 Mar. 1784. 100 acres.
Hoof, James. Va. Corporal. 6 Apr. 1786. 400 acres.
Hoof, Samuel. Ga. ———. 17 May 1784. ———.
Hoofer, John. Va. Private. 19 Sep. 1783. 200 acres.
Hooffer, Samuel. Va. Private. 7 Dec. 1784. 100 acres.
Hoofnagle, George. Pa. Private. 30 Aug. 1782. 200 acres.
Hook, George. N.C. Private. 11 Jul. 1785. 274 acres.
Hook, James. Va. Captain. 18 Apr. 1823. 200 acres.
Hook, James. Va. Captain. 18 Apr. 1823. 200 acres.
Hook, James. Va. Captain. 18 Apr. 1823. 200 acres.
Hook, James. Va. Captain. 18 Apr. 1823. 200 acres.
Hook, James. Va. Captain. 18 Apr. 1823. 200 acres.
Hook, James. Va. Captain. 18 Apr. 1823. 200 acres.
Hook, James. Va. Captain. 18 Apr. 1823. 200 acres.
Hook, James. Va. Captain. 18 Apr. 1823. 200 acres.
Hook, James. Va. Captain. 18 Apr. 1823. 200 acres.
Hook, James. Va. Captain. 18 Apr. 1823. 200 acres.
Hook, James. Va. Captain. 18 Apr. 1823. 200 acres.
Hook, James. Va. Captain. 18 Apr. 1823. 200 acres.
Hook, James. Va. Captain. 18 Apr. 1823. 200 acres.
Hook, James. Va. Captain. 18 Apr. 1823. 200 acres.
Hook, James. Va. Captain. 18 Apr. 1823. 200 acres.
Hook, James. Va. Captain. 18 Apr. 1823. 200 acres.
Hook, James. Va. Captain. 18 Apr. 1823. 200 acres.
Hook, James. Va. Captain. 18 Apr. 1823. 200 acres.
Hook, James. Va. Captain. 18 Apr. 1823. 200 acres.
Hook, James. Va. Captain. 18 Apr. 1823. 200 acres.
Hook, James. Va. Captain. 19 Jul. 1867. 1227 7/9 acres.
Hooker, Evan. N.C. ———. 30 Sep. 1785. 1000 acres to heirs.
Hooker, Hannah. Conn. Sufferer. Norwalk. 211.13.9.
Hooker, John. N.Y. ———. 13 Sep. 1790. 500 acres to heirs.
Hooker, John. N.C. Private. 5 Dec. 1796. 274 acres.
Hooker, William. Pa. Private. 7 Aug. 1787. 200 acres.
Hookes, Ephraim. N.C. Private. 29 Sep. 1784. 228 acres.
Hooks, Asa. Ga. ———. 15 Mar. 1784. 250 acres.
Hooks, John. N.C. Private. 10 Aug. 1785. 640 acres.
Hooks, John. N.C. Private. 14 Sep. 1820. 228 acres.
Hooks, William. N.C. Private. 30 Sep. 1785. 640 acres to heirs.
Hooks, William. Va. Private. 5 Feb. 1785. 100 acres.
Hoole, Joseph. Md. Private. ———. 50 acres.
Hoomes, Thomas Claiborne. Va. Lieutenant. 4 Nov. 1782. 2666 2/3 acres.
Hooms, Benjamin. Va. Captain. 7 Sep. 1796. 1333 1/3 acres.
Hooper, Absalom. Ga. ———. 15 Mar. 1784. 250 acres.
Hooper, Absolam. S.C. Soldier. 5 May 1800. 200 acres.
Hooper, Enos. N.C. Private. 15 Feb. 1797. 274 acres.
Hooper, James. Virginia. Private. 20 May 1829. 200 acares.
Hooper, Jeremiah. Md. Private. ———. 50 acres.
Hooper, R. Jacob. N. Y. Private. 8 Jul. 1790. 600 acres.
Hooper, Richard. Virginia. Captain. 7 Nov. 1811. 1000 acres.
Hooper, Richard. Virginia. Captain. 7 Nov. 1811. 1000 acres.
Hooper, Richard. Virginia. Captain. 7 Nov. 1811. 1000 acres.
Hooper, Richard. Virginia. Captain. 7 Nov. 1811. 1000 acres.
Hooper, Thomas. Va.-Ind. Private. 108 acres.

Hooper, Walter. Virginia. Private. 12 Dec. 1783. 200 acres.
Hoops, Adam. Md. Captain. ———. 200 acres.
Hoover, Anthony. Pa. Private. ———. 200 acres.
Hoover, Jacob. N.C. Private. 25 May 1820. 185 acres.
Hoover, John. Pa. Private. 28 Feb. 1787. 200 acres.
Hope, Ralph. Md. Private. ———. 50 acres.
Hope, William. Md. Private. ———. 50 acres.
Hopewell, George. N.C. Private. 30 Sep. 1785. 640 acres to heirs.
Hopewell, Thomas. Virginia. Private. 12 Apr. 1784. 100 acres.
Hopkins, David. Md. Major. ———. 200 acres.
Hopkins, David. Virginia. Major. 6 Jul. 1782. 5333 1/3 acres.
Hopkins, David. Virginia. Major. 28 Sep. 1808. 1000 acres.
Hopkins, David. Virginia. Major. 28 Sep. 1808. 1073 acres.
Hopkins, Francis. Md. Private. ———. 50 acres.
Hopkins, Isaac. N.C. Private. 8 Mar. 1785. 274 acres.
Hopkins, James. Md. ———. ———. 50 acres.
Hopkins, James. Pa. Sergeant. 23 Jul. 1787. 250 acres.
Hopkins, John. Md. Private. ———. 50 acres.
Hopkins, John. N.C. Private. 30 Sep. 1785. 640 acres to heirs.
Hopkins, John. Pa. Private. ———. 200 acres.
Hopkins, Jonathan. N.C. Corporal. 22 Feb. 1785. 1000 acres.
Hopkins, Lambeth. Ga. ———. 29 Jul. 1784. 287 1/2 acres.
Hopkins, Patrick. Virginia. Private. 7 Nov. 1783. 100 acres.
Hopkins, Richard. Mass. Corporal. 1 May 1832. 200 acres to heirs.
Hopkins, Richard. N.C. Private. 29 Sep. 1784. 228 acres.
Hopkins, Samuel. Va. Lieutenant Colonel. 17 May 1783. 7000 acres.
Hopkins, Samuel. Va. Lieutenant Colonel. 29 Aug. 1807. 833 1/3 acres.
Hopkins, Thomas. Ga. Private. 1784. 250 acres.
Hopkins, Thomas. N.C. Private. 16 Aug. 1821. 640 acres.
Hopkins, Thomas. Va. Private. 18 Apr. 1783. 200 acres.
Hopkins, Thomas. Conn. Sufferer. New London. 198.17.9.
Hopkins, William. Ga. ———. 29 Jul. 1784. 287 1/2 acres.
Hopkins, William. Pa. ———. 20 Nov. 1803. 200 acres to Isaac Grigg & Oliver Ormsby, assignees.
Hopkins, William. Pa. Private. ———. 200 acres.
Hopkinstock, Christopher. Va. Private. 22 Aug. 1783. 200 acres.
Hopper, Henry. Pa. ———. 4 Mar. 1806. 200 acres to Hannah Hopper, widow.
Hopper, John. Va. Private. ca. Feb. 1784. 100 acres.
Hopper, John. Va. Corporal. 31 Dec. 1784. 400 acres.
Hopper, John. Va. Corporal. 27 Apr. 1785. 400 acres.
Hopper, Peter. N. Y. Private. 8 Jul. 1790. 600 acres.
Hopper, Thomas. Va. Captain. 24 Dec. 1813. 500 acres.
Hopper, Thomas. Va. Captain. 24 Dec. 1813. 500 acres.
Hopper, Thomas. Va. Captain. 24 Dec. 1813. 500 acres.
Hopper, Thomas. Va. Captain. 24 Dec. 1813. 500 acres.
Hopper, Thomas. Va. Captain. 24 Dec. 1813. 500 acres.
Hopper, Thomas. Va. Captain. 24 Dec. 1813. 500 acres.
Hopper, Thomas. Va. Captain. 24 Dec. 1813. 500 acres.
Hopper, Thomas. Va. Captain. 24 Dec. 1813. 500 acres.
Hopper, William. N.C. Private. 22 Apr. 1785. 228 acres.
Hoppings, Ephraim. N. Y. ———. ———. 333 1/3 acres.
Hopston, John. N.C. Private. 24 Nov. 1796. 640 acres to heirs.
Hord, James. Va. Ensign. 3 Feb. 1834. 1333 1/3 acres.
Hord, James. Va. Ensign. 3 Feb. 1834. 1333 1/3 acres.

Hord, Thomas. Va. Captain. 20 May 1783. 4666 2/3 acres.
Horde, Thomas. Va. Captain. 8 Jul. 1808. 555 acres.
Horfield, Thomas. Va. Sergeant. 23 Jun. 1783. 400 acres.
Horn, Absolom. Ga. Soldier. 17 Aug. 1784. —— acres to widow and four children.
Horn, Henry. Va. Private. 11 Nov. 1814. 100 acres.
Horn, Jacob. Ga. ———. 17 May 1784. 287 1/2 acres.
Horn, Jesse. Ga. ———. 14 Sep. 1784. 287 1/2 acres.
Horn, John. Ga. ———. 17 May 1784. ———.
Horn, Phanton. N. Y. Private. 7 Jul. 1790. 600 acres.
Horn, Ralph. Va. Private. 27 Mar. 1784. 100 acres.
Horn, Ralph. Va. Seaman. 10 Apr. 1835. 100 acres.
Horn, Ralph R. Va. Private. 16 Dec. 1809. 131 1/2 acres.
Horne, Roddam. N.C. Private. 7 Dec. 1797. 640 acres.
Horner, Francis. N. Y. Matross. 9 Jul. 1790. 600 acres.
Horner, Isaac. S.C. ———. 4 Dec. 1786. 200 acres.
Horner, John. Ga. Soldier. 5 Sep. 1785. ———.
Horner, John. Pa. Private. ———. 200 acres.
Horney, William. Md. Private. ———. 50 acres.
Hornsby, John. Va. Seaman. 19 Jun. 1833. 100 acres.
Hornsby, Levi. Va. Private. 27 Mar. 1812. 200 acres.
Hornsby, Philip. Ga. Refugee. 26 Oct. 1784. 575 acres.
Horry, Peter. S.C. Colonel. 21 Jan. 1785. 500 acres.
Horsfield, Joseph. Md. Private. ———. 50 acres.
Horsford, Joseph. N. Y. Private. 8 Jul. 1790. 600 acres.
Horsley, James. Va. Private. 15 Oct. 1785. 200 acres.
Horsom, David. Me. Private. 8 Aug. 1838. 200 acres. Berwick.
Horton, Elisha. Mass. Sergeant. 5 Feb. 1833. 200 acres to heirs.
Horton, Hugh. Ga. ———. 17 Dec. 1784. ———.
Horton, James. N.C. Private. 29 Apr. 1784. 640 acres to Sarah Horton, heiress.
Horton, John. N.C. Private. 12 Dec. 1796. 640 acres.
Horton, Mary. Conn. Sufferer. New/East Haven. 5.14.9.
Horton, Samuel. N.C. Private. 10 Mar. 1788. 640 acres to heirs.
Horton, Samuel. Va. Private. 12 Aug. 1793. 200 acres.
Horton, Samuel. Conn. Sufferer. New/East Haven. 77.6.6.
Horton, William. N.C. Private. 7 Dec. 1797. 640 acres to heirs.
Hosea, Samuel. Va. Private. 5 Dec. 1833. 100 acres.
Hosick, William. Va. Private. 2 Feb 1820. 100 acres.
Hoskins, Joseph. Va. Private. 4 Jan. 1784. 100 acres.
Hoskins, Randolph. Md. Private. ———. 50 acres.
Hoskins, Thomas. N.Y. ———. 13 Sep. 1790. 500 acres heirs.
Hostings, Ebenezer. N. Y. Matross. 9 Jul. 1790. 600 acres.
Hostory, Henry. N.C. Private. 1 Dec. 1789. 182 acres.
Hotchkiss, Amos. Conn. Sufferer. New/East Haven. 34.3.9.
Hotchkiss, Caleb. Conn. Sufferer. New/East Haven. 9.7.6.
Hotchkiss, Enos. Conn. Sufferer. New/East Haven. 3.17.8.
Hotchkiss, Hannah. Conn. Sufferer. New/East Haven. 4.12.0.
Hotchkiss, Jonah. Conn. Sufferer. New/East Haven. 19.6.2.
Hotchkiss, Nehemiah. Conn. Sufferer. New/East Haven. 14.11.6.
Hotchkiss, Obadiah. Conn. Sufferer. New/East Haven. 69.3.7.
Hotchkiss, Silas. Conn. Sufferer. New/East Haven. 3.1.0.
Hotchkiss, Stephen. Conn. Sufferer. New/East Haven. 4.7.0.
Hotchkiss, Susannah. Conn. Sufferer. New/East Haven. 14.8.6.
Hotchkiss, William. N.Y. ———. 13 Sep. 1790. 500 acres to heirs.
Houchings, Bernard. Va. Private. 12 May 1810. 100 acres.

Hougan, Silvester. Pa. Private. ———. 200 acres.
Hough, Thomas. Va. Private. 4 Nov. 1784. 100 acres.
Houghman, Lewis. Ga. Soldier. 7 Jun. 1785. 230 acres to heirs.
Houghton, Joshua. Ga. ———. 20 Dec. 1785. 287 1/2 acres.
Hounam, James. Conn. Sufferer. Greenwich. 208.17.0.
Houragin, Patrick. Va. Private. 10 Mar. 1784. 100 acres.
Hours, Christian. Pa. Private. 1 Dec. 1786. 200 acres to Stephen Loudon, assignee.
House, Andrew. Va.-Ind. Private. 108 acres.
House, Brittan. Ga. ———. 17 May 1784. ———.
House, Christian. N. Y. ———. 5 Jul. 1794. 600 acres.
House, Henry. N. Y. Private. 8 Jul. 1790. 500 acres.
House, Jacob. N. Y. ———. 5 Jul. 1794. 600 acres.
House, John. Ga. Private. 7 Sep. 1784. ———.
House, John. N. Y. Private. 7 Jul. 1790. 600 acres.
House, Laurance. Va. Captain. 13 Feb. 1834. 4000 acres.
House, Lawrence. Ga. ———. 17 May 1784. 230 acres.
House, William. Va. Gunner. 9 Dec. 1783. 100 acres.
House, William. Va. Gunner. 30 May 1831. 1283 1/3 acres.
House, William. Va. Gunner. 30 May 1831. 320 5/6 acres.
House, William. Va. Gunner. 30 May 1831. 320 5/6 acres.
House, William. Va. Gunner. 30 May 1831. 320 5/6 acres.
House, William. Va. Gunner. 30 May 1831. 320 5/6 acres.
Houseford, James. N.C. Private. 18 Dec. 1793. 640 acres.
Householder, Jacob. Pa. Private. 9 Feb. 1789. 200 acres.
Houseman, George. N.Y. ———. 13 Sep. 1790. 500 acres to heirs.
Housley, John. Md. Private. ———. 50 acres.
Housley, Newdigate. Ga. ———. 17 May 1784. ———.
Housley, Newel. Ga. ———. 250 acres. ———.
Housley, Thomas. Ga. ———. ———. 287 1/2 acres.
Housley, Welden. Ga. Sergeant. 17 May 1784. ———.
Housley, William. Ga. ———. 17 May 1784. ———.
Housman, Conrad. Pa. Private. ———. 200 acres.
Houston, Henry. Ga. Minute Man. 17 May 1784. ———.
Houston, James. Pa. Sergeant. 21 Sep. 1787. 200 acres.
Houston, John. Me. ———. 4 Aug. 1834. 200 acres. Sanford.
Houston, Samuel. Me. Non-commissioned Officer. 22 Jun. 1835. 200 acres to widow Sarah Houston. Belfast.
Houston, William. Ga. Surgeon. 17 May 1784. ———.
Houston, William. N.C. Private. 15 Nov. 1793. 640 acres to heirs.
Houston, William. Pa. Lieutenant & Adjutant. 2 Aug. 1787. 200 acres to Susanna Houston, widow.
Houston, William. Pa. Adjutant. 2 Aug. 1787. 200 acres to widow.
Houstoun, James. Ga. Surgeon. 19 Mar. 1784. ———.
Hover, Henry. N.C. Private. 2 Feb. 1786. 640 acres to heirs.
How, Baxter. N. Y. Lieutenant. 13 Sep. 1790. 1000 acres to heirs.
How, Isaac. Mass. Corporal. 2 Aug. 1833. 200 acres.
Howard, Austen. Md. Private. ———. 50 acres.
Howard, Benjamin. Ga. ———. 17 May 1784. ———.
Howard, Benjamin. N.C. Private. 3 Feb. 1785. 274 acres.
Howard, Charles. Ga. Minute Man. 4 May 1785. 287 1/2 acres.
Howard, Charles. Va. Private. 10 Mar. 1786. 200 acres.
Howard, Cornelius. Md. Sergeant. ———. 50 acres.
Howard, David. Ga. Minute Man. 12 Feb. 178-. 287 1/2 acres.
Howard, Edward. N.C. Private. 24 Oct. 1783. 228 acres.
Howard, George. N.C. Private. 22 Dec. 1796. 274 acres.

Howard, Henry. Ga. ———. ———. 287 1/2 acres.
Howard, Ignatius. Va. Private. 16 Feb. 1801. 100 acres.
Howard, Isaac. N.C. Private. 20 Apr. 1784. 274 acres.
Howard, James. N.C. Private. 30 Sep. 1785. 640 acres to heirs.
Howard, James. Va. Private. 5 Apr. 1787. 200 acres.
Howard, John. Ga. Minute Man. 19 Jul. 1784. 287 1/2 acres.
Howard, John. Md. Matross. ———. 50 acres.
Howard, John. Md. Private. ———. 50 acres.
Howard, John. N.C. Private. 12 Dec. 1796. 640 acres to heirs.
Howard, John. Va. Private. 1 Oct. 1783. 100 acres.
Howard, John Egar. Md. Lieutenant Colonel. ———. 200 acres.
Howard, Joseph. Me. ———. 21 Jul. 1835. 200 acres. Brownfield.
Howard, Joseph. N.C. Private. 22 Oct. 1783. 274 acres.
Howard, Julius. Ga. ———. 17 May 1784. ———.
Howard, Peregrine. Md. Private. ———. 50 acres.
Howard, Peter. Md. Private. ———. 50 acres.
Howard, Peter. Va. Private. 5 Apr. 1784. 200 acres.
Howard, Rhesa. Ga. ———. 15 Mar. 1784. 250 acres.
Howard, Richard. N.C. Private. 9 Sep. 1785. 640 acres to heirs.
Howard, Robert. Va. Private. 20 Jun. 1783. 100 acres.
Howard, Samuel. Ga. ———. 17 May 1784. ———.
Howard, Solomon. N.C. Private. 29 Apr. 1784. 228 acres.
Howard, Thomas. Va. Midshipman. 16 May 1834. 2666 2/3 acres.
Howard, Vachel D. Va. Captain. 14 Jun. 1820. 3333 1/3 acres.
Howard, Vachel D. Va. Captain. 15 Dec. 1820. 666 2/3 acres.
Howard, William. Ga. ———. 30 Sep. 1784. ———.
Howard, William. N.C. Private. 2 Feb. 1786. 640 acres to heirs.
Howe, Azor. Mass. Private. 27 Mar. 1833. 200 acres.
Howe, Banister. Va. Sailing Master. 14 Aug. 1834. 2000 acres.
Howe, Banister. Va. Sailing Master. 14 Aug. 1834. 666 2/3 acres.
Howe, Daniel. Md. Private. ———. 50 acres.
Howe, Darius. Mass. Sergeant. 20 Feb. 1833. 200 acres.
Howe, Ebenezer. Conn. Sufferer. Greenwich. 13.12.4.
Howe, Hannah. Conn. Sufferer. New/East Haven. 13.3.6.
Howe, Isaac. Conn. Sufferer. Greenwich. 83.19.7.
Howe, Jacob. Me. ———. 15 Jun. 1835. 200 acres to widow Betty Howe. Sumner.
Howe, John. N. Y. Private. 8 Jul. 1790. 500 acres.
Howe, John. Va. Sergeant. 2 Jun. 1827. 200 acres.
Howe, Robert. Ga. Lieutenant. 5 Jan. 1784. 460 acres to heirs.
Howe, Robert. N.C. Major General. 19 Jun. 1820. 16,000 acres to heirs.
Howe, Sarah. Conn. Sufferer. New/East Haven. 14.7.1.
Howe, Walter. Md. Private. ———. 50 acres.
Howe, William. Md. Private. ———. 50 acres.
Howe, William. Pa. Matross. ———. 200 acres.
Howell, Aaron. N. Y. Private. 8 Jul. 1790. 600 acres.
Howell, Abemeleck. N.C. Drum Major. 22 Dec. 1796. 1000 acres.
Howell, Abner. Va. Private. 8 Apr. 1784. 100 acres.
Howell, Caleb. Ga. ———. 6 Feb. 1784. 250 acres.
Howell, Caleb. Ga. Major. 11 Feb. 1784. 600 acres.
Howell, Caleb. N.C. Private. 17 Feb. 1824. 640 acres.
Howell, Daniel. Ga. Captain. 6 Feb. 1784. 500 acres.
Howell, Daniel. N.C. Private. 10 Aug. 1785. 640 acres to heirs.
Howell, David. Ga. ———. 15 Mar. 1784. 250 acres.

Howell, David. Va. Private. 21 Apr. 1784. 100 acres.
Howell, Edward. N.C. Corporal. 2 Sep. 1820. 357 acres.
Howell, Ezekiel. Pa. ———. 2 Feb. 1787. 200 acres.
Howell, Ezekiel. Pa. Lieutenant. 2 Feb. 1785. 200 acres.
Howell, Frederick. N.C. Private. 9 Nov. 1784. 640 acres to John Howell, heir.
Howell, George. N. Y. Sergeant. 8 Jul. 1790. 600 acres.
Howell, Henry. N.C. Private. 10 Dec. 1788. 640 acres to heirs.
Howell, James. Ga. ———. 17 May 1784. ———.
Howell, James. N.C. Private. 12 Sep. 1785. 640 acres to heirs.
Howell, Jehiel. N.Y. ———. 13 Sep. 1790. 500 acres to heirs.
Howell, John. Md. Private. ———. 50 acres.
Howell, John. N.C. Private. 24 Oct. 1783. 640 acres to Edward Howell.
Howell, John. N.C. Private. 9 Nov. 1784. 640 acres.
Howell, John. N.C. Private. 30 Sep. 1785. 640 acres to heirs.
Howell, John, Sr. Ga. ———. 15 Mar. 1784. 250 acres.
Howell, Joseph. Conn. Sufferer. New/East Haven. 75.12.5.
Howell, Lewis. Va. Private. 13 May 1834. 100 acres.
Howell, Nathan. Conn. Sufferer. New/East Haven. 10.8.1 1/2.
Howell, Nathaniel. Ga. ———. 17 May 1784. ———.
Howell, Peter. N.C. Private. 12 Sep. 1785. 640 acres to heirs.
Howell, Phillison. Va. Corporal. 17 Apr. 1783. 400 acres.
Howell, Robert. N.C. Private. 2 Feb. 1786. 274 acres.
Howell, Robert. Va. Private. 13 Feb. 1809. 100 acres.
Howell, Samuel. Conn. Sufferer. New/East Haven. 39.5.3.
Howell, Seth. N. Y. Private. 8 Jul. 1790. 600 acres.
Howell, Stephen. N.C. Private. 24 Jul. 1820. 640 acres to heirs.
Howell, T. N.C. Private. 10 Aug. 1785. 640 acres.
Howell, Tallifaro. N.C. Fifer. 22 Dec. 1796. 1000 acres to heirs.
Howell, Thomas. Pa. Private. 13 Oct. 1786. 200 acres.
Howell, Vincent. Va. Private. 19 Feb. 1784. 100 acres.
Howell, Vincent. Va. Subaltern. 25 Dec. 1784. 2666 2/3 acres.
Howington, William. N.C. Private. 17 Feb. 1824. 640 acres.
Howle, Thomas. Va. Private. 30 Aug. 1799. 100 acres.
Hoy, John. Va. Private. 18 Dec. 1827. 100 acres.
Hoye, Alexander. Va. Private. 4 Jul. 1786. 200 acres.
Hoye, Thomas. Md. Private. ———. 50 acres.
Hoyman, Henry. Ga. Refugee. 17 May 1784. ———.
Hoyman, Stephen. Ga. Refugee. 26 May 1784. 287 1/2 acres.
Hoyman, Stouton. Ga. Refugee. 17 May 1784. ———.
Hoyt, Caleb. Conn. Sufferer. Danbury. 4.13.4.
Hoyt, Comfort. Conn. Sufferer. Danbury. 50.7.0.
Hoyt, Comfort, Jr. Conn. Sufferer. Danbury. 478.15.7.
Hoyt, Eleazer. Conn. Sufferer. Danbury. 1.19.8.
Hoyt, Henry. N. Y. Private. 8 Jul. 1790. 600 acres.
Hoyt, Justus. Conn. Sufferer. Danbury. 2.5.0.
Hoyt, Noah. Conn. Sufferer. Danbury. 3.5.4.
Hubbard, Benjamin. Ga. ———. 15 Mar. 1784. 250 acres.
Hubbard, Charles. Va. Sailor. 27 Jul. 1784. 100 acres.
Hubbard, Elias. Va. Private. 30 Jan. 1784. 100 acres.
Hubbard, Eppa. Va. Sergeant. 24 Mar. 1784. 200 acres.
Hubbard, Isaac. Va. Private. 7 Jun. 1785. 100 acres.
Hubbard, Jacob. Ga. Refugee. 14 Apr. 1784. ———.
Hubbard, James. N.C. Private. 23 Dec. 1818. 640 acres to heirs.
Hubbard, James. Va. Private. 21 Feb. 1784. 200 acres.

Hubbard, John. Ga. Refugee. 30 Jul. 1784. 287 1/2 acres.
Hubbard, John. N. Y. Private. 8 Jul. 1790. 600 acres.
Hubbard, John. Va. Midshipman. 1 Dec. 1787. 2666 2/3 acres.
Hubbard, Mary. Conn. Sufferer. New/East Haven. 5.17.11.
Hubbard, Matthew. Va. Private. 16 Aug. 1797. 100 acres.
Hubbard, Nathaniel. Conn. Sufferer. Greenwich. 3.2.6.
Hubbard, Russell. Conn. Sufferer. New London. 1,012.0.3.
Hubbard, Samuel. Va. Sergeant. 20 Oct. 1795. 533 1/3 acres.
Hubbard, Warburton. N.C. Sergeant. 9 Sep. 1785. 1000 acres to heirs.
Hubbard, William. Va. Sailor. 15 Oct. 1788. 200 acres.
Hubbard, William. Va. Sergeant. 8 Sep. 1797. 200 acres.
Hubbard, William. Conn. Sufferer. Greenwich. 16.2.3.
Hubbart, Elisha. N.C. Private. 4 Aug. 1821. 640 acres.
Hubbell, Abigail. Conn. Sufferer. Fairfield. 176.13.4.
Hubbell, Isaac. Conn. Sufferer. Fairfield. 18.16.0.
Hubbell, Jabez. Conn. Sufferer. Fairfield. 32.16.9.
Hubbert, John. N. Y. Engisn. 13 Sep. 1790. 1000 acres.
Hubble, Isaac. N. Y. Private. 8 Jul. 1790. 600 acres.
Hubble, Isaac. N. Y. Lieutenant. 6 Jul. 1790 1200 acres.
Hubby, Benjamin. Conn. Sufferer. Greenwich. 34.13.5.
Hubby, Ebenezer. Conn. Sufferer. Greenwich. 39.11.11.
Hubby, Joseph, Jr. Conn. Sufferer. Greenwich. 31.9.0.
Hubby, Nathaniel. Conn. Sufferer. Greenwich. 12.0.0.
Hubert, George & Michael Zeller. Pa. 8 Feb. 1807. 200 acres. [Are these veterans?]
Hubert, Matthew. Ga. ———. 17 May 1784. ———.
Hubert, Paul. N. Y. ———. ———. 500 acres.
Hubert, Peter. N. Y. ———. ———. 500 acres.
Hubley, Adam. Pa. Lieutenant Colonel. 20 Oct. 1785. 500 acres.
Hubley, Adam. Pa. Lieutenant Colonel. 20 Nov. 1785. 500 acres.
Hubley, Bernard. Pa. ———. 500 acres.
Huddleston, John. Va. Private. 1 May 1783. 100 acres.
Hudgall, Nicholas. N. Y. Private. 8 Jul. 1790. 600 acres.
Hudgin, Holder. N.C. ———. 13 Jun. 1785. 640 acres to heir.
Hudgins, Moses. Va. Private. 17 May 1783. 100 acres.
Hudgins, Samuel. Va. Private. 21 Jun. 1784. 100 acres.
Hudlen, Joseph. N.C. Private. 9 Feb. 1796. 640 acres to heirs.
Hudler, John. N.C. Private. 3 Mar. 1784. 640 acres.
Hudler, Joseph. N.C. Private. 3 Mar. 1784. 274 acres.
Hudler, Joseph. N.C. Private. 3 Mar. 1784. 274 acres.
Hudler, Joseph. N.C. Private. 30 Mar. 1820. 366 acres to heir David Hudler.
Hudler, Lemuel. N.C. Private. 3 Mar. 1784. 274 acres.
Hudler, Lemuel. N.C. Private. 30 Mar. 1820. 366 acres to heir Kenan Hudler.
Hudlestone, Robert. N.C. Private. 2 Aug. 1784. 640 acres.
Hudlestone, William. N.C. Private. 2 Aug. 1784. 640 acres.
Hudnall, James. Va. Private. 8 Dec. 1796. 200 acres.
Hudnall, Thomas. Va. Private. 29 Oct. 1784. 200 acres.
Hudson, Chamberlain. N.C. Private. 9 Nov. 1784. 640 acres.
Hudson, Charles. Va. Private. 22 Mar. 1833. 100 acres.
Hudson, Cuthburt. Ga. ———. 15 Mar. 1784. 250 acres.
Hudson, Ezekiel. N.C. Private. 8 Sep. 1804. 640 acres to heirs.
Hudson, George. N.C. Private. 9 Nov. 1784. 640 acres to heir.
Hudson, Jacob. Ga. ———. 17 May 1784. ———.
Hudson, James. Ga. ———. 27 Jan. 1784. 250 acres.

Hudson, James. Ga. ———. 29 Jan. 1784. 250 acres.
Hudson, James. Md. Private. ———. 50 acres.
Hudson, James. Pa. Matross. 19 May 1787. 200 acres.
Hudson, Joachim. Ga. ———. 17 Dec. 1784. ———.
Hudson, John. Ga. Private. 10 Dec. 1784. 250 acres.
Hudson, John. Md. Private. ———. 50 acres.
Hudson, John. N. Y. Private. 8 Jul. 1790. 600 acres.
Hudson, John. Va. Captain. 15 Jul. 1783. 4000 acres.
Hudson, John. Va. Private. 7 Aug 1783. 200 acres.
Hudson, John. Va. Private. 18 Dec. 1783. 100 acres.
Hudson, John. Va. Captain. 30 Dec. 1851. 482 acres.
Hudson, John. Va. Captain. 30 Dec. 1851. 241 acres.
Hudson, John. Va. Captain. 30 Oct. 1852. 482 acres.
Hudson, John. Va. Captain. 30 Oct. 1852. 241 acres.
Hudson, Joseph. Ga. Refugee. 15 Mar. 1784. 250 acres.
Hudson, Melus. N.C. Private. Nov. 1788. 274 acres.
Hudson, Nathaniel. Ga. Refugee. 26 May 1784. 287 1/2 acres.
Hudson, Robert. Ga. Refugee. 14 Jan. 1784. 287 1/2 acres.
Hudson, Rush. Va. Corporal. 28 Oct. 1783. 400 acres.
Hudson, Samuel. Ga. Private. 26 Oct. 1784. 287 1/2 acres.
Hudson, Stephen. Mass. Private. 18 Oct. 1833. 200 acres.
Hudson, William. N. Y. Private. 8 Jul. 1790. 500 acres.
Hudson, William. Va. Lieutenant. 4 Sep. 1807. 500 acres.
Hudson, William. Va. Lieutenant. 4 Sep. 1807. 500 acres.
Hudson, William. Va. Lieutenant. 4 Sep. 1807. 866 2/3 acres.
Hudson, William. Va. Lieutenant. 4 Sep. 1807. 800 acres.
Hudspeth, Charles. Ga. ———. 17 Dec. 1784. ———.
Huel, William. N.C. Lieutenant. 5 Sep. 1821. 2560 acres,
Huelet, Robert. N.C. Sergeant. 2 Dec. 1796. 1000 acres.
Hueston, Hugh. N.C. Private. 29 Apr. 1784. 274 acres.
Huey, John. Va. Private. 9 Dec. 1783. 100 acres.
Huff, John. Pa. Private. 11 Jun. 1785. 200 acres.
Huff, Moses. Me. Seaman. 9 Jul. 1835. 200 acres. Edgecomb.
Huff, Robert. N.C. Private. 5 Dec. 1796. 640 acres.
Huff, Samuel. Ga. ———. 15 Mar. 1784. 250 acres.
Huffman, Aaron. N. Y. Private. 8 Jul. 1790. 600 acres.
Huffman, Andrew. N. Y. Private. 8 Jul. 1790. 500 acres.
Huffman, Philip. Va. Lieutenant. 10 Mar. 1783. 2666 2/3 acres.
Hufman, Reuben. Va. Private. 24 May 1813. 100 acres.
Huger, Isaac. S.C. Brigadier General. 16 Jul. 1784. 400 acres.
Huger, Isaac. S.C. Brigadier General. 15 Oct. 1784. 450 acres.
Huges, Benjamin. Va. Private. 25 Oct. 1783. 100 acres.
Huges, Nathaniel. Va. Private. 24 Apr. 1783. 100 acres.
Hugg, Daniel. Me. ———. 16 May 1835. 200 acres. Edgecomb.
Huggens, Richard. Md. Sergeant. ———. 50 acres.
Huggin, Jeff. N.C. Private. 17 Feb. 1824. 640 acres.
Huggins, Andrew. S.C. ———. 2 Oct. 1786. 200 acres to John Huggins, heir.
Huggins, Benjamin. S.C. Ensign. 16 Jul. 1784. 150 acres.
Huggins, Ebenezer. Conn. Sufferer. New/ East Haven. 47.12.8.
Huggins, James. N.C. Private. 11 Sep. 1820. 640 acres.
Huggins, James. S.C. ———. 3 Sep. 1787. 200 acres to John Huggins, heir.
Huggins, John. S.C. ———. 4 Sep. 1786. 200 acres.
Huggins, Robert. Ga. Minute Man. 4 Nov. 1785. ———.
Huggins, Samuel. Md. ———. ———. 50 acres.

Huggins, Samuel. Conn. Sufferer. New/ East Haven. 91.16.9.
Huggins, William. S.C. ———. 2 Oct. 1787. 200 acres.
Hughes, Abigail. Conn. Sufferer. New/East Haven. 37.12.5.
Hughes, Bartly. N.C. Private. 22 Dec. 1796. 640 acres.
Hughes, Burrell. N.C. Private. 16 Aug. 1821. 640 acres.
Hughes, George. Va. Sergeant. 9 Dec. 1784. 400 acres.
Hughes, Henry. N.C. Private. 20 May 1784. 640 acres.
Hughes, Henry. Va. Subaltern. 27 Oct. 1784. 2666 2/3 acres.
Hughes, Henry F. Conn. Sufferer. New/ East Haven. 38.1.0.
Hughes, Isaac. Ga. Minute Man. 26 Jul. 1784. 287 1/2 acres.
Hughes, Jacob. Va. Sergeant. 15 Oct. 1785. 200 acres.
Hughes, James. Pa. Private. 22 Jan. 1787. 200 acres.
Hughes, James. Va. Sergeant. 10 Sep. 1783. 400 acres.
Hughes, James. Va. Bombardier. 29 Dec. 1796. 100 acres.
Hughes, Jasper. Va. Colonel. 9 Mar. 1784. 2666 2/3 acres.
Hughes, Jasper. Va. Cornet. 12 Nov. 1796. 444 1/2 acres.
Hughes, Jesse. Va. Private. 13 Sep. 1783. 100 acres.
Hughes, Jesse. Va. Private. 7 Apr. 1838. 100 acres.
Hughes, John. Ga. Minute Man. 17 Dec. 1784. ———.
Hughes, John. Va.-Ind. Private. 108 acres.
Hughes, John. Md. Private. ———. 50 acres.
Hughes, John. N.C. Sergeant. 17 Dec. 1785. 428 acres.
Hughes, John. Pa. Captain. 20 Mar. 1786. 500 acres to Alexander Power, assignee.
Hughes, John. Pa. Lieutenant. 17 Oct. 1786. 200 acres.
Hughes, John. Va. Captain. 9 Mar. 1784. 4666 2/3 acres.
Hughes, John. Va. Sergeant Major. 5 Jul. 1806. 200 acres.
Hughes, Michael. Md. Matross. ———. 50 acres.
Hughes, Nathaniel. Ga. Soldier. 22 Mar. 1784. —— acres to heir, Elizabeth Watson.
Hughes, Nicholas. Ga. Minute Man. 15 Mar. 1784. 250 acres.
Hughes, Pratt. Va. Lieutenant. 5 Jun. 1783. 3110 2/3 acres.
Hughes, Reuben. Va. Private. 19 Jun. 1783. 100 acres.
Hughes, Samuel. Md. Private. ———. 50 acres.
Hughes, Samuel. Md. Private. ———. 50 acres.
Hughes, Thomas. N. Y. ———. 11 Sep. 1806. 200 acres.
Hughes, William. Md. Private. ———. 50 acres.
Hughes, William. Pa. Private. ———. 200 acres.
Hughes, William. Va. Gunner's Mate. 4 Aug. 1835. 2666 2/3 acres.
Hughes, William. Va. Private. 20 Feb. 1845. 100 acres.
Hughey, Robert. S.C. ———. 2 Nov. 1801. 27 acres to John Boyd, administrator.
Hughey, Robert. S.C. ———. 3 Aug. 1801. 50 acres to James Timms, administrator.
Hughey, Robert. S.C. ———. 3 Aug. 1801. 50 acres to James Timms, administrator.
Hughlet, Charles. N.C. Private. 9 Feb. 1796. 640 acres to heirs.
Hughlett, Jeremiah. N.C. Private. 19 Jan. 1786. 640 acres.
Hughlett, John. Va. Midshipman. 1 Aug. 1788. 2666 2/3 acres.
Hughs, Burwell. N.C. Private. 30 Sep. 1785. 640 acres to heirs.
Hughs, David. N.C. Private. 30 Sep. 1785. 640 acres to heirs.
Hughs, George. N.C. Private. 30 Sep. 1785. 640 acres to heirs.
Hughs, John. N.C. Private. 9 Dec. 1797. 274 acres.
Hughs, John. Pa. Lieutenant. 17 Oct. 1786. 200 acres.
Hughs, John. Va. Private. 3 Mar. 1785. 200 acres.
Hughs, Joseph. Va. Private. 28 Jun. 1783. 100 acres.
Hughs, Nathaniel. N.C. Private. 18 Oct. 1783. 316 acres.
Hughs, Zacheriah. N.C. Private. 2 Feb. 1786. 640 acres to heirs.

Hugon, Thomas B. Md. Captain. ———. 200 acres.
Hukell, Joseph. Md. Private. ———. 50 acres.
Hulbert, Aaron. N. Y. Private. 8 Jul. 1790. 600 acres.
Hulet, John. Md. Private. ———. 50 acres.
Hull, Anna. Conn. Sufferer. Fairfield. 64.16.6.
Hull, Becham. Va. Private. 29 Dec. 1785. 200 acres.
Hull, David. Va. Private. 10 Sep. 1783. 100 acres.
Hull, David. Conn. Sufferer. New/East Haven. 19.14.0.
Hull, Ebenezer. Conn. Sufferer. New/East Haven. 5.5.0.
Hull, Edwin. Va. Captain. 13 Feb. 1809. 1000 acres.
Hull, Edwin. Va. Captain. 13 Feb. 1809. 1000 acres.
Hull, Edwin. Va. Captain. 13 Feb. 1809. 500 acres.
Hull, Edwin. Va. Captain. 13 Feb. 1809. 500 acres.
Hull, Edwin. Va. Captain. 13 Feb. 1809. 500 acres.
Hull, Edwin. Va. Captain. 13 Feb. 1809. 500 acres.
Hull, Hezekiah. Conn. Sufferer. Fairfield. 10.0.0.
Hull, Hopewell. Va. Private. 2 Dec. 1785. 100 acres.
Hull, James. Conn. Sufferer. New/East Haven. 9.6.0.
Hull, John. Md. Drummer. ———. 50 acres.
Hull, John. Va. Sergeant. 23 Jun. 1783. 400 acres.
Hull, Nathaniel. Md. Private. ———. 50 acres.
Hull, Samuel. N.Y. ———. 21 Sep. 1796. 600 acres to trustees David Hull and Samuel Sayre.
Hull, Thomas. Va. Private. 2 Dec. 1785. 100 acres.
Hulling, James. Va. Private. 23 Jun. 1783. 200 acres.
Hulls, John. Md. Private. ———. 50 acres.
Huls, James. Va. Private. 2 Aug. 1783. 100 acres.
Hulse, William. Va. Sergeant. 24 Oct. 1783. 200 acres.
Humphlett, Thomas. Va. Lieutenant. 14 Jun. 1832. 4000 acres.
Humphlett, William. Va. Seaman. 22 Nov. 1783. 100 acres.
Humphress, Randolph. N.C. Private. 8 May 1784. 640 acres.
Humphrey, Alexander. N. Y. Sergeant. 8 Jul. 1790. 500 acres.
Humphrey, James. N. Y. Private. 8 Jul. 1790. 600 acres.
Humphrey, John. N. Y. Private. 8 Jul. 1790. 600 acres.
Humphrey, John. Pa. Lieutenant. 21 Sep. 1787. 200 acres.
Humphrey, John. S.C. Soldier. 21 Jan. 1785. 200 acres.
Humphreys, George. Va. Private. 16 Dec. 1837. 200 acres.
Humphreys, Jacob. Pa. Captain. 17 Oct. 1786. 500 acres.
Humphreys, James. Va. Seaman. 4 Apr. 1838. 200 acres.
Humphreys, John. Va. Private. 2 Dec. 1783. 100 acres.
Humphreys, Joseph. Pa. Private. 14 Oct. 1786. 200 acres to Alexander Harry, Assignee.
Humphreys, Reuben. Va. Private. 20 Mar. 1783. 100 acres.
Humphreys, Robert. Pa. Private. 29 Sep. 1787. 200 acres.
Humphreys, Samuel. Va. Seaman. 27 Nov. 1783. 100 acres.
Humphreys, Samuel. Va. Private. 14 Aug. 1834. 100 acres.
Humphreys, Samuel. Va. Master at Arms. 3 Apr. 1838. 1283 acres.
Humphreys, Samuel. Va. Master at Arms. 3 Apr. 1838. 641 1/3 acres.
Humphreys, Samuel. Va. Master at Arms. 3 Apr. 1838. 641 1/3 acres.
Humphries Thomas. Va. Sergeant. 12 Jun. 1784. 200 acres.
Humphries, Daniel. N.C. Private. 6 Jan. 1784. 228 acres.
Humphries, Henry. N.C. Private. 30 Sep. 1785. 640 acres to heirs.
Humphries, James. Md. Private. ———. 50 acres.
Humphries, James. N.C. Private. 1 Dec. 1789. 182 acres.
Humphries, John. Pa. Lieutenant. 21 Sep. 1787. 200 acres.

Humphries, John. Va. Lieutenant. 12 Dec. 1783. 2666 2/3 acres.
Humphries, John. Va. Private. 31 Jan. 1784. 100 acres.
Humphries, John. Va. Lieutenant. 27 Mar. 1840. 101 3/4 acres.
Humphries, John. Va. Lieutenant. 27 Mar. 1840. 101 3/4 acres.
Humphries, John. Va. Lieutenant. 27 Mar. 1840. 203 1/2 acres.
Humphries, John. Va. Lieutenant. 26 Oct. 1842. 271 1/3 acres.
Humphries, John. Va. Lieutenant. 26 Oct. 1842. 135 2/3 acres.
Humphries, Joseph. N.C. Private. 29 Sep. 1784. 640 acres to heirs.
Humphries, Ralph. Va. Private. 11 May 1784. 100 acres.
Humphries, Robert. Va. Private. 8 May 1784. 100 acres.
Humphries, Robert. Va. Private. 15 Apr. 1853. 100 acres.
Humphries, William. N.C. Private. 2 Dec. 1785. 640 acres.
Humphries, Willis. N.C. Private. 29 Sep. 1785. 640 acres.
Humphris, Samuel. Va.-Ind. Private. 108 acres.
Humpton, Richard. Pa. Colonel. 17 Oct. 1785. 300 acres.
Humpton, Richard. Pa. Colonel. ———. 500 acres.
Hundley, Joshua. Va. Private. 3 Sep. 1783. 100 acres.
Hundon, Benjamin. Ga. ———. 17 May 1784. ———.
Hungarius, Gabriel. Pa. Private. 2 Oct. 1786. 200 acres.
Hungerford, David. N.Y. ———. 13 Sep. 1790. 500 acres to heirs.
Hungerford, Thomas. Va. Lieutenant. 11 Apr. 1800. 1000 acres.
Hungerford, Thomas. Va. Lieutenant. 11 Apr. 1800. 1000 acres.
Hungerford, Thomas. Va. Lieutenant. 11 Apr. 1800. 666 2/3 acres.
Hungerford, Thomas. Va. Lieutenant. 11 Dec. 1807. 1222 acres.
Hunnewell, Thomas. Me. ———. 20 May 1835. 200 acres to widow Elizabeth Colby. Emden.
Hunney, Calis. Va. Private. 19 Jun. 1783. 100 acres.
Hunt, David. N.C. Private. 12 Mar. 1785. 640 acres to heirs.
Hunt, Elijah. Pa. Private. 5 May 1787. 200 acres.
Hunt, Elisha. N.C. Private. 22 Oct. 1783. 640 acres.
Hunt, Fitzmaurice. Ga. Refugee. 17 May 1784. ———.
Hunt, Glover. Pa. Private. 13 May 1794. 200 acres to son Richard Hunt.
Hunt, Glover. Pa. Private. 13 May 1794. 200 acres to son Richard Hunt.
Hunt, Hardy. N.C. Private. 9 Feb. 1796. 640 acres to heirs.
Hunt, Ichabod. Me. Private. 3 Jun. 1835. 200 acres to widow Eunich Hunt. Unity.
Hunt, Jacob. Md. Private. ———. 50 acres.
Hunt, James. Va. Private. 16 Jun. 1783. 100 acres.
Hunt, John. S.C. ———. 1 Aug. 1785. 200 acres.
Hunt, John. S.C. ———. 2 Oct. 1786. 200 acres.
Hunt, John S. Md. Private. ———. 50 acres.
Hunt, Joseph. N. Y. Matross. 9 Jul. 1790. 500 acres.
Hunt, Joshua. N. Y. Private. 8 Jul. 1790. 600 acres.
Hunt, Memucan. Va. Private. 15 Jun. 1785. 100 acres.
Hunt, Samuel. Va. Private. 12 Jan. 1784. 233 1/3 acres.
Hunt, Sarah. Conn. Sufferer. New/East Haven. 3.4.0.
Hunt, Thomas. Ga. Soldier. 4 Oct. 1785. ———.
Hunt, Thomas. N. Y. Lieutenant. 9 Jul. 1790. 1200 acres.
Hunt, Thomas. Va. Private. 23 Oct. 1784. 200 acres.
Hunt, William. Ga. ———. 28 Feb. 1784. 500 acres.
Hunt, William. N. Y. Private. 8 Jul. 1790. 500 acres.
Hunt, William. Pa. Private. ———. 200 acres.
Hunt, William. Va. Private. 20 Aug. 1783. 200 acres.
Hunt, William, Jr. Ga. ———. 25 May 1784. 287 1/2 acres.
Hunter, Benjamin. Pa. Private. ———. 200 acres.

Hunter, Benjamin. Pa. Private. 14 Oct. 1785. 200 acres.

Hunter, Cherry. N.C. Corporal. 9 Dec. 1797. 428 acres.

Hunter, Elisha. N.C. Private. 30 Nov. 1785. 640 acres.

Hunter, Ezekiel. N.Y. ———. 13 Sep. 1790. 500 acres to heirs.

Hunter, George. Va. Surgeon. 29 Jul. 1831. 5000 acres.

Hunter, George. Va. Surgeon. 29 Jul. 1831. 1000 acres.

Hunter, George. Va. Surgeon. 13 Apr. 1838. 1227 1/3 acres.

Hunter, George. Va. Surgeon. 13 Apr. 1838. 613 2/3 acres.

Hunter, Jesse. Ga. ———. 17 May 1784. ———.

Hunter, John. Ga. ———. 17 May 1784. ———.

Hunter, John. S.C. Soldier. 21 Jan. 1785. 200 acres.

Hunter, Joseph. Mass. Private. 15 Jan. 1834. 200 acres.

Hunter, Miles. Ga. ———. 17 May 1784. ———.

Hunter, Philip. Ga. ———. 17 May 1784. ———.

Hunter, Robert. N. Y. Lieutenant. 9 Jul. 1790. 1200 acres.

Hunter, Samuel. Ga. ———. 17 May 1784. ———.

Hunter, Solomon. N.C. Sergeant. 7 Jan. 1786. 1000 acres to heirs.

Hunter, Timothy. N.C. Private. 30 Sep. 1785. 640 acres to heirs.

Hunter, William. Va. Private. 9 Mar. 1785. 100 acres.

Huntley, Thomas. N. Y. Private. 8 Jul. 1790. 600 acres.

Hunton, Jonathan. Me. ———. 14 Sep. 1835. 200 acres to widow Hannah Hunton. Wiscasset.

Hunton, Thomas. Va. Lieutenant. 1 Mar. 1851. 1500 acres.

Hunton, Thomas. Va. Lieutenant. 1 Mar. 1851. 1000 acres.

Hunton, Thomas. Va. Lieutenant. 1 Mar. 1851. 1000 acres.

Hunton, Thomas. Va. Lieutenant. 1 Mar. 1851. 500 acres.

Huntsman, Michael. Ga. ———. 1784. 250 acres.

Huntsman, William. Ga. Refugee. 15 Mar. 1784. 250 acres.

Hupp, Philip. Va. Private. 6 Apr. 1784. 100 acres.

Hupp, Philip. Va. Private. 21 Mar. 1807. 200 acres.

Hurdle, Lawrence. Md. Private. ———. 50 acres.

Hurlburt, Daniel. Conn. Sufferer. New London. 126.14.7.

Hurlburt, Mary. Conn. Sufferer. New London. 212.13.0.

Hurlburt, Titus. Conn. Sufferer. New London. 1,961.3.0.

Hurlbut, Joseph. Conn. Sufferer. New London. 965.8.3.

Hurley, Arthur. N. Y. Private. 8 Jul. 1790. 600 acres.

Hurley, Edward. Md. Private. ———. 50 acres.

Hurley, John. Md. Private. ———. 50 acres.

Hurley, John. N.C. Private. 25 Oct. 1783. 640 acres.

Hurley, John. N.C. Private. 13 Sep. 1820. 640 acres.

Hurley, Josiah. Md. Private. ———. 50 acres.

Hurley, Matthew. Va. Private. 23 Jun. 1783. 200 acres.

Hurley, William. Md. Private. ———. 50 acres.

Hursk, Thomas. N.C. Private. 10 Aug. 1785. 640 acres.

Hurson, Matthew. Ga. Soldier. 5 Dec. 1785. 230 acres.

Hurst, Samuel. Md. Private. ———. 50 acres.

Hurt, James. Va. Private. 19 Dec. 1807. 100 acres.

Hurt, John. Va. Brigade Chaplain. 13 Jan. 1784. 7000 acres.

Hurt, John. Va. Brigade Chaplain. 22 May 1792. 777 2/3 acres.

Hurt, West. Va. Private. 25 Jun. 1783. 100 acres.

Hurt, William. N.C. ———. 21 May 1784. 640 acres to heirs.

Hurteigh, John. N. Y. Private. 8 Jul. 1790. 600 acres.

Hurtsock, Valentine. Pa. Private. 9 Oct. 1786. 200 acres.

Huse, Samuel. N.C. Private. 12 Dec. 1796. 640 acres.

Hussar, Francis. N.C. Private. 17 Feb. 1824. 640 acres.
Huster, Nicholas. Md. Private. ———. 50 acres.
Hustler, Thomas. Pa. Sergeant. 5 Apr. 1787. 250 acres.
Huston, John. Ga. Citizen. 10 Dec. 1783. 250 acres.
Huston, Neil. N.C. Private. 25 Oct. 1783. 640 acres to Daniel Huston, heir.
Huston, Philip. Md. Private. ———. 50 acres.
Hutchcraft, Thomas. Md. Private. ———. 50 acres.
Hutchens, Edward. N.C. Sergeant. 30 Sep. 1785. 1000 acres.
Hutchens, James. N.C. Private. 28 May 1784. 640 acres.
Hutcherson, Charles. Va. Sergeant. 17 May 1783. 200 acres.
Hutcherson, John. Va. Private. 7 Aug. 1813. 200 acres.
Hutcherson, Thomas. Va. Sergeant. 23 Oct. 1783. 200 acres.
Hutcheson, William. Md. Private. ———. 50 acres.
Hutchings, Charles. Va. Private. 17 Jul. 1783. 200 acres.
Hutchings, Hercules. Md. Private. ———. 50 acres.
Hutchings, Hezekiah. Mass. Corporal. 18 Oct. 1833. 200 acres.
Hutchins, Amos. N. Y. ———. ———. 500 acres to his representatives.
Hutchins, Eastman. Me. ———. 14 May 1835. 200 acres to widow Betsey Hutchins. Alfred.
Hutchins, Edward. N.C. Private. 10 Sep. 1821. 274 acres to heirs.
Hutchins, Jesse. N.C. Private. 6 Dec. 1815. 274 acres.
Hutchins, Levi. Me. ———. 14 May 1835. 200 acres. Alfred.
Hutchins, Robert. N.C. Private. 26 Aug. 1785. 640 acres to heirs.
Hutchins, Simeon. Me. Private. 16 Mar. 1836. 200 acres. Kennebunk.
Hutchinson, Ebenezer. N.Y. Surgeon's Mate. 6 Jul. 1790. 1300 acres.
Hutchinson, Israel. Me. Private. 11 Aug. 1838. 200 acres. Hallowell.
Hutchinson, James. Va. Private. 3 Nov. 1784. 200 acres.
Hutchinson, John. Pa. Private. 30 Jul. 1787. 200 acres.
Hutchinson, John. Pa. Private. 8 Dec. 1786. 200 acres.
Hutchinson, John. Va. Private. 1 Sep. 1786. 100 acres.
Hutchinson, Jonathan. Ga. ———. 17 May 1784. ———.
Hutchinson, Joseph. Ga. ———. 17 May 1784. ———.
Hutchinson, Joseph. Va. Sergeant. 14 May 1789. 200 acres.
Hutchinson, Joseph. Va. Sergeant. 9 Jun. 1857. 200 acres.
Hutchinson, Richard. Pa. Private. ———. 200 acres.
Hutchinson, Thomas. Va. Corporal. 29 Jun. 1784. 200 acres.
Hutchinson, William. Pa. Private. 6 Nov. 1786. 200 acres.
Hutchison, John. Va. Private. 15 Jun. 1807. 100 acres.
Hutchison, Thomas. Va. Sergeant. 6 Mar. 1834. 200 acres.
Hutson, Isaac. N.C. Sergeant. 24 Nov. 1783. 357 acres.
Hutson, Isaac. N.C. Private. 23 Apr. 1785. 640 acres to heirs.
Hutson, John. Md. Private. ———. 50 acres.
Hutson, John. N.C. Private. 12 Mar. 1785. 640 acres to heirs.
Hutson, Thomas. N.C. Sergeant. 23 Jun. 1820. 1000 acres to heirs.
Hutson, Thomas. N.C. Private. 8 Aug. 1821. 640 acres.
Hutson, William. Va. Private. 5 Jun. 1783. 100 acres.
Hutt, Elijah. Md. Private. ———. 50 acres.
Hutt, John. Va. Private. 30 May 1831. 100 acres.
Hutt, Read. Va. Private. 29 Jul. 1783. 100 acres.
Hutto, Henry. S.C. ———. 1 Oct. 1787. 200 acres.
Hutton, Christopher. N. Y. Lieutenant. 8 Jul. 1790. 1200 acres.
Hutton, James. Md. Sergeant. ———. 50 acres.
Hutton, James. Pa. Private. 9 May 1794. 200 acres.
Hutton, James. Pa. Private. ———. 200 acres.

Hutton, William. Md. Corporal. ———. 50 acres.

Hutts, Jacob. Va. Private. 25 Jul. 1783. 200 acres.

Hutts, John. Ga. Minute Man. 1784. 287 1/2 acres.

Hutts, Joseph. Conn. Sufferer. New/East Haven. 1.5.0.

Hutts, Leonard. Va. Private. 25 Jul. 1783. 200 acres.

Huver, John. N.C. Private. 7 Jan. 1786. 640 acres to heirs.

Hyatt, Abraham. N. Y. Lieutenant. 7 Jul. 1790. 1200 acres.

Hyatt, Daniel. Conn. Sufferer. Norwalk. 85.6.7.

Hyatt, Daniel. Conn. Sufferer. Norwalk. 9.0.6.

Hyatt, Ebenezer. Conn. Sufferer. Norwalk. 76.15.6.

Hyatt, Gershom. Conn. Sufferer. Norwalk. 32.5.0.

Hyatt, Minnah. N. Y. Private. 8 Jul. 1790. 500 acres.

Hyatt, Nathan, Jr. Conn. Sufferer. Norwalk. 29.19.11.

Hyde, Andrew. N.C. Private. 22 Dec. 1796. 274 acres.

Hyde, John. Md. Private. ———. 50 acres.

Hyde, John. Conn. Sufferer. Fairfield. 47.11.3.

Hyde, John, Jr. Conn. Sufferer. Fairfield. 7.6.3.

Hyde, Joseph. Conn. Sufferer. Fairfield. 35.0.0.

Hyde, Thomas. N. Y. Private. 8 Jul. 1790. 600 acres.

Hyde, Westwood. N.C. Private. 7 Dec. 1797. 365 acres.

Hyer, Alexander. N. Y. Private. 8 Jul. 1790. 600 acres.

Hyer, Jacob. N. Y. Private. 8 Jul. 1790. 600 acres.

Hyer, John. Pa. Sergeant. 29 Sep. 1787. 250 acres.

Hyle, Conradt. N.Y. ———. 13 Sep. 1790. 500 acres to heirs.

Hyman, Joseph. N.C. Private. 5 Sep. 1821. 640 acres.

Hynear, Thomas. N.C. Private. 9 Feb. 1796. 640 acres to heirs.

Hynes, James. Va. Private. 25 Aug. 1783. 200 acres.

Hynes, Robert. Ga. ———. 25 May 1784. 287 1/2 acres.

Hyrne, Henry. S.C. Lieutenant. 21 Jan. 1785. 200 acres.

Hyslop, Abner. Va. Private. 15 Jun. 1807. 200 acres.

Hyslop, Levin. Va. Private. 15 Jun. 1807. 200 acres.

Hyslop, Smyth. Va. Private. 27 Apr. 1811. 200 acres.

Idole, Henry. Ga. Soldier. 4 Oct. 1785. ———.

Igle, John. Ga. Refugee. 20 Feb. 1784. 500 acres.

Igley, Samuel. N.C. Private. 30 Sep. 1785. 640 acres to heirs.

Ijams, Frederick. Md. Private. ———. 50 acres.

Iler, Philip. Pa. Private. ———. 200 acres.

Imhoff, John Lewis Peyer. S.C. Captain. 21 Jan. 1795. 300 acres.

Imonds, William. N.C. Private. 10 Feb. 1796. 640 acres to heirs.

Impson, Henry. Pa. Private. 14 Jan. 1789. 200 acres.

Ingalls, Phineas. Me. Artificer. 5 Nov. 1835. 200 acres. Bridgton.

Ingersoll, Anne. Conn. Sufferer. Greenwich. 14.15.6.

Ingersoll, Elizabeth. Conn. Sufferer. Greenwich. 68.14.4.

Ingersoll, Jared. Conn. Sufferer. New/East Haven. 2.0.0.

Ingersoll, Nathaniel. Conn. Sufferer. Greenwich. 59.16.7.

Ingles, John. Ga. Soldier. 4 Oct. 1785. ———.

Ingles, John. N.C. Captain. 10 Nov. 1783. 3840 acres.

Ingles, William. Md. Private. ———. 50 acres.

Inglis, Charles. N.C. Private. 14 Feb. 1796. 274 acres.

Inglish, Joseph. N.C. Musician. 22 May 1820. 360 acres to heirs.

Ingraham, George. N.C. Private. 30 Sep. 1785. 640 acres to heirs.

Ingram, James. N.C. Private. 17 Dec. 1785. 640 acres to heirs.

Ingram, John. N.C. Sergeant. 27 Jul. 1785. 797 acres.

Ingram, John. N.C. Sergeant. 14 Sep. 1820. 1000 acres.

Ingram, Richard. Ga. ———. 17 May 1784. ———.
Ingram, Thomas. N.Y. ———. 13 Sep. 1790. 500 acres to heirs.
Injoins, William. Ga. Soldier. 7 Jun. 1785. 230 acres.
Inloe, Thomas. Va. Private. 17 Apr. 1792. 100 acres.
Inlow, Potter. Ga. Minute Man. 17 May 1784. ———.
Inlow, Sebastian. Ga. ———. 16 Jul. 1784. 287 1/2 acres.
Inman, Joshua. Ga. Captain. 6 Feb. 1784. 500 acres.
Inman, Joshua. Ga. ———. 6 Feb. 1784. 250 acres.
Inman, Shadrack. Ga. Captain. 17 May 1784. —— acres to wife and daughter, Elizabeth Inman and Mary Inman.
Inmon, William. N.C. Private. 13 Dec. 1796. 320 acres.
Innes, James. Va. Colonel. 27 Dec. 1783. 6666 2/3 acres.
Innis, Rice. Va. Private. 31 Aug. 1830. 100 acres.
Irby, David. Va. Private. 6 Jan. 1834. 200 acres.
Irby, Douglass. Va. Sergeant. 2 May 1827. 200 acres.
Irby, Douglass. Va. Sergeant. 2 May 1827. 200 acres.
Irby, Hardyman. Va. Sergeant. 27 May 1783. 200 acres.
Irby, James. Va.-Ind. Sergeant. 216 acres. [possibly Irley].
Irby, William. Va. Private. 14 Jun. 1787. 100 acres.
Ireland, Job. Conn. Sufferer. Greenwich. 0.4.1.
Ireland, John. Md. Matross. ———. 50 acres.
Ireson, George. Va. Private. 24 Apr. 1784. 100 acres.
Irick, Michael. Pa. Private. 23 May 1804. 200 acres.
Irish, Nathaniel. Pa. Captain. 28 Aug. 1787. 500 acres.
Ironmunger, Robert. Va. Fife Major. 17 Jun. 1783. 200 acres.
Irons, John. Md. Private. ———. 50 acres.
Irons, William. Ga. Soldier. 7 Jun. 1785. 230 acres.
Irvine, Abram. Md. Private. ———. 50 acres.
Irvine, Alexader. Ga. ———. 6 Feb. 1784. 500 acres.
Irvine, Hugh. Ga. ———. 6 Feb. 1784. 250 acres.
Irvine, James. Pa. Lieutenant. ———. 200 acres.
Irvine, Jared. Ga. ———. 17 Feb. 1784. 250 acres.
Irvine, John. Ga. ———. 17 May 1784. ———.
Irvine, John. Pa. Captain. 5 Mar. 1787. 500 acres.
Irvine, John. Va. Private. 18 Jun. 1788. 100 acres.
Irvine, Matthew. Pa. Surgeon. ———. 300 acres.
Irvine, Matthew. Pa. Surgeon. 19 May 1787. 300 acres.
Irvine, Matthew. Va. Surgeon. 16 Apr. 1807. 1000 acres.
Irvine, Matthew. Va. Surgeon. 16 Apr. 1807. 1000 acres.
Irvine, Matthew. Va. Surgeon. 16 Apr. 1807. 1000 acres.
Irvine, Matthew. Va. Surgeon. 16 Apr. 1807. 1000 acres.
Irvine, Matthew. Va. Surgeon. 16 Apr. 1807. 500 acres.
Irvine, Matthew. Va. Surgeon. 16 Apr. 1807. 500 acres.
Irvine, Matthew. Va. Surgeon. 16 Apr. 1807. 500 acres.
Irvine, Matthew. Va. Surgeon. 16 Apr. 1807. 500 acres.
Irvine, Matthew. Va. Surgeon. 28 Sep. 1808. 2333 1/3 acres.
Irvine, William. Ga. ———. 17 Feb. 1784. 250 acres.
Irvine, William. Pa. Brigadier General. 25 Feb. 1943. 50 acres to J. D. Sargeant, assignee.
Irvine, William. Pa. Brigadier General. 19 Apr. 1787. 500 acres.
Irvine, William. Pa. Brigadier General. 19 Apr. 1787. 500 acres.
Irving, William. Va. Sergeant. 31 Jan. 1784. 200 acres.
Irwin, Andrew. Pa. Captain. 13 Nov. 1786. 500 acres.
Irwin, Charles. Pa. Private. 15 Nov. 1786. 200 acres.
Irwin, Christopher. Pa. Private. 28 Aug. 1787. 200 acres.

Irwin, Henry. N.C. Lieutenant Colonel. 28 Sep. 1785. 5760 acres to heir Henry Irwin.

Irwin, James. Pa. Lieutenant. 10 Apr. 1787. 200 acres.

Irwin, John. Conn. Sufferer. New London. 800.0.0.

Isaac, Benjamin. Conn. Sufferer. Norwalk. 406.8.9 to his heirs.

Isaacs, James. Md. Private. ———. 50 acres.

Isaacs, Jesse. Ga. Refugee. 6 Aug. 1785. ———.

Isaacs, John. Va.-Ind. Private. 108 acres.

Isaacs, John. Va. Private. 14 Jun. 1787. 200 acres.

Isaacs, Joseph. Md. Private. ———. 50 acres.

Isbell, Daniel. Va. Private. 14 Jun. 1784. 100 acres.

Isdell, Thomas. Va. Private. 14 Feb. 1784. 100 acres.

Isdell, Thomas. Va. Private. 12 Jan. 1842. 100 acres.

Isement, Peter. N. Y. ———. ———. 500 acres.

Isipise, George. Pa. Private. ———. 200 acres.

Island, Absalom. Ga. ———. 15 Mar. 1784. 250 acres.

Island, John. Ga. ———. 17 May 1784. 250 acres. ———.

Ison, George. Va. Corporal. 13 Jan. 1813. 200 acres.

Israel, Isaac. Va. Captain. 25 Feb. 1807. 4000 acres.

Issable, Robert. Md. Sergeant. ———. 50 acres.

Issbell, Thomas. Va. Private. 25 May 1785. 100 acres.

Ives, James. N.C. Private. 20 Apr. 1784. 640 acres.

Ives, Levi. Conn. Sufferer. New/East Haven. 46.1.4.

Ivey, Curtis. N.C. Lieutenant. 23 Oct. 1783. 2560 acres.

Ivey, David. N.C. Private. 10 May 1784. 274 acres.

Ivey, David. N.C. Musician. 21 Aug. 1820. 154 acres.

Ivorey, William. N.Y. ———. 13 Sep. 1790. 500 acres to heirs.

Ivy, Elisha. N.C. Private. 30 Sep. 1785. 640 acres to heirs.

Ivy, William. Va. Captain. 21 Mar. 1834. 4000 acres.

Ivy, William. Va. Captain. 14 Apr. 1835. 1333 1/3 acres.

Ivy, William. Va. Captain. 10 Mar. 1854. 995 6/9 acres.

Jabine, John. N. Y. Drummer. 8 Jul. 1790. 500 acres.

Jack, Francis. N.C. Private. 20 Sep. 1821. 640 acres.

Jack, John. Ga. ———. 17 May 1784. ———.

Jack, Samuel. Ga. Refugee. 30 Jan. 1784. 250 acres.

Jack, Samuel. Ga. Colonel. 2 Feb. 1784. 800 acres.

Jackman, Richard. Me. ———. 24 Apr. 1835. 200 acres. Wayne.

Jackson, Abraham. Ga. ———. 17 May 1784. ———.

Jackson, Absalom. Ga. Citizen. 5 Apr. 1785. 287 1/2 acres.

Jackson, Baziel. N.C. Private. 15 Dec. 1802. 84 acres.

Jackson, Benjamin. Ga. ———. 17 May 1784. ———.

Jackson, Charles. N.C. Private. 14 Dec. 1797. 640 acres to heirs.

Jackson, Daniel. Ga. Refugee. 25 Feb. 1784. 500 acres.

Jackson, Daniel. Conn. Sufferer. Norwalk. 53.2.5.

Jackson, David. Ga. ———. 17 May 1784. ———.

Jackson, Drury. Ga. Citizen Private. 10 Dec. 1784. 250 acres.

Jackson, Ed. Md. Private. ———. 50 acres.

Jackson, Edmon. N.C. Private. 10 Dec. 1788. 320 acres to heirs.

Jackson, Edmund. N.C. Private. Jan. 1795. 640 acres to heirs.

Jackson, Edward. Va. Private. 13 Dec. 1786. 100 acres.

Jackson, Francis. N.Y. Quartermaster Sergeant. 8 Jul. 1790. 600 acres.

Jackson, Frederick. N.C. Private. 15 Jul. 1785. 640 acres to heirs.

Jackson, Henry. Ga. ———. 17 May 1784. ———.

Jackson, Henry. Me. ———. 22 Sep. 1835. 200 acres to widow Sarah Jackson. Raymond.

Jackson, Hezekiah. Va. Private. 19 Dec. 1786. 100 acres.

Jackson, Isaac. Ga. Major. 15 Mar. 1784. 650 acres.

Jackson, Isaac. Ga. ———. 30 Apr. 1785. ———.

Jackson, Isaac. Pa. Sergeant. 6 Sep. 1787. 250 acres.

Jackson, Isaac. Va. Private. 4 Dec. 1783. 200 acres.

Jackson, Jacob. N.C. Private. 19 Dec. 1809. 640 acres to heirs.

Jackson, James. Ga. Lieuenant Colonel. 15 Mar. 1784. 1500 acres.

Jackson, James. Md. Sergeant. ———. 50 acres.

Jackson, James. N.C. Private. 27 Jul. 1785. 228 acres.

Jackson, James. Va. Sergeant. 4 Nov. 1784. 400 acres.

Jackson, Jeremiah. N.C. Private. 20 Jan. 1785. 640 acres to heirs.

Jackson, Jeremiah. Pa. Captain. 25 Feb. 1943. 500 acres.

Jackson, Job. Ga. ———. 17 May 1784. ———.

Jackson, Job. N.C. Private. 30 Sep. 1785. 640 acres to heirs.

Jackson, John. Ga. Private. 1784. 287 1/2 acres.

Jackson, John. Md. Private. ———. 50 acres.

Jackson, John. N.C. Private. 7 Dec. 1783. 274 acres.

Jackson, John. S.C. ———. 5 Mar. 1787. 200 acres.

Jackson, John. Va. Private. 10 Dec. 1783. 200 acres.

Jackson, John. Va. Sergeant. 30 Jun. 1784. 200 acres.

Jackson, Jonathan. N.C. Private. 2 Jun. 1813. 640 acres to heirs.

Jackson, Joseph. Ga. Citizen. 5 Apr. 1785. 287 1/2 acres.

Jackson, Joseph. Pa. Private. 17 Aug. 1787. 200 acres.

Jackson, Josiah. N.C. Private. 11 May 1785. 640 acres.

Jackson, Josiah. N.C. Private. 30 Sep. 1785. 640 acres to heirs.

Jackson, Michael. Ga. Soldier. 24 Dec. 178-. ———.

Jackson, Michael. Va. Private. 20 Feb. 1784. 100 acres.

Jackson, Nathan. Ga. ———. 4 May 1785. 287 1/2 acres.

Jackson, Nathan. Va. Private. 24 Dec. 1784. 200 acres.

Jackson, Nathaniel. Ga. ———. 5 Sep. 1785. 287 1/2 acres.

Jackson, Nathaniel. Me. Corporal. 15 Sep. 1835. 200 acres to widow Rosanna Jackson. Jay.

Jackson, Patton. N. Y. Lieutenant. 9 Jul. 1790. 1200 acres.

Jackson, Peter. Ga. ———. 17 May 1784. ———.

Jackson, Philip. N.C. Private. 12 Sep. 1785. 640 acres to heirs.

Jackson, Philip. S.C. Soldier. 7 Dec. 1801. 200 acres.

Jackson, Randolph. Ga. ———. 17 May 1784. ———.

Jackson, Reuben. Va. Private. 3 Sep. 1796. 200 acres.

Jackson, Reubin. Ga. Private. 22 Mar. 1785. 250 acres.

Jackson, Roberson. N.C. Private. 28 Sep. 1785. 640 acres to heirs.

Jackson, Robert. Ga. Soldier. ———. ———.

Jackson, Robert. N.C. Private. 2 Dec. 1785. 276 acres.

Jackson, Samuel. Va. Private. 19 Dec. 1783. 100 acres.

Jackson, Simon. Ga. Soldier. 10 Dec. 1784. 230 acres.

Jackson, Thomas. Ga. ———. 17 May 1784. ———.

Jackson, Thomas. N. Y. Private. 8 Jul. 1790. 600 acres.

Jackson, Thomas. N.C. Private. 2 Dec. 1785. 640 acres to heirs.

Jackson, Thomas. Va. Private. 23 Jun. 1783. 200 acres.

Jackson, Thomas Tredwell. N.Y. Lieutenant. 16 Jul. 1800. 1000 acres.

Jackson, William. Ga. ———. 30 Sep. 1784. 287 1/2 acres.

Jackson, William. Ga. ———. 5 Apr. 1785. 287 1/2 acres.

Jackson, William. N. Y. Private. 8 Jul. 1790. 600 acres.

Jackson, William. N.C. Private. 23 Oct. 1783. 274 acres.

Jackson, William. N.C. Private. 27 Nov. 1783. 274 acres.

Jackson, William. Va. Private. 29 Jan. 1784. 200 acres.

Jackson, William. Va. Private. 16 Feb. 1784. 100 acres.

Jackson, William. Va. Private. 1 Dec. 1785. 100 acres.

Jackson, William. Va. Sergeant. 21 Nov. 1795. 200 acres.

Jackson, William. Va. Private. 2 Dec. 1837. 100 acres.

Jackson, Wilson. N.C. Private. 6 Dec. 1796. 460 acres to heirs.

Jackson, Zacheriah. N.C. Sergeant. 27 Nov. 1800. 428 acres.

Jaco, William. Va. Private. 14 Oct. 1783. 100 acres.

Jacob, John. N.C. Lieutenant. 17 Feb. 1824. 2560 acres.

Jacobas, Ambrose. N.C. Private. 19 Jan. 1786. 640 acres.

Jacobi, Michael. Pennsylvania. ———. 4 Mar. 1803. 200 acres.

Jacobi, Philip. Pa. Lieutenant. 30 Sep. 1787. 200 acres.

Jacobs [or Jacobson], Cornelius. N.Y. Private. 13 Sep. 1790. 500 acres.

Jacobs, Abel. N. Y. Matross. 9 Jul. 1790. 600 acres.

Jacobs, Benjamin. N.C. Private. 28 Oct. 1783. 274 acres.

Jacobs, Benjamin. S.C. ———. 4 Jul. 1791. 137 acres.

Jacobs, Benjamin. Va. Private. 15 Oct. 1785. 100 acres.

Jacobs, Benjamin. Va. Private. 19 Feb. 1818. 100 acres.

Jacobs, Daniel. N.C. Sergeant. 22 Apr. 1785. 1000 acres.

Jacobs, George. Me. Lieutenant. 27 Apr. 1838. 600 acres to widow Hepsibah Jacobs. Sanford.

Jacobs, Henry. Md. Private. ———. 50 acres.

Jacobs, Jesse. Md. Sergeant. ———. 50 acres.

Jacobs, John. Me. ———. 7 Sep. 1835. 200 acres. Mount Vernon.

Jacobs, John. N. Y. Sergeant. 8 Jul. 1790. 600 acres.

Jacobs, John. N.Y. ———. 13 Sep. 1790. 500 acres to heirs.

Jacobs, John. Pa. Private. 11 Sep. 1789. 200 acres.

Jacobs, John. Va. Private. 8 Dec. 1784. 200 acres.

Jacobs, Joseph. Pa. Private. 12 Oct. 1786. 200 acres.

Jacobs, Joshua. N.C. Private. 17 Dec. 1785. 640 acres.

Jacobs, Peter. N.C. Private. 9 Nov. 1784. 640 acres.

Jacobs, Roley. Va. Private. 20 Jun. 1783. 100 acres.

Jacobs, Samuel. Va. Private. 17 Jun. 1784. 100 acres.

Jacobs, William. N.C. Private. 24 Nov. 1796. 640 acres to heirs.

Jacobs, William. Va. Private. 20 Jun. 1783. 100 acres.

Jacobs, William. Conn. Sufferer. Greenwich. 60.0.0.

Jacobs, Zacheriah. Md. Private. ———. 50 acres.

Jacobson, Noble. Ga. Refugee. 6 Aug. 1785. ———.

Jacobus, Abraham. N.C. Private. 9 Sep. 1785. 640 acres to heirs.

Jacoby, David. Pa. Private. 19 Oct. 1786. 200 acres.

Jacoby, Nicholas. Pa. ———. 31 Dec. 1802. 200 acres.

Jacques, John. N. Y. Sergeant. 8 Jul. 1790. 500 acres.

Jacquet, Joseph. Pa. Lieutenant. 6 Apr. 1794. 200 acres to Susanna Jacquet, widow.

Jacquett, Joseph. Pa. LIeutenant. 6 Apr. 1794. 200 acres to heirs.

Jaison, Thomas. N.C. Private. 18 Nov. 1788. 640 acres to heirs.

Jakins, William. N.C. Private. 27 Jul. 1785. 274 acres.

James, Abraham. Va.-Ind. Private. 108 acres.

James, Benjamin. S.C. ———. 2 Jan. 1792. 100 acres.

James, David. N.C. Private. 10 Feb. 1796. 640 acres to heirs.

James, Ebenezer. N. Y. Corporal. 8 Jul. 1790. 600 acres.

James, Edwin. N.C. Private. 13 Jan. 1823. 228 acres.

James, Elijah. Ga. ———. 5 Sep. 1785. 287 1/2 acres.

James, Elisha. Va. Private. 2 Jul. 1783. 100 acres.

James, Henry. Va. Steward. 14 Feb. 1838. 1333 1/3 acres.
James, Henry. Va. Steward. 14 Feb. 1838. 1333 1/3 acres.
James, Henry. Va. Steward. 10 Nov. 1848. 1333 1/3 acres.
James, John. Ga. Soldier. 1 May 1785. ———.
James, John. N.C. Private. 12 Sep. 1785. 640 acres to heirs.
James, Michael. Va. Lieutenant. 3 Aug. 1784. 2666 2/3 acres.
James, Michael. Va. Lieutenant. 25 May 1852. 1333 1/3 acres.
James, Michael. Va. Lieutenant. 10 Aug. 1833. 148 1/9 acres.
James, Michael. Va. Lieutenant. 10 Aug. 1833. 148 1/9 acres.
James, Michael. Va. Lieutenant. 10 Aug. 1833. 148 1/9 acres.
James, Michael. Va. Lieutenant. 10 Aug. 1833. 42 2/7 acres.
James, Michael. Va. Lieutenant. 10 Aug. 1833. 42 2/7 acres.
James, Michael. Va. Lieutenant. 10 Aug. 1833. 42 2/7 acres.
James, Michael. Va. Lieutenant. 10 Aug. 1833. 42 2/7 acres.
James, Michael. Va. Lieutenant. 10 Aug. 1833. 42 2/7 acres.
James, Michael. Va. Lieutenant. 10 Aug. 1833. 42 2/7 acres.
James, Michael. Va. Lieutenant. 10 Aug. 1833. 42 2/7 acres.
James, Michael. Va. Lieutenant. 10 Aug. 1833. 148 1/9 acres.
James, Michael. Va. Lieutenant. 10 Aug. 1833. 148 1/9 acres.
James, Michael. Va. Lieutenant. 10 Aug. 1833. 148 1/9 acres.
James, Michael. Va. Lieutenant. 10 Aug. 1833. 59 1/5 acres.
James, Michael. Va. Lieutenant. 10 Aug. 1833. 59 1/5 acres.
James, Michael. Va. Lieutenant. 10 Aug. 1833. 59 1/5 acres.
James, Michael. Va. Lieutenant. 10 Aug. 1833. 59 1/5 acres.
James, Michael. Va. Lieutenant. 10 Aug. 1833. 59 1/5 acres.
James, Michael. Va. Lieutenant. 10 Aug. 1833. 148 1/9 acres.
James, Michael. Va. Lieutenant. 10 Aug. 1833. 59 1/5 acres.
James, Michael. Va. Lieutenant. 10 Aug. 1833. 98 2/3 acres.
James, Michael. Va. Lieutenant. 10 Aug. 1833. 98 2/3 acres.
James, Michael. Va. Lieutenant. 10 Aug. 1833. 296 2/9 acres.
James, Michael. Va. Lieutenant. 10 Aug. 1833. 296 2/9 acres.
James, Michael. Va. Lieutenant. 10 Aug. 1833. 98 2/3 acres.
James, Michael. Va. Lieutenant. 26 Aug. 1835. 98 2/3 acres.
James, Noah. N.C. Corporal. 19 Dec. 1809. 428 acres.
James, Peter. Va. Private. 4 Jul. 1783. 100 acres.
James, William. N.C. Private. 18 May 1784. 640 acres.
James, William. Va. Private. 17 Nov. 1784. 100 acres.
James, Willoughby. N.C. Private. 9 Dec. 1797. 640 acres.
Jameson, Adam. Md. Private. ———. 50 acres.
Jameson, David. Va. Private. 16 Feb. 1801. 100 acres.
Jameson, John. Va. Lieutenant Colonel. 19 Mar. 1783. 6000 acres.
Jameson, John. Va. Lieutenant Colonel. 19 Jun. 1784. 1000 acres.
Jameson, John. Va. Lieutenant Colonel. 6 Feb. 1808. 416 2/3 acres.
Jameson, Samuel. Va. Private. 16 Feb. 1801. 100 acres.
Jamieson, Jonathan. Ga. ———. 5 Sep. 1786. ———.
Jamieson, Richard. Pa. Private. 30 Sep.1787. 200 acres.
Jamison, Adam. Md. Lieutenant. ———. 200 acres.
Jamison, John. Pa. Private. 15 Jan. 1787. 200 acres.
Janney, Thomas. Pa. ———. 27 Feb. 1794. 200 acres.
Jansen, T. Cornelius. N. Y. Captain. 9 Jul. 1790. 1800 acres.
January, James. Va.-Ind. Private. 108 acres.
Janus, Charles. N.C. Private. 2 Feb. 1786. 640 acres to heirs.
Jaque, Louis. N. Y. ———. ———. 500 acres.
Jaquett, Peter. Va. Private. 8 Nov. 1832. 4000 acres.

Jarman, William. N.C. Private. 12 Dec. 1796. 640 acres.
Jarmany, Peter. N.C. Private. 29 Sep. 1785. 640 acres.
Jarrald, James. Va.-Ind. Private. 108 acres.
Jarratt, Robert. Ga. ———. 25 May 1784. 287 1/2 acres.
Jarrell, Soloman. Va. Private. 19 Mar. 1783. 100 acres.
Jarret, Andrew. Pa. Private. 29 Nov. 1786. 200 acres to Samuel Benezet, assignee.
Jarrett, Jacob. N.C. Private. 24 Nov. 1796. 640 acres to heirs.
Jarvis, Daniel. Md. Private. ———. 50 acres.
Jarvis, Francis. Va. Private. 2 Feb. 1819. 100 acres.
Jarvis, Isaac. Conn. Sufferer. Fairfield. 23.10.9.
Jarvis, Issac. Conn. Sufferer. Fairfield. 0.0.0. to be deducted.
Jarvis, Joel. N.C. Private. 30 Sep. 1785. 640 acres to heirs.
Jarvis, John. Md. ———. ———. 50 acres.
Jarvis, John. N.C. Private. 2 Sep. 1820. 640 acres.
Jarvis, John. N.C. Captain. 15 Aug. 1823. 1920 acres to heirs.
Jarvis, Levi. N.C. Private. 29 Nov. 1800. 228 acres.
Jarvis, Lewis. N.C. Private. 22 Dec. 1796. 228 acres.
Jarvis, Nathan. Conn. Sufferer. Norwalk. 279.7.6.
Jarvis, Nathaniel. N.Y. ———. 17 Sep. 1792. 500 acres to heirs.
Jarvis, Nicholas. Ga. Refugee. 17 May 1784. —— acres to heirs.
Jarvis, Patrick. Ga. ———. 17 May 1784. ———.
Jarvis, Stephen. Conn. Sufferer. Danbury. 43.8.6.
Jarvis, Thomas. N.C. ———. 5 Dec. 1797. 1000 acres.
Jarvis, William. N.C. Private. 21 May 1784. 274 acres.
Jarvis, William. Va. Seaman. 4 Jan. 1834. 100 acres.
Jason, Henry. N.C. Private. 5 Sep. 1821. 640 acres.
Jasper, William. S.C. Sergeant. 4 Jan. 1790. 200 acres to William Jasper, heir at law.
Javiss, Betty. Conn. Sufferer. Norwalk. 2.8.6.
Jay, Isaac. N.C. Private. 7 Dec. 1797. 640 acres to heirs.
Jay, Simmon. N.C. Private. 8 Dec. 1795. 640 acres to heirs.
Jay, William. Pa. Matross. 9 Apr. 1787. 200 acres.
Jealentine, Daniel. N.C. Private. 10 Feb. 1796. 640 acres to heirs.
Jeans, Joseph. Md. Sergeant. ———. 50 acres.
Jeans, William. Ga. ———. 1 May 1785. ———.
Jeff, James. Ga. ———. 30 Sep. 1784. ———.
Jeff, Robert. Pa. Private. 2 Dec. 1786. 200 acres.
Jeffcoat, John. Va. Private. 20 Dec. 1785. 100 acres.
Jefferies, Littlebury. S.C. ———. 5 Jul. 1790. 200 acres.
Jeffers, Allen. S.C. ———. 5 Jul. 1790. 200 acres.
Jeffers, Allen. S.C. ———. 2 May 1785. 200 acres.
Jeffers, George. S.C. Soldier. 21 Jan. 1785. 200 acres.
Jeffers, Jacob. Md. Private. ———. 50 acres.
Jeffers, John. N. Y. Private. 8 Jul. 1790. 500 acres.
Jeffers, Osborn. S.C. ———. 7 Feb. 1791. 200 acres.
Jefferson, Isaac. Ga. Refugee. Sep. 1785. ———.
Jefferson, Joel. N.C. Private. 30 Sep. 1785. 640 acres to heirs.
Jefferson, Samuel, Sr. N.C. Private. 17 Dec. 1796. 320 acres to heirs.
Jeffres, John. N.C. Private. 28 Sep. 1785. 640 acres to heirs.
Jeffrey, Edward. Conn. Sufferer. Groton. 158.5.4.
Jeffrey, Moses. Conn. Sufferer. New London. 36.3.6.
Jeffreys, John. N.C. Private. 27 Nov. 1783. 274 acres.
Jeffries, Benjamin G. N.C. Sergeant. 22 Dec. 1796. 1000 acres to heirs.
Jeffries, Elisha. Va. Private. 6 Dec. 1783. 100 acres.
Jeffries, Gowin. Va. Private. 1 Jul. 1819. 100 acres.

Jeffries, Isaac. Va. Ensign. 12 Dec. 1792. 2666 2/3 acres.
Jeffries, Isaac. Va. Ensign. 4 Apr. 1850. 363 acres.
Jeffries, Isaac. Va. Ensign. 4 Apr. 1850. 363 acres.
Jeffries, James. Ga. Refugee. 8 Jun. 1784. 250 acres.
Jeffries, James. Va. Private. 5 Aug. 1784. 100 acres.
Jeffries, John. Pa. Drummer. ———. 200 acres.
Jeffries, Mourning. Va. Private. 19 Aug. 1835. 200 acres.
Jeffries, Nathaniel. Ga. ———. 17 May 1784. ———.
Jeffries, Thomas. N.C. Private. 16 Aug. 1821. 640 acres.
Jeffries, Thomas. Va. Sergeant. 26 Apr. 1783. 200 acres.
Jeffries, William. Va. Private. 16 Sep. 1785. 200 acres.
Jelie, Joseph. N. Y. ———. ———. 500 acres.
Jemmason, Thomas. N.C. Private. 18 May 1784. 228 acres.
Jemminson, James. N.C. Private. 23 Apr. 1784. 640 acres.
Jemmison, Roger. N.C. Private. 14 Dec. 1796. 357 acres.
Jenkins, Abraham. Va. Private. 1 Nov. 1787. 100 acres.
Jenkins, Arthur. Ga. ———. 17 May 1784. ———.
Jenkins, Benjamin. Ga. Refugee. 17 Feb. 1784. 250 acres.
Jenkins, Edward. Va. Private. 21 Jan. 1799. 100 acres.
Jenkins, Elijah. Ga. Refugee. Sep. 1785. ———.
Jenkins, Elijah. N.C. Private. 16 Aug. 1821. 640 acres.
Jenkins, Enoch. Mass. ———. 22 Sep. 1828. 200 acres.
Jenkins, Francis. Ga. Refugee. 17 May 1784. ———.
Jenkins, George. Ga. Minute Man. 3 Sep. 1785. ———.
Jenkins, Isaac. Va. Private. 1 Nov. 1787. 100 acres.
Jenkins, James. N.C. Private. 1 Jan. 1794. 640 acres to heirs.
Jenkins, James. Va. Private. 16 Dec. 1796. 200 acres.
Jenkins, Job. Va. Private. 12 Aug. 1785. 100 acres.
Jenkins, Joel. Mass. Ensign. 10 Sep. 1831. 200 acres to heirs.
Jenkins, John. Ga. ———. 5 Dec. 1785. ———.
Jenkins, John. Va. Private. 9 Jun. 1785. 200 acres.
Jenkins, John. Va. Private. 28 Mar. 1837. 200 acres.
Jenkins, John. Va. Private. 28 Mar. 1837. 200 acres.
Jenkins, John. Va. Private. 21 Dec. 1833. 200 acres.
Jenkins, Joseph. Md. Private. ———. 50 acres.
Jenkins, Joshua. Va. Sergeant. 26 Jun. 1797. 400 acres.
Jenkins, Josiah. N.C. Private. 30 Sep. 1785. 640 acres to heirs.
Jenkins, Lewis. N.C. Private. 13 Nov. 1795. 374 acres.
Jenkins, Peter. Ga. ———. 5 Dec. 1785. ———.
Jenkins, Reason. S.C. ———. 6 Oct. 1799. 180 acres to James Timms, administrator.
Jenkins, Reason. S.C. ———. 6 Oct. 1794. 20 acres to James Timms, administrator.
Jenkins, Richard. Ga. ———. 17 May 1784. ———.
Jenkins, Richard. Va. Sergeant. 2 Oct. 1783. 200 acres.
Jenkins, Richard. Va. Private. 21 Nov. 1783. 100 acres.
Jenkins, Robert. Ga. Soldier. 15 Apr. 1785. 250 acres.
Jenkins, Robert. N.C. Private. 27 Nov. 1819. 228 acres.
Jenkins, Samuel. Md. ———. ———. 50 acres.
Jenkins, Sherwood. Ga. Minute Man. 3 Apr. 1785. ———.
Jenkins, Sterling. Ga. ———. 15 Mar. 1784. 250 acres.
Jenkins, Thomas. Ga. Refugee. Sep. 1785. ———.
Jenkins, William. Ga. Soldier. 30 Apr. 1785. ———.
Jenkins, William. Va. Sergeant. 20 Jun. 1783. 200 acres.
Jenkins, William. Va. Private. 19 Jan. 1785. 100 acres.

Jenkins, William. Va. Private. 17 Jan. 1789. 200 acres.
Jenkins, William. Va. Sergeant. 29 Aug. 1807. 200 acres.
Jenkinson, Robert. Ga. Soldier. 5 May 1785. ———.
Jennerett, Elias. S.C. ———. 5 Mar. 1792. 200 acres.
Jennet, Samuel. N.C. Private. 29 Sep. 1784. 274 acres.
Jennett, Lewis. N.C. Sergeant. 28 Sep. 1785. 1000 acres.
Jennings, Aaron. Conn. Sufferer. Fairfield. 100.0.0.
Jennings, Abigail. Conn. Sufferer. Fairfield. 49.16.1.
Jennings, Andrew. Conn. Sufferer. Fairfield. 210.0.0.
Jennings, Daniel. Conn. Sufferer. Fairfield. 32.2.1.
Jennings, David. Conn. Sufferer. Fairfield. 27.18.10.
Jennings, David, 2d. Conn. Sufferer. Fairfield. 255.3.5.
Jennings, Edward. Pa. ———. 11 Mar. 1803. 200 acres.
Jennings, Ephraim. Conn. Sufferer. Fairfield. 6.9.6.
Jennings, George. Md. Private. ———. 50 acres.
Jennings, George. N.C. Private. 16 Feb. 1822. 640 acres to heirs.
Jennings, Hezekiah. Conn. Sufferer. Fairfield. 1.1.0.
Jennings, Isaac. Conn. Sufferer. Fairfield. 281.1.4.
Jennings, Jacob. Conn. Sufferer. Norwalk. 22.5.6.
Jennings, James. N.C. Private. 16 Aug. 1821. 640 acres.
Jennings, James. Va. Seaman. 28 Feb. 1840. 100 acres.
Jennings, Jeremy. Conn. Sufferer. Fairfield. 196.12.11.
Jennings, John. Ga. ———. 17 May 1784. ———.
Jennings, John. Pa. ———. 2 May 1787. 200 acres to Barbara Isiprice, widow.
Jennings, John. Va. Sailing Master. 14 Oct. 1783. 2666 2/3 acres.
Jennings, Justin. Conn. Sufferer. Fairfield. 31.7.0.
Jennings, Lyman. Conn. Sufferer. Fairfield. 5.10.6.
Jennings, Martha. Conn. Sufferer. Fairfield. 27.18.0.
Jennings, Miles. Ga. ———. 17 May 1784. ———.
Jennings, Moses. Conn. Sufferer. Fairfield. 599.12.4.
Jennings, Peter. Conn. Sufferer. Fairfield. 7.8.3.
Jennings, Priscilla. Ga. ———. 17 May 1784. ———.
Jennings, Rebecca. Conn. Sufferer. Fairfield. 127.0.4.
Jennings, Soloman. Va. Sergeant. 18 Dec. 1783. 200 acres.
Jennings, Solomon. N. Y. Private. 8 Jul. 1790. 600 acres.
Jennings, Stephen. Conn. Sufferer. Fairfield. 195.5.5.
Jennings, Thomas. N.C. Corporal. 31 Aug. 1820. 428 acres to heirs.
Jennings, Thomas. N.C. Corporal. 15 Jan. 1821. 113 acres.
Jennings, Thomas. N.C. Private. 15 Jan. 1821. 274 acres to heirs.
Jennings, Thomas. Pa. Private. 16 Oct. 1786. 200 acres.
Jennings, Thomas. Va. Sailor. 21 Nov. 1783. 100 acres.
Jennings, William. N.C. Private. 16 Feb. 1822. 640 acres to heirs.
Jennings, William. Va. Sailor. 21 Nov. 1783. 100 acres.
Jennings, William. Va. Sailor. 22 Feb. 1861. 100 acres.
Jennings, William. Va. Captain. 28 Mar. 1834. 4000 acres.
Jennings, William. Va. Captain. 26 Nov. 1860. 1333 1/3 acres.
Jenny, Abel. N.C. Sergeant. 10 Feb. 1796. 1000 acres.
Jenny, Thomas. Pa. Lieutenant. 3 Jan. 1787. 200 acres.
Jenny, Thomas. Pa. Lieutenant. ———. 200 acres.
Jeremiah, John. N.Y. ———. 13 Sep. 1790. 500 acres to heirs.
Jermany, Thomas. N.C. Private. 30 Sep. 1785. 640 acres.
Jernagan, Gardner. N.C. Private. 25 Jun. 1785. 274 acres.
Jerow, Jacob. Va. Private. 13 Oct. 1783. 100 acres.
Jerrell, Ezekiel. N.Y. ———. 13 Sep. 1790. 500 acres to heirs.

Jerrell, John. Va. Private. 4 Nov. 1819. 100 acres.
Jervis, John. N. Y. ———. ———. 500 acres.
Jessey, Turner. Va. Sergeant. 11 Feb. 1784. 200 acres.
Jessop, Issac. N.C. Private. 19 Nov. 1796. 274 acres.
Jessop, Stephen. N.C. Private. 30 Sep. 1785. 640 acres to heirs.
Jessup, Amos. Conn. Sufferer. Greenwich. 20.6.0.
Jessup, Ebenezer. Conn. Sufferer. Fairfield. 282.19.3.
Jessup, Ebenezer. Conn. Sufferer. Fairfield. 3.1.6.
Jester, John. Va. Seaman. 7 Mar. 1834. 100 acres.
Jeter, John. Ga. Soldier. 5 May 1785. 230 acres.
Jeter, Joseph. Ga. ———. 1 Oct. 1784. 287 1/2 acres.
Jeter, Thomas. Ga. Soldier. 5 May 1785. 230 acres.
Jeth, Tanner. N.C. Private. 12 Sep. 1785. 640 acres to heirs.
Jethro, Josiah. N.C. Private. 6 Dec. 1797. 640 acres to heirs.
Jett, James. Ga. ———. 17 May 1784. ———.
Jett, Jeremiah. N.C. Private. 10 Aug. 1785. 640 acres to heirs.
Jett, John. Va. Seaman. 29 May 1783. 100 acres.
Jett, John. Va. Seaman. 31 Oct. 1856. 100 acres.
Jett, Peter. N.C. ———. 10 Aug. 1785. 640 acres to heirs.
Jewel, Samuel. N.C. Private. 3 Jul. 1792. 640 acres to heirs.
Jiles, Richard. Pa. ———. 1 Apr. 1803. 200 acres to Mary Woodrow, devisee.
Jinkins, Abraham. N.C. Sergeant. 6 Jan. 1784. 357 acres.
Jinkins, Asa. N.C. Private. 25 Jun. 1785. 274 acres.
Jinkins, Burwell. N.C. Private. 27 Jul. 1785. 274 acres.
Jinkins, Demcey. N.C. Private. 22 Oct. 1783. 320 acres.
Jinkins, John. N.C. Private. 14 Dec. 1796. 640 acres to heirs.
Jinkins, Levi. N.C. Private. 30 Sep. 1785. 640 acres to heirs.
Jinkins, William. Md. Private. ———. 50 acres.
Jinkins, William. N.C. Private. 26 Aug. 1785. 640 acres to heirs.
Jinnngs, John. N.C. Private. 12 May 1784. 365 acres.
Jitt, Jesse. N.C. Corporal. 28 Sep. 1785. 1000 acres to heirs.
Jocelyn, Amaziah. Conn. Sufferer. New/East Haven. 25.16.3.
Jocelyn, Simeon. Conn. Sufferer. New/East Haven. 10.5.6.
John, Johnston. N.C. Private. 7 Dec. 1796. 228 acres.
Johns, James. Ga. Soldier. 30 Apr. 1785. ———.
Johns, James. Va. Private. 1 Sep. 1789. 100 acres.
Johns, Peter. Ga. Refugee. Sep. 1785. ———.
Johns, Thomas. Md. Private. ———. 50 acres.
Johns, Ware. Ga. Soldier. 4 Oct. 1785. ———.
Johnson, Abraham. Conn. Sufferer. New/East Haven. 5.16.10.
Johnson, Andrew. Me. ———. 2 May 1838. 200 acres. Stow.
Johnson, Bailey. Va. Sergeant. 30 Oct. 1812. 400 acres.
Johnson, Comfort. Mass. Sergeant. 26 Nov. 1832. 200 acres.
Johnson, David. N.C. Private. 15 Nov. 1793. 640 acres to heirs.
Johnson, Edward. Va. Private. 27 May 1783. 200 acres.
Johnson, Edward. Va. Private. 19 Jul. 1784. 100 acres.
Johnson, Ellis. Va. Private. 22 Oct. 1789. 100 acres.
Johnson, Enos. Conn. Sufferer. New/East Haven. 1.17.9.
Johnson, Jabez. Conn. Sufferer. New/East Haven. 13.9.4.
Johnson, Jacob. Va. Private. 27 May 1793. 100 acres.
Johnson, Jacob. Va. Private. 1 Aug. 1799. 200 acres.
Johnson, James. Me. ———. 18 Aug. 1835. 200 acres to widow Hannah Johnson. Augusta.
Johnson, James. Me. Private. 18 Aug. 1835. 200 acres to widow Hannah Johnson. Augusta.

Johnson, James. Va. Private. 23 Jun. 1783. 200 acres.
Johnson, James. Va. Private. 28 Feb. 1785. 200 acres.
Johnson, James. Va. Private. 11 Feb. 1814. 200 acres.
Johnson, James. Va. Private. 29 Jul. 1836. 100 acres.
Johnson, Jasper. Me. Sergeant. 27 Aug. 1835. 200 acres to widow Rebecca Johnson. Pownal.
Johnson, John. Va.-Ind. Private. 108 acres.
Johnson, John. Mass. Corporal. 19 Nov. 1832. 200 acres.
Johnson, John. Pa. Private. 20 Sep. 1787. 200 acres to Robert Whitehall, assignee.
Johnson, John. Va. Private. 12 Apr. 1784. 100 acres.
Johnson, John. Va. Private. 20 May 1823. 100 acres.
Johnson, John. Va. Seaman. 30 Jul. 1831. 100 acres.
Johnson, John. Va. Captain. 30 May 1838. 2666 2/3 acres.
Johnson, John. Va. Captain. 30 May 1838. 666 2/3 acres.
Johnson, John. Va. Captain. 30 May 1838. 666 2/3 acres.
Johnson, John. Va. Captain. 27 Mar. 1849. 666 2/3 acres.
Johnson, John. Va. Captain. 23 Jun. 1851. 666 2/3 acres.
Johnson, John B. Va. Captain. 13 Dec. 1783. 4000 acres.
Johnson, John B. Va. Captain. 3 Feb. 1809. 666 2/3 acres.
Johnson, Joseph. Va. Private. 28 Apr. 1783. 200 acres.
Johnson, Joshua. Va. Boatswain. 14 Dec. 1833. 200 acres.
Johnson, Joshua. Va. Boatswain. 30 May 1840. 1233 1/3 acres.
Johnson, Joshua. Va. Boatswain. 7 Jul. 1840. 411 7/9 acres.
Johnson, Joshua. Va. Boatswain. 7 Jul. 1840. 822 2/9 acres.
Johnson, Joshua. Va. Boatswain. 28 Mar. 1837. 200 acres.
Johnson, Joshua. Va. Boatswain. 25 Jan. 1833. 444 1/9 acres.
Johnson, Lawrence. Mass. Private. 20 Feb. 1833. 200 acres to heirs.
Johnson, Lydia. Conn. Sufferer. New/East Haven. 5.7.0.
Johnson, Mabel. Conn. Sufferer. New/East Haven. 6.0.0.
Johnson, Major. Va. Private. 15 Jun. 1807. 200 acres.
Johnson, Matthew. Va. Private. 22 Feb. 1799. 200 acres.
Johnson, Moses. Va. Private. 20 Jun. 1783. 100 acres.
Johnson, Nathan. Me. Private. 25 Jun. 1835. 200 acres to widow Mary Johnson. Cumberland.
Johnson, Orange. Mass. Private. 19 Nov. 1832. 200 acres.
Johnson, Peter. Conn. Sufferer. New/East Haven. 20.18.9.
Johnson, Philip. Va. Private. 23 Dec. 1819. 100 acres.
Johnson, Randolph. Va. Private. 6 Jan. 1812. 100 acres.
Johnson, Richard. Va. Corporal. 14 Dec. 1783. 200 acres.
Johnson, Richard. Conn. Sufferer. New/ East Haven. 11.8.6.
Johnson, Samuel. N. Y. Private. 8 Jul. 1790. 600 acres.
Johnson, Samuel. Va. Sergeant. 14 Dec. 1809. 200 acres.
Johnson, Samuel. Va. Drum Major. 5 Sep. 1821. 400 acres.
Johnson, Sarah. Conn. Sufferer. Norwalk. 33.18.10.
Johnson, Solomon. N.C. Private. 22 May 1820. 640 acres to heirs.
Johnson, Stephen. Va. Private. 15 Dec. 1783. 200 acres.
Johnson, Stephen. Conn. Sufferer. New/ East Haven. 14.3.9.
Johnson, Thomas. Va. Captain. 20 Jan. 1834. 2666 2/3 acres.
Johnson, Thomas. Va. ———. 18 Jul. 1835. 1333 1/3 acres.
Johnson, Thomas. Conn. Sufferer. Greenwich. 41.15.1.
Johnson, Timothy K. S.C. ———. 3 Mar. 1788. 200 acres.
Johnson, William. N. Y. Private. 8 Jul. 1790. 600 acres.
Johnson, William. Va. Sailor. 19 Dec. 1783. 100 acres.
Johnson, William. Va. Captain. 23 Dec. 1783. 4666 2/3 acres.
Johnson, William. Va. Noncommissioned Officer. 17 May 1784. 200 acres.

Johnson, William. Va. Private. 31 Dec. 1784. 100 acres.
Johnson, William. Va. Corporal. 13 Dec. 1830. 200 acres.
Johnson, William. Conn. Sufferer. Greenwich. 8.0.0.
Johnston, Abel. N.C. Private. 15 Feb. 1797. 320 acres.
Johnston, Andrew. Pa. Lieutenant. 27 Oct. 1786. 200 acres.
Johnston, Andrew. Pa. Lieutenant. 27 Oct. 1786. 200 acres.
Johnston, Archibald. Md. Sergeant. ———. 50 acres.
Johnston, Archibald. N.C. Private. 30 Sep. 1785. 640 acres to heirs.
Johnston, Arthur. N.C. Private. 5 Dec. 1796. 640 acres.
Johnston, Benedict. Md. Matross. ———. 50 acres.
Johnston, Benjamin. Md. Fifer. ———. 50 acres.
Johnston, Benjamin. N.C. Private. 22 Oct. 1783. 390 acres.
Johnston, Benjamin. N.C. Private. 20 Sep. 1784. 228 acres.
Johnston, Benjamin. N.C. Private. 22 Sep. 1795. 640 acres to heirs.
Johnston, Benjamin. N.C. Private. 23 Nov. 1797. 228 acres.
Johnston, Benjamin. Va. Private. 27 May 1793. 200 acres.
Johnston, Britain. N.C. Private. 2 Aug. 1784. 640 acres.
Johnston, Brutus. N.C. Musician. 21 Aug. 1820. 1000 acres.
Johnston, Caleb. Ga. ———. 15 Sep. 287 1/2 acres.
Johnston, Charles. N.C. Private. 10 Feb. 1796. 640 acres to heirs.
Johnston, Cornelius. Va. Private. 5 Mar. 1785. 100 acres.
Johnston, Craffar. N.C. Private. 20 Apr. 1784. 640 acres.
Johnston, Croffield. N.C. Private. 22 Dec. 1796. 640 acres.
Johnston, Daniel. Ga. Sergeant. 17 May 1784. ———.
Johnston, Daniel. N. Y. Private. 8 Jul. 1790. 600 acres.
Johnston, Daniel. N.C. Private. 29 Apr. 1784. 274 acres.
Johnston, David. Ga. Minute Man. 3 Apr. 1785. ———.
Johnston, David. N. Y. Corporal. 8 Jul. 1790. 500 acres.
Johnston, Drury. N.C. Private. 8 Dec. 1796. 640 acres to heirs.
Johnston, Drury. S.C. ———. 6 Jan. 1794. 22 acres to William Johnston, heir at law.
Johnston, Drury. S.C. ———. 6 Jan. 1794. 21 acres to William Johnston, heir at law.
Johnston, Drury. S.C. ———. 6 Jan. 1794. 123 acres to William Johnston, heir at law.
Johnston, Drury. S.C. ———. 6 Jan. 1794. 34 acres to William Johnston, heir at law.
Johnston, Edward. Va.-Ind. Private. 108 acres.
Johnston, Edward. Va. Private. 8 Jun. 1787. 100 acres.
Johnston, Francis. Md. Matross. ———. 50 acres.
Johnston, Francis. Pa. Colonel. 12 Oct. 1786. 500 acres.
Johnston, Francis. Pa. Colonel. 28 Feb. 1794. 500 acres.
Johnston, Francis. Pa. Colonel. ———. 500 acres.
Johnston, George. N.C. Private. 23 Apr. 1785. 640 acres to heirs.
Johnston, George. Va. Lieutenant Colonel. 20 Jul. 1786. 6000 acres.
Johnston, George. Va. Private. 5 Feb. 1820. 100 acres.
Johnston, Gideon. Va. Captain. 29 May 1783. 4000 acres.
Johnston, Gideon. Va. Brigade Quartermaster. 5 Jun. 1851. 1777 2/3 acres.
Johnston, Gideon. Va. Brigade Quartermaster. 5 Jun. 1851. 889 acres.
Johnston, Gideon. Va. Brigade Quartermaster. 5 Jun. 1851. 889 acres.
Johnston, Gideon. Va. Brigade Quartermaster. 5 Jun. 1851. 889 acres.
Johnston, Gideon. Va. Brigade Quartermaster. 5 Jun. 1851. 889 acres.
Johnston, Hardy. N.C. Private. 23 Apr. 1785. 640 acres to heirs.
Johnston, Harmon. N.C. Private. 30 Sep. 1785. 640 acres to heirs.
Johnston, Harper. N.C. Private. 30 Sep. 1785. 640 acres to heirs.
Johnston, Henry. Ga. ———. 30 Sep. 1784. ———.

Johnston, Henry. N.C. Private. 14 Oct. 1783. 640 acres.

Johnston, Henry. N.C. Private. 21 Apr. 1784. 640 acres.

Johnston, Henry. N.C. Private. 7 Dec. 1797. 640 acres to heirs.

Johnston, Holland. N.C. Sergeant. 21 Apr. 1784. 428 acres.

Johnston, Howell. N.C. Private. 2 Feb. 1786. 640 acres.

Johnston, Isaac. Ga. Minute Man. 4 Feb. 1785. ———.

Johnston, Isaac. Md. Private. ———. 50 acres.

Johnston, Isaac. N. Y. Matross. 9 Jul. 1790. 500 acres.

Johnston, Jacob. Ga. ———. 17 May 1784. 250 acres.

Johnston, Jacob. S.C. Soldier. 4 Oct. 1790. 200 acres.

Johnston, James. Ga. Sergeant. 15 Mar. 1784. 250 acres.

Johnston, James. N. Y. Lieutenant. 3 Jul. 1790. 1200 acres.

Johnston, James. N.Y. ———. 13 Sep. 1790. 500 acres to heirs.

Johnston, James. N.C. Sergeant. 28 May 1784. 1000 acres.

Johnston, James. N.C. Private. 20 Oct. 1792. 640 acres to heirs.

Johnston, James. Pa. Private. 24 Apr. 1787. 200 acres.

Johnston, James. Va. Private. 26 May 1786. 100 acres.

Johnston, James. Va. Major. 26 Jan. 1810. 5333 1/3 acres.

Johnston, James. Va. Private. 14 Dec. 1811. 100 acres.

Johnston, Jesse. Ga. ———. 17 May 1784. ———.

Johnston, Job. Ga. Soldier. 20 Dec. 1785. 920 acres.

Johnston, John. Ga. ———. 24 May 1784. 287 1/2 acres.

Johnston, John. Md. Private. ———. 50 acres.

Johnston, John. Md. Private. ———. 50 acres.

Johnston, John. Md. Private. ———. 50 acres.

Johnston, John. N. Y. Matross. 9 Jul. 1790. 600 acres.

Johnston, John. N. Y. Captain. 9 Jul. 1790. 1800 acres.

Johnston, John. N.C. Private. 2 Feb. 1785. 640 acres to heir.

Johnston, John. Pa. Private. ———. 200 acres.

Johnston, John. Va. Private. 20 Jun. 1783. 100 acres.

Johnston, John. Va. Private. 22 Mar. 1836. 200 acres.

Johnston, John Hutchins. Ga. ———. 15 Mar. 1784. 250 acres.

Johnston, Joseph. Md. Private. ———. 50 acres.

Johnston, Joseph. N.C. Lieutenant. 24 Nov. 1796. 2560 acres.

Johnston, Joseph. Pa. ———. 5 Nov. 1812. 200 acres.

Johnston, Joseph. Pa. Sergeant. ———. 250 acres.

Johnston, Levy. Ga. Minute Man. 4 Feb. 1785. ———.

Johnston, Littleton. N.C. Sergeant. 16 Aug. 1821. 1000 acres.

Johnston, Lydia. Conn. Sufferer. New London. 21.15.0.

Johnston, Martin. N.C. Private. 3 Dec. 1797. 640 acres to heirs.

Johnston, Matthew. Ga. ———. 17 May 1784. ———.

Johnston, Nicholas. N. Y. Private. 8 Jul. 1790. 600 acres.

Johnston, Peter. N.C. Private. 12 Sep. 1785. 640 acres to heirs.

Johnston, Phillip. Va. Sergeant. 23 Oct. 1784. 200 acres.

Johnston, Reuben. N.C. Private. 2 Nov. 1795. 640 acres.

Johnston, Rice. N.C. Private. 27 Nov. 1789. 274 acres.

Johnston, Richard. Ga. ———. 30 Jan. 1784. 500 acres.

Johnston, Richard. N.C. Sergeant. 22 Mar. 1784. 428 acres.

Johnston, Richard. N.C. ———. 29 Apr. 1784. 640 acres to Snoden Johnston, heir.

Johnston, Richard. Pa. Lieutenant of Rangers. 2 Jul. 1789. 200 acres.

Johnston, Richard. Pa. Private. 3 Apr. 1787. 200 acres to Rachel Johnston, widow.

Johnston, Richard. Pa. Lieutenant. 2 Jul. 1787. 200 acres.

Johnston, Richard. Va. Private. 21 Jan. 1785. 100 acres.

Johnston, Robert. Md. Private. ———. 50 acres.
Johnston, Robert. Md. Private. ———. 50 acres.
Johnston, Robert. Pa. Surgeon. 31 Mar. 1803. 300 acres.
Johnston, Robert. Pa. Matross. ———. 200 acres.
Johnston, Robert. Pa. Surgeon. 31 May 1803. 300 acres.
Johnston, Samuel. N.C. Private. 2 Aug. 1784. 185 acres.
Johnston, Silas. Ga. Minute Man. 3 Apr. 1785. ———.
Johnston, Silas. Va. Private. 21 Apr. 1785. 100 acres.
Johnston, Stephen. Ga. Captain. 15 Mar. 1784. 750 acres.
Johnston, Stephen. Ga. ———. 17 May 1784. ———.
Johnston, Thomas. Ga. Lieutenant. 15 Mar. 1784. 350 acres.
Johnston, Thomas. Ga. ———. 25 May 1784. 287 1/2 acres.
Johnston, Thomas. Md. ———. ———. 50 acres.
Johnston, Thomas. N.C. Private. 9 Nov. 1784. 274 acres.
Johnston, Thomas. N.C. Private. 12 Sep. 1785. 640 acres to heirs.
Johnston, Thomas. N.C. Private. 17 Dec. 1801. 274 acres.
Johnston, Thomas. N.C. Private. 14 Sep. 1820. 640 acres.
Johnston, Thomas. Va. Private. 18 Nov. 1783. 200 acres.
Johnston, Thomas. Va. Private. 2 Sep. 1784. 100 acres.
Johnston, Uriah. N.Y. Corporal. 13 Sep. 1790. 500 acres to heirs.
Johnston, William. Ga. ———. 26 May 1784. 287 1/2 acres.
Johnston, William. Ga. Lieutenant. 19 Mar. 1784. 400 acres to widow Amey Johnston.
Johnston, William. Md. Sergeant. ———. 50 acres.
Johnston, William. Md. Sergeant. ———. 50 acres.
Johnston, William. N.C. Private. 7 Jan. 1786. 640 acres to heirs.
Johnston, William. Pa. Corporal. 13 Sep. 1787. 200 acres.
Johnston, William. Pa. Private. 26 Apr. 1787. 200 acres.
Johnston, William. S.C. ———. 5 Feb. 1787. 133 acres.
Johnston, William. Va. Captain. 6 Oct. 1783. 2000 acres.
Johnston, William. Va. Captain. 6 Oct. 1783. 2000 acres.
Johnston, William. Va. Surgeon. 29 Aug. 1851. 6000 acres.
Johnston, William. Va. Surgeon. 23 Apr. 1853. 1000 acres.
Johnston, William. Va. Surgeon. 23 Apr. 1853. 1000 acres.
Johnston, William. Va. Surgeon. 23 Apr. 1853. 1000 acres.
Johnston, William. Va. Surgeon. 26 Apr. 1853. 1500 acres.
Johnston, William. Va. Surgeon. 5 May 1853. 1500 acres.
Johnston, Willis. N.C. Private. Dec. 1802. 182 acres.
Johnston, Zebulen. N.C. Private. 10 Feb. 1796. 274 acres.
Johnstone, James. Conn. Sufferer. Greenwich. 8.10.0.
Johnstone, Peter. Va. Lieutenant. 23 Feb. 1784. 2666 2/3 acres.
Joice, David. N.C. Private. 2 Feb. 1786. 640 acres.
Joice, Joseph. N.Y. ———. 13 Sep. 1790. 500 acres to heirs.
Joice, William. Md. Private. ———. 50 acres.
Joice, William. Md. Private. ———. 50 acres.
Joiner, Benjamin. Ga. Refugee. 15 Mar. 1784. 250 acres.
Joiner, Freeman. N.C. Private. 30 Sep. 1785. 640 acres to heirs.
Joiner, John. S.C. Captain. 4 Jul. 1785. 300 acres.
Joiner, John. S.C. Captain. 4 Jul. 1785. 200 acres.
Joiner, Samuel. S.C. ———. 4 Dec. 1786. 200 acres.
Joiner, Thomas. Ga. ———. 15 Mar. 1784. 250 acres to heirs.
Joines, John. Va. Sergeant. 17 Jul. 1784. 200 acres.
Joinner, Hugh. N.C. Private. 2 Feb. 1786. 640 acres to heirs.
Joins, Levin. Va. Lieutenant Colonel Commandant. 24 Apr. 1784. 3000 acres.

Joins, Levin. Va. Lieutenant Colonel Commandant. 24 Apr. 1784. 1000 acres.
Joins, Levin. Va. Lieutenant Colonel Commandant. 24 Apr. 1784. 1000 acres.
Joins, Levin. Va. Lieutenant Colonel Commandant. 24 Apr. 1784. 1000 acres.
Jolley, Menoah. N.C. Private. 2 Feb. 1786. 274 acres.
Jollibois, Jacque. N. Y. Lieutenant. ———. 100 acres.
Jolliff, John. Va. Lieutenant. 14 Jun. 1783. 2666 2/3 acres.
Jolly, Joseph. Va. Private. 11 May 1810. 200 acres.
Jolly, Luke. Pa. Private. 20 Nov. 1786. 200 acres.
Jolly, Richard. N.Y. Private. 13 Sep. 1790. 500 acres to heirs.
Jolly, Thomas. Ga. Soldier. 5 Aug. 1785. ———.
Jones, Aaron. Md. Private. ———. 50 acres.
Jones, Aaron. N.C. Private. 12 Sep. 1785. 640 acres to heirs.
Jones, Abel. Ga. Soldier. 1 May 1785. ———.
Jones, Abel. N.C. Private. 6 Dec. 1797. 640 acres to heirs.
Jones, Abraham. Ga. Refugee. 15 Mar. 1784. 250 acres.
Jones, Abraham. N.C. Private. 26 May 1784. 640 acres.
Jones, Abraham. Va. Private. 19 Feb. 1818. 100 acres.
Jones, Absalom. N.C. Private. 30 Sep. 1785. 640 acres to heirs.
Jones, Absalom. Va. Private. 2 May 1831. 66 2/3 acres.
Jones, Absalom. Va. Private. 2 May 1831. 66 2/3 acres.
Jones, Adam. Ga. ———. 17 May 1784. ———.
Jones, Adam. Va. Private. 25 Jan. 1805. 100 acres.
Jones, Albridgton. Va. Lieutenant. 5 Jun. 1783. 2666 2/3 acres.
Jones, Albridgton. Va. Lieutenant. 17 Apr. 1807. 741 acres.
Jones, Alexander. Va. Private. 7 Jun. 1783. 200 acres.
Jones, Ambrose. Va. Private. 22 Apr. 1784. 100 acres.
Jones, Arthur. N.C. Private. 2 Feb. 1786. 640 acres to heirs.
Jones, Aventon. Ga. Minute Man. 3 Sep. 1785. ———.
Jones, Bedford. N.C. Private. 8 Dec. 1795. 640 acres.
Jones, Benjamin. Mass. Private. 20 Feb. 1833. 200 acres to heirs.
Jones, Benjamin. N.C. Private. 7 Jan. 1786. 320 acres.
Jones, Benjamin. S.C. Soldier. 2 May 1785. 200 acres.
Jones, Benjamin. Va. Private. 11 Jul. 1786. 100 acres.
Jones, Benjamin, Sr. ———. Ga. 1784. 287 1/2 acres.
Jones, Binns. Va. Private. 2 Dec. 1833. 2666 2/3 acres.
Jones, Birtton. Va. Private. 5 Dec. 1833. 100 acres.
Jones, Brinson. N.C. Corporal. 3 Aug. 1820. 360 acres to heirs.
Jones, Brison. N.C. Private. 12 May 1784. 640 acres to Abram Jones, heir.
Jones, Britain. N.C. Private. 13 Dec. 1796. 640 acres.
Jones, Broton. N.C. Private. 20 Sep. 1821. 640 acres.
Jones, Cadwallader. Va. Captain. 21 Feb. 1784. 2000 acres.
Jones, Cadwallader. Va. Captain. 21 Feb. 1784. 1000 acres.
Jones, Cadwallader. Va. Captain. 21 Feb. 1784. 1000 acres.
Jones, Cadwallader. Va. Major. 1 Jun. 1839. 444 4/9 acres.
Jones, Cadwallader. Va. Major. 1 Jun. 1839. 444 4/9 acres.
Jones, Cadwallader. Va. Major. 1 Jun. 1839. 444 4/9 acres.
Jones, Charles. Va.-Ind. Private. 108 acres.
Jones, Charles. Md. Private. ———. 50 acres.
Jones, Charles. N.C. Private. 19 Dec. 1808. 640 acres to heirs.
Jones, Charles. Va. Lieutenant. 31 Jul. 1783. 2666 2/3 acres.
Jones, Charles. Va. Lieutenant. 5 Mar. 1784. 444 acres.
Jones, Charles. Va. Sergeant. 11 Nov. 1788. 200 acres.
Jones, Churchill. Va. Captain. 29 Jan. 1784. 4000 acres.
Jones, Churchill. Va. Captain. 6 Feb. 1808. 611 acres.

Jones, Clemmons. N.C. Private. 9 Dec. 1797. 640 acres to heirs.
Jones, Daniel. N.C. Captain. 29 Sep. 1784. 1234 acres.
Jones, Daniel. S.C. ———. 7 Apr. 1806. 200 acres.
Jones, David. Ga. Minute Man. 19 Jul. 1785. 287 1/2 acres.
Jones, David. Va.-Ind. Private. 108 acres.
Jones, David. Md. Corporal. ———. 50 acres.
Jones, David. N.C. Corporal Commandant. 15 Dec. 1783. 1000 acres.
Jones, David. N.C. Corporal. 27 Nov. 1789. 1000 acres to heirs.
Jones, David. N.C. Private. 5 Sep. 1821. 640 acres.
Jones, David. Pa. Chaplain. ———. 300 acres.
Jones, David. Pa. Chaplain. 13 May 1794. 300 acres.
Jones, David. Pa. Chaplain. ———. 300 acres.
Jones, David. Va. Private. 18 Nov. 1814. 100 acres.
Jones, Davis. N.C. Lieutenant. 29 Sep. 1784. 1096 acres.
Jones, Dyal. Ga. Minute Man. 3 Sep. 1785. ———.
Jones, Ebenezer. Conn. Sufferer. Ridgefield. 5.4.8.
Jones, Edward. Ga. Refugee. ———. 575 acres.
Jones, Edward. Va. Private. 24 Jun. 1783. 200 acres.
Jones, Elias. Ga. ———. 25 May 1784. 287 1/2 acres.
Jones, Elisha. N.C. Private. 5 Dec. 1796. 274 acres.
Jones, Elisha. Va. Private. 18 Mar. 1784. 100 acres.
Jones, Evans. N. Y. Private. 8 Jul. 1790. 600 acres.
Jones, Ezekiel. Mass. Private. 16 Jan. 1833. 200 acres.
Jones, Francis. Pa. Private. 29 Sep. 1787. 200 acres.
Jones, Frederick. Ga. ———. 17 May 1784. ———.
Jones, Frederick. N.C. Private. 13 Jan. 1792. 640 acres to heirs.
Jones, Frederick. Va. Private. 5 Dec. 1833. 100 acres.
Jones, Gabriel. Va. Captain. 12 Apr. 1784. 4000 acres.
Jones, Gabriel. Va. Captain. 20 Dec. 1838. 208 2/3 acres.
Jones, Gabriel. Va. Captain. 20 Dec. 1838. 208 2/3 acres.
Jones, George. Md. Private. ———. 50 acres.
Jones, George. Va. Private. 11 Mar. 1784. 200 acres.
Jones, Gideon. Mass. Corporal. 9 Jan. 1833. 200 acres to heirs.
Jones, Godfrey. Va. Private. 10 Dec. 1783. 100 acres.
Jones, Griffin. N. Y. Private. 8 Jul. 1790. 600 acres.
Jones, Hardy. N.C. Private. 23 Oct. 1783. 360 acres.
Jones, Henry. Va. Private. 15 Jun. 1807. 100 acres.
Jones, Hezekiah. N.C. Private. 30 Sep. 1785. 228 acres.
Jones, Holmes. Va. Sergeant. 18 Apr. 1801. 200 acres.
Jones, Hugh. Ga. ———. 15 Mar. 1784. 250 acres.
Jones, Hugh. Ga. ———. 15 Mar. 1784. 250 acres.
Jones, Hugh. Pa. Private. 8 Mar. 1787. 200 acres.
Jones, Isaac. Conn. Sufferer. New/East Haven. 148.19.9.
Jones, Jacob. Ga. Soldier. 4 Oct. 1785. ———.
Jones, Jacob. N. Y. Private. 8 Jul. 1790. 500 acres.
Jones, Jacob. N.C. Private. 30 Sep. 1785. 640 acres to heirs.
Jones, Jacob. N.C. Private. 23 Nov. 1797. 228 acres.
Jones, James. Ga. Minute Man. 3 Apr. 1785. 287 1/2 acres.
Jones, James. Ga. Soldier. 3 Oct. 1785. 230 acres.
Jones, James. Ga. ———. ———. 287 1/2 acres to heirs.
Jones, James. N. Y. Private. 7 Jul. 1790. 600 acres.
Jones, James. N.C. Private. 9 Nov. 1784. 274 acres.
Jones, James. Pa. Surgeon. ———. 300 acres.
Jones, James. Pa. Sergeant. 30 Jun. 1787. 300 acres.

Jones, James. Va. Private. 11 Mar. 1784. 200 acres.
Jones, James. Va. Bombardier. 11 Nov. 1791. 100 acres.
Jones, James. Va. Private. 21 Dec. 1788. 100 acres.
Jones, James. Va. Corporal. 13 Jan. 1810. 200 acres.
Jones, James. Va. Private. 8 Nov. 1822. 50 acres.
Jones, James. Va. Private. 8 Nov. 1822. 50 acres.
Jones, Jesse. Ga. Minute Man. 19 Jul. 1784. 287 1/2 acres.
Jones, Jesse. N.C. Private. 12 Sep. 1785. 640 acres to heirs.
Jones, Jesse. Va. Private. 11 Jun. 1783. 100 acres.
Jones, Joel. Va. Private. 29 Jul. 1784. 200 acres.
Jones, John. Ga. ———. 15 Mar. 1784. 250 acres.
Jones, John. Va.-Ind. Private. 108 acres.
Jones, John. Md. Private. ———. 50 acres.
Jones, John. Md. Private. ———. 50 acres.
Jones, John. N.C. Private. 22 Oct. 1783. 274 acres.
Jones, John. N.C. Sergeant. 21 Apr. 1784. 1000 acres to Evan Jones, heir.
Jones, John. N.C. Private. 20 Dec. 1784. 640 acres to William Jones, heir.
Jones, John. N.C. Private. 9 Sep. 1785. 640 acres to heirs.
Jones, John. N.C. Private. 1 Dec. 1797. 640 acres to heir Thomas Jones.
Jones, John. Pa. Quartermaster Sergeant. 12 Mar. 1787. 250 acres.
Jones, John. Pa. Private. 26 Sep. 1787. 200 acres.
Jones, John. Pa. Private. 31 Jul. 1787. 200 acres.
Jones, John. S.C. ———. 1 Apr. 1793. 143 acres.
Jones, John. S.C. ———. 1 Apr. 1793. 12 1/2 acres.
Jones, John. S.C. ———. 3 Oct. 1791. 60 acres.
Jones, John. Va. Private. 9 Jul. 1783. 200 acres.
Jones, John. Va. Private. 27 Aug. 1783. 200 acres.
Jones, John. Va. Private. 4 Feb. 1784. 200 acres.
Jones, John. Va. Private. 2 May 1785. 100 acres.
Jones, John. Va. Private. 22 Jun. 1786. 100 acres.
Jones, John. Va. Private. 5 Feb. 1798. 100 acres.
Jones, John. Va. Private. 9 Aug. 1799. 100 acres.
Jones, John. Va. Private. 9 Aug. 1799. 200 acres.
Jones, John. Va. Private. 19 Dec. 1807. 100 acres.
Jones, John. Va. Private. 28 Mar. 1834. 200 acres.
Jones, John. Va. Captain. 24 Dec. 1839. 2000 acres.
Jones, John. Va. Captain. 8 Nov. 1841. 1200 acres.
Jones, John. Va. Captain. 18 Mar. 1842. 800 acres.
Jones, John Courts. Md. Captain. ———. 200 acres.
Jones, John Paul. Va. Captain. 21 Dec. 1838. 600 acres.
Jones, John Paul. Va. Captain. 21 Dec. 1838. 382 acres.
Jones, John Paul. Va. Captain. 21 Dec. 1838. 3000 4/5 acres.
Jones, John Paul. Va. Captain. 9 Dec. 1839. 2325 1/20 acres.
Jones, John Paul. Va. Captain. 9 Dec. 1839. 5231 29/80 acres.
Jones, John Paul. Va. Captain. 9 Dec. 1839. 1743 63/80 acres.
Jones, John Paul. Va. Captain. 14 Nov. 1839. 500 acres.
Jones, John Paul. Va. Captain. 14 Nov. 1839. 2503 4/5 acres.
Jones, John Paul. Va. Captain. 26 Dec. 1839. 2325 1/20 acres.
Jones, John, Sr. Md. Private. ———. 50 acres.
Jones, Jonathan. Ga. ———. 15 Mar. 1784. 250 acres.
Jones, Jonathan. N.C. Corporal. 17 Dec. 1804. 427 acres.
Jones, Joseph. Md. Private. ———. 50 acres.
Jones, Joseph. N. Y. Private. 8 Jul. 1790. 600 acres.
Jones, Joseph. Pa. Private. 27 Oct. 1787. 200 acres.
Jones, Joshua. Me. Private. 11 May 1835. 200 acres. Durham.

Jones, Joshua. N.C. Private. 23 Apr. 1785. 640 acres to heirs.
Jones, Josiah. N.C. Drummer. 29 Apr. 1784. 1000 acres,
Jones, Josiah. N.C. Private. 30 Sep. 1785. 228 acres.
Jones, Julius. N.C. Private. 9 Dec. 1797. 640 acres to heirs.
Jones, Kedar. N.C. Private. 12 Sep. 1785. 640 acres to heirs.
Jones, Lazarus. Me. ———. 15 Jun. 1835. 200 acres. Brighton.
Jones, Lazarus. N.C. Private. 21 Apr. 1784. 352 acres.
Jones, Lewelling. Va. Captain. 8 Sep. 1804. 2000 acres.
Jones, Lewelling. Va. Captain. 8 Sep. 1804. 500 acres.
Jones, Lewelling. Va. Captain. 8 Sep. 1804. 400 acres.
Jones, Lewelling. Va. Captain. 8 Sep. 1804. 1100 acres.
Jones, Lewis. Va. Master's Mate. 21 Jun. 1783. 2666 2/3 acres.
Jones, Lewis. Va. ———. 27 Jul. 1839. 508 acres.
Jones, Lewis. Va. ———. 27 Jul. 1839. 423 acres.
Jones, Lewis. Va. ———. 27 Jul. 1839. 100 7/12 acres.
Jones, Lewis. Va. Lieutenant. 3 Sep. 1839. 50 7/24 acres.
Jones, Lewis. Va. Lieutenant. 3 Sep. 1839. 50 7/24 acres.
Jones, Lewis. Va. Lieutenant. 28 Aug. 1851. 202 acres.
Jones, Lewis, Jr. Va. Lieutenant. 21 Jun. 1783. 2666 2/3 acres.
Jones, Littleton. N.C. Private. 13 Sep. 1820. 640 acres.
Jones, Mark. Ga. ———. 17 May 1784. ———.
Jones, Martin. N.C. Sergeant. 12 Sep. 1785. 1000 acres to heirs.
Jones, Mathew. Va.-Ind. Private. 108 acres.
Jones, Matthew. Ga. Refugee. 15 Mar. 1784. 250 acres.
Jones, Michael. Ga. Captain. 29 Jan. 1784. 250 acres.
Jones, Miles. N.C. Private. 8 Dec. 1795. 640 acres to heirs.
Jones, Nathan. Ga. ———. 15 Mar. 1784. 250 acres.
Jones, Nealy. Md. Private. ———. 50 acres.
Jones, Nicholas. Va. Private. 1 Oct. 1810. 100 acres.
Jones, Noel. Ga. Minute Man. 14 Jun. 1785. ———.
Jones, Oliver. N.C. Private. 2 Nov. 1795. 640 acres to heirs.
Jones, Peter. Ga. Minute Man. 3 Sep. 1785. ———.
Jones, Peter. N.C. ———. 8 Mar. 1785. 640 acres to heirs.
Jones, Peter. Va. Corporal. 2 Sep. 1783. 200 acres.
Jones, Peter. Va. Captain. 17 Oct. 1783. 4000 acres.
Jones, Peter. Va. Private. 30 Nov. 1785. 100 acres.
Jones, Philip. Ga. ———. 25 May 1784. 287 1/2 acres.
Jones, Philip. Md. Matross. ———. 50 acres.
Jones, Philip. N.C. Captain Lieutenant. 27 Oct. 1783. 2560 acres.
Jones, Philip. N.C. Private. 29 Sep. 1784. 640 acres.
Jones, Philip. N.C. Private. 22 Dec. 1796. 274 acres.
Jones, Raymond. N.C. Private. 12 Dec. 1796. 640 acres to heirs.
Jones, Richard. Ga. Minute Man. Sep. 1784. 287 1/2 acres.
Jones, Richard. N.C. Private. 2 Sep. 1820. 228 acres.
Jones, Richard. S.C. Lieutenant. 21 Jan. 1785. 200 acres.
Jones, Richard. Va. Sergeant. 21 Aug. 1783. 400 acres.
Jones, Richard. Va. Private. 21 Jan. 1784. 100 acres.
Jones, Richard. Va. Private. 21 Jan. 1784. 200 acres.
Jones, Richard. Va. Private. 12 Nov. 1784. 100 acres.
Jones, Richard. Va. Private. 31 Dec. 1788. 100 acres.
Jones, Richard. Va. Private. 17 Jul. 1797. 100 acres.
Jones, Robert. Ga. Soldier. 13 Sep. 1784. 287 1/2 acres.
Jones, Robert. N.C. Private. 17 Feb. 1824. 640 acres.
Jones, Robert. Pa. Private. ———. 200 acres.

Jones, Robert. Pa. Private. 9 Mar. 1795. 200 acres to John Nicholson, assingee.
Jones, Robert. Va. Sergeant. 22 Aug. 1783. 200 acres.
Jones, Runard. N.C. Private. 10 Aug. 1785. 640 acres.
Jones, Russell. Ga. Soldier. 23 Apr. 1785. 230 acres.
Jones, Samuel. N. Y. Private. 7 Jul. 1790. 600 acres.
Jones, Samuel. N.C. Ensign. 22 Oct. 1783. 2560 acres to Nathaniel Jones, heir.
Jones, Samuel. N.C. Captain. 23 Oct. 1783. 3840 acres.
Jones, Samuel. N.C. Private. 23 Apr. 1785. 640 acres to heirs.
Jones, Samuel. Va. Captain. 14 Dec. 1782. 4000 acres.
Jones, Samuel. Va. Corporal. 12 Nov. 1783. 200 acres.
Jones, Samuel. Va. Private. 4 Feb. 1786. 200 acres.
Jones, Samuel Paine. Mass. Sergeant. 18 Sep. 1834. 200 acres to widow Pamelia Jones.
Jones, Seaborn. Ga. Refugee. 17 May 1784. ———.
Jones, Seth. N. Y. Private. 8 Jul. 1790. 500 acres.
Jones, Simeon. Ga. ———. 1784. 287 1/2 acres.
Jones, Singleton. N.C. Private. 22 Dec. 1796. 640 acres to heirs.
Jones, Soloman. Va. Private. 26 Nov. 1783. 200 acres.
Jones, Solomon. Ga. Minute Man. 3 Sep. 1785. ———.
Jones, Solomon. N.C. Private. 8 Dec. 1795. 640 acres to heirs.
Jones, Stephen. N.C. Private. 10 Dec. 1788. 640 acres to heirs.
Jones, Strother. Va. Captain. 3 Jan. 1783. 4000 acres.
Jones, Taylor. N.C. Private. 12 Sep. 1785. 640 acres to heirs.
Jones, Theophilus. N.C. Private. 30 Sep. 1785. 640 acres to heirs.
Jones, Thomas. Ga. ———. 23 Jul. 1784. 287 1/2 acres.
Jones, Thomas. Me. Private. 28 Jan. 1836. 200 acres to widow Mary Jones. Hope.
Jones, Thomas. Md. Private. ———. 50 acres.
Jones, Thomas. Md. Private. ———. 50 acres.
Jones, Thomas. Md. Private. ———. 50 acres.
Jones, Thomas. Md. Private. ———. 50 acres.
Jones, Thomas. Md. Private. ———. 50 acres.
Jones, Thomas. N. Y. Sergeant. 8 Jul. 1790. 600 acres.
Jones, Thomas. N. Y. Corporal. 8 Jul. 1790. 600 acres.
Jones, Thomas. N.C. Private. 21 Apr. 1784. 640 acres to Evan Jones, heir.
Jones, Thomas. N.C. Private. 29 Sep. 1784. 228 acres.
Jones, Thomas. Pa. Private. 5 Apr. 1787. 200 acres.
Jones, Thomas. Va. Private. 23 Jun. 1783. 200 acres.
Jones, Thomas. Va. Private. 21 Jan. 1784. 100 acres.
Jones, Thomas. Va. Private. 3 May 1784. 100 acres.
Jones, Thomas. Va. Private. 28 Aug. 1784. 200 acres.
Jones, Thomas. Va. Corporal. 30 Nov. 1785. 100 acres.
Jones, Thomas. Va. Sergeant. 5 Feb. 1808. 200 acres.
Jones, Thomas. Conn. Sufferer. New London. 40.4.10.
Jones, Thomas (Son of Wm). Ga. ———. ———. 287 1/2 acres.
Jones, Timothy & William Jones. Conn. Sufferers. New/East Haven. 167.13.6.
Jones, Timothy, Jr. Conn. Sufferer. New/ East Haven. 38.4.11.
Jones, Turner. Ga. Soldier. 4 Oct. 1785. ———.
Jones, Underhill. N.C. Private. 8 Dec. 1795. 640 acres to heirs.
Jones, William. Ga. Sergeant. 26 May 1784. 230 acres.
Jones, William. Ga. 13 Sep. 1784. 287 1/2 acres.
Jones, William. Md. Private. ———. 50 acres.
Jones, William. Md. Private. ———. 50 acres.
Jones, William. Md. Private. ———. 50 acres.
Jones, William. N.C. Private. 6 Dec. 1783. 274 acres.

Jones, William. N.C. Private. 20 Dec. 1784. 411 acres.
Jones, William. N.C. Private. 7 Dec. 1797. 274 acres.
Jones, William. Pa. Private. 4 Sep. 1789. 200 acres.
Jones, William. S.C. ———. 4 Jul. 1785. 200 acres.
Jones, William. Va. Private. 22 Apr. 1783. 200 acres.
Jones, William. Va. Private. 9 Jul. 1783. 200 acres.
Jones, William. Va. Corporal. 31 Oct. 1783. 400 acres.
Jones, William. Va. Sergeant. 16 Feb. 1784. 100 acres.
Jones, William. Va. Sergeant. 3 Aug. 1784. 400 acres.
Jones, William. Va. Private. 24 Dec. 1784. 100 acres.
Jones, William. Va. Private. 23 Nov. 1797. 200 acres.
Jones, William. Va. Seaman. 9 Nov. 1832. 100 acres.
Jones, William. Va. Seaman. 9 Nov. 1832. 100 acres.
Jones, Winn. N.C. Private. 10 Feb. 1796. 640 acres to heirs.
Jones, Wood. Va. Lieutenant. 26 Nov. 1824. 2666 2/3 acres.
Jones, Woode. N.C. Private. 22 Mar. 1785. 274 acres.
Jones, Zachariah. Va. Private. 10 Jun. 1783. 100 acres.
Jonns, William. N.C. Private. 7 Dec. 1797. 640 acres to heirs.
Joperton, Taylor. N.C. Private. 12 Sep. 1785. 640 acres to heirs.
Jopling, Ralph. Va. Ensign. 22 May 1827. 1333 1/3 acres.
Jopling, Ralph. Va. Ensign. 22 May 1827. 1333 1/3 acres.
Jordain, John. Va. Private. 6 Nov. 1783. 100 acres.
Jordan, Baxton. Ga. ———. 15 Mar. 1784. 250 acres.
Jordan, Caleb. N.C. Private. 19 May 1784. 640 acres.
Jordan, Charles. Ga. ———. ———. 250 acres.
Jordan, David. Me. Private. 7 May 1835. 200 acres. Albany.
Jordan, Demsey. Ga. ———. 15 Mar. 1784. 250 acres.
Jordan, Edward. Mass. Private. 9 Jul. 1834. 200 acres.
Jordan, Fountain. N.C. Private. 29 Apr. 1784. 640 acres.
Jordan, George. Va. Private. 20 May 1823. 100 acres.
Jordan, George. Va. Sergeant. 16 Nov. 1824. 100 acres.
Jordan, Hezekiah. Me. ———. 18 Jun. 1835. 200 acres to widow Eunice Jordan. Raymond.
Jordan, Humphrey. Me. ———. 16 May 1835. 200 acres to widow Johannah Jordan. Danville.
Jordan, Jacob. Ga. Refugee. 15 Mar. 1784. 250 acres.
Jordan, James. Me. ———. 25 Sep. 1835. 200 acres to widow Hannah Jordan. Monroe.
Jordan, James. Va. Private. 5 Jun. 1786. 100 acres.
Jordan, Jeremiah. N.C. Private. 30 Sep. 1785. 640 acres to heirs.
Jordan, John. Md. Captain. ———. 200 acres.
Jordan, John. Md. Quartermaster Sergeant. ———. 50 acres.
Jordan, John. N.C. Private. 18 Dec. 1802. 640 acres to heirs.
Jordan, John. Pa. ———. 16 Mar. 1803. 200 acres.
Jordan, John. Va. Captain. 17 Feb. 1784. 4666 2/3 acres.
Jordan, John. Va. Captain. 3 Mar. 1808. 500 acres.
Jordan, John. Va. Cornet. 24 Jun. 1830. 2666 2/3 acres.
Jordan, Joseph. N.C. Private. 30 Sep. 1785. 640 acres to heirs.
Jordan, Nathan. N.C. Private. 13 Sep. 1820. 640 acres.
Jordan, Needam. Ga. Lieutenant. 3 Apr. 1784. 400 acres.
Jordan, Pilate. N.C. Private. 30 Sep. 1785. 640 acres to heirs.
Jordan, Robert. N.C. Private. 12 May 1784. 640 acres.
Jordan, Samuel. Ga. ———. 14 Jul. 1784. 287 1/2 acres.
Jordan, Solomon. Me. Corporal. 5 Aug. 1836. 200 acres to Sarah Jordan. Cape Elizabeth.
Jordan, Sterling. Ga. ———. 17 May 1784. ———.

Jordan, Thomas. N.C. Private. 1 Sep. 1785. 640 acres to heirs.
Jordan, William. Ga. ———. 26 May 1784. 460 acres.
Jordan, William. N.C. ———. 18 Aug. 1784. 640 acres to John Jordan, heir.
Jordon, John. Pa. Captain. 16 Nov. 1786. 500 acres.
Joseph, Reubin. N.Y. ———. 13 Sep. 1790. 500 acres to heirs.
Joslin, David. Ga. Soldier. 3 May 1785. 230 acres.
Josling, Daniel. Ga. Refugee. 26 May 1784. 287 1/2 acres.
Jouitt, Matthew. Va. Captain. 26 Apr. 1783. 4000 acres.
Jouitt, Robert. Va. Lieutenant. 3 Mar. 1784. 2666 2/3 acres.
Jourdan, Ptolemy. N.C. Private. 22 Dec. 1796. 640 acres.
Jourdan, Reuben. Ga. ———. 17 May 1784. ———.
Jourdine, Lewis. Ga. ———. 17 May 1748. ———.
Jourdon, Michael. Va. Private. 28 Apr. 1783. 200 acres.
Joy, Richard. Va. Private. 18 Dec. 1783. 200 acres.
Joyce, Charles. Pa. Private. 13 Feb. 1787. 200 acres.
Joyce, James. N.Y. Private. 26 Sep. 1792. 500 acres to heirs.
Joyner, Benjamin. N.C. Private. 27 Oct. 1783. 640 acres.
Joyner, David. N.C. Captain. 18 Dec. 1802. 3840 acres to heirs.
Joyner, Joel. N.C. Private. 28 May 1784. 640 acres.
Joyner, Lewis. N.C. Private. 30 Sep. 1785. 640 acres to heirs.
Joyner, Matthew. N.C. Private. 23 Aug. 1820. 185 acres.
Joyner, Stephen. N.C. Private. 15 Jul. 1785. 640 acres to heirs.
Joyner, Thomas. N.C. Lieutenant. 2 Feb. 1786. 2560 acres to heirs.
Joynes, Charles. Va. Private. 14 Feb. 1834. 100 acres.
Joynes, Edward. Va. Seaman. 5 Jun. 1833. 100 acres.
Joynes, John. Va.-Ind. Private. 108 acres.
Joynes, John. Va. Sergeant. 13 Apr. 1833. 400 acres.
Joynes, Levin. Va. Lieutenant Colonel. 4 Jun. 1798. 1000 acres.
Joynes, Levin. Va. Lieutenant Colonel. 8 Sep. 1808. 833 1/3 acres.
Joynes, Levin. Va. Colonel. 17 Sep. 1850. 435 acres.
Joynes, Levin. Va. Colonel. 27 Dec. 1850. 217 1/2 acres.
Joynes, Levin. Va. Colonel. 12 Feb. 1851. 217 1/2 acres.
Joynes, Reuben. Va. Lieutenant. 15 Jan. 1808. 2666 2/3 acres.
Jucket, Elijah. Mass. Private. 13 Jan. 1831. 200 acres.
Judah, Barnard, Jr. N.C. Private. 13 Dec. 1796. 640 acres.
Judah, David. Conn. Sufferer. Norwalk. 9.19.0.
Judah, Michael. Conn. Sufferer. Norwalk. 13.9.6.
Judah, Michael. Conn. Sufferer. Norwalk. 0.2.0.
Judd, Bethiah. Conn. Sufferer. Danbury. 1.9.0.
Judd, David. Conn. Sufferer. Danbury. 9.16.0.
Jude, George. Va. Private. 1 Dec. 1826. 100 acres.
Jude, George. Va. Private. 30 Dec. 1839. 100 acres.
Judge, James. N.C. Private. 29 Sep. 1784. 228 acres.
Judges, William. Pa. ———. 14 Oct. 1786. 200 acres to George Ingram, assignee.
Julian, John. Va. Surgeon. 6 Feb. 1834. 6833 1/3 acres.
Julian, John. Va. Surgeon. 1 Oct. 1858. 580 1/2 acres.
Jump, George. Va. Lieutenant. 27 Mar. 1840. 229 3/5 acres.
Jump, George. Va. Lieutenant. 27 Mar. 1840. 114 4/5 acres.
Jump, George. Va. Lieutenant. 27 Mar. 1840. 57 2/5 acres.
Jump, George. Va. Lieutenant. 27 Mar. 1840. 114 4/5 acres.
Jump, George. Va. Lieutenant. 27 Mar. 1840. 93 3/5 acres.
Jump, George. Va. Lieutenant. 27 Mar. 1840. 114 4/5 acres.
Jump, George. Va. Lieutenant. 27 Mar. 1840. 38 2/5 acres.
Jump, George. Va. Lieutenant. 27 Mar. 1840. 19 1/5 acres.

Jump, George. Va. Lieutenant. 27 Mar. 1840. 19 1/5 acres.
Jump, George. Va. Lieutenant. 27 Mar. 1840. 142 3/5 acres.
Jump, George. Va. Lieutenant. 26 Oct. 1842. 114 2/3 acres.
Jump, George. Va. Lieutenant. 26 Oct. 1842. 57 1/3 acres.
Jump, George. Va. Lieutenant. 5 Apr. 1854. 114 2/3 acres.
Jump, George. Va. Lieutenant. 5 Apr. 1854. 57 1/2 acres.
Jump, George. Va. Lieutenant. 12 Aug. 1854. 172 1/10 acres.
Jump, George. Va. Lieutenant. 1 Jun. 1868. 2152 1/3 acres.
Jumper, Richard. N.C. Private. 17 Feb. 1824. 640 acres.
Junial, Anthony. Va. Private. 13 Jul. 1785. 100 acres.
Jupeter, Silas. N. Y. Private. 8 Jul. 1790. 600 acres.
Justice, Dempsy. Ga. ———. 17 May 1784. ———.
Justice, George. Va. Private. 15 Jun. 1807. 100 acres.
Justice, Isaac. Ga. ———. 1 Aug. 1785. 287 1/2 acres.
Justice, Jacob. Pa. Private. 6 Jul. 1789. 200 acres.
Justice, John. S.C. ———. 7 Aug. 1786. 200 acres.
Justice, John, Jr. S.C. ———. 4 Sep. 1786. 200 acres.
Justice, John, Sr. S.C. ———. 7 Aug. 1786. 200 acres.
Justice, John, Sr. S.C. ———. 4 Sep. 1786. 95 acres.
Justice, Peter. Pa. ———. 30 Mar. 1805. 200 acres.
Kader, John. N. Y. Private. 8 Jul. 1790. 600 acres.
Kaghnatshon, Nicholas. N.Y. Lieutenant. 29 Jan. 1791. 100 acres. [an Indian].
Kahektotow, Cornelius. N.Y. Lieutenant. 29 Jan. 1791. 1200 acres. [an Indian].
Kaighn, Michael. Pa. Sergeant. ———. 250 acres to Mary Kaighn, widow.
Kail, John. N.C. Private. 7 Sep. 1820. 228 acres to heirs.
Kain, John. N. Y. Private. 24 Aug. 1790. 500 acres.
Kain, Matthew. Pa. Private. 6 Apr. 1787. 200 acres to Mary Kain.
Kairns, John. Va. Corporal. 26 Jun. 1783. 400 acres.
Kairns, Michael. Va. Private. 23 Jun. 1783. 200 acres.
Kalkoffen, John Jacob. S.C. Sergeant. 6 Sep. 1790. 200 acres.
Kallum, Reuben. N. Y. Private. 8 Jul. 1790. 600 acres.
Kaltieson, Michael. S.C. Captain. 21 Jan. 1785. 300 acres.
Kanard, James. Va. Private. 24 Feb. 1784. 100 acres.
Kanard, Joshua. Va. Private. 24 Feb. 1784. 100 acres.
Kapple, Jacob. Pa. Ranger. ———. 200 acres.
Karney, Thomas. N. Y. Private. 13 Sep. 1790. 500 acres.
Karns, Benjamin. Md. Private. ———. 50 acres.
Karr, Alexander. N.C. Private. 13 Dec. 1796. 320 acres.
Karr, James. Va. Private. 23 Jun. 1783. 200 acres.
Kasey, Stephen. Ga. Refugee. 15 Mar. 1784. 250 acres.
Kator, James. N.Y. ———. 13 Sep. 1790. 500 acres to heirs.
Kautzman, John. Va. Lieutenant. 7 May 1784. 2666 2/3 acres.
Kautzman, John V. Va. Lieutenant. 24 Mar. 1847. 1333 1/3 acres.
Kays, Robert. Va. Lieutenant. 7 May 1783. 2666 2/3 acres.
Keader, Adam. N. Y. Private. 8 Jul. 1790. 600 acres.
Kean, Jacob. N.C. Private. 5 Dec. 1804. 640 acres to heirs.
Kearney, Black. N.C. Private. 5 Dec. 1796. 640 acres.
Kearns, Francis. Md. Private. ———. 50 acres.
Kearns, John. Va. Private. 20 Dec. 1784. 100 acres.
Kearns, Thomas. Md. ———. ———. 50 acres.
Kearny, William. N.C. Private. 12 Apr. 1808. 640 acres.
Kearsey, Edward. Md. Private. ———. 50 acres.
Kearsey, John. Pa. Private. ———. 200 acres.
Keath, Ethel. Ga. ———. 16 May 1784. ———.

Keating, Ignatius. Pa. Private. 20 Sep. 1787. 200 acres.
Keating, Thomas. N. Y. Corporal. 9 Jul. 1790. 500 acres.
Keaton, John. Pa. Private. 6 Feb. 1787. 200 acres to Richard Leedom, assignee.
Keay, Jonathan. N.C. Private. 11 May 1785. 228 acres.
Kebble, William. Va. Corporal. 4 Oct. 1783. 200 acres.
Keckland, James. Md. Private. ———. 50 acres.
Kedwell, Elisha. N.C. Private. 22 Dec. 1796. 274 acres.
Keech, Walter. Md. Private. ———. 50 acres.
Keel, Hardy. N.C. Private. 1 Sep. 1785. 640 acres to heirs.
Keelan, John. Pa. Private. 5 Apr. 1787. 200 acres.
Keeler, Benjamin. Conn. Sufferer. Norwalk. 10.19.4.
Keeler, Isaac. Conn. Sufferer. Ridgefield. 194.0.0.
Keeler, Jacob. Mass. Private. 24 Jan. 1832. 200 acres to his cousin and heir at law Joseph Tobias.
Keeler, James. Conn. Sufferer. Norwalk. 8.4.8.
Keeler, Jemima. Conn. Sufferer. Ridgefield. 0.18.8.
Keeler, John. Conn. Sufferer. Ridgefield. 23.0.4.
Keeler, Margaret. Conn. Sufferer. Fairfield. 13.2.1.
Keeler, Martha. Conn. Sufferer. Ridgefield. 2.2.4.
Keeler, Matthew. Conn. Sufferer. Norwalk. 165.10.10.
Keeler, Matthew. Conn. Sufferer. Ridgefield. 6.16.8.
Keeler, Nathan. Conn. Sufferer. Norwalk. 3.7.0.
Keeler, Robert. N.C. Private. 12 Dec. 1797. 274 acres.
Keeler, Samuel. Conn. Sufferer. Norwalk. 30.14.0.
Keeler, Samuel. Conn. Sufferer. Ridgefield. 4.13.0.
Keeler, Samuel, 2d. Conn. Sufferer. Ridgefield. 1.7.8.
Keeler, Stephen. Conn. Sufferer. Norwalk. 25.1.3.
Keeler, Thaddeus. Conn. Sufferer. Norwalk. 2.5.10.
Keeler, Timothy, 2d. Conn. Sufferer. Ridgefield. 51.9.0.
Keelock, Ebenezer. Ga. Soldier. 27 Apr. 1784. 287 1/2 acres.
Keelock, John. Ga. Soldier. 27 Apr. 1784. 287 1/2 acres.
Keemar, Nicholas. Pa. Private. 19 Nov. 1786. 200 acres.
Keen, John. Va. Private. 23 Oct. 1784. 200 acres.
Keen, Lawrence. Pa. Aide de Camp. 16 Jul. 1787. 500 acres.
Keenan, John. Pa. Private. 7 Nov. 1786. 200 acres.
Keenan, Roger. Pa. Private. 7 Apr. 1785. 200 acres.
Keene, Samuel Y. Md. Surgeon's Mate. ———. 200 acres.
Keep, James. Va. Private. 28 Jun. 1783. 200 acres.
Keernes, John. Va. Private. 26 Jan. 1785. 100 acres.
Kees, David. Pa. Private. 9 Mar. 1795. 200 acres to John Nicholson, assignee.
Kees, Joseph. N.C. Private. 3 Aug. 1821. 228 acres.
Keeth, Isham. Va. Private. 26 May 1784. 2666 2/3 acres.
Keeton, Edmund. Va. Private. 27 Nov. 1784. 100 acres.
Keeton, William. Va. Private. 27 Nov. 1784. 200 acres.
Kein, Thomas. Va. Private. 28 Jun. 1783. 233 1/3 acres.
Keith, Alexander. Va. Sergeant. 18 Nov. 1818. 400 acres.
Keith, Alexander. Va. Lieutenant. 30 Aug. 1830. 2666 2/3 acres.
Keith, Cornelius. Me. ———. 20 May 1835. 200 acres to widow Lydia Keith. Bath.
Keith, Daniel. Va. Private. 13 Dec. 1783. 200 acres.
Keith, Daniel. Va. Private. 20 Jan. 1812. 100 acres.
Keith, David. Ga. ———. 16 Apr. 1784. 287 1/2 acres.
Keith, John. N.C. Private. 10 Dec. 1788. 640 acres to heirs.
Keith, John. S.C. ———. 4 May 1789. 200 acres.

Keith, Lyman. Ga. ———. ———. 287 1/2 acres.
Keith, Samuel, Jr. Ga. ———. 23 Apr. 1784. 287 1/2 acres.
Keith, Samuel, Sr. Ga. ———. 23 Apr. 1784. 287 1/2 acres.
Keith, Thomas. Va. Captain & Commissary. 13 May 1848. 1777 2/3 acres.
Keith, Thomas. Va. Captain & Commissary. 13 May 1848. 592 1/2 acres.
Keith, Thomas. Va. Captain & Commissary. 13 May 1848. 592 1/2 acres.
Keith, Thomas. Va. Captain & Commissary. 13 May 1848. 592 1/2 acres.
Keith, Thomas. Va. Captain & Commissary. 13 May 1848. 592 1/2 acres.
Keith, Thomas. Va. Captain & Commissary. 13 May 1848. 592 1/2 acres.
Keith, Thomas. Va. Captain & Commissary. 13 May 1848. 395 acres.
Keith, Thomas. Va. Captain & Commissary. 13 May 1848. 197 acres.
Keith, Thomas. Va. ———. 3 Jun. 1852. 1333 1/3 acres.
Keith, Thomas. Va. ———. 3 Jun. 1852. 2666 2/3 acres.
Keiton, James. N.C. Private. 6 Sep. 1821. 640 acres.
Kelbe, James. N.C. Matchmaker. 13 Jan. 1823. 274 acres.
Kell [?], Upton. Ga. ———. 4 Oct. 1785. ———.
Kell, Archibald. Ga. ———. 22 Sep. 1784. 287 1/2 acres.
Kellar, Abraham. Va.-Ind. Captain. Jul. 1785. 3234 acres.
Kellar, Abraham. Va. Captain. 8 Jul. 1784. 4000 acres.
Kellar, Conard. Pa. Private. ———. 200 acres.
Kellar, Francis. Pa. Private. 11 Apr. 1787. 200 acres.
Kellar, George. Pa. Private. 16 Oct. 1786. 200 acres.
Kellar, Isaac. Va.-Ind. Sergeant. 216 acres.
Keller, Edward. Pa. Private. ———. 200 acres.
Keller, Frederick. S.C. ———. 6 Apr. 1789. 17 acres.
Keller, John. N. Y. Private. 8 Jul. 1790. 600 acres.
Keller, Leonard. N.C. Private. 8 Dec. 1795. 640 acres to heirs.
Kelley, Charles. N.C. Sergeant. 7 Jan. 1784. 580 acres.
Kelley, John. N.C. Private. 22 Feb. 1784. 640 acres.
Kelley, John. Pa. ———. 13 Aug. 1787. 200 acres.
Kelley, John. Va. Private. 25 Feb. 1783. 100 acres.
Kelley, Patrick. N.C. Private. 21 Aug. 1820. 640 acres.
Kelley, Peter. Va. Private. 7 Jun. 1811. 200 acres.
Kelley, Thomas. N.C. Private. 21 May 1784. 274 acres.
Kelley, William. S.C. ———. 6 Nov. 1786. 200 acres.
Kellock, David. Me. ———. 11 May 1835. 200 acres. Warren.
Kellog, John. Conn. Sufferer. Norwalk. 76.9.0.
Kellogg, Elijah. Me. ———. 25 Apr. 1835. 200 acres. Portland.
Kellogg, Jarvis. Conn. Sufferer. Norwalk. 2.3.9.
Kellon, Edward. Pa. Private. 18 Aug. 1787. 200 acres.
Kellow, William. Md. Sergeant. ———. 50 acres.
Kelly, Andrew. Va. Private. 3 Feb. 1784. 200 acres.
Kelly, Barney. N.Y. ———. 13 Sep. 1790. 500 acres to heirs.
Kelly, Benjamin. Va. Private. 22 Apr. 1783. 200 acres.
Kelly, Benjamin. Va. Private. 30 Apr. 1783. 100 acres.
Kelly, Christian. N.Y. ———. 13 Sep. 1790. 500 acres to heirs.
Kelly, David. Md. Private. ———. 50 acres.
Kelly, David. N. Y. Private. 8 Jul. 1790. 600 acres.
Kelly, Dennis. Md. Sergeant. ———. 50 acres.
Kelly, Dugald. N.C. Private. 31 Jan. 1795. 640 acres to heirs.
Kelly, Edmond. N. Y. Private. 8 Jul. 1790. 500 acres.
Kelly, Edward. Ga. ———. 15 Mar. 1784. 250 acres.
Kelly, Edward. N.C. Private. 21 Aug. 1820. 640 acres.
Kelly, Edward. Pa. Private. 10 Aug. 1787. 200 acres.

Kelly, Gordon. Va. Private. 21 Jan. 1786. 100 acres.
Kelly, Jacob. Ga. Refugee. 22 Apr. 1784. 287 1/2 acres.
Kelly, Jacob. Md. Private. ———. 50 acres.
Kelly, James. Ga. ———. 20 Apr. 1784. 287 1/2 acres.
Kelly, James. Md. Private. ———. 50 acres.
Kelly, James. Md. Corporal. ———. 50 acres.
Kelly, James. N.C. Private. 21 Aug. 1820. 640 acres.
Kelly, Jesse. Va. Private. 20 Nov. 1783. 200 acres.
Kelly, John. Ga. Refugee. 26 May 1784. 287 1/2 acres.
Kelly, John. N. Y. Matross. 9 Jul. 1790. 600 acres.
Kelly, John. N.Y. Matross. 13 Sep. 1790. 500 acres to heirs.
Kelly, John. N.C. Private. 12 Dec. 1785. 640 acres to heirs.
Kelly, John. Pa. Private. 5 Feb. 1787. 200 acres.
Kelly, John. Pa. Private. 16 Aug. 1787. 200 acres.
Kelly, John. Va. Private. 20 Jun. 1783. 100 acres.
Kelly, Joshua. N. Y. Private. 8 Jul. 1790. 600 acres.
Kelly, Jospeh. N.C. Private. 30 Sep. 1785. 274 acres.
Kelly, Matthew. Md. Private. ———. 50 acres.
Kelly, Patrick. Pa. Private. 11 Oct. 1786. 200 acres.
Kelly, Robert. N. Y. Corporal. 8 Jul. 1790. 600 acres.
Kelly, Thaddeus. Va. Captain. 10 Mar. 1783. 4000 acres.
Kelly, Thomas. Ga. ———. 27 Apr. 1784. 250 acres.
Kelly, Thomas. Pa. Private. ———. 200 acres.
Kelly, Timothy. Pa. Private. 25 Feb. 1903. 200 acres.
Kelly, Timothy. Pa. Private. ———. 200 acres to Alexander Powers.
Kelly, Timothy. Va. Private. 31 Jan. 1785. 100 acres.
Kelly, Wiliiam. Va. Captain. 15 Nov. 1838. 5777 acres.
Kelly, William. N.C. Private. 8 Dec. 1796. 640 acres to heirs.
Kelly, William. Pa. Private. ———. 200 acres.
Kelly, William. Pa. Private. ———. 200 acres.
Kelly, William. Pa. Private. ———. 200 acres.
Kelly, William. Va. Private. 8 Nov. 1784. 200 acres.
Kelly, William. Va. Captain. 8 Jan. 1839. 1777 acres.
Kelly, William. Va. Captain. 8 Jan. 1839. 2000 acres.
Kelly, William. Va. Captain. 8 Jan. 1839. 1000 acres.
Kelly, William. Va. Captain. 8 Jan. 1839. 1000 acres.
Kelly, William, Jr. Ga. ———. 27 Apr. 1784. 287 1/2 acres.
Kelly, William, Sr. Ga. ———. 16 Apr. 1784. 287 1/2 acres.
Kelly, Woodford. S.C. ———. 1 Aug. 1785. 200 acres.
Kelp, John. Pa. Private. 6 Mar. 1787. 200 acres.
Kelsey, Hugh. Ga. Sergeant. 25 Feb. 1784. 250 acres.
Kelsey, Thomas. Ga. Minute Man Private. 26 Feb. 1785. 250 acres to brother Hugh Kelsey of Camden Dist., S.C.
Kelso, Benjamin. N. Y. Private. 8 Jul. 1790. 500 acres.
Kelso, John. Pa. Sergeant. 19 Dec. 1786. 250 acres.
Kelson, George. Md. Private. ———. 50 acres.
Kelty, John. Va. Captain. 9 Jun. 1855. 740 2/3 acres.
Kelty, John. Va. Captain. 9 Jun. 1855. 370 1/3 acres.
Keltz, Nicholas. N. Y. Private. 8 Jul. 1790. 600 acres.
Kemble, Benjamin. Ga. ———. 1784. 278 1/2 acres.
Kemble, Stephen. Md. Private. ———. 50 acres.
Kemble, William. Ga. ———. 1784. 278 1/2 acres.
Kemp, David. N.C. Private. 30 Sep. 1785. 640 acres to heirs.
Kemp, James. Va. Ensign. 8 Mar. 1784. 2666 2/3 acres.

Kemp, James. Va. Private. 11 Mar. 1788. 100 acres.
Kemp, Joseph, Jr. Ga. ———. 27 Apr. 1784. 287 1/2 acres.
Kemp, Peter. Va. Captain. 20 Mar. 1783. 4000 acres.
Kemp, Peter. Va. Private. 6 Mar. 1784. 100 acres.
Kemp, Thomas. Ga. ———. 27 Apr. 1784. 287 1/2 acres.
Kemp, Thomas. Va. Surgeon's Mate. 13 Nov. 1832. 2666 2/3 acres.
Kemp, Thomas. Va. Surgeon's Mate. 10 Mar. 1833. 1333 1/3 acres.
Kemp, William. Ga. Refugee. 8 Apr. 1784. ———.
Kemp, William. Va. Private. 13 Aug. 1784. 200 acres.
Kempe, James. Va. Brigade Quartermaster. 31 Dec. 1851. 3555 2/3 acres.
Kempe, James. Va. Brigade Quartermaster. 31 Dec. 1851. 1777 2/3 acres.
Kempin, William. Va. Private. 18 Mar. 1785. 200 acres.
Kenady, Anthony. N.C. Private. 19 Jan. 1786. 640 acres.
Kenady, James. N.C. Private. 24 Nov. 1796. 640 acres.
Kenady, Joab. N.C. Private. 24 Nov. 1796. 640 acres to heirs.
Kenady, Ruben. N.C. Private. 24 Nov. 1796. 640 acres to heirs.
Kenaston, John. Pa. Private. 13 Oct 1786. 200 acres.
Kendall, Benjamin. Va.-Ind. Private. 108 acres.
Kendall, Custis. Va. Captain. 13 Apr. 1784. 4666 2/3 acres.
Kendall, George. Va. Private. 2 May 1783. 200 acres.
Kendall, Jeremiah. Ga. ———. 15 Apr. 1784. 287 1/2 acres.
Kendall, Jeremiah. Va. Private. 31 Mar. 1810. 100 acres.
Kendall, Jeremiah. Va. Sergeant. 10 Oct. 1812. 100 acres.
Kendall, Jesse. Va. Private. 27 Sep. 1786. 100 acres.
Kendall, William. Va.-Ind. Private. 108 acres.
Kendall, William. Me. Private. 8 Aug. 1836. 200 acres to widow Abigail Kendall. Fairfield.
Kendrick, Daniel. Va. Private. 3 Jun. 1783. 100 acres.
Kendrick, Hezekiah. Ga. Refugee. 16 Apr. 1784. 287 1/2 acres.
Kendrick, John. Ga. ———. 27 Apr. 1784. 287 1/2 acres.
Kendrick, Nathaniel. Ga. ———. 27 Apr. 1784. 287 1/2 acres.
Kenedy, John. S.C. ———. 4 Jul. 1791. 200 acres.
Kenedy, Moses. Va. Private. 26 Apr. 1783. 200 acres.
Kenenbrew, Jacob. Ga. Soldier. 1784. 287 1/2 acres.
Kenerson, John. Me. Private. 4 Feb. 1845. 200 acres to widow Betsey (Fall) Kenerson. Denmark. Surname also appears as Kenison and Keniston.
Kenly, John, Jr. Ga. ———. 17 May 1784. ———.
Kennady, Andrew. Va. Private. 19 Sep. 1787. 100 acres.
Kennady, John. Va. Private. 21 May 1784. 200 acres.
Kennan, John. N.C. Private. 10 Feb. 1796. 640 acres.
Kennard, John. Md. ———. ———. 50 acres.
Kennebrew, John. Ga. ———. 22 Apr. 1784. 287 1/2 acres.
Kennedy, Andrew. Pa. Private. ———. 200 acres.
Kennedy, Archibald. N.C. Sergeant. 16 Aug. 1821. 1000 acres.
Kennedy, Benjamin. N.C. Sergeant. 23 Dec. 1792. 500 acres.
Kennedy, Benjmain. N.C. Private. 17 Feb. 1824. 640 acres.
Kennedy, Daniel. Pa. Adjutant. 12 Sep. 1789. 500 acres.
Kennedy, David. Md. ———. ———. 50 acres.
Kennedy, Dennis. Pa. Private. 19 Sep. 1787. 200 acres.
Kennedy, James. S.C. Lieutenant. 16 Jul. 1784. 200 acres.
Kennedy, James. Va. Lieutenant. 20 Dec. 1782. 2666 2/3 acres.
Kennedy, James. Va. Lieutenant. 14 Apr. 1858. 818 acres.
Kennedy, James. Va. Lieutenant. 3 Dec. 1853. 2666 2/3 acres.
Kennedy, John. Ga. ———. 28 Feb. 1784. 287 1/2 acres.

Kennedy, John. N. Y. Private. 6 Jul. 1790. 600 acres.
Kennedy, Robert. Conn. Sufferer. New London. 350.0.0.
Kennedy, Samuel. Pa. Captain. 14 Oct. 1786. 500 acres to Thomas Pinkerton, assignee.
Kennedy, William. Md. Private. ———. 50 acres.
Kennedy, William. N.C. Sergeant. 5 Sep. 1821. 1000 acres.
Kennedy, William. S.C. ———. 2 Jul. 1792. 100 acres.
Kennedy, William. Va. Private. 12 Nov. 1783. 100 acres.
Kennedy, William. Va. Ensign. 18 Mar. 1840. 1333 1/3 acres.
Kennedy, William. Va. Ensign. 27 Feb. 1841. 333 1/3 acres.
Kennehan, Richard. Pa. Private. 26 Jun. 1787. 200 acres.
Kennehorn, William. Va. Private. 15 Jun. 1807. 100 acres.
Kennelly, John. N. Y. Drummer. 13 Sep. 1790. 600 acres.
Kenner, Howson. Va. Midshipman. 28 Mar. 1785. 2666 2/3 acres.
Kenner, Jonathan. N. Y. Private. 8 Jul. 1790. 600 acres.
Kenner, Rodham. Va. Sailor. 3 May 1784. 100 acres.
Kenner, Rodham. Va. Private. 17 Mar. 1785. 100 acres.
Kenner, Rodham. Va. Gunner. 30 Dec. 1851. 2566 2/3 acres.
Kennerly, John. Ga. ———. 27 Apr. 1784. 500 acres.
Kenney, Archelus. Mass. ———. 21 Sep. 1829. 200 acres.
Kenney, Benjamin. Me. Private. 8 Jun. 1835. 200 acres to widow Elizabeth Kenney. Freedom.
Kenney, Peter. Pa Private. 28 Aug. 1787. 200 acres to William Turnbull, assignee.
Kenney, Robert. N.C. Private. 10 Feb. 1796. 640 acres to heirs.
Kennon, John. Va. Lieutenant. 11 May 1784. 2666 2/3 acres.
Kennon, John. Va. Captain. 7 Jun. 1784. 1333 1/3 acres.
Kennon, Richard. Va. Captain. 23 May 1800. 1000 acres.
Kennon, Richard. Va. Captain. 23 May 1800. 1000 acres.
Kennon, Richard. Va. Captain. 23 May 1800. 500 acres.
Kennon, Richard. Va. Captain. 23 May 1800. 500 acres.
Kennon, Richard. Va. Captain. 23 May 1800. 500 acres.
Kennon, Richard. Va. Captain. 23 May 1800. 500 acres.
Kennon, Richard. Va. Captain. 29 Aug. 1807. 1166 1/2 acres.
Kenny, Richard. Va. Private. 7 Oct. 1783. 233 1/3 acres.
Kent, Alexander. Va. Private. 21 Apr. 1784. 100 acres.
Kent, Daniel. Va. Ensign. 21 May 1833. 2666 2/3 acres.
Kent, Edwin. Va. Midshipman. 17 Mar. 1838. 1777 4/9 acres.
Kent, Edwin. Va. Midshipman. 17 Mar. 1838. 444 4/9 acres.
Kent, Edwin. Va. Midshipman. 17 Mar. 1838. 444 4/9 acres.
Kent, Jesse. Va. Midshipman. 4 Aug. 1786. 2666 2/3 acres.
Kent, Joshua. Va. Seaman. 9 Apr. 1835. 100 acres.
Kent, Moso. Conn. Sufferer. Fairfield. 185.0.7.
Kent, Smith. Va. Sergeant. 23 Oct. 1783. 200 acres.
Kent, Thomas. N.C. Private. 12 Mar. 1785. 640 acres to heirs.
Kent, Thomas. N.C. Private. 6 Sep. 1821. 640 acres.
Kent, Thomas. Va. Sailor. 24 Oct. 1786. 100 acres.
Kent, William. Va. Sailor. 24 Oct. 1786. 100 acres.
Kenton, Simon. Va.-Ind. Private. 108 acres.
Kephart, Adam. Md. Private. ———. 50 acres.
Kepp, Amos. N. Y. Private. 8 Jul. 1790. 600 acres.
Kerby, William. N.C. Private. 22 Dec. 1796. 274 acres.
Kerdendawl, John. N.C. Private. 2 Nov. 1795. 640 acres to heirs.
Kerk, John. N.C. Private. 4 May 1784. 274 acres.
Kernes, William. Va. Private. 29 Sep. 1807. 100 acres.
Kerney, Arthur. N.C. Private. 20 Sep. 1784. 274 acres.

Kerney, John. Va. Captain. 12 Jun. 1783. 1000 acres.

Kerney, John. Va. Captain. 12 Jun. 1783. 1500 acres.

Kerney, John. Va. Captain. 12 Jun. 1783. 1500 acres.

Kerney, John. Va. Captain. 9 Oct. 1830. 888 2/3 acres.

Kernon, Michael. Md. Private. ———. 50 acres.

Kerns, Godfrey. Pa. ———. 18 Jan. 1803. 200 acres.

Kerr, John. N.C. Private. 10 Dec. 1788. 640 acres.

Kerr, John. Pa. ———. 23 Feb. 1789. 200 acres to Mary Coleman, widow.

Kerr, Mark. N. Y. Corporal. 8 Jul. 1790. 600 acres.

Kerrick, Benjamin H. Md. Private. ———. 50 acres.

Kerrick, Joseph. Md. Corporal. ———. 50 acres.

Kersey, Isaac. S.C. ———. 2 Jan. 1792. 204 acres.

Kersey, Stephen. Ga. Refugee. 15 Mar. 1784. 250 acres.

Kersey, Stephen, Jr. ———. 17 May 1784. ———.

Kersey, William. Va. Private. 20 Sep. 1784. 100 acres.

Kertiller, Abraham. Va. Private. 11 Jun. 1784. 100 acres.

Kervin, Thomas. N.C. Private. 6 Dec. 1783. 274 acres.

Kesler, Henry. Pa. Private. 21 May 1787. 200 acres.

Keslow, John. Va. Private. 27 Nov. 1833[?]. 100 acres.

Kesor, Richard. N.C. Sergeant. 9 Dec. 1797. 428 acres.

Ketchum, Elizabeth. Conn. Sufferer. Norwalk. 45.10.6.

Ketchum, Joshua. N. Y. Gunner. 9 Jul. 1790. 600 acres.

Ketchum, Samuel. Conn. Sufferer. Norwalk. 4.1.6.

Ketchum, Timothy. Conn. Sufferer. Danbury. 23.6.6.

Kettle [or Kite], George. Pa. ———. 12 Oct. 1786. 200 acres.

Kettle, Abram. Md. Private. ———. 50 acres.

Kettle, David. Md. Private. ———. 50 acres.

Key, George. Va.-Ind. Private. 108 acres.

Key, George. Va. Private. 13 Jun. 1783. 100 acres.

Key, George. Va. Private. 20 May 1829. 50 acres.

Key, George. Va. Private. 20 May 1829. 50 acres.

Key, Price. Va. Corporal. 22 Jul. 1824. 400 acres.

Key, Thomas. Va.-Ind. Sergeant. 216 acres.

Keyes, Ebenezer. Me. Private. 28 Apr. 1835. 200 acres. Jay.

Keys, Johnston. N.C. Private. 9 Dec. 1797. 640 acres to heirs.

Keysor, William. Va. Private. 12 May 1784. 100 acres.

Kidd, Alexander. N. Y. Private. 8 Jul. 1790. 600 acres.

Kidd, Alexander. Conn. Sufferer. Groton. 9.5.11.

Kidd, Benjamin. Va. Private. 14 Apr. 1783. 100 acres.

Kidd, Benjamin. Va. Private. 30 May 1831. 100 acres.

Kidd, John. Md. Private. ———. 50 acres.

Kidd, William. Va. Private. 4 Jan. 1834. 100 acres.

Kidder, Benjamin. Pa. Private. 10 Aug. 1787. 200 acres.

Kidwell, Elijah. N.C. Private. 21 Apr. 1784. 640 acres.

Kiel, Hardy. N.C. Private. 1 Dec. 1797. 428 acres.

Kilborn, John. Mass. Sergeant. 15 Jan. 1833. 200 acres.

Kilbourn, Zaccheus. N. Y. Private. 8 Jul. 1790. 600 acres.

Kilbourne, Benjamin. Pa. Private. 10 Sep. 1787. 200 acres to heirs.

Kilburn, John. Mass. Private. 11 Mar. 1834. 200 acres.

Kilby, John. Pa. Corporal. ———. 200 acres.

Kilby, Marak. Conn. Sufferer. New/East Haven. 0.2.6.

Kildee, John. Md. Private. ———. 50 acres.

Kile, Charles. N.C. Private. 24 Nov. 1796. 640 acres to heirs.

Kile, Christopher. N. Y. Matross. 9 Jul. 1790. 600 acres.

Kile, Dempsey. N.C. Private. 24 Nov. 1796. 640 acres to heirs.

Kilgore, Henry. S.C. ———. 6 Aug. 1787. 200 acres to James Kilgore, his brother & heir at law.

Kilgore, James. S.C. ———. 6 Aug. 1787. 200 acres.

Kilgore, James. S.C. ———. 6 Aug. 1787. 200 acres.

Kilgore, John. Ga. ———. 23 Apr. 1784. 287 1/2 acres.

Kilgore, Ralph. Ga. ———. 15 Mar. 1784. 250 acres.

Kilgore, Robert. Ga. ———. 27 Apr. 1784. 287 1/2 acres.

Kilgore, Thomas. Ga. ———. 25 May 1784. 287 1/2 acres.

Kilgore, William. Ga. ———. 21 Apr. 1784. 287 1/2 acres.

Killagan, James. Md. Private. ———. 50 acres.

Killen, John. Pa. Private. ———. 200 acres.

Killer, Frederick. N. Y. Private. 8 Jul. 1790. 500 acres.

Killingworth, John. N.C. Private. 30 Mar. 1784. 714 acres.

Killman, Edward. Md. Private. ———. 50 acres.

Killom, John. N.C. Private. 26 May 1784. 640 acres.

Killon, John. Pa. Matross. 28 Aug. 1787. 200 acres.

Killpatrick, John. N.C. Private. 30 Mar. 1785. 298 acres.

Killsa, James. Me. Private. 20 Jun. 1835. 200 acres to widow Lydia Killsa. Thornton.

Kilpatrick, Hugh. N.C. Private. 15 Feb. 1797. 274 acres.

Kilpatrick, Robert. N.C. Musician. 21 Aug. 1820. 1000 acres to heirs.

Kilpatrick, Thomas. Ga. Refugee. 26 May 1784. 287 1/2 acres.

Kilsdorf, John. Pa. Private. 9 Oct. 1786. 200 acres.

Kilson, George. S.C. Soldier. 21 Jan. 1785. 200 acres.

Kilty, John. Md. Captain. ———. 200 acres.

Kilty, John. Va. Captain. 11 Apr. 1793. 4000 acres.

Kilty, William. Md. Surgeon. ———. 200 acres.

Kimball, Joseph. Me. ———. 21 Oct. 1835. 200 acres. Bridgeton.

Kimball, Nathan. Me. ———. 17 Jul. 1835. 200 acres to widow Lydia Kimball. South Berwick.

Kimball, Rufus. Me. Private. 20 Aug. 1838. 200 acres to widow Lucy Kimball. Hollis.

Kimberley, Azael. Conn. Sufferer. New/East Haven. 52.10.0.

Kimberley, Azel. Conn. Sufferer. New/East Haven. 32.16.6.

Kimberley, Lydia. Conn. Sufferer. New/East Haven. 21.8.9.

Kimberley, Mary. Conn. Sufferer. New/East Haven. 20.0.0.

Kimberley, Nathaniel. Conn. Sufferer. New/East Haven. 2.13.0.

Kimberley, Sarah. Conn. Sufferer. New/East Haven. 27.16.0.

Kimberley, Silas. Conn. Sufferer. New/East Haven. 9.18.6.

Kimberley, Silas. Conn. Sufferer. New/East Haven. 193.16.0.

Kimberlye, Mary. Conn. Sufferer. New/East Haven. 18.10.0.

Kimble, Robert. Va. Private. 13 Oct. 1783. 100 acres.

Kimbrough, John. Ga. Lieutenant. 25 Feb. 1784. 250 acres.

Kimbrough, Shadrack. Ga. Soldier. 5 May 1785. ———.

Kimbrough, William. Ga. ———. 25 Feb. 1784. 250 acres.

Kimmsey, Jonathan. N.C. ———. 21 Nov. 1804. 251 acres.

Kimmy, Isaac. Va. Private. 20 Sep. 1797. 100 acres.

Kimpsey, Patrick. Pa. Private. 6 Feb. 1787. 200 acres.

Kincade, John. Md. ———. ———. 50 acres.

Kincaid, Andrew. Pa. ———. 13 Nov. 1786. 200 acres to John Donnell, assignee.

Kincaid, John. Va. Private. 9 Apr. 1838. 200 acres.

Kincaid, Joseph. Va. Ensign. 31 Mar. 1838. 444 4/9 acres.

Kincaid, Joseph. Va. Ensign. 31 Mar. 1838. 444 4/9 acres.

Kincaid, Joseph. Va. Ensign. 31 Mar. 1838. 444 4/9 acres.

Kincaid, Joseph. Va. Ensign. 31 Mar. 1838. 444 4/9 acres.

Kincaid, Joseph. Va. Ensign. 31 Mar. 1838. 444 4/9 acres.

Kincaid, Joseph. Va. Ensign. 31 Mar. 1838. 444 4/9 acres.

Kincaid, William. N. Y. ———. 16 Nov. 1806. 200 acres.

Kinch, Widow. Conn. Sufferer. Greenwich. 8.10.0.

Kinch, William. Conn. Sufferer. Greenwich. 5.14.2.

Kindle, William. Md. Private. ———. 50 acres.

Kindrick, Hezekiah. Ga. ———. 17 Feb. 1784. 250 acres.

King, Andrew. N.C. Private. 30 Sep. 1785. 640 acres to heirs.

King, Anthony. N.C. Private. 30 Sep. 1785. 640 acres to heirs.

King, Charles. Va. Sergeant. 3 Nov. 1787. 200 acres.

King, Charles. Va. Lieutenant. 19 Nov. 1783. 2666 2/3 acres.

King, Christian. Pa. Corporal. 11 Apr. 1787. 200 acres.

King, Christopher. S.C. ———. 6 Nov. 1786. 200 acres.

King, Edmund. N.C. Private. 19 May 1784. 640 acres.

King, Elijah. Conn. Sufferer. New/East Haven. 11.19.10.

King, Elisha. Va. Lieutenant. 19 Feb. 1818. 333 acres.

King, Enoch. N.C. Private. 22 Mar. 1785. 640 acres.

King, Enoch. N.C. Private. 2 Dec. 1785. 640 acres.

King, Ephaphroditus. N.C. Private. 30 Sep. 1785. 640 acres to heirs.

King, Francis. Pa. Private. ———. 200 acres.

King, Francis. Va. Private. 1 Apr. 1783. 100 acres.

King, Francis. Va. Private. 27 Oct. 1783. 200 acres.

King, Frederick. S.C. ———. 4 May 1789. 200 acres.

King, George. N.C. ———. 30 Apr. 1784. 640 acres to Robert King, heir.

King, Henry. Ga. Minute Man. 16 Sep. 1785. 287 1/2 acres.

King, Jacob. N.C. Private. 24 Nov. 1796. 640 acres to heirs.

King, James. N.C. ———. 7 May 1784. 640 acres to Julias King, heiress.

King, James. N.C. Captain. 20 Jan. 1785. 3840 acres to heirs.

King, James. N.C. Private. 15 Feb. 1797. 640 acres to heirs.

King, James. N.C. Private. 6 Dec. 1809. 640 acres to heirs.

King, James. Va. Sergeant. 24 Jun. 1784. 200 acres.

King, Joel. Ga. ———. 15 Mar. 1784. 250 acres.

King, John. Ga. Private. 27 Apr. 1784. 450 acres.

King, John. Md. Private. ———. 50 acres.

King, John. Md. Private. ———. 50 acres.

King, John. N. Y. Corporal. 7 Jul. 1790. 600 acres.

King, John. N.C. Private. 19 May 1784. 274 acres.

King, John. N.C. Private. 28 Sep. 1785. 457 acres to heirs.

King, John. Pa. Dragoon. ———. 200 acres.

King, John. Va. Private. 8 Mar. 1783. 100 acres.

King, John. Va. Private. 24 Sep. 1783. 100 acres.

King, John. Va. Private. 18 Jun. 1783. 200 acres.

King, John. Va. Private. 13 Jul. 1797. 100 acres.

King, Joseph. N.C. Private. 26 Apr. 1784. 274 acres.

King, Josiah. Mass. Private. 22 Oct. 1830. 200 acres.

King, Miles. Va. Surgeon's Mate. 2 Mar. 1784. 2666 2/3 acres.

King, Miles. Va. Surgeon's Mate. 11 Aug. 1856. 389 4/9 acres.

King, Miles. Va. Surgeon's Mate. 11 Aug. 1856. 833 1/3 acres.

King, Miles. Va. Surgeon's Mate. 5 Oct. 1860. 83 1/3 acres.

King, Moses. Me. ———. 23 Jun. 1835. 200 acres to widow Mary Brainard. Pittston.

King, Nicholas. Va. Private. 17 Jul. 1784. 200 acres.

King, Peter. Ga. Soldier. 4 Oct. 1785. ———.

King, Philip. N. Y. Private. 8 Jul. 1790. 600 acres.

King, Richard. Ga. ———. 21 Apr. 1784. 300 acres.

King, Richard. N.C. Private. 30 Sep. 1785. 640 acres to heirs.
King, Samuel. Ga. Private. 29 Jun. 1784. 250 acres.
King, Samuel. Conn. Sufferer. Fairfield. 5.7.0.
King, Thomas. Md. Private. ———. 50 acres.
King, Vincent. N.C. Private. 15 Feb. 1797. 228 acres.
King, William. Md. Private. ———. 50 acres.
KIng, William. N.C. Private. 10 Jan. 1794. 640 acres.
King, William. N.C. Private. 7 Dec. 1796. 640 acres to heirs.
King, William. Va. Private. 17 Mar. 1784. 100 acres.
King, Zachariah. Va. Private. 12 Jul. 1783. 100 acres.
Kingore, William. Va. Private. 20 Jun. 1783. 100 acres.
Kingsbury, John. N.C. Captain Commandant. 15 Dec. 1783. 4800 acres.
Kingsmill, Robert. N.C. Private. 14 Feb. 1796. 640 acres.
Kink, William. N.C. Private. 13 Jan. 1823. 640 acres.
Kinkade, Peter. Md. Private. ———. 50 acres.
Kinkaid, William. N.C. Private. 6 Sep. 1821. 640 acres.
Kinkead, John. Pa. ———. 7 Apr. 1802. 200 acres.
Kinkead, John. Pa. ———. 10 Aug. 1805. 200 acres.
Kinkead, John Pa. Private. 7 Sep. 1803. 200 acres.
Kinley, Benjamin. Va. Captain. 5 Mar. 1784. 4000 acres.
Kinley, Benjamin. Va. Captain. 16 Jan. 1834. 4000 acres.
Kinnaird, David. Va. Private. 8 Dec. 1795. 100 acres.
Kinnard, Joseph. Pa. Private. 29 May 1795. 200 acres to Henry Spring, assignee.
Kinneday, David. N.C. Private. 19 May 1784. 640 acres.
Kinney, Charles. N. Y. Private. 8 Jul. 1790. 600 acres.
Kinsley, Daniel. Me. Sergeant. 4 Jul. 1835. 200 acres. Minot.
Kinton, Mark. Va. Private. 6 Nov. 1783. 233 1/3 acres.
Kipp, Peter. N. Y. Sergeant. 3 Jul. 1790. 600 acres.
Kippey, Peter. N.C. Musician. 5 Sep. 1821. 1000 acres.
Kirby, John. Va. Drummer. 19 Mar. 1783. 200 acres.
Kirk, Edward. Md. Private. ———. 50 acres.
Kirk, George. N. Y. Private. 8 Jul. 1790. 600 acres.
Kirk, James. Pa. Private. 12 Oct. 1786. 200 acres.
Kirk, James, Sr. Ga. ———. 17 May 1784. ———.
Kirk, Robert. Va. Lieutenant. 17 Jul. 1783. 2666 2/3 acres.
Kirk, Robert. Va. Lieutenant. 25 Feb. 1807. 444 1/3 acres.
Kirk, Robert. Va. Lieutenant. 29 Aug. 1807. 370 acres.
Kirk, Thomas. Ga. Soldier. 20 Apr. 1784. 345 acres.
Kirk, William. N.C. Private. 28 Sep. 1785. 640 acres to heirs.
Kirkham, Joseph. Ga. Soldier. 27 Apr. 1784. 287 1/2 acres.
Kirkindall, Samuel. N.C. Private. 2 Feb. 1786. 274 acres.
Kirkland, William. N.C. ———. 26 Aug. 1785. 640 acres to heirs.
Kirkpatrick, Abraham. Va. Captain. 29 Nov. 1783. 4666 2/3 acres.
Kirkpatrick, David. Va. Captain. 28 Nov. 1868. 1000 acres.
Kirkpatrik, James. Va. Private. 22 Aug. 1783. 200 acres.
Kirkwood, Hugh. S.C. Soldier. 16 Jul. 1784. 200 acres to John Bowie, executor, for the deceased's children.
Kirkwood, Robert. Va. Captain. 8 Nov. 1832. 4000 acres.
Kirley, Stephen. N.C. Private. 22 Dec. 1796. 274 acres.
Kirpatrick, David. Va. Captain. 24 Jul. 1824. 2000 acres.
Kirpatrick, David. Va. Captain. 24 Jul. 1824. 2000 acres.
Kisby, Richard. Md. Private. ———. 50 acres.
Kiser, Jacob. Md. Private. ———. 50 acres.
Kisselbaugh, Oswald. Pa. Private. 18 Oct. 1786. 200 acres to Alexander Power, assignee.

Kissinger, Charles. Pa. Private. 8 May 1787. 200 acres.
Kitcham, Joseph. N. Y. Corporal. 8 Jul. 1790. 600 acres.
Kitchem, John. N. Y. Private. 8 Jul. 1790. 600 acres.
Kitchen, James. Va. Private. 16 Feb. 1801. 100 acres.
Kitchen, John. Ga. Soldier. 25 Apr. 1784. 287 1/2 acres.
Kite, William. N.C. Private. 30 Sep. 1785. 640 acres to heirs.
Kitely, Francis. Md. Private. ———. 50 acres.
Kites, Charles. N.C. Private. 7 Dec. 1796. 274 acres.
Kittle, Jacob. N.C. Private. 16 Aug. 1821. 640 acres.
Kittle, Thomas P. Md. Private. ———. 50 acres.
Kitts, Charles. Pa. Private. 9 Oct. 1786. 200 acres.
Kitts, John. Ga. Soldier. 27 Apr. 1784. 287 1/2 acres.
Kitts, Samuel. N.C. Private. 9 Dec. 1797. 640 acres to heirs.
Kizor, Edward. N. Y. Private. 8 Jul. 1790. 600 acres.
Kizor, Joseph. N. Y. Private. 8 Jul. 1790. 500 acres.
Kleckner, Christian. Pa. Ensign. ———. 300 acres.
Klinger, Philip. Pa. Private. 8 Nov. 1786. 200 acres.
Klung, Henry. Va. Private. 26 Jun. 1783. 200 acres.
Knapp, Aaron. N.Y. ———. 13 Sep. 1790. 500 acres to heirs.
Knapp, Aaron. Conn. Sufferer. Danbury. 4.18.0.
Knapp, Abraham. Conn. Sufferer. Greenwich. 2.6.0.
Knapp, Caleb. N. Y. Private 8 Jul. 1790. 600 acres.
Knapp, Charles. Conn. Sufferer. Greenwich. 11.2.9.
Knapp, Ebenezer. Conn. Sufferer. Greenwich. 147.17.6.
Knapp, Eunice. Conn. Sufferer. Greenwich. 14.15.3.
Knapp, Ezekiel. Conn. Sufferer. Greenwich. 25.7.5.
Knapp, Horace. Conn. Sufferer. Danbury. 2.15.0.
Knapp, Israel, Jr. Conn. Sufferer. Greenwich. 4.15.5.
Knapp, James. N. Y. Drummer. 8 Jul. 1790. 600 acres.
Knapp, John. Conn. Sufferer. Greenwich. 23.3.7.
Knapp, John. Conn. Sufferer. Danbury. 6.10.0.
Knapp, Jonah. Conn. Sufferer. Greenwich. 44.13.7.
Knapp, Jonathan. Conn. Sufferer. Greenwich. 26.9.7.
Knapp, Joshua. Conn. Sufferer. Greenwich. 125.9.3.
Knapp, Joshua. Conn. Sufferer. Danbury. 43.3.8.
Knapp, Moses. Conn. Sufferer. Danbury. 4.6.8.
Knapp, Nathaniel. Conn. Sufferer. Greenwich. 15.8.0.
Knapp, Samuel. N. Y. Corporal. 9 Jul. 1790. 600 acres.
Knapsnyder, John. Pa. Private. 7 Mar. 1813. 200 acres to heirs.
Kneal, Patrick. Ga. Soldier. 25 May 1784. 230 acres.
Knell, William. N.C. Private. 14 Feb. 1796. 640 acres.
Knight, Andrew. Va. Private. 19 Dec. 1783. 100 acres.
Knight, Daniel. Me. ———. 2 Jun. 1835. 200 acres. Norway.
Knight, Howard. Pa. Private. ———. 200 acres.
Knight, Jacob. Md. Private. ———. 50 acres.
Knight, James. Va. Private. 20 Jun. 1783. 100 acres.
Knight, James. Va. Private. 14 Dec. 1833. 100 acres.
Knight, James. Va. Sergeant. 6 Dec. 1784. 200 acres.
Knight, Jesse. N.C. Private. 22 Oct. 1783. 640 acres to Mary Knight, relict.
Knight, Jesse. N.C. Private. 21 Aug. 1820. 274 acres.
Knight, John. Me. ———. 12 Aug. 1835. 200 acres. Windham.
Knight, John. Va. Surgeon's Mate. 31 Mar. 1783. 2000 acres.
Knight, John. Va. Surgeon's Mate. 31 Mar. 1783. 2000 acres.
Knight, John. Va. Private. 25 Jul. 1783. 100 acres.

Knight, John. Va. Private. 25 Jul. 1783. 100 acres.
Knight, John. Va. Surgeon's Mate. 11 Mar. 1800. 444 1/4 acres.
Knight, John. Va. Surgeon's Mate. 5 Aug. 1876. 222 2/9 acres.
Knight, Jonathan. Me. Private. 29 Jun. 1835. 200 acres. Windham.
Knight, Joseph. Me. Sergeant. 16 Sep. 1835. 200 acres. Alfred.
Knight, Michael. Pa. Private. 19 Sep. 1787. 200 acres.
Knight, Miles. N.C. Sergeant. 25 Oct. 1783. 1000 acres.
Knight, Miles. N.C. Sergeant. 7 Dec. 1783. 1000 acres.
Knight, Morgan. N.C. Private. 23 Dec. 1809. 640 acres to heirs.
Knight, Peter. N.C. Private. 12 Sep. 1785. 640 acres to heirs.
Knight, Reubin. N.C. Fifer. 13 Nov. 1795. 357 acres.
Knight, Richard. Ga. ———. 17 May 1784. ———.
Knight, Richard. Pa. Drummer. 24 Feb. 1787. 200 acres to Catharine Knight, widow.
Knight, Samuel. N.C. Private. 25 Oct. 1783. 274 acres.
Knight, William. Va. Private. 27 Nov. 1784. 100 acres.
Knight, William. Va. Private. 30 May 1831. 100 acres.
Knights, William. N. Y. Private. 8 Jul. 1790. 600 acres.
Knote, William. N.C. Lieutenant. 24 Oct. 1787. 1882 acres.
Knott, James. Md. Private. ———. 50 acres.
Knott, Nathaniel. Md. Private. ———. 50 acres.
Knowles, Richard. N.C. Private. 19 Jan. 1786. 640 acres.
Knowles, Timothy. Pa. Private. 31 Mar. 1787. 200 acres to Hannah Knowles, widow.
Knox, Allison. N.C. Private. 29 Sep. 1784. 640 acres to William Knox, heir.
Knox, Archibald. S.C. ———. 2 Mar. 1789. 200 acres.
Knox, George. Va. Private. 1 Dec. 1787. 100 acres.
Knox, James. Va. Major. 5 Dec. 1783. 5333 1/3 acres.
Knox, James. Va. Major. 1 Jun. 1805. 888 2/3 acres.
Knox, James. Va. Major. 29 Aug. 1807. 740 acres.
Knox, John. Md. Private. ———. 50 acres.
Knox, John. Md. Private. ———. 50 acres.
Knox, Jonathan. Me. Private. 8 Aug. 1838. 200 acres. Berwick.
Knox, Matthew. Pa. Lieutenant. 9 Jun. 1813. 200 acres.
Knox, Matthew. Pa. Lieutenant. 10 Jun. 1813. 200 acres.
Knox, Samuel. Ga. ———. 27 Apr. 1784. 650 acres.
Knox, Thomas. Va. Private. 2 Apr. 1784. 100 acres.
Knox, William. N.C. Captain. 29 Sep. 1784. 3840 acres to John Knox, heir.
Koch, Ludwick. Pa. ———. 16 Mar. 1803. 200 acres to Matthew Koch & Magdalena Keaffer, heirs.
Koen, Caleb. N.C. Lieutenant. 6 Sep. 1821. 2560 acres.
Koen, John. N.C. Corporal. 12 May 1784. 571 acres.
Kolb, George. Ga. ———. 27 Apr. 1784. 287 1/2 acres.
Kolb, Josiah. S.C. ———. 2 Oct. 1786. 200 acres.
Kolb, Peter. Ga. ———. 27 Apr. 1784. 287 1/2 acres.
Koockoojaei, Samuel. Pa. ———. 10 Mar. 1808. 200 acres.
Kook, Robert. Ga. Soldier. 4 Oct. 1785. ———.
Kouts, Jacob. Va. Private. 28 Jun. 1783. 233 1/3 acres.
Krack, Gotlib. N. Y. Private. 8 Jul. 1790. 600 acres.
Kramer, Francis. Pa. Private. ———. 200 acres.
Kronkhite, John. N. Y. Fifer. 8 Jul. 1790. 600 acres.
Kronkhite, Patrick. N. Y. Private. 8 Jul. 1790. 600 acres.
Kuhn, Christian. Pa. Dragoon. 7 Jun. 1787. 200 acres.
Kuntz, Henry. Pa. Private. 16 Jul. 1787. 200 acres.
Kurtz, Michael. Pa. Corporal. ———. 200 acres.
Kurz, Michael. Pa. Private. 16 Aug. 1787. 200 acres.

Kycenceder, Martin. Va. Private. 23 Jun. 1848. 100 acres.
Kycenceder, Martin. Va. Private. 23 Jun. 1848. 100 acres.
Kynion, William. N.Y. Sergeant. 13 Sep. 1790. 500 acres to heirs.
Labe, Francis. N. Y. ———. ———. 500 acres.
Labe, Joseph. N. Y. ———. ———. 500 acres.
Labelle, William. N. Y. ———. ———. 500 acres.
Labiel, Francis. N.C. Private. 17 Feb. 1824. 640 acres.
Labonte, John Baptiste. N. Y. Captain. ———. 1000 acres.
Labonte, John Baptiste. N. Y. ———. ———. 500 acres.
LaBonte, Pierre. N. Y. ———. ———. 500 acres.
Lacey, Joshua. S.C. Captain. 3 Apr. 1786. 300 acres.
Lackey, Christopher. N.C. Lieutenant. 7 Dec. 1802. 2560 acres.
Lackey, James. N. Y. Matross. 3 Jul. 1790. 600 acres.
Lackey, John. N.C. Private. 30 Sep. 1785. 640 acres to heirs.
Lackey, Robert. Pa. Private. 27 Jun. 1789. 200 acres.
Lackey, Thomas. Ga. ———. 15 Mar. 1784. 250 acres.
Lackey, William. Ga. Refugee. 15 Mar. 1784. 250 acres.
Lackhouse, Nicholas. Va. Private. 3 Nov. 1838. 200 acres.
Lackhouse, Nicholas. Va. Private. 27 Mar. 1855. 200 acres.
Lacklin, William. Ga. ———. 21 Apr. 1784. 250 acres.
Lackneir, John. N. Y. Matross. 9 Jul. 1790. 500 acres.
Lacky, Hugh. N. Y. Private. 8 Jul. 1790. 600 acres.
Lacron, John. Pa. Private. 7 Sep. 1787. 200 acres.
Lacy, Henry R. Va. Private. 17 Feb. 1784. 100 acres.
Lacy, John. Ga. Soldier. 7 Jun. 1785. 230 acres.
Lacy, John Richard. N.C. ———. 26 Dec. 1792. 852 acres.
Ladd, James. Va. Private. 9 Nov. 1808. 100 acres.
Ladley, William. Pa. Private. 13 Jan. 1787. 200 acres.
Ladow, Ambrose. N. Y. Matross. 9 Jul. 1790. 600 acres.
Lafferty, John. N. Y. Private. 3 Jul. 1790. 600 acres.
Lafferty, John. N.C. Private. 7 Sep. 1820. 274 acres.
LaFleur, Pierre. Va. Private. 10 Dec. 1838. 100 acres.
LaFleur, Pierre. Va. Private. 27 Mar. 1855. 100 acres.
LaFlour, Joseph. Va. Private. 14 Jul. 1835. 100 acres.
LaFlour, Paul. Va. Private. 31 Dec. 1851. 100 acres.
LaFlour, Paul. Va. Private. 21 Apr. 1856. 100 acres.
LaFlour, Pierre. Va. Private. 2 May 1856. 100 acres.
Laflure, John. N. Y. Matross. 9 Jul. 1790. 500 acres.
Lahaw, David. Va. Private. 20 Jun. 1783. 100 acres.
Lahaw, Jeremiah. Va. Private. 20 Jun. 1783. 100 acres.
Laighton, William. N.C. Private. 9 Nov. 1784. 274 acres.
Lain, Abram. N.C. Private. 30 Sep. 1785. 640 acres to heirs.
Lain, James. N.C. Private. 30 Sep. 1785. 640 acres to heirs.
Lain, Jethro. N.C. Private. 10 Jan. 1794. 640 acres to heir Jonathan Lain.
Lain, John. N.C. Sergeant. 3 Feb. 1795. 1000 acres to heirs.
Lain, William. N.C. Private. 10 Dec. 1788. 640 acres to heirs.
Laine, John. Va. Private. 5 Nov. 1811. 100 acres.
Laine, Thomas. N.C. Private. 2 Dec. 1785. 640 acres.
LaJennesse, Prudent. N. Y. ———. ———. 500 acres.
LaJeunesse, John Baptiste. N. Y. ———. ———. 500 acres.
LaLancett, John. N. Y. Private. 7 Jul. 1790. 600 acres.
Lamachs, Samuel. Ga. ———. 22 Apr. 1784. 287 1/2 acres.
Lamar, Basil. Ga. ———. 15 Mar. 1784. 250 acres.
Lamar, Benjamin. Ga. ———. 5 Sep. 1785. 575 acres.

Lamar, Gideon. Ga. Soldier. 5 Dec. 1785. ———.

Lamar, Joel. Ga. Private. 10 Dec. 1784. 250 acres.

Lamar, John. Ga. ———. 22 Apr. 1784. 287 1/2 acres.

Lamar, John. Ga. ———. 22 Apr. 1784. 1000 acres.

Lamar, Luke. Ga. Minute Man. 27 Apr. 1784. 287 1/2 acres.

Lamar, Samuel. Ga. ———. 15 Apr. 1784. 287 1/2 acres.

Lamar, Thomas. Ga. ———. 27 Apr. 1784. 287 1/2 acres.

Lamar, William. Ga. ———. 15 Apr. 1784. 287 1/2 acres.

Lamar, William. Md. Captain. ———. 200 acres.

Lamar, Zacheriah. Ga. Refugee. 15 Mar. 1784. 250 acres.

Lamarch, Beauvard. Va. Private. 2 May 1856. 100 acres.

Lamarch, Beauvard. Va. Private. 14 Jul. 1836. 100 acres.

Lamarch, Jacques. Va. Private. 31 Dec. 1851. 100 acres.

Lamarche, J. B. Va. Private. 2 May 1856. 100 acres.

Lamarche, Jacques. Va. Private. 9 Apr. 1856. 100 acres.

Lamarche, John B. Va. Private. 14 Jul. 1835. 100 acres.

Lamb, Abner. N.C. Lieutenant. 14 May 1784. 2560 acres.

Lamb, Abraham. Ga. ———. 21 Apr. 1784. 287 1/2 acres.

Lamb, Arthur. N. Y. Private. 8 Jul. 1790. 500 acres.

Lamb, B. C.[?]. Ga. ———. 26 May 1784. 287 1/2 acres to heirs.

Lamb, Gibbs. N.C. Private. 25 Oct. 1783. 640 acres.

Lamb, Gideon. N.C. Colonel. 21 May 1784. 6171 acres to heir.

Lamb, Gideon. N.C. Lieutenant Colonel. 19 Dec. 1803. 1029 acres to heirs.

Lamb, Isaac. N.Y. ———. 13 Sep. 1790. 500 acres to heirs.

Lamb, John. N. Y. Colonel. 7 Jul. 1790. 3000 acres.

Lamb, John. N.C. Private. 22 Apr. 1785. 640 acres to heirs.

Lamb, Joseph. Pa. Private. 9 Oct. 1786. 200 acres.

Lamb, Michael. Pa. Private. 7 Feb. 1789. 200 acres.

Lamb, Nathan. N.C. Private. 30 Sep. 1785. 640 acres to heirs.

Lambert, Abraham. N. Y. ———. 8 Oct. 1792. 600 acres.

Lambert, C. De. Pa. ———. ———. 200 acres.

Lambert, Charles. Va. Private. 6 Dec. 1785. 200 acres.

Lambert, Chevalier D. Pa. Lieutenant. 30 May 1787. 200 acres.

Lambert, Christopher. Md. Private. ———. 50 acres.

Lambert, George. Va. Captain. 21 May 1823. 4000 acres.

Lambert, Henry. N.C. Private. 1 Sep. 1785. 640 acres to heirs.

Lambert, John. N. Y. Private. 8 Jul. 1790. 600 acres.

Lambert, John. Va. Sergeant. 28 Apr. 1783. 400 acres.

Lambert, Ronald. N.C. Private. 15 Feb. 1797. 274 acres.

Lambert, Samuel. Conn. Sufferer. Danbury. 3.19.4.

Lamberth, Charles. Va. Private. 8 Sep. 1813. 100 acres.

Lambertson, Simon. N. Y. Private. 6 Jul. 1790. 600 acres.

Lambrecht, John. Ga. Refugee. 29 Jan. 1784. 250 acres.

Lambreck, James. N.C. Private. 30 Sep. 1785. 640 acres to heirs.

Lamkin, John. Va. Private. 21 Jan. 1786. 100 acres.

Lamkin, Peter. Va. Sergeant. 25 Jan. 1805. 200 acres.

Lamme, Nathan. Va. Captain. 30 Dec. 1785. 4000 acres.

Lamphier, James. Conn. Sufferer. New London. 233.9.0.

Lamphier, James, Jr. Conn. Sufferer. New London. 42.0.7.

Lampier, Francis. N. Y. Private. 3 Jul. 1790. 600 acres.

Lampkin, William. Va. Private. 8 Sep. 1812. 100 acres.

Lamrche, Lewis. Va. Private. 2 May 1856. 100 acres.

Lanahan, Darby. Md. Private. ———. 50 acres.

Lancaster, Joseph. Me. ———. 23 Apr. 1835. 200 acres. Richmond.

Lancaster, Levi. Ga. ———. 20 Apr. 1784. 287 1/2 acres.
Lancaster, Rowland. Ga. Soldier. 28 Sep. 1784. 230 acres to heirs.
Lancaster, William. Ga. ———. 15 Sep. 1784. 230 acres.
Land, Lewis. Va. Private. 20 Nov. 1785. 100 acres.
Land, Lewis. Va. Private. 15 Apr. 1853. 100 acres.
Landerkin, Daniel. Me. Marine. 27 Jan. 1838. 200 acres. Boothbay.
Landers, Abraham. Ga. ———. 15 Mar. 1784. 250 acres.
Landers, Jacob. Ga. Soldier. 15 Mar. 1784. 250 acres.
Landers, Jacob. Ga. Refugee. 27 Apr. 1784. 575 acres.
Landers, Roger. Md. Private. ———. 50 acres.
Landis, David. Pa. Private. ———. 200 acres.
Landman, Newman. Va. Private. 19 Feb. 1818. 100 acres.
Landrom, John. Ga. ———. 1784. 287 1/2 acres.
Landrom, Josiah. Ga. Soldier. 7 Jun. 1785. 230 acres.
Landrom, Zachariah. Ga. ———. 30 Jul. 1784. 287 1/2 acres.
Landrum, Samuel. Va. Sergeant. 12 Dec. 1796. 400 acres.
Landrum, Thomas. Va. Private. 26 May 1783. 100 acres.
Landrum, Thomas. Va. Surgeon's Mate. 19 Mar. 1834. 4000 acres.
Landwick, William. Va. Private. 3 Mar. 1784. 200 acres.
Lane, Charles. Ga. ———. 19 Apr. 1784. 350 acres.
Lane, Ebenezer. Mass. Private. 19 Nov. 1832. 200 acres.
Lane, Jacob. N.C. Private. 28 May 1784. 274 acres.
Lane, James. Ga. Soldier. 17 Jan. 1785. 230 acres.
Lane, James. Pa. Private. 11 Oct. 1786. 200 acres.
Lane, James. Va. Quartermaster Sergeant. 23 Jun. 1783. 400 acres.
Lane, James. Conn. Sufferer. New/East Haven. 9.6.10.
Lane, Jesse. N.C. Private. 14 May 1784. 640 acres.
Lane, John. Me. ———. 23 May 1835. 200 acres. Buxton.
Lane, John. Va. Private. 31 Dec. 1851. 100 acres.
Lane, Joseph. Ga. Major. 31 Dec. 1783. 800 acres.
Lane, Richard. Ga. ———. 19 Apr. 1784. 600 acraes.
Lane, Thomas. Ga. Refugee. 24 Jan. 1784. 250 acres.
Lane, Thomas. N.C. Private. 29 Sep. 1784. 274 acres.
Lane, Timothy. Pa. Corporal. 5 Sep. 1789. 200 acres.
Lane, William. Ga. Soldier. ———. 230 acres to heirs.
Lane, William. Mass. Matross. 10 Sep. 1832. 200 acres.
Lane, Zachariah. Va. Private. 22 Nov. 1783. 100 acres.
Lang, Alexander. Va. Boatswain. 26 Feb. 1831. 2666 2/3 acres.
Lang, John. Ga. ———. 17 May 1784. ———.
Lang—, Samuel. N.C. Private. 10 Feb. 1796. 640 acres to heirs.
Langbourn, William. Va. Major. 17 Nov. 1824. 6224 acres.
Langdon, Benjamin. N. Y. Private. 8 Jul. 1790. 600 acres.
Langdon, Jonathan. Va. Captain. 31 May 1839. 4000 acres.
Langfit, Philip. Va. Private. 18 Apr. 1823. 233 1/3 acres.
Langfitt, Philip. Va. Private. 23 Oct. 1783. 100 acres.
Langfitt, Thomas. Va. Private. 23 Oct. 1783. 100 acres.
Langford, Daniel. S.C. ———. 2 Oct. 1786. 200 acres.
Langford, Euclid. Va. Private. 24 May 1783. 100 acres.
Langford, John. Ga. ———. 17 May 1784. ———.
Langford, Jonathan. Ga. 18 Jun. 1784. 287 1/2 acres.
Langford, Joseph. Ga. ———. 17 May 1784. ———.
Langford, Peter. N.C. Private. 12 Sep. 1785. 640 acres to heirs.
Langham, Elias. Va. Lieutenant. 15 Jul. 1783. 2666 2/3 acres.
Langham, Elias. Va. Lieutenant. 19 Aug. 1809. 333 1/3 acres.

Langrel, Timothy. Md. Private. ———. 50 acres.
Langsdon, Charles. Va. Private. 16 Sep. 1785. 200 acres.
Langsdon, Daniel. Va. Private. 16 Sep. 1785. 200 acres.
Langsdon, William. Va. Private. 16 Sep. 1785. 200 acres.
Langston, Elisha. N.C. Private. 20 Jan. 1785. 640 acres to heirs.
Langston, George. Va. Private. 24 Jan. 1817. 100 acres.
Langston, John. N.C. Private. 10 Aug. 1785. 640 acres to heirs.
Langston, Josiah. N.C. Private. 1 Sep. 1785. 640 acres to heirs.
Langston, Samuel. Ga. ———. 27 Apr. 1784. 287 1/2 acres.
Langston, Timothy. Va. Private. 5 Dec. 1833. 200 acres.
Langston, William. Va. Private. 17 Feb. 1786. 100 acres.
Langton, David. Ga. Soldier. 4 Feb. 1785. ———.
Langworthy, Edward. Ga. ———. 27 Apr. 1784. 1000 acres.
Lanham, Kinsey. Md. Private. ———. 50 acres.
Lanier, Benjamin. Ga. Refugee. 1784. 250 acres.
Lanier, Clement. Ga. Refugee. 6 Feb. 1784. 500 acres.
Lanier, James. N.C. Ensign. 3 Mar. 1784. 2560 acres.
Lanier, Lemuel. Ga. Refugee. 1784. 250 acres.
Lanier, Peter. N.C. Private. 30 Sep. 1785. 640 acres to heirs.
Lanier, Robert. N.C. Private. 12 Sep. 1785. 640 acres to heirs.
Lanier, Samuel. Ga. ———. 17 May 1784. ———.
Lanier, Thomas. Va. Ensign. 8 Jul. 1808. 1250 acres.
Lanier, Thomas. Va. Ensign. 8 Jul. 1808. 1416 2/3 acres.
Lanieve, Samuel. Va. Sergeant. 25 Apr. 1837. 333 1/3 acres.
Lank, John. Va. Private. 9 Dec. 1783. 100 acres.
Lankford, Josiah. Ga. ———. 17 May 1784. 230 acres.
Lankford, Moses. Ga. Soldier. 17 May 1784. 230 acres.
Lanon, James. N.C. Private. 22 Dec. 1796. 274 acres.
Lansdale, Thomas. Md. Major. ———. 200 acres.
Lansing, Garret. N. Y. Ensign. 9 Jul. 1790. 1150 acres.
Lantern, Thomas. Ga. ———. 23 Apr. 1784. 287 1/2 acres.
Laperche, Louis. Va. Private. 31 Dec. 1851. 100 acres.
Laperche, Louis. Va. Private. 21 Apr. 1856. 100 acres.
Laperche, Peter. Va. Private. 31 Dec. 1851. 100 acres.
Laperche, Peter. Va. Private. 9 Apr. 1856. 100 acres.
Lapeure, Francis. Va. Private. 31 Dec. 1851. 100 acres.
Lapeure, Francis. Va. Private. 21 Apr. 1856. 100 acres.
Lapine, Paul. Md. Private. ———. 50 acres.
Lapsely, Samuel. Va. Captain. 23 Apr. 1783. 4000 acres.
Lapsley, John. Va. Lieutenant. 23 Apr. 1783. 2666 2/3 acres.
Lara, James. Me. ———. 28 Jun. 1835. 200 acres. Turner.
Laramore, John. Ga. ———. 22 Apr. 1784. 250 acres.
Lard, Lemon. N.C. Private. 9 Dec. 1797. 640 acres to heirs.
Lardner, Edward. Pa. ———. ———. 200 acres.
Largrent, James. Va. Private. 21 Dec. 1784. 100 acres.
Larkin, Edward. Va. Private. 24 Mar. 1787. 200 acres.
Larkins, Edward. Conn. Sufferer. New/East Haven. 21.3.0.
Larkins, James. Pa. ———. 4 Apr. 1803. 250 acres.
Larkins, Stephen. N.C. Private. 5 Dec. 1796. 274 acres.
Larner, Robert. Pa. Private. 6 Dec. 1786. 200 acres.
LaRochella, Michael. Va. Private. 2 Jun. 1788. 100 acres.
Larouse, Joshua. N.C. Private. 9 Sep. 1785. 640 acres to heirs.
Larrabee, Jonathan. Mass. ———. 10 Jun. 1828. 200 acres to assignee John P. Dundee.

Larraby, Elias. N. Y. Private. 7 Jul. 1790. 500 acres.
Larrimore, John. N.C. Private. 17 Dec. 1796. 640 acres to heirs.
Larrimore, Marmaduke. N.C. Private. 12 Oct. 1795. 640 acres to heirs.
Larrimore, Thomas. Md. Private. ———. 50 acres.
Larrimore, William. N.C. Private. 14 Dec. 1796. 640 acres to heirs.
Larty, John. Va. Captain. 24 Jan. 1784. 4000 acres.
Lasceteer, Josiah. N.C. Private. 19 Jan. 1786. 640 acres.
Lasciter, Shadrach. N.C. Lieutenant. 6 Jan. 1784. 731 acres.
Lasdell, Asa. Me. Private. 12 May 1835. 200 acres. Burnham.
Laselle, James. N. Y. Matross. 9 Jul. 1790. 500 acres.
Lasitur, James. N.C. Sergeant. 1 Dec. 1796. 1000 acres.
Laslie, John. Pa. Private. 20 Oct. 1787. 200 acres.
Lasouch, Louis. N. Y. ———. ———. 500 acres.
Lassell, Caleb. Me. ———. 14 May 1835. 200 acres. Waterboro.
Lassister, Jethro. N.C. Lieutenant. 5 Sep. 1821. 2560 acres.
Lassiter, Benjamin. Va. Private. 21 Jan. 1834. 100 acres.
Lassiter, Dempsey. Va. Private. 21 Jan. 1834. 100 acres.
Lassiter, Jacob. N.C. ———. 29 Apr. 1784. 640 acres to Demsey Lassiter, heir.
Lassiter, Samuel. N.C. Private. 30 Sep. 1785. 640 acres to heirs.
Lassiter, Thaddeus. S.C. ———. 4 Jul. 1785. 200 acres.
Lassiter, Thomas. N.C. Private. 29 Apr. 1784. 640 acres.
Laster, James. N.C. Private. 30 Sep. 1785. 640 acres to heirs.
Laster, Josiah. N.C. Private. 30 Sep. 1785. 640 acres to heirs.
Lath, Abner. N.C. Private. 19 Jan. 1786. 640 acres.
Latham, A., Widow. Conn. Sufferer. Groton. 36.19.0.
Latham, Edward, Capt. Conn. Sufferer. Groton. 4.8.7.
Latham, Elizabeth. Conn. Sufferer. Groton. 15.12.6.
Latham, John. Conn. Sufferer. Groton. 94.18.9.
Latham, Jonathan. Conn. Sufferer. Groton. 3.4.8.
Latham, Lydia. Conn. Sufferer. Groton. 92.4.6.
Latham, Mary. Conn. Sufferer. Groton. 4.0.0.
Latham, Phineas. N.C. Sergeant. 21 Apr. 1784. 1000 acres.
Latham, William, Capt. Conn. Sufferer. Groton. 45.2.2.
Lathers, Ezekiel. N. Y. Private. 8 Jul. 1790. 500 acres.
Lathrop, John. Conn. Sufferer. New/East Haven. 71.17.2
Lathrop, John. Conn. Sufferer. New London. 1.11.9.
Latimer, Henry. Va. Private. 5 Jan. 1786. 200 acres.
Laton, John. Md. Private. ———. 50 acres.
Laton, John. N.C. ———. 21 Apr. 1784. 640 acres to William Laton, heir.
Lattemore, Edward. Va. Lieutenant. 16 Mar. 1847. 666 2/3 acres.
Lattimer, Lydia. Conn. Sufferer. New London. 27.8.6.
Lattimer, Peter. Conn. Sufferer. New London. 317.1.6.
Lattimer, Pickett. Conn. Sufferer. New London. 565.7.8.
Lattimer, Richard. Conn. Sufferer. New London. 26.19.8.
Lattimer, Samuel. Conn. Sufferer. New London. 910.19.5.
Lattimer, Samuel. Conn. Sufferer. New London. 24.7.6.
Lattimore, Edward. Va. Lieutenant. 24 Apr. 1838. 2666 2/3 acres.
Lattimore, Edward. Va. Lieutenant. 24 Apr. 1838. 666 2/3 acres.
Lattimore, Edward. Va. Lieutenant. 24 Apr. 1838. 666 2/3 acres.
Lattimore, Matthew. Va. Private. 27 Nov. 1792. 200 acres.
Lattimore, Richard. Pa. Matross. ———. 200 acres.
Latuma, Joseph. N. Y. ———. ———. 500 acres.
Lauderdale, John. Ga. Refugee. 26 May 1784. 287 1/2 acres.

Laughingham, Thomas. N.C. Private. 17 Dec. 1807. 274 acres to heirs.
Laughlin, Cornelius. N.C. Private. 10 Feb. 1796. 640 acres to heirs.
Laughlin, John M. Md. Private. ———. 50 acres.
Laughlin, Richard. N.C. Fifer. 22 Dec. 1796. 1000 acres to heirs.
Laurance, Nathaniel. N.C. Lieutenant. 10 Aug. 1785. 2560 acres.
Laurance, Zebulon. N.C. Private. 17 Dec. 1796. 320 acres.
Laurence, John. Va. Private. 1 Mar. 1806. 200 acres.
Laurence, John. Va. Private. 17 May 1834. 100 acres.
Laurence, Joshua. N.C. Private. 30 Sep. 1785. 640 acres to heirs.
Laurence, Nathaniel. N.C. Private. 29 Nov. 1783. 2560 acres.
Laurence, Peter. Md. Matross. ———. 50 acres.
Laurence, Thomas. Va. Sergeant. 21 May 1783. 200 acres.
Laurence, William. Va. Private. 21 Jan. 1834. 100 acres.
Laurent, Joseph. N. Y. ———. ———. 500 acres.
Lavender, John. Md. Private. ———. 50 acres.
Lavers, Richard. Pa. Private. 18 Oct. 1794. 200 acres.
Lavery, James. N.C. Private. 11 Feb. 1796. 640 acres to heirs.
Lavis, Thomas D. Conn. Sufferer. Groton. 0.13.10.
Lavyne, Jacque. N. Y. ———. ———. 500 acres.
Law, Ezekiel. Pa. Private. 30 Dec. 1786. 200 acres.
Law, France. N.C. Non Commissioned Officer. 19 May 1784. 1000 acres.
Law, George. Ga. Private. 22 Mar. 1785. 287 1/2 acres.
Law, Gilbert. S.C. ———. 5 Nov. 1792. 200 acres to heir at law, Richard Law.
Lawell, Thomas. Va. Steward. 20 Jan. 1834. 2666 2/3 acres.
Lawler, Michael. Md. Private. ———. 50 acres.
Lawless, Austin. Va. Private. 23 Jun. 1783. 100 acres.
Lawless, Austin. Va. Private. 20 Dec. 1786. 100 acres.
Lawless, Austin. Va. Private. 14 Dec. 1833. 100 acres.
Lawless, Matthew. N.C. Private. 26 Aug. 1785. 640 acres to heirs.
Lawrecy, Daniel. N.C. Private. 30 Sep. 1785. 640 acres to heirs.
Lawrence, Benjamin. N. Y. Sergeant. 8 Jul. 1790. 600 acres.
Lawrence, Jacob. N. Y. Private. 6 Jul. 1790. 500 acres.
Lawrence, John. Ga. ———. 17 May 1784. ———.
Lawrence, John. Me. Private. 29 Jan. 1836. 200 acres. North Yarmouth.
Lawrence, John. Pa. Private. 7 Nov. 1786. 200 acres.
Lawrence, Jonathan, Jr. N.Y. Lieutenant. 13 Sep. 1790. 1200 acres.
Lawrence, Peter. Ga. Minute Man. 3 Apr. 1785. ———.
Lawrence, Rosman. Conn. Sufferer. New London. 54.0.0.
Laws, David. N.C. Private. 23 Apr. 1784. 640 acres.
Laws, George. Md. Private. ———. 50 acres.
Laws, Henry. Md. Private. ———. 50 acres.
Laws, John. N.C. Sergeant. 11 Jan. 1822. 1000 acres to heirs.
Laws, Richard. N.C. Private. 23 Dec. 1792. 274 acres.
Laws, Timothy. Va. ———. 20 Jun. 1838. 296 acres.
Laws, Timothy. Va. ———. 20 Jun. 1838. 148 acres.
Laws, Timothy. Va. Gunner. 4 May 1838. 1185 acres.
Laws, Timothy. Va. Gunner. 3 Apr. 1860. 1185 acres.
Laws, Timothy. Va. Gunner. 4 May 1838. 592 acres.
Laws, Timothy. Va. Gunner. 3 Apr. 1860. 296 acres.
Laws, Timothy. Va. Gunner. 13 Nov. 1843. 222 2/9 acres.
Laws, Timothy. Va. Gunner. 13 Nov. 1843. 222 2/9 acres.
Laws, William. Md. Private. ———. 50 acres.
Lawson, Andrew. Ga. Refugee. 20 Feb. 1784. 250 acres.
Lawson, Andrew. Ga. Private. 16 Apr. 1784. 287 1/2 acres to heirs.

Lawson, Andrew. Va. Private. 13 May 1783. 100 acres.
Lawson, Benjamin. Va. Lieutenant. 1 Jan. 1782. 2666 2/3 acres.
Lawson, Benjamin. Va. Private. 11 Mar. 1784. 100 acres.
Lawson, Benjamin. Va. Lieutenant. 14 Feb. 1840. 166 1/2 acres.
Lawson, Claiborne. Va. Captain. 1 Jan. 1783. 4000 acres.
Lawson, Henry. Va. Private. 19 Jan. 1785. 100 acres.
Lawson, Hugh. Ga. Soldier. 18 Oct. 1783. 250 acres.
Lawson, Hugh. Ga. Captain. 26 Dec. 1783. 500 acres.
Lawson, John. N.C. Private. 25 Jun. 1785. 274 acres.
Lawson, John. Va. Private. 3 Mar. 1784. 200 acres.
Lawson, John, Sr. Ga. Refugee Private. 26 Jun. 1784. 250 acres.
Lawson, John, Sr. Va. Private. 10 May 1784. 100 acres.
Lawson, Richard. N.C. Private. 4 Sep. 1820. 640 acres to heirs.
Lawson, Robert. Va. Briagdier General. 20 Nov. 1783. 10,000 acres.
Lawson, Roger, Jr. Ga. Refugee. 20 Feb. 1784. 250 acres.
Lawson, Thomas. Ga. Soldier. 16 Apr. 1784. 287 1/2 acres.
Lawson, William. N.C. Private. 26 Aug. 1785. 640 acres to heirs.
Lawyer, Christopher. N. Y. Private. 8 Jul. 1790. 500 acres.
Laydon, Thomas. N.C. Private. 21 May 1784. 274 acres.
Layman, William. Pa. Private. 4 Jan. ——. 200 acres.
Layne, John. Va. Private. 28 Jun. 1783. 200 acres.
Layne, John. Va. Midshipman. 28 Jul. 1834. 2666 2/3 acres.
Layne, John. Va. Midshipman. 17 Mar. 1836. 1333 1/3 acres.
Layne, John. Va. Midshipman. 17 Mar. 1836. 1333 1/3 acres.
Layne, Josiah. Va. Private. 14 Feb. 1784. 100 acres.
Layne, William. Va. Private. 26 Feb. 1785. 100 acres.
Layton, Reuben. Va. Private. 20 Apr. 1784. 100 acres.
Layton, Robert. Va. Captain. 19 Dec. 1831. 400 acres.
Lazarus, Frederick. Pa. Private. 19 Nov. 1788. 200 acres to Walter Stewart, assignee.
Lazarus, Nicholas. Ga. Private. 21 Apr. 1784. 200 acres.
Lazear, Hayette. Va. Private. 21 Mar. 1807. 200 acres.
Leach, Andrew. Va. Private. 24 Mar. 1831. 100 acres.
Leach, Christopher. N. Y. Matross. 9 Jul. 1790. 600 acres.
Leach, George. Va. Private. 30 Mar. 1831. 100 acres.
Leach, Valentine. Va. Sergeant. 23 Mar. 1818. 200 acres.
Leach, William. Va. Private. 24 Jan. 1809. 200 acres.
Leach, William. Va. Private. 24 Jan. 1809. 200 acres.
Leadingham, Isaac. N.C. Private. 13 Jan. 1792. 274 acres.
Leadon, John. N.C. ———. 29 Apr. 1784. 640 acres to Robert Leadon, heir.
Leago, Charles. Md. Private. ———. 50 acres.
League, James. Va. Private. 14 Aug. 1783. 200 acres.
Leakins, William. Md. Private. ———. 50 acres.
Leaming, Pomp. Conn. Sufferer. Norwalk. 14.10.0.
Lean, Charles. Ga. ———. 17 May 1784. ———.
Leapham, Abraham. Ga. ———. 17 May 1784. ———.
Leapham, Frederick. Ga. Lieutenant. 22 Apr. 1784. 460 acres.
Leapham, Moses. Ga. ———. 27 Apr. 1784. 287 1/2 acres.
Lear, George. Va. Private. 18 Nov. 1784. 200 acres.
Lear, John. Va. Private. 24 Jan. 1784. 200 acres.
Leare, William. Va.-Ind. Private. 108 acres.
Learey, Keadey. N.Y. ———. 13 Sep. 1790. 500 acres to heirs.
Learned, Amasa. Conn. Sufferer. New London. 18.1.0.
Learwood, Josiah. Va. Private. 11 Aug. 1783. 100 acres.
Leary, Dennis. Md. Private. ———. 50 acres.

Leary, Patrick. N.C. Private. 10 Dec. 1788. 640 acres to heirs.
Leary, William. Pa. Private. 2 Jan. 1787. 200 acres.
Leath, James. Ga. ———. 20 Apr. 1784. 287 1/2 acres.
Leath, John. Ga. ———. 27 Apr. 1784. 287 1/2 acres.
Leath, Peter. Va. Private. 19 Oct. 1785. 100 acres.
Leatham, John. N.Y. ———. 13 Sep. 1790. 500 acres to heirs.
Leathers, Moses. N.C. Corporal. 20 Sep. 1784. 357 acres.
Leava, Lewis. Va. Private. 27 Mar. 1855. 200 acres.
Leava, Louis. Va. Private. 3 Nov. 1838. 200 acres.
Leavenworth, Jesse. Conn. Sufferer. New/East Haven. 143.9.0.
Leavenworth, Mark. Conn. Sufferer. New/East Haven. 7.1.6.
Leavitt, William. Me. Private. 20 May 1839. 200 acres to Betsey Levitt. Alfred.
Leaycraft, George. N, Y. Lieutenant. 9 Jul. 1790. 1200 acres.
Leaycraft, William. N. Y. Lieutenant. 9 Jul. 1790. 1200 acres.
LeBumbard, Joseph. N. Y. ———. ———. 500 acres.
LeClive, Francis. N. Y. ———. ———. 500 acres.
Leconte, Lewis. Va. Private. 31 Dec. 1851. 100 acres.
Leconte, Lewis. Va. Private. 21 Apr. 1856. 100 acres.
Lecotte, Francis. N. Y. ———. ———. 500 acres.
Lecotte, John. N. Y. ———. ———. 500 acres.
LeCroise, Michael. N. Y. ———. ———. 500 acres.
Ledbetter, Frederick. Ga. ———. 20 Feb. 1784. 250 acres.
Ledbetter, John. Ga. Refugee. 25 May 1784. 287 1/2 acres.
Ledington, Peter. Md. Private. ———. 50 acres.
Ledyard, Anne. Conn. Sufferer. Groton. 142.7.10.
Ledyard, Benjamin & Caleb Ledyard. Conn. Sufferers. Groton. 200.0.0.
Ledyard, Bridgett. Conn. Sufferer. Groton. 397.14.5.
Ledyard, Ebenezer. Conn. Sufferer. Groton. 1,151.3.4.
Ledyard, Isaac. N.Y. Physician & Surgeon. 26 Sep. 1792. 2400 acres.
Ledyard, Youngs. Conn. Sufferer. Groton. 75.0.0 to his heirs.
Lee, Andrew. Ga. Refugee. 25 Feb. 1784. 250 acres.
Lee, Andrew. Pa. Private. 6 Apr. 1787. 200 acres.
Lee, Andrew. Pa. Lieutenant. 6 Apr. 1787. 200 acres.
Lee, Andrew. Va. Private. 14 Feb. 1834. 100 acres.
Lee, Bartlett. Va. Private. 27 Jul. 1792. 200 acres.
Lee, Bryan. N.C. Private. 17 Feb. 1824. 640 acres.
Lee, Charles. N.C. Private. 17 Feb. 1824. 640 acres.
Lee, Charles. Va. Major General. 20 Feb. 1834. 3750 acres.
Lee, Charles. Va. Major General. 20 Feb. 1834. 1875 acres.
Lee, Charles. Va. Major General. 20 Feb. 1834. 1875 acres.
Lee, Charles. Va. Major General. 20 Feb. 1834. 1875 acres.
Lee, Charles. Va. Major General. 20 Feb. 1834. 1875 acres.
Lee, Charles. Va. Major General. 20 Feb. 1834. 2812 1/2 acres.
Lee, Charles. Va. Major General. 20 Feb. 1834. 2812 1/2 acres.
Lee, Daniel. N. Y. Private. 8 Jul. 1790. 600 acres.
Lee, Dudley. Md. Private. ———. 50 acres.
Lee, Edgcomb. Conn. Sufferer. New London. 48.4.7.
Lee, Edward. Pa. Private. 12 Sep. 1787. 200 acres to William Lee, administrator.
Lee, Edward. Pa. Sergeant. 3 Apr. 1805. 250 acres to heirs.
Lee, Edward. Va. Private. 26 Apr. 1783. 200 acres.
Lee, Gilbert. Ga. ———. 23 Apr. 1784. 287 1/2 acres.
Lee, Greenbury. Ga. ———. 15 Mar. 1784. 250 acres.
Lee, Hardy. N.C. Private. 30 Sep. 1785. 640 acres to heirs.

Lee, Henry. Va. Lieutenant Colonel Commandant. 30 Oct. 1783. 7777 2/3 acres.
Lee, Henry. Va. Lieutenant Colonel Commandant. 3 Jul. 1807. 462 2/3 acres.
Lee, James. Pa. Private. 9 Jul. 1787. 200 acres.
Lee, James. Va. Private. 20 Aug. 1783. 100 acres.
Lee, James. Va. Private. 4 Jan. 1785. 100 acres.
Lee, James. Va. Private. 3 May 1822. 100 acres.
Lee, Jeptha. N. Y. Matross. 9 Jul. 1790. 600 acres.
Lee, Jeremiah. Md. Private. ———. 50 acres.
Lee, Jesse. N.C. Private. 12 Sep. 1785. 640 acres to heirs.
Lee, Jesse. Va. Private. 1 Jul. 1784. 100 acres.
Lee, John. Md. Private. ———. 50 acres.
Lee, John. N.Y. ———. 13 Sep. 1790. 500 acres to heirs.
Lee, John. N.C. Private. 19 May 1784. 640 acres.
Lee, John. Va. Major. 29 Apr. 1783. 5333 1/3 acres.
Lee, John. Va. Private. 22 May 1784. 100 acres.
Lee, John. Va. Corporal. 5 Oct. 1789. 200 acres.
Lee, John. Va. Private. 29 Jun. 1784. 100 acres.
Lee, Joseph. N. Y. Matross. 9 Jul. 1790. 600 acres.
Lee, Joshua. Ga. ———. 15 Mar. 1784. 250 acres.
Lee, Peter. N.C. Private. 28 Sep. 1785. 274 acres to heirs.
Lee, Peter. Va. Private. 8 Nov. 1790. 100 acres.
Lee, Philip Richard Francis. Va. Captain. 27 Mar. 1840. 164 2/3 acres.
Lee, Philip Richard Francis. Va. Captain. 27 Mar. 1840. 184 2/3 acres.
Lee, Philip Richard Francis. Va. Captain. 27 Mar. 1840. 174 1/3 acres.
Lee, Philip Richard Francis. Va. Captain. 21 Jun. 1784. 4000 acres.
Lee, Philip Richard Francis. Va. Captain. 1 Oct. 1798. 4000 acres.
Lee, Philip Richard Francis. Va. Captain. 25 Jan. 1847. 61 2/3 acres.
Lee, Philip Richard Francis. Va. Captain. 25 Jan. 1847. 30 5/6 acres.
Lee, Randolph. Va. Private. 14 Nov. 1783. 100 acres.
Lee, Richard. Ga. Soldier. 3 May 1785. 230 acres.
Lee, Richard. Va. Private. 12 Jul. 1783. 200 acres.
Lee, Richard Francis. Va. Captain. 16 Oct. 1846. 123 1/3 acres.
Lee, Richeson. Va. Corporal. 23 Oct. 1783. 200 acres.
Lee, Simmons. Va. Private. 23 Jun. 1784. 100 acres.
Lee, Thomas. N. Y. Captain. 9 Jul. 1790. 1500 acres.
Lee, Timothy. Ga. Refugee. 19 Jul. 1784. 287 1/2 acres.
Lee, Timothy. N.C. Private. 30 Sep. 1785. 640 acres to heirs.
Lee, William. Md. Private. ———. 50 acres.
Lee, William. Md. Private. ———. 50 acres.
Lee, William. N. Y. Corporal. 7 Jul. 1790. 600 acres.
Lee, William. N.C. Musician. 11 May 1812. 1000 acres to heirs.
Lee, William. Pa. Sergeant. 12 Apr. 1794. 250 acres.
Lee, William. Conn. Sufferer. Greenwich. 7.10.0.
Leech, George. Va. Private. 4 Oct. 1783. 100 acres.
Leech, James. Pa. Private. 14 Jun. 1805. 200 acres to Henry Leech, heir.
Leech, John. N.C. Private. 19 May 1784. 640 acres.
Leech, Joseph. S.C. ———. 7 Apr. 1794. 200 acres.
Leeds, Anne. Conn. Sufferer. Groton. 57.15.2.
Leeds, Edward Dickson. Ga. ———. 17 May 1784. ———
Leeds, William. Conn. Sufferer. Groton. 360.7.8.
Leedum, John. N.C. Ensign. 16 Aug. 1821. 2560 acres.
Leek, Henry. N.C. Private. 7 Jan. 1786. 640 acres to heirs.
Leet, Daniel. Va. Brigadier General. 5 May 1838. 5333 1/3 acres.

Leet, Mehitabel. Conn. Sufferer. New London. 124.0.0.
Leethizer, George. Pa. Private. 2 Aug. 1804. 200 acres to Catharine Leethizer, widow.
Leetor, Andrew. N.C. Private. 2 Feb. 1786. 640 acres.
Lefecy, Shadrach. Va. Private. 13 May 1785. 100 acres.
Leffingwell, Christopher. Conn. Sufferer. New London. 25.0.0.
LeFountaine, Joseph. N. Y. ———. ———. 500 acres.
LeFrais, Peter. N. Y. ———. ———. 500 acres.
LeFrambois, Nicholas. N. Y. ———. ———. 500 acres.
LeFramboise, Jacque. N. Y. ———. ———. 500 acres.
LeFramboise, John Baptiste. N. Y. ———. ———. 500 acres.
LeFramboise, John Baptiste, Jr. N. Y. ———. ———. 500 acres.
Leftwich, Joel. Va. Private. 22 Sep. 1783. 100 acres.
Leftwich, John. Va. Sergeant. 21 May 1784. 200 acres.
Lega [alias Leagea], Peter. Pa. ———. ———. 200 acres.
Legare, James. N.C. Private. 27 May 1784. 365 acres.
Legare, James. S.C. Lieutenant. 21 Jan. 1785. 200 acres.
Legg, Edward. Md. Private. ———. 50 acres.
Legg, John. Va. Private. 15 May 1783. 100 acres.
Legg, Robert. Md. Private. ———. 50 acres.
Legget, Abraham. N. Y. Lieutenant. 9 Jul. 1790. 1200 acres.
Legget, Elias. S.C. ———. 4 Jul. 1785. 200 acres.
Leggett, Abner. Ga. Refugee. 15 Mar. 1784. 250 acres.
Leggett, Elisha. N.C. Private. 30 Sep. 1785. 640 acres to heirs.
Leggett, John. Ga. Minute Man. 27 Apr. 1784. 287 1/2 acres.
Leggit, Owen. Va. Private. 1 May 1783. 200 acres.
Leglise, Dominique. N. Y. ———. ———. 500 acres.
Legrave, Michael. Va. Private. 31 Dec. 1851. 100 acres.
Legrave, Michael. Va. Private. 21 Apr. 1856. 100 acres.
Leigh, Benjamin. Ga. ———. 17 Apr. 1784. 450 acres.
Leigh, John. Va. Sergeant. 15 Feb. 1783. 200 acres.
Leigh, John. Va. Lieutenant. 20 Feb. 1784. 2466 2/3 acres.
Leigh, Lewis. N.C. Sergeant. 4 Sep. 1820. 1000 acres to heirs.
Leigh, Walter. Ga. ———. 13 Apr. 1784. 400 acres.
Leighton, William. N.C. Private. 16 Mar. 1795. 640 acres to heirs.
Leisner, George. Mass. Corporal. 30 Nov. 1835. 200 acres to his heirs Charles Leisner, William Leisner, George Leisner, Caleb Leisner, James Leisner, Mary Leisner, Ruth Benner, and Catharine Groton.
Leister, Joshua. Md. Private. ———. 50 acres.
Leitch, Andrew. Va. Major. 29 Jun. 1784. 5333 1/3 acres.
Leitch, Andrew. Va. Major. 16 Mar. 1840. 1554 acres.
Leitch, George. Va. Sergeant. 8 Nov. 1786. 200 acres.
Leitch, James. Va. Corporal. 24 Sep. 1783. 400 acres.
Leitchfield, Thomas. Va. Sailor. 7 Dec. 1830. 100 acres.
Leland, Ebenezer. Me. Ensign. 13 Aug. 1835. 200 acres to widow Mary Leland. Castine.
Leland, Francis. Pa. Private. 29 Mar. 1805. 200 acres.
Leland, Henry. Me. ———. 27 Apr. 1838. 200 acres to widow Sarah Leland. Sangerville.
Leman, Dedrick. Va. Private. 4 Dec. 1783. 100 acres.
Lemarche, Lewis. Va. Private. 14 Jul. 1835. 100 acres.
Lemare, Lewis. N.C. Private. 30 Sep. 1785. 274 acres.
Lemaster, James. Va. Private. 1 Apr. 1784. 100 acres.
LeMaster, Joseph. Va. Sergeant. 20 Nov.1814. 200 acres.
Lemay, John. Va. Private. 2 Jan. 1786. 100 acres.

Lemmon, Barney. Md. Private. ———. 50 acres.
Lemmon, Ephraim. N.C. Private. Jan. 1795. 640 acres to heirs.
Lemmon, Francis. Mass. Matross. 30 Dec. 1831. 200 acres to his brother Samuel Lemmon.
Lemmon, James. Va. Captain. 13 Apr. 1838. 1723 1/3 acres.
Lemmon, James. Va. Captain. 13 Apr. 1838. 1723 1/3 acres.
Lemmon, James. Va. Captain. 13 Apr. 1838. ——— acres.
Lemmon, James. Va. Captain. 13 Apr. 1838. 689 acres.
Lemmon, James. Va. Captain. 13 Apr. 1838. 689 acres.
Lemmon, James. Va. Captain. 13 Apr. 1838. 690 acres.
Lemmon, James. Va. Captain. 13 Apr. 1838. 689 acres.
Lemmon, John. Pa. Private. 21 Oct. 1786. 200 acres.
Lemmon, John. Va. Private. 6 Aug. 1784. 200 acres.
Lemmon, Samuel. Va. Private. 23 Jun. 1783. 200 acres.
Lemon, Ephraim. N.C. ———. 20 Apr. 1784. 1000 acres to heir.
Lemon, John. Va.-Ind. Private. 108 acres.
Lemon, Michael. Pa. Private. 1 Feb. 1787. 200 acres.
Lemon, William. N. Y. Matross. 9 Jul. 1790. 600 acres.
Lemot, Edward. Ga. ———. 2 May 1785. ———.
LeNashu, John. Md. Lieutenant. ———. 200 acres.
Lenn, Thomas. Ga. ———. 1 Oct. 1784. 287 1/2 acres.
Lennis, Francis. Va. Lieutenant. 24 Mar. 1834. 4000 acres.
Lenoir, Charles. N.C. Private. 10 Feb. 1796. 640 acres to heirs.
Lenoir, Thomas, Jr. N.C. Private. 10 Feb. 1796. 640 acres to heirs.
Lenoir, Thomas, Sr. N.C. Private. 10 Feb. 1796. 640 acres to heirs.
Lenox, James. Ga. ———. 26 May 1784. 287 1/2 acres.
Lensey, Walter. N.C. Private. 22 Dec. 1796. 274 acres.
Lent, Abraham. N.Y. ———. 13 Sep. 1790. 500 acres to heirs.
Lent, Hendrick. N.Y. ———. 13 Sep. 1790. 500 acres to heirs.
Lent, Hercules. N. Y. Private. 8 Jul. 1790. 600 acres.
Lent, Moses. N. Y. Private. 17 Aug. 1790. 600 acres.
Lent, William. Va. Private. 18 Nov. 1818. 100 acres.
Lenwick, Samuel. Va. Corporal. 7 Feb. 1784. 200 acres.
Leonard, Adam. Pa. Private. 6 Dec. 1786. 200 acres.
Leonard, Edward. N. Y. Private. 8 Jul. 1790. 600 acres.
Leonard, Elijah. Ga. ———. 27 Apr. 1784. 287 1/2 acres.
Leonard, Jacob. Mass. Sergeant. 2 Mar. 1833. 200 acres.
Leonard, John. Pa. Private. 30 Nov. 1786. 200 acres.
Leonard, Patrick. Pa. Matross. 5 Mar. 1787. 200 acres.
Leonard, Richard. Pa. Private. 15 Nov. 1786. 200 acres to John Donnell, assignee.
Leonard, Robert. N. Y. Private. 8 Jul. 1790. 500 acres.
Leonard, Robert. Va. Private. 17 Nov. 1783. 233 1/3 acres.
Leonard, William. Ga. Soldier. 20 Dec. 1785. 230 acres.
Leonard, William. Va. Sailor. 21 Nov. 1783. 100 acres.
Leonnerd, Locklin. S.C. ———. 5 Mar. 1787. 200 acres.
Lepherd, John. N. Y. Private. 7 Jul. 1790. 600 acres.
LePierre, Thomas. N. Y. ———. ———. 500 acres.
Leplong, Joseph. Va. Corporal. 12 Apr. 1783. 400 acres.
LePuis, Jacque. N. Y. ———. ———. 500 acres.
LeRoy, George. Pa. Lieutenant. 3 Apr. 1787. 200 acres.
LeRoy, George. Pa. Lieutenant. 5 Dec. 1786. 200 acres.
Lerr, James. N.C. Private. 10 Dec. 1788. 640 acres to heirs.
Lesley, John. Md. Private. ———. 50 acres.
Lesley, Joseph. Ga. ———. 27 Apr. 1784. 287 1/2 acres.

Lesperance, Joseph. N. Y. ———. ———. 500 acres.
Lesseaux, Augustine. N. Y. Captain. ———. 1000 acres.
Lessemby, Timothy. N.C. Private. 9 Feb. 1796. 228 acres.
Lesshly, William. N.C. Private. 24 Dec. 1796. 274 acres.
Lessna, John. Ga. ———. 27 Apr. 1784. 200 acres.
Lester, Amos. Conn. Sufferer. New London. 12.11.9.
Lester, Benajah. Conn. Sufferer. Groton. 0.2.7.
Lester, Ebenezer. Conn. Sufferer. New London. 8.12.0.
Lester, Guy. N. Y. Matross. 9 Jul. 1790. 600 acres.
Lester, Jesse. Pa. Private. 14 Nov. 1786. 200 acres to Stephen Loudon, assignee.
Lester, John. Conn. Sufferer. New London. 35.19.7.
Lester, Thomas. Ga. Soldier. 20 Dec. 1783. 200 acres.
Lestick, Charles. Ga. Soldier. 7 Jun. 1785. 230 acres.
Letchmore, Watson. N.C. Private. 22 Dec. 1796. 640 acres to heirs.
Lett, James. Ga. Private. 15 Mar. 1784. 250 acres to widow Hannah Lett and children.
Lett, James. N.C. Private. 22 Oct. 1783. 274 acres.
Lett, Patrick. Ga. Soldier. ———. ———.
Lett, Reuben. Ga. Minute Man. 6 Feb. 1784. 287 1/2 acres.
Letters, James. N.Y. ———. 13 Sep. 1790. 500 acres to heirs.
Lettman, William. Md. Private. ———. 50 acres.
Lettrell, James. Va. Sergeant. 29 Apr. 1785. 400 acres.
Lettrell, Joseph. Va. Private. 29 Apr. 1785. 200 acres.
Levalle, Anthony. N. Y. ———. ———. 500 acres.
Levant, Anthony. N. Y. ———. ———. 500 acres.
Levell, Henry. Va. Private. 13 Nov. 1784. 200 acres.
Levellin, James. Ga. Minute Man. 27 Apr. 1784. 287 1/2 acres.
Levellin, William. Ga. Minute Man. 27 Apr. 1784. 287 1/2 acres.
Leveret, Aaron. Ga. Soldier. 27 Apr. 1784. 250 acres.
Leveret, Henry. Ga. Refugee. 27 Apr. 1784. 250 acres.
Leveret, John. Ga. Soldier. 17 Sep. 1784. 287 1/2 acres to heirs.
Leveret, Robert. Ga. Refugee. 15 Mar. 1784. 250 acres.
Leveret, Thomas. Ga. ———. 17 May 1784. 250 acres.
Leveret, William. Ga. ———. 27 Apr. 1784. 287 1/2 acres.
Levering, J. Pa. ———. 14 Jun. 1803. 200 acres to Abel Levering et al.
Levering, Wickard. Pa. Private. 20 Jun. 1787. 200 acres.
Leveringhouse, Christopher. Pa. ———. 2 Mar. 1803. 200 acres.
Levi, Alexander. Md. Private. ———. 50 acres.
Levi, Matthew. N.C. Private. 9 Sep. 1785. 640 acres to heirs.
Levick, Caleb. Va. Sergeant. 9 Jan. 1819. 400 acres.
Levillivant, James. Va. Private. 1 Mar. 1784. 100 acres.
Levines, Henry. N.Y. ———. 13 Sep. 1790. 500 acres to heirs.
Levingston, George. Va.-Ind. Private. 108 acres.
Levins, Richard. Ga. Refugee. 26 May 1784. 862 1/2 acres.
Levitre, Mary Anne. N. Y. ———. ———. 666 2/3 acres.
Levitt, David. Mass. Private. 25 Oct. 1830. 200 acres.
Levoy, Augustine. N. Y. ———. ———. 500 acres.
Levoy, Pierre. N. Y. ———. ———. 500 acres.
Levoye, Louis. N. Y. ———. ———. 500 acres.
Lewellin, Thomas. N.C. Private. 6 Jan. 1784. 274 acres.
Lewin, John. Md. Private. ———. 50 acres.
Lewis , Charles. Va. Colonel. 28 Dec. 1795. 6000 acres.
Lewis, Abijah. Me. ———. 14 Sep. 1835. 200 acres to widow Elizabeth Lewis. Hiram.
Lewis, Abraham. Pa. Private. 19 Apr. 1787. 200 acres to Ann Lewis, widow.

Lewis, Addison. Va. Captain. 25 Apr. 1783. 4000 acres.
Lewis, Ambrose. Va. Sailor. 1 Nov. 1783. 100 acres.
Lewis, Ambrose. Va. Seaman. 15 Aug. 1834. 100 acres.
Lewis, Amos. N.C. Private. 20 Dec. 1784. 228 acres.
Lewis, Andrew. Va. Lieutenant. 3 Jun. 1783. 2666 2/3 acres.
Lewis, Benjamin. Ga. Refugee. 15 Apr. 1784. 287 1/2 acres.
Lewis, Charles. N.C. ———. 14 Jun. 1785. 640 acres to heirs.
Lewis, Charles. Va. Colonel. 13 Nov. 1832. 666 2/3 acres.
Lewis, Charles. Va. Colonel. 18 Sep. 1833. 666 2/3 acres.
Lewis, Charles. Va. Seaman. 15 Aug. 1834. 100 acres.
Lewis, Charles. Va. Colonel. 9 Jun. 1855. 2690 acres.
Lewis, Daniel. Va. Private. 10 Jul. 1787. 200 acres.
Lewis, Daniel. Va. Seaman. 9 Dec. 1833. 100 acres.
Lewis, David. Ga. Refugee. 20 Apr. 1784. 287 1/2 acres to widow Kesiah Lewis.
Lewis, David. N.C. Private. 30 Sep. 1785. 640 acres to heirs.
Lewis, David, Jr. Ga. Refugee. 15 Mar. 1784. 250 acres.
Lewis, Edward. N.C. Private. 21 Aug. 1820. 640 acres.
Lewis, Eleazer. Ga. ———. 20 Feb. 1784. 500 acres.
Lewis, Elijah. Ga. Refugee Private. 26 May 1784. 250 acres.
Lewis, Elisha. N.C. Private. 17 Feb. 1824. 640 acres.
Lewis, Evan. Ga. Surgeon's Mate. 17 May 1784. 690 acres to heirs.
Lewis, Francis. N.C. Private. 23 Apr. 1784. 640 acres.
Lewis, George. Va. Captain. 17 Apr. 1783. 4000 acres.
Lewis, Hezekiah. Ga. ———. 17 May 1784. ———.
Lewis, Hines. N.C. Private. 6 Dec. 1797. 640 acres to heirs.
Lewis, Isaac. N.C. Private. 19 May 1784. 640 acres.
Lewis, Isaac, Rev. Conn. Sufferer. Norwalk. 5.1.4.
Lewis, Jacob. Ga. Refugee. 15 Mar. 1784. 250 acres.
Lewis, James. Ga. ———. 20 Apr. 1784. 575 acres.
Lewis, James. N. Y. Matross. 9 Jul. 1790. 600 acres.
Lewis, James. Va. Private. 23 Apr. 1784. 200 acres.
Lewis, Joel. Ga. Refugee. 27 Apr. 1784. 287 1/2 acres to heirs.
Lewis, Joel. N.C. Lieutenant. 21 Oct. 1783. 1463 acres.
Lewis, John. N.C. Private. 23 Apr. 1785. 640 acres to heirs.
Lewis, John. Va. Private. 28 Jun. 1783. 200 acres.
Lewis, John. Va. Private. 20 Dec. 1783. 100 acres.
Lewis, John. Va. Private. 6 Mar. 1784. 100 acres.
Lewis, John. Va. Captain. 6 Feb. 1832. 4495 acres.
Lewis, John. Va. Captain. 6 Feb. 1832. 112 1/5 acres.
Lewis, John. Va. Captain. 27 Feb. 1832. 499 6/9 acres.
Lewis, Jonathan. Md. Private. ———. 50 acres.
Lewis, Jonathan. N.C. Private. 22 Mar. 1785. 274 acres.
Lewis, Jonathan. Conn. Sufferer. Fairfield. 921.11.7.
Lewis, Joseph. Ga. Refugee Private. 8 Jun. 1784. 250 acres.
Lewis, Joseph. Md. Private. ———. 50 acres.
Lewis, Joseph. N. Y. Private. 7 Jul. 1790. 600 acres.
Lewis, Joseph. Va. Private. 3 May 1784. 200 acres.
Lewis, Joshua. N.C. Private. 23 Apr. 1785. 640 acres to heirs.
Lewis, Joshua. N.C. Private. 13 Dec. 1796. 640 acres to heirs.
Lewis, Joshua. N.C. Private. 3 Dec. 1797. 1000 acres to heirs.
Lewis, Josiah. Ga. Chaplain. 15 Apr. 1784. 287 1/2 acres to his brother Benjamin Lewis in trust for the heirs, the widow Susannah Lewis and children Jonathan Rees Lewis, Benjamin Thomas Lewis, Susanna Lewis, and Josiah Lewis.

Lewis, Lathrop. Conn. Sufferer. Fairfield. 27.5.2.
Lewis, Lockhard. N. Y. Private. 3 Jul. 1790. 600 acres.
Lewis, Mary. Conn. Sufferer. New London. 5.12.0.
Lewis, Matthew. Va. Carpenter's Mate. 9 Mar. 1837. 2666 2/3 acres.
Lewis, Matthew. Va. Seaman. 22 Nov. 1783. 100 acres.
Lewis, Matthew. Va. Carpenter's Mate. 20 Jun. 1833. 2666 2/3 acres.
Lewis, Micajah. N.C. Captain. 21 Oct. 1783. 3840 acres to William Terrell Lewis, heir.
Lewis, Morgan. N.C. Private. 15 Jul. 1785. 640 acres to heirs.
Lewis, Richard. Md. Sergeant. ———. 50 acres.
Lewis, Richard. N.C. Private. 12 Oct. 1795. 640 acres to heirs.
Lewis, Sampson. N.C. Private. 22 Oct. 1783. 640 acres to Martha Lewis, relict.
Lewis, Samuel. N. Y. Lieutenant. 17 Jul. 1790. 1200 acres.
Lewis, Samuel. Pa. ———. 9 Mar. 1795. 200 acres to John Nicholson.
Lewis, Samuel. Pa. Private. 29 July 1789. 200 acres.
Lewis, Samuel W. N.C. Private. 6 Sep. 1821. 640 acres.
Lewis, Stephen. Pa. Private. 11 Apr. 1787. 200 acres.
Lewis, Stephen. Va. Lieutenant. 6 Apr. 1784. 2666 2/3 acres.
Lewis, Sturges. Conn. Sufferer. Fairfield. 52.11.2.
Lewis, Thomas. Ga. Captain. 1784. 575 acres.
Lewis, Thomas. Md. Private. ———. 50 acres.
Lewis, Thomas. N.C. Private. 1 Dec. 1796. 640 acres.
Lewis, Thomas. Va. Lieutenant. 28 Jul. 1786. 1333 1/3 acres.
Lewis, Thomas. Va. Lieutenant. 28 Jul. 1786. 1333 1/3 acres.
Lewis, Thomas, Jr. Ga. Refugee. [20 Feb. 1784]. 287 1/2 acres.
Lewis, William. N.C. Private. 22 Oct. 1783. 274 acres.
Lewis, William. N.C. Private. 12 Dec. 1785. 640 acres to heir.
Lewis, William. N.C. Lieutenant. 31 Jul. 1820. 823 acres to Crowell Lewis who said he was the heir.
Lewis, William. N.C. Musician. 21 Aug. 1820. 427 acres.
Lewis, William. N.C. Musician. 4 Sep. 1820. 427 acres to heirs.
Lewis, William. Va. Major. 30 Nov. 1782. 6222 acres.
Lewis, William. Va. Private. 1 Dec. 1783. 200 acres.
Lewis, William. Va. Major. 10 Oct. 1806. 888 2/3 acres.
Lewis, William. Va. Lieutenant. 20 Mar. 1840. 1049 1/3 acres.
Lewis, William. Va. Lieutenant. 20 Mar. 1840. 699 5/9 acres.
Lewis, William. Va. Lieutenant. 20 Mar. 1840. 699 5/9 acres.
Lewis, William. Va. Lieutenant. 20 Mar. 1840. 699 5/9 acres.
Lewis, William Terrell. N.C. Lieutenant. 21 Oct. 1783. 1463 acres.
Lewis, Zachariah. Va. Sergeant. 19 Nov. 1783. 200 acres.
Lezear, Peter. Va. Private. 2 Feb. 1819. 100 acres.
Libbincut, John. N.C. Private. 30 Sep. 1785. 640 acres to heirs.
Libby, Allison. Me. ———. 29 Oct. 1835. 200 acres to widow Sarah Small. Limington.
Libby, Benjamin. Me. ———. 7 May 1835. 200 acres to widow Hannah Libby. Whitefield.
Libby, Edward. Me. Private. 17 Jun. 1835. 200 acres. Gorham.
Libby, Francis. Me. ———. 29 May 1835. 200 acres. Buxton.
Libby, James. Me. ———. 15 May 1835. 200 acres to widow Sally Libby. Poland.
Libby, Jonathan. Me. Lieutenant. 4 Oct. 1838. 600 acres to widow Abigail Libby. Scarborough.
Libby, Luke. Me. ———. 2 Jun. 1836. 200 acres to widow Dolly (McKenny) Libby. Danville.
Libby, Simeon. Me. Soldier. 25 Jun. 1835. 200 acres to widow Ann Libby. Gorham.
Libby, Solomon. Me. ———. 30 Apr. 1835. 200 acres to widow Sally Libby. Saco.
Libby, Thomas. Me. Sergeant. 28 May

1835. 200 acres to widow Mary Libby. Gorham.
Lickner, John Simon. Va. Private. 31 Jan. 1786. 200 acres.
Liddle, George. S.C. Captain. 16 Jul. 1784. 300 acres.
Lidell, Richard. N.C. Private. 29 Sep. 1784. 274 acres.
Liebert, Philip. N. Y. Captain. ———. 1000 acres.
Ligget, Thomas. Pa. Private. ———. 200 acres.
Liggins, William. Pa. Private. ———. 200 acres.
Liggins, William. Pa. ———. 22 Mar. 1810. 200 acres in trust. [He is probably not the veteran.]
Light, John. N. Y. Private. 7 Jul. 1790. 500 acres.
Lightburen, Stafford. Va. Lieutenant. 28 Jan. 1858. 142 6/7 acres.
Lightburn, Richard. Va. Lieutenant. 21 Jun. 1783. 2666 2/3 acres.
Lightburn, Stafford. Va. Lieutenant. 16 May 1838. 2928 3/7 acres.
Lightburn, Stafford. Va. Lieutenant. 16 May 1838. 571 4/7 acres.
Lightburn, Stafford. Va. Lieutenant. 16 May 1838. 500 acres.
Lightburne, Richard. Va. Lieutenant. 20 Sep. 1845. 2666 2/3 acres.
Lightburne, Richard. Va. Lieutenant. 1 Dec. 1845. 328 1/3 acres.
Lightburne, Richard. Va. Lieutenant. 1 Dec. 1845. 1005 acres.
Lightburne, Richard. Va. Lieutenant. 25 Sep. 1854. 296 8/27 acres.
Lightburne, Richard. Va. Lieutenant. 25 Sep. 1854. 207 8/27 acres.
Lightburne, Richard. Va. Lieutenant. 25 Sep. 1854. 92 16/27 acres.
Lightburne, Richard. Va. Lieutenant. 25 Sep. 1854. 197 43/81 acres.
Lightburne, Richard. Va. Lieutenant. 25 Sep. 1854. 74 2/27 acres.
Lightburne, Richard. Va. Lieutenant. 25 Sep. 1854. 232 62/81 acres.
Lightburne, Richard. Va. Lieutenant. 25 Sep. 1854. 116 31/81 acres.
Lightburne, Richard. Va. Lieutenant. 25 Sep. 1854. 116 31/81 acres.
Lightburne, Richard. Va. Lieutenant. 11 Nov. 1854. 311 86/243 acres.
Lightburne, Richard. Va. Lieutenant. 11 Nov. 1854. 77 21/243 acres.
Lightburne, Richard. Va. Lieutenant. 11 Nov. 1854. 77 21/243 acres.
Lightburne, Richard. Va. Lieutenant. 20 Sep. 1845. 592 16/27 acres.
Lightburne, Richard. Va. Lieutenant. 20 Sep. 1845. 148 11/27 acres.
Lightburne, Richard. Va. Lieutenant. 20 Sep. 1846. 394 80/81 acres.
Lightburne, Richard. Va. Lieutenant. 20 Sep. 1845. 414 16/27 acres.
Lightburne, Richard. Va. Lieutenant. 20 Sep. 1845. 110 16/27 acres.
Lightburne, Richard. Va. Lieutenant. 25 Sep. 1845. 222 1/6 acres.
Lightburne, Richard. Va. Lieutenant. 25 Sep. 1845. 266 1/6 acres.
Lightburne, Richard. Va. Lieutenant. 29 Nov. 1845. 561 1/3 acres.
Lightburne, Stafford. Va. Lieutenant. 25 Oct. 1852. 480 acres.
Lightburne, Stafford. Va. Lieutenant. 25 Oct. 1852. 1200 acres.
Lightburne, Stafford. Va. Lieutenant. 25 Oct. 1852. 480 acres.
Lightburne, Stafford. Va. Lieutenant. 25 Oct. 1852. 480 acres.
Lightburne, Stafford. Va. Lieutenant. 25 Oct. 1852. 480 acres.
Lightburne, Stafford. Va. Lieutenant. 25 Oct. 1852. 20 acres.
Lightburne, Stafford. Va. Lieutenant. 25 Oct. 1852. 91 4/7 acres.
Lightburne, Stafford. Va. Lieutenant. 25 Oct. 1852. ——— acres,
Lightburne, Stafford. Va. Lieutenant. 15 Apr. 1853. 120 acres.
Lightburne, Stafford. Va. Lieutenant. 15 Apr. 1853. 120 acres.
Lightburne, Stafford. Va. Lieutenant. 15 Apr. 1853. 120 acres.
Lightburne, Stafford. Va. Lieutenant. 11 Jan. 1858. 3428 2/7 acres.
Lightburne, Stafford. Va. Lieutenant. 8 Feb. 1858. 142 6/7 acres.
Lightburne, Stafford. Va. Lieutenant. 8 Feb. 1858. 142 6/7 acres.
Lightfoot, Francis. Ga. ———. 19 Jul. 1784. 500 acres.
Lightfoot, John. N.C. Private. 9 Feb. 1796. 228 acres.
Lightfoot, Philip. Va. Corporal. 19 Jun. 1783. 200 acres.

Lightfoot, Philip. Va. Lieutenant. 11 Jul. 1835. 2666 2/3 acres.
Lighthall, James. N. Y. Private. 8 Jul. 1790. 600 acres.
Lighthall, John. N. Y. Private. 8 Jul. 1790. 600 acres.
Lighthall, Lancaster. N. Y. Corporal. 8 Jul. 1790. 600 acres.
Lighthall, William. N.Y. Lieutenant. 21 Aug. 1800. 1000 acres.
Liles, Elijah. Va. Private. 24 Feb. 1784. 100 acres.
Liles, Henry. Ga. ———. 20 Apr. 1784. 350 acres.
Lilley, John. N.C. Private. 30 Sep. 1785. 640 acres to heirs.
Lilley, John. N.C. Private. 5 Dec. 1796. 274 acres.
Lillie, Josiah. N.C. Corporal. 14 Sep. 1821. 1000 acres to heirs.
Lilliston, John. Va. Private. 15 Jun. 1807. 100 acre.
Lilliston, William. Va. Private. 15 Jun. 1807. 100 acres.
Lilly, John. Pa. Private. 26 Mar. 1787. 200 acres.
Lilly, John. Va. Private. 21 Nov. 1783. 100 acres.
Lilly, Thomas. Va. Captain. 26 Apr. 1784. 5333 1/3 acres.
Lilly, William. Md. Private. ———. 50 acres.
Limbacker, John. N. Y. Private. 8 Jul. 1790. 600 acres.
Linam, George. Ga. ———. 27 Apr. 1784. 750 acres.
Linch, John. N.C. Lieutenant. 6 Sep. 1821. 2560 acres to heirs.
Linch, Lacie. N.C. Private. 5 Sep. 1821. 640 acres.
Lind, Arthur. Va. Captain. 29 Nov. 1782. 4000 acres.
Linden, Joseph. Ga. Sergeant. 18 Apr. 1784. 450 acres to heirs.
Linden, Michael. Pa. Private. ———. 200 acres.
Lindersmith, George. Pa. Private. 6 Jun. 1787. 200 acres.
Lindsay, Arthur. Va.-Ind. Private. 108 acres.
Lindsay, Daniel. Ga. ———. 27 Apr. 1784. 1000 acres.
Lindsay, Dennis. Ga. Refugee. 28 Feb. 1784. 250 acres.
Lindsay, John. Ga. Refugee Major. 15 Mar. 1784. 250 acres.
Lindsay, John. Md. Private. ———. 50 acres.
Lindsay, Theophilus. Md. Private. ———. 50 acres.
Lindsay, William. Va. Captain. 21 Jun. 1783. 4000 acres.
Lindsey, David. Va. Private. 2 Apr. 1784. 100 acres.
Lindsey, Hezekiah. Va. Private. 23 Jun. 1783. 100 acres.
Lindsey, Peter. Va. Private. 23 Jun. 1783. 100 acres.
Line, William. Ga. Soldier. 7 Jun. 1785. 287 1/2 acres.
Lines, Ebenezer. Conn. Sufferer. New/East Haven. 20.11.6.
Lines, John. Va.-Ind. Private. 108 acres.
Lines, John. Va. Private. 27 Sep. 1786. 100 acres.
Lines, Major. Conn. Sufferer. New/East Haven. 14.8.6.
Lingan, James M. Md. Captain. ———. 200 acres.
Lingard, Nehemiah. Md. Private. ———. 50 acres.
Lingo, Henry. Pa. Private. 5 Sep. 1787. 200 acres.
Lingo, Robinson. Va. Private. 18 Sep. 1807. 133 1/3 acres.
Lingo, Thomas. Va. Private. 30 Dec. 1808. 261 acres.
Lining, Charles. S.C. Captain. 15 Oct. 1784. 300 acres.
Link, John. Va. Private. 20 May 1783. 100 acres.
Linkon, John. Md. Private. ———. 50 acres.
Linn, Charles. Ga. ———. 23 Apr. 1784. 550 acres.
Linn, James. Va. Private. 30 Oct. 1797. 100 acres.
Linn, John. Ga. Soldier. 1 Oct. 1784. 230 acres to heirs.
Linn, Jonathan. N.C. Private. 10 Feb. 1796. 640 acres to heirs.
Linn, Michael. Pa. Private. 31 May 1796. 200 acres to John Lawson in right of.
Linn, Robert. Ga. Soldier. 4 Oct. 1785. ———.
Linn, Robert. N.C. Private. 24 Oct. 1783. 274 acres.

Linn, Stephen. N.C. Sergeant. 23 Apr. 1784. 1000 acres.
Linn, Thomas. Ga. ———. 30 Sep. 1784. 287 1/2 acres.
Linnigar, John. N. Y. Private. 8 Jul. 1790. 600 acres.
Linscott, Theodore. Me. ———. 14 May 1836. 200 acres. Sanford.
Linsey, Edward. Va. Private. 16 Oct. 1784. 100 acres.
Linsey, Isaac. N.C. Private. 8 Dec. 1795. 274 acres to heirs.
Lintner, Edward. Va. Private. 7 Dec. 1784. 100 acres.
Linton, George. Md. Private. ———. 50 acres.
Linton, Hezekiah, Sr. N.C. Private. 24 Oct. 1783. 640 acres to Hezekiah Linton, heir.
Linton, Jehu. N.C. Private. 27 Nov. 1819. 640 acres to heirs.
Linton, Jesse. N.C. Sergeant. 21 Apr. 1784. 1000 acres to Hezekiah Linton, heir.
Linton, John. Ga. Soldier. 4 Aug. 1784. ———.
Linton, John. N.C. Private. 21 Apr. 1784. 640 acres to Hezekiah Linton, heir.
Linton, John. Va. Lieutenant. 28 Jan. 1784. 2666 2/3 acres.
Linton, John. Va. Lieutenant. 5 Feb. 1784. 440 acres.
Linton, Michael. Va. Private. 18 Dec. 1782. 100 acres.
Linton, Roger. N.C. Private. 10 Feb. 1796. 640 acres to heirs.
Linton, Silas. N.C. Private. 12 May 1784. 640 acres.
Linton, William. N.C. Captain. 21 Apr. 1784. 1427 acres.
Linturn, John. Ga. Soldier. 7 Jun. 1785. 230 acres.
Lion, Jacob. Md. Sergeant. ———. 50 acres.
Lipford, Henry. Va. Private. 31 Aug. 1830. 100 acres.
Lipky, Henry. Pa. Private. 29 May 1787. 200 acres.
Lipner, Jacob. Pa. Private. ———. 200 acres.
Lippencutt, William. N.C. ———. 9 Dec. 1805. 360 acres to Thomas Crecy.
Lippment, William. N.C. Private. 8 Dec. 1796. 640 acres.
Lipscomb, Archibald. Va. Private. 13 Dec. 1783. 100 acres.
Lipscomb, Benjamin. Va. Private. 19 Mar. 1783. 100 acres.
Lipscomb, Benoni. Va. Private. 21 Jun. 1797. 100 acres.
Lipscomb, Bernard. Va. Captain Lieutenant. Dec. 1782. 4000 acres.
Lipscomb, Daniel. Va. Lieutenant. 25 Jul. 1835. 2666 2/3 acres.
Lipscomb, Daniel. Va. Lieutenant. 15 Jun. 1836. 2666 2/3 acres.
Lipscomb, Henry. Va. Fifer. 27 Jun. 1783. 200 acres.
Lipscomb, James. Va. Sergeant. 7 Mar. 1789. 200 acres.
Lipscomb, James. Va. Sergeant. 31 Oct. 1856. 200 acres.
Lipscomb, Joel. Ga. ———. 27 Apr. 1784. 500 acres.
Lipscomb, John. Va. Corporal. 27 May 1783. 200 acres.
Lipscomb, Major. Va. Sergeant. 6 Jan. 1786. 200 acres.
Lipscomb, Mourning. Va. Private. 1 Aug. 1783. 100 acres.
Lipscomb, Nathan. Ga. ———. 27 Apr. 1784. 250 acres.
Lipscomb, Reuben. Va. Captain. 31 Dec. 1782. 4000 acres.
Lipscomb, Reuben. Va. Captain. 25 May 1837. 370 2/3 acres.
Lipscomb, Reuben. Va. Captain. 25 May 1837. 740 acres.
Lipscomb, Thomas. Va. Private. 1 Aug. 1783. 100 acres.
Lipscomb, Thomas. Va. Ensign. 8 Feb. 1808. 1000 acres.
Lipscomb, Thomas. Va. Ensign. 8 Feb. 1808. 333 1/3 acres.
Lipscomb, Thomas. Va. Ensign. 8 Feb. 1808. 666 2/3 acres.
Lipscomb, Thomas. Va. Ensign. 8 Feb. 1808. 666 2/3 acres.
Lipscomb, Yancey. Va. Captain Lieutenant. Dec. 1782. 4000 acres.
Liscomb, John. N.C. Ensign. 16 Aug. 1821. 2560 acres.
Liscomb, Wilson. N.C. Private. 24 Oct. 1787. 274 acres.
Liscombe, Willis. N.C. Private. 13 Jan. 1823. 228 acres.
Lisembert, Anthony. N. Y. ———. ———. 500 acres.

Lisk, James. N.C. Private. 19 May 1784. 640 acres.
Lisk, Peter. Pa. Private. 27 Nov. 1786. 200 acres.
Lisle, Richard. Ga. ———. 17 May 1784. ———.
List, John. N. Y. Private. 8 Jul. 1790. 600 acres.
Litchfield, Francis. Va. Private. 3 Nov. 1787. 100 acres.
Litchworth, Andrew. N.C. Private. 30 Sep. 1785. 640 acres to heirs.
Litford, Robert. Pa. Private. 9 Oct. 1786. 200 acres.
Lithco, William. N.C. Private. 28 Sep. 1785. 640 acres to heirs.
Lithgore, Andrew, Jr. Minute Man. Ga. 22 Apr. 1784. 287 1/2 acres.
Lithgore, Andrew, Sr. Minute Man. Ga. 22 Apr. 1784. 287 1/2 acres.
Lithgore, Robert. Minute Man. Ga. 15 Apr. 1784 287 1/2 acres.
Litten, Abel. N.C. Noncomissioned Officer. 30 Nov. 1802. 428 acres.
Litten, Abel. N.C. Drummer. 7 May 1804. 429 acres.
Litteral, Jeremiah. N.C. Private. 17 Dec. 1785. 640 acres to heirs.
Litterall, John. N.C. Lieutenant Colonel. 13 May 1784. 2262 acres to John Umstead, heir.
Little, Archibald. Ga. Refugee. 25 May 1784. 287 1/2 acres.
Little, Deodat. Conn. Sufferer. New London. 207.5.0.
Little, James. Ga. Refugee. 15 Mar. 1784. 250 acres.
Little, James. N. Y. Sergeant. 3 Jul. 1790. 600 acres.
Little, Jonas. N.C. Private. 10 Feb. 1795. 640 acres to heirs.
Little, Moses. Va. Private. 9 Dec. 1783. 100 acres.
Little, Samuel. Conn. Sufferer. New/East Haven. 11.8.1.
Little, Thomas. N.C. Private. 6 Sep. 1821. 640 acres.
Little, Thomas. Pa. Private. 24 Mar. 1813. 200 acres.
Little, William. Ga. Refugee. 25 May 1784. 287 1/2 acres.
Little, William. Md. Private. ———. 50 acres.
Littlefield, John. Me. Ensign. 7 May 1838. 600 acres to widow Miriam Littlefield. Wells.
Littlefield, Moses. Me. Private. 5 Feb. 1839. 200 acres. Frankort.
Littlepage, John. Va. Private. 26 Oct. 1785. 200 acres.
Littleton, Mark. Ga. ———. 20 Apr. 1784. 287 1/2 acres.
Litton, Lemuel. N.C. Private. 12 Dec. 1797. 274 acres.
Liveley, Godrell. Va. Private. 9 Dec. 1800. 200 acres.
Lively, Matthew. N.C. Private. 9 Sep. 1785. 640 acres to heirs.
Livesay, William. Conn. Sufferer. Fairfield. 152.0.0.
Livingston, Aaron. Ga. ———. 23 Apr. 1784. 287 1/2 acres.
Livingston, Abraham. Ga. ———. ———. 287 1/2 acres.
Livingston, Abraham. N. Y. Captain. 13 Sep. 1790. 1800 acres.
Livingston, Abraham. N. Y. Captain. ———. 1000 acres.
Livingston, H. Robert. N. Y. Lieutenant. 9 Jul. 1790. 1200 acres.
Livingston, James. Ga. ———. 22 Apr. 1784. 600 acres.
Livingston, James. N. Y. Colonel. 13 Sep. 1790. 3000 acres.
Livingston, James. N. Y. Colonel. ———. 1000 acres.
Livingston, James, Jr. N. Y. ———. ———. 500 acres.
Livingston, John. N. Y. ———. ———. 500 acres.
Livingston, John, Jr. N. Y. ———. ———. 500 acres.
Livingston, Justice. V. Surgeon. 22 Jul. 1783. 2000 acres.
Livingston, Justice. Va. Surgeon. 22 Jul. 1783. 2000 acres.
Livingston, Justice. Va. Surgeon. 22 Jul. 1783. 2000 acres.
Livingston, Justice. Va. Surgeon. 22 Jul. 1783. 2000 acres.
Livingston, Moses. S.C. ———. 3 Jul. 1786. 200 acres.
Livingston, Richard. N.Y. Lieutenant Colonel. 29 Jan. 1791. 2250 acres.
Livingston, Richard. N. Y. Lieutenant Colonel. ———. 1000 acres.

Livingston, Richard, Jr. N. Y. ———. ———. 500 acres.
Livingston, Robert. Ga. ———. 19 Apr. 1784. 300 acres.
Livingston, Robert. Md. Matross. ———. 50 acres.
Livingston, Thomas. Ga. ———. 21 Apr. 1784. 400 acres.
Livingston, William. Ga. ———. 27 Apr. 1784. 287 1/2 acres to heirs.
Livingston, William. N.Y. ———. 13 Sep. 1790. 500 acres to heirs.
Lizotte, Louis. N. Y. ———. ———. 500 acres.
Lloyd, Benjamin. S.C. Lieutenant. 2 May 1785. 200 acres.
Lloyd, Edward. S.C. Lieutenant. 21 Jan. 1785. 200 acres.
Lloyd, James. Pa. Captain. 11 Jun. 1795. 200 acres.
Lloyd, James. Pa. Captain Lieutenant. 28 Aug. 1787. 200 acres.
Lloyd, Michael. Md. Private. ———. 50 acres.
Lloyd, Stephen. Ga. Soldier. 20 Dec. 1785. 230 acres.
Lloyd, Thomas. Ga. Soldier. 20 Dec. 1785. 230 acres.
Lock, John. N.C. Sergeant. 21 Apr. 1784. 357 acres.
Lock, John. N.C. Private. 23 Nov. 1797. 228 acres.
Lock, William. N.C. Private. 19 May 1784. 640 acres.
Lock, William. Va. Private. 12 Apr. 1783. 200 acres.
Lockart, John. Va. Private. 23 Jun. 1783. 200 acres.
Lockart, Pleasant. Va.-Ind. Private. 108 acres. [Lockett].
Locke, John. N. Y. Matross. 9 Jul. 1790. 600 acres.
Locke, John. Va. Corporal. 6 Dec. 1784. 400 acres.
Locke, Joseph. Va. Private. 25 Apr. 1783. 100 acres.
Lockeleare, Jonathan. N.C. Private. 2 Feb. 1786. 640 acres.
Locker, Jesse. Md. Private. ———. 50 acres.
Lockerey, Michael. Pa. Private. ———. 200 acres.
Lockett, Archibald. Va. Private. 5 Jun. 1807. 100 acres.
Lockett, Benjamin. Va. Private. 11 Aug. 1784. 100 acres.
Lockett, Benjamin. Va. Private. 2 Dec. 1785. 100 acres.
Lockett, Benjamin. Va. Private. 17 Jul. 1797. 100 acres.
Lockett, Jacob. Va. Private. 26 Mar. 1784. 100 acres.
Lockhart, Benjamin. Ga. ———. 27 Apr. 1784. 287 1/2 acres.
Lockhart, Charles. S.C. Soldier. 21 Jan. 1785. 200 acres.
Lockhart, Isaac. Ga. Refugee. 1784. 500 acres.
Lockhart, James. Va. Private. 2 Dec. 1783. 100 acres.
Lockhart, Joel. Ga. ———. 22 Apr. 1784. 200 acres.
Lockhart, John. N.Y. ———. 13 Sep. 1790. 500 acres to heirs.
Lockhart, William. Ga. Minute Man. 22 Mar. 1785. 250 acres.
Lockhart, William. Va. Private. 20 Dec. 1784. 200 acres.
Lockheart, John. N.C. Quartermaster Sergeant. 20 Apr. 1784. 321 acres.
Lockheart, Samuel. N.C. Lieutenant Colonel. 20 Apr. 1784. 5760 acres.
Lockley, Daniel. Va. Private. 19 Sep. 1787. 100 acres.
Lockwood, Abraham. Conn. Sufferer. Greenwich. 0.0.0.
Lockwood, Abraham. Conn. Sufferer. Norwalk. 2.12.0.
Lockwood, Ebenezer. Conn. Sufferer. Norwalk. 82.2.2.
Lockwood, Eliphalet. Conn. Sufferer. Norwalk. 721.8.11 1/2.
Lockwood, Eliphalet. Conn. Sufferer. Norwalk. 23.18.0.
Lockwood, Enos. Conn. Sufferer. Greenwich. 13.15.0.
Lockwood, Ezekiel. Conn. Sufferer. Greenwich. 9.13.1.
Lockwood, Hannah. Conn. Sufferer. Greenwich. 29.4.10.
Lockwood, Hannah. Conn. Sufferer. Danbury. 2.13.8.
Lockwood, Hezekiah. Conn. Sufferer. Norwalk. 176.4.7 3/4.
Lockwood, Israel. Conn. Sufferer. Greenwich. 51.4.10.
Lockwood, John. Conn. Sufferer. Norwalk. 9.12.8.

Lockwood, John, 3d. Conn. Sufferer. Norwalk. 218.4.0.

Lockwood, John, Jr. Conn. Sufferer. Norwalk. 249.14.0 1/2.

Lockwood, Joseph. Conn. Sufferer. Greenwich. 30.19.6.

Lockwood, Mary. Conn. Sufferer. Norwalk. 2.8.6.

Lockwood, Nathaniel. Conn. Sufferer. Danbury. 7.14.3 1/2.

Lockwood, Philip. Conn. Sufferer. Greenwich. 0.0.0.

Lockwood, Samuel. Conn. Sufferer. Greenwich. 108.14.4.

Lockwood, Stephen. Conn. Sufferer. Norwalk. 18.12.0.

Lockwood, Thaddeus. Conn. Sufferer. Greenwich. 54.18.5.

Lockwood, Theophilus. Conn. Sufferer. Greenwich. 2.0.0.

Lockwood, Timothy. Conn. Sufferer. Greenwich. 10.4.8.

Lockwood, William. Conn. Sufferer. Greenwich. 18.19.2.

Locust, Arthur. N.C. Private. 2 Dec. 1796. 640 acres to heirs.

Locust, Francis. N.C. Private. 2 Dec. 1796. 640 acres to heirs.

Locust, Thomas. N.C. Private. 30 Sep. 1785. 640 acres to heirs.

Lodder, William. N. Y. Private. 8 Jul. 1790. 600 acres.

Loden, Benjamin. Va. Private. 12 Jun. 1784. 200 acres.

Loden, Jesse. Va. Private. 16 Apr. 1783. 200 acres.

Loden, William. Va. Private. 6 Aug. 1783. 200 acres.

Loder, Daniel. N. Y. Private. 7 Jul. 1790. 600 acres.

Lodge, Benjamin. Pa. Lieutenant. ———. 200 acres.

Lodge, Benjamin. Pa. ———. ———. 200 acres.

Lodge, Lewis. N.C. Private. 27 Nov. 1789. 640 acres.

Loe, George. N.C. Private. 27 Jun. 1788. 294 acres.

Loffman, Benjamin. Md. Private. ———. 50 acres.

Lofman, John. N.C. Private. 17 Dec. 1785. 274 acres.

Lofton, Cornelius. Ga. ———. 21 Apr. 1784. 287 1/2 acres.

Lofton, John. Ga. ———. 21 Apr. 1784. 250 acres.

Logan, Alexander. S.C. ———. 1 Aug. 1785. 200 acres.

Logan, David. S.C. ———. 1 Aug. 1785. 200 acres.

Logan, John. Ga. Soldier. 20 Dec. 1785. 230 acres.

Logan, John. Pa. Private. 29 Dec. 1794. 200 acres to children Samuel Logan, Anne Logan, and Mary Logan.

Logan, John. S.C. ———. 2 Oct. 1786. 200 acres.

Logan, John. Va. Private. 6 Mar. 1834. 200 acres.

Logan, Philip. Ga. Refugee. 1784. 287 1/2 acres.

Logan, Philip. N.C. Private. 6 Sep. 1817. 640 acres.

Logan, Samuel. N. Y. Major. 9 Sep. 1790. 2400 acres.

Logan, Thomas. S.C. ———. 2 Oct. 1786. 200 acres to John Logan, heir at law.

Logan, William. Ga. Soldier. 20 Dec. 1785. 230 acres.

Logan, William. N.C. Private. 16 Apr. 1821. 640 acres.

Logan, William. Va. Private. 6 Mar. 1834. 100 acres.

Logee, Charles. N.C. Drummer. 6 Dec. 1797. 640 acres.

Loggins, Martin. Va. Corporal. 20 Feb. 1837. 80 acres.

Loggins, Martin. Va. Corporal. 7 Jan. 1842. 120 acres.

Loggins, Martin. Va. Corporal. 2 Mar. 1847. 40 acres.

Loggins, Martin. Va. Corporal. 2 Mar. 1847. 40 acres.

Loggins, Martin. Va. Corporal. 2 Mar. 1847. 40 acres.

Loghman, Charles. S.C. ———. 4 Jul. 1785. 200 acres.

Loghman, John. S.C. ———. 4 Jul. 1785. 300 acres.

Lomack, William. N.C. Private. 17 Dec. 1785. 274 acres.

Lomas, Jacob. N. Y. Private. 7 Jul. 1790. 500 acres.

Lomas, Samuel. Ga. ———. 250 acres. ———.

Lomax, Theophilus. Md. Sergeant. ———. 50 acres.

Lomax, William. N.C. Private. 27 Apr. 1784. 274 acres.
Lombard, Caleb. Me. ———. 2 May 1835. 200 acres to widow Hannah Lumbard. Turner.
Lombard, Jedediah. Me. ———. 12 Aug. 1835. 200 acres. Standish.
Lombard, Nathaniel. Me. ———. 22 Jul. 1835. 200 acres. Milburn.
Lonass, John. Md. Private. ———. 50 acres.
London, Moses. Va. Private. 16 May 1810. 100 acres.
London, William. Va. Private. 19 Jun. 1783. 100 acres.
Long, Andrew. Va. Private. 8 May 1784. 100 acres.
Long, Armistead. Va. Sergeant. 19 Dec. 1792. 200 acres.
Long, Daniel. Va. Private. 5 Jun. 1784. 100 acres.
Long, David. Ga. Private. 10 Dec. 1784. 250 acres.
Long, Evans. Va. Private [Sergeant]. 19 Feb. 1784. 100 [200] acres.
Long, Francis. Md. Private. ———. 50 acres.
Long, Gabriel. Ga. ———. 15 Apr. 1784. 1000 acres.
Long, Gabriel. Virginia. Captain. 23 Dec. 1783. 4000 acres.
Long, George. Va. Private. 27 Feb. 1797. 100 acres.
Long, Haywood. N.C. Private. 30 Sep. 1785. 640 acres to heirs.
Long, Henry. Ga. Lieutenant. 26 May 1784. 460 acres.
Long, James. Mass. ———. 8 Jul. 1833. 200 acres to widow Elizabeth Long.
Long, James. N.C. Private. 30 Sep. 1785. 640 acres to heirs.
Long, John. Ga. Minute Man. 15 Mar. 1784. 250 acres.
Long, John. Ga. Lieutenant. 26 May 1784. 460 acres to heirs.
Long, John. N.C. Private. 24 Nov. 1797. 640 acres to heirs.
Long, John. N.C. Ensign. 4 Aug. 1820. 1097 acres to heirs.
Long, Joseph. Md. Private. ———. 50 acres.
Long, Levi. Va. Private. 15 Nov. 1786. 200 acres.
Long, Nehemiah. N.C. Captain. 22 Oct. 1783. 1785 acres.
Long, Nicholas. Va. Private [Sergeant]. 19 Feb. 1784. 100 [200] acres.
Long, Nicholas, Jr. Ga. ———. 15 Apr. 1784. 1000 acres.
Long, Reuben. Va. Lieutenant. 14 Aug. 1783. 2666 2/3 acres.
Long, Reuben. Va. Private. 6 Dec. 1784. 100 acres.
Long, Richard. Va. Corporal. 19 Mar. 1784. 200 acres.
Long, Robert. Ga. ———. 27 Apr. 1784. 287 1/2 acres.
Long, Solomon. S.C. ———. 6 Nov. 1786. 200 acres to Mary Long, widow.
Long, Thomas. Md. Private. ———. 50 acres.
Long, William. N.C. Private. 24 May 1784. 640 acres.
Long, William. Va. Captain. 14 Feb. 1783. 4000 acres.
Longchamps, Louis. N. Y. ———. ———. 500 acres.
Longdon, John. Va. Sergeant. 13 Jun. 1808. 605 acres.
Longest, Daniel. Md. Private. ———. 50 acres.
Longest, James. Va. Private. 19 Dec. 1798. 200 acres.
Longford, Alloway. N.C. Lieutenant. 7 May 1804. 2560 acres to heirs.
Longley, Asa. Me. Private. 30 Apr. 1835. 200 acres. St. Albans.
Longley, Joseph. Mass. ———. 22 Jul. 1833. 200 acres.
Longley, Zacheriah. Me. Private. 6 Jul. 1835. 200 acres to widow Betsey Longley. Dover.
Longwith, Burgess. Va. Gunner. 28 Nov. 1783. 2666 2/3 acres.
Longwith, John. Va. Seaman. 28 Nov. 1783. 100 acres.
Looker, John. N.C. Private. 10 Feb. 1796. 640 acres to heirs.
Loomes, Jonathan. N.C. Surgeon. 25 Apr. 1784. 3942 acres.
Loomis, Roger. Me. Private. 12 May 1835. 200 acres to widow Isabella Loomis. Westport.
Looney, Daniel. N.C. Private. 6 Dec. 1797. 228 acres.
Looney, Michael. N.C. Private. 6 Sep. 1821. 640 acres.

Looney, Moses. N.C. Private. 2 Nov. 1795. 640 acres to heirs.
Looney, Robert. S.C. Soldier. 15 Oct. 1784. 200 acres.
Loper, Joshua. Ga. ———. 27 Apr. 1784. 200 acres.
Lor, Henry. N. Y. ———. ———. 500 acres.
Lorain, Henry. N.C. Sergeant. 28 Aug. 1820. 1000 acres.
Lord, Adam. Me. ———. 17 Sep. 1836. 200 acres to widow Olive Stone. Limington.
Lord, Esther. Conn. Sufferer. Fairfield. 7.4.0.
Lord, Levi. Md. Private. ———. 50 acres.
Lord, Nathan. Me. Private. 29 May 1835. 200 acres to widow Sarah Lord. Lebanon.
Lord, Richard. Me. Private. 7 Jan. 1836. 200 acres to widow Mary Lord. South Berwick.
Lord, Roberson. Va. Private. 5 Jun. 1783. 200 acres.
Lord, Simeon. Me. Captain. 30 Jan. 1839. 600 acres to widow Polly Lord. North Berwick.
Lorde, John. Va. Sergeant. 1 May 1783. 400 acres.
Lorden, George. Pa. Private. 19 Sep. 1787. 200 acres.
Loring, Benjamin. N. Y. Drummer. 9 Jul. 1790. 500 acres.
Lott, George. N.C. Private. 9 Nov. 1784. 640 acres.
Lott, Jeremiah. Pa. Private. 10 Jul. 1787. 200 acres.
Lott, Job. N.C. Private. 21 Aug. 1820. 640 acres.
Lott, William. S.C. Soldier. 21 Jan. 1785. 200 acres.
Loucks, Andrew. N. Y. Private. 8 Jul. 1790. 500 acres.
Loudon, Adam. Va. Private. 2 Apr. 1784. 200 acres.
Loudon, John. Conn. Sufferer. Greenwich. 7.10.0.
Loudon, Stephen. Pa. Sergeant. 4 Oct. 1786. 250 acres.
Loughmiller, Wilcome. Va. Private. 23 Jun. 1784. 100 acres.
Lougrage, William. Pa. Private. 28 Oct. 1786. 200 acres.
Loumber, John. S.C. Soldier. 15 Oct. 1784. 200 acres.
Lounsberry, Edward. N.Y. Captain. 10 Aug. 1792. 1500 acres.
Loury, Lewis. Va. Corporal. 8 Mar. 1809. 694 acres.
Loury, William. Va. Sailor. 30 Jun. 1784. 100 acres.
Loux, Hendrick. N. Y. Private. 8 Jul. 1790. 600 acres.
Love, David. Md. Sergeant. ———. 50 acres.
Love, David. N.C. Surgeon. 27 Nov. 1783. 2057 acres.
Love, Davis. N. Y. Private. 8 Jul. 1790. 600 acres.
Love, Jesse. Ga. Minute Man. 22 Mar. 1785. 250 acres.
Love, John. Ga. Minute Man. 14 Feb. 1785. ———.
Love, John. Md. Private. ———. 50 acres.
Love, John. Va. Sergeant. 26 Apr. 1783. 400 acres.
Love, Michael. Conn. Sufferer. New London. 23.0.0.
Love, Samuel. N.C. Private. 12 Dec. 1796. 640 acres.
Love, Samuel. Va. Sergeant. 14 Aug. 1835. 200 acres.
Love, Samuel. Va. Sergeant. 5 Mar. 1840. 22 2/9 acres.
Love, Thomas. N.C. Private. 22 Dec. 1796. 274 acres.
Love, William. Mass. Corporal. 10 Sep. 1832. 200 acres.
Love, William. N.C. Private. 2 Dec. 1785. 640 acres.
Loveday [or Lovely], Thomas. Md. Drummer. ———. 50 acres.
Loveday, John. Md. Private. ———. 50 acres.
Lovel, Richard. Va. Private. 17 Jul. 1784. 200 acres.
Lovel, Robert. Va. Lieutenant. 17 Nov. 1789. 2666 2/3 acres.
Loveless, Archibald. Ga. Soldier. 5 Dec. 1785. 230 acres.
Lovell, James. Va. Lieutenant. 27 Jun. 1795. 2666 2/3 acres.
Lovell, John. N.C. Private. 10 Feb. 1796. 640 acres to heirs.
Lovell, Richard. Ga. ———. 22 Apr. 1784. 287 1/2 acres.

Lovell, Richard. Va.-Ind. Private. 108 acres.
Lovell, William L. Va. Captain. 20 Nov. 1782. 4000 acres.
Lovely, John. Pa. Sergeant. 16 Oct. 1815. 250 acres.
Lovely, Joshua. Md. Matross. ———. 50 acres.
Lovering, Samuel. Mass. Private. 15 Jan. 1833. 200 acres to assignee James Mellen.
Lovett, John. N. Y. Private. 3 Jul. 1790. 600 acres.
Lovey, John. N.C. Private. 17 Dec. 1796. 640 acres.
Loving, Richard. Va. Private. 17 Dec. 1830. 200 acres.
Low, Abraham. N.C. Private. 10 Aug. 1785. 640 acres to heirs.
Low, James. Va. Private. 23 Jun. 1783. 200 acres.
Low, John. N.C. Lieutenant. 5 Sep. 1821. 2560 acres to heirs.
Low, Jonathan. N.C. Private. 15 Jun. 1785. 640 acres.
Low, Pleasant. N.C. Private. 7 Dec. 1797. 640 acres to heirs.
Lowdon, William. N. Y. Drum Major. 7 Jul. 1790. 600 acres.
Lowe, Beverly. Ga. ———. 27 Apr. 1784. 287 1/2 acres.
Lowe, Daniel. Ga. Minute Man. 23 Apr. 1784. 575 acres.
Lowe, Isaac, Sr. Ga. ———. 20 Feb. 1784. 250 acres.
Lowe, Jacob. Md. Sergeant. ———. 50 acres.
Lowe, James. Va. Private. 16 Nov. 1844. 200 acres.
Lowe, James. Va. Private. 16 Nov. 1844. 200 acres.
Lowe, John. Ga. ———. 15 Mar. 1784. 250 acres.
Lowe, John. Va. Private. 9 Aug. 1783. 100 acres.
Lowe, John. Va. Private. 4 Dec. 1783. 200 acres.
Lowe, John Tolson. Md. Lieutenant. ———. 200 acres.
Lowe, Obediah. Ga. Refugee. 20 Feb. 1784. 250 acres.
Lowe, Philip. Ga. Major. 1784. 920 acres.
Lowe, Thomas. Va. Sergeant. 9 Aug. 1783. 200 acres.
Lowe, William. Ga. ———. 27 Apr. 1784. 1000 acres.
Lowe, William. N.C. Fife Major. 12 Sep. 1785. 427 acres.
Lowe, William. Pa. Private. 17 Oct. 1786. 200 acres.
Lowell, Beniah. Maine. ———. 24 Oct. 1835. 200 acres to widow Elizabeth Lowell. Standish.
Lowell, Benjamin. Me. Matross. 24 Jul. 1835. 200 acres to widow Lydia Lowell. Bucksport.
Lowell, James. N.C. Private. 30 Sep. 1785. 640 acres to heirs.
Lowell, Paul. Me. Private. 5 Jun. 1835. 200 acres. Turner.
Lowerman, John. S.C. ———. 7 Jul. 1788. 200 acres.
Lowman, Mark. N.C. Private. 30 Sep. 1785. 640 acres to heirs.
Lowman, Peter. N. Y. Private. 8 Jul. 1790. 600 acres.
Lowman, Philip. Pa. Private. 10 Mar. 1795. 200 acres to Clement Biddle, assignee.
Lowrance, John. Ga. ———. 21 Apr. 1784. 500 acres.
Lowry, James. Md. Private. ———. 50 acres.
Lowry, John. Ga. ———. 27 Apr. 1784. 200 acres.
Lowry, John. Md. Private. ———. 50 acres.
Lowry, Matthew. S.C. ———. 4 Jul. 1785. 200 acres.
Lowry, Thomas. S.C. ———. 4 Dec. 1786. 200 acres.
Lows, John. Va. Private. 19 Nov. 1784. 100 acres.
Loyal, John. Va. Private. 24 Dec. 1784. 100 acres.
Loyd, Abemeleck. N.C. Private. 10 Feb. 1796. 640 acres to heirs.
Loyd, Burrel. N.C. Private. 2 Jan. 1810. 640 acres to heirs.
Loyd, George. Va. Sergeant. 31 May 1783. 200 acres.
Loyd, George. Va. Private. 27 Jun. 1783. 100 acres.
Loyd, Henry. N.C. Private. 25 Aug. 1813. 640 acres to heirs.
Loyd, James. Ga. ———. 2 May 1785. 287 1/2 acres.
Loyd, James. Va. Private. 6 Nov. 1787. 100 acres.

Loyd, John. Ga. ———. Aug. 1785. 287 1/2 acres.
Loyd, John C. N.C. Private. 30 Sep. 1785. 640 acres to heirs.
Loyd, Leonard. N.C. Private. 22 Oct. 1783. 640 acres to Thomas Loyd, heir.
Loyd, Leonard. N.C. Private. 28 Oct. 1783. 640 acres to heir.
Loyd, Markhum. N.C. Private. 14 Dec. 1796. 640 acres to heirs.
Loyd, Morris. Va. Gunner's Mate. 30 May 1788. 2666 2/3 acres.
Loyd, Thomas. N.C. Sergeant. 5 Sep. 1821. 1000 acres.
Loyd, Thomas. Va. Private. 3 Mar. 1784. 100 acres.
Loyd, William. Va. Private. 19 Feb. 1784. 100 acres.
Lozelton, Ferman. N. Y. ———. ———. 500 acres.
Lozier, Helebrand. Va. Private. 2 Feb. 1819. 100 acres.
Lozier, Oliver. N. Y. Bombardier. 9 Jul. 1790. 600 acres.
Lucas, Ball. N.C. Private. 24 Dec. 1796. 640 acres to heirs.
Lucas, Billing. N.C. Private. 2 Sep. 1820. 640 acres.
Lucas, Henry. Pa. Private. 29 Aug. 1787. 200 acres.
Lucas, Humphrey. Va. Private. 17 Aug. 1785. 200 acres.
Lucas, James. Ga. ———. 23 Apr. 1784. 287 1/2 acres.
Lucas, James. Va. Major. 20 Feb. 1784. 5333 1/3 acres.
Lucas, John. Ga. Captain. 5 Sep. 1783. 600 acres.
Lucas, John. Md. Private. ———. 50 acres.
Lucas, Matthew. N.C. Private. 2 Dec. 1796. 640 acres to heirs.
Lucas, Nathaniel. Va. Captain. 18 Jun. 1784. 4000 acres.
Lucas, Nathaniel. Va. Captain. 10 Mar. 1840. 106 1/7 acres.
Lucas, Nathaniel. Va. Captain. 10 Mar. 1840. 106 1/7 acres.
Lucas, Nathaniel. Va. Captain. 10 Mar. 1840. 106 1/7 acres.
Lucas, Nathaniel. Virginia. Captain. 10 Mar. 1840. 106 1/7 acres.
Lucas, Nathaniel. Va. Captain. 10 Mar. 1840. 210 2/7 acres.
Lucas, Nathaniel. Va. Captain. 11 Dec. 1855. 158 5/7 acres.
Lucas, Richard. N.C. Private. 6 Sep. 1821. 640 acres.
Lucas, Samuel. Va. Fife Major. 1 May 1783. 400 acres.
Lucas, Samuel. Va. Private. 9 Dec. 1783. 100 acres.
Lucas, Thomas. Va. Private. 5 May 1783. 200 acres.
Lucas, Thomas. Va. Captain. 19 May 1823. 4000 acres.
Lucas, Valentine. N.C. Private. 30 Apr. 1784. 288 acres.
Lucas, William. Ga. Refugee. 25 May 1784. 287 1/2 acres.
Lucas, William. Md. Private. ———. 50 acres.
Lucas, William. Va. Private. 8 Apr. 1784. 100 acres.
Lucay, Peter. Ga. Minute Man. 14 Feb. 1785. ———.
Lucis, Benjamin. N.C. Private. 30 Sep. 1785. 640 acres.
Luck, Asa. Ga. Soldier. 25 May 1784. 230 acres to heirs.
Luck, John. Ga. Soldier. 25 May 1784. 230 acres to heirs.
Luckars, James. N.C. Private. 13 Dec. 1796. 640 acres to heirs.
Luckars, Richard. N.C. Private. 13 Dec. 1796. 640 acres to heirs.
Luckett, David. Md. Captain. ———. 200 acres.
Luckett, Thomas H. Md. Captain. ———. 200 acres.
Luckett, Thomas H. Va. Captain. 6 Jan. 1838. 5500 acres.
Lucky, Thomas. Ga. ———. 17 May 1784. ———.
Lucy, Burrell. N.C. Private. 22 Feb. 1784. 640 acres.
Lucy, Frederick. N.C. Private. 22 Dec. 1796. 640 acres to heirs.
Lucy, Isham. N.C. Private. 6 Dec. 1796. 640 acres.
Lucy, William. N.C. Private. 6 Dec. 1796. 228 acres.
Luddington, Elam. Conn. Sufferer. New/ East Haven. 408.6.7.
Ludeman, J. William. Va. Lieutenant. 13 Jun. 1783. 2666 2/3 acres.
Ludlum, Daniel. N. Y. Sergeant. 7 Jul. 1790. 500 acres.

Ludlum, John. N. Y. Private. 7 Jul. 1790. 500 acres.
Ludwick, John M. Pa. Sergeant. 12 Feb. 1803. 250 acres to widow Elizabeth Ludwick.
Ludwick, Nicholas. Pa. Private. 16 Mar. 1787. 200 acres to Stephen Louden, assignee.
Luff, Thomas [or John]. Md. Private. ———. 50 acres.
Luke, Gad. Conn. Sufferer. New/East Haven. 27.11.4.
Luke, Henry. N. Y. Private. 8 Jul. 1790. 500 acres.
Lumb, Joseph. Va. Private. 3 Feb. 1784. 200 acres.
Lumber, Thomas. Va. Gunner's Mate. 5 May 1831. 444 1/3 acres.
Lumber, Thomas. Va. Gunner's Mate. 5 May 1831. 444 1/3 acres.
Lumber, Thomas. Va. Gunner's Mate. 5 May 1831. 444 1/3 acres.
Lumber, Thomas. Va. Gunner's Mate. 5 May 1831. 444 1/3 acres.
Lumber, Thomas. Va. Gunner's Mate. 5 May 1831. 444 1/3 acres.
Lumber, William. Va. Gunner. 7 Dec. 1830. 444 1/3 acres.
Lumber, William. Va. Gunner. 7 Dec. 1830. 444 1/3 acres.
Lumber, William. Va. Gunner. 7 Dec. 1830. 444 acres.
Lumber, William. Va. Gunner. 7 Dec. 1830. 444 acres.
Lumber, William. Va. Gunner. 7 Dec. 1830. 444 acres.
Lumber, William. Va. Gunner. 5 May 1831. 444 1/3 acres.
Lumblies, David. N.C. Private. 14 Dec. 1796. 640 acres to heirs.
Lumblies, Simon. N.C. Private. 14 Dec. 1796. 640 acres to heirs.
Lumkin, Moore. Va. Private. 2 Mar. 1812. 200 acres.
Lunceford, Elias. Va. Sailor. 13 Feb. 1784. 100 acres.
Luncie, Jesse. Ga. ———. 27 Apr. 1784. 287 1/2 acres.
Lundy, Nathaniel. Ga. Refugee. 23 Apr. 1784. 500 acres.
Lundy, Theophilus. Ga. Refugee. 26 May 1784. 575 acres.
Luney, John. S.C. Soldier. 2 May 1785. 200 acres.
Lunn, Frederick. S.C. Surgeon. 21 Jan. 1785. 300 acres.
Lunney, Philip. N.Y. ———. 13 Sep. 1790. 500 acres to heirs.
Lunsford, George. Va.-Ind. Private. 108 acres.
Lunsford, Lewis. Va. Cornet. 30 Jun. 1784. 2666 2/3 acres.
Lunsford, Mason. Va.-Ind. Private. 108 acres.
Lunsford, Mason. Va. Private. 20 Jan. 1834. 100 acres.
Lunsford, Moses. Va.-Ind. Private. 108 acres.
Lunsford, Moses. Va. Private. 9 Nov. 1791. 200 acres.
Lunt, Amos. Me. ———. 25 Apr. 1835. 200 acres. Brunswick.
Lunt, Amos. Me. ———. 25 Apr. 1835. 200 acres. Brunswick.
Lunt, Job. Mass. Private. 8 Jul. 1833. 200 acres to widow Mary Lunt.
Lurton, Levin. Va. Private. 15 Jun. 1807. 100 acres.
Lurton, William. Va. Private. 15 Jun. 1807. 100 acres.
Lurty, John. Va. Captain. 20 Jan. 1855. 684 4/27 acres.
Lurty, John. Va. Captain. 26 Feb. 1855. 333 1/3 acres.
Lurty, John. Va. Captain. 16 May 1855. 111 1/9 acres.
Lurty, John. Va. Captain. 28 May 1855. 63 31/63 acres.
Lurvey, William. Mass. Private. 27 Oct. 1834. 200 acres to widow Ruth Hull.
Lusader, Abraham. Va.-Ind. Private. 108 acres.
Lusk, John. N. Y. Private. 8 Jul. 1790. 600 acres.
Lusk, William. N.C. Private. 15 Nov. 1793. 640 acres to heirs.
Lusk, William. Pa. Captain. 4 Oct. 1786. 500 acres.
Luster, John. N. Y. Private. 8 Jul. 1790. 600 acres.
Luster, William. Va. Private. 20 Nov. 1784. 100 acres.
Luton, Lemuel. N.C. Private. 2 Dec. 1796. 640 acres.
Luton, Lemuel. N.C. Corporal. 23 Jun. 1820. 1000 acres to heirs.
Luts, John. N.C. Corporal. 22 May 1820. 1000 acres to heirs.

Lutteral, James. N.C. Private. 9 Dec. 1797. 640 acres to heirs.
Lutterell, Richard. Va.-Ind. Private. 108 acres.
Luttrell, Rodham. Va. Seaman. 7 Jun. 1851. 100 acres.
Lutzell, John. N.C. Lieutenant Colonel. 17 Feb. 1824. 5760 acres.
Lybea, John. N. Y. Private. 8 Jul. 1790. 600 acres.
Lykes, Solomon. Ga. ———. 5 Dec. 1785. ———.
Lyle, Charles. Va. Private. 19 Jun. 1783. 100 acres.
Lyles, Benjamin. N.C. Private. 22 Apr. 1785. 640 acres.
Lyles, William. Ga. Soldier. 5 Sep. 1785. ———.
Lyles, Zachariah. Md. Private. ———. 50 acres.
Lylliecrap, John. Pa. Private. 13 Oct. 1786. 200 acres.
Lyman, Daniel. Conn. Sufferer. New/East Haven. 368.7.8.
Lymus, John. N.C. Private. 30 Sep. 1785. 640 acres to heirs.
Lynam, George. Ga. ———. 17 May 1784. ———.
Lynch, George. N.C. Private. 30 Sep. 1785. 640 acres to heirs.
Lynch, James. Va. Private. 19 Jul. 1783. 200 acres.
Lynch, John. Ga. Soldier. 17 May 1784. 230 acres.
Lynch, John. Md. Major. ———. 200 acres.
Lynch, John. Md. Private. ———. 50 acres.
Lynch, John. Md. Private. ———. 50 acres.
Lynch, John. N.C. Private. 17 Dec. 1785. 640 acres to heirs.
Lynch, John. Pa. Private. ———. 200 acres.
Lynch, Owin. N.Y. ———. 13 Sep. 1790. 500 acres to heirs.
Lynch, Patrick. Va. Private. 9 Jun. 1783. 100 acres.
Lynch, Stephen. N.C. Private. 5 Dec. 1796. 640 acres.
Lynch, Thomas. N.C. Private. 6 Sep. 1821. 640 acres to heirs.
Lynch, Timothy. Va. Private. 29 Apr. 1783. 200 acres.
Lynch, William. Md. Private. ———. 50 acres.
Lynch, William. N. Y. Private. 8 Jul. 1790. 600 acres.
Lyndes, James. Conn. Sufferer. New/East Haven. 4.17.6.
Lyne, Barnabas. Va. Private. 3 Feb. 1784. 100 acres.
Lyne, John. Va. Private. 29 Jul. 1785. 100 acres.
Lyne, Joseph. Va.-Ind. Private. 108 acres.
Lyner, Philip. Va. Private. 15 Dec. 1786. 100 acres.
Lynn, Charles. Ga. ———. 20 Dec. 1785. 287 1/2 acres.
Lynn, Curtis. Ga. Soldier. 17 Jan.1785. 230 acres. Of Sussex Co., Va.
Lynn, David. Md. Captain. ———. 200 acres.
Lynn, John. Ga. Soldier. 30 Sep. 1784. 287 1/2 acres.
Lynn, John. Md. Lieutenant. ———. 200 acres.
Lynn, John. Pa. Private. 21 Jun. 1806. 200 acres.
Lynn, Michael. Pa. Drummer. 26 Jul. 1787. 200 acres.
Lynn, William. Va.-Ind. Major. 4312 acres.
Lyon, Amos. Conn. Sufferer. Greenwich. 19.5.4.
Lyon, Caleb. Conn. Sufferer. Greenwich. 9.9.11.
Lyon, Caleb, Jr. Conn. Sufferer. Greenwich. 29.7.9.
Lyon, Gilbert. Conn. Sufferer. Greenwich. 16.17.5.
Lyon, James. Ga. ———. 16 Apr. 1784. 500 acres.
Lyon, James. Va. Private. 24 May 1783. 100 acres.
Lyon, James. Conn. Sufferer. Greenwich. 58.12.5.
Lyon, James, Jr. Conn. Sufferer. Greenwich. 7.10.0.
Lyon, John. Va. Surgeon's Mate. 28 Mar. 1834. 1333 1/3 acres.
Lyon, John. Va. Surgeon's Mate. 16 May 1834. 1333 1/3 acres.
Lyon, Joseph. Ga. ———. 17 May 1784. ———.
Lyon, Joseph. Conn. Sufferer. Fairfield. 31.15.9.
Lyon, Nicholas. Ga. ———. 15 Jul. 1784. 550 acres.

Lyon, Thomas. N. Y. Lieutenant. 14 Jun. 1793. 1000 acres.
Lyon, Thomas. Va. Sergeant. 25 Apr. 1783. 400 acres.
Lyon, Thomas. Va. Private. 14 May 1789. 100 acres.
Lyon, William. Va. Private. 27 Dec. 1834. 100 acres.
Lyon, William. Conn. Sufferer. New/East Haven. 92.2.5.
Lyons, Edward. Pa. Private. 10 Sep. 1789. 200 acres.
Lyons, John. Va. Surgeon's Mate. 17 Dec. 1834. 666 acres.
Lyons, John. Va. Surgeon's Mate. 22 Dec. 1834. 666 acres.
Lyons, Moses. Pa. Private. 28 Oct. 1786. 200 acres.
Lyons, Peter. Ga. ———. 25 Apr. 1784. 200 acres.
Lyons, Thomas. Va. Private. 9 Jun. 1857. 100 acres.
Lytle, Andrew. N.C. Private. 27 Oct. 1783. 640 acres to William Lytle, heir.
Lytle, Andrew. N.C. Sergeant. 7 Dec. 1797. 360 acres to heirs.
Lytle, Andrew. Pa. Lieutenant. 7 Apr. 1787. 200 acres.
Lytle, Andrew. Pa. Private. 7 Apr. 1787. 200 acres.
Lytle, Archibald. N.C. Lieutenant Colonel Commandant. 14 Oct. 1783. 7200 acres.
Lytle, James. Pa. Private. 21 July 1789. 200 acres.
Lytle, William. N.C. Captain. 14 Oct. 1783. 3840 acres.
Mabane, Matthew. Ga. Minute Man. 20 Apr. 1784. 287 1/2 acres.
Mabane, William. Ga. Minute Man. 20 Apr. 1784. 287 1/2 acres. Of Rutherford Co., N.C. in 1786.
Mabin, James. Va. Captain. 25 Mar. 1783. 4000 acres.
Mabon, James. Va. Captain. 21 Jan. 1784. 666 2/3 acres.
Mabon, James. Va. Captain. 3 Jul. 1807. 500 acres.
Mabry, Gray. N.C. Private. 7 Jan. 1786. 228 acres.
Mabry, John. N.C. Private. 7 Jan. 1786. 228 acres.
Mabry, Reps. Ga. Sergeant. 17 Jan. 1785. 870 acres.
Mabry, Robert. Va. Lieutenant. 26 Mar. 1831. 2666 2/3 acres.
Macanally, John. Md. Private. ———. 50 acres.
Macarty, William. N. Y. ———. ———. 500 acres.
Maccroll, James. Va. Private. 27 May 1783. 200 acres.
MacFarland, Alexander. N.C. Private. 7 Jan. 1786. 640 acres to heirs.
MacGee, John. S.C. Soldier. 21 Jan. 1785. 200 acres.
Mack, Bazaliel. N. Y. Matross. 9 Jul. 1790. 600 acres.
Mackelway, John. N.C. Drummer. 19 Feb. 1784. 1000 acres.
Mackey, William. Pa. Captain. 28 Feb. 1794. 500 acres.
Macklin, James. Va. Private. 10 Jul. 1783. 100 acres.
Maclain, William. N.C. Surgeon's Mate. 27 Nov. 1789. 2400 acres.
Maclaine, Jerome. N.C. Captain. 13 Jan. 1823. 3840 acres to heirs.
Macomber, John. Va. Corporal. 28 Jun. 1783. 400 acres.
Macomber, Zenas. Va. Private. 22 Oct. 1787. 100 acres.
Macomes, Aquila. N.C. Private. 29 Sep. 1784. 640 acres to John Poteate, heir.
Macon, James. N.C. ———. 9 Nov. 1784. 640 acres to John Macon, Jr., heir.
Macon, John. N.C. Captain. 23 Oct. 1783. 1097 acres.
Macon, William. N.C. ———. 9 Nov. 1784. 640 acres to John Macon, Jr., heir.
Madden, Benjamin. Ga. ———. 5 Dec. 1785. 287 1/2 acres.
Madden, David. Ga. ———. 15 Mar. 1784. 250 acres.
Madden, Dennis. Ga. Minute Man. 1 Aug. 1785. ———.
Madden, John. Me. Sergeant. 19 May 1835. 200 acres. Waldo.
Madden, Michael. Pa. Corporal. ———. 200 acres.
Madden, Samuel. Ga. ———. 5 Dec. 1785. 287 1/2 acres.
Madden, William. Ga. ———. 5 Dec. 1785. 287 1/2 acres.
Madder, Martin. Va. Private. 19 Jan. 1785. 200 acres.

Maddin, Bryan. N.C. Private. 17 Feb. 1824. 640 acres.
Maddin, Thomas. Va. Private. 10 Mar. 1784. 100 acres.
Maddin, Thomas. Va. Private. 19 Sep. 1797. 100 acres.
Maddocks, Samuel. Me. Non-commissoned Officer. 9 May 1844. 200 acres. Ellsworth.
Maddon, Thomas. Pa. Private. 14 May 1804. 200 acres.
Maddox, Alexander. Va. Private. 7 Aug. 1834. 100 acres.
Maddox, Claiborne. Va. Sergeant. 5 Jun. 1786. 200 acres.
Maddox, John. Ga. Private. 20 Feb. 1784. 250 acres.
Maddox, John. Va. Private. 24 Jan. 1784. 200 acres.
Maddox, John. Va. Private. 11 Mar. 1788. 100 acres.
Maddox, Notley. Va. Private. 1 Aug. 1783. 200 acres.
Maddox, Notley. Va. Sergeant. 13 Aug. 1834. 400 acres.
Maddox, William. Ga. Private. 24 May 1784. 287 1/2 acres.
Maddox, William. Va. Private. 12 Aug. 1785. 100 acres.
Maden, David. Ga. Lieutenant. 15 Mar. 1784. 350 acres.
Maden, Robert. Va. Private. 5 Aug. 1783. 200 acres.
Maderia, Samuel. Pa. ———. 12 Dec. 1803. 200 acres.
Maderris, John. N.C. Captain. 16 Oct. 1783. 3290 acres.
Maderson, John. Va. Private. 26 May 1783. 100 acres.
Madery, William. N.C. Private. 21 May 1784. 357 acres.
Madison, Ambrose. Va. Captain. 3 Feb. 1834. 4000 acres.
Madison, Ambrose. Va. Captain. 11 Apr. 1838. 481 1/3 acres.
Madison, Ambrose. Va. Captain. 11 Apr. 1838. 481 acres.
Madison, Henry. Ga. ———. 17 May 1784. ———.
Madison, John. N.C. Private. 14 Dec. 1796. 640 acres.
Madison, Rowland. Va. Captain. 19 Jan. 1810. 4000 acres.
Madison, William. Va. Private. 3 Mar. 1783. 100 acres.
Madison, William. Va. Private. 22 Apr. 1784. 100 acres.
Madison, William. Va. Lieutenant. 6 Jan. 1838. 1333 1/3 acres.
Madison, William. Va. Lieutenant. 6 Jan. 1838. 1333 1/3 acres.
Madkins, William. Ga. ———. 17 May 1784. ———.
Madrid, Elisha. Va. Private. 7 Dec. 1785. 100 acres.
Madrid, Elisha. Va. Private. 18 Sep. 1807. 100 acres.
Madry, Bryan. N.C. Private. 16 Aug. 1821. 640 acres.
Madry, Darling. N.C. Private. 29 Sep. 1784. 228 acres.
Madry, John. N.C. Corporal. 29 Apr. 1784. 333 acres.
Madry, Moses. N.C. Private. 2 Dec. 1785. 640 acres to heirs.
Maffet, William. Va. Private. 3 Jan. 1833. 200 acres.
Magaw, Robert. Pa. Colonel. 28 Aug. 1787. 500 acres.
Magaw, William. Pa. Surgeon. ———. 300 acres.
Magby, Robert. N.C. Private. 30 Sep. 1785. 640 acres to heirs.
Magee, Peter. N. Y. Lieutenant. 9 Jul. 1790. 1200 acres.
Magee, Peter. N.C. Sergeant. 8 Nov. 1784. 1000 acres to heirs.
Magee, Robert. Pa. Private. 15 Nov. 1786. 200 acres.
Magill, Charles. Va. Major. 6 Nov. 1783. 2000 acres.
Magill, Charles. Va. Major. 6 Nov. 1783. 1000 acres.
Magill, Charles. Va. Major. 6 Nov. 1783. 1000 acres.
Magill, Charles. Va. Major. 6 Nov. 1783. 1000 acres.
Magill, Charles. Va. Major. 6 Nov. 1783. 333 1/3 acres.
Magill, Charles. Va. Major. 2 Oct. 1830. 889 8/9 acres.
Magill, John. Pa. Private. 9 Oct. 1786. 200 acres to Reading Howell, assignee.
Maglin, John. Md. Private. ———. 50 acres.
Magraw, Christopher. Md. Drummer. ———. 50 acres.

Magraw, James. Md. Private. ———. 50 acres.
Magraw, Stephen. Md. Private. ———. 50 acres.
Maguire, Michael. Md. Private. ———. 50 acres.
Maguire, Peter. Md. Private. ———. 50 acres.
Mahaffy, James. Pa. Private. 5 Oct. 1786. 200 acres.
Mahan, Patrick. N. Y. Private. 8 Jul. 1790. 600 acres.
Mahanes, Tapley. Va. Major. 5 Aug. 1783. 100 acres.
Mahans, Samuel. N.C. Corporal. 29 Oct. 1821. 640 acres to heirs.
Mahon, Archibald. Ga. Minute Man. 15 Mar. 1784. 250 acres.
Mahon, Arthur. Pa. Private. ———. 200 acres.
Mahon, John. Va. Marine. 26 Mar. 1831. 100 acres.
Mahon, Samuel. Ga. ———. 16 Apr. 1784. 287 1/2 acres.
Mahon, Susannah. Conn. Sufferer. New/ East Haven. 1.6.8.
Mahoney, Edward. Md. Private. ———. 50 acres.
Mahoney, Florence. Va.-Ind. Private. 108 acres.
Mahoney, Florence. Va. Private. 23 Oct. 1786. 100 acres.
Mahoney, James. Pa. Private. 28 Aug. 1787. 200 acres.
Mahoney, James. Va. Private. 15 Oct. 1783. 200 acres.
Mahoney, Joseph. Va. Private. 19 Jun. 1783. 200 acres.
Mahoney, Thomas. Md. Private. ———. 50 acres.
Mahoney, Thomas. Md. Private. ———. 50 acres.
Mahoon, Ralph. N.C. Private. 7 Dec. 1797. 640 acres to heirs.
Mahorn, Patrick. Md. Private. ———. 50 acres.
Mahorn, Robeson. Va. Private. 7 Mar. 1834. 100 acres.
Mahun, David. Ga. Soldier. 6 Apr. 1785. ———.
Maine, Philip. Va. Private. 23 Jan. 1786. 100 acres.
Mainer, John. Ga. ———. 15 Mar. 1784. 250 acres.
Maines, Francis. Va. Private. 23 Jun. 1783. 200 acres.
Mains, Thomas. Va. Quartermaster. 14 Dec. 1784. 100 acres.
Mains, William. N.C. Private. 17 Dec. 1785. 274 acres.
Maise, John. Ga. Soldier. 17 May 1784. 230 acres.
Mait, Wilmore. Va. Private. 28 Dec. 1787. 100 acres.
Maitre, O. John. N. Y. Private. 8 Jul. 1790. 500 acres.
Major, Ironmonger. Va. Private. 2 Aug. 1783. 100 acres.
Major, James. Va. Private. 29 Apr. 1785. 200 acres.
Major, John. Va. Private. 26 Apr. 1785. 100 acres.
Majors, John. Md. Private. ———. 50 acres.
Makains, William. N.C. Private. 17 Dec. 1785. 274 acres.
Maker, Burton. Mass. ———. 20 Mar. 1832. 200 acres to heirs.
Malbone, Solomon. Va. Private. 8 May 1833. 200 acres.
Malborn, David. N.C. Private. 20 Apr. 1784. 274 acres.
Malborn, David. N.C. Sergeant. 9 Sep. 1820. 154 acres.
Malborn, Solomon. N.C. Sergeant. 20 Apr. 1784. 1000 acres.
Malcolm, William. N. Y. Colonel. 9 Jul. 1790. 3000 acres.
Malebey, William. N.C. Private. 26 Aug. 1785. 640 acres to heirs.
Maljei, James. Pa. Private. 18 Oct. 1786. 200 acres.
Mallaby, James. N.C. Private. 24 Dec. 1785. 640 acres.
Mallery, Joseph. N.C. Private. 30 Sep. 1785. 640 acres to heirs.
Mallery, Levi. Conn. Sufferer. Fairfield. 21.18.6.
Mallery, Matthew. Conn. Sufferer. Norwalk. 87.4.11.
Mallett, Stephen. Va. Private. 29 Jan. 1784. 100 acres.
Mallihorn, Thomas. Va. Private. 20 Nov. 1784. 100 acres.
Mallory, Giles. Conn. Sufferer. Norwalk. 12.4.10.
Mallory, John. Va. Sergeant. 28 Feb. 1783. 200 acres.

Mallory, John. Va. Private. 3 Mar. 1783. 100 acres.
Mallory, Nathan. Conn. Sufferer. Norwalk. 157.12.0.
Mallory, Philip. Va. Captain. Dec. 1782. 4000 acres.
Mallory, Philip. Va. Captain. 15 Dec. 1807. 611 acres.
Mallow, George. Va. Private. 5 Nov. 1811. 200 acres.
Malone, Archibald. Pa. Private. ———. 200 acres.
Malone, Jacob. N.C. Private. 22 Dec. 1796. 640 acres to heirs.
Malone, John. Pa. Private. 10 Jan. 1786. 200 acres.
Malone, John. Pa. Private. 28 Mar. 1808. 200 acres to heirs.
Malone, John. Va. Private. 1 Jun. 1785. 100 acres.
Malone, Martin. Ga. Citizen. 5 Apr. 1785. 287 1/2 acres.
Malone, Patrick. Pa. Private. ———. 200 acres.
Maloney, Daniel. N. Y. Bombardier. 9 Jul. 1790. 600 acres.
Maloney, Richard. Pa. ———. 7 May 1804. 200 acres to Moses McIlvain, assignee.
Maloney, Thomas. Md. Private. ———. 50 acres.
Malony, John. Pa. Private. ———. 200 acres.
Maloy, Edward. Conn. Sufferer. New/East Haven. 265.18.9.
Maloy, James. Va. Private. 26 Mar. 1784. 100 acres.
Malpus, Ezekiel. S.C. Soldier. 21 Jan. 1785. 200 acres.
Malpus, Henry. N.C. Private. 12 Oct. 1795. 640 acres to heirs.
Maltby, Jonathan. Conn. Sufferer. Fairfield. 47.5.10.
Manadue, Henry. Ga. Refugee Captain. 16 Apr. 1784. 575 acres.
Managa, Joseph. Md. Private. ———. 50 acres.
Manen, Joseph. Ga. ———. 15 Mar. 1784. 250 acres.
Maner, Samuel. Ga. ———. 17 May 1784. ———.
Mangers. Nicholas. Md. Captain. ———. 200 acres.
Mangold, Thomas. N.C. Private. 8 Dec. 1796. 640 acres.
Manifee, David. N.C. Private. 8 Dec. 1795. 274 acres.
Manifee, John. N.C. Sergeant. 28 Nov. 1795. 357 acres.
Manifee, Jonas. Va.-Ind. Private. 108 acres.
Maning, John. N.C. Private. 20 Jan. 1785. 640 acres to heirs.
Manley, Allen. N.C. Private. 29 Apr. 1784. 640 acres to Jane Manley, heiress.
Manley, John. Md. Private. ———. 50 acres.
Manley, Mark. N.C. Private. 25 Oct. 1783. 640 acres to Libba Archer, heiress.
Manley, Solomon. N.C. Private. 22 Oct. 1783. 640 acres to Anna Manley, relict.
Manley, William. N.C. Private. 22 Oct. 1783. 274 acres.
Manly, William. Md. Private. ———. 50 acres.
Mann, Arnold. N.C. Private. 12 Sep. 1789. 228 acres.
Mann, Claiborne. Va. Private. 15 Dec. 1784. 200 acres.
Mann, Daniel. Md. Private. ———. 50 acres.
Mann, David. Va. Lieutenant. 10 Dec. 1782. 2666 2/3 acres.
Mann, Francis. N.C. Private. 7 Jan. 1786. 640 acres to heirs.
Mann, George. Mass. Sergeant. 8 Jul. 1833. 200 acres.
Mann, John. Ga. Refugee. 21 Apr. 1784. 287 1/2 acres.
Mann, John. N.C. ———. 29 Apr. 1784. 640 acres to Nathan Mann, heir.
Mann, Luke. Ga. ———. 21 Apr. 1784. 900 acres.
Mann, Robert. N.C. Private. 30 Sep. 1785. 640 acres.
Mann, Thomas. N.C. Private. 2 Dec. 1785. 640 acres.
Mann, William. Md. Private. ———. 50 acres.
Mann, William. Md. Private. ———. 50 acres.
Mannen, James. Ga. ———. 17 May 1784. 287 1/2 acres.
Manner, Joshua. Ga. Citizen. 19 Dec. 1785. 287 1/2 acres.
Manner, Timothy. N.C. Private. 10 Mar. 1788. 228 acres.

Manning, Abraham. Md. Private. ———. 50 acres.
Manning, Adam. Ga. ———. 17 May 1784. ———.
Manning, Adam. Ga. ———. 15 Apr. 1784. 287 1/2 acres.
Manning, Christian. Pa. Private. ———. 200 acres to Stephen Loudon, assignee.
Manning, Drury. Ga. ———. 17 May 1784. 250 acres.
Manning, Jesse. Va. Private. 12 May 1783. 200 acres.
Manning, John. Ga. Soldier. 15 Mar. 1784. 250 acres.
Manning, Laurence. Va. Lieutenant. 28 Sep. 1808. 2666 2/3 acres.
Manning, Lawrence. Pa. Lieutenant. 21 Apr. 1796. 200 acres.
Manning, Lawrence. Pa. Lieutenant. 21 Apr. 1787. 200 acres.
Manning, Pierce. Pa. Private. ———. 200 acres.
Manning, Robert. Ga. Refugee. 15 Apr. 1784. 287 1/2 acres.
Manning, Samuel. Va. Private. 26 Apr. 1783. 200 acres.
Manning, William. Ga. Private. 10 Dec. 1784. 250 acres.
Mans, Matthew. Pa. Surgeon. 14 Oct. 1786. 300 acres to Moses Bartram, assignee.
Mans, Matthew. Pa. Surgeon. ———. 300 acres.
Mansfield, Daniel. Conn. Sufferer. New/ East Haven. 11.17.6.
Mansfield, Esther. Conn. Sufferer. New/ East Haven. 299.5.4.
Mansfield, George. Va. Private. 20 May 1785. 200 acres.
Mansfield, Hannah. Conn. Sufferer. New/ East Haven. 8.17.0.
Mansfield, Henry. Md. Private. ———. 50 acres.
Mansfield, Kirsted. Conn. Sufferer. New/ East Haven. 10.13.9.
Mansfield, Moses. Conn. Sufferer. New/ East Haven. 6.3.0.
Mansfield, Nathan. Conn. Sufferer. New/ East Haven. 3.10.6.
Mansfield, Thomas. Va. Private. 1 Apr. 1783. 100 acres.
Mansfield, Thomas. Va. Private. 26 Apr. 1783. 200 acres.
Mansfield, William. Md. Private. ———. 50 acres.
Mansfield, William. Conn. Sufferer. New/ East Haven. 47.17.9.
Manshare, George. N.C. Private. 2 Feb. 1786. 640 acres.
Manson, Ebenezer. Conn. Sufferer. Danbury. 23.6.8.
Manson, John. N.C. Private. 30 Sep. 1785. 640 acres to heirs.
Manson, John. Pa. Private. 9 Mar. 1795. 200 acres to John Nicholson, assignee.
Mantle, George. Md. Private. ———. 50 acres.
Mantle, John. Md. Sergeant. ———. 50 acres.
Manwaring, David. Conn. Sufferer. New London. 51.3.0.
Manwaring, Robert. Conn. Sufferer. New London. 21.8.8.
Mapes, John. Va. Private. 13 Apr. 1838. 200 acres.
Mapes, Phineas. N. Y. Private. 8 Jul. 1790. 500 acres.
Maples, Marmaduke. N.C. Private. 14 Dec. 1787. 278 acres.
Maples, Marmaduke. N.C. Corporal. 18 Nov. 1820. 482 acres.
Mapps, John. N.Y. Private. 13 Sep. 1790. 500 acres to heirs.
Marberry, Joseph. Md. Captain. ———. 200 acres.
Marbery, Jesse. N.C. Private. 30 Sep. 1785. 640 acres to heirs.
Marble, Henry. Mass. Private. 8 Sep. 1830. 200 acres.
Marbury, Horatio. Ga. Refugee. 16 Apr. 1784. 287 1/2 acres.
Marbury, Leonard. Ga. Colonel. ———. 1150 acres.
Marbury, Leonard, Sr. Ga. Private. ———. 250 acres.
Marbury, Thomas. Ga. Refugee. 26 May 1784. 287 1/2 acres.
Marcey, John. N.C. Private. 10 Aug. 1785. 640 acres to heirs.
March, Febreas. N.C. Private. 30 Sep. 1785. 640 acres to heirs.
March, John. Va. Private. 5 Dec. 1833. 200 acres.
March, William. Va. Midshipman. 12 Sep. 1787. 2666 2/3 acres.
Marchment, John. N.C. Private. 6 Dec. 1797. 640 acres to heirs.
Marcus, Daniel. Ga. Minute Man. 22 Mar. 1785. 250 acres.

Marcus, Eli. Ga. ———. ———. 287 1/2 acres.

Marcus, John. Ga. ———. 17 May 1784. ———.

Mardera, James. N.C. Private. 30 Sep. 1785. 640 acres to heirs.

Mardis, William. Va. Private. 20 Jun. 1783. 100 acres.

Margan, Richard. N.C. Private. 9 Nov. 1784. 640 acres.

Margery, Jonathan. Me. Private. 19 Oct. 1835. 200 acres to widow Sarah Margery. Scarbrough.

Mariner, Suthey. N.C. Private. 7 Dec. 1797. 640 acres to heirs.

Marion, Francis. S.C. ———. Lieutenant Colonel Commandant. 5 Sep. 1785. 302 acres.

Marius, Jacob. N. Y. Bombardier. 9 Jul. 1790. 600 acres.

Marker, Andrew. Pa. Private. ———. 200 acres.

Markham, Ebenezer. N. Y. ———. ———. 333 1/3 acres.

Markham, James. Va. Private. 29 Oct. 1783. 4000 acres.

Markham, James. Va. Captain. 29 Oct. 1783. 2222 acres.

Markham, James. Va. Captain. 25 Jan. 1812. 277 3/4 acres.

Markham, James. Va. Captain. 8 Jun. 1832. 91 1/4 acres.

Markland, John. Pa. Private. 11 Jun. 1795. 200 acres.

Markland, John. Pa. Lieutenant. 11 Apr. 1787. 200 acres.

Markle, Charles. Va. Captain. 31 Dec. 1839. 1333 1/3 acres.

Markle, Charles. Va. Captain. 31 Dec. 1839. 666 2/3 acres.

Markle, Charles. Va. Captain. 31 Dec. 1839. 1333 1/3 acres.

Markle, Charles. Va. Captain. 31 Dec. 1839. 666 2/3 acres.

Markley, Andrew. S.C. ———. 7 Sep. 1789. 24 acres.

Markley, Andrew. S.C. ———. 7 Sep. 1789. 63 acres.

Markley, Andrew. S.C. ———. 7 Sep. 1789. 13 acres.

Markley, Andrew. S.C. ———. 7 Sep. 1789. 100 acres.

Marks, George. Pa. Private. 2 Apr. 1794. 200 acres to Elizabeth Marks, widow.

Marks, Isaiah. Va. Captain. 30 Aug. 1783. 4000 acres.

Marks, John. N.C. Private. 17 Dec. 1807. 640 acres to heirs.

Marks, John. Va. Captain. 3 Sep. 1782. 4000 acres.

Marks, John. Va. Sailor. 26 Jun. 1784. 100 acres.

Marleau, Andrew. Va. Private. 31 Dec. 1851. 100 acres.

Marleau, Andrew. Va. Private. 8 Apr. 1856. 100 acres.

Marleau, Gabriel. Va. Private. 31 Dec. 1851. 100 acres.

Marleau, Gabriel. Va. Private. 21 Apr. 1856. 100 acres.

Marler, John. N.C. Private. 29 Oct. 1821. 640 acres to heirs.

Marler, William. Ga. ———. 22 Apr. 1784. 287 1/2 acres.

Marlet, Baptiste. N. Y. ———. ———. 500 acres.

Marley, Dempsey. N.C. Private. 11 Jul. 1785. 640 acres to heirs.

Marlin, Robert. N.C. Private. 20 Sep. 1784. 428 acres.

Marlin, William. Va. Private. 2 Feb. 1785. 100 acres.

Marlo, Robert. N.C. Private. 19 May 1784. 640 acres.

Marlow, William. Md. Sergeant. ———. 50 acres.

Marman, George. Pa. Private. ———. 200 acres.

Marney, Louis. N. Y. ———. ———. 500 acres.

Marney, Louis, Jr. N. Y. ———. ———. 500 acres.

Marony, Florence. N. Y. Sergeant. 8 Jul. 1790. 600 acres.

Marquis, Joseph. S.C. ———. 3 Oct. 1796. 123 acres.

Marquis, Joseph. S.C. ———. 3 Oct. 1796. 39 acres.

Marquis, Joseph. S.C. ———. 3 Oct. 1796. 22 acres.

Marquis, Joseph. S.C. ———. 3 Oct. 1796. 16 acres.

Marquis, Samuel. S.C. ———. 3 Oct. 1796. 169 acres to Joseph Marquis, heir at law.

Marquis, Samuel. S.C. ———. 3 Oct. 1796. 27 acres to Joseph Marquis, heir at law.

Marr, John. N.C. ———. 29 Apr. 1784. 640 acres to James Marr, heir.
Marr, John, Sr. N.C. Sergeant. 29 Apr. 1784. 335 acres.
Marr, Patrick. Va.-Ind. Private. 108 acres.
Marriner, Jeffrey. Va. Private. 8 Jun. 1839. 100 acres.
Marriner, Laban. Va. Seaman. 9 Dec. 1833. 100 acres.
Marriner, Levin. Va. Seaman. 19 Nov. 1833. 100 acres.
Marrow, Robert. Va. Captain. 26 May 1783. 4000 acres.
Mars, Barnabas. Va. Private. 4 Jun. 1783. 100 acres.
Mars, Timothy. N.C. Private. 1 Sep. 1785. 640 acres to heirs.
Marsden, Humphry. N. Y. Private. 3 Jul. 1790. 600 acres.
Marselas, Garret. N. Y. ———. 5 Jul. 1794. 600 acres.
Marsh, Benjamin. Md. Private. ———. 50 acres.
Marsh, Charles. Md. Private. ———. 50 acres.
Marsh, Eli. N.C. Private. 8 Dec. 1795. 640 acres to heirs.
Marsh, Elijah. Ga. ———. 17 Sep. 1784. 287 1/2 acres.
Marsh, Ephraim. N.Y. ———. 13 Sep. 1790. 500 acres to heirs.
Marsh, John. Ga. ———. 17 Sep. 1784. 287 1/2 acres.
Marsh, John. N. Y. Ensign. 9 Jul. 1790. 1150 acres.
Marsh, Joseph. Mass. Private. 18 Oct. 1834. 200 acres to widow Mary Marsh.
Marsh, Nathan. Ga. ———. 17 Sep. 1784. 287 1/2 acres.
Marsh, Noah. Me. ———. 14 Feb. 1843. 200 acres to widow Hannah Marsh. Cornwell.
Marshal, William. Md. Corporal. ———. 50 acres.
Marshall, Abraham. Ga. Chaplain. 2 Jan. 1784. 747 1/2 acres.
Marshall, Abraham. Ga. ———. 17 May 1784. —— acres to heirs.
Marshall, Andrew. Conn. Sufferer. Greenwich. 26.14.3.
Marshall, Benjamin. Pa. Private. ———. 200 acres.
Marshall, Benjamin. Pa. Private. 21 May 1787. 200 acres.
Marshall, Benjamin. Va. Master at Arms. 28 Oct. 1784. 200 acres.
Marshall, Benjamin. Va. ———. 29 Aug. 1835. 2466 2/3 acres.
Marshall, Benjamin. Va. ———. 22 Jun. 1837. ———.
Marshall, Benjamin. Va. ———. 22 June 1837. ———.
Marshall, Benjamin. Va. ———. 22 June 1837. ———.
Marshall, Charles. N.C. Private. 2 Feb. 1786. 640 acres to heirs.
Marshall, Daniel. Ga. Citizen. 2 Jan. 1784. 250 acres.
Marshall, Daniel. Conn. Sufferer. Greenwich. 22.1.4.
Marshall, Daniel, Sr. Ga. Citizen. 3 Jan. 1784. 250 acres.
Marshall, David. Pa. Lieutenant. ———. 200 acres.
Marshall, David. Pa. Lieutenant. 9 Jun. 1787. 200 acres.
Marshall, David. Pa. ———. ———. 250 acres.
Marshall, David. Va. Private. 30 Jul. 1783. 100 acres.
Marshall, Dixon. N.C. Lieutenant. 9 Nov. 1784. 2560 acres.
Marshall, Elihu. N. Y. Captain. 6 Jul. 1790. 1800 acres.
Marshall, Emanuel. N.C. Private. Nov. 1788. 640 acres to heirs.
Marshall, Ezra. Conn. Sufferer. Greenwich. 0.0.0.
Marshall, Ezra. Conn. Sufferer. Greenwich. 56.1.9.
Marshall, George. N.C. Private. 14 May 1784. 228 acres.
Marshall, Gilbert. Conn. Sufferer. Greenwich. 0.0.0.
Marshall, Henry. Va. Sergeant. 19 Jun. 1783. 400 acres.
Marshall, Henry. Va. Sergeant. 19 Jun. 1783. 200 acres.
Marshall, Henry. Conn. Sufferer. Greenwich. 35.12.0.
Marshall, Humphrey. Va. Captain. 14 Dec. 1782. 4000 acres.
Marshall, James. Va. Captain. 13 Nov. 1830. 2000 acres.
Marshall, James. Va. Captain. 27 Nov. 1830. 333 1/3 acres.
Marshall, James. Va. Captain. 13 Nov. 1830. 1000 acres.

Marshall, James. Va. Captain. 27 Nov. 1830. 166 2/3 acres.
Marshall, James. Va. Captain. 13 Nov. 1830. 1000 acres.
Marshall, James. Va. Captain. 27 Nov. 1830. 166 2/3 acres.
Marshall, James. Va. Midshipman. 2 May 1838. 1777 7/9 acres.
Marshall, James. Va. Midshipman. 21 Sep. 1841. 592 16/27 acres.
Marshall, James. Va. Midshipman. 21 Sep. 1841. 292 8/27 acres.
Marshall, James Markham. Va. Lieutenant. 3 Feb. 1784. 2666 2/3 acres.
Marshall, Jenifer. Va. Sailing Master. 7 Dec. 1830. 2666 2/3 acres.
Marshall, John. Ga. ———. 25 May 1784. 287 1/2 acres.
Marshall, John. Pa. ———. ———. 200 acres to widow.
Marshall, John. Pa. Captain. ———. 500 acres.
Marshall, John. Va. Captain. 30 Nov. 1782. 4000 acres.
Marshall, John. Va. Boatswain. 30 Dec. 1783. 200 acres.
Marshall, John. Va. Boatswain. 28 Aug. 1835. 2466 2/3 acres.
Marshall, John. Va. ———. 22 Jun. 1837. ———.
Marshall, John. Va. ———. 22 Jun. 1837. ———.
Marshall, John. Va. ———. 22 Jun. 1837. ———.
Marshall, Joseph. Ga. Citizen. 2 Jan. 1784. 250 acres.
Marshall, Joseph. Ga. Soldier. 7 Jun. 1785. 230 acres to heirs.
Marshall, Joseph. Va. Sailing Master. 3 Mar. 1851. 2666 2/3 acres.
Marshall, Levy. Ga. Citizen. 5 Apr. 1785. 287 1/2 acres.
Marshall, Matthew. Ga. ———. 23 Apr. 1784. 287 1/2 acres.
Marshall, Moses. Ga. Citizen. 2 Jan. 1784. 250 acres.
Marshall, Rachel. Conn. Sufferer. Greenwich. 10.5.5.
Marshall, Richard. Va. Corporal. 28 Nov. 1783. 466 2/3 acres.
Marshall, Richard. Va. Private. 8 Dec. 1784. 200 acres.
Marshall, Robert. N. Y. Private. 3 Jul. 1790. 600 acres.
Marshall, Silas. N.C. Private. 10 Feb. 1796. 640 acres.
Marshall, Solomon. Ga. Citizen. 25 May 1784. 287 1/2 acres.
Marshall, Thomas. N. Y. Corporal. 8 Jul. 1790. 500 acres.
Marshall, Thomas. Va. Sergeant Major. 8 Jul. 1783. 400 acres.
Marshall, Thomas. Va. Colonel. 26 Jun. 1783. 6666 2/3 acres.
Marshall, Thomas. Va. Sergeant. 15 Dec. 1795. 200 acres.
Marshall, Thomas. Va. Colonel. 26 Mar. 1831. 1388 2/3 acres.
Marshall, Thomas. Va. Sergeant. 19 Mar. 1834. 200 acres.
Marshall, Thomas, Jr. Va. Captain. 14 Dec. 1782. 4000 acres.
Marshall, William. Conn. Sufferer. Greenwich. 14.16.11.
Marshall, Willis. N.C. Private. 16 Aug. 1821. 640 acres.
Marshall, Zacharias. Ga. ———. 17 May 1784. ———.
Marshall, Zackheus. Ga. Citizen. 2 Jan. 1784. 250 acres.
Marston, John. Va. Lieutenant. 29 Apr. 1783. 2666 2/3 acres.
Marston, John. Va. Lieutenant. 29 Jan. 1848. 500 acres.
Marston, John. Va. Lieutenant. 29 Jan. 1848. 1966 2/3 acres.
Marston, John. Va. ———. 21 Jan. 1851. 200 acres.
Marston, Nathaniel. Me. ———. 14 May 1838. 200 acres to widow Jane Marston Gardiner.
Marston, Nathaniel. S.C. Lieutenant. 21 Jan. 1785. 300 acres.
Martain, James. Va. Corporal. 28 Apr. 1783. 400 acres.
Martain, John. Va. Private. 13 Jun. 1783. 100 acres.
Martial, Solomon. N.C. Private. 25 Nov. 1795. 640 acres to heirs.
Martin, Alexander. N.C. Colonel. 14 Oct. 1783. 2314 acres.
Martin, Alexander. Pa. Matross. 13 Jul. 1787. 200 acres.
Martin, Alexander. Va. Drummer. 25 Apr. 1783. 200 acres.
Martin, Anthony. N. Y. ———. ———. 500 acres.

Martin, Archibald. N.C. Private. 12 May 1784. 297 acres.
Martin, Austin. Ga. ———. 26 May 1784. 287 1/2 acres.
Martin, Baptiste. N. Y. ———. ———. 500 acres.
Martin, Bartlett. Ga. ———. 17 May 1784. ———.
Martin, Charles. Ga. ———. 16 Apr. 1784. 1000 acres.
Martin, Charles. Va.-Ind. Private. 108 acres.
Martin, Charles. Pa. Private. 15 Jul. 1812. 200 acres.
Martin, Charles. Pa. ———. 15 Jul. 1812. 200 acres.
Martin, Claudius. Pa. Private. ———. 200 acres.
Martin, Cornelius. Ga. Minute Man. 16 Sep. 1785. 287 1/2 acres.
Martin, David. Me. ———. 14 Jul. 1835. 200 acres. Bridgeton.
Martin, Edmond. Ga. Refugee Lieutenant. 15 Apr. 1784. 350 acres.
Martin, Francis. N. Y. ———. ———. 500 acres.
Martin, Francis, Jr. N. Y. ———. ———. 500 acres.
Martin, Gannaway. Ga. Refugee. 25 Feb. 1784. 250 acres.
Martin, George. N.C. Private. 30 Sep. 1785. 640 acres to heirs.
Martin, George. Pa. ———. 14 Dec. 1808. 200 acres to Mary Martin, widow.
Martin, Godfrey. Ga. ———. 21 Apr. 1784. 700 acres.
Martin, Henry. N.C. Private. 2 Jan. 1784. 640 acres.
Martin, Hudson. Va. Lieutenant. 5 May 1838. 2666 2/3 acres.
Martin, Hugh. Pa. Surgeon. 22 Aug. 1787. 300 acres to John Dunlap et al, executors.
Martin, Hugh. Pa. Surgeon. 22 Aug. 1787. 300 acres to John Dunlap et al., executors.
Martin, Jacob. Ga. ———. 1784. 287 1/2 acres.
Martin, Jacob. N.C. Private. 7 Jan. 1786. 620 acres.
Martin, James. Ga. Lieutenant Colonel. 25 Feb. 1784. 800 acres.
Martin, James. Ga. ———. 14 Sep. 1784. 287 1/2 acres.
Martin, James. Ga. Colonel. 20 Feb. 1784. 250 acres.
Martin, James. Ga. ———. 15 Mar. 1784. 250 acres.
Martin, James. N.C. Captain. 22 Oct. 1783. 1462 acres.
Martin, James. N.C. Private. 25 Nov. 1783. 274 acres.
Martin, James. N.C. Private. 2 Jun. 1813. 228 acres to heirs.
Martin, James. S.C. ———. 6 Nov. 1786. 150 acres to Rachel Martin, widow.
Martin, James. S.C. ———. 6 Nov. 1786. 50 acres to Rachel Martin, widow.
Martin, James. S.C. Surgeon. 16 Jul. 1784. 300 acres.
Martin, James. Va. Private. 15 Jun. 1807. 100 acres.
Martin, Joel. N.C. Private. 8 Aug. 1821. 640 acres.
Martin, Joel. N.C. Private. 8 Feb. 1823. 640 acres to heirs.
Martin, John. Ga. Colonel. 24 May 1784. 977 1/2 acres.
Martin, John. Ga. ———. ———. 287 1/2 acres.
Martin, John. Me. Drummer. 6 Apr. 1836. 200 acres to widow Lydia Martin. Monmouth.
Martin, John. Md. Private. ———. 50 acres.
Martin, John. Md. Private. ———. 50 acres.
Martin, John. N. Y. Matross. 6 Jul. 1790. 600 acres.
Martin, John. N.C. Private. 9 Sep. 1785. 640 acres to heirs.
Martin, John. S.C. Soldier. 21 Jan. 1785. 200 acres.
Martin, John. Va. Private. 27 May 1783. 200 acres.
Martin, John. Va. Private. 15 Oct. 1783. 200 acres.
Martin, John. Va. Sergeant. 12 Feb. 1784. 200 acres.
Martin, John. Va. Private. 20 Jun. 1786. 100 acres.
Martin, John H. Ga. ———. ———. 287 1/2 acres.
Martin, John, Jr. Ga. Refugee. 20 Feb. 1784. 250 acres.
Martin, Joseph. N. Y. ———. ———. 500 acres.

Martin, Joseph P. Me. Private. 28 Jan. 1839. 200 acres. Prospect.
Martin, Joshua. N.C. Private. 20 Oct. 1783. 274 acres.
Martin, Josiah. Va. Private. 28 May 1784. 200 acres.
Martin, Lewis D. S.C. Captain. 5 Sep. 1785. 300 acres.
Martin, Martin. S.C. ———. 4 Jun. 1787. 12 acres.
Martin, Martin. S.C. ———. 4 Jun. 1787. 60 acres.
Martin, Martin. S.C. ———. 4 Jun. 1787. 16 acres.
Martin, Martin. S.C. ———. 4 Jun. 1787. 67 acres.
Martin, Martin. S.C. ———. 4 Jun. 1787. 25 acres.
Martin, Matthew. Ga. Private. 17 May 1784. ———.
Martin, Miles. N.C. Private. 25 Nov. 1795. 640 acres to heirs.
Martin, Nicholas. N.C. Private. 2 Feb. 1786. 640 acres to heirs.
Martin, Norman. S.C. Soldier. 21 Jan. 1785. 200 acres.
Martin, Patrick. N.C. Sergeant. 13 Jun. 1785. 1000 acres to heirs.
Martin, Patrick. Va. Private. 12 Dec. 1783. 200 acres.
Martin, Patrick. Va. Private. 17 Mar. 1784. 100 acres.
Martin, Peter. Pa. Private. 6 Apr 1794. 200 acres to Sarah Martin, widow.
Martin, Peter. Pa. Lieutenant. 6 Apr. 1794. 200 acres to Sarah Martin, widow.
Martin, Pierre. Va. Private. 14 Jul. 1835. 100 acres.
Martin, Pierre. Va. Private. 2 May 1856. 100 acres.
Martin, Richard. N.C. Private. 20 Apr. 1784. 228 acres.
Martin, Richard. N.C. Private. 6 Sep. 1821. 640 acres.
Martin, Robert. Me. ———. 14 Jul. 1835. 200 acres. Sebago.
Martin, Robert. Pa. Private. 30 Sep. 1787. 200 acres.
Martin, Robert. Pa. Lieutenant. 30 Sep. 1787. 200 acres.
Martin, Robert. Va. Private. 27 Mar. 1812. 200 acres.
Martin, Samuel. N.C. Private. 5 Dec. 1796. 228 acres.
Martin, Simon. Ga. ———. 17 May 1784. ———.
Martin, Thomas. N.C. Private. 2 Aug. 1784. 228 acres.
Martin, Thomas. Va. Lieutenant. 31 Jan. 1784. 1000 acres.
Martin, Thomas. Va. Lieutenant. 31 Jan. 1784. 1666 2/3 acres.
Martin, Thomas. Va. Lieutenant. 23 Jun. 1784. 444 2/3 acres.
Martin, Thomas. Va. Private. 20 Nov. 1784. 200 acres.
Martin, Thomas. Va. Captain. 1 Jun. 1805. 1555 2/3 acres.
Martin, Thomas. Va. Captain. 29 Aug. 1807. 555 acres.
Martin, William. Ga. First Lieutenant. 19 Apr. 1784. 460 acres to Betty Martin for the heirs.
Martin, William. Md. Corporal. ———. 50 acres.
Martin, William. N.C. Infirm. 20 Sep. 1784. 640 acres.
Martin, William. Pa. Sergeant. 26 Apr. 1786. 250 acres.
Martin, William. Pa. Captain. 7 Sep. 1787. 500 acres.
Martin, William. S.C. Soldier. 21 Jan. 1785. 200 acres.
Martin, William. Va. ———. 25 Jan. 1834. 100 acres.
Martin, William. Va. Private. 23 Jun. 1783. 200 acres.
Martin, William. Va. Private. 30 Jun. 1783. 200 acres.
Martindale, John. Md. Fife Major. ———. 50 acres.
Marting, Lawrence. Conn. Sufferer. New London. 55.18.6.
Martingly, John. Va. Private. 26 May 1783. 100 acres.
Martling, Deliverence. N.Y. Private. 13 Sep. 1790. 600 acres.
Marvin, Isaiah. Conn. Sufferer. Norwalk. 158.10.1.
Marvin, Matthew. Conn. Sufferer. Norwalk. 19.0.8.
Marvin, Samuel. Conn. Sufferer. Norwalk. 319.3.10.
Masey, Zebulon. N.C. Private. 17 Dec. 1785. 640 acres.
Mash, John. Ga. ———. 17 Sep. 1784. 287 1/2 acres.

Mash, Thomas. Ga. Minute Man. 16 Sep. 1785. 287 1/2 acres.
Mash, Thomas. Va. Private. 9 Feb. 1784. 100 acres.
Mashburn, Edward. N.C. Private. 10 Sep. 1821. 84 acres to heirs.
Maskall, Thomas. S.C. Captain. 21 Jan. 1785. 300 acres.
Mason, Caleb. Md. Ensign. ———. 200 acres.
Mason, Christopher. N.C. Private. 15 Feb. 1797. 640 acres to heirs.
Mason, Daniel. Va. Private. 11 Feb. 1784. 100 acres.
Mason, David. Va. Captain. 6 Feb. 1807. 2500 acres.
Mason, David. Va. Captain. 6 Feb. 1807. 1500 acres.
Mason, David. Va. Colonel. 31 May 1839. 237 acres.
Mason, David. Va. Colonel. 7 Oct. 1846. 119 1/7 acres.
Mason, David. Va. Colonel. 7 Oct. 1846. 195 1/7 acres.
Mason, David. Va. Colonel. 12 Apr. 1849. 95 1/4 acres.
Mason, David. Va. Colonel. 12 Apr. 1849. 95 1/4 acres.
Mason, David. Va. Colonel. 12 Apr. 1849. 95 1/4 acres.
Mason, David. Va. Colonel. 12 Apr. 1849. 95 1/4 acres.
Mason, David. Va. Colonel. 12 Apr. 1849. 95 1/4 acres.
Mason, David. Va. Colonel. 12 Apr. 1849. 95 1/4 acres.
Mason, David. Va. Colonel. 12 Apr. 1849. 95 1/4 acres.
Mason, David. Va. Colonel. 12 Apr. 1849. 95 1/4 acres.
Mason, David. Va. Colonel. 12 Apr. 1849. 95 1/4 acres.
Mason, David. Va. Colonel. 12 Apr. 1849. 95 1/4 acres.
Mason, David. Va. Colonel. 6 Nov. 1849. 172 acres.
Mason, David. Va. Colonel. 6 Nov. 1849. 214 acres.
Mason, David. Va. Colonel. ———. 172 acres.
Mason, David. Va. Colonel. 20 Jun. 1851. 114 2/3 acres.
Mason, David. Va. Colonel. 20 Jun. 1851. 57 1/3 acres.
Mason, David. Va. Colonel. 20 Jun. 1851. 172 acres.
Mason, David. Va. Colonel. 20 Jun. 1851. 172 acres.
Mason, David. Va. Colonel. 8 Jul. 1851. ———.
Mason, David. Va. Colonel. 8 Jul. 1851. 47 1/2 acres.
Mason, David. Va. Colonel. 8 Jul. 1851. 143 1/3 acres.
Mason, David. Va. Colonel. 8 Jul. 1851. 143 1/3 acres.
Mason, David. Va. Colonel. 8 Jul. 1851. 86 acres.
Mason, David. Va. Colonel. 25 Mar. 1852. 396 2/3 acres.
Mason, David. Va. Colonel. 25 Mar. 1852. 79 1/3 acres.
Mason, George. S.C. ———. 2 Oct. 1786. 100 acres.
Mason, Henry. Conn. Sufferer. Groton. 27.18.0.
Mason, Isachea. Md. Corporal. ———. 50 acres.
Mason, James. Md. Private. ———. 50 acres.
Mason, James. Va. Sergeant. 4 Nov. 1793. 200 acres.
Mason, James. Va. Captain. 9 Mar. 1831. 4000 acrres.
Mason, John. N. Y. Chaplain. 3 Jul. 1790. 2000 acres.
Mason, John. N.C. Private. 4 May 1785. 640 acres to heirs.
Mason, John. Va. Private. 17 Jun. 1784. 200 acres.
Mason, Littlebury. Va. Paymaster. 8 Nov. 1832. 4000 acres.
Mason, Nathaniel. Va. Captain. 9 Mar. 1840. 666 2/3 acres.
Mason, Nathaniel. Va. Captain. 9 Mar. 1840. 133 1/3 acres.
Mason, Nathaniel. Va. Captain. 9 Mar. 1840. 666 2/3 acres.
Mason, Nathaniel. Va. Captain. 9 Mar. 1840. 133 1/3 acres.
Mason, Nathaniel. Va. Captain. 19 Feb. 1845. 666 2/3 acres.
Mason, Nathaniel. Va. Captain. 19 Feb. 1845. 133 1/3 acres.
Mason, Nathaniel. Va. Captain. 19 Feb. 1845. 666 2/3 acres.
Mason, Nathaniel. Va. Captain. 19 Feb. 1845. 133 1/3 acres.

Mason, Nathaniel. Va. Captain. 7 Mar. 1849. 80 acres.
Mason, Nathaniel. Va. Captain. 7 Mar. 1849. 80 acres.
Mason, Nathaniel. Va. Captain. 7 Mar. 1849. 80 acres.
Mason, Nathaniel. Va. Captain. 7 Mar. 1849. 80 acres.
Mason, Nathaniel. Va. Captain. 7 Mar. 1849. 80 acres.
Mason, Nathaniel. Va. Captain. 7 Mar. 1849. 80 acres.
Mason, Nathaniel. Va. Captain. 7 Mar. 1849. 80 acres.
Mason, Nathaniel. Va. Captain. 7 Mar. 1849. 80 acres.
Mason, Nathaniel. Va. Captain. 7 Mar. 1849. 80 acres.
Mason, Nathaniel. Va. Captain. 7 Mar. 1849. 80 acres.
Mason, Nathaniel. Va. Captain. 12 Dec. 1845. 222 2/9 acres.
Mason, Nathaniel. Va. Captain. 7 Oct. 1846. 222 2/9 acres.
Mason, Nathaniel. Va. Captain. 7 Oct. 1846. 222 2/9 acres.
Mason, Philip. N.C. Drum Major. 26 Aug. 1785. 1000 acres.
Mason, Philip. N.C. Private. 30 Sep. 1785. 640 acres to heirs.
Mason, Richard. S.C. Captain. 1 May 1786. 100 acres to William Mason, heir at law.
Mason, Richard. S.C. Captain. 4 Sep. 1786. 200 acres to William Mason, heir at law.
Mason, Thomas. Md. Captain. ———. 200 acres.
Mason, Thomas. N.Y. ———. 13 Sep. 1790. 500 acres to heirs.
Mason, Thomas. Va. Private. 16 Oct. 1783. 200 acres.
Mason, William. Pa. Private. ———. 200 acres.
Mason, William. Va. Private. 17 Apr. 1793. 200 acres.
Massenburg, Alexander. Va. Master. 1 Mar. 1851. 2666 23/ acres.
Massenburg, Nicholas. Va. Lieutenant. 19 Dec. 1792. 2666 2/3 acres.
Massenburg, Nicholas. Va. Lieutenant. 23 Feb. 1861. 595 2/3 acres.
Massey, ———. N.C. ———. 23 Oct. 1783. 640 acres to Thomas Massey, heir.
Massey, ———. N.C. ———. 23 Oct. 1783. 640 acres to Reuben Massey, heir.
Massey, Caleb. Va. Private. 15 Jun. 1807. 100 acres.
Massey, Dade. Va. Private. 22 Jun. 1784. 100 acres.
Massey, Hezekiah. Md. Sergeant. ———. 50 acres.
Massey, John. N.C. Private. 31 Dec. 1806. 228 acres.
Massey, John. Va. Private. 20 Dec. 1786. 200 acres.
Massey, John. Va. Cornet. 10 Apr. 1835. 1777 7/9 acres.
Massey, John. Va. Cornet. 26 May 1835. 889 8/9 acres.
Massey, Joseph. N.C. Private. 26 May 1784. 640 acres.
Massey, Joseph. N.C. Private. 14 Dec. 1797. 640 acres to heirs.
Massey, Taliaferro. Va. Private. 22 Jun. 1784. 100 acres.
Massey, Theodorick. Va. Private. 15 Apr. 1783. 4000 acres.
Massey, Thomas. N.C. Sergeant. 25 Aug. 1820. 360 acres to heirs.
Massey, Thomas. Va. Major. 24 Jun. 1783. 5333 1/3 acres.
Massey, William. Va. Fife Major. 25 May 1832. 400 acres.
Massey, Zacheriah. N.C. Private. 24 Nov. 1796. 640 acres to heirs.
Masson, Thomas. N. Y. Private. 6 Jul. 1790. 600 acres.
Masters, John. Va. Private. 13 Jun. 1826. 200 acres.
Masters, Jonathan. N. Y. Private. 8 Jul. 1790. 600 acres.
Masterson, Philip. Md. Matross. ———. 50 acres.
Masterson, Thomas. Va. Midshipman. 15 Aug. 1834. 1333 1/3 acres.
Masterson, Thomas. Va. Midshipman. 15 Aug. 1835. 1333 1/3 acres.
Matchett, Edward. N.C. Private. 9 Nov. 1784. 640 acres to heir.
Matchin, Thomas. N. Y. Captain. 9 Jul. 1790. 1800 acres.
Mathews, Daniel. Va. Private. 3 May 1838. 100 acres.
Mathews, George. Va. Colonel. 14 Sep. 1807. 1019 acres.

Mathews, H. Pa. Captain. 27 Feb. 1794. 500 acres to Mary Mathews, widow.

Mathews, Henry. Pa. Captain. 26 Oct. 1791. 500 acres to widow.

Mathews, James. N.C. Private. 16 Sep. 1820. 228 acres.

Mathews, James. Pa. ———. ———. 200 acres.

Mathews, Richard. N.C. Private. 12 Mar. 1785. 640 acres to heirs.

Mathews, William. N.C. Private. 9 Sep. 1785. 640 acres to heirs.

Mathews, William. Va. Corporal. 2 Dec. 1837. 171 3/7 acres.

Matlock, John. N.C. Sergeant. 21 Apr. 1784. 428 acres.

Matth ews, William. Va. Corporal. 7 Oct. 1783. 200 acres.

Matthew, Peter. N. Y. Private. 8 Jul. 1790. 500 acres.

Matthewes, John. N.C. ———. 8 Mar. 1785. 640 acres to heirs.

Matthews, Benjamin. Va. Private. 15 Dec. 1783. 100 acres.

Matthews, Charles. N.C. Private. 24 Nov. 1796. 640 acres to heirs.

Matthews, Daniel. Ga. Minute Man. 15 Apr. 1784. 287 1/2 acres.

Matthews, Daniel, Jr. Ga. Minute Man. 17 May 1784. ———.

Matthews, George. Ga. ———. 20 Dec. 1785. 690 acres.

Matthews, George. Va. Colonel. 22 Nov. 1783. 7777 2/3 acres.

Matthews, Gilbert. N.C. Private. 25 Nov. 1795. 640 acres.

Matthews, Isham. Ga. Minute Man. 23 Apr. 1784. 287 1/2 acres.

Matthews, Jacob. N.C. Private. 10 Nov. 1783. 640 acres.

Matthews, James. Ga. ———. 17 May 1784. ———.

Matthews, James. Md. Corporal. ———. 50 acres.

Matthews, James. Conn. Sufferer. New London. 29.19.2.

Matthews, John. Ga. ———. 23 Apr. 1784. 287 1/2 acres.

Matthews, John. Md. Sergeant. ———. 50 acres.

Matthews, John. Md. Private. ———. 50 acres.

Matthews, John. N.C. Private. 30 Sep. 1785. 640 acres.

Matthews, John. Pa. Private. 3 Jan. 1787. 200 acres to Murlock Sullivan, administrator.

Matthews, Joseph. Ga. Citizen. 19 Dec. 1785. 287 1/2 acres.

Matthews, Meshack. Ga. ———. 26 May 1784. 287 1/2 acres.

Matthews, Moses. Ga. ———. 15 Apr. 1784. 287 1/2 acres.

Matthews, Paul. Ga. Soldier. 7 Jun. 1785. 230 acres.

Matthews, Price. N.C. Private. 8 Dec. 1796. 640 acres.

Matthews, Reubin. Ga. Minute Man. 16 Apr. 1784. 287 1/2 acres.

Matthews, Robert. Md. Corporal. ———. 50 acres.

Matthews, Robert. N.C. Private. 12 Dec. 1785. 640 acres.

Matthews, Robert. Conn. Sufferer. New/ East Haven. 8.3.0.

Matthews, Thomas. Ga. ———. 17 May 1784. ———.

Matthews, Thomas. Md. Corporal. ———. 50 acres.

Matthews, Thomas. Md. Private. ———. 50 acres.

Matthews, Thomas. Va. Lieutenant Colonel. ———. 6000 acres.

Matthews, William. Ga. Minute Man. 25 May 1784. 287 1/2 acres.

Matthews, William. Ga. Captain. 26 May 1784. 287 1/2 acres.

Matthews, William. Ga. Refugee. May 1784. 287 1/2 acres.

Matthews, William. Md. Private. ———. 50 acres.

Matthewson, Alexander. Md. Private. ———. 50 acres.

Matthias, Griffith. Va. Private. 21 Apr. 1785. 100 acres.

Mattingly, Joseph. Md. Private. ———. 50 acres.

Mattison, Samuel. N.Y. ———. 13 Sep. 1790. 500 acres to heirs.

Mattlemore, William. N.C. Private. 13 Dec. 1796. 640 acres.

Mattox, Benjamin. Ga. Minute Man. 20 Apr. 1784. 287 1/2 acres.

Mattox, John. Ga. Minute Man. 20 Apr. 1784. 287 1/2 acres.

Maubley, William. Pa. Private. 31 May 1787. 200 acres.

Maughan, Mathias. Va. ———. 12 Aug. 1833. 100 acres.
Maughon, George. Va. Seaman. 28 Nov. 1783. 100 acres.
Mauldin, Miles. N.C. Private. 12 Dec. 1785. 640 acres to heirs.
Maupin, Gabriel. Va. Captain. 16 Jun. 1784. 4000 acres.
Maupin, Gabriel. Va. Captain. 19 Mar. 18—. 1338 2/3 acres. [warrant 24 Jul. 1856 1333 1/3 acres].
Maury, Abraham. Va. Lieutenant. Jan. 1783. 2666 2/3 acres.
Maxen, William. Pa. Private. 8 Jun. 1787. 200 acres.
Maxwell, Anthony. N. Y. Lieutenant. 17 Aug. 1790. 1200 acres.
Maxwell, Bazil. Ga. Soldier. ———. ———.
Maxwell, Cornelius. N. Y. Sergeant. 8 Jul. 1790. 600 acres.
Maxwell, David. Ga. ———. 17 Apr. 1784. 200 acres.
Maxwell, Edward. Ga. ———. 16 Apr. 1784. 200 acres.
Maxwell, George. Ga. ———. 15 Sep. 1784. 230 acres.
Maxwell, Henry. Pa. Private. 28 Apr. 1789. 200 acres.
Maxwell, James. Ga. Private. 22 May 178-. 287 1/2 acres.
Maxwell, James. Md. Corporal. ———. 50 acres.
Maxwell, James. Pa. Private. 9 Feb. 1808. 200 acres.
Maxwell, James. Pa. ———. 8 Dec. 1802. 200 acres.
Maxwell, James. Va. Captain. 9 Dec. 1833. 5333 1/3 acres.
Maxwell, James. Va. Captain. 25 Aug. 1835. 1066 3/5 acres.
Maxwell, James. Va. Captain. 25 Aug. 1835. 4266 2/5 acres.
Maxwell, John. Md. Private. ———. 50 acres.
Maxwell, Josiah. Ga. Lieutenant. 24 Jan. 1784. 400 acres.
Maxwell, Richard. Md. Private. ———. 50 acres.
Maxwell, Thomas. Ga. Major. 25 Jun. 1784. 600 acres.
Maxwell, Thomas. Ga. Refugee. ———. 250 acres.
Maxwell, William. Va. Private. 25 Apr. 1783. 200 acres.
May, Abraham. N.C. Sergeant. 12 Sep. 1785. 1000 acres to heirs.
May, Baily. Ga. Minute Man. 1784. 287 1/2 acres.
May, Beckham. Ga. Citizen. 5 Apr. 1785. 287 1/2 acres.
May, Coleman. Va. Private. 16 Oct. 1813. 100 acres.
May, Humphrey. Va. Sergeant. 21 Dec. 1833. 200 acres.
May, Jacob. Pa. Private. 15 Aug. 1787. 200 acres to James Martin, assignee.
May, John. Ga. ———. 24 May 1784. 287 1/2 acres.
May, John. Me. ———. 24 Jul. 1835. 200 acres to widow Hepsibay May. Poland.
May, Joseph. Ga. Soldier. 5 Dec. 1785. 230 acres.
May, Major. N.C. Private. 29 Apr. 1784. 640 acres.
May, Major. N.C. Corporal. 6 Sep. 1820. 360 acres to heirs.
May, Moses. Ga. ———. 17 May 1784. ———.
May, Thomas. N.C. Private. 29 Apr. 1784. 274 acres.
May, Thomas. Va. Corporal. 28 Aug. 1784. 400 acres.
May, William. Ga. Minute Man. 20 Feb. 1784. 250 acres.
May, William. Va. Private. 20 May 1784. 200 acres.
May, William. Va. Sergeant. 30 May 1821. 200 acres.
Mayberry, William. Me. ———. 13 Jun. 1835. 200 acres. Raymond.
Mayberry, William. Me. ———. 1835. 200 acres. Raymond.
Mayberry, William. Pa. Fifer. ———. 200 acres.
Mayberry, William, Sr. Pa. Private. 28 Oct. 1786. 200 acres to William Power, assignee.
Maybury, Thomas. Pa. Private. 4 Jan. 1787. 200 acres.
Mayes, George. Ga. ———. 17 May 1784. ———.
Mayfield, Henry. Va. Private. 28 Jan. 1784. 200 acres.
Mayfield, John. Va. Private. 28 Jan. 1784. 200 acres.

Mayfield, Micajah. Va.-Ind. Private. 108 acres.
Mayfield, Micajah. Va. Private. 17 Jul. 1784. 100 acres.
Mayhew, James. Me. Private. 17 Apr. 1844. 200 acres. Hermon.
Mayhew, Jonathan. Md. Corporal. ———. 50 acres.
Maynard, Nathaniel. Va. Corporal. 11 Feb. 1784. 200 acres.
Maynor, Henry. Va. Private. 18 Nov. 1784. 100 acres.
Maynor, Peter. Md. Fifer. ———. 50 acres.
Maynor, Peter, Sr. Md. Matross. ———. 50 acres.
Mayo, Henry. N.C. ———. 13 Jun. 1785. 640 acres to heirs.
Mayo, James. N.C. Corporal. 9 Dec. 1797. 420 acres.
Mayo, John. N.C. Private. 30 Sep. 1785. 640 acres to heirs.
Mays, William. Pa. Private. 30 Sep. 1787. 200 acres.
Mayson, Luke. S.C. Lieutenant. 7 Nov. 1785. 125 acres to James Mayson, Jr., his brother.
Mayton, Ezekiel. N.C. Private. 15 Feb. 1797. 274 acres.
Mazaret, John. Va. Major. 30 Nov. 1784. 3000 acres.
Mazaret, John. Va. Major. 30 Nov. 1784. 1333 1/3 acres.
Mazyck, Daniel. S.C. Captain. 4 Apr. 1785. 300 acres.
Mazyck, Stephen. S.C. Lieutenant. 2 May 1785. 200 acres.
McAdam, John. Va. Lieutenant. 30 Jun. 1784. 2666 2/3 acres.
McAdam, John. Va. Captain. 15 Jan. 1808. 1278 acres.
McAdam, John. Va. Captain. 15 Jan. 1808. 851 1/3 acres.
McAdam, John. Va. Captain. 15 Jan. 1808. 150 acres.
McAdam, John. Va. Captain. 15 Jan. 1808. 276 acres.
McAdam, Joseph. Va. Surgeon's Mate. 26 Feb. 1784. 2666 2/3 acres.
McAdam, Joseph. Va. Surgeon's Mate. 3 Nov. 1859. 888 2/3 acres.
McAdam, Joseph. Va. Surgeon's Mate. 14 May 1860. 296 2/3 acres.
McAdam, Joseph. Va. Surgeon's Mate. 14 May 860. 148 acres.
McAdam, Joseph. Va. Surgeon's Mate. 28 Feb. 1861. 444 1/3 acres.
McAdam, Joseph. Va. Surgeon's Mate. 28 Feb. 1861. 444 1/3 acres.
McAdams, Alexander. Va. Private. 9 May 1785. 100 acres.
McAdoe, Jonah. N.C. Private. 8 Mar. 1796. 640 acres to heirs.
Mcafee, Azariah. N.C. Private. 28 May 1784. 640 acres.
McAfee, Matthew. Pa. Private. 30 Sep. 1787. 200 acres.
McAlister, John. N.C. Private. 8 Dec. 1795. 274 acres.
Mcallen, Richard. N.C. Private. 28 May 1784. 365 acres.
McAllister, Archibald. Pa. Private. 5 Mar. 1787. 200 acres to Isaac Pomeroy, assignee.
McAllister, Daniel. Va. Private. 14 Feb. 1834. 200 acres.
McAllister, John. N.C. Private. 19 May 1784. 274 acres.
McAllister, John. Pa. Private. 29 Aug. 1788. 200 acres.
McAllister, John. Pa. Private. 28 May 1795. 200 acres to William R. Hanna & Alexander Fowler, assignees.
McAllister, William. N. Y. Sergeant. 8 Jul. 1790. 600 acres.
McAllister, William. Pa. ———. 29 May 1787. 200 acres.
McAltree, Barnabus. N.C. Private. 17 Feb. 1824. 640 acres.
McAndrews, Andrew. N.C. Private. 19 Jan. 1786. 640 acres.
McAnelley, William. Pa. ———. 14 Aug. 1787. 200 acres to Caspar Schnider, assignee.
McAnneley, John. Ga. Citizen. 7 Jun. 1785. 287 1/2 acres.
McArthur, Alexander. N. Y. Lieutenant. 9 Jul. 1790. 1200 acres.
McArthur, Alexander. N.C. Private. 10 Jan. 1794. 274 acres.
McAtee, Joseph. Md. Private. ———. 50 acres.
McAuley, Auley. Conn. Sufferer. Norwalk. 30.19.3.
McAuley, Daniel. Conn. Sufferer. Norwalk. 248.7.0.
McAway, Christopher. Md. Private. ———. 50 acres.

McBane, Daniel. N.C. Sergeant. 15 Nov. 1821. 357 acres.
McBeth, George. S.C. Soldier. 16 Jul. 1784. 200 acres.
McBride, Andrew. Ga. ———. 17 May 1784. ———.
McBride, Duncan. N.C. Private. 8 Dec. 1795. 640 acres to heirs.
McBride, Duncan. N.C. Corporal. 11 Jan. 1822. 1000 acres to heirs.
McBride, Edward. Ga. Soldier. 29 Oct. 1784. ———.
McBride, Isaac. Va.-Ind. Private. 108 acres.
McBride, James. N.C. Private. 24 Dec. 1785. 640 acres.
McBride, John. Md. Private. ———. 50 acres.
McBride, John. S.C. Soldier. 6 Nov. 1786. 200 acres.
McBride, Peter. Pa. Private. 14 Oct. 1786. 200 acres to George Savile, assignee.
McBurnet, Daniel. Ga. ———. 20 Apr. 1784. 250 acres.
McCabe, Joshua. N.C. Private. 7 Dec. 1796. 640 acres to heirs. He was of Tyrrell County.
McCabe, Michael. Va. Private. 2 Apr. 1784. 200 acres.
McCabe, Peter. N.C. Private. 30 Sep. 1785. 640 acres to heirs.
McCain, John. Ga. Refugee. 24 Feb. 1784. ———.
McCaleb, James. N.C. Private. 30 Nov. 1807. 640 acres to heirs.
McCaliff, John. Md. Drummer. ———. 50 acres.
McCall, Angus. Conn. Sufferer. Greenwich. 13.2.7.
McCall, Samuel. Va. Sergeant. 2 Jun. 1783. 200 acres.
McCall, Thomas. Ga. Refugee. 19 Apr. 1784. 287 1/2 acres.
McCalla, Thomas. Pa. Surgeon. ———. 300 acres.
McCalla, Thomas. Pa. Surgeon. 16 Oct. 1786. 300 acres.
McCallester, Daniel. N.C. Private. 14 Dec. 1796. 456 acres.
McCalley, Hugh. N. Y. Sergeant. 7 Jul. 1790. 600 acres.
McCally, Edward. Pa. Private. 30 Jul. 1787. 200 acres.
McCalpin, Alexander. Ga. Refugee. 15 Mar. 1784. 250 acres.
McCalvey, John. Ga. Minute Man. 2 Apr. 1784. ———.
McCalvey, William. Ga. Soldier. 10 Oct. 1789. 287 1/2 acres.
McCandliss, John. Va. Private. 15 Jun. 1820. 200 acres.
McCann, Francis. Md. Private. ———. 50 acres.
McCann, Hugh. N.C. Private. 19 May 1784. 640 acres.
McCann, Hugh. N.C. Private. 22 Apr. 1785. 640 acres to heirs.
McCann, John. Md. Private. ———. 50 acres.
McCann, John. N.C. Lieutenant. 24 Oct. 1783. 2560 acres to Nathaniel McCann, heir.
McCann, Michael. Md. Private. ———. 50 acres.
McCannon, Christopher. Va. Sergeant. 4 Dec. 1783. 400 acres.
McCannon, Christopher. Va. Private. 3 Sep. 1783. 100 acres.
McCannon, Christopher. Va. Private. 1 Nov. 1792. 100 acres.
McCant, James. Va. Private. 18 Dec. 1783. 200 acres.
McCardvery, Cornelius. Ga. Minute Man. 23 Apr. 1784. 287 1/2 acres. Alias McCardell.
McCargo, Stephen. Va. Private. 26 Apr. 1784. 200 acres.
McCarlty, Michael. Pa. Private. 2 May 1787. 200 acres.
McCarmick, George. Va. Captain. 12 Jun. 1820. 2000 acres.
McCarmick, George. Va. Captain. 12 Jun. 1820. 2000 acres.
McCarracher, James. Pa. Private. 27 Aug. 1787. 200 acres.
McCarrell, John. N.C. Private. 10 Feb. 1796. 228 acres.
McCarron, Daniel. N.C. Private. Nov. 1788. 640 acres to heirs.
McCartey, John. Ga. Minute Man. 25 May 1784. 287 1/2 acres.
McCarthy, John. Pa. ———. 14 Jan. 1796. 200 acres to Daniel Richards, executor.
McCartney, David. Pa. Private. ———. 200 acres.
McCartney, Dennis. Pa. Private. ———. 200 acres to widow.
McCartney, Peter. Va. Private. 23 Jun. 1783. 200 acres.

McCartney, Peter. Va. Private. 31 Oct. 1783. 100 acres.
McCartney, Richard. Pa. ———. ———. 200 acres to Elizabeth Lebeck, assignee.
McCarty, Charles. Va. Private. 22 Apr. 1783. 200 acres.
McCarty, Daniel. Ga. Refugee. 15 Mar. 1784. 250 acres.
McCarty, Daniel. S.C. ———. 7 Nov. 1791. 130 acres.
McCarty, Dennis. N. Y. Private. 8 Jul. 1790. 600 acres.
McCarty, Dennis. Va. Private. 28 Jun. 1784. 100 acres.
McCarty, James. Md. Private. ———. 50 acres.
McCarty, Jeremiah. Pa. Private. ———. 200 acres.
McCarty, John. Ga. Adjutant. 25 May 1784. 460 acres.
McCarty, Owen. Pa. Sergeant. 9 Oct. 1786. 250 acres.
McCarty, Richard. Va.-Ind. Captain. Apr. 1784. 3234 acres.
McCarty, Richard. Pa. Private. ———. 200 acres.
McCarty, Richard. Va. Captain. 22 Apr. 1784. 4000 acres.
McCarty, Timothy. Va. Drummer. 4 Jul. 1786. 200 acres.
McCary, Richard. Ga. ———. 17 May 1784. ———.
McCary, Robert. Ga. ———. 15 Mar. 1784. 250 acres.
McCaslin, Patrick. Pa. Private. 2 Feb. 1787. 200 acres.
McCastleton, Samuel D. Pa. Sergeant. 12 Sep. 1789. 200 acres.
McCathey, Flourance. N.C. Lieutenant. 27 Aug. 1784. 822 acres.
McCaul, Alexander. N.C. Private. 26 May 1784. 640 acres.
McCaul, Archibald. N.C. Private. 26 May 1784. 640 acres.
McCauley, John. N.C. Private. 10 Feb. 1796. 640 acres to heirs.
McCauly, Matthew. N.C. Lieutenant. 22 Oct. 1783. 761 acres.
McCausland, Henry. Me. Private. 4 Jun. 1835. 200 acres to widow Abiah McCausland. Gardiner.
McCausland, James. Me. ———. 29 Apr. 1835. 200 acres to widow Mary McCausland. Gardiner.
McCawley, James. N. Y. Private. 8 Jul. 1790. 600 acres.
McCawly, John. Va. Private. 14 Dec. 1784. 200 acres.
McCay, John. Md. Sergeant. ———. 50 acres.
McCernan, Thomas. Md. Corporal. ———. 50 acres.
McChoud, Archibald. Va. Private. 26 Aug. 1784. 233 1/3 acres.
McChristie, Michael M. Pa. Private. 19 Apr. 1787. 200 acres.
McChristy, Michael. Pa. Private. 28 Feb. 1794. 200 acres.
McClain, Arthur. Md. Sergeant. ———. 50 acres.
McClain, Enoch. Md. Sergeant. ———. 50 acres.
McClain, John. Md. Private. ———. 50 acres.
McClain, Thomas. Va. Private. 16 Jun. 1783. 100 acres.
McClain, Thomas. Va. Private. 25 Jan. 1786. 100 acres.
McClammey, Joseph. N.C. Lieutenant. 10 Aug. 1785. 2560 acres.
McClanachan, Elijah. Va. Armourer. 1 Apr. 1783. 100 acres.
McClannahan, Alexander. Va. Colonel. 5 Jun. 1784. 6666 2/3 acres.
McClannahan, Elijah. Va. Private. 30 Sep. 1783. 200 acres.
McClannahan, Elijah. Va. ———. 28 Aug. 1835. 2566 2/3 acres.
McClannell, John. Ga. Citizen. 7 Jun. 1785. 287 1/2 acres.
McClarin, Thomas. Pa. Sergeant. 24 Aug. 1787. 250 acres.
McClarney, Henry. N.C. Private. 17 Dec. 1785. 640 acres to heirs.
McClarning, David. N.Y. ———. 13 Sep. 1790. 500 acres to heirs.
McClarran, Daniel, Sr. Va. Private. 8 Dec. 1860. 33 1/3 acres.
McClarran, Daniel, Sr. Va. Private. 26 Feb. 1861. ——.
McClarren, Daniel. Va. Private. 13 Jun. 1832. 66 2/3 acres.
McClasky, George. N.C. Private. 19 Jan. 1786. 640 acres.
McClaughery, John. N. Y. Lieutenant. 13 Sep. 1790. 1600 acres to heirs.
McClean, Alexander. Pa. ———. 18

Feb. 1803. 200 acres to Mary Alexander, widow.

McClean, Archibald. Pa. Private. 4 Jan. 1787. 200 acres.

McClean, Jacob. Pa. Private. 2 Jun. 1791. 200 acres.

McClean, James. Pa. Private. 19 Sep. 1787. 200 acres.

McClean, James. Pa. Sergeant. 9 Mar. 1795. 250 acres to John Nicholson, assignee.

McClean, Laughlin. Va. Private. 23 Jun. 1783. 200 acres.

McClean, Thomas. Pa. Private. ———. 200 acres.

McClellan, John. Me. ———. 6 Jun. 1838. 200 acres. Glenburn.

McClellan, John. N.C. Sergeant. 13 Dec. 1796. 714 acres.

McClellan, John. Pa. Captain. ———. 500 acres.

McClelland, David. Pa. Private. 12 Mar 1787. 200 acres.

McClelland, Hugh. Pa. Private. 18 Jan. 1787. 200 acres.

McClelland, James. N.C. Sergeant. 27 Oct. 1783. 429 acres.

McClelland, John. Pa. Private. 4 Sep. 1789. 200 acres.

McClemy, John. Ga. ———. 15 Mar. 1784. 250 acres.

McClendon, Dennis. Ga. ———. 16 Jul. 1784. 287 1/2 acres.

McClendon, Isaac. Ga. ———. 21 Apr. 1784. 287 1/2 acres.

McClendon, Jacob. Ga. ———. 21 Apr. 1784. 287 1/2 acres.

McClendon, James. Ga. ———. 19 Dec. 1786. 287 1/2 acres.

McClendon, Joseph. Ga. Minute Man. 3 Oct. 1783. ———.

McClendon, Samuel. Ga. ———. 21 Apr. 1784. 287 1/2 acres.

McClendon, Travis. Ga. Refugee. 21 Apr. 1784. 287 1/2 acres.

McClenen, Thomas. Va. Private. 28 Aug. 1835. 100 acres.

McClennen, Thomas. Va. Private. 8 May 1833. 100 acres.

McClintock, Alexander. Pa. Private. 27 Oct. 1786. 200 acres to Sarah McClintock, widow.

McClintock, Alexander. Pa. Lieutenant. 27 Oct. 1786. 200 acres to Sarah McClintock, widow.

McCloskey, Samuel. Pa. Surgeon. ———. 300 acres.

McCloud, Alexander. N.C. Private. 22 Apr. 1785. 640 acres to heirs.

McCloud, Daniel. N.C. Private. 9 Sep. 1785. 640 acres to heirs.

McCloud, Daniel. N.C. Private. 22 Dec. 1796. 274 acres.

McCloud, Daniel. Pa. Matross. 13 Jun. 1787. 200 acres.

McCloud, John. N. Y. Matross. 9 Jul. 1790. 600 acres.

McCloy, William. Va. Private. 3 Jul. 1784. 200 acres.

McClum, Sampson. Ga. Minute Man. 5 May 1785. 287 1/2 acres.

McClurdy, Lazarus. N.C. Private. 10 Feb. 1796. 640 acres to heirs.

McClure, Hardaman. N.C. Private. 14 Feb. 1796. 640 acres.

McClure, John. Pa. Sergeant. 21 Mar. 1787. 250 acres to William Read, assignee.

McClure, John. Pa. Captain. 12 Oct. 1786. 500 acres.

McClure, Michael. N.C. Private. 7 Jan. 1786. 640 acres to heirs.

McClure, William. N.C. Surgeon. 29 Apr. 1784. 4800 acres.

McClure, William. Va. Private. 24 May 1784. 200 acres.

McClurg, James. Va. Director of Hospitals. 20 Oct. 1783. 6000 acres.

McClurg, Walter. Va. Surgeon. 20 Apr. 1784. 6000 acres.

McCluskey, Peter. N.Y. Fifer. 13 Sep. 1790. 500 acres to heirs.

McColgan, John. Md. Private. ———. 50 acres.

McColister, James. N.C. ———. 2 Aug. 1784. 640 acres to Jesse McColister, heir.

McCollister, John. Va. Sergeant. 5 Jan. 1788. 200 acres.

McCollum, Reuben. N. Y. Private. 8 Jul. 1790. 600 acres.

McColm, Samuel. N. Y. Private. 8 Jul. 1790. 600 acres.

McComeskry, Moses. Va. Private. 2 Apr. 1784. 100 acres.

McConnel, Samuel. Md. Sergeant. ———. 50 acres.

McConnell, Charles. Pa. Corporal. ———. 200 acres.
McConnell, Matthew. Pa. ———. 12 Oct. 1786. 500 acres.
McConnell, Philip. N.C. Private. 27 Jul. 1820. 640 acres to heirs.
McConnell, Robert. Pa. Lieutenant. 8 Jan. 1787. 200 acres to Jane McConnell, administratrix.
McConnell, Robert. Pa. Lieutenant. 8 Feb. 1787. 200 acres to widow.
McConnell, William. N. Y. Private. 8 Jul. 1790. 600 acres.
McConnell, William. Pa. Sergeant. 12 Jan. 1787. 250 acres.
McConnical, Patrick. N.C. Private. 7 Jan. 1786. 640 acres to heirs.
McConnikin, John. Md. Private. ———. 50 acres.
McConnolly, Hugh. N. Y. Fifer. 8 Jul. 1790. 600 acres.
McConnough, Abraham. N.C. Corporal. 30 Sep. 1785. 1000 acres to heirs.
McConnough, Dugald. N.C. Private. 9 Sep. 1785. 640 acres to heirs.
McConnough, Samuel. N.C. Private. 9 Sep. 1785. 640 acres to heirs.
McCord, Isaiah. Pa. Private. ———. 200 acres.
McCord, Mark. Pa. Private. 6 Apr 1794. 200 acres to Catherine McCord, widow.
McCord, Samuel. Va. Private. 23 Jun. 1783. 200 acres.
McCorkle, Andrew. Va. Private. 2 Jul. 1784. 100 acres.
McCorkle, Samuel. Va. Private. 2 Jul. 1784. 100 acres.
McCormack, Adam. Va. Private. 22 Aug. 1783. 200 acres.
McCormack, Benjamin. Ga. Refugee. 15 Mar. 1784. 250 acres.
McCormack, John. Ga. ———. 15 Mar. 1784. 250 acres.
McCormack, John. N.C. Private. 30 Nov. 1785. 640 acres to heirs.
McCormack, Joseph. Ga. Refugee. 15 Mar. 1784. 250 acres.
McCormack, Reuben. N.C. Private. 8 Dec. 1795. 640 acres to heirs.
McCormack, Thomas. Ga. ———. 15 Mar. 1784. 250 acres.
McCormack, William. Va. Private. 23 Jan. 1788. 200 acres.
McCormick, Dennis. Md. Corporal. ———. 50 acres.
McCormick, Hugh. Pa. Private. ———. 200 acres.
McCormick, James. Va. Private. 13 Feb. 1786. 100 acres.
McCormick, John. N. Y. Private. 3 Jul. 1790. 600 acres.
McCormick, John. Pa. Private. ———. 200 acres.
McCormick, Patrick. Pa. Private. 12 Oct. 1786. 200 acres.
McCormick, William. Pa. ———. 19 Mar. 1808. 200 acres.
McCoskey, Samuel. Pa. Surgeon. 13 Nov. 1786. 300 acres.
McCowen, Daniel. Ga. ———. 15 Mar. 1784. 250 acres.
McCowen, Duncan. Ga. ———. 5 Apr. 1785. 278 1/2 acres.
McCowen, Nobel. Ga. Citizen. 5 Apr. 1785. 287 1/2 acres.
McCowen, William. Ga. Citizen. 5 Apr. 1785. 287 1/2 acres.
McCown, James. Va. Private. 17 Mar. 1784. 100 acres.
McCown, Malcom. Va. Sergeant. 16 Feb. 1801. 200 acres.
McCoy, Alexander. N. Y. Private. 8 Jul. 1790. 500 acres.
McCoy, Alexander. N.C. Private. 10 Feb. 1796. 640 acres to heirs.
McCoy, Daniel. N.C. Private. 17 Oct. 1783. 549 acres.
McCoy, Daniel. N.C. Private. 10 Dec. 1788. 640 acres to heirs.
McCoy, Dugald. N.C. Private. 22 Apr. 1785. 640 acres to heirs.
McCoy, Hugh. Md. Private. ———. 50 acres.
McCoy, James. Ga. Captain. 21 Apr. 1784. 575 acres.
McCoy, James. N. Y. Private. 8 Jul. 1790. 600 acres.
McCoy, James A. N.C. Private. 8 Dec. 1795. 640 acres.
McCoy, John. Md. Lieutenant. ———. 200 acres.
McCoy, John. Md. Private. ———. 50 acres.
McCoy, John. N.C. Sergeant. 4 May 1784. 1000 acres.
McCoy, John. N.C. Private. 28 May 1784. 640 acres.

McCoy, John, Jr. N.C. Private. 23 Apr. 1785. 640 acres to heirs.
McCoy, Michael. Pa. Private. ———. 200 acres.
McCoy, Morris. N.C. Private. 30 Sep. 1785. 640 acres to heirs.
McCoy, Patrick. N.C. Private. 8 Dec. 1795. 640 acres.
McCoy, Reubin. N.C. Private. 13 Dec. 1796. 640 acres.
McCoy, Roderick. Pa. ———. 23 Jun. 1787. 200 acres.
McCoy, Roger. N.C. Private. 16 Mar. 1795. 640 acres to heirs.
McCoy, Samuel. Va. Private. 26 Oct. 1819. 100 acres.
McCoy, Samuel. Va. Private. 22 Jan. 1834. 100 acres.
McCoy, William. Pa. Private. 19 Oct. 1786. 200 acres to Alexander Power, assignee.
McCoy, William. Pa. Private. 15 Nov. 1786. 200 acres to Stephen Loudon, assignee.
McCracken, Allen. Pa. ———. 29 Feb. 1804. Resurvey 192 acres.
McCracken, David. N.C. Private. 10 Feb. 1796. 640 acres to heirs.
McCracken, James. Va. Private. 24 Jan. 1820. 200 acres.
McCracken, John. N.C. Private. 10 Feb. 1796. 640 acres to heirs.
McCrakin, Jamer. Md. Private. ———. 50 acres.
McCraw, Francis. Va. Private. 8 Feb. 1786. 200 acres.
McCraw, John. Va. Private. 12 Dec. 1783. 100 acres.
McCraw, William. Va. Deputy Quartermaster General. 5 Nov. 1812. 4000 acres.
McCraw, William. Va. Deputy Quartermaster. 5 Dec. 1856. 127 1/5 acres.
McCraw, William. Va. Deputy Quartermaster. 5 Dec. 1856. 127 1/5 acres.
McCraw, William. Va. Deputy Quartermaster. 5 Dec. 1856. 127 1/5 acres.
McCraw, William. Va. Deputy Quartermaster. 5 Dec. 1856. 127 1/5 acres.
McCraw, William. Va. Deputy Quartermaster. 5 Dec. 1856. 127 1/5 acres.
McCraw, William. Va. Deputy Quartermaster. 5 Dec. 1856. 317 acres.
McCrea, Stephen. N.Y. Physician & Surgeon. 26 Sep. 1792. 2700 acres.
McCree, Charles. N.C. Private. 30 Sep. 1785. 640 acres to heirs.
McCree, John. S.C. Soldier. 21 Jan. 1785. 200 acres.
McCrory, James. N.C. Ensign. 4 Aug. 1820. 2560 acres.
McCrossan, Patrick. Pa. Private. 24 Jun. 1794. 200 acres to Beatty Excurius, assignee.
McCrum, Michael. Va. Sergeant. 15 Mar. 1806. 400 acres.
McCubbins, Isaac. N.C. Private. 22 Apr. 1785. 640 acres.
McCue, Henry. Va. Private. 3 Jun. 1783. 100 acres.
McCuller, Joseph. N.C. Sergeant. 21 Aug. 1820. 360 acres.
McCuller, Joseph. N.C. Private. 1 Sep. 1820. 360 acres to heir Moore McCuller.
McCulloch, James. Pa. ———. 1 Mar. 1809. 200 acres to John McCulloch, devisee.
McCulloch, John. Ga. Refugee. 22 Mar. 1785. 250 acres.
McCulloch, Joseph. N.C. Private. 22 Apr. 1785. 640 acres to heirs.
McCulloch, Patrick. Ga. Minute Man. 16 Apr. 1784. 286 1/2 acres.
McCulloch, Roger. Ga. Minute Man. 3 Apr. 1785. ———.
McCulloch, Roger. Pa. Private. 10 Sep. 1794. 200 acres to George Donaker, assignee.
McCulloch, Samuel. Ga. Sergeant. 15 Apr. 1784. 287 1/2 acres.
McCullock, Alexander. N.C. Private. 20 Apr. 1784. 640 acres to Robert McCullock, heir.
McCullock, John. N.C. Private. 20 Sep. 1784. 274 acres.
McCullock, John. N.C. Private. 22 Dec. 1796. 274 acres.
McCullom, John. Pa. Lieutenant. ———. 200 acres.
McCullom, Jonathan. Pa. Private. ———. 200 acres.
McCullouch, James. Pa. ———. 1 Feb. 1803. 200 acres to heirs.
McCullouch, John. S.C. ———. 5 Sep. 1791. 200 acres.
McCullough, John. Pa. Lieutenant. 1 Feb. 1803. 200 acres to heirs.

McCully, George. Pa. Captain. 19 Dec. 1786. 500 acres.
McCully, Robert. Pa. ———. 16 May 1809. 300 acres to Abraham Todhunter, assignee.
McCumber, David. N.C. Private. 10 Feb. 1796. 640 acres to heirs.
McCumber, Jeremiah. Conn. Sufferer. New/East Haven. 20.5.8.
McCumbes, Humphrey. N.C. Sergeant. 13 Dec. 1796. 1000 acres.
McCune, Patrick. Va. Private. 30 Jun. 1783. 100 acres.
McCune, Patrick. Va. Sergeant. 5 Apr. 1784. 200 acres.
McCune, William. Pa. Private. ———. 200 acres.
McCurdy, Andrew. N.C. Private. 10 Feb. 1796. 274 acres.
McCurdy, James. Pa. ———. 29 Jan. 1799. 200 acres.
McCurdy, John. Conn. Sufferer. New London. 1,128.0.0.
McCurdy, Moses. Pa. Private. 25 Jul. 1787. 200 acres to Margaret Hughes, widow.
McCurdy, Moses. Pa. ———. 2 Aug. 1803. 200 acres to Peggy Hughes, widow.
McCurdy, Robert. Pa. Private. 21 Sep. 1787. 200 acres.
McCurdy, William. Pa. Captain. 18 Dec. 1786. 500 acres.
McCurney, Stephen. N.Y. ———. 13 Sep. 1790. 500 acres to heirs.
McCutchen, George. Mass. Private. 2 Feb. 1831. 200 acres.
McDade, James. Va. Private. 31 Dec. 1787. 100 acres.
McDade, Philip. Va. Private. 22 Feb. 1799. 100 acres.
McDaniel, Alexander. N.C. Captain. 29 Sep. 1784. 1000 acres.
McDaniel, Alexander. N.C. Private. 28 Nov. 1795. 640 acres to heirs.
McDaniel, Allen. N.C. Private. 30 Sep. 1785. 640 acres to heirs.
McDaniel, Andrew. N.C. Private. 6 Dec. 1796. 640 acres to heirs.
McDaniel, Andrew. Va. Private. 31 Jul. 1784. 100 acres.
McDaniel, Daniel. N.C. Private. 2 Dec. 1785. 640 acres to heirs.
McDaniel, Enamias. Va. Private. 2 Oct. 1800. 100 acres.
McDaniel, George. N.C. Private. 9 Dec. 1796. 274 acres.
McDaniel, Hugh. N.C. Sergeant. 29 Apr. 1784. 1000 acres to heirs.
McDaniel, James. Me. ———. 14 Jan. 1837. 200 acres to widow Susanna McDaniel. York.
McDaniel, James. Mass. Private. 13 Feb. 1833. 200 acres to assignee Edward Augustus Emerson.
McDaniel, James. Va. Private. 18 Apr. 1801. 200 acres.
McDaniel, John. Ga. ———. 26 May 1784. 287 1/2 acres.
McDaniel, John. N.C. Private. 30 Sep. 1785. 640 acres to heirs.
McDaniel, Joseph. N.C. Private. 13 Sep. 1820. 274 acres.
McDaniel, Joseph. N.C. Private. 16 Aug. 1821. 640 acres.
McDaniel, Larkin. N.C. Private. 25 Apr. 1785. 640 acres to heirs.
McDaniel, Malcolm. N.C. Private. 4 Aug. 1821. 640 acres.
McDaniel, Thomas. N.C. Private. 24 Dec. 1785. 274 acres.
McDaniel, Zakiah. Ga. Minute Man. 22 Mar. 1785. 250 acres.
McDash, John. N.C. Private. 2 Feb. 1786. 274 acres.
McDaw, Daniel. Va. Private. 1 Apr. 1783. 100 acres.
McDermet, Francis. Va.-Ind. Private. 108 acres.
McDermond, John. Pa. Private. 18 Oct. 1786. 200 acres.
McDermot, Francis. Va. Private. 19 Jan. 1786. 200 acres.
McDermott, Francis. Va. Private. 13 Aug. 1834. 200 acres.
McDermott, Francis. Va. Private. 16 Aug. 1838. 100 acres.
McDermott, Francis. Va. Private. 16 Aug. 1838. 100 acres.
McDeton, Joseph. N.C. Private. 2 Feb. 1786. 274 acres.
McDewell, Stephen. N.C. Private. 30 Sep. 1785. 640 acres to heirs.
McDonal, David. Va. Private. 10 Jun. 1836. 133 1/3 acres.
McDonal, David. Va. Private. 10 Jun. 1836. 66 2/3 acres.
McDonald, Abner. Me. ———. 8 Sep. 1835. 200 acres to widow Polly

Johnson. Windham. Surname also spelled McDaniel.

McDonald, Alexander. N.C. Corporal. 30 Aug. 1819. 1000 acres to heirs.

McDonald, Alexander. Va. Sergeant. 24 Jan. 1820. 200 acres.

McDonald, Alexander. Va. Sergeant. 19 Apr. 1820. 200 acres.

McDonald, Angus. Va. Private. 21 Apr. 1785. 100 acres.

McDonald, Archibald. N.C. Private. 30 Sep. 1785. 640 acres to heirs.

McDonald, Archibald. N.C. Private. 16 Mar. 1795. 640 acres to heirs.

McDonald, Archibald. Pa. Private. ———. 200 acres.

McDonald, Archibald. S.C. ———. 1 Jun. 1789. 200 acres.

McDonald, Arthur. N.C. Private. 19 May 1784. 640 acres.

McDonald, Benjamin. Va. Private. 4 Dec. 1783. 200 acres.

McDonald, Benjamin. Va. Private. 22 Apr. 1784. 100 acres.

McDonald, Charles. Pa. Private. 27 Oct. 1786. 200 acres.

McDonald, Colin. N.C. Private. 8 Jan. 1794. 640 acres to heirs.

McDonald, David. Va.-Ind. Private. 108 acres.

McDonald, David. Va. Private. 11 Jul. 1835. 200 acres.

McDonald, Edward. Va. Private. 23 Jun. 1783. 200 acres.

McDonald, Finlay. N.C. Private. 28 Mar. 1837. 640 acres to Daniel McDonald.

McDonald, Francis. Pa. Private. 28 May 1787. 200 acres.

McDonald, George. Md. Private. ———. 50 acres.

McDonald, George. N.C. Noncomissioned Officer. 21 Dec. 1803. 83 acres.

McDonald, Godfrey. Pa. Private. 9 Oct. 1786. 200 acres.

McDonald, Henry. S.C. ———. 4 Jun. 1798. 100 acres.

McDonald, Hugh. Ga. Minute Man. 15 Apr. 1785. 500 acres.

McDonald, Hugh. N.C. Private. 24 Dec. 1818. 640 acres.

McDonald, James. Md. Private. ———. 50 acres.

McDonald, James. N. Y. Corporal. 3 Jul. 1790. 600 acres.

McDonald, James. Pa. Private. 17 Aug. 1805. 200 acres.

McDonald, John. Ga. ———. 26 May 1784. 287 1/2 acres.

McDonald, John. Md. Fifer. ———. 50 acres.

McDonald, John. Md. Sergeant. ———. 50 acres.

McDonald, John. Pa. Sergeant. ———. 250 acres.

McDonald, John. Pa. Private. 9 Jan. 1787. 200 acres.

McDonald, John. S.C. ———. 4 Mar. 1793. 80 acres.

McDonald, John. S.C. ———. 4 Mar. 1793. 86 acres.

McDonald, John. S.C. ———. 4 Mar. 1793. 40 acres.

McDonald, Jonathan. N.C. Private. 2 Sep. 1820. 640 acres.

McDonald, Marmaduke. Md. Private. ———. 50 acres.

McDonald, Martin. Conn. Sufferer. Greenwich. 4.10.0.

McDonald, Pelatiah. Me. ———. 20 Oct. 1835. 200 acres. Standish.

McDonald, Reuben. Va. Private. 5 Jun. 1784. 100 acres.

McDonald, Reynold. N. Y. Private. 8 Jul. 1790. 500 acres.

McDonald, Robert. Pa. Private. 29 May 1787. 200 acres.

McDonald, Terence. Va. Private. 28 May 1783. 100 acres.

McDonald, Thomas. N.C. Private. 20 Feb. 1784. 640 acres.

McDonald, William. N.C. Private. 17 Dec. 1785. 640 acres to heirs.

McDonald, William. Pa. Sergeant. 29 Nov. 1786. 200 acres with George North, Lieutenant.

McDonald, William. Pa. Lieutenant. ———. 200 acres.

McDonald, William. Pa. Private. 15 Oct. 1787. 200 acres.

McDonald, William. Pa. Sergeant. 13 Oct. 1786. 250 acres to Eleanor McDonald, widow.

McDonald, William. Pa. Private. 10 Aug. 1786. 200 acres to daughter.

McDonald, William. Pa. Private. ———. 200 acres.

McDonald, William. Va. Private. 24 Jan. 1820. 200 acres.

McDonel, David. N.C. Private. 17 Feb. 1824. 640 acres.
McDonley, John. N.C. Private. 5 Dec. 1797. 274 acres.
McDonnell, John. Pa. Sergeant. 31 Oct. 1786. 250 acres.
McDonnell, Thomas. Ga. ———. 17 May 1784. ———.
McDorman, Daniel. Va. Private. 20 Nov. 1784. 200 acres.
McDorman, Daniel. Va. Matross. 6 Jan. 1834. 200 acres.
McDorman, David. Va. Private. 7 Jul. 1791. 200 acres.
McDorman, James. Va. Private. 20 May 1783. 100 acres.
McDorman, James. Va. Private. 17 Aug. 1832. 200 acres.
McDorman, James. Va. Private. 17 Aug. 1832. 100 acres.
McDormet, Cornelius. N. Y. Private. 3 Jul. 1790. 600 acres.
McDougall, Alexander. N.Y. Major General. 3 Jul. 1790. 5500 acres.
McDougall, Stephen. N. Y. Aide-de-Camp Major. 3 Jul. 1790. 2000 Acres.
McDougle, Alexander. Ga. ———. 15 Mar. 1784. 250 acres.
McDougle, John. Md. Private. ———. 50 acres.
McDowell, David. N.C. Private. 6 Dec. 1797. 640 acres to heirs.
McDowell, Hugh. Md. Matross. ———. 50 acres.
McDowell, James. Ga. Private. 5 Apr. 1785. 230 acres.
McDowell, John. N. Y. Private. 8 Jul. 1790. 500 acres.
McDowell, John. Pa. Surgeon. ———. 300 acres.
McDowell, John. Pa. Surgeon. ———. 300 acres.
McDowell, John. Va. Lieutenant. 14 Jun. 1783. 2666 2/3 acres.
McDowell, John. Va. Private. 7 Jan. 1834. 200 acres.
McDowell, John. Va. Private. 5 Apr. 1784. 233 1/3 acres.
McDowell, John. Va. Private. 12 Oct. 1796. 200 acres.
McDowell, John. Va. Private. 12 Oct. 1796. 100 acres.
McDowell, John, Jr. N.C. Private. 7 Dec. 1797. 640 acres to heirs.
McDowell, Matthew. Va. Private. 17 Jun. 1783. 100 acres.
McDowell, Michael. Pa. Private. 21 Nov. 1786. 200 acres to James Mchaffey, assignee.
McDowell, Thomas. Ga. Lieutenant. ———. ———.
McDowell, Thomas. Ga. Minute Man. 19 Jul. 1784. 287 1/2 acres.
McDowell, William. Pa. Lieutenant. ———. 200 acres.
McDowg, Samuel. N.C. Private. 1 Aug. 1821. 640 acres.
McDowl, Thomas. Mass. ———. 11 Sep. 1829. 200 acres to widow Mary McDowl.
McDown, John. N.C. Private. 14 Dec. 1796. 640 acres to heirs.
McDuell, Willis. N.C. Private. 30 Sep. 1785. 640 acres to heirs.
McDuffy, John. Ga. ———. 28 Feb. 1784. 250 acres.
McDugal, John. Va. Drummer. 1 Apr. 1783. 100 acres.
McElbey, John. Ga. ———. 17 May 1784. ———.
McElhaney, John. Ga. ———. 17 May 1784. ———.
McElhatton, William. Pa. Captain. ———. 500 acres to William Richards, assignee.
McElhoes, Isaac. Pa. Private. ———. 200 acres.
McElrevy, Hugh. Pa. Private. 17 Aug. 1787. 200 acres.
McElroy, John. Pa. Fife Major. 28 Aug. 1787. 200 acres.
McElroy, Samuel. N.C. Private. 16 Aug. 1821. 640 acres.
McElroy, William. Va. Private. 19 Jan. 1785. 100 acres.
McElroy, William. Va. Private. 15 Dec. 1808. 100 acres.
McElvain, James. Pa. Private. 3 May 1787. 200 acres.
McElvain, John. Pa. ———. 6 Apr. 1794. 200 acres.
McElvaine, Thomas. Pa. Private. 19 Sep. 1787. 200 acres.
McElwin, Thomas. Va. Drummer. 23 Jun. 1783. 200 acres.
McEntee, Thomas. Pa. Private. 11 Sep. 1789. 200 acres to Benjamin Dubois, assignee.

McEntee, Thomas. Pa. Private. 1 Sep. 1787. 200 acres.
McEuen, John. N. Y. Ensign. 17 Aug. 1790. 1000 acres.
McEver, James. Conn. Sufferer. New London. 600.0.0 to heirs.
McEvers, John. N.Y. Sergeant. 13 Sep. 1790. 500 acres to heirs.
McFadden, James. Md. Captain. ———. 200 acres.
McFaddon, James. Va. Captain. 28 Jul. 1830. 4000 acres.
McFalter, Daniel. N.C. Private. 19 May 1784. 640 acres.
McFaren, Andrew. S.C. ———. 3 Nov. 1788. 200 acres.
McFarlan, James. Pa. ———. 27 Jan. 1801. 200 acres to Andrew McFarlan, heir.
McFarlan, John. N. Y. Private. 7 Jul. 1790. 600 acres.
McFarland, Andrew. Pa. Dragoon. 9 Dec. 1786. 200 acres to widow.
Mcfarland, Benjamin. N.C. Private. 14 Dec. 1796. 274 acres.
McFarland, Elijah. Me. ———. 7 May 1835. 200 acres to widow Sarah McFarland. Fairfield.
McFarland, Hosea. N.Y. ———. 13 Sep. 1790. 500 acres to heirs.
McFarland, James. Ga. ———. 20 Feb. 1784. 250 acres.
McFarland, James. Pa. Lieutenant. 6 Jun. 1787. 200 acres.
McFarland, John. Ga. ———. 17 Apr. 1784. 287 1/2 acres.
McFarland, John. N.C. Private. 9 Feb. 1796. 228 acres.
McFarland, John, Jr. Ga. ———. 17 May 1784. ———.
McFarland, Lettice. Ga. ———. 19 Jul. 1784. 1000 acres.
McFarland, William. Ga. 1 Aug. 1785. 690 acres to heirs.
McFarlin, Morgan. N.C. Private. 8 Nov. 1784. 640 acres to heir.
McFarlin, Walter. N.C. Private. 9 Sep. 1785. 640 acres to heirs.
McFarling, Andrew. S.C. ———. 2 Oct. 1786. 200 acres.
McFarson, Duncan. N.C. Private. 30 Sep. 1785. 640 acres to heirs.
McFarson, Roger. N.C. Private. 17 Dec. 1796. 640 acres to heirs.
McFashions, Henry. N.C. Private. 30 Sep. 1785. 640 acres to heirs.
McFashon, Caleb. N.C. Private. 30 Sep. 1785. 640 acres to heirs.
McFeely, John. Va. Private. 3 Aug. 1785. 100 acres.
McField, William. Ga. ———. 17 May 1784. ———.
McFirney, Alexander. N.C. Private. 30 Sep. 1785. 640 acres to heirs.
McFoy, Morris. N.C. Private. 30 Sep. 1785. 640 acres to heirs.
McGahan, John. Pa. Private. ———. 200 acres to Charles Stockton, assignee.
McGahey, John. Pa. Private. 18 Sep. 1787. 200 acres.
McGall, John. Md. Private. ———. 50 acres.
McGann John. Va.-Ind. Private. 108 acres.
McGann, James. Va. Private. 11 Nov. 1783. 200 acres.
McGannon, Darby. Va. Sergeant. 10 Apr. 1784. 200 acres.
McGarey, Edward. Ga. Refugee. 16 Jul. 1784. 575 acres.
McGarr, Owen. Ga. ———. 22 Apr. 1784. 287 1/2 acres.
McGarriche, Edward. N. Y. Private. 7 Jul. 1790. 600 acres.
McGauran, Francis. Md. Sergeant. ———. 50 acres.
McGavock, Hugh. Va. Lieutenant. 16 Jun. 1831. 2000 acres.
McGavock, Hugh. Va. Lieutenant. 16 Jun. 1831. 666 2/3 acres.
McGaw, Robert. Pa. Colonel. 28 Aug. 1787. 500 acres.
McGaw, William. Pa. Surgeon. 3 Apr. 1787. 300 acres.
McGeary, Neal. Pa. Private. 6 Jul. 1787. 200 acres.
McGeary, Robert. Ga. Minute Man. 1784. 250 acres.
McGee, Archibald. Va. Private. 15 Jun. 1807. 200 acres.
McGee, Daniel. Pa. Matross. 2 Feb. 1787. 200 acres.
McGee, Hugh. Ga. Captain. 6 Feb. 1784. 500 acres.
McGee, Lewis. Ga. Refugee. 17 May 1784. ———.
McGee, Neil. Me. ———. 29 Nov. 1842. 200 acres to widow Susannah Ryan, late widow of James Ryan. Brooksville.

McGee, Thomas. Ga. ———. 13 Sep. 1784. 287 1/2 acres.
McGee, William. Md. Private. ———. 50 acres.
McGenty, Robert. Ga. ———. 15 Mar. 1784. 250 acres.
McGeorge, William. Va. Private. 31 Mar. 1814. 100 acres.
McGibban, Neil. N.C. Private. 17 Feb. 1824. 640 acres.
McGibbon, Patrick. N.C. Lieutenant. 27 Nov. 1783. 1920 acres.
McGill, Daniel. Va. Private. 5 Apr 1784. 200 acres.
McGill, John. Ga. Minute Man. 22 Apr. 1784. 287 1/2 acres.
McGill, John. Pa. Private. 14 Oct. 1786. 200 acres.
McGilton, James. Ga. Refugee. 25 May 1784. 287 1/2 acres.
McGilton, Vance. Ga. Private. 21 Apr. 1784. 200 acres to heirs.
McGilton, William. Pa. Sergeant. 1 Dec. 1786. 250 acres to Francis Murray, assignee.
McGinley, John. Pa. Private. 13 Jul. 1787. 200 acres to Alexander McGinley, executor.
McGinnes, Ambrose. Va. Private. 10 Dec. 1785. 100 acres.
McGinnes, John. Pa. Private. 11 Oct. 1786. 200 acres.
McGinnis, Arthur. N. Y. Matross. 9 Jul. 1790. 500 acres.
McGinnis, Daniel. Pa. Private. 24 May 1787. 200 acres.
McGinnis, John. Pa. Private. 29 Mar. 1787. 200 acres.
McGinnis, Robert. Pa. Private. 28 Aug. 1787. 200 acres to Samuel McCoy, assignee.
McGlasky, James. Ga. ———. 17 May 1784. ———.
McGlaughlin, John. N.C. Private. 12 May 1784. 274 acres.
McGlauhan, Jeremiah. N.C. Private. 3 Dec. 1797. 640 acres to heirs.
McGlochlin, James. Va. Private. 18 Apr. 1801. 100 acres.
McGlocklin, Amos. Ga. ———. 19 Apr. 1784. 1000 acres.
McGlouchlin, Alexander. N.C. Private. 22 Apr. 1785. 640 acres to heirs.
McGound, Thomas. N.C. Private. 13 Dec. 1796. 640 acres to heirs.
McGovern, James. Va. Private. 29 Jun. 1784. 200 acres.
McGowan, Jeremiah. N. Y. Private. 8 Jul. 1790. 600 acres.
McGowan, John. Pa. ———. 24 Feb. 1815. 250 acres.
McGowan, John. Pa. Captain. 4 Apr. 1789. 500 acres.
McGowen, James. Md. Matross. ———. 50 acres.
McGowen, James. S.C. ———. 4 Jul. 1785. 200 acres.
McGowen, William. Va. Private. 1 Mar. 1787. 200 acres.
McGower, Michael. Md. Private. ———. 50 acres.
McGown, James. N.C. Private. 13 Dec. 1804. 640 acres to heirs.
McGown, James. S.C. ———. 2 May 1785. 200 acres.
McGown, John. N.C. Private. 12 Dec. 1797. 640 acres.
McGran, John. Md. Private. ———. 50 acres.
McGraves, Richard, Jr. N.C. Private. 17 Dec. 1796. 274 acres.
McGraw, James. Va. Private. 24 Jan. 1785. 100 acres.
McGraw, James. Va. Private. 6 Apr. 1787. 100 acres.
McGraw, James. Va. Private. 18 Apr. 1788. 100 acres.
McGraw, Joseph. N.C. Private. 17 Feb. 1824. 640 acres.
McGregor, Alexander. Ga. ———. 17 May 1784. ———.
McGregor, Malcomb. Va. Private. 20 Sep. 1806. 100 acres.
McGrew, Peter. S.C. Soldier. 2 Oct. 1786. 200 acres.
McGrey, Robert. Ga. Soldier. 3 Jan. 1785. ———.
McGruder, Ninian Offut. Ga. ———. 17 May 1784. ———.
McGruder, Zadock. Ga. ———. 28 Jul. 1784. 287 1/2 acres.
McGruen, Andrew. Ga. Minute Man. 22 Mar. 1785. ———.
McGuichen, Andrew. Pa. Private. 14 Jun. 1787. 200 acres.
McGuigan, Michael. N. Y. Sergeant. 8 Jul. 1790. 600 acres.

McGuinis, John. Md. Private. ———. 50 acres.
McGuire, Andrew. Pa. Private. ———. 200 acres.
McGuire, Andrew. Va. Private. 4 Aug. 1783. 233 1/3 acres.
McGuire, Elijah. S.C. ———. 4 Dec. 1786. 200 acres.
McGuire, James. Va. Private. 25 Jan. 1806. 100 acres.
McGuire, John. Pa. Private. 31 Oct. 1786. 200 acres.
McGuire, Matthew. Pa. Captain Lieutenant. ———. 200 acres.
McGuire, Matthew. Pa. Private. ———. 200 acres to Alexander Power, assignee.
McGuire, Merry. S.C. ———. 2 Oct. 1786. 150 acres.
McGuire, Merry. S.C. ———. 2 Oct. 1786. 15 acres.
McGuire, Michael. N.C. Private. 9 Nov. 1784. 640 acres to heirs.
McGuire, Michael. S.C. ———. 4 Jan. 1790. 200 acres.
McGuire, Peter. Ga. Citizen. 5 Dec. 1785. 287 1/2 acres.
McGuire, Silas. N.C. Private. 9 Nov. 1784. 640 acres to heir.
McGuy, Bennett. Va. Private. 26 Jun. 1783. 200 acres.
McHaffee, Benjamin. Md. Private. ———. 50 acres.
McHainey, Terry. Ga. Soldier. 7 Mar. 1785. 230 acres.
McHene, John. Va. Private. 1 Apr. 1783. 100 acres.
McHenry, Edward. Pa. Private. ———. 200 acres.
McHenry, Henry. N.Y. ———. 13 Sep. 1790. 500 acres to heirs.
McHenry, Thomas. Ga. ———. 5 Sep. 1785. ———.
McIlehany, John. Va. Captain. 25 Dec. 1783. 4000 acres.
McIlhaney, James. Va. Captain. 14 Mar. 1834. 4000 acres.
McIlhany, James. Va. Private. 9 Nov. 1784. 100 acres.
McIlhatton, William. Pa. ———. 27 Aug. 1806. 200 acres to George Armstrong, assignee.
McIlhatton, William. Pa. Private. 30 Sep. 1787. 200 acres.
McIlwee, James. S.C. ———. 2 May 1785. 200 acres.
McIntire, Alexander. Va.-Ind. Private. 108 acres.
McIntire, Daniel. Pa. Private. 26 Sep. 1787. 200 acres.
McIntire, James. Md. Private. ———. 50 acres.
McIntire, James. N.C. Private. 1 Oct. 1840. 640 acres to heirs.
McIntire, Thomas. Pa. Captain. 6 Aug. 1787. 500 acres.
McIntire, William. Pa. Private. 16 Mar. 1789. 200 acres.
McIntire, William. Va. Sergeant. 27 Nov. 1783. 200 acres.
McIntire, Willliam. N.C. Private. 26 Apr. 1784. 640 acres.
McIntosh, Alexander. Va. Private. 23 Jun. 1783. 200 acres.
McIntosh, John. Ga. Lieutenant Colonel Commandant. 25 May 1784. 575 acres.
McIntosh, John. Md. Private. ———. 50 acres.
McIntosh, John. N. Y. Private. 8 Jul. 1790. 600 acres.
McIntosh, Lachlan. Ga. Major. 13 Sep. 1783. 800 acres to administrator William McIntosh.
McIntosh, Lachlan. Ga. Major General. 19 Mar. 1784. 500 acres.
McIntosh, Lachlan. Ga. Brigadier General. 25 May 1783. 927 1/2 acres.
McIntosh, Lachlan. Ga. Lieutenant. 25 May 1784. 460 acres.
McIntosh, Peter. Ga. Soldier. 7 Jul. 1785. 287 1/2 acres.
McIntosh, Peter. Va. Private. 21 Apr. 1820. 100 acres.
McIntosh, Thomas. Va. Private. 13 Apr. 1822. 100 acres.
McIntosh, William. Ga. Captain. 9 Sep. 1783. 600 acres.
McIntosh, William. Va. Private. 8 Jul. 1783. 100 acres.
McIntosh, William. Va. Private. 22 Jul. 1783. 233 1/3 acres.
McIntosh, William. Va. Private. 6 Mar. 1834. 100 acres.
McIntyre, Barny. N. Y. Private. 8 Jul. 1790. 500 acres.
McKain, Peter. S.C. ———. 2 Oct. 1786. 200 acres.

McKain, Thomas. Ga. ———. 26 May 1784. 287 1/2 acres.
McKall, Michael. N.C. Private. 9 Nov. 1784. 342 acres.
McKann, Daniel. Pa. Private. 11 Sep. 1787. 200 acres.
McKannon, Christopher. Va. Sergeant. 3 May 1792. 400 acres.
McKay, Daniel. Ga. ———. 15 Apr. 1784. 287 1/2 acres.
McKay, Dougald. N.C. Sergeant. 8 Nov. 1784. 1000 acres to heir.
McKay, Eneas. Pa. Colonel. 28 Aug. 1787. 500 acres to Mary Adams, widow.
McKay, Eneas. Pa. Colonel. 20 May 1797. 500 acres to Mary Adams in trust for him.
McKay, Eneas. Pa. Colonel. 28 Aug. 1787. 500 acres to heirs.
McKay, Eneas. Va. Private. 23 Jun. 1783. 200 acres.
McKay, James. Ga. ———. 6 Feb. 1784. 250 acres.
McKay, John. N.C. Private. 30 May 1820. 640 acres to heirs.
McKean, John. N.C. Private. 23 May 1821. 640 acres.
McKean, John. Pa. ———. 24 Sep. 1794. 200 acres to George Donnaker, assignee.
McKee, Andrew. Pa. ———. 26 Jan. 1804. 200 acres.
McKee, James. Pa. Private. 28 Mar. 1809. 200 acres to Eleanor McKee, widow.
McKee, John. S.C. ———. 4 Dec. 1786. 200 acres.
McKee, Richard. Va. Private. 1 Nov. 1782. 200 acres.
McKee, William. Va. Captain. 6 Dec. 1806. 4000 acres.
McKeel, Joshua. N.C. Private. 2 Feb. 1786. 640 acres to heirs.
McKeel, Thomas. N.C. Private. 29 Oct. 1821. 640 acres to heirs.
McKeen, William. Ga. ———. 15 Mar. 1784. 250 acres.
McKellup, Abram. N. Y. Sergeant. 9 Jul. 1790. 600 acres.
McKelvey, Robert. S.C. Captain. 4 Jul. 1786. 170 acres.
McKelvey, Robert. S.C. Captain. 7 Nov. 1785. 123 acres.
McKelvey, Thomas. Pa. Private. 9 Mar. 1795. 200 acres to John Nicholson, assignee.
McKelvey, William. Ga. Minute Man. 3 Oct. 1783. ———.
McKennan, Martin. Va. Sergeant. 14 Aug. 1786. 400 acres.
McKenney, Abner. Me. ———. 14 Feb. 1838. 200 acres to widow Sarah McKenney. Saco.
McKenney, Daniel. Va. Private. 29 Nov. 1783. 100 acres.
McKenney, James. Va. Private. 9 May 1785. 100 acres.
McKenney, Jeremiah. Me. ———. 4 Aug. 1835. 200 acres to widow Anna McKenney. Saco.
McKenney, John. Pa. Lieutenant. ———. 200 acres.
McKenney, William. Me. Lieutenant. 2 Jun. 1838. 600 acres to widow Miriam McKenney. Auburn.
McKenny, Charles. N. Y. Sergeant. 8 Jul. 1790. 600 acres.
McKenny, Charles. N. Y. Private. 8 Jul. 1790. 600 acres.
McKenny, Francis. Ga. ———. 17 May 1784. ———.
McKenny, Henry. Ga. Refugee. 28 Feb. 1784. 250 acres.
McKenny, John. Ga. ———. 24 Feb. 1784. 250 acres.
McKenny, John. Va. Private. 23 Jun. 1783. 100 acres.
McKenny, Joseph. Me. ———. 18 Jun. 1835. 200 acres. Green.
McKenny, Matthew. Ga. Minute Man. 20 Apr. 1784. 287 1/2 acres.
McKenny, Nathan. Ga. Minute Man. ———. 287 1/2 acres.
McKenny, Thomas. Ga. Minute Man. 19 Jun. 1784. 287 1/2 acres.
McKenny, Travis. Ga. ———. 24 Feb. 1784. 250 acres.
McKenny, William. Ga. Minute Man. 19 Jul. 1784. 287 1/2 acres.
McKenzie, John. N. Y. Matross. 9 Jul. 1790. 600 acres.
McKenzie, William. N.C. Private. 13 Jan. 1792. 640 acres.
McKessick, Thomas. N.C. Private. 24 Oct. 1783. 640 acres.
McKew, John. N. Y. Matross. 6 Jul. 1790. 600 acres.

McKewn, James. Pa. Private. 21 Oct. 1786. 200 acres.

McKey, Bennet. Va. Private. 30 Mar. 1831. 200 acres.

McKillen, Edward. Pa. Private. 7 Feb. 1787. 200 acres.

McKillip, Robert. Pa. Private. ———. 200 acres to widow.

McKimm, John. Pa. Private. 20 Oct. 1786. 200 acres. to Sarah McKimm, widow.

McKimmons, John. Pa. Private. 3 Jan. 1786. 200 acres.

McKindrick, Archibald. Pa. Private. 9 Mar. 1795. 200 acres to John Nicholson, assignee.

McKiney, Hugh. N.C. Private. 22 Apr. 1785. 640 acres to heirs.

McKinley, Alexander. Pa. Private. 11 Jun. 1787. 200 acres.

McKinley, Alexander. Va. Private. 11 Nov. 1784. 100 acres.

McKinley, Charles. Va. Private. 19 Jan. 1785. 100 acres.

McKinley, Daniel. N.C. Sergeant. 17 Feb. 1824. Balance of 360 acres.

McKinley, John. N.C. Private. 21 Aug. 1820. 228 acres.

McKinley, John. Pa. Sergeant. 3 Nov. 1786. 250 acres.

McKinley, John. Va. Private. 29 Jul. 1783. 233 1/3 acres.

McKinley, John. Va. Lieutenant. 21 Feb. 1810. 500 acres.

McKinley, John. Va. Lieutenant. 21 Feb. 1810. 500 acres.

McKinley, John. Va. Lieutenant. 21 Feb. 1810. 500 acres.

McKinley, John. Va. Lieutenant. 21 Feb. 1810. 500 acres.

McKinley, John. Va. Lieutenant. 21 Feb. 1810. 666 2/3 acres.

McKinley, Peter. Pa. Private. 17 Aug. 1787. 200 acres.

McKinley, William. Md. Private. ———. 50 acres.

McKinly, Daniel. N.C. Private. 29 Sep. 1784. 640 acres to Andrew Caenahan, heir.

McKinne, Timothy. N.C. Private. 7 Jan. 1786. 640 acres to heirs.

McKinney, Andrew. Pa. Private. 28 Nov. 1786. 200 acres.

McKinney, Charles. N.C. Private. 12 May 1784. 640 acres.

McKinney, Daniel. N.C. Private. 5 Dec. 1796. 640 acres.

McKinney, Dennis. Va. Private. 21 Dec. 1784. 100 acres.

McKinney, James. N.Y. ———. 13 Sep. 1790. 500 acres to heirs.

McKinney, John. Pa. Private. ———. 200 acres.

McKinney, John. Va. Drummer. 7 Apr. 1838. 400 acres.

McKinney, John. Va. Drummer. 7 Apr. 1838. 400 acres.

McKinney, Roger, Sr. S.C. ———. 2 Oct. 1786. 200 acres to Roger McKinney, Jr., heir.

McKinney, Timothy. S.C. ———. 2 Feb. 1789. 100 acres.

McKinney, William. N.C. Private. 19 May 1784. 640 acres.

McKinnie, Robert. N.C. Private. 19 May 1784. 640 acres.

McKinnis, John. N.C. Private. 9 Sep. 1785. 640 acres to heirs.

McKinny, John. Pa. Lieutenant. ———. 200 acres.

McKinsey, Alexander. Va. Sergeant. 26 Jun. 1784. 400 acres.

McKinsey, Hannah. Conn. Sufferer. Fairfield. 1.4.0.

McKinsey, Jesse. Md. Private. ———. 50 acres.

McKinsey, Joshua. Md. Private. ———. 50 acres.

McKinsey, Moses. Md. Private. ———. 50 acres.

McKinsey, Patrick. Md. Private. ———. 50 acres.

McKinsey, Roderick. Md. Private. ———. 50 acres.

McKinsey, Thomas. Md. Private. ———. 50 acres.

McKinsey, William. N.C. Private. 25 Oct. 1783. 640 acres.

McKinstry, John. N. Y. ———. 3 May 1808. 300 acres.

McKinzey, Allisander. N.C. Private. 2 Dec. 1785. 640 acres.

McKinzie, Malcolm. N.Y. ———. 13 Sep. 1790. 500 acres to heirs.

McKnight, Benjamin. Va. Private. 2 Apr. 1784. 100 acres.

McKnight, Charles. N.Y. Physician & Surgeon. 10 Aug. 1792. 2700 acres.

McKnight, David. Pa. Lieutenant. 9 Apr. 1787. 200 acres.
McKnight, David. Pa. Private. 9 Apr. 1787. 200 acres.
McKnight, Patrick. N.C. Private. 5 Dec. 1796. 640 acres.
McKnight, William. Va. Private. 20 Jun. 1783. 100 acres.
McLain, James. Ga. Refugee. 25 May 1784. 287 1/2 acres.
McLain, Jeremiah. N.C. Private. 27 Jul. 1785. 640 acres.
McLain, John. Ga. Refugee. 24 Feb. 1784. 250 acres.
McLain, Thomas. Pa. Fifer. 8 Nov. 1804. 200 acres.
McLamar, Timothy. Md. Private. ———. 50 acres.
McLane, Allen. Va. Major. 30 May 1820. 250 acres.
McLane, Allen. Va. Major. 30 May 1820. 250 acres.
McLane, Allen. Va. Major. 30 May 1820. 250 acres.
McLane, Allen. Va. Major. 30 May 1820. 250 acres.
McLane, Allen. Va. Major. 30 May 1820. 250 acres.
McLane, Allen. Va. Major. 30 May 1820. 250 acres.
McLane, Allen. Va. Major. 30 May 1820. 250 acres.
McLane, Allen. Va. Major. 30 May 1820. 250 acres.
McLane, Allen. Va. Major. 30 May 1820. 250 acres.
McLane, Allen. Va. Major. 30 May 1820. 250 acres.
McLane, Allen. Va. Major. 30 May 1820. 250 acres.
McLane, Allen. Va. Major. 30 May 1820. 250 acres.
McLane, Allen. Va. Major. 30 May 1820. 250 acres.
McLane, Allen. Va. Major. 30 May 1820. 250 acres.
McLane, Allen. Va. Major. 30 May 1820. 250 acres.
McLane, Allen. Va. Major. 30 May 1820. 250 acres.
McLane, Allen. Va. Major. 30 May 1820. 250 acres.
McLane, Allen. Va. Major. 30 May 1820. 250 acres.
McLane, Allen. Va. Major. 30 May 1820. 250 acres.
McLane, Allen. Va. Major. 30 May 1820. 250 acres.
McLane, Allen. Va. Major. 30 May 1820. 250 acres.
McLane, Allen. Va. Major. 30 May 1820. 250 acres.
McLane, John. N. Y. Sergeant. 8 Jul. 1790. 600 acres.
McLane, John. N. Y. Matross. 9 Jul. 1790. 500 acres.
McLardy, Alexander. Va. Corporal. 25 Jun. 1783. 200 acres.
Mclary, Thomas. N.C. Fifer. 30 Sep. 1785. 1000 acres to heirs.
McLaughlin, Amos. Ga. ———. 17 May 1784. ———.
McLaughlin, Cornelius. Md. Private. ———. 50 acres.
McLaughlin, George. Pa. Private. 30 Jan. 1787. 200 acres.
McLaughlin, Hugh. N.C. Private. 6 Dec. 1797. 640 acres to heirs.
McLaughlin, Hugh. Va. Private. 14 Dec. 1833. 100 acres.
McLaughlin, John. Ga. ———. 21 Apr. 1784. 250 acres.
McLaughlin, Owen. Pa. Private. 28 Aug. 1787. 200 acres.
McLaughlin, Patrick. Pa. Private. 29 Aug. 1787. 200 acres.
McLaughlin, William. Md. Private. ———. 50 acres.
McLean, Angus. N. Y. Private. 29 Jan. 1791. 600 acres.
McLean, Daniel. N.Y. ———. 8 Oct. 1792. 500 acres to heirs.
McLean, Jacob. Pa. ———. 9 Mar. 1795. 200 acres to John Nicholson.
McLean, James. Pa. Lieutenant. 3 Jan. 1787. 200 acres.
McLean, James. Pa. Private. 6 Jan. 1787. 200 acres.
McLean, John. N. Y. Private. 7 Jul. 1790. 600 acres.
McLean, John. N. Y. ———. 21 Sep. 1804. 600 acres.
McLean, John. Conn. Sufferer. Danbury. 528.7.1.
McLean, Lewis. Ga. Private. 28 Feb. 1784. 287 1/2 acres.
McLean, Neal. N. Y. Private. 8 Jul. 1790. 600 acres.

McLean, Uriah. Mass. Private. 13 Dec. 1831. 200 acres to his children William McLean, John McLean, Rensselaer McLean, Abner McLean, Philander McLean, Nancy the wife of Martin Goff, and Jane the wife of Thomas Wright.

McLemore, John. N.C. Private. 31 Aug. 1795. 640 acres to heirs.

McLochlin, John. Va. Private. 24 Jun. 1789. 100 acres.

McLung, John. Ga. Citizen. 6 Apr. 1785. 287 1/2 acres.

McMahan, Andrew. Va. Sergeant. 2 Feb. 1785. 400 acres.

McMahan, Andrew. Va. Private. 1 Apr. 1785. 100 acres.

McMahan, Daniel. S.C. ———. 6 Nov. 1786. 200 acres to Luke McMahan, heir.

McMahan, John. S.C. ———. 2 Jul. 1787. 200 acres.

McMahan, Patrick. Va. Private. 4 Dec. 1793. 100 acres.

McMahon, John. Pa. Sergeant. ———. 250 acres.

McMahon, Peter. Pa. Dragoon. 21 Jul. 1787. 200 acres.

McMahon, Roger. Va. Private. 26 Nov. 1783. 100 acres.

McMahon, Timothy. Md. Private. ———. 50 acres.

McManey, John. Va. Private. 3 Apr. 1784. 100 acres.

McManiard, Nicholas. Md. Private. ———. 50 acres.

McMann, Matthew. Ga. Minute Man. 16 Apr. 1784. 287 1/2 acres.

McMann, William. Pa. Matross. 20 Jan. 1787. 200 acres.

McManus, Barney. Md. Private. ———. 50 acres.

McManus, George. Va.-Ind. Private. 108 acres.

McManus, Hugh. Pa. Private. 11 Sep. 1789. 200 acres.

McManus, John. Me. ———. 27 Apr. 1835. 200 acres. Brunswick.

McManus, John. Me. ———. 27 Apr. 1835. 200 acres. Brunswick.

McManus, John. Pa. Private. ———. 200 acres.

McManus, John, Jr. Va.-Ind. Private. 108 acres.

McManus, John, Sr. Va.-Ind. Private. 108 acres.

McMaster, Alexander. N. Y. Private. 8 Jul. 1790. 500 acres.

McMasters, Michael. Va. Private. 25 Jun. 1783. 100 acres.

McMath, Joseph. Ga. ———. 1784. 287 1/2 acres.

McMeans, William. Va. Private. 23 Jun. 1783. 100 acres.

McMechen, Robert. Va. Private. 26 Nov. 1783. 100 acres.

McMechen, William. Va. Surgeon. 20 Oct. 1783. 6000 acres.

McMeekin, Joseph. Va. Drum Major. 2 Jun. 1783. 200 acres.

McMellin, Michael. N.C. Private. Jan. 1795. 274 acres.

McMichael, James. Pa. Lieutenant. 1 Nov. 1786. 200 acres.

McMichael, James. Pa. Private. 1 Nov. 1787. 200 acres.

McMichel, John. Pa. Private. 24 Nov. 1787. 200 acres.

McMillan, Hugh. Md. Sergeant. ———. 50 acres.

McMullen, Daniel. Pa. ———. 15 Aug. 1787. 200 acres.

McMullen, James. N.C. Drummer. 29 Sep. 1784. 309 acres.

McMullen, James. Pa. Private. 17 Aug. 1805. 200 acres.

McMullen, James. Va. Private. 19 Jan. 1785. 100 acres.

McMullen, Jeremiah. N.C. Private. 22 Dec. 1796. 274 acres.

McMullen, Jerome. N.C. Private. 6 Sep. 1821. 640 acres.

McMullen, John. Pa. Private. 10 Sep. 1789. 200 acres.

McMullen, Michael. Pa. Private. 4 Aug. 1787. 200 acres.

McMullen, Patrick. Ga. Minute Man. 16 Jul. 1784. 287 1/2 acres.

McMullen, Robert. Ga. ———. 17 May 1784. ———.

McMullen, Samuel. Va.-Ind. Private. 108 acres.

McMullin, Isaac. N.C. Private. 30 Sep. 1785. 640 acres to heirs.

McMullin, William. Pa. Private. ———. 200 acres.

McMunn, John. Ga. ———. 25 May 1784. 287 1/2 acres.

McMurdy, Robert. Pa. Chaplain. 10 Apr. 1787. 300 acres.
McMurphy, Daniel. Ga. Refugee. 29 Jan. 1784. 250 acres.
McMurray, David. Ga. ———. 25 Feb. 1784. 250 acres.
McMurray, Frederick. Soldier. ———. 287 1/2 acres.
McMurray, John. Ga. Minute Man. 22 Apr. 1784. 287 1/2 acres.
McMurray, Robert. Pa. Chaplain. ———. 300 acres.
McMurray, William. Ga. Minute Man. 26 Oct. 1784. 287 1/2 acres.
McMurray, William. S.C. ———. 2 Oct. 1786. 200 acres.
McMurtry, William. N.C. Private. 30 Sep. 1785. 640 acres to heirs.
McNabb, Robert. Ga. ———. 250 acres. ———.
McNable, Charles. Md. Sergeant. ———. 50 acres.
McNair, Archibald. Pa. ———. 3 May 1811. 200 acres.
McNair, Daniel. Ga. Soldier. 20 Feb. 1784. 250 acres.
McNair, John. Pa. Private. 12 Sep. 1787. 200 acres.
McNamara, Darby. Md. Private. ———. 50 acres.
McNamara, Joseph. Md. Private. ———. 50 acres.
McNamara, Timothy. Va. Private. 22 Aug. 1783. 200 acres.
McNames, Charles. N.Y. ———. 13 Sep. 1790. 500 acres to heirs.
McNatt, Solomon. Ga. Minute Man. ———. 287 1/2 acres.
McNaughton, Peter. Md. Sergeant. ———. 50 acres.
McNeal, Charles. N. Y. Private. 8 Jul. 1790. 600 acres.
McNeal, David. Va. Private. 3 Feb. 1784. 100 acres.
McNeal, Lewis. Ga. ———. 21 Apr. 1784. 287 1/2 acres.
McNeal, Peter. Va. Private. 23 Jun. 1784. 100 acres.
McNeal, William. Md. Corporal. ———. 50 acres.
McNeel, John. N.C. Private. 30 Sep. 1785. 640 acres to heirs.
McNeel, Zebulon. N.C. Corporal. 2 Feb. 1786. 1000 acres to heirs.
McNeely, Daniel. Ga. Soldier. 16 Apr. 1784. 287 1/2 acres.
McNeely, Daniel. Ga. Refugee. 16 Apr. 1784. 287 1/2 acres. [There are two Daniels]
McNeely, Hugh. Ga. ———. 16 Apr. 1784. 287 1/2 acres.
McNeese, John. N.C. Captain. 27 Nov. 1783. 3840 acres.
McNeill, John. Md. Private. ———. 50 acres.
McNell, Absalom. N.C. Private. 2 Feb. 1786. 640 acres.
McNichol, John. Va. Surgeon. 30 Apr. 1846. 857 1/7 acres.
McNichol, John. Va. Surgeon. 30 Apr. 1846. 857 1/7 acres.
McNichol, John. Va. Surgeon. 30 Apr. 1846. 857 1/7 acres.
McNichol, John. Va. Surgeon. 30 Apr. 1846. 857 1/7 acres.
McNichol, John. Va. Surgeon. 30 Apr. 1846. 857 1/7 acres.
McNichol, John. Va. Surgeon. 30 Apr. 1846. 857 1/7 acres.
McNichol, John. Va. Surgeon. 30 Apr. 1846. 857 1/7 acres.
McNickle, John. Va. Surgeon. 19 Mar. 1834. 1000 acres.
McNickle, John. Va. Surgeon. 19 Mar. 1834. 4000 acres.
McNickle, John. Va. Surgeon. 19 Mar. 1834. 1000 acres.
McNickle, John. Va. Surgeon. 17 Oct. 1842. 857 1/7 acres.
McNickle, John. Va. Surgeon. 17 Oct. 1842. 857 1/7 acres.
McNickle, John. Va. Surgeon. 17 Oct. 1842. 857 1/7 acres.
McNickle, John. Va. Surgeon. 17 Oct. 1842. 857 1/7 acres.
McNickle, John. Va. Surgeon. 17 Oct. 1842. 857 1/7 acres.
McNickle, John. Va. Surgeon. 17 Oct. 1842. 857 1/7 acres.
McNickle, John. Va. Surgeon. 17 Oct. 1842. 857 1/7 acres.
McNiel, Archibald. Ga. Refugee. 1784. 250 acres to his heirs.
McNiel, Daniel. Ga. ———. 1784. 250 acres.
McNiel, Daniel, Jr. Ga. ———. 1784. 287 1/2 acres.

McNiel, Daniel, Sr. Ga. ———. 1784. 287 1/2 acres.
McNiel, Duncan. Ga. ———. 17 May 1784. ———.
McNiel, James. Ga. ———. 1784. 250 acres.
McNiel, James. Ga. Colonel. 17 Feb. 1784. 650 acres.
McNiel, Jesse. Ga. ———. 17 May 1784. ———.
McNiel, Michael. Ga. Soldier. 1784. 250 acres.
McNight, John. Md. Fifer. ———. 50 acres.
McNolly, Michel. Va. Private. 20 Jun. 1783. 100 acres.
McNulty, John. N.C. Private. 31 Aug. 1795. 640 acres to heirs.
McNutt, James. Va.-Ind. Private. 108 acres.
McNutt, James. Va. Lieutenant. 29 Dec. 1798. 2666 2/3 acres.
McNutten, Daniel. Va. Private. 21 Feb. 1786. 100 acres.
McPariss, Charles. N.C. Sergeant. 8 Dec. 1795. 1000 acres.
McPeck, Dennis. N.Y. Corporal. 13 Sep. 1790. 500 acres to heirs.
McPheatridge, Daniel. Pa. ———. 22 Aug. 1787. 200 acres.
McPherson, Abel. N.C. Sergeant. 8 Mar. 1785. 1000 acres.
McPherson, James. Pa. Lieutenant. 5 Apr. 1787. 200 acres.
McPherson, James. Pa. Lieutenant. ———. 200 acres.
McPherson, John. Pa. Lieutenant. 29 Feb. 1804. 200 acres to Richard Allison, assignee.
McPherson, Mark. Md. Lieutenant. ———. 200 acres.
McPherson, Murdock. N. Y. Lieutenant. ———. 1000 acres.
McPherson, Samuel. Md. Captain. ———. 200 acres.
McPherson, William. Md. Private. ———. 50 acres.
McPherson, William. Pa. Major. 10 Sep. 1789. 300 acres To R. B. Rogers, assignee.
McPherson, William. Pa. Major. 10 Sep. 1789. 300 acres to John B. Rodgers, assignee.
McPike, Richard. Pa. Private. 26 Mar. 1787. 200 acres.
McQueen, Joshua. Va. Sergeant. 20 May 1823. 400 acres.
McQuellin, James. Pa. Private. ———. 200 acres.
McQuiddy, Thomas. Va. Private. 11 Jul. 1835. 100 acres.
McQuillen, Robert. Va. Private. 20 Jan. 1783. 200 acres.
McQuillin, Walter. N.C. Private. 19 Nov. 1804. 640 acres to heirs.
McQuillon, William. N.C. Private. 24 Nov. 1796. 640 acres to heirs.
McQuire, William. Va. Lieutenant. 14 Feb. 1784. 2666 2/3 acres.
McQuiston, John. N.C. Private. 10 Feb. 1796. 640 acres.
McRae, Ruebin. N.C. Sergeant. 14 Dec. 1796. 640 acres to heirs.
McRaee, Roger. N.C. Private. 19 May 1784. 640 acres.
McRee, Griffith John. N.C. Major. 20 Apr. 1784. 4800 acres.
McRenels, Robert. N.C. Ensign. 17 Feb. 1824. 2560 acres.
McReynolds, Thomas. Va. Lieutenant. 3 Mar. 1833. 2666 2/3 cres.
McReynolds, Thomas. Va. Captain. 31 Dec. 1833. 1333 1/3 acres.
McReynolds, Thomas. Va. Captain. 9 Nov. 1852. 592 2/3 acres.
McReynolds, Thomas. Va. Captain. 9 Nov. 1852. 500 acres.
McRory, Arthur. N.C. Private. 8 Dec. 1795. 640 acres to heirs.
McRory, Thomas. N.C. Captain. 20 Oct. 1783. 3840 acres to James McRory, heir at law.
McShehe, Miles. N.C. Lieutenant. 28 May 1784. 2560 acres.
McSwain, Edward. Va. Sergeant. 11 Aug. 1783. 200 acres.
McSwain, George. Pa. Private. 27 Jul. 1787. 200 acres to Griffith Levering, assignee.
McSwain, Malcolm. N.C. Private. 24 Nov. 1796. 640 acres.
McTear, Frizzel. Va. Sergeant. 6 Dec. 1783. 200 acres.
McTear, William. Va. Sergeant. 6 Dec. 1783. 200 acres.
McValley, James. Va. Private. 1 May 1783. 200 acres.
McVeey, John. N.C. Private. 26 May 1784. 640 acres.

McVey, Charles. N.C. Private. 7 Dec. 1797. 640 acres to heirs.

McVey, Eli. N.C. Private. 27 Oct. 1783. 640 acres.

McVey, John. N.C. ———. 27 Oct. 1783. 640 acres to Eli McVey, heir.

McVicars, Daniel. Ga. Soldier. 11 Oct. 1783. 200 acres to widow Christian McVicars.

McWilliams, James. Va. Private. 12 Mar. 1834. 200 acres.

McWilliams, John. Va. Private. 21 Apr. 1784. 100 acres.

McWilliams, Joshua. Va. Midshipman. 5 Jul. 1783. 2666 2/3 acres.

McWilliams, Joshua. Va. Midshipman. 15 Nov. 1843. 2666 2/3 acres.

McWilliston, ———, Rev. Conn. Sufferer. New/East Haven. 21.8.0.

McYea, John. N.C. Drummer. 29 Sep. 1784. 1000 acres to William McIlyea, heir.

Meacham, Henry. Va. Private. 18 Apr. 1801. 100 acres.

Meacham, William. Va. Sergeant. 11 Jun. 1784. 200 acres.

Mead, Abigail. Conn. Sufferer. Greenwich. 6.0.0.

Mead, Abraham. Conn. Sufferer. Greenwich. 17.19.5.

Mead, Amos, Dr. Conn. Sufferer. Greenwich. 180.4.8.

Mead, Andrew. Conn. Sufferer. Greenwich. 36.0.0.

Mead, Azor. Conn. Sufferer. Norwalk. 36.6.8.

Mead, Benjamin. Conn. Sufferer. Greenwich. 111.5.8.

Mead, Caleb. Conn. Sufferer. Greenwich. 33.17.7.

Mead, Caleb, 2d. Conn. Sufferer. Greenwich. 76.11.7.

Mead, Charles. Conn. Sufferer. Greenwich. 0.4.10.

Mead, Deliverance. Conn. Sufferer. Greenwich. 39.0.3.

Mead, Deliverance & Jared Mead. Conn. Sufferers. Greenwich. 200.0.0.

Mead, Ebenezer. Conn. Sufferer. Greenwich. 5.18.4.

Mead, Edmond. Conn. Sufferer. Greenwich. 11.9.11.

Mead, Eliphalet. Conn. Sufferer. Greenwich. 5.2.8.

Mead, Eliphalet & Jehiel Mead. Conn. Sufferers. Greenwich. 85.0.0.

Mead, Eliphalet, Jr. Conn. Sufferer. Greenwich. 95.10.6.

Mead, Elizabeth. Conn. Sufferer. Greenwich. 13.14.8.

Mead, Elkanah. Conn. Sufferer. Greenwich. 7.10.11.

Mead, Enos. Conn. Sufferer. Greenwich. 12.12.5.

Mead, Everard. Va. Major. 20 Feb. 1784. 5333 1/3 acres.

Mead, Hannah. Conn. Sufferer. Greenwich. 2.15.0.

Mead, Henry. Conn. Sufferer. Greenwich. 105.4.2

Mead, Ichiel. Conn. Sufferer. Greenwich. 5.12.10.

Mead, James. Md. Drum Major. ———. 50 acres.

Mead, Jared. Conn. Sufferer. Greenwich. 68.0.7.

Mead, Jemima. Conn. Sufferer. Greenwich. 18.8.8.

Mead, Jeremiah, Jr. Conn. Sufferer. Greenwich. 92.15.7.

Mead, Jerusha. Conn. Sufferer. Greenwich. 7.0.0.

Mead, Jesse. Conn. Sufferer. Greenwich. 22.8.5.

Mead, John. Va. Private. 20 Jun. 1783. 100 acres.

Mead, John. Conn. Sufferer. Greenwich. 162.9.9.

Mead, John, Jr. Conn. Sufferer. Greenwich. 54.16.3.

Mead, Jonah. Conn. Sufferer. Greenwich. 24.12.0.

Mead, Jonas. Conn. Sufferer. Greenwich. 20.4.1.

Mead, Jonathan. N. Y. Gunner. 9 Jul. 1790. 600 acres.

Mead, Joseph. Ga. Soldier. 7 Jun. 1785. 230 acres.

Mead, Joseph. N.C. Private. 12 Dec. 1797. 274 acres.

Mead, Joseph. Conn. Sufferer. Greenwich. 39.15.3.

Mead, Joshua. Conn. Sufferer. Greenwich. 11.8.4.

Mead, Jotham. Conn. Sufferer. Greenwich. 26.10.6.

Mead, Mahlon. Va. Private. 22 Dec. 1783. 100 acres.

Mead, Matthew. Conn. Sufferer. Greenwich. 61.12.8.
Mead, Matthew, Col. Conn. Sufferer. Norwalk. 4.19.4.
Mead, Nathaniel, 3d. Conn. Sufferer. Greenwich. 18.3.5.
Mead, Nehemiah. Conn. Sufferer. Greenwich. 55.6.2.
Mead, Nehemiah, Jr. Conn. Sufferer. Greenwich. 9.8.3.
Mead, Peter. Conn. Sufferer. Greenwich. 138.19.9.
Mead, Peter, Jr. Conn. Sufferer. Greenwich. 41.4.10.
Mead, Richard Kidder. Va. Lieutenant Colonel. 19 Jun. 1783. 6000 acres.
Mead, Sarah. Conn. Sufferer. Greenwich. 71.5.4.
Mead, Shadrack. Conn. Sufferer. Greenwich. 42.0.0.
Mead, Silas. Conn. Sufferer. Greenwich. 62.8.7.
Mead, Sybil. Conn. Sufferer. Greenwich. 86.12.0.
Mead, Thornton. Va. Private. 10 Apr. 1832. 100 acres.
Mead, Titus. Conn. Sufferer. Greenwich. 95.5.2.
Mead, William. Ga. ———. 20 Apr. 1784. 1000 acres.
Mead, William. Va. Ensign. 23 Apr. 1785. 2666 2/3 acres.
Mead, Zacheus. Conn. Sufferer. Greenwich. 9.14.7.
Meade, Richard K. Va. Private. 28 Mar. 1834. 200 acres.
Meaders, Jonas. Ga. ———. 17 May 1784. ———.
Meadow, Thomas. Va. Private. 13 Dec. 1811. 200 acres.
Meadows, David. Md. Private. ———. 50 acres.
Meadows, Francis. Va. Private. 18 Apr. 1823. 100 acres.
Meadows, Israel. Va. Private. 21 May 1823. 100 acres.
Meadows, Jacob. S.C. ———. 6 Oct. 1794. 17 1/2 acres to James Timms, administrator.
Meadows, Jacob. S.C. ———. 6 Oct. 1794. 17 1/2 acres to James Timms, administrator.
Meadows, Jacob. S.C. ———. 1 Jun. 1795. 97 acres to James Timms, administrator.
Meadows, Jacob. S.C. ———. 2 Mar. 1795. 34 1/2 acres to James Timms, administrator.
Meadows, John. S.C. ———. 6 Oct. 1794. 8 acres to James Timms, administrator.
Meadows, John. S.C. ———. 6 Oct. 1794. 33 acres to James Timms, administrator.
Meadows, John. S.C. ———. 6 Oct. 1794. 8 acres to James Timms, administrator.
Meadows, John. S.C. ———. 6 Oct. 1794. 23 1/2 acres to James Timms, administrator.
Meadows, John. S.C. ———. 6 Oct. 1794. 150 acres to James Timms, administrator.
Mealing, Henry. Ga. ———. 17 May 1784. ———.
Meals, Samuel. Va. Seaman. 12 Jan. 1784. 100 acres.
Meanley, John. Ga. Lieutenant. 20 Sep. 1783. 400 acres.
Meanly, John. Va. Lieutenant. 19 Nov. 1808. 1333 1/3 acres.
Meanly, John. Va. Lieutenant. 19 Nov. 1808. 1333 1/3 acres.
Meanly, Robert. Va. Private. 20 May 1783. 100 acres.
Means, Hugh. Pa. ———. 6 Apr. 1794. 300 acres.
Means, John. Va. Corporal. 18 Dec. 1784. 200 acres.
Means, Thomas. Me. ———. 2 Nov. 1835. 200 acres to widow Eleanor Means. Freeport.
Means, Thomas. Pa. ———. 26 Mar. 1813. 200 acres.
Means, Thomas. Pa. Private. 28 Mar. 1803. 200 acres.
Mears, Abraham. N.C. Sergeant. 12 Sep. 1785. 1000 acres to heirs.
Mears, Bartholomew. Va. Gunner. 18 Jan. 1806. 1333 1/3 acres.
Mears, Bartholomew. Va. Gunner. 18 Jan. 1806. 1333 1/3 acres.
Mears, John. N.C. Private. 12 Sep. 1785. 640 acres to heirs.
Mears, Timothy. N.C. Private. 16 Feb. 1784. 640 acres.
Mears, Willis. N.C. Private. 28 Sep. 1785. 640 acres.
Meazles, Micajah. N.C. Private. 30 Sep. 1785. 640 acres to heirs.

Mebane, Robert, Sr. N.C. Colonel Commandant. 23 Oct. 1783. 7200 acres to William Mebane, heir.
Mechea, George. Va. Sergeant. 23 Jun. 1784. 200 acres.
Mecker, Solomon. N. Y. Private. 7 Jul. 1790. 600 acres.
Medaris, Abraham. N.C. Private. 3 Feb. 1785. 274 acres.
Medgett, Jacob. N.C. Private. 28 Sep. 1785. 640 acres.
Medicis, Cesimo de. N.C. Captain. 18 Nov. 1788. 1872 acres.
Medler, Boston. Md. Drummer. ———. 50 acres.
Medler, Christopher. N. Y. Matross. 9 Jul. 1790. 600 acres.
Medlin, Henry. N.C. Private. 30 Mar. 1820. 640 acres to heir John Medlin.
Medlock, Nathaniel. N.C. Private. 17 Feb. 1824. 640 acres.
Medum, John. N.C. Private. 17 Feb. 1824. 640 acres.
Meed, John. Va. Sergeant. 10 Feb. 1784. 400 acres.
Meeker, Benjamin. Conn. Sufferer. Fairfield. 15.17.4.
Meeker, Seth. Conn. Sufferer. Fairfield. 22.5.8.
Meeks, Robert. N.C. Private. 20 Apr. 1784. 274 acres.
Meeks, William. N.C. ———. 10 Aug. 1785. 228 acres.
MeGee, Charles. Md. Private. ———. 50 acres.
Megginson, William. Va. Captain. 11 Dec. 1834 [1833]. 3500 acres.
Megginson, William. Va. Captain. 22 Jun. 1835. 500 acres.
Megruder, Ningin Offet. Ga. ———. 15 Mar. 1784. 250 acres.
Meham, Nicholas. Ga. Minute Man. 22 Mar. 1785. 250 acres.
Melally, Michael. Conn. Sufferer. New London. 94.4.7.
Melcham, Joseph. Pa. Private. 19 Jul. 1787. 200 acres.
Melcher, John. Va. Private. 2 Apr. 1784. 100 acres.
Melloy, William. N.C. Private. 8 Dec. 1796. 640 acres.
Melone, Peter. N.C. Private. 10 Aug. 1785. 640 acres to heirs.
Melson, Charles. Va. Private. 14 Feb. 1829. 60 acres.
Melson, Charles. Va. Private. 22 Sep. 1857. 20 acres.
Melson, Charles. Va. Private. 22 Sep. 1857. 20 acres.
Melson, Levin. Va. Carpenter's Mate. 9 Dec. 1830. 666 2/3 acres.
Melson, Levin. Va. Carpenter's Mate. 9 Dec. 1830. 666 2/3 acres.
Melson, Levin. Va. Carpenter's Mate. 9 Dec. 1830. 666 2/3 acres.
Melson, Levin. Va. Carpenter's Mate. 9 Dec. 1830. 666 2/3 acres.
Melson, Levin. Va. Carpenter's Mate. 19 Jul. 1831. 666 2/3 acres.
Melson, Levin. Va. Carpenter's Mate. 19 Jul. 1831. 666 2/3 acres.
Melson, Levin. Va. Carpenter's Mate. 19 Jul. 1831. 666 2/3 acres.
Melson, Levin. Va. Carpenter's Mate. 19 Jul. 1831. 166 2/3 acres.
Melson, Levin. Va. Carpenter's Mate. 19 Jul. 1831. 166 2/3 acres.
Melson, Levin. Va. Carpenter's Mate. 19 Jul. 1831. 166 2/3 acres.
Melson, Levin. Va. Carpenter's Mate. 19 Jul. 1831. 166 2/3 acres.
Melton, Hardy. Va. Private. 3 Sep. 1783. 100 acres.
Melton, Isham. Va. Private. 21 Nov. 1783. 100 acres.
Melton, James. Va. Private. 21 Nov. 1783. 100 acres.
Melton, James. Va. Private. 20 May 1834. 100 acres.
Melton, John. Pa. Drum Major. 7 Nov. 1786. 250 acres.
Melton, John. Va. Private. 21 Nov. 1783. 100 acres.
Melton, Jonathan. N.C. Private. 25 Nov. 1796. 228 acres.
Melton, Thomas. Va. Private. 25 Aug. 1821. 100 acres.
Melton, William. N.C. Corporal. 21 Aug. 1820. 360 acres.
Melvany, Patrick. Pa. Private. 9 Mar. 1795. 200 acres to John Nicholson, assignee.
Melven, George. Ga. Captain. 19 Mar. 1784. 600 acres.
Melville, Aleard. Md. Private. ———. 50 acres.
Melville, James. Pa. Sergeant. 19 Nov.

1786. 250 acres to Joseph Johnston, assignee.
Melvin, Peter. Md. Private. ———. 50 acres.
Melvin, Richard. Pa. Private. 5 Apr. 1787. 200 acres.
Mendenhall, Joseph. N.C. Private. 7 Jan. 1786. 640 acres to heirs.
Menico, Abraham. N.C. Private. 7 Sep. 1820. 640 acres to heirs.
Menshew, Micajah. N.C. Private. 10 Dec. 1788. 640 acres to heirs.
Menter, Barker. Va. Private. 25 May 1785. 200 acres.
Mentges, Christian. Pa. Private. 9 May 1795. 200 acres to Michael Ferrick, assignee.
Mentges, Francis. Pa. Colonel. 4 Oct. 1786. 250 acres.
Menzies, John. Ga. ———. 17 May 1784. ———.
Mercer, Asa. Ga. ———. 23 Apr. 1784. 287 1/2 acres.
Mercer, George. Pa. Private. 30 Aug. 1787. 200 acres.
Mercer, Hugh. Va. Brigadier General. 10 Jun. 1783. 10,000 acres.
Mercer, Hugh. Va. Brigadier General. 20 Feb. 1834. 1873 acres.
Mercer, Hugh. Va. Brigadier General. 1 Feb. 1838. 884 acres.
Mercer, Isaac. Va. Master. 19 Sep. 1786. 1333 1/3 acres.
Mercer, Isaac. Virginia. Master. 19 Sep. 1786. 1333 1/3 acres.
Mercer, Jacob. Ga. ———. 22 Apr. 1784. 287 1/2 acres.
Mercer, James. Ga. ———. 22 Apr. 1784. 287 1/2 acres.
Mercer, John. N.C. Private. 7 Jan. 1786. 274 acres.
Mercer, John F. Va. Captain. 27 Dec. 1783. 4000 acres.
Mercer, Joshua. Ga. ———. 1784. —— acres to heir Samuel Crabb.
Mercer, Julian. Va. Private. 31 Dec. 1851. 100 acres.
Mercer, Peter. N.C. Private. 20 Dec. 1796. 640 acres to heirs.
Mercer, Silas. Ga. Chaplain. 24 Feb. 1784. 650 acres.
Merchand, Bernard. N. Y. ———. ———. 500 acres.
Merchant, Caleb. N.C. Private. 12 May 1784. 274 acres.
Mercier, Hubert. Va. Private. 31 Dec. 1851. 100 acres.
Mercier, Hubert. Va. Private. 21 Apr. 1856. 100 acres.
Mercier, John B. Va. Private. 31 Dec. 1851. 100 acres.
Mercier, John B. Va. Private. 9 Apr. 1856. 100 acres.
Mercier, John D. N. Y. ———. ———. 500 acres.
Mercier, Julian. Va. Private. 21 Apr. 1856. 100 acres.
Meredith, Benjamin. N.C. Private. 26 Nov. 1796. 640 acres to heirs.
Meredith, William. Va. Captain. 27 Dec. 1782. 4000 acres.
Meredith, William. Va. Captain. 1 Jun. 1805. 466 2/3 acres.
Merewether, Thomas. Va. Major. 25 Nov. 1782. 5333 2/3 acres.
Merewether, William. Va. Lieutenant. 17 Feb. 1834. 2666 2/3 acres.
Mericle, Samuel. N. Y. Private. 8 Jul. 1790. 600 acres.
Meriwether, David. Va. Lieutenant. ———. 2666 2/3 acres.
Meriwether, David. Va. Lieutenant. 21 Jan. 1803. 444 1/3 acres.
Meriwether, James. Va. Lieutenant. 17 Jul. 1783. 2666 2/3 acres.
Meriwether, James. Va. Lieutenant. 27 Aug. 1783. 2666 2/3 acres.
Meriwether, James. Va. Lieutenant. 11 Feb. 1784. 2666 2/3 acres.
Merlet, Hardoin. N. Y. ———. ———. 333 1/3 acres.
Mero, Amariah. Me. Private. 11 May 1835. 200 acres. Union.
Merret, Joel. N.C. Private. 12 Dec. 1806. 640 acres to heirs.
Merrett, Benjamin. N.C. ———. 19 May 1784. 640 acres to Stephen Merrett.
Merrick, John. Va. Private. 21 Nov. 1787. 200 acres.
Merril, Benjamin. Conn. Sufferer. Norwalk. 5.0.0.
Merrill, Daniel. Me. Captain. 2 May 1838. 600 acres to widow Sarah Merril. Kennebunkport.
Merrill, Moses. Me. Private. 28 Jun. 1836. 200 acres to widow Elizabeth Merrill. Portland.

Merriman, Luke. Md. Private. ———. 50 acres.
Merriman, Silas. Conn. Sufferer. New/East Haven. 2.2.6.
Merriman, William. Pa. Private. 24 Oct. 1786. 200 acres.
Merrit, Reuben. Conn. Sufferer. Greenwich. 25.7.9.
Merritt, Archelaus. Va. Private. 25 Jun. 1783. 100 acres.
Merritt, Daniel. Me. ———. 2 Jun. 1835. 200 acres to widow Hannah Merritt, now wife of William Merritt. Addison.
Merritt, Daniel. Conn. Sufferer. Greenwich. 36.6.9.
Merritt, Major. Va. Private. 17 Sep. 1793. 200 acres.
Merritt, Nathan. Conn. Sufferer. Greenwich. 46.13.4.
Merritt, Samuel. Va. Private. 25 Aug. 1783. 100 acres.
Merritt, William. Me. ———. 14 Sep. 1835. 200 acres. Addison.
Merritt, William. N. Y. Matross. 9 Jul. 1790. 500 acres.
Merritt, William. N.C. Private. 15 Jul. 1785. 640 acres to heirs.
Merriweather, James. Va.-Ind. Lieutenant. Jan. 1784. 2156 acres.
Merriweather, William. Va.-Ind. Sergeant. 216 acres.
Merrow, William. Me. ———. 18 Mar. 1837. 200 acres to widow Margaret Merrow. Standish.
Merrow, William. Pa. ———. 21 May 1794. 200 acres to John McEwen, assignee.
Merryman, Francis. Va. Private. 17 Jun. 1784. 100 acres.
Merryman, Thomas. Va. Sergeant. 3 Aug. 1809. 200 acres.
Merryman, Thomas. Va. Private. 18 Feb. 1834. 100 acres.
Merryweather, James. ———. Ga. 17 May 1784. ———.
Merryweather, John. Ga. ———. 17 May 1784. ———.
Merryweather, Thomas. Ga. ———. 17 May 1784. ———.
Mershimer, Sebastian. Pa. Private. 28 Dec. 1786. 200 acres.
Mershorn, Nathaniel. Va.-Ind. Private. 108 acres.
Mesnard, John. Conn. Sufferer. Greenwich. 14.0.0.
Mesnard, John, Jr. Conn. Sufferer. Greenwich. 6.0.0.
Mesnard, Thomas. Conn. Sufferer. Greenwich. 6.7.6.
Messaw, Joseph. Va. Private. 30 Apr. 1783. 200 acres.
Messer, Benjamin. N.C. Private. 20 Apr. 1784. 274 acres.
Messer, Jeremiah. N.C. Private. 8 Aug. 1821. 640 acres.
Messer, Thomas. Ga. ———. 15 Mar. 1784. 250 acres.
Messersmith, Peter. Pa. Private. 6 Apr. 1787. 200 acres.
Messick, Jacob. N.C. Lieutenant. 20 Apr. 1784. 2560 acres to Jacob Messick, heir.
Metcalf, Anthony. Ga. Lieutenant. 19 Apr. 1784. 460 acres.
Metcalf, Danza. Ga. Soldier. 25 May 1784. 250 acres.
Metcalf, Gordon. Va. ———. 6 Jun. 1838. 2466 2/3 acres.
Metcalf, Thomas. Va. Private. 15 Jun. 1807. 100 acres.
Metcalf, Walter. Va. Sailor. 5 Jul. 1786. 100 acres.
Metcalf, Walter. Va. Private. 15 Jun. 1807. 200 acres.
Metcalf, William. Ga. Soldier. 25 May 1784. 250 acres.
Metcalf, William. N. Y. Private. 8 Jul. 1790. 600 acres.
Metts, Willis. N.C. Private. 1 Sep. 1785. 640 acres to heirs.
Mewshaw, John. N.C. Private. 20 Jan. 1785. 640 acres to heirs.
Michael, Conrod. Va. Private. 31 Aug. 1786. 100 acres.
Michael, Frederick. Ga. Soldier. 20 Apr. 1785. ———.
Michael, John. Pa. Private. 16 Apr. 1806. 200 acres.
Micham, John. Va. Private. 25 Apr. 1785. 100 acres.
Michaux, Joseph. Va. Captain. 20 Apr. 1738. 4000 acres.
Michell, Aaron. Md. Private. ———. 50 acres.
Mick, John. Md. Private. ———. 50 acres.
Micou, Henry. Va. Ensign. 9 Nov. 1832. 2666 2/3 acres.

Middlebrook, John. Va. Private. 23 Jul. 1784. 200 acres.
Middlebrook, John. Va. Private. 8 Feb. 1810. 100 acres.
Middlebrook, Jonathan. Conn. Sufferer. Fairfield. 4.4.10.
Middlebrook, Samuel. Conn. Sufferer. Norwalk. 14.9.11.
Middletof, Zacheriah. N.C. Private. 5 Dec. 1797. 640 acres to heirs.
Middleton, Basil. Va. Surgeon. 30 Oct. 1783. 6000 acres.
Middleton, Basil. Va. Surgeon. 3 Jul. 1807. 1750 acres.
Middleton, Benedict. Ga. 19 Jul. 1784. 287 1/2 acres.
Middleton, Daniel. N.C. Private. 8 Dec. 1796. 640 acres.
Middleton, Hatton. Ga. Captain. 16 Apr. 1784. 575 acres.
Middleton, Holland. Ga. ———. 15 Apr. 1784. 287 1/2 acres.
Middleton, Holland, Sr. Ga. ———. 15 Apr. 1784. 287 1/2 acres.
Middleton, James. Ga. ———. 25 May 1784. 287 1/2 acres.
Middleton, John. Va. Private. 1 Jun. 1785. 100 acres.
Middleton, Nathaniel. Ga. ———. 26 May 1784. 287 1/2 acres.
Middleton, Riley. Va. Private. 27 Nov. 1832. 100 acres.
Middleton, Robert. Ga. Captain. 15 Apr. 1784. 575 acres.
Middleton, Robert. Ga. ———. 19 Jul. 1784. 287 1/2 acres.
Middleton, Salathel. Va. Private. 14 Feb. 1834. 100 acres.
Middleton, Samuel. N.C. Sergeant. 9 Nov. 1784. 1000 acres.
Middleton, Smallwood. Ga. ———. 19 Jul. 1784. 287 1/2 acres.
Middleton, Solomon. N.C. Private. 19 May 1784. 640 acres.
Middleton, William. Ga. ———. 15 Apr. 1784. 287 1/2 acres.
Mie, Thomas. Md. Private. ———. 50 acres.
Mighel, Moses. Me. Private. 28 Sep. 1838. 200 acres to widow Elizabeth Mighel. Parsonsfield.
Milan, Abraham. N.C. Private. 6 Dec. 1797. 640 acres to heirs.
Milburn, Nicholas. Md. Private. ———. 50 acres.
Milcher, Paul. N.Y. ———. 13 Sep. 1790. 500 acres to heirs.
Miles, Alliss. Conn. Sufferer. New/East Haven. 5.8.0.
Miles, Elnathan. N. Y. Matross. 9 Jul. 1790. 600 acres.
Miles, Frederick. Md. Corporal. ———. 50 acres.
Miles, Jacob. N.C. Private. 17 Dec. 1785. 640 acres to heirs.
Miles, James. Ga. ———. 17 May 1784. ———.
Miles, James. Va. Private. 26 Apr 1783. 100 acres.
Miles, John. Md. Corporal. ———. 50 acres.
Miles, John. N. Y. Lieutenant. 9 Jul. 1790. 1200 acres.
Miles, John. Va. Private. 5 Jun. 1783. 100 acres.
Miles, John. Conn. Sufferer. New/East Haven. 48.5.9.
Miles, Joseph. N.C. Private. 6 Sep. 1821. 640 acres.
Miles, Mary. Conn. Sufferer. New/East Haven. 2.12.0.
Miles, Michael. Va.-Ind. Sergeant. 216 acres.
Miles, Michael. Va. Sergeant. 14 Aug. 1784. 400 acres.
Miles, Walter. Md. Corporal. ———. 50 acres.
Miles, William. Va. Private. 5 Jun. 1783. 100 acres.
Miles, William. Va. Seaman. 9 Dec. 1833. 100 acres.
Miles, William. Conn. Sufferer. New/East Haven. 5.19.8.
Mill, James. Va. Private. 30 Jan. 1822. 100 acres.
Millar, Abraham. Va.-Ind. Private. 108 acres.
Millard, Major. N.C. Private. 7 Sep. 1820. 640 acres.
Milledge, John. Ga. ———. 17 May 1784. ———.
Miller, Abraham. S.C. ———. 5 Sep. 1791. 200 acres.
Miller, Adam. S.C. ———. 2 May 1785. 200 acres.
Miller, Alexander. Ga. ———. 25 Feb. 1784. 250 acres.

Miller, Benjamin. N. Y. Private. 8 Jul. 1790. 600 acres.
Miller, C. Jeremiah. N. Y. Ensign. 9 Jul. 1790. 1000 acres.
Miller, Caspar. N. Y. Private. 8 Jul. 1790. 600 acres.
Miller, Charles. Ga. Minute Man. 20 Apr. 1784. 287 1/2 acres.
Miller, Charles. Pa. Private. 25 Oct. 1786. 200 acres.
Miller, Christian. Pa. Private. ———. 200 acres.
Miller, Christopher. N.C. Private. 15 Feb. 1797. 228 acres.
Miller, Conrad. Pa. ———. ———. 200 acres.
Miller, Daniel. Ga. ———. 15 Mar. 1784. 250 acres.
Miller, Daniel. Ga. Private. 1 Jun. 1784. 250 acres.
Miller, Daniel. N.C. Private. 20 Apr. 1784. 640 acres to Daniel Hargett, devisee.
Miller, Daniel. Pa. Private. 29 Sep.1787. 200 acres.
Miller, Daniel. Va. Private. 16 Jul. 1818. 100 acres.
Miller, Daniel. Va. Private. 20 Dec. 1825. 100 acres.
Miller, David. Ga. ———. Jul. 1784. 287 1/2 acres.
Miller, David. N.Y. ———. 13 Sep. 1790. 500 acres to heirs.
Miller, David. Va. Lieutenant. 9 Apr. 1783. 3110 2/3 acres.
Miller, David. Va. Lieutenant. 27 Feb. 1810. 370 2/3 acres.
Miller, David. Va. Lieutenant. 31 May 1843. 370 2/3 acres.
Miller, Elisha. Ga. Captain. 16 Mar. 1784. 600 acres.
Miller, Elisha. Mass. Private. 28 May 1832. 200 acres.
Miller, Elisha. N. Y. Private 8 Jul. 1790. 600 acres.
Miller, Ezekiel. Ga. ———. 28 Feb. 1784. 250 acres.
Miller, Francis. Pa. ———. 15 May 1813. 250 acres.
Miller, Francis. Va. Private. 24 Jul. 1784. 200 acres.
Miller, Gavin. Pa. Private. ———. 200 acres.
Miller, George. Ga. Minute Man. 5 May 1785. 287 1/2 acres.
Miller, George. Md. Private. ———. 50 acres.
Miller, George. Pa. Private. 3 Apr. 1787. 200 acres.
Miller, George, Jr. Ga. Minute Man. May 1784. 287 1/2 acres.
Miller, Gilbert. N.C. Private. 1 Aug. 1821. 640 acres.
Miller, Henry. N. Y. Private. 8 Jul. 1790. 600 acres.
Miller, Henry. N.C. Non Commissioned Officer. 19 May 1784. 1000 acres.
Miller, Henry. Pa. Private. 24 Oct. 1786. 200 acres to heirs.
Miller, Henry. Pa. Private. 19 Oct. 1786. 200 acres.
Miller, Henry. Pa. Private. ———. 200 acres to heirs.
Miller, Isaac. Pa. Private. 30 Jan. 1787. 200 acres.
Miller, Jacob. Pa. ———. ———. 200 acres.
Miller, Jacob. S.C. ———. 5 Sep. 1791. 200 acres.
Miller, James. Ga. ———. 23 Apr. 1784. 287 1/2 acres.
Miller, James. N.C. Private. 9 Sep. 1785. 640 acres to heirs.
Miller, James. Va. Private. 12 Apr. 1783. 200 acres.
Miller, James. Conn. Sufferer. New London. 93.8.6.
Miller, Javan. Va. Private. 22 Aug. 1783. 3110 2/3 acres.
Miller, Jeremiah. Conn. Sufferer. New London. 2,535.18.10.
Miller, Jesse. Ga. ———. 28 Feb. 1784. 250 acres.
Miller, John. Md. Private. ———. 50 acres.
Miller, John. N. Y. Private. 8 Jul. 1790. 600 acres.
Miller, John. N. Y. ———. 3 Dec. 1806. 500 acres to representatives Peter Miller and James Miller.
Miller, John. N.C. Private. 20 Sep. 1784. 640 acres to heir.
Miller, John. N.C. Corporal. 21 Aug. 1820. 360 acres.
Miller, John. Pa. ———. 13 Nov. 1802. 200 acres.
Miller, John. Pa. Private. 22 Nov. 1788. 200 acres.

Miller, John. Pa. Private. ———. 200 acres.
Miller, John. Pa. ———. 5 Nov. 1806. 200 acres.
Miller, John. Pa. Captain. 30 Dec. 1786. 500 acres to Margaret Miller, widow.
Miller, John. S.C. ———. 5 Sep. 1791. 200 acres.
Miller, John. S.C. ———. 2 Apr. 1798. 20 acres.
Miller, John. S.C. ———. 2 Apr. 1798. 29 acres.
Miller, John. S.C. ———. 2 Apr. 1798. 25 acres.
Miller, John. S.C. ———. 2 Apr. 1798. 14 acres.
Miller, John. S.C. ———. 2 Apr. 1798. 40 acres.
Miller, John. S.C. ———. 2 Apr. 1798. 70 acres.
Miller, John. Va. Private. 13 Sep. 1783. 200 acres.
Miller, John. Va. Private. 12 May 1835. 100 acres.
Miller, John C. Md. Private. ———. 50 acres.
Miller, John M. Pa. ———. 14 Dec. 1808. 200 acres.
Miller, John Peter. Pa. Private. 2 Jun. 1789. 200 acres.
Miller, Jonathan. Ga. ———. 17 May 1784. ———.
Miller, Jonathan. N.C. Private. 30 Sep. 1785. 640 acres to heirs.
Miller, Joseph. Ga. ———. 28 Feb. 1784. 250 acres.
Miller, Joshua. Ga. ———. 28 Feb. 1784. 250 acres.
Miller, Josiah. N.C. Private. 8 Aug. 1821. 640 acres.
Miller, Justus. N.Y. ———. 13 Sep. 1790. 500 acres to heirs.
Miller, Lemuel. Me. Lieutenant. 2 May 1838. 600 acres. Kennebunkport.
Miller, Lodowick. Va. Private. 18 Dec. 1783. 100 acres.
Miller, Martin. N.C. Private. 23 Nov. 1797. 274 acres.
Miller, Michael. Md. Private. ———. 50 acres.
Miller, Moses. Ga. Refugee. 17 Feb. 1784. 250 acres.
Miller, Nicholas. Ga. Refugee. 27 Sep. 1784. 287 1/2 acres.
Miller, Phebe. Conn. Sufferer. New/East Haven. 15.5.2.
Miller, Philip. S.C. ———. 2 Oct. 1786. 200 acres to William Miller, heir at law.
Miller, Robert. Va. Private. 11 Feb. 1784. 100 acres.
Miller, Robert. Va. Private. 18 Mar. 1833. 200 acres.
Miller, Samuel. Ga. Refugee. 15 Mar. 1784. 500 acres to widow Mary Miller and son Morris Miller.
Miller, Samuel. Ga. Soldier. 19 Jul. 1784. 287 1/2 acres.
Miller, Samuel. Pa. Private. ———. 200 acres.
Miller, Samuel. Pa. Captain. 24 Jul. 1795. 500 acres to heirs.
Miller, Samuel. Pa. Captain. ———. 500 acres.
Miller, Smith. Ga. Soldier. 24 Dec. 178-. ———.
Miller, Solomon. N.C. Private. 30 Sep. 1785. 640 acres to heirs.
Miller, Thomas. N. Y. Private. 8 Jul. 1790. 600 acres.
Miller, Thomas. Va. Lieutenant. 29 Nov. 1784 [1783]. 2666 2/3 acres.
Miller, William. Ga. Refugee. ———. 287 1/2 acres.
Miller, William. N.C. Private. 2 Sep. 1820. 274 acres.
Miller, William. Pa. Private. 28 Aug. 1787. 200 acres.
Miller, William. Pa. Corporal. 6 Dec. 1786. 200 acres.
Miller, William. Pa. Captain. 24 Feb. 1789. 500 acres.
Miller, William. S.C. ———. 6 Feb. 1792. 200 acres.
Miller, William. Va. Captain Lieutenant. 27 Feb. 1783. 4000 acres.
Miller, William. Va. Private. 6 Apr. 1787. 100 acres.
Miller, William. Va. Captain Lieutenant. 17 Oct. 1799. 666 2/3 acres.
Miller, William. Va. Captain Lieutenant. 11 Sep. 1807. 388 2/3 acres.
Millesock, Augustus. Pa. Private. 7 May 1795. 200 acres to George Dannacker, assignee.
Millet, Abraham. Mass. Private. 28 Feb. 1832. 200 acres to heirs.
Milligan, Jacob. S. C. Captain. 15 Oct. 1784. 450 acres.

Milligan, James. N.C. Lieutenant. 8 Oct. 1814. 2560 acres to heir Joseph Milligan.
Milligan, James. Pa. Lieutenant. 25 May 1796. 200 acres.
Milligan, James. Pa. Private. 25 May 1796. 200 acres.
Milligan, James. Pa. Lieutenant. 11 Apr. 1787. 200 acres.
Milligan, James. Pa. Lieutenant. 6 Apr. 1794. 200 acres.
Milligan, John. Va. Private. 11 Feb. 1786. 200 acres.
Milligan, John. Va. Private. 11 Feb. 1786. 100 acres.
Milligin, Hugh. Ga. ———. 15 Mar. 1784. 250 acres.
Milliken, Daniel. Mass. Sergeant. 2 Mar. 1833. 200 acres.
Milliken, Joel. Me. ———. 26 Jun. 1835. 200 acres. Scarborough.
Milliken, Josiah. Me. ———. 12 Sep. 1835. 200 acres to widow Sarah Milliken. Limington.
Milliner, Henry. Va. Sergeant. 15 Jun. 1807. 200 acres.
Milliner, Robert. Va. Lieutenant. 7 Dec. 1830. 363 2/3 acres.
Milliner, Robert. Va. Lieutenant. 7 Dec. 1830. 363 2/3 acres.
Milliner, Robert. Va. Lieutenant. 7 Dec. 1830. 362 2/3 acres.
Milliner, Robert. Va. Lieutenant. 7 Dec. 1830. 363 2/3 acres.
Milliner, Robert. Va. Lieutenant. 7 Dec. 1830. 363 2/3 acres.
Milliner, Robert. Va. Lieutenant. 7 Dec. 1830. 363 2/3 acres.
Milliner, Robert. Va. Lieutenant. 7 Dec. 1830. 363 2/3 acres.
Milliner, Robert. Va. Lieutenant. 7 Dec. 1830. 182 2/3 acres.
Milliner, Robert. Va. Lieutenant. 7 Dec. 1830. 363 2/3 acres.
Milliner, Robert. Va. Lieutenant. 7 Dec. 1830. 727 1/3 acres.
Milliner, Robert. Va. Lieutenant. 7 Dec. 1830. 182 2/3 acres.
Milliner, Robert. Va. Lieutenant. 12 Mar. 1831. 182 acres.
Milling, Hugh. S.C. Captain. 15 Oct. 1784. 300 acres.
Millirons, Henry. Va. Private. 6 Jul. 1784. 100 acres.
Millirons, William. Va. Private. 10 Jun. 1785. 100 acres.
Millott, Farrell. N. Y. Matross. 9 Jul. 1790. 500 acres.
Mills, Alexander. N. Y. Private. 8 Jul. 1790. 600 acres.
Mills, Andrew. N. Y. Corporal. 8 Jul. 1790. 600 acres.
Mills, Anthony. Va. Sergeant. 24 Feb. 1791. 200 acres.
Mills, Benjamin. N.C. Captain. 9 Nov. 1784. 1142 acres.
Mills, Daniel. N.C. Private. 30 Sep. 1785. 640 acres to heirs.
Mills, Elijah. N.C. Private. 29 Sep. 1784. 640 acres to William Mills, heir.
Mills, Elisha. N.C. Private. 21 Aug. 1820. 274 acres to heirs.
Mills, Francis. Va. Sergeant. 30 May 1823. 200 acres.
Mills, George. Ga. Refugee. 13 May 1784. 500 acres.
Mills, Gilbert. S.C. ———. 1 Jan. 1787. 200 acres.
Mills, James. N.C. Captain. 20 Apr. 1784. 3840 acres.
Mills, John. Me. Private. 30 Jul. 1835. 200 acres to widow Mary Mills. Belgrade.
Mills, John. Md. Private. ———. 50 acres.
Mills, John. Md. Private. ———. 50 acres.
Mills, John. N. Y. Private. 8 Jul. 1790. 500 acres.
Mills, John. N.C. Private. 30 Sep. 1785. 640 acres to heirs.
Mills, John. Pa. Private. 26 Mar. 1787. 200 acres.
Mills, John. S.C. ———. 2 Jul. 1787. 200 acres.
Mills, John. Va. Lieutenant. 31 Mar. 1783. 1300 acres.
Mills, John. Va. Lieutenant. 31 Mar. 1783. 1366 2/3 acres.
Mills, John. Va. Private. 5 Jun. 1783. 100 acres.
Mills, Joseph. N.C. Private. 7 Dec. 1797. 640 acres to heirs.
Mills, Moses. Va. Private. 30 Mar. 1785. 100 acres.
Mills, Nicholas. Va. Private. 26 May 1783. 100 acres.
Mills, Peter. N. Y. Captain. 8 Apr. 1803. 1500 acres.
Mills, William. Ga. ———. 15 Mar. 1784. 250 acres.

Mills, William. Mass. ———. 17 Jun. 1820. 200 acres.
Mills, William. N.C. Corporal. 29 Sep. 1784. 285 acres.
Mills, Zacheriah. Md. Private. ———. 50 acres.
Millson, Daniel. Conn. Sufferer. Danbury. 0.13.4.
Millsook, Augustus. Pa. Private. ———. 200 acres.
Milner, John. Ga. Refugee. 21 Apr. 1784. 287 1/2 acres.
Milner, Samuel. N.C. Private. 10 Feb. 1796. 640 acres to heirs.
Milowee, Martin. Ga. Private. 22 Mar. 1785. 250 acres.
Milstead, John. Md. Private. ———. 50 acres.
Milton, Charles. Va. Private. 2 Oct. 1784. 100 acres.
Milton, Daniel. N.C. Private. 18 Aug. 1784. 640 acres.
Milton, Daniel. N.C. Private. 20 Jan. 1785. 640 acres.
Milton, John. Ga. Major. 17 May 1784. 690 acres.
Milton, John. N.C. Private. 29 Sep. 1784. 640 acres to heirs.
Milton, John. Pa. Private. 1 Nov. 1786. 200 acres.
Milton, Nathaniel. Ga. ———. 26 May 1784. 287 1/2 acres.
Milton, Thomas. Va. Private. 24 Feb. 1784. 100 acres.
Milton, William. N.C. Private. 20 Sep. 1784. 640 acres to heirs.
Mimms, Drury. Ga. ———. 21 Apr. 1784. 287 1/2 acres.
Mimms, Frederick. Ga. ———. ———. 250 acres.
Mimms, John. Ga. ———. 21 Apr. 1784. 287 1/2 acres.
Mimms, Joseph. Ga. ———. 21 Apr. 1784. 287 1/2 acres.
Mimms, Josiah. Ga. ———. ———. 17 May 1784.
Mimms, Martin. Ga. ———. 21 Apr. 1784. 287 1/2 acres.
Mimms, Shadrach. Ga. ———. 20 Apr. 1784. 287 1/2 acres.
Mimms, William. Ga. ———. 21 Apr. 1784. 287 1/2 acres.
Minal, Diar. Ga. ———. 5 Dec. 1785. ———.
Minard, Antoine. N. Y. ———. ———. 500 acres.
Minard, Francis. N. Y. ———. ———. 500 acres.
Minema, Daniel. N. Y. Surgeon. 6 Jul. 1790. 1900 acres.
Mines, Peter. Va. Private. 5 Feb. 1808. 100 acres.
Minich, Peter. Pa. Private. 28 Sep. 1787. 200 acres.
Minick, Henry. N. Y. Private. 8 Jul. 1790. 600 acres.
Minikee, Gifford. Md. Private. ———. 50 acres.
Miniken, Humphrey. Md. Private. ———. 50 acres.
Minner, Moses. N.Y. Private. 13 Sep. 1790. 500 acres to heirs.
Minnes, Callohill. Va. Captain. 12 Feb. 1783. 4666 2/3 acres.
Minnes, Holman. Va. Captain. 13 Jun. 1797. 666 2/3 acres.
Minnes, John. Va. Private. 26 Jun. 1783. 200 acres.
Minnis, Benjamin. Va. Sergeant. 10 Mar. 1808. 200 acres.
Minnis, Callohill. Va. Captain. 3 Mar. 1808. 500 acres.
Minnis, Francis. Va. Captain. 6 Jun. 1783. 4666 2/3 acres.
Minnis, Holman. Va. Captain. 3 Mar. 1808. 945 acres.
Minns, Holman. Va. Captain. 12 Feb. 1783. 4000 acres.
Minor, Ephraim. Conn. Sufferer. New London. 348.17.4.
Minor, James. Conn. Sufferer. New London. 7.10.7.
Minor, Lewis. Conn. Sufferer. New London. 71.7.4.
Minor, Peter. Va. Captain. 11 Aug. 1804. 2000 acres.
Minor, Peter. Va. Captain. 11 Aug. 1804. 1000 acres.
Minor, Peter. Va. Captain. 11 Aug. 1804. 500 acres.
Minor, Peter. Va. Captain. 11 Aug. 1804. 500 acres.
Minor, Peter. Va. Captain. 17 Apr. 1807. 1221 acres.
Minor, Prudence. Conn. Sufferer. Groton. 17.19.10.
Minor, Rebecca. Conn. Sufferer. Groton. 1.6.11.

Minor, Thomas. Va. Captain. 12 Jun. 1830. 5333 1/3 acres.
Minory, George. N.C. Private. 9 Sep. 1785. 640 acres to heirs.
Minshaw, Micajah. N.C. ———. 15 Jun. 1785. 640 acres to heir William Minshaw.
Minshew, Richard. N.C. Private. 10 Aug. 1785. 640 acres to heirs.
Minson, Mason. N.C. Private. 17 Feb. 1824. 640 acres.
Minter, James. Va. Seaman. 25 Aug. 1835. 100 acres.
Mintges, Francis. Pa. Lieutenant Colonel. 4 Oct. 1785. 500 acres.
Minton, Ebenezer. Va. Private. 17 Aug. 1807. 200 acres.
Minton, John. Va. Private. 7 Apr. 1784. 200 acres.
Mintor, John. N.C. Private. 14 Dec. 1796. 640 acres.
Minzies, George. Va. Ensign. 11 May 1799. 1000 acres.
Minzies, George. Va. Ensign. 11 May 1799. 1000 acres.
Minzies, George. Va. Ensign. 11 May 1799. 666 2/3 acres.
Mires, John. N.C. Private. 11 May 1784. 274 acres.
Mirrian, Philip. N.C. Private. 3 Feb. 1800. 640 acres.
Miscampbell, Robert. S.C. Lieutenant. 2 May 1785. 200 acres.
Miskell, John. Va. Sergeant. 25 May 1787. 200 acres.
Miskell, Jonathan. Va. Sergeant. 25 May 1787. 200 acres.
Mitcalf, Gordon. Va. Quartermaster. 1 Dec. 1785. 200 acres.
Mitchel, Thomas. Va. Private. 20 Jun. 1783. 100 acres.
Mitchell, Abraham. N.C. Private. 22 Apr. 1785. 228 acres.
Mitchell, Anthony. Conn. Sufferer. New London. 23.11.6.
Mitchell, Archelaus. Va. Noncommissioned Officer. 14 Feb. 1809. 200 acres.
Mitchell, Arthur. N.C. Private. 17 Feb. 1824. 640 acres.
Mitchell, Bethro. N.C. Private. 17 Feb. 1824. 640 acres.
Mitchell, Charles. Ga. ———. 17 May 1784. ———.
Mitchell, David. Ga. Minute Man. 21 Apr. 1784. 287 1/2 acres.
Mitchell, David. Va. Private. 19 Jun. 1783. 100 acres.
Mitchell, Edward. N. Y. Private. 8 Jul. 1790. 600 acres.
Mitchell, Ephraim. S.C. Major. 16 Jul. 1784. 400 acres.
Mitchell, George. Va. Sergeant. 11 Nov. 1783. 200 acres.
Mitchell, Henry. Pa. Sergeant. ———. 250 acres.
Mitchell, Jacob. N.C. Private. 30 Sep. 1785. 640 acres to heirs.
Mitchell, James. Pa. Sergeant. 19 Oct. 1786. 250 acres.
Mitchell, James. Pa. Sergeant. 20 Mar. 1807. 250 acres.
Mitchell, James. S.C. Captain. 16 Jul. 1784. 300 acres.
Mitchell, James. Va. Corporal. 30 Apr. 1783. 400 acres.
Mitchell, James. Va. Private. 7 Dec. 1786. 100 acres.
Mitchell, James, Sr. N.C. Private. 10 Feb. 1796. 640 acres to heirs.
Mitchell, Job. N.C. Private. 5 Sep. 1821. 640 acres.
Mitchell, John. Ga. Lieutenant. 24 Jan. 1784. 400 acres.
Mitchell, John. Ga. ———. 28 Feb. 1784. 250 acres.
Mitchell, John. Ga. ———. 14 Jul. 1784. 200 acres.
Mitchell, John. Md. Captain. ———. 200 acres.
Mitchell, John. N.C. Private. 30 Apr. 1784. 640 acres to Reuben Mitchell, heir.
Mitchell, John. Va. Sergeant. 13 Oct. 1783. 400 acres.
Mitchell, John. Va. Private. 12 Jul. 1786. 100 acres.
Mitchell, Joseph. N. Y. Private. 8 Jul. 1790. 500 acres.
Mitchell, Joseph. Va. Captain. 24 Jul. 1824. 144 acres.
Mitchell, Joseph. Va. Captain. 24 Jul. 1824. 1000 acres.
Mitchell, Joseph. Va. Captain. 24 Jul. 1824. 1000 acres.
Mitchell, Joseph. Va. Captain. 24 Jul. 1824. 1000 acres.
Mitchell, Joseph. Va. Captain. 24 Jul. 1824. 856 acres.

Mitchell, Joshua. Me. ———. 1 Oct. 1835. 200 acres to widow Tamesin Mitchell. Bath. Surname also appears as Michaels.
Mitchell, Jospeh. N.C. Private. 22 Oct. 1783. 274 acres.
Mitchell, Mark. Va. Private. 4 Jun. 1783. 100 acres.
Mitchell, Nathaniel. Va. Major. 6 Jan. 1834. 5333 1/3 acres.
Mitchell, Nathaniel. Va. Major. 3 Feb. 1835. 1333 1/12 acres.
Mitchell, Nathaniel. Va. Major. 3 Feb. 1835. 1333 1/12 acres.
Mitchell, Nathaniel. Va. Major. 3 Feb. 1835. 1333 1/12 acres.
Mitchell, Nathaniel. Va. Major. 3 Feb. 1835. 1333 1/12 acres.
Mitchell, Ralph. Va. Private. 3 Aug. 1835. 200 acres.
Mitchell, Reaps. Va. Sergeant. 26 Jun. 1783. 400 acres.
Mitchell, Reaps. Va. Sergeant. 18 Dec. 1818. 466 2/3 acres.
Mitchell, Richard. Md. Private. ———. 50 acres.
Mitchell, Richard. Va. Midshipman. 28 Mar. 1834. 1333 1/3 acres.
Mitchell, Richard. Va. Midshipman. 9 May 1834. 1333 1/3 acres.
Mitchell, Richard. Va. Midshipman. 22 Dec. 1834. 1333 1/3 acres.
Mitchell, Richard. Va. Midshipman. 22 Dec. 1834. 1333 1/3 acres.
Mitchell, Robert. Ga. Refugee. 27 Sep. 1784. 287 1/2 acres.
Mitchell, Robert. Md. Private. ———. 50 acres.
Mitchell, Robert. Pa. Private. ———. 200 acres.
Mitchell, Robert. Va. Drummer. 30 Jan. 1813. 266 2/3 acres.
Mitchell, Samuel. Me. ———. 22 Apr. 1835. 200 acres. Bowdoin.
Mitchell, Samuel. N.Y. ———. 13 Sep. 1790. 500 acres to heirs.
Mitchell, Samuel. N.C. Private. 2 Feb. 1786. 640 acres to heirs.
Mitchell, Theophilus. N.C. Private. 21 Aug. 1820. 640 acres to heirs.
Mitchell, Thomas. Ga. ———. 15 Mar. 1784. 250 acres.
Mitchell, Thomas. Va. Sailor. 29 Jan. 1788. 100 acres.
Mitchell, Thomas. Va. Private. 18 Nov. 1811. 100 acres.
Mitchell, William. Ga. Refugee. 26 May 1784. 287 1/2 acres.
Mitchell, William. Ga. Soldier. 11 Oct. 1783. 200 acres.
Mitchell, William. Md. Private. ———. 50 acres.
Mitchell, William. N.C. Drummer. 22 Oct. 1783. 1000 acres.
Mitchell, William. N.C. Private. 30 May 1820. 228 acres to heirs.
Mitchell, William. Pa. Private. 6 Apr. 1787. 200 acres.
Mitchell, William. S.C. Captain. 4 Apr. 1785. 300 acres to James Mitchell in trust for the heirs.
Mitchell, William. S.C. Captain. 4 Apr. 1785. 300 acres to James Mitchell in trust for the heirs.
Mitchell, William. Va. Corporal. 17 Jun. 1783. 200 acres.
Mitchell, William. Va. Private. 27 Jan. 1810. 200 acres.
Mitchell, William. Va. Captain. 29 Apr. 1839. 555 5/9 acres.
Mitchell, William. Va. Captain. 29 Apr. 1839. 555 5/9 acres.
Mitchell, William. Va. Captain. 29 Apr. 1839. 555 5/9 acres.
Mitchell, William. Va. Captain. 29 Apr. 1839. 333 1/3 acres.
Mitchell, William. Va. Captain. 18 Mar. 1844. 250 acres.
Mitchell, William. Va. Captain. 18 Mar. 1844. 187 1/2 acres.
Mitchell, William. Va. Captain. 18 Mar. 1844. 187 1/2 acres.
Mitchell, William. Va. Captain. 18 Mar. 1844. 187 1/2 acres.
Mitchell, William. Va. Captain. 18 Mar. 1844. 187 1/2 acres.
Mites, Isaac. Pa. Private. ———. 200 acres.
Mitts, Peter. N.C. Private. 28 Sep. 1785. 640 acres to heirs.
Mix, Elisha. Conn. Sufferer. New/East Haven. 25.7.4.
Mix, Hannah. Conn. Sufferer. New/East Haven. 36.4.3.
Mix, John. Conn. Sufferer. New/East Haven. 37.10.9.
Mix, John, Jr. Conn. Sufferer. New/East Haven. 9.19.6.

Mix, Jonah. Conn. Sufferer. New/East Haven. 15.19.0.
Mix, Joseph. Conn. Sufferer. New/East Haven. 11.15.10.
Mix, Nathaniel. Conn. Sufferer. New/East Haven. 10.13.0.
Mix, Patuna. Conn. Sufferer. New/East Haven. 20.19.1.
Mix, Stephen. N. Y. Matross. 9 Jul. 1790. 600 acres.
Mix, Timothy. N. Y. Lieutenant. 9 Jul. 1790. 1200 acres.
Mix, Timothy, Dr. Conn. Sufferer. New/East Haven. 16.12.3.
Mixom, Charles. N.C. Ensign. 16 Aug. 1821. 2560 acres.
Moade, William. Md. Private. ———. 50 acres.
Moates, Eleazer. Ga. ———. 21 Apr. 1784. 287 1/2 acres.
Moates, Levi. Ga. ———. 15 Mar. 1784. 250 acres.
Moates, Repser. Ga. ———. 21 Apr. 1784. 287 1/2 acres.
Moates, Silas. Ga. ———. 15 Mar. 1784. 250 acres.
Moates, Simeon. Ga. ———. 15 Mar. 1784. 250 acres.
Moates, Simon. Ga. ———. 23 Apr. 1784. 287 1/2 acres.
Moates, William. Ga. ———. 23 Apr. 1784. 287 1/2 acres.
Mobley, John. Ga. ———. 13 Sep. 1784. 287 1/2 acres.
Mocock, Henry. Ga. Minute Man. 17 May 1784. ———.
Modlin, Benjamin. N.C. Private. 29 Nov. 1810. 640 acres.
Modlin, Elisha. N.C. Private. 9 Nov. 1784. 640 acres.
Modlin, Elisha. N.C. Private. 20 Mar. 1785. 274 acres.
Modlin, Ezekiel. N.C. Private. 27 Dec. 1792. 640 acres to heirs.
Modlin, Jeremiah. N.C. Private. 6 Sep. 1821. 640 acres.
Modlin, Shadrack. N.C. Private. 22 Dec. 1796. 228 acres.
Modlin, Thomas. N.C. Private. 9 Nov. 1784. 365 acres.
Modlin, Zebod. N.C. Private. 9 Nov. 1784. 640 acres.
Moe, James. Conn. Sufferer. Greenwich. 32.6.2.
Moffett, Thomas. Ga. Soldier. 2 Feb. 1784. ———.
Moffett, William. Va. Private. 19 Jan. 1785. 100 acres.
Mogelin, Freeman. N.C. Private. 19 Apr. 1820. 228 acres.
Moglin, Stephen. N.C. Private. 8 Dec. 1795. 640 acres to heirs.
Moho, John. Mass. Private. 18 Jan. 1834. 200 acres to assignee Abner Coburn.
Mohon, James. N.C. Private. 2 Dec. 1796. 640 acres.
Molborn, Solomon. N.C. Sergeant. 22 Dec. 1796. 1000 acres to heirs.
Mollohon, Patrick. Md. Private. ———. 50 acres.
Molloy, James. Pa. Private. 19 Sep. 1787. 200 acres.
Moncieff, Thomas. N.C. Private. 21 May 1784. 274 acres.
Moncrief, Josiah. Ga. ———. 22 Apr. 1784. 700 acres.
Moncrief, Massey. Ga. ———. 22 Apr. 1784. 200 acres.
Moncrief, Sampson. Ga. ———. 28 Jul. 1784. 287 1/2 acres to heirs.
Monday, Edward. Va. Private. 18 Mar. 1840. 100 acres.
Monday, Thomas. Pa. Private. 3 Mar. 1787. 200 acres.
Money, John. Ga. ———. 17 May 1784. ———.
Monk, Israel. N.C. Private. 2 Dec. 1796. 640 acres to heirs.
Monk, James. N.C. Private. 20 Feb. 1835. 640 acres.
Monk, Joseph. Va. Sergeant. 27 Aug. 1783. 200 acres.
Monk, Notingham. N.C. Private. 29 Sep. 1784. 274 acres.
Monro, George. Va. Surgeon. 22 Aug. 1783. 6000 acres.
Monroe, Alexander. Va. Sergeant. 15 Feb. 1817. 200 acres.
Monroe, James. Va.-Ind. Private. 108 acres.
Monroe, James. Va. Major. 2 Feb. 1784. 5333 1/2 acres.
Monroe, James. Va. Lieutenant Colonel. 16 Sep. 1850. 1087 1/3 acres.
Monroe, James. Va. Lieutenant Colonel. 16 Sep. 1850. 587 1/3 acres.
Monroe, James. Va. Lieutenant Colonel. 16 Sep. 1850. 500 acres.

Monroe, James. Va. ———. 6 Jul. 1860. 2666 2/3 acres.
Monroe, James. Va. ———. 6 Jul. 1860. 1333 1/3 acres.
Monroe, James. Va. ———. 6 Jul. 1860. 1333 1/3 acres.
Monroe, John. Va. Sergeant. 13 Jun. 1809. 200 acres.
Monroe, Solomon. Mass. Private. 18 Oct. 1833. 200 acres.
Monroe, William. Va. Private. 5 Jun. 1784. 100 acres.
Monson, Amos. Conn. Sufferer. New/East Haven. 1.0.0.
Montague, Bryan. N.C. Private. 20 Sep. 1821. 640 acres.
Montague, Samuel. N.C. Private. 20 Sep. 1821. 640 acres.
Montaigut, David. Ga. ———. 17 May 1784. ———.
Montaque, Richard. Va. Lieutenant. 11 May 1838. 1333 1/3 acres.
Monteith, James. N.Y. ———. 13 Sep. 1790. 500 acres to heirs.
Montford, Joseph. N.C. Captain. 27 Nov. 1783. 3840 acres.
Montford, Robert. Ga. ———. 22 Apr. 1784. 500 acres.
Montgomery, Hugh. Va. Private. 31 Dec. 1806. 100 acres.
Montgomery, Hugh. Va. Private. 6 Jan. 1808. 100 acres.
Montgomery, James. Ga. Refugee. 1 Jul. 1784. ———.
Montgomery, James. Va.-Ind. Lieutenant. Mar. 1784. 2156 acres.
Montgomery, James. Pa. Captain. 9 Sep. 1789. 500 acres.
Montgomery, James. Pa. Private. 10 Aug. 1787. 200 acres.
Montgomery, James. Va. Lieutenant. 3 Mar. 1784. 2666 2/3 acres.
Montgomery, John. Va.-Ind. Lieutenant Colonel. 4851 acres.
Montgomery, John. Va.-Ind. Private. 108 acres.
Montgomery, John. Pa. Private. ———. 200 acres.
Montgomery, John. Va. Lieutenant Colonel. 3 Mar. 1784. 6000 acres.
Montgomery, John. Va. Private. 6 Jan. 1808. 100 acres.
Montgomery, Samuel. Pa. Captain. 28 Feb. 1797. 500 acres.
Montgomery, Thomas, Jr. N.C. Private. 14 Dec. 1797. 228 acres.
Montgomery, William. N.C. Private. 18 Aug. 1784. 640 acres.
Monty, Amable. N. Y. ———. ———. 500 acres.
Monty, Enfant. N. Y. ———. ———. 500 acres.
Monty, Francis. N. Y. Lieutenant. ———. 1000 acres.
Monty, Francis, Jr. N. Y. ———. ———. 500 acres.
Monty, Glaud. N. Y. ———. ———. 500 acres.
Monty, Glaud, Jr. N. Y. ———. ———. 500 acres.
Monty, Jacque. N. Y. ———. ———. 500 acres.
Monty, Joseph. N. Y. ———. ———. 500 acres.
Moodie, Andrew. N. Y. Captain. 9 Jul. 1790. 1800 acres.
Moody, Daniel. Me. ———. 12 Jun. 1835. 200 acres to widow Lucy Moody. Minot.
Moody, Edward. Va. Captain. 10 Dec. 1782. 4666 2/3 acres.
Moody, Elijah. Va. Private. 14 Mar. 1810. 222 acres.
Moody, George. Me. ———. 17 Oct. 1835. 200 acres. Limington.
Moody, James. Va. Captain. 12 Aug. 1783. 2000 acres.
Moody, James. Va. Captain. 12 Aug. 1783. 2000 acres.
Moody, James. Va. Captain. 28 Mar. 1840. 1000 acres.
Moody, William. Va. Private. 21 Oct. 1783. 200 acres.
Moody, William. Va. Private. 17 Nov. 1784. 100 acres.
Moody, William. Va. Private. 5 Feb. 1785. 200 acres.
Moon, Archibald. Ga. ———. 17 May 1784. ———.
Moon, Archibald. Va. Captain. 10 Feb. 1809. 1000 acres.
Moon, Archibald. Va. Captain. 10 Feb. 1809. 1000 acres.
Moon, Archibald. Va. Captain. 10 Feb. 1809. 1000 acres.
Moon, Archibald. Va. Captain. 10 Feb. 1809. 1000 acres.

Moon, Jacob. Va. Lieutenant. 5 Nov. 1808. 666 2/3 acres.
Moon, Jacob. Va. Lieutenant. 5 Nov. 1808. 666 2/3 acres.
Moon, Jacob. Va. Lieutenant. 5 Nov. 1808. 666 2/3 acres.
Moon, Jacob. Va. Lieutenant. 5 Nov. 1808. 666 2/3 acres.
Moon, Jacob. Va. Captain Lieutenant. 26 Apr. 1838. 595 acres.
Moon, Jacob. Va. Lieutenant. 24 Mar. 1848. 595 acres.
Moon, Samuel. Ga. ———. 20 Apr. 1784. 287 1/2 acres.
Moon, William. Ga. ———. 17 May 1784. ———.
Mooney, Henry. Pa. Private. 10 Sep. 1787. 200 acres.
Mooney, Isaac. Va. Private. 7 Jan. 1784. 100 acres.
Mooney, Joseph. Ga. ———. 19 Jul. 1784. 287 1/2 acres.
Mooney, William. N. Y. Private. 8 Jul. 1790. 600 acres.
Moonie, Martin. Va. Private. 3 May 1822. 100 acres.
Moor, Alexander. Va. Private. 20 Jun. 1785. 200 acres.
Moore, Abraham. N.Y. ———. 13 Sep. 1790. 500 acres to heirs.
Moore, Alexander. Ga. Refugee. 26 May 1784. 287 1/2 acres.
Moore, Alexander. S.C. ———. ———. 200 acres.
Moore, Alexander. Va. Midshipman. 21 Feb. 1783. 2000 acres.
Moore, Alexander. Va. Private. 1 Aug. 1834. 200 acres.
Moore, Alexander. Va. Midshipman. 11 Jul. 1853. 666 2/3 acres.
Moore, Alfred, Sr. N.C. Captain. 10 Dec. 1821. 1097 acres to heirs.
Moore, Andrew. Md. Private. ———. 50 acres.
Moore, Andrew. Va. Captain. 23 Jun. 1808. 4000 acres.
Moore, Benjamin. N.C. Private. 30 Sep. 1785. 640 acres to heirs.
Moore, Burgess. Ga. Private. 21 Apr. 1784. 200 acres.
Moore, Burrus. Va. Private. 15 Apr. 1812. 100 acres.
Moore, Cleon. Va. Captain. 16 Jun. 1784. 4000 acres.
Moore, Daniel. N.C. Private. 5 Dec. 1796. 274 acres.
Moore, Demsey. N.C. Lieutenant. 25 Oct. 1783. 780 acres.
Moore, Edmund. Mass. Private. 25 Nov. 1833. 200 acres to widow Persis Moore to assignee Abner Coburn.
Moore, Elijah. N.C. Captain. 20 Oct. 1783. 3840 acres.
Moore, Elijah. N.C. Captain. 25 Oct. 1783. 3840 acres.
Moore, Elizabeth. Conn. Sufferer. Greenwich. 7.2.0.
Moore, Elizabeth. Conn. Sufferer. Groton. 62.10.9.
Moore, Francis. Ga. ———. 17 May 1784. 920 acres to heirs.
Moore, Frederick. N. Y. Private. 6 Jul. 1790. 600 acres.
Moore, Frederick. N.C. Private. 12 Mar. 1785. 274 acres.
Moore, Frederick. Conn. Sufferer. Groton. 269.2.0.
Moore, George. Ga. ———. ———. 287 1/2 acres.
Moore, Henly. Va. Sergeant. 2 Dec. 1788. 200 acres.
Moore, Henry. N.Y. Surgeon's Mate. 26 Sep. 1792. 1800 acres.
Moore, Henry. S.C. Captain. 21 Jan. 1785. 300 acres.
Moore, Isaac. N.C. Captain. 28 May 1784. 3840 acres.
Moore, Jacob. N.C. Private. 4 Aug. 1821. 640 acres.
Moore, Jacob. Va. Ensign. 5 Sep. 1811. 800 acres.
Moore, Jacob. Va. Ensign. 5 Sep. 1811. 800 acres.
Moore, Jacob. Va. Ensign. 5 Sep. 1811. 1066 2/3 acres.
Moore, James. Ga. ———. 25 May 1784. 287 1/2 acres.
Moore, James. Md. Gunner. ———. 50 acres.
Moore, James. N. Y. Matross. 9 Jul. 1790. 600 acres.
Moore, James. N.C. General. 17 Oct. 1783. 12,000 acres to James Moore, heir at law.
Moore, James. N.C. Lieutenant. 20 Apr. 1784. 2560 acres.
Moore, James. N.C. Private. 9 Nov. 1784. 274 acres.

Moore, James. N.C. Private. 1 Oct. 1792. 228 acres.
Moore, James. N.C. Private. 31 Dec. 1833. 640 acres.
Moore, James. Pa. Major. 11 Jul. 1787. 300 acres.
Moore, James. Pa. Private. ———. 200 acres.
Moore, James. Pa. Sergeant. 18 Sep. 1787. 250 acres.
Moore, James. Pa. Major. 11 Jul. 1787. 300 acres.
Moore, James. Pa. Private. 14 Jan. 1796. 200 acres.
Moore, James. Va. Private. 3 Dec. 1785. 100 acres.
Moore, Jesse. N.C. Private. 15 Feb. 1797. 228 acres.
Moore, Jesse. Pa. Private. 26 Sep. 1787. 200 acres.
Moore, John. Ga. Sergeant. 24 May 1784. 345 acres.
Moore, John. Ga. ———. ———. 287 1/2 acres.
Moore, John. Va.-Ind. Sergeant. 216 acres.
Moore, John. Va.-Ind. Private. 108 acres.
Moore, John. Md. Sergeant. ———. 50 acres.
Moore, John. Md. Private. ———. 50 acres.
Moore, John. Md. Private. ———. 50 acres.
Moore, John. Md. Private. ———. 50 acres.
Moore, John. Md. Private. ———. 50 acres.
Moore, John. N. Y. Fifer. 7 Jul. 1790. 600 acres.
Moore, John. N. Y. Private. 8 Jul. 1790. 500 acres.
Moore, John. N. Y. Private. 8 Jul. 1790. 600 acres.
Moore, John. N.C. Lieutenant. 16 Aug. 1821. 2560 acres.
Moore, John. Pa. Private. 29 Sep. 1787. 200 acres to widow.
Moore, John. Pa. Private. 18 Sep. 1787. 200 acres.
Moore, John. S.C. Captain. 2 May 1785. 300 acres.
Moore, John. Va. Master. 4 Nov. 1783. 2666 2/3 acres.
Moore, John. Va. Private. 26 Nov. 1783. 100 acres.
Moore, John. Va. Sergeant. 6 Aug. 1784. 400 acres.
Moore, John. Va. Private. 18 Dec. 1784. 100 acres.
Moore, John. Va. Private. 25 Jun. 1787. 100 acres.
Moore, John. Va. Ensign. 20 Jan. 1807. 2666 2/3 acres.
Moore, John. Va. Lieutenant. 29 Dec. 1851. 1333 1/3 acres.
Moore, John Davis. N.C. Private. 8 Mar. 1796. 640 acres to heirs.
Moore, Jonas. Ga. ———. 17 Apr. 1784. 287 1/2 acres.
Moore, Joseph. N.C. Musician. 9 Sep. 1820. 1000 acres to heirs.
Moore, Joshua. Me. ———. 14 Apr. 1835. 200 acres. Vienna.
Moore, Levi. Va. Private. 15 Jun. 1807. 100 acres.
Moore, Lewis. Va. Private. 26 Apr. 1783. 200 acres.
Moore, Major. Ga. Major. 27 Dec. 1783. 400 acres to heirs John Moore et. al.
Moore, Marmaduke. N.C. Private. 21 May 1784. 640 acres.
Moore, Martin. Ga. ———. 13 Apr. 1784. 287 1/2 acres.
Moore, Mary. Conn. Sufferer. Groton. 10.15.6.
Moore, Matthew. Md. Private. ———. 50 acres.
Moore, Matthew. Md. Private. ———. 50 acres.
Moore, Maurice. N.C. Lieutenant. 10 Dec. 1821. 2560 acres to heirs.
Moore, Michael. Va. Private. 9 Dec. 1783. 100 acres.
Moore, Michael. Va. Private. 31 Jan. 1786. 200 acres.
Moore, Mordecai. Ga. ———. 15 Mar. 1784. 250 acres.
Moore, Morris. N.C. Private. 15 Jul. 1785. 640 acres to heirs.
Moore, Moses. N.C. Private. 30 Sep. 1785. 640 acres to heirs.
Moore, Nancy. Conn. Sufferer. Groton. 30.10.2.
Moore, Nicholas. N.C. Private. 9 Sep. 1785. 640 acres to heirs.
Moore, Nicholas. Va. Private. 25 Nov. 1783. 200 acres.
Moore, Nicholas. Va. Private. 6 Jan. 1785. 200 acres.

Moore, Patrick. N.C. Private. 7 Dec. 1797. 640 acres to heirs.
Moore, Peter. Va. Lieutenant. 13 Feb. 1784. 2666 2/3 acres.
Moore, Peter. Va. Private. 28 May 1784. 200 acres.
Moore, Peter. Va. Captain. 6 Oct. 1830. 853 1/3 acres.
Moore, Peter. Va. Captain. 6 Oct. 1830. 480 acres.
Moore, Peter. Va. Captain. 5 Jul. 1860. 447 acres.
Moore, Peter. Va. Captain. 5 Jul. 1860. 447 acres.
Moore, Peter. Va. Captain. 12 Mar. 1861. 447 acres.
Moore, Peter. Va. Captain. 22 Jan. 1834. 666 2/3 acres.
Moore, Peter. Va. Captain. 22 Jan. 1834. 666 2/3 acres.
Moore, Ralph. N.C. Private. 13 Sep. 1820. 640 acres.
Moore, Ralph. Va. Corporal. 26 Aug. 1783. 400 acres.
Moore, Richard. Ga. Minute Man. 24 May 1784. 287 1/2 acres.
Moore, Richard. N. Y. Private. 8 Jul. 1790. 500 acres.
Moore, Richard. Va. Corporal. 24 Jan. 1785. 200 acres.
Moore, Sampson. N.C. Private. 10 Feb. 1796. 320 acres.
Moore, Samuel. Ga. ———. 19 Dec. 1785. 575 acres.
Moore, Samuel. N.C. Private. 23 Apr. 1785. 640 acres to heirs.
Moore, Samuel. N.C. Private. 24 Nov. 1796. 640 acres to heirs.
Moore, Stephen. Ga. Sergeant. 21 Jul. 1785. —— acres to widow Mary Moore.
Moore, Stephen. Va. Private. 15 Jun. 1807. 100 acres.
Moore, Stephen. Va. Seaman. 6 Mar. 1834. 100 acres.
Moore, Temerance. Conn. Sufferer. New London. 24.3.0.
Moore, Thomas. Ga. ———. Jul. 1784. 287 1/2 acres.
Moore, Thomas. Va.-Ind. Private. 108 acres.
Moore, Thomas. N. Y. Private. 8 Jul. 1790. 600 acres.
Moore, Thomas. N.C. Private. 23 Oct. 1783. 274 acres.
Moore, Thomas. N.C. Private. 14 Apr. 1800. 228 acres.
Moore, Thomas. Pa. Private. ———. 200 acres.
Moore, Thomas. S.C. Soldier. 2 May 1785. 200 acres.
Moore, Thomas. Va. Private. 8 Feb. 1783. 100 acres.
Moore, Thomas. Va. Private. 23 Jun. 1783. 200 acres.
Moore, Thomas. Va. Captain. 28 Dec. 1810. 500 acres.
Moore, Thomas. Va. Captain. 28 Dec. 1810. 500 acres.
Moore, Thomas. Va. Captain. 28 Dec. 1810. 500 acres.
Moore, Thomas. Va. Captain. 28 Dec. 1810. 500 acres.
Moore, Thomas. Va. Captain. 28 Dec. 1810. 500 acres.
Moore, Thomas. Va. Captain. 28 Dec. 1810. 500 acres.
Moore, Thomas. Va. Captain. 28 Dec. 1810. 500 acres.
Moore, Thomas. Va. Captain. 28 Dec. 1810. 500 acres.
Moore, Thomas L. Pa. Major. 5 Jul. 1787. 300 acres.
Moore, Thomas L. Pa. Major. 5 Jul. 1787. 300 acres.
Moore, Truman. N.C. Private. 20 Dec. 1796. 640 acres to heirs.
Moore, William. Ga. Minute Man. 26 Jul. 1784. 287 1/2 acres.
Moore, William. Ga. ———. 22 Apr. 1784. 1000 acres.
Moore, William. Md. Private. ———. 50 acres.
Moore, William. Md. Private. ———. 50 acres.
Moore, William. Md. Private. ———. 50 acres.
Moore, William. N.C. Private. 9 Nov. 1784. 640 acres.
Moore, William. N.C. Private. 30 Sep. 1785. 640 acres to heirs.
Moore, William. N.C. ———. 4 Mar. 1800. 1280 acres.
Moore, William. Pa. Lieutenant. 30 Sep. 1787. 200 acres.
Moore, William. Pa. Lieutenant. 30 Sep. 1787. 200 acres.

Moore, William. Pa. ———. 23 Oct. 1786. 200 acres.
Moore, William. Va. Sergeant. 2 May 1783. 400 acres.
Moore, William. Va. Private. 12 Jul. 1783. 100 acres.
Moore, William. Va. Lieutenant. 3 Oct. 1783. 2666 2/3 acres.
Moore, William. Va. Private. 29 Jan. 1784. 100 acres.
Moore, William. Va. Lieutenant. 12 Apr. 1796. 2666 2/3 acres.
Moore, William Daniel. Va. Private. 2 Dec. 1785. 100 acres.
Moore, Zedekiah. Md. Lieutenant. ———. 200 acres.
Moorehead, Charles. Va. Sergeant. 4 Apr. 1784. 400 acres.
Mopp, James. Ga. ———. 23 Apr. 1784. 287 1/2 acres.
Moran, Benjamin. Md. Private. ———. 50 acres.
Moran, Charles. N. Y. ———. ———. 500 acres.
Moran, John. N.C. Sergeant. 26 Aug. 1785. 1000 acres to heir Ambrose Bull.
Morarity, Dennis. Pa. ———. 6 Apr. 1794. 200 acres to Daniel Stever, assignee.
Morehead, James. N.C. Lieutenant. 15 Sep. 1784. 944 acres.
Morehead, John. Pa. Private. 24 Jul. 1787. 200 acres to John Ebert, assignee.
Morehouse, Andrew. Conn. Sufferer. Norwalk. 1.16.0.
Morehouse, Ebenezer. Conn. Sufferer. Fairfield. 83.8.3.
Morehouse, Eunice. Conn. Sufferer. Fairfield. 68.7.0.
Morehouse, Gideon. Conn. Sufferer. Fairfield. 66.10.6.
Morehouse, Grummon. Conn. Sufferer. Fairfield. 6.11.6.
Morehouse, Hannah. Conn. Sufferer. Fairfield. 33.18.8.
Morehouse, Jesse. Conn. Sufferer. Fairfield. 16.6.2.
Morehouse, John. Conn. Sufferer. Fairfield. 233.11.5.
Morehouse, John. Conn. Sufferer. Fairfield. 15.13.0.
Morehouse, Michael. Conn. Sufferer. Norwalk. 4.3.0.
Morehouse, Michael, Jr. Conn. Sufferer. Norwalk. 7.7.4.
Morehouse, Sarah. Conn. Sufferer. Norwalk. 6.4.4.
Morehouse, Sarah. Conn. Sufferer. Ridgefield. 100.6.9.
Morehouse, Solomon. Conn. Sufferer. Norwalk. 5.11.0.
Morehouse, Thaddeus. Conn. Sufferer. Norwalk. 2.3.0.
Moreland, Bartlett. N.C. Private. 5 Sep. 1821. 640 acres.
Moremouth, Joseph. Ga. ———. ———. 250 acres.
Morewise, Jacob. N. Y. Private. 8 Jul. 1790. 600 acres.
Morgan, Andrew. Va. Sergeant. 8 Sep. 1783. 200 acres.
Morgan, Asa. Ga. ———. 25 Feb. 1784. 250 acres.
Morgan, Bennet. N.C. Sergeant. 4 Dec. 1783. 1000 acres.
Morgan, Bryan. N.C. Private. 6 Dec. 1796. 640 acres to heirs.
Morgan, Charles. Va.-Ind. Sergeant. 216 acres.
Morgan, Charles. N.C. Sergeant. 14 Sep. 1820. 356 acres.
Morgan, Charles. Va. Private. 23 Jun. 1783. 200 acres.
Morgan, Christopher. Ga. Private. 20 Apr. 1784. 287 1/2 acres.
Morgan, Daniel. Ga. ———. 19 Apr. 1784. 300 acres.
Morgan, Daniel. Va. Brigadier General. 7 Nov. 1782. 5000 acres.
Morgan, Daniel. Va. Brigadier General. 7 Nov. 1783. 6666 2/3 acres.
Morgan, Daniel. Va. Brigadier General. 21 Jun. 1783. 11,666 2/3 acres.
Morgan, David. Md. Lieutenant. ———. 200 acres.
Morgan, David. Va. Private. 28 Jun. 1783. 200 acres.
Morgan, Drewry. N.C. Private. 30 Sep. 1785. 640 acres to heirs.
Morgan, Elisha. Conn. Sufferer. Groton. 7.13.0.
Morgan, George. Pa. Private. 29 Sep. 1787. 200 acres to Thomas Carpenter, assignee.
Morgan, Griffin. N.C. Private. 30 Sep. 1785. 640 acres to heirs.
Morgan, Haynes. Va. Colonel. 22 Mar. 1838. 6666 2/3 acres.

Morgan, Haynes. Va. Colonel. 10 Jul. 1838. 740 acres.
Morgan, Haynes. Va. Colonel. 10 Jul. 1838. 1482 acres.
Morgan, Haynes. Va. Colonel. 10 Jul. 1838. 740 acres.
Morgan, Haynes. Va. Colonel. 10 Jul. 1838. 1482 acres.
Morgan, Haynes. Va. Colonel. 10 Jul. 1838. 444 acres.
Morgan, Haynes. Va. Colonel. 10 Jul. 1838. 1778 acres.
Morgan, Humphrey. N.C. Private. 30 Sep. 1785. 640 acres to heirs.
Morgan, Isham. Ga. ———. 17 May 1784. ———.
Morgan, Isham. N.C. Private. 30 Sep. 1785. 640 acres to heirs.
Morgan, Jacob. N.C. Private. 12 Sep. 1785. 640 acres to heirs.
Morgan, James. N.C. Private. 30 Sep. 1785. 640 acres to heirs.
Morgan, James. N.C. Private. 24 Dec. 1785. 274 acres.
Morgan, James. Va. Private. 19 Jun. 1783. 200 acres.
Morgan, Jeremiah. Ga. Refugee. 16 Nov. 1784. 287 1/2 acres.
Morgan, Jeremiah. Va. Ensign. 1 Apr. 1820. 2666 2/3 acres.
Morgan, Jesse. Ga. Refugee. 17 May 1784. 287 1/2 acres.
Morgan, John. Ga. Refugee. 19 Jun. 1784. 287 1/2 acres. Of Mecklenburg Co., Va. 1784.
Morgan, John. N.C. Private. 9 Nov. 1784. 274 acres.
Morgan, John. N.C. Musician. 11 Aug. 1820. 1000 acres to heirs.
Morgan, John. Pa. Private. 27 Oct. 1786. 200 acres to William Power, assignee.
Morgan, John. Va. Private. 27 Nov. 1782. 200 acres.
Morgan, John. Va. Sergeant. 26 Nov. 1783. 200 acres.
Morgan, John. Va. Ensign. 9 May 1785. 2666 2/3 acres.
Morgan, John. Va. Ensign. 18 Jun. 1832. 2666 2/3 acres.
Morgan, Jonas. Va. Private. 7 Apr. 1787. 200 acres.
Morgan, Joseph. N. Y. Sergeant. 8 Jul. 1790. 600 acres.
Morgan, Joseph. Pa. Sergeant. 10 Jul. 1794. 250 acres.
Morgan, Joshua & Isaac Morgan. Conn. Sufferers. Groton. 4.10.0.
Morgan, Lewis. N.C. Private. 30 Sep. 1785. 640 acres to heirs.
Morgan, Luke. Ga. ———. 25 Feb. 1784. 250 acres.
Morgan, Luke John. Ga. ———. 26 May 1784. 287 1/2 acres.
Morgan, Malachi. Ga. Refugee. 22 Apr. 1784. 287 1/2 acres.
Morgan, Morriss. N.C. Private. 21 Oct. 1783. 640 acres.
Morgan, Peter. N.C. Private. 10 Dec. 1788. 640 acres to heirs.
Morgan, Philip. Ga. Soldier. 17 May 1784. 230 acres.
Morgan, Robert. Ga. ———. 30 Sep. 1784. 287 1/2 acres to heirs.
Morgan, Simon. Va. Captain. 25 Feb. 1784. 4666 2/3 acres.
Morgan, Simon. Va. Captain. 20 Sep. 1806. 666 2/3 acres.
Morgan, Spencer. Va. Ensign. 28 Jun. 1783. 2666 2/3 acres.
Morgan, Stephen. Ga. ———. 30 Sep. 1784. 287 1/2 acres.
Morgan, Thomas. Md. Private. ———. 50 acres.
Morgan, William. Ga. Lieutenant. 19 Apr. 1784. 287 1/2 acres.
Morgan, William. N.C. Sergeant. 28 May 1784. 1000 acres.
Morgan, William. N.C. Private. 9 Nov. 1784. 274 acres.
Morgan, William. N.C. Private. 30 Sep. 1785. 640 acres to heirs.
Morgan, William. N.C. Private. 29 Nov. 1792. 640 acres.
Morgan, William. Va. Private. 12 Aug. 1783. 233 1/3 acres.
Morgan, William. Va. Private. 11 Dec. 1833. 200 acres.
Morganson, A-sa. Ga. ———. 15 Apr. 1784. 287 1/2 acres.
Morhouse, Daniel. N.C. Private. 26 Aug. 1785. 640 acres to heirs.
Morning, John. N.C. Private. 6 Sep. 1821. 640 acres.
Moroney, Joseph. N. Y. Matross. 9 Jul. 1790. 600 acres.
Morphet, James. Ga. ———. 15 Apr. 1784. 287 1/2 acres.

Morphet, Thomas. Ga. Refugee. 15 Mar. 1784. 250 acres.
Morphet, William. N.Y. ———. 13 Sep. 1790. 500 acres to heirs.
Morphey, Daniel. N.Y. Private. 13 Sep. 1790. 500 acres to heirs.
Morphis, John. N.C. Ensign. 6 Sep. 1820. 2560 acres.
Morpus, John. N.C. Private. 12 Oct. 1795. 640 acres to heirs.
Morrell, Joseph. N. Y. Lieutenant. 9 Jul. 1790. 1200 acres.
Morrell, William. N, Y. Private. 6 Jul. 1790. 600 acres.
Morrill, Isaac. N. Y. Sergeant. 8 Jul. 1790. 600 acres.
Morrill, Jacob. Me. ———. 3 Sep. 1835. 200 acres to widow Olive Morrill. Greenbush.
Morrill, John. N. Y. Sergeant. 8 Jul. 1790. 600 acres.
Morris, Abraham. Pa. ———. 31 Oct. 1795. 200 acres to Rachel Morris, widow.
Morris, Amos. Conn. Sufferer. New/East Haven. 1,235.15.4.
Morris, Benjamin. N.C. Private. 9 Nov. 1784. 640 acres to John Morris, heir.
Morris, Benjamin. N.C. Private. 9 Nov. 1784. 640 acres to John Morris, heir.
Morris, Benjamin. Pa. Dragoon. ———. 200 acres to Richard Leedom, assignee.
Morris, Claiborne. Va. Private. 18 Jan. 1814. 100 acres.
Morris, David. Pa. Private. 12 Jan. 1787. 200 acres.
Morris, Edmond. N. Y. Private. 8 Jul. 1790. 600 acres.
Morris, George. Pa. Fifer. ———. 200 acres.
Morris, James. Ga. Minute Man. 1784. 287 1/2 acres.
Morris, James. N.C. Private. 9 Nov. 1784. 640 acres to John Morris, heir.
Morris, James. N.C. Private. 9 Nov. 1784. 640 acres to John Morris, heir.
Morris, John. Ga. ———. 22 Apr. 1784. 287 1/2 acres.
Morris, John. Md. Captain. ———. 200 acres.
Morris, John. Md. Corporal. ———. 50 acres.
Morris, John. Md. Private. ———. 50 acres.
Morris, John. N.C. Private. 22 Apr. 1785. 640 acres to heirs.
Morris, John. N.C. Private. 14 Jul. 1820. 228 acres to heirs.
Morris, John. Pa. Sergeant Dragoons. 1 Feb. 1787. 250 acres.
Morris, John. Pa. Private. 6 Jul. 1808. 200 acres.
Morris, John. Va. Private. 18 Apr. 1783. 200 acres.
Morris, John. Va. Private. 4 Jun. 1783. 200 acres.
Morris, John. Va. ———. 18 Nov. 1783. 100 acres.
Morris, John. Va. Private. 9 Jan. 1813. 200 acres.
Morris, John. Conn. Sufferer. New London. 29.16.0.
Morris, M. Henry. N.Y. ———. 13 Sep. 1790. 500 acres to heirs.
Morris, Moses. Va. Private. 16 Apr. 1784. 100 acres.
Morris, Nathaniel. N.C. Private. 10 Dec. 1788. 640 acres to heirs.
Morris, Nathaniel. Va. Private. 17 Jan. 1797. 200 acres.
Morris, Nathaniel G. Va. Captain. 15 Apr. 1809. 100 acres.
Morris, Nathaniel G. Va. Captain. 15 Apr. 1809. 100 acres.
Morris, Nathaniel G. Va. Captain. 15 Apr. 1809. 100 acres.
Morris, Nathaniel G. Va. Captain. 15 Apr. 1809. 100 acres.
Morris, Nathaniel G. Va. Captain. 15 Apr. 1809. 100 acres.
Morris, Nathaniel G. Va. Captain. 15 Apr. 1809. 100 acres.
Morris, Nathaniel G. Va. Captain. 15 Apr. 1809. 100 acres.
Morris, Nathaniel G. Va. Captain. 15 Apr. 1809. 100 acres.
Morris, Nathaniel G. Va. Captain. 15 Apr. 1809. 100 acres.
Morris, Nathaniel G. Va. Captain. 15 Apr. 1809. 100 acres.
Morris, Nathaniel G. Va. Captain. 15 Apr. 1809. 200 acres.
Morris, Nathaniel G. Va. Captain. 15 Apr. 1809. 200 acres.
Morris, Nathaniel G. Va. Captain. 15 Apr. 1809. 200 acres.
Morris, Nathaniel G. Va. Captain. 15 Apr. 1809. 200 acres.

Morris, Nathaniel G. Va. Captain. 15 Apr. 1809. 200 acres.
Morris, Nathaniel G. Va. Captain. 15 Apr. 1809. 200 acres.
Morris, Nathaniel G. Va. Captain. 15 Apr. 1809. 200 acres.
Morris, Nathaniel G. Va. Captain. 15 Apr. 1809. 200 acres.
Morris, Nathaniel G. Va. Captain. 15 Apr. 1809. 200 acres.
Morris, Nathaniel G. Va. Captain. 15 Apr. 1809. 200 acres.
Morris, Nathaniel G. Va. Captain. 15 Apr. 1809. 500 acres.
Morris, Nathaniel G. Va. Captain. 15 Apr. 1809. 500 acres.
Morris, Nathaniel G. Va. Captain. 15 Apr. 1809. 500 acres.
Morris, Nathaniel G. Va. Captain. 15 Apr. 1809. 500 acres.
Morris, Nathaniel G. Va. Captain. 15 Apr. 1809. 221 acres.
Morris, Patrick. Ga. Private. Jul. 1784. 287 1/2 acres.
Morris, Philip. N.C. Private. 10 Dec. 1788. 640 acres to heirs.
Morris, Rees. Ga. 19 Jul. 1784. 287 1/2 acres.
Morris, Richard. N.C. Private. 23 Dec. 1792. 228 acres.
Morris, Robert. N. Y. Matross. 9 Jul. 1790. 600 acres.
Morris, Robert. Va. Private. 31 May 1783. 100 acres.
Morris, Samuel. Va. Private. 13 Sep. 1793. 100 acres.
Morris, Samuel. Va. Sergeant. 28 Sep. 1801. 400 acres.
Morris, Shadrack. N.C. Private. 5 Dec. 1804. 640 acres.
Morris, Thomas. Ga. ———. 17 May 1784. 690 acres to heirs.
Morris, Thomas. S.C. ———. 6 Feb. 1792. 173 acres.
Morris, Thomas. S.C. ———. 6 Feb. 1792. 37 acres.
Morris, Thomas. Va. Private. 23 Jul. 1824. 100 acres.
Morris, William. Ga. Sergeant. 26 May 1784. 345 acres.
Morris, William. Ga. ———. 26 May 1784. 287 1/2 acres.
Morris, William. N.C. Private. 28 May 1784. 640 acres.
Morris, William. N.C. Private. 28 Sep. 1785. 640 acres to heirs.
Morris, William. N.C. Sergeant. 24 Dec. 1785. 1000 acres.
Morris, William W. N. Y. Lieutenant. 8 Jul. 1790. 1200 acres.
Morrisett, Henry. N.C. Private. 21 Jan. 1818. 640 acres.
Morrisett, Peter. N.C. Corporal. 23 Feb. 1820. 1000 acres to heirs.
Morrison, Alexander. N.C. Sergeant. 14 Oct. 1783. 1000 acres.
Morrison, Anthony. Va. Seaman. 9 Aug. 1834. 200 acres.
Morrison, David. N. Y. Sergeant. 8 Jul. 1790. 500 acres.
Morrison, Hugh. Va. Sergeant. 3 Oct. 1783. 200 acres.
Morrison, James. Pa. Lieutenant. 10 Aug. 1787. 200 acres.
Morrison, James. Pa. Lieutenant. 10 Aug. 1787. 200 acres.
Morrison, James. Pa. Private. ———. 200 acres.
Morrison, Joel. N.C. Private. 12 Dec. 1785. 640 acres.
Morrison, John. Ga. Lieutenant. 15 Jul. 1784. 575 acres.
Morrison, John. Ga. Captain. 23 Nov. 1784. 690 acres.
Morrison, John. Md. Fifer. ———. 50 acres.
Morrison, John. N.C. Private. 20 Sep. 1784. 640 acres.
Morrison, John. N.C. Private. 23 Apr. 1785. 640 acres to heirs.
Morrison, John. Pa. Sergeant. 1 Mar. 1787. 250 acres.
Morrison, John. Va. Private. 23 Jun. 1783. 200 acres.
Morrison, Larkin. Pa. Private. 18 Oct. 1786. 200 acres.
Morrison, Michael. Pa. Private. 6 Nov. 1786. 200 acres to James W. Smith.
Morrison, Moses. Me. ———. 15 Apr. 1835. 200 acres. Philipsburgh.
Morrison, Richard. N. Y. Private. 3 Jul. 1790. 600 acres.
Morrison, Robert. N.C. Private. 23 Apr. 1784. 640 acres.
Morrison, William. Va. Sergeant. 30 Jun. 1784. 200 acres.
Morriss, Gilson. Va. Private. 7 Jun. 1784. 100 acres.

Morriss, Isaac. Va. Private. 3 Jan. 1784. 200 acres.
Morriss, Phillimon. N.C. Private. 21 Apr. 1784. 274 acres.
Morriss, Reuben. Va. Private. 7 Jun. 1784. 100 acres.
Morriss, Shadrack. Conn. Sufferer. Danbury. 10.6.8.
Morriss, Thomas. N.C. Private. 28 Nov. 1795. 274 acres.
Morrisson, Duncan. N.C. Private. 16 Mar. 1795. 640 acres to heirs.
Morrough, George. Va. Private. 23 Dec. 1784. 100 acres.
Morrow, John. S.C. ———. 7 Jan. 1788. 43 acres.
Morrow, John. S.C. ———. 7 Jan. 1788. 155 acres.
Morrow, Matthew. S.C. ———. 7 Jul. 1788. 200 acres.
Morrow, Patrick. N. Y. Matross. 6 Jul. 1790. 600 acres.
Morrow, Robert. S.C. ———. 7 Jul. 1788. 200 acres.
Morrow, Robert. Va. Captain. 15 Mar. 1803. 666 2/3 acres.
Morrow, Robert. Va. Captain. 2 Oct. 1807. 555 acres.
Morrow, Samuel. N.C. Private. 30 Sep. 1785. 640 acres to heirs.
Morrow, Thomas. N.C. Private. 10 Dec. 1788. 640 acres to heirs.
Morrow, William. Pa. ———. ———. 200 acres to heirs.
Morse, Anthony. Me. ———. 9 May 1835. 200 acres to widow Susa Morse. Brunwick.
Morse, Benjamin. Mass. Private. 8 Sep. 1830. 200 acres.
Morse, Cornelius. Mass. Private. 24 Feb. 1834. 200 acres.
Morse, Elisha. Mass. Private. 19 Sep. 1833. 200 acres.
Morse, Farrell. N.C. Private. 19 Jul. 1808. 640 acres to heirs.
Morse, John. Mass. Sergeant. 10 Sep. 1832. 200 acres to heirs.
Morse, Ozias. Mass. Corporal. 17 Feb. 1835. 200 acres to widow Lucy Morse.
Mortimer, James. N. Y. Matross. 9 Jul. 1790. 500 acres.
Morton, Archibald. Md. Private. ———. 50 acres.
Morton, Edmund. Va. Lieutenant. 6 Mar. 1838. 575 acres.
Morton, Edmund. Va. Lieutenant. 6 Mar. 1838. 575 acres.
Morton, Edmund. Va. Lieutenant. 16 Mar. 1847. 575 acres.
Morton, Hezekiah. Va. Captain. 20 Jan. 1783. 4000 acres.
Morton, Hezekiah. Va. Captain. 30 Apr. 1808. 500 acres.
Morton, James. Va. Lieutenant. 26 Dec. 1782. 2666 2/3 acres.
Morton, James. Va. Lieutenant. 18 Mar. 1797. 444 1/2acres.
Morton, James. Va. Lieutenant. 16 Oct. 1807. 370 acres.
Morton, John. Va. Captain. 7 May 1838. 500 acres.
Morton, John. Va. Captain. 13 Apr. 1853. 500 acres.
Morton, John. Va. Captain. 19 Dec. 1853. 71 3/7 acres.
Morton, John. Va. Captain. 27 Jul. 1854. 500 acres.
Morton, Jones. N.C. Private. 27 Jul. 1785. 274 acres.
Morton, Thomas. Me. Private. 24 Jun. 1835. 200 acres. Gorham.
Morton, William. N.C. Sergeant. 23 Apr. 1785. 1000 acres to heirs.
Mosby, Charles. Ga. Soldier. 6 Apr. 1785. 230 acres to heirs.
Mosby, Charles. Va. Private. 29 Jul. 1831. 100 acres.
Mosby, Littleberry. Va. Captain. 21 May 1823. 1000 acres.
Mosby, Littleberry. Va. Captain. 21 May 1823. 1000 acres.
Mosby, Littleberry. Va. Major. 21 May 1823. 1000 acres.
Mosby, Littleberry. Va. Major. 21 May 1823. 1000 acres.
Mosby, Robert. Va. Lieutenant. 14 Jun. 1831. 1333 1/3 acres.
Mosby, Robert. Va. Lieutenant. 14 Jun. 1831. 1333 1/3 acres.
Mosby, Samuel. Va. Sergeant. 31 Aug. 1830. 200 acres.
Mosby, William. Va. Private. 12 Dec. 1783. 200 acres.
Mosby, William. Va. Captain. 27 Nov. 1810. 4000 acres.
Moseby, Benjamin. Va. Lieutenant. 13 Dec. 1782. 2666 2/3 acres.

Moseby, Littleberry. Ga. Captain. 23 Apr. 1784. 690 acres.
Moseby, Robert. Ga. Lieutenant. 17 May 1784. 460 acres.
Moseley, Benjamin. Ga. ———. 18 Jun. 1784. 287 1/2 acres.
Moseley, Benjamin. Va. Lieutenant. 12 Mar. 1783. 2666 2/3 acres.
Moseley, Brantly. Ga. ———. 18 Jun. 1784. 287 1/2 acres.
Moseley, Isaac. Conn. Sufferer. New London. 500.0.0.
Moseley, John. Ga. Soldier. 13 Feb. 1784. ———.
Moseley, Thomas. N.C. Private. 29 Sep. 1784. 640 acres to heir.
Moseley, Thomas, Jr. Ga. ———. 17 May 1784. ———.
Moseley, William. Ga. Refugee. 15 Apr. 1784. 287 1/2 acres.
Moseley, William. N.C. Private. 10 Dec. 1817. 648 acres to heirs.
Moseley, William. Va. Major. 7 Feb. 1783. 5333 1/3 acres.
Moseley, William. Va. Major. 18 Nov. 1796. 888 2/3 acres.
Moseley, William. Va. Major. 2 Oct. 1807. 740 acres.
Moseley, William H. Ga. ———. 17 May 1784. ———.
Mosely, George. Va. Private. 27 Feb. 1797. 100 acres.
Mosely, John. N.C. Private. 8 Dec. 1795. 640 acres.
Moser, Cruise. Md. Private. ———. 50 acres.
Moser, Samuel. Pa. Private. 22 Feb. 1787. 200 acres.
Moses, Jacob. Md. Private. ———. 50 acres.
Moses, Jacob. Md. Private. ———. 50 acres.
Mosir, Francis. N.C. Private. 28 Sep. 1785. 640 acres to heirs.
Mosir, Samuel. N.C. Private. 28 Sep. 1785. 640 acres to heirs.
Mosland, John. N.C. Private. 2 Feb. 1786. 640 acres.
Moss, David. N. Y. Private. 8 Jul. 1790. 600 acres.
Moss, Edmund. Va. Lieutenant. 11 Jul. 1835. 2666 2/3 acres.
Moss, Francis. Va. Armourer. 22 Jul. 1835. 2666 2/3 acres.
Moss, Francis. Va. Armourer. 22 Jun. 1837. 444 acres.
Moss, Francis. Va. Armourer. 22 Jun. 1837. 444 acres.
Moss, Francis. Va. Armourer. 22 Jun. 1837. 222 acres.
Moss, Francis. Va. Armourer. 22 Jun. 1837. 222 acres.
Moss, Francis. Va. Armourer. 22 Jun. 1837. 444 acres.
Moss, Francis. Va. Armourer. 22 Jun. 1837. 444 acres.
Moss, Francis. Va. Armourer. 22 Jun. 1837. 148 1/2 acres.
Moss, Francis. Va. Armourer. 22 Jun. 1837. 148 1/2 acres.
Moss, Francis. Va. Armourer. 22 Jun. 1837. 148 1/2 acres.
Moss, Henry. Va. Captain. 21 May 1783. 4000 acres.
Moss, Henry. Va. Private. 10 Jun. 1783. 100 acres.
Moss, Henry. Va. Captain. 2 Dec. 1796. 666 2/3 acres.
Moss, Henry. Va. Captain. 14 Aug. 1807. 555 acres.
Moss, John. S.C. ———. 4 Jul. 1791. 200 acres.
Moss, John. Va. Major. 5 Nov. 1808. 5333 1/3 acres.
Moss, Julius. Va. Private. 22 Jan. 1788. 100 acres.
Moss, Leonard. Ga. Soldier. 17 May 1784. ———.
Moss, Robert. N.C. Private. 7 Dec. 1796. 640 acres to heirs.
Moss, Starke. Va. Carpenter. 9 Nov. 1831. 444 4/9 acres.
Moss, Starke. Va. Carpenter. 9 Nov. 1831. 444 4/9 acres.
Moss, Starke. Va. Carpenter. 9 Nov. 1831. 222 2/9 acres.
Moss, Starke. Va. Carpenter. 9 Nov. 1831. 222 2/9 acres.
Moss, Starke. Va. Carpenter. 9 Nov. 1831. 444 4/9 acres.
Moss, Starke. Va. Carpenter. 9 Nov. 1831. 371 1/3 acres.
Moss, Starke. Va. Carpenter. 9 Nov. 1831. 172 1/3 acres.
Moss, Starke. Va. Carpenter. 9 Nov. 1831. 172 1/3 acres.
Moss, Starke. Va. Carpenter. 9 Nov. 1831. 172 1/3 acres.

Moss, William. Ga. ———. 17 May 1784. ———.
Mosses, John. Va. Private. 26 Apr. 1783. 200 acres.
Mosslander, Abel. N.C. ———. 13 May 1784. 2560 acres to heirs.
Mossum, David. Va. Captain. 16 Arp. 1833. 666 2/3 acres.
Mossum, David. Va. Captain. 16 Apr. 1833. 666 2/3 acres.
Mossum, David. Va. Captain. 16 Apr. 1833. 500 acres.
Mossum, David. Va. Captain. 16 Apr. 1833. 500 acres.
Mossum, David. Va. Captain. 16 Apr. 1833. 166 2/3 acres.
Mossum, David. Va. Captain. 16 Apr. 1833. 166 2/3 acres.
Mossum, David. Va. Captain. 16 Apr. 1833. 380 20/21 acres.
Mossum, David. Va. Captain. 16 Apr. 1833. 380 20/21 acres.
Mossum, David. Va. Captain. 16 Apr. 1833. 95 5/21 acres.
Mossum, David. Va. Captain. 16 Apr. 1833. 95 5/21 acres.
Mossum, David. Va. Captain. 3 Jan. 1844. 190 10/21 acres.
Mossum, David. Va. Captain. 3 Jan. 1844. 190 10/21 acres.
Mossum, David. Va. Captain. 17 May 1867. 571 3/7 acres.
Mossum, David. Va. Captain. 17 May 1867. 571 3/7 acres.
Mossum, David. Va. Captain. 17 May 1867. 571 3/7 acres.
Mossum, David. Va. Captain. 17 May 1867. 571 3/7 acres.
Mossum, David. Va. Captain. 17 May 1867. 573 3/7 acres.
Mossum, David. Va. Captain. 17 May 1867. 571 3/7 acres.
Mossum, David. Va. Captain. 17 May 1867. 114 2/7 acres.
Mossum, David. Va. Captain. 17 May 1867. 457 1/7 acres.
Mosure, Francis. N.C. Private. 2 Dec. 1785. 640 acres.
Mothershead, Nathaniel. Va. Sergeant. 27 Oct. 1783. 200 acres.
Motley, David. Va. Private. 9 Dec. 1833. 100 acres.
Mott, Abraham. N.C. Private. 9 Sep. 1785. 640 acres to heirs.
Mott, Benjamin. N.C. Non Commissioned Officer. 19 May 1784. 1000 acres.
Mott, Daniel. N.C. Private. 23 Nov. 1790. 640 acres to heir Benjamin Mott.
Mott, Ebenezer. N. Y. Lieutenant. 9 Jul. 1790. 1200 acres.
Mott, Edge. N.C. Private. 30 Sep. 1785. 640 acres to heirs.
Mott, Gershom. N. Y. Captain. 9 Jul. 1790. 1800 acres.
Mott, Noah. N. Y. Private. 8 Jul. 1790. 600 acres.
Mott, Samuel. N. Y. Corporal. 8 Jul. 1790. 600 acres.
Mott, Thomas. Va. Sailor. 17 Nov. 1784. 100 acres.
Mott, William. Conn. Sufferer. Norwalk. 10.14.6.
Motte, Charles. S.C. Major. 21 Jan. 1785. 400 acres to heirs.
Motte, Edgerton. N.C. Private. 19 May 1784. 640 acres.
Motte, Joseph. Ga. ———. 20 Feb. 1784. 250 acres.
Motte, Uriah. Ga. ———. 24 Feb. 1784. 250 acres.
Motte, William. Ga. ———. 20 Feb. 1784. 250 acres.
Motte, Zephaniah. Ga. ———. 24 Feb. 1784. 250 acres.
Moughan, Matthew. Va. Private. 17 Nov. 1784. 100 acres.
Moulden, Thomas. Va. Corporal. 12 Mar. 1783. 200 acres.
Moulton, Simeon. Me. ———. 14 Aug. 1838. 200 acres to Sally Moulton. Newfield.
Moulton, William. N. Y. ———. 3 Dec. 1803. 1000 acres.
Moultrie, William. S.C. Major General. 16 Jul. 1784. 1100 acres.
Mounger, Sampson. Ga. ———. 6 Aug. 1787. 287 1/2 acres.
Mount, Matthew. Va. Private. 21 Apr. 1784. 100 acres.
Mount, Richard. N.C. Private. 28 Sep. 1785. 274 acres.
Mountague, Richard. Va. Lieutenant. 27 Jul. 1783. 2666 2/3 acres.
Mountjoy, Alvin. Va. Lieutenant. 25 Oct. 1798. 2666 2/3 acres.
Mountjoy, John. Va. Captain. 15 Apr. 1800. 4000 acres.

Mountjoy, John. Va. Captain. 11 Sep. 1807. 555 acres.
Mountjoy, William. Va. Captain. 16 Jun. 1784. 4000 acres.
Mounty, John D. Pa. Matross. ———. 200 acres.
Moura, Christian. Pa. Private. ———. 200 acres.
Moveal, Henry. N.C. Private. 30 Sep. 1785. 640 acres to heirs.
Mowra, Jacob. N.C. Private. Dec. 1802. 274 acres.
Moxley, George. Va. Corporal. 22 Mar. 1784. 400 acres.
Moxley, Rhodam. Va. Subaltern. 17 Apr. 1784. 2666 2/3 acres.
Moye, Gardner. N.C. Corporal. 29 Sep. 1784. 428 acres.
Moye, George. N.C. Private. 13 Dec. 1783. 228 acres.
Moye, John. N.C. ———. 25 Jun. 1785. 2560 acres to heirs.
Moyer, John. Pa. Private. 28 May 1785. 200 acres to William R. Hanna and Alexander Forster, executors.
Moylan, Stephen. Pa. Colonel in Cavalry. 12 Jul. 1787. 500 acres.
Moylan, Stephen. Pa. Colonel. 12 Jul. 1787. 500 acres.
Muckleroth, Elizabeth. Ga. ———. 17 Sep. 1784. 287 1/2 acres.
Muckleroy, John. N.C. Private. 12 Dec. 1785. 274 acres.
Muckleroy, William. N.C. Private. 22 Aug. 1820. 640 acres to heirs.
Mudd, Bennett. Md. Sergeant. ———. 50 acres.
Mudd, Jeremiah. Md. Sergeant. ———. 50 acres.
Mudd, Richard. Md. Sergeant. ———. 50 acres.
Muhlenberg, Peter. Va. Brigadier General. 29 Aug. 1807. 1528 acres.
Muhlenburg, Peter. Va. Brigadier General. 10 Mar. 1783. 11,666 2/3 acres.
Muir, Francis. Va. Captain. 1 Aug. 1783. 4000 acres.
Muir, John. Va. Midshipman. 10 Mar. 1784. 2666 2/3 acres.
Muire, James. Va. Private. 8 Sep. 1813. 100 acres.
Muiritt, Charles. Md. Matross. ———. 50 acres.
Mulcaster, John. S.C. Soldier. 21 Jan. 1785. 200 acres.
Mulford, David. Conn. Sufferer. New/East Haven. 7.16.6.
Mulford, Portis. N.C. Private. 30 Sep. 1785. 640 acres to heirs.
Mulhering, Charles, Jr. S.C. ———. 3 Sep. 1787. 200 acres.
Mulhering, Charles, Sr. S.C. ———. 3 Sep. 1787. 183 acres.
Mulholland, James. N. Y. Private. 8 Jul. 1790. 500 acres.
Mulins, Anthony. Va. Private. 21 Aug. 1783. 200 acres.
Mulkey, John. N.C. Private. 30 Sep. 1785. 640 acres to heirs.
Mullen, Daniel. Pa. Private. 11 Sep. 1787. 200 acres to Abraham Smith, assignee.
Mullen, Michael. N.C. Private. 26 May 1784. 640 acres.
Mullen, William. N. Y. Private. 8 Jul. 1790. 600 acres.
Mullen, William. N.C. Private. 28 May 1784. 365 acres.
Mulliken, John. Va. Private. 20 May 1823. 100 acres.
Mullin, John. Va. Sergeant. 13 May 1783. 200 acres.
Mullin, John. Va. Sergeant. 13 May 1783. 400 acres.
Mulliner, Moses. N. Y. Private. 8 Jul. 1790. 500 acres.
Mullins, David. Va. Private. 1 Oct. 1783. 100 acres.
Mullins, Melone. N.C. Private. 16 Oct. 1783. 228 acres.
Mullis, James. N.C. Private. 14 Dec. 1796. 640 acres to heirs.
Mulloy, Martin. Md. Private. ———. 50 acres.
Mulroi, Francis. N. Y. ———. ———. 500 acres.
Mulvaney, John. Pa. Private. 11 May 1789. 200 acres.
Mumford, David. Conn. Sufferer. New London. 318.5.9.
Mumford, Giles. Conn. Sufferer. New London. 44.0.0.
Mumford, Thomas. Ga. Soldier. 25 Apr. 1785. ———.
Mumford, Thomas. Conn. Sufferer. Groton. 604.16.0.
Mumpower, Nicholas. Va. Private. 11 Feb. 1784. 100 acres.

Munday, Thomas. Va. Private. 5 Mar. 1784. 100 acres.
Munden, Edward. Va. Private. 1 Apr. 1783. 200 acres.
Mundine, Joseph. N.C. Private. 30 Sep. 1785. 640 acres to heirs.
Mundine, Reubin. N.C. Private. 30 Sep. 1785. 640 acres to heirs.
Mundine, Zebulon. N.C. Private. 30 Sep. 1785. 640 acres to heirs.
Mundon, John. N. Y. Sergeant. 24 Aug. 1790. 500 acres.
Mundy, James. N. Y. Corporal. 3 Jul. 1790. 600 acres.
Munford, William Green. Va. Colonel. 7 Dec. 1808. 6666 2/3 acres.
Munro, Alexander. N. Y. Private. 8 Jul. 1790. 600 acres.
Munro, Ebenezer. Conn. Sufferer. Fairfield. 1.15.0.
Munrow, John. Va. Private. 9 May 1788. 100 acres.
Munson, Amos. Conn. Sufferer. New/East Haven. 18.15.6.
Munson, David. Conn. Sufferer. New/East Haven. 2.8.6.
Munson, Ebenezer, Jr. Conn. Sufferer. Danbury. 21.8.0.
Munson, Israel. Conn. Sufferer. New/East Haven. 27.6.6.
Munson, Joseph. Conn. Sufferer. New/East Haven. 10.14.6.
Munson, Samuel. Conn. Sufferer. New/East Haven. 41.17.10.
Munson, Stephen. Conn. Sufferer. New/ East Haven. 22.12.4.
Munson, William. Ga. ———. 17 May 1784. ———.
Munson, William. Conn. Sufferer. New/ East Haven. 73.6.8.
Murbee, Patrick. N.C. Private. 13 Dec. 1796. 640 acres.
Murch, Mathias. Me. ———. 13 Aug. 1835. 200 acres. Gorham.
Murden, Peter. Va. Private. 12 Jul. 1783. 200 acres.
Murdoch, William. Md. Lieutenant. ———. 200 acres.
Murdock, Allen. N.C. Private. 30 Sep. 1785. 640 acres to heirs.
Murdock, Jonathan, Rev. Conn. Sufferer. Greenwich. 79.14.4.
Murdock, Joseph. Va. Private. 20 Jun. 1783. 100 acres.
Murdock, McCloud. N.C. Private. 30 Sep. 1785. 640 acres to heirs.
Murfree, Hardy. N.C. Colonel. 24 Dec. 1785. 640 acres.
Murfree, Hardy. N.C. Colonel. 24 Dec. 1785. 640 acres.
Murfree, Richard E. N.C. Private. 17 Dec. 1796. 640 acres to heirs.
Murfrey, John. Va. Private. 25 Nov. 1783. 100 acres.
Murlat, Abraham. Va. Private. 14 Jun. 1785. 200 acres.
Murley, Dennis. Md. Private. ———. 50 acres.
Murphey, Archibald. N.C. Private. 7 Feb. 1795. 640 acres to heirs.
Murphey, Charles. Va. Private. 26 Nov. 1783. 100 acres.
Murphey, Hardy. N.C. Lieutenant Colonel. 22 Oct. 1783. 5760 acres.
Murphey, James. N.C. Private. 14 Nov. 1820. 640 acres to heirs.
Murphey, James. Pa. Private. 5 Oct. 1786. 200 acres.
Murphey, John. Va. Private. 23 Jun. 1783. 100 acres.
Murphey, John Manning. Va. Private. 26 Mar. 1803. 200 acres.
Murphey, Joseph. Md. Private. ———. 50 acres.
Murphey, Leander. Va. Private. 29 Mar. 1784. 100 acres.
Murphey, Michael. S.C. ———. 6 Oct. 1788. 200 acres.
Murphey, Michael. Va. Private. 23 Jun. 1783. 200 acres.
Murphey, Owen. Va. Private. 23 Jun. 1783. 100 acres.
Murphey, Patrick. N.C. Sergeant. 6 Dec. 1783. 1000 acres.
Murphey, Patrick. N.C. Private. 30 Nov. 1785. 640 acres.
Murphey, Samuel. Va. Private. 15 Nov. 1783. 100 acres.
Murphy, Andrew. Pa. Private. ———. 200 acres.
Murphy, Archibald. Pa. Sergeant. ———. 250 acres.
Murphy, Charles. Md. Sergeant. ———. 50 acres.
Murphy, Daniel. Md. Private. ———. 50 acres.
Murphy, Edward. Ga. ———. 25 May 1784. 287 1/2 acres.

Murphy, Edward. S.C. ———. 4 Jul. 1785. 200 acres.
Murphy, Gabriel. Va. Private. 15 Dec. 1838. 100 acres.
Murphy, James. Md. Private. ———. 50 acres.
Murphy, James. N.C. Private. 22 Aug. 1820. 640 acres.
Murphy, James. Pa. Matross. 28 Aug. 1787. 200 acres to William Turnbull, assignee.
Murphy, John. Va.-Ind. Private. 108 acres.
Murphy, John. N. Y. Matross. 7 Jul. 1790. 600 acres.
Murphy, John. Va. Private. 30 Aug. 1784. 100 acres.
Murphy, John. Va. Private. 5 Nov. 1811. 200 acres.
Murphy, John. Va. Private. 15 Aug. 1834. 100 acres.
Murphy, Lawrence. Pa. Private. 20 Feb. 1787. 200 acres.
Murphy, Lemuel. Va. Private. 6 Mar. 1833. 25 acres.
Murphy, Lemuel. Va. Private. 6 Mar. 1833. 25 acres.
Murphy, Martin. Va. Sergeant. 30 Jul. 1783. 400 acres.
Murphy, Michael. Pa. Private. 5 Sep. 1787. 200 acres to Robert Galbraith, assignee.
Murphy, Michael. S.C. ———. 1 Aug. 1791. 200 acres.
Murphy, Michael. Va. Private. 10 Sep. 1783. 200 acres.
Murphy, Miles. Ga. Refugee. 6 Feb. 1784. 500 acres.
Murphy, Morris. Ga. ———. 17 May 1784. ———.
Murphy, Patrick. Va. Private. 28 Jun. 1783. 100 acres.
Murphy, Thomas. Md. Private. ———. 50 acres.
Murphy, Thomas. N.C. Private. 14 Sep. 1820. 640 acres.
Murphy, William. S.C. ———. 7 Sep. 1789. 200 acres.
Murrah, George. Va. Private. 21 Jul. 1783. 100 acres.
Murray, Daniel. Va. Private. 23 Jan. 1784. 200 acres.
Murray, David. Va. Sailing Master's Mate. 9 Dec. 1830. 2666 2/3 acres.
Murray, Edward. Va. Private. 23 May 1835. 100 acres.
Murray, Francis. Pa. Lieutenant Colonel. 28 Feb. 1794. 250 acres.
Murray, Francis. Pa. Lieutenant Colonel. ———. 500 acres.
Murray, Francis. Va. Private. 28 Apr. 1783. 200 acres.
Murray, George. Va. Private. 27 Jun. 1783. 100 acres.
Murray, James. Va. Private. 8 Dec. 1783. 200 acres.
Murray, James. Conn. Sufferer. New/East Haven. 9.14.4.
Murray, John. Ga. ———. 17 May 1784. ———.
Murray, John. Md. Private. ———. 50 acres.
Murray, John. Md. Private. ———. 50 acres.
Murray, John. N.C. Private. 7 Dec. 1797. 428 acres.
Murray, John. Pa. Lieutenant Colonel. ———. 250 acres.
Murray, John. Pa. ———. 200 acres to John Nicholson.
Murray, John. Pa. Colonel. 23 Apr. 1787. 500 acres.
Murray, Joshua. N.C. Private. 29 Sep. 1785. 640 acres.
Murray, Patrick. Pa. Private. ———. 200 acres.
Murray, Ralph. Va. Private. 30 Aug. 1783. 100 acres.
Murray, Richard. Va. Private. 12 Sep. 1783. 100 acres.
Murray, Samuel. N.C. Private. 7 Jan. 1786. 274 acres.
Murray, Thomas. N.C. Private. 26 Nov. 1796. 640 acres to heirs.
Murray, Thomas. Pa. Private. 11 Jun. 1794. 200 acres to James Snodgrass and William Snodgrass, assignees.
Murray, Valentine. Md. Corporal. ———. 50 acres.
Murray, William. N.C. Sergeant. 9 Dec. 1797. 428 acres.
Murray, William. Pa. ———. 9 Oct. 1786. 200 acres.
Murray, William. Pa. Private. 30 Sep. 1787. 200 acres.
Murray, William. Va. Private. 19 Jun. 1783. 100 acres.
Murray, William. Va. Private. 29 Dec. 1796. 100 acres.

Murrell, Henry. N.C. Private. 30 Sep. 1785. 640 acres to heirs.
Murrell, Jacob. N.C. Private. 15 Jul. 1785. 640 acres to heirs.
Murrell, Matthew. N.C. Private. 23 Apr. 1785. 640 acres to heirs.
Murren, Wiliam. Pa. Lieutenant. ———. 200 acres.
Murren, William. Pa. Lieutenant. 26 Dec. 1786. 200 acres.
Murry, Charles. N.C. Sergeant. 25 Jun. 1785. 357 acres.
Murry, Daniel. Pa. Private. 5 Oct. 1786. 200 acres to Joseph Junkin, assignee.
Murry, Duncan. Va. Private. 17 May 1783. 200 acres.
Murry, Edward. Va.-Ind. Private. 108 acres.
Murry, James. N. Y. Private. 8 Jul. 1790. 600 acres.
Murry, James. N.C. Private. 23 Apr. 1785. 640 acres to heirs.
Murry, John. N. Y. Matross. 9 Jul. 1790. 600 acres.
Murry, Matthew. Va. Private. 18 Apr. 1801. 100 acres.
Murry, William. N. Y. Private. 8 Jul. 1790. 600 acres.
Murthwait, Richard. Pa. Sergeant. ———. 250 acres.
Murtis, Zedekiah. N.C. Private. 30 Sep. 1785. 640 acres to heirs.
Murtz, Thomas. Pa. Private. 28 Feb. 1794. 200 acres to George Knopler, assignee.
Muse, George. Va. Sergeant. 30 Jun. 1783. 200 acres.
Muse, Jesse. Va. Midshipman. 28 Oct. 1783. 2666 2/3 acres.
Muse, Richard. Va. Lieutenant. 8 Mar. 1838. 381 acres.
Muse, Richard. Va. Lieutenant. 8 Mar. 1838. 381 acres.
Muse, Richard. Va. Lieutenant. 8 Mar. 1838. 570 1/3 acres.
Muse, Richard. Va. Lieutenant. 8 Mar. 1838. 570 1/3 acres.
Muse, Richard. Va. Lieutenant. 8 Mar. 1838. 191 acres.
Muse, Richard. Va. Lieutenant. 8 Mar. 1838. 191 acres.
Muse, Richard. Va. Lieutenant. 8 Mar. 1838. 191 acres.
Muse, Richard. Va. Lieutenant. 8 Mar. 1838. 191 acres.
Muse, Walker. Md. Captain. ———. 200 acres.
Muse, Walker. Va. Captain. 1 Mar. 1851. 4000 acres.
Musgrove, William. Va. Private. 20 Jun. 1783. 100 acres.
Musgrove, William. Va. Corporal. 31 May 1783. 200 acres.
Mush, Robert. Va. Private. 6 Aug. 1783. 200 acres.
Mushler, Adam. Md. Private. ———. 50 acres.
Muss, John. N.C. Private. 30 Sep. 1785. 640 acres to heirs.
Musteen, William. Ga. Private. 3 Oct. 1785. ———.
Muter, George. Va. Colonel. 9 Dec. 1782. 6666 2/3 acres.
Muter, George. Va. Colonel. 2 Apr. 1834. 1810 acres.
Muter, George. Va. Colonel. 9 Apr. 1840. 514 acres.
Mutlow, William. Va. Private. 20 Dec. 1796. 100 acres.
Mutt, William. N. Y. Private. 8 Jul. 1790. 500 acres.
Myer, Christopher. Va. Lieutenant. 6 Nov. 1788. 2666 2/3 acres.
Myers, Casper. Va. Private. 19 Aug. 1820. 50 acres.
Myers, Casper. Va. Private. 19 Aug. 1820. 50 acres.
Myers, Christian. Md. Private. ———. 50 acres.
Myers, Henry. N. Y. Private. 8 Jul. 1790. 500 acres.
Myers, Jacob. Md. Private. ———. 50 acres.
Myers, Jacob. N.C. ———. 10 Aug. 1785. 640 acres.
Myers, John. Pa. Private. 19 Jan. 1787. 200 acres to Dorothy Myers, widow.
Myers, Lawrence. Md. Lieutenant. ———. 200 acres.
Myers, Peter. Pa. Private. 9 Mar. 1795. 200 acres to John Nicholson, assignee.
Myers, Robert. Md. Matross. ———. 50 acres.
Myers, Thomas. Ga. Refugee. 15 Mar. 1784. 250 acres.
Myers, Thomas. Ga. Private on a galley. 27 Jan. 1784. 200 acres.
Myers, William. Va.-Ind. Private. 108 acres.

Myers, William. N.C. Private. 22 Apr. 1785. 640 acres to heirs.
Mygatt, Eli. Conn. Sufferer. Danbury. 542.7.11.
Myham, William. N.C. Private. 2 Feb. 1786. 640 acres to heirs.
Myngas, Moses. N. Y. Private. 8 Jul. 1790. 600 acres.
Myres, Christain. Md. Captain. ———. 200 acres.
Myrick, William. S.C. Soldier. 21 Jan. 1785. 200 acres.
Mytinger, Jacob. Pa. Lieutenant. ———. 200 acres.
Mytinger, Jacob. Pa. Lieutenant. ———. 200 acres.
Nabb, Charles. Md. Private. ———. 50 acres.
Nabb, Joseph. Md. Private. ———. 50 acres.
Nace, George. Pa. ———. ———. 200 acres.
Naffee, Garrit. N. Y. Private. 8 Jul. 1790. 600 acres.
Nagle, Christian. Pa. Sergeant. 10 Jan. 1787. 250 acres.
Nagle, Henry. Pa. Sergeant. 29 Nov. 1786. 250 acres.
Nail, Aquilla. Ga. ———. ———. 287 1/2 acres.
Nail, Benjamin. Ga. Sergeant. 27 Apr. 1784. 287 1/2 acres.
Nail, Bradley. Ga. ———. 13 Sep. 1784. 287 1/2 acres.
Nail, Henry. Ga. Refugee. 26 May 1784. 575 acres.
Nail, James. Ga. ———. 27 Apr. 1784. 250 acres to heirs.
Nail, John. Ga. Minute Man. 3 Sep. 1785. ———.
Nail, John. Va. Sergeant. 28 Mar. 1834. 400 acres.
Nail, John. Va. Ensign. 29 Dec. 1851. 2994 acres.
Nail, Joseph. Ga. Captain. 15 Mar. 1784. 500 acres.
Nail, Joseph. Ga. ———. 15 Mar. 1784. 248 acres to heirs.
Nail, Julian. Ga. ———. 27 Apr. 1784. 287 1/2 acres.
Nail, Matthew. N.C. Private. 9 Dec. 1797. 640 acres to heirs.
Nail, Nicolas. N.C. Private. 9 Dec. 1797. 640 acres to heirs.
Nail, Reuben. Ga. Refugee. 29 Jul. 1784. 287 1/2 acres.
Nail, Richard. Ga. ———. ———. 250 acres.
Nailor, William. Md. Private. ———. 50 acres.
Nance, David. N.C. Lieutenant. 15 Jul. 1785. 1097 acres.
Nance, Frederick. Va. Sergeant. 23 Apr. 1784. 200 acres.
Nance, Zacheriah. Va. Private. 3 May 1784. 100 acres.
Napper, Caleb. Ga. ———. 27 Apr. 1784. 287 1/2 acres.
Napper, Thomas Ga. ———. 17 May 1784. 1000 acres.
Narvel, James. Md. Fifer. ———. 50 acres.
Narvell, Aquilla. Va. Sergeant. 15 May 1783. 200 acres.
Nash, Clement. Ga. Captain. 28 Oct. 1783. 600 acres to widow Mary Nash.
Nash, Francis. N.C. ———. 16 Feb. 1784. 640 acres.
Nash, Francis. N.C. Brigadier General. 29 Apr. 1784. 12,000 acres.
Nash, Francis. Conn. Sufferer. Greenwich. 646.7.5.
Nash, Jacob. Mass. Matross. 19 Mar. 1834. 200 acres.
Nash, John. N.C. Sergeant. 22 Oct. 1783. 428 acres.
Nash, John. N.C. Private. 12 Dec. 1796. 228 acres.
Nash, John, Jr. Va. Private. 15 Apr. 1853. 100 acres.
Nash, Michael. N.C. Private. 23 Apr. 1784. 640 acres.
Nash, Rebecca. Conn. Sufferer. Fairfield. 6.7.5.
Nash, Richard. N.C. Private. 17 Dec. 1785. 640 acres to heirs.
Nash, Thomas. Va. Private. 22 Nov. 1791. 100 acres.
Nash, William. Va. Private. 20 Nov. 1784. 100 acres.
Nason, David. Mass. Sergeant. 22 Dec. 1832. 200 acres to children Nathaniel Nason, David Nason, Merebeth Bliven, Abby Nason, Rebecca Hunt, Daniel Nason, Eliza Tanner, Harriet Hazard, and Catharine Spink and grand-daughter Sally Austin, the daughter of Anstis Austin, deceased.

Nathan, Andrew. N.C. Private. 2 Feb. 1786. 274 acres.
Nations, John. N.C. Private. 30 Sep. 1785. 640 acres to heirs.
Natson, George. Ga. ———. 17 May 1784. ———.
Nave, John. Md. Private. ———. 50 acres.
NcNulty, John. N.C. Private. 17 Feb. 1824. 640 acres.
Neagell, Morris. Md. Private. ———. 50 acres.
Neal, Benjamin. S.C. ———. 2 Oct. 1786. 200 acres.
Neal, Charles. Va. Sergeant. 2 Mar. 1784. 200 acres.
Neal, Charles. Va. Private. 22 Apr. 1820. 200 acres.
Neal, Daniel. Md. Matross. ———. 50 acres.
Neal, Edward. N.C. Private. 7 Dec. 1797. 640 acres to heirs.
Neal, George. Va. Private. 29 May 1819. 100 acres.
Neal, James. Mass. Gunner. 14 Jan. 1833. 200 acres.
Neal, James. S.C. ———. 6 Aug. 1787. 200 acres.
Neal, James. Va. Captain. 25 Oct. 1806. 2000 acres.
Neal, James. Va. Captain. 25 Oct. 1806. 2000 acres.
Neal, Owen. Conn. Sufferer. New London. 91.14.6.
Neal, Presley. Va. Midshipman. 26 Apr. 1838. 2666 2/3 acres.
Neal, Thomas. Ga. ———. 27 Apr. 1784. 600 acres.
Neal, William. Va. Private. 6 May 1784. 100 acres.
Neale, James. Md. Matross. ———. 50 acres.
Neale, Joseph. Md. Private. ———. 50 acres.
Neale, Presley. Va. Midshipman. 10 Nov. 1848. 1333 1/3 acres.
Neale, Presley. Va. Midshipman. 10 Nov. 1848. 1333 1/3 acres.
Neale, Richard. Va. Private. 30 May 1837. 200 acres.
Neale, William. Va. Private. 1 Nov. 1842. 100 acres.
Neall, James. Pa. Sergeant. 6 Dec. 1786. 250 acres.
Neary, John. Md. Sergeant. ———. 50 acres.
Needham, Isaac. Va. Private. 9 Feb. 1784. 200 acres.
Needham, John. N.C. Private. 16 Aug. 1821. 640 acres.
Needham, Thomas. N.C. Sergeant. 5 Sep. 1821. 1000 acres to heirs.
Needham, Thomas. Pa. Private. 29 Sep. 1787. 200 acres to John Stewart, executor.
Needhand, William A. Md. Sergeant. ———. 50 acres.
Neely, Abraham. N. Y. Captain. 24 Aug. 1790. 1800 acres.
Neely, David. Pa. Private. 21 Dec. 1785. 200 acres to heirs.
Neely, Richard. Ga. 3 May 1785. 287 1/2 acres.
Neidlinger, John Godlieb. Ga. Refugee. 29 Jan. 1784. 250 acres.
Neighbours, John. Md. Private. ———. 50 acres.
Neil, Nicholas. Va. Sergeant. 1 Apr. 1783. 466 2/3 acres.
Neill, Nicholas. Pa. Sergeant. 12 Mar. 1787. 250 acres.
Neill, Thomas. Md. Private. ———. 50 acres.
Neilly, Benjamin. Pa. Lieutenant. 30 Sep. 1787. 200 acres.
Neilly, Benjamin. Pa. Lieutenant. 30 Sep. 1787. 200 acres.
Neilson, John. N. Y. Fifer. 9 Jul. 1790. 500 acres.
Neilson, John. N. Y. Matross. 9 Jul. 1790. 500 acres.
Nellson, Thomas. N. Y. Matross. 9 Jul. 1790. 600 acres.
Nelly, John. Ga. Minute Man. 27 Apr. 1784. 287 1/2 acres.
Nelme, Samuel J. Md. ———. ———. 50 acres.
Nelms, Charles. N.C. Private. 29 Sep. 1784. 274 acres.
Nelms, Charles. Va. Sergeant. 1 Mar. 1784. 200 acres.
Nelms, Jesse. N.C. Private. 9 Sep. 1785. 640 acres to heirs.
Nelms, John. N.C. Private. 9 Dec. 1797. 274 acres.
Nelms, Meredith. Va. Seaman. 2 Sep. 1783. 100 acres.

Nelson, ——— Widow. Conn. Sufferer. New London. 63.10.0.
Nelson, Abraham. Ga. ——— 27 Apr. 1784. 200 acres.
Nelson, Alexander. N.C. Lieutenant. 23 Oct. 1783. 763 acres.
Nelson, Andrew. Pa. Sergeant. 25 Oct. 1786. 250 acres.
Nelson, Arthur. N.C. Private. 15 Mar. 1813. 640 acres to heirs.
Nelson, Arthur. N.C. Private. 10 Jul. 1820. 640 acres to heirs.
Nelson, Collins. N.C. Private. 19 Jan. 1786. 640 acres.
Nelson, Enoch. Va.-Ind. Private. 108 acres.
Nelson, Estridge. N.C. Private. 7 Jan. 1786. 640 acres to heirs.
Nelson, George. Ga. ———. 27 Apr. 1784. 200 acres.
Nelson, George. Va. Sergeant. 25 Mar. 1785. 200 acres.
Nelson, Giles. N.C. Private. 9 Nov. 1784. 274 acres.
Nelson, James. Ga. Minute Man. 1784. 287 1/2 acres.
Nelson, James. Va. Private. 14 Feb. 1834. 100 acres.
Nelson, Jesse. N.C. Private. 22 Jan. 1784. 640 acres.
Nelson, Jesse. N.C. Private. 29 Sep. 1784. 640 acres to heir.
Nelson, John. Ga. Refugee. 15 Mar. 1784. 250 acres.
Nelson, John. Md. Lieutenant. ———. 200 acres.
Nelson, John. Md. Private. ———. 50 acres.
Nelson, John. N.C. Major. 21 Oct. 1783. 4800 acres.
Nelson, John. N.C. Private. 26 Aug. 1785. 640 acres to heirs.
Nelson, John. Va. Major. 25 Sep. 1783. 5333 1/3 acres.
Nelson, John. Va. Captain. 12 Jan. 1784. 4000 acres.
Nelson, John. Va. Captain. 1 Aug. 1799. 666 2/3 acres.
Nelson, John. Va. Captain. 11 Sep. 1807. 500 acres.
Nelson, John. Va. Private. 25 May 1813. 100 acres.
Nelson, Jonathan. N.Y. ———. 13 Sep. 1790. 500 acres to heirs.
Nelson, Nathaniel. N.C. Private. 26 Aug. 1785. 640 acres to heirs.
Nelson, Provost. Va. Private. 8 May 1833. 200 acres.
Nelson, Richard. Md. Private. ———. 50 acres.
Nelson, Robert. N.C. Sergeant. 27 Oct. 1783. 357 acres.
Nelson, Robert. Va. Sergeant. 15 Jun. 1807. 200 acres.
Nelson, Roger. Md. Lieutenant. ———. 200 acres.
Nelson, Roger. Va. Lieutenant. 29 Mar. 1784. 1000 acres.
Nelson, Roger. Va. Lieutenant. 29 Mar. 1784. 1666 2/3 acres.
Nelson, Solomon. Ga. ———. 4 Oct. 1785. ———.
Nelson, Thomas. Ga. ———. 20 Feb. 1784. 250 acres.
Nelson, Thomas. Va. Captain. 13 Feb. 1834. 4000 acres.
Nelson, William. Ga. Soldier. 27 Apr. 1784. 287 1/2 acres.
Nelson, William. N.C. Private. 22 Jan. 1784. 640 acres.
Nelson, William. N.C. Private. 29 Sep. 1784. 640 acres to heirs.
Nelson, William. Va. Lieutenant Colonel. 27 Dec. 1783. 6000 acres.
Nelson, William. Va. Lieutenant. 1 Mar. 1797. 2666 2/3 acres.
Nelson, William. Va. Lieutenant. 11 Mar. 1842. 777 7/9 acres.
Nelson, William. Va. Lieutenant. 23 Apr. 1853. 388 8/9 acres.
Nelson, William. Va. Lieutenant. 23 Apr. 1853. 388 8/9 acres.
Nephew, James. Ga. Refugee. 15 Mar. 1784. 250 acres.
Nepier, James. Va. Sergeant. 19 Apr. 1783. 400 acres.
Nesler, Adam. Ga. Refugee. 19 Jul. 1784. 575 acres.
Nestell, George. N. Y. Matross. 9 Jul. 1790. 600 acres.
Nestell, Martin. N. Y. Matross. 9 Jul. 1790. 600 acres.
Nestell, Peter. N. Y. Lieutenant. 9 Jul. 1790. 1200 acres.
Nettles, Abraham. Va. Private. 13 Mar. 1797. 100 acres.
Nettles, Elisha. Ga. Minute Man. 15 Apr. 1784. 287 1/2 acres.

Nettles, Jesse. N.C. Private. 16 Aug. 1821. 640 acres.
Neucom, Solomon. Va. Private. 1 Aug. 1783. 200 acres.
Neven, Daniel. N. Y. Captain. 9 Jul. 1790. 1800 acres.
Never, David. N.C. Private. 30 Sep. 1785. 640 acres to heirs.
Nevil, Peter. Ga. Minute Man. 14 Jul. 1785. ———.
Nevil, Thomas. Ga. Minute Man. 3 Oct. 1783. ———.
Nevill, John. Va. Colonel. 7 Nov. 1783 [1782]. 7777 2/3 acres.
Nevill, John. Va. Colonel. 17 Aug. 1807. 1388 3/4 acres.
Nevill, Presley. Va. Lieutenant Colonel. 7 Nov. 1782. 7000 acres.
Neville, Presley. Va. Lieutenant Colonel. 23 Nov. 1841. 97 4/18 acres.
Neville, Presley. Va. Lieutenant Colonel. 23 Nov. 1841. 48 11/18 acres.
Neville, Presley. Va. Lieutenant Colonel. 18 Mar. 1840. 194 4/9 acres.
Neville, Presley. Va. Lieutenant Colonel. 18 Mar. 1840. 97 2/9 acres.
Neville, Presley. Va. Lieutenant Colonel. 18 Mar. 1840. 29 7/60 acres.
Neville, Presley. Va. Lieutenant Colonel. 18 Mar. 1840. 116 7/15 acres.
Neville, Presley. Va. Lieutenant Colonel. 18 Mar. 1840. 97 4/18 acres.
Neville, Presley. Va. Lieutenant Colonel. 18 Mar. 1840. 48 11/18 acres.
Neville, Presley. Va. Lieutenant Colonel. 26 Oct. 1842. 97 acres.
Neville, Presley. Va. Lieutenant Colonel. 26 Oct 1842. 48 acres.
Neville, Presley. Va. Lieutenant. ———. 96 acres.
Nevin, James. S.C. Soldier. 21 Jan. 1785. 200 acres.
Nevit, John. Md. Private. ———. 50 acres.
Nevy, Frederick. N.C. Private. 17 Feb. 1824. 640 acres.
New, Jesse. Va. Private. 26 Apr. 1783. 100 acres.
Newall, John. N.C. Private. 20 Jan. 1785. 640 acres to heirs.
Newberry, Mary. Conn. Sufferer. New London. 14.5.0.
Newberry, William. Ga. ———. 17 May 1784. 250 acres.
Newberry, William. N.C. Private. 30 Sep. 1785. 640 acres to heirs.
Newbey, Matthew. N.C. Private. 17 Mar. 1784. 640 acres.
Newborn, Thomas. N.C. Private. 12 Dec. 1806. 228 acres to heirs.
Newby, Jesse. Va. Sergeant. 16 Sep. 1850. 200 acres.
Newby, John. Va. Private. 2 Aug. 1783. 100 acres.
Newby, Leroy. Va. Sergeant. 16 Dec. 1784. 200 acres.
Newby, Matthew. N.C. Sergeant. 4 Aug. 1821. 1000 acres.
Newby, Peter. Ga. Minute Man. 3 Sep. 1785. ———.
Newby, Robert. N.C. Private. 3 Feb. 1785. 640 acres.
Newby, Thomas. Va. Private. 2 Jun. 1783. 100 acres.
Newby, William. Va. Marine. 26 Mar. 1831. 100 acres.
Newby, William. Va. Carpenter. 3 May 1838. 1283 1/3 acres.
Newby, William. Va. Carpenter. 3 May 1838. 427 7/9 acres.
Newby, William. Va. Carpenter. 3 May 1838. 855 5/9 acres.
Newcomb, Elizabeth. Conn. Sufferer. New London. 12.0.0.
Newcomb, George. Conn. Sufferer. New London. 238.1.9.
Newcomb, Joseph. Va. Private. 9 Jun. 1813. 66 2/3 acres.
Newcomb, Kinner. N. Y. Private. 8 Jul. 1790. 600 acres.
Newcomb, Richard. Va. Private. 9 Jun. 1813. 100 acres.
Newcomb, Thomas. Va. Corporal. 19 Sep. 1787. 200 acres.
Newdigate, John. Ga. Captain. ———. 690 acres.
Newel, James. N. Y. Matross. 16 Jan. 1795. 500 acres.
Newell, John. Va. Sergeant. 8 Sep. 1783. 200 acres.
Newell, Nathan. N.C. Private. 17 Feb. 1824. 640 acres.
Newell, Samuel. Mass. Private. 19 Nov. 1833. 200 acres.
Newell, Thomas. Ga. ———. 6 May 1785. 287 1/2 acres.
Newell, William. Va. Private. 2 Apr. 1810. 100 acres.

Newens, Nehemiah. Pa. Sergeant. 2 Dec. 1786. 250 acres.
Newham, Francis. N.C. Private. 10 Dec. 1788. 640 acres to heirs.
Newingham, Daniel. Pa. Private. 6 Dec. 1804. 200 acres to heirs.
Newinham, Thomas. N.C. Private. 14 Dec. 1797. 365 acres.
Newkins, Joseph. N.C. Private. 1 Sep. 1785. 640 acres to heirs.
Newkirk, Charles. N.Y. Captain Lieutenant. 9 Jul. 1790. 1200 acres.
Newland, John. Va. Private. 28 Apr. 1786. 200 acres.
Newley, John. Pa. Dragoon. ———. 200 acres.
Newlin, Matthew. Va. Private. 21 Jun. 1785. 200 acres.
Newly, William. Va. ———. 13 Nov. 1848. 427 7/9 acres.
Newman, Edward. N.C. Private. 31 Aug. 1795. 640 acres to heirs.
Newman, Edward. Va. Sergeant. 5 Jan. 1812. 200 acres.
Newman, George. Va. Private. 19 Dec. 1785. 100 acres.
Newman, John. Ga. Soldier. 17 May 1784. 230 acres.
Newman, Joseph. Va. Private. 10 Mar. 1784. 200 acres.
Newman, Joseph, Sr. Va. Private. 24 Nov. 1789. 100 acres.
Newman, Owen. Va. Sergeant. 21 Nov. 1783. 466 2/3 acres.
Newman, Reuben. N.C. Private. 21 Aug. 1820. 228 acres.
Newman, Samuel. Ga. ———. 15 Mar. 1784. 250 acres.
Newman, Thomas. Va. Sergeant. 25 Apr. 1783. 200 acres.
Newman, Thomas. Va. Private. 3 Feb. 1784. 100 acres.
Newman, William. Ga. Minute Man. 25 May 1784. 287 1/2 acres.
Newshan, Aaron. N.C. Private. 20 Jan. 1785. 640 acres to heir.
Newsom, Clayborn. Ga. ———. 20 Feb. 1784. 250 acres.
Newsom, Crawford. N.C. Private. 10 Dec. 1788. 640 acres to heirs.
Newsom, Hardy. Ga. ———. 27 Apr. 1784. 287 1/2 acres.
Newsom, Moses. N.C. Private. 27 Nov. 1789. 640 acres.
Newsom, Randolph. N.C. Private. 2 Sep. 1820. 274 acres.
Newsom, Reubin. Ga. ———. 23 Apr. 1784. 287 1/2 acres.
Newsom, Robert. N.C. Private. 21 Feb. 1822. 274 acres to heirs.
Newsom, Solomon. Ga. ———. 15 Mar. 1784. 250 acres.
Newson, Benjamin. S.C. Lieutenant. 21 Jan. 1785. 200 acres.
Newson, William. N.C. Private. 9 Dec. 1797. 640 acres to heirs.
Newton, Edward. N.C. Private. 26 May 1784. 640 acres.
Newton, Estridge. N.C. Sergeant. 17 Dec. 1785. 1000 acres.
Newton, Henry. N.C. Private. 10 Dec. 1788. 640 acres to heirs.
Newton, Hezekiah. Mass. Sergeant. 17 Mar. 1831. 200 acres.
Newton, John. Md. Private. ———. 50 acres.
Newton, John. Md. Private. ———. 50 acres.
Newton, Joseph, Sr. N.C. Private. 24 Nov. 1796. 640 acres to heirs.
Newton, Levy. Ga. 15 Sep. 1784. 287 1/2 acres.
Newton, Peter. Va.-Ind. Private. 108 acres.
Newton, Richard. Ga. ———. 18 Sep. 1784. 287 1/2 acres.
Newton, Stephen. N.C. Private. 30 Sep. 1785. 274 acres.
Newton, Thomas. Va. Private. 2 Jul. 1784. 100 acres.
Newton, William. Md. Private. ———. 50 acres.
Newton, William. Va. Sergeant. 4 Mar. 1819. 200 acres.
Newton, William. Va. Sergeant. 23 May 1842. 200 acres.
Niblet, William. Md. Private. ———. 50 acres.
Nice, John. Pa. Captain. 21 Oct. 1786. 500 acres.
Nichola, Lewis. Pa. Colonel. 26 Oct. 1786. 500 acres to Major McConnell, assignee.
Nicholas, Charles. S.C. Soldier. 16 Jul. 1784. 200 acres.
Nicholas, George. N.C. Private. 6 Sep. 1821. 640 acres.
Nicholas, George. Va. Lieutenant Colonel. 26 Mar. 1834. 6000 acres.

Nicholas, James. Pa. Private. 18 Aug. 1787. 200 acres.
Nicholas, John. N. Y. Sergeant. 8 Jul. 1790. 600 acres.
Nicholas, John. Va. Ensign. 29 Apr. 1807. 500 acres.
Nicholas, John. Va. Ensign. 29 Apr. 1807. 500 acres.
Nicholas, John. Va. Ensign. 29 Apr. 1807. 500 acres.
Nicholas, John. Va. Ensign. 29 Apr. 1807. 500 acres.
Nicholas, John. Va. Ensign. 29 Apr. 1807. 666 2/3 acres.
Nicholas, John. Va. Captain. 1 Dec. 1807. 4000 acres.
Nicholas, Ningerman. Pa. Private. ———. 200 acres to widow.
Nicholas, Stephen. N. Y. Corporal. 8 Jul. 1790. 600 acres.
Nicholass, Hancock. N.C. Private. 23 Apr. 1784. 640 acres.
Nicholls, Asael. Md. Private. ———. 50 acres.
Nicholls, Issac. Md. Private. ———. 50 acres.
Nicholls, Thomas. Va. Private. 2 Jul. 1784. 100 acres.
Nichols, Bela. Me. Lieutenant. 6 May 1837. 200 acres to widow Dorcas Nichols. Prospect.
Nichols, Benjamin. Ga. ———. 27 Apr. 1784. 286 1/2 acres.
Nichols, Charles. Va. Private. 5 Apr. 1784. 100 acres.
Nichols, Charles. Va. Private. 12 Jun. 1797. 200 acres.
Nichols, Eli. N. Y. Matross. 6 Jul. 1790. 600 acres.
Nichols, Hancock. N.C. Private. 24 Nov. 1796. 640 acres to heirs.
Nichols, Hezekiah. Conn. Sufferer. Fairfield. 394.10.7.
Nichols, John. N.C. Private. 13 Sep. 1784. 640 acres.
Nichols, John. N.C. Private. 2 Dec. 1785. 640 acres to heirs.
Nichols, John. Va. Private. 20 Aug. 1783. 100 acres.
Nichols, John. Va. Private. 3 Feb. 1784. 200 acres.
Nichols, Lewis. Pa. Colonel. 26 Oct. 1786. 500 acres to Matthew Connell, assignee.
Nichols, N. Thompson. Conn. Sufferer. Fairfield. 67.18.0.
Nichols, Samuel. N.C. Private. 30 Apr. 1784. 1000 acres to heirs.
Nichols, William, Jr. Ga. ———. 24 May 1784. 287 1/2 acres.
Nichols, William, Jr. N.C. Private. 20 Oct. 1787. 640 acres.
Nicholson, Benjamin. Ga. Minute Man. 27 Apr. 1784. 287 1/2 acres.
Nicholson, C. George. N.Y. Major. 13 Sep. 1790. 2400 acres to heirs.
Nicholson, George. Md. ———. ———. 50 acres.
Nicholson, Henry. Md. Corporal. ———. 50 acres.
Nicholson, Henry. Va. Cornet. 19 Mar. 1834. 2666 2/3 acres.
Nicholson, Henry. Va. Brigade Quartermaster. Dec. 1851/31 Jan. 1853. 2000 acres.
Nicholson, Henry. Va. Brigade Quartermaster. Dec. 1851/31 Jan. 1853. 1778 acres.
Nicholson, Henry. Va. Brigade Quartermaster. Dec. 1851/31 Jan. 1853. 1555 1/3 acres.
Nicholson, Isaac. N.C. Private. 22 Dec. 1796. 640 acres to heirs.
Nicholson, Isaac. N.C. Private. 22 Dec. 1796. 640 acres.
Nicholson, Jesse. Va. Private. 22 Mar. 1786. 100 acres.
Nicholson, Jesse. Va. Private. 21 Feb. 1812. 200 acres.
Nicholson, John. Ga. ———. 27 Apr. 1784. 850 acres.
Nicholson, John. Md. Private. ———. 50 acres.
Nicholson, John. N.C. Private. 13 Dec. 1796. 640 acres to heirs.
Nicholson, John. Pa. Sergeant. 4 Apr. 1787. 250 acres.
Nicholson, John. S.C. Soldier. 16 Jul. 1784. 174 acres.
Nicholson, John. Va. Captain. 30 Dec. 1851. 5333 1/3 acres.
Nicholson, Nicholas. Md. Sergeant. ———. 50 acres.
Nicholson, Robert. N.C. Lieutenant. 14 Sep. 1820. 807 acres.
Nicholson, Robert. Va. Surgeon. 27 Mar. 1834. 4000 acres.
Nicholson, Stephen. Md. Sergeant. ———. 50 acres.

Nicholson, Watkins. Ga. ———. 23 Apr. 1784. 287 1/2 acres.
Nicholson, William. Pa. Private. ———. 200 acres.
Nicholson, William. Pa. Private. ———. 200 acres.
Nickelson, James. N.C. Private. 30 Sep. 1785. 640 acres to heirs.
Nickens, Edward. Va. Sailor. 28 Nov. 1783. 100 acres.
Nickens, Hezekiah. Va. Seaman. 9 Apr. 1835. 100 acres.
Nickens, James. Va. Private. 9 Nov. 1832. 200 acres.
Nickens, Nathaniel. Va. Sailor. 1 Aug. 1786. 100 acres.
Nickens, Richard. Va. Seaman. 2 Aug. 1783. 100 acres.
Nickerson, Edward. Mass. Private. 20 May 1836. 200 acres.
Nickerson, Reuben. Me. ———. 8 Jul. 1835. 200 acres. Frankfort.
Nickes, Edward. N.C. Private. 14 Dec. 1796. 640 acres to heirs.
Nicking, James. Va. Sailor. 27 Jul. 1783. 100 acres.
Nickins, William. Va. Drummer. 15 Apr. 1783. 200 acres.
Nickles, Isaac. N.C. Private. 12 Dec. 1796. 274 acres.
Nickleson, William. Va. Private. 18 Apr. 1783. 200 acres.
Nickols, Nathan T. Conn. Sufferer. Fairfield. 81.16.0.
Nickson, Archibald. Ga. Minute Man. 22 Mar. 1785. 250 acres.
Niclett, John. N.C. Private. 30 Sep. 1785. 640 acres to heirs.
Nicolas, Richard. N.C. Private. 13 Dec. 1796. 640 acres to heirs.
Nicols, James. N.C. Private. 17 Dec. 1804. 228 acres.
Nicolson, Robert. Va. ———. 19 Mar. 1836. 3750 acres.
Nicolson, Robert. Va. ———. 19 Mar. 1836. 2250 acres.
Niel, Daniel. N.C. Private. 17 Feb. 1824. 640 acres.
Niel, George. Ga. ———. 28 Feb. 1784. 250 acres.
Niel, George. Ga. Soldier. 6 Apr. 1785. 230 acres.
Niel, Thomas. Ga. ———. 28 Feb. 1784. 250 acres.
Niel, William. N.C. Lieutenant. 5 Sep. 1821. 2560 acres.
Niell, John. N.C. Private. 21 Jul. 1820. 640 acres to heirs.
Nielson, Allen. N.Y. Private. 8 Jul. 1790. 500 acres.
Night, James. N.C. Private. 12 Sep. 1785. 640 acres to heirs.
Night, Richard. Ga. ———. 21 Apr. 1784. 200 acres.
Nightingale, Matthew. Va. Boatswain. 30 Jun. 1784. 200 acres.
Nightingale, Matthew. Va. ———. 11 Jan. 1838. 2466 2/3 acres.
Nightshade, Henry. N.C. Private. 22 Dec. 1796. 640 acres to heirs.
Nilherhouse, Daniel. Pa. Private. 14 Nov. 1786. 200 acres.
Nipper, James. S.C. ———. 6 May 1793. 200 acres.
Nisbet, Sanders. N.C. Private. 22 Dec. 1796. 640 acres.
Nisbitt, Joseph. N. Y. Private. 8 Jul. 1790. 600 acres.
Nison, Benjamin. Ga. Citizen Private. 10 Dec. 1784. 250 acres.
Nivel, Peter. Ga. Minute Man. 14 Jul. 1785. ———.
Nix, George. Ga. Private. 23 Feb. 1785. ———.
Nixon, Andrew. Va. Captain. 2 May 1783. 4000 acres.
Nixon, Andrew. Va. Captain. 19 Feb. 1845. 207 acres.
Nixon, Hugh Alexander. S.C. ———. 21 Jan. 1785. 200 acres.
Nixon, John. S.C. ———. 21 Jan. 1785. 200 acres.
Nixon, Mervin [Marvin]. Pa. Private. 29 Sep. 1787. 200 acres.
Nixon, Robert. N.C. Private. 7 Jan. 1786. 640 acres to heirs.
Nixon, Solomon. Ga. Minute Man. 3 Sep. 1785. ———.
Nixon, Thomas, Sr. N.C. Captain. 15 Sep. 1820. 3840 acres to heirs.
Nobland, William. N.C. Private. 2 Feb. 1786. 640 acres.
Noble, Martin. Md. ———. ———. 50 acres.
Noble, William. N.C. Sergeant. 9 Nov. 1784. 500 acres.
Noble, William. Pa. ———. 15 May 1816. 200 acres to heirs.

Nobles, Hezekiah. N.C. Private. 3 Dec. 1796. 228 acres.
Nobles, John. N.C. Private. 10 Dec. 1788. 640 acres to heirs.
Nobles, Lewis. Ga. ———. 26 May 1784. 287 1/2 acres.
Nobles, Meredith. Ga. Minute Man. 3 Sep. 1785.
Nobles, Robert. N.C. Private. 30 Sep. 1785. 274 acres.
Nock, George. Va. Private. 15 Jun. 1807. 100 acres.
Nock, William. Va. Private. 15 Jun. 1807. 100 acres.
Nocks, Asel. N.C. Private. 26 May 1784. 640 acres.
Noe, John. Pa. Private. 13 Apr. 1787. 200 acres.
Noel, Archilles. Va. Sergeant. 31 Jan. 1784. 200 acres.
Noel, Lambert. Pa. Private. 12 Feb. 1803. 200 acres.
Noell, Richard. Va. Corporal. 31 Jan. 1784. 200 acres.
Nolan, Patrick. Md. Private. ———. 50 acres.
Noland, Michael. Md. Private. ———. 50 acres.
Noland, Pierce. Va. Lieutenant. 7 Oct. 1783. 2666 2/3 acres.
Nolley, Dixson. N.C. Private. 29 Sep. 1784. 640 acres to heirs.
Nolly, Anderson. N.C. Private. 30 Sep. 1785. 640 acres to heirs.
Nooning, William. N.C. Private. 13 Sep. 1820. 640 acres.
Norman, Basil. Md. Private. ———. 50 acres.
Norman, John. Me. ———. 31 Jul. 1835. 200 acres to widow Sally Norman.
Norman, Levi. N.C. Private. 7 Dec. 1796. 640 acres to heirs. He was of Tyrrell County.
Norman, Thomas. N.C. Private. 12 Dec. 1785. 365 acres.
Norman, William. Va. Seaman. 28 Nov. 1783. 100 acres.
Normly, Job. N.C. Private. 9 Dec. 1797. 640 acres to heirs.
Norrel, Hugh. Va. Private. 28 Mar. 1812. 100 acres.
Norrell, Samuel. Ga. ———. 21 Apr. 1784. 287 1/2 acres.
Norress, David. N.C. Private. 30 Sep. 1785. 640 acres to heirs.
Norris, Bazaleel. Va. Private. 23 Apr. 1791. 200 acres.
Norris, Daniel. S.C. Soldier. 2 May 1785. 200 acres.
Norris, George. N.C. Private. 30 Sep. 1785. 640 acres.
Norris, George. Pa. Lieutenant. ———. 200 acres.
Norris, George. Pa. Lieutenant. 16 Oct. 1786. 200 acres.
Norris, Jacob. Md. Captain. ———. 200 acres.
Norris, James. Pa. ———. 10 Feb. 1808. 200 acres.
Norris, James. Pa. Private. 10 Feb. 1808. 200 acres.
Norris, Martin. Va. Sergeant. 30 Jul. 1830. 200 acres.
Norris, Martin. Va. Lieutenant. 26 Feb. 1834. 2466 2/3 acres.
Norris, Moses. N.C. Fifer. 9 Dec. 1797. 1000 acres.
Norris, Neal. Md. Private. ———. 50 acres.
Norris, Stephen. Conn. Sufferer. Ridgefield. 3.0.0.
Norris, Thomas. S.C. ———. 7 Jul. 1788. 200 acres.
Norris, Thomas. Va. Ensign. 14 Aug. 1834. 2666 2/3 acres.
Norris, William. N.C. Private. 24 Dec. 1796. 640 acres.
Norsworthy, James. N.C. Sergeant. 12 Dec. 1806. 428 acres.
Norsworthy, Samuel. N.C. Private. 6 Sep. 1821. 640 acres.
North, Caleb. Pa. Lieutenant Colonel. 8 May 1787. 500 acres.
North, Caleb. Pa. Lieutenant Colonel. 8 May 1787. 250 acres.
North, George. Pa. Lieutenant. 29 Nov. 1786. 200 acres with William McDonald, Sergeant.
North, George. Pa. Lieutenant. ———. 200 acres.
North, John. Ga. ———. ———. 287 1/2 acres.
Northam, Miles. Va. Seaman. 9 Dec. 1833. 100 acres.
Northbush, William. Pa. Private. ———. 200 acres.

Northrop, Amos. Conn. Sufferer. Danbury. 2.9.0.
Northrop, Anne. Conn. Sufferer. Danbury. 3.8.0.
Northrop, Benjamin. Conn. Sufferer. Ridgefield. 159.7.6.
Northrop, David. Conn. Sufferer. Danbury. 3.14.8.
Northrop, David. Conn. Sufferer. Danbury. 4.6.8.
Northrop, Gamaliel. Conn. Sufferer. Ridgefield. 87.13.7.
Northrop, James. Conn. Sufferer. Ridgefield. 53.17.4.
Northrop, John. Conn. Sufferer. Ridgefield. 142.17.5.
Northrop, Prue. Conn. Sufferer. Ridgefield. 4.4.0.
Northrum, Timothy. Conn. Sufferer. Danbury. 2.6.8.
Northware, George. N. Y. Private. 8 Jul. 1790. 600 acres.
Norton, George. N. Y. Sergeant. 8 Jul. 1790. 600 acres.
Norton, Henry. N.Y. ———. 13 Sep. 1790. 500 acres to heirs.
Norton, Jacob. N.C. Private. 21 Aug. 1820. 640 acres.
Norton, Jeremiah. N.C. Private. 13 Dec. 1796. 640 acres to heirs.
Norton, Nathaniel. N. Y. Captain. 9 Jul. 1790. 1800 acres.
Norton, Patrick. Pa. Private. 17 Oct. 1786. 200 acres.
Norton, Thomas. Ga. ———. 15 Mar. 1784. 250 acres.
Norton, William. N.C. Private. 30 Nov. 1785. 640 acres to heirs.
Norton, William. N.C. Private. 1 Jul. 1801. 640 acres to heiress Winney Norton.
Norton, William. Pa. Private. 29 Aug. 1787. 200 acres.
Norvall, Henry Holdcraft. Va. Sergeant. 12 Jun. 1783. 200 acres.
Norvell, George. Va. Cornet. 2 Feb. 1810. 2666 2/3 acres.
Norvell, John. Va. Sergeant. 2 Feb. 1810. 400 acres.
Norvell, Lipscomb. Va. Lieutenant. 10 Feb. 1808. 148 acres.
Norwood, Daniel. S.C. Soldier. 15 Oct. 1784. 200 acres to John Norwood, heir at law.
Norwood, John. Ga. ———. 23 Apr. 1784. 1000 acres.
Norwood, Joseph. Va. Private. 18 Jun. 1783. 100 acres.
Norwood, Richard. Ga. Minute Man. 5 May 1785. 287 1/2 acres.
Norwood, Samuel. S.C. ———. 2 May 1785. 200 acres.
Norwood, Theophilus. N.C. Private. 14 Dec. 1796. 640 acres to heirs.
Norwood, Theopilis. S.C. ———. 4 Dec. 1786. 200 acres.
Norwood, William. N.C. Private. 7 Jan. 1786. 640 acres to heirs.
Nott, Nathaniel. Md. ———. ———. 50 acres.
Nouvester, John. N.C. Private. 22 Dec. 1796. 320 acres.
Nowe, Lewis. N. Y. Sergeant. 8 Jul. 1790. 600 acres.
Nowell, James. N.C. Private. 30 Sep. 1785. 640 acres to heirs.
Nowell, Josiah. N.C. Private. 8 Dec. 1823. 182 acres.
Nowell, Lipscomb. Va. Lieutenant. 10 Apr. 1783. 2666 2/3 acres.
Nowell, William. N.C. Private. 1 Sep. 1785. 640 acres to heirs.
Nowell, Zacheriah. Me. ———. 29 Dec. 1835. 200 acres. Portland.
Nowland, Jesse. N.C. Private. 22 Dec. 1796. 640 acres to heirs.
Nowland, John. Pa. Private. 26 Jan. 1787. 200 acres.
Nowland, Philip. Ga. ———. 15 Apr. 1784. 287 1/2 acres.
Nowland, William. Pa. Private. 14 Dec. 1786. 200 acres.
Noyes, Bela. Me. Private. 8 May 1835. 200 acres to widow Elizabeth Noyes. Greenwood.
Noyes, Dudley. Mass. Sergeant. 10 Sep. 1832. 200 acres to heirs.
Noyes, Jonathan. Mass. Private. 9 Aug. 1830. 200 acres.
Noyes, Paul. Conn. Sufferer. New/East Haven. 2.18.11.
Noyes, William. N. Y. Sergeant. 3 Jul. 1790. 600 acres.
Noyes, William. Conn. Sufferer. New/East Haven. 11.14.0.
Nucomb, Joseph. Va. Private. 12 Dec. 1833. 200 acres.

Nucum, Aaron. N.C. ———. 14 Jun. 1785. 640 acres to heir.

Nugan, Michael. Ga. Private. 28 Sep. 1784. 230 acres.

Null, Jacob. Va. Private. 14 May 1812. 100 acres.

Numery, Andrewson. N.C. Private. 10 Aug. 1785. 640 acres to heirs.

Nunally, Daniel. Va. Private. 24 Apr. 1786. 100 acres.

Nunally, John. Va. Sergeant. 25 Feb. 1784. 400 acres.

Nunally, Joseph. Va. Private. 25 Feb. 1784. 100 acres.

Nunally, Obadiah. Va. Private. 12 Nov. 1783. 100 acres.

Nunn, James. Va. Private. 19 Feb. 1818. 100 acres.

Nunn, Richard. Va. Private. 19 Feb. 1818. 100 acres.

Nunnamaker, John. Va. Private. 1 Apr. 1785. 100 acres.

Nunnemaker, Lewis. Va. Private. 27 Nov. 1783. 100 acres.

Nunnery, Henry. N.C. Private. 27 Nov. 1789. 228 acres.

Nusum, Etheldred. N.C. Private. 16 Feb. 1784. 640 acres.

Nutt, John. Va. Private. 19 Apr. 1797. 200 acres.

Nutt, Robert. Conn. Sufferer. Greenwich. 14.16.4.

Nutt, Thomas. Va. Sailor. 30 Jun. 1784. 100 acres.

Nuttal, Iverson. Va. Midshipman. 2 Sep. 1783. 2666 2/3 acres.

Nuttall, John. Va. Gunner's Mate. 19 Mar. 1835. 100 acres.

Nuttall, John. Va. ———. 27 Aug. 1835. 2566 2/3 acres.

Nutting, Abel. Me. Private. 23 Nov. 1835. 200 acres to widow Rhoda Green. Lisbon.

O'Banion, Thomas. Va. Private. 8 Jun. 1787. 200 acres.

O'Barn, William. Ga. Minute Man. 22 Mar. 1785. 250 acres.

O'Brian, James. Va. Private. 9 Feb. 1786. 100 acres.

O'Brian, John. Md. Private. ———. 50 acres.

O'Brian, Michael. Md. Bugler. ———. 50 acres.

O'Brian, Philip. Md. Corporal. ———. 50 acres.

O'Brien, Dennis. Pa. Lieutenant. ———. 200 acres.

O'Brien, Martin. Pa. Private. 4 Aug. 1787. 200 acres to Moses Barnett, executor.

O'Brien, Philip. Pa. Private. 11 Oct. 1786. 200 acres.

O'Brien, Thomas. N. Y. Private. 29 Jan. 1791. 600 acres.

O'Brien, William. Pa. Private. 28 Sep. 1787. 200 acres.

O'Brion, Samuel. N.C. Private. 9 Dec. 1797. 640 acres.

O'Bryan, Daniel. Pa. Private. ———. 200 acres.

O'Bryan, Duncan. Ga. Minute Man. 23 Apr. 1784. 287 1/2 acres.

O'Bryan, James. Ga. Private. 29 Jan. 1784. 200 acres.

O'Bryan, John. N. Y. Private. 7 Jul. 1790. 600 acres.

O'Bryan, Thomas. N. Y. Private. 3 Jul. 1790. 500 acres.

O'Bryan, William. N.C. Private. 12 Dec. 1820. 640 acres.

O'Bryon, James. Pa. Private. 17 Aug. 1787. 200 acres.

O'Conner, Edmond. Ga. ———. 18 Apr. 1784. 200 acres.

O'Connor, Timothy. Va. Private. 2 Aug. 1784. 100 acres.

O'Donnally, Benjamin. N.C. Private. 17 Feb. 1824. 640 acres.

O'Donohy, Patrick. N. Y. Private. 8 Jul. 1790. 600 acres.

O'Farrel, Michael. Md. Matross. ———. 50 acres.

O'Hara, Francis. Pa. ———. 17 Jan. 1803. 200 acres.

O'Hara, Joseph. Pa. ———. 9 Dec. 1803. 200 acres to his heirs.

O'Harrow, Michael. Va.-Ind. Private. 108 acres.

O'Hearn, Josiah. Ga. Refugee. 6 Feb. 1784. 250 acres.

O'Kain, James. Pa. Private. 6 Sep. 1789. 200 acres.

O'Kelly, Patrick. N.C. Private. 16 Aug. 1821. 640 acres.

O'Neal, Archibald. N.C. Private. 30 Sep. 1785. 640 acres to heirs.

O'Neal, Axom. Ga. ———. 21 Apr. 1784. 287 1/2 acres.

O'Neal, Edmond. Ga. ———. 15 Sep. 1784. 287 1/2 acres.

O'Neal, James. Pa. Private. 28 Oct. 1786. 200 acres to Stephen Loudon, assignee.

O'Neal, James. Pa. Private. 19 Mar. 1787. 200 acres to Stephen Loudon, assignee.

O'Neal, John. Pa. Sergeant. 7 Sep. 1787. 250 acres.

O'Neal, Mathias. N.C. Private. 30 Sep. 1785. 640 acres to heirs.

O'Neal, Nathaniel. Ga. ———. 15 Mar. 1784. 250 acres.

O'Neal, William. Ga. Private. Sep. 1785. 250 acres.

O'Neally, Abraham. Ga. Minute Man. 3 Sep. 1785.

O'Neally, John. Ga. Minute Man. 3 Sep. 1785.

O'Neill, Edward. Pa. Private. 18 Jun. 1787. 200 acres.

O'Niel, John. Ga. ———. 27 Apr. 1784. 287 1/2 acres.

O'Quinn, Daniel. Md. Private. ———. 50 acres.

O'Quynn, Richard. Md. Private. ———. 50 acres.

Oakes, Nathan. Conn. Sufferer. New/East Haven. 19.6.4.

Oakes, Robert. N.C. Drummer. 10 Feb. 1796. 1000 acres to heirs.

Oakley, Elijah. Md. Private. ———. 50 acres.

Oakley, Erasmus. Va. Sergeant. 31 Aug. 1830. 200 acres.

Oakley, George. Va. Sergeant. 11 Feb. 1784. 200 acres.

Oakley, John. Va.-Ind. Private. 108 acres.

Oakley, John. N. Y. Private. 3 Jul. 1790. 600 acres.

Oakley, Jonathan. N. Y. Private. 8 Jul. 1790. 500 acres.

Oakley, Thomas. N. Y. Matross. 7 Jul. 1790. 500 acres.

Oakman, William. Ga. Fife Major. 11 Feb. 1784. 200 acres.

Oakman, William. Va. Private. 6 May 1786. 100 acres.

Oaks, John. Me. ———. 12 May 1835. 200 acres. Exeter.

Oast, James. Va. Private. 15 Mar. 1832. 100 acres.

Oate, Daniel. N.C. Private. 30 Sep. 1785. 640 acres to heirs.

Oates, Jeremiah. Ga. ———. 21 Apr. 1784. 450 acres.

Oates, Richard. Ga. ———. 27 Apr. 1784. 287 1/2 acres.

Obarr, Daniel. N.C. Private. 9 Nov. 1784. 457 acres.

Obarr, Michael. N.C. Private. 22 Apr. 1785. 640 acres.

Obarr, Robert. N.C. Private. 9 Nov. 1784. 457 acres.

Obinion, William. N.C. Private. 21 Apr. 1784. 274 acres.

Obrian, Dennis. S.C. Soldier. 2 May 1785. 200 acres.

Obrian, Tide. N.C. Corporal. 30 Sep. 1785. 1000 acres to heirs.

Ocarrel, Henry. N.C. Corporal. 14 Feb. 1796. 1000 acres to heirs.

Oconner, Sullivan. N.C. Private. 22 Dec. 1796. 274 acres.

Odam, Harman. N.C. Private. 9 Dec. 1797. 640 acres.

Odam, Lewis. N.C. Private. 30 Sep. 1785. 640 acres to heirs.

Odell, Reuben. Va. Private. 29 Apr. 1785. 100 acres.

Oderbaugh, Peter. Pennsylvania. Private. 31 Aug. 1787. 200 acres.

Oderkirk, Myndert. N. Y. Private. 8 Jul. 1790. 600 acres.

Odgen, Daniel. Conn. Sufferer. Greenwich. 115.15.2.

Odin, Robert. N.C. Private. 2 Jun. 1813. 640 acres to heirs.

Odinsells, Charles. Ga. Captain. 25 May 1784. 575 acres.

Odonally, Hugh. N.C. Private. 21 Aug. 1820. 640 acres.

Odum, Dickenson. N.C. Private. 13 Dec. 1796. 640 acres to heirs.

Odum, Uriah. Ga. Minute Man. 27 Apr. 1784. 287 1/2 acres.

Offutt, Ezekiel. Ga. Refugee Captain. 26 May 1784. 287 1/2 acres.

Offutt, Jesse. Ga. Refugee. 27 Apr. 1784. 287 1/2 acres.

Offutt, John. Ga. 13 Sep. 1784. 287 1/2 acres.

Offutt, Nathaniel. Ga. Refugee. 27 Apr. 1784. 287 1/2 acres.

Ogan, Thomas. Va. Private. 12 Aug. 1785. 200 acres.

Ogden, Daniel. N. Y. Private. 8 Jul. 1790. 600 acres.

Ogden, David. N. Y. Private. 8 Jul. 1790. 600 acres.
Ogden, John. N. Y. Private. 8 Jul. 1790. 600 acres.
Ogden, Matthew. Va. Private. 22 Aug. 1783. 200 acres.
Ogden, Sarah. Conn. Sufferer. Fairfield. 19.6.1.
Oggden, Dempsy. N.C. Private. 22 Dec. 1796. 640 acres to heirs.
Ogier, George. S.C. Lieutenant. 2 May 1785. 175 acres.
Ogier, Lewis. S.C. Captain. 4 Sep. 1786. 300 acres.
Ogilsby, Robert. Va. Private. 31 Aug. 1786. 100 acres.
Ogle, Charles. N.C. Private. 15 Feb. 1797. 274 acres.
Ogle, Thomas. Va. Sergeant. 15 Dec. 1790. 200 acres.
Ogleby, George. Pa. Sergeant. 19 Jan. 1802. 250 acres to Elizabeth Ogleby, widow.
Ogleby, Nehemiah. N.C. Private. 22 Dec. 1796. 640 acres.
Oglesbey, Richard. N.C. Private. 9 Sep. 1785. 640 acres to heirs.
Ohlin, G. Henry. N. Y. Sergeant. 8 Jul. 1790. 600 acres.
Oile, Christian. Pa. Matross. 27 Jun. 1787. 200 acres to Caspar Snyder, assignee.
Oile, Nicholas. Pa. Matross. 21 Mar. 1787. 200 acres to heirs.
Oknoyata, Cornelius. N.Y. Lieutenant. 10 Aug. 1792. 1000 acres.
Oldham, Conway. Va. Captain. 8 Nov. 1782. 4000 acres.
Oldham, Edward. Md. Captain. ———. 200 acres.
Oldham, George. Va. Lieutenant. 15 Jun. 1807. 2666 2/3 acres.
Oldham, George. Va. Lieutenant. 2 Jul. 1840. 519 acres.
Oldridge, William. N.C. Private. 13 Jan. 1823. 228 acres.
Oldwin, Barney. Pa. Dragoon. 25 Jul. 1787. 200 acres.
Olendorph, Leonard. N. Y. Private. 8 Jul. 1790. 600 acres.
Olfin, Thomas. Va. Private. 21 Feb. 1784. 100 acres.
Olifer, Niell. N.C. Private. 14 Feb. 1796. 640 acres to heirs.
Oligood, Henry. N.C. Private. 17 Feb. 1824. 640 acres.
Olinger, Peter. N.C. Private. 7 Dec. 1796. 228 acres.
Oliphant, Benjamin. Va. Private. 2 Dec. 1785. 100 acres.
Oliphant, William. N. Y. Private. 8 Jul. 1790. 600 acres.
Oliver, Abisha. N.C. Private. 16 Aug. 1821. 640 acres.
Oliver, Dionysius. Ga. ———. 15 Mar. 1784. 250 acres.
Oliver, Isaac. Conn. Sufferer. New London. 40.7.3.
Oliver, James. Ga. ———. 27 Apr. 1784. 287 1/2 acres.
Oliver, John. Ga. Soldier. 15 Jul. 1785. 287 1/2 acres.
Oliver, John. Va. Private. 29 Apr. 1783. 200 acres.
Oliver, John. Va. Private. 27 Feb. 1833. 100 acres.
Oliver, Joseph. Pa. Sergeant. 14 Oct. 1786. 250 acres.
Oliver, Moses. Va. Private. 12 Aug. 1785. 200 acres.
Oliver, Nicholas. Va. Private. 12 May 1819. 200 acres.
Oliver, Peter. Ga. ———. 22 Apr. 1784. 250 acres.
Oliver, Samuel. S.C. ———. 4 Sep. 1786. 200 acres to Elizabeth Oliver, heir.
Oliver, Samuel. S.C. ———. 2 Oct. 1786. 200 acres.
Oliver, Stephen. Pa. Private. ———. 200 acres.
Oliver, William. Va. Captain Lieutenant. 30 May 1783. 4000 acres.
Oliver, William. Va. Private. 26 Jun. 1784. 100 acres.
Oliver, William. Va. Private. 19 Mar. 1835. 100 acres.
Olivier, Laurence. N. Y. Captain. ———. 1000 acres.
Olliver, Elijah. N.C. Private. 9 Nov. 1784. 640 acres to heir.
Olmstead, David. Conn. Sufferer. Ridgefield. 36.2.0.
Olmstead, Ebenezer. Conn. Sufferer. Ridgefield. 5.1.4.
Olmstead, James. Conn. Sufferer. Norwalk. 7.9.0.
Olmstead, James Small. Conn. Sufferer. Norwalk. 2.18.8.

Olmstead, Joseph. Conn. Sufferer. Norwalk. 2.8.0.
Olmstead, Samuel. Conn. Sufferer. Ridgefield. 74.18.9.
Olmstead, Samuel, 3d. Conn. Sufferer. Ridgefield. 23.16.7.
Olmsted, John. N. Y. ———. 16 Jan. 1795. 500 acres.
Olphin, William. N.C. Private. 1 Jul. 1825. 640 acres.
Olvis, Emanuel. Va. Private. 20 Dec. 1796. 100 acres.
Olyphant, David. S.C. Director General Hospital. 15 Oct. 1784. 850 acres.
Omenate, John. Va. Private. 10 Dec. 1783. 100 acres.
Omery, Owen. N.C. Private. 11 May 1785. 640 acres to Richard Omery, heir.
Onants, James. Md. Private. ———. 50 acres.
Oneal, Charles. N.C. Lieutenant. 26 Apr. 1784. 853 acres.
Oneal, Farrell. Va. Sergeant. 21 Aug. 1783. 400 acres.
Oneal, Ferdinand. Va. Captain. 17 Jul. 1783. 4000 acres.
Oneal, Ferdinand. Va. Captain. 7 Jan. 1802. 666 2/3 acres.
Oneal, Isham. N.C. Private. 30 Sep. 1785. 640 acres to heirs.
Oneal, James. N.C. ———. 21 May 1784. 640 acres to heirs.
Oneal, John. N.C. Private. 22 Dec. 1796. 274 acres.
Oneal, John. Va. Private. 29 Jan. 1784. 200 acres.
Oneal, William. Va. Private. 29 Sep. 1783. 100 acres.
Onion, John. Md. Fifer. ———. 50 acres.
Onions, Selby. Va. Private. 15 Jan. 1807. 200 acres.
Onooles, Isham. N.C. Private. 30 Sep. 1785. 640 acres to heirs.
Onslow, David. N.C. Private. 10 Feb. 1796. 228 acres.
Onslow, George. Ga. Minute Man. 3 Sep. 1785. ———.
Onslow, John. N.C. Private. 10 Feb. 1796. 274 acres.
Oosterhoudt, Peter. N.Y. ———. 13 Sep. 1790. 500 acres to heirs.
Oothoudt, Tilman. N.Y. ———. 13 Sep. 1790. 500 acres to heirs.
Oram, Henry. Va. Private. 20 Jun. 1783. 100 acres.
Oram, James. N.C. Private. 22 Sep. 1795. 640 acres to heirs.
Oram, John. N.C. Private. 13 Sep. 1820. 640 acres.
Oram, Samuel. Md. Private. ———. 50 acres.
Orange, William. N.C. Private. 26 Aug. 1785. 640 acres to heirs.
Ord, John. N.C. Private. 15 Feb. 1797. 640 acres to heirs.
Ordon, Peter. N.C. Private. 10 Dec. 1788. 640 acres to heirs.
Oreer, Daniel. Va.-Ind. Private. 108 acres.
Oreer, Jesse. Va.-Ind. Private. 108 acres.
Oreer, John. Va.-Ind. Sergeant. 216 acres.
Oreer, William. Va.-Ind. Private. 108 acres.
Organ, Cornelious. Va. Private. 18 Sep. 1797. 100 acres.
Organ, John. Pa. Private. ———. 200 acres to Matthew Organ, administrator.
Organ, John. Pa. Private. 7 Oct. 1786. 200 acres.
Organ, Matthew. Pa. Private. ———. 200 acres.
Orgin, Isaac. Mass. ———. 17 May 1829. 200 acres.
Orish, James. Va. Private. 23 Jun. 1783. 200 acres.
Orme, Charles. Md. Private. ———. 50 acres.
Ornsby, Daniel. Ga. Fife Major. 17 May 1784. 230 acres to heirs, widow Mary Berry & daughter Isabella Ornsby.
Orr, Alexander. Me. Lieutenant. 4 Dec. 1838. 600 acres to widow Deborah Ames. Camden.
Orr, Baltus. N. Y. Private. 7 Jul. 1790. 600 acres.
Orr, Charles. N.C. ———. 7 May 1784. 640 acres to Nathan Orr, heir.
Orr, Charles. N.C. Corporal. 1 Aug. 1820. 360 acres to heirs.
Orr, Charles. S.C. ———. 2 Apr. 1798. 60 acres.
Orr, Charles. S.C. ———. 3 Feb. 1800. 17 1/2 acres.
Orr, Charles. S.C. ———. 8 May 1798. 60 acres.
Orr, Daniel. N. Y. Private. 8 Jul. 1790. 600 acres.
Orr, James. N.C. Private. 30 Sep. 1785. 640 acres to heirs.

Orr, John. Pa. Sergeant. 19 Dec. 1786. 250 acres.
Orr, Samuel. N.C. Private. 23 Apr. 1785. 640 acres to heirs.
Orr, Samuel. Va. Private. 21 Sep. 1782. 100 acres.
Orr, William. N. Y. Private. 8 Jul. 1790. 600 acres.
Orrell, Thomas. N.C. Lieutenant. 29 Sep. 1784. 1144 acres.
Orwick, James. Ga. Soldier. 20 Feb. 1784. 250 acres.
Orwie, James. Ga. Soldier. 7 Jan. 1784. ———.
Osborn, Aaron. N. Y. Corporal. 8 Jul. 1790. 600 acres.
Osborn, Abigail. Conn. Sufferer. Fairfield. 106.9.9.
Osborn, Benjamin. Conn. Sufferer. Fairfield. 152.0.0 to heirs.
Osborn, Daniel. Conn. Sufferer. Fairfield. 135.5.0.
Osborn, Daniel. Conn. Sufferer. Fairfield. 0.13.6.
Osborn, David. Conn. Sufferer. Fairfield. 21.9.0.
Osborn, David. Conn. Sufferer. New/East Haven. 30.14.5.
Osborn, Eleazer, Jr. Conn. Sufferer. Fairfield. 181.2.9.
Osborn, Hugh. Me. Private. 5 May 1835. 200 acres. Rome.
Osborn, James. Me. ———. 29 Jul. 1835. 200 acres. Kennebunk.
Osborn, Mabel. Conn. Sufferer. Fairfield. 605.0.2
Osborn, Mehitabel. Conn. Sufferer. New/ East Haven. 3.12.3.
Osborn, Samuel. Conn. Sufferer. Fairfield. 36.13.6.
Osborne, Jesse. N.C. Private. 15 Feb. 1797. 640 acres to heirs.
Osbourn, Jeremiah. N. Y. Sergeant. 9 Jul. 1790. 600 acres.
Osburn, Ebenezer. Va.-Ind. Private. 108 acres.
Osburn, Elijah. Va. Private. 24 Sep. 1783. 200 acres.
Osburn, George. Va. Private. 18 Feb. 1786. 100 acres.
Osburn, John. Md. Private. ———. 50 acres.
Osburn, Samuel. Va. Private. 23 Jun. 1783. 200 acres.
Osgood, Asa. Me. ———. 23 Oct. 1835. 200 acres to widow Hannah Osgood. Hiram.
Osgood, John. Ga. Refugee. 8 Jun. 1784. 250 acres.
Osgood, Josiah. Ga. Private. 8 Jun. 1784. 250 acres.
Osmun, John. N. Y. Sergeant. 3 Jul. 1790. 600 acres.
Ossey, Francis. N.Y. ———. 8 Jul. 1790. 500 acres.
Osten [or Austin], Henry. Md. Private. ———. 50 acres.
Osterhoudt, Peter. N. Y. Private. 8 Jul. 1790. 600 acres.
Osterhout, Isaac. N. Y. Private. 7 Jul. 1790. 600 acres.
Oston, William. N.C. Private. 10 Dec. 1788. 640 acres to heirs.
Ostrander, Thomas. N. Y. Lieutenant. 9 Jul. 1790. 1000 acres.
Ostrander, W. Peter. N. Y. Corporal. 7 Jul. 1790. 600 acres.
Oswald, Joseph. Ga. Refugee. 23 Apr. 1784. 250 acres.
Oswald, Thomas. Ga. Refugee. 23 Apr. 1784. 250 acres.
Otaawightow, John. N.Y. Captain. 29 Jan. 1791. 1800 acres. [an Indian].
Ott, Elias. Pa. ———. 2 Mar. 1803. 200 acres.
Oundsley, Charles. Va.-Ind. Private. 108 acres. [Houndsler].
Ouram, Timothy. N.C. Private. 8 Dec. 1796. 640 acres to heirs.
Ouse, Jonathan. N.C. Private. 13 Dec. 1796. 640 acres to heirs.
Ousler, Faramon. N.C. Private. 22 Dec. 1796. 640 acres.
Ousley, Thomas. N.C. Private. 8 Dec. 1796. 640 acres.
Ousley, Thomas. Va. Private. 25 Jul. 1821. 200 acres.
Ousley, Welden. Ga. ———. 21 Apr. 1784. 287 1/2 acres.
Oust, George. Va. Corporal. 21 Jul. 1783. 400 acres.
Outerbridge, Leonard. Md. Private. ———. 50 acres.
Outhouse, Peter. Md. Private. ———. 50 acres.
Outlaw, Edward. Ga. ———. 26 Feb. 1784. 250 acres.

Outlaw, Jesse. N.C. Private. 9 Dec. 1797. 342 acres.
Outlaw, John. N.C. Private. 22 Dec. 1796. 640 acres to heirs.
Outlaw, Lewis. N.C. Private. 5 Sep. 1821. 640 acres.
Outlaw, Ludwick. Ga. Refugee. 24 May 1784. 287 1/2 acres to heir son James Outlaw.
Outlaw, Moses. N.C. Private. 9 Dec. 1797. 640 acres.
Outlow, Aaron. N.C. Private. 30 Sep. 1785. 640 acres to heirs.
Oven, John. N.C. Private. 22 Dec. 1796. 640 acres to heirs.
Overall, Marmaduke. N.C. Private. 13 Dec. 1796. 640 acres to heirs.
Overall, Nathaniel. Va. Private. 30 Sep. 1812. 100 acres.
Overcreek, Joseph. Md. Private. ———. 50 acres.
Overlin, William. Va. Private. 23 Jun. 1783. 200 acres.
Overman, Henry. Pa. ———. 7 May 1796. 200 acres to Jacob Miley, assignee.
Overman, Henry. Pa. Private. 8 Dec. 1786. 200 acres.
Overstreet, Benoni. Va. Sergeant. 24 Apr. 1784. 200 acres.
Overstreet, John. Ga. ———. 2 Jan. 1786. ———.
Overstreet, John. N.C. Private. 30 Sep. 1785. 640 acres to heirs.
Overstreet, John. Va. Private. 15 Jun. 1785. 100 acres.
Overton, Caleb. N.C. Private. 11 Aug. 1820. 274 acres to heirs.
Overton, Daniel. N.C. Private. 11 Aug. 1820. 274 acres to heirs.
Overton, James. N.C. Private. 12 May 1784. 365 acres.
Overton, Jerry. N.C. Private. 9 Dec. 1797. 274 acres.
Overton, Joab. N.C. Private. 8 Jun. 1792. 640 acres.
Overton, John. N.C. Private. 17 Dec. 1785. 274 acres.
Overton, John. N.C. Private. 11 Aug. 1820. 640 acres to heirs.
Overton, John. Va. Captain. 25 Dec. 1783. 4000 acres.
Overton, John. Va. Captain. 5 May 1800. 666 2/3 acres.
Overton, Lemuel. N.C. Private. 11 Aug. 1820. 274 acres.
Overton, Nathaniel. Conn. Sufferer. New London. 27.9.0.
Overton, Samuel. N.C. Private. 6 Dec. 1796. 274 acres.
Overton, Solomon. N.C. Sergeant. 30 Sep. 1785. 1000 acres to heirs.
Overton, Thomas. Va. Lieutenant. 6 Dec. 1782. 2666 2/3 acres.
Overton, Thomas. Va. Captain. 18 Nov. 1783. 1333 1/3 acres.
Overton, Thomas. Va. Captain. 1 Jun. 1805. 666 2/3 acres.
Overton, Thomas. Va. Captain. 29 Aug. 1807. 555 acres.
Owel, James. N.C. Private. 30 Sep. 1785. 274 acres.
Owel, John. N.C. Private. 30 Sep. 1785. 640 acres to heirs.
Owen, Charles. Va. Private. 9 May 1783. 200 acres.
Owen, Evans. Va. Private. 28 Apr. 1785. 100 acres.
Owen, Francis. N.C. Private. 25 Oct. 1783. 278 acres.
Owen, Herbert. Va. Private. 16 Aug. 1797. 100 acres.
Owen, John. Pa. Private. 10 Aug. 1787. 200 acres.
Owen, Joseph. Conn. Sufferer. New London. 75.18.6.
Owen, Philip. Me. Private. 17 Apr. 1835. 200 acres. Brunswick.
Owen, Richard M. Va. Lieutenant. 24 Dec. 1830. 2666 2/3 acres.
Owen, Samuel. Va. Private. 27 Nov. 1832. 200 acres.
Owen, Vincent. Va. Private. 8 Dec. 1783. 100 acres.
Owen, William. Va. Private. 14 Jun. 1787. 100 acres.
Owens, Aaron. Ga. Soldier. 1 May 1785. ———.
Owens, Christopher. Va. Sergeant. 25 Mar. 1784. 200 acres.
Owens, Daniel. N. Y. Sergeant. 8 Jul. 1790. 600 acres.
Owens, David. N.C. Private. 27 Nov. 1789. 640 acres to heirs.
Owens, Ephraim. Ga. ———. 27 Apr. 1784. 287 1/2 acres.
Owens, Ephraim. Va. Corporal. 30 Dec. 1784. 200 acres.

Owens, Jacob. Md. Matross. ———. 50 acres.
Owens, Jacob. N.C. Private. 26 Sep. 1821. 185 acres.
Owens, James. Md. Private. ———. 50 acres.
Owens, John. Md. Private. ———. 50 acres.
Owens, John. N.C. Private. 18 Nov. 1800. 274 acres.
Owens, John E. N.C. Private. 10 Feb. 1796. 640 acres to heirs.
Owens, Joseph. Md. Private. ———. 50 acres.
Owens, Maberry. N. Y. Private. 8 Jul. 1790. 500 acres.
Owens, Robert. Ga. Refugee. 25 Feb. 1784. 250 acres.
Owens, Samuel. Md. Private. ———. 50 acres.
Owens, Stephen. Md. Private. ———. 50 acres.
Owens, Stephen. N.C. Lieutenant. 10 Jan. 1794. 1097 acres.
Owens, Thomas. Ga. ———. 13 Apr. 1784. 287 1/2 acres.
Owens, Thomas. N.Y. ———. 13 Sep. 1790. 500 acres to heirs.
Owens, Thomas E. N.C. Private. 10 Feb. 1796. 640 acres to heirs.
Owens, Uriah. N. Y. Private. 8 Jul. 1790. 500 acres.
Owens, William. Ga. Soldier. 15 Jul. 1785. ———.
Owens, William. N.C. Private. 26 Aug. 1785. 640 acres to heirs.
Owl, Robert. Va. Private. 11 Aug. 1783. 200 acres.
Owles, Piram. N.C. Private. 16 Sep. 1820. 274 acres to heirs.
Owsley, Abraham. Ga. Minute Man. 3 Sep. 1785. ———.
Owsley, John. Ga. ———. ———. 287 1/2 acres.
Owsley, Robert. Ga. 16 Jul. 1784. 287 1/2 acres.
Oxx, Michael. Pa. Private. 15 Aug. 1787. 200 acres.
Oyler, John. N.C. Private. 13 Jan. 1823. 274 acres.
Pace, Barnard. Ga. ———. 30 Apr. 1784. 287 1/2 acres.
Pace, Demsey. N.C. Private. 15 Jul. 1785. 640 acres to heir.
Pace, Thomas. Ga. Refugee. 26 Jul. 1784. 287 1/2 acres.
Pace, William. Va. Private. 20 Oct. 1783. 200 acres.
Pack, James. Md. ———. ———. 50 acres.
Packard, Nehemiah. Me. Private. 29 Jun. 1835. 200 acres. Minot.
Packetts, Richard. Va. Private. 4 Sep. 1783. 100 acres.
Packwood, Joseph. Conn. Sufferer. New London. 817.5.4.
Packwood, William. Conn. Sufferer. New London. 12.6.0.
Padder, John. N. Y. Private. 3 Jul. 1790. 600 acres.
Paddin, Thomas. N.C. ———. 18 Jun. 1785. 640 acres to heirs.
Padgett, Thomas. N.C. Private. 29 Sep. 1784. 640 acres.
Padrick, John. N.Y. ———. 13 Sep. 1790. 500 acres to heirs.
Pafford, William. N.C. Private. 30 Apr. 1784. 640 acres.
Pagan, David. Va.-Ind. Private. 108 acres.
Page, Abraham. Me. Second Sergeant. ———. 200 acres. Belgrade.
Page, Abraham. N.C. Private. 20 Jan. 1785. 640 acres to heirs.
Page, Carter. Va. Captain. 26 May 1784. 4000 acres.
Page, Daniel. Me. ———. 1 May 1835. 200 acres. Fairfield.
Page, Ichabod. Conn. Sufferer. New/East Haven. 59.9.6.
Page, James. Pa. Private. 11 Oct. 1786. 200 acres.
Pagram, William. Md. Private. ———. 50 acres.
Pain, Armon. N.C. Private. 10 Dec. 1788. 640 acres to heirs.
Pain, Charles. Mass. Corporal. 14 Jun. 1830. 200 acres.
Pain, John. N.C. Private. 10 Dec. 1788. 640 acres to heirs.
Paine, John. Md. Matross. ———. 50 acres.
Paine, Samuel. Ga. Minute Man. 15 Apr. 1784. 287 1/2 acres.
Paine, Thomas. Me. ———. 19 Aug. 1835. 200 acres. Pownal.
Paine, William. Pa. Private. 26 Oct. 1784. 200 acres.

Pains, Peter. N.C. Private. 30 Sep. 1785. 640 acres to heirs.
Painter, Edward. N. Y. Private. 8 Jul. 1790. 600 acres.
Painter, Elijah. Conn. Sufferer. New/East Haven. 14.0.0.
Painter, George. Va. Sergeant. 4 Nov. 1819. 400 acres.
Painter, Lamberton. Conn. Sufferer. New/East Haven. 11.12.0.
Painter, Lamberton. Conn. Sufferer. New/East Haven. 24.0.0.
Paintree, John. Va.-Ind. Private. 108 acres.
Pair, George. Va. Private. 20 May 1783. 200 acres.
Pair, George. Va. Private. 12 Aug. 1785. 200 acres.
Paivel, James. Md. ———. ———. 50 acres.
Pale, William. N.C. Private. 14 Dec. 1796. 640 acres to heirs.
Pall, Jacob. N.C. Private. 12 Dec. 1796. 640 acres to heirs.
Palmer, ——— Widow. Conn. Sufferer. New London. 48.0.0.
Palmer, Abigail. Conn. Sufferer. Groton. 6.19.4.
Palmer, Andrew. Pa. Private. 15 Nov. 1786. 200 acres.
Palmer, Andrew. Conn. Sufferer. New London. 105.10.0.
Palmer, Benjamin. N.C. Private. 30 Sep. 1785. 640 acres to heirs.
Palmer, Charles. Va. Private. 12 Apr. 1785. 100 acres.
Palmer, Daniel. Conn. Sufferer. Greenwich. 35.19.2.
Palmer, David. Va. Corporal. 26 Apr. 1783. 200 acres.
Palmer, Denham. Conn. Sufferer. Greenwich. 2.6.8.
Palmer, Elisha. N.C. Private. 10 Dec. 1788. 640 acres to heirs.
Palmer, George. Ga. ———. 23 Apr. 1784. 287 1/2 acres.
Palmer, Jeffery. Va. Private. 20 Apr. 1784. 100 acres.
Palmer, Jeremiah & John Wood Palmer. Conn. Sufferers. Greenwich. 9.9.3.
Palmer, John. Ga. Minute Man. 25 May 1784. 287 1/2 acres.
Palmer, John. Conn. Sufferer. Greenwich. 4.2.0.
Palmer, Joseph. N.C. Private. 30 Sep. 1785. 640 acres.
Palmer, Joseph. Pa. Private. 5 Mar. 1787. 200 acres.
Palmer, Joseph. Conn. Sufferer. Greenwich. 100.9.1..
Palmer, Robert. N.C. Private. 5 Sep. 1821. 640 acres.
Palmer, Samuel. Conn. Sufferer. Greenwich. 77.4.2.
Palmer, Simeon. Me. Private. 13 Apr. 1838. 200 acres. Windsor.
Palmer, Stephen. Conn. Sufferer. Greenwich. 6.16.1.
Palmer, Thomas. Va. Private. 20 Mar. 1783. 100 acres.
Palmer, Titus. Conn. Sufferer. Greenwich. 3.0.0.
Palmer, William. Va. Corporal. 5 Apr. 1783. 200 acres.
Palmer, William. Va. Sergeant. 17 Jan. 1809. 200 acres.
Palmer, Winans. Conn. Sufferer. Greenwich. 6.14.2.
Palmeter, John. N. Y. Private. 7 Jul. 1790. 600 acres.
Palmeter, Joseph. N.Y. ———. 13 Sep. 1790. 500 acres to heirs.
Palmetier, Isaac. N. Y. Private. 7 Jul. 1790. 500 acres.
Palmetier, William. N. Y. Private. 13 Sep. 1790. 500 acres.
Palmier, John. Va. Private. 8 Apr. 1856. 100 acres.
Palmiers, John. Va. Private. 31 Dec. 1851. 100 acres.
Palmore, Jonathan. N. Y. Private. 8 Jul. 1790. 600 acres.
Palmour, Solomon. Ga. Soldier. 25 Feb. 1784. 250 acres.
Pangburn, John. N. Y. Private. 8 Jul. 1790. 600 acres.
Pangburn, William. N. Y. Private. 8 Jul. 1790. 500 acres.
Pannell, David. Va. Captain. 27 Nov. 1834. 2550 acres.
Pannell, David. Va. Captain. 27 Nov. 1834. 850 acres.
Pannell, David. Va. Captain. 26 Mar. 1842. 166 2/3 acres.
Pannell, David. Va. Captain. 25 Jun. 1844. 250 acres.
Pannell, Evan. N.C. Private. 14 Dec. 1797. 274 acres.

Pannier, Peter. N. Y. Private. 8 Jul. 1790. 600 acres.
Pannill, David. Va. ———. 23 Mar. 1835. 200 acres.
Pannill, Joseph. Ga. Lieutenant Colonel. 31 Jan. 1784. 900 acres.
Papin, Joseph. Va. Private. 31 Dec. 1851. 100 acres.
Papin, Joseph. Va. Private. 8 Apr. 1856. 100 acres.
Parakee, Emanuel. N.C. Private. 17 Dec. 1785. 640 acres to heirs.
Paramore, Amos. N.C. Corporal. 6 Dec. 1802. 428 acres.
Pardo, Joseph. Pa. Private. ———. 200 acres.
Pardy, Benjamin. Conn. Sufferer. New/East Haven. 88.12.0.
Pardy, Jacob and Abijah Pardy. Conn. Sufferers. New/East Haven. 402.8.2.
Pardy, Levi. Conn. Sufferer. New/East Haven. 3.15.0.
Pardy, Mary. Conn. Sufferer. New/East Haven. 134.14.0.
Pardy, Mary & Lydia Pardy. Conn. Sufferers. New/East Haven. 40.8.4.
Pardy, Moses. Conn. Sufferer. New/East Haven. 15.14.0.
Parent, Henry. N. Y. ———. ———. 500 acres.
Parham, Drury. N.C. Private. 28 Nov. 1795. 228 acres.
Parham, Richard. Ga. Soldier. 17 Jan. 1785. 230 acres to heirs.
Paris, Anthony. N. Y. Matross. 9 Jul. 1790. 600 acres.
Paris, Peter. Ga. ———. 17 Apr. 1784. 287 1/2 acres.
Parish, Abraham. N.C. Private. 23 Nov. 1797. 640 acres to heirs.
Parish, Booker. N.C. Private. 15 Dec. 1797. 640 acres.
Parish, Johnston. N.C. Private. 15 Dec. 1797. 640 acres to heirs.
Parish, Moses. Va. Private. 20 Jan. 1798. 100 acres.
Parish, Peter. Va. Sergeant. 25 Nov. 1783. 200 acres.
Parish, William. Va. Sergeant. 4 Oct. 1783. 200 acres.
Parish, William. Va. Pilot. 17 Sep. 1850. 750 acres.
Parish, William. Va. Pilot. 17 Sep. 1850. 500 acres.
Parish, William. Va. Pilot. 17 Sep. 1850. 500 acres.
Parish, William. Va. Pilot. 17 Sep. 1850. 277 1/3 acres.
Parish, William. Va. Pilot. 17 Sep. 1850. 638 2/3 acres.
Park, John. Mass. Matross. 7 Jan. 1834. 200 acres to widow Lucy Park.
Parker, Alexander. Pa. Captain. 27 Jun. 1789. 500 acres.
Parker, Alexander. Va. Captain. 15 Oct. 1783. 5333 1/3 acres.
Parker, Allen. Ga. Refugee. ———. 250 acres.
Parker, Anderson. Va. Private. 14 Feb. 1834. 100 acres.
Parker, Arthur. N.C. Private. 6 Dec. 1783. 228 acres.
Parker, Arthur. N.C. Lieutenant. 17 Sep. 1785. 1000 acres to heirs.
Parker, Benjamin. N.C. Private. 14 Dec. 1787. 640 acres.
Parker, Caleb. Va. Private. 15 Jun. 1807. 200 acres.
Parker, Charles. Ga. ———. 250 acres. ———.
Parker, Charles. N.C. Private. 15 Feb. 1797. 365 acres.
Parker, Daniel. Ga. ———. 23 Apr. 1784. 287 1/2 acres.
Parker, Ebenezer. N. Y. Private. 8 Jul. 1790. 500 acres.
Parker, Edmond. N. Y. Corporal. 9 Jul. 1790. 600 acres.
Parker, Edmund. Me. ———. 18 Apr. 1835. 200 acres. Norridgewock.
Parker, Edward. Va.-Ind. Sergeant. 216 acres.
Parker, Elisha. N. Y. Private. 7 Jul. 1790. 600 acres.
Parker, Ephraim. N.C. Private. 8 Dec. 1796. 274 acres.
Parker, George. Ga. Refugee Private. ———. 500 acres.
Parker, George. Md. Private. ———. 50 acres.
Parker, George. Pa. Private. 18 Oct. 1787. 200 acres.
Parker, Hillary. N.C. Private. 1 Jan. 1794. 640 acres to heirs.
Parker, Isum. N.C. Private. 30 Sep. 1785. 640 acres to heirs.
Parker, J. Richard. N. Y. Drummer. 8 Jul. 1790. 600 acres.

Parker, Jackson. N. Y. Matross. 9 Jul. 1790. 600 acres.
Parker, James. Ga. Refugee Private. 10 Dec. 1784. 250 acres.
Parker, James. N. Y. Sergeant. 7 Jul. 1790. 600 acres.
Parker, James. N.C. Private. 24 Nov. 1796. 228 acres.
Parker, Jeptha. N.C. Sergeant. 22 Oct. 1783. 1000 acres.
Parker, Jeremiah. Va. Sergeant. 11 Aug. 1783. 200 acres.
Parker, Jesse. N.C. Sergeant. 21 Aug. 1820. 1000 acres.
Parker, Jesse. Va. Private. 31 Aug. 1830. 100 acres.
Parker, John. Ga. Soldier. 27 Apr. 1784. 287 1/2 acres.
Parker, John. Ga. Refugee Lieutenant. ———. ———.
Parker, John. Me. Private. 14 Jan. 1836. 200 acres to widow Anne Parker. Westbrook.
Parker, John. N.C. Private. 8 Dec. 1796. 640 acres to heirs.
Parker, John. Pa. Sergeant. 11 Aug. 1787. 250 acres.
Parker, John. Va. Private. 1 Nov. 1791. 200 acres.
Parker, Joseph. Ga. ———. 28 Feb. 1784. 250 acres.
Parker, Joseph. N.C. Sergeant. 20 Jan. 1785. 1000 acres to heirs.
Parker, Joseph. Va. Corporal. 30 Sep. 1783. 200 acres.
Parker, Josiah. Va. Colonel. 21 Nov. 1783. 6666 2/3 acres.
Parker, Leonard. N.C. Sergeant. 16 Aug. 1821. 1000 acres.
Parker, Levin. Va. Private. 15 Jun. 1807. 100 acres.
Parker, Nicholas. Va. Lieutenant. 17 Jun. 1783. 2666 2/3 acres.
Parker, Phineas. Ga. ———. 1784. 287 1/2 acres.
Parker, Richard. Va. Colonel. 4 Jun. 1783. 6666 2/3 acres.
Parker, Richard. Va. Lieutenant. 31 Mar. 1831. 1000 acres.
Parker, Richard. Va. Lieutenant. 30 Mar. 1831. 3000 acres.
Parker, Richard. Va. Lieutenant. 12 Dec. 1831. 1000 acres.
Parker, Richard. Va. Lieutenant. 12 Dec. 1831. 1000 acres.
Parker, Richard. Va. Lieutenant. 12 Dec. 1831. 1000 acres.
Parker, Richard. Va. Colonel. 18 Mar. 1834. 678 acres.
Parker, Richard. Va. Colonel. 26 Mar. 1838. 2361 acres.
Parker, Robert. Pa. Lieutenant. ———. 200 acres.
Parker, Robert. Pa. Captain/Lieutenant. 28 Feb. 1794. 200 acres.
Parker, Robert. Va. Corporal. 10 Jun. 1783. 200 acres.
Parker, Samuel. Mass. Matross. 25 Feb. 1833. 200 acres.
Parker, Samuel. N.C. Captain. 23 Oct. 1783. 3840 acres to Kedar Parker, heir.
Parker, Samuel. N.C. Private. 16 Aug. 1821. 640 acres.
Parker, Simon. N.C. Private. 20 Apr. 1784. 640 acres.
Parker, Thomas. N.C. Private. 1 Jan. 1794. 640 acres.
Parker, Thomas. Pa. Private. 25 Aug. 1787. 200 acres to Hannah Newan, widow.
Parker, Thomas. Va. Captain. 4 Jun. 1783. 4000 acres.
Parker, Thomas. Va. Captain. 27 Apr. 1784. 4000 acres.
Parker, Thomas. Va. Captain. 27 Apr. 1784. 666 2/3 acres.
Parker, Thomas. Va. Private. 13 Jun. 1786. 100 acres.
Parker, Thomas. Va. Captain. 29 Aug. 1807. 555 acres.
Parker, Thomas. Va. Captain. 30 Dec. 1808. 555 acres.
Parker, Thomas. Va. Midshipman. 22 Jul. 1834. 2666 2/3 acres.
Parker, Warren. Va. Sergeant. 24 Sep. 1783. 400 acres.
Parker, Watts. Va. Sergeant. 4 Nov. 1783. 200 acres.
Parker, William. Ga. ———. 22 Apr. 1784. 550 acres.
Parker, William. N.C. Private. 1 Sep. 1785. 640 acres to heirs.
Parker, William. N.C. Sergeant. 29 Nov. 182-. 1000 acres to heirs.
Parker, William. Va. Private. 3 May 1823. 200 acres.
Parker, William H. V. Lieutenant. 5 Aug. 1831. 1333 1/3 acres.

Parker, William Harway. Va. Lieutenant. 20 May 1783. 2666 2/3 acres.
Parker, Wyatt. Va. Private. 13 Jun. 1783. 100 acres.
Parkes, Hugh. N.C. Private. 26 May 1784. 274 acres.
Parkes, James. N.C. Private. 15 Feb. 1797. 228 acres.
Parkes, Solomon. N.C. Ensign. 24 Dec. 1785. 733 acres.
Parkes, William. N.C. Private. 17 Dec. 1785. 640 acres.
Parkeson, James. N.C. Lieutenant. 25 Oct. 1783. 2560 acres.
Parkhurst, Nathan. Me. ———. 6 Mar. 1843. 200 acres to widow Sarah Parkhurst. Unity.
Parkinson, John. Md. Private. ———. 50 acres.
Parks, Andrew. N.C. Private. 17 Feb. 1824. 640 acres.
Parks, Charles. Ga. ———. 20 Apr. 1784. 287 1/2 acres.
Parks, Charles, Sr. Ga. ———. 27 Apr. 1784. 287 1/2 acres.
Parks, Henry. Va. Private. 2 May 1783. 200 acres.
Parks, James. Va. Lieutenant. 10 Apr. 1798. 2666 2/3 acres.
Parks, John. Ga. Lieutenant. 15 Mar. 1784. 350 acres.
Parks, John. N. Y. Private. 13 Sep. 1790. 600 acres.
Parks, John. Pa. Private. ———. 200 acres.
Parks, Samuel. N.C. Private. 30 Sep. 1785. 640 acres to heirs.
Parks, Solomon. N.C. Private. 12 Sep. 1785. 640 acres to heirs.
Parks, Solomon. Va. Private. 15 Jun. 1807. 200 acres.
Parler, James. Va. Private. 23 Jun. 1783. 200 acres.
Parmaley, Ephraim. N.C. Private. 2 Dec. 1785. 640 acres.
Parmely, Hezekiah. Conn. Sufferer. New/East Haven. 109.5.1.
Parmely, Jeremiah. Conn. Sufferer. New/East Haven. 18.17.0.
Parmely, Sarah. Conn. Sufferer. New/East Haven. 8.17.2.
Parmenter, Levi. Mass. Private. 21 Mar. 1834. 200 acres to assignee Abner Coburn.
Parmenter, Luther. Mass. Private. 18 Oct. 1833. 200 acres.
Parmer, George. Ga. ———. 17 May 1784. ———.
Parmer, John. Ga. ———. 17 May 1784. ———.
Parmer, Jonathan. Ga. ———. ———. 287 1/2 acres.
Parmer, Solomon, Sr. Ga. ———. ———. 287 1/2 acres.
Parmer, Thomas. Ga. ———. 30 Sep. 1784. ———.
Parnal, James. S.C. ———. 7 Oct. 1793. 120 acres.
Parnal, James. S.C. ———. 7 Oct. 1793. 80 acres.
Parnal, Joshua. N.C. Private. 12 Sep. 1785. 640 acres to heirs.
Parnel, Abraham. N.C. Private. 13 Jan. 1823. 640 acres.
Parnel, Benjamin. Va. Private. 6 Jan. 1808. 100 acres.
Parnel, Joseph. Va. Private. 6 Jan. 1808. 100 acres.
Parnold, James. S.C. ———. 7 Sep. 1795. 65 acres.
Parnold, James. S.C. ———. 7 Sep. 1795. 35 acres.
Parnold, James. S.C. ———. 7 Sep. 1795. 80 acres.
Parnold, James. S.C. ———. 7 Sep. 1795. 20 acres.
Parr, Caleb. N.C. Private. 1 Dec. 1797. 274 acres.
Parr, Isaiah. N.C. Private. 6 Jan. 1784. 274 acres.
Parr, Isaiah. N.C. Sergeant. 1 May 1826. 154 acres to heirs.
Parr, James. Pa. Major. ———. 300 acres to Thomas Denton, assignee.
Parr, James. Pa. Major. 21 Oct. 1786. 300 acres to Thomas Denton, assignee.
Parr, James. Va. Private. 22 Mar. 1839. 200 acres.
Parr, Matthias. N. Y. Private. 8 Jul. 1790. 600 acres.
Parr, Noah. N.C. Private. 6 Jan. 1784. 640 acres.
Parr, William. N.C. Private. 21 May 1784. 274 acres.
Parramore, Thomas. Va. Captain. 20 Dec. 1822. 4000 acres.
Parramore, Thomas. Va. Captain. 15 Jan. 1823. 666 2/3 acres.

Parriott, John. Va. Private. 24 Oct. 1821. 100 acres.
Parrish, Henry. N.C. Private. 3 Feb. 1785. 274 acres.
Parrish, Henry. Va. Sergeant. 7 Feb. 1786. 200 acres.
Parrish, John. N.C. Private. 29 Sep. 1784. 280 acres.
Parrish, John. Va. Pilot. 6 Jul. 1850. 400 acres.
Parrish, John. Va. Pilot. 6 Jul. 1850. 400 acres.
Parrish, John. Va. Pilot. 6 Jul. 1850. 1422 2/3 acres.
Parrish, John. Va. Pilot. 6 Jul. 1850. 177 2/3 acres.
Parrish, John. Va. Pilot. 18 Jan. 1853. 88 2/3 acres.
Parrish, John. Va. Pilot. 18 Jan. 1853. 177 acres.
Parrish, Mark. N.C. Corporal. 30 Sep. 1785. 1000 acres to heirs.
Parrish, Mark. Va. Pilot. 17 Sep. 1850. 480 acres.
Parrish, Mark. Va. Pilot. 17 Sep. 1850. 480 acres.
Parrish, Mark. Va. Pilot. 17 Sep. 1850. 480 acres.
Parrish, Mark. Va. Pilot. 17 Sep. 1850. 257 acres.
Parrish, Mark. Va. Pilot. 17 Sep. 1850. 889 2/3 acres.
Parrish, Mark. Va. Pilot. 17 Sep. 1850. 80 acres.
Parrish, Mark. Va. Pilot. 26 Jan. 1858. 2666 2/3 acres.
Parrish, Nicholas. N.C. Private. 3 Feb. 1785. 640 acres.
Parrish, William. Va. Pilot. 21 Dec. 1852. 80 acres.
Parrish, William. Va. Pilot. 26 Jan. 1858. 2666 2/3 acres.
Parrison, Peter. Pa. ———. 29 Mar. 1787. 200 acres to Peter Gully, assignee.
Parrot, John. N.C. Private. 17 Dec. 1785. 640 acres to heirs.
Parrott, Abraham. Conn. Sufferer. Fairfield. 4.14.0.
Parrott, Benjamin. N.C. Private. 22 Dec. 1796. 640 acres to heirs.
Parrott, James. Va. Private. 31 Jul. 1784. 100 acres.
Parrott, John. S.C. ———. 1 Jun. 1789. 200 acres to Bartholomew Whittington, heir at law.
Parrott, John. Conn. Sufferer. Fairfield. 86.9.8.
Parrott, Joseph. Va. Lieutenant. 3 Apr. 1813. 1333 acres.
Parrott, Joseph. Va. Lieutenant. 3 Apr. 1813. 1333 2/3 acres.
Parrott, Martin. Conn. Sufferer. New/East Haven. 27.18.8.
Parry, Francis. N.C. Private. 15 Feb. 1797. 640 acres to heirs.
Parry, Moses. Va. Sergeant. 13 Oct. 1784. 200 acres.
Parrymore, James. N.C. Private. 20 Jan. 1785. 640 acres to heirs.
Parsmore, John. N.C. Private. 1 Sep. 1785. 640 acres to heirs.
Parson, Solomon. Mass. Private. 1 Oct. 1832. 200 acres to heirs.
Parsons Nathan. Me. Ensign. 23 Apr. 1838. 600 acres to widow Susan Parsons. Bangor.
Parsons, Charles. N. Y. Captain. 9 Jul. 1790. 1800 acres.
Parsons, George. Va. Private. 26 Nov. 1783. 100 acres.
Parsons, Henry. Ga. Citizen. 19 Dec. 1785. 287 1/2 acres.
Parsons, John. Md. Private. ———. 50 acres.
Parsons, John. N.Y. ———. 13 Sep. 1790. 500 acres to heirs.
Parsons, John. Pa. ———. 23 Jul. 1787. 200 acres to Caspar Schneider, assignee.
Parsons, John. Conn. Sufferer. Fairfield. 22.1.2.
Parsons, Moses. Mass. ———. 22 Jul. 1833. 200 acres.
Parsons, Nathaniel. Conn. Sufferer. Fairfield. 86.7.7.
Parsons, Philip. Mass. ———. 22 Jul. 1833. 200 acres.
Parsons, Samuel. N. Y. Matross. 9 Jul. 1790. 600 acres.
Parsons, Sarah. Conn. Sufferer. Greenwich. 5.16.4.
Parsons, Sylvanus. Mass. ———. 22 Jul. 1833. 20 acres.
Parsons, Thomas. Va. Private. 23 Jun. 1783. 100 acres.
Parsons, Thomas. Va. Lieutenant. 26 Feb. 1834. 2666 2/3 acres.

Parsons, Thomas. Va. Lieutenant. 30 Jul. 1835. 2000 acres.
Parsons, Thomas. Va. Lieutenant. 30 Jul. 1835. 666 2/3 acres.
Parsons, Thomas. Va. Lieutenant. 20 Aug. 1835. 666 2/3 acres.
Parsons, William. S.C. Captain. 4 Jul. 1785. 300 acres.
Parsons, William. Va. Captain. ———. 4000 acres.
Parsons, William. Va. Captain. 18 Mar. 1840. 250 acres.
Parsons, William. Va. Captain. 28 Mar. 1840. 250 acres.
Parsons, William. Va. Captain. 18 Mar. 1840. 250 acres.
Parsons, Williby. Va. Private. 21 Feb. 1784. 100 acres.
Parsons, Williby. Va. Private. 12 Jan. 1842. 100 acres.
Parteer, James. Conn. Sufferer. New London. 21.19.0.
Partin, John. Ga. Refugee. 15 Mar. 1784. 250 acres.
Partin, Peter. Pa. Lieutenant. ———. ———.
Partridge, David. Me. Private. 5 Dec. 1835. 200 acres to widow Mary Partridge. Poland.
Parum, Peter. Ga. ———. 21 Apr. 1784. 287 1/2 acres.
Paschall, Jeremiah. Pa. Sergeant. 12 Mar. 1787. 250 acres.
Paskill, George. Va. Private. 15 Nov. 1785. 200 acres.
Paskins, Hugh. Ga. Soldier. 4 Feb. 1785. ———.
Pasley, Joel. Va. Private. 22 Nov. 1783. 100 acres.
Pasley, Thomas. Va. Private. 18 Nov. 1818. 200 acres.
Pasmore, Enoch. N.C. Private. 22 Apr. 1785. 640 acres to heirs.
Pasmore, Joshua. N.C. Private. 2 Feb. 1786. 640 acres.
Pasmore, Oliver. N.C. Private. 8 Dec. 1795. 640 acres to heirs.
Passmore, David. N.C. Private. 7 Jan. 1784. 365 acres.
Pasteur, Bluitt. Va. Seaman. 22 Nov. 1783. 100 acres.
Pasture, John. Va. Captain. 29 Mar. 1834. 5333 1/3 acres.
Pasture, Thomas. N.C. Lieutenant. 10 Nov. 1783. 2560 acres.
Patchen, Martin. Conn. Sufferer. New/East Haven. 31.0.6.
Pate, Enos. Ga. ———. 17 May 1784. ———.
Pate, Matthew. Va. Private. 7 Jun. 1783. 100 acres.
Pate, William. N.C. Private. 21 Apr. 1784. 274 acres.
Patillo, James. Va. Sergeant. 14 Oct. 1783. 200 acres.
Patman, William. Va. Sergeant. 10 Jul. 1783. 200 acres.
Patmore, William. Ga. Soldier. 3 May 1785. 230 acres.
Patrick, Daniel. N.C. Private. 21 Feb. 1822. 274 acres to heirs.
Patrick, George. Md. Private. ———. 50 acres.
Patrick, James. Ga. ———. 17 May 1784. ———.
Patridge, John. Pa. Private. 11 Aug. 1789. 200 acres.
Patten, Alexander. Va. Private. 24 Feb. 1784. 100 acres.
Patten, Henry. Va. Private. 25 May 1785. 100 acres.
Patten, James. Va.-Ind. Private. 108 acres.
Patten, James. Mass. Private. 2 Mar. 1833. 200 acres.
Patten, Lewis. Pa. Private. 4 Oct. 1786. 200 acres to widow.
Patten, Philip. N.C. Private. 9 Dec. 1797. 365 acres.
Patten, William. Va. Private. 22 Apr. 1785. 100 acres.
Patterson, Andrew. Pa. Private. 20 Mar. 1807. 200 acres.
Patterson, George. S.C. ——— 1 Dec. 1794. 200 acres.
Patterson, Gideon. Ga. Lieutenant. 19 Apr. 1784. 400 acres.
Patterson, Gideon. Ga. Refugee. 19 Apr. 1784. 287 1/2 acres.
Patterson, Hezekiah. N. Y. Private. 7 Jul. 1790. 600 acres.
Patterson, Hugh. N.C. ———. 11 Jul. 1785. 640 acres to heirs.
Patterson, Isaac. Ga. Minute Man. 16 Mar. 1785. ———.
Patterson, James, 1st. N. Y. Private. 8 Jul. 1790. 500 acres.

Patterson, James, 2d. N. Y. Private. 8 Jul. 1790. 600 acres.
Patterson, Jesse. N.C. Private. 7 Jan. 1786. 320 acres.
Patterson, John. Ga. Lieutenant. 20 Feb. 1784. 500 acres.
Patterson, John. N. Y. Gunner. 9 Jul. 1790. 600 acres.
Patterson, John. N.C. Private. 17 Dec. 1785. 640 acres to heirs.
Patterson, John. N.C. Private. 28 Sep. 1805. 274 acres.
Patterson, John. Pa. Captain. ———. 500 acres to John Christie, assignee.
Patterson, John. Va. Sergeant Major. 28 May 1783. 400 acres.
Patterson, John. Va. Midshipman. 23 Jul. 1835. 2666 2/3 acres.
Patterson, John, Jr. Ga. Refugee. 26 May 1784. 575 acres.
Patterson, Jonathan. N.Y. Private. 8 Jul. 1790. 600 acres.
Patterson, Joseph. Me. ———. 20 Jan. 1836. 200 acres to widow Lucretia Patterson. Saco.
Patterson, Philip. Va. Private. 22 Aug. 1835. 100 acres.
Patterson, Robert. Ga. Refugee. 20 Feb. 1784. 500 acres.
Patterson, Robert. Va.-Ind. Sergeant. 216 acres.
Patterson, Robert. Pa. Private. ———. 200 acres.
Patterson, Samuel. Ga. ———. 17 May 1784. ———.
Patterson, Thomas. Md. Private. ———. 50 acres.
Patterson, Tilman. Va. Sergeant. 16 Jan. 1784. 400 acres.
Patterson, William. Ga. Soldier. 27 Apr. 1784. 287 1/2.
Patterson, William. N. Y. Private. 7 Jul. 1790. 500 acres.
Patterson, William. N. Y. Private. 13 Sep. 1790. 500 acres.
Patterson, William. Pa. Private. 14 Apr. 1787. 200 acres.
Patteson, Thomas. Va. Captain. 8 Mar. 1784. 4000 acres.
Patteson, Thomas. Va. Captain. 23 Dec. 1833. 1000 acres.
Pattillo, John. Ga. Soldier. ———. 230 acres to heir James Pattillo of Brunswick Co., Fa.
Patton, James. Pa. Dragoon. 24 Oct. 1786. 200 acres to Thomas Patton, administrator.
Patton, John. N.C. Colonel. 29 Nov. 1783. 7200 acres.
Patton, John. Pa. Private. 3 Feb. 1789. 200 acres to Stephen Loudon, assignee.
Patton, Robert. Pa. Captain. 20 Oct. 1786. 500 acres.
Patton, Thomas. Ga. ———. 16 Jul. 1784. 287 1/2 acres.
Pattron, Samuel. Ga. ———. 19 Apr. 1784. 200 acres.
Paul, ———. S.C. ———. 7 May 1787. 200 acres to William Paul, his father. Veteran died in the service.
Paul, Arthur. N. Y. Private. 17 Aug. 1790. 600 acres.
Paul, Daniel. N.C. Private. 14 Feb. 1796. 640 acres to heirs.
Paul, Edward. Va. Private. 23 Jun. 1783. 200 acres.
Paul, Hugh. Mass. Private. 19 Nov. 1832. 200 acres to heirs.
Paul, James. N.C. Private. 17 Dec. 1785. 640 acres to heirs.
Paul, John. Va.-Ind. Private. 108 acres.
Paul, Morris. N.C. Private. 8 Dec. 1796. 640 acres.
Paul, Robert. N. Y. ———. ———. 500 acres.
Paul, Stephen. N.C. Private. 17 Dec. 1785. 640 acres to heirs.
Paul, William. Md. Private. ———. 50 acres.
Paul, William. S.C. Soldier. 21 Jan. 1785. 200 acres.
Paulent, Amable. N. Y. ———. ———. 500 acres.
Paulent, Antoine. N. Y. Captain. ———. 1000 acres.
Paulett, Jesse. Va. Ensign. 17 Mar. 1834. 2666 2/3 acres.
Paulett, Jesse. Va. Ensign. 20 Dec. 1834. 1333 1/3 acres.
Paulett, Jesse. Va. Ensign. 20 Dec. 1834. 1333 1/3 acres.
Paulett, Richard. Va. Lieutenant. 24 Feb. 1834. 2666 2/3 acres.
Paulier, Clement. N. Y. ———. ———. 500 acres.
Paulier, Joseph. N. Y. ———. ———. 500 acres.

Paulk, Joseph. Ga. ——— . 27 Apr. 1784. 287 1/2 acres.

Paulk, Micajah. Ga. Soldier. 20 Feb. 1784. 250 acres.

Pawling, Henry. N. Y. Captain. 6 Jul. 1790. 1800 acres.

Pawlk, John. Ga. ———. 20 Feb. 1784. 250 acres.

Paxton, William. Ga. Lieutenant. 25 May 1784. 287 1/2 acres.

Paxton, William. Ga. Sergeant. 1784. ——— acres to widow Mary Hooper.

Payford, William. N.C. Musician. 22 Dec. 1807. 360 acres.

Paylor, William. Va. Private. 19 Feb. 1784. 100 acres.

Payn, William. Me. Private. 20 May 1835. 200 acres. Anson.

Payne, Charles. Va. Private. 16 Dec. 1784. 100 acres.

Payne, Jacob. Va. Sergeant. 21 Nov. 1783. 200 acres.

Payne, John. Ga. ———. 21 Apr. 1784. 350 acres.

Payne, John. Va. Private. 2 Dec. 1783. 200 acres.

Payne, John. Va. Master. 9 Dec. 1833. 2666 2/3 acres.

Payne, Joseph. Ga. ———. 17 May 1784. ———.

Payne, Joseph. Va. Lieutenant. 22 Aug. 1783. 1000 acres.

Payne, Joseph. Va. Lieutenant. 22 Aug. 1783. 1000 acres.

Payne, Joseph. Va. Lieutenant. 22 Aug. 1783. 666 2/3 acres.

Payne, Joseph. Va. Lieutenant. 22 Jul. 1837. 60 66/100 acres.

Payne, Joseph. Va. Lieutenant. 22 Jul. 1837. 60 66/100 acres.

Payne, Joseph. Va. Lieutenant. 22 Jul. 1837. 60 66/100 acres.

Payne, Joseph. Va. Lieutenant. 22 Jul. 1837. 60 66/100acres.

Payne, Joseph. Va. Lieutenant. 22 Jul. 1837. 60 66/100 acres.

Payne, Joseph. Va. Lieutenant. 22 Jul. 1837. 60 66/100 acres.

Payne, Joseph. Va. Lieutenant. 22 Jul. 1837. 60 66/100 acres.

Payne, Joseph. Va. Lieutenant. 22 Jul. 1837. 60 66/100 acres.

Payne, Joseph. Va. Lieutenant. 22 Jul. 1837. 60 66/100 acres.

Payne, Joseph. Va. Lieutenant. 22 Jul. 1837. 60 66/100 acres.

Payne, Joseph. Va. Lieutenant. 22 Jul. 1837. 60 66/100 acres.

Payne, Josiah. Va. Subaltern. 3 Mar. 1784. 2666 2/3 acres.

Payne, Merriman. Va. Lieutenant. 8 Nov. 1832. 4000 acres.

Payne, Moses. Ga. ———. 21 Apr. 1784. 200 acres.

Payne, Nathaniel. Ga. ———. 21 Apr. 1784. 200 acres.

Payne, Peter. N.C. Private. 12 Sep. 1785. 640 acres to heirs.

Payne, Samuel, Jr. Ga. ———. 27 Apr. 1784. 287 1/2 acres.

Payne, Tarlton. Va. Captain. 31 May 1783. 4666 2/3 acres.

Payne, Tarlton. Va. Captain. 28 Feb. 1810. 777 1/2 acres.

Payne, Thomas. Ga. Lieutenant. 20 Sep. 1783. 400 acres.

Payne, Thomas. Ga. ———. 21 Apr. 1784. 250 acres.

Payne, Thomas. Va. Captain. 16 Dec. 1782. 4000 acres.

Payne, Thomas. Va. Captain. 29 Jul. 1794. 666 2/3 acres.

Payne, Thomas. Va. Captain. 21 Jun. 1808. 500 acres.

Payne, Thomas, Jr. Ga. ———. 21 Apr. 1784. 500 acres.

Payne, William. Ga. ———. 27 Apr. 1784. 287 1/2 acres.

Payne, William. Me. Private. 20 May 1835. 200 acres. Anson.

Payne, William. Va. Captain. 29 Nov. 1784. 4000 acres.

Pea, Thomas. Va. Private. 10 Dec. 1810. 100 acres.

Peace, Samuel. Va. Sergeant. 20 May 1783. 200 acres.

Peacock, Hugh. N. Y. Lieutenant. 17 Aug. 1790. 1200 acres.

Peacock, John. N.C. Private. 16 Feb. 1822. 274 acres to heirs.

Peacock, Neal. Md. Private. ———. 50 acres.

Peacock, Robert. S.C. ———. 7 Aug. 1786. 200 acres.

Peacock, Thomas. Md. Private. ———. 50 acres.

Peak, John. Ga. ———. 20 Feb. 1784. 250 acres.

Peak, Nathan. Md. Sergeant. ———. 50 acres.
Peak, William. N. Y. Private. 7 Jul. 1790. 500 acres.
Peak, William. Va. Quartermaster Sergeant. 30 Oct. 1797. 400 acres.
Peal, John. Ga. Refugee. 16 Apr. 1784. 287 1/2 acres.
Peal, Pearson. N.C. Sergeant. 5 Sep. 1821. 428 acres to heirs.
Peany, John. Md. Drummer. ———. 50 acres.
Pearce, Aquilla. Md. Drummer. ———. 50 acres.
Pearce, Hardy. N.C. ———. 29 Apr. 1784. 640 acres to John Pearce, heir.
Pearce, James. N.C. ———. 29 Apr. 1784 640 acres to John Pearce, heir.
Pearce, Lovell. Va. Sergeant. 30 Apr. 1838. 200 acres.
Pearce, Nathaniel. Ga. Lieutenant. 24 Jun. 1784. 750 acres.
Pearce, Theopilus. N.C. Private. 27 May 1784. 640 acres.
Pearce, Thomas. N.C. Private. 7 Dec. 1797. 640 acres to heirs.
Pearce, William. N.C. Private. 1 Jul. 1820. 640 acres to heirs.
Pearcy, Nehemiah. N.C. Private. 19 May 1784. 640 acres.
Pearl, James. N.C. Captain. 30 Sep. 1785. 3860 acres.
Pearman, Harrison. Va. Private. 22 Aug. 1783. 200 acres.
Pearman, Thomas. Va. Private. 21 Feb. 1784. 200 acres.
Pearse, John. N. Y. Private. 7 Jul. 1790. 500 acres.
Pearson, George. Pa. Ranger. 16 Jul. 1787. 200 acres.
Pearson, John. Md. Matross. ———. 50 acres.
Pearson, John. Pa. Colonel. 6 Jul. 1789. 500 acres to Mary Pearson, devisee.
Pearson, John. Pa. Private. 14 Apr. 1787. 200 acres.
Pearson, Thomas. Va. Lieutenant. 20 Jun. 1783. 2666 2/3 acres.
Pearson, Thomas. Va. Lieutenant. 1 Jun. 1805. 444 2/3 acres.
Pearson, Thomas. Va. Lieutenant. 11 Sep. 1807. 333 acres.
Pease, John. Md. Sergeant. ———. 50 acres.
Pease, John. Conn. Sufferer. New/East Haven. 18.13.4.
Pease, Mary. Conn. Sufferer. New/East Haven. 2.2.0.
Peavy, Abraham. Ga. Private. 2 Jan. 1784. 250 acres.
Peavy, Dyal. Ga. Citizen. 20 Apr. 1784. 287 1/2 acres.
Peavy, John. Ga. Soldier. 20 Feb. 1784. 250 acres.
Peavy, Joseph. Ga. ———. 27 Apr. 1784. 287 1/2 acres.
Peavy, Peter. Ga. Citizen. 5 Apr. 1785. 287 1/2 acres.
Peavy, Thomas. N.C. Private. 16 Aug. 1821. 640 acres.
Peay, Elias. Va. Sergeant. 29 Jun. 1785. 200 acres.
Peay, Thomas. Va. Corporal. 29 Jun. 1785. 200 acres.
Pecar, Alexander. N. Y. ———. ———. 500 acres.
Peck, Benjamin. N. Y. Drummer. 9 Jul. 1790. 600 acres.
Peck, Benjamin. Conn. Sufferer. Greenwich. 26.16.9.
Peck, Catherine. Conn. Sufferer. Greenwich. 16.0.0.
Peck, Charles. Conn. Sufferer. Danbury. 6.8.4.
Peck, Ebenezer. Conn. Sufferer. New/East Haven. 23.2.2.
Peck, Eliphalet. Conn. Sufferer. Danbury. 1.5.0.
Peck, Frederick. N.C. Private. 13 Sep. 1820. 274 acres.
Peck, Henry. Ga. ———. 22 Apr. 1784. 600 acres.
Peck, Henry. Conn. Sufferer. Danbury. 2.2.8.
Peck, Heth. Conn. Sufferer. Greenwich. 9.0.11.
Peck, Hiel. N. Y. Lieutenant. 9 Jul. 1790. 1200 acres.
Peck, James. Pa. Private. 2 Nov. 1786. 200 acres.
Peck, John. N. Y. Private. 8 Jul. 1790. 600 acres.
Peck, John. Conn. Sufferer. Danbury. 2.3.4.
Peck, John C. Ga. Soldier. 22 Apr. 1784. 800 acres.
Peck, Joshua. Me. ———. 4 May 1835. 200 acres to widow Diadamas C. Peck. Clinton.

Peck, Lucy. Ga. ———. 22 Apr. 1784. 500 acres.
Peck, Mary. Conn. Sufferer. Greenwich. 8.8.5.
Peck, Phineas. Conn. Sufferer. Danbury. 1.4.1 1/2.
Peck, Sarah. Conn. Sufferer. Danbury. 1.9.4.
Peck, Simeon. Conn. Sufferer. New London. 19.16.0.
Peck, Theophilus, Jr. Conn. Sufferer. Greenwich. 50.6.4.
Pecker, William. Md. Private. ———. 50 acres.
Pediford, Edward. Va. Private. 12 Jan. 1784. 200 acres.
Pedon, Thomas. N.C. Private. 17 Dec. 1785. 640 acres to heirs.
Peebles, Andrew. Va. Private. 8 Jul. 1868. 100 acres.
Peebles, Robert. Pa. Lieutenant. ———. 200 acres.
Peebles, Robert. Pa. Private. 17 May 1787. 200 acres.
Peek, Jesse. Va. Private. 2 Nov. 1824. 200 acres.
Peel, Daniel. N.C. Private. 29 Sep. 1784. 640 acres to James Peel, heir.
Peers, Thomas. Va. Fifer. 12 May 1783. 100 acres.
Peers, Thomas. Va. Private. 16 Dec. 1811. 200 acres.
Peers, Valentine. Va. Major. 19 May 1923. 5333 1/3 acres.
Peers, William. Va. Drummer. 6 Aug. 1795. 100 acres.
Peet, John. N. Y. Matross. 9 Jul. 1790. 500 acres.
Peevil, John. N.C. Private. 17 Feb. 1824. 640 acres.
Pegman, Matthew. Va. Private. 2 Jun. 1800. 200 acres.
Peigher, John. N.C. Private. 18 Dec. 1797. 274 acres.
Peirce, Amos. Mass. Private. 5 Oct. 1833. 200 acres.
Peirce, Joseph. N.C. Private. 20 Dec. 1796. 640 acres to heirs.
Peirce, Shadrack. N.C. Private. 7 Dec. 1797. 365 acres.
Peircy, Thomas. N.C. Private. 7 Dec. 1797. 365 acres.
Pelette, Charles. Va. Private. 14 Jul. 1835. 100 acres.
Pelette, Charles. Va. Private. 2 May 1856. 100 acres.
Pelette, Lewis. Va. Private. 31 Dec. 1851. 100 acres.
Pelette, Lewis. Va. Private. 9 Apr. 1856. 100 acres.
Pelette, Michael. Va. Private. 31 Dec. 1851. 100 acres.
Pelette, Michael. Va. Private. 21 Apr. 1856. 100 acres.
Pelham, Charles. Va. Major. 3 Apr. 1783. 6222 acres.
Pelham, Charles. Va. Major. 20 Feb. 1809. 666 2/3 acres.
Pelham, William. Va. Surgeon. 11 Aug. 1808. 1200 acres.
Pelham, William. Va. Surgeon. 11 Aug. 1808. 1200 acres.
Pelham, William. Va. Surgeon. 11 Aug. 1808. 1200 acres.
Pelham, William. Va. Surgeon. 11 Aug. 1808. 1200 acres.
Pelham, William. Va. Surgeon. 11 Aug. 1808. 1200 acres.
Pell, Joseph S. Va. Surgeon. 22 Mar. 1834. 7045 acres.
Pell, Salle. Conn. Sufferer. Danbury. 6.13.4.
Pell, T. Samuel. N. Y. Captain. 9 Jul. 1790. 1800 acres.
Pelt, Isaac. N.C. Private. 30 Sep. 1785. 640 acres to heirs.
Pelton, Benjamin. N. Y. Captain. 9 Jul. 1790. 1800 acres.
Pemberton, Bennet. Va. Private. 22 Feb. 1833. 100 acres.
Pemberton, Reuben. Va. Private. 18 Dec. 1792. 200 acres.
Pemberton, Reuben. Va. Private. 12 Jan. 1842. 200 acres.
Pemberton, Thomas. N. Y. Private. 8 Jul. 1790. 600 acres.
Pemberton, Thomas. Va. Captain. 20 Jan. 1783. 4000 acres.
Pemberton, Thomas. Va. Captain. 14 Nov. 1795. 666 2/3 acres.
Pembroke, David, Jr. N. Y. Matross. 9 Jul. 1790. 500 acres.
Pembroke, David, Sr. N. Y. Matross. 9 Jul. 1790. 500 acres.
Pembroke, James. N. Y. Matross. 9 Jul. 1790. 600 acres.
Pembroke, John. N.C. Private. 9 Dec. 1797. 640 acres.

Pen, Lewis. N.C. Private. 26 Aug. 1785. 640 acres to heirs.

Penchback, Thomas. Va. Sergeant. 16 Feb. 1784. 200 acres.

Pendall, John. Ga. ———. 26 May 1784. 287 1/2 acres.

Pender, Benjamin. N.C. Private. 30 Sep. 1785. 640 acres to heirs.

Pendergast, William. Md. Lieutenant. ———. 200 acres.

Pendergrass, David. N.C. Private. 29 Sep. 1784. 228 acres.

Pendergrass, Job. N.C. Private. 22 Oct. 1783. 274 acres.

Pendergrass, John. N.C. Private. 27 Oct. 1783. 274 acres.

Pendergrass, John. N.C. Private. 25 Jun. 1785. 640 acres.

Pendergrass, Raleigh. N.C. Private. 7 Dec. 1797. 640 acres to heirs.

Pendergrass, Robert. Pa. Sergeant. ———. 250 acres.

Pendergrass, Robert. Pa. Sergeant. 11 Aug. 1789 to Stephen Loudon, assignee. 300 acres.

Pendergrass, William. N.C. Private. 17 Dec. 1785. 640 acres heirs.

Pendleton, Benjamin. N.C. Private. 10 Sep. 1821. 640 acres to heirs.

Pendleton, Edward. N.C. Private. 4 Aug. 1821. 640 acres.

Pendleton, James. Va. Captain. 24 Jan. 1783. 4666 2/3 acres.

Pendleton, James. Va. Captain. 8 Feb. 1808. 555 acres.

Pendleton, James. Va. Captain. 10 Jan. 1809. 555 1/3 acres.

Pendleton, Nathaniel. Va. Captain. 18 Jul. 1783. 4666 2/3 acres.

Pendleton, Nathaniel. Va. Captain. 20 May 1808. 944 acres.

Pendleton, Richard. Va. Captain. 16 Mar. 1838. 2000 acres.

Pendleton, Richard. Va. Captain. 16 Mar. 1838. 2000 acres.

Pendleton, Solomon. N. Y. Lieutenant. 9 Jul. 1790. 1000 acres.

Penfield, James. Conn. Sufferer. Fairfield. 6.12.0.

Penfield, Mary. Conn. Sufferer. Fairfield. 139.14.1.

Penfield, Samuel. Conn. Sufferer. Fairfield. 1,065.9.4.

Penfield, Sarah. Conn. Sufferer. Fairfield. 15.16.0.

Penkerton, Andrew. Pa. Private. 1 Sep. 1789. 200 acres.

Penn, John. Va. Sailor. 8 Sep. 1783. 100 acres.

Penn, William. Va. Lieutenant. 23 Dec. 1785. 2666 2/3 acres.

Penniman, James. Conn. Sufferer. New London. 137.10.7.

Pennington, Job. Pa. Private. 25 Feb. 1807. 200 acres.

Pennington, Robert. Md. Private. ———. 50 acres.

Pennington, Stephen. Ga. ———. 5 May 1785. 287 1/2 acres.

Pennington, Thomas. Ga. ———. 17 Apr. 1784. 287 1/2 acres.

Pennington, William. N. Y. Lieutenant. 9 Jul. 1790. 1200 acres.

Pennwert, John. Conn. Sufferer. New London. 223.8.6.

Penny, George. Me. ———. 1 May 1835. 200 acres to widow Abigail Penny. Wells.

Penny, John. Va. Private. 30 Apr. 1838. 100 acres.

Penny, Jonathan. N. Y. Private. 8 Jul. 1790. 600 acres.

Penny, Salathiel. Me. ———. 18 Apr. 1835. 200 acres. Waterville.

Pennyback, Conrad. Va. Fife Major. 26 Mar. 1826. 400 acres.

Pennyfield, Thomas. Md. Private. ———. 50 acres.

Penson, William. Ga. ———. ———. 287 1/2 acres.

Penticost, Dancy. N.C. Sergeant. 21 Aug. 1820. 356 acres.

Penticost, Dancy. N.C. Sergeant. 17 Feb. 1824. 644 acres to heirs.

Penticost, William. Va. Private. 5 Nov.1811. 100 acres.

Penton, Aaron. Pa. Private. 10 Nov. 1786. 200 acres.

Penury, Robert. Va. Private. 1 Jun. 1785. 100 acres.

Peokins, Titus. N.Y. ———. 13 Sep. 1790. 500 acres to heirs.

Peoples, William. N.C. Private. 12 Sep. 1820. 228 acres.

Peoples, William. Pa. Captain. 1 Sep. 1789. 500 acres to heirs.

Pepin, Andrew. N. Y. Lieutenant. ———. 1000 acres.

Pepper, Elijah. Md. Private. ———. 50 acres.

Peraull, Michael. Va. Captain. 3 Mar. 1784. 4000 acres.

Perault, Michael. Va.-Ind. Lieutenant. Mar. 1784. 2156 acres.

Percy, William. N.C. Private. 30 Sep. 1785. 640 acres to heirs.

Peres, Peter. Pa. Surgeon. 24 Jul. 1787. 300 acres.

Peres, Peter. Pa. Surgeon. 24 Jul. 1787. 300 acres.

Perius, Dimmick. N.Y. ———. 8 Oct. 1792. 500 acres to heirs.

Perkenson, Drury. N.C. Private. 16 Aug. 1821. 640 acres.

Perkenson, John. N.C. Sergeant. 27 Mar. 1821. 428 acres to heirs.

Perker, Edward. N. Y. Private. 7 Jul. 1790. 600 acres.

Perkeson, James. Va. Private. 3 Sep. 1784. 200 acres.

Perkhoff, Frederick. N. Y. Private. 7 Jul. 1790. 600 acres.

Perkins, Abraham. Ga. ———. 27 Apr. 1784. 287 1/2 acres.

Perkins, Adam. Ga. ———. 27 Apr. 1784. 287 1/2 acres.

Perkins, Adams. N.C. Private. 22 Apr. 1785. 274 acres.

Perkins, Archelaus. Va. Lieutenant. 3 Feb. 1784. 2666 2/3 acres.

Perkins, Benjamin. Ga. Minute Man. 24 Aug. 1785. 250 acres.

Perkins, Elisha. Ga. ———. ———. 250 acres.

Perkins, Ephraim. Ga. Minute Man. 3 Sep. 1785. ———.

Perkins, Isaac. Ga. Minute Man. 3 Sep. 1785. ———.

Perkins, Isaac. N.C. Private. 17 Dec. 1785. 274 acres.

Perkins, James. N. Y. Private. 8 Jul. 1790. 600 acres.

Perkins, Jesse. N.C. Private. 17 Dec. 1785. 640 acres to heirs.

Perkins, John. Ga. ———. 25 May 1784. 287 1/2 acres.

Perkins, Joseph. N. Y. Sergeant. 8 Jul. 1790. 600 acres.

Perkins, Joseph. Va. Private. 30 Jun. 1783. 200 acres.

Perkins, Nimrod. N.C. Private. 6 Dec. 1797. 640 acres.

Perkins, Nimrod. Va. Drummer. 9 Dec. 1830. 2666 2/3 acres.

Perkins, Nimrod. Va. Drummer. 17 Sep. 1831. 100 acres.

Perkins, Peter. Ga. ———. 30 Sep. 1784. ———.

Perkins, Richard. Ga. ———. 17 May 1784. ———.

Perkins, Richard. N.C. Private. 14 Sep. 1820. 640 acres.

Perkins, Samuel. Me. Private. 21 Dec. 1835. 200 acres to widow Mehitabel Perkins. Paris.

Perkins, Stephen. N.C. Private. 30 Sep. 1785. 640 acres to heirs.

Perkins, William. Ga. ———. 27 Apr. 1784. 287 1/2 acres.

Perkins, Zedekiah. N.C. Private. 30 Sep. 1785. 640 acres to heirs.

Perkinson, Jacob. N.C. Private. 13 Jan. 1823. 640 acres.

Perkinton, William. Va. Sergeant. 27 Jun. 1783. 200 acres.

Perkison, Beverley. N.C. Private. 22 Apr. 1785. 640 acres to heirs.

Pero, Baptiste. N. Y. ———. ———. 500 acres.

Perpeany, Simon. Mass. ———. 24 Feb. 1832. 200 acres to heir Ann Packnett.

Perren, John. Va. Private. 6 Dec. 1784. 100 acres.

Perritt, John. Ga. ———. 27 Apr. 1784. 575 acres.

Perritt, Robert. Ga. Minute Man. 27 Apr. 1784. 287 1/2 acres.

Perritt, William. Ga. ———. 15 Mar. 1784. 250 acres.

Perry, Burwell. Ga. ———. 20 Apr. 1784. 1000 acres.

Perry, Caleb. Pa. Lieutenant Colonel. 25 Aug. 1787. 250 acres to Elizabeth Perry, widow.

Perry, Caleb. Pa. Lieutenant Colonel. 25 Aug. 1787. 500 acres to Elizabeth Perry, widow.

Perry, David. Conn. Sufferer. Ridgefield. 3.2.0.

Perry, Henry. Va. Private. 1 Aug. 1783. 100 acres.

Perry, Hildey. Va. Sergeant. 26 Apr. 1783. 400 acres.

Perry, Isaac. Ga. ———. 20 Apr. 1784. 287 1/2 acres.
Perry, Isaac. N.C. Private. 30 Sep. 1785. 640 acres to heirs.
Perry, Jabez. Conn. Sufferer. Fairfield. 2.18.0.
Perry, Jeremiah. Ga. ———. 23 Apr. 1784. 1000 acres.
Perry, Jeremiah. N.C. Private. 20 Apr. 1784. 228 acres.
Perry, Jesse. Me. ———. 15 May 1835. 200 acres to widow Mary Perry. Steuben.
Perry, John. N.C. Private. 8 Mar. 1785. 228 acres.
Perry, John. Va. Cornet. 21 Aug. 1783. 2666 2/3 acres.
Perry, John. Conn. Sufferer. Fairfield. 6.17.0.
Perry, Jonathan. Mass. Private. 25 Nov. 1833. 200 acres.
Perry, Joseph. N.C. Private. 17 Dec. 1785. 640 acres to heirs.
Perry, Joseph. Pa. Private. ———. 200 acres.
Perry, Joshua. Ga. ———. 20 Apr. 1784. 400 acres.
Perry, Peter. Conn. Sufferer. New London. 9.18.0.
Perry, Robert. N.C. Private. 30 Nov. 1785. 640 acres.
Perry, Simon. Md. Private. ———. 50 acres.
Perry, Thomas. Md. Private. ———. 50 acres.
Perry, William. N.C. Private. 30 Sep. 1785. 640 acres to heirs.
Perry, William. Pa. Private. 3 May 1791. 200 acres to widow.
Perry, William. Va. Drummer. 30 May 1783. 100 acres.
Perry, William. Va. Private. 30 Jun. 1783. 100 acres.
Perryman, Benone. Va. Fifer. 11 Aug. 1783. 100 acres.
Perryman, Daniel. Va. Private. 15 Oct. 1783. 100 acres.
Perryman, Philip. Va. Private. 16 Jun. 1783. 100 acres.
Persett, John. Ga. Refugee. 24 Apr. 1784. 287 1/2 acres.
Persey, John. N.C. Private. 30 Sep. 1785. 640 acres to heirs.
Person, Jesse. N.C. Private. 29 Sep. 1784. 640 acres.
Person, Nathan. N.C. Private. 29 Sep. 1784. 640 acres to heirs.
Person, Roger. N.C. Private. 29 Sep. 1784. 640 acres to heirs.
Persons, Jones. Ga. Refugee. 25 May 1784. 287 1/2 acres.
Persythe, Joseph. N.C. Private. 9 Sep. 1785. 640 acres to heirs.
Pertie, Benjamin. Ga. ———. 19 Apr. 1784. 575 acres.
Pervall, John. N.C. Private. 30 Sep. 1785. 1000 acres to heirs.
Pervie, James. N.C. Private. 30 Sep. 1785. 640 acres to heirs.
Pervines, Dempsey. N.C. Private. 9 Feb. 1796. 228 acres.
Peteet, Richard. Ga. ———. 22 Apr. 1784. 350 acres.
Peter, Daniel. N.C. Private. 30 Sep. 1785. 274 acres.
Peters, Abraham. N.C. Private. 12 Sep. 1785. 640 acres to heirs.
Peters, Anthony. Va. Private. 29 Dec. 1796. 200 acres.
Peters, Bernard. N.C. Private. 15 Feb. 1797. 640 acres to heirs.
Peters, Elias. Pa. Private. ———. 200 acres to widow.
Peters, Elijah. Ga. ———. 24 May 1784. 287 1/2 acres.
Peters, Elisha. Ga. Minute Man. 14 Feb. 1785. ———.
Peters, Gabriel. Md. Private. ———. 50 acres.
Peters, Isaac. Ga. Minute Man. 3 Apr. 1785. ———.
Peters, Jacob. Pa. Private. ———. 200 acres.
Peters, James. Va. Sailor. 19 Sep. 1787. 100 acres.
Peters, John. Ga. Minute Man. 3 Sep. 1785. 250 acres.
Peters, John. Va.-Ind. Private. 108 acres.
Peters, John. N. Y. Private. 3 Jul. 1790. 600 acres.
Peters, John. N.C. Private. 12 Sep. 1785. 640 acres to heirs.
Peters, Jonathan. Ga. Refugee. Sep. 1785. ———.
Peters, Joseph. Md. ———. ———. 50 acres.

Peters, Solomon. Ga. Minute Man. 3 Sep. 1785. ———.
Peters, Thomas. Va. Private. 11 Jul. 1783. 100 acres.
Peters, Titus. N.C. Private. 30 Sep. 1785. 640 acres to heirs.
Peters, William. Md. Private. ———. 50 acres.
Peterson, Conrod. Va. Private. 30 Jun. 1784. 100 acres.
Peterson, Duncan. N.C. Private. 13 Sep. 1820. 640 acres.
Peterson, Gabriel. Pa. Lieutenant. 12 Apr. 1787. 200 acres.
Peterson, Gabriel. Pa. Lieutenant. 11 Apr. 1787. ———.
Peterson, Hardy. N.C. Private. 22 Apr. 1785. 640 acres.
Peterson, Israel. Va. Private. 7 Aug. 1783. 200 acres.
Peterson, James. Ga. Soldier. 5 Aug. 1785. ———.
Peterson, John. Ga. Minute Man. 3 Sep. 1785. ———.
Peterson, Simon. N. Y. Private. 13 Sep. 1790. 500 acres.
Pethosell, Thomas. N.C. Private. 17 Feb. 1824. 640 acres.
Petler, John. Va. Private. 14 Jul. 1835. 100 acres.
Petman, Isham. N.C. Private. 30 Sep. 1785. 640 acres to heirs.
Petre, Arnold. Pa. Private. ———. 200 acres.
Petree, Anthony. Pa. Private. ———. 200 acres.
Petrie, Alexander. Va. Sergeant. 8 Jan. 1784. 200 acres.
Petter, Alfonse. Va. Private. 31 Dec. 1851. 100 acres.
Petter, Alfonse. Va. Private. 8 Apr. 1856. 100 acres.
Petter, Joseph. Va. Private. 2 May 1856. 100 acres.
Petter, Michael. Va. Private. 8 Apr. 1856. 100 acres.
Petter, Michael. Va. Private. 31 Dec. 1851. 100 acres.
Petters, William. N. Y. Ensign. 7 Jul. 1790. 1000 acres.
Pettes, James. N.C. Private. 15 Feb. 1797. 274 acres.
Pettet, Benjamin. Ga. Minute Man. ———. ———.
Pettiford, Drury. Va. Private. 24 Nov. 1784. 100 acres.
Pettiford, Elias. Va. Private. 24 Nov. 1784. 100 acres.
Pettigrew. John. Va. Lieutenant. 26 Feb. 1831. 1333 1/3 acres.
Pettigrew, Gavin. Va. Seaman. 26 Feb. 1831. 100 acres.
Pettigrew, Hance. N.C. Non Commissioned Officer. 10 Aug. 1785. 1080 acres.
Pettigrew, James. Pa. Lieutenant. 30 Sep. 1787. 200 acres.
Pettigrew, James. Pa. Lieutenant. 30 Sep. 1787. 200 acres.
Pettigrew, John. Va. Lieutenant. 26 Feb. 1831. 1333 1/3 acres.
Pettigrew, John. Va. Lieutenant. 26 Feb. 1831. 1333 1/3 acres.
Pettigrew, John. Va. Lieutenant. 22 Sep. 1831. 2000 acres.
Pettigrew, John. Va. Lieutenant. 22 Sep. 1831. 250 acres.
Pettigrew, John. Va. Lieutenant. 22 Sep. 1831. 250 acres.
Pettigrew, John. Va. Lieutenant. 22 Sep. 1831. 250 acres.
Pettigrew, John. Va. Lieutenant. 22 Sep. 1831. 250 acres.
Pettigrew, John. Va. Lieutenant. 22 Sep. 1831. 250 acres.
Pettigrew, John. Va. Lieutenant. 22 Sep. 1831. 250 acres.
Pettigrew, John. Va. Lieutenant. 22 Sep. 1831. 250 acres.
Pettigrew, John. Va. Lieutenant. 22 Sep. 1831. 250 acres.
Pettijohn, Thomas. N.C. Private. 24 Dec. 1785. 640 acres to heirs.
Pettis, Stephen. N.C. Private. 20 Jan. 1785. 640 acres to heirs.
Pettit, Gideon. N.C. Fifer. 14 Jul. 1784. 428 acres.
Pettit, Gideon. N.C. Private. 8 Dec. 1795. 640 acres to heirs.
Pettit, Jabez. N. Y. Matross. 9 Jul. 1790. 500 acres.
Pettit, James. Va. Private. 30 Dec. 1823. 100 acres.
Pettit, Samuel. N. Y. Private. 7 Jul. 1790. 500 acres.
Pettit, Samuel. N. Y. Private. 7 Jul. 1790. 600 acres.
Pettit, Thomas. Md. Private. ———. 50 acres.

Pettus, John. Va. Captain. 6 Feb. 1784. 1000 acres.
Pettus, John. Va. Captain. 6 Feb. 1784. 1000 acres.
Pettus, John. Va. Captain. 6 Feb. 1784. 2000 acres.
Pettus, Samuel O. Va. Lieutenant. 9 Nov. 1792. 2666 2/3 acres.
Pettus, Thomas. Va. Private. 12 Mar. 1840. 200 acres.
Petty, Abiel. N. Y. Sergeant. 9 Jul. 1790. 500 acres.
Petty, Francis. Ga. ———. 27 Apr. 1784. 200 acres.
Petty, John. N.C. ———. 13 Jun. 1785. 228 acres.
Petty, William. Ga. Minute Man. 22 Apr. 1784. 287 1/2 acres.
Petty, William. Va. Private. 27 May 1786. 100 acres.
Pettygrew, Richard. Va. Seaman. 29 Jul. 1834. 100 acres.
Pettyjohn, Thomas. N.C. Private. 22 Mar. 1785. 640 acres.
Pettyjohn, Thomas. N.C. Corporal. 27 Nov. 1819. 1000 acres to heirs.
Pettyshall, Joshua. N.C. Sergeant. 14 Dec. 1797. 1000 acres to heirs.
Pettyshall, Thomas. N.C. Private. 12 Dec. 1797. 640 acres to heirs.
Pettyway, Micajah. N.C. Private. 3 Feb. 1785. 228 acres.
Petyon, Francis. Va. Private. 7 Oct. 1783. 100 acres.
Pevey, Nehemiah. N.C. Fifer. 12 Oct. 1795. 1000 acres.
Pew, Arthur. N.C. ———. 29 Apr. 1784. 640 acres to David Pew, heir.
Pew, David. Va. Private. 12 Apr. 1784. 200 acres.
Pew, John. N.C. Private. 12 Sep. 1785. 640 acres to heirs.
Peyton, Charles. Va. Private. 24 Nov. 1784. 100 acres.
Peyton, Dade. Va. Lieutenant. 29 Jun. 1784. 2666 2/3 acres.
Peyton, George. Va. Ensign. 20 Apr. 1784. 2666 2/3 acres.
Peyton, George. Va. Ensign. 11 May 1838. 169 1/2 acres.
Peyton, Henry. Va. Major. 26 Jun. 1784. 5333 1/3 acres.
Peyton, James. Va. Private. 8 Dec. 1783. 100 acres.
Peyton, John. Va. Captain. 16 Dec. 1782. 4000 acres.
Peyton, John. Va. Captain. 12 Jan. 1808. 815 acres.
Peyton, John. Va. Captain. 12 Jan. 1808. 407 acres.
Peyton, Robert. Va. Lieutenant. 12 Dec. 1783. 2666 2/3 acres.
Peyton, Valentine. Va. Captain. 27 Jun. 1783. 4000 acres.
Peyton, Valentine. Va. Captain. 18 Mar. 1834. 139 acres.
Peyton, Valentine. Va. ———. 4 Mar. 1836. 139 acres.
Peyton, Valentine. Va. ———. 4 Mar. 1836. 139 acres.
Peyton, Valentine. Va. ———. 4 Mar. 1836. 139 acres.
Peyton, Valentine. Va. Captain. 6 Jan. 1848. 69 3/4 acres.
Pfifer, Martin. N.C. Captain. 17 Oct. 1783. 1149 acres.
Phelps, Benjamin. Md. Private. ———. 50 acres.
Phelps, David. Ga. Lieutenant. 15 Mar. 1784. 250 acres.
Phelps, David. Ga. Sergeant. 20 Feb. 1784. 250 acres.
Phelps, Garrett. N.C. Private. 20 Oct. 1787. 640 acres to heirs.
Phelps, George. Va. Private. 23 Jun. 1783. 200 acres.
Phelps, James. N.C. Fifer. 2 Feb. 1784. 1000 acres.
Phelps, Jesse. N.C. Drummer. 22 Dec. 1796. 1000 acres.
Phelps, Josiah. Va.-Ind. Private. 108 acres.
Phelps, Kedar. N.C. Drummer. 2 Feb. 1784. 1000 acres.
Phelps, Stephen. N.C. Private. 30 Sep. 1785. 640 acres to heirs.
Pheney, Lacklin. Ga. Private. 17 May 1784. 230 acres.
Pherson, Joseph. Md. Corporal. ———. 50 acres.
Pherson, William. Md. Private. ———. 50 acres.
Phew, Richard. N.C. Private. 12 Sep. 1785. 640 acres to heirs.
Philbrook, David. Me. Private. 17 Jul. 1835. 200 acres to Catharine Philbrook. Hallowell.
Philips, Abial. Conn. Sufferer. Danbury. 6.11.4.

Philips, Burwell. Ga. Private. ———. 250 acres.
Philips, David. Ga. Lieutenant. 15 Mar. 1784. 350 acres.
Philips, David. N. Y. Drummer. 6 Jul. 1790. 600 acres.
Philips, Dempsey. Ga. ———. 1 Oct. 1784. 287 1/2 acres.
Philips, Henry. Ga. ———. 21 Apr. 1784. 287 1/2 acres.
Philips, Isaac. Ga. ———. ———. 250 acres.
Philips, Isaiah. Ga. ———. 22 Apr. 1784. 287 1/2 acres.
Philips, Isham. Ga. ———. 27 Apr. 1784. 287 1/2 acres.
Philips, Jacob. Va. Private. 31 Aug. 1786. 100 acres.
Philips, James. Ga. ———. 21 Apr. 1784. 287 1/2 acres to heirs.
Philips, Joel. Ga. Refugee. 15 Mar. 1784. 250 acres.
Philips, Joel, Jr. Ga. ———. 17 May 1784. ———.
Philips, Joel, Jr. Ga. Refugee. 22 Apr. 1784. 575 acres.
Philips, John. Ga. Minute Man. 22 Feb. 1785. 287 1/2 acres.
Philips, John. Va. Private. 30 Dec. 1784. 100 acres.
Philips, Jonathan. N.Y. ———. 13 Sep. 1790. 500 acres to heirs.
Philips, Joseph. Ga. ———. 15 Mar. 1784. 250 acres.
Philips, Joseph. Ga. Minute Man. 22 Mar. 1785. 250 acres.
Philips, Joseph. Ga. Minute Man. 17 May 1784. —— acres to widow Cassandra Philips and son Isham Philips.
Philips, Joseph, Jr. Ga. Refugee. 5 Mar. 1784. ———.
Philips, Joshua. N. Y. Private. 6 Jul. 1790. 600 acres.
Philips, Josiah. Ga. ———. 17 May 1784. ———.
Philips, Larkin. Va. Private. 25 Feb. 1783. 100 acres.
Philips, Leonard. Ga. ———. 19 Apr. 1784. 750 acres.
Philips, Levi. Ga. ———. 22 Apr. 1784. 300 acres.
Philips, Mark. Ga. Refugee. 19 Jul. 1784. 575 acres.
Philips, Philip. Va. Private. 9 Jun. 1789. 100 acres.
Philips, Reuben. Ga. Refugee. 15 Mar. 1784. 250 acres.
Philips, Richard. Ga. ———. 19 Apr. 1784. 300 acres.
Philips, Robert. Ga. ———. 20 Dec. 1785. 287 1/2 acres.
Philips, Samuel. Ga. ———. ———. 287 1/2 acres.
Philips, Samuel. Va. Ensign. 9 Nov. 1782. 2666 2/3 acres.
Philips, Wilder. Ga. Citizen. 22 Mar. 1785. 250 acres.
Philips, William. Ga. ———. 15 Mar. 1784. 250 acres.
Philips, William. Ga. ———. 22 Apr. 1784. 200 acres.
Philips, William. Va. Private. 23 Jul. 1808. 200 acres.
Philips, William (son of Zachery). Ga. ———. 22 Apr. 1784. 575 acres.
Philips, Zachariah. Ga. Captain. 15 Mar.1784. 575 acres.
Phillips, Andrew. N.C. Private. 25 Oct. 1783. 360 acres.
Phillips, Andrew. N.C. Private. 22 Dec. 1796. 274 acres.
Phillips, Benjamin. Va. Private. 28 Apr. 1783. 200 acres.
Phillips, Bush. N.C. Private. 6 Aug. 1785. 640 acres to Thomas Phillips, heir.
Phillips, Charles. Va. Private. 15 Jun. 1807. 100 acres.
Phillips, Craven. N.C. Private. 9 Dec. 1797. 640 acres to heirs.
Phillips, David. N.C. Private. 16 Oct. 1783. 228 acres.
Phillips, Dennis. Pa. Private. 28 Feb. 1794. 200 acres to Joseph Egg, assignee.
Phillips, Elijah. Va. Private. 15 Jun. 1807. 100 acres.
Phillips, George. Md. Private. ———. 50 acres.
Phillips, George. Mass. Private. 1 Mar. 1833. 200 acres.
Phillips, George. N.C. Private. 23 Oct. 1783. 640 acres.
Phillips, Henry. Md. Private. ———. 50 acres.
Phillips, Henry. N.C. Private. 5 Dec. 1804. 640 acres to heirs.
Phillips, Jacob. Va. Boatswain. 24 Mar. 1831. 2666 2/3 acres.

Phillips, Jairus. Me. Private. 3 Jun. 1835. 200 acres to widow Silence Turner. Turner.
Phillips, James. Md. Private. ———. 50 acres.
Phillips, James. Conn. Sufferer. Greenwich. 20.0.0.
Phillips, John. N.C. Private. 15 Jul. 1785. 640 acres to heirs.
Phillips, John. Va. Private. 23 Jun. 1783. 200 acres.
Phillips, John. Va. Private. 19 Mar. 1784. 100 acres.
Phillips, John. Va. Corporal. 9 Jun. 1784. 2000 [sic] i.e. 200 acres.
Phillips, John. Va. Private. 10 Dec. 1785. 100 acres.
Phillips, John. Va. Private. 3 Dec. 1811. 100 acres.
Phillips, Jonas. Md. Matross. ———. 50 acres.
Phillips, Joseph. N.C. Captain. 25 Oct. 1783. 1280 acres.
Phillips, Joseph. N.C. Private. 10 Jul. 1820. 274 acres to heirs.
Phillips, Lambert. Md. Private. ———. 50 acres.
Phillips, Levi. Va. Private. 19 Feb. 1798. 100 acres.
Phillips, Mark. N.C. Private. 23 Apr. 1785. 640 acres to heirs.
Phillips, Matthew. Pa. Private. 10 Mar. 1787. 200 acres.
Phillips, Matthias. Va. Private. 15 Jun. 1807. 100 acres.
Phillips, Michael. N.C. Private. 30 Sep. 1785. 640 acres.
Phillips, Newton. Va. Private. 3 May 1784. 100 acres.
Phillips, Richard. N.C. Private. 25 Oct. 1783. 274 acres.
Phillips, Richard. N.C. Private. 26 May 1784. 640 acres.
Phillips, Richard. N.C. Private. 22 Dec. 1796. 274 acres.
Phillips, William. N.C. Private. 26 May 1784. 640 acres.
Phillips, William. N.C. Private. 23 Apr. 1785. 640 acres to heirs.
Phillips, William. N.C. Private. 24 Dec. 1785. 640 acres.
Phillips, William. Va. Seaman. 24 Mar. 1831. 100 acres.
Phillips, Zebulon. N.C. Private. 10 Dec. 1788. 640 acres to heirs.
Philps, Israel. N. Y. Private. 8 Jul. 1790. 500 acres.
Philsby, Richard. N.C. Private. 20 Sep. 1784. 274 acres.
Phippeny, Nehemiah. Conn. Sufferer. Fairfield. 12.12.0.
Phipps, David. Conn. Sufferer. New/East Haven. 7.6.6.
Phipps, George. Va. Private. 26 Apr. 1783. 200 acres.
Phipps, Jedediah. Mass. Private. 18 Oct. 1833. 200 acres.
Phipps, Solomon. Conn. Sufferer. New/ East Haven. 43.10.0.
Phipps, Thomas. Md. Private. ———. 50 acres.
Phips, John. N.C. Private. 26 Nov. 1796. 640 acres to heirs.
Phremer, Philip. Pa. Sergeant. 23 Jul. 1787. 250 acres.
Piborn, William. N.C. Private. 16 Sep. 1820. 640 acres to heirs.
Picard, Pierre. N. Y. ———. ———. 500 acres.
Pickens, Samuel. Va.-Ind. Private. 108 acres.
Pickering, John. Md. Private. ———. 50 acres.
Picket, John. Va. Private. 20 Oct. 1783. 100 acres.
Pickett, Abial. Conn. Sufferer. Danbury. 3.14.6.
Pickett, Deborah. Conn. Sufferer. Norwalk. 22.0.0.
Pickett, Francis. Va. Drummer. 26 Apr. 1783. 400 acres.
Pickett, George. Va. Drummer. 26 Apr. 1783. 200 acres.
Pickett, Jeremiah. Va. Private. 4 Jun. 1813. 100 acres.
Pickle, Henry. N. Y. Private. 8 Jul. 1790. 500 acres.
Pickle, Jonas. N.C. Private. 17 Dec. 1796. 228 acres.
Pickle, Richard. N.C. Private. 28 Sep. 1785. 274 acres to heirs.
Pickrel, Samuel. Va. Drummer. 12 Jul. 1783. 100 acres.
Pickrens, Spencer M. Va. Sailor. 30 Jun. 1784. 100 acres.
Pier, Earnest John. N. Y. Private. 8 Jul. 1790. 600 acres.

Pierce, Abraham. Ga. ———. 23 Apr. 1784. 287 1/2 acres.
Pierce, Daniel Conn. Sufferer. Danbury. 3.12.0.
Pierce, George. Md. Private. ———. 50 acres.
Pierce, Israel. N.C. Private. 10 Feb. 1796. 640 acres to heirs.
Pierce, Jacob. N.C. Private. 22 Apr. 1809. 640 acres.
Pierce, James. Mass. Private. 23 Dec. 1831. 200 acres.
Pierce, Jesse. Ga. Minute Man. 12 Feb. 178-. 287 1/2 acres.
Pierce, John. Ga. Minute Man. 12 Feb. 178-. 287 1/2 acres.
Pierce, John. Mass. ———. 25 Nov. 1831. 200 acres to heirs.
Pierce, John. Va. Midshipman. 17 Aug. 1832. 2666 2/3 acres.
Pierce, Joshua. Md. Private. ———. 50 acres.
Pierce, Lovell. Va. Sergeant. 30 Apr. 1838. 200 acres.
Pierce, Reubin. N.C. Private. 19 Dec. 1808. 640 acres to heirs.
Pierce, Theophilus. N.C. Private. 15 Feb. 1808. 640 acres to heirs.
Pierce, Thomas. Pa. Private. 12 Oct. 1786. 200 acres.
Pierce, Thomas. Va. Private. 19 Dec. 1783. 100 acres.
Pierce, William. Ga. Minute Man. 12 Feb. 178-. 287 1/2 acres.
Pierce, William. Ga. ———. 16 Jul. 1784. 650 acres.
Pierce, William. N.C. Private. 8 Nov. 1784. 640 acres to heir.
Pierce, William. Va. Captain. 9 Feb. 1784. 4666 2/3 acres.
Pierce, William. Va. Captain. 28 Jul. 1810. 222 acres.
Piercy, Henry. Pa. Lieutenant. 25 Jul. 1787. 200 acres.
Piercy, Henry. Pa. Lieutenant. 25 Jul. 1787. 200 acres.
Pierpoint, John. N. Y. Gunner. 9 Jul. 1790. 600 acres.
Pierpont, John. Conn. Sufferer. New/East Haven. 18.8.0.
Pierson, Charles. Va. Corporal. 14 Jun. 1820. 400 acres.
Pierson, John. N. Y. Private. 13 Sep. 1790. 500 acres.
Pierson, Mesheck. Va. Private. 18 Nov. 1818. 100 acres.
Pierson, Samuel. N.C. Private. 11 Apr. 1784. 640 acres.
Pierson, Shadrack. Va. Private. 29 Aug. 1807. 100 acres.
Pierson, Thomas. N.C. Private. 6 Sep. 1821. 640 acres.
Pigman, Zachariah. Va. Sergeant. 21 Jan. 1799. 400 acres.
Pigott, Abraham. Va. Private. 20 Nov. 1783. 100 acres.
Pike, John. Mass. ———. 22 Jul. 1833. 200 acres.
Pike, Samuel. Mass. Corporal. 19 Nov. 1832. 200 acres.
Pike, Samuel. N.C. Captain. 7 Mar. 1785. 3840 acres to heirs.
Pike, William. Va. Sergeant. 29 May 1821. 400 acres.
Pikes, Josiah. Ga. ———. 250 acres. ———.
Pile, Benjamin. Va. Private. 20 Jun. 1785. 200 acres.
Pile, Richard. Va. Sergeant. 9 Dec. 1783. 200 acres.
Pile, Richard. Va. Corporal. 20 Jun. 1785. 400 acres.
Piles, William. Va. Private. 5 Oct. 1787. 100 acres.
Pilgrit, Henry. N. Y. Private. 3 Jul. 1790. 600 acres.
Pilkerton, Michael. Md. Private. ———. 50 acres.
Pillsbury, Nathan. Me. ———. 20 Aug. 1835. 200 acres to widow Lucy Pillsbury. Thomaston.
Pilotte, Simeon. N. Y. ———. ———. 500 acres.
Pimple, Paul. Pa. Private. ———. 200 acres.
Pinckney, Charles Cotesworth. S.C. Brigadier General. 16 Jul. 1784. 850 acres.
Pinckney, Jonathan. N. Y. Private. 7 Jul. 1790. 600 acres.
Pinckney, Thomas. S.C. Major. 15 Oct. 1784. 400 acres.
Pindell, Richard. Md. Surgeon. ———. 200 acres.
Pinder, Thomas. Md. Private. ———. 50 acres.
Pine, John. Pa. Matross. 29 Apr. 1795. 200

acres to Isaac Gregg and Jeremiah Baker in his right.
Piner, James. N.C. Private. 5 Sep. 1821. 640 acres.
Piner, Jesse. Va.-Ind. Private. 108 acres.
Piner, Thomas. N.C. Private. 30 Sep. 1785. 640 acres.
Pinkerton, Elijah. Ga. ———. 5 Dec. 1785. 287 1/2 acres.
Pinkerton, Isham. Ga. ———. 5 Dec. 1785. ———.
Pinkerton, John. Ga. ———. 5 Dec. 1785. 287 1/2 acres.
Pinks, James. Pa. Private. 26 Sep. 1787. 200 acres.
Pinkstone, Shadrack. Va. Private. 19 Nov. 1785. 100 acres.
Pinson, Isaac. Ga. ———. 28 Feb. 1784. 250 acres.
Pinto, Jacob. Conn. Sufferer. New/East Haven. 22.13.11.
Piott, Edward. N.C. Private. 7 Dec. 1797. 640 acres.
Piper, James. Pa. Lieutenant. 27 Mar. 1787 500 acres to widow.
Piper, James. Pa. Colonel. 9 May 1796. 250 acres to Lucinda Piper, widow.
Piper, John. Va. Lieutenant. 27 May 1795. 2666 2/3 acres.
Piper, Lewis. N. Y. Private. 3 Jul. 1790. 600 acres.
Piper, William. Va. Sergeant. 30 Jul. 1783. 200 acres.
Pipkin, William. N.C. Private. 23 May 1821. 640 acres to heirs.
Pipkin, Willis. N.C. Private. 30 Sep. 1785. 640 acres to heirs.
Pippen, Bannister. Va. Sailor. 15 Oct. 1792. 100 acres.
Pique, William. Va. Sergeant. 17 Jul. 1784. 400 acres.
Pite, Edward. Ga. ———. 1784. 250 acres.
Pitkington, Drury. Va. Private. 30 Nov. 1787. 100 acres.
Pitman, Buckner. Va. Sergeant. 17 Jul. 1784. 200 acres.
Pitman, George. Va. Sergeant. 29 Nov. 1783. 200 acres.
Pitman, Isaac. Va. Sergeant. 7 Nov. 1783. 200 acres.
Pitman, John. Ga. ———. 14 Sep. 1784. 287 1/2 acres.
Pitman, John. N.C. Private. 8 Dec. 1796. 640 acres.
Pitman, Philip. Ga. ———. 15 Mar. 1784. 250 acres.
Pitman, Timothy. Ga. ———. 21 Apr. 1784. 287 1/2 acres.
Pitnon, John. N.C. Private. 15 Jul. 1785. 640 acres to heir.
Pitt, John. Va. Surgeon. 14 Mar. 1831. 6000 acres.
Pittman, Buckner. Va.-Ind. Sergeant. 216 acres.
Pittman, James. Conn. Sufferer. New London. 145.8.4.
Pitts, Bradley. Va. Private. 28 Jul. 1784. 100 acres.
Pitts, David. Va. Private. 28 Jul. 1784. 100 acres.
Pitts, John. S.C. ———. 1 Dec. 1788. 200 acres.
Pitts, Matthias. N.C. Private. 2 Dec. 1785. 640 acres.
Pixley, John. N. Y. Private. 8 Jul. 1790. 600 acres.
Plage, John. Va. Private. 19 Jan. 1804. 200 acres.
Plaine, Jacob. Md. ———. ———. 50 acres.
Plaisted, John. Me. ———. 11 Aug. 1835. 200 acres to widow Lydia Plaisted.
Plant, James. Conn. Sufferer. New/East Haven. 94.17.10.
Platen, Benjamin. Ga. Minute Man. 22 Mar. 1785. 250 acres.
Plato, Thomas. N. Y. Private. 7 Jul. 1790. 600 acres.
Platt, Anne. Conn. Sufferer. New/East Haven. 10.11.3.
Platt, John. N.C. Private. 19 May 1784. 640 acres.
Platt, John. Conn. Sufferer. Norwalk. 0.15.6.
Platt, Richard. N. Y. Major. 9 Jul. 1790. 3000 acres.
Platt, Samuel. N.C. Surgeon's Mate. 17 Feb. 1824. 2560 acres.
Pleasants, Samuel. Md. Private. ———. 50 acres.
Plimley, Henry. N. Y. Private. 8 Jul. 1790. 600 acres.
Plimmaist, William. Conn. Sufferer. New/East Haven. 32.14.11.
Plimpton, Oliver. Mass. Corporal. 19 Nov. 1833. 200 acres to widow Lydia Plimpton.

Plodd, John. Va. Private. 11 Jul. 1810. 200 acres.
Plomendon, Joseph. N. Y. ———. ———. 500 acres.
Plugh, Nicholas. N.Y. ———. 8 Oct. 1792. 500 acres to heirs.
Plumb, Elizabeth. Conn. Sufferer. New London. 197.19.0.
Plumb, Green. Conn. Sufferer. New London. 43.19.3
Plumb, Joseph. Conn. Sufferer. New London. 24.16.0.
Plumley, George. Md. Private. ———. 50 acres.
Plumley, George. N.C. Private. 29 Sep. 1784. 640 acres to Lucy Plumley, heiress.
Plummer, Armistead. Va. Private. 22 Aug. 1783. 100 acres.
Plummer, Cupid. Md. Private. ———. 50 acres.
Plummer, Edward. Me. ———. 21 Apr. 1835. 200 acres. Albion.
Plummer, Isaac. Me. ———. 11 Aug. 1835. 200 acres to widow Esther Plummer. Gorham.
Plummer, Joseph. Ga. Refugee. 28 Feb. 1784. 250 acres.
Plummer, Obediah. Md. Private. ———. 50 acres.
Plummer, William. Me. ———. 22 Jul. 1835. 200 acres. Danville.
Plummer, William. Va. Sergeant. 30 Aug. 1783. 200 acres.
Plumpus, Timothy. N.C. Private. 20 Sep. 1821. 640 acres.
Plunket, Reuben. Va. Corporal. 13 Oct. 1783. 200 acres.
Plunkett, James. Va. Private. 1 Aug. 1799. 100 acres.
Plunkett, John. Va. Private. 7 May 1784. 200 acres.
Pock, James. Ga. Minute Man. 16 Sep. 1785. ———.
Poe, Daniel. N.C. Private. 24 Nov. 1796. 640 acres to heirs.
Poe, Jesse. Va. Private. 12 Jun. 1821. 100 acres.
Poe, John. N.C. Private. 23 Dec. 1792. 640 acres to heirs.
Poe, John. Va. Private. 30 Aug. 1796. 200 acres.
Poe, John. Va. Private. 17 Dec. 1818. 100 acres.
Poe, Thomas. Va. Private. 19 Jun. 1783. 100 acres.
Poe, Virgil. Va. Private. 18 Nov. 1818. 100 acres.
Poe, William. Va. Private. 13 Jul. 1783. 100 acres.
Poe, William. Va. Private. 14 Jun. 1820. 100 acres.
Pogue, Andrew. Pa. Private. 29 Nov. 1786. 200 acres.
Pogue, Joseph. Md. Matross. ———. 50 acres.
Poin, John. Va. Private. 1 Dec. 1801. 100 acres.
Poiner, Peter. N.C. Private. 30 Sep. 1785. 640 acres.
Pointer, William. Ga. ———. 23 Apr. 1784. 750 acres.
Pointer, William. Va. Lieutenant. 25 Mar. 1783. 2666 2/3 acres.
Poland, Joseph. Me. Corporal. 14 May 1838. 200 acres to widow Hannah Poland. Cumberland.
Poland, William. Md. Private. ———. 50 acres.
Polk, John. Ga. Soldier. 23 Apr. 1784. 287 1/2 acres.
Polk, John. N.C. Private. 9 Sep. 1785. 640 acres to heirs.
Polk, Thomas. N.C. Ensign. 22 Oct. 1783. 2191 acres.
Polk, William. N.C. Major. 23 Oct. 1783. 1888 acres.
Pollard, Absalom. Va. Corporal. 11 May 1784. 200 acres.
Pollard, Barton. Me. Sergeant. 21 Nov. 1838. 200 acres to widow Mary (Phillips) Pollard. Albion.
Pollard, Benjamin. Va. Captain. 18 Nov. 1830. 1000 acres.
Pollard, Benjamin. Va. Captain. 18 Nov. 1830. 1000 acres.
Pollard, Benjamin. Va. Captain. 18 Nov. 1830. 1000 acres.
Pollard, Benjamin. Va. Captain. 18 Nov. 1830. 1000 acres.
Pollard, Braxton. Va. Corporal. 28 Apr. 1783. 400 acres.
Pollard, Demsey. Ga. Soldier. 4 Feb. 1785. ———.
Pollard, John. N.C. Private. 21 Aug. 1820. 274 acres.
Pollard, Matthew. N.C. Private. 20 Jan. 1785. 640 acres to heirs.

Pollard, Richard. S.C. Captain. 21 Jan. 1785. 300 acres.
Pollard, Robert. Ga. ———. 1784. 287 1/2 acres.
Pollard, Seth. Mass. Sergeant. 13 Dec. 1833. 200 acres to heirs.
Pollard, Thomas. N. Y. Private. 8 Jul. 1790. 600 acres.
Pollard, Thomas. Va. Captain. 7 Mar. 1834. 4000 acres.
Pollard, William. Ga. ———. 5 Jun. 1787. 200 acres.
Pollard, William. N.C. Private. 17 Feb. 1824. 640 acres.
Pollett, John. Va. Private. 15 Aug. 1809. 100 acres.
Polley, Hugh. N. Y. Gunner. 9 Jul. 1790. 600 acres.
Pollhouse, Thomas. Md. Private. ———. 50 acres.
Pollock, Benjamin. N.C. Private. 23 Apr. 1785. 640 acres to heirs.
Pollock, Jacob. N.C. Captain. 6 Dec. 1796. 3840 acres to heirs.
Pollock, Micajah. Ga. ———. 23 Apr. 1784. 287 1/2 acres.
Pollock, Thomas. Va. Sergeant. 8 Feb. 1798. 200 acres.
Polock, Thomas. Va. Private. 20 Jun. 1783. 100 acres.
Polson, John. N.C. Private. 30 Sep. 1785. 228 acres.
Polson, John. N.C. Corporal. 11 Aug. 1820. 128 acres.
Polston, Emanuel. Md. ———. ———. 50 acres.
Pomeroy, Joseph. Pa. Private. ———. 200 acres.
Pomeroy, Sarah. Conn. Sufferer. New/East Haven. 27.16.0.
Pond, John. N.C. Private. 29 Sep. 1784. 274 acres.
Pond, Joseph. N.C. Private. 15 Dec. 1797. 640 acres to heirs.
Pondale, John. Ga. ———. 5 Dec. 1785. ———.
Ponder, Thomas. N.C. Private. 17 Dec. 1785. 640 acres to heirs.
Ponder, William. N.C. Private. 22 Oct. 1783. 318 acres.
Ponds, Zacheriah. N.C. Private. 30 Sep. 1785. 640 acres.
Poney, Francis. N.C. Drummer. 30 Sep. 1785. 1000 acres to heirs.
Ponton, Thomas. Pa. Private. 100 acres. 14 Mar. 1787 to Hester Stromey, administratrix.
Pooe, David. N.C. Private. 28 May 1784. 640 acres.
Pool, Baxter. Va. Private. 28 Oct. 1783. 100 acres.
Pool, Charles. Ga. ———. 5 Dec. 1785. ———.
Pool, Edward. Va. Corporal. 19 Dec. 1783. 200 acres.
Pool, John. N.C. Private. 10 Aug. 1785. 640 acres to heirs.
Pool, Peter. Va. Private. 10 Dec 1784. 100 acres.
Pool, Robert. Va. Private. 28 May 1783. 100 acres.
Poole, Abraham. N.C. Private. 27 Nov. 1789. 640 acres.
Poole, James. Md. Private. ———. 50 acres.
Poole, James. N.C. Private. 19 Jan. 1786. 640 acres.
Poole, Sarah. Conn. Sufferer. New London. 4.19.0.
Poole, Thomas. Me. Sergeant. 13 May 1835. 200 acres to widow Rebecca Poole. Brunswick.
Poor, John. N.C. Private. 30 Nov. 1785. 640 acres to heirs.
Poor, William. N.C. Private. 22 Dec. 1796. 640 acres to heirs.
Poor, William. Pa. Private. ———. 200 acres.
Poore, Thomas. N.C. Private. 15 Sep. 1820. 640 acres.
Pope, Burwell. Ga. ———. 27 Apr. 1784. 500 acres.
Pope, Charles. Conn. Sufferer. Norwalk. 7.10.7.
Pope, Charles. Conn. Sufferer. Norwalk. 6.0.0.
Pope, Fortunatus. Va. Sergeant. 8 Sep. 1783. 200 acres.
Pope, Henry. Ga. ———. 14 Jul. 1784. 550 acres.
Pope, John. N. Y. ———. 29 Mar. 1804. 450 acres.
Pope, John. Va. Private. 26 Mar. 1819. 200 acres.
Pope, Matthew. Va. Regimental Surgeon. 27 May 1856. 2175 acres.
Pope, Matthew. Va. Regimental Surgeon. 8 Apr. 1833. 6000 acres.

Pope, Peter. N.C. Private. 12 Sep. 1785. 640 acres to heirs.
Pope, Rueben. N.C. Private. 5 Dec. 1796. 274 acres.
Pope, Samuel. N.C. Private. 25 Jul. 1784. 274 acres.
Pope, Samuel. N.C. Private. 2 Nov. 1795. 640 acres to heirs.
Pope, Thomas. Va. Private. 27 Sep. 1797. 100 acres.
Pope, Thomas. Va. Private. 18 Jun. 1833. 200 acres.
Pope, Wilie. Ga. ———. 27 Apr. 1784. 350 acres.
Pope, William. N.C. Private. 30 Nov. 1785. 365 acres.
Pope, William. Va. Midshipman. 31 Jul. 1834. 888 8/9 acres.
Pope, William. Va. Midshipman. 31 Jul. 1834. 740 7/9 acres.
Pope, William. Va. Midshipman. 31 Jul. 1834. 740 7/9 acres.
Pope, William. Va. Midshipman. 31 Jul. 1834. 296 2/3 acres.
Pope, William. Va. Private. 19 Oct. 1784. 100 acres.
Pope, Willis. Ga. ———. 27 Apr. 1784. 300 acres.
Popes, Christian. Pa. Private. 22 Dec. 1786. 200 acres.
Popham, Francis. Md. Matross. ———. 50 acres.
Popham, William. N. Y. Aide-de-camp with rank of Major. 9 Jul. 1790. 2300 acres.
Poplar, Hack. Va. Seaman. 7 Nov. 1783. 100 acres.
Popp, John. Va. Private. 22 Feb. 1799. 100 acres.
Poram, Jonas. N.C. Private. 8 Dec. 1795. 640 acres.
Porks, Walter. N.Y. ———. 13 Sep. 1790. 500 acres to heirs.
Porter, Andrew. Pa. Colonel. 26 Oct. 1786. 500 acres.
Porter, Andrew. Pa. Colonel. 26 Oct. 1786. 500 acres.
Porter, Asa. Mass. ———. 8 Jul. 1833. 200 acres.
Porter, Benjamin. Ga. Major. 25 May 1784. 920 acres.
Porter, Benjamin. Va. Major. 6 Oct. 1810. 5333 1/3 acres.
Porter, Benjamin Jones. Me. Surgeon. 30 Jan. 1848. 600 acres to sons, Charles R. Porter, Rufus K. J. Porter, Benjamin J. Porter, and ——— Porter.
Porter, Calvert. Va. Sergeant. 23 Apr. 1783. 200 acres.
Porter, Daniel. Va. Sergeant. 16 Apr. 1783. 400 acres.
Porter, David. Va. Private. 5 Apr. 1784. 100 acres.
Porter, Elisha. Va. Private. 23 Jun. 1784. 100 acres.
Porter, James. Pa. Private. 1 Mar. 1787. 200 acres.
Porter, John. N.C. Private. 8 Dec. 1796. 640 acres.
Porter, John. Conn. Sufferer. Danbury. 2.0.0.
Porter, Joshua. N.C. ———. 13 Jun. 1785. 640 acres to heirs.
Porter, Oliver. Ga. ———. 21 Apr. 1784. 300 acres.
Porter, Robert. Ga. Lieutenant. ———. 460 acres.
Porter, Robert. Pa. Lieutenant. 27 Oct. 1786. 200 acres.
Porter, Robert. Pa. Lieutenant. ———. 200 acres.
Porter, Robert. Pa. Sergeant. 26 Jun. 1787. 250 acres to widow Elizabeth Porter.
Porter, Sampson. Ga. Soldier. 4 Feb. 1785. ———.
Porter, Samuel. N.C. Private. 7 Jan. 1786. 320 acres.
Porter, Thomas. Ga. Lieutenant. 16 Feb. 1785. ———.
Porter, Thomas. Md. Private. ———. 50 acres.
Porter, Thomas. Va. Sergeant. 5 Apr. 1784. 200 acres.
Porter, Thomas. Va. Captain. 6 Oct. 1810. 4666 2/3 acres.
Porter, William. Md. Private. ———. 50 acres.
Porter, William. N.C. ———. 13 Jun. 1785. 640 acres to heirs.
Porter, William. Va. Private. 28 Apr. 1783. 200 acres.
Porter, William. Va. Lieutenant. 29 May 1783. 2666 2/3 acres.
Porter, William. Va. Subaltern. 6 Apr. 1784. 2666 2/3 acres.
Porter, William. Va. Lieutenant. 25 Jul. 1797. 444 2/3 acres.

Porter, William. Va. Lieutenant. 27 Jan. 1813. 444 acres.
Porter, William. Va. Lieutenant. 27 Jan. 1813. 444 acres.
Porter, William May. Va. Private. 20 Aug. 1810. 100 acres.
Porterfield, Charles. Va. Lieutenant Colonel. 29 Nov. 1782. 2666 2/3 acres.
Porterfield, Charles. Va. Captain. 2 Oct. 1807. 4000 acres.
Porterfield, Charles. Va. Lieutenant Colonel. 19 May 1837. 2333 acres.
Porterfield, Charles. Va. Lieutenant Colonel. 1 Apr. 1853. 2333 acres.
Porterfield, Dempsey. N.C. Captain. 21 Oct. 1783. 3840 acres to heir James Porterfield.
Porterfield, Robert. Va. Captain. 29 Nov. 1782. 4000 acres.
Porterfield, Robert. Va. Captain. 1 Jun. 1805. 666 2/3 acres.
Porterfield, Robert. Va. Captain. 29 Aug. 1807. 555 acres.
Portis, Kirby. Va. Private. 27 Dec. 1796. 100 acres.
Portlock, Caleb. N.C. Private. 3 Dec. 1787. 274 acres.
Portress, John. N.C. Private. 25 Aug. 1813. 640 acres to heirs.
Portrus, Simon. Ga. Minute Man. 22 Mar. 1785. 250 acres.
Portwood, Loyd. Va. Private. 20 Feb. 1837. 100 acres.
Portwood, Loyd. Va. Private. 10 Jul. 1838. 100 acres.
Posey, Richard. Ga. ———. 21 Apr. 1784. 700 acres.
Posey, Thomas. Va. Lieutenant Colonel. 31 Mar. 1783. 7000 acres.
Posey, Thomas. Va. Lieutenant Colonel. 29 Aug. 1807. 833 1/3 acres.
Posey, Zaphaniah. Va. Private. 19 Apr. 1784. 100 acres.
Post, Anthony. N. Y. Captain. 13 Sep. 1790. 1800 acres.
Post, Henry. N. Y. Private. 8 Jul. 1790. 600 acres.
Postell, Francis. S.C. ———. 3 Aug. 1795. 40 acres.
Potan, Matthew. N. Y. Ensign. 16 Apr. 1794. 1000 acres.
Pothill, Jeremiah. Ga. Soldier. 4 Feb. 1785. ———.
Potin, John Matthew. N. Y. Lieutenant. ———. 500 acres.
Potter, Abigail. Conn. Sufferer. New/East Haven. 25.9.3.
Potter, Abigail. Conn. Sufferer. New London. 573.4.11.
Potter, Daniel. N.C. Private. 30 Sep. 1785. 228 acres.
Potter, Daniel. N.C. Private. 15 Feb. 1797. 228 acres.
Potter, Ephraim. S.C. ———. 2 Mar. 1789. 200 acres.
Potter, Francis. N.C. Private. 5 Dec. 1796. 228 acres.
Potter, Isaac. N.Y. ———. 13 Sep. 1790. 500 acres to heirs.
Potter, John. N.C. Private. 16 Oct. 1783. 228 acres.
Potter, John. N.C. Sergeant. 9 Dec. 1797. 1000 acres.
Potter, John. Va. Private. 15 Jun. 1807. 100 acres.
Potter, John. Conn. Sufferer. New London. 83.13.3.
Potter, Joshua. Conn. Sufferer. New London. 8.14.5.
Potter, Nathaniel. Va. Private. 26 Mar. 1787. 100 acres.
Potter, Richard. Conn. Sufferer. New London. 382.2.3.
Potter, Samuel. N. Y. Privtate. 7 Jul. 1790. 500 acres.
Potter, Samuel. N.C. Private. 13 Sep. 1820. 640 acres.
Potter, Thomas. Md. Fifer. ———. 50 acres.
Potts, David. Va. Private. 30 Aug. 1784. 100 acres.
Potts, Jesse. N.C. Captain. 9 Sep. 1820. 3840 acres.
Potts, John. Ga. Minute Man. 20 Apr. 1784. 287 1/2 acres.
Potts, John. Va. Private. 12 Dec. 1783. 100 acres.
Potts, Jonathan. Va. Private. 30 Aug. 1784. 100 acres.
Potts, Joseph. Pa. Captain. 9 Jun. 1812. 500 acres to heirs.
Potts, Joshua. N.C. Captain. 21 Dec. 1820. 3840 acres.
Pough, Michael. Va. Private. 30 Nov. 1784. 100 acres.
Poulson, John. Va. Major. 3 Jan. 1783. 6222 acres.

Poulson, John. Va. Major. 8 Jun. 1809. 740 acres.
Poulson, Michael. N. Y. Private. 7 Jul. 1790. 500 acres.
Pound, Reubin. Ga. Private. 22 Jul. 1784. 230 acres.
Pound, Samuel. Ga. Refugee. 27 Apr. 1784. 287 1/2 acres.
Pound, William. Va. Corporal. 19 Mar. 1783. 200 acres.
Pound, William. Va. Private. 24 Jul. 1824. 50 acres.
Pound, William. Va. Private. 24 Jul. 1824. 50 acres.
Powell, Aaron. Va. Sergeant. 10 Jun. 1783. 200 acres.
Powell, Benjamin. Ga. Minute Man. 16 Apr. 1784. 287 1/2 acres.
Powell, Benjamin. N.C. Private. 2 Apr. 1784. 640 acres.
Powell, Benjamin. Va. Private. 31 Dec. 1785. 200 acres.
Powell, Cader. Ga. ———. 21 Apr. 1784. 287 1/2 acres.
Powell, Charles. Va. Sergeant. 30 Aug. 1783. 200 acres.
Powell, Edward. Ga. ———. 17 May 1784. ———.
Powell, Francis. N.C. Private. 23 Apr. 1785. 640 acres to heirs.
Powell, Francis. Va. Second Midshipman. 11 Aug. 1834. 2666 2/3 acres.
Powell, George. Ga. ———. 16 Jul. 1784. 287 1/2 acres.
Powell, Jacob. S.C. ———. 4 Jun. 1787. 200 acres.
Powell, James. Ga. Surgeon. 20 Feb. 1784. 500 acres.
Powell, John. N.C. Private. 29 Sep. 1784. 228 acres.
Powell, John. Va. Private. 26 Apr. 1783. 200 acres.
Powell, John. Va. Sergeant. 10 Jun. 1784. 400 acres.
Powell, Joshua. Ga. ———. 16 Jun. 1785. 287 1/2 acres.
Powell, Josiah. Ga. Refugee. 20 Feb. 1784. 250 acres.
Powell, Josiah. Ga. ———. 17 May 1784. ———.
Powell, Leven. Va. Lieutenant Colonel. 18 Jun. 1784. 6000 acres.
Powell, Leven. Va. Lieutenant Colonel. 11 Oct. 1855. 6000 acres.
Powell, Leven. Va. Private. 29 Dec. 1784. 200 acres.
Powell, Leven. Va. Lieutenant Colonel. 17 Aug. 1784. 2000 acres.
Powell, Leven. Va. Major. 17 Aug. 1784. 2000 acres.
Powell, Leven. Va. Major. 17 Aug. 1784. 2000 acres.
Powell, Lewis. Ga. Soldier. 1784. 287 1/2 acres.
Powell, Lewis. N.C. Private. 17 Feb. 1824. 640 acres.
Powell, Lloyd. Pa. Private. ———. 200 acres.
Powell, Mark. S.C. Soldier. 21 Jan. 1785. 200 acres.
Powell, Matthew. N.C. Private. 25 Nov. 1795. 640 acres to heirs.
Powell, Moses. N.C. Private. 23 Apr. 1785. 640 acres to heirs.
Powell, Moses, Jr. Ga. Citizen. 21 Apr. 1784. 287 1/2 acres.
Powell, Nicholas. N.C. Private. 23 Apr. 1785. 640 acres to heirs.
Powell, Peter. N.C. Private. 30 Sep. 1785. 640 acres to heirs.
Powell, Peyton. Va. Lieutenant. 22 Jul. 1783. 1666 2/3 acres.
Powell, Peyton. Va. Lieutenant. 22 Jul. 1783. 1000 acres.
Powell, Peyton. Va. Lieutenant. 19 Jul. 1797. 444 2/3 acres.
Powell, Peyton. Va. Lieutenant. 11 Aug. 1807. 333 1/3 acres.
Powell, Richard. Va. Private. 15 Sep. 1785. 100 acres.
Powell, Richard. Va. Private. 20 May 1823. 100 acres.
Powell, Robert. Va. Captain. 20 Jun. 1783. 4000 acres.
Powell, Robert. Va. Major. 9 May 1834. 259 acres.
Powell, Robert. Va. Major. 9 May 1834. 259 acres.
Powell, Robert. Va. Major. 29 Apr. 1844. 259 acres.
Powell, Robert. Va. Major. 29 Apr. 1844. 259 acres.
Powell, Robert. Va. Major. 22 Jun. 1844. 259 acres.
Powell, Robert. Va. Major. 11 Jan. 1861. 259 acres.
Powell, Robert, Sr. Va. Captain. 20 Nov. 1818. 666 2/3 acres.

Powell, Solomon. Va. Seaman. 24 Mar. 1831. 2666 2/3 acres.
Powell, Solomon. Va. Seaman. 21 Oct. 1831. 100 acres.
Powell, Solomon. Va. Quartermaster. 31 Dec. 1851. 1283 1/3 acres.
Powell, Solomon. Va. Quartermaster. 31 Dec. 1851. 1283 1/3 acres.
Powell, Stephen. N. Y. Private. 8 Jul. 1790. 600 acres.
Powell, Stephen. N.C. Private. 23 Apr. 1785. 640 acres to heirs.
Powell, Thomas. N.C. Private. 22 Oct. 1783. 320 acres.
Powell, Thomas. Pa. ———. ———. 200 acres.
Powell, Thomas. S.C. Soldier. 15 Oct. 1784. 200 acres.
Powell, Thomas. Va. Lieutenant. 29 May 1783. 2666 2/3 acres.
Powell, Thomas. Va. Surgeon. 13 Feb. 1834. 4800 acres.
Powell, Thomas. Va. ———. 27 Jul. 1836. 900 acres.
Powell, Thomas. Va. ———. 27 Jul. 1836. 300 acres.
Powell, Thomas. Va. ———. 15 Oct. 1836. 1200 acres.
Powell, Thomas. Va. ———. 15 Oct. 1836. 1200 acres.
Powell, Thomas. Va. ———. 15 Oct. 1836. 1200 acres.
Powell, Thomas. Va. ———. 15 Oct. 1836. 300 acres.
Powell, Thomas. Va. ———. 15 Oct. 1836. 300 acres.
Powell, Thomas. Va. ———. 15 Oct. 1836. 300 acres.
Powell, Thomas. Va. ———. 15 Oct. 1836. 300 acres.
Powell, William. N.C. Private. 22 Oct. 1783. 440 acres.
Powell, William. Pa. ———. 24 Aug. 1787. 200 acres to Mary Powell, widow.
Powell, William. Va. Lieutenant. 14 Dec. 1832. 2666 2/3 acres.
Power, Alexander. Pa. Quartermaster. 2 Oct. 1787. 200 acres.
Power, Alexander. Pa. Private. 2 Oct. 1787. 200 acres.
Power, Robert. Va. Cornet. 19 Sep. 1783. 3110 2/3 acres.
Power, William. Pa. Captain. 28 Oct. 1786. 500 acres.
Power, William. Pa. Private. 30 Aug. 1787. 200 acres to Sarah Power, widow.
Powers, Caleb. N.C. Private. 19 Dec. 1808. 274 acres.
Powers, David. Ga. Minute Man. 3 Apr. 1785. ———.
Powers, David. Mass. ———. 22 Jul. 1833. 200 acres.
Powers, David. N.C. Private. 7 Dec. 1796. 640 acres to heirs. He was of Tyrrell County.
Powers, Ichabod. Conn. Sufferer. New London. 620.8.0.
Powers, Ichabod, Jr. Conn. Sufferer. New London. 188.16.6.
Powers, James. N.C. Lieutenant. 29 Sep. 1784. 1200 acres.
Powers, Jesse. Md. Private. ———. 50 acres.
Powers, John. Ga. Soldier. 27 Apr. 1784. 200 acres.
Powers, John. Va. Private. 16 May 1785. 100 acres.
Powers, Joseph. Ga. Minute Man. 3 Apr. 1785. ———.
Powers, Joshua. Conn. Sufferer. New London. 4.17.0.
Powers, Lewis. Va. Private. 23 Sep. 1809. 100 acres.
Powers, Mancefield. N.C. Private. 20 Dec. 1803. 640 acres to heirs.
Powers, Robert. N.C. Private. 30 Sep. 1785. 640 acres to heirs.
Powers, Stephen. Mass. Private. 6 Mar. 1834. 200 acres.
Powers, William. N.C. Private. 14 Sep. 1820. 274 acres.
Powers, William. Va. Private. 15 Dec. 1783. 100 acres.
Powers, William. Va. Private. 19 Feb. 1784. 200 acres.
Powle, William. Va. Private. 21 Jun. 1783. 100 acres.
Poyas, John Ernest. S.C. Surgeon. 15 Oct. 1784. 300 acres.
Poyner, Peter. N.C. Private. 21 May 1784. 274 acres.
Poyner, William. Va. Lieutenant. 7 Nov. 1811. 500 acres.
Poyner, William. Va. Lieutenant. 7 Nov. 1811. 500 acres.
Poyner, William. Va. Lieutenant. 7 Nov. 1811. 500 acres.

Poyner, William. Va. Lieutenant. 7 Nov. 1811. 500 acres.
Poyner, William. Va. Lieutenant. 7 Nov. 1811. 666 2/3 acres.
Poynter, John. N.C. Captain. 30 Sep. 1785. 1508 acres.
Poythress, Francis. Va. Sergeant. 24 Jun. 1786. 400 acres.
Poythress, William. Va. Captain Lieutenant. 1783. 4000 acres.
Poyton, James. Pa. ———. 28 Dec. 1786. 200 acres to the heirs.
Prall, Edward. Md. Captain. ———. 200 acres.
Prather, Daniel. Ga. ———. 26 May 1784. 287 1/2 acres.
Prather, Edward. Ga. ———. 13 Apr. 1784. 287 1/2 acres.
Prather, Henry. Va.-Ind. Private. 108 acres.
Prather, William. Md. Fifer. ———. 50 acres.
Pratt, James. N.C. Private. 13 Dec. 1796. 274 acres.
Pratt, John. N. Y. Matross. 9 Jul. 1790. 600 acres.
Pratt, John. Pa. Lieutenant. ———. 200 acres.
Pratt, John. Pa. Lieutenant. 11 Jan. 1787. 200 acres.
Pratt, John. Va. Private. 25 May 1785. 100 acres.
Pratt, Peter. N.C. Private. 26 Aug. 1785. 640 acres to heirs.
Pratt, Shubale. Va. Surgeon. 15 May 1783. 6000 acres.
Pratt, Shubale. Va. Surgeon. 10 Jul. 1838. 400 acres.
Pratt, Zebulon. N.C. Private. 22 Mar. 1785. 274 acres.
Praull, David. Pa. ———. 25 Oct. 1786. 200 acres.
Pray, Job. Ga. Captain. 23 Apr. 1784. 600 acres.
Prayles, John. Va. Sailor. 23 Jan. 1788. 100 acres.
Prentice, Amos. Conn. Sufferer. Groton. 566.1.6.
Prentice, John. Conn. Sufferer. New London. 3.16.0.
Prentice, Jonas. Conn. Sufferer. New/East Haven. 27.17.6.
Prescot, Jonathan. N.C. Private. 24 Nov. 1796. 640 acres to heirs.
Prescot, Willoughby. N.C. Private. 3 Feb. 1785. 365 acres.
Prescote, Aaron. N.C. Private. 26 Sep. 1800. 640 acres to heirs.
Prescote, Austin. N.C. Private. 12 Dec. 1785. 640 acres.
Prescote, Charles. N.C. Private. 24 Nov. 1796. 640 acres to heirs.
Prescote, Isaac. N.C. Private. 15 Feb. 1797. 640 acres to heirs.
Prescote, Thomas. N.C. Sergeant. 30 Sep. 1785. 1000 acres.
Prescott, Aaron. N.C. Private. 12 Dec. 1796. 640 acres to heirs.
Prescott, James. Conn. Sufferer. New/East Haven. 26.3.6.
Prescott, Thomas. Va. Private. 15 Jun. 1807. 200 acres.
Prestage, John. Ga. ———. 17 May 1784. ———.
Preston, Amariah. Mass. Private. 18 Oct. 1833. 200 acres.
Preston, Andrew. Md. ———. ———. 50 acres.
Preston, Benjamin. N. Y. Private. 8 Jul. 1790. 600 acres.
Preston, Nathan. Va. Private. 15 Jun. 1785. 100 acres.
Preston, Othniel. N. Y. Private. 8 Jul. 1790. 600 acres.
Preston, Patrick. Pa. Sergeant. 16 Oct. 1786. 250 acres to Alexander Power, assignee.
Preston, Robert. Va. Private. 23 Jul. 1824. 200 acres.
Preston, Stephen. Md. Private. ———. 50 acres.
Preston, Zuriah. Conn. Sufferer. New London. 21.13.0.
Preton, George. N.C. Private. 30 Sep. 1785. 640 acres to heirs.
Preuit, Benjamin. Ga. Soldier. ———. ———.
Preuit, William. N.C. Private. 15 Feb. 1797. 228 acres.
Preuitt, Lacy. N.C. Private. 9 Dec. 1797. 274 acres.
Prevatt, James. Ga. ———. 27 Apr. 1784. 200 acres.
Prewett, Joshua. Va. Private. 10 May 1838. 100 acres.
Prewite, Ransom. N.C. Private. 20 Apr. 1784. 274 acres.

Pribble, Samuel. N. Y. Corporal. 3 Jul. 1790. 600 acres.
Price, Adam. N. Y. Private. 8 Jul. 1790. 600 acres.
Price, Anjer. Va. Sergeant. 31 Oct. 1811. 200 acres.
Price, Benjamin. Md. Captain. ———. 200 acres.
Price, Benjamin. N.Y. ———. 13 Sep. 1790. 500 acres to heirs.
Price, Burdett. Va. Private. 26 Nov. 1784. 200 acres.
Price, Casper. Ga. ———. 15 Apr. 1784. 230 acres.
Price, Darrington. Pa. Sergeant. 20 Sep.1787. 250 acres.
Price, David. Va. Sergeant. 22 Aug. 1783. 400 acres.
Price, Ebenezer. Va. Quartermaster. 20 Jun. 1787. 2666 2/3 acres.
Price, Ebenezer. Va. Quartermaster. 15 Apr. 1853. 2666 2/3 acres.
Price, Elijah. N. Y. Matross. 9 Jul. 1790. 600 acres.
Price, Elijah. S.C. Soldier. 21 Jan. 1785. 200 acres.
Price, George. Va. Private. 2 Jul. 1784. 100 acres.
Price, George. Va. Private. 21 Apr. 1784. 100 acres.
Price, Jacob. Va. Private. 13 Mar. 1797. 100 acres.
Price, James. N. Y. ———. ———. 500 acres.
Price, James. N.C. Private. 17 Sep. 1785. 274 acres to heirs.
Price, James. Va. Captain. 18 Oct. 1811. 4000 acres.
Price, James. Va. Captain. 5 Mar. 1859. 1185 2/3 acres.
Price, Job. Ga. ———. 19 Jul. 1784. 287 1/2 acres.
Price, John. Ga. ———. 13 Sep. 1784. 460 acres.
Price, John. Va. Private. 9 Jan. 1812. 100 acres.
Price, John. Va. Private. 9 Jan. 1812. 200 acres.
Price, Micajah. N.C. Private. 30 Sep. 1785. 640 acres to heirs.
Price, Nathaniel. Md. Private. ———. 50 acres.
Price, Nathaniel. N. Y. Gunner. 9 Jul. 1790. 500 acres.
Price, Rice. N.C. Private. 12 Sep. 1785. 640 acres to heirs.
Price, Samuel. N.C. Private. 30 Sep. 1785. 640 acres.
Price, Samuel. N.C. Private. 1 Dec. 1796. 640 acres.
Price, Stephen. Md. Private. ———. 50 acres.
Price, Thomas. Md. Lieutenant. ———. 200 acres.
Price, Thomas. Md. ———. ———. 50 acres.
Price, Thomas. N.C. Private. 3 Feb. 1785. 274 acres.
Price, Thomas. Pa. Sergeant. 26 Jul. 1805. 250 acres.
Price, Thomas. Va. Private. 24 Jun. 1784. 100 acres.
Price, William. N.C. Private. 19 May 1784. 640 acres.
Price, William. N.C. Private. 24 Dec. 1785. 640 acres.
Price, William. Va. Lieutenant. 3 Jul. 1809. 500 acres.
Price, William. Va. Lieutenant. 3 Jul. 1809. 500 acres.
Price, William. Va. Lieutenant. 3 Jul. 1809. 500 acres.
Price, William. Va. Lieutenant. 3 Jul. 1809. 500 acres.
Price, William. Va. Lieutenant. 3 Jul. 1809. 200 acres.
Price, William. Va. Lieutenant. 3 Jul. 1809. 200 acres.
Price, William. Va. Lieutenant. 3 Jul. 1809. 100 acres.
Price, William. Va. Lieutenant. 3 Jul. 1809. 166 2/3 acres.
Price, William. Va. Lieutenant. 25 Oct. 1809. 740 acres.
Price, William. Va. Lieutenant. 10 Jun. 1828. 246 2/3 acres.
Price, William. Va. Lieutenant. 10 Jun. 1828. 246 2/3 acres.
Price, William. Va. Lieutenant. 10 Jun. 1828. 246 acres, 1 rod, 64 poles.
Prichard, Clement. N.C. Private. 9 Sep. 1785. 640 acres to heirs.
Prichard, George.. Va. Private. 14 Dec. 1808. 200 acres.
Prichard, Jesse. N.C. Sergeant. 2 Dec. 1785. 428 acres.
Prickett, Thomas. Va. Gunner. 12 Sep. 1796. 100 acres.

Prickett, William. Va. Sergeant. 13 Aug. 1834. 400 acres.
Pridal, John. Ga. ———. 17 May 1784. ———.
Priddy, John. Ga. ———. 22 Apr. 1784. 850 acres.
Priddy, Richard. Va. Sergeant. 22 Dec. 1784. 200 acres.
Pride, William. Va. Lieutenant. 3 Jun. 1783. 2666 2/3 acres.
Pridgen, Thomas. N.C. Noncomissioned Officer. 1 Jan. 1801. 1000 acres to heirs.
Pridgeon, William. N.C. Private. 25 Jul. 1784. 274 acres.
Pridgeon, Zacheriah. N.C. Private. 10 Aug. 1785. 640 acres.
Pridgon, Marmaduke. N.C. Private. 9 Feb. 1796. 640 acres to heirs.
Priest, John. Mass. Private. 19 Nov. 1832. 200 acres.
Priest, Joseph. Mass. Private. 29 Jan. 1833. 200 acres to heirs.
Priest, Peter. Va.-Ind. Private. 108 acres.
Prigin, Ezekiel. N.C. Private. 28 Sep. 1785. 640 acres.
Primm, Abraham. N.C. Sergeant. 12 Mar. 1785. 1000 acres to heirs.
Primm, James. Va. Quartermaster Sergeant. 29 Jul. 1835. 200 acres.
Prince, Christopher. Conn. Sufferer. New London. 512.4.3.
Prince, John. Ga. ———. 19 Dec. 1785. 575 acres.
Prince, Robert. S.C. ———. 4 Jul. 1785. 200 acres.
Prince, Thomas. S.C. Lieutenant. 15 Oct. 1784. 200 acres to Robert Prince, heir.
Prindle, Charles. Conn. Sufferer. New/East Haven. 47.4.6.
Prindle, Jones Enos. N.Y. Sergeant Major. 9 Jul. 1790. 500 acres.
Prindle, Jotham. N. Y. Private. 8 Jul. 1790. 600 acres.
Prindle, Silas. N.C. Private. 9 Feb. 1796. 228 acres.
Prior, Abner. N. Y. Surgeon's Mate. 7 Jul. 1790. 1300 acres.
Prior, Elisha. Conn. Sufferer. Groton. 34.12.11.
Prior, John. Va. Captain. 30 Dec. 1782. 4000 acres.
Prior, William. Md. Private. ———. 50 acres.
Prisley, Daniel. Ga. ———. ———. 575 acres.
Pritchard Jesse. N.C. Sergeant. 11 Aug. 1820. 572 acres to heirs.
Pritchard, James. Md. ———. ———. 50 acres.
Pritchard, James. N.C. Private. 26 Aug. 1785. 640 acres to heirs.
Pritchard, James. Va. Private. 24 Sep. 1783. 200 acres.
Pritchard, James. Va. Private. 18 Oct. 1785. 200 acres.
Pritchard, Thomas. Va. Private. 25 Feb. 1785. 100 acres.
Pritchard, William. Va.-Ind. Sergeant. 216 acres.
Pritchet, Arthur. Md. Private. ———. 50 acres.
Pritchet, Edward. N.C. Private. 1 Aug. 1792. 640 acres.
Pritchett, John. N.Ca. Private. 12 Dec. 1796. 228 acres.
Pritchett, John. Va. Sergeant. 23 Apr. 1783. 200 acres.
Pritchett, Peter. Va. Sergeant. 7 May 1784. 200 acres.
Privale, Miles. N.C. Private. 17 Feb. 1824. 640 acres.
Proby, John. S.C. Soldier. 7 Oct. 1799. 125 acres to Mary Proby, widow.
Proby, John. S.C. ———. 7 Oct. 1799. 70 acres to Mary Proby, widow.
Proby, Minson. Va. Sergeant. 24 Apr. 1832. 200 acres.
Proctor, Francis. Pa. Major. 28 Aug. 1787. 300 acres.
Proctor, Francis. Pa. Major. 28 Aug. 1787. 300 acres to trustees.
Proctor, Isaac. Va. Private. 27 Sep. 1796. 200 acres.
Proctor, John. Va. Sergeant. 12 Jul. 1783. 200 acres.
Proctor, Joshua. N.C. Private. 10 Aug. 1785. 640 acres to heirs.
Proctor, Richard. Md. Private. ———. 50 acres.
Proctor, Samuel. Me. Private. 27 May 1835. 200 acres to widow Joanna Thompson. Wayne.
Proctor, William. N.C. Private. 3 Feb. 1785. 228 acres.
Proctor, William. N.C. Sergeant. Jan. 1795. 500 acres.

Profit, Pleasant. Ga. ———. 27 Apr. 1784. 200 acres.
Propper, Frederick. N. Y. Private. 8 Jul. 1790. 600 acres.
Proud, Charles. Pa. ———. ———. 200 acres.
Prouse, Germaine. N. Y. ———. ———. 500 acres.
Prout, John. Md. Matross. ———. 50 acres.
Prouth, Degory. N. Y. Private. 8 Jul. 1790. 600 acres.
Prouty, Eli. Mass. Corporal. 17 Feb. 1834. 200 acres to widow Rebekah Prouty.
Provaux, Adrian. S.C. Captain. 2 May 1785. 300 acres.
Province, John. N.C. Private. 14 Dec. 1796. 640 acres to heirs.
Provoost, Robert. N. Y. Ensign. 9 Jul. 1790. 1000 acres.
Prowdford, John. N.C. Private. 2 Aug. 1784. 640 acres.
Prowdford, John. N.C. Private. 22 Dec. 1796. 274 acres.
Pruden, Henry. Va. Sergeant. 22 Jan. 1834. 200 acres.
Pruder, Henry. Va. Sergeant. 12 Feb. 1785. 200 acres.
Pruite, Joshua. N.C. Private. 20 Apr. 1784. 274 acres.
Pruitt, Josiah. Va.-Ind. Private. 108 acres.
Pryce, Thomas. Pa. Captain. 27 Mar. 1787. 500 acres to widow.
Pryor, John. Ga. ———. 15 Apr. 1784. 200 acres.
Pryor, John. Va. Captain Lieutenant. 3 Jul. 1807. 323 2/3 acres.
Pryor, John. Va. Captain Lieutenant. 3 Jul. 1807. 231 1/3 acres.
Pucket, Reason. N.C. Private. 23 Nov. 1797. 274 acres to heirs.
Pucket, Thomas. N.C. Musician. 6 Dec. 1797. 428 acres.
Puckett, Josiah. Va. Private. 11 Feb. 1785. 200 acres.
Puckett, Womack. Va. Private. 27 Aug. 1782. 100 acres.
Pugh, David. N.C. Private. 1 Sep. 1785. 640 acres to heirs.
Pugh, Elijah. Ga. ———. 20 Apr. 1784. 287 1/2 acres.
Pugh, Francis. Ga. ———. 25 May 1784. 287 1/2 acres.
Pugh, Frederick. N.C. Private. 28 Sep. 1785. 640 acres to heirs.
Pugh, James. Ga. Refugee. 6 Feb. 1784. 250 acres.
Pugh, James, Jr. Ga. Refugee. 17 Feb. 1784. 250 acres.
Pugh, Jehu. Ga. ———. 21 Apr. 1784. 287 12/ acres.
Pugh, Jesse. Ga. ———. 21 Apr. 1784. 287 1/2 acres.
Pugh, Jonathan. Pa. Lieutenant & Adjutant. 13 Aug. 1787 to 200 acres to Catherine Pugh, widow.
Pugh, Jonathan. Pa. Lieutenant & Adjutant. 13 Aug. 1787. 200 acres to heirs.
Pugh, Joseph. Va. Lieutenant. 14 Jun. 1820. 1333 1/3 acres.
Pugh, Joseph. Va. Lieutenant. 14 Jun. 1820. 1333 1/3 acres.
Pugh, Lewis. Va. Private. 27 Jun. 1783. 200 acres.
Pugh, William. Ga. ———. 17 Feb. 1784. 250 acres.
Pugh, Willis. Va. Ensign. 3 Oct. 1782. 2666 2/3 acres.
Pulford, John. Va.-Ind. Private. 108 acres.
Pulham, John. Va. Private. 5 Jun. 1783. 100 acres.
Pulle, Harmon. N.C. Private. 17 Dec. 1796. 640 acres.
Pullen, Henry. Va. Private. 5 Feb. 1834. 200 acres.
Pullen, John. Me. Private. 28 May 1835. 200 acres to widow Amy Pullen. Waterville.
Pullen, Samuel. Pa. ———. 200 acres.
Pullen, William. Va. Sergeant. 8 Sep. 1783. 200 acres.
Pullen, William. Va. Lieutenant. 5 Nov. 1811. 500 acres.
Pullen, William. Va. Lieutenant. 5 Nov. 1811. 500 acres.
Pullen, William. Va. Lieutenant. 5 Nov. 1811. 500 acres.
Pullen, William. Va. Lieutenant. 5 Nov. 1811. 500 acres.
Pullen, William. Va. Lieutenant. 5 Nov. 1811. 666 2/3 acres.
Pullen, William. Va. Private. 9 Nov. 1818. 100 acres.
Puller, John. Va. Private. 21 Apr. 1785. 100 acres.
Pulles, John. N. Y. Private. 8 Jul. 1790. 600 acres.

Pulley, Benjamin. N.C. Private. 12 Sep. 1785. 640 acres to heirs.
Pulley, George. N.C. Private. 30 Sep. 1785. 640 acres to heirs.
Pulley, Isham. N.C. Private. 17 Dec. 1785. 274 acres.
Pulley, James. N.C. Private. 29 Apr. 1784. 228 acres.
Pulley, James. N.C. Private. 28 Sep. 1785. 640 acres.
Pulley, William. Va. Private. 14 Jun. 1784. 100 acres.
Pulliam, Joseph. Ga. ———. 24 May 1784. 287 1/2 acres.
Pulliam, William. Ga. Refugee. 24 May 1784. 287 1/2 acres.
Pulliam, William. Ga. ———. 24 May 1784. 287 1/2 acres.
Pullin, George. Va. Private. 18 Feb. 1784. 100 acres.
Pulman, Salter. N. Y. Private. 3 Jul. 1790. 600 acres.
Pumpilly, Bennet. Me. Private. 29 Sep. 1835. 200 acres to widow Elizabeth Pumpilly. Turner.
Pumpshin, Daniel. N.Y. ———. 13 Sep. 1790. 500 acres to heirs.
Punang, John. N.C. Private. 7 Jan. 1786. 640 acres to heirs.
Punch, Patrick. Va. Private. 6 Mar. 1788. 200 acres.
Punchard, William. Conn. Sufferer. New/East Haven. 20.1.9.
Punchard, William. Conn. Sufferer. New/East Haven. 26.13.0.
Punderson, Thomas. Conn. Sufferer. New/East Haven. 2.18.3.
Punderson, Thomas, Jr. Conn. Sufferer. New/East Haven. 14.15.7.
Punter, Henry. Va. Sergeant. 14 Apr. 1783. 200 acres.
Purcell, George. Va. Lieutenant. 6 Oct. 1819. 2666 2/3 acres.
Purcell, Henry. S.C. Chaplain. 21 Jan. 1785. 450 acres.
Purcell, Henry D. Pa. Lieutenant. 12 Oct. 1786. 200 acres.
Purcell, Henry D. Pa. Lieutenant. 12 Oct.1786. 200 acres.
Purcell, John. Va. Private. 20 Aug. 1783. 200 acres.
Purcell, Robert. Va. Private. 12 Nov. 1783. 100 acres.
Purcell, Thomas. Va. Private. 5 Jun. 1802. 200 acres.
Purcell, William. Va.-Ind. Private. 108 acres.
Purchase, William. Md. Corporal. ———. 50 acres.
Purdey, James. N. Y. Matross. 9 Jul. 1790. 500 acres.
Purdy, Edward. Md. ———. ———. 50 acres.
Purdy, Henry. Md. Private. ———. 50 acres.
Purdy, James. N.C. Private. 22 Oct. 1783. 281 acres.
Purdy, John. Md. Private. ———. 50 acres.
Purdy, John. Conn. Sufferer. Greenwich. 10.7.1.
Purdy, Joseph. Md. Drum Major. ———. 50 acres.
Purdy, Solomon. Conn. Sufferer. Greenwich. 83.18.9.
Purkett, Henry. Mass. ———. 27 Feb. 1813. 200 acres.
Purkins, Abraham. N.C. Private. 21 Apr. 1784. 640 acres to James Purkins, heir.
Purkins, Adam. N.C. Private. 29 Apr. 1784. 640 acres.
Purkins, Joshua. Va. Private. 18 Apr. 1832. 100 acres.
Purky, Henry. S.C. ———. 7 May 1787. 200 acres.
Pursar, William. Va. Seaman. 14 Jun. 1833. 100 acres.
Purse, Thomas. N.C. ———. 29 Apr. 1784. 640 acres to Jeremiah Purse, heir.
Pursell, William. Md. Private. ———. 50 acres.
Pursely, William. Va. Sergeant. 5 May 1783. 200 acres.
Purser, Joseph. N.C. Private. 17 Feb. 1824. 640 acres.
Pursley, Lawrence. Va. Private. 30 Aug. 1783. 100 acres.
Pursly, John. N.C. Private. 30 Sep. 1785. 640 acres to heirs.
Purtle, John. Pa. Private. 18 Oct. 1786. 200 acres.
Purton, Ellexana. N.C. Private. 30 Sep. 1785. 640 acres to heirs.
Purviance, John. Ga. ———. 27 Apr. 1784. 400 acres.
Purvice, Barnett. N.C. Private. 30 Sep. 1785. 640 acres to heirs.

Purvice, James. N.C. Private. 10 Dec. 1788. 640 acres to heirs.
Purvis, James. Va. Captain. 2 Dec. 1784. 4000 acres.
Purvis, William. Va. Private. 26 Nov. 1783. 100 acres.
Puryear, Jesse. Va. Private. 1 Sep. 1783. 100 acres.
Puryear, Reuben. Va. Private. 3 Dec. 1812. 100 acres.
Puryear, Thomas. Va. Private. 16 Jun. 1783. 100 acres.
Pusley, David. Ga. Soldier. 24 Dec. 178-. ———.
Putman, Randal. N.C. Private. 30 Sep. 1785. 640 acres to heirs.
Putnall, Christopher. Ga. ———. 20 Apr. 1784. 287 1/2 acres to heirs.
Putnall, William. N.C. Private. 30 Sep. 1785. 640 acres to heirs.
Putnam, William. N. Y. Private. 8 Jul. 1790. 600 acres.
Pyatt, Benjamin. Va. Sergeant. 9 May 1785. 200 acres.
Pyeatt, Peter. N.C. Sergeant. 27 Nov. 1783. 428 acres.
Pyle, William. Va. Lieutenant. 4 Apr. 1797. 2666 2/3 acres.
Pyot, Thomas. N.C. Private. 6 Sep. 1821. 640 acres.
Quackenboss, Benjamin. N.Y. ———. 13 Sep. 1790. 500 acres to heirs.
Quackenboss, Jacobus. N.Y. ———. 13 Sep. 1790. 500 acres to heirs.
Quackenboss, John. N.Y. ———. 13 Sep. 1790. 500 acres to heirs.
Quail, John. Va. Private. 25 Oct. 1784. 100 acres.
Qualfarge, Peter. N. Y. ———. ———. 500 acres.
Qualls, Peter. Ga. ———. 26 May 1784. 287 1/2 acres.
Quarles, Abner. Va. Private. 27 Jun. 1783. 200 acres.
Quarles, Henry. Va. Captain. 28 May 1783. 4000 acres.
Quarles, James. Va. Captain. 31 Dec. 1782. 4000 acres.
Quarles, James. Va. Major. 26 Feb. 1783. 1333 1/3 acres.
Quarles, John. Va. Captain Lieutenant. 2 Feb. 1784. 4000 acres.
Quarles, John. Va. Lieutenant. 6 Apr. 1784. 2666 2/3 acres.
Quarles, Moses. Va. Private. 25 May 1785. 200 acres.
Quarles, Moses. Va. Private. 4 May 1858. 200 acres.
Quarles, Nathaniel. Va. Sergeant. 28 Feb. 1783. 200 acres.
Quarles, Robert. Va. Lieutenant. 3 Feb. 1784. 2666 2/3 acres.
Quarles, Thomas. Va. Lieutenant. 13 Jun. 1783. 2666 2/3 acres.
Quarles, Wharton. Va. Lieutenant. 18 Nov. 1830. 2666 2/3 acres.
Quarles, Wharton. Va. Brigade Quartermaster. 30 Dec. 1851. 3555 2/3 acres.
Quarles, Wharton. Va. Brigade Quartermaster. 30 Dec. 1851. 1777 2/3 acres.
Quarles, William P. Va. Lieutenant. 21 Feb. 1784. 2000 acres.
Quarles, William P. Va. Lieutenant. 21 Feb. 1784. 666 2/3 acres.
Quarls, Roger. Ga. ———. 15 Mar. 1784. 250 acres.
Quarrel, James. Pa. Sergeant. 3 Nov. 1786. 250 acres.
Quarterman, Thomas. Ga. Refugee. 3 Apr. 1784. 250 acres.
Quarterman, William. Ga. Refugee. 22 Feb. 1785. ———.
Quay, James. Md. Private. ———. 50 acres.
Queen, Christopher. N. Y. Private. 8 Jul. 1790. 600 acres.
Queen, William. Ga. Soldier. 27 Apr. 1784. 287 1/2 acres.
Querns, John. Ga. Citizen. 15 Mar. 1784. 250 acres.
Quick, Cornelius. N. Y. Private. 8 Jul. 1790. 600 acres.
Quick, Jacob. N. Y. Private. 8 Jul. 1790. 500 acres.
Quick, John. Md. Sergeant. ———. 50 acres.
Quigly, Edward. Pa. Private. 20 Jan. 1787. 200 acres.
Quillen, Daniel. N.C. Private. 10 Dec. 1788. 640 acres to heirs.
Quillin, Robert. Va. Private. 2 Apr. 1807. 200 acres.
Quin, Patrick. Va. Private. 29 Jul. 1783. 200 acres.
Quinby, Eleazer. N.C. Private. 21 Feb. 1821. 274 acres to heirs.
Quinley, William. Va. Sergeant. 28 Feb. 1784. 200 acres.

Quinlin, Joseph. Va. Surgeon. 25 Mar. 1834. 6000 acres.

Quinn, John. Md. Matross. ———. 50 acres.

Quinn, John. Va. Private. 15 Dec. 1808. 100 acres.

Quinn, John. Va. Private. 15 Mar. 1832. 100 acres.

Quinn, Joseph. Md. Private. ———. 50 acres.

Quinn, Michael. N.C. Captain. 29 Sep. 1784. 2102 acres.

Quinn, Patrick. Md. Private. ———. 50 acres.

Quinn, Thomas. N.C. Private. 10 Sep. 1821. 274 acres to heirs.

Quintard, Peter. Conn. Sufferer. Norwalk. 401.0.0.

Quintin, William. Md. Private. ———. 50 acres.

Quirk, Thomas. Va.-Ind. Major. Jul. 1783. 4312 acres.

Quirk, Thomas. Va. Major. 9 Jul. 1783. 1000 acres.

Quirk, Thomas. Va. Major. 9 Jul. 1783. 1000 acres.

Quirk, Thomas. Va. Captain. 9 Jul. 1783. 3333 1/3 acres.

Rabey, Cader. Va. Private. 11 Aug. 1834. 100 acres.

Raborne, George. N.C. Private. 20 May 1801. 274 acres.

Raby, Adam. N.C. Private. 12 Dec. 1806. 640 acres to heirs.

Race[?], John. ———. 28 Jul. 1784. 287 1/2 acres.

Racine, Charles. N. Y. ———. ———. 500 acres.

Racine, Peter. N. Y. ———. ———. 500 acres.

Raden, George. Ga. ———. 17 May 1784. ———.

Rader, Samuel. Va. Private. 5 Mar. 1833. 100 acres.

Radford, William. Va. Sergeant. 17 Sep. 1788. 400 acres.

Radley, Berriman. N.C. Private. 27 Jul. 1785. 640 acres.

Radley, Jonas. N.C. Private. 24 Nov. 1796. 640 acres to heirs.

Radly, John. Md. Sergeant. ———. 50 acres.

Rae, James. Ga. Deputy Comissary General of Purchases. 15 Apr. 1784. 287 1/2 acres.

Rafferty, Michael. Ga. Refugee. 21 Apr. 1784. 287 1/2 acres.

Ragan, Daniel. Va. Sergeant. 11 Feb. 1784. 200 acres.

Ragan, Ezekiel. Ga. ———. 2 Jan. 1786. ———.

Ragan, Felix. Ga. Refugee. 27 Apr. 1784. 287 1/2 acres.

Ragan, John. Ga. ———. 22 Apr. 1784. 287 1/2 acres.

Ragan, Jonathan. Ga. ———. 22 Apr. 1784. 287 1/2 acres.

Ragland, Benjamin. Ga. Refugee. 30 Jul. 1784. 575 acres.

Ragland, Evan. Ga. Lieutenant. 15 Mar. 1784. 350 acres.

Ragland, John. Ga. ———. 21 Apr. 1784. 300 acres.

Ragor, Bartholomew. Va. Private. 20 Jun. 1783. 100 acres.

Ragsdale, Drury. Va. Captain. 20 Jan. 1783. 4000 acres.

Ragsdale, Drury. Va. Captain. 22 Oct. 1807. 555 acres.

Rague, John. Pa. Surgeon's Mate. 31 May 1787. 300 acres to Thomas Forrest, assignee.

Raiborne, George. Va. Fifer. 12 Dec. 1796. 200 acres.

Raiford, John. N.C. Lieutenant. 29 Sep. 1784. 635 acres.

Raiford, Robert. N.C. Captain. 15 Sep. 1784. 3840 acres.

Railey, Isaac. N.C. Private. 12 Dec. 1796. 640 acres to heirs.

Rainer, John. N.C. Private. 30 Sep. 1785. 640 acres to heirs.

Raines, Adam. Md. Private. ———. 50 acres.

Rainey, James. N.C. Private. 27 Oct. 1783. 640 acres to Joel Lewis, assignee.

Rainey, James. N.C. Private. 22 Apr. 1785. 320 acres.

Rainey, Peter. N.C. Sergeant. 27 Oct. 1783. 1000 acres to Joel Lewis, assignee.

Rainey, Peter. N.C. Private. 28 May 1784. 640 acres.

Rains, Ephraim. N.C. ———. 14 Jun. 1785. 640 acres to heirs.

Rains, Henry. Va. Private. 29 Dec. 1784. 100 acres.

Rains, John. N.C. ———. 14 Jun. 1785. 640 acres to heirs.
Rains, John. Va. Private. 31 Jul. 1783. 100 acres.
Rains, Peter. N.C. Private. 15 Feb. 1797. 274 acres.
Rains, Robert. Va. Private. 7 Feb. 1785. 200 acres.
Rains, William. N.C. Private. 6 Dec. 1797. 640 acres to heirs.
Raison, William. Md. Lieutenant. ———. 200 acres.
Raleigh, William. Va. Private. 15 Jun. 1807. 200 acres.
Ralja, John. N. Y. Private. 8 Jul. 1790. 500 acres.
Ralls, Nathaniel. Va. Sergeant. 22 Dec. 1783. 200 acres.
Ralph, Ephraim. Va. Lieutenant. 24 Jan. 1786. 2666 2/3 acres.
Ralph, John. N.C. Private. 2 Dec. 1785. 640 acres.
Ralph, Lewis. N.C. Private. 22 Apr. 1785. 228 acres.
Ralston, Andrew. Pa. Sergeant. 20 Nov. 1788. 250 acres.
Ramage, Alexander. N.C. Private. 8 May 1784. 640 acres.
Ramage, Thomas. N.C. Private. 19 Dec. 1808. 640 acres to heirs.
Ramble, Samuel. Va. Private. 11 Aug. 1783. 200 acres.
Rampson, Philip. Pa. Private. 2 Dec. 1786. 200 acres.
Ramsay, Isaac, Jr. Ga. Minute Man. 23 Apr. 1784. 287 1/2 acres.
Ramsay, Isaac, Sr. Ga. Private. 23 Apr. 1784. 287 1/2 acres.
Ramsay, John. Ga. Minute Man. 17 Apr. 1784. 287 1/2 acres.
Ramsay, John. Va. Surgeon. 17 Feb. 1809. 6000 acres.
Ramsay, John. Va. Surgeon. 25 Mar. 1840. 500 acres.
Ramsay, John. Va. ———. 10 Jul. 1838. 600 acres.
Ramsay, John. Va. ———. 10 Jul. 1838. 493 acres.
Ramsay, Joseph. Va. Lieutenant. 26 Feb. 1834. 2666 2/3 acres.
Ramsay, Joseph Hall. S.C. Surgeon. 2 May 1785. 300 acres.
Ramsay, Mills. N.C. ———. 29 Apr. 1784. 640 acres to John Ramsay, heir.
Ramsay, Randol. Ga. Soldier. 23 Apr. 1784. 287 1/2 acres.
Ramsay, Samuel. Ga. Soldier. 27 Apr. 1784. 287 1/2 acres.
Ramsay, Samuel. Ga. ———. 27 Apr. 1784. 287 1/2 acres to heirs.
Ramsay, Thomas. Ga. Private. 23 Apr. 1784. 287 1/2 acres.
Ramsay, William. Ga. ———. 27 Apr. 1784. 287 1/2 acres.
Ramsay, William. Va. Surgeon's Mate. 15 Mar. 1838. 3277 1/2 acres.
Ramsay, William. Va. Surgeon's Mate. 15 Mar. 1838. 1092 1/2 acres.
Ramsdell, James. Me. ———. 2 Feb. 1836. 200 acres to widow Juda Robinson. Luke.
Ramsey, Allen. N.C. Captain. 22 Oct. 1783. 1097 acres.
Ramsey, Andrew. N.C. Private. 30 Sep. 1785. 640 acres to heirs.
Ramsey, Francis. Va. Private. 12 Nov. 1783. 200 acres.
Ramsey, Henry. N.C. Private. 10 Dec. 1788. 640 acres to heirs.
Ramsey, James. Va.-Ind. Private. 108 acres.
Ramsey, James. Va. Private. 6 May 1786. 100 acres.
Ramsey, James. Va. Private. 31 Oct. 1791. 200 acres.
Ramsey, Joel. N.C. Private. 29 Apr. 1784. 274 acres.
Ramsey, Joel. N.C. Private. 18 Jan. 1792. 274 acres.
Ramsey, John. Va. Surgeon. 17 Mar. 1838. 1093 acres.
Ramsey, Matthew. N.C. Captain. 22 Oct. 1783. 2697 acres.
Ramsey, Mills. N.C. Private. 30 Sep. 1785. 640 acres to heirs.
Ramsey, Nathan. N. Y. ———. 9 Jul. 1790. 600 acres.
Ramsey, Nathaniel. Md. Colonel. ———. 200 acres.
Ramsey, Solomon. N.C. Sergeant. 30 Sep. 1785. 1000 acres to heirs.
Ramsey, William. Pa. Private. ———. 200 acres to James McDonald, assignee.
Ramson, Jacob. N. Y. Private. 8 Jul. 1790. 600 acres.
Randall, Abraham. N.C. Sergeant. 7 Jan. 1784. 1000 acres to Caty Randall, heiress.

Randall, Henry. N.Y. ———. 13 Sep. 1790. 500 acres to heirs.
Randall, John. Mass. Private. 10 Sep. 1832. 200 acres to heirs.
Randall, John. N.C. Private. 26 Aug. 1785. 640 acres to heirs.
Randall, Obediah. Ga. Soldier. 7 Nov. 1783. ———.
Randell, Jeremiah. N. Y. Matross. 9 Jul. 1790. 600 acres.
Randle, Timothy. N.C. Private. 24 Nov. 1796. 640 acres to heirs.
Randolph, Adam. Va. Private. 26 Apr. 1783. 200 acres.
Randolph, Henry. Va. Corporal. 21 Feb. 1784. 200 acres.
Randolph, John. Pa. Lieutenant. 29 Dec. 1788. 200 acres.
Randolph, John. Va. Private. 13 Sep. 1783. 100 acres.
Randolph, Joseph. N.C. Private. 24 Dec. 1796. 228 acres.
Randolph, Robert. Va. Captain. 27 May 1783. 4000 acres.
Ranfier, John. N. Y. Private. 8 Jul. 1790. 600 acres.
Range, James. Va. Private. 16 Jan. 1812. 100 acres.
Range, James. Va. Private. 2 Jan. 1833. 100 acres.
Ranger, Joseph. Va. Sailor. 4 Jun. 1783. 100 acres.
Ranger, Joseph. Va. Sailor. 24 Oct. 1786. 100 acres.
Rankin, James. N. Y. Private. 8 Jul. 1790. 600 acres.
Rankin, John. N.C. Private. 14 Feb. 1796. 320 acres.
Rankin, Robert. Va. Lieutenant. 8 Mar. 1783. 2666 2/3 acres.
Rankin, Robert. Va. Lieutenant. 22 Nov. 1796. 444 1/2 acres.
Rankin, Thomas. N. Y. Fifer. 7 Jul. 1790. 600 acres.
Rankins, Benjamin. Va. Private. 11 Feb. 1784. 100 acres.
Rankins, James. Me. Private. 19 Dec. 1838. 200 acres to widow Sarah Rankins. Lebanon.
Rankins, James. Va. Private. 19 Jan. 1785. 100 acres.
Rankins, Robert. Va. Sergeant. 2 Aug. 1783. 200 acres.
Rankins, William. Va. Private. 2 Aug. 1783. 100 acres.
Rann, Francis. Ga. ———. 21 Apr. 1784. 287 1/2 acres.
Ransdall, Thomas. Va. Captain. 4 Mar. 1783. 4000 acres.
Ransdell, Thomas. Va. Captain. 6 Feb. 1808. 944 acres.
Ransom, Job. Mass. Private. 9 Jul. 1834. 200 acres.
Ransome, Thomas. Va. Seaman. 30 Mar. 1840. 100 acres.
Ransone, Ambrose. Ga. ———. 27 Apr. 1784. 200 acres.
Ransone, Henry. Ga. ———. 23 Apr. 1784. 287 1/2 acres.
Ransone, Robert. Va. Private. 22 Aug. 1783. 100 acres.
Ransone, Thomas. Va. Lieutenant. 27 Jan. 1851. 444 1/2 acres.
Ransone, Thomas. Va. Lieutenant. 27 Jan. 1851. 444 1/2 acres.
Ransone, Thomas. Va. Lieutenant. 27 Jan. 1851. 444 1/2 acres.
Ransone, Thomas. Va. Lieutenant. 27 Jan. 1851. 444 1/2 acres.
Ransone, Thomas. Va. Lieutenant. 27 Jan. 1851. 888 acres.
Ransone, Thomas. Va. Lieutenant. 24 Feb. 1854. 592 2/3 acres.
Ransone, Thomas. Va. Lieutenant. 8 Mar. 1854. 296 acres.
Ransone, Thomas. Va. ———. 20 Apr. 1854. 197 2/3 acres.
Ransone, Thomas. Va. ———. 20 Apr. 1854. 98 2/3 acres.
Ransone, Thomas. Va. Lieutenant. 15 May 1854. 246 2/3 acres.
Ransone, Thomas. Va. Lieutenant. 15 May 1854. 123 1/3 acres.
Ransone, Thomas. Va. ———. 17 May 1854. 98 2/3 acres.
Ransone, Thomas. Va. ———. 17 May 1854. 49 1/3 acres.
Ransone, Thomas. Va. Lieutenant. 21 Jun. 1854. 444 1/3 acres.
Ransone, Thomas. Va. Lieutenant. 18 Jul. 1854. 66 acres.
Ransone, Thomas. Va. Lieutenant. 24 Oct. 1854. 98 2/3 acres.
Ransone, Thomas. Va. Lieutenant. 7 Nov. 1854. 148 1/3 acres.
Ransone, Thomas. Va. Lieutenant. 7 Nov. 1854. 49 1/3 acres.

Rape, Francis. N.C. Private. 1 Sep. 1785. 640 acres to heirs.
Raper, Caleb. N.C. Private. 28 Nov. 1795. 640 acres to heirs.
Raper, John. N.C. Private. 13 Jan. 1792. 274 acres.
Raper, Robert. N.C. Private. 13 Jan. 1792. 503 acres.
Rasco, Teagle. N.C. Private. 12 Dec. 1797. 640 acres to heirs.
Ratcliff, Francis. Va. Corporal. 26 Mar. 1803. 200 acres.
Ratcliff, James. Ga. Private. 2 May 1785. 250 acres.
Rath, Frederick. Va. Private. 15 Jul. 1784. 200 acres.
Rattee, Charles. N. Y. ———. ———. 500 acres.
Ravenscraft, Francis. Va. Private. 10 Jun. 1788. 100 acres.
Ravenscraft, Thomas. Va. Private. 10 Jun. 1783. 100 acres.
Ravenscraft, Thomas. Va. Lieutenant. 16 Feb. 1852. 88 acres.
Ravenscroft, Thomas. Va. Lieutenant. 16 Feb. 1852. 88 acres.
Ravenscroft, Thomas. Va. Lieutenant. 13 Feb. 1834. 1333 1/3 acres.
Ravenscroft, Thomas. Va. Lieutenant. ———. 342 2/3 acres.
Ravenscroft, Thomas. Va. Lieutenant. 26 Nov. 1836. 266 2/3 acres.
Ravenscroft, Thomas. Va. Lieutenant. 10 Dec. 1850. 88 2/3 acres.
Ravot, Abraham. Ga. Refugee. 19 Jul. 1784. 287 1/2 acres.
Rawan, John. Pa. Private. ———. 200 acres.
Rawlings, Bennet. Md. Private. ———. 50 acres.
Rawlings, Isaac. Md. Lieutenant. ———. 200 acres.
Rawlings, Moses. Va. Colonel. 14 Mar. 1834. 9055 acres.
Rawlins, Moses. Va. Private. 24 Nov. 1784. 200 acres.
Rawlins, Thomas. Va. Private. 10 Oct. 1812. 100 acres.
Raws, Laurance. N.C. Private. 11 Feb. 1796. 640 acres to heirs.
Ray, Ambrose. Ga. Refugee. 15 Mar. 1784. 250 acres.
Ray, Andre. Va. Surgeon. 28 Mar. 1834. 1800 acres.
Ray, Andre. Va. Surgeon. 13 May 1834. 300 acres.
Ray, Andre. Va. Surgeon. 20 May 1834. 1200 acres.
Ray, Andre. Va. Surgeon. 29 Mar. 1839. 500 acres.
Ray, Andre. Va. Surgeon. 29 Mar. 1839. 250 acres.
Ray, Andre. Va. Surgeon. 29 Mar. 1839. 250 acres.
Ray, Andre. Va. Surgeon. 29 Mar. 1839. 250 acres.
Ray, Andre. Va. Surgeon. 29 Mar. 1839. 250 acres.
Ray, Andre. Va. Surgeon. 29 Mar. 1839. 1000 acres.
Ray, Andre. Va. Surgeon. 29 Mar. 1839. 1000 acres.
Ray, Andre. Va. Surgeon. 29 Mar. 1839. 1000 acres.
Ray, Andre. Va. Surgeon. 29 Mar. 1839. 500 acres.
Ray, Andre. Va. Surgeon. 29 Mar. 1839. 1000 acres.
Ray, Andrew. Ga. Citizen. 6 Apr. 1784. 287 1/2 acres.
Ray, Archibald. N.C. Private. 22 Apr. 1785. 640 acres to heirs.
Ray, Archibald. N.C. Private. 30 Sep. 1785. 640 acres.
Ray, Benjamin. Ga. ———. 27 Apr. 1784. 287 1/2 acres.
Ray, Benjamin. N.C. Private. 29 Sep. 1784. 640 acres.
Ray, Caleb. N. Y. Corporal. 9 Jul. 1790. 600 acres.
Ray, Daniel. N.C. Private. 30 Sep. 1785. 640 acres to heirs.
Ray, David. Va. Private. 20 Jun. 1783. 100 acres.
Ray, David. Va. Private. 25 Jun. 1784. 100 acres.
Ray, George. Ga. ———. 27 Apr. 1784. 287 1/2 acres.
Ray, James. N. Y. Private. 8 Jul. 1790. 600 acres.
Ray, James. N.C. Private. 17 Dec. 1785. 640 acres to heirs.
Ray, John. Ga. Citizen. 6 Apr. 1785. 287 1/2 acres.
Ray, Joseph. N. Y. ———. ———. 500 acres.
Ray, Martin. Conn. Sufferer. New/East Haven. 70.15.6.

Ray, Stephen. N.C. ———. 29 Apr. 1784. 640 acres to Elizabeth Ray, heiress.
Ray, Stephen. N.C. Private. 18 Nov. 1800. 640 acres to heirs.
Ray, Thomas. Va. Private. 30 Dec. 1784. 100 acres.
Ray, Thomas. Va. Captain. 3 Nov. 1814. 1000 acres.
Ray, Thomas. Va. Captain. 3 Nov. 1814. 1000 acres.
Ray, Thomas. Va. Captain. 3 Nov. 1814. 1000 acres.
Ray, Thomas. Va. Captain. 3 Nov. 1814. 1000 acres.
Ray, William. Ga. Soldier. 18 Sep. 1784. 287 1/2 acres.
Ray, William. Va.-Ind. Private. 108 acres.
Ray, William. Va. Private. 21 Nov. 1782. 100 acres.
Ray, Zachary. Ga. ———. 27 Apr. 1784. 287 1/2 acres.
Raybolt, Jacob. Md. Lieutenant. ———. 200 acres.
Rayfield, Caleb. N.C. Private. 12 Dec. 1796. 640 acres to heirs.
Rayfield, Spencer. Ga. ———. 15 Sep. 1784. 230 acres.
Rayfield, Spencer. N.C. Private. 3 Feb. 1785. 228 acres.
Rayford, Maurice. N.C. Private. 29 Sep. 1784. 236 acres.
Raymond, Abigail. Conn. Sufferer. Norwalk. 144.4.3.
Raymond, Clapp. Conn. Sufferer. Norwalk. 34.3.10.
Raymond, Eliakim. Conn. Sufferer. Norwalk. 297.7.11.
Raymond, Eliakim, Capt. Conn. Sufferer. Norwalk. 80.17.4.
Raymond, Hezekiah. Conn. Sufferer. Norwalk. 152.14.4.
Raymond, Jabez. Conn. Sufferer. Norwalk. 293.13.0.
Raymond, Jabez. Conn. Sufferer. Norwalk. 38.16.0.
Raymond, Jedediah. Conn. Sufferer. Norwalk. 10.18.3.
Raymond, Jedediah. Conn. Sufferer. Norwalk. 15.0.0.
Raymond, Jesse. Conn. Sufferer. Norwalk. 147.2.2.
Raymond, John & E. Cooley. Conn. Sufferers. Fairfield. 56.2.7.
Raymond, Josiah. Conn. Sufferer. Norwalk. 239.9.3.
Raymond, Moses. Conn. Sufferer. Norwalk. 5.0.0.
Raymond, Nathaniel. Conn. Sufferer. Norwalk. 4.4.0.
Raymond, Nathaniel, Jr. Conn. Sufferer. Norwalk. 144.5.1 3/4.
Raymond, Simeon. Conn. Sufferer. Norwalk. 428.7.3 1/2.
Raymond, Simeon. Conn. Sufferer. Norwalk. 14.0.0.
Raymond, Uriah. Conn. Sufferer. Norwalk. 124.11.1 3/4.
Raymond, William. Conn. Sufferer. Norwalk. 5.0.0.
Raymond, Zuriel. Mass. Private. 19 Nov. 1832. 200 acres to heirs.
Raymore, Daniel. N.C. Private. 9 Sep. 1785. 640 acres to heirs.
Raynor, Amos. N.C. Private. 30 Sep. 1785. 640 acres to heirs.
Raynor, Francis. Ga. ———. 17 May 1784. ———.
Raynor, John. Va. Private. 18 Apr. 1783. 200 acres.
Razer, Isaac. Ga. Refugee. 21 Apr. 1784. 287 1/2 acres.
Razor, John. N.C. Private. 13 Sep. 1820. 274 acres.
Rea, Adam. Pa. Sergeant. ———. 250 acres.
Rea, James. Ga. ———. 17 May 1784. ———.
Reab, George. Mass. ———. 17 Apr. 1829. 200 acres.
Read, Abijah. Mass. Sergeant. 18 Oct. 1833. 200 acres.
Read, Alexander. Va. Sergeant. 6 Apr. 1784. 466 2/3 acres.
Read, Benjamin. Conn. Sufferer. Norwalk. 42.14.6.
Read, Clement. Va. Lieutenant. 6 Dec. 1782. 2666 2/3 acres.
Read, David. Conn. Sufferer. Norwalk. 126.7.4.
Read, Edmund. Va. Captain. 26 Apr. 1838. 1225 acres.
Read, Eli. Conn. Sufferer. Norwalk. 58.10.11.
Read, Henry. Va. Private. 5 Mar. 1807. 200 acres.
Read, Isaac. Va. Colonel. 3 Dec. 1782. 6666 2/3 acres.

Read, Isaac. Va. Colonel. 10 Jan. 1839. 1766 acres.
Read, James. N.C. Captain. 25 Oct. 1783. 3840 acres.
Read, Jesse. Conn. Sufferer. Norwalk. 3.11.6.
Read, John. Ga. ———. 23 Apr. 1784. 287 1/2 acres.
Read, John. Va. Lieutenant. 6 Jul. 1850. 3009 2/3 acres.
Read, John. Va. Lieutenant. 5 Feb. 1853. 1004 2/3 acres.
Read, John. Va. Lieutenant. 5 Feb. 1853. 500 acres.
Read, John. Va. Lieutenant. 5 Feb. 1853. 1504 2/3 acres.
Read, John. Conn. Sufferer. Norwalk. 9.10.11.
Read, Mary. Conn. Sufferer. Norwalk. 47.17.0.
Read, Richard. Ga. ———. 27 Apr. 1784. 200 acres.
Read, William. Ga. Physician & Surgeon General. 25 May 1784. 920 acres.
Read, William. N.C. Private. 25 Jun. 1785. 640 acres to heir.
Read, William. Pa. Private. 18 Jul. 1787. 200 acres.
Read, William. Va. Corporal. 22 Jul. 1783. 200 acres.
Read, Zachariah. Conn. Sufferer. New/East Haven. 3.7.0.
Reade, Edmund. Va. Captain. 14 Dec. 1782. 4000 acres.
Readen, George. Ga. ———. 15 Apr. 1784. 287 1/2 acres.
Reading, Benjamin. Ga. ———. 17 May 1784. —— acres to heirs.
Ready, Hezekiah. N.C. Private. 30 Sep. 1785. 640 acres to heirs.
Ready, James. N. Y. Private. 8 Jul. 1790. 500 acres.
Realey, Abraham. N.C. Private. 10 Aug. 1785. 640 acres to heirs.
Reamer, John George. N.Y. ———. 13 Sep. 1790. 500 acres to heirs.
Reamer, Philip. Pa. Private. 15 Nov. 1786. 200 acres to Thomas Bible, assignee.
Reams, William. N.C. Private. 15 Feb. 1797. 228 acres.
Rearden, Jeremiah. N.C. Private. 22 Dec. 1796. 274 acres.
Reardon, Dudley. N.C. ———. 29 Apr. 1784. 640 acres to Nancy Reardon & Elizabeth Reardon, coheiresses.
Reardon, George. Va. Sergeant. 5 Apr. 1783. 200 acres.
Reardon, George. Va. Sergeant. 25 Apr. 1783. 400 acres.
Reardon, Jeremiah. N.C. Private. 29 Apr. 1784. 274 acres.
Reardon, John. N.C. Private. 14 Dec. 1796. 274 acres.
Reardon, William. N.C. Sergeant. 23 Apr. 1784. 1000 acres to Dennis Reardon, heir.
Reasen, Reuben. Va. Private. 27 Mar. 1787. 100 acres.
Reason, Amos. Ga. ———. 5 May 1786. ———.
Reason, Caleb. Ga. Refugee. 6 Aug. 1785. ———.
Reason, Edward. Ga. Refugee. 6 Aug. 1785. ———.
Reason, John. Ga. Refugee. 6 Aug. 1785. ———.
Reason, Peter. Ga. Refugee. 6 Aug. 1785. ———.
Reason, Thomas. N.C. Private. 28 May 1784. 274 acres.
Reason, William. N.C. Private. 25 Oct. 1783. 412 acres.
Reasons, John. N.C. Private. 13 Dec. 1796. 640 acres.
Reasons, William. N.C. Private. 10 Feb. 1796. 640 acres to heirs.
Reasons, William. Va. Private. 19 Feb. 1784. 100 acres.
Reaves, Benjamin. N.C. Private. 28 May 1784. 640 acres.
Reaves, David. N.C. Private. 30 Sep. 1785. 640 acres to heirs.
Reaves, James. Ga. Minute Man. 17 Jan. 1785. 287 1/2 acres.
Reaves, James. Va. Sailor. 13 Feb. 1789. 100 acres.
Reaves, John. N.C. Private. 22 Apr. 1785. 228 acres.
Reaves, Nehemiah. N.C. Private. 27 Jul. 1785. 228 acres.
Reaves, Samuel. N.C. Private. 22 Dec. 1796. 270 acres.
Reaves, William. N.C. Private. 30 Sep. 1785. 640 acres to heirs.
Reavis, Samuel. N.C. Private. 14 Dec. 1796. 228 acres.

Rector, Maximilian. Va. Private. 1 Nov. 1811. 100 acres.
Rector, Maximilion. Va. Private. 21 Apr. 1784. 100 acres.
Red, Henry. Ga. Soldier. 20 Jul. 1785. ———.
Red, James. Ga. ———. 20 Apr. 1784. 287 1/2 acres.
Red, John. Ga. Minute Man. 3 Apr. 1785. ———.
Red, Peter. Ga. Minute Man. 3 Apr. 1785. ———.
Red, Samuel. Ga. ———. 21 Apr. 1784. 287 1/2 acres.
Redcross, John. Va. Private. 22 Jun. 1784. 200 acres.
Reddick, Isaac. N.C. Private. 9 Nov. 1784. 640 acres to Joseph Reddick.
Reddick, Isaac. N.C. Private. 30 Sep. 1785. 640 acres to heirs.
Reddick, Jason. Va. Captain. 9 Jun. 1784. 4000 acres.
Reddick, Peter. N.C. Private. 12 Sep. 1785. 640 acres to heirs.
Reddick, Thomas. N.C. Private. 30 Sep. 1785. 640 acres to heirs.
Reddick, William. Pa. Private. 6 Nov. 1787. 200 acres.
Reddick, Willis. Va. Captain. 9 Jun. 1784. 4000 acres.
Reddin, John. N.C. Private. 29 Apr. 1784. 228 acres.
Reddit, Samuel. N.C. Private. 20 Oct. 1787. 366 acres.
Reddy, Dennis. Va. Sergeant. 3 Dec. 1782. 200 acres.
Reddy, Dennis. Va. Sergeant. 14 Sep. 1811. 400 acres.
Redfield, Lucretia. Conn. Sufferer. Fairfield. 28.3.4.
Redfield, Sarah. Conn. Sufferer. Fairfield. 28.15.6.
Redhair, Frederick. Pa. Matross. 12 Jan. 1787. 200 acres.
Redin, Absalom. Ga. ———. 16 Apr. 1784. 287 1/2 acres.
Redington, Asa. Me. ———. 28 Aug. 1838. 200 acres. Waterville.
Redkin, Henry. Pa. Captain. 18 Oct. 1786. 500 acres.
Redman, John. Pa. Private. 17 Aug. 1787. 200 acres.
Redman, Martin. Va. Private. 3 Jan. 1833. 100 acres.
Redman, Michael. Pa. Sergeant. 4 Oct. 1786. 250 acres.
Redman, Solomon. Va. Private. 13 Dec. 1786. 100 acres.
Redman, Thomas. Md. Private. ———. 50 acres.
Redman, William. Ga. Soldier. 20 Jul. 1785. ———.
Redner, George. N.C. Musician. 4 Aug. 1821. 1000 acres.
Redwood, John. Va. Private. 25 Feb. 1784. 100 acres.
Redy, Jacob. N.C. Private. 9 Sep. 1785. 640 acres to heirs.
Reed, Ajonadab. Ga. ———. 22 Apr. 1784. 500 acres.
Reed, Alexander. Conn. Sufferer. Groton. 60.18.1.
Reed, Amaziah. Me. ———. 19 Sep. 1836. 200 acres to widow Jediah Reed. Weld.
Reed, Benjamin. N.C. Private. 22 Oct. 1783. 640 acres.
Reed, Ebenezer. N.C. Private. 17 Dec. 1796. 640 acres to heirs.
Reed, Francis. Va. Midshipman. 12 Aug. 1834. 2666 2/3 acres.
Reed, George. Mass. Private. 1 Mar. 1833. 200 acres.
Reed, Guilford. N.C. Private. 11 Feb. 1796. 640 acres to heirs.
Reed, Jacob. N. Y. Captain. 9 Jul. 1790. 1800 acres.
Reed, James. Ga. ———. 21 Apr. 1784. 300 acres.
Reed, James. N.C. Private. 11 Aug. 1820. 274 acres to heirs.
Reed, James. Pa. Major. 22 Aug. 1787. 300 acres.
Reed, James. Pa. Major. 28 Aug. 1787. 300 acres.
Reed, Jesse. N.C. Captain. 10 Nov. 1783. 3840 acres.
Reed, John. N. Y. Lieutenant. 9 Jul. 1790. 1200 acres.
Reed, Joseph. N.C. Private. 30 Sep. 1785. 640 acres to heirs.
Reed, Joseph. N.C. Sergeant. 25 Aug. 1813. 1000 acres to heirs.
Reed, Moses. N.C. Private. 23 Aug. 1821. 640 acres to heirs.
Reed, Nathan. Va. Captain. 20 May 1783. 4000 acres.
Reed, Nathaniel. N.Y. ———. 13 Sep. 1790. 500 acres to heirs.

Reed, Peter. Pa. Sergeant. 15 Nov. 1786. 250 acres to Matthew McConnell, assignee.

Reed, Philip. Md. Captain. ———. 200 acres.

Reed, Reuben. Ga. ———. 22 Apr. 1784. 200 acres.

Reed, Samuel. Ga. ———. 24 May 1784. 900 acres.

Reed, Samuel. Pa. Lieutenant. 23 Aug. 1787. 200 acres to Thomas Reed, administrator.

Reed, Samuel. Pa. Lieutenant. 23 Aug. 1787. 200 acres.

Reed, Stephen. N.C. Private. 12 Sep. 1785. 640 acres to heirs.

Reed, Thomas. Ga. ———. 18 Sep. 1784. 287 1/2 acres.

Reed, Thomas. N. Y. Surgeon. 17 Aug. 1790. 1900 acres.

Reed, Watson. N.C. Private. 8 Mar. 1796. 640 acres to heirs.

Reed, William. N.C Private. 22 Jan. 1793. 640 acres to heirs.

Reed, William. N.C. Private. 22 Dec. 1796. 640 acres.

Reed, William. Pa. Private. 12 Jan. 1787. 200 acre.

Reeder, James. Ga. Soldier. 20 Jul. 1785. ———.

Reeder, William. Ga. Soldier. 20 Jul. 1785. ———.

Reel, James. N.C. Private. 9 Sep. 1785. 640 acres to heirs.

Rees, David. Ga. Deputy Judge Advocate. 5 Mar. 1784. 600 acres.

Rees, David. Pa. Private. 29 Nov. 1786. 200 acres.

Rees, Hugh. Ga. ———. 27 Apr. 1784. 300 acres.

Rees, Joel. Ga. ———. 20 Apr. 1784. 200 acres.

Rees, Martin. N. Y. Private. 8 Jul. 1790. 600 acres.

Rees, Philip. Pa. Private. 21 Oct. 1786. 200 acres.

Reese, John. N.C. Private. 25 Oct. 1783. 274 acres.

Reese, Jonathan. Ga. Minute Man. 14 Jul. 1785. ———.

Reese, Joshua. Pa. Private. 17 Oct. 1786. 200 acres.

Reese, Roger. N.C. Private. 25 Oct. 1783. 274 acres.

Reeve, Israel. N. Y. ———. 8 Apr. 1803. 500 acres.

Reeves, Benjamin. S.C. ———. 3 Jan. 1791. 200 acres.

Reeves, Burgess. S.C. ———. 1 Jun. 1789. 200 acres.

Reeves, David. Ga. Corporal. 15 Apr. 1784. 187 1/2 acres.

Reeves, Enos. Pa. Lieutenant. 28 Sep. 1787. 200 acres.

Reeves, Enos. Pa. Lieutenant. 28 Sep. 1787. 200 acres.

Reeves, Frederick. N.C. Private. 21 Apr. 1784. 228 acres.

Reeves, Joseph. N.Y. ———. 13 Sep. 1790. 500 acres to heirs.

Reeves, Spencer. Ga. ———. 13 Sep. 1784. 287 1/2 acres.

Reeves, Thomas. Ga. ———. 13 Sep. 1784. 287 1/2 acres.

Regan, Darby. Ga. ———. 23 Apr. 1784. 287 1/2 acres.

Regans, John. N.C. Private. 29 Sep. 1784. 640 acres to Mary Regans, heiress.

Rehm, Frederick. Ga. Surgeon. 21 Jan. 1784. 750 acres.

Reickert, Peter. Pa. ———. 19 Mar. 1810. 200 acres.

Reid, Alexander. Va. Private. 18 Apr. 1823. 100 acres.

Reid, John. N. Y. Private. 8 Jul. 1790. 500 acres.

Reid, John H. Va. Private. 16 Mar. 1822. 100 acres.

Reid, Nathan. Va. Captain. 7 Sep. 1808. 555 acres.

Reiley, James. N. Y. Private. 3 Jul. 1790. 600 acres.

Reiley, John. Pa. Fifer. 27 Sep. 1787. 200 acres.

Reiley, Lewis. N.Y. ———. 13 Sep. 1790. 500 acres to heirs.

Reiley, Patrick. Pa. Matross. 19 Dec. 1786. 200 acres.

Reily, Job. Pa. Private. 1 Feb. 1804. 200 acres to William Kelly in trust &c.

Reily, Job. Pa. Private. ———. 200 acres.

Reily, John. Pa. Captain. 12 Oct. 1786. 500 acres.

Reim, Nicholas. Pa. Sergeant. 2 Apr. 1804. 250 acres. Alias Rheam.

Reindicker, Samuel. Pa. Private. 29 Sep. 1787. 200 acres.

Reins, John. N. Y. ———. 9 Jul. 1790. 600 acres.

Reins, John. Va. Private. 18 Apr. 1823. 100 acres.

Rench, John. Ga. Minute Man. 27 Apr. 1784. 287 1/2 acres.

Reniston, John. Me. ———. 14 Feb. 1843. 200 acres to widow Betsey Bean.

Renn, Aaron. N.C. Private. 12 Sep. 1785. 640 acres to heirs.

Renn, Jesse. N.C. Private. 12 Sep. 1785. 640 acres to heirs.

Rennce, Coral. N.Y. ———. 13 Sep. 1790. 500 acres to heirs.

Renshaw, Bennet. Pa. Corporal. 20 Sep. 1787. 200 acres.

Repeto, William. Ga. ———. 27 Apr. 1784. 287 1/2 acres.

Resco, Mary. Conn. Sufferer. Norwalk. 2.19.0.

Resner, John. Va. Private. 27 Apr. 1785. 200 acres.

Restin, William. N. Y. Private. 8 Jul. 1790. 600 acres.

Revell, John. Va. Gunner's Mate. 15 Mar. 1832. 2222 1/3 acres.

Revell, John. Va. Gunner's Mate. 15 Mar. 1832. 444 1/3 acres.

Revelle, Holladay. Va. Private. 30 Jul. 1831. 100 acres.

Revelle, Holliday. Va. Private. 10 Jul. 1838. 100 acres.

Revely, Francis. Md. Captain. ———. 200 acres.

Revere, John. N. Y. ———. 9 Jul. 1790. 500 acres.

Revers, Benjamin. N.C. Private. 9 Sep. 1785. 640 acres to heirs.

Revers, John. N.C. Private. 9 Sep. 1785. 640 acres to heirs.

Revice, John. N.C. Private. 25 Jun. 1785. 274 acres.

Reviere, Wyatt. Va. ———. 29 Jul. 1831. 2566 2/3 acres.

Revilea, Lewis. N.Y. ———. 13 Sep. 1790. 500 acres to heirs.

Revill, Elijah. N.C. Private. 30 Sep. 1785. 640 acres to heirs.

Rexford, Philip. Conn. Sufferer. New/East Haven. 15.17.3.

Reyley, John. N.C. Private. 30 Sep. 1785. 640 acres to heirs.

Reymond, Daniel. N.C. Private. 19 May 1784. 640 acres.

Reynolds, Aaron. Va. Corporal. 30 Jun. 1784. 200 acres.

Reynolds, Allan. Ga. ———. 2 Jan. 1786. ———.

Reynolds, Ambrose & Jonathan Reynolds. Conn. Sufferers. Greenwich. 18.1.7.

Reynolds, Anne. Conn. Sufferer. Greenwich. 22.2.9.

Reynolds, Benedict. Md. Private. ———. 50 acres.

Reynolds, Bernard. Va. Private. 16 Apr. 1783. 200 acres.

Reynolds, Charles. Ga. ———. 27 Apr. 1784. 287 1/2 acres.

Reynolds, Charles. Md. Sergeant. ———. 50 acres.

Reynolds, Coleman. Ga. ———. 15 Apr. 1784. 287 1/2 acres.

Reynolds, Daniel. Me. ———. 24 Jun. 1835. 200 acres to widow Thankful Reynolds. Burnham.

Reynolds, David. Me. Private. 25 Oct. 1838. 200 acres to widow Rebecca Reynolds. Dennysville.

Reynolds, Eliphalet. Me. Private. 8 Oct. 1838. 200 acres. Addison.

Reynolds, George. Ga. ———. 29 Jul. 1784. 287 1/2 acres.

Reynolds, George. N.C. Sergeant Commandant. 15 Dec. 1783. 1000 acres.

Reynolds, Hamilton. Ga. ———. 29 Jul. 1784. 287 1/2 acres.

Reynolds, Horton. Conn. Sufferer. Greenwich. 65.15.10.

Reynolds, Jaems. N.C. Private. 23 Feb. 1820. 274 acres to heirs.

Reynolds, James. Va. Private. 23 Jun. 1783. 200 acres.

Reynolds, Joanna. Conn. Sufferer. Greenwich. 12.2.0.

Reynolds, John. N.C. Private. 26 Dec. 1792. 228 acres.

Reynolds, John. Va. Ensign. 28 Jun. 1822. 1333 1/3 acres.

Reynolds, John. Va. Ensign. 28 Jun. 1822. 1333 1/3 acres.

Reynolds, John. Va. Surgeon. 28 Mar. 1834. 6000 acres.

Reynolds, John. Va. Surgeon. 27 Jul. 1836. 6000 acres.

Reynolds, Johnston. N.C. Private. 14 Dec. 1796. 640 acres.

Reynolds, Jonathan. Conn. Sufferer. Greenwich. 18.0.0.

Reynolds, Joseph. Pa. Private. 20 Sep. 1787. 200 acres to Martha Reynolds, widow.

Reynolds, Martin. Pa. Private. ———. 200 acres.

Reynolds, Mathias. N.C. Corporal. 13 Dec. 1796. 1000 acres.

Reynolds, Nathaniel. Conn. Sufferer. Greenwich. 47.15.6.

Reynolds, Nathaniel, Jr. Conn. Sufferer. Greenwich. 10.10.4.

Reynolds, Silvester. N.C. Private. 22 Dec. 1796. 640 acres to heirs.

Reynolds, Susannah. Conn. Sufferer. Greenwich. 18.16.4.

Reynolds, Thomas. Ga. ———. 2 Jan. 1786. ———.

Reynolds, Timothy. N. Y. Private. 8 Jul. 1790. 600 acres.

Reynolds, William. N.C. Private. 26 May 1784. 640 acres.

Reynolds, William. Pa. Private. 29 Sep. 1787. 200 acres to William Banquett, assignee.

Reynolds, William. Va. Sergeant. 31 Dec. 1782. 200 acres.

Reynolds, William. Va. Lieutenant. 24 Jan. 1787. 2666 2/3 acres.

Rhaney, William. Ga. Soldier. 27 Apr. 1784. 287 1/2 acres.

Rhea, Matthew. Va. Lieutenant. 31 Jul. 1783. 2666 2/3 acres.

Rheinick, Christian. Pa. Surgeon's Mate. 26 Jul. 1834. 300 acres to Catherine Rheinick, daughter.

Rhem, Peter. N.C. Sergeant. 20 Apr. 1784. 428 acres.

Rhine, Lazarus. Va. Private. 21 Mar. 1807. 200 acres.

Rhoades, Henry. N.C. Private. 24 Dec. 1785. 640 acres to heirs.

Rhoades, Joseph. N. Y. Private. 6 Jul. 1790. 500 acres.

Rhoads, John. Va. Private. 26 Apr. 1783. 200 acres.

Rhoads, William. N.C. Sergeant. 24 Dec. 1785. 640 acres to heirs.

Rhoads, William. Va. Corporal. 7 Aug. 1783. 466 2/3 acres.

Rhoads, William. Va. Private. 16 Aug. 1783. 100 acres.

Rhodes, Benjamin. Ga. ———. 20 Apr. 1784. 650 acres.

Rhodes, Charles. N.C. Sergeant. 11 Sep. 1820. 356 acres to heirs.

Rhodes, Cornelius. N.Y. ———. 13 Sep. 1790. 500 acres to heirs.

Rhodes, Elijah. Va. Private. 7 May 1784. 100 acres.

Rhodes, Hope. Conn. Sufferer. Ridgefield. 7.10.0.

Rhodes, Isaac. N.C. Private. 29 Apr. 1784. 228 acres.

Rhodes, Jacob. N.C. Private. 2 Feb. 1786. 640 acres to heirs.

Rhodes, John. Ga. ———. 13 Apr. 1784. 287 1/2 acres.

Rhodes, Joseph Thomas. N.C. Captain. 21 Apr. 1784. 3840 acres.

Rhodes, Michael. Va. ———. 8 Aug. 1836. 200 acres.

Rhone, John. N.C. Private. 10 Aug. 1785. 640 acres to heirs.

Rhytmire, Michael. Md. Private. ———. 50 acres.

Riant, Joseph. Me. Private. 6 Sep. 1838. 200 acres. Farmington.

Riblet, Abraham. Pa. Private. 6 Jul. 1787. 200 acres.

Riblet, Peter. Pa. Dragoon. 15 Jan. 1787. 200 acres.

Ricard, Paul. N. Y. ———. ———. 500 acres.

Rice, Basdiel. Va. Private. 17 Mar. 1784. 100 acres.

Rice, David. Ga. ———. 5 May 1785. 287 1/2 acres.

Rice, David. N.C. Private. 27 Oct. 1783. 640 acres.

Rice, David. Va. Sergeant Major. 23 Dec. 1808. 400 acres.

Rice, Ezra. Mass. ———. 22 Jul. 1833. 200 acres.

Rice, George. Va. Captain. 17 Jun. 1783. 4000 acres.

Rice, George. Va. Corporal. 1 Aug. 1783. 400 acres.

Rice, Hezekiah. N.C. Captain. 4 Aug. 1821. 3840 acres.

Rice, Holman. Va. Captain. 17 Jan. 1834. 3600 acres.

Rice, Holman. Va. Captain. 17 Jan. 1834. 400 acres.

Rice, Isaac. Va. Private. 29 Jan. 1788. 100 acres.

Rice, James. Conn. Sufferer. New/East Haven. 64.9.2.

Rice, Jeptha. N.C. Ensign. 6 Sep. 1821. 640 acres to heirs.
Rice, John. Ga. Minute Man. 22 Apr. 1784. 287 1/2 acres.
Rice, John. N. Y. ———. 8 Oct. 1792. 500 acres.
Rice, John. N.C. Private. 20 Sep. 1784. 640 acres.
Rice, John. N.C. Private. 22 Dec. 1796. 274 acres.
Rice, John. N.C. Lieutenant. 19 Dec. 1808. 731 acres.
Rice, John. Va. Private. 15 Aug. 1834. 100 acres.
Rice, Michael. Pa. Private. ———. 200 acres.
Rice, Nathan. Ga. Minute Man. 17 Jan. 1785. 287 1/2 acres.
Rice, Nathaniel. Va. Lieutenant. 3 Jan. 1783. 2666 2/3 acres.
Rice, Peter. Ga. Minute Man. 14 Jul. 1785. ———.
Rice, Richard. Va. Private. 3 Dec. 1795. 100 acres.
Rice, Roger. N.C. Private. 22 Dec. 1796. 274 acres.
Rice, Thomas. N.C. Sergeant. 19 Aug. 1820. 1000 acres to heirs.
Rice, William. Pa. Captain. 6 Nov. 1786. 500 acres.
Rice, William. Va. Sergeant. 5 Aug. 1783. 200 acres.
Rice, William. Va. Private. 24 Feb. 1784. 100 acres.
Rich, Hannah. Conn. Sufferer. Greenwich. 9.0.0.
Rich, James. N.C. ———. 10 Aug, 1785. 640 acres.
Rich, John. Conn. Sufferer. Greenwich. 21.3.0.
Rich, John. Conn. Sufferer. Norwalk. 72.6.0.
Rich, Mary. Conn. Sufferer. Greenwich. 44.2.0.
Rich, Thomas. Conn. Sufferer. Greenwich. 45.15.9.
Rich, Timothy. N.C. Private. 30 Sep. 1785. 640 acres to heirs.
Rich, William. Va. Private. 6 Aug. 1783. 100 acres.
Richard, Thomas. Va. Private. 19 Jan. 1785. 100 acres.
Richards, ———. S.C. Soldier. 21 Jan. 1785. 100 acres to Mary Richards, widow.
Richards, Ann. Conn. Sufferer. New London. 224.15.10.
Richards, Boswell. Va. Private. 10 Mar. 1786. 100 acres.
Richards, Charles. N.C. Private. 5 Sep. 1821. 640 acres.
Richards, Clement. Va. Private. 19 Jun. 1786. 100 acres.
Richards, Daniel. Conn. Sufferer. Norwalk. 12.5.1.
Richards, David. Conn. Sufferer. New London. 1.4.9.
Richards, Edward. Va. Private. 10 Dec. 832. 200 acres.
Richards, George. N.C. Musician. 20 Sep. 1821. 1000 acres.
Richards, Gershom. Conn. Sufferer. Norwalk. 31.13.1.
Richards, Gilbert. N. Y. Private. 8 Jul. 1790. 600 acres.
Richards, Guy & sons. Conn. Sufferers. New London. 811.8.0.
Richards, Henry. N.C. Private. 30 Sep. 1785. 640 acres to heirs.
Richards, Isaac. Conn. Sufferer. Norwalk. 44.10.10.
Richards, Jabez. Conn. Sufferer. New London. 4.4.0.
Richards, Jacob. Ga. Minute Man. 22 Mar. 1785. 250 acres.
Richards, Jacob. N.C. Private. 25 Oct. 1783. 342 acres.
Richards, James. N.C. Sergeant. 14 Jun. 1785. 640 acres.
Richards, James. Va. Sergeant. 23 Jul. 1824. 400 acres.
Richards, Jesse. N.C. ———. 10 Aug. 1785. 640 acres.
Richards, John. N.C. Private. 10 Aug. 1785. 640 acres to heirs.
Richards, John. Va. Steward. 21 Feb. 1784. 100 acres.
Richards, John. Va. Private. 15 Jan. 1808. 100 acres.
Richards, John. Va. Steward & Clerk. 2 Jun. 1835. 2666 2/3 acres.
Richards, John. Conn. Sufferer. Norwalk. 7.6.8.
Richards, John. Conn. Sufferer. New/East Haven. 13.6.0.
Richards, Jonathan. N.C. Private. 7 Jan. 1784. 274 acres.

Richards, Joseph. Me. ———. 9 May 1835. 200 acres. Saco.

Richards, Joseph. N.C. Private. 25 Nov. 1796. 640 acres to heirs.

Richards, Lewis. N.C. Private. 10 Sep. 1821. 640 acres to heirs.

Richards, Mary. Conn. Sufferer. New London. 258.17.0.

Richards, Preeson. Va. Private. 15 Jan. 1808. 261 acres.

Richards, Thomas. Va. Sergeant. 13 Jun. 1783. 200 acres.

Richards, Thomas. Va. Sergeant. 8 Aug. 1783. 200 acres.

Richards, William. N.C. Private. 4 Apr. 1821. 228 acres.

Richards, William. Va. Private. 15 Jan. 1808. 100 acres.

Richardson, Alexander. N.Y. ——. 13 Sep. 1790. 500 acres to heirs.

Richardson, Alexander. N.C. Private. 14 Dec. 1797. 640 acres.

Richardson, Charles. Va. Private. 15 Jun. 1807. 100 acres.

Richardson, Daniel. Va. Lieutenant. 7 Oct. 1784. 2666 2/3 acres.

Richardson, Daniel. Va. Private. 15 Jun. 1807. 200 acres.

Richardson, Daniel. Va. Lieutenant. ———. 1333 1/3 acres.

Richardson, Edward. Md. Private. ———. 50 acres.

Richardson, Enos. Ga. ———. 19 Jul. 1784. 287 1/2 acres.

Richardson, Ezekiel. Pa. Private. 9 Sep.1789. 200 acres.

Richardson, Isham. Ga. ———. 22 Apr. 1784. 900 acres.

Richardson, James. N.C. Private. 30 Sep. 1785. 640 acres to heirs.

Richardson, James. N.C. Private. 30 Sep. 1785. 640 acres to heirs.

Richardson, John. N.C. Private. 15 Dec. 1783. 274 acres.

Richardson, John. N.C. Ensign. 16 Aug. 1821. 2560 acres.

Richardson, John. Va. Private. 7 Jun. 1831. 100 acres.

Richardson, John. Va. Private. 5 Feb. 1834. 200 acres.

Richardson, Joseph. Ga. ———. 20 Feb. 1784. 250 acres.

Richardson, Moses. N.C. Private. 17 Dec. 1785. 640 acres to heirs.

Richardson, Mourning. Va. Private. 15 Mar. 1785. 100 acres.

Richardson, Richard. S.C. ———. 5 Sep. 1785. 150 acres.

Richardson, Richard. S.C. ———. 5 Sep. 1785. 50 acres.

Richardson, Richard. Va. Private. 25 Nov. 1783. 200 acres.

Richardson, Robert. Md. Private. ———. 50 acres.

Richardson, Robert. Mass. Private. 6 Jul. 1832. 200 acres to heirs who assigned it to Abner Coburn.

Richardson, Robert. Va. Private. 12 Jan. 1784. 100 acres.

Richardson, Robert. Va. Private. 5 Feb. 1784. 100 acres.

Richardson, Walker. Ga. ———. 27 Apr. 1784. 1000 acres.

Richardson, William. Md. Private. ———. 50 acres.

Richardson, William. N.C. Private. 22 Feb. 1784. 640 acres.

Richardson, William. Va. Private. 10 Feb. 1784. 100 acres.

Richardson, William. Va. Private. 15 Jun. 1807. 100 acres.

Richardson, William. Va. Seaman. 7 Mar. 1834. 100 acres.

Richardson, Zorobabel. Va. Private. 15 Jun. 1807. 200 acres.

Riche, William. Ga. Citizen. 19 Dec. 1785. 287 1/2 acres.

Richee, James. Va. Private. 22 Mar. 1784. 100 acres.

Richeson, Holt. Va. Lieutenant Colonel. 17 Feb. 1784. 6000 acres.

Richeson, Holt. Va. Colonel. 31 Dec. 1851. 666 2/3 acres.

Richeson, Holt. Va. Colonel. 6 Jul. 1860. 6000 acres.

Richeson, James. Va. Sergeant. 31 May 1783. 400 acres.

Richeson, John. Va. Private. 23 Jun. 1783. 200 acres.

Richeson, Walker. Va. Lieutenant. 19 Jun. 1783. 2666 2/3 acres.

Richey, Abram. N.C. Private. 11 Feb. 1796. 640 acres to heirs.

Richey, John. N.Y. ———. 13 Sep. 1790. 500 acres to heirs.

Richey, John. Pa. Sergeant. 1 Nov. 1786. 250 acres.

Richey, John. Va. Private. 11 Jan. 1834. 300 acres.
Richey, Thomas. N.C. Corporal. 8 Dec. 1795. 1000 acres to heirs.
Richie, John. Ga. Lieutenant. 2 Feb. 1784. 400 acres.
Richmond, Christopher. Md. Captain. ———. 200 acres.
Richmond, John. N.C. Private. 19 Nov. 1800. 640 acres.
Richmond, William. Va. Private. 16 Feb. 1801. 100 acres.
Rickerson, Marmaduke. Ga. ———. 27 Apr. 1784. 287 1/2 acres.
Rickerson, Timothy. Ga. ———. 15 Apr. 1784. 287 1/2 acres.
Rickerson, Timothy, Sr. Ga. ———. 27 Apr. 1784. 287 1/2 acres.
Rickeson, Jesse. N.C. Private. 27 Jul. 1785. 320 acres.
Rickets, Nicholas. Va. Lieutenant. 15 Nov. 1822. 1333 1/3 acres.
Rickets, Nicholas. Va. Lieutenant. 15 Nov. 1822. 200 acres.
Rickets, Nicholas. Va. Lieutenant. 15 Nov. 1822. 200 acres.
Rickets, Nicholas. Va. Lieutenant. 15 Nov. 1822. 200 acres.
Rickets, Nicholas. Va. Lieutenant. 15 Nov. 1822. 200 acres.
Rickets, Nicholas. Va. Lieutenant. 15 Nov. 1822. 533 1/3 acres.
Rickett, Ezra. Conn. Sufferer. Norwalk. 82.11.5 1/4.
Ricketts, Nicholas. Md. Lieutenant. ———. 200 acres.
Ricketts, William. Va. Private. 1 Apr. 1783. 100 acres.
Rickey, Jeremiah. N. Y. Private. 8 Jul. 1790. 600 acres.
Rickman, William. Va. Colonel & Director General of Hospitals. 12 Jan. 1784. 6666 2/3 acres.
Rickow, Abraham. N. Y. ———. 22 Apr. 1806. 200 acres to representatives Elizabeth Miller and Mary Dean.
Ricks, Lewis. N.C. Private. 30 Sep. 1785. 640 acres to heirs.
Ridden, Robert. Va. Private. 1 Apr. 1783. 100 acres.
Riddin, James. Va. Private. 29 Jan. 1808. 100 acres.
Riddle, Charles. Md. Private. ———. 50 acres.
Riddle, William. Ga. Minute Man. 20 Apr. 1784. 287 1/2 acres.
Riddle, William. S.C. ———. 7 May 1787. 200 acres.
Riddle, William Powell. S.C. ———. 1 Aug. 1785. 200 acres.
Riden, Benjamin. Ga. ———. 17 Apr. 1784. 287 1/2 acres to heirs.
Rideout, Abraham. Me. Private. 5 Aug. 1835. 200 acres. Kennebunkport.
Rideout, William. Me. Soldier. 19 Jun. 1835. 200 acres to widow Ruth Rideout. Cumberland.
Rider, Adam. Va. Private. 1 Apr. 1784. 100 acres.
Rider, Asa. Mass. Private. 1 Feb. 1833. 200 acres to heirs.
Rider, George. N. Y. Private. 8 Jul. 1790. 600 acres.
Rider, Isaac. Ga. Minute Man. 3 Apr. 1785. ———.
Rider, Jacob. Ga. Minute Man. 3 Apr. 1785. ———.
Rider, Peter. Ga. Minute Man. 3 Apr. 1785. ———.
Rider, William. Ga. Soldier. 20 Jul. 1785. ———.
Ridgeway, Isaac. Mass. Private. 30 Dec. 1831. 200 acres.
Ridin, Joseph Scott. Ga. Refugee. 26 May 1784. 287 1/2 acres.
Riding, George. Ga. Refugee. 19 Feb. 1784. ———.
Ridley, David. Me. ———. 11 May 1835. 200 acres to his guardian Gideon Barton.
Ridley, George. Me. Private. 2 May 1835. 200 acres to widow Mary Rogers. Bowdoin.
Ridley, Hardy. N.C. Private. 5 Sep. 1821. 640 acres.
Ridley, John. Va. Sergeant. 10 Jul. 1783. 200 acres.
Ridley, Thomas. Va. Major. 6 Jun. 1783. 5333 1/3 acres.
Ridley, Thomas. Va. Major. 3 Dec. 1795. 888 2/3 acres.
Ridley, Thomas. Va. Major. 26 Mar. 1808. 666 1/3 acres.
Ridsey, Alexander. Va. Private. 11 Feb. 1784. 100 acres.
Rieley, John. Pa. Private. 20 Oct. 1786. 200 acres.

Riely, Edmund. N.C. Private. 17 Dec. 1796. 640 acres to heirs.
Riely, Edward. Md. Private. ———. 50 acres.
Riely, Ezekiel. N.C. Sergeant. 22 Apr. 1785. 428 acres.
Riely, William. Md. Captain. ———. 200 acres.
Riffet, John. Pa. Private. ———. 200 acres.
Rigbey, Ezekiel. N.C. Private. 30 Sep. 1785. 640 acres to heirs.
Rigby, John. Pa. ———. 4 May 1795. 200 acres to Alexander Power, assignee.
Riggan, William. Va. Private. 10 May 1788. 100 acres.
Riggan, William. Va. Private. 27 Feb. 1840. 100 acres.
Riggans, Powell. N.C. Private. 29 Jun. 1820. 274 to heir James Riggins.
Riggin, Darby. Ga. Citizen. 5 Apr. 1785. 287 1/2 acres.
Riggins, Powell. N.C. Private. 25 Oct. 1783. 274 acres.
Riggs, Andrew. Md. Private. ———. 50 acres.
Riggs, Daniel. N. Y. Private. 8 Jul. 1790. 500 acres.
Riggs, George B. Va. Seaman. 9 Dec. 1833. 100 acres.
Riggs, George B. Va. Seaman. 28 Mar. 1837. 100 acres.
Riggs, George B. Va. Seaman. 28 Mar. 1837. 100 acres.
Riggs, Jacob. Va. Private. 31 Dec. 1785. 200 acres.
Riggs, John. Ga. ———. 27 Apr. 1784. 200 acres.
Riggs, John. N.C. Private. 19 Dec. 1808. 274 acres.
Riggs, Joshua. Va. Private. 18 Sep. 1807. 100 acres.
Riggs, William. Va. Private. 18 Apr. 1822. 100 acres.
Right, Thomas. N.C. Private. 5 May 1784. 274 acres.
Rigins, Joel. N.C. Private. 28 Sep. 1785. 228 acres.
Rigless, William. Pa. ———. 4 May 1795. 200 acres to Alexander Power, assignee.
Rigsbey, Frederick. N.C. Private. 29 Apr. 1784. 274 acres.
Rilea, Richard. Va. Private. 16 Aug. 1834. 100 acres.
Rileet, Noel. N.C. Private. 26 May 1784. 640 acres.
Riley, Barnard. Ga. Minute Man. 5 May 1785. 287 1/2 acres.
Riley, Daniel. Va. Private. 6 Apr. 1784. 200 acres.
Riley, John. Ga. Minute Man. 14 Jul. 1785. ———.
Riley, John. N.C. Private. 22 Apr. 1785. 640 acres to heirs.
Riley, John. Va. Private. 23 Jun. 1783. 200 acres.
Riley, Joseph. Ga. ———. 22 Apr. 1784. 287 1/2 acres.
Riley, William. Ga. ———. 25 May 1784. 287 1/2 acres.
Rinder, Christian. N. Y. Private. 7 Jul. 1790. 600 acres.
Rinehart, Joshua. N.C. Private. 2 Dec. 1785. 640 acres.
Ring, James. N.C. Musician. 28 Aug. 1820. 1000 acres.
Ring, James, Sr. N.C. Private. 4 Aug. 1821. 640 acres.
Ring, William. N.C. Private. 12 Sep. 1785. 640 acres to heirs.
Rings, Burtus. Va. Private. 12 Apr. 1783. 200 acres.
Ringstaff, Andrew. N.C. Private. 6 Dec. 1797. 640 acres to heirs.
Rinker, Edward. Va. Private. 29 Jul. 1831. 100 acres.
Rinker, Jesse. Va. Private. 4 Nov. 1784. 100 acres.
Rinkin, Edward. Va. Sergeant. 18 Dec. 1783. 200 acres.
Ripley, Hezekiah, Rev. Conn. Sufferer. Fairfield. 368.19.2.
Ripley, John. Va. Sergeant. 14 Dec. 1813. 400 acres.
Ripley, Peter. Pa. ———. 14 Jan. 1796. 200 acres to Daniel Richards, executor.
Ripley, Peter. Pa. Private. ———. 200 acres.
Rippeto, William. Va. Sergeant. 14 Apr. 1795. 400 acres.
Risby, Zaddock. N.C. Private. 30 Sep. 1785. 640 acres to heirs.
Risdale, William. N. Y. Private. 8 Jul. 1790. 600 acres.
Rise, Robert. Md. Private. ———. 50 acres.
Risk, William. N.C. Private. 6 Sep. 1821. 640 acres.

Risley, David. N. Y. ———. 9 Jul. 1790. 600 acres.

Risly, Samuel. N.C. Private. 7 Jan. 1786. 640 acres to heirs.

Risly, Thomas. N.C. Private. 7 Jan. 1786. 640 acres to heirs.

Rison, David. N.C. Private. 22 Apr. 1785. 640 acres to heirs.

Rissell, Jacob. Ga. ———. ———. 230 acres.

Ritchie, Abraham. Va. Private. 19 Jan. 1785. 100 acres.

Ritchie, John. S.C. ———. 2 May 1796. 170 acres.

Ritchie, John. Va. Private. 3 Jul. 1784. 100 acres.

Ritchie, William. Va. ———. 19 Jan. 1785. 100 acres.

Rivere, Wyatt. Va. Armourer. 13 Oct. 1783. 100 acres.

Rivers, Benjamin. N.C. Private. 19 May 1784. 640 acres.

Rives, Foster. N.C. Private. 30 Sep. 1785. 640 acres to heirs.

Rixford, Henry. Mass. Private. 5 Oct. 1833. 200 acres.

Roach, James. N.C. Private. 28 Sep. 1785. 502 acres.

Roach, John. Va. Corporal. 4 Oct. 1783. 200 acres.

Roach, Richard. Va. Private. 23 Jun. 1783. 200 acres.

Roach, William. Va. Corporal. 26 Jun. 1783. 466 2/3 acres.

Roan, Abraham Johnston. N.C. Corporal. 22 Dec. 1796. 1000 acres to heirs.

Roan, James. Ga. ———. 19 Apr. 1784. 287 1/2 acres.

Roan, Tudstall. Ga. ———. 22 Apr. 1784. 287 1/2 acres.

Roane, Christopher. Va. Captain. 19 Dec. 1782. 4000 acres.

Roane, Christopher. Va. Captain. 30 Sep. 1783. 666 2/3 acres.

Roark, William. N.C. Musician. 5 Sep. 1821. 1000 acres.

Roase, Jacob. N. Y. Private. 8 Jul. 1790. 500 acres.

Roase, Peter. N. Y. Private. 8 Jul. 1790. 600 acres.

Robb, William. N.C. Corporal. 23 Oct. 1783. 357 acres.

Robbins, Ephraim. Conn. Sufferer. Fairfield. 106.14.10.

Robbins, Otis. Me. ———. 19 Aug. 1835. 200 acres. Thomaston.

Robbins, Thomas. Mass. Private. 16 Sep. 1834. 200 acres.

Robecheau, James. N. Y. Captain. 13 Sep. 1790. 1500 acres.

Roberds, William. Va. Private. 25 Feb. 1784. 100 acres.

Roberge, Pierre. N. Y. Captain. ———. 500 acres.

Roberson, Elijah. N.C. Commissary. 13 May 1784. 960 acres.

Roberson, James. N.C. Private. 25 Nov. 1795. 640 acres.

Roberson, John. N.C. Private. 18 Aug. 1784. 640 acres.

Roberson, Jonathan. N.C. Private. 7 Dec. 1797. 640 acres to heirs.

Roberson, Willoughby. N.C. Private. 28 Sep. 1785. 640 acres to heirs.

Roberts, Absalom. Ga. Soldier. 1 May 1785. ———.

Roberts, Ambrose. Va. Private. 28 Jun. 1783. 100 acres.

Roberts, Amon. Ga. ———. 1784. 287 1/2 acres.

Roberts, Anthony. Va. Private. 28 Apr. 1783. 200 acres.

Roberts, Benjamin. Va. Captain. 28 Jul. 1830. 4000 acres.

Roberts, Caleb. N. Y. Private. 8 Jul. 1790. 600 acres.

Roberts, Cyrus L. Va. Captain. 28 Mar. 1834. 4207 acres.

Roberts, Daniel. Va. Private. 21 Jun. 1784. 100 acres.

Roberts, David. Conn. Sufferer. New London. 17.16.0.

Roberts, Elijah. N.C. Private. 7 Jan. 1786. 640 acres to heirs.

Roberts, Francis. Ga. Soldier. 27 Apr. 1784. 287 1/2 acres.

Roberts, Francis. N.C. Private. 18 Dec. 1797. 640 acres.

Roberts, George. Va. Sergeant. 8 Dec. 1785. 200 acres.

Roberts, Gerrard. Va. Sergeant. 29 May 1783. 200 acres.

Roberts, Griffith. Pa. Private. 11 Sep. 1789. 200 acres.

Roberts, Hardy. N.C. Private. 30 Sep. 1785. 640 acres to heirs.

Roberts, Harris. Ga. Soldier. 4 Feb. 1785. ———.

Roberts, Horatio. Md. Private. ———. 50 acres.
Roberts, Isaac. N.C. Private. 5 Sep. 1821. 640 acres.
Roberts, James. Ga. Refugee. 25 May 1784. 575 acres.
Roberts, James. N.C. Private. 20 Dec. 1784. 274 acres.
Roberts, John. Ga. Refugee. 25 May 1784. 287 1/2 acres.
Roberts, John. Ga. Soldier. 7 Jun. 1785. 230 acres to heirs.
Roberts, John. N.C. Private. 30 Sep. 1785. 640 acres to heirs.
Roberts, John. N.C. Private. 12 Sep. 1789. 372 acres.
Roberts, John. N.C. Lieutenant. 16 Aug. 1821. 2560 acres.
Roberts, John. Va. Surgeon. Jan. 1783. 6000 acres.
Roberts, John. Va. Private. 20 Aug. 1783. 100 acres.
Roberts, John. Va. Private. 11 Jun. 1784. 100 acres.
Roberts, John. Va. Sergeant. 5 Feb. 1785. 400 acres.
Roberts, John. Va. Surgeon. 20 Nov. 1818. 750 acres.
Roberts, John. Va. Surgeon. 20 Nov. 1818. 750 acres.
Roberts, John. Va. Major. 18 Nov. 1831. 5333 1/3 acres.
Roberts, John. Va. Major. 25 Mar. 1840. 1151 1/2 acres.
Roberts, Jonas. Ga. ———. 17 May 1784. ———.
Roberts, Joseph. N.C. Private. 7 Jan. 1786. 228 acres.
Roberts, Joseph. Pa. Private. 5 Apr. 1787. 200 acres.
Roberts, Joshua. N.C. Private. 30 Sep. 1785. 640 acres to heirs.
Roberts, Kinchin. N.C. ———. 29 Sep. 1784. 640 acres to Ishmael Roberts, heir.
Roberts, Obedience. Va. Private. 21 Aug. 1783. 200 acres.
Roberts, Owen. S.C. Colonel. 21 Jan. 1785. 500 acres to Richard Brooke Roberts, heir.
Roberts, Patrick. Pa. Private. 1 Aug. 1787. 200 acres.
Roberts, Richard. N.C. Private. 19 May 1784. 640 acres.
Roberts, Richard. N.C. Private. 13 Sep. 1820. 274 acres.
Roberts, Richard Brooke. S.C. Captain. 16 Jul. 1784. 300 acres.
Roberts, Rubin. N.C. Private. 9 Nov. 1784. 228 acres.
Roberts, Sampson. N.C. Private. 30 Sep. 1785. 640 acres to heirs.
Roberts, Samuel. N.C. Musician. 4 Sep. 1820. 1000 acres to heirs.
Roberts, Samuel. Conn. Sufferer. New London. 94.6.10.
Roberts, Shadrach. N.C. Private. 13 Jun. 1785. 228 acres.
Roberts, Thomas. Ga. ———. 16 Apr. 1784. 287 1/2 acres.
Roberts, Thomas. Ga. ———. 22 Apr. 1784. 400 acres.
Roberts, Thomas. Va. Sergeant. 13 Apr. 1784. 200 acres.
Roberts, Thomas W. N.C. Private. 10 Feb. 1796. 640 acres to heirs.
Roberts, Vinson. N.C. Private. 20 Jan. 1785. 308 acres.
Roberts, William. Md. Private. ———. 50 acres.
Roberts, William. Pa. Sergeant. 26 Feb. 1787. 200 acres.
Roberts, William. Va. Private. 19 Jan. 1785. 100 acres.
Roberts, William. Va. Private. 26 Aug. 1786. 100 acres.
Roberts, William. Va. Ensign. 9 Mar. 1831. 380 20/21 acres.
Roberts, William. Va. Ensign. 9 Mar. 1831. 380 20/21 acres.
Roberts, William. Va. Ensign. 20 Oct. 1831. 76 4/21 acres.
Roberts, William. Va. Ensign. 20 Oct. 1831. 76 4/16 acres.
Roberts, William. Va. Ensign. 20 Oct. 1831. 76 4/21 acres.
Roberts, William. Va. Ensign. 20 Oct. 1831. 76 4/21 acres.
Roberts, William. Va. Ensign. ———. 380 20/100 acres.
Roberts, William. Va. Ensign. 15 Nov. 1831. 76 4/21 acres.
Roberts, William. Va. Ensign. 13 Jul. 1832. 1142 16/21 acres.
Roberts, William. Va. Ensign. 9 Mar. 1831. 1056 6/7 acres.
Roberts, William. Va. Ensign. 29 Aug. 1835. 380 1/3 acres.

Roberts, William. Va. Ensign. 17 Jun. 1833. 53 16/21 acres.

Roberts, William. Va. ———. 26 Jul. 1836. 190 acres.

Roberts, William. Va. ———. 30 Jul. 1836. 95 1/4 acres.

Robertson, Alexander. Ga. Soldier. 24 Jan. 1784. 200 acres.

Robertson, Archibald. Ga. ———. 27 Apr. 1784. 287 1/2 acres.

Robertson, Benjamin. Va. Sergeant. 19 Dec. 1785. 200 acres.

Robertson, Cornelius. N.C. Private. 6 Dec. 1797. 274 acres.

Robertson, David. Ga. Lieutenant Colonel. 27 Apr. 1784. 805 acres.

Robertson, David. Va. Private. 30 Sep. 1783. 200 acres.

Robertson, David, Jr. Ga. Minute Man. 27 Apr. 1784. 287 1/2 acres.

Robertson, Elisha. Ga. Citizen. 7 Jun. 1785. 287 1/2 acres.

Robertson, Elisha. Va. Private. 9 Jun. 1785. 200 acres.

Robertson, Gardener. N.C. Private. 12 Sep. 1785. 640 acres to heirs.

Robertson, George. Va. Private. 23 May 1783. 100 acres.

Robertson, George. Va. Private. 21 Jan. 1784. 100 acres.

Robertson, Hannah. Conn. Sufferer. Danbury. 2.6.8.

Robertson, Henry. N.C. Musician. 4 Sep. 1820. 360 acres to heirs.

Robertson, Hezekiah. Ga. Soldier. 6 Apr. 1785. 230 acres.

Robertson, Hooker. N.C. Private. 2 Feb. 1786. 274 acres.

Robertson, Hugh. Va. Sergeant. 5 Aug. 1783. 200 acres.

Robertson, Isaac. N.C. Private. 30 Sep. 1785. 640 acres to heirs.

Robertson, James. Va.-Ind. Lieutenant. Aug. 1783. 2156 acres.

Robertson, James. N. Y. Private. 8 Jul. 1790. 500 acres.

Robertson, James. N.C. ———. 13 Jun. 1785. 640 acres to his heirs. He was a son of John Robertson.

Robertson, James. S.C. Soldier. 21 Jan. 1785. 200 acres.

Robertson, James. Va. Lieutenant. 26 Aug. 1783. 2666 2/3 acres.

Robertson, James. Va. Private. 26 Mar. 1784. 100 acres.

Robertson, Jehu. Conn. Sufferer. New/East Haven. 26.15.2.

Robertson, John. Ga. ———. 21 Apr. 1784. 300 acres.

Robertson, John. Md. Private. ———. 50 acres.

Robertson, John. N. Y. Excellency's Guards. 8 Jul. 1790. 500 acres.

Robertson, John. N.Y. ———. 13 Sep. 1790. 500 acres to heirs.

Robertson, John. N.C. Private. 7 Dec. 1797. 274 acres.

Robertson, John. Va. Private. 17 Feb. 1785. 100 acres.

Robertson, John. Va. Private. 6 Dec. 1834. 100 acres.

Robertson, Jonathan. Ga. Refugee. 27 Apr. 1784. 287 1/2 acres to heirs.

Robertson, Joseph. Ga. Private. 20 Apr. 1784. 287 1/2 acres.

Robertson, Joseph. N.C. Private. 7 Jan. 1786. 640 acres to heirs.

Robertson, Joseph. Va. Private. 1 Mar. 1784. 200 acres.

Robertson, Matthew. N.C. Private. 10 Dec. 1788. 640 acres to heirs.

Robertson, Mordecai. Va. Private. 9 Dec. 1783. 100 acres.

Robertson, Samuel. Ga. ———. 23 Apr. 1784. 287 1/2 acres.

Robertson, Servie. N.C. Private. 12 Sep. 1785. 640 acres to heirs.

Robertson, Silvanus. Ga. ———. 27 Apr. 1784. 287 1/2 acres.

Robertson, Thomas. Ga. ———. 27 Apr. 1784. 200 acres.

Robertson, William. Ga. Soldier. 21 Apr. 1784. 400 acres.

Robertson, William. Va. Lieutenant. 24 Apr. 1783. 2666 2/3 acres.

Robertson, William. Va. Lieutenant. 18 Sep. 1807. 889 1/3 acres.

Robertson, Zadock. Ga. ———. 20 Apr. 1784. 287 1/2 acres.

Robeson, Edward. N.C. Sergeant. Jan. 1795. 1000 acres to heirs.

Robeson, Hardy. N.C. Private. 1 Sep. 1785. 640 acres to heirs.

Robeson, Jacob. N.C. Private. 22 Dec. 1796. 274 acres.

Robeson, Noah. N.C. Private. 18 Dec. 1817. 640 acres to heirs.

Robeson, Thomas. N.C. Private. 4 May 1784. 274 acres.
Robinett, Joseph. Va. Private. 15 Oct. 1783. 233 1/3 acres.
Robins, James. N.C. Private. 30 Sep. 1785. 640 acres to heirs.
Robins, Jesse. N.C. Private. 22 Apr. 1785. 274 acres.
Robins, John. N.C. Private. 30 Sep. 1785. 640 acres to heirs.
Robins, John. Va. Lieutenant. 11 Oct. 1783. 2666 2/3 acres.
Robins, John. Va. Midshipman. 29 Oct. 1784. 200 acres.
Robins, John. Va. Lieutenant. 9 Sep. 1797. 444 2/3 acres.
Robins, John. Va. Midshipman. 23 Jan. 1834. 2466 2/3 acres.
Robins, William. Va. Private. 24 May 1784. 100 acres.
Robinson, Alexander. Pa. ———. 200 acres to his widow.
Robinson, Andrew. Pa. ———. ———. 200 acres.
Robinson, Andrew. Pa. Lieutenant. 30 May 1787. 200 acres.
Robinson, Andrew. Va. Private. 24 Mar. 1786. 100 acres.
Robinson, Benjamin. N.C. Private. 29 Sep. 1784. 274 acres.
Robinson, Charles. Va. Private. 23 Jun. 1783. 200 acres.
Robinson, Cole. Va. Sergeant. 31 May 1783. 200 acres.
Robinson, Cole. Va. Ensign. 29 Oct. 1790. 2666 2/3 acres.
Robinson, Cole. Va. Ensign. 9 Nov. 1843. 2666 2/3 acres.
Robinson, Cole. Va. Ensign. 9 Nov. 1843. 1333 1/3 acres.
Robinson, Cole. Va. Ensign. 9 Nov. 1843. 1333 1/3 acres.
Robinson, Cole. Va. Ensign. 31 Jan. 1850. 666 2/3 acres.
Robinson, Cole. Va. Ensign. 31 Jan. 1850. 666 2/3 acres.
Robinson, Cornelius. N.C. Private. Aug. 1787. 274 acres.
Robinson, David. N. Y. Matross. 8 Jul. 1790. 600 acres.
Robinson, Edmund. N. Y. Private. 8 Jul. 1790. 600 acres.
Robinson, Edward. N.C. Private. 27 Jun. 1789. 640 acres to heirs.
Robinson, Francis. Pa. Private. 28 Aug. 1787. 200 acres.
Robinson, George. Ga. Private. 10 Dec. 1784. 250 acres.
Robinson, George. Me. ———. 15 Oct. 1835. 200 acres to widow Isabella Robinson. Hollis.
Robinson, Green. Va. Private. 6 Oct. 1783. 200 acres.
Robinson, Henry. N.C. Private. 4 May 1785. 640 acres to heirs.
Robinson, Hezekiah. Va. Private. 31 Aug. 1830. 100 acres.
Robinson, Isaac. Mass. Fifer. 19 Nov. 1832. 200 acres to heirs.
Robinson, Jacob. N.C. Sergeant. 20 Apr. 1784. 428 acres.
Robinson, James. N. Y. Private. 3 Jul. 1790. 600 acres.
Robinson, James. Pa. Private. ———. 200 acres.
Robinson, James. Pa. Private. ———. 200 acres.
Robinson, James. Pa. Private. ———. 200 acres.
Robinson, James. Pa. Sergeant. 14 Oct. 1785. 250 acres.
Robinson, James. Pa. Private. 29 May 1787. 200 acres.
Robinson, James. Va. Corporal. 23 Jun. 1783. 200 acres.
Robinson, James. Va. Private. 15 Jan. 1808. 100 acres.
Robinson, Jesse. N.C. Private. 26 Apr. 1784. 640 acres to John Robinson, heir.
Robinson, Jesse. N.C. Corporal. 12 May 1784. 1000 acres to John Robinson, heir.
Robinson, Joel. N.C. Private. 9 Nov. 1784. 640 acres.
Robinson, John. Me. ———. 11 Aug. 1835. 200 acres to widow Phebe Robinson. Sebago.
Robinson, John. Me. Private. 5 Oct. 1835. 200 acres to widow Deborah Robinson. Limington.
Robinson, John. N. Y. Private. 3 Jul. 1790. 500 acres.
Robinson, John. N.C. Private. 4 Sep. 1820. 640 acres to heirs.
Robinson, John. Va. Private. 23 Jun. 1783. 200 acres.
Robinson, John. Va. Lieutenant. 6 Dec. 1783. 2666 2/3 acres.

Robinson, John. Va. Private. 11 Aug. 1834. 100 acres.

Robinson, Maximilion. Va. Private. 17 Apr. 1784. 100 acres.

Robinson, Mordecai. Va. Private. 11 Oct. 1783. 200 acres.

Robinson, Nathaniel. Va. Private. 31 Aug. 1830. 100 acres.

Robinson, Patrick. N.C. Private. 9 Nov. 1784. 640 acres to heir.

Robinson, Patrick. Conn. Sufferer. New London. 3.0.0.

Robinson, Peter. Conn. Sufferer. New London. 81.12.2.

Robinson, Richard. N. Y. Private. 7 Jul. 1790. 600 acres.

Robinson, Robert. N. Y. Private. 8 Jul. 1790. 600 acres.

Robinson, Robert. S.C. ———. 6 May 1793. 108 acres.

Robinson, Samuel. Me. ———. 29 Dec. 1835. 200 acres to widow Betsey Robinson. Portland.

Robinson, Samuel. Conn. Sufferer. New/ East Haven. 9.16.2.

Robinson, Simon. Pa. Private. 29 Aug. 1787. 200 acres.

Robinson, Stephen. N. Y. Private. 8 Jul. 1790. 600 acres.

Robinson, Thomas. Pa. Captain. 19 Sep. 1787. 500 acres.

Robinson, Thomas. Pa. Lieutenant Colonel. 6 Oct. 1786. 250 acres.

Robinson, Thomas. Pa. Lieutenant Colonel. 6 Oct. 1786. 500 acres to Francis Johnston, assignee.

Robinson, Tuly. Va. Captain. 1 Jun. 1832. 4000 acres.

Robinson, William. Me. ———. 22 Apr. 1835. 200 acres to widow Sarah Robinson. York.

Robinson, William. N. Y. ———. 9 Jul. 1790. 600 acres.

Robinson, William. Pa. Private. 9 Oct. 1786. 200 acres.

Robinson, William. Va. Private. 31 May 1783. 200 acres.

Robinson, William. Va. Sergeant. 25 Nov. 1783. 400 acres.

Robisheaux, James. N. Y. Captain. ———. 1000 acres.

Robison, George. N. Y. Private. 8 Jul. 1790. 500 acres.

Robison, Robert. S.C. ———. 6 Oct. 1794. 28 acres.

Robison, Robert. S.C. ———. 6 Oct. 1794. 25 acres.

Robison, Robert. S.C. ———. 1 Dec. 1794. 40 acres.

Robson, Green. Va. Private. 19 Jun. 1783. 100 acres.

Roch, Sadler. Pa. Private. 29 Sep. 1787. 200 acres.

Rochel, John. N.C. Captain. 16 Aug. 1821. 1600 acres to heir Allen Rochell.

Rochele, George. N.C. Private. 12 Dec. 1806. 640 acres to heirs.

Rochell, Isaiah. N.C. ———. 29 Apr. 1784. 640 acres to Jacob Rochell, heir.

Rochester, William. N.C. Corporal. 16 Aug. 1821. 1000 acres.

Rock, Jack. N.C. Private. 27 Mar. 1821. 640 acres.

Rock, James. Ga. Minute Man. 6 May 1785. 287 1/2 acres.

Rock, John. Md. Private. ———. 50 acres.

Rock, John. Va. Private. 31 Oct. 1783. 200 acres.

Rock, John. Va. Private. 18 Oct. 1784. 200 acres.

Rock, William. Ga. ———. 27 Apr. 1784. 200 acres.

Rock, William. Md. Private. ———. 50 acres.

Rock, William. Va. Private. 5 Mar. 1784. 200 acres.

Rocke, Moses. N.C. Private. 30 Sep. 1785. 640 acres to heirs.

Rockwell, Abijah. Conn. Sufferer. Ridgefield. 3.5.2.

Rockwell, Abraham. Conn. Sufferer. Ridgefield. 10.4.4.

Rockwell, David. Conn. Sufferer. Ridgefield. 8.4.8.

Rockwell, David, 2d. Conn. Sufferer. Ridgefield. 3.2.10.

Rockwell, Jabez. Conn. Sufferer. Danbury. 158.10.9.

Rockwell, John. Conn. Sufferer. Norwalk. 5.16.0.

Rockwell, Thaddeus. Conn. Sufferer. Ridgefield. 26.18.0.

Rodden, John. Va. Private. 6 Aug. 1783. 200 acres.

Rodes, Jacob. Va. Private. 5 Jan. 1811. 200 acres.

Rodes, Jeremiah. Md. Private. ———. 50 acres.
Rodes, Lewis. N.C. Private. 30 Sep. 1785. 640 acres to heirs.
Rodgers, Andrew. Va. Lieutenant. 20 May 1823. 1000 acres.
Rodgers, Andrew. Va. Lieutenant. 20 May 1823. 1000 acres.
Rodgers, Andrew. Va. Lieutenant. 20 May 1832. 666 2/3 acres.
Rodgers, Henry. Va. Seaman. 29 Nov. 1832. 100 acres.
Rodgers, Jacob. S.C. ———. 4 Nov. 1793. 66 acres to James Timms, administrator.
Rodgers, John. Va.-Ind. Captain. Feb. 1783. 3234 acres.
Rodgers, John R. B. Pa. Surgeon. ———. 300 acres.
Rodgers, Joseph. Va. Lieutenant. 5 Mar. 1838. 3258 acres.
Rodgers, Wiliam. N.C. Private. 24 Dec. 1785. 640 acres to heirs.
Rodman, William. Pa. Private. 16 Dec. 1786. 200 acres.
Rodridge, Emanuel. N. Y. ———. ———. 500 acres.
Roe, Andrew. Ga. ———. 27 Apr. 1784. 287 1/2 acres.
Roe, James. Ga. Refugee. 16 Apr. 1784. 278 1/2 acres.
Roe, John. Va. Private. 20 Aug. 1783. 200 acres.
Roe, Joseph. Pa. ———. 18 Feb. 1803. 200 acres.
Roe, Lemuel. N.C. Private. 24 Jan. 1800. 274 acres.
Roe, Lyman. N. Y. Private. 8 Jul. 1790. 500 acres.
Roe, Ormond. Ga. Private. 23 Apr. 1784. 287 1/2 acres to heirs.
Roe, Robert. Ga. Soldier. 4 Oct. 1785. ———.
Roe, Samuel. N.C. Private. 24 Jan. 1800. 228 acres.
Roe, Terry. N.C. Private. 8 Dec. 1796. 640 acres to heirs.
Roe, Walter. Ga. Minute Man. 24 Apr. 1784. ———.
Roe, William. N.C. Private. 10 Feb. 1796. 640 acres to heirs.
Roe, William. Va. Private. 19 Feb. 1784. 100 acres.
Roe, William. Va. Surgeon's Mate. 22 Jun. 1786. 2666 2/3 acres.
Roe, William. Va. Surgeon's Mate. 8 Mar. 1853. 666 2/3 acres.
Roe, William. Va. Surgeon's Mate. 8 Mar. 1853. 222 1/4 acres.
Roe, William. Va. Surgeon's Mate. 8 Mar. 1853. 444 1/4 acres.
Rogan, Thomas. Pa. ———. ———. 200 acres to Richard Hunt, assignee.
Rogers, ———. Pa. Private. ———. 200 acres to widow Elizabeth Rogers.
Rogers, Absalom. N.C. Private. 12 Sep. 1785. 640 acres to heirs.
Rogers, Alexander. S.C. ———. 2 May 1785. 200 acres.
Rogers, Amos. Conn. Sufferer. New London. 31.1.8.
Rogers, Andrew. Pa. Private. 7 Dec. 1786. 200 acres.
Rogers, Arthur. N.C. Private. 12 Mar. 1785. 640 acres to heirs.
Rogers, Austin. N.C. Private. 24 Dec. 1796. 228 acres.
Rogers, Benjamin. Conn. Sufferer. New London. 9.19.5.
Rogers, Bernard. Va. Private [Sergeant]. 19 Feb. 1784. 100 [200] acres.
Rogers, Bowling. Va. Private. 11 Feb. 1786. 200 acres.
Rogers, Britain. Ga. Refugee. 21 Apr. 1784. 287 1/2 acres.
Rogers, Burwell. Ga. ———. 21 Apr. 1784. 287 1/2 acres.
Rogers, Daniel. N.C. Private. 1 Sep. 1785. 640 acres to heirs.
Rogers, David. Ga. Refugee. 6 Aug. 1785. ———.
Rogers, David. N.C. Private. 26 Nov. 1796. 640 acres to heirs.
Rogers, David. Va. Colonel. 6 Feb. 1851. 1631 7/24 acres.
Rogers, David. Va. Colonel. 6 Feb. 1851. 1631 7/24 acres.
Rogers, David. Va. Colonel. 6 Feb. 1851. 833 acres.
Rogers, David. Va. Colonel. 6 Feb. 1851. 833 acres.
Rogers, David. Va. Colonel. 6 Feb. 1851. 833 acres.
Rogers, David. Va. Colonel. 6 Feb. 1851. 905 5/12 acres.
Rogers, Dread. Ga. Refugee. 21 Apr. 1784. 287 1/2 acres.
Rogers, Drury. Ga. ———. 21 Apr. 1784. 287 1/2 acres.

Rogers, Edward. Ga. Minute Man. 3 Sep. 1785. ———.
Rogers, Edward. Ga. ———. 27 Apr. 1784. 287 1/2 acres.
Rogers, Eli. N.C. Private. 13 Sep. 1820. 274 acres.
Rogers, Elisha. N.C. Private. 3 Feb. 1785. 640 acres.
Rogers, Elizabeth. Conn. Sufferer. Norwalk. 228.14.0.
Rogers, Elizabeth 2d. Conn. Sufferer. Norwalk. 1.5.0.
Rogers, Ephraim. N.C. Private. 2 Apr. 1784. 274 acres.
Rogers, George. Va. Captain. 15 Apr. 1833. 4000 acres.
Rogers, George. Va. Captain. 13 Jun. 1833. 1333 1/3 acres.
Rogers, George. Conn. Sufferer. New London. 14.14.0.
Rogers, Harris. Conn. Sufferer. New London. 128.13.10.
Rogers, Henry. Mass. Sergeant. 19 Nov. 1832. 200 acres to heirs.
Rogers, Jacob. S.C. ———. 4 Jul. 1796. 15 1/2 acres to Robert Coleman, assignee of James Timms, administrator.
Rogers, Jacob. S.C. ———. 4 Nov. 1793. 39 acres to James Timms, administrator.
Rogers, Jacob. S.C. ———. 4 Nov. 1793. 25 acres to James Timms, administrator.
Rogers, Jacob. Va. Private. 13 Apr. 1833. 200 acres.
Rogers, James. N.C. Private. 30 Sep. 1785. 640 acres to heirs.
Rogers, James. S.C. ———. 5 Jun. 1797. 54 acres to James Timms, administrator, in trust for the heirs.
Rogers, James. Va. Private. 26 Feb. 1833. 100 acres.
Rogers, James. Va. Private. 25 Oct. 1833. 100 acres.
Rogers, James. Conn. Sufferer. New London. 455.16.5.
Rogers, James. Conn. Sufferer. New London. 1.16.0.
Rogers, Jeremiah. Ga. ———. 27 Apr. 1784. 287 1/2 acres.
Rogers, Jesse. N.C. Private. 12 Sep. 1785. 640 acres to heirs.
Rogers, John. Ga. Minute Man. 20 Apr. 1784. 287 1/2 acres to heirs.
Rogers, John. Ga. Refugee. 27 Apr. 1784. 287 1/2 acres.
Rogers, John. N.C. Private. 23 Feb. 1820. 640 acres.
Rogers, John. Va. Captain. 2 Dec. 1782. 3000 acres.
Rogers, John. Va. Captain. 2 Dec. 1784. 1000 acres.
Rogers, John. Va. Private. 31 Jan. 1784. 200 acres.
Rogers, John. Va. Captain. 4 Feb. 1834. 1333 1/3 acres.
Rogers, John. Va. Captain. 4 Feb. 1834. 1333 1/3 acres.
Rogers, John. Va. ———. 25 Jun. 1835. 2666 2/3 acres.
Rogers, John. Va. Captain. 23 Sep. 1856. 818 1/8 acres.
Rogers, John. Va. Captain. 23 Sep. 1856. 818 1/8 acres.
Rogers, John. Conn. Sufferer. Norwalk. 41.1.9.
Rogers, John. Conn. Sufferer. New London. 31.8.10.
Rogers, John R. B. Pa. Surgeon. 13 Oct. 1786. 300 acres.
Rogers, Joseph. Ga. ———. 19 Dec. 1785. 575 acres.
Rogers, Joseph. Va. Lieutenant. 10 Jul. 1838. 500 acres.
Rogers, Joseph. Va. Lieutenant. 10 Jul. 1838. 500 acres.
Rogers, Joseph. Va. Lieutenant. 10 Jul. 1838. 500 acres.
Rogers, Joseph. Va. Lieutenant. 10 Jul. 1838. 500 acres.
Rogers, Joseph. Va. Lieutenant. 10 Jul. 1838. 500 acres.
Rogers, Joseph. Va. Lieutenant. 10 Jul. 1838. 500 acres.
Rogers, Joseph. Va. Lieutenant. 10 Jul. 1838. 258 acres.
Rogers, Joseph Thompson. N.C. Drum Major. 22 Dec. 1796. 1000 acres to heirs.
Rogers, Joshua. N.C. Private. 27 Aug. 1784. 640 acres.
Rogers, Joshua. Conn. Sufferer. Norwalk. 14.15.3.
Rogers, Mark. N.C. Private. 7 Jan. 1786. 640 acres to heirs.
Rogers, Mary. Conn. Sufferer. New London. 8.13.0.
Rogers, Michael. N.C. Private. 3 Feb. 1785. 274 acres.

Rogers, Parker. N.C. Fifer. 29 Sep. 1784. 319 acres.
Rogers, Parker. N.C. Fifer. 25 Nov. 1796. 681 acres.
Rogers, Patrick. N.C. Lieutenant. 12 Dec. 1785. 2560 acres to heirs.
Rogers, Peleg. Ga. ———. 23 Apr. 1784. 287 1/2 acres.
Rogers, Peter. Ga. Minute Man. 27 Apr. 1784. 287 1/2 acres.
Rogers, Peter. Conn. Sufferer. New London. 16.2.4.
Rogers, Peter, Jr. Conn. Sufferer. New London. 1.12.9.
Rogers, Reuben. Ga. ———. 21 Apr. 1784. 287 1/2 acres.
Rogers, Robert. Va. Private. 14 Feb. 1834. 100 acres.
Rogers, Solomon. Ga. Minute Man. ———. ———.
Rogers, Solomon. Conn. Sufferer. New London. 101.4.3.
Rogers, Stephen. Mass. Private. 12 Sep. 1832. 200 acres to widow Lydia Rogers.
Rogers, Stephen. N.C. Private. 23 Dec. 1792. 356 acres.
Rogers, Sylvester. N.C. Private. 10 Dec. 1821. 274 acres to heirs.
Rogers, Thomas. Ga. Soldier. 5 Aug. 1785. ———.
Rogers, Tully. Va. Private. 23 May 1809. 260 acres.
Rogers, Uriah, Dr. Conn. Sufferer. Norwalk. 225.0.0 to his heirs.
Rogers, William. Ga. Refugee. 27 Apr. 1784. 287 1/2 acres.
Rogers, William. Md. Private. ———. 50 acres.
Rogers, William. N.C. Private. 9 Sep. 1820. 274 acres.
Rogers, William. Pa. Chaplain. 11 Oct. 1786. 300 acres.
Rogers, William. Pa. Chaplain. 12 Oct. 1786. 300 acres.
Rogers, William. Va. Captain. 18 Jun. 1783. 4000 acres.
Rogers, William. Va. Captain. 29 Aug. 1807. 500 acres.
Rogers, William. Va. Captain. 29 Aug. 1807. 500 acres.
Rogers, William. Va. Captain. 29 Aug. 1807. 111 acres.
Rogers, William. Va. Seaman. 25 Mar. 1833. 80 acres.
Rogers, William. Conn. Sufferer. New London. 18.3.0.
Rogers, William. Conn. Sufferer. New London. 4.19.0.
Rogester, Nicholas. N.C. Corporal. 9 Nov. 1784. 1000 acres to heir.
Roggerson, John. N.C. Private. 27 Jun. 1788. 360 acres.
Rolan, James. N.C. Private. 17 Dec. 1785. 274 acres.
Rolan, Samuel. N.C. Private. 17 Dec. 1785. 640 acres.
Roland, Burwell. Va. Private. 18 Sep. 1799. 100 acres.
Rolin, Godfrey. N.C. Private. 17 Dec. 1796. 640 acres to heirs.
Rolin, Robert. N.C. Sergeant. 12 Nov. 1821. 1000 acres.
Rolins, James. N.C. Private. 6 Jan. 1784. 274 acres.
Rollance, John. N.C. Private. 22 Dec. 1796. 640 acres to heirs.
Rollen, Henry. N.C. Sergeant. 22 Apr. 1785. 1000 acres.
Rollen, James. N.C. Private. 22 Apr. 1785. 640 acres to heirs.
Rollen, William. N.C. Private. 22 Oct. 1783. 649 acres to heirs.
Rollins, Bernard. Ga. Minute Man. ———. ———.
Rollins, Daniel. Va. Private. 27 Sep. 1786. 100 acres.
Rollins, David. Ga. Minute Man. 3 Oct. 1783. ———.
Rollins, Eliphalet. Me. ———. 27 Apr. 1835. 200 acres. Hallowell.
Rollins, John. Me. Private. 7 May 1835. 200 acres. Augusta.
Rollins, John, Jr. Ga. Minute Man. 3 Oct. 1783. ———.
Rollins, John, Sr. Ga. Minute Man. 3 Oct. 1783. ———.
Rollins, Patrick. N.C. Private. 8 Dec. 1796. 640 acres to heirs.
Rollins, William. N.C. Private. 16 Dec. 1797. 640 acres to heirs.
Rolston, Isaac. N.C. Lieutenant. 21 May 1784. 1240 acres.
Rolston, Robert. N.C. Captain. 24 May 1784. 1097 acres.
Roney, John. Va. Lieutenant. 12 Jan. 1784. 3110 2/3 acres.
Roods, William. Va. Private. 3 Aug. 1798. 200 acres.

Roody, Patrick. Pa. Private. 28 Aug 1787. 200 acres to Matthew McConnell, assignee.

Rook, Ternon. Pa. ———. 22 Nov. 1786. 250 acres to Francis White, assignee.

Rooke, John. Va. Private. 23 Jun. 1783. 200 acres.

Rooksberry, Edward. Ga. Soldier. 7 Jun. 1785. 200 acres to heirs.

Rooksberry, Jacob. Ga. Soldier. 7 June 1785. 230 acres.

Roome, Benjamin. N. Y. Private. 3 Jul. 1790. 600 acres.

Roomer, William. N. Y. Private. 8 Jul. 1790. 500 acres.

Rootes, John. Va. ———. 30 Dec. 1784. 3000 acres.

Roper, James. N.C. Private. 17 Sep. 1785. 274 acres to heirs.

Roper, James. N.C. Private. 6 Sep. 1821. 640 acres.

Roper, Patrick. N.C. Private. 2 Feb. 1786. 274 acres.

Roper, Richard. N.C. Private. 15 Jul. 1785. 228 acres.

Roper, Stephen. N.C. Sergeant. 7 Jan. 1786. 1000 acres to heirs.

Roquemore, James. Ga. ———. 24 May 1784. 287 1/2 acres.

Roquemore, Peter. Ga. Lieutenant. 19 Jul. 1784. 575 acres.

Roscrow, Henry. Pa. Private. 16 Jul. 1787. 200 acres.

Rose, Albert. N. Y. Private. 8 Jul. 1790. 600 acres.

Rose, Alexander. Va. Captain. 3 Nov. 1785. 2000 acres.

Rose, Alexander. Va. Captain. 3 Nov. 1785. 2000 acres.

Rose, Alexander. Va. Captain. 6 Feb. 1807. 666 2/3 acres.

Rose, Alexander. Va. Captain. 29 Aug. 1807. 444 acres.

Rose, Andrew. N. Y. Private. 3 Jul. 1790. 600 acres.

Rose, Andrew. N.C. Private. 5 Dec. 1796. 640 acres.

Rose, Archibald. Va. Sergeant. 2 Oct. 1783. 400 acres.

Rose, Archibald. Va. Sergeant. 13 Aug. 1853. 400 acres.

Rose, Arry. N.Y. ———. 13 Sep. 1790. 500 acres to heirs.

Rose, Benjamin. Me. ———. 29 Apr. 1835. 200 acres. Hartland.

Rose, Christian. Conn. Sufferer. Danbury. 0.18.4.

Rose, David. N.C. Sergeant. 22 Apr. 1785. 1000 acres.

Rose, Enoch. Mass. ———. 3 Jul. 1837. 200 acres to assignee William M. Lathrop.

Rose, George. Va. Private. 17 Apr. 1783. 200 acres.

Rose, George. Va. Private. 27 Feb. 1797. 200 acres.

Rose, Henry. Ga. ———. 27 Apr. 1784. 287 1/2 acres.

Rose, Isaac. Va. Corporal. 17 Apr. 1784. 200 acres.

Rose, James. N. Y. Private. 3 Jul. 1790. 600 acres.

Rose, James. N.C. Private. 22 Dec. 1796. 228 acres.

Rose, James. Va. Private. 16 Dec. 1837. 100 acres.

Rose, Jesse. Va. Private. 18 Apr. 1783. 100 acres.

Rose, Jesse. Va. Sergeant. 3 May 1823. 100 acres.

Rose, John. Ga. ———. 27 Apr. 1784. 287 1/2 acres.

Rose, John. Pa. Lieutenant. 19 Apr. 1787. 200 acres.

Rose, John. Pa. Lieutenant. 19 Apr. 1787. 200 acres.

Rose, Reuben. Va. Private. 1 Aug. 1799. 100 acres.

Rose, Richard. N.C. Private. 29 Sep. 1785. 640 acres to heirs.

Rose, Robert. Va. Surgeon. 1 Nov. 1783. 7000 acres.

Rose, Robert. Va. Surgeon. 22 Sep. 1809. 1000 acres.

Rose, Samuel. N.C. Private. 2 Feb. 1786. 640 acres to heirs.

Rose, Thomas. Ga. ———. 27 Apr. 1784. 287 1/2 acres.

Rose, Thomas. Va. Private. 22 Mar. 1827. 200 acres.

Rose, William. Va. Private. 18 Apr. 1783. 100 acres.

Roseborough, George. Ga. Soldier. 28 Feb. 1784. 250 acres to heirs.

Roseborough, William. Ga. ———. 21 Apr. 1784. 287 1/2 acres.

Rosekrans, James. N. Y. Major. 3 Jul. 1790. 2400 acres.
Rosewill, Jacob. Pa. Private. 9 Oct. 1786. 200 acres.
Ross, Abram. N.C. Private. 6 Sep. 1784. 640 acres to Francis Ross, heir.
Ross, Cristian. Md. Private. ———. 50 acres.
Ross, David. Va. Private. 20 Dec. 1796. 100 acres.
Ross, Elijah. N.C. Private. 9 Dec. 1797. 640 acres.
Ross, Elijah. Va. Private. 7 May 1785. 100 acres.
Ross, Elijah. Va. Private. 15 Jun. 1807. 100 acres.
Ross, George. Mass. Private. 18 Oct. 1833. 200 acres.
Ross, James. N.C. Private. 9 Dec. 1797. 228 acres.
Ross, James. Va. Private. 30 Jan. 1786. 100 acres.
Ross, John. Ga. ———. 250 acres. ———.
Ross, John. N. Y. ———. 3 Jul. 1790. 600 acres.
Ross, John. N. Y. Private. 24 Aug. 1790. 600 acres.
Ross, John. N.C. Private. 26 Aug. 1785. 640 acres to heirs.
Ross, John. N.C. Private. 27 Nov. 1789. 182 acres.
Ross, John. Pa. Private. 13 Oct. 1786. 200 acres to Mary Ross, widow.
Ross, John. Va. Private. 21 May 1783. 200 acres.
Ross, John. Va. Private. 15 Jun. 1807. 100 acres.
Ross, Joseph. Va.-Ind. Private. 108 acres.
Ross, Oliver. Pa. Private. 27 Jul. 1787. 200 acres.
Ross, Robert. Conn. Sufferer. Fairfield. 2.17.0.
Ross, Samuel. N.C. Private. 30 Sep. 1785. 640 acres to heirs.
Ross, Samuel. N.C. Private. 30 Nov. 1785. 640 acres to heirs.
Ross, Valentine. Va. Private. 22 Aug. 1783. 200 acres.
Ross, William. Va. Private. 7 Dec. 1793. 100 acres.
Rosse, Thomas. Ga. ———. 15 Mar. 1784. 250 acres.
Rosser, John. Va. Private. 4 Mar. 1784. 100 acres.
Rosson, William. Va. Private. 7 Jun. 1785. 100 acres.
Rotchester, William. N.C. Private. 22 Apr. 1785. 640 acres to heirs.
Roth, Philip. Pa. Musician. 15 Nov. 1786. 200 acres.
Roth, Philip. Va. Master Musician. 4 Nov. 1819. 200 acres.
Rothwell, David. N.C. Private. 28 Oct. 1783. 640 acres to heirs.
Rothwell, William. N.C. Private. 28 Oct. 1783. 640 acres to heir.
Rougett, Stephen. Conn. Sufferer. New London. 37.6.1.
Rough, Ludwick. Pa. Private. 7 Jan. 1806. 200 acres.
Rough, Peter. N.C. Private. 27 Mar. 1821. 360 acres.
Roundtree, Andrew. N.C. Private. 9 Dec. 1797. 640 acres to heirs.
Roundtree, Archer. N.C. Private. 7 Jan. 1786. 640 acres to heirs.
Roundtree, Jesse. Refugee. Ga. 27 Apr. 1784. 287 1/2 acres.
Roundtree, Job. Ga. Refugee. 27 Apr. 1784. 287 1/2 acres to heirs.
Roundtree, John. N.C. Private. 7 Dec. 1797. 640 acres to heirs.
Roundtree, Joseph. Ga. ———. 17 May 1784. ——— to heirs.
Roundtree, Reubin. N.C. Lieutenant. 15 Dec. 1783. 1144 acres.
Roundtree, Samuel. Va. Private. 18 Nov. 1818. 100 acres.
Rourk, Martin. Me. ———. 29 Jul. 1842. 200 acres to widow Elizabeth Rourk. Durham.
Rourk, Timothy. Pa. Private. 3 Feb. 1787. 200 acres.
Rouse, Jacob. Pa. Private. 3 May 1787. 200 acres.
Rouse, Jacque. N. Y. ———. ———. 500 acres.
Rouse, Thomas. Md. Lieutenant. ———. 200 acres.
Rouse, Thomas. Pa. ———. 22 Dec. 1803. 200 acres.
Rouse, William. Pa. Private. 22 Dec. 1802. 200 acres.
Routledge, William. N.C. Lieutenant. 24 Oct. 1783 2560 acres to Sarah Routledge, heir.

Routon, Richard. Va. Corporal. 23 Jun. 1783. 200 acres.
Routt, Richard. Va. Lieutenant. 28 Feb. 1837. 888 1/3 acres.
Routt, Richard. Va. Lieutenant. 28 Feb. 1837. 444 1/2 acres.
Routt, Richard. Va. Lieutenant. 28 Feb. 1837. 444 1/2 acres.
Routt, Richard. Va. Lieutenant. 28 Feb. 1837. 444 1/2 acres.
Routt, Richard. Va. Lieutenant. 28 Feb. 1837. 444 1/2 acres.
Routt, Richard. Va. Lieutenant. 19 Mar. 1849. 888 1/3 acres.
Roux, Anthony Lee. Va. Private. 23 Feb. 1784. 200 acres.
Row, George. N.C. Private. 20 Apr. 1784. 640 acres.
Row, James. N.C. Fifer. 23 Apr. 1784. 1000 acres.
Row, James. Va. Corporal. 15 Mar. 1784. 200 acres.
Row, Jesse. N.C. Drummer. 11 Apr. 1784. 428 acres.
Row, Walton. Ga. Soldier. 3 Jan. 1785. ———.
Row, William. Ga. ———. ———. 287 1/2 acres.
Rowan, John. S.C. ———. 2 Mar. 1789. 200 acres.
Rowan, Simon. N.C. Private. 2 Feb. 1786. 640 acres to heirs.
Rowe, Dempsey. N.C. Private. 30 Sep. 1785. 640 acres.
Rowe, Jesse. N.C. Private. 30 Sep. 1785. 640 acres.
Rowe, John. Va. Private. 26 Apr. 1783. 200 acres.
Rowe, Samuel. Mass. Sergeant. 22 Jul. 1833. 200 acres.
Rowe, Webber. Me. Private. 3 Sep. 1835. 200 acres. Baldwin.
Rowe, William. Va. Private. 21 Oct. 1785. 100 acres.
Rowell, Andrew. N.C. Private. 23 Apr. 1785. 640 acres to heirs.
Rowell, Edward. Ga. ———. 27 Apr. 1784. 500 acres.
Rowell, Howell. Ga. ———. 27 Apr. 1784. 287 1/2 acres.
Rowell, Howell. N.C. Private. 30 Sep. 1785. 228 acres.
Rowell, Jesse. N.C. Private. 27 Mar. 1821. 640 acres.
Rowlan, Dyal. Ga. Refugee. Sep. 1785. ———.
Rowland, Andrew. Ga. ———. 17 May 1784. ———.
Rowland, Andrew. Conn. Sufferer. Fairfield. 1,568.15.11.
Rowland, George. Ga. ———. 27 Apr. 1784. 287 1/2 acres.
Rowland, George. Pa. Private. ———. 200 acres.
Rowland, George, Jr. Ga. ———. 27 Apr. 1784. 200 acres.
Rowland, James. N.C. Private. 20 Sep. 1784. 640 acres.
Rowland, James. Pa. ———. 24 Nov. 1787. 200 acres to Joseph Johnston, assignee.
Rowland, John. N.C. Private. 3 Dec. 1796. 640 acres to heirs.
Rowland, John. Pa. ———. 28 Feb. 1794. 200 acres to Walter Stewart, assignee.
Rowland, John. Pa. Private. 21 Dec. 1786. 200 acres to widow.
Rowland, Samuel. Ga. Minute Man. 20 Apr. 1784. 287 1/2 acres.
Rowland, Samuel. Conn. Sufferer. Fairfield. 476.10.7.
Rowland, William. N.C. Private. 20 Dec. 1800. 640 acres to heirs.
Rowland, William. Va. Private. 5 Feb. 1798. 200 acres.
Rowles, William. Md. Private. ———. 50 acres.
Rowley, John. Ga. Minute Man. 22 Mar. 1785. 250 acres.
Rowley, Timothy. N. Y. Private. 8 Jul. 1790. 600 acres.
Rowling, David, Sr. Ga. Minute Man. 17 Jan. 1785. 287 1/2 acres.
Rowling, John, Jr. Ga. Minute Man. 22 Mar. 1785. 250 acres.
Rowling, John, Sr. Ga. Minute Man. 2 Feb. 1785. 287 1/2 acres.
Rows, John. N.C. Private. 9 Nov. 1784. 274 acres.
Rowse, William. N.C. Sergeant. 17 Dec. 1785. 420 acres.
Rowsel, Thomas. Va. Private. 6 Mar. 1784. 100 acres.
Rowsing, Jeremiah. Pa. ———. 20 Dec. 1788. 200 acres to Frederick Snider, assignee.
Roxburgh, Alexander. Md. Major. ———. 200 acres.

Roy, Beverly. Va. Captain. 3 Mar. 1783. 4000 acres.
Roy, Beverly. Va. Captain. 24 Nov. 1796. 666 2/3 acres.
Royal, Grief. Va. Private. 16 Jun. 1783. 100 acres.
Royal, James. N.C. Private. 20 Feb. 1784. 640 acres to heir.
Royal, Joseph. N.C. Private. 28 May 1784. 640 acres.
Royall, Francis. Va. Private. 19 Jun. 1783. 100 acres.
Royall, William. Va. Captain. 9 Nov. 1808. 4889 acres.
Royster, John. Va. Sergeant. 9 Oct. 1783. 200 acres.
Rozar, William. S.C. ———. 5 May 1788. 200 acres.
Rozer, Amos. Ga. Minute Man. 22 Mar. 1785. 250 acres.
Rozer, Caleb. Ga. Refugee. ———. 500 acres.
Rozer, Darby. Ga. Citizen. 22 Mar. 1785. 250 acres.
Rozer, Edward. Ga. Private. 10 Dec. 1784. 250 acres.
Rozer, Jacob. Ga. Minute Man. 3 Apr. 1785. ———.
Rozer, John. Ga. Private. 10 Dec. 1784. 250 acres.
Rozer, Shadrach. Ga. ———. 13 Apr. 1784. 600 acres.
Rozier, Jordan. N.C. Private. 24 Nov. 1796. 640 acres to heirs.
Ruark, James. N.C. Private. 21 Aug. 1820. 640 acres.
Ruark, Nicholas. N.C. Private. 21 Aug. 1820. 274 acres.
Rubey, William. Va.-Ind. Sergeant. 216 acres.
Rubey, William. Va.-Ind. Private. 108 acres.
Rucker, Angus. Va. Captain. 20 Jan. 1783. 4000 acres.
Rucker, Angus. Va. Captain. 5 Apr. 1838. 140 acres.
Rucker, Angus. Va. Captain. 5 Apr. 1838. 421 acres.
Rucker, Elliott. Va. Lieutenant. 20 Feb. 1783. 2666 2/3 acres.
Rucker, Jacob. Va. Private. 23 Jun. 1783. 200 acres.
Rucks, Benjamin. Va. Private. 23 Apr. 1798. 100 acres.
Rudd, Benjamin. Va. Sailor. 19 Dec. 1783. 100 acres.
Rudd, Thomas. Ga. Soldier. 20 Jul. 1785. ———.
Ruddell, Isaac. Va.-Ind. Captain. Mar. 1784. 3234 acres.
Rudder, Epaphroditus. Va. Lieutenant. 13 Feb. 1783. 2666 2/3 acres.
Ruddle, Cornelius. Va.-Ind. Private. 108 acres.
Rude, William. N. Y. Private. 8 Jul. 1790. 600 acres.
Rudolph, Christopher. N. Y. Private. 8 Jul. 1790. 600 acres.
Rudolph, David. N. Y. ———. 9 Jul. 1790. 600 acres.
Rudolph, John. Md. Major. ———. 200 acres.
Rudolph, Joseph. Pa. Lieutenant. 29 Dec.1788. 200 acres.
Rudolph, Michael. Md. Captain. ———. 200 acres.
Rudpeth, John. N.C. Lieutenant. 22 Oct. 1783. 2560 to Elizabeth Rudpeth, widow.
Rudulph, John. Va. Major. 30 Mar. 1819. 5333 1/3 acres.
Rudulph, John. Va. Major. 14 Mar. 1868. 2078 1/3 acres.
Rudulph, John. Va. Major. 30 Jun. 1868. 807 22/27 acres.
Rudulph, Michael. Va. Captain. 30 Mar. 1819. 4000 acres.
Rudulph, Michael. Va. ———. 14 Mar. 1868. 615 acres.
Rue, Charles. N.C. Private. 17 Dec. 1785. 640 acres.
Ruff, Jonathan. N. Y. ———. 9 Jul. 1790. 600 acres.
Ruff, Peter. N.C. Private. 22 Dec. 1796. 274 acres.
Ruffin, Thomas. Va. Captain. 4 Jun. 1808. 4000 acres.
Ruger, John. N. Y. Private. 8 Jul. 1790. 600 acres.
Rukie, Robert. N.C. Drummer. 7 Dec. 1797. 471 acres.
Ruland, Ezekiel. N.Y. ———. 13 Sep. 1790. 500 acres to heirs.
Rulison, William. Va.-Ind. Private. 108 acres. [Rollison].
Rullerton, Richard. Pa. Lieutenant. 10 Nov. 1787. 200 acres.

Rullins, William. N.Y. ———. 13 Sep. 1790. 500 acres to heirs.
Rumage, David. Va. Private. 20 Jun. 1783. 100 acres.
Rumar, Cornelius. N.C. Corporal. 21 Aug. 1820. 1000 acres.
Rumblo, Thomas. N. Y. Matross. 9 Jul. 1790. 600 acres.
Rumley, Nathaniel. Ga. Citizen. 5 Apr. 1785. 287 1/2 acres.
Rumney, William. Va. Surgeon. 9 Apr. 1838. 1500 acres.
Rumney, William. Va. Surgeon. 9 Apr. 1838. 1125 acres.
Rumney, William. Va. Surgeon. 9 Apr. 1838. 1125 acres.
Rumney, William. Va. Surgeon. 9 Apr. 1838. 1125 acres.
Rumney, William. Va. Surgeon. 9 Apr. 1838. 1125 acres.
Rumrill, Joseph. Mass. Private. 18 Jan. 1834. 200 acres.
Rumrill, Thomas. Mass. Private. 18 Oct. 1833. 200 acres.
Rumsey, Benjamin. Conn. Sufferer. Fairfield. 0.15.0.
Runalds, Flourence. N.C. Private. 6 Dec. 1797. 365 acres.
Rundal, Samuel. Conn. Sufferer. Greenwich. 4.6.4.
Rundall, Abigail. Conn. Sufferer. Greenwich. 3.2.0.
Rundall, Amy. Conn. Sufferer. Greenwich. 4.15.0.
Rundall, Reuben. Conn. Sufferer. Greenwich. 44.2.0.
Rundall, Shubael. Conn. Sufferer. Greenwich. 9.12.6.
Rundall, Solomon. Conn. Sufferer. Greenwich. 39.19.6.
Rundall, Timothy. Conn. Sufferer. Greenwich. 7.11.8.
Rundall, William. Conn. Sufferer. Greenwich. 81.7.1.
Rundell, Hannah. Conn. Sufferer. Greenwich. 45.0.0.
Runnalls, Frederick. Ga. ———. 21 Apr. 1784. 287 1/2 acres.
Runnals, Richard. Ga. ———. 2 Jan. 1786. ———.
Runnell, Philip. Pa. Private. 6 Feb. 1787. 200 acres.
Runnels, Coleman. Ga. Refugee. 15 Mar. 1784. 250 acres.
Runnels, Enos. Mass. Corporal. 19 Sep. 1834. 200 acres.
Runnels, George. Ga. Minute Man. 29 Jul. 1784. 287 1/2 acres.
Runnels, Hamilton. Ga. Soldier. 29 Jul. 1784. 287 1/2 acres.
Runnels, John. Me. ———. 23 Apr. 1836. 200 acres to widow Rhoda Runnels. Portland.
Runnels, Joseph. N.C. Corporal. 10 Sep. 1821. 1000 acres to heirs.
Runnels, Thomas. Me. Private. 20 Aug. 1838. 200 acres. Portland.
Runnion, Benjamin. N. Y. Private. 7 Jul. 1790. 600 acres.
Rupert, Adam. Pa. ———. 5 May 1807. 200 acres to Mary Eckert et al., devisees.
Rupert, George. Va. Private. 17 Jul. 1784. 200 acres.
Ruroy, James. Ga. Minute Man. 22 Mar. 1785. 250 acres.
Rush, Thomas. Pa. Private. 13 Apr. 1787. 200 acres.
Rush, William. N.C. Private. 30 Sep. 1785. 640 acres to heirs.
Rushing, Malachi. Ga. ———. 15 Mar. 1784. 250 acres.
Rushing, Matthew. Ga. Refugee. 26 May 1784. 287 1/2 acres.
Rushman, William. Pa. Sergeant. 30 Oct. 1786. 250 acres.
Russau, William. Ga. ———. 23 Apr. 1784. 650 acres.
Russel, Solomon. Va. Private. 15 Jun. 1807. 100 acres.
Russell, Albert. Va. Lieutenant. 31 Mar. 1783. 2666 2/3 acres.
Russell, Albert. Va. Lieutenant. 5 Aug. 1808. 407 acres.
Russell, Andrew. Me. ———. 22 Apr. 1835. 200 acres. Madison.
Russell, Andrew. Me. ———. 22 Apr. 1835. 200 acres. Madison.
Russell, Andrew. N.C. Private. 30 Sep. 1785. 640 acres to heirs.
Russell, Andrew. Va. Major. 28 Dec. 1784. 2666 1/3 acres.
Russell, Andrew. Va. Major. 28 Dec. 1784. 2666 2/3 acres.
Russell, Andrew. Va. Major. 27 Mar. 1840. 494 acres.
Russell, Andrew. Va. Major. 27 Mar. 1840. 246 3/4 acres.

Russell, Andrew. Va. Major. 17 Sep. 1840. 246 11/12 acres.
Russell, Andrew. Va. Major. 17 Sep. 1840. 494 acres.
Russell, Cannon. N.C. Private. 13 Dec. 1796. 640 acres.
Russell, Charles. Va. Lieutenant. 1 Apr. 1783. 2666 2/3 acres.
Russell, David. Ga. ———. 21 Apr. 1784. 400 acres.
Russell, Ephraim. Va. Private. 31 Jul. 1784. 200 acres.
Russell, Hannah. Conn. Sufferer. New/East Haven. 17.17.6.
Russell, James. N. Y. Private. 8 Jul. 1790. 500 acres.
Russell, James. N.C. Sergeant. 13 May 1784. 357 acres.
Russell, James. Va. Sergeant. 23 Jun. 1783. 200 acres.
Russell, Jeffry. Va. Private. 31 Oct. 1811. 100 acres.
Russell, John. N. Y. ———. 9 Jul. 1790. 600 acres.
Russell, John. N.C. Private. 23 Apr. 1785. 640 acres to heirs.
Russell, John. N.C. Private. 28 Jul. 1804. 640 acres to heirs.
Russell, John. Va. Lieutenant. 19 Mar. 1783. 2666 2/3 acres.
Russell, John. Va. Private. 29 Aug. 1835. 100 acres.
Russell, John. Va. Private. 20 Apr. 1847. 86 2/3 acres.
Russell, Jonathan. N. Y. Private. 8 Jul. 1790. 500 acres.
Russell, Major. N.C. Private. 28 Jul. 1804. 640 acres.
Russell, Malachi. N.C. Private. 23 Apr. 1784. 640 acres.
Russell, Nicholas. N.C. Private. 8 Mar. 1796. 228 acres.
Russell, Nicholas. Va. Private. 25 Oct. 1783. 100 acres.
Russell, Oliver. N.C. Private. 8 Dec. 1796. 640 acres to heirs.
Russell, Rachel. Conn. Sufferer. New/East Haven. 3.18.10.
Russell, Robert. Va. Private. 9 Aug. 1834. 100 acres.
Russell, Samuel. Va. Sergeant. 15 Jun. 1807. 200 acres.
Russell, Thomas. N. Y. Private. 8 Jul. 1790. 600 acres.
Russell, Thomas. N.Y. ———. 13 Sep. 1790. 500 acres to heirs.
Russell, Thomas. S.C. Lieutenant Commander. 16 Jul. 1784. 200 acres.
Russell, Thomas. Va. Private. 19 Apr. 1783. 200 acres.
Russell, Thomas. Va. Private. 1 Jun. 1785. 100 acres.
Russell, Uriah. N.C. Private. 28 Sep. 1785. 640 acres to heirs.
Russell, William. Ga. Minute Man. 22 Mar. 1785. 250 acres.
Russell, William. N. Y. Private. 8 Jul. 1790. 600 acres.
Russell, William. N.C. Private. 5 Aug. 1820. 640 acres to heirs.
Russell, William. Va. Colonel. 19[?] Dec. 1783. 6666 2/3 acres.
Russell, William. Va. Private. 23 Feb. 1786. 100 acres.
Russell, William. Va. Colonel. 15 Jun 1807. 1111 acres.
Russwurm, William. N.C. Lieutenant. 17 Feb. 1824. 735 acres to heir John S. Russwurm.
Russwurm, William. N.C. Lieutenant. 15 Feb. 1841. 1825 acres to heir John S. Russwurm.
Rust, Benjamin. Va. Lieutenant. 27 Jul. 1783. 2666 2/3 acres.
Rust, Benjamin. Va. Lieutenant. 7 Jul. 1832. 1333 1/3 acres.
Rust, George. Va. Private. 25 Oct. 1784. 200 acres.
Rust, Vincent. Va. Private. 25 Oct. 1784. 200 acres.
Rusters, David. N.C. Private. 30 Sep. 1785. 640 acres to heirs.
Rutan, Petria. N. Y. Lieutenant. 13 Sep. 1790. 1000 acres.
Ruth, Abraham. N.C. Private. 11 Feb. 1796. 320 acres.
Ruth, Edward. N.C. Private. 10 Dec. 1788. 640 acres.
Ruth, John. N.C. Private. 11 Feb. 1796. 640 acres.
Rutherford, Alexander. Md. Private. ———. 50 acres.
Rutherford, John. Ga. ———. 21 Apr. 1784. 450 acres.
Rutherford, Julius. Va. Private. 3 Jan. 1784. 100 acres.
Rutherford, Robert. Ga. ———. 27 Apr. 1784. 1000 acres.

Rutherford, Samuel. Ga. ———. 27 Apr. 1784. 450 acres.
Rutherford, Thomas. N.C. Private. 10 Dec. 1788. 640 acres.
Rutherford, Thomas Brooks. Ga. ———. 27 Apr. 1784. 200 acres.
Rutledge, Joshua. Md. Lieutenant. ———. 200 acres.
Rutler, Joseph. N.C. Private. 30 Apr. 1784. 640 acres to Thomas Rutler, heir.
Rutter, Adam. Va. Private. 2 Sep. 1783. 200 acres.
Ryal, William. N.C. Private. 19 May 1784. 640 acres.
Ryal, William. N.C. Private. 12 Oct. 1795. 640 acres.
Ryall, Richard. Ga. Soldier. 4 Oct. 1785. ———.
Ryalls, James. Va. Private. 1 Feb. 1791. 200 acres.
Ryals, John. N.C. Private. 8 Dec. 1796. 640 acres.
Ryals, Joseph. N.C. Private. 1 Aug. 1792. 640 acres.
Ryan, Albert. N. Y. Private. 8 Jul. 1790. 500 acres.
Ryan, George. Va. Private. 9 Dec. 1783. 100 acres.
Ryan, George. Va. Sergeant. 30 Dec. 1812. 400 acres.
Ryan, Harcules. N.C. Private. 4 Aug. 1821. 640 acres.
Ryan, James. Ga. Minute Man. 22 Apr. 1784. 287 1/2 acres.
Ryan, James. Pa. Private. 19 Jul. 1787. 200 acres.
Ryan, Jeffrey. N.C. Private. 24 Dec. 1796. 228 acres.
Ryan, John. Ga. ———. 23 Apr. 1784. 287 1/2 acres.
Ryan, John. N. Y. ———. 9 Jul. 1790. 600 acres.
Ryan, Partrick. N.C. Sergeant. 10 Nov. 1783. 1000 acres.
Ryan, Patrick. N.C. Private. 22 Dec. 1796. 274 acres.
Ryan, Patrick. N.C. Sergeant. 21 Aug. 1820. 726 acres.
Ryan, Richard. Ga. ———. 22 Apr. 1784. 287 1/2 acres.
Ryan, Robert. N. Y. Private. 8 Jul. 1790. 500 acres.
Ryan, Thomas. N.C. Musician. 23 Jun. 1820. 356 acres to heirs.
Rybecker, John. Pa. Private. 5 Mar. 1807. 200 acres.
Ryckman, Wilhelmus. N. Y. Lieutenant. 9 Jul. 1790. 1200 acres.
Rycroft, Thomas. Va. Private. 13 Jun. 1783. 100 acres.
Rydman, John. Va. Gunner. 14 Jun. 1783. 2666 2/3 acres.
Rye, Robert. N.C. Private. 12 Dec. 1796. 228 acres.
Ryecroft, George. Pa. Private. 27 Aug. 1787. 200 acres to William Powers, assignee.
Ryker, Abraham. N. Y. Captain. 13 Sep. 1790. 1500 acres to heirs.
Ryland, John. Va. Corporal. 31 Jan. 1784. 400 acres.
Ryly, James. Md. Private. ———. 50 acres.
Rynan, George. Ga. ———. Soldier. ———.
Rynders, James. N. Y. ———. 30 May 1803. 500 acres.
Rynor, Ichabod. N.Y. ———. 13 Sep. 1790. 500 acres to heirs.
Ryon, Cornelius. N.C. Private. 15 Dec. 1783. 640 acres.
Ryon, Cornelius. N.C. Private. 19 May 1784. 640 acres.
Sabin, Charles. Conn. Sufferer. New/East Haven. 29.5.6.
Sabin, Hezekiah. Conn. Sufferer. New/East Haven. 79.8.9.
Sabin, Hezekiah, Jr. Conn. Sufferer. New/East Haven. 21.10.6.
Sabin, Jonathan. Conn. Sufferer. New/East Haven. 64.18.6.
Sackett, Hannah. Conn. Sufferer. New/East Haven. 5.7.6.
Sackett, Joseph. Conn. Sufferer. Greenwich. 13.12.6.
Sackett, Justus. Conn. Sufferer. Greenwich. 223.16.5.
Sackett, Samuel. N. Y. Captain. 13 Sep. 1790. 1500 acres to heirs.
Saddore, Stephen. N. Y. ———. 8 Oct. 1792. 500 acres.
Sadler, Robert. Va. Private. 25 Mar. 1840. 100 acres.
Sadler, Robert. Va. Private. 28 Oct. 1852. 100 acres.
Sadusky, Jonathan. Va. Private. 30 Nov. 1784. 100 acres.

Saffold, Daniel. Ga. ———. 14 Sep. 1784. 287 1/2 acres.
Sage, Edward. N.C. Private. 30 Sep. 1785. 640 acres.
Sage, Francis. Conn. Sufferer. New/East Haven. 34.1.10.
Sager, John. N. Y. Private. 8 Jul. 1790. 500 acres.
Sager, Thomas. N.Y. ———. 13 Sep. 1790. 500 acres to heirs.
Saggerson, James. Pa. Private. 29 Aug. 1787. 200 acres.
Sagoharase, John. N.Y. Lieutenant. 29 Jan. 1791. 1200 acres. [an Indian].
Sailor, Martin. Va. Sergeant. 8 Apr. 1796. 200 acres.
Sailor, Peter. Pa. Private. 1 Jun. 1787. 200 acres.
Sale, John. Va. Private. 17 Oct. 1799. 100 acres.
Salier, Zaccheus. N. Y. Private. 8 Jul. 1790. 600 acres.
Salinger, Abraham. N.C. Private. 9 Dec. 1797. 640 acres to heirs.
Salisbury, Casper. N. Y. Private. 8 Jul. 1790. 600 acres.
Salisbury, John. N. Y. Private. 8 Jul. 1790. 600 acres.
Salisbury, Thomas. Ga. Soldier. 17 May 1784. 230 acres.
Salitor, Levy. S.C. Soldier. 21 Jan. 1785. 200 acres.
Salladay, Daniel. Pa. Private. 8 Jun. 1787. 200 acres.
Sallards, Eliphalet. Va. Private. 8 Dec. 1783. 100 acres.
Sallet, Robert. Ga. Refugee. 26 May 1784. 575 acres.
Salley, Thomas. N.C. Private. 7 Jan. 1786. 640 acres to heirs.
Sallis, John. Ga. ———. 17 May 1784. ———.
Salmon, George. Va. Private. 12 Aug. 1783. 400 acres.
Salmon, John. Md. Private. ———. 50 acres.
Salmon, Joseph. Pa. ———. 10 Apr. 1807. 300 acres.
Salmon, Vincent. N.C. Corporal. 25 Oct. 1783. 1000 acres.
Salmon, William. N. Y. Matross. 9 Jul. 1790. 600 acres.
Salmons, Henry. Va. Private. 12 Jun. 1784. 100 acres.
Salsbury, S. Barent. N. Y. Lieutenant. 9 Jul. 1790. 1200 acres.
Salsbury, Thomas. Md. Private. ———. 50 acres.
Salter, Jacob. S.C. ———. 7 Aug. 1786. 200 acres.
Salter, John. N.C. Private. 15 Jun. 1785. 457 acres.
Saltonstall, Gurdon. Conn. Sufferer. New London. 1,440.0.0.
Saltonstall, Nathaniel. Conn. Sufferer. New London. 146.9.6.
Saltonstall, Roswell. Conn. Sufferer. New London. 1,800.0.0.
Saltonstall, Winthrop. Conn. Sufferer. New London. 1,181.16.8.
Saltsman, Peter. N. Y. Private. 7 Jul. 1790. 600 acres.
Salusbury, Newman. Va. Private. 8 Dec. 1784 [1783]. 200 acres.
Sames, Joseph. Va. Private. 30 May 1821. 100 acres.
Sammons, Charles. Va. Private. 16 Aug. 1797. 100 acres.
Sammons, John. Va. Private. 26 Nov. 1783. 100 acres.
Sample, James. Va. Private. 26 Jun. 1783. 200 acres.
Sample, Robert. Pa. Captain. 29 May 1787. 500 acres.
Sample, Robert. Pa. Captain. 17 Oct. 1786. 500 acres.
Sampson, Abner. Mass. Private. 19 Sep. 1833. 200 acres.
Sampson, David. N.C. Private. 2 Feb. 1786. 640 acres to heirs.
Sampson, Dred. N.C. Private. 2 Feb. 1786. 640 acres to heirs.
Sampson, George. Va. Private. 22 Jul. 1789. 100 acres.
Sampson, Henry. N. Y. Private. 29 Jan. 1791. 600 acres.
Sampson, Isaac. N. Y. Private. 6 Jul. 1790. 600 acres.
Sampson, Jacob. N.C. Private. 2 Feb. 1786. 640 acres.
Sampson, Samuel. Pa. Private. 16 Mar. 1789. 200 acres.
Samson, Ezekiel. N.Y. Lieutenant. 13 Sep. 1790. 1000 acres.
Samson, Reubin. N.C. Private. 7 Dec. 1797. 228 acres.
Samuel, Gray. Va. Sergeant. 10 Dec. 1784. 200 acres.

Samuel, Jeremiah. Va. Sergeant. 24 Jan. 1810. 200 acres.

Sanborn, Simeon. Me. ———. 9 May 1835. 200 acres to widow Hannah Sanborn. Greenwood.

Sandall, John. Md. Matross. ———. 50 acres.

Sandefer, Samuel. Va. Private. 22 Nov. 1783. 100 acres.

Sanderford, Amos. N.C. Private. 13 Sep. 1820. 640 acres.

Sanderford, Samuel. Va. Private. 1 May 1783. 200 acres.

Sanderlin, Isaac. N.C. Private. 30 Sep. 1785. 640 acres.

Sanderlin, Isaac. N.C. Private. 13 Nov. 1795. 640 acres.

Sanderlin, Levi. N.C. Private. 2 Dec. 1785. 228 acres.

Sanderling, Levi. N.C. Private. 1 Dec. 1797. 640 acres.

Sanders, Applewhite. N.C. Private. 30 Sep. 1785. 640 acres to heirs.

Sanders, Benjamin. Mass. Private. 18 Oct. 1833. 200 acres.

Sanders, Daniel. Va. Private. 23 Mar. 1793. 200 acres.

Sanders, George. Md. Private. ———. 50 acres.

Sanders, James. Va. Private. 15 Jun. 1820. 100 acres.

Sanders, John. Ga. Refugee. 22 Apr. 1784. 287 1/2 acres.

Sanders, John. Md. Private. ———. 50 acres.

Sanders, John. S.C. ———. 2 Oct. 1786. 200 acres.

Sanders, John. Va. Private. 11 Jun. 1784. 200 acres.

Sanders, Joseph. N.C. Private. 9 Dec. 1796. 640 acres.

Sanders, Joseph. N.C. Corporal. 3 Aug. 1820. 428 acres to heirs.

Sanders, Joseph. N.C. Corporal. 3 Aug. 1820. 428 acres to heirs.

Sanders, Joseph. Va. Lieutenant. 27 Jul. 1783. 2666 2/3 acres.

Sanders, Joseph. Va. Lieutenant. 26 Oct. 1842. 296 acres.

Sanders, Joseph. Va. Lieutenant. 26 Oct. 1842. 296 acres.

Sanders, Joseph. Va. Lieutenant. 26 Oct. 1842. 296 acres.

Sanders, Mark. Ga. ———. 22 Apr. 1784. 287 1/2 acres.

Sanders, Presley. Va. Sergeant. 29 Jul. 1783. 200 acres.

Sanders, Robert. N.C. Private. 9 Dec. 1805. 640 acres.

Sanders, Robert. S.C. ———. 7 Aug. 1787. 39 acres.

Sanders, Robert. S.C. ———. 6 Nov. 1797. 20 acres.

Sanders, Robert. S.C. ———. 3 Feb. 1800. 70 acres.

Sanders, Robert. S.C. ———. 3 Feb. 1800. 10 acres 23 poles.

Sanders, Robert. S.C. ———. 6 Apr. 1801. 51 acres.

Sanders, Simon. Ga. Minute Man. 17 Jan. 1785. 287 1/2 acres.

Sanders, Thomas. Md. Private. ———. 50 acres.

Sanders, Thomas. N.C. Private. 2 Dec. 1796. 640 acres to heirs.

Sanders, Thomas. Va. Private. 23 Mar. 1793. 200 acres.

Sanders, William. N.C. Lieutenant. 21 Oct. 1783. 2560 acres.

Sanderson, Caleb. N.C. Private. 11 Aug. 1820. 640 acres to heirs.

Sanderson, Samuel. Va. Private. 3 Jul. 1784. 100 acres.

Sanderson, William. N.C. Private. 24 Nov. 1796. 640 acres to heirs.

Sandford, John. N. Y. Private. 8 Jul. 1790. 500 acres.

Sandford, John. N. Y. Captain. 9 Jul. 1790. 1800 acres.

Sandford, John. Va. Private. 25 Apr. 1783. 200 acres.

Sandidge, John. Ga. ———. 19 Apr. 1784. 200 acres.

Sandridge, Austin. Va. Lieutenant. 9 Sep. 1841. 333 1/3 acres.

Sandridge, Austin. Va. Lieutenant. 22 May 1851. 333 1/3 acres.

Sandridge, Austin. Va. Lieutenant. 9 Sep. 1841. 333 1/3 acres.

Sandridge, Austin. Va. Lieutenant. 9 Sep. 1841. 333 1/3 acres.

Sandridge, Austin. Va. Lieutenant. 16 Jul. 1852. 333 1/3 acres.

Sandridge, Austin. Va. Lieutenant. 9 Sep. 1841. 333 1/3 acres.

Sandridge, Austin. Va. Lieutenant. 9 Sep. 1841. 666 2/3 acres.

Sandridge, Austin. Va. Lieutenant. 8 Nov. 1853. 666 2/3 acres.
Sandridge, Austin. Va. Lieutenant. 29 Jul. 1854. 66 3/5 acres.
Sandridge, Austin. Va. Lieutenant. 23 Jun. 1855. 83 1/3 acres.
Sandridge, Austin. Va. Lieutenant. 23 Jun. 1855. 83 1/3 acres.
Sandridge, Austin. Va. Lieutenant. 23 Jun. 1855. 83 1/3 acres.
Sandridge, Austin. Va. Lieutenant. 23 Jun. 1855. 83 1/3 acres.
Sands, Andrew. Pa. Sergeant. 12 Oct. 1786. 250 acres.
Sandy, Thomas. Va. Private. 12 Sep. 1796. 100 acres.
Sanford, Benjamin. Conn. Sufferer. New/ East Haven. 32.5.11.
Sanford, Jacob. N.C. Sergeant. 15 Feb. 1797. 1000 acres.
Sanford, William. Va. Captain. 25 Sep. 1807. 746 acres.
Sanford, William. Va. Captain. 25 Sep. 1807. 746 acres.
Sanford, William. Va. Captain. 25 Sep. 1807. 746 acres.
Sanford, William. Va. Captain. 25 Sep. 1807. 746 acres.
Sanford, William. Va. Captain. 25 Sep. 1807. 746 acres.
Sanford, William. Va. Captain. 25 Sep. 1807. 746 acres.
Sanford, William. Va. Captain. 25 Sep. 1807. 746 acres.
Sanford, Zachariah. Conn. Sufferer. Fairfield. 2.5.0.
Sankey, John. Md. ———. ———. 50 acres.
Sansom, James. Ga. ———. 17 May 1784. ———.
Sansom, Jean. S.C. ———. 7 May 1787. 200 acres.
Sanson, Luke. Md. Private. ———. 50 acres.
Sansouci, Guilliame. N. Y. ———. ———. 500 acres.
Sansum, Philip. Va. Captain. 14 Dec. 1782. 4000 acres.
Sansum, Philip. Va. Captain. 1 Sep. 1796. 666 2/3 acres.
Santee, Ceasar. N.C. Private. 19 May 1784. 640 acres.
Santee, Ceasar. N.C. Private. 15 Feb. 1797. 640 acres.
Santee, Michael. N.C. Private. 16 Dec. 1801. 640 acres.
Santee, William. Va. Private. 15 Dec. 1783. 100 acres.
Sapp, Dill. Ga. ———. 22 Apr. 1784. 287 1/2 acres.
Sapp, Elijah. Ga. ———. 21 Apr. 1784. 287 1/2 acres.
Sapp, Emanuel. Ga. ———. 21 Apr. 1784. 287 1/2 acres.
Sapp, John. Ga. ———. 21 Apr. 1784. 287 1/2 acres.
Sapp, William. Ga. ———. 21 Apr. 1784. 287 1/2 acres.
Sappington, James. Md. Private. ———. 50 acres.
Sappington, Thomas. Md. Sergeant. ———. 50 acres.
Saratoga, John. N. Y. ———. ———. 500 acres.
Sargent, Charles. Me. ———. 23 Jul. 1835. 200 acres. South Berwick.
Sargent, Paul Dudley. Me. Colonel. 20 Sep. 1838. 600 acres to widow Lucy Sargent who assigned it to her daughter Mary Sargent. Sullivan.
Sarlet, William. Pa. Private. 7 Aug. 1807. 200 acres.
Sartine, John. Va.-Ind. Private. 108 acres.
Sartine, Page. Va.-Ind. Private. 108 acres.
Satchell, George. Va. Private. 14 Feb. 1834. 200 acres.
Satchell, William. Va. Private. 14 Feb. 1834. 200 acres.
Satterwhite, John. Va. Sergeant. 6 Aug. 1783. 400 acres.
Satterwhite, John. Va. Private. 19 Aug. 1819. 100 acres.
Satterwhite, Robert. Va. Private. 18 Aug. 1835. 100 acres.
Satterwhite, William. Va. Sergeant. 30 Sep. 1786. 200 acres.
Satterwhite, Willilam. Ga. ———. 20 Apr. 1784. 287 1/2 acres.
Saucier, John B. Va. Private. 31 Dec. 1851. 100 acres.
Saucier, John B. Va. Private. 21 Apr. 1856. 100 acres.
Saulsbury, Moses. Va. Armourer. 24 Mar. 1831. 2666 2/3 acres.
Saulsbury, Moses. Va. Armourer. ———. 177 77/100 acres.
Saulsbury, Moses. Va. Armourer. ———. 177 77/100 acres.

Saulsbury, Moses. Va. Armourer. ———. 177 77/100 acres.
Saulsbury, Moses. Va. Armourer. ———. 177 77/100 acres.
Saulsbury, Moses. Va. Armourer. ———. 177 77/100 acres.
Saulsbury, Moses. Va. Armourer. ———. 222 22/100 acres.
Saulsbury, Moses. Va. Armourer. ———. 222 22/100 acres.
Saulsbury, Moses. Va. Armourer. ———. 111 11/100 acres.
Saulsbury, Moses. Va. Armourer. ———. 111 11/100 acres.
Saulsbury, Moses. Va. Armourer. ———. 222 22/100 acres.
Saulsbury, Moses. Va. Armourer. ———. 444 44/100 acres.
Saulsbury, Moses. Va. Armourer. ———. 444 44/100 acres.
Saulsbury, Moses. Va. Armourer. 17 Jun. 1833. 29 63/100 acres.
Saulsbury, Moses. Va. Armourer. 17 Jun. 1833. 29 63/100 acres.
Saulsbury, Moses. Va. Armourer. 17 Jun. 1833. 29 63/100 acres.
Saulsbury, Moses. Va. Armourer. 17 Jun. 1833. 29 63/100 acres.
Saulsbury, Moses. Va. Armourer. 17 Jun. 1833. 29 63/100 acres.
Saulsbury, Moses. Va. Armourer. 17 Jun. 1833. 29 63/100 acres.
Saulsbury, Thomas. Va. Private. 14 Feb. 1834. 100 acres.
Saulters, Simon. Ga. Soldier. 23 Apr. 1784. 287 1/2 acres.
Saunderlain, Thomas. N.C. Private. 29 Sep. 1785. 640 acres
Saunders, Alleck. Va. Private. 15 Jun. 1812. 100 acres.
Saunders, Andrew. N.C. Corporal. 29 Sep. 1784. 428 acres.
Saunders, Benjamin. N.C. Private. 7 Dec. 1797. 640 acres to heirs.
Saunders, Celey. Va. Captain. 12 Mar. 1783. 4666 2/3 acres.
Saunders, Celey. Va. Captain. 18 Mar. 1834. 1601 5/9 acres.
Saunders, Celey. Va. Captain. 9 Apr. 1840. 480 acres.
Saunders, Daniel. N.C. Drummer. 9 Dec. 1796. 1000 acres.
Saunders, Isaac. Mass. Private. 6 May 1831. 200 acres.
Saunders, Isaac. N.C. Private. 30 Sep. 1785. 640 acres to heirs.
Saunders, Jabez. Conn. Sufferer. Norwalk. 31.13.11.
Saunders, Jacob. N.C. Private. 8 Dec. 1795. 640 acres to heirs.
Saunders, James. N.C. Private. 9 Nov. 1784. 640 acres to heir.
Saunders, Jesse. Ga. ———. 17 Apr. 1784. 750 acres.
Saunders, Job. N.C. Private. 20 Jan. 1785. 640 acres to heirs.
Saunders, John. Va.-Ind. Private. 108 acres.
Saunders, John. N.C. Private. 22 Apr. 1785. 640 acres to heirs.
Saunders, John. N.C. Private. 30 Sep. 1785. 640 acres to heirs.
Saunders, John. Conn. Sufferer. Norwalk. 241.18.10.
Saunders, Joseph. Va. Lieutenant. 28 Jul. 1830. 2666 2/3 acres.
Saunders, Joseph. Va. Lieutenant. 24 Jan. 1843. 296 acres.
Saunders, Joseph. Va. Lieutenant. 24 Jan. 1843. 148 acres.
Saunders, Joshua. Ga. ———. 24 Feb. 1784. 250 acres.
Saunders, Peter. N.C. Private. 17 Dec. 1785. 640 acres to heirs.
Saunders, Reuben. Va. Sergeant. 1 Aug. 1799. 400 acres.
Saunders, Richard. N.C. Private. 17 Dec. 1785. 640 acres to heirs.
Saunders, Richard. Va. Midshipman. 1 Oct. 1783. 2666 2/3 acres.
Saunders, Robert. N. Y. Fifer. 9 Jul. 1790. 600 acres.
Saunders, Robert H. Va. Lieutenant. 8 Oct. 1832. 2666 2/3 acres.
Saunders, William. N.C. Private. 29 Sep. 1784. 274 acres.
Saunders, William. Va. Captain. 20 May 1783. 4000 acres.
Saunders, William. Va. Captain. 21 Jun. 1786. 666 2/3 acres.
Saunders, William. Va. Captain. 19 Mar. 1834. 944 acres.
Saunders, William. Va. Captain. 23 Mar. 1840. 758 1/2 acres.
Saunders, William. Va. Captain. 23 Mar. 1840. 284 1/2 acres.
Saunders, William. Va. Captain. 23 Mar. 1840. 95 acres.

Saunders, Zachariah. Va. Private. 10 Nov. 1787. 100 acres.

Saunford, Thomas. Va. Private. 25 Dec. 1784. 100 acres.

Savage, Elias. N.C. Private. 30 Sep. 1785. 640 acres to heirs.

Savage, George. Va. Private. 29 Jun. 1786. 100 acres.

Savage, James. N.C. Private. 30 Sep. 1785. 640 acres.

Savage, Joseph. N. Y. Captain. 9 Jul. 1790. 1800 acres.

Savage, Joseph. N.C. Private. 30 Sep. 1785. 640 acres to heirs.

Savage, Joseph. Va. Surgeon's Mate. 25 Feb. 1784. 2666 2/3 acres.

Savage, Joseph. Va. Surgeon's Mate. 10 Apr. 1858. 222 1/6 acres.

Savage, Joseph. Va. Surgeon's Mate. 15 Feb. 1858. 222 1/6 acres.

Savage, Joseph. Va. Surgeon's Mate. 15 Feb. 1858. 222 1/6 acres.

Savage, Joseph. Va. Surgeon's Mate. 15 Feb. 1858. 222 1/6 acres.

Savage, Joseph. Va. Surgeon's Mate. 15 Feb. 1858. 222 1/6 acres.

Savage, Lovelace. Ga. Chaplain. 22 Apr. 1784. 747 1/2 acres.

Savage, Micajah. N.C. Private. 28 Sep. 1785. 228 acres.

Savage, Michael. N.C. Private. 19 Aug. 1820. 228 acres to heirs.

Savage, Nathaniel. Va. Lieutenant. Feb. 1783. 2666 2/3 acres.

Savage, Ransom. N.C. Private. 22 Oct. 1783. 560 acres.

Savage, Ransom. N.C. Private. 28 Sep. 1785. 357 acres.

Savage, Richard. Va. Private. 5 Jan. 1811. 200 acres.

Savage, Robert. Ga. ———. 22 Apr. 1784. 287 1/2 acres.

Saveall, James. Va. Private. 23 Jun. 1783. 200 acres.

Savoy, John. Va. Private. 6 Feb. 1784. 200 acres.

Savoy, Philip. Md. Private. ———. 50 acres.

Sawyer, Henry. N.C. Private. 29 Sep. 1800. 640 acres to heirs.

Sawyer, Josiah. Me. Private. 30 Apr. 1835. 200 acres. Steuben.

Sawyer, Miller. N.C. Fifer. 27 Nov. 1783. 1000 acres.

Sawyer, Miller. N.C. Private. 17 Dec. 1785. 274 acres.

Sawyer, Paul. Mass. ———. 28 Feb. 1832. 200 acres to his children Uriah H. Sawyer, Louisa Vinon, Borzleel Sawyer, Soloma Handy, Joseph Sawyer, and Elmiclia Rummer.

Sawyer, Richard. N.C. Private. 17 Dec. 1808. 274 acres to heirs.

Sawyer, Thomas. N.C. Private. 11 May 1784. 274 acres.

Sawyer, Willis. N.C. Private. 18 Dec. 1793. 640 acres to heirs.

Sawyer, Willis. N.C. Private. 24 Nov. 1797. 640 acres to heirs.

Sawyers, James. Va. Corporal. 4 Dec. 1799. 400 acres.

Sawyers, John. Ga. ———. 21 Apr. 1784. 287 1/2 acres.

Saxburry, William. N.Y. ———. 8 Oct. 1792. 500 acres to heirs.

Saxon, James. S.C. ———. 2 Oct. 1786. 200 acres.

Saxon, Samuel. S.C. ———. 2 Oct. 1786. 128 acres.

Saxon, William. S.C. ———. 2 Oct. 1786. 184 acres.

Saxton, John. Va. Private. 3 Jan. 1784. 100 acres.

Sayers, Robert. Va. Captain. 18 Dec. 1784. 1000 acres.

Sayers, Robert. Va. Captain. 18 Dec. 1784. 1000 acres.

Sayers, Robert. Va. Captain. 18 Dec. 1784. 1000 acres.

Sayers, Robert. Va. Captain. 18 Dec. 1784. 1000 acres.

Sayers, Robert. Va. Captain. 1 Jun. 1805. 666 2/3 acres.

Sayers, Robert. Va. Captain. 29 Aug. 1807. 555 acres.

Saylors, Jacob. N.Y. Private. 13 Sep. 1790. 500 acres to heirs.

Saymore, William. Va. Private. 24 Feb. 1784. 100 acres.

Scaits, James. N. Y. Corporal. 8 Jul. 1790. 500 acres.

Scalp, James. N.C. Private. 30 Sep. 1785. 640 acres to heirs.

Scandlit, James. N.C. Private. 21 Feb. 1822. 274 acres to heirs.

Scans, Peter. Va. Private. 25 Oct. 1820. 200 acres.

Scantland, John. Va. Private. 25 Aug. 1835. 100 acres.
Scantlin, Michael. N.C. Private. 23 May 1821. 640 acres.
Scantlin, William. N.C. Private. 5 Sep. 1821. 640 acres.
Scantlin, William. Va. Sergeant. 31 Aug. 1789. 200 acres.
Scantling, Patrick. N,C. Private. 6 Feb. 1823. 274 acres.
Scarborough, Nathan. N.C. Private. 10 Dec. 1788. 640 acres to heirs.
Scarbrough, John. Va. Lieutenant. 26 Aug. 1784. 2666 2/3 acres.
Scarburg, John. Va. Lieutenant. 4 Jun. 1798. 444 1/3 acres.
Scarf, John. N.C. Private. 21 Apr. 1784. 297 acres.
Scarff, Joseph. S.C. Soldier. 2 May 1785. 200 acres.
Scarlet, James. N.C. Private. 26 May 1784. 640 acres.
Sceodore, John. N.Y. ———. 13 Sep. 1790. 500 acres to heirs.
Schaffer, Andrew. Pa. Private. 11 Jan. 1787. 200 acres to Barbara Schaffer, widow.
Schaw, Duncan. N.C. Private. 13 Jan. 1792. 640 acres to heirs.
Schick, Frederick. Ga. Lieutenant. 30 Dec. 1784. 460 acres.
Schindler, John. Mass. Private. 21 Aug. 1835. 200 acres to heir Mary McConnell, wife of John McConnell of Philadelphia, Pa., innkeeper.
Schneider, Andrew. Ga. Refugee. 26 May 1784. 287 1/2 acres.
Schneider, Frederick. Pa. Private. 22 Aug. 1787. 200 acres.
Schockee, Abraham. Md. Private. ———. 50 acres.
Schooler, William. Va. Sergeant. 17 May 1822. 400 acres.
Schoolfield, Benjamin. N.C. Private. 13 Sep. 1820. 640 acres.
Schoonmaker, Daniel. N. Y. 8 Jul. 1790. 600 acres.
Schoudrick, Charles. Md. Corporal. ———. 50 acres.
Schrawder, Philip. Pa. Captain. 23 Feb. 1787. 500 acres.
Schreeder, J. John. N. Y. Private. 8 Jul. 1790. 600 acres.
Schryver, Christian. N. Y. Private. 8 Jul. 1790. 600 acres.
Schuyler, Derick. N. Y. Ensign. 7 Jul. 1790. 1000 acres.
Schuyler, Nicholas. N.Y. Surgeon. 17 Aug. 1790. 1900 acres.
Scofield, Nathaniel. N. Y. Matross. 9 Jul. 1790. 600 acres.
Scofield, Stephen. Conn. Sufferer. Danbury. 6.5.4.
Scoggins, Ephraim. Va. Private. 18 Apr. 1801. 100 acres.
Scoggins, John. Va. Private. 18 Apr. 1801. 100 acres.
Scoggins, Willis. N.C. Private. 12 Dec. 1796. 640 acres.
Scollar, Isaac. N.C. Private. 23 Feb. 1820. 640 acres to heirs.
Scone, George. Md. Corporal. ———. 50 acres.
Scotland, Thomas. Pa. Sergeant. 18 Oct. 1786. 250 acres.
Scott, Abraham. Ga. ———. 19 Apr. 1784. 287 1/2 acres.
Scott, Abraham. Va. Private. 29 Dec. 1796. 200 acres.
Scott, Adam. N.C. Private. 19 Dec. 1812. 640 acres to heirs.
Scott, Alexander. Ga. Chaplain. 24 May 1784. 862 1/2 acres.
Scott, Alexander. Va. Private. 24 Jun. 1833. 200 acres.
Scott, Benjamin. Ga. ———. 23 Apr. 1784. 287 1/2 acres.
Scott, Charles. Md. Private. ———. 50 acres.
Scott, Charles. Va. General. 29 Nov. 1782. 11,666 2/3 acres.
Scott, Charles. Va. Major General. 5 Dec. 1783. 1666 2/3 acres.
Scott, Charles. Va. Cornet. 10 Feb. 1784. 2666 2/3 acres.
Scott, Charles. Va. Brigadier General. 8 Feb. 1808. 277 2/3 acres.
Scott, Charles. Va. Brigadier General. 9 Nov. 1808. 1666 2/3 acres.
Scott, Cornelius. Ga. Minute Man. 23 Apr. 1784. 287 1/2 acres.
Scott, David. Va. Captain. 1 Mar. 1806. 1000 acres.
Scott, David. Va. Captain. 1 Mar. 1806. 1000 acres.
Scott, David. Va. Captain. 1 Mar. 1806. 1000 acres.

Scott, David. Va. Captain. 1 Mar. 1806. 1000 acres.
Scott, Drury. N.C. Private. 16 Dec. 1810. 274 acres.
Scott, Drury. Va. Private. 24 Jan. 1784. 200 acres.
Scott, Eleazer. Conn. Sufferer. Norwalk. 16.0.9.
Scott, George. Va. Private. 22 Nov. 1784. 100 acres.
Scott, Henry. Va. Sergeant. 5 Sep. 1810. 200 acres.
Scott, Isaac. Va. Private. 10 Sep. 1787. 100 acres.
Scott, James. Ga. ———. 17 Apr. 1784. 1000 acres.
Scott, James. Md. Sergeant. ———. 50 acres.
Scott, James. N. Y. Fifer. 8 Jul. 1790. 600 acres.
Scott, James. N.C. Private. 16 Aug. 1821. 640 acres.
Scott, James. S.C. ———. 2 May 1785. 200 acres.
Scott, James. S.C. ———. 7 Aug. 1786. 188 acres.
Scott, James. Va. Private. 1 May 1783. 200 acres.
Scott, James. Va. Private. 22 Nov. 1783. 100 acres.
Scott, James. Conn. Sufferer. Ridgefield. 2.12.8.
Scott, John. Md. Drummer. ———. 50 acres.
Scott, John. N.C. Private. 22 Apr. 1785. 640 acres to heirs.
Scott, John. Va. Private. 22 Aug. 1783. 200 acres.
Scott, John. Va. Captain Lieutenant. 16 Oct. 1783. 4000 acres.
Scott, John. Va. Private. 20 Feb. 1784. 100 acres.
Scott, John. Va. Subaltern. 24 Feb. 1784. 2666 2/3 acres.
Scott, John. Va. Subaltern. 21 Jun. 1784. 2666 2/3 acres.
Scott, John. Va. Sailor. 26 Jun. 1784. 100 acres.
Scott, John. Va. Private. 11 Dec. 1819. 100 acres.
Scott, John. Conn. Sufferer. New/East Haven. 7.0.9.
Scott, John E. Va. Lieutenant. 18 Nov. 1811. 2333 2/3 acres.
Scott, John E. Va. Lieutenant. 18 Nov. 1811. 333 acres.
Scott, John, Jr. Ga. Minute Man. 23 Apr. 1784. 287 1/2 acres.
Scott, John, Sr. Ga. Minute Man. 23 Apr. 1784. 287 1/2 acres.
Scott, Joseph. Ga. Soldier. 21 Apr. 1784. 287 1/2 acres.
Scott, Joseph. Va. Private. 20 Feb. 1784. 100 acres.
Scott, Joseph. Va. Captain. 1 Jun. 1820. 333 1/3 acres.
Scott, Joseph, Jr. Va. Captain. 17 Oct. 1783. 4000 acres.
Scott, Joseph, Sr. Va. Captain. 14 Dec. 1782. 4666 2/3 acres.
Scott, Joseph, Sr. Va. Captain. 29 Aug. 1807. 777 2/3 acres.
Scott, Levi. Md. Drummer. ———. 50 acres.
Scott, Littleberry. Va. Private. 22 Apr. 1784. 200 acres.
Scott, Matthew. Va. Sergeant. 25 May 1784. 200 acres.
Scott, Nathan. N.C. Private. 25 Dec. 1812. 640 acres to heirs.
Scott, Overstreet. N.C. Private. 15 Jul. 1785. 640 acres to heirs.
Scott, Patrick. Md. Private. ———. 50 acres.
Scott, Peter. Ga. Sergeant. 17 May 1784. ———.
Scott, Reuben. Md. Matross. ———. 50 acres.
Scott, Robert. Va. Corporal. 20 Sep. 1783. 200 acres.
Scott, Sacker. Va. Private. 15 Jun. 1807. 100 acres.
Scott, Samuel. Md. Private. ———. 50 acres.
Scott, Samuel. N.C. Private. 4 Aug. 1821. 640 acres.
Scott, Stephen. Va. Private. 23 Jan. 1793. 200 acres.
Scott, Thomas. N.C. Private. 20 Apr. 1784. 388 acres.
Scott, Walter. Va. Lieutenant. 26 Sep. 1783. 2666 2/3 acres.
Scott, William. Ga. Captain. 1784. 287 1/2 acres.
Scott, William. Ga. Minute Man. 1784. 287 1/2 acres.
Scott, William. N.C. Private. 22 Dec. 1796. 228 acres.

Scott, William. N.C. Private. 15 Feb. 1797. 220 acres.
Scott, William. Pa. Private. 28 Feb. 1794. 200 acres to Richard Leedom, assignee.
Scott, William. Pa. Private. 29 Sep. 1787. 200 acres.
Scott, William. Pa. ———. 8 Jan. 1803. 200 acres.
Scott, William. Pa. Private. 30 Mar. 1787. 200 acres.
Scott, William. S.C. Lieutenant Colonel. 21 Jan. 1785. 450 acres.
Scott, William. Va. Sergeant. 9 May 1783. 200 acres.
Scott, William. Va. Drummer. 28 Jun. 1783. 233 1/3 acres.
Scott, William. Va. Private. 9 Dec. 1783. 100 acres.
Scott, William. Va. Captain. 16 Nov. 1824. 1000 acres.
Scott, William. Va. Captain. 16 Nov. 1824. 1000 acres.
Scott, William. Va. Captain. 16 Nov. 1824. 1000 acres.
Scott, William. Va. Captain. 16 Nov. 1824. 1000 acres.
Scott, William, Jr. Ga. Minute Man. 23 Apr. 1784. 287 1/2 acres.
Scoudrick, Thomas. Md. Private. ———. 50 acres.
Scovil, ——— Widow. Conn. Sufferer. New/East Haven. 7.0.0.
Scrabbles, Jeremiah. Md. Private. ———. 50 acres.
Screven, Hester. Ga. ———. ———. 1000 acres.
Screven, Mary. Ga. ———. ———. 1000 acres.
Scriber, Jacob. N. Y. Private. 8 Jul. 1790. 500 acres.
Scriber, Peter. N. Y. Private. 8 Jul. 1790. 600 acres.
Scriviner, Robert. Md. Sergeant. ———. 50 acres.
Scrouse, John. Pa. Matross. 31 Mar. 1787. 200 acres to George Tucker, assignee.
Scrugg, Philip. N.C. Private. 16 Apr. 1821. 640 acres to heirs.
Scrugg, Sigg. N.C. Private. 16 Apr. 1821. 640 acres to heirs.
Scruggs, Gross. Va. Major. 2 Oct. 1810. 5333 1/3 acres.
Scruggs, James. Va. Private. 9 Jun. 1831. 100 acres.
Scruggs, James. Va. Private. 20 Aug. 1844. 100 acres.
Scruggs, John. Va. Private. 9 Jun. 1831. 100 acres.
Scruggs, John. Va. Private. 20 Aug. 1844. 100 acres.
Scruggs, Samuel. Va. Private. 4 May 1810. 100 acres.
Scruggs, Timothy. Va. Private. 20 Aug. 1831. 200 acres.
Scudder, Isaac. Conn. Sufferer. Norwalk. 661.16.0.
Scudder, William. N. Y. Lieutenant. 3 Jul. 1790. 1200 acres.
Scull, John Gambier. N.C. Lieutenant. 29 Sep. 1784. 1127 acres.
Scull, Joseph. N.C. Private. 30 Sep. 1785. 640 acres to heirs.
Sculley, James. Va. Private. 2 Jul. 1791. 200 acres.
Scurlock, James. N.C. Private. 22 Oct. 1783. 2560 acres.
Scurlock, William. S.C. ———. 2 May 1785. 200 acres.
Scutchins, Meredy. N.C. Private. 30 Spe. 1785. 640 acres to heirs.
Scutchins, Samuel. N.C. Private. 15 Jul. 1785. 640 acres to heirs.
Seaburn, John. Va. Private. 11 Dec. 1798. 100 acres.
Seaburn, Joseph. N.C. Private. 9 Nov. 1784. 274 acres.
Seabury, Elizabeth. Conn. Sufferer. Groton. 177.11.0.
Seabury, Nathaniel. Conn. Sufferer. Groton. 3.18.0.
Seagraves, John, Jr. N.C. Private. 12 Dec. 1796. 640 acres to heirs.
Sealf, Abel. N.C. Private. 11 Feb. 1796. 640 acres to heirs.
Seals, Francis. N.C. Private. 27 Nov. 1789. 182 acres.
Seals, John. N.C. Private. 28 Aug. 1820. 640 acres to heirs.
Searcey, Luke. N.C. Private. 14 May 1784. 640 acres to heirs.
Searchwell, Joshua. N.C. Private. 12 Sep. 1785. 640 acres to heirs.
Searls, Thomas. N.C. Private. 5 Sep. 1820. 640 acres to heirs.
Sears, Arthur. N.C. Private. 2 Feb. 1786. 640 acres.
Sears, John. Md. Lieutenant. ———. 200 acres.

Sears, John. N.C. Private. 23 Dec. 1819. 640 acres to heirs.
Sears, John. Va. Lieutenant Colonel. 24 Jan. 1783. 6000 acres.
Sears, Joseph. Va. Private. 6 Jan. 1786. 200 acres.
Sears, Moses. N. Y. Private. 8 Jul. 1790. 600 acres.
Sears, Noah. Md. Private. ———. 50 acres.
Sears, Seth. Conn. Sufferer. New London. 13.19.7.
Sears, Thomas. Va. Private. 18 Jul. 1783. 100 acres.
Sears, Thomas. Va. Private. 6 Feb. 1784. 2666 2/3 acres.
Seavron, John. N.C. Private. 9 Sep. 1785. 640 acres to heirs.
Seawalls, Daniel. N.C. Private. 10 Dec. 1821. 640 acres to heirs.
Seay, Jacob. Va. Private. 17 Mar. 1784. 100 acres.
Seay, John. Ga. ———. 16 Apr. 1784. 200 acres.
Seay, Reuben. Va. Private. 21 Jan. 1784. 100 acres.
Seay, William. Ga. ———. 16 Apr. 1784. 200 acres.
Seayres, John. Va. Lieutenant Colonel. 4 Apr. 1850. 531 1/4 acres.
Seayres, John. Va. Lieutenant Colonel. 4 Apr. 1850. 531 1/4 acres.
Seayres, John. Va. Lieutenant Colonel. 13 Feb. 1851. 531 1/4 acres.
Seayres, John. Va. Lieutenant Colonel. 13 Feb. 1851. 531 1/4 acres.
Seayres, John. Va. Lieutenant. 29 Jul. 1852. 417 acres.
Seayres, John. Va. Lieutenant. 29 Jul. 1852. 114 1/4 acres.
Sebastian, Benjamin. Va. Private. 27 Mar. 1784. 233 1/3 acres.
Sebaston, Stephen. N.C. Private. 30 Sep. 1785. 640 acres to heirs.
Sebert, John. Ga. Refugee. 21 Apr. 1784. 250 acres.
Sebley, John. S.C. -———. 2 Jun. 1788. 200 acres.
Sebley, William. S.C. ———. 2 Jun. 1788. 200 acres.
Sebolt, Christain. Pa. Private. 29 Sep. 1787. 200 acres to William Banquett, assignee.
Sebry, William. Va. Private. 5 Mar. 1784. 200 acres.
Seburn, Jacob. Va. Private. 1 Dec. 1785. 100 acres.
Sechler, Michael. Pa. Private. 29 Aug. 1811. 200 acres.
Sedgwick, John. Pa. ———. 28 Feb. 1794. 200 acres.
Sedmon, John. Ga. ———. 1784. 287 1/2 acres.
Sedwick, John. Pa. Private. 26 Apr. 1787. 200 acres.
Seeberry, Alstone. N.C. Private. 29 Sep. 1784. 640 acres to Mary Seeberry, heiress.
Seeds, Edward Dixon. Ga. ———. 30 Sep. 1784. ———.
Seeds, George. N.Y. ———. 13 Sep. 1790. 500 acres to heirs.
Seeley, George. Pa. Sergeant. 19 Oct. 1786. 250 acres.
Seeley, Isaac. Pa. Captain. 22 Mar. 1803. 500 acres to heirs.
Seener, Peter. N.C. Private. 27 Nov. 1789. 182 acres.
Seers, Robert. N.C. Private. 19 May 1784. 640 acres.
Segraves, John. N.C. Private. 6 Dec. 1796. 640 acres.
Segrove, John. N.C. Private. 21 Apr. 1784. 228 acres.
Seigle, Frederick. Va. Surgeon. 26 Jun. 1797. 6000 acres.
Seigle, Frederick. Va. Surgeon. 23 Nov. 1868. 1838 2/3 acres.
Selden, Joseph. Va. Lieutenant. 5 Mar. 1833. 2666 2/3 acres.
Selden, Joseph. Va. Lieutenant. 24 May 1834. 178 1/3 acres.
Selden, Joseph. Va. Lieutenant. 8 May 1833. 296 acres.
Selden, Joseph. Va. Lieutenant. 8 May 1833. 296 acres.
Selden, Joseph. Va. Lieutenant. 8 May 1833. 296 acres.
Selden, Joseph. Va. Lieutenant. 13 Aug. 1833. 888 2/3 acres.
Selden, Joseph. Va. Lieutenant. 8 May 1834. 888 2/3 acres.
Selden, Joseph. Va. Lieutenant. 11 Jun. 1833. 88 1/2 acres.
Selden, Joseph. Va. Lieutenant. 5 Aug. 1833. 444 1/3 acres.

Selden, Joseph. Va. Lieutenant. 5 Aug. 1833. 444 1/3 acres.

Selden, Joseph. Va. Lieutenant. 13 Aug. 1833. 267 2/3 acres.

Selden, Joseph. Va. Lieutenant. 20 Mar. 1834. 88 8/9 acres.

Selden, Samuel. Va. Lieutenant. 26 Jan. 1784. 2666 2/3 acres.

Selden, Samuel. Va. Lieutenant. 15 Feb. 1784. 2666 2/3 acres.

Selden, Wilson C. Va. Surgeon. 22 Nov. 1833. 2000 acres.

Selden, Wilson C. Va. Surgeon. 22 Nov. 1833. 2000 acres.

Selden, Wilson C. Va. Surgeon. 22 Nov. 1833. 2000 acres.

Selden, Wilson C. Va. Surgeon. 24 Aug. 1835. 1000 acres.

Selden, Wilson C. Va. Surgeon. 24 Aug. 1835. 5000 acres.

Seley, Lewis. N. Y. Matross. 9 Jul. 1790. 600 acres.

Self, Larkin. Va. Private. 17 Feb. 1784. 200 acres.

Self, Samuel. N.C. Private. 8 Dec. 1796. 640 acres.

Selkirk, James. N. Y. Sergeant. 8 Jul. 1790. 600 acres.

Sell, George. Va. Private. 27 Jun. 1783. 200 acres.

Sell, Thomas. N.C. Private. 17 Feb. 1824. 640 acres.

Sellars, Daniel. N.C. Private. 8 Nov. 1784. 640 acres to heir.

Sellars, John. N.C. Private. 30 Sep. 1785. 640 acres to heirs.

Sellars, Robert. N.C. Private. 30 Sep. 1785. 640 acres to heirs.

Sellers, Henry. N.C. Private. 22 Dec. 1796. 640 acres.

Sellers, Michael. Va. Private. 5 Feb. 1785. 200 acres.

Sellers, William. Va. Private. 1 Aug. 1835. 100 acres.

Sellich, Gold John. Conn. Sufferer. Greenwich. 13.18.0.

Sellman, Jonathan. Md. Major. ———. 200 acres.

Selman, Joseph. Va. Private. 29 Aug. 1786. 100 acres.

Sergeant, Thomas. Md. Private. ———. 50 acres.

Serjeant, Jeremiah. Va. Private. 18 Jan. 1822. 100 acres.

Serjeson, William. N. Y. Drummer. 3 Jul. 1790. 600 acres.

Serrett, Samuel. N.C. Private. 23 Nov. 1790. 640 acres.

Servant, Richard. Va. Lieutenant. 18 Nov. 1830. 4000 acres.

Seskon, Thomas. N.C. Private. 8 May 1784. 640 acres.

Sessoms, William. Ga. Private. 26 May 1784. 287 1/2 acres.

Sessums, Abell. N.C. Private. 31 Aug. 1795. 640 acres to heirs.

Sessums, William, Sr. Ga. ———. 26 May 1784. 230 acres.

Setchell, Sarah. Conn. Sufferer. New London. 56.16.0.

Setgreaves, Jacob. N.C. Private. 10 Aug. 1785. 640 acres.

Setgreaves, John. N.C. Private. 10 Aug. 1785. 640 acres.

Settle, Benjamin. Va. Corporal. 12 Apr. 1784. 200 acres.

Settle, Strother. Va. Lieutenant. 31 Mar. 1784. 2666 2/3 acres.

Settle, Strother G. Va. Captain. 14 May 1812. 4000 acres.

Settlemeyer, Godfrey. Pa. Private. 25 Aug. 1787. 200 acres.

Sevan, John. Va. Captain. 3 May 1784. 4666 2/3 acres.

Seven, Joseph. N.C. Private. 30 Sep. 1785. 640 acres to heirs.

Severance, Caleb. Me. Private. 15 Sep. 1836. 200 acres. Brewer.

Severance, Ephraim. Me. Private. 17 Mar. 1836. 200 acres to widow Ruth Severance. Knox.

Severman, Philip. Pa. Private. 18 Oct. 1786. 200 acres.

Severns, Ebenezer. Va.-Ind. Private. 108 acres.

Severns, John. Va.-Ind. Private. 108 acres.

Sevey, Joseph. N. Y. Private. 8 Jul. 1790. 600 acres.

Sewall, Henry. Me. Captain. 1 Jun. 1838. 600 acres. Augusta.

Sewall, James. Md. Private. ———. 50 acres.

Seward, William, Rev. Conn. Sufferer. Greenwich. 25.8.0.

Sewell, Thomas. Va. Sergeant. 20 Dec. 1785. 200 acres.

Sexton, Jeremiah. N.C. Private. 12 May 1784. 640 acres.

Sexton, Jonathan. N.C. Private. 13 Dec. 1796. 640 acres.
Sexton, William. N.C. Private. 11 May 1784. 640 acres.
Sexton, William. Va. Private. 3 Mar. 1784. 100 acres.
Seymore, Christopher. Md. Private. ———. 50 acres.
Seymore, Edmund. N.C. ———. 10 Aug. 1785. 640 acres to heirs.
Seymore, Philip. N.C. Private. 2 Sep. 1820. 274 acres.
Seymore, Solomon. N.C. Private. 22 Oct. 1783. 228 acres.
Seymore, William. N.C. Private. 22 Oct. 1783. 228 acres.
Seymour, Anne. Conn. Sufferer. Norwalk. 3.1.6.
Seymour, Anne. Conn. Sufferer. Norwalk. 6.17.5.
Seymour, Daniel. Conn. Sufferer. Norwalk. 11.18.10.
Seymour, Daniel, Jr. Conn. Sufferer. Norwalk. 87.16.5.
Seymour, David. Conn. Sufferer. Norwalk. 3.19.0.
Seymour, Drake. Conn. Sufferer. Greenwich. 123.19.5.
Seymour, Hannah. Conn. Sufferer. Ridgefield. 18.7.3.
Seymour, John. Conn. Sufferer. Norwalk. 345.5.0.
Seymour, John, Jr. Conn. Sufferer. Norwalk. 161.19.9 1/2.
Seymour, Samuel. Conn. Sufferer. Greenwich. 195.15.3.
Seymour, Seth. Conn. Sufferer. Norwalk. 157.4.1 to his heirs.
Seymour, Thomas. Conn. Sufferer. Ridgefield. 65.16.6.
Seymour, William. Conn. Sufferer. Norwalk. 93.1.9.
Shabbiso, Peter. N.C. Private. 22 Dec. 1796. 274 acres.
Shackleford, Alexander. Va. Private. 20 Nov. 1784. 100 acres.
Shackleford, Henry. Va. Private. 15 Dec. 1783. 100 acres.
Shackleford, John. Ga. Refugee. 20 Feb. 1784. 500 acres.
Shackleford, Mag. Va. Private. 15 Dec. 1783. 100 acres.
Shackleford, Richard. Va. Private. 19 Mar. 1832. 100 acres.
Shackleford, William. Va. Lieutenant. 30 Mar. 1784. 2666 2/3 acres.
Shackler, Phillip. N.C. Private. 7 Dec. 1783. 640 acres.
Shacklett, Edward. Va. Private. 2 Dec. 1785. 100 acres.
Shackley, Joseph. Me. ———. 3 Aug. 1835. 200 acres. Lyman.
Shaddock, Charles. N.C. Private. 7 Jan. 1794. 640 acres to heirs.
Shaddock, Thomas. Ga. Refugee. 15 Apr. 1784. 575 acres.
Shaddon, David. S.C. ———. 5 Feb. 1787. 200 acres.
Shaffer, David. Ga. ———. 19 Apr. 1784. 287 1/2 acres.
Shaffer, George. N. Y. Private. 8 Jul. 1790. 600 acres.
Shaffer, Henry. N.C. Private. 30 Sep. 1785. 640 acres to heirs.
Shaffner, Casper. Pa. Cornet. 23 May 1803. 300 acres.
Shafford, Joel. N.C. Private. 30 Sep. 1785. 640 acres to heirs.
Shakleford, John. Ga. ———. 22 Apr. 1784. 287 1/2 acres.
Shall, John. N.Y. ———. 13 Sep. 1790. 500 acres to heirs.
Shane, Richard. Me. Private. 16 Nov. 1835. 200 acres to widow Susannah Shane. Raymond.
Shaneberger, Philip. Pa. Private. 31 Aug. 1789. 200 acres.
Shaner, George. Va. Private. 29 Jul. 1785. 100 acres.
Shanklin, James. N.C. Private. 15 Feb. 1797. 320 acres.
Shanklin, John. N.C. Drummer. 14 Dec. 1797. 500 acres.
Shanks, James. N.C. Private. 12 Sep. 1785. 640 acres to heirs.
Shanks, James. Va. Private. 2 Apr. 1784. 100 acres.
Shanks, John. Md. Private. ———. 50 acres.
Shanks, John. Va. Private. 3 May 1823. 200 acres.
Shannon, David. Pa. Trumpeteer. 1 Sep. 1787. 200 acres.
Shannon, John. Ga. ———. 19 Jul. 1784. 287 1/2 acres.
Shannon, Owen. Ga. ———. 24 May 1784. 287 1/2 acres.

Shannon, Patrick. Va. Sergeant. 23 Jun. 1783. 200 acres.
Shannon, Robert. N. Y. Private. 8 Jul. 1790. 600 acres.
Shannon, Thomas. Ga. ———. 13 Apr. 1784. 287 1/2 acres.
Shantze, Christian. N. Y. Private. 8 Jul. 1790. 600 acres.
Shapley, Adam. Conn. Sufferer. New London. 20.17.16.
Shapley, Eliza. Conn. Sufferer. New London. 382.5.0.
Shappo, Anthony. Mass. Private. 8 Dec. 1835. 200 acres to heirs.
Sharbond, Joseph. N.C. Private. 8 Dec. 1796. 640 acres.
Sharp, Anthony. N.C. Captain. 21 Oct. 1783. 3840 acres.
Sharp, Benjamin. N.C. Sergeant. 21 Oct. 1783. 1000 acres.
Sharp, Bishop. N.C. Private. 17 Feb. 1824. 640 acres.
Sharp, James Boyd. Ga. Surgeon's Mate. 17 Apr. 1784. 690 acres.
Sharp, Jesse. N.C. Private. 7 Dec. 1797. 640 acres to heirs.
Sharp, Jesse. N.C. Private. 14 Dec. 1797. 408 acres.
Sharp, John, Jr. Ga. ———. 23 Apr. 1784. 287 1/2 acres.
Sharp, John, Sr. Ga. ———. 25 May 1784. 287 1/2 acres.
Sharp, Joseph. N.C. Private. 26 Apr. 1784. 428 acres.
Sharp, Joshua. Ga. ———. 23 Apr. 1784. 287 1/2 acres.
Sharp, Josiah. Va. Private. 25 May 1789. 100 acres.
Sharp, Michael. Ga. ———. 23 Apr. 1784. 287 1/2 acres.
Sharp, Thomas. Va. Private. 4 Nov. 1820. 200 acres.
Sharp, William. Md. Corporal. ———. 50 acres.
Sharp, William. Va. Private. 4 Nov. 1820. 200 acres.
Sharpe, Jonas. N.C. Private. 30 Sep. 1785. 640 acres to heirs.
Sharpe, Thomas. Pa. Private. 23 Aug. 1787. 200 acres.
Sharpless, David. Pa. ———. 17 Aug. 1811. 200 acres to heirs.
Sharpless, John. Va. Surgeon. 5 Jun. 1783. 6000 acres.
Sharpless, John. Va. Surgeon. 14 Dec. 1850. 1402 1/3 acres.
Sharpless, Robert. Md. Corporal. ———. 50 acres.
Sharpley, John. N.C. Private. 13 Sep. 1820. 640 acres.
Sharrow, Richard. Va. Private. 23 Jun. 1783. 200 acres.
Shattuck, Joseph. Mass. Corporal. 19 Mar. 1834. 200 acres.
Shaur, James. Md. Private. ———. 50 acres.
Shaver, Frederick. Va. Private. 30 Sep. 1793. 200 acres.
Shaver, George. Va. Private. 10 May 1785. 100 acres.
Shaver, John. Va. Private. 10 May 1785. 100 acres.
Shavers, John. N.C. ———. 12 Dec. 1806. 213 acres to heirs.
Shaw, Abraham. Pa. Private. ———. 200 acres.
Shaw, Basil. Md. Sergeant. ———. 50 acres.
Shaw, Daniel. Ga. ———. 27 Apr. 1784. 400 acres.
Shaw, Daniel. N.C. Lieutenant. 25 Apr. 1785. 2560 acres.
Shaw, David. Ga. Minute Man. 3 Apr. 1785. ———.
Shaw, Ephraim. Me. Private. 5 Sep. 1835. 200 acres to widow Rebecca Shaw. New Vineyard.
Shaw, Herman. N.C. Private. 14 Dec. 1796. 228 acres.
Shaw, John. Me. ———. 29 Aug. 1835. 200 acres. Woolwich.
Shaw, John. Md. ———. ———. 50 acres.
Shaw, John. N. Y. Lieutenant. 8 Jul. 1790. 1200 acres.
Shaw, John. N.Y. ———. 13 Sep. 1790. 500 acres to heirs.
Shaw, John. N.C. Private. 7 Jan. 1786. 640 acres to heirs.
Shaw, John. Pa. Private. 31 Oct. 1795. 200 acres to John Lanson, assignee.
Shaw, John. Pa. Private. 4 Apr. 1787. 200 acres.
Shaw, John R. Pa. Sergeant. ———. 250 acres.
Shaw, Matthew. Va. Private. 31 Jan. 1786. 200 acres.

Shaw, Michael. N. Y. Private. 8 Jul. 1790. 600 acres.
Shaw, Michael. Pa. Matross. 28 Dec. 1786. 200 acres.
Shaw, Michael. Pa. Private. 9 Mar. 1795. 200 acres to John Nicholson, assignee.
Shaw, Nathaniel. Me. ———. 11 May 1835. 200 acres to widow Polly Shaw. Portland.
Shaw, Nathaniel & Thomas Shaw. Conn. Sufferers. New London. 2,834.5.0.
Shaw, Thomas. Conn. Sufferer. Groton. 1.1.6.
Shaw, Thomas, Jr. Ga. Minute Man. 22 Apr. 1784. 287 1/2 acres.
Shaw, Thomas, Sr. Ga. 17 May 1784. Sergeant. ———.
Shaw, William. Va. Private. 10 May 1785. 100 acres.
Shaw, Zackeus. N.C. Private. 12 Mar. 1785. 640 acres to heirs.
Shay, Dennis. Va. Private. 7 Aug. 1783. 200 acres.
Shear, George. Pa. Private. ———. 200 acres.
Shearer, Michael. S.C. ———. 5 Feb. 1787. 100 acres.
Shearman, Duke. Va. Private. 26 Mar. 1808. 100 acres.
Shearman, Martin. Va. Midshipman. 2 Sep. 1783. 2666 2/3 acres.
Shearman, Peter. N. Y. Private. 8 Jul. 1790. 600 acres.
Shearman, Robert. Ga. ———. 22 Apr. 1784. 600 acres.
Shearman, Robert. Va. Fife Major. 21 May 1783. 200 acres.
Sheat, John. Va. Private. 23 Jun. 1783. 200 acres.
Shed, Lemuel. Me. ———. 1835. 200 acres to widow Ruth Shed. Norway.
Shed, Nathan. Mass. Private. 15 Jan. 1834. 200 acres.
Shee, Murphy. Md. Private. ———. 50 acres.
Sheehane, Thomas. N. Y. Matross. 9 Jul. 1790. 500 acres.
Sheener, Matthias. Va. Sergeant. 19 Jan. 1785. 200 acres.
Sheets, Caspar. Pa. Private. 12 Jan. 1787. 200 acres.
Sheets, William. Pa. Private. 15 May 1787. 200 acres to Stephen Loudon, assignee.
Sheffer, John. Md. Private. ———. 50 acres.
Sheffield, Charles. Mass. Private. 22 Oct 1830. 200 acres.
Sheffield, Mark. Ga. ———. 17 May 1784. ———.
Sheffield, Peter. Va. Private. 26 Apr. 1783. 200 acres.
Sheffield, Thomas. Va. Private. 28 Jun. 1783. 100 acres.
Sheftall, Mark. Ga. Refugee. 13 Apr. 1784. 575 acres.
Sheftall, Mordicai. Ga. ———. 22 Jul. 1784. 1150 acres.
Sheftall, Shefftall. Ga. ———. 22 Jul. 1784. 575 acres.
Sheftall, William. Ga. Refugee. 13 Apr. 1784. 575 acres.
Sheidner, Philip. Pa. ———. 200 acres.
Sheilds, James. Pa. Private. 4 Aug. 1787. 200 acres.
Sheken, Daniel. Pa. Private. 9 Oct. 1786. 200 acres.
Shelby, James. Va.-Ind. Captain. 3234 acres.
Shelby, James. Va. Captain. 12 May 1838. 1000 acres.
Shelby, James. Va. Captain. 12 May 1838. 1000 acres.
Shelby, James. Va. Captain. 12 May 1838. 1000 acres.
Shelby, James. Va. Captain. 12 May 1838. 1000 acres.
Sheldon, Joseph. N. Y. Private. 8 Jul. 1790. 600 acres.
Sheldon, Peter E. Va. Fifer. 1 Jan. 1785. 200 acres.
Sheldon, Simeon. Mass. Corporal. 13 Feb. 1833. 200 acres to heirs.
Sheldon, Thomas. Va. Fife Major. 12 Nov. 1783. 533 1/3 acres.
Shell, Elisha. N. Y. Matross. 9 Jul. 1790. 500 acres.
Shell, George. N. Y. Private. 8 Jul. 1790. 600 acres.
Shell, William. Va. Private. 20 Dec. 1813. 100 acres.
Shelly, Cyrus. N. Y. Private. 8 Jul. 1790. 500 acres.
Shelly, John. N.Y. ———. 13 Sep. 1790. 500 acres to heirs.
Shelton, Clough. Va. Captain. Jan. 1783. 4000 acres.

Shelton, Clough. Va. Captain. 10 Feb. 1784. 666 2/3 acres.

Shelton, David. Va. Private. 10 Sep. 1783. 100 acres.

Shelton, Henry. Ga. ———. 17 May 1784. ———.

Shelton, Thomas. Va. Private. 1 May 1783. 200 acres.

Shelton, Thomas. Va. Private. 31 Oct. 1854. 266 2/3 acres.

Shelton, Thomas. Va. Private. 6 Dec. 1854. 300 acres.

Shelton, Thomas. Va. Private. 17 Dec. 1855. 300 acres.

Shepard, Edward. Va. Private. 9 Nov. 1811. 100 acres.

Shepard, George. Va.-Ind. Private. 108 acres.

Shepard, Peter. Va.-Ind. Private. 108 acres.

Shepard, William. N.C. Private. 5 Sep. 1821. 640 acres.

Shephard, Abraham. Va. Captain. 6 Mar. 1807. 1333 1/3 acres.

Shephard, John. Conn. Sufferer. Danbury. 1.1.0.

Shepherd, Abraham. Va. Captain. 3 Apr. 1783. 4000 acres.

Shepherd, Abraham. Va. Captain. 22 Aug. 1807. 277 2/3 acres.

Shepherd, Benjamn. Ga. ———. 21 Apr. 1784. 1000 acres.

Shepherd, David. Va. Private. 30 Jan. 1784. 100 acres.

Shepherd, David. Va. Private. 25 Aug. 1784. 100 acres.

Shepherd, James. Ga. ———. 17 May 1784. ———.

Shepherd, James. Me. ———. 1835. 200 acres to widow Mary Shepherd. Jefferson.

Shepherd, James. Md. Private. ———. 50 acres.

Shepherd, James. Va. Sergeant. 5 Feb. 1784. 200 acres.

Shepherd, John. N. Y. Captain. 13 Sep. 1790. 1350 acres.

Shepherd, John. N.C. Private. 3 Aug. 1820. 640 acres to heirs.

Shepherd, John. Conn. Sufferer. New London. 76.14.0.

Shepherd, Lewis. Me. Private. 26 Aug. 1835. 200 acres to widow Elizabeth Shepherd. Portland.

Shepherd, Peter. Va. Corporal. 9 May 1784. 200 acres.

Shepherd, Robert. Pa. Sergeant. 20 Dec. 1786. 250 acres.

Shepherd, Stephen. Ga. Minute Man. 13 Apr. 1784. 287 1/2 acres.

Sheppard, Abram. N.C. Colonel. 2 Feb. 1786. 2571 acres.

Sheppard, John. N.C. Private. 19 May 1784. 640 acres.

Sheppard, John. N.C. Major. 6 May 1792. 1714 acres.

Sheppard, Valentine. N.C. Private. 30 Sep. 1785. 640 acres to heirs.

Sheppard, William. N.C. Captain. 2 Feb. 1786. 1252 acres.

Shepperd, Anne. Conn. Sufferer. Danbury. 8.2.0.

Sheridan, Bartholomew. Md. ———. ———. 50 acres.

Sheridan, James. Md. Private. ———. 50 acres.

Sheridan, James. Pa. Private. 28 Oct. 1786. 200 acres.

Sheridan, Martin. Pa. Private. 12 Sep. 1786. 200 acres.

Sheridan, Thomas. Md. Private. ———. 50 acres.

Sherkley, Thomas. N.C. Fifer. 14 Feb. 1796. 1000 acres.

Sherley, Bennet. Md. Private. ———. 50 acres.

Sherley, William. Md. Private. ———. 50 acres.

Sherman, Adonijah. Conn. Sufferer. New/ East Haven. 29.15.0.

Sherman, Amos. Conn. Sufferer. New/East Haven. 34.12.8.

Sherman, Edmond. N. Y. Sergeant. 9 Jul. 1790. 600 acres.

Sherman, James. Me. Sergeant. 19 Oct. 1836. 200 acres to widow Margaret Sherman. Freeport.

Sherman, James. Conn. Sufferer. New/East Haven. 7.1.0.

Sherman, John. Ga. Minute Man. 3 Sep. 1785. ———.

Sherman, William. Conn. Sufferer. New/ East Haven. 37.3.3.

Sherman, William. Conn. Sufferer. New/ East Haven. 23.2.10.

Sherod, Robert. N.C. ———. 10 Aug. 1785. 640 acres to heirs.

Sherrard, Richard. N.C. Private. 10 Dec. 1821. 640 acres to heirs.
Sherril, David. Ga. Refugee. 18 May 1784. ———.
Sherrin, Joseph. N.C. Private. 3 Dec. 1802. 640 acres.
Sherrin, Joseph. N.C. Corporal. 5 Aug. 1820. 360 acres to heirs.
Sherriner, Lodwick. N. Y. Sergeant. 7 Jul. 1790. 600 acres.
Sherrod, Thomas. N.C. Private. 30 Sep. 1785. 640 acres to heirs.
Sherry, Henry. Pa. Private. 27 Apr. 1789. 200 acres.
Sherwood, Andrew. N. Y. Matross. 9 Jul. 1790. 600 acres.
Sherwood, Ebenezer. Conn. Sufferer. Fairfield. 2.0.0.
Sherwood, Ebenezer. Conn. Sufferer. Ridgefield. 5.13.4.
Sherwood, Edmund. N.C. ———. 8 Mar. 1785. 640 acres to heirs.
Sherwood, Gilbert. Conn. Sufferer. Greenwich. 7.13.8.
Sherwood, Isaac. N.Y. Lieutenant. 13 Sep. 1790. 1200 acres to heirs.
Sherwood, Jabez. Conn. Sufferer. Greenwich. 47.3.5.
Sherwood, James. N. Y. Private. 8 Jul. 1790. 500 acres.
Sherwood, Jehiel. Conn. Sufferer. Fairfield. 4.14.0.
Sherwood, Joseph. Conn. Sufferer. Fairfield. 9.15.6.
Sherwood, Micajah. N.Y. Private. 8 Oct. 1792. 500 acres to heirs.
Sherwood, Nathan. N. Y. Private. 8 Jul. 1790. 600 acres.
Sherwood, Nehemiah. N. Y. Private. 8 Jul. 1790. 600 acres.
Sherwood, Oliver. Conn. Sufferer. Greenwich. 10.0.0.
Sherwood, William. N.C. Private. 7 Jan. 1786. 640 acres to heirs.
Shesehan, Thomas. Pa. Private. 2 Feb. 1787. 200 acres.
Shibler, Frederick. Va. Private. 23 Jan. 1786. 100 acres.
Shield, John. Va. Captain. 26 Nov. 1782. 4000 acres.
Shields, Andrew. Ga. Soldier. 21 Jun. 1784. 287 1/2 acres.
Shields, Daniel. N. Y. Private. 8 Jul. 1790. 600 acres.
Shields, James. Va. Private. 24 Jun. 1783. 100 acres.
Shields, William. N.C. Private. 16 Aug. 1821. 640 acres.
Shields, William, Jr. Ga. Refugee. 21 Apr. 1784. 287 1/2 acres.
Shields, William, Sr. Ga. ———. 21 Apr. 1784. 287 1/2 acres.
Shilkes, Lewis. N.C. Private. 27 Aug. 1784. 640 acres.
Shine, James. N.C. Lieutenant. 26 Dec. 1821. 731 acres to heir W. E. Shine.
Shipherd, Solomon. Va. Private. 6 Mar. 1810. 200 acres.
Shipley, Robert. Md. Private. ———. 50 acres.
Shipman, Elias. Conn. Sufferer. New/East Haven. 10.19.6.
Shires, Nicholas. Va. Private. 31 Jan. 1784. 200 acres.
Shirley, James. Va. Private. 19 Dec. 1783. 100 acres.
Shirley, Martin. Ga. ———. 26 Jul. 1784. 287 1/2 acres.
Shirlock, John. N. Y. Private. 7 Jul. 1790. 600 acres.
Shirts, ———. N. Y. ———. 18 Nov. 1806. 200 acres to David Shirts, John Shirts, Henry Shirts, Peter Shirts, Andries Shirts, Jacob Shirts, Catherine Shirts, Lenah Shirts, Anna Shirts, and Eve Shirts.
Shirts, Peter. N. Y. Private. 8 Jul. 1790. 600 acres.
Shitten, Henry. Ga. ———. 250 acres. ———.
Shivers, James. N.C. Private. 12 Dec. 1806. 274 acres to heirs.
Shivers, James. N.C. ———. 19 Dec. 1808. 366 acres to heirs.
Shivers, William. N.C. Private. 30 Sep. 1785. 640 acres to heirs.
Shives, Robert. Ga. Soldier. 4 Oct. 1785. ———.
Shoalders, William. N.C. Private. 13 Sep. 1820. 274 acres.
Shockey, Christian. Pa. ———. 16 Apr. 1787. 250 acres.
Shockley, Isaac. N.C. ———. 13 Jun. 1785. 640 acres to heirs.
Shoebrick, Philip. Md. Invalid. ———. 50 acres.
Shoecroft, Abram. N.C. Private. 1 Sep. 1785. 640 acres to heirs.

Shoemaker, Jacob. Md. Ensign. ———. 200 acres.
Shoemaker, John. N.C. Private. 7 Dec. 1797. 640 acres to heirs.
Shoemaker, Peter. Md. ———. ———. 50 acres.
Shoemaker, Samuel F. Md. Private. ———. 50 acres.
Shoffle, William. Ga. ———. 17 May 1784. ———.
Sholes, Jabez. Conn. Sufferer. Groton. 0.9.9.
Sholes, Lucretia. Conn. Sufferer. Groton. 4.9.0.
Sholes, Nathan. Conn. Sufferer. Groton. 0.15.3.
Shomaker, David. Ga. Refugee. Sep. 1785. ———.
Shoop, Frederick. Pa. Private. 23 Feb. 1787. 200 acres.
Shoope, John. Va. Sergeant. 7 Feb. 1810. 200 acres.
Shores, David. N.C. Private. 21 Nov. 1805. 228 acres.
Shores, Thomas. Va. Private. 23 Jun. 1783. 100 acres.
Shormantine, Hezekiah. N.C. Private. 13 Jan. 1792. 228 acres.
Short, Abraham. N.C. Private. 30 Sep. 1785. 640 acres to heirs.
Short, Charles. N.C. Musician. 10 Sep. 1821. 1000 acres to heirs.
Short, David. N.C. Private. 30 Sep. 1785. 640 acres to heirs.
Short, Henry. N.C. Private. 10 Sep. 1821. 640 acres to heirs.
Short, Isham. N.C. Private. 30 Sep. 1785. 640 acres to heirs.
Short, Joanna. Conn. Sufferer. New London. 276.14.0.
Short, Jonathan. Md. Sergeant. ———. 50 acres.
Short, Richard. Pa. Private. 14 May 1784. 200 acres.
Short, Thomas. N.C. Private. 1 Dec. 1789. 182 acres.
Short, William. N.C. Private. 30 Sep. 1785. 640 acres to heirs.
Short, William. N.C. Private. 15 Feb. 1797. 274 acres.
Shorter, Roger. Md. Private. ———. 50 acres.
Shot, Richard. Pa. Private. 9 Oct. 1786. 200 acres.
Shouell, John. Md. Private. ———. 50 acres.
Shoup, Lewis. Pa. Private. 2 May 1787. 200 acres.
Shoup, William. Va. Sergeant. 21 Dec. 1784. 400 acres.
Shouse, Samuel. Va. Private. 30 Nov. 1784. 100 acres.
Shove, Benjamin. Conn. Sufferer. Danbury. 2.11.10 1/2.
Shove, Seth. Conn. Sufferer. Danbury. 5.14.4.
Showers, Adam. Ga. ———. 3 May 1785. 287 1/2 acres.
Showers, David. Ga. Minute Man. 3 Sep. 1785. ———.
Showers, Peter. Ga. Minute Man. 3 Sep. 1785. ———.
Shows, Adam. Ga. ———. 17 Apr. 1784. 287 1/2 acres.
Shows, John. Ga. ———. 15 Apr. 1784. 287 1/2 acres.
Shraeter, Israel. Pa. Dragoon. ———. 200 acres.
Shreeves, William. Va. Private. 3 Jun. 1812. 200 acres.
Shrink, Andrew. Md. Matross. ———. 50 acres.
Shriver, Frederick. Pa. Private. 16 Nov. 1786. 200 acres.
Shrofe, Adam. Pa. Private. 18 Aug. 1789. 200 acres.
Shubrick, Jacob. S.C. Captain. 21 Jan. 1785. 300 acres.
Shubrick, Richard. S.C. Captain. 21 Jan. 1785. 300 acres to heirs.
Shubrick, Thomas. S.C. Captain. 21 Jan. 1785. 300 acres.
Shuffel, John. Ga. ———. 25 May 1784. 287 1/2 acres.
Shugart, Martin. Md. Lieutenant. ———. 200 acres.
Shull, John. Va. Private. 16 Feb. 1801. 100 acres.
Shultz, Christopher. N. Y. Fifer. 9 Jul. 1790. 600 acres.
Shultz, John. N. Y. Private. 7 Jul. 1790. 600 acres.
Shultz, Peter. N.Y. ———. 13 Sep. 1790. 500 acres to heirs.
Shuman, Adam. Pa. Private. 3 Feb. 1803. 200 acres.
Shures, John. Ga. ———. 17 May 1784. ———.

Shurls, Benjamin. Va. Private. 14 Jun. 1783. 100 acres.
Shute, Jesse. N.C. Private. 21 Apr. 1784. 640 acres.
Shute, Samuel. N.C. Private. 12 Sep. 1785. 640 acres to heirs.
Shute, Thomas. N.C. Ensign. 28 Nov. 1795. 731 acres.
Shute, William. N.C. Private. 2 Apr. 1784. 640 acres.
Sickels, Abraham. N. Y. Private. 8 Jul. 1790. 600 acres.
Sickle, Charles. Md. Private. ———. 50 acres.
Siddle, Jesse. N.C. Private. 16 Aug. 1821. 640 acres.
Sidebotham, John. Va. Private. 20 May 1823. 100 acres.
Sidham, John. Ga. ———. 22 Apr. 1784. 287 1/2 acres.
Sidney, Joseph. Md. Private. ———. 50 acres.
Sigman, John. Ga. ———. 27 Apr. 1784. 450 acres.
Sikes, James. N.C. Private. 30 Sep. 1785. 640 acres to heirs.
Sikes, Sampson. N.C. Private. 19 May 1784. 640 acres.
Sikes, William. Ga. ———. 17 Apr. 1784. 400 acres.
Sikes, William. N.C. Private. 19 Dec. 1808. 274 acres.
Sikes, Zedekiah. N.C. Private. 21 Apr. 1784. 274 acres.
Silas, Samuel. Pa. ———. 17 Jan. 1787. 200 acres to Elias Phillips, assignee.
Sillard, Thomas. N.C. Private. 16 Aug. 1821. 640 acres.
Sillinaver, John. N.C. Gunner. 15 Dec. 1783. 640 acres.
Sillman, John. Md. Matross. ———. 50 acres.
Sills, John. Ga. ———. 23 Apr. 1784. 287 1/2 acres.
Silsby, Sarah. Conn. Sufferer. Ridgefield. 2.13.8.
Silver, George. Md. Private. ———. 50 acres.
Silvester, Joseph. Mass. Private. 1 Mar. 1833. 200 acres to heirs.
Silvester, Luke. N.C. Private. 17 Dec. 1785. 640 acres to heirs.
Silwood, William. Md. Private. ———. 50 acres.
Simmers, John. Pa. Private. 26 Mar. 1787. 200 acres.
Simmonds, Ann. Conn. Sufferer. New London. 13.18.0.
Simmonds, James. Md. Matross. ———. 50 acres.
Simmonds, John. N. Y. Private. 8 Jul. 1790. 600 acres.
Simmonds, Richard. N.C. Private. 1 Dec. 1789. 182 acres.
Simmons, Alanson. N.C. Sergeant. 22 Apr. 1785. 1000 acres.
Simmons, Anthony. N.C. Private. 4 Aug. 1821. 640 acres.
Simmons, Benjamin. Ga. Private. 22 Apr 1784. 287 1/2 acres.
Simmons, Benjamin. N.C. Sergeant. 23 Feb. 1784. 428 acres.
Simmons, Bryan. Va. Private. 20 Jun. 1783. 100 acres.
Simmons, Chapman. Conn. Sufferer. New London. 22.18.0.
Simmons, Charles. Ga. Refugee. 30 Jan. 1784. 250 acres.
Simmons, Edward. Ga. Private. ———. 250 acres.
Simmons, Ephraim. N.Y. ———. 13 Sep. 1790. 500 acres to heirs.
Simmons, Felix. N.C. Private. 20 Apr. 1784. 274 acres.
Simmons, George. Va. Private. 9 May 1783. 100 acres.
Simmons, Gideon. N.C. Private. 19 Dec. 1812. 274 acres to heirs.
Simmons, Holdin. N.C. Private. 28 Nov. 1795. 640 acres to heirs.
Simmons, Holmes. N.C. Private. 8 Dec. 1796. 640 acres to heirs.
Simmons, Isaac. N.C. Private. 12 Sep. 1785. 640 acres to heirs.
Simmons, Isles. N.C. Sergeant. 12 Dec. 1785. 428 acres.
Simmons, Isles. Pa. Sergeant. 15 Aug. 1787. 250 acres.
Simmons, James. Ga. Refugee. 10 Dec. 1784. 500 acres.
Simmons, James. Ga. Minute Man. 20 Apr. 1784. 287 1/2 acres.
Simmons, James. Va. Private. 27 Jun. 1783. 200 acres.
Simmons, James. Va. Private. 2 Nov. 1787. 100 acres.
Simmons, James Mason. Ga. ———. 17 May 1784. ———.

Simmons, Joel. Me. ———. 17 May 1835. 200 acres to widow Artemisa Packard. Minot.

Simmons, John. Ga. ———. 21 Apr. 1784. 287 1/2 acres.

Simmons, John. N.C. Private. 3 Feb. 1785. 274 acres.

Simmons, Joshua. N. Y. Private. 8 Jul. 1790. 600 acres.

Simmons, Joshua. Va. Fife Major. 27 Jun. 1783. 400 acres.

Simmons, Malbourn. Ga. ———. 15 Mar. 1784. 250 acres.

Simmons, Mellica. N.C. Private. 27 Jul. 1785. 640 acres to heir.

Simmons, Noble. Md. ———. ———. 50 acres.

Simmons, Patterson. Ga. ———. 5 Sep. 1785. 287 1/2 acres.

Simmons, Perez. Mass. Sergeant. 18 Jul. 1832. 200 acres.

Simmons, Peter. N.C. Private. 22 Mar. 1785. 640 acres.

Simmons, Phillip. Ga. Refugee. 22 Mar. 1785. 250 acres.

Simmons, Richard. Ga. Minute Man. 4 Oct. 1785. 287 1/2 acres.

Simmons, Robert. Ga. Refugee. 22 Mar. 1785. 250 acres.

Simmons, Samuel. N.C. Private. 6 Dec. 1808. 640 acres to heirs.

Simmons, Solomon. Ga. Refugee. 6 Aug. 1785. ———.

Simmons, Spratley. Va. Sergeant. 12 Oct. 1797. 100 acres.

Simmons, Sterns. Ga. ———. 21 Apr. 1784. 287 1/2 acres.

Simmons, Thomas. Ga. Minute Man. 21 Apr. 1784. 287 1/2 acres.

Simmons, William. Ga. Private. 10 Dec. 1784. 230 acres.

Simmons, William. Md. Private. ———. 50 acres.

Simmons, William. N.C. Private. 17 Dec. 1785. 640 acres to heirs.

Simmons, William. Va. Sergeant. 25 Feb. 1807. 200 acres.

Simmons, Williamson. Va. Private. 28 Jun. 1783. 233 1/3 acres.

Simms, Charles. Va. Lieutenant Colonel. 14 Apr. 1783. 6000 acres.

Simms, Drewry. N.C. Private. 30 Sep. 1785. 640 acres to heirs.

Simms, Edward. Va. Sergeant. 19 Mar. 1783. 200 acres.

Simms, Edward. Va. Sergeant. 18 Jul. 1854. 200 acres.

Simms, Isaac. Va. Private. 27 Jun. 1783. 200 acres.

Simms, James. Md. Sergeant. ———. 50 acres.

Simms, John. Ga. Soldier. 3 May 1785. 230 acres.

Simms, Mann. Ga. Soldier. 17 May 1784. ———.

Simms, William. Ga. ———. 23 Apr. 1784. 287 1/2 acres.

Simol, Edward. Ga. ———. 2 May 1785. 287 1/2 acres.

Simol, Robert. Ga. ———. 2 May 1785. 287 1/2 acres.

Simonds, Martin. N. Y. Private. 8 Jul. 1790. 600 acres.

Simonds, Robert. N. Y. Matross. 9 Jul. 1790. 500 acres.

Simons, Jesse. Md. Corporal. ———. 50 acres.

Simons, John. N.C. Private. 30 Sep. 1785. 640 acres to heirs.

Simons, Joshua. N.C. Private. 30 Sep. 1785. 640 acres to heirs.

Simonson, Isaac. Ga. ———. 1784. 287 1/2 acres.

Simonton, Alexander. Pa. ———. 17 Dec. 1808. 250 acres.

Simonton, Alexander. Pa. Sergeant. 23 May 1804. 250 acres.

Simonton, Walter. Me. Private. 17 Nov. 1838. 200 acres to widow Lucy (Sawyer) Simonton.

Simpkins, Christopher. Md. Private. ———. 50 acres.

Simpkins, Garrett. Va. Private. 3 Jan. 1785. 100 acres.

Simpkins, Gideon. N. Y. Private. 8 Jul. 1790. 600 acres.

Simpkins, James. Va. Private. 4 Jan. 1785. 100 acres.

Simpkins, Joseph. N.C. Private. 22 Dec. 1796. 640 acres to heirs.

Simpkins, Reubin. Va. Private. 25 May 1785. 200 acres.

Simpkins, William. Va. Private. 4 Jan. 1787. 100 acres.

Simpson James. Ga. Soldier. 20 Feb. 1784. 250 acres.

Simpson, Aaron. Pa. Private. 12 Sep. 1789. 200 acres.
Simpson, Alexander. Va. Private. 18 Aug. 1835. 100 acres.
Simpson, Alexander. Va. Private. 16 Aug. 1837. 100 acres.
Simpson, Andrew. N.C. Sergeant. 1 Mar. 1784. 1000 acres.
Simpson, Benjamin. N.C. Private. 6 Dec. 1797. 640 acres to heirs.
Simpson, Charles. Md. Private. ———. 50 acres.
Simpson, Daniel. Va. Corporal. 15 Sep. 1785. 200 acres.
Simpson, Drummond. Va. Private. 15 Jun. 1807. 100 acres.
Simpson, Elisha. Va. Fifer. 15 Jun. 1807. 100 acres.
Simpson, Elisha. Va. Seaman. 8 Jun. 1833. 100 acres.
Simpson, Hancock. Va. Coxswain. 7 Dec. 1830. 2666 2/3 acres.
Simpson, Jack. N.C. Drummer. 22 Dec. 1796. 1000 acres to heirs.
Simpson, Jeremiah. Va. Sergeant. 7 Dec. 1830. 200 acres.
Simpson, John. N.C. Private. 21 Oct. 1783. 640 acres.
Simpson, John. N.C. Private. 18 Dec. 1804. 640 acres to heirs.
Simpson, John. Pa. ———. ———. 200 acres.
Simpson, John. Va. Private. 30 Aug. 1783. 100 acres.
Simpson, Laurence. Md. Private. ———. 50 acres.
Simpson, Michael. Pa. Captain. 14 Nov. 1788. 500 acres.
Simpson, Moses. N.C. Private. 26 Aug. 1785. 640 acres to heirs.
Simpson, Nathaniel. Pa. Private. 15 Jul. 1812. 200 acres to John Brown, assignee.
Simpson, Salathiel. Va. Seaman. 20 Jan. 1834. 100 acres.
Simpson, Salathiel. Va. Master at Arms. 17 Sep. 1851. 1711 acres.
Simpson, Salathiel. Va. Master at Arms. 17 Sep. 1851. 855 acres.
Simpson, Samuel. Ga. Soldier. 1784. 230 acres.
Simpson, Samuel. N.C. Private. 19 May 1784. 640 acres.
Simpson, Smith. N.C. Private. 17 Dec. 1785. 640 acres to heirs.
Simpson, Spencer. Va. Private. 22 Dec. 1783. 100 acres.
Simpson, Thomas. Ga. ———. ———. 250 acres.
Simpson, Thomas. Va.-Ind. Private. 108 acres.
Simpson, William. Mass. Private. 18 Oct. 1833. 200 acres.
Simpson, William. Va. Seaman. 8 Jun. 1833. 100 acres.
Sims, Edward. Va. Private. 26 Feb. 1831. 200 acres.
Sims, Robert. Ga. Soldier. 23 Jun. 1785. 640 acres.
Sims, Thomas. Ga. ———. Soldier. 5 Dec. 1785. ———.
Sims, Thomas. N.C. Private. 26 Aug. 1785. 640 acres to heirs.
Sims, Thomas. Va. Sergeant. 26 Mar. 1784. 200 acres.
Sinah, John. Va. Private. 8 Dec. 1784. 100 acres.
Sinclair, Joshua. Me. Private. 18 Oct. 1842. 200 acres. Bangor.
Sinclair, William. Md. Private. ———. 50 acres.
Sinclear, Thomas. N.C. Private. 30 Apr. 1784. 640 acres to heirs.
Singleton, Anthony. Va. Captain. 15 Sep. 1792. 666 2/3 acres.
Singleton, Anthony. Va. Captain. 13 Dec. 1783. 4000 acres.
Singleton, Anthony. Va. Captain. 20 Jun. 1807. 222 acres.
Singleton, Benjamin. S.C. ———. 14 Dec. 1789. 200 acres.
Singleton, Frederick. Va. Private. 24 Jan. 1787. 200 acres.
Singleton, Henry. N.C. Private. 14 May 1784. 640 acres.
Singleton, John. Pa. ———. ———. 200 acres to Samuel Smith, assignee.
Singleton, Joshua. Va. Lieutenant. 12 May 1783. 2666 2/3 acres.
Singleton, Joshua. Va. Sergeant. 14 Oct. 1783. 200 acres.
Singleton, Joshua. Va. Lieutenant. 16 Apr. 1831. 1334 acres.
Singleton, Richard, Jr. S.C. ———. 4 Jul. 1791. 200 acres.
Singleton, Robert. N.C. Ensign. 5 Sep. 1821. 2560 acres.

Sinn, George. Pa. Private. 13 Mar. 1789. 200 acres.
Sinnot, Patrick. N. Y. Sergeant Major. 8 Jul. 1790. 600 acres.
Sinquefield, Aaron. Ga. ———. 21 Apr. 1784. 287 1/2 acres.
Sinquefield, Moses. Ga. ———. 21 Apr. 1784. 287 1/2 acres.
Sinquefield, Samuel. Ga. Refugee. 21 Apr. 1784. 287 1/2 acres.
Sinquefield, William. Ga. Private. 2 May 1785. 250 acres.
Siscat, Desire. Conn. Sufferer. Norwalk. 8.7.6.
Siscat, Obediah. Conn. Sufferer. Norwalk. 3.0.0.
Sisk, James. N.C. Corporal. 21 Aug. 1820. 1000 acres.
Sisk, John. Pa. Private. 6 Nov. 1786. 200 acres.
Sisson, Frederick. Ga. ———. 21 Apr. 1784. 900 acres.
Sisson, Richard. Va. Private. 30 May 1837. 100 acres.
Sisson, Robert. Va. Sergeant. 26 May 1795. 400 acres.
Sitten, John. Ga. ———. 23 Apr. 1784. 287 1/2 acres to heirs.
Sitton, Isaac. N.C. Private. 24 Nov. 1796. 274 acres.
Sitzer, John. Va.-Ind. Private. 108 acres.
Sitzer, Michael. Va.-Ind. Private. 108 acres.
Sivel, Daniel. N.C. Private. 25 Nov. 1789. 640 acres to heirs.
Sizeland, William. Md. Private. ———. 50 acres.
Sizemore, Isaac. Ga. Minute Man. 3 Sep. 1785. ———.
Sizemore, William. Ga. Minute Man. 1784. 287 1/2 acres.
Skarrett, Clement. Va. Lieutenant. 9 Nov. 1832. 2666 2/3 acres.
Skarrett, Clement. Va. Lieutenant. 9 Nov. 1833. 2666 2/3 acres.
Skarrett, Clement. Va. Captain Lieutenant. 28 Nov. 1868. 666 2/3 acres.
Skarrett, Clement. Va. Lieutenant. 9 Nov. 1833. 2666 2/3 acres.
Skeehan, Jeremiah. N. Y. Private. 7 Jul. 1790. 500 acres.
Skeen, John. N.C. Private. 15 Dec. 1783. 640 acres.
Skeeton, Joseph. N.C. Private. 10 Aug. 1785. 640 acres to heirs.
Skelton, John. S.C. Soldier. 21 Jan. 1785. 200 acres.
Skerlock, Dempsy. N.C. Private. 22 Dec. 1796. 640 acres.
Skerrett, Clement. Va. Captain Lieutenant. 4 Apr. 1838. 1000 acres.
Skerrett, Clement. Va. Captain Lieutenant. 4 Apr. 1838. 333 acres.
Skerrilt, Clement. Md. Captain. ———. 200 acres.
Skiffington, John. N. Y. Sergeant. 8 Jul. 1790. 500 acres.
Skilling, John. Pa. ———. 7 Oct. 1807. 200 acres.
Skilton, Jonathan. Pa. Private. 25 Oct. 1787. 200 acres.
Skinner, Alexander. Va. Regimental Surgeon. 4 Jun. 1783. 6000 acres.
Skinner, Alexander. Va. Surgeon. 21 Jun. 1784. 1000 acres.
Skinner, Alexander. Va. Surgeon. 7 Jul. 1807. 750 acres.
Skinner, Bathsheba. Conn. Sufferer. New London. 180.0.0.
Skinner, Evan. N.C. Private. 5 Dec. 1796. 640 acres.
Skinner, Henry. Va. Private. 23 Jun. 1783. 200 acres.
Skinner, Isaac. Ga. Captain. 20 Feb. 1784. 500 acres.
Skinner, John. Me. Sergeant. 23 May 1835. 200 acres. Lewiston.
Skinner, John. N.C. Private. 12 Sep. 1785. 640 acres to heirs.
Skinner, John. N.C. Private. 4 Sep. 1820. 228 acres to heirs.
Skinner, Richard. Va. Private. 3 Jun. 1783. 100 acres.
Skinner, Thomas. N.C. Private. 30 Nov. 1807. 640 acres to heirs.
Skinner, William. N.C. Private. 30 Nov. 1807. 640 acres to heirs.
Skinner, William. Va. Captain. 8 Nov. 1832. 5333 1/3 acres.
Skinner, William. Conn. Sufferer. New London. 15.0.11.
Skipper, Benjamin. N.C. Private. 15 Feb. 1797. 640 acres.
Skipper, Ezekiel. N.C. Private. 30 Sep. 1785. 640 acres to heirs.
Skipper, George. N.C. Private. 13 Sep. 1820. 274 acres.
Skipper, Hardy. N.C. Private. 30 Sep. 1785. 640 acres to heirs.

Skipper, Joseph. N.C. Private. 29 Sep. 1784. 640 acres to heir.
Skipper, Joseph. N.C. Private. 13 Sep. 1820. 274 acres.
Skipper, Nathan. N.C. Private. 29 Sep. 1784. 640 acres to heir.
Skipton, Andrew. N.C. Private. 30 Sep. 1785. 640 acres to heirs.
Slack, Henry. Md. Sergeant. ———. 50 acres.
Slack, James. N. Y. Matross. 6 Jul. 1790. 600 acres.
Slack, John. Md. Sergeant. ———. 50 acres.
Slack, William. Va.-Ind. Private. 108 acres.
Slade, Nathaniel. N.C. Private. 30 Sep. 1785. 640 acres to heirs.
Slade, Stepehn. N.C. Lieutenant. 22 Mar. 1784. 2560 acres.
Slade, Thomas. Md. Private. ———. 50 acres.
Slade, William. N.C. Lieutenant. 11 Apr. 1784. 1607 acres.
Slaitor, George. S.C. Soldier. 21 Jan. 1785. 200 acres.
Slaitor, John, Jr. S.C. ———. 21 Jan. 1785. 200 acres.
Slate, James. Va. Corporal. 6 Aug. 1783. 400 acres.
Slate, John. Va. Corporal. 25 Nov. 1783. 200 acres.
Slaton, Major. S.C. Soldier. 15 Oct. 1784. 200 acres.
Slaughter, Augustin. Va. Surgeon. 14 Nov. 1838. 562 1/2 acres.
Slaughter, Augustin. Va. Surgeon. 14 Nov. 1838. 375 acres.
Slaughter, Augustin. Va. Surgeon. 14 Nov. 1838. 562 1/2 acres.
Slaughter, Augustin. Va. Surgeon. 25 Jan. 1853. 562 1/3 acres.
Slaughter, Augustin. Va. Surgeon. 4 Nov. 1784. 3000 acres.
Slaughter, Augustin. Va. Surgeon. 4 Nov. 1784. 3000 acres.
Slaughter, Constantine. N.C. Private. 30 Sep. 1785. 640 acres to heirs.
Slaughter, Francis L. Va. Private. 16 Mar. 1822. 200 acres.
Slaughter, Francis Lightfoot. Va. Private. 31 May 1784. 200 acres.
Slaughter, George. Va. Major. 16 Nov. 1784. 2500 acres.
Slaughter, George. Va. Major. 16 Nov. 1784. 1000 acres.
Slaughter, George. Va. Major. 16 Nov. 1784. 1833 1/3 acres.
Slaughter, George. Va. Private. 18 Sep. 1850. 100 acres.
Slaughter, John. N.C. Captain. 2 Sep. 1820. 3840 acres.
Slaughter, John. Va. Private. 26 May 1783. 100 acres.
Slaughter, John. Va. Subaltern. 14 Feb. 1784. 2666 2/3 acres.
Slaughter, John. Va. Private. 11 Feb. 1788. 100 acres.
Slaughter, John. Va. Private. 5 Mar. 1819. 100 acres.
Slaughter, John. Va. Lieutenant. 9 Dec. 1848. 2666 2/3 acres.
Slaughter, John. Va. Lieutenant. 7 Jan. 1851. 410 1/4 acres.
Slaughter, John. Va. Lieutenant. 7 Jan. 1851. 410 1/4 acres.
Slaughter, John. Va. Lieutenant. 7 Jan. 1851. 410 1/4 acres.
Slaughter, John. Va. Lieutenant. 7 Jan. 1851. 410 1/4 acres.
Slaughter, John. Va. Lieutenant. 7 Jan. 1851. 410 1/4 acres.
Slaughter, John. Va. Lieutenant. 7 Jan. 1851. 410 1/4 acres.
Slaughter, John. Va. Lieutenant. 7 Jan. 1851. 205 1/4 acres.
Slaughter, John. Va. Lieutenant. 22 Dec. 1852. 410 1/4 acres.
Slaughter, John. Va. Lieutenant. 22 Dec. 1852. 410 acres.
Slaughter, John. Va. Lieutenant. 22 Dec. 1852. 410 acres.
Slaughter, John. Va. Lieutenant. 22 Dec. 1852. 410 acres.
Slaughter, John. Va. Lieutenant. 22 Dec. 1852. 205 1/6 acres.
Slaughter, John. Va. Lieutenant. 21 Feb. 1853. 410 1/4 acres.
Slaughter, Lawrence. Va.-Ind. Lieutenant. Apr. 1783. 2156 acres.
Slaughter, Lawrence. Va. Lieutenant. 1 Apr. 1783. 2666 2/3 acres.
Slaughter, Nathaniel. Va. Private. 20 Dec. 1783. 100 acres.
Slaughter, Philip. Va. Captain. 21 Dec. 1782. 4000 acres.
Slaughter, Philip. Va. Captain. 30 Jul. 1830. 1000 acres.

Slaughter, Philip. Va. Paymaster. 30 Dec. 1851. 4000 acres.
Slaughter, Robert. Va. Lieutenant. 20 Nov. 1818. 2666 2/3 acres.
Slaughter, Thomas. Va. Lieutenant. 28 Feb. 1850. 2666 2/3 acres.
Slaughter, William. Va. Lieutenant. 31 Mar. 1783. 2666 2/3 cres.
Slaughter, William. Va. Lieutenant. 12 May 1784. 666 2/3 acres.
Slaughter, William. Va. Ensign. 14 Dec. 1833. 2666 2/3 acres.
Slaughter, William. Va. Ensign. 20 Feb. 1837. 2666 2/3 acres.
Slaven, Cornelius. Va. Private. 17 Nov. 1783. 100 acres.
Slaven, John. Va. Private. 29 Jan. 1808. 100 acres.
Slaven, Samuel. N.C. Musician. 13 Sep. 1820. 1000 acres.
Slawson, Ebenezer. N. Y. Private. 13 Sep. 1790. 500 acres.
Slawson, Ezekiel. N.C. Private. 30 Sep. 1785. 640 acres to heirs.
Slayden, Daniel. Va. Private. 13 Dec. 1782. 100 acres.
Slayers, Martin. N.C. Private. 16 Aug. 1821. 640 acres.
Slayton, Joseph. Ga. ———. 17 May 1784. ———.
Sledd, Seaton. Va. Private. 13 Apr. 1784. 100 acres.
Sledd, Seaton. Va. Sergeant. 14 Apr. 1785. 300 acres.
Sleeker, George. Ga. Minute Man. 24 May 1784. 287 1/2 acres.
Sleeker, William. S.C. ———. 6 Oct. 1794. 200 acres.
Sliter, John. N.Y. ———. 13 Sep. 1790. 500 acres to heirs.
Sloan, David. Mass. Private. 5 Nov. 1832. 200 acres.
Sloan, David. N.C. ———. 11 Jul. 1785. 640 acres to heirs.
Sloan, David. Pa. Lieutenant. 26 Sep. 1785. 200 acres to heirs.
Sloan, David. Pa. Lieutenant. 29 Sep. 1787. 200 acres to Mary Sloan, widow.
Sloan, John. Pa. Private. ———. 200 acres.
Sloan, Lawrence. Pa. Private. 24 Nov. 1786. 200 acres to Joseph Johnston, assignee.
Slocumb, Seth. Ga. Refugee. 20 Feb. 1784. 287 1/2 acres to heir Samuel Slocumb.
Slomelk, Henry. Pa. Matross. 21 Mar. 1786. 200 acres.
Slone, Arthur. N.C. Private. 24 Nov. 1796. 640 acres to heirs.
Slonkerman, Christian. Pa. Private. 9 Mar. 1787. 200 acres.
Sloop, John. Md. ———. ———. 50 acres.
Sloop, Joseph. Md. Private. ———. 50 acres.
Slouter, Andrew. N. Y. Private. 8 Jul. 1790. 500 acres.
Slouter, Evert. N. Y. Private. 8 Jul. 1790. 600 acres.
Sloutter, John. N. Y. Private. 8 Jul. 1790. 600 acres.
Slutt, Peter. N. Y. Private. 8 Jul. 1790. 500 acres.
Sluyter, Jacob. N. Y. Private. 8 Jul. 1790. 500 acres.
Sly, William. Md. Corporal. ———. 50 acres.
Slyter, Nicholas. N. Y. Sergeant. 7 Jul. 1790. 600 acres.
Small, Abraham. N.C. Private. 13 Dec. 1796. 320 acres.
Small, Daniel. Me. Private. 15 Aug. 1835. 200 acres. Limington.
Small, Henry. Va. Private. 9 Dec. 1783. 100 acres.
Small, James. Me. ———. 8 May 1835. 200 acres. Scarborough.
Smallwood, H. Va. ———. 29 Dec. 1838. 154 1/3 acres.
Smallwood, H. Va. ———. 29 Dec. 1838. 308 2/3 acres.
Smallwood, H. Va. ———. 29 Dec. 1838. 61 3/5 acres.
Smallwood, H. Va. ———. 29 Dec. 1838. 123 2/5 acres.
Smallwood, H. Va. ———. 29 Dec. 1838. 154 1/3 acres.
Smallwood, H. Va. ———. 29 Dec. 1838. 308 2/3 acres.
Smallwood, Heaberd. Va. Captain. 21 Mar. 1840. 61 13/18 acres.
Smallwood, Heaberd. Va. Captain. 21 Mar. 1840. 61 13/18 acres.
Smallwood, Heaberd. Va. Captain. 21 Mar. 1840. 61 13/18 acres.
Smallwood, Heaberd. Va. Captain. 18 Oct. 1849. 246 2/3 acres.

Smallwood, Heaberd. Va. Captain. 18 Oct. 1849. 123 1/3 acres.
Smallwood, Heaberd. Va. Captain. 18 Oct. 1849. 123 1/3 acres.
Smallwood, Heaberd. Va. Captain. 18 Oct. 1849. 62 1/2 acres.
Smallwood, Heaberd. Va. Captain. 18 Oct. 1849. 123 1/3 acres.
Smallwood, Heaberd. Va. Captain. 18 Oct. 1849. 62 1/2 acres.
Smallwood, Heabird. Va. Captain. 13 Apr. 1838. 370 1/3 acres.
Smallwood, Heabird. Va. Captain. 13 Apr. 1838. 740 2/3 acres.
Smallwood, Heabird. Va. Captain. 13 Apr. 1838. 185 1/6 acres.
Smallwood, Heabird. Va. Captain. 13 Apr. 1838. 370 1/3 acres.
Smallwood, Heabird. Va. Captain. 13 Apr. 1838. 92 1/2 acres.
Smallwood, Heabird. Va. Captain. 13 Apr. 1838. 185 1/4 acres.
Smallwood, Heabird. Va. Captain. 13 Apr. 1838. 31 acres.
Smallwood, Heabird. Va. Captain. 13 Apr. 1838. 62 acres.
Smallwood, Heabird. Va. Captain. 13 Apr. 1838. 55 1/5 acres.
Smallwood, Heabird. Va. Captain. 13 Apr. 1838. 111 acres.
Smallwood, John. Md. Private. ———. 50 acres.
Smallwood, John. Md. Private. ———. 50 acres.
Smallwood, Walter B. Md. Private. ———. 50 acres.
Smallwood, William. Md. Major General. ———. 200 acres.
Smally, James. N.C. Private. 12 Sep. 1785. 640 acres to heirs.
Smally, Michael. Ga. ———. 16 Apr. 1784. 287 1/2 acres.
Smally, Thomas. N. Y. Private. 8 Jul. 1790. 500 acres.
Smart, John. N.C. Private. 2 Feb. 1786. 640 acres to heirs.
Smart, Richard. Va. Master's Mate. 19 May 1783. 2666 2/3 acres.
Smart, Robert. Ga. Minute Man. 20 Apr. 1784. 287 1/2 acres.
Smart, Thomas. N.C. Private. 30 Sep. 1785. 640 acres to heirs.
Smaw, John. Va. Sergeant. 13 May 1783. 200 acres.
Smaw, John. Va. Sergeant. 16 Dec. 1783. 200 acres.
Smedis, John. N.Y. Surgeon's Mate. 14 Jun. 1793. 1500 acres.
Smedley, John. Conn. Sufferer. Fairfield. 763.10.4.
Smedley, Samuel. Conn. Sufferer. Fairfield. 415.19.7.
Smick, Reynard. Pa. Sergeant. 5 Mar. 1787. 250 acres.
Smile, Thompson. N.C. Private. 11 Feb. 1796. 640 acres to heirs.
Smiler, Jonathan. N.C. Private. 30 Sep. 1785. 640 acres to heirs.
Smith, ———. S.C. ———. 2 Oct. 1786. 53 acres to Margaret Smith.
Smith, Aaron. S.C. Lieutenant. 15 Oct. 1784. 200 acres.
Smith, Aaron. Va. Private. 15 Mar. 1783. 200 acres.
Smith, Abijah. Conn. Sufferer. Ridgefield. 16.14.0.
Smith, Abraham. Ga. Minute Man. 27 Jul. 1785. ———.
Smith, Alexander. Ga. ———. 5 Dec. 1785. 287 1/2 acres.
Smith, Alexander. Md. Surgeon's Mate. ———. 200 acres.
Smith, Alexander. N.C. ———. 29 Sep. 1784. 640 acres to Ann Cox, heir.
Smith, Alexander L. Md. Major. ———. 200 acres.
Smith, Alexander [or Andrew]. Md. Private. ———. 50 acres.
Smith, Amos. Mass. Private. 13 Dec. 1831. 200 acres to heirs.
Smith, Andrew. S.C. ———. 5 Feb. 1787. 200 acres.
Smith, Andrew. Va. Private. 24 Feb. 1784. 100 acres.
Smith, Andrew. Conn. Sufferer. New/East Haven. 14.7.0.
Smith, Anthony. Md. Drummer. ———. 50 acres.
Smith, Aquilla. Md. Private. ———. 50 acres.
Smith, Archibald. N. Y. Private. 8 Jul. 1790. 500 acres.
Smith, Archibald. N.C. Private. 7 Jan. 1786. 640 acres to heirs.
Smith, Arthur. Ga. Refugee. 24 May 1784. 287 1/2 acres.
Smith, Arthur. N.C. Private. 10 Aug. 1785. 640 acres to heirs.

Smith, Arthur. Va. Captain. 3 Mar. 1808. 1500 acres.
Smith, Arthur. Va. Captain. 3 Mar. 1808. 1500 acres.
Smith, Arthur. Va. Captain. 3 Mar. 1808. 1000 acres.
Smith, Austin. Va. Private. 1 May 1838. 200 acres.
Smith, B. Egbert. N.Y. ———. 13 Sep. 1790. 500 acres to heirs.
Smith, Ballard. Va. Lieutenant. 26 Mar. 1783. 2666 2/3 acres.
Smith, Ballard. Va. Lieutenant. 22 May 1810. 185 acres.
Smith, Bathsheba. Conn. Sufferer. New London. 465.14.10.
Smith, Benjamin. Ga. ———. 21 Apr. 1784. 250 acres.
Smith, Benjamin. Md. Private. ———. 50 acres.
Smith, Benjamin. N. Y. Private. 8 Jul. 1790. 600 acres.
Smith, Benjamin. N.C. Sergeant. 23 Apr. 1784. 428 acres.
Smith, Benjamin. N.C. Private. 28 May 1784. 274 acres.
Smith, Benjamin. N.C. Private. 22 Mar. 1785. 274 acres. He was of Pasquotank County.
Smith, Benjamin. N.C. Private. 1 Jul. 1820. 640 acres to heirs.
Smith, Benjamin. Va. Private. 21 May 1823. 100 acres.
Smith, Benjamin. Conn. Sufferer. New/East Haven. 3.0.0.
Smith, Benjamin. Conn. Sufferer. Ridgefield. 4.14.0.
Smith, Bryant. N.C. Private. 22 Oct. 1783. 342 acres.
Smith, Burwell. Ga. Major. 25 May 1784. 747 1/2 acres.
Smith, Burwell. N.C. Sergeant. 26 May 1784. 1000 acres.
Smith, Caleb. Ga. ———. Refugee. 6 Aug. 1785.
Smith, Caleb. N. Y. Private. 8 Jul. 1790. 600 acres.
Smith, Caleb. N.C. Private. 23 Apr. 1800. 640 acres.
Smith, Charles. Ga. ———. 21 Apr. 1784. 1000 acres.
Smith, Charles. N.C. Private. 23 Apr. 1785. 640 acres to heirs.
Smith, Charles. N.C. Private. 30 Sep. 1785. 640 acres.
Smith, Charles. S.C. ———. 4 Nov. 1793. 200 acres.
Smith, Charles. Va. Private. 13 Oct. 1786. 100 acres.
Smith, Charles. Va. Private. 22 Mar. 1838. 200 acres.
Smith, Christopher. N. Y. Private. 8 Jul. 1790. 500 acres.
Smith, Christopher [or Christian]. Md. Private. ———. 50 acres.
Smith, Clement. N.C. Private. 21 Apr. 1784. 640 acres to Thomas Smith, heir.
Smith, Conrad. Md. Private. ———. 50 acres.
Smith, Conrad. Pa. Private. 7 Feb. 1787. 200 acres to widow.
Smith, Cornelius. Ga. Refugee. 1784. 287 1/2 acres.
Smith, Daniel. Ga. Citizen. 6 Apr. 1785. 287 1/2 acres.
Smith, Daniel. Md. Private. ———. 50 acres.
Smith, Daniel. Md. Private. ———. 50 acres.
Smith, Daniel. N.C. Private. 1 Dec. 1797. 640 acres to heirs.
Smith, Daniel. Pa. Dragoon. 1 Aug. 1789. 200 acres.
Smith, Daniel. Conn. Sufferer. Greenwich. 76.3.4.
Smith, Daniel. Conn. Sufferer. Norwalk. 99.5.1 1/2.
Smith, Daniel. Conn. Sufferer. Ridgefield. 183.4.6.
Smith, Daniel & Joshua Smith. Conn. Sufferers. Greenwich. 218.12.6.
Smith, Daniel, 2d. Conn. Sufferer. Ridgefield. 2.13.4.
Smith, Daniel, 3d. Conn. Sufferer. Ridgefield. 30.19.10.
Smith, David. Ga. ———. 15 Mar. 1784. 250 acres.
Smith, David. Md. Private. ———. 50 acres.
Smith, David. N. Y. Corporal. 8 Jul. 1790. 600 acres.
Smith, David. N. Y. Private. 8 Jul. 1790. 600 acres.
Smith, David. N.C. Private. 31 Mar. 1810. 640 acres.
Smith, Duncan. N. Y. Drummer. 8 Jul. 1790. 600 acres.

Smith, Ebenezer. Ga. Refugee. 19 Apr. 1784. 287 1/2 acres.
Smith, Ebenezer. Me. Captain. 18 Oct. 1839. 600 acres to widow Jennet Smith. Richmond.
Smith, Edmond. Conn. Sufferer. New/East Haven. 4.17.1.
Smith, Edward. Va. Lieutenant. 3 Mar. 1808. 2666 2/3 acres.
Smith, Edward. Va. Lieutenant. 3 Mar. 1808. 400 acres.
Smith, Edward M. Md. Lieutenant. ———. 200 acres.
Smith, Eichael. Md. Private. ———. 50 acres.
Smith, Eliakim. Conn. Sufferer. Norwalk. 203.16.4.
Smith, Elias. Md. Private. ———. 50 acres.
Smith, Elias. N.C. Private. 5 Sep. 1821. 640 acres to heirs.
Smith, Elijah. Md. Private. ———. 50 acres.
Smith, Elijah. Va. Private. 22 Jul. 1783. 100 acres.
Smith, Enock. Va. Gunner. 28 May 1856. 200 acres.
Smith, Ezekiel. S.C. Soldier. 15 Oct. 1784. 200 acres.
Smith, Fountain. Conn. Sufferer. Norwalk. 158.15.10.
Smith, Francis. Ga. ———. ———. 287 1/2 acres.
Smith, Francis. Pa. Private. 18 Oct. 1786. 200 acres.
Smith, Francis. Va. Lieutenant. 27 Dec. 1782. 2666 2/3 acres.
Smith, Francis. Va. Fifer. 21 Jun. 1783. 100 acres.
Smith, Francis. Va. Private. 10 May 1784. 100 acres.
Smith, Francis. Va. Lieutenant. 20 Oct. 1807. 333 acres.
Smith, Frederick. Pa. Matross. 6 Apr. 1787. 200 acres.
Smith, George. Ga. ———. 22 Apr. 1784. 287 1/2 acres.
Smith, George. Va.-Ind. Private. 108 acres.
Smith, George. N. Y. Lieutenant. 28 Mar. 1791. 1200 acres.
Smith, George. N.C. Private. 25 Apr. 1784. 274 acres.
Smith, George. Pa. ———. 9 Mar. 1795. 200 acres to John Nicholson, assignee.
Smith, George. Va. Private. 20 Jun. 1783. 100 acres.
Smith, George. Conn. Sufferer. New/East Haven. 20.1.6.
Smith, Gershom. N. Y. Private. 8 Jul. 1790. 600 acres.
Smith, Godfrey. Va. Private. 14 Aug. 1834. 200 acres.
Smith, Granvill. Va. Ensign. 13 Apr. 1784. 2666 2/3 acres.
Smith, Gregory. Va. Colonel. 10 Feb. 1783. 6666 2/3 acres.
Smith, Grey. Ga. ———. 17 May 1784. ———.
Smith, Guy. Ga. ———. 22 Apr. 1784. 550 acres.
Smith, Henry. N.C. Private. 15 Oct. 1783. 640 acres.
Smith, Hezekiah. N.C. Private. 27 Jul. 1785. 228 acres.
Smith, Ignatius. Md. Private. ———. 50 acres.
Smith, Isaac. Mass. Private. 9 Apr. 1834. 200 acres.
Smith, Isaac. N. Y. Lieutenant. 8 Jul. 1790. 1200 acres.
Smith, Isaac. Va. Private. 18 Mar. 1784. 100 acres.
Smith, Isaac. Va. Sergeant. 28 Jun. 1783. 200 acres.
Smith, Isaac. Va. Private. 25 Sep. 1788. 100 acres.
Smith, Israel. Ga. ———. 22 Jul. 1784 287 1/2 acres.
Smith, Israel. N. Y. Captain. 9 Jul. 1790. 1800 acres.
Smith, Jacob. Ga. Soldier. 17 Apr. 1784. 287 1/2 acres.
Smith, Jacob. N.C. Private. 8 Dec. 1796. 640 acres to heirs.
Smith, Jacob. Pa. Private. 20 Aug. 1787. 200 acres.
Smith, Jacob. Pa. Private. 30 Sep. 1787. 200 acres. Alias Lindersmith.
Smith, Jacob. Pa. ———. 9 Mar. 1795. 200 acres.
Smith, Jacob. Va. Private. 31 Jul. 1783. 100 acres.
Smith, Jahleel. N.C. Private. 30 Mar. 1785. 914 acres.
Smith, James. Ga. Refugee. 25 May 1784. 287 1/2 acres.
Smith, James. Md. Captain. ———. 200 acres.

Smith, James. Md. Private. ———. 50 acres.
Smith, James. Md. Private. ———. 50 acres.
Smith, James. Md. Private. ———. 50 acres.
Smith, James. N.C. Private. 29 Apr. 1784. 640 acres.
Smith, James. N.C. Private. 13 Jan. 1792. 640 acres to heirs.
Smith, James. Pa. Private. 5 Jan. 1787. 200 acres.
Smith, James. Pa. Lieutenant. ———. 200 acres.
Smith, James. Pa. Private. 12 Jan. 1787. 200 acres to Jane Smith, widow.
Smith, James. S.C. Soldier. 2 May 1785. 200 acres to Catharine Smith, heir.
Smith, James. S.C. ———. 5 Sep. 1791. 200 acres.
Smith, James. Va. Private. 23 Jun. 1783. 200 acres.
Smith, James. Va. Private. 22 Aug. 1783. 200 acres.
Smith, James. Va. Private. 24 Mar. 1785. 100 acres.
Smith, James. Va. Corporal. 5 Jan. 1786. 200 acres.
Smith, James. Va. Corporal. 24 Dec. 1834. 200 acres.
Smith, James. Va. Sergeant. 31 May 1791. 400 acres.
Smith, James. Va. Private. 31 Jan. 1792. 100 acres.
Smith, James. Va. Lieutenant. 8 Jan. 1807. 3111 1/3 acres.
Smith, James. Va. Lieutenant. 22 Dec. 1807. 370 acres.
Smith, James. Conn. Sufferer. Norwalk. 21.13.0.
Smith, James. Conn. Sufferer. New London. 4.7.8.
Smith, James. Conn. Sufferer. Groton. 6.2.0.
Smith, Jeremiah. Mass. Corporal. 13 Dec. 1832. 200 acres to heirs.
Smith, Jeremiah. N. Y. Gunner. 9 Jul. 1790. 600 acres.
Smith, Jeremiah. N.C. Private. 20 Apr. 1784. 274 acres.
Smith, Jeremiah. N.C. Private. 14 Sep. 1820. 640 acres.
Smith, Jesse. Ga. ———. 5 Dec. 1785. 287 1/2 acres.
Smith, Jesse. Me. ———. 27 Feb. 1842. 200 acres to widow Lucy Smith. Bangor.
Smith, Jesse. Me. ———. 27 Feb. 1842. 200 acres to widow Lucy Smith. Bangor.
Smith, Jesse. N. Y. Sergeant. 6 Jul. 1790. 600 acres.
Smith, Jesse. S.C. ———. 6 Feb. 1797. 200 acres.
Smith, Jesse. Va. Private. 14 Aug. 1834. 100 acres.
Smith, Joal. N.C. Private. 30 Sep. 1785. 640 acres to heirs.
Smith, Job. N.C. Sergeant. 13 Nov. 1795. 355 acres.
Smith, John. Ga. Minute Man. 21 Apr. 1784. 287 1/2 acres.
Smith, John. Md. Captain. ———. 200 acres.
Smith, John. Md. Captain. ———. 200 acres.
Smith, John. Md. Private. ———. 50 acres.
Smith, John. Md. Private. ———. 50 acres.
Smith, John. Md. Corporal. ———. 50 acres.
Smith, John. Md. Corporal. ———. 50 acres.
Smith, John. Md. Private. ———. 50 acres.
Smith, John. Md. Matross. ———. 50 acres.
Smith, John. Md. Sergeant. ———. 50 acres.
Smith, John. Mass. Private. 13 Sep. 1830. 200 acres.
Smith, John. N. Y. Sergeant Major. 8 Jul. 1790. 600 acres.
Smith, John. N. Y. Private. 8 Jul. 1790. 600 acres.
Smith, John. N. Y. Private. 7 Jul. 1790. 600 acres.
Smith, John. N. Y. Private. 8 Jul. 1790. 600 acres.
Smith, John. N. Y. Corporal. 9 Jul. 1790. 500 acres.
Smith, John. N. Y. Sergeant. 9 Jul. 1790. 600 acres.
Smith, John. N. Y. Lieutenant. 3 Jul. 1790. 1000 acres.
Smith, John. N.Y. ———. 13 Sep. 1790. 500 acres to heirs.

Smith, John. N.Y. Sergeant. 13 Sep. 1790. 500 acres to heirs.
Smith, John. N.Y. ———. 13 Sep. 1790. 500 acres to heirs.
Smith, John. N.Y. Fifer. 13 Sep. 1790. 500 acres to heirs.
Smith, John. N. Y. ———. 17 Nov. 1806. 200 acres.
Smith, John. N.C. Private. 17 Mar. 1784. 640 acres.
Smith, John. N.C. Private. 20 Apr. 1784. 640 acres.
Smith, John. N.C. Private. 28 May 1784. 640 acres.
Smith, John. N.C. Private. 28 May 1784. 640 acres.
Smith, John. N.C. Private. 29 Sep. 1784. 388 acres.
Smith, John. N.C. Private. 9 Nov. 1784. 640 acres. He was of Bladen County.
Smith, John. N.C. Trooper. 27 Nov. 1789. 182 acres.
Smith, John. N.C. Private. 22 Dec. 1796. 274 acres.
Smith, John. N.C. Musician. 3 Aug. 1820. 1000 acres to heirs.
Smith, John. Pa. Private. 28 Aug. 1787. 200 acres.
Smith, John. Pa. Private. 21 Oct. 1785. 200 acres.
Smith, John. Pa. Private. 11 Sep. 1789. 200 acres.
Smith, John. Pa. Private. 24 Aug. 1787. 200 acres.
Smith, John. Pa. Private. ———. 200 acres.
Smith, John. Pa. Private. 24 Aug. 1787. 200 acres.
Smith, John. Pa. Captain. ———. 200 acres.
Smith, John. Pa. Private. 20 Dec. 1786. 200 acres.
Smith, John. Pa. Private. 24 Aug. 1787. 200 acres to William Powers, assignee.
Smith, John. Pa. Private. 9 Oct. 1787. 200 acres.
Smith, John. S.C. ———. 2 Jan. 1797. 110 acres to George Smith, heir at law.
Smith, John. S.C. ———. 7 Nov. 1796. 146 acres.
Smith, John. S.C. ———. 3 Sep. 1792. 200 acres.
Smith, John. S.C. Soldier. 15 Oct. 1784. 200 acres.
Smith, John. S.C. ———. 3 Mar. 1798. 200 acres.
Smith, John. Va. Private. 20 Jun. 1783. 100 acres.
Smith, John. Va. Drummer. 23 Jun. 1783. 200 acres.
Smith, John. Va. Private. 4 Aug. 1783. 200 acres.
Smith, John. Va. Private. 8 Sep. 1783. 100 acres.
Smith, John. Va. Seaman. 20 Nov. 1783. 100 acres.
Smith, John. Va. Private. 17 Mar. 1784. 100 acres.
Smith, John. Va. Private. 12 Apr. 1784. 100 acres.
Smith, John. Va. Private. 2 Jul. 1784. 100 acres.
Smith, John. Va. Sergeant. 30 Jun. 1785 [1784]. 200 acres.
Smith, John. Va. Private. 6 Apr. 1787. 100 acres.
Smith, John. Va. Private. 3 Oct. 1793. 100 acres.
Smith, John. Va. Private. 12 Mar. 1833. 200 acres.
Smith, John. Conn. Sufferer. Ridgefield. 13.7.2.
Smith, John Carraway. S.C. Major. 21 Jan. 1785. 400 acres.
Smith, John Kilby. Me. Captain. 17 May 1838. 600 acres. Portland.
Smith, John, Jr. N. Y. Private. 8 Jul. 1790. 500 acres.
Smith, John, Jr. S.C. Soldier. 5 May 1800. 200 acres.
Smith, John, Sr. Ga. Private. 10 Dec. 1784. 250 acres.
Smith, Jonah. Conn. Sufferer. Greenwich. 70.4.3.
Smith, Jonathan. Va. Lieutenant. 13 Feb. 1783. 2666 2/3 acres.
Smith, Jonathan. Va. Lieutenant. 20 May 1829. 889 1/2 acres.
Smith, Joseph. Ga. Refugee. 25 May 1784. 287 1/2 acres.
Smith, Joseph. Md. Captain. ———. 200 acres.
Smith, Joseph. Md. Private. ———. 50 acres.
Smith, Joseph. N. Y. Corporal. 8 Jul. 1790. 500 acres.
Smith, Joseph. N. Y. Matross. 6 Jul. 1790. 600 acres.

Smith, Joseph. N. Y. ———. ———. 500 acres.
Smith, Joseph. N.C. Private. 25 Oct. 1783. 604 acres.
Smith, Joseph. N.C. Private. 14 May 1784. 640 acres to James Smith, heir.
Smith, Joseph. N.C. Private. 9 Nov. 1784. 640 acres.
Smith, Joseph. Va. Private. 10 Jun. 1784. 100 acres.
Smith, Joseph. Va. Captain. 31 May 1806. 3111 2/3 acres.
Smith, Joseph. Va. Captain. 31 May 1806. 1000 acres.
Smith, Joseph. Va. Captain. 31 May 1806. 555 acres.
Smith, Joseph S. Va. Cornet. 8 Nov. 1832. 2666 2/3 acres.
Smith, Joseph, 3d. Conn. Sufferer. New/East Haven. 12.8.10.
Smith, Joshua. Conn. Sufferer. Greenwich. 149.7.4.
Smith, Josiah. Md. Sergeant. ———. 50 acres.
Smith, Larkin. Va. Captain. 22 May 1783. 4000 acres.
Smith, Larkin. Va. Captain. 6 Dec. 1836. 166 1/3 acres.
Smith, Larkin. Va. Captain. 19 May 1838. 57 3/4 acres.
Smith, Larkin. Va. ———. 1 Sep. 1838. 224 acres.
Smith, Larkin. Va. ———. 9 Oct. 1838. 224 acres.
Smith, Larkin. Va. ———. 9 Oct. 1838. 224 acres.
Smith, Lawrence. Va. Paymaster. 28 Jun. 1858/29 Dec. 1851. 4000 acres.
Smith, Leonard. Md. Private. ———. 50 acres.
Smith, Leonard. Pa. Private. ———. 200 acres.
Smith, Levy. Md. Sergeant. ———. 50 acres.
Smith, Major. Va. Private. 20 Aug. 1786. 100 acres.
Smith, Major. Va. Private. 1 May 1838. 200 acres.
Smith, Mary. Conn. Sufferer. Norwalk. 17.5.0.
Smith, Mary. Conn. Sufferer. Fairfield. 16.14.3.
Smith, Mathias. Pa. Private. 13 Aug. 1787. 200 acres.
Smith, Matthew. S.C. ———. 7 Mar. 1791. 100 acres.
Smith, Matthew. Va. Captain. 18 Dec. 1784. 4000 acres.
Smith, Micajah. N.C. Private. 29 Sep. 1785. 640 acres to heirs.
Smith, Michael. Ga. ———. 23 Apr. 1784. 287 1/2 acres.
Smith, Michael. Md. Private. ———. 50 acres.
Smith, Michael. N.C. Private. 23 Apr. 1784. 640 acres.
Smith, Michael. Pa. Private. 5 Apr. 1787. 200 acres to Catherine Smith, administratrix.
Smith, Michael. Va. Sergeant. 7 Jun. 1783. 200 acres.
Smith, Michael. Va. Private. 23 Jun. 1783. 200 acres.
Smith, Minor. Va. Private. 11 Nov. 1784. 200 acres.
Smith, Moses. Ga. Refugee. 5 May 1785. 287 1/2 acres.
Smith, Moses. Me. ———. 7 May 1835. 200 acres. Prospect.
Smith, Moses. N. Y. Private. 8 Jul. 1790. 500 acres.
Smith, Nahum. Mass. Private. 19 Nov. 1833. 200 acres to widow Ruth Smith.
Smith, Nathan. Ga. ———. 15 Mar. 1784. 250 acres.
Smith, Nathan. Ga. Refugee. 22 Apr. 1784. 287 1/2 acres.
Smith, Nathan. Va. Surgeon's Mate. 17 Apr. 1784. 2666 2/3 acres.
Smith, Nathan. Va. Surgeon's Mate. 29 Jun. 1854. 950 acres.
Smith, Nathan. Va. Surgeon's Mate. 19 Jan. 1858. 191 2/3 acres.
Smith, Nathan. Va. Surgeon's Mate. 7 Sep. 1858. 191 2/3 acres.
Smith, Nathan. Conn. Sufferer. New/East Haven. 9.15.6.
Smith, Nathaniel. Ga. Refugee. 22 Apr. 1784. 287 1/2 acres.
Smith, Nathaniel. Ga. ———. 15 Mar. 1784. 350 acres.
Smith, Nathaniel. Md. Private. ———. 50 acres.
Smith, Nathaniel. Pa. Lieutenant. 19 Dec. 1786. 200 acres.
Smith, Nathaniel. Pa. Lieutenant. 19 Dec. 1786. 200 acres.

Smith, Nehemiah. N.C. Private. 30 Sep. 1785. 640 acres to heirs.
Smith, Nehemiah. Conn. Sufferer. New/East Haven. 9.12.0.
Smith, Nicholas. N. Y. Matross. 9 Jul. 1790. 600 acres.
Smith, Noah. Conn. Sufferer. Norwalk. 89.11.10.
Smith, Obadiah. Va. Lieutenant. 27 May 1783. 2666 2/3 acres.
Smith, Owen. N.C. ———. 15 Jun. 1785. 640 acres to heirs.
Smith, Patrick. Pa. Private. 29 Aug. 1787. 200 acres to Sarah Smith, widow.
Smith, Peleg. Me. Private. 1 Jun. 1836. 200 acres to widow Lucy Ann Smith. Hope.
Smith, Peter. Ga. Minute Man. 3 Sep. 1785. ———.
Smith, Peter. Md. Sergeant. ———. 50 acres.
Smith, Peter. Pa. Quartermaster & Lieutenant. 17 Sep. 1787. 200 acres to Myer Hart, assignee.
Smith, Peter. Pa. Private. 10 Sep. 1787. 200 acres.
Smith, Peter. Pa. Quartermaster Sergeant. 17 Sep. 1787. 200 acres to Myar Hart, assignee.
Smith, Philemon. Conn. Sufferer. New/East Haven. 53.0.3.
Smith, Philip. N. Y. ———. ———. 500 acres.
Smith, Ralph. S.C. ———. 7 Mar. 1796. 200 acres.
Smith, Rebecca. Conn. Sufferer. Norwalk. 3.2.9.
Smith, Redick. Ga. Private. 10 Dec. 1784. 250 acres.
Smith, Redick. N.C. Private. 29 Sep. 1784. 640 acres.
Smith, Reed. N.C. Private. 17 Dec. 1796. 274 acres.
Smith, Reuben. Md. Private. ———. 50 acres.
Smith, Reuben. N. Y. ———. 16 Jan. 1795. 500 acres.
Smith, Reuben. N.C. Private. 7 Jan. 1784. 640 acres.
Smith, Richard. Ga. Refugee. 6 Aug. 1785. ———.
Smith, Richard. Md. Sergeant. ———. 50 acres.
Smith, Richard. N. Y. Corporal. 8 Jul. 1790. 600 acres.
Smith, Richard. N.C. Private. 3 Aug. 1821. 640 acres to heirs. Served in Mills's company.
Smith, Richard. N.C. Private. 3 Aug. 1821. 640 acres to heirs. Served in Carter's company.
Smith, Richard. Va. Private. 20 Dec. 1784. 200 acres.
Smith, Richard. Va. Private. 13 Oct. 1786. 100 acres.
Smith, Richard. Conn. Sufferer. Danbury. 6.6.0.
Smith, Robert. Md. Matross. ———. 50 acres.
Smith, Robert. Mass. Private. 9 Jan. 1833. 200 acres to his children Levi Smith, Melinda French, and Triphene Hodges.
Smith, Robert. N. Y. Sergeant. 8 Jul. 1790. 600 acres.
Smith, Robert. N.C. Captain. 24 Oct. 1783. 1828 acres.
Smith, Robert. Conn. Sufferer. New London. 24.18.0.
Smith, Roland. Me. ———. 27 Apr. 1835. 200 acres. Augusta.
Smith, S. William. N. Y. Lieutenant Colonel. 3 Jul. 1790. 2600 acres.
Smith, Samuel. Ga. Refugee. 19 Apr. 1784. 287 1/2 acres.
Smith, Samuel. N. Y. Private. 8 Jul. 1790. 500 acres.
Smith, Samuel. N.C. Corporal. 23 Oct. 1783. 429 acres.
Smith, Samuel. N.C. Private. 29 Nov. 1810. 640 acres to heirs.
Smith, Samuel. Pa. Private. 5 Feb. 1806. 200 acres.
Smith, Samuel. Pa. Captain. 17 Oct. 1785. 500 acres.
Smith, Samuel. Va. Private. 23 Jun. 1783. 200 acres.
Smith, Samuel. Va. Surgeon. 16 Feb. 1801. 6000 acres.
Smith, Samuel. Conn. Sufferer. Fairfield. 19.16.9.
Smith, Samuel. Conn. Sufferer. Ridgefield. 18.15.2.
Smith, Samule. Me. Private. 28 Apr. 1835. 200 acres. Monroe.
Smith, Seth. Conn. Sufferer. Fairfield. 56.7.0.
Smith, Shorter. N. Y. Private. 8 Jul. 1790. 600 acres.

Smith, Simon. Ga. Sergeant. 22 Apr. 1784. 287 1/2 acres.
Smith, Simon. N.C. Private. 29 Sep. 1784. 274 acres.
Smith, Stephen. Me. Private. 8 May 1835. 200 acres. Freedom.
Smith, Stephen. N.C. Private. 26 May 1784. 640 acres.
Smith, Stephen. N.C. Private. 23 Apr. 1785. 640 acres to heirs.
Smith, Stephen. N.C. Private. 10 Dec. 1788. 640 acres to heirs.
Smith, Stephen. N.C. Private. Jan. 1802. 640 acres to heir Cullen Smith.
Smith, Stephen. Va. Private. 25 Sep. 1783. 100 acres.
Smith, Stephen. Va. Private. 12 Jun. 1787. 200 acres.
Smith, Stephen. Conn. Sufferer. Norwalk. 48.2.11.
Smith, Stephen. Conn. Sufferer. Ridgefield. 8.5.0.
Smith, Susannah. Ga. ———. 21 Apr. 1784. 250 acres.
Smith, Thaddeus. N. Y. ———. 13 Aug. 1794. 500 acres.
Smith, Theophilus. N.C. Private. 8 Dec. 1796. 640 acres to heirs.
Smith, Theophilus. N.C. Private. 13 Dec. 1796. 640 acres to heirs.
Smith, Thomas. Ga. ———. 22 Apr. 1784. 287 1/2 acres.
Smith, Thomas. Ga. Private. 22 Apr. 1784. 287 1/2 acres.
Smith, Thomas. Md. Private. ———. 50 acres.
Smith, Thomas. Md. Private. ———. 50 acres.
Smith, Thomas. Md. Private. ———. 50 acres.
Smith, Thomas. Md. Matross. ———. 50 acres.
Smith, Thomas. N. Y. Corporal. 9 Jul. 1790. 600 acres.
Smith, Thomas. N.C. Private. 10 Nov. 1783. 640 acres.
Smith, Thomas. N.C. Private. 21 Apr. 1784. 274 acres.
Smith, Thomas. N.C. Private. 8 Nov. 1784. 640 acres.
Smith, Thomas. N.C. Sergeant. 9 Nov. 1784. 465 acres to Samuel Reed, administrator.
Smith, Thomas. N.C. Sergeant. 8 Feb. 1802. 1000 acres.
Smith, Thomas. Pa. Private. 12 Jan. 1787. 200 acres.
Smith, Thomas. Va. Private. 28 Nov. 1783. 100 acres.
Smith, Thomas. Va. Drum Major. 7 Mar. 1786. 400 acres.
Smith, Thomas. Va. Private. 23 Sep. 1796. 200 acres.
Smith, Thomas. Conn. Sufferer. New London. 11.0.0.
Smith, Thomas, Jr. Minute Man. Ga. 22 Apr. 1784. 287 1/2 acres.
Smith, Underwood. Va. Private. 3 May 1783. 100 acres.
Smith, Uriah. Conn. Sufferer. Norwalk. 35.9.0.
Smith, Uriah. Conn. Sufferer. Norwalk. 4.0.0.
Smith, Valentine. Md. Private. ———. 50 acres.
Smith, Wait. N. Y. Matross. 6 Jul. 1790. 600 acres.
Smith, Weedon. Va. Private. 17 Dec. 1784. 100 acres.
Smith, Weedon. Va. Private. 23 Jan. 1810. 100 acres.
Smith, William. Ga. ———. 22 Apr. 1784. 287 1/2 acres.
Smith, William. Ga. Soldier. 5 Dec. 1785. 230 acres.
Smith, William. Va.-Ind. Private. 108 acres.
Smith, William. Md. Private. ———. 50 acres.
Smith, William. Md. Private. ———. 50 acres.
Smith, William. Md. Drummer. ———. 50 acres.
Smith, William. Md. ———. ———. 50 acres.
Smith, William. Md. ———. ———. 50 acres.
Smith, William. Massachusetts. ———. 7 Jan. 1829. 200 acres.
Smith, William. N. Y. Private. 8 Jul. 1790. 600 acres.
Smith, William. N.C. Private. 13 Dec. 1783. 640 acres.
Smith, William. N.C. Private. 29 Sep. 1784. 480 acres.
Smith, William. N.C. Private. 29 Sep. 1784. 640 acres to Simon Smith, heir.

Smith, William. N.C. Sergeant. 9 Nov. 1784. 1000 acres.
Smith, William. N.C. Private. 18 Aug. 1792. 274 acres.
Smith, William. N.C. Private. 23 Nov. 1797. 640 acres to heirs.
Smith, William. N.C. Private. 28 Nov. 1800. 274 acres.
Smith, William. N.C. Sergeant. 10 Jul. 1805. 1000 acres to heirs.
Smith, William. Pa. Private. 9 Feb. 1787. 200 acres.
Smith, William. S.C. ———. 3 Jan. 1791. 200 acres.
Smith, William. S.C. ———. 6 Nov. 1786. 200 acres.
Smith, William. S.C. ———. 3 Mar. 1788. 200 acres.
Smith, William. Va. Private. 25 Apr. 1783. 200 acres.
Smith, William. Va. Private. 23 Jun. 1783. 200 acres.
Smith, William. Va. Sergeant. 27 Jul. 1783. 200 acres.
Smith, William. Va. Drummer. 17 Sep. 1783. 200 acres.
Smith, William. Va. Lieutenant. 27 May 1783. 2666 2/3 acres.
Smith, William. Va. Private. 22 Jun. 1784. 100 acres.
Smith, William. Va. Private. 17 Jul. 1784. 200 acres.
Smith, William. Va. Boatswain. 8 Nov. 1784. 100 acres.
Smith, William. Va. Sergeant. 28 Apr. 1785. 200 acres.
Smith, William. Va. Private. 31 Aug. 1786. 100 acres.
Smith, William. Va. Lieutenant. 17 Nov. 1787. 2666 2/3 acres.
Smith, William. Va. Boatswain. 26 Nov. 1832. 2566 2/3 acres.
Smith, William. Va. Private. 25 Mar. 1839. 100 acres.
Smith, William. Va. Boatswain. 11 Jan. 1861. 1083 2/3 acres.
Smith, William. Va. Boatswain. 11 Jan. 1861. 200 acres.
Smith, William. Va. Boatswain. 11 Jan. 1861. 1283 acres.
Smith, William Pitt. N.Y. Surgeon's Mate. ———. 1800 acres.
Smith, William S. Va. Lieutenant. 29 Nov. 1782. 2666 2/3 acres.
Smith, William S. Va. Lieutenant. 16 Oct. 1807. 333 acres.
Smith, Willis. N.C. Private. 21 May 1784. 640 acres.
Smith, Wyatt. Va. Private. 19 Dec. 1795. 200 acres.
Smithard, John. Md. Private. ———. 50 acres.
Smither, Benjamin. Va. Private. 22 Dec. 1785. 100 acres.
Smither, Benjamin. Va. Private. 22 Dec. 1785. 100 acres.
Smithers, Stephen. Va. Sergeant. 22 Aug. 1783. 466 2/3 acres.
Smithick, Edward. N.C. Private. 2 Aug. 1784. 640 acres to heir John Smithwick.
Smithson, Samuel. N.C. Private. 12 Dec. 1797. 640 acres.
Smithwick, James. N.C. Private. 26 Aug. 1785. 640 acres.
Smithwick, William. N.C. Corporal. 28 Aug. 1820. 1000 acres to heirs.
Smithy, Benjamin. Va. Private. 27 Jun. 1783. 100 acres.
Smithy, George. N.C. Private. 7 Jan. 1786. 640 acres to heirs.
Smithy, Robert. Va. Private. 26 May 1783. 100 acres.
Smock, Jacob. Va. Sergeant. 23 Jun. 1783. 200 acres.
Smoot, William. Md. Lieutenant. ———. 200 acres.
Smothers, William. Va. Private. 6 Mar. 1784. 200 acres.
Smythe, Joel. N.C. Private. 30 Sep. 1785. 640 acres to heirs.
Snale, Thomas. Va. Lieutenant. 11 Jun. 1833. 4000 acres.
Snale, Thomas. Va. Lieutenant. 11 Jun. 1833. 4000 acres.
Snead, Charles. Ga. ———. 17 May 1784. ———.
Snead, Charles. Va. Captain. 18 Aug. 1823. 4666 2/3 acres.
Snead, Dudley. Ga. Refugee. 17 May 1784. ———.
Snead, Holman. Va. Private. 12 Jul. 1783. 100 acres.
Snead, John. Ga. ———. 5 Sep. 1785. 287 1/2 acres.
Snead, Philip. Va. Sergeant. 5 Dec. 1809. 200 acres.
Snead, Smith. Va. Major. 24 Jun. 1783. 6222 acres.

Snead, Smith. Va. Major. 8 Jun. 1809. 740 acres.
Snead, Thomas. Va. Major. 23 Jun. 1808. 2000 acres.
Snead, Thomas. Va. Major. 23 Jun. 1808. 1000 acres.
Snead, Thomas. Va. Major. 23 Jun. 1808. 1000 acres.
Snead, Thomas. Va. Major. 23 Jun. 1808. 1333 1/3 acres.
Sneed, Christopher. Va. Private. 23 Sep. 1784. 100 acres.
Sneed, Ellick. N.C. Private. 30 Sep. 1785. 640 acres to heirs.
Sneed, George. Va. Private. 15 Jun. 1807. 100 acres.
Sneed, John. N.C. Private. 30 Sep. 1785. 640 acres to heirs.
Sneed, John. Va. Private. 18 Feb. 1784. 100 acres.
Sneed, Robert. Va. Surgeon. 7 Dec. 1830. 4500 acres.
Sneed, Robert. Va. Surgeon. 7 Dec. 1830. 1500 acres.
Sneed, Thomas. Va. Private. 16 Jun. 1783. 100 acres.
Snell, David. Ga. ———. 17 May 1784. ———.
Snell, James. N.C. Private. 22 Mar. 1785. 274 acres.
Snell, James. N.C. Private. 1 Dec. 1797. 274 acres.
Snelling, John. Md. Private. ———. 50 acres.
Snelson, James. Ga. ———. 23 Apr. 1784. 287 1/2 acres.
Snelson, Samuel. Ga. ———. 30 Jul. 1784. 287 1/2 acres.
Snelson, Thomas, Jr. Ga. Sergeant. 15 Apr. 1784. 287 1/2 acres.
Snelson, Thomas, Sr. Ga. ———. 15 Apr. 1784. 287 1/2 acres.
Snidecker, Moses. N. Y. Private. 7 Jul. 1790. 600 acres.
Snider, Drury. N.C. Private. 22 Apr. 1785. 640 acres to heirs.
Sniffen, Amos. N. Y. Private. 8 Jul. 1790. 600 acres.
Sniffin, Nehemiah. N. Y. Private. 8 Jul. 1790. 500 acres.
Snither, Andrew. Ga. ———. 6 Feb. 1784. 250 acres.
Snither, Peter. N.C. Corporal. 30 Sep. 1785. 1000 acres to heirs.
Snodgrass, John. N.C. Private. 11 Feb. 1796. 228 acres.
Snow, Charles. Md. Private. ———. 50 acres.
Snow, Ephraim. N. Y. Lieutenant. 9 Jul. 1790. 1200 acres.
Snow, George. Va.-Ind. Private. 108 acres.
Snow, Paul M. Me. ———. 29 May 1835. 200 acres to widow Mary Snow. Saco.
Snow, Solomon. Mass. ———. 22 Jul. 1833. 200 acres.
Snowden, Cato. Md. Private. ———. 50 acres.
Snowden, John. N. Y. Private. 8 Jul. 1790. 600 acres.
Snowden, Nathaniel. N.C. Lieutenant. 25 Dec. 1820. 2560 acres to heirs.
Snowden, Thomas. Pa. Sergeant. 6 Jul. 1787. 250 acres.
Snowdon, Jonathan. Va. Lieutenant. 13 Dec. 1800. 1000 acres.
Snowdon, Jonathan. Va. Lieutenant. 13 Dec. 1800. 1666 2/3 acres.
Snuckle, Peter. Pa. Private. 18 Oct. 1786. 200 acres.
Snyder, Andrew. Pa. Private. 24 May 1784. 200 acres.
Snyder, Jacob. N. Y. Private. 8 Jul. 1790. 600 acres.
Soles, William. Va. Private. 15 Dec. 1783. 100 acres.
Solesberry, Benjamin. N.C. Private. 15 Feb. 1797. 228 acres.
Sollers, William. Va. Private. 20 Jun. 1783. 100 acres.
Solloman, George. Va. Private. 20 Jun. 1783. 100 acres.
Solomon, Henry. Pa. Private. ———. 200 acres.
Solomon, James. Va. Private. 25 Jul. 1835. 100 acres.
Solomon, Michael. Pa. Private. 4 May 1795. 200 acres to Alexander Power, assignee.
Solomon, Richard. Va. Private. 25 Jul. 1835. 50 acres.
Solomon, Richard. Va. Private. 12 Jan. 1853. 50 acres.
Solomon, Stephen. N.C. Private. 20 Dec. 1796. 640 acres to heirs.
Somerford, Jacob. Ga. Minute Man. 24 May 1784. 287 1/2 acres.
Somerford, Richard. Ga. Minute Man. 24 May 1784. 287 1/2 acres.

Somers, William. Va. Corporal. 23 Sep. 1783. 200 acres.
Somerville, James. Md. Captain. ———. 200 acres.
Sommerhill, James. Ga. ———. ———. 287 1/2 acres.
Sommerhill, Philip. Ga. ———. ———. 287 1/2 acres.
Sommers, Simon. Va. Adjutant. 25 Nov. 1784. 4000 acres.
Sommers, Simon. Va. Captain. 1 Mar. 1817. 666 2/3 acres.
Sommerville, John. Pa. Private. ———. 200 acres.
Son, Anthony. Va. Sergeant. 3 Jul. 1783. 400 acres.
Sorrell, Elisha. Va. Private. 15 Jun. 1820. 100 acres.
Sorrell, James. Va. Private. 9 Dec. 1783. 100 acres.
Sorrell, Richard. Va. Private. 24 May 1784. 100 acres.
Sorrell, Thomas. N.C. Private. 30 Sep. 1785. 640 acres to heirs.
Sorrell, Thomas. Va. Private. 15 Jun. 1820. 100 acres.
Soso, Lewis. N.Y. ———. 8 Jul. 1790. 500 acres.
Soucer, Henry. N. Y. Private. 8 Jul. 1790. 500 acres.
Soule, Charles. Mass. Sergeant. 19 Nov. 1832. 200 acres to heirs.
Soulter, John. Ga. Minute Man. 28 Apr. 1785. ———.
Sours, Michael. Md. Private. ———. 50 acres.
Southall, Joseph. Md. Private. ———. 50 acres.
Southall, Stephen. Va. Lieutenant. 21 Jan. 1784. 2666 2/3 acres.
Southard, John. N. Y. Private. 8 Jul. 1790. 600 acres.
Southerland, George. N.C. Private. 20 Jan. 1785. 274 acres.
Southerland, George. N.C. Private. 2 Feb. 1786. 274 acres.
Southerland, James. N.C. Private. 29 Sep. 1784. 274 acres.
Southerland, John. N.C. Private. 25 Oct. 1783. 274 acres.
Southerland, John. N.C. Private. 5 Sep. 1821. 640 acres.
Southerland, Roger. Conn. Sufferer. Greenwich. 14.12.2.
Southerland, William. N.C. Private. 20 Jan. 1785. 640 acres to heirs.
Southerland, William. Va. Private. 3 May 1784. 200 acres.
Southworth, Thomas. Va. Private. 28 Jun. 1783. 200 acres.
Sowell, John. N.C. Private. 12 Dec. 1806. 640 acres to heirs.
Sowell, Lewis. N.C. Private. 26 May 1784. 640 acres.
Sowell, Obadiah. N.C. Private. 30 Sep. 1785. 640 acres to heirs.
Sowell, Zadock. N.C. Private. 2 Aug. 1784. 228 acres.
Space, John. N. Y. Drummer. 8 Jul. 1790. 600 acres.
Spaerpoint, Joseph. N.C. Private. 22 Dec. 1796. 640 acres.
Spaight, Joseph. N.C. Private. 20 Oct. 1792. 640 acres.
Spain, Austin. N.C. Sergeant. Aug. 1787. 428 acres.
Spain, Epes. N.C. Sergeaent. Aug. 1787. 1000 acres.
Spain, Thomas. N.C. Fifer. Aug. 1787. 1000 acres.
Spain, William. N.C. Fifer. Aug. 1787. 1000 acres.
Spalding, Aaron. Md. Sergeant. ———. 50 acres.
Spalding, Charles. Va. Private. 21 Apr. 1785. 100 acres.
Spalding, Edmund. N.C. Private. 30 Sep. 1785. 640 acres to heirs.
Spalding, Grace. Conn. Sufferer. Fairfield. 90.4.4.
Spalding, John. Pa. Private. 17 May 1795. 200 acres to George Vannadeer, assignee.
Spalding, John. Pa. Drummer. 9 Nov. 1786. 200 acres to Stephen Loudon, assignee.
Spalding, Samuel. Me. Private. 24 Dec. 1839. 200 acres. Frankfort.
Span, James. Va. Private. 8 Aug. 1783. 100 acres.
Span, Richard. Va. Private. 8 Aug. 1783. 100 acres.
Spang, David. Va. Private. 29 Jul. 1785. 100 acres.
Spann, Charles. Ga. ———. 13 Apr. 1787. 450 acres.
Spann, George. Ga. ———. 16 Apr. 1787. 287 1/2 acres.

Spann, James. N.C. Private. 2 Dec. 1785. 228 acres.
Spann, Willis. N.C. Private. 19 May 1784. 228 acres.
Sparkes, Joseph. N.C. Private. 12 Sep. 1785. 640 acres to heirs.
Sparkman, Edward. N.C. Private. 30 Sep. 1785. 640 acres to heirs.
Sparkman, William. N.C. Private. 30 Sep. 1785. 640 acres to heirs.
Sparks, Samuel. Va. Private. 20 Jun. 1783. 200 acres.
Sparks, Solomon. Pa. ———. 17 Dec. 1802. 200 acres.
Speak, Nathan. Md. Private. ———. 50 acres.
Speak, William. Va. Private. 27 Dec. 1813. 100 acres.
Speake, Joseph. Va. Lieutenant. 4 Apr. 1835. 2000 acres.
Speake, Joseph. Va. Lieutenant. 4 Apr. 1835. 666 2/3 acres.
Speake, Joseph. Va. Lieutenant. 30 Apr. 1835. 1000 acres.
Speake, Joseph. Va. Lieutenant. 30 Apr. 1835. 1000 acres.
Speake, Joseph. Va. Lieutenant. 30 Apr. 1835. 1000 acres.
Speake, Joseph. Va. Lieutenant. 30 Apr. 1835. 1000 acres.
Speakman, Henry. Va. Private. 14 Feb. 1834. 100 acres.
Spear, David. N.C. Sergeant. 24 Jul. 1820. 428 acres.
Spear, Edward. Pa. Lieutenant. 11 Jun. 1795. 200 acres to John Cadwalader in trust.
Spear, Edward. Pa. Lieutenant. ———. 200 acres.
Spear, Edward. Pa. Lieutenant. ———. 200 acres.
Spear, Jacob. Va.-Ind. Private. 108 acres.
Spear, John. N.C. Private. 24 Jul. 1821. 640 acres to heirs.
Spear, John. Pa. Sergeant. 13 Oct. 1786. 250 acres.
Spear, Seth. N.C. Private. 2 Feb. 1786. 640 acres.
Spearman, James. Va. Sergeant. 7 Oct. 1783. 200 acres.
Spearpoint, John. N.C. Private. 20 Apr. 1784. 640 acres.
Spears, John. N. Y. Corporal. 7 Jul. 1790. 600 acres.
Speider, Jacob. Pa. ———. 2 Jul. 1812. 200 acres.
Speight, Francis. N.C. Private. 30 Sep. 1785. 640 acres to heirs.
Speigle, Laurence. Pa. ———. 5 Jan. 1803. 200 acres.
Speirs, Thomas. N.C. Private. 5 Dec. 1796. 640 acres.
Spells, Henry. N.C. Private. 13 Sep. 1820. 228 acres.
Spelmon, Simon. N.C. Private. 13 Dec. 1796. 640 acres.
Spelmore, Jacob. N.C. Private. 17 Feb. 1824. 640 acres.
Spelsbury, Jacob. N.Y. ———. 13 Sep. 1790. 500 acres to heirs.
Spence, David. Pa. Private. 21 Aug 1787. 200 acres.
Spence, Henry. Va. Private. 18 Jun. 1783. 100 acres.
Spence, Incel. N.C. Private. 17 Feb. 1824. 640 acres.
Spence, James. N.C. Private. 22 Apr. 1785. 228 acres.
Spence, James. Pa. Private. 23 Oct. 1942. 200 acres.
Spence, James. Pa. Private. 16 Mar. 1803. 200 acres to Thomas Shields, assignee.
Spence, Jobe. N.C. Private. 17 Dec. 1785. 274 acres.
Spence, John. S.C. Soldier. 16 Jul. 1784. 200 acres.
Spence, Robert. S.C. ———. 7 Aug. 1786. 110 acres.
Spence, William. N.C. Private. 30 Sep. 1785. 640 acres to heirs.
Spencer, Abraham. Va. Private. 1783. 200 acres.
Spencer, Amos. Va. Private. 11 Dec. 1798. 100 acres.
Spencer, Benjamin. Va. Private. 19 Jun. 1783. 200 acres.
Spencer, Beverley. Va. Private. 30 Jan. 1784. 100 acres.
Spencer, Calvin. S.C. Captain. 2 Nov. 1789. 300 acres.
Spencer, Gideon. Va. Lieutenant. 26 Dec. 1832. 2666 2/3 acres.
Spencer, Humphrey. Md. Sergeant. ———. 50 acres.
Spencer, John. Va. Lieutenant. 23 Mar. 1784. 2666 2/3 acres.
Spencer, John. Va. Private. 14 Jun. 1784. 100 acres.

Spencer, John. Conn. Sufferer. New London. 58.8.0.
Spencer, Joseph. Va. Captain. 20 May 1823. 1000 acres.
Spencer, Joseph. Va. Captain. 20 May 1823. 1000 acres.
Spencer, Joseph. Va. Captain. 20 May 1823. 1000 acres.
Spencer, Joseph. Va. Captain. 20 May 1823. 1000 acres.
Spencer, Joseph H. Md. Sergeant. ———. 50 acres.
Spencer, Moses. Va. Private. 21 Apr. 1785. 100 acres.
Spencer, Robert. N.C. Private. 17 Feb. 1824. 640 acres.
Spencer, Solomon. Me. ———. 1 May 1835. 200 acres. Hartford.
Spencer, Tamerlane. Md. ———. ———. 50 acres.
Spencer, Thomas. Va. Lieutenant. 2 Mar. 1833. 2666 2/3 acres.
Spencer, Thomas J. Va. Lieutenant. 16 Feb. 1836. 380 1/6 acres.
Spencer, Thomas J. Va. Lieutenant. 16 Feb. 1836. 380 1/6 acres.
Spencer, Thomas J. Va. Lieutenant. 16 Feb. 1836. 380 1/6 acres.
Spencer, Thomas J. Va. Lieutenant. 16 Feb. 1836. 380 1/6 acres.
Spencer, Thomas J. Va. Lieutenant. 16 Feb. 1836. 380 1/6 acres.
Spencer, Thomas J. Va. Lieutenant. 16 Feb. 1836. 380 1/6 acres.
Spencer, Thomas J. Va. Lieutenant. 16 Feb. 1836. 380 1/6 acres.
Spencer, William. Ga. Refugee. 26 May 1784. 287 1/2 acres.
Spencer, William. Va. Lieutenant. 11 Feb. 1784. 2666 2/3 acres.
Spencer, William. Va. Private. 22 May 1786. 100 acres.
Spencer, William. Va. Private. 23 Jan. 1788. 200 acres.
Spencer, William. Va. Subaltern. 3 Mar. 1808. 1333 1/3 acres.
Spencer, William. Va. Subaltern. 3 Mar. 1808. 888 8/9 acres.
Spendler, Boston. N.C. Private. 22 Dec. 1796. 274 acres.
Spering, John. Pa. Private. 10 Dec. 1808. 200 acres to Samuel Cochran, assignee.
Sperry, Benjamin. Conn. Sufferer. Danbury. 113.4.2.
Sperry, Timothy. Conn. Sufferer. New/East Haven. 30.13.2.
Spicely, James. Va. Private. 17 Jun. 1833. 200 acres.
Spicer, Jacob. N. Y. Private. 8 Jul. 1790. 500 acres.
Spicer, John. N.C. Private. 3 Dec. 1800. 640 acres to heir William Spicer.
Spicer, John. N.C. Paymaster. 5 Aug. 1821. 1920 acres to heirs.
Spickard, George. Va. Private. 22 Jul. 1824. 100 acres.
Spieglar, Henry. N. Y. Private. 8 Jul. 1790. 600 acres.
Spiers, Caleb. Va. Private. 14 Feb. 1834. 100 acres.
Spiers, Jonathan. N. Y. Private. 7 Jul. 1790. 500 acres.
Spiers, Spencer. N.C. Private. 19 May 1784. 640 acres.
Spikes, Elias. Ga. Minute Man. 22 Mar. 1785. 250 acres.
Spikes, Joseph. Ga. Private. 5 Sep. 1785. 250 acres.
Spikes, Nathan. Ga. Private. 10 Dec. 1784. 250 acres.
Spiller, Benjamin. Va. Captain. 1 Mar. 1785. 4000 acres.
Spiller, Cave. Va. Private. 29 Dec. 1808. 100 acres.
Spiller, William. Va. Captain. 20 Jan. 1783. 4000 acres.
Spiller, William. Va. Captain. 4 Apr. 1831. 222 1/3 acres.
Spiller, William. Va. Captain. 4 Apr. 1831. 222 1/3 acres.
Spiller, William. Va. Captain. 4 Apr. 1831. 222 1/3 acres.
Spilman, Francis. Va.-Ind. Private. 108 acres.
Spilman, James. Va.-Ind. Private. 108 acres.
Spinck, Lydia. Conn. Sufferer. New London. 9.13.9.
Spinks, Joseph. Md. Private. ———. 50 acres.
Spinks, Rawling. Md. Matross. ———. 50 acres.
Spinner, Richard. Va. Private. 24 Aug. 1784. 100 acres.
Spire, John. Md. Private. ———. 50 acres.
Spires, Absalom. N.C. Private. 22 Oct. 1783. 360 acres.

Spires, Richard. Md. Private. ———. 50 acres.
Spitfatham, John. Va. Ensign. 5 Jul. 1809. 1233 1/3 acres.
Spitfatham, John. Va. Ensign. 5 Jul. 1809. 1233 1/3 acres.
Spitfatham, John. Va. Ensign. 14 Dec. 1809. 259 acres.
Spitfathom, John. Va. Ensign. 14 Dec. 1809. 259 acres.
Spitzfathem, John. Va. Sergeant. 5 Feb. 1785. 200 acres.
Spivey, Moses. N.C. Private. 12 Dec. 1796. 640 acres.
Splann, Thomas. Va. Private. 5 Jul. 1783. 100 acres.
Splendor, Boston. N.C. Private. 10 Jan. 1794. 640 acres.
Spoolman, William. N.C. Sergeant. 22 Apr. 1785. 1000 acres.
Spooner, Judas P. Conn. Sufferer. New London. 21.12.0.
Spooner, William. Mass. Bombardier. 1 Feb. 1833. 200 acres to heirs.
Spotswood, Alexander. Va. Colonel. 25 Nov. 1795. 6000 acres.
Spotswood, Alexander. Va. Brigadier General. 28 Mar. 1834. 6777 1/3 acres.
Spotswood, Alexander. Va. ———. 11 May 1836. 904 acres.
Spotswood, Alexander. Va. ———. 11 May 1836. 904 acres.
Spotswood, Alexander. Va. ———. 11 May 1836. 904 acres.
Spotswood, Alexander. Va. ———. 11 May 1836. 904 acres.
Spotswood, Alexander. Va. ———. 11 May 1836. 904 acres.
Spotswood, Alexander. Va. Brigadier General. 3 May 1855. 150 1/2 acres.
Spotswood, Alexander. Va. Brigadier General. 7 Nov. 1856. 225 acres.
Spotswood, Alexander. Va. ———. 19 Aug. 1836. 603 acres.
Spotswood, Alexander. Va. ———. 19 Aug. 1836. 301 acres.
Spotswood, John. Va. Captain. 15 Apr. 1783. 4000 acres.
Spotswood, John. Va. Captain. 2 Oct. 1807. 333 1/3 acres.
Spotswood, John. Va. Captain. 2 Oct. 1807. 333 1/3 acres.
Spottswood, Alexander. Va. ———. 18 Mar. 1835. 1129 1/3 acres.
Spottswood, Alexander. Va. ———. 18 Mar. 1835. 564 2/5 acres.
Spottswood, Alexander. Va. ———. 18 Mar. 1835. 564 2/5 acres.
Spottswood, Alexander. Va. ———. 18 Mar. 1835. 4519 1/3 acres.
Sprague, Joseph. Conn. Sufferer. Fairfield. 2.3.8.
Sprague, Lazarus. N. Y. Private. 8 Jul. 1790. 600 acres.
Sprague, William. S.C. Navy Captain's Clerk. 21 Jan. 1785. 200 acres.
Spraphon, William. Pa. Private. 15 Feb. 1787. 200 acres.
Sprat, Charles. N.C. Private. 9 Dec. 1797. 228 acres.
Spratley, Richard. Va. Corporal. 2 May 1783. 200 acres.
Spratley, Richard. Va. Corporal. 6 Mar. 1839. 200 acres.
Spratlin, James. Ga. ———. 23 Apr. 1784. 750 acres.
Sprig, Nathan. Va. Sailor. 10 Sep. 1787. 100 acres.
Spriggs, John. Md. Private. ———. 50 acres.
Spring, Henry. N. Y. Private. 7 Jul. 1790. 500 acres.
Spring, Josiah. Me. Soldier. 14 Aug. 1835. 200 acres. Brownfield.
Springer, Jacob. Va. Lieutenant. 23 Mar. 1783. 1300 acres.
Springer, Jacob. Va. Lieutenant. 23 Mar. 1783. 1366 2/3 acres.
Springer, Jacob. Va. Lieutenant. 6 Mar. 1807. 444 2/3 acres.
Springer, John. Conn. Sufferer. New London. 17.19.0.
Springer, Philip. Pa. Private. 12 Dec. 1786. 200 acres.
Springer, Silvester. S.C. Surgeon's Mate. 3 Jul. 1786. 200 acres.
Springer, Uriah. Va. Captain. 31 Mar. 1783. 2000 acres.
Springer, Uriah. Va. Captain. 31 Mar. 1783. 2000 acres.
Springer, Uriah. Va. Captain. 11 Mar. 1800. 666 2/3 acres.
Springs, Sedgwick. N.C. Private. 26 Dec. 1821. 228 acres.
Springsteen, Abraham. N. Y. Private. 8 Jul. 1790. 600 acres.
Springsteen, George. N. Y. Private. 8 Jul. 1790. 600 acres.

Sprout, William. Pa. Captain. 2 Mar. 1797. 500 acres to heirs.
Spruce, John. Va. Private. 28 May 1783. 100 acres.
Spruell, Richard. N.C. Private. 30 Sep. 1785. 640 acres to heirs.
Spur, John. Va. Sergeant. 18 Nov. 1788. 200 acres.
Spurlock, Robert. Ga. Private. 21 Apr. 1784. 287 1/2 acres to heirs.
Spurrier, Edward. Md. Captain. ———. 200 acres.
Spyers, William. Md. ———. ———. 50 acres.
Squire, Ann. Conn. Sufferer. New London. 7.10.0.
Squire, Benjamin. Conn. Sufferer. Fairfield. 1.7.0.
Squire, Ebenezer. Conn. Sufferer. Fairfield. 14.14.4.
Squire, John, Jr. Conn. Sufferer. Fairfield. 15.16.8.
Squire, Joseph. Conn. Sufferer. Fairfield. 65.0.6.
Squire, Joshua and Samuel Burr. Conn. Sufferers. Fairfield. 35.17.6.
Squire, Samuel. Conn. Sufferer. Fairfield. 412.15.4.
Squire, Samuel, 2d. Conn. Sufferer. Fairfield. 83.6.8.
Squires, Andrew. N.C. Private. 28 Nov. 1795. 640 acres to heirs.
Squires, John. N.C. Private. 4 Dec. 1783. 320 acres.
Squires, Thomas. N.C. Private. 28 Aug. 1820. 640 acres to heirs.
Squirrel, Jacob. N. Y. Sergeant. 8 Jul. 1790. 500 acres.
St.Lawrence, George. N. Y. Corporal. 3 Jul. 1790. 600 acres.
St.Clair, George. N. Y. Matross. 9 Jul. 1790. 600 acres.
St.Lawrence, Etienne. N. Y. ———. ———. 500 acres.
St.Pierre, John Baptiste. N. Y. ———. ———. 500 acres.
St.Clair, Daniel. Pa. Lieutenant. 28 Feb. 1794. 200 acres.
St.John, John. Pa. Private. 6 Oct. 1786. 200 acres.
St.Clair, Arthur. Pa. General. 28 Feb. 1794. 500 acres.
St.Clair, Daniel. Pa. ———. 23 Feb. 1785. 200 acres.
St.Clair, Daniel. Pa. Lieutenant. 21 Aug. 1787. 200 acres.
St.Clair, Arthur. Pa. Major General. 21 Aug. 1787. 500 acres.
St.Clair, Arthur. Pa. Major General. 21 Aug. 1787. 500 acres.
St. Clair, Arthur. Pa. Major General. 21 Aug. 1787. 500 acres.
St.Clair, Daniel. Pa. Lieutenant. 27 Aug. 1787. 200 acres.
St.Clair, Arthur. Pa. Major General. 21 Aug. 1787. 500 acres.
St.Marie, Levacher de. S.C. Captain. 21 Jan. 1785. 300 acres.
St.Leger, William. Va. Private. 2 Sep. 1783. 100 acres.
St.John, John. Conn. Sufferer. Norwalk. 51.16.3.
St.John, William. Conn. Sufferer. Norwalk. 318.11.0.
St.John, Nehemiah. Conn. Sufferer. Norwalk. 89.9.6.
St.John, Stephen, Col. Conn. Sufferer. Norwalk. 713.6.7.
St.John, Stephen. Conn. Sufferer. Norwalk. 20.1.0.
St.John, Moses. Conn. Sufferer. Norwalk. 3.5.0.
St.John, Nehemiah, 2nd. Conn. Sufferer. Norwalk. 6.11.0.
St.John, Esther. Conn. Sufferer. Norwalk. 2.2.0.
St.John, Stephen and Hooker St.John. Conn. Sufferers. Norwalk. 30.1.6.
St.John, William. Conn. Sufferer. Norwalk. 35.12.0.
Stacey, John. Va. Private. 2 Sep. 1783. 100 acres.
Stacey, Simon. Va. Private. 6 Dec. 1783. 100 acres.
Stacey, Stephen. Va. Private. 4 Mar. 1784 100 acres.
Stack, Abraham. Ga. ———. 23 Apr. 1784. 500 acres.
Stack, Richard. Pa. Fife Major. 11 Apr. 1787. 200 acres to Stephen Loudon, assignee.
Stackhouse, John. Md. Private. ———. 50 acres.
Stackhouse, John. Va. Private. 4 Nov. 1784. 100 acres.
Stackpale, James. Va. Private. 23 Jun. 1783. 200 acres.

Stacy, William. Pa. Private. ———. 200 acres.
Stadelman, John. Pa. Private. 16 Oct. 1785. 200 acres.
Stader, George. N.C. Sergeant. 11 Jul. 1785. 1000 acres.
Stafford, David. Va. Private. 18 Apr. 1801. 100 acres.
Stafford, John. N.C. Private. 17 Feb. 1824. 640 acres.
Stafford, Josiah. N.C. Private. 20 Dec. 1784. 274 acres.
Stafford, Samuel. Ga. ———. 13 Apr. 1784. 287 1/2 acres.
Stafford, William. Ga. ———. 17 May 1784. ———.
Stagg, Jasper. N. Y. Private. 3 Jul. 1790. 600 acres.
Stagg, John. N. Y. Private. 3 Jul. 1790. 600 acres.
Stagg, John. N.Y. ———. 13 Sep. 1790. 500 acres to heirs.
Stagg, John, Jr. N. Y. Lieutenant. 9 Jul. 1790. 1200 acres.
Stags, Richard. Va. Private. 24 Nov. 1817. 200 acres.
Stake, Jacob. Pa. Captain. 30 Jul. 1787. 500 acres.
Stake, John. N. Y. Cornet. 6 Jul. 1790. 1150 acres.
Stalker, William. Md. Matross. ———. 50 acres.
Stall, George. Pa. Private. 12 July 1787. 200 acres.
Stall, John C. N.Y. ———. 13 Sep. 1790. 500 acres to heirs.
Stallings, Abraham. Md. Drummer. ———. 50 acres.
Stallings, Ezekiel. Ga. Refugee. 20 Feb. 1784. 287 1/2 acres.
Stallings, Frederick. Ga. Captain. 21 Apr. 1784. 575 acres to heirs.
Stallings, Frederick. Ga. ———. 21 Apr. 1784. 287 1/2 acres to heirs.
Stallings, James. Ga. Lieutenant. 21 Apr 1784. 402 1/2 acres.
Stallings, James. Ga. Refugee. 24 Dec. 1783. 250 acres.
Stallings, Jesse. Ga. Soldier. 22 Apr. 1784. 287 1/2 acres.
Stallings, John. Ga. Refugee. 23 Apr. 1784. 287 1/2 acres.
Stallings, Malachi. Ga. ———. 17 May 1784. ———.
Stallions, James. N.C. Private. 22 Apr. 1785. 640 acres to heir.
Stalman, William. Pa. Matross. 20 Feb. 1787. 200 acres.
Stammers, John. Pa. Private. 27 June 1789. 200 acres.
Stamper, Daniel. Ga. ———. 30 Jul. 1784. 287 1/2 acres.
Stamper, Powell. Ga. ———. 21 Apr. 1784. 287 1/2 acres.
Stamper, Robert. Ga. ———. 30 Jul. 1784. 287 1/2 acres.
Stamps, Timothy. Ga. ———. 17 May 1784. ———.
Stanaland, James. N.C. Private. 29 Sep. 1784. 640 acres to Benjamin Stanaland, Jr., heir.
Stanaland, Robert. N.C. Sergeant. 29 Sep. 1784. 1000 acres to Benjamin Stanaland, Jr., heir.
Stanback, Littleberry. Va. Sailor. 23 Jun. 1784. 100 acres.
Stancil, Peter. N.C. Private. 22 Dec. 1796. 640 acres to heirs.
Standen, John. N.C. Private. 12 Sep. 1789. 502 acres.
Standfast, William. N.C. Private. 14 Dec. 1796. 640 acres to heirs.
Standley, Handcock. N.C. Private. 30 Sep. 1785. 640 acres to heirs.
Standley, Jacob. Md. Private. ———. 50 acres.
Standley, James. N.C. Private. 28 May 1784. 274 acres.
Standley, John, Jr. Md. Matross. ———. 50 acres.
Standley, Jonathan. N.C. Private. 29 Sep. 1784. 274 acres.
Standley, Moses. Va. Private. 22 Jun. 1784. 100 acres.
Standley, Moses. Va. Private. 22 Jun. 1810. 100 acres.
Standley, Peter. Pa. Private. ———. 200 acres.
Standley, Robert. N.C. Sergeant. 28 May 1784. 428 acres.
Standley, Robert. N.C. Private. 14 Dec. 1796. 640 acres to heirs.
Standley, Sand. Ga. ———. 21 Apr. 1784. 1000 acres.
Standley, Thomas. Md. Matross. ———. 50 acres.
Standley, William. Md. Private. ———. 50 acres.

Standly, Michael. Md. Private. ———. 50 acres.
Stanford, John. Ga. ———. 15 Apr. 1784. 287 1/2 acres.
Stanford, John. Me. ———. 16 Apr. 1836. 200 acres. Cape Elizabeth.
Stanford, Moses. Mass. Private. 9 Jul. 1834. 200 acres.
Stanford, William. Ga ———. 30 Sep. 1784. 287 1/2 acres.
Stanley, Adin. Me. Private. 11 May 1835. 200 acres. Winthrop.
Stanley, Dempsey. Ga. ———. 19 Jul. 1784. 287 1/2 acres.
Stanley, John. Ga. ———. 21 Apr. 1784. 200 acres.
Stanley, Shadrack. Ga. ———. 21 Apr. 1784. 500 acres.
Stanley, Shadrack. Ga. ———. ———. 250 acres.
Stanley, Solady. Md. Private. ———. 50 acres.
Stanley, William. Pa. Lieutenant. 9 Oct. 1786. 200 acres.
Stanley, William. Pa. Lieutenant. 11 Oct.1786. 200 acres.
Stanley, William. Va. Private. 5 Dec. 1783. 100 acres.
Stanly, James. N.C. Private. 3 Aug. 1821. 640 acres to heirs.
Stanniker, Francis. N.C. Private. 20 Dec. 1796. 640 acres to heirs.
Stansbury, Luke. N.C. Private. 22 Dec. 1796. 274 acres.
Stanton, John. Md. Private. ———. 50 acres.
Stanton, John. N.C. Sergeant. 5 Aug. 1820. 1000 acres to heirs.
Stanton, Thankful. Conn. Sufferer. Groton. 0.8.9.
Stape, Thomas. Va. Drummer. 28 Jan. 1784. 200 acres.
Stapler, John. Ga. ———. 21 Apr. 1784. 287 1/2 acres.
Stapler, Thomas. Ga. ———. 21 Apr. 1784. 287 1/2 acres.
Staples, Joseph. Me. ———. 2 Jun. 1835. 200 acres to widow Louisa Staples. Beddiford.
Staples, Joseph. Me. ———. 2 Jun. 1835. 200 acres to widow Louisa Staples. Biddeford.
Staples, Joseph. Va. Sergeant. 30 Dec. 1784. 200 acres.
Staples, Robert. N.C. Private. 27 Jun. 1788. 228 acres.
Staples, Robert. N.C. Musician. 18 Nov. 1820. 772 acres to heirs.
Staples, Stephen. Me. Soldier. 17 Oct. 1835. 200 acres to widow Charity (Coombs) Staples. Lisbon.
Staples, Thomas. Conn. Sufferer. Fairfield. 247.4.7.
Starbird, Samuel. Me. ———. 27 Apr. 1835. 200 acres. Lisbon.
Stark, Richard. Va. ———. 15 Feb. 1783. 2666 2/3 acres.
Stark, Thomas. Ga. ———. 22 Apr. 1784. 287 1/2 acres.
Stark, William. Conn. Sufferer. New London. 17.9.10.
Starke, Richard. Va. Lieutenant. 8 Dec. 1796. 444 1/2 acres.
Starke, William. Va. Lieutenant. 9 Feb. 1784. 2666 2/3 acres.
Starkey, John. Md. Private. ———. 50 acres.
Starkey, William. N.C. Private. 6 May 1784. 640 acres.
Starlings, Palishia. Ga. Citizen. 6 Apr. 1785. 287 1/2 acres.
Starnbaragh, Elijah. N. Y. Private. 8 Jul. 1790. 500 acres.
Starr & Tallman. Conn. Sufferer. New London. 150.0.0.
Starr, Abigail. Conn. Sufferer. New/East Haven. 14.1.0.
Starr, Christianna. Conn. Sufferer. Danbury. 6.1.2.
Starr, Ezra. Conn. Sufferer. Danbury. 1,214.11.4.
Starr, Hance. N.C. Private. 30 Nov. 1785. 640 acres to heirs.
Starr, John. Conn. Sufferer. Groton. 0.19.6.
Starr, Jonathan & J. Starr. Conn. Sufferers. New London. 53.2.3.
Starr, Joshua. Conn. Sufferer. Danbury. 4.16.0.
Starr, Joshua. Conn. Sufferer. New London. 1,250.11.1.
Starr, Josiah. Conn. Sufferer. Danbury. 9.3.8.
Starr, Josiah. Conn. Sufferer. Danbury. 13.5.8.
Starr, Lucy. Conn. Sufferer. New London. 5.9.8.
Starr, Matthew. Conn. Sufferer. Danbury. 2.12.0.

Starr, Nathaniel. Conn. Sufferer. Danbury. 4.7.4.
Starr, Thomas. Conn. Sufferer. Danbury. 9.5.1.
Statt, John. Ga. Minute Man. 4 May 1785. 287 1/2 acres.
Statt, Peter. Ga. Minute Man. 19 Dec. 1786. 287 1/2 acres.
Statten, Joseph. Ga. ———. 22 Apr. 1784. 287 1/2 acres.
Stauffer, Henry. Pa. Private. 12 Jul. 1787. 200 acres.
Staves, William. Va. Private. 26 Apr. 1783. 200 acres.
Steadham, Tobias. N.C. Private. 30 Sep. 1785. 640 acres to heirs.
Steagall, John Potter. Ga. ———. 26 Jul. 1784. 200 acres.
Steagle, Conrad. Va. Private. 14 Mar. 1840. 100 acres.
Stearn, Moses. N.C. Private. 23 May 1821. 640 acres.
Stearn, Peter. N.C. Private. 2 Feb. 1786. 640 acres to heirs.
Stebbins, Ebenezer. Conn. Sufferer. Ridgefield. 1.19.8.
Stebbins, Joseph. Conn. Sufferer. Ridgefield. 19.16.0.
Stedham, Isaiah. N.C. Private. 30 Sep. 1785. 640 acres to heirs.
Stedman, Benjamin. N.C. Captain. 16 Aug. 1821. 3840 acres.
Stedman, James. Ga. Lieutenant. 16 Mar. 1784. 400 acres to heirs.
Stedman, John. Ga. Soldier. 8 Dec. 1784. ———.
Stedman, Sarah. Conn. Sufferer. Groton. 0.14.2.
Stedmore, James. N.C. Private. 30 Sep. 1785. 640 acres to heirs.
Stedmore, John. N.C. Private. 30 Sep. 1785. 640 acres.
Stedmore, Peter. N.C. Private. 30 Sep. 1785. 640 acres to heirs.
Stedom, John. Ga. ———. 1784. 287 1/2 acres.
Steed, Edward. Ga. Minute Man. 17 Jan. 1785. 287 1/2 acres.
Steed, Jesse. N.C. Sergeant. 20 Apr. 1784. 357 acres.
Steed, John. Va. Captain. 13 Jun. 1783. 4000 acres.
Steed, John. Va. Captain. 12 Dec. 1798. 666 2/3 acres.
Steed, Philip. Ga. Soldier. 20 Apr. 1784. 287 1/2 acres.
Steede, Jesse. N.C. Lieutenant. 21 Oct. 1783. 2560 acres.
Steedinger, John. Pa. Private. 20 Aug. 1787. 200 acres.
Steedwell, Thomas. Conn. Sufferer. Greenwich. 2.6.4.
Steel, Charles. S.C. ———. 4 Jul. 1785. 200 acres.
Steel, David. Va. Captain. 25 Oct. 1806. 2000 acres.
Steel, David. Va. Captain. 25 Oct. 1806. 2000 acres.
Steel, Franics. Pa. Private. 15 Nov. 1786. 200 acres.
Steel, John. Ga. ———. 20 Apr. 1784. 460 acres.
Steel, John. Va. Lieutenant. 20 May 1783. 2666 2/3 acres.
Steel, John. Va. Lieutenant. 8 Feb. 1808. 388 2/3 acres.
Steel, John Philip. Pa. Private. 19 Sep. 1787. 200 acres.
Steel, Thomas. Pa. Private. 20 Aug. 1787. 200 acres.
Steel, William. Va. Lieutenant. 26 Aug. 1783. 1000 acres.
Steel, William. Va. Lieutenant. 26 Aug. 1783. 1666 2/3 acres.
Steele, James. N. Y. Private. 8 Jul. 1790. 600 acres.
Steele, John. Pa. Captain. 28 Aug. 1787. 500 acres.
Steele, Nicholas. Ga. Minute Man. 3 Apr. 1785. ———.
Steele, William. Va. Lieutenant. 25 Jan. 1841. 1333 1/3 acres.
Steell, John. N.C. Private. 2 Feb. 1786. 640 acres to heirs.
Steelley, Jeremiah. N.C. Private. 2 Feb. 1786. 640 acres.
Steem [or Stumm], George. Md. Private. ———. 50 acres.
Stein, Edward. Pa. Private. 29 Sep. 1787. 200 acres.
Stemm, William. N.C. Private. 8 Aug. 1821. 640 acres.
Step, Abraham. N.C. Sergeant. 7 Jan. 1786. 1000 acres to heirs.
Step, Henry. N.C. Private. 2 Nov. 1795. 640 acres to heirs.
Stephard, Edward. Va. Private. 23 Jun. 1783. 200 acres.

Stephen, John. Va. Private. 26 Jan. 1820. 100 acres.

Stephens, Alexander. Pa. Private. 26 Sep. 1787. 200 acres to William Banquett, assignee.

Stephens, Barnaby. N.C. Private. 9 Feb. 1796. 228 acres.

Stephens, Benjamin. Ga. Minute Man. 4 May 1785. 287 1/2 acres.

Stephens, Gabriel. Va. Private. 18 Dec. 1818. 100 acres.

Stephens, Henry. N.C. Private. 30 Sep. 1785. 640 acres to heirs.

Stephens, James. Ga. ———. ———. 287 1/2 acres.

Stephens, Jesse. S.C. ———. 5 May 1788. 200 acres.

Stephens, Jesse. Conn. Sufferer. New/East Haven. 18.17.4.

Stephens, John. Ga. Soldier. 13 Apr. 1784. 287 1/2 acres.

Stephens, John. N.C. Private. 31 Jan. 1795. 640 acres to heirs.

Stephens, John. N.C. Private. 16 Dec. 1814. 274 acres.

Stephens, John. Va. Sergeant. 9 Oct. 1783. 200 acres.

Stephens, John. Va. Private. 22 Dec. 1784. 100 acres.

Stephens, John. Va. Private. 21 Dec. 1790. 200 acres.

Stephens, Joseph. Ga. ———. ———. 287 1/2 acres.

Stephens, Joseph. N.C. Private. 17 Dec. 1785. 640 acres to heirs.

Stephens, Joseph. S.C. Soldier. 5 Sep. 1785. 200 acres.

Stephens, Moses. Ga. ———. 22 Apr. 1784. 287 1/2 acres.

Stephens, Oliver. Md. Private. ———. 50 acres.

Stephens, Peter. Md. Private. ———. 50 acres.

Stephens, Richard. Va. Private. 5 Feb. 1784. 100 acres.

Stephens, Simon. Va. Seaman. 5 Jun. 1833. 100 acres.

Stephens, Stephen. Ga. ———. 5 Dec. 1785. 287 1/2 acres.

Stephens, Stephen. Va. Seaman. 5 Jun. 1833. 100 acres.

Stephens, Theodore. N. Y. Matross. 9 Jul. 1790. 500 acres.

Stephens, Thomas. N.C. Private. 8 May 1784. 640 acres.

Stephens, Thomas. Va. Corporal. 21 Jul. 1783. 466 2/3 acres.

Stephens, William. Mass. Private. 1 Mar. 1833. 200 acres.

Stephenson, Alexander. Md. Drummer. ———. 50 acres.

Stephenson, Benjamin. N.C. Private. 10 Sep. 1821. 640 acres to heirs.

Stephenson, David. Va. Major. 16 Apr. 1783. 6222 acres.

Stephenson, David. Va. Major. 18 Sep. 1807. 777 acres.

Stephenson, George. Pa. Private. 28 Mar. 1784. 200 acres.

Stephenson, Hugh. Va. Colonel. 21 Apr. 1784. 6666 2/3 acres.

Stephenson, Hugh. Va. Colonel. 18 Dec. 1838. 1003 acres.

Stephenson, James. N.C. Sergeant. 12 Dec. 1797. 1000 acres to heirs.

Stephenson, John. N.C. Private. 26 Aug. 1785. 640 acres to heirs.

Stephenson, John. Va. Major. 17 Apr. 1821. 3555 1/3 acres.

Stephenson, John. Va. Major. 17 Apr. 1821. 1777 2/3 acres.

Stephenson, John R. N.C. Private. 8 Dec. 1795. 640 acres to heirs.

Stephenson, Jonathan. N.C. Private. 15 Feb. 1797. 640 acres to heirs.

Stephenson, Peter. N.C. Private. 2 Feb. 1786. 274 acres.

Stephenson, Samuel. Va.-Ind. Private. 108 acres.

Stephenson, Silas S. N.C. Captain. 29 Dec. 1821. 1097 acres to James Hart of Carteret Co.

Stephenson, William. Ga. ———. 19 Apr. 1784. 1000 acres.

Stephenson, William. N.C. Private. 10 Sep. 1821. 274 acres to heirs.

Stepp, John. N.C. Private. 9 Nov. 1784. 640 acres to heir.

Sterling, Isaac. N.C. Sergeant. 9 Jun. 1820. 1000 acres to heirs.

Sterling, Isaac. Va. Private. 27 Nov. 1832. 100 acres.

Sterling, Levi. N. Y. Sergeant. 8 Jul. 1790. 600 acres.

Sterling, Richard. Va. Private. 15 Jun. 1807. 100 acres.

Sterling, William. Md. Private. ———. 50 acres.
Sterling, William. Va. Private. 15 Jun. 1807. 100 acres.
Stern, Charles. Va. Sergeant. 13 Aug. 1783. 200 acres.
Stern, David. Va. Sergeant. 9 Jul. 1792. 400 acres.
Sterret, Alexander. Pa. ———. 26 Jul. 1805. 200 acres.
Stetson, Jezekiah. Me. Private. 9 Dec. 1836. 200 acres to widow Chloe Stetson. Hartford.
Steuben, Baron. Pa. General. ———. 500 acres.
Steuben, Baron. Pa. General. ———. 500 acres.
Steuben, Baron. Pa. Major General. 11 Oct. 1786. 500 acres.
Steuben, Baron. Pa. Major General. 12 Oct. 1787. 500 acres.
Steuben, Baron von. Va. Major General. 30 Jan. 1783. 15,000 acres.
Stevens, Daniel. Conn. Sufferer. Danbury. 2.12.0.
Stevens, Ebenezer. N. Y. Lieutenant Colonel. 3 Jul. 1790. 2700 acres.
Stevens, Edward. Va. Brigadier General. 20 Nov. 1783. 5000 acres.
Stevens, Edward. Va. Brigadier General. 20 Nov. 1783. 3000 acres.
Stevens, Edward. Va. Brigadier General. 20 Nov. 1783. 2000 acres.
Stevens, Edward. Va. Sergeant. 3 Jul. 1784. 200 acres.
Stevens, Edward. Va. Private. 5 Feb. 1820. 100 acres.
Stevens, Ezra. Conn. Sufferer. Danbury. 3.4.0.
Stevens, James. Ga. Soldier. 6 Apr. 1785. 230 acres.
Stevens, James. Va. Private. 3 Mar. 1784. 100 acres.
Stevens, Jervis Henry. S.C. Captain. 2 May 1785. 300 acres.
Stevens, John. N.C. Private. 10 Mar. 1788. 228 acres.
Stevens, John. Va. Private. 18 Dec. 1783. 100 acres.
Stevens, John. Va. Private. 22 Mar. 1784. 100 acres.
Stevens, John. Va. Captain. 4 May 1840. 888 8/9 acres.
Stevens, John. Va. Captain. 4 May 1840. 888 8/9 acres.
Stevens, John. Va. Captain. 4 May 1840. 888 8/9 acres.
Stevens, John. Va. Captain. 4 May 1840. 888 8/9 acres.
Stevens, John. Va. Captain. 30 Jul. 1842. 888 8/9 acres.
Stevens, John. Va. Captain. 30 Jul. 1842. 888 8/9 acres.
Stevens, John. Va. ———. 9 Apr. 1855. 444 4/9 acres.
Stevens, John. Va. Captain. 12 May 1853. 888 8/9 acres.
Stevens, Jonas. Me. Sergeant. 7 May 1835. 200 acres to widow Mary Stevens. Norway.
Stevens, Joseph. S.C. ———. 4 Jul. 1785. 200 acres.
Stevens, Joseph. S.C. ———. 4 Jul. 1785. 196 acres.
Stevens, Joseph. Va. Sergeant. 21 Nov. 1789. 200 acres.
Stevens, Joshua. N.C. Private. 30 Sep. 1785. 640 acres to heirs.
Stevens, Leveret. Conn. Sufferer. New/East Haven. 3.0.0.
Stevens, Lewis. N.C. Private. 30 Nov. 1785. 228 acres.
Stevens, Nathaniel. Conn. Sufferer. Danbury. 3.8.0.
Stevens, Peleg. Mass. ———. 24 Feb. 1832. 200 acres to only son William Stevens.
Stevens, Peter. Va. Sergeant. 10 Aug. 1784. 200 acres.
Stevens, Richard. Va. Captain. 23 Jul. 1824. 307 acres 2 10/13 rods.
Stevens, Richard. Va. Captain. 23 Jul. 1824. 307 acres 2 10/13 rods.
Stevens, Richard. Va. Captain. 23 Jul. 1824. 307 acres 2 10/13 rods.
Stevens, Richard. Va. Captain. 23 Jul. 1824. 307 acres 2 10/13 rods.
Stevens, Richard. Va. Captain. 23 Jul. 1824. 307 acres 2 10/13 rods.
Stevens, Richard. Va. Captain. 23 Jul. 1824. 307 acres 2 10/13 rods.
Stevens, Richard. Va. Captain. 23 Jul. 1824. 307 acres 2 10/13 rods.
Stevens, Richard. Va. Captain. 23 Jul. 1824. 307 acres 2 10/13 rods.
Stevens, Richard. Va. Captain. 23 Jul. 1824. 307 acres 2 10/13 rods.

Stevens, Richard. Va. Captain. ———. 1230 acres.
Stevens, Richard. Va. Captain. 16 Nov. 1840 237 1/3 acres.
Stevens, Richard. Va. Captain. 21 Sep. 1833. 1093 43/100 acres.
Stevens, Robert. Ga. ———. 4 Oct. 1785. ———.
Stevens, Samuel. Me. Private. 19 May 1835. 200 acres to widow Amey Stevens. Mercer.
Stevens, Sarah. Conn. Sufferer. New/East Haven. 4.11.0.
Stevens, Shep. Va.-Ind. Private. 108 acres.
Stevens, Thomas. Ga. Refugee. 8 Jun. 1784. 250 acres.
Stevens, Warrington. Va. Private. 29 Dec. 1784. 100 acres.
Stevens, William. N. Y. Captain. 9 Jul. 1790. 1800 acres.
Stevens, William. S.C. ———. 7 Dec. 1789. 200 acres.
Stevens, William. Va. Lieutenant. 25 Dec. 1784. 2666 2/3 acres.
Stevens, William. Va. Lieutenant. 11 Oct. 1824. 370 acres.
Stevens, William Smith. S.C. Surgeon. 15 Oct. 1784. 300 acres.
Stevenson, Hugh. N.C. Private. 2 Feb. 1785. 365 acres.
Stevenson, James. N.C. Private. 2 Feb. 1786. 640 acres to heirs.
Stevenson, Michael. N.C. Private. 15 Feb. 1797. 640 acres.
Stevenson, Stephen. Pa. Captain. 13 Nov. 1786. 500 acres.
Stevenson, William. Pa. Dragoon. 21 Dec. 1786. 200 acres.
Stevenson, William. Va. Lieutenant. 8 Mar. 1838. 315 acres.
Stevenson, William. Va. Lieutenant. 5 Apr. 1786. 2666 2/3 acres.
Steves, Philip. N. Y. Sergeant. 8 Jul. 1790. 600 acres.
Steward, Benjamin. Me. Private. 20 May 1835. 200 acres to widow Sally Steward. Newport.
Steward, Benjamin. Md. Private. ———. 50 acres.
Steward, Benjamin. Conn. Sufferer. Norwalk. 14.19.7.
Steward, Edward. Va. Private. 23 Jul. 1784. 100 acres.
Steward, Ephraim. Conn. Sufferer. Norwalk. 5.4.4.
Steward, Simeon, Jr. Conn. Sufferer. Norwalk. 8.6.0.
Steward, William. Md. Fifer or Private. ———. 50 acres.
Stewart, Alexander. Pa. Surgeon. 27 Feb. 1787. 300 acres.
Stewart, Alexander. Pa. Surgeon. 27 Feb. 1787. 250 acres.
Stewart, Alexander. Conn. Sufferer. Danbury. 5.17.4.
Stewart, Andrew. Md. Private. ———. 50 acres.
Stewart, Andrew. N.C. Private. 2 Feb. 1786. 274 acres.
Stewart, Benjamin. Mass. Private. 12 Dec. 1834. 200 acres.
Stewart, Benjamin. Va. Private. 13 Oct. 1783. 233 1/3 acres.
Stewart, Charles. N.C. Captain. 30 Sep. 1785. 3840 acres to legatee, George Wolfenden.
Stewart, Charles. N.C. Sergeant. 16 Aug. 1821. 1000 acres.
Stewart, Charles. Va. Private. 6 Feb. 1797. 100 acres.
Stewart, Charles. Va. Ensign. 21 Jan. 1817. 2666 2/3 acres.
Stewart, Christopher. Pa. Lieutenant Colonel. 10 Nov. 1786. 500 acres.
Stewart, Christopher. Pa. Sergeant. 10 Nov. 1786. 250 acres.
Stewart, Daniel. N.C. ———. 22 Apr. 1785. 640 acres to heirs.
Stewart, George. N.C. Sergeant. 20 Oct. 1787. 1000 acres to heirs.
Stewart, George. Va. Master. 31 Dec. 1851. 2666 2/3 acres.
Stewart, Henry. Ga. ———. 19 Dec. 1785. 287 1/2 acres.
Stewart, Henry. Va. Private. 14 Nov. 1791. 200 acres.
Stewart, Hugh. Pa. Private. 23 Aug. 1787. 200 acres.
Stewart, Jacob. Ga. ———. 7 Jun. 1785. 287 1/2 acres.
Stewart, James. Md. Private. ———. 50 acres.
Stewart, James. Md. Private. ———. 50 acres.
Stewart, James. N. Y. Captain. 6 Jul. 1790. 1800 acres.

Stewart, James. N. Y. Captain. ———. 1000 acres.

Stewart, James. N.C. Private. Dec. 1802. 274 acres.

Stewart, James. Va. Private. 31 Aug. 1793. 200 acres.

Stewart, James. Va. Private. 27 Feb. 1797. 100 acres.

Stewart, James. Conn. Sufferer. New London. 13.18.6.

Stewart, Jeremiah. S.C. Soldier. 21 Jan. 1785. 200 acres.

Stewart, John. Md. Lieutenant Colonel. ———. 200 acres.

Stewart, John. N.C. Private. 20 Feb. 1784. 274 acres.

Stewart, John. Pa. Sergeant. ———. 250 acres.

Stewart, John. S.C. ———. 5 Sep. 1791. 200 acres.

Stewart, John. Va. Private. 18 Feb. 1784. 100 acres.

Stewart, Marks. Va. Private. 12 Mar. 1785. 100 acres.

Stewart, Maxey. Va. Private. 22 Jul. 1824. 100 acres.

Stewart, Patrick. Va. Private. 6 Aug. 1783. 100 acres.

Stewart, Philip. Va. Lieutenant. 31 Jan. 1784. 2666 2/3 acres.

Stewart, Philip William. Pa. Private. 4 Mar. 1795. 200 acres.

Stewart, Robert. Va. Private. 27 May 1786. 100 acres.

Stewart, Samuel. Ga. Minute Man. 16 Sep. 1785. ———.

Stewart, Samuel. N.C. Private. 22 Dec. 1796. 228 acres.

Stewart, Samuel. Conn. Sufferer. Norwalk. 12.2.0.

Stewart, Simeon. Conn. Sufferer. Norwalk. 69.10.10.

Stewart, Solomon. Va. Private. 1 Apr. 1783. 100 acres.

Stewart, Thomas. Pa. ———. 18 Nov. 1803. 200 acres.

Stewart, Walter. Pa. Colonel. 10 May 1787. 500 acres.

Stewart, Walter. Pa. Colonel. 10 May 1787. 500 acres.

Stewart, William. Ga. ———. 20 Apr. 1784. 350 acres.

Stewart, William. N.C. Private. 23 Apr. 1784. 640 acres.

Stewart, William. N.C. Private. 20 Sep. 1821. 640 acres.

Stewart, William. Pa. Lieutenant. 1 Nov. 1785. 200 acres.

Stewart, William. Pa. Ranger. 12 Sep. 1787. 200 acres.

Stewart, William. Pa. Lieutenant. ———. 200 acres.

Stewart, William. Va. Private. 9 Dec. 1782. 100 acres.

Stickley, Moses. N.C. Private. 9 Dec. 1797. 640 acres.

Stickly, John. N.C. Private. 9 Dec. 1797. 320 acres.

Stiff, William. Ga. Soldier. 17 Apr. 1784. 230 acres.

Stiles, Moses. N. Y. Corporal. 7 Jul. 1790. 600 acres.

Still, John. Va. Sergeant. 4 Apr. 1838. 400 acres.

Stillman, Elizabeth. Conn. Sufferer. New/ East Haven. 26.15.6.

Stillwell, David. N.C. Private. 29 Sep. 1784. 403 acres.

Stillwell, Jeremiah. N.C. Private. 17 Dec. 1785. 640 acres to heirs.

Stillwell, Joseph. Va. Private. 6 Apr. 1787. 100 acres.

Stillwell, Mary. Conn. Sufferer. New/East Haven. 13.10.6.

Stillwell, Semon. N.C. Private. 30 Sep. 1785. 640 acres to heirs.

Stilts, Garret. N.C. Private. 7 Dec. 1797. 640 acres to heirs.

Stilwell, Jacob. N.C. Fifer. 25 Oct. 1783. 264 acres.

Stinson, John. N.C. Private. 12 Sep. 1785. 640 acres to heirs.

Stinson, Samuel. Me. ———. 3 Aug. 1835. 200 acres. Deer Isle.

Stirk, Samuel. Ga. ———. 13 Apr. 1784. 287 1/2 acres.

Stith, John. Va. Captain. 29 Nov. 1782. 4000 acres.

Stith, John. Va. Captain. 13 Oct. 1783. 4000 acres.

Stith, John. Va. Captain. 1 Nov. 1798. 666 2/3 acres.

Stith, John. Va. Captain. 14 Aug. 1807. 500 acres.

Stive, William. Ga. ———. 4 Oct. 1785. ———.

Stivers, Reuben. Va. Private. 22 Jul. 1824. 200 acres.

Stoakes, Christopher. Va. Sergeant. 13 Dec. 1783. 200 acres.
Stoakes, Zachariah. Va. Private. 14 Jul. 1784. 100 acres.
Stoboth, James. N.C. Private. 2 Feb. 1786. 640 acres.
Stock, George. N. Y. Corporal. 7 Jul. 1790. 500 acres.
Stockbridge, John. N. Y. Matross. 9 Jul. 1790. 600 acres.
Stockdell, John. Va. Private. 31 Mar. 1784. 100 acres.
Stocker, Seth. N. Y. Sergeant. 9 Jul. 1790. 600 acres.
Stocker, William. N. Y. Private. 8 Jul. 1790. 600 acres.
Stockham, Seth. Ga. Minute Man. 17 Jan. 1784. 287 1/2 acres.
Stockley, Charles. Va. Lieutenant. 8 Aug. 1783. 444 acres.
Stockley, Jehu. N.C. Private. 15 Jul. 1785. 228 acres.
Stockley, Richard. N.C. Corporal. 9 Dec. 1797. 1000 acres.
Stockly, Charles. Va. Lieutenant. 23 Apr. 1810. 370 acres.
Stocks, Bentley. Ga. ———. 19 Apr. 1784. 287 1/2 acres.
Stocks, Isaac. Ga. Citizen. 19 Dec. 1785. 287 1/2 acres.
Stocks, Joshua. N.C. Private. 6 Sep. 1821. 640 acres.
Stockwell, Levi. N. Y. Lieutenant. 9 Jul. 1790. 1000 acres.
Stockwell, Peter. Ga. Minute Man. 14 Feb. 1785. ———.
Stockwell, Thomas. Ga. Minute Man. 6 Jun. 1785. ———.
Stoddard, Nathaniel. Me. Private. 6 Sep. 1836. 200 acres to widow Hannah Stoddard. Perry.
Stoddard, Samuel. Mass. Private. 13 Dec. 1833. 200 acres to daughter Sarah Packard.
Stoddart, William T. Md. Lieutenant. ———. 200 acres.
Stoffee, Frederick. Md. Private. ———. 50 acres.
Stoffle, John. Md. ———. ———. 50 acres.
Stokeley, Nehemiah. Pa. Captain. 18 May 1812. 500 acres to Susanna Stokeley, widow.
Stokely, Charles. Va. Lieutenant. 3 Jan. 1783. 2666 2/3 acres.
Stokely, Thomas. Pa. Captain. 11 Oct. 1786. 500 acres.
Stoker, Edward. Va. Private. 7 May 1801. 100 acres.
Stokes, Armistead. Ga. ———. 17 May 1784. ———.
Stokes, George. Ga. ———. 23 Apr. 1784. 200 acres.
Stokes, Henry. N.C. Private. 17 Feb. 1824. 640 acres.
Stokes, Joel. N.C. Private. 21 Aug. 1820. 640 acres.
Stokes, John. Ga. ———. 23 Apr. 1784. 200 acres.
Stokes, John. N.C. Private. 22 Apr. 1785. 640 acres to heirs.
Stokes, John. Va. Captain. 19 Jul. 1783. 4666 2/3 acres.
Stokes, John. Va. Private. 30 Nov. 1784. 100 acres.
Stokes, John. Va. Captain. 2 May 1812. 100 acres.
Stokes, John. Va. Captain. 2 May 1812. 100 acres.
Stokes, John. Va. Captain. 2 May 1812. 100 acres.
Stokes, John. Va. Captain. 2 May 1812. 100 acres.
Stokes, John. Va. Captain. 2 May 1812. 100 acres.
Stokes, Marcus. Ga. ———. 22 Apr. 1784. 900 acres.
Stokes, Peter. N.C. Private. 7 Jan. 1786. 640 acres to heirs.
Stokes, Robert. Va. Private. 20 Jun. 1783. 200 acres.
Stokes, Silvanus. Va. Private. 26 Feb. 1784. 100 acres.
Stokes, Thomas. Md. Private. ———. 50 acres.
Stokes, William. Ga. ———. 22 Apr. 1784. 1000 acres.
Stokley, Alexander. N.C. Sergeant. 7 Jan. 1786. 1000 acres to heirs.
Stole, Daniel. Conn. Sufferer. New London. 27.14.0.
Stoleman, David. Ga. ———. ———. 250 acres.
Stone, Aaron. Conn. Sufferer. Danbury. 2.11.0.
Stone, Charles. Ga. Minute Man. 15 Apr. 1784. 287 1/2 acres.

Stone, David. Ga. Minute Man. 26 May 1784. 287 1/2 acres.
Stone, Dotson. S.C. ———. 7 May 1792. 200 acres.
Stone, George. Me. ———. 18 Jul. 1835. 200 acres. Limington.
Stone, Hugh. N. Y. Private. 8 Jul. 1790. 500 acres.
Stone, Joel. N.C. Private. 30 Sep. 1785. 640 acres to heirs.
Stone, John. Me. ———. 1835. 200 acres. Parsonsfield.
Stone, John. N. Y. Private. 6 Jul. 1790. 600 acres.
Stone, John. N.C. Private. 30 Sep. 1785. 640 acres to heirs.
Stone, John. Conn. Sufferer. Danbury. 4.16.8.
Stone, John H. Md. Colonel. ———. 200 acres.
Stone, Jonathan. Me. Soldier. 17 Jun. 1835. 200 acres to widow Damaris Stone. Gorham.
Stone, Joseph. S.C. ———. 6 Oct. 1794. 81 acres to James Gore, administrator.
Stone, Joseph. S.C. ———. 6 Oct. 1794. 26 acres to James Gore, administrator.
Stone, Joseph. S.C. ———. 7 Sep. 1795. 79 acres to James Gore, administrator.
Stone, Joseph. S.C. ———. 6 Nov. 1797. 2 1/2 acres to James Gore, administrator.
Stone, Joseph. S.C. ———. 6 Nov. 1797. 14 acres to James Gore, administrator.
Stone, Joseph. S.C. ———. 6 Nov. 1797. 36 acres to James Gore, administrator.
Stone, Joseph. S.C. ———. 6 Nov. 1797. 23 1/2 acres to James Gore, administrator.
Stone, Joshua. Ga. Minute Man. 17 Jan. 1785. 287 1/2 acres.
Stone, Littleberry. N.C. Private. 7 Jan. 1786. 640 acres to heirs.
Stone, Reuben. S.C. ———. 7 May 1787. 200 acres.
Stone, Richard. Pa. Private. 30 Nov. 1786. 200 acres.
Stone, Sylvanus. N.C. Private. 8 Dec. 1795. 640 acres to heirs.
Stone, Thomas. Ga. ———. 24 May 1784. 287 1/2 acres.
Stone, William. Va. Private. 5 Dec. 1783. 100 acres.
Stone, William. Conn. Sufferer. Danbury. 7.2.6.
Stone, Zedekiah. N.C. Private. 30 Sep. 1785. 640 acres to heirs.
Stoneham, Henry. Va. Corporal. 21 Jul. 1783. 400 acres.
Stoner, Jacob. Pa. Private. 30 Jul. 1787. 200 acres.
Stoner, John. N. Y. Drummer. 8 Jul. 1790. 600 acres.
Stoner, Nicholas. N. Y. Fifer. 8 Jul. 1790. 500 acres.
Stonestreet, William. Md. Private. ———. 50 acres.
Stonnell, Richard. Va. Private. 6 Apr. 1786. 200 acres.
Storer, Ebenezer. Me. First Lieutenant & Paymaster. 9 Jun. 1838. 600 acres. Gorham.
Storer, Hannah. Conn. Sufferer. New/East Haven. 5.0.0.
Storer, John. Conn. Sufferer. New/East Haven. 55.11.0.
Storer, Joseph. Me. ———. 20 Jun. 1835. 200 acres to widow Joanna Storer. Westbrook.
Storer, William. Me. Private. 24 Aug. 1835. 200 acres to widow Sarah Storer. Hiram.
Storey, Richard. N.C. Private. 9 Dec. 1797. 640 acres.
Storm, Andrew. N.C. Private. 8 Dec. 1795. 640 acres to heirs.
Stormer, Henry. N.C. Corporal. 30 Sep. 1785. 1000 acres to heirs.
Storms, Abraham. N. Y. Private. 13 Sep. 1790. 500 acres.
Storms, John. N. Y. Private. 8 Jul. 1790. 600 acres.
Storrer, Henry. S.C. ———. 2 Oct. 1786. 200 acres.
Story, Boswell. Ga. ———. 5 Apr. 1785. 287 1/2 acres.
Story, Caleb. N.C. ———. 14 May 1784. 640 acres to John Story, heir.
Story, Edmond. Ga. ———. 5 Apr. 1785. 287 1/2 acres.
Story, Isaiah. N.C. Private. 2 Feb. 1786. 274 acres.
Story, John. N.C. Private. 20 Jan. 1785. 640 acres.
Story, John. Va. Private. 24 Nov. 1784. 100 acres.
Story, John. Va. Private. 12 Dec. 1812. 100 acres.

Story, John. Va. Private. 18 Nov. 1818. 200 acres.
Story, Parker. Mass. Private. 11 Jul. 1837. 200 acres to assignee Samuel Cook.
Story, Richard. Ga. ———. 5 Apr. 1785. 287 1/2 acres.
Story, William. N.C. ———. 14 May 1784. 640 acres to heirs.
Stotesburg, John. Pa. Captain. 20 Nov. 1786. 500 acres.
Stotherd, Thomas. Va. Private. 20 Jun. 1783. 100 acres.
Stott, William. Va. Lieutenant. 3 Apr. 1784. 2666 2/3 acres.
Stott, William. Va. Lieutenant. 21 Nov. 1834. 666 acres.
Stott, William. Va. Lieutenant. 17 Dec. 1834. 666 acres.
Stott, William. Va. Boatswain. 26 Aug. 1835. 226 2/3 acres.
Stott, William. Va. Boatswain. 26 Aug. 1835. 226 2/3 acres.
Stott, William. Va. Boatswain. 25 Feb. 1851. 222 acres.
Stott, William. Va. Boatswain. 25 Feb. 1851. 222 acres.
Stott, William. Va. Boatswain. 25 Feb. 1851. 222 acres.
Stott, William. Va. Boatswain. 25 Feb. 1851. 222 acres.
Stott, William. Va. Boatswain. 25 Feb. 1851. 222 acres.
Stott, William. Va. Boatswain. 25 Feb. 1851. 222 acres.
Stott, William. Va. Boatswain. 25 Feb. 1851. 166 2/3 acres.
Stott, William. Va. Boatswain. 4 Apr. 1851. 89 acres.
Stott, William. Va. Boatswain. 4 Apr. 1851. 89 acres.
Stott, William. Va. Boatswain. 4 Apr. 1851. 44 1/2 acres.
Stott, William. Va. Boatswain. 4 Apr. 1851. 44 1/2 acres.
Stott, William. Va. Boatswain. 12 Sep. 1851. 266 acres.
Stott, William. Va. Boatswain. 25 Mar. 1853. 166 2/3 acres.
Stott, William. Va. Boatswain. 23 Jun. 1854. 666 2/3 acres.
Stott, William. Va. Boatswain. 23 Jun. 1854. 666 2/3 acres.
Stott, William. Va. Boatswain. 23 Jun. 1854. 666 2/3 acres.
Stott, William. Va. Boatswain. 23 Jun. 1854. 666 2/3 acres.
Stoud, Lott. N.C. Private. 9 Mar. 1801. 228 acres.
Stout, David. Ga. Minute Man. 16 Sep. 1785. 287 1/2 acres.
Stoutenger, George. N. Y. Private. 8 Jul. 1790. 600 acres.
Stouterbaugh, Michael. Pa. Private. ———. 200 acres.
Stoveall, John. N.C. Private. 2 Aug. 1784. 640 acres to heir.
Stover, Christopher. Me. Private. 28 Feb. 1836. 200 acres to widow Catherine Stover. Appleton.
Stoverlate, Nicholas. Pa. Private. 16 Oct. 1786. 200 acres to George Ingram, administrator.
Stow, John. Me. ———. 13 Jun. 1835. 200 acres. Parsonsfield.
Stowbridge, John. N.C. Private. 22 Dec. 1796. 640 acres.
Stowers, John. Pa. Private. 15 Mah 1787. 200 acres.
Stoy, John. Pa. Lieutenant. 31 Oct. 1792. 200 acres.
Stoy, John. Pa. Captain. ———. 200 acres.
Stoy, John. Pa. Lieutenant. 4 Oct. 1786. 200 acres.
Strachan, William. N. Y. Lieutenant. 8 Jul. 1790. 1200 acres.
Stradford, John. N.C. Private. 14 Dec. 1796. 228 acres.
Stradley, Edward. N.C. Private. 30 Nov. 1785. 640 acres.
Stradley, James. N.C. Private. 28 Jul. 1784. 640 acres.
Strahan, John. Md. ———. ———. 50 acres.
Stram, James. Ga. Minute Man. 3 Oct. 1783. 287 1/2 acres.
Strand, John. N.C. Private. 30 Sep. 1785. 640 acres to heirs.
Strange, Ephraim. Ga. Soldiers. 7 Nov. 1783. ———.
Strange, James. N.C. Private. 27 Nov. 1783. 274 acres.
Strange, James. N.C. Private. 22 Jan. 1784. 274 acres.
Strange, John. Ga. Minute Man. 3 Sep. 1785. ———.
Strange, William. Va. Private. 24 Feb. 1784. 100 acres.

Stratin, Joab. N.C. Private. 2 Feb. 1786. 640 acres.
Stratton, Cornelius. Conn. Sufferer. Fairfield. 1.5.3.
Stratton, David. Mass. Private. 16 Dec. 1831. 200 acres.
Stratton, Hussey. N. Y. Private. 8 Jul. 1790. 600 acres.
Stratton, John. Conn. Sufferer. Fairfield. 1.13.5.
Stratton, Seth. Va. Private. 29 Apr. 1785. 200 acres.
Straughan, John. Va. Private. 26 Jun. 1783. 100 acres.
Straughan, Presley. Va. Private. 27 Oct. 1783. 100 acres.
Straughon, Richard. N.C. Private. 19 May 1784. 640 acres.
Streaton, John. Pa. Private. 24 Aug. 1787. 200 acres.
Street, David. Pa. Private. 2 Jan. 1787. 200 acres.
Street, John. Va. Private. 17 Apr. 1784. 100 acres.
Street, Nathaniel. Conn. Sufferer. Norwalk. 33.12.9.
Street, Samuel. Md. Fifer. ———. 50 acres.
Street, Samuel. N. Y. Private. 8 Jul. 1790. 500 acres.
Streets, Robert. Md. Private. ———. 50 acres.
Strength, John. Ga. ———. 15 Mar. 1784. 250 acres.
Stribling, Segismond. Va. Captain. 21 Jun. 1783. 4666 2/3 acres.
Stribling, Segismond. Va. Captain. 23 Oct. 1807. 833 acres.
Stribling, William. Va. Sergeant. 22 Oct. 1784. 400 acres.
Stricher, John. Pa. Lieutenant. 24 Nov. 1786. 200 acres.
Stricker, Jacob. Pa. Private. 27 Oct. 1786. 200 acres.
Stricker, John. Pa. Lieutenant. 11 Nov. 1786. 200 acres.
Stricker, John. Pa. Lieutenant. 2 Feb. 1787. 200 acres.
Stricker, Martin. N.C. Private. 6 Jan. 1784. 228 acres.
Strickland, John. N.C. Private. 1 Jul. 1820. 228 acres to heirs.
Strickler, John. Pa. Lieutenant. 24 Nov. 1786. 200 acres.
Stricklin, Marmaduke. N.C. Private. 18 Dec. 1802. 640 acres to heirs.
Strickling, Alexander. Va. Private. 6 Jan. 1834. 200 acres.
Stringer, George. N.C. Private. 20 Sep. 1784. 411 acres.
Stringer, John. Ga. Minute Man. 22 Apr. 1784. 287 1/2 acres.
Stringer, John. N.C. Private. 19 May 1784. 640 acres.
Stringer, Josiah. N.C. Private. 13 Aug. 1784. 274 acres.
Stringer, Lemage. N.C. Private. 17 Dec. 1785. 640 acres to heirs.
Stringer, Samuel. N.Y. Director General of the Hospital & Physician. 3 Sep. 1792. 4250 acres.
Stringer, Samuel. N.C. Sergeant. 28 May 1784. 571 acres.
Stringerlandt, Peter. N.Y. ——. 13 Sep. 1790. 500 acres to heirs.
Stringfellow, David. Va. Sergeant. 3 May 1784. 400 acres.
Stringfellow, Henry. Va. Private. 8 Dec. 1784. 200 acres.
Stringham, Henry. N. Y. Private. 8 Jul. 1790. 500 acres.
Stripes, Dempsey. N.C. Private. 10 Dec. 1788. 640 acres to heirs.
Stripland, William. S.C. ———. 4 Dec. 1786. 200 acres.
Striplin, Newton. N.C. Private. 12 Mar. 1785. 640 acres to heirs.
Striplin, Newton. N.C. Private. 17 Dec. 1785. 640 acres to heirs.
Stripling, Francis. Ga. ———. 14 Sep. 1784. 287 1/2 acres.
Strode, Samuel. Va.-Ind. Sergeant. 216 acres.
Strohager, Rudolph. Ga. Refugee. 20 Apr. 1784. 287 1/2 acres.
Strong, George. N.C. Private. 17 Dec. 1796. 640 acres to heirs.
Strong, John. Ga. ———. 15 Mar. 1784. 500 acres.
Strong, Moses. Conn. Sufferer. New/East Haven. 9.10.0.
Strong, Nathan. N. Y. Captain. 7 Jul. 1790. 1800 acres.
Strong, William. Va. Corporal. 20 Apr. 1785. 200 acres.
Strosier, Peter. Ga. Refugee. 15 Mar. 1784. 250 acres.

Strother, Benjamin. Va. Midshipman. 21 Oct. 1831. 533 1/3 acres.
Strother, Benjamin. Va. Midshipman. 21 Oct. 1831. 533 1/3 acres.
Strother, Benjamin. Va. Midshipman. 21 Oct. 1831. 533 1/3 acres.
Strother, Benjamin. Va. Midshipman. 21 Oct. 1831. 177 1/3 acres.
Strother, Benjamin. Va. Midshipman. 21 Oct. 1831. 177 1/3 acres.
Strother, Benjamin. Va. Midshipman. 21 Oct. 1831. 533 1/3 acres.
Strother, Benjamin. Va. Midshipman. 21 Oct. 1831. 177 1/3 acres.
Strother, Benjamin. Va. Midshipman. 21 Oct. 1831. 177 1/3 acres.
Strother, James. Va. Sergeant. 16 Feb. 1819. 200 acres.
Strother, William. N.C. Private. 9 Nov. 1784. 640 acres.
Strother, William. N.C. Private. 7 Dec. 1797. 640 acres to heirs.
Strother, William. Va. Sergeant. 19 Feb. 1784. 400 acres.
Stroud, Cleyborn. Ga. ———. ———. 250 acres.
Stroud, Jacob. Pa. ———. 27 Mar. 1807. 200 acres to James Hollingshead et al., assignees.
Stroud, John. N.C. Private. 7 Dec. 1797. 640 acres to heirs.
Stroud, Richard. Conn. Sufferer. New London. 23.15.0.
Strout, Isaac. Me. Private. 15 Oct. 1835. 200 acres to widow Mary Strout. Limington.
Stryon, Samuel. N.C. Private. 8 Mar. 1785. 640 acres.
Stuart, Amos. Ga. ———. 17 May 1784. ———.
Stuart, Charles. Ga. Lieutenant. 18 Apr. 1784. 287 1/2 acres.
Stuart, Clement. Ga. Minute Man. 18 Apr. 1784. 287 1/2 acres.
Stuart, Colwell. N.C. Private. 19 Aug. 1815. 640 acres to heirs.
Stuart, Isaac. Ga. ———. 20 Apr. 1784. 287 1/2 acres.
Stuart, James. Ga. Refugee. 26 May 1784. 287 1/2 acres.
Stuart, James, Sr. Ga. Refugee. 15 Mar. 1784. 250 acres.
Stuart, John. Ga. Colonel. 18 Apr. 1784. 920 acres.
Stuart, John. Ga. Refugee. 18 Apr. 1784. 287 1/2 acres to heirs.
Stuart, John. Ga. ———. 21 Apr. 1784. 300 acres. Of Strostown. [verify if of Stroker's Town or Stroke's Town]
Stuart, Robert. Ga. ———. 250 acres. ———.
Stuart, Samuel. Ga. Minute Man. 19 Jul. 1784. 287 1/2 acres to heirs.
Stuart, Stuart. Ga. ———. 15 Mar. 1784. 250 acres.
Stuart, Thomas. Ga. ———. 21 Apr. 1784. 400 acres.
Stuart, William. Ga. Private. 10 Dec. 1784. 250 acres.
Stuart, William. Ga. ———. 23 Apr. 1784. 287 1/2 acres.
Stubblefield, Beverley. Va. Captain. 26 Jun. 1783. 4000 acres.
Stubblefield, Beverley. Va. Captain. 1 Aug. 1799. 666 2/3 acres.
Stubblefield, Beverley. Va. Captain. 11 Sep. 1807. 500 acres.
Stubblefield, George, Jr. Va. Ensign. 25 Jun 1783. 2666 2/3 acres.
Stubblefield, Peter. Ga. ———. 22 Apr. 1784. 1000 acres.
Stubblefield, Seth. Ga. ———. 17 May 1784. ———.
Stubbs, Allen. Va. Private. 23 Mar. 1784. 200 acres.
Stubbs, Allen. Va. Private. 23 Aug. 1784. 100 acres.
Stubbs, Benjamin. Va. Private. 28 Mar. 1812. 100 acres.
Stubbs, Francis. Va. Private. 21 May 1783. 100 acres.
Stubbs, James. Ga. ———. 17 May 1784. ———.
Stubbs, James. Ga. ———. 17 May 1784. ———.
Stubbs, John. Va. Midshipman. 23 Oct. 1847. 1333 1/3 acres.
Stubbs, John. Va. Midshipman. 23 Oct. 1847. 1333 1/3 acres.
Stubbs, John. Va. Midshipman. 24 Jun. 1848. 700 acres.
Stubbs, John. Va. Midshipman. 24 Jun. 1848. 300 acres.
Stubbs, John. Va. Midshipman. 24 Jun. 1848. 333 1/3 acres.
Stubbs, John. Va. Midshipman. 24 Jun. 1848. 700 acres.

Stubs, Robert. Pa. Private. 12 Aug. 1788. 200 acres.
Studstall, John. Ga. Minute Man. 3 Oct. 1783. 387 1/2 acres.
Studwell, Henry. Conn. Sufferer. Greenwich. 85.17.6.
Studwell, Thomas. Conn. Sufferer. Greenwich. 2.6.4.
Stuffle, John. Ga. ———. 23 Apr. 1784. 287 1/2 acres.
Stull, Anthony. N.C. Private. 17 Feb. 1824. 640 acres.
Stump, John. N. Y. Private. 6 Jul. 1790. 600 acres.
Stump, Michel. Va. Private. 20 Jun. 1783. 100 acres.
Stumps, Peter. Ga. ———. 4 Oct. 1785. ———.
Stumps, Peter. Ga. Soldier. ———. ———.
Stur, Thomas. Va. Sailor. 1 Aug. 1783. 100 acres.
Sturdevant, Joel. Va. Captain. 26 Sep. 1834. 888 88/100 acres.
Sturdevant, Joel. Va. Captain. 26 Sep. 1834. 197 1/2 acres.
Sturdevant, Joel. Va. Captain. 26 Sep. 1834. 252 96/100 acres.
Sturdevant, Joel. Va. Captain. 26 Sep. 1834. 507 92/100 acres.
Sturdevant, Joel. Va. Captain. 24 Feb. 1835. 493 80/100 acres.
Sturdevant, Joel. Va. Captain. 13 Jul. 1835. 265 acres.
Sturdevant, John. Conn. Sufferer. Danbury. 4.11.0.
Sturdivan, John. Va. Private. 11 Aug. 1784. 200 acres.
Sturdivant, John. Va. Captain. 25 Jun. 1856. 2727 acres.
Sturdivant, John. Va. Lieutenant. 15 Jul. 1818. 666 2/3 acres.
Sturdivant, John, Jr. Va. Lieutenant. 15 Jul. 1818. 666 2/3 acres.
Sturdivant, John, Jr. Va. Lieutenant. 15 Jul. 1818. 666 2/3 acres.
Sturdivant, John, Jr. Va. Lieutenant. 15 Jul. 1818. 666 2/3 acres.
Sturdivant, John, Jr. Va. Lieutenant. 25 Jun. 1856. 120 acres.
Sturdivant, John, Jr. Va. Lieutenant. 25 Jun. 1856. 120 acres.
Sturdivant, John, Jr. Va. Lieutenant. 25 Jun. 1856. 120 acres.
Sturdivant, John, Jr. Va. Lieutenant. 25 Jun. 1856. 120 acres.
Sturdivant, John, Jr. Va. Lieutenant. 25 Jun. 1856. 120 acres.
Sturdivant, John, Jr. Va. Lieutenant. 25 Jun. 1856. 120 acres.
Sturdivant, John, Jr. Va. Lieutenant. 25 Jun. 1856. 120 acres.
Sturdivant, John, Jr. Va. Lieutenant. 25 Jun. 1856. 120 acres.
Sturdivant, John, Jr. Va. Lieutenant. 25 Jun. 1856. 120 acres.
Sturdivant, John, Jr. Va. Lieutenant. 25 Jun. 1856. 120 acres.
Sturdivant, John, Jr. Va. Lieutenant. 25 Jun. 1856. 13 1/2 acres.
Sturetevant, Seth. Me. Corporal. 18 May 1835. 200 acres. Canton.
Sturges, Andrew. Ga. ———. 5 Mar. 1787. 690 acres.
Sturges, Andrew. Conn. Sufferer. Fairfield. 13.18.0.
Sturges, Daniel. Conn. Sufferer. Norwalk. 1.15.8.
Sturges, Ebenezer. Conn. Sufferer. Fairfield. 89.4.3.
Sturges, Elizabeth. Conn. Sufferer. Fairfield. 150.0.0.
Sturges, Hezekiah. Conn. Sufferer. Fairfield. 532.8.3.
Sturges, James. Conn. Sufferer. Ridgefield. 10.11.8.
Sturges, Jonathan. Conn. Sufferer. Fairfield. 748.2.6.
Sturges, Joseph. Conn. Sufferer. Fairfield. 339.15.2 to heirs.
Sturges, Judson. Conn. Sufferer. Fairfield. 128.16.7.
Sturges, Peter. Conn. Sufferer. Norwalk. 0.14.0.
Sturges, Samuel. Conn. Sufferer. Fairfield. 234.18.1.
Sturges, Seth. Conn. Sufferer. Fairfield. 431.0.1.
Sturges, Solomon. Conn. Sufferer. Fairfield. 319.3.9.
Sturgess, William. Ga. ———. 19 Apr. 1784. 1000 acres.
Sturlivant, Barnabas. N.C. Private. 13 Sep. 1820. 274 acres.
Sturtevant, Asa. Me. Private. 30 Apr. 1835. 200 acres. Dover.

Sturtevant, Francis. Me. ———. 26 May 1835. 200 acres to widow Mary Sturtevant. Paris.
Sturtevant, Isaac. Mass. Sergeant. 19 Sep. 1834. 200 acres to his widow Hannah Sturtevant.
Sturtevant, Lot. Me. ———. 15 Jun. 1835. 200 acres. Waterville.
Sturton, Robert. Md. Private. ———. 50 acres.
Stymets, Isaac. N. Y. Matross. 9 Jul. 1790. 600 acres.
Stymets, Jasper. N. Y. Matross. 9 Jul. 1790. 600 acres.
Suart, James. Va. Private. 20 Aug. 1783. 200 acres.
Sublett, Benjamin. Va. Sergeant. 17 Jun. 1783. 200 acres.
Suddeth, William. Va. Sergeant. 26 Jan. 1809. 200 acres.
Suddoth, John. Va. Private. 11 May 1784. 100 acres.
Suddoth, William. Va. Private. 8 Mar. 1784. 100 acres.
Suddoth, William. Va. Corporal. 3 Nov. 1784. 200 acres.
Sudlow, Samuel. N. Y. Private. 8 Jul. 1790. 600 acres.
Sudthard, John. Va. Private. 20 Oct. 1796. 200 acres.
Suffield, John. Ga. ———. 17 May 1784. ———.
Sugan, James. Va. Private. 20 May 1823. 100 acres.
Sugg, John. N.C. Private. 27 Nov. 1783. 274 acres.
Sugg, John. N.C. Private. 22 Jan. 1784. 274 acres.
Sugg, Michael. N.C. Private. 2 Feb. 1786. 274 acres.
Suggs, George. Va. Private. 10 Sep. 1784. 100 acres.
Sugins, Joseph. N.C. Private. 13 Sep. 1820. 640 acres.
Suite, Jesse. Md. Sergeant. ———. 50 acres.
Sullers, Samuel. Ga. Soldier. 4 Oct. 1785. ———.
Sullins, William. Va. Private. 20 Nov. 1784. 200 acres.
Sullivan, Abel. N.C. Private. 25 Nov. 1795. 640 acres to heirs.
Sullivan, Craven. Va. Private 30 Jun. 1784. 100 acres.
Sullivan, Daniel. N.C. Private. 26 Jul. 1820. 185 acres to heir Daniel Sullivan.
Sullivan, Daniel. Pa. Private. 29 Sep. 1787. 200 acres.
Sullivan, Darby. Md. Private. ———. 50 acres.
Sullivan, Frederick. Va. Private. 23 Jul. 1784. 100 acres.
Sullivan, James. Md. Private. ———. 50 acres.
Sullivan, James. N.C. Private. 10 Dec. 1788. 640 acres to heirs.
Sullivan, Jeremiah. Md. Private. ———. 50 acres.
Sullivan, Jeremiah. N.C. Private. 26 Jul. 1820. 640 acres to heir Daniel Sullivan.
Sullivan, John. N.Y. ———. 13 Sep. 1790. 500 acres to heirs.
Sullivan, John. N.C. Private. 26 May 1784. 640 acres.
Sullivan, John. Pa. Private. ———. 200 acres.
Sullivan, John. Pa. Dragoon. 8 Dec. 1786. 200 acres.
Sullivan, John. Va. Corporal. 8 Jul. 1783. 200 acres.
Sullivan, Mark. Ga. ———. 15 Mar. 1784. 250 acres.
Sullivan, Martick. Pa. Private. 28 Mar. 1786. 200 acres to Philip Boehn, assignee.
Sullivan, Murtoch. Pa. ———. 8 Dec. 1835. 100 acres to William Alsworth. 24 May 1837. 97 acres to William McGinnis.
Sullivan, Owen. Ga. Minute Man. 22 Apr. 1784. 287 1/2 acres.
Sullivan, Owen. Pa. Private. 25 Oct. 1786. 200 acres.
Sullivan, Pat. N.C. Private. 22 Dec. 1796. 640 acres to heirs.
Sullivan, Patrick. Ga. Soldier. 6 Sep. 1785. 230 acres.
Sullivan, Patrick. N.C. Private. 26 Jul. 1820. 185 acres to heir Daniel Sullivan.
Sullivan, Patrick. Pa. Private. 25 May 1789. 200 acres.
Sullivan, Perry. Md. Private. ———. 50 acres.
Sullivan, Solomon. Md. Private. ———. 50 acres.
Sullivan, Thomas. Ga. ———. 23 Apr. 1784. 287 1/2 acres.

Sullivan, Thomas. Pa. Sergeant. 16 Jul. 1787. 250 acres.
Sullivan, William. Ga. Refugee. 22 Apr. 1784. 287 1/2 acres.
Sullivan, William. Md. Private. ———. 50 acres.
Sullivan, Wilson. N.C. Private. 13 Dec. 1796. 640 acres to heirs.
Sullivant, William. Ga. Private. 19 Apr. 1784. 287 1/2 acres.
Sulser, Matthew. Va. Private. 24 Nov. 1784. 100 acres.
Summeral, James. N.C. Sergeant. 15 Nov. 1793. 1000 acres to heirs.
Summerford, Jacob. Ga. Minute Man. 24 May 1784. 287 1/2 acres.
Summerford, Richard. Ga. Minute Man. 24 May 1784. 287 1/2 acres.
Summerlin, James. Ga. Refugee. 1785. 500 acres.
Summerlin, William. Ga. ———. 13 Sep. 1784. 287 1/2 acres.
Summers, Dempsey. Ga. Minute Man. 16 Sep. 1785. 287 1/2 acres.
Summers, Farrel. N. Y. Corporal. 9 Jul. 1790. 600 acres.
Summers, Francis. N.C. Private. 30 Sep. 1785. 640 acres to heirs.
Summers, George. N.C. Sergeant. 28 Sep. 1785. 228 acres.
Summers, George. Pa. Private. 11 Oct. 1786. 200 acres.
Summers, James. N.C. Sergeant. 25 Nov. 1783. 857 acres.
Summers, James. Va. Private. 26 Apr. 1783. 200 acres.
Summers, John. Ga. Minute Man. 16 Sep. 1785. ———.
Summers, John. Md. Private. ———. 50 acres.
Summers, John. N.C. Captain. 25 Oct. 1783. 3840 acres.
Summers, John. N.C. Captain. 29 Nov. 1783. 3840 acres.
Summers, Leven. N.C. Private. 10 Dec. 1821. 274 acres to heirs.
Summers, Samuel. Ga. Minute Man. 17 Jan. 1785. 287 1/2 acres.
Summers, Solomon. Md. Private. ———. 50 acres.
Summers, Thomas. Md. Private. ———. 50 acres.
Summersett, Thomas. Va. Private. 27 Jul. 1797. 100 acres.
Summerson, Gawin. Va. Midshipman. 18 Aug. 1783. 2666 2/3 acres.
Summerson, George. Va. Private. 23 Oct. 1783. 200 acres.
Summerson, George. Va. Seaman. 19 May 1835. 100 acres.
Summerson, George. Va. Seaman. 18 Apr. 1838. 100 acres.
Summerville, George. Md. ———. ———. 50 acres.
Sumner, Edward. Ga. Refugee. 3 Apr. 1784. 250 acres.
Sumner, Francis. N.C. Private. 28 May 1784. 274 acres.
Sumner, Jacob. N.C. Private. 30 Sep. 1785. 640 acres to heirs.
Sumner, Jethro. N.C. Brigadier General. 23 Oct. 1783. 12,000 acres.
Sumner, Jethro. N.C. Private. 17 Dec. 1796. 640 acres to heirs.
Sumner, Julias. N.C. Private. 14 Feb. 1796. 640 acres to heirs.
Sumner, Solomon. Ga. Minute Man. 3 Sep. 1785. ———.
Sunderland, John. N. Y. Matross. 9 Jul. 1790. 600 acres.
Sures, John. Ga. Minute Man. 15 Apr. 1784. 287 1/2 acres.
Surlock, Ephraim. N.C. ———. 14 Jun. 1785. 640 acres to heirs.
Surls, Joseph. N.C. Private. 12 Sep. 1785. 640 acres to heirs.
Susong, Andrew. Va. Private. 30 Jun. 1785 [i.e. 1784]. 100 acres.
Suster, Martin. Pa. Private. 20 Mar. 1789. 200 acres.
Sute, Edward. Md. Corporal. ———. 50 acres.
Sutherland, Daniel. N. Y. Private. 8 Jul. 1790. 600 acres.
Sutherland, John. Ga. ———. 4 Oct. 1785. ———.
Sutherland, Thomas. Ga. Minute Man. 20 Apr. 1784. 287 1/2 acres.
Sutton, Abraham. Md. ———. ———. 50 acres.
Sutton, Benjamin. Va. Corporal. 19 Feb. 1784. 200 acres.
Sutton, Benjamin. Conn. Sufferer. Greenwich. 5.11.2.
Sutton, Charles. Md. Sergeant. ———. 50 acres.
Sutton, James. Ga. Soldier. 7 Jun. 1785. 230 acres to heirs.

Sutton, Jeremiah. N.C. Sergeant. 27 Jun. 1788. 1000 acres.
Sutton, Jesse. Conn. Sufferer. Greenwich. 6.8.9.
Sutton, John. Ga. Soldier. 7 Jun. 1785. 230 acres to heirs.
Sutton, John. Me. ———. 5 Oct. 1835. 200 acres to widow Lois Sutton. Limington.
Sutton, John. Pa. Private. 24 Aug. 1787. 200 acres.
Sutton, John. S.C. ———. 4 Jul. 1785. 200 acres.
Sutton, John. Va. Captain. 26 Mar. 1833. 4000 acres.
Sutton, Martin. Va. Private. 30 Oct. 1787. 100 acres.
Sutton, Philip. Ga. ———. 22 Apr. 1784. 287 1/2 acres.
Sutton, Ralph. Ga. Corporal. 24 May 1784. 230 acres to heirs.
Sutton, Robert. N.C. Private. 9 Dec. 1797. 640 acres.
Sutton, Rowland. Va. Private. 19 Feb. 1784. 100 acres.
Sutton, William. Va. Private. 26 May 1797. 100 acres.
Swagot, George. N.C. Private. 26 Aug. 1785. 640 acres to heirs.
Swails, John. N. Y. Private. 7 Jul. 1790. 600 acres.
Swain, Edward. Pa. Sergeant. 25 Jun. 1804. 250 acres to devisee Mary Madaen alias Rockhill alias Swain.
Swain, Hezekiah. N.C. Private. 6 Dec. 1797. 640 acres to heirs.
Swan, Charles. Va. Private. 25 Mar. 1839. 100 acres.
Swan, James. Ga. ———. 30 Sep. 1784. ———.
Swan, John. Lawrence. Va.-Ind. Lieutenant. 2156 acres.
Swan, John. Md. Major. ———. 200 acres.
Swan, John. Va. Captain. 3 May 1784. 4666 2/3 acres.
Swan, John. Va. Major. 6 Feb. 1808. 1555 1/3 acres.
Swan, Joshua. Pa. Private. 1 Feb. 1787. 200 acres.
Swan, Leonard. Md. Private. ———. 50 acres.
Swan, Timothy. Pa. Corporal. 4 Sep. 1789. 200 acres.
Swan, William. Va.-Ind. Private. 108 acres.
Swancot, Benjamin. N.C. Private. 8 Dec. 1796. 640 acres.
Swann, Joshua. Mass. Private. 17 Apr. 1834. 200 acres.
Swann, Nimrod. N.C. Sergeant. 24 Dec. 1785. 351 acres.
Swann, Thomas. N.C. Private. 17 Dec. 1785. 640 acres to heirs.
Swanson, John. N.C. Private. 30 Nov. 1785. 640 acres to heirs.
Swanson, William. Ga. ———. 17 Apr. 1784. 1000 acres.
Swartwout, Abraham. N. Y. Captain. 7 Jul. 1790. 1800 acres.
Swartwout, Barnardus. N. Y. Ensign. 7 Jul. 1790. 1150 acres.
Swartwout, Cornelius. N. Y. Private. 8 Jul. 1790. 600 acres.
Swartwout, Cornelius. N. Y. Lieutenant. 7 Jul. 1790. 1200 acres.
Swartwout, Henry. N. Y. Lieutenant. 9 Jul. 1790. 1200 acres.
Swartz, Godfrey. Pa. Private. 9 Oct. 1785. 200 acres.
Swartz, Godfrey. Pa. Private. 9 Oct. 1786. 200 acres.
Swartz, Philip. Pa. Private. 3 Apr. 1789. 200 acres.
Swearingen, Joseph. Va. Captain. 31 Mar. 1783. 4000 acres.
Swearingen, Joseph. Va. Captain. 17 Nov. 1789. 666 2/3 acres.
Swearingen, Joseph. Va. Captain. 23 Jan. 1805. 666 2/3 acres.
Swearingen, Joseph. Va. Captain. 18 Nov. 1807. 277 acres.
Swearingen, Van. Va.-Ind. Private. 108 acres.
Swearingham, Van. N.C. Private. 8 Dec. 1796. 640 acres to heirs.
Sweat, David. N.C. Private. 19 May 1784. 640 acres.
Sweat, William. N.C. Private. 27 Nov. 1783. 228 acres.
Sweeney, Edward. N. Y. Bombardier. 9 Jul. 1790. 500 acres.
Sweeney, Thomas. Va. Private. 20 Jun. 1793. 200 acres.
Sweeny, Hugh. Pa. Private. 30 Jul. 1787. 200 acres.
Sweeny, James. Md. Private. ———. 50 acres.

Sweeny, Richard. Md. Private. ———. 50 acres.
Sweet, Caleb. N. Y. Surgeon. 9 Jul. 1790. 1900 acres.
Sweet, Israel. Me. ———. 29 Jun. 1835. 200 acres. Cape Elizabeth.
Sweet, John. Me. ———. 22 Sep. 1835. 200 acres. Windham.
Sweet, Roger. N.Y. ———. 13 Sep. 1790. 500 acres to heirs.
Sweets, Jacob. N. Y. Private. 8 Jul. 1790. 500 acres.
Sweney, James. Pa. Corporal. ———. 200 acres.
Swepston, John. Va. Private. 7 Apr. 1838. 100 acres.
Swift, Isaac. Mass. ———. 28 Feb. 1832. 200 acres to daughter Hannah Cowell and grandchildren Stephen Capey and Hannah Boston.
Swift, John White. N. Y. ———. ———. 333 1/3 acres.
Swindle, Jesse. N.C. Private. 12 Dec. 1804. 640 acres to heirs.
Swiney, William. N.C. Private. 15 Feb. 1797. 640 acres.
Swinson, William. N.C. Private. 4 Sep. 1820. 228 acres to heirs.
Swint, John. Ga. ———. 28 Feb. 1784. 250 acres.
Switz, Walter. N.Y. Lieutenant. 13 Sep. 1790. 1000 acres to heirs.
Switzer, Henry. S.C. ———. 3 Mar. 1788. 117 acres.
Switzer, Henry. S.C. ———. 7 Apr. 1788. 76 acres.
Switzer, Leonard. Ga. ———. 21 Apr. 1784. 287 1/2 acres.
Swope, John. Va. Surgeon. Dec. 1782. 1000 acres.
Swope, John. Va. Surgeon. Dec. 1782. 5000 acres.
Sword, Francis D. Conn. Sufferer. Fairfield. 3.3.6.
Sword, John. S.C. Soldier. 21 Jan. 1785. 200 acres.
Sworden, Jonathan. Va.-Ind. Private. 108 acres.
Swords, James. Ga. Minute Man. 20 Apr. 1784. 287 1/2 acres.
Swords, James. S.C. Soldier. 21 Jan. 1785. 200 acres.
Swords, William. N.C. Matchmaker. 6 Feb. 1823. 640 acres.
Swords, William. S.C. ———. 2 Oct. 1786. 192 acres.
Sykes, Adam. N.C. Private. 4 Aug. 1821. 640 acres.
Sykes, Daniel. Ga. Refugee. 15 Mar. 1784. 500 acres.
Sykes, George. Va. Private. 31 May 1783. 100 acres.
Sykes, William. Ga. ———. 17 May 1784. ———.
Sykes, William. Md. Private. ———. 50 acres.
Sylvester, Job. Md. Private. ———. 50 acres.
Sylvester, Thomas. Md. Private. ———. 50 acres.
Symmons, James. N.C. Private. 15 Oct. 1783. 640 acres.
Symonds, Jonas. Pa. Captain. 17 Aug. 1787. 500 acres.
Syndor, Fortunatus. Va. Private. 21 May 1784. 200 acres.
Syng, Abraham. Pa. Private. 26 Jun. 1787. 200 acres.
Sypeart, Robert. N.C. Private. 27 Nov. 1789. 228 acres.
Sypress, Robert. N.C. Sergeant. 6 Feb. 1823. 129 acres.
Sytes, Christopher. N.Y. ———. 13 Sep. 1790. 500 acres to heirs.
Sytez, George. N. Y. Captain. 9 Jul. 1790. 1800 acres.
Tabb, Augustine. Va. Captain. 11 Apr. 1783. 4000 acres.
Tabb, Thomas, Jr. Ga. ———. 15 Apr. 1784. 800 acres.
Tabor, Thomas. N. Y. Private. 8 Jul. 1790. 500 acres.
Tachal, James. N.C. Private. 21 Aug. 1820. 640 acres.
Talbert, William. N. Y. Corporal. 8 Jul. 1790. 600 acres.
Talbot, Jeremiah. Pa. ———. 20 Apr. 1796. 300 acres to John Davis, assignee.
Talbot, Jeremiah. Pa. Major. 19 Nov. 1786. 300 acres.
Talbot, John. Ga. ———. 27 Apr. 1784. 700 acres.
Talbot, William. Ga. ———. 27 Apr. 1784. 200 acres.
Talbott, Levi. Va. Private. 5 Mar. 1819. 100 acres.
Talcott, Bartlett. Conn. Sufferer. Ridgefield. 5.10.10.

Talcott, George. Conn. Sufferer. Ridgefield. 12.17.4.
Taliaferro, Benjamin. Va. Captain. 8 May 1783. 4666 2/3 acres.
Taliaferro, Nicholas. Va. Lieutenant. 17 Jun. 1783. 2666 2/3 acres.
Taliaferro, Nicholas. Va. Lieutenant. 20 Feb. 1809. 370 acres.
Taliaferro, Richard. Va. Captain. 20 Jan. 1834. 4000 acres.
Taliaferro, William. Va. Lieutenant Colonel. 16 Jun. 1783. 6000 acres.
Taliaferro, William. Va Lieutenant Colonel. 18 Mar. 1834. 1500 acres.
Taliaferro, William. Va. Lieutenant Colonel. 16 Mar. 1838. 391 1/2 acres.
Taliaferro, William. Va. Lieutenant Colonel. 16 Mar. 1838. 130 1/2 acres.
Taliaferro, William. Va. Lieutenant Colonel. 15 Aug. 1839. 195 3/4 acres.
Taliaferro, William. Va. Lieutenant. 23 Aug. 1854. 195 3/4 acres.
Taliaferro, William. Va. Lieutenant Colonel. 25 Apr. 1855. 130 1/2 acres.
Taliaferro, William. Va. Lieutenant Colonel. 25 Apr. 1855. 65 1/4 acres.
Talley, John. Va.-Ind. Private. 108 acres.
Talley, John, Jr. Va. Private. 1 Apr. 1785. 200 acres.
Talley, John, Sr. Va. Private. 1 Apr. 1785. 200 acres.
Talley, Thomas. Va. Private. 18 Apr. 1788. 100 acres.
Talliday, John. N. Y. Private. 8 Jul. 1790. 600 acres.
Tallifarro, Richard. N.C. Private. 30 Sep. 1785. 640 acres to heirs.
Tallmadge, Samuel. N. Y. Lieutenant. 9 Jul. 1790. 1200 acres.
Tallman, Bethiah. Conn. Sufferer. New London. 63.5.0.
Tallman, James. Va. Private. 25 Jan. 1812. 200 acres.
Tallman, Peter. N. Y. Captain. 9 Jul. 1790. 1800 acres.
Tally, Anthony. Va. Private. 21 Jan. 1817. 200 acres.
Talmadge, Timothy. Conn. Sufferer. New/ East Haven. 37.19.6.
Talton, James. N.C. Private. 28 Sep. 1785. 640 acres to heirs.
Talton, Thomas. N.C. Private. 30 Sep. 1785. 640 acres to heirs.
Talton, William. N.C. Private. 16 Aug. 1821. 640 acres.
Tame, John. N.C. Private. 8 Dec. 1796. 640 acres to acres.
Tankard, John. Va. Surgeon. 16 Sep. 1850. 6000 acres.
Tankersfield, John. Ga. ———. 17 Sep. 1784. 287 1/2 acres.
Tankersley, John. Ga. ———. 27 Apr. 1784. 1000 acres.
Tankesley, William. N.C. Private. 17 Feb. 1824. 640 acres.
Tann, Ephraim. N.C. ———. 8 Mar. 1785. 640 acres to heirs.
Tann, James. N.C. Private. 16 Aug. 1821. 640 acres to heirs.
Tann, Joseph. N.C. ———. 8 Mar. 1785. 640 acres to heirs.
Tannehill, Admomson. Md. Captain. ———. 200 acres.
Tannehill, Josiah. Md. Lieutenant. ———. 200 acres.
Tannehill, Josiah. Va. Lieutenant. 31 Mar. 1783. 1333 1/3 acres.
Tannehill, Josiah. Va. Lieutenant. 31 Mar. 1783. 1333 1/3 acres.
Tannehill, Thomas. Va. Sergeant. 23 Jun. 1783. 400 acres.
Tanner, Edward. Md. Private. ———. 50 acres.
Tanner, Jacob. Pa. Private. 29 Sep. 1787. 200 acres.
Tanner, Joel. Ga. ———. ———. 287 1/2 acres.
Tanner, John. N.C. Private. 30 Sep. 1785. 640 acres to heirs.
Tanner, John. Va. Private. 13 May 1786. 100 acres.
Tanner, Paul. Va. Private. 21 Feb. 1840. 100 acres.
Tanner, Thomas. Md. Private. ———. 50 acres.
Tanner, William. Va. Private. 7 Apr. 1784. 100 acres.
Tannyhill, John. Ga. Minute Man. 25 May 1784. 287 1/2 acres.
Tapley, Thomas. Va. Private. 22 Aug. 1783. 200 acres.
Tapp, Venet. Va. Private. 20 Jun. 1783. 100 acres.
Tapp, Vincent. Va. Sergeant Major. 3 Jun. 1783. 200 acres.
Tappar, William. S.C. ———. 4 Dec. 1786. 200 acres.

Tappen, Daniel. N. Y. Sergeant. 8 Jul. 1790. 600 acres.

Tappen, Peter. N. Y. Lieutenant. 7 Jul. 1790. 1200 acres.

Tapperwine, Christian. N.Y. ———. 16 Jan. 1795. 600 acres.

Tapscott, Ezekial. Va. Sailor. 27 Jul. 1783. 100 acres.

Tapscott, Ezekial. Va. Sailor. 12 Jan. 1842. 100 acres.

Tapscott, John. Va. Sailor. 27 Jul. 1783. 100 acres.

Tapscott, John. Va. Sailor. 12 Jan. 1842. 100 acres.

Tapscott, John. Va. Sergeant. 10 Sep. 1787/ 5 May 1791. 200 acres.

Tarbarra, Samuel. N.C. Private. 14 Sep. 1820. 640 acres.

Tarbell, David. Mass. Sergeant. 5 Feb. 1833. 200 acres.

Tarbell, Joseph. Me. ———. 18 Apr. 1835. 200 acres to widow Miriam Tarbell. Norridgewock.

Tarborough, John. Ga. ———. 5 Dec. 1785. 287 1/2 acres.

Tardwell, Abram. N.C. Private. 24 Nov. 1796. 230 acres.

Tarrant, Manlove. N.C. Captain. 20 Apr. 1784. 1371 acres.

Tarrant, Manlove. Va. Sergeant. 16 Dec. 1784. 400 acres.

Tarvin, George. Ga. ———. 21 Apr. 1784. 287 1/2 acres.

Tasco, Richard. Md. Private. ———. 50 acres.

Tasker, James. Va. Private. 22 Dec. 1783. 100 acres.

Tate, Adam. Va. Fifer. 26 Apr. 1783. 200 acres.

Tate, Enos. Ga. ———. 19 Apr. 1784. 650 acres.

Tate, James. Ga. ———. 19 Apr. 1784. 750 acres.

Tate, James. N.C. Chaplain. 21 Oct. 1783. 1553 acres.

Tate, James. Va. Private. 28 Dec. 1785 [?1784]. 100 acres.

Tate, James. Va. Sergeant. 29 Mar. 1806. 200 acres.

Tate, John. N.C. Private. 20 Feb. 1818. 640 acres to heirs.

Tate, Joseph. N.C. Captain. 26 Apr. 1784. 3840 acres to Adam Tate, heir.

Tate, Mathew. Va. Private. 8 May 1838. 100 acres.

Tate, Mathew. Va. Private. 8 May 1838. 100 acres.

Tate, Richard. Ga. Citizen. 22 Mar. 1785. 250 acres.

Tate, Robert. Va. Private. 20 Nov. 1784. 100 acres.

Tate, Robert. Va. Sailor. 29 Jan. 1788. 100 acres.

Tate, Thomas. N.C. Private. 7 Jan. 1786. 640 acres.

Tate, William. N.C. Trooper. 21 Oct. 1783. 274 acres.

Tate, William. S.C. Captain Lieutenant. 16 Jul. 1784. 300 acres.

Tatom, Abner. Ga. ———. 20 Apr. 1784. 350 acres.

Tatom, Bernard. N.C. Private. 22 Apr. 1785. 228 acres.

Tatom, Peter. Ga. ———. 3 Oct. 1785. 287 1/2 acres.

Tatum, Christopher. S.C. ———. 3 Mar. 1788. 200 acres.

Tatum, Henry. Va. Lieutenant. 24 Dec. 1802. 1000 acres.

Tatum, Henry. Va. Lieutenant. 24 Dec. 1802. 1000 acres.

Tatum, Henry. Va. Lieutenant. 24 Dec. 1802. 666 2/3 acres.

Tatum, Henry. Va. Lieutenant. 8 Jan. 1807. 444 1/3 acres.

Tatum, Henry. Va. Lieutenant. 10 Feb. 1808. 296 acres.

Tatum, Howell. N.C. Captain. 27 Nov. 1783. 3565 acres.

Tatum, James. N.C. Lieutenant. 27 Nov. 1783. 2560 acres.

Tatum, John. N.C. Private. 21 Apr. 1784. 274 acres.

Tatum, Zacheriah. Va. Sulaltern. 28 Feb. 1784. 2666 2/3 acres.

Taunt, Jesse. N.C. Drummer. 21 Apr. 1784. 1000 acres.

Taunt, Thomas. N.C. Private. 21 Apr. 1784. 640 acres.

Taybourn, Joel. N.C. Private. 19 May 1784. 640 acres.

Tayler, Charels. Va. Surgeon. 3 Jun. 1839. 563 acres.

Tayler, Charles. Va. Surgeon. 3 Jun. 1839. 563 acres.

Tayler, Charles. Va. Surgeon. 3 Jun. 1839. 187 acres.

Tayler, Charles. Va. Surgeon. 3 Jun. 1839. 563 acres.
Tayler, Charles. Va. Surgeon. 3 Jun. 1839. 187 acres.
Tayler, Charles. Va. Surgeon. 3 Jun. 1839. 187 acres.
Tayler, Zebediah. Conn. Sufferer. Greenwich. 10.0.0.
Taylor, Aaron. N.C. Musician. 14 Jul. 1820. 1000 acres to heirs.
Taylor, Abraham. Va.-Ind. Private. 108 acres.
Taylor, Abraham. N.C. Private. 29 Sep. 1784. 274 acres.
Taylor, Archibald. Va. Private. 20 Aug. 1783. 200 acres.
Taylor, Ayres. Va. Seaman. 9 Dec. 1833. 100 acres.
Taylor, Bartholomew. Va. Private. 14 Apr. 1783. 200 acres.
Taylor, Benjamin. Ga. Minute Man. 27 Apr. 1784. 200 acres.
Taylor, Benjamin. N.C. Corporal. 24 Jul. 1821. 1000 acres to heirs.
Taylor, Benjamin. Va. Midshipman. 13 May 1783. 2666 2/3 acres.
Taylor, Benjamin. Va. Private. 14 Feb. 1834. 100 acres.
Taylor, Benjamin. Conn. Sufferer. Danbury. 2.15.4.
Taylor, Caleb. N.C. Private. 20 Sep. 1821. 640 acres to heirs.
Taylor, Cawfield. Va. Sergeant. 1 Oct. 1811. 200 acres.
Taylor, Charles. Va. Private. 9 Dec. 1783. 100 acres.
Taylor, Charles. Va. Surgeon. 10 Mar. 1838. 750 acres.
Taylor, Charles. Va. Surgeon. 10 Mar. 1838. 1500 acres.
Taylor, Charles. Va. Surgeon. 10 Mar. 1838. 750 acres.
Taylor, Charles. Va. Surgeon. 10 Mar. 1838. 750 acres.
Taylor, Charles. Va. Surgeon. 10 Mar. 1838. 750 acres.
Taylor, Charles. Va. Surgeon. 10 Mar. 1838. 750 acres.
Taylor, Charles. Va. Surgeon. 3 Jun. 1839. 563 acres.
Taylor, Charles. Va. Surgeon. 3 Jun. 1839. 187 acres.
Taylor, Charles. Va. Surgeon. 28 Jul./29 Aug. 1848. 887 1/2 acres.
Taylor, Charles. Va. Surgeon. 28 Jul./29 Aug. 1848. 887 1/2 acres.
Taylor, Charles. Va. Surgeon. 10 Jul. 1838. 375 acres.
Taylor, Charles. Va. Surgeon. 10 Jul. 1838. 1125 acres.
Taylor, Charles. Va. Surgeon. 16 Mar. 1841. 562 1/2 acres.
Taylor, Charles. Va. Surgeon. 16 Mar. 1841. 562 1/2 acres.
Taylor, Charles. Va. Surgeon. 22 Sep. 1848. 592 acres.
Taylor, Charles. Va. Surgeon. 22 Sep. 1848. 295 acres.
Taylor, Charles. Va. Surgeon. 18 Oct. 1847. 322 acres.
Taylor, Charles. Va. Surgeon. 18 Oct. 1847. 80 1/2 acres.
Taylor, Charles. Va. Surgeon. 18 Oct. 1847. 80 1/2 acres.
Taylor, Charles. Va. Surgeon. 26 Oct. 1847. 185 acres.
Taylor, Charles. Va. Surgeon. 19 Apr. 1856. 563 acres.
Taylor, Christian. Pa. Surgeon. ———. 300 acres.
Taylor, Daniel. Va. Seaman. 8 Jun. 1833. 100 acres.
Taylor, Daniel. Conn. Sufferer. Danbury. 656.0.1 1/4.
Taylor, Edward. N. Y. Private. 8 Jul. 1790. 500 acres.
Taylor, Elias. Conn. Sufferer. Danbury. 4.2.0.
Taylor, Elijah. N.C. Private. 2 Feb. 1786. 274 acres.
Taylor, Elizabeth. Ga. ———. 27 Apr. 1784. 500 acres.
Taylor, Ephraim. Me. Private. 10 May 1835. 200 acres. New Castle.
Taylor, Ferguson. Va. Fifer. 5 Aug. 1783. 100 acres.
Taylor, Francis. Md. Private. ———. 50 acres.
Taylor, Francis. Va. Major. 22 Nov. 1783. 5333 1/3 acres.
Taylor, Francis. Va. Major. 1 Oct. 1800. 888 2/3 acres.
Taylor, Francis. Va. Major. 11 Sep. 1807. 888 2/3 acres.
Taylor, Francis. Va. Colonel. 16 Sep. 1850. 1876 1/3 acres.
Taylor, Francis. Va. ———. 16 Apr. 1851. 625 1/3 acres.

Taylor, Francis. Va. ———. 16 Apr. 1851. 1251 acres.
Taylor, George. Md. Private. ———. 50 acres.
Taylor, Giles. Va. Private. 14 Feb. 1834. 200 acres.
Taylor, Giles. Va. Private. 9 Aug. 1841. 200 acres.
Taylor, Hannah. Conn. Sufferer. Fairfield. 40.4.0.
Taylor, Henry. Ga. ———. 17 Apr. 1784. 287 1/2 acres.
Taylor, Henry. N.C. Private. 12 Sep. 1785. 640 acres to heirs.
Taylor, Humphrey. Va. Private. 28 May 1783. 100 acres.
Taylor, Isaac. Va.-Ind. Captain. 3234 acres.
Taylor, Isaac. Va. Sergeant. 26 Jun. 1783. 466 2/3 acres.
Taylor, Isaac. Va. Captain. 3 Mar. 1784. 4000 acres.
Taylor, Jabez. Va. ———. 30 May 1840. 411 1/9 acres.
Taylor, Jabez. Va. ———. 30 May 1840. 822 2/9 acres.
Taylor, Jabez. Va. ———. 30 May 1840. 154 3/18 acres.
Taylor, Jabez. Va. ———. 30 May 1840. 154 3/18 acres.
Taylor, Jabez. Va. Boatswain's Mate. 28 Mar. 1842. 89 acres.
Taylor, Jabez. Va. Boatswain's Mate. 4 Apr. 1842. 125 acres.
Taylor, Jabez. Va. Boatswain. 2 Dec. 1853. 411 1/9 acres.
Taylor, Jabez. Va. Boatswain. 2 Dec. 1853. 57 7/8 acres.
Taylor, Jabez. Va. Boatswain. 2 Dec. 1853. 102 7/9 acres.
Taylor, Jabez. Va. Boatswain. 2 Dec. 1853. 51 7/9 acres.
Taylor, Jabez. Va. Boatswain. 2 Dec. 1853. 102 7/9 acres.
Taylor, Jabez. Va. Boatswain's Mate. 14 Dec. 1833. 200 acres.
Taylor, James. Ga. Captain. 27 Apr. 1784. 575 acres.
Taylor, James. N.C. Sergeant. 20 Apr. 1784. 535 acres.
Taylor, James. N.C. Corporal. 10 Jul. 1820. 154 acres to heirs.
Taylor, James. Va. Sergeant. 5 Aug. 1783. 200 acres.
Taylor, James. Va. Private. 31 Jan. 1784. 100 acres.
Taylor, James. Va. Sergeant. 6 Feb. 1784. 200 acres.
Taylor, James. Va. Private. 5 Apr. 1784. 200 acres.
Taylor, James. Va. Drum Major. 9 Dec. 1785. 100 acres.
Taylor, James. Va. Private. 26 Oct. 1793. 200 acres.
Taylor, James. Va. Lieutenant. 19 Jul. 1837. 1333 acres.
Taylor, James, Sr. N.C. Private. 17 Feb. 1824. 640 acres.
Taylor, Jesse. Ga. Minute Man. 14 Feb. 1785. ———.
Taylor, Jesse. N.C. Private. 22 Jul. 1784. 640 acres.
Taylor, John. Ga. Minute Man. 13 May 1784. 287 1/2 acres.
Taylor, John. Ga. ———. 27 Apr. 1784. 200 acres.
Taylor, John. Md. Private. ———. 50 acres.
Taylor, John. Md. Private. ———. 50 acres.
Taylor, John. Mass. Drummer. 30 Nov. 1832. 200 acres.
Taylor, John. N. Y. Matross. 9 Jul. 1790. 500 acres.
Taylor, John. N.C. Private. 10 Dec. 1788. 640 acres.
Taylor, John. N.C. Private. 10 Dec. 1788. 640 acres to heirs.
Taylor, John. N.C. Private. 13 Jan. 1792. 640 acres.
Taylor, John. N.C. Private. 22 Dec. 1796. 274 acres.
Taylor, John. N.C. Paymaster. 17 Feb. 1824. 2560 acres.
Taylor, John. N.C. Musician. 17 Feb. 1824. 640 acres.
Taylor, John. S.C. ———. 2 Oct. 1786. 200 acres.
Taylor, John. Va. Private. 15 Dec. 1785. 100 acres.
Taylor, John. Va. Major. 9 Aug. 1799. 5333 1/3 acres.
Taylor, John. Va. Sergeant. 5 Oct. 1811. 200 acres.
Taylor, John. Va. Private. 20 Mar. 1832. 200 acres.
Taylor, John. Va. Lieutenant. 13 Nov. 1832. 2666 2/3 acres.

Taylor, John. Conn. Sufferer. Danbury. 11.3.8.
Taylor, Jonathan. Conn. Sufferer. Danbury. 6.1.6.
Taylor, Joseph. N.C. Private. 10 Jul. 1820. 228 acres to heirs.
Taylor, Josiah. Ga. ———. 21 Apr. 1784. 287 1/2 acres.
Taylor, Josiah, Jr. Conn. Sufferer. Norwalk. 4.9.10.
Taylor, Judith. Conn. Sufferer. Danbury. 1.8.0.
Taylor, Knevit. Va. Private. 9 Dec. 1833. 200 acres.
Taylor, Levin. Va. Seaman. 27 Nov. 1832. 100 acres.
Taylor, Major. Va. Private. 14 Apr. 1783. 200 acres.
Taylor, Major. Conn. Sufferer. Danbury. 462.12.2.
Taylor, Mary. Conn. Sufferer. New London. 26.15.10.
Taylor, Matthew. Conn. Sufferer. Danbury. 23.19.6.
Taylor, Nathan, 3d. Conn. Sufferer. Danbury. 15.5.0.
Taylor, Nathan, Jr. Conn. Sufferer. Danbury. 4.0.8.
Taylor, Noah. Me. ———. 18 Jun. 1835. 200 acres. Sanford.
Taylor, Oliver. Conn. Sufferer. Danbury. 4.16.10.
Taylor, Philip. N.C. Captain. 24 Oct. 1783. 1759 acres.
Taylor, Philip. N.C. Captain. 1 Jul. 1825. 24 acres.
Taylor, Reuben. Mass. Private. 18 Oct. 1833. 200 acres.
Taylor, Reuben. Va. Captain. 22 Nov. 1783. 4000 acres.
Taylor, Richard. Md. Private. ———. 50 acres.
Taylor, Richard. Va. Captain. 19 Feb. 1783. 5333 1/3 acres.
Taylor, Richard. Va. Lieutenant Colonel. 8 Sep. 1783. 6000 acres.
Taylor, Richard. Va. Lieutenant Colonel. 20 Apr. 1799. 1000 acres.
Taylor, Richard. Va. Lieutenant Colonel. 1 Aug. 1799. 1000 acres.
Taylor, Richard. Va. Lieutenant Colonel. 11 Sep. 1807. 166 2/3 acres.
Taylor, Richard. Va. Lieutenant. 15 Sep. 1810. 2666 2/3 acres.
Taylor, Richard. Va. Captain. 26 Feb. & 1 Mar. 1834. 2000 acres.
Taylor, Richard C. Va. Private. 30 Dec. 1828. 100 acres.
Taylor, Robert. Ga. ———. 27 Apr. 1784. 287 1/2 acres.
Taylor, Robert. Md. Sergeant. ———. 50 acres.
Taylor, Robert. Va. Private. 24 Jul. 1784. 200 acres.
Taylor, Robert. Va. Private. 30 Jun. 1784. 100 acres.
Taylor, Robeson. Va. Private. 14 Feb. 1834. 100 acres.
Taylor, Roland. Ga. ———. 27 Apr. 1784. 200 acres.
Taylor, Samuel. Ga. ———. 27 Apr. 1784. 800 acres.
Taylor, Samuel. Md. Private. ———. 50 acres.
Taylor, Samuel. S.C. Major. 16 Jul. 1784. 400 acres.
Taylor, Samuel. Va. Private. 14 Apr. 1783. 100 acres.
Taylor, Samuel. Conn. Sufferer. Fairfield. 9.17.0.
Taylor, Samuel. Conn. Sufferer. Danbury. 22.1.2.
Taylor, Selby. Va. Private. 9 Dec. 1833. 200 acres.
Taylor, Stephen. Mass. Sergeant. 9 Jul. 1834. 200 acres.
Taylor, Thomas. Ga. ———. 27 Apr. 1784. 287 1/2 acres.
Taylor, Thomas. Va. Seaman. 9 Dec. 1833. 100 acres.
Taylor, Thomas. Va. ———. 28 Mar. 1837. 100 acres.
Taylor, Thomas. Conn. Sufferer. Danbury. 11.18.3.
Taylor, Thomas. Conn. Sufferer. Danbury. 32.5.4.
Taylor, Thomas, Jr. Conn. Sufferer. Danbury. 10.2.0.
Taylor, Thornton. Va. Lieutenant. 20 Sep. 1784. 2666 2/3 acres.
Taylor, William. Ga. ———. 27 Apr. 1784. 287 1/2 acres.
Taylor, William. Va.-Ind. Private. 108 acres. [Tyler].
Taylor, William. Md. Private. ———. 50 acres.
Taylor, William. Md. Private. ———. 50 acres.

Taylor, William. N.C. Private. 22 Feb. 1784. 274 acres.

Taylor, William. N.C. Private. 8 Dec. 1796. 640 acres.

Taylor, William. N.C. Private. 17 Dec. 1796. 274 acres.

Taylor, William. Va. Major. 19 Feb. 1783. 5333 1/3 acres.

Taylor, William. Va. Sergeant. 25 Dec. 1784. 200 acres.

Taylor, William. Va. Private. 11 Jan. 1786. 200 acres.

Taylor, William. Va. Major. 15 Apr. 1800. 889 acres.

Taylor, William. Va. Major. 11 Sep. 1807. 888 2/3 acres.

Taylor, William, Jr. Md. Private. ———. 50 acres.

Taylor, Zacheriah. Va. Private. 18 Nov. 1819. 100 acres.

Teackle, Severn. Va. Captain. 15 Jan. 1808. 1221 acres.

Teagle, Severn. Va. Captain. 4 Jun. 1792. 4000 acres.

Teague, John. S.C. ———. 2 May 1785. 200 acres.

Teakle, Arthur. Va. Lieutenant. 18 Apr. 1823. 3111 17/160 acres.

Teal, Jacob. N.C. Private. 12 Oct. 1795. 640 acres to heirs.

Teall, Levi. Va.-Ind. Private. 108 acres.

Teas, William. Va. Cornet. 14 Dec. 1832. 2666 2/3 acres.

Teasley, John. N.C. Private. 11 Sep. 1820. 640 acres to heirs.

Tebbs, Thomas. Va. Captain. 4 Jul. 1783. 4000 acres.

Teddrick, James. N.C. Private. 6 Dec. 1797. 640 acres to heirs.

Teel, Jeremiah. Pa. Private. 2 Apr. 1787. 200 acres.

Teer, William. N.C. Private. 23 Apr. 1784. 640 acres.

Tees, Charles. Ga. ———. 27 Apr. 1784. 550 acres.

Telfair, Edward. Ga. ———. 27 Apr. 1784. 575 acres.

Telkins, John. Va. Private. 29 Oct. 1783. 100 acres.

Tellier, Charles. N. Y. ———. ———. 500 acres.

Temple, Alexander. Va. Sailor. 20 Nov. 1784. 100 acres.

Temple, Alexander. Va. Seaman. 15 Apr. 1803. 100 acres.

Temple, Benjamin. Va. Lieutenant Colonel. 6 Feb. 1784. 6000 acres.

Temple, Benjamin. Va. Lieutenant Colonel. 8 Dec. 1785. 1000 acres.

Temple, Benjamin. Va. Colonel. 2 Oct. 1807. 555 1/2 acres.

Temple, Ebenezer. N. Y. Matross. 9 Jul. 1790. 600 acres.

Temple, Humphrey. Va. Mate. 19 May 1838. 500 acres.

Temple, Humphrey. Va. Mate. 19 May 1838. 2166 2/3 acres.

Temple, Humphrey. Va. Mate. 16 Mar. 1847. 500 acres.

Temple, Jacob. S.C. ———. 2 Mar. 1789. 100 acres.

Temple, John. Ga. ———. 20 Dec. 1785. 575 acres.

Temple, John. Mass. Lieutenant. 2 Mar. 1833. 200 acres.

Temple, John. Va. Private. 30 Jun. 1784. 100 acres.

Temple, Peter. S.C. ———. 2 Mar. 1789. 100 acres.

Temple, Thomas. N.Y. ———. 13 Sep. 1790. 500 acres to heirs.

Templeston, William. N.C. Drummer. 30 Sep. 1785. 1000 acres to heirs.

Templeton, Andrew. Ga. Captain. 17 May 1784. 690 acres.

Templeton, Thomas. N.C. Sergeant. 30 Mar. 1785. 428 acres.

Tenant, Caesar. Va. Pilot. 1 Aug. 1831. 2666 2/3 acres.

TenBrook, Adam. N. Y. Ensign. 9 Jul. 1790. 1150 acres.

TenBrook, C. John. N. Y. Captain. 9 Jul. 1790. 1800 acres.

TenEyck, Abraham. N. Y. Lieutenant. 9 Jul. 1790. 1200 acres.

TenEyck, D. P. John. N. Y. Captain. 13 Sep. 1790. 1800 acres.

TenEyck, Henry. N. Y. Captain. 13 Oct. 1802. 1000 acres.

TenEyck, John. N.Y. ———. 13 Sep. 1790. 500 acres to heirs.

TenEyck, Joseph. N. Y. Private. 6 Jul. 1790. 600 acres.

Tennell, Francis. Ga. Lieutenant. 27 Apr. 1784. 460 acres.

Tennell, George. Va. Private. 28 Aug. 1784. 200 acres.

Tenville, Alexis. N. Y. ———. ———. 500 acres.
Ternan, Dennis. Md. Private. ———. 50 acres.
Terrel, Ruebin. N.C. Private. 14 Dec. 1797. 640 acres to heirs.
Terrell, Aaron. N.C. Private. 15 Feb. 1797. 320 acres.
Terrell, Harry. Va. Colonel. 30 Dec. 1851. 600 acres.
Terrell, Harry. Va. Colonel. 30 Dec. 1851. 600 acres.
Terrell, Harry. Va. Colonel. 30 Dec. 1851. 1200 acres.
Terrell, Harry. Va. Colonel. 30 Dec. 1851. 1200 acres.
Terrell, Harry. Va. Colonel. 30 Dec. 1851. 153 1/3 acres.
Terrell, John. N.C. Private. 17 Feb. 1824. 640 acres.
Terrell, Joseph. N.C. Private. 18 Dec. 1797. 640 acres.
Terrell, Nimrod. N.C. Drummer. 15 Feb. 1797. 1000 acres.
Terrell, Presley. Va. Colonel. 25 Aug. 1821. 200 acres.
Terrell, Richard. N.C. Private. 6 Feb. 1823. 640 acres.
Terrell, Sampson. N.C. Private. 11 Feb. 1796. 640 acres.
Terrell, William. Ga. ———. 22 Apr. 1784. 1000 acres.
Terrell, William. Va. Corporal. 16 Jul. 1783. 400 acres.
Terrell, William. Va. Lieutenant. 2 Sep. 1808. 500 acres.
Terrell, William. Va. Lieutenant. 2 Sep. 1808. 500 acres.
Terrell, William. Va. Lieutenant. 2 Sep. 1808. 1000 acres.
Terrell, William. Va. Lieutenant. 2 Sep. 1808. 666 2/3 acres.
Terrell, William, Jr. Ga. ———. 22 Apr. 1784. 250 acres.
Terrems, John. Ga. Soldier. 6 Dec. 1785. 460 acres.
Terril, Edmund. Va. Sergeant. 26 Nov. 1783. 200 acres.
Terril, Henry. N.C. Private. 14 Dec. 1797. 228 acres.
Terrill, David. Ga. ———. 5 Apr. 1785. 287 1/2 acres.
Terrill, Harry. Va. Major. 7 Aug. 1813. 3999 1/3 acres.
Terrill, Harry. Va. Major. 7 Aug. 1813. 444 2/3 acres.
Terrill, Harry. Va. Major. 7 Aug. 1813. 444 2/3 acres.
Terrill, Harry. Va. Major. 7 Aug. 1813. 444 2/3 acres.
Terrill, Joel. Ga. ———. 22 Apr. 1784. 500 acres.
Terrill, Peter. Ga. ———. 22 Apr. 1784. 250 acres.
Terrill, Simon. N.C. Private. 9 Dec. 1797. 640 acres.
Terry, James. Md. Private. ———. 50 acres.
Terry, James. Va. Private. 3 Sep. 1784. 100 acres.
Terry, Nathaniel. Va. Captain. 23 Feb. 1784. 4666 2/3 acres.
Terry, Nathaniel. Va. Captain. 22 Dec. 1809. 500 acres.
Terry, Obediah. Va. Private. 18 Apr. 1823. 100 acres.
Terry, Oliver. N.C. Private. 17 Dec. 1785. 640 acres to heirs.
Terry, Samuel. N.Y. ———. 13 Sep. 1790. 500 acres to heirs.
Terry, Sarah. Ga. ———. 20 Apr. 1784. 200 acres.
Terry, Stephen. Va. Corporal. 8 Feb. 1783. 200 acres.
Terry, Thomas. Va. Private. 14 Oct. 1818. 100 acres.
Terry, Thomas. Va. Private. 4 Nov. 1819. 100 acres.
Tessier, Charles. N. Y. ———. ———. 500 acres.
Tessier, Jean. N. Y. ———. ———. 500 acres.
Tewahangaraghkan, Hanyere. N.Y. Captain. 29 Jan. 1791. 1800 acres. [an Indian].
Tewahongarahken, Hanyost. N.Y. Lieutenant. 29 Jan. 1791. 1200 acres. [an Indian].
Thacker, Stephen. N. Y. Matross. 9 Jul. 1790. 500 acres.
Thackery, Thomas. Pa. Private. 16 Dec. 1808. 200 acres to Juliana Thackery, widow.
Thacknill, Rezin. Md. Private. ———. 50 acres.
Thackston, James. N.C. Lieutenant Colonel Commandant. 25 Oct. 1783. 4352 acres.
Thankfield, Daniel. N.C. Private. 13 Dec. 1796. 640 acres to heirs.

Tharp, Elkanah. Va. Sergeant. 24 Jan. 1784. 466 2/3 acres.
Tharp, Job. N.C. Private. 20 Dec. 1803. 640 acres.
Tharp, Jonathan. Va. Private. 9 Dec. 1833. 200 acres.
Tharpwell, William. Pa. 11 Nov. 1788. ——— to Stephen Loudon, assignee.
Thatch, Daniel. Conn. Sufferer. Norwalk. 215.17.0 to his heirs.
Thatcher, David. N.C. Private. 6 Feb. 1823. 640 acres.
Thatcher, Josiah. Conn. Sufferer. Norwalk. 400.6.5 1/2.
Thatcher, Josiah, Capt. Conn. Sufferer. Norwalk. 16.7.4.
Thatcher, Josiah, Jr. Conn. Sufferer. Norwalk. 193.17.8.
Thatcher, Stephen G. Conn. Sufferer. Norwalk. 13.1.5.
Thayar, William. Va. Sergeant Major. 22 Aug. 1783. 466 2/3 acres.
Thayer, Caleb. Mass. Corporal. 13 Jul. 1835. 200 acres.
Thayer, Cornelius. Conn. Sufferer. New/ East Haven. 3.17.8.
Thayer, John. N. Y. Matross. 9 Jul. 1790. 600 acres.
Thayer, Levi. Mass. Private. 16 Sep. 1833. 200 acres.
Thayer, William. Va. Sergeant Major. 22 Jan. 1834. 400 acres.
Thayer, William. Va. Sergeant Major. 3 Mar. 1853. 200 acres.
Thayer, William. Va. Sergeant Major. 3 Mar. 1853. 200 acres.
Theel, Levi. Va. Private. 17 Jul. 1784. 100 acres.
Thegott, John. Ga. Minute Man. 22 Mar. 1785. 250 acres.
Thelaball, Robert. Va. Lieutenant. 2 Sep. 1811. 1333 1/3 acres.
Thelaball, Robert. Va. Lieutenant. 2 Sep. 1811. 500 acres.
Thelaball, Robert. Va. Lieutenant. 2 Sep. 1811. 500 acres.
Thelaball, Robert. Va. Lieutenant. 2 Sep. 1811. 333 1/3 acres.
Therrell, Abraham. N.C. Private. 24 Dec. 1785. 640 acres to heirs.
Therrogood, Francis. N.C. Corporal. 11 May 1784. 773 acres.
Theus, Simeon. S.C. Captain. 21 Jan. 1785. 300 acres.
Thickling, John. Conn. Sufferer. Fairfield. 20.8.9.
Thirman, David. Ga. ———. 15 Mar. 1784. 250 acres.
Thirmon, John. Ga. ———. 15 Mar. 1784. 250 acres.
Tholly, William. Pa. ———. 200 acres to Joseph Stout, assignee.
Thom, John. Pa. ———. 14 Jan. 1796. 200 acres to Daniel Richards, executor.
Thomas [or Thompson], Giles. Md. Private. ———. 50 acres.
Thomas, Amos. Va. Private. 2 May 1783. 200 acres.
Thomas, Asa. N.C. Private. 29 Sep. 1784. 228 acres.
Thomas, Augustin. Ga. ———. 23 Apr. 1784. 400 acres.
Thomas, Benajah. Conn. Sufferer. New/ East Haven. 7.6.7.
Thomas, Benjamin. Ga. Minute Man. 20 Apr. 1784. 287 1/2 acres.
Thomas, Benjamin. Ga. Sergeant. 23 Apr. 1784. 200 acres.
Thomas, Benjamin. N.C. Private. 30 Apr. 1784. 640 acres.
Thomas, Benjamin. N.C. Private. 7 Dec. 1796. 640 acres.
Thomas, Brittain. N.C. ———. 14 Jun. 1785. 640 acres to heir.
Thomas, Caleb. N.C. Private. 19 May 1784. 640 acres.
Thomas, Charles. N.C. Sergeant. 14 Dec. 1796. 428 acres.
Thomas, Daniel. Va. Private. 4 Jun. 1783. 200 acres.
Thomas, Daniel. Va. Private. 25 Jul. 1834. 100 acres.
Thomas, Demcy. N.C. Private. 8 Dec. 1796. 640 acres.
Thomas, Dempsey. S.C. ———. 1 Aug. 1785. 200 acres.
Thomas, Elisha. Va. Private. 14 Oct. 1784. 100 acres.
Thomas, Evan. Md. Private. ———. 50 acres.
Thomas, Evan. Pa. Private. 4 Oct. 1786. 200 acres to Elizabeth Thomas, widow.
Thomas, Ezekiel. N. Y. Sergeant. 8 Jul. 1790. 600 acres.
Thomas, George. Ga. Minute Man. 3 Sep. 1785. ———.
Thomas, George. Va. Private. 9 Nov. 1811. 100 acres.

Thomas, Gideon. Ga. ———. 23 Apr. 1784. 287 1/2 acres.

Thomas, Gilshot. Ga. ———. 21 Apr. 1784. 575 acres.

Thomas, Henry. N. Y. Private. 8 Jul. 1790. 600 acres.

Thomas, Henry. Va. Private. 5 Apr. 1784. 100 acres.

Thomas, Jacob. Va. Private. 17 Feb. 1784. 100 acres.

Thomas, James. Ga. Minute Man. 21 Apr. 1784. 287 1/2 acres.

Thomas, James. Ga. ———. 22 Apr. 1784. 200 acres.

Thomas, James. Va. Private. 4 Mar. 1819. 100 acres.

Thomas, James. Va. Boatswain. 21 Mar. 1840. 1333 1/3 acres.

Thomas, James. Va. Boatswain. 21 Mar. 1840. 1333 1/3 acres.

Thomas, James. Va. Boatswain. 30 Jun. 1856. 1333 1/3 acres.

Thomas, James, Jr. Md. Private. ———. 50 acres.

Thomas, James, Sr. Md. Sergeant. ———. 50 acres.

Thomas, Jeremiah. N.C. ———. 8 Mar. 1785. 640 acres to heirs.

Thomas, Jeremiah. N.C. Private. 30 Sep. 1785. 640 acres to heirs.

Thomas, Jesse. Ga. Minute Man. 21 Apr. 1784. 800 acres.

Thomas, John. Ga. ———. 15 Mar. 1784. 250 acres.

Thomas, John. Md. Private. ———. 50 acres.

Thomas, John. Md. Sergeant. ———. 50 acres.

Thomas, John. Md. Private. ———. 50 acres.

Thomas, John. N. Y. Corporal. 9 Jul. 1790. 600 acres.

Thomas, John. N.Y. ———. 13 Sep. 1790. 500 acres to heirs.

Thomas, John. N.C. Private. 29 Sep. 1784. 297 acres.

Thomas, John. N.C. Private. 30 Sep. 1785. 640 acres to heirs.

Thomas, John. N.C. Ensign. 1 Jul. 1825. 1280 acres.

Thomas, John. Pa. Matross. 9 Nov. 1786. 200 acres to John Longstreth, assignee.

Thomas, John. Va. Captain. 13 Jan. 1786. 4000 acres.

Thomas, John. Va. Captain. 2 Nov. 1830. 4000 acres.

Thomas, John. Va. Captain. 8 Jun. 1832. 1333 1/3 acres.

Thomas, John. Va. Captain. 23 Apr. 1860. 894 acres.

Thomas, John German. Md. ———. 50 acres.

Thomas, Joseph. N. Y. Captain. 9 Jul. 1790. 1800 acres.

Thomas, Joseph. Va. Private. 6 May 1784. 100 acres.

Thomas, Joseph. Va. Private. 14 Oct. 1784. 100 acres.

Thomas, Josiah. Pa. Private. 19 Jun. 1794. 200 acres to Jacob Stroud.

Thomas, Josiah. Pa. Private. ———. 200 acres to Jacob Stroud, assignee.

Thomas, Lemuel. N.C. Private. 22 Feb. 1784. 640 acres.

Thomas, Levin. Md. Private. ———. 50 acres.

Thomas, Lewis. Va. Private. 10 Mar. 1784. 4000 acres.

Thomas, Mark. Va. Captain. 26 Mar. 1831. 3000 acres.

Thomas, Mark. Va. Captain. 26 Mar. 1831. 1000 acres.

Thomas, Mark. Va. Captain. 2 Dec. 1833. 125 acres.

Thomas, Mark. Va. Captain. 2 Dec. 1833. 125 acres.

Thomas, Mark. Va. Captain. 2 Dec. 1833. 125 acres.

Thomas, Mark. Va. Captain. 2 Dec. 1833. 125 acres.

Thomas, Mark. Va. Captain. 2 Dec. 1833. 125 acres.

Thomas, Mark. Va. Captain. 2 Dec. 1833. 125 acres.

Thomas, Mark. Va. Captain. 2 Dec. 1833. 125 acres.

Thomas, Mark. Va. Captain. 2 Dec. 1833. 125 acres.

Thomas, Martin. N.C. Private. 2 Feb. 1786. 640 acres.

Thomas, Masey. Va. Private. 18 Feb. 1784. 100 acres.

Thomas, Peter. Ga. Refugee. 15 Mar. 1784. 500 acres.

Thomas, Peter. Va. Private. 20 Oct. 1796. 200 acres.

Thomas, Philip. Ga. ———. 23 Apr. 1784. 450 acres.

Thomas, Philip. N.C. Private. 4 Aug. 1821. 640 acres.

Thomas, Philip. N.C. Private. 1 May 1826. 640 acres to heirs.

Thomas, Reuben. Va. Sergeant. 12 Jan. 1819. 200 acres.

Thomas, Richard. N.C. Private. 5 May 1784. 228 acres.

Thomas, Robert. N.C. Sergeant. 28 May 1784. 428 acres.

Thomas, Ross. N.C. Private. 17 Dec. 1785. 274 acres.

Thomas, Samuel. Ga. Refugee. 26 May 1784. 287 1/2 acres.

Thomas, Thomas. N.C. Private. 30 Sep. 1785. 640 acres to heirs.

Thomas, William. Ga. ———. 27 Apr. 1784. 200 acres.

Thomas, William. N.C. Private. 7 Jan. 1784. 640 acres.

Thomas, William. Pa. Private. ———. 200 acres.

Thomas, William. Pa. Ranger. 17 Mar. 1789. 200 acres.

Thomas, William. S.C. ———. 6 Nov. 1786. 200 acres.

Thomas, William. Va. Corporal. 1 May 1783. 400 acres.

Thomas, William. Va. Private. 2 May 1783. 200 acres.

Thomas, William. Va. Private. 9 Dec. 1783. 100 acres.

Thomas, William. Va. Private. 17 Apr. 1784. 100 acres.

Thomas, Zebulon. N.C. Private. 19 Jan. 1786. 640 acres.

Thomasson, John. N.C. Private. 23 Apr. 1784. 640 acres.

Thomlin, Thomas. S.C. ———. 3 Dec. 1792. 115 acres.

Thompson, Abigail. Conn. Sufferer. Fairfield. 8.10.0.

Thompson, Abraham. Conn. Sufferer. New/ East Haven. 5.2.2.

Thompson, Ahab. N.C. Private. 2 Feb. 1786. 640 acres.

Thompson, Alexander. Ga. ———. 27 Apr. 1784. 200 acres.

Thompson, Alexander. Me. Private. 1 May 1835. 200 acres to widow Lydia Thompson. Topsham.

Thompson, Alexander. N. Y. Lieutenant. 8 Jul. 1790. 1200 acres.

Thompson, Andrew. N. Y. Lieutenant. 13 Sep. 1790. 1200 acres.

Thompson, Archibald. N.Y. ——. 13 Sep. 1790. 500 acres to heirs.

Thompson, Ayler. N.C. Private. 10 Dec. 1788. 640 acres to heirs.

Thompson, Benjamin. Ga. Refugee. 22 Apr. 1784. 575 acres.

Thompson, Benjamin. Me. Lieutenant. 23 Mar. 1843. 600 acres to his widow Rhoda (Ham) Thompson. Topsham.

Thompson, Benjamin. N. Y. Private. 8 Jul. 1790. 500 acres.

Thompson, Benjamin. N. Y. Lieutenant. ———. 666 2/3 acres.

Thompson, Benjamin, Jr. Ga. Refugee. 22 Apr. 1784. 287 1/2 acres.

Thompson, Clanders. Va. Corporal. 23 Jul. 1783. 400 acres.

Thompson, Daniel. N.C. Private. 22 Oct. 1783. 274 acres.

Thompson, Daniel. Va. Private. 28 May 1783. 100 acres.

Thompson, David. N.C. Private. 30 Sep. 1785. 640 acres to heirs.

Thompson, Drury. Ga. Refugee. 23 Apr. 1784. 287 1/2 acres.

Thompson, Edward. N.C. Private. 10 Dec. 1821. 640 acres to heirs.

Thompson, Elias. N. Y. Private. 8 Jul. 1790. 600 acres.

Thompson, Ezekiel. N.C. Private. 5 Dec. 1797. 274 acres.

Thompson, Francis. Md. Private. ———. 50 acres.

Thompson, Francis. Va. Private. 22 Jun. 1814. 100 acres.

Thompson, George. Pa. Private. 27 Oct. 1786. 200 acres.

Thompson, George. Va. Lieutenant. 12 Feb. 1784. 2666 2/3 acres.

Thompson, George. Va. Private. 20 Nov. 1784. 100 acres.

Thompson, George. Va. Sergeant. 22 Jun. 1814. 200 acres.

Thompson, Goodwin. N.C. Private. 22 Dec. 1796. 640 acres to heirs.

Thompson, Henry. Va. Private. 3 Jul. 1783. 100 acres.

Thompson, Hugh. Pa. Sergeant. 21 Aug. 1789. 250 acres.

Thompson, Isaac. Conn. Sufferer. New/ East Haven. 2.16.4.

Thompson, Isaiah. N. Y. Lieutenant. 9 Jul. 1790. 1200 acres.
Thompson, Isaiah. Pa. Private. ———. 200 acres.
Thompson, Isham. Ga. Refugee. 23 Apr. 1784. 287 1/2 acres.
Thompson, Jacob. Va. Private. 25 Jan. 1812. 200 acres.
Thompson, Jacob. Conn. Sufferer. New/ East Haven. 60.19.2.
Thompson, James. Ga. ———. 21 Apr. 1784. 287 1/2 acres.
Thompson, James. Ga. Refugee. 1785. 500 acres.
Thompson, James. Me. ———. 3 Aug. 1835. 200 acres. Kennebunkport.
Thompson, James. Me. ———. 29 Jul. 1844. 200 acres to widow Hannah (Fossett) Thompson. Calais.
Thompson, James. N. Y. Private. 8 Jul. 1790. 600 acres.
Thompson, James. Va. Private. 20 Jun. 1783. 100 acres.
Thompson, James. Va. Lieutenant. 16 Feb. 1801. 2666 2/3 acres.
Thompson, James. Conn. Sufferer. New/ East Haven. 0.19.0.
Thompson, James. Conn. Sufferer. New London. 350.0.7.
Thompson, Jesse. Ga. Minute Man. 22 Apr. 1785. 287 1/2 acres.
Thompson, Jesse. Md. Sergeant. ———. 50 acres.
Thompson, John. Ga. Refugee. 21 Apr. 1784. 287 1/2 acers.
Thompson, John. Ga. ———. 6 Apr. 1785. 287 1/2 acres to heirs.
Thompson, John. N. Y. Private. 8 Jul. 1790. 500 acres.
Thompson, John. N. Y. Sergeant. 8 Jul. 1790. 500 acres.
Thompson, John. N.C. Private. 9 Sep. 1785. 640 acres to heirs.
Thompson, John. Pa. Sergeant. ———. 250 acres.
Thompson, John. Pa. Private. ———. 200 acres.
Thompson, John. Pa. Private. 9 Oct. 1786. 200 acres.
Thompson, John. S.C. ———. 6 Nov. 1786. 200 acres.
Thompson, John. Va. Sergeant. 18 Feb. 1784. 200 acres.
Thompson, John. Va. Private. 23 Mar. 1784. 100 acres.
Thompson, John. Va. Corporal. 12 Jun. 1786. 400 acres.
Thompson, John. Va. Private. 18 Apr. 1801. 100 acres.
Thompson, John. Va. Private. 23 Mar. 1821. 200 acres.
Thompson, John. Va. Private. 13 Jul. 1822. 200 acres.
Thompson, John. Conn. Sufferer. New London. 59.16.9.
Thompson, John Farley. Ga. Refugee. 20 Apr. 1784. 250 acres.
Thompson, Joseph. Me. ———. 25 Apr. 1835. 200 acres to widow Happy Thompson. Bangor.
Thompson, Joseph. Md. Sergeant. ———. 50 acres.
Thompson, Joseph. Pa. Private. 11 Sep. 1789. 200 acres.
Thompson, Joseph. Pa. Surgeon Mate. ———. 300 acres.
Thompson, Joseph. Conn. Sufferer. New/ East Haven. 12.14.0.
Thompson, Joshua. Ga. ———. 22 Apr. 1784. 287 1/2 acres.
Thompson, Joshua. N.C. Private. 12 Sep. 1785. 640 acres to heirs.
Thompson, Laban. Ga. ———. 1 Apr. 1784. 287 1/2 acres.
Thompson, Laurance. N.C. Captain. 4 May 1784. 1806 acres.
Thompson, Littleberry. Va. Private. 1 Apr. 1783. 100 acres.
Thompson, Moses. Mass. ———. 5 Feb. 1833. 200 acres.
Thompson, Moses. Conn. Sufferer. New/ East Haven. 6.0.0.
Thompson, Nathan. N.C. Private. 6 Dec. 1797. 274 acres.
Thompson, Ned. N.C. Private. 17 Dec. 1785. 640 acres.
Thompson, Patrick. Va. Sergeant. 9 Dec. 1783. 200 acres.
Thompson, Peter. Ga. ———. 23 Apr. 1784. 287 1/2 acres.
Thompson, Reubin. Ga. ———. 15 Mar. 1784. 250 acres.
Thompson, Richard. Me. Private. 18 May 1835. 200 acres to widow Bathsheba Thompson. Wales.
Thompson, Robert. Ga. Refugee. 17 Apr. 1784. 287 1/2 acres.

Thompson, Robert. Va. Private. 28 Jun. 1783. 200 acres.
Thompson, Royal. Va. Private. 9 Feb. 1784. 100 acres.
Thompson, Samuel. N.C. Private. 22 Dec. 1796. 428 acres.
Thompson, Samuel. Pa. Private. 5 Dec. 1786. 200 acres.
Thompson, Smith. Va. Private. 22 Apr. 1784. 100 acres.
Thompson, Stanley. N. Y. Private. 8 Jul. 1790. 600 acres.
Thompson, Stephen. Va. Private. 14 Oct. 1818. 200 acres.
Thompson, Thaddeus. N. Y. Bombardier. 9 Jul. 1790. 600 acres.
Thompson, Thankful. Conn. Sufferer. New/ East Haven. 23.7.8.
Thompson, Thomas. Md. Private. ———. 50 acres.
Thompson, Thomas. N. Y. Lieutenant. 13 Sep. 1790. 1100 acres.
Thompson, Thomas. N. Y. Lieutenant. ———. 1000 acres.
Thompson, Thomas. N.C. Private. 8 May 1784. 640 acres.
Thompson, Thomas. Va. Private. 25 Jun. 1783. 100 acres.
Thompson, William. Ga. Refugee. 17 Apr. 1784. 287 1/2 acres.
Thompson, William. Ga. ———. 25 Feb. 1784. 500 acres.
Thompson, William. Va.-Ind. Private. 108 acres.
Thompson, William. Me. ———. 22 Apr. 1835. 200 acres to widow Joanna Thompson. Wayne.
Thompson, William. N. Y. Sergeant. 9 Jul. 1790. 600 acres.
Thompson, William. N.Y. ———. 13 Sep. 1790. 500 acres to heirs.
Thompson, William. N.C. Private. 8 May 1784. 640 acres to heirs.
Thompson, William. N.C. Sergeant. 21 May 1784. 428 acres.
Thompson, William. N.C. Private. 12 Dec. 1785. 228 acres. He was of Halifax County.
Thompson, William. Pa. General. 14 Feb. 1787. 500 acres to heirs.
Thompson, William. Pa. Lieutenant. 28 Mar. 1789. 200 acres.
Thompson, William. Pa. Ranger. 6 Apr. 1787. 200 acres.
Thompson, William. Pa. Brigadier General. 13 Oct. 1786. 500 acres to widow.
Thompson, William. Pa. Brigadier General. 18 Oct. 1786. 500 acres to his widow.
Thompson, William. Pa. Brigadier General. ———. 500 acres to widow & heirs.
Thompson, William. Va. Corporal. 17 Jul. 1784. 200 acres.
Thompson, William. Va. Private. 30 May 1821. 200 acres.
Thompson, Willis. N.C. Private. 17 Dec. 1804. 640 acres to heirs.
Thompson, Willoughby. N.C. Private. 17 Dec. 1785. 640 acres to heirs.
Thompson, Zacheriah. Ga. ———. 21 Apr. 1784. 287 1/2 acres.
Thomson, Ebenezer. Pa. Private. 16 Jan. 1789. 200 acres to Robert Shepherd, assignee.
Thomson, John. Md. Private. ———. 50 acres.
Thomson, Samuel. N.C. Private. 10 Aug. 1785. 640 acres.
Thomson, William. Pa. Lieutenant. 27 Mar. 1789. 200 acres.
Thomson, William. Va. Captain. 9 Dec. 1782. 4000 acres.
Thomspon, John. Ga. ———. 7 Jun. 1785. 230 acres to heirs.
Thorbury, Francis. Pa. ———. 28 Feb. 1794. 200 acres to Walter Stewart.
Thorn, David. Ga. Refugee. 26 May 1784. 575 acres.
Thorn, Ica. N.C. Private. 11 Feb. 1796. 640 acres to heirs.
Thorn, Richard. Va. Private. 8 Nov. 1784. 200 acres.
Thorn, Samuel. N.Y. ———. 13 Sep. 1790. 500 acres to heirs.
Thorn, William. Ga. Soldier. 26 May 1784. 575 acres.
Thornall, John. N.C. Private. 12 Sep. 1785. 640 acres to heirs.
Thornburg, Francis. Pa. Lieutenant. 15 Dec. 1786. 200 acres to Samuel Alexander, assignee.
Thornburn, John. Va. Private. 2 Jul. 1783. 200 acres.
Thornbury, Francis. Pa. Lieutenant. 15 Dec. 1786. 200 acres to Samuel Alexander, assignee.
Thornhill, Thomas. Va. Private. 30 Jun. 1784. 200 acres.

Thornman, Levin. Va. Private. 20 Nov. 1809. 100 acres.
Thornton, James. N. Y. Private. 8 Jul. 1790. 600 acres.
Thornton, James. Pa. Drummer. 25 Aug. 1787. 200 acres.
Thornton, James. Va. Private. 15 Jun. 1807. 100 acres.
Thornton, Jesse. Va. Fife Major. 19 Feb. 1814. 400 acres.
Thornton, John. Ga. ———. 27 Apr. 1784. 287 1/2 acres.
Thornton, John. Pa. Private. ———. 200 acres.
Thornton, John. Va. Lieutenant Colonel. 24 Apr. 1833. 6000 acres.
Thornton, John. Va. Lieutenant Colonel. 5 Sep. 1855. 1666 2/3 acres.
Thornton, John. Va. Lieutenant Colonel. 21 Dec. 1855. 111 1/3 acres.
Thornton, John. Va. Colonel. 19 Sep. 1833. 6000 acres.
Thornton, Joseph. Va.-Ind. Private. 108 acres.
Thornton, Patrick. Va. Private. 23 Jun. 1783. 200 acres.
Thornton, Presley. Va. Captain. 17 Jun. 1783. 4000 acres.
Thornton, Presley. Va. Captain. 29 Mar. 1796. 666 2/3 acres.
Thornton, Samuel. Ga. ———. 27 Apr. 1784. 287 1/2 acres.
Thornton, Solomon. Ga. ———. 20 Apr. 1784. 287 1/2 acres.
Thornton, William. Ga. ———. 24 May 1784. 287 1/2 acres.
Thornton, William. N. Y. Matross. 9 Jul. 1790. 600 acres.
Thornton, William. Va. Private. 6 Dec. 1783. 200 acres.
Thornycraft, Joseph. Pa. Private. 20 Sep. 1787. 200 acres.
Thorp, Eliphalet. Conn. Sufferer. Fairfield. 401.6.1.
Thorp, Gershom. Conn. Sufferer. Fairfield. 9.0.0.
Thorp, Jabez. Conn. Sufferer. Fairfield. 147.18.0.
Thorp, James. Va. Boatswain's Mate. 7 Feb. 1798. 200 acres.
Thorp, James. Va. Boatswain's Mate. 22 Sep. 1856. 673 acres.
Thorp, James. Va. Boatswain's Mate. 22 Sep. 1856. 673 acres.
Thorp, James. Va. Boatswain's Mate. 15 Sep. 1857. 1120 2/3 acres.
Thorp, John. Ga. Soldier. 2 Aug. 1784. ———.
Thorp, John. Va. Private. 29 Sep. 1809. 200 acres.
Thorp, Nathaniel. Conn. Sufferer. New London. 3.13.5.
Thorp, Ruel. Conn. Sufferer. Fairfield. 6.6.0.
Thorp, Stephen. Conn. Sufferer. Fairfield. 515.1.8.
Thorp, Thomas. N. Y. Matross. 9 Jul. 1790. 600 acres.
Thorp, Thomas. Va. Private. 7 Aug. 1813. 200 acres.
Thorp, William. Va. Private. 29 Sep. 1809. 200 acres.
Thorp, William. Conn. Sufferer. Fairfield. 24.18.0.
Thorp, William. Conn. Sufferer. Fairfield. 3.0.0.
Thow, Thomas. N.C. Private. 6 Aug. 1785. 640 acres to heirs.
Thrall, John. Va. Lieutenant. 4 Aug. 1786. 2666 2/3 acres.
Thrall, John. Va. Lieutenant. 13 Nov. 1832. 1333 1/3 acres.
Thrash, Jacob. Ga. ———. 19 Apr. 1784. 600 acres.
Threadgill, George. Ga. ———. ———. 230 acres.
Threadgill, Thomas. Ga. Captain. 17 Jan. 1785. 690 acres.
Threat, Frederick. N.C. Private. 6 Dec. 1809. 228 acres.
Thrift, Abraham. N.C. Private. 27 Jul. 1785. 274 acres.
Thrift, Miles. N.C. Private. 23 Nov. 1797. 640 acres to heirs.
Thrift, Miles. N.C. ———. 7 Dec. 1797. ——— acres to heirs.
Thrift, Solomon. N.C. Private. 27 Jul. 1785. 640 acres to heir.
Throckmorton, Albion. Va. Subaltern. 23 Jun. 1784. 1000 acres.
Throckmorton, Albion. Va. Subaltern. 23 Jun. 1784. 1666 2/3 acres.
Throckmorton, Robert. Va. Private. 14 Jun. 1806. 100 acres.
Throckmorton, William. Va. Private. 3 Jun. 1797. 100 acres.
Throop, Josiah. N. Y. Lieutenant Colonel. ———. 1000 acres.

Throop, R. John. N. Y. Lieutenant. 9 Jul. 1790. 1200 acres.
Thruston, Charles M. Va. Colonel. 19 Nov. 1833. 6666 2/3 acres.
Thruston, Charles M. Va. Colonel. 22 Oct. 1835. 3333 1/3 acres.
Thruston, Charles M. Va. Colonel. 22 Oct. 1835. 833 1/3 acres.
Thruston, Charles M. Va. Colonel. 22 Oct. 1835. 833 1/3 acres.
Thruston, Charles M. Va. Colonel. 22 Oct. 1835. 833 1/3 acres.
Thruston, Charles M. Va. Colonel. 22 Oct. 1835. .0048 acres.
Thruston, Charles M. Va. Colonel. 22 Oct. 1835. .0048 acres.
Thruston, John. Va. Cornet. 30 Aug. 1830. 2666 2/3 acres.
Thruston, John. Va. Cornet. 22 Aug. 1831. 296 1/3 acres.
Thruston, John. Va. Cornet. 22 Aug. 1831. 296 1/3 acres.
Thruston, John. Va. Cornet. 22 Aug. 1831. 296 1/3 acres.
Thruston, John. Va. Cornet. 22 Aug. 1831. 296 1/3 acres.
Thruston, John. Va. Cornet. 22 Aug. 1831. 296 1/3 acres.
Thruston, John. Va. Cornet. 22 Aug. 1831. 196 1/3 acres.
Thruston, John. Va. Cornet. 22 Aug. 1831. 296 1/3 acres.
Thruston, John. Va. Cornet. 22 Aug. 1831. 296 1/3 acres.
Thruston, John. Va. Cornet. 22 Aug. 1831. 98.78 acres.
Thruston, John. Va. Cornet. 22 Aug. 1831. 98.78 acres.
Thruston, John. Va. Cornet. 22 Aug. 1831. 98.78 acres.
Thruston, Robert. Va. Lieutenant. 18 Jun. 1833. 2666 2/3 acres.
Thurman, Absalom. Ga. ———. 20 Apr. 1784. 287 1/2 acres.
Thurman, Charles. V. Sergeant. 18 Dec. 1833. 400 acres.
Thurman, David. Ga. ———. 19 Apr. 1784. 575 acres.
Thurman, John. Ga. ———. 15 Apr. 1784. 1000 acres.
Thurmond, John. Ga. ———. 27 Apr. 1784. 300 acres.
Thurmond, Richard. Ga. ———. 17 May 1784. ———.
Thurmond, Robert. Ga. ———. 27 Apr. 1784. 300 acres.
Thurmond, William. Va. Surgeon Major. 20 Nov. 1834 [?1833]. 3426 acres.
Thurmond, William. Va. ———. 29 Nov. 1838. 57 1/7 acres.
Thurrell, Abraham. N.C. Private. 16 Mar. 1795. 640 acres to heirs.
Thurstein, William. Va. Private. 30 Nov. 1785. 100 acres.
Thurston, Jacob. Me. ———. 28 Dec. 1835. 200 acres to widow Ann B. Piper.
Thurston, John. Ga. ———. 21 Apr. 1784. 450 acres.
Thurston, John. Va.-Ind. Cornet. Aug. 1831. 2156 acres.
Thurston, Michael. Pa. Private. 12 Jan. 1787. 200 acres.
Thurston, William. N.C. Private. 15 Jul. 1785. 228 acres.
Thust, William. N.C. Private. 30 Sep. 1785. 640 acres to heirs.
Thuston, Thomas. S.C. Soldier. 21 Jan. 1785. 200 acres.
Thuttle, William. N. Y. Private. 8 Jul. 1790. 600 acres.
Thweatt, Thomas. Va. Captain. 27 Mar. 1783. 4000 acres.
Tibbets, Giles. Me. Private. 16 May 1835. 200 acres to widow Susan Tibbets. Boothbay.
Tibbs, John. Va. Lieutenant. 15 Apr. 1800. 3111 acres.
Tibbs, John. Va. Lieutenant. 11 Sep. 1807. 370 acres.
Tibbs, John. Va. Captain. 3 Sep. 1847. 519 acres.
Tibo, Micahel. N. Y. ———. ———. 500 acres.
Tibout, Henry. N. Y. Captain. 9 Jul. 1790. 1800 acres.
Tice, John. N. Y. Private. 8 Jul. 1790. 600 acres.
Tiel, Leonard. Pa. Private. 28 Oct. 1786. 200 acres to Andrew Beelner, assignee.
Tiffen, Thomas. N.C. Private. 25 Oct. 1783. 570 acres.
Tigner, James. Md. Private. ———. 50 acres.
Tilden, John Bell. Pa. Lieutenant. 28 Sep. 1787. 200 acres.
Tilden, John Bell. Pa. Lieutenant. 28 Sep. 1787. 200 acres.

Tilghman, Bellitha. N.C. Sergeant. 28 May 1784. 1000 acres.
Tilghman, John. N.C. Private. 28 May 1784. 274 acres.
Tilghman, Tench. Pa. Colonel. 16 Jul. 1787. 250 acres.
Tilghman, Tench. Pa. Lieutenant Colonel. 12 Jul. 1787. 500 acres.
Tilghman, William. N.C. Private. 28 May 1784. 640 acres.
Tilghman, William. N.C. Private. 19 Jun. 1801. 274 acres.
Tillard, Edward. Md. Lieutenant Colonel. ———. 200 acres.
Tiller, Andrew. N.C. Private. 22 Dec. 1796. 640 acres to heirs.
Tiller, William. Va. Corporal. 8 Jun. 1784. 200 acres.
Tillery, John. N.C. Lieutenant. 4 Aug. 1821. 2560 acres.
Tillery, John. Va. Private. 31 Jul. 1783. 200 acres.
Tillery, Richard. N.C. Private. 9 Dec. 1796. 640 acres to heirs.
Tilley, James. Conn. Sufferer. New London. 1,533.10.3.
Tilley, John. Conn. Sufferer. New London. 6.12.6.
Tilley, Lewis. N.C. Private. 17 Dec. 1796. 274 acres.
Tilley, Lewis. N.C. Private. 22 Dec. 1796. 274 acres.
Tilly, John. Ga. Soldier. 5 Dec. 1785. 230 acres.
Tilton, Richard. N.C. Private. 30 Sep. 1785. 640 acres to heirs.
Timber, James. Pa. ———. ———. 200 acres.
Timberlake, Benjamin. Va. Captain. 1 May 1838. 2666 2/3 acres.
Timberlake, Benjamin. Va. Captain. 1 May 1838. 1333 1/3 acres,
Timberlake, Joseph. Va. Private. 26 Jun. 1783. 233 1/3 acres.
Timbrel, John. N.C. Private. 17 Feb. 1824. 640 acres.
Times, Peter. Va. Private. 31 Jan. 1786. 200 acres.
Timmons, John. Va. Sergeant. 24 Jun. 1784. 200 acres.
Timms, Edward. Md. Private. ———. 50 acres.
Timpany, Michael C. Conn. Sufferer. Greenwich. 76.14.8.
Timpson, Samuel. Va. ———. 25 Jul. 1832. 4000 acres.
Tims, Peter. Pa. Private. 9 Oct. 1805. 200 acres.
Tindall, John. Ga. ———. 27 Apr. 1784. 287 acres.
Tindall, Samuel. Md. Sergeant. ———. 50 acres.
Tindall, William. Ga. Soldier. 19 Apr. 1784. 287 1/2 acres.
Tine, Henry. Ga. ———. 27 Apr. 1784. 230 acres.
Tiner, William. N.C. Private. 30 Sep. 1785. 640 acres to heirs.
Tinker, Daniel. Conn. Sufferer. New London. 22.17.6.
Tinker, John. N.C. Private. 7 Sep. 1820. 640 acres.
Tinkham, Hezekiah. Mass. ———. 10 Aug. 1829. 200 acres.
Tinsley, Jonathan. Va. Private. 22 Aug. 1783. 200 acres.
Tinsley, Samuel. Va. Cornet. 5 Dec. 1783. 2666 2/3 acres.
Tinsley, William. Va. Private. 6 Feb. 1808. 100 acres.
Tipper, John. N.C. Private. 25 Oct. 1783. 228 acres.
Tippet, George. N.C. Private. 12 Dec. 1796. 640 acres to heirs.
Tippet, Natley. Md. Private. ———. 50 acres.
Tippet, Peter. Md. Private. ———. 50 acres.
Tipton, Abraham. Va. Captain. 18 May 1789. 4000 acres.
Tipton, Abraham. Va. Captain. 19 Jun. 1855. 4000 acres.
Tisdale, Christopher. N.C. Sergeant. 7 Dec. 1797. 471 acres.
Tison, Aron. N.C. Private. 10 Dec. 1788. 640 acres to heirs.
Tison, Edmund. N.C. Private. 29 Sep. 1785. 640 acres.
Tison, James. N.C. Private. 25 Jun. 1785. 274 acres.
Tison, John. Ga. ———. 27 Apr. 1784. 250 acres.
Tite, James. Md. Private. ———. 50 acres.
Titus, Jonathan. N. Y. Private. 8 Jul. 1790. 600 acres.
Titus, Jonathan. N. Y. Captain. 9 Jul. 1790. 1800 acres.

Titus, Martin. N.C. Private. 30 Sep. 1785. 640 acres.

Toaff, Henry. Pa. Private. 9 Jan. 1787. 200 acres.

Tobias, Jacob. N.Y. ———. 13 Sep. 1790. 500 acres to heirs.

Tobias, Job. Mass. Private. 24 Jan. 1832. 200 acres to son Joseph Tobias.

Tobin, Edward. N. Y. Private. 29 Jan. 1791. 500 acres.

Toby, John. Me. Private. 3 Aug. 1835. 200 acres to widow Margaret Toby. Portland.

Toby, William. N.C. Private. 10 Sep. 1821. 274 acres to heirs.

Todd, Archibald. Mass. Corporal. 18 Mar. 1834. 200 acres.

Todd, Caleb. Ga. ———. 21 Apr. 1784. 500 acres.

Todd, Ephraim. N.C. Private. 7 Dec. 1797. 640 acres to heirs.

Todd, James. N.C. Private. 21 Nov. 1805. 640 acres.

Todd, John. N. Y. Private. 8 Jul. 1790. 500 acres.

Todd, John. N.C. Private. 30 Sep. 1785. 640 acres to heirs.

Todd, Josiah. N.C. ———. 8 Mar. 1785. 640 acres to heirs.

Todd, Levi. Lawrence. Va.-Ind. Lieutenant. 2156 acres.

Todd, Michael. Conn. Sufferer. New/East Haven. 73.16.11.

Todd, Robert. Va.-Ind. Captain. Feb. 1784. 3234 acres.

Todd, Robert. Va. Captain. 21 Feb. 1784. 4000 acres.

Todd, Thomas. N.C. Musician. 7 Dec. 1797. 1000 acres to heirs.

Todd, William. Ga. Citizen. 5 Apr. 1785. 287 1/2 acres.

Todd, William. N.C Private. 30 Sep. 1785. 640 acres to heirs.

Toland, William. Md. Private. ———. 50 acres.

Tolar, Daniel. N.C. Private. 9 Nov. 1784. 640 acres.

Tolbert, Samuel. Pa. Captain. 14 Jan. 1787. 500 acres.

Toler, Dempsy. Ga. ———. 27 Apr. 1784. 287 1/2 acres.

Toler, William. Va. Corporal. 25 Jun. 1783. 200 acres.

Tolin, Elias. Va. Sergeant. 20 Jun. 1783. 200 acres.

Tolley, Jonas. N.C. Private. 14 Feb. 1796. 640 acres.

Tolock, Arthur. N.C. Private. 2 Feb. 1786. 640 acres.

Tom, John. Pa. Private. 27 Jul. 1787. 200 acres to William Banquet, assignee.

Tomberlin, John. Ga. ———. 13 Sep. 1784. 230 acres.

Tomerlain, Thomas. S.C. ———. 2 May 1785. 200 acres.

Tominey, Andrew. S.C. ———. 3 Dec. 1798. 200 acres.

Tomkies, Charles. Va. ———. 21 Aug. 1834. 500 acres.

Tomlin, John. Md. Private. ———. 50 acres.

Tomlin, John. Va. Private. 20 Jun. 1783. 100 acres.

Tomlin, Stephen. Va. Corporal. 31 Oct. 1796. 200 acres.

Tomlin, William. Va. Sergeant. 13 Feb. 1784. 200 acres.

Tomlinson, David. Ga. Minute Man. 22 Apr. 1784. 287 1/2 acres.

Tomlinson, Harbert. Va. Private. 29 Jun. 1784. 100 acres.

Tomlinson, Joseph. Va. Private. 29 Jun. 1784. 100 acres.

Tomlinson, Littleberry. Va. Private. 29 Jun. 1784. 100 acres.

Tomlinson, William. Pa. Private. ———. 200 acres.

Tomme, Joseph. Ga. ———. 27 Apr. 1784. 287 1/2 acres.

Tommoss, James. Ga. ———. 23 Apr. 1784. 287 1/2 acres.

Tompkies, Charles. Va. Captain. 14 Mar. 1834. 1166 2/3 acres.

Tompkies, Charles. Va. Captain. 14 Mar. 1834. 583 1/3 acres.

Tompkies, Charles. Va. Captain. 23 Jul. 1834. 1166 1/3 acres.

Tompkies, Charles. Va. Captain. 18 Aug. 1834. 583 1/3 acres.

Tompkins, Abraham. N. Y. Corporal. 8 Jul. 1790. 600 acres.

Tompkins, Christopher. Va. Subaltern. 24 Oct. 1783. 2666 2/3 acres.

Tompkins, Christopher. Va. Lieutenant. 14 Nov. 1791. 2666 2/3 acres.

Tompkins, Christopher. Va. Lieutenant. 5 Aug. 1831. 1333 1/3 acres.

Tompkins, Daniel. Va. Lieutenant. 2 Mar. 1784. 1000 acres.

Tompkins, Daniel. Va. Lieutenant. 2 Mar. 1784. 1666 2/3 acres.

Tompkins, Henry. Va. Ensign. 25 Apr. 1783. 2666 2/3 acres.

Tompkins, Joshua. Pa. ———. ———. 200 acres.

Tompkins, Nathaniel. N. Y. Private. 8 Jul. 1790. 600 acres.

Tompkins, Oliver. Conn. Sufferer. Greenwich. 7.14.6.

Tompkins, Robert. Va. Lieutenant. 25 Apr. 1783. 2666 2/3 acres.

Tompkins, Robert. Va. Captain. 14 Nov. 1791. 4000 acres.

Tompkins, Robert. Va. Captain. 20 Mar. 1834. 1333 1/3 acres.

Tompkins, Robert. Va. Captain. 20 May 1859. 1259 acres.

Tompson, Andrew. N.C. Private. 29 Nov. 1796. 274 acres.

Tompson, Bartholomew. Md. Private. ———. 50 acres.

Tompson, Lambert. Md. Private. ———. 50 acres.

Tomson, Cornelius. Md. Private. ———. 50 acres.

Tomson, Nathan. N.C. Private. 29 Apr. 1784. 640 acres.

Ton, Christopher. N.C. Private. 12 Dec. 1785. 640 acres to heirs.

Toney, Anthony. N.C. Private. 21 Oct. 1783. 640 acres.

Toney, Archibald. Va. Private. 9 Nov. 1785. 100 acres.

Toney, John. N.C. Private. 8 Aug. 1821. 640 acres.

Toney, Reuben. Va. Private. 9 Nov. 1785. 100 acres.

Toney, Vincent. Va. Private. 3 Feb. 1784. 100 acres.

Tongue, George. N.Y. ———. 13 Sep. 1790. 500 acres to heirs.

Tood, Levi. Va. Lieutenant. 17 Feb. 1834. 2666 2/3 acres.

Tool, Richard. Va. Gunner. 19 Aug. 1835. 2566 2/3 acres.

Tool, Richard. Va. Gunner. 8 Jun. 1833. 100 acres.

Toole, John. N.Y. ———. 13 Sep. 1790. 500 acres to heirs.

Toombs, Gabriel. Ga. ———. 21 Apr. 1784. 600 acres.

Toombs, Robert. Ga. ———. 21 Apr. 1784. 250 acres.

Toomer, Joseph. N.C. Private. 12 Sep. 1785. 640 acres to heirs.

Toomes, William. Va. Private. 5 Aug. 1813. 200 acres.

Toops, Lawrence. Pa. Private. ———. 200 acres.

Toot, Edward. Pa. ———. 27 May 1953. 200 acres.

Toot, Joseph. Va. Private. 1 Jun. 1785. 200 acres.

Toothaker, Seth. Me. ———. 24 Apr. 1835. 200 acres. Harpswell.

Topp, George. N.C. Private. 14 Oct. 1783. 640 acres.

Topping, John. Va. Sergeant. 15 Jun. 1807. 200 acres.

Topping, Major. Va. Private. 8 Jan. 1833. 200 acres.

Topping, Peter. Md. Private. ———. 50 acres.

Torey, William. N. Y. Lieutenant. ———. 1000 acres.

Torrence, John. Ga. Refugee. 19 Apr. 1784. 287 1/2 acres.

Torrentine, Alexander. N.C. Private. 12 May 1784. 640 acres to John Torrentine, heir.

Torrey, Samuel. N. Y. Sergeant. 13 Sep. 1790. 600 acres.

Totevine, Coleburn. N.C. Sergeant. 28 May 1784. 1000 acres to Simon Totevine, heir.

Totevine, [?]ender. N.C. Private. 28 May 1784. 640 acres to Simon Totevine, heir.

Totty, Thomas. N.C. Private. 14 Feb. 1796. 640 acres.

Touchstone, Christopher. Md. Private. ———. 50 acres.

Tourtilott, Abraham. Me. Captain. 16 Apr. 1835. 200 acres to widow Leah Tourtilott. Howland.

Tow, Christopher. N.C. Private. 3 Aug. 1820. 640 acres to heirs.

Towell, Ambrose. N.C. Private. 28 Oct. 1783. 640 acres.

Towell, Stephen. N.C. Private. 26 May 1784. 640 acres.

Towers, John. Va. Private. 11 Jan. 1783. 100 acres.

Towers, John. Va. Private. 20 May 1783. 200 acres.

Towler, Abraham. N.C. Private. 22 Oct. 1783. 640 acres.
Towles, Oliver. S. C. Captain. 21 Jan. 1785. 300 acres.
Towles, Oliver. Va. Lieutenant Colonel. 10 Jun. 1783. 6000 acres.
Towles, Oliver. Va. Lieutenant Colonel. 9 Aug. 1799. 1000 acres.
Towles, Oliver. Va. Lieutenant Colonel. 11 Sep. 1807. 750 acres.
Towlin, John. Md. ———. 50 acres.
Town, John. Conn. Sufferer. Greenwich. 15.4.10.
Town, Mary. Conn. Sufferer. Greenwich. 4.10.0.
Town, William. Conn. Sufferer. Greenwich. 3.3.0.
Townen, James. N.C. Private. 12 Mar. 1785. 640 acres.
Townes, John. Ga. Minute Man. 20 Apr. 1784. 287 1/2 acres.
Townes, John. Ga. ———. 23 Apr. 1784. 900 acres.
Towning, Solomon. N.C. Private. 24 Nov. 1796. 640 acres to heirs.
Townley, Henry. Md. Private. ———. 50 acres.
Townly, William. N.C. Private. 4 Aug. 1821. 640 acres.
Towns, John. Va. Lieutenant. 28 Nov. 1783. 2662 2/3 acres.
Townsend, Aaron. Md. Private. ———. 50 acres.
Townsend, Allen. Md. Private. ———. 50 acres.
Townsend, Daniel. Me. Private. 5 Oct. 1835. 200 acres to widow Sarah Sawtell. Sidney.
Townsend, Ebenezer. Conn. Sufferer. New/ East Haven. 9.5.0.
Townsend, Ewel. Va. Corporal. 7 Dec. 1784. 200 acres.
Townsend, Henry. Ga. ———. 17 Sep. 1784. 287 1/2 acres.
Townsend, Isaac. Conn. Sufferer. New/East Haven. 11.16.10
Townsend, Jeremiah. Conn. Sufferer. New/ East Haven. 36.7.8.
Townsend, John. Ga. ———. 22 Apr. 1784. 550 acres.
Townsend, John. Va. Private. 6 Apr. 1785. 200 acres.
Townsend, John. Conn. Sufferer. New/East Haven. 3.0.0.
Townsend, John. Conn. Sufferer. New/East Haven. 16.14.2.
Townsend, Platt. Conn. Sufferer. Norwalk. 2.17.0.
Townsend, Robert. Conn. Sufferer. New/ East Haven. 15.19.6.
Townsend, Samuel. N. Y. Private. 8 Jul. 1790. 600 acres.
Townsend, Samuel. N. Y. Paymaster. 13 Sep. 1790. 1500 acres.
Townsend, Thomas. Ga. ———. 20 Apr. 1784. 287 1/2 acres.
Townsend, Timothy. Conn. Sufferer. New/ East Haven. 11.5.8.
Townsend, William. Md. Private. ———. 50 acres.
Townsend, William. Va. Private. 16 Jul. 1783. 200 acres.
Townshend, George. Va. Private. 1 Apr. 1783. 100 acres.
Towson, William. Md. Lieutenant. ———. 200 acres.
Toy, John. Pa. Private. 4 Oct. 1786. 200 acres.
Trabue, John. Va. Lieutenant. 3 Feb. 1784. 2666 2/3 acres.
Trabue, William. Va. Sergeant. 6 Mar. 1784. 200 acres.
Traby, Ansel. Conn. Sufferer. Fairfield. 96.11.7.
Tracey, James. N.C. Private. 20 Sep. 1784. 274 acres.
Tracey, Joseph. N.C. Private. 8 Dec. 1808. 640 acres.
Tracy, John. N.C. Private. 17 Feb. 1824. 640 acres
Tracy, John. Pa. Private. 28 Feb. 1794. 200 acres to Francis Murray, assignee.
Tracy, John. Pa. Private. ———. 200 acres.
Tracy, Solomon. Va. Private. 21 Jun. 1808. 100 acres.
Trader, George. N.C. Private. 13 Sep. 1820. 640 acres.
Trahon, Etienne. N. Y. ———. ———. 500 acres.
Trammel, Jarrott. Ga. ———. 22 Apr. 1784. 200 acres.
Trammell, Dennis. Ga. Refugee. 26 May 1784. 287 1/2 acres.
Tramwell, Dennis. Md. Private. ———. 50 acres.
Trantham, Martin. N.C. Private. 17 Feb. 1824. 640 acres.

Trapp, Elijah. N.C. Private. 24 Nov. 1797. 640 acres to heirs.
Trapp, Elijah. N.C. ———. 3 Dec. 1797. 1000 acres to heirs.
Trapp, John. Ga. ———. 22 Apr. 1784. 287 1/2 acres.
Trapp, John. N.C. Private. 20 Dec. 1796. 640 acres to heirs.
Trapp, Joseph. Ga. Private. 1784. 250 acres.
Trapp, Martin. N.C. Private. 20 Apr. 1784. 640 acres.
Trask, Jonathan. Mass. Sergeant. 18 Feb. 1833. 200 acres to heirs.
Traverse, Andrew. Pa. Private. ———. 200 acres.
Traverse, Joseph. N. Y. ———. ———. 333 1/3 acres.
Travice, Abraham. N. Y. Private. 8 Jul. 1790. 600 acres.
Travice, Scott. N. Y. Private. 8 Jul. 1790. 600 acres.
Travis, Edward. Va. Captain. 28 Feb. 1784. 5333 1/3 acres.
Travis, Edward. Va. Captain. 3 Mar. 1851. 1415 acres.
Travis, Jacob. N.Y. ———. 13 Sep. 1790. 500 acres to heirs.
Travis, James. Va. Private. 27 Feb. 1833. 100 acres.
Travis, Joseph. N. Y. Gunner. 3 Jul. 1790. 600 acres.
Travis, Miles. Va. Private. 20 Mar. 1786. 100 acres.
Travis, Sylvanus. N. Y. Private. 13 Sep. 1790. 600 acres.
Trayner, Alexander. N.C. Private. 11 Feb. 1796. 640 acres.
Trayner, James. N.C. Private. 28 Oct. 1783. 640 acres to heirs.
Traywick, Francis. Ga. Soldier. 27 Apr. 1784. 287 1/2 acres.
Treacle, Dawson. Va. Private. 28 May 1783. 100 acres.
Treacle, John. Va. Private. 28 May 1783. 100 acres.
Treacle, William. Va. Private. 29 May 1783. 100 acres.
Treacle, William. Va. Private. 31 Oct. 1856. 100 acres.
Treacle, William. Va. Private. 31 Jan. 1784. 100 acres.
Treat, Malachi. N.Y. Physician & Surgeon. 13 Apr. 1792. 2700 acres.
Trebel, Augustine. N. Y. ———. ———. 500 acres.
Treekle, John. Va. Private. 17 May 1783. 100 acres.
Trego, James. Md. Private. ———. 50 acres.
Trent, Beverly. Va.-Ind. Sergeant. 216 acres.
Trent, Laurence. Va. Captain. 28 May 1783. 4000 acres.
Trent, Thomas. Va. Sergeant. 3 Feb. 1784. 200 acres.
Trenton, Thomas. N.C. Private. 17 Dec. 1785. 640 acres to heirs.
Trewilliger, James. N. Y. Private. 8 Jul. 1790. 600 acres.
Treyham, John. N.C. Private. 13 Dec. 1796. 640 acres to heirs.
Trezvant, John. Va. Surgeon. 3 Feb. 1784. 6000 acres.
Tribell, John. Pa. Private. 28 Mar. 1787. 200 acres to John Philips, executor.
Trice, Dabney. Va. Private. 20 Nov. 1784. 100 acres.
Trice, Dabney. Va. Private. 15 Apr. 1853. 100 acres.
Trice, John. Ga. ———. 20 Apr. 1784. 350 acres.
Trice, William. Va. Private. 20 Nov. 1784. 100 acres.
Trice, William. Va. Private. 15 Apr. 1853. 100 acres.
Trickle, Jonathan. N.C. Private. 8 Dec. 1796. 640 acres to heirs.
Trickle, Jonathan. Pa. Matross. 1 Jul. 1787. 200 acres.
Trigg, Samuel. Md. Private. ———. 50 acres.
Trimble, Moses. Ga. ———. 19 Jul. 1784. 287 1/2 acres.
Trimmins, Abner. N. Y. Private. 8 Jul. 1790. 600 acres.
Trimnal, Dennis. N.C. Private. 8 Dec. 1795. 640 acres to heirs.
Triplett, Daniel. Va. Sergeant. 19 Apr. 1783. 200 acres.
Triplett, Francis. Ga. ———. 27 Apr. 1784. 287 1/2 acres.
Triplett, George. Va. Lieutenant. 1 Apr. 1783. 2666 2/3 acres.
Triplett, Hedgman. Va. Lieutenant. 14 Jun. 1820. 1333 1/3 acres.
Triplett, Hedgman. Va. Lieutenant. 14 Jun. 1820. 1333 1/3 acres.

Triplett, Nathaniel. Va. Sergeant. 9 Dec. 1783. 400 acres.
Triplett, Peter. Va. Private. 8 Sep. 1812. 100 acres.
Triplett, Reuben. Va. Midshipman. 19 Mar. 1834. 242 4/11 acres.
Triplett, Reuben. Va. Midshipman. 19 Mar. 1834. 242 4/11 acres.
Triplett, Reuben. Va. Midshipman. 19 Mar. 1834. 242 4/11 acres.
Triplett, Reuben. Va. Midshipman. 19 Mar. 1834. 242 4/11 acres.
Triplett, Reuben. Va. Midshipman. 19 Mar. 1834. 242 4/11 acres.
Triplett, Reuben. Va. Midshipman. 19 Mar. 1834. 242 4/11 acres.
Triplett, Reuben. Va. Midshipman. 19 Mar. 1834. 242 4/11 acres.
Triplett, Reuben. Va. Midshipman. 19 Mar. 1834. 242 4/11 acres.
Triplett, Reuben. Va. Midshipman. 19 Mar. 1834. 242 4/11 acres.
Triplett, Reuben. Va. Midshipman. 19 Mar. 1834. 242 4/11 acres.
Triplett, Reuben. Va. Midshipman. 19 Mar. 1834. 242 4/11 acres.
Triplett, Reuben. Va. ———. 4 Apr. 1838. 242 4/11 acres.
Triplett, Roger. Va. Lieutenant. 21 Jul. 1791. 1000 acres.
Triplett, Roger. Va. Lieutenant. 21 Jul. 1791. 1000 acres.
Triplett, Roger. Va. Lieutenant. 21 Jul. 1791. 666 2/3 acres.
Triplett, Thomas. Va. Captain. 10 Feb. 1817. 4666 2/3 acres.
Triplett, William. Ga. ———. 14 Apr. 1784. 250 acres.
Triplett, William. Va. Sergeant. 4 Jun. 1783. 200 acres.
Triplett, William. Va. Lieutenant. 28 Jan. 1786. 2666 2/3 acres.
Triplett, William. Va. Captain. 6 Oct. 1810. 1000 acres.
Triplett, William. Va. Captain. 6 Oct. 1810. 1000 acres.
Triplett, William. Va. Captain. 6 Oct. 1810. 1000 acres.
Triplett, William. Va. Captain. 6 Oct. 1810. 1000 acres.
Triplett, William. Va. Captain. 6 Oct. 1810. 666 2/3 acres.
Triplett, William. Va. Captain. 14 Nov. 1811. 200 acres.
Triplett, William. Va. Captain. 14 Nov. 1811. 100 acres.
Triplett, William. Va. Captain. 14 Nov. 1811. 100 acres.
Triplett, William. Va. Captain. 14 Nov. 1811. 100 acres.
Triplett, William. Va. Captain. 14 Nov. 1811. 100 acres.
Triplett, William. Va. Captain. 14 Nov. 1811. 166 2/3 acres.
Tripner, George. Pa. Private. 10 Sep. 1789. 200 acres.
Tripp, James. Mass. Private. 5 Feb. 1833. 200 acres to heirs.
Tripp, John. N.C. Private. 30 Sep. 1785. 640 acres to heirs.
Tripps, Adam. Va. Sergeant. 26 Apr. 1784. 200 acres.
Troop, John R. Conn. Sufferer. New/East Haven. 7.2.0.
Trotier, Francis. Va. Private. 31 Dec. 1851. 100 acres.
Trotier, Francis. Va. Private. 21 Apr. 1856. 100 acres.
Trotier, Paul. Va. Private. 31 Dec. 1851. 100 acres.
Trotier, Paul. Va. Private. 9 Apr. 1856. 100 acres.
Trotter, John. Va. Private. 5 Apr. 1784. 200 acres.
Troublefield, Benjamin. N.C. Private. 30 Sep. 1785. 640 acres to heirs.
Troublefield, John. S.C. ———. 1 Feb. 1790. 100 acres.
Trout, Daniel. Ga. ———. 1 Aug. 1785. 575 acres.
Trout, Michael. N. Y. Private. 8 Jul. 1790. 600 acres.
Trouter, Thomas. N.C. Private. 2 Feb. 1786. 640 acres to heirs.
Trowbridge, Caleb. Conn. Sufferer. New/East Haven. 125.15.3.
Trowbridge, James. Conn. Sufferer. Danbury. 7.1.4.
Trowbridge, Jeremiah, Jr. Conn. Sufferer. New/East Haven. 7.3.3.
Trowbridge, John. Conn. Sufferer. New/East Haven. 17.13.8.
Trowbridge, Joseph. Conn. Sufferer. New/East Haven. 10.1.0.
Trowbridge, Stephen. Conn. Sufferer. Danbury. 7.0.4.
Trowbridge, Stephen. Conn. Sufferer. New/East Haven. 8.0.10.

Trowbridge, William. Conn. Sufferer. New/ East Haven. 12.19.6.

Trowbridge, William. Conn. Sufferer. New/ East Haven. 7.4.0.

Troy, James. N.C. Private. 17 Feb. 1824. 640 acres.

Troy, John. Ga. Minute Man. 26 May 1784. 287 1/2 acres.

Troysmitt [?], John. Ga. ———. 23 Apr. 1784. 575 acres.

Truce, Brandick. Ga. ———. ———. 230 acres.

Trudell, Joseph. N. Y. ———. ———. 333 1/3 acres.

True, Obadiah. Me. ———. 20 Nov. 1785. 200 acres. Denmark.

Trueluck, George. N.C. Private. 30 Sep. 1785. 640 acres to heirs.

Trueman, Alexander. Md. Major. ———. 200 acres.

Trueman, John. Md. Lieutenant. ———. 200 acres.

Truhit, Stephen. N.C. Private. 26 Dec. 1800. 640 acres.

Truit, Peter. N.C. Private. 10 Dec. 1788. 640 acres to heirs.

Truit, Stephen. N.C. Private. 2 Apr. 1784. 640 acres.

Truit, William. Va. Private. 18 Dec. 1832. 200 acres.

Truitt, Franklin. N.C. ———. 26 Apr. 1784. 640 acres to John Eckland, heir.

Truitt, Solomon. N.C. Private. 17 Dec. 1785. 640 acres to heirs.

Truluck, Sutton. N.C. Private. 9 Nov. 1784. 274 acres.

Truman, Daniel. Conn. Sufferer. New London. 6.0.0.

Trusty, John. Md. Private. ———. 50 acres.

Tryal, Christopher. N.C. Private. 26 Aug. 1785. 640 acres to heirs.

Tryon, William. Mass. ———. 13 Jan. 1830. 200 acres.

Tucker, Anthony. Md. Private. ———. 50 acres.

Tucker, Daniel. N. Y. Quartermaster. ———. 1000 acres.

Tucker, Daniel. Va. Private. 25 Jul. 1835. 100 acres.

Tucker, Edward. Conn. Sufferer. New London. 25.15.9.

Tucker, George. Ga. Refugee. 22 Apr. 1784. 287 1/2 acres.

Tucker, George. Va. Private. 1 Jun. 1799. 200 acres.

Tucker, Gray. N.C. Private. 30 Sep. 1785. 640 acres to heirs.

Tucker, Henry. Md. Sergeant. ———. 50 acres.

Tucker, Isaac. Conn. Sufferer. Fairfield. 68.17.0.

Tucker, James. N.C. Private. 19 May 1784. 640 acres.

Tucker, James. Va. Sergeant. 11 Aug. 1783. 200 acres.

Tucker, John. Md. Private. ———. 50 acres.

Tucker, John. N.Y. ———. 13 Sep. 1790. 500 acres to heirs.

Tucker, Joshua. N. Y. Private. 8 Jul. 1790. 500 acres.

Tucker, Luke. N.C. Private. 7 Jan. 1786. 640 acres to heirs.

Tucker, Michael. Va. Sergeant. 20 Apr. 1784. 200 acres.

Tucker, Noah. Conn. Sufferer. New/East Haven. 99.17.4.

Tucker, Paschal. Ga. Private. 30 Apr. 1785. 230 acres.

Tucker, Reuben. Va. Private. 22 Sep. 1786. 100 acres.

Tucker, Richard. N.C. Private. 15 Aug. 1823. 640 acres to heirs.

Tucker, Robert. Ga. ———. 27 Apr. 1784. 287 1/2 acres.

Tucker, Samuel. N.C. Private. 17 Dec. 1785. 640 acres.

Tucker, Silas. Va. Prize Master. 18 Mar. 1795. 2666 2/3 acres.

Tucker, Thomas. Ga. Refugee. 21 Apr. 1784. 287 1/2 acres.

Tucker, Thomas. N.C. Corporal. 5 Sep. 1821. 1000 acres.

Tucker, Thomas Tuder. S.C. Director. 4 Jul. 1785. 450 acres.

Tucker, Thomas, Sr. Ga. ———. 22 May 1784. 287 1/2 acres.

Tucker, Willey. N.C. Private. 12 Sep. 1785. 640 acres to heirs.

Tucker, William. N.C. ———. 14 Jun. 1785. 640 acres to heir.

Tucker, William. Pa. Private. 7 Sep. 1787. 200 acres.

Tucker, William. Va. Private. 21 May 1783. 100 acres.

Tucker, Woody. N.C. Private. 1 May 1826. 640 acres to heirs.

Tudor, George. Pa. Major. ———. 300 acres.
Tudor, George. Pa. Major. 28 Feb. 1794. 300 acres to Walter Stewart, assignee.
Tuff, John. Md. Private. ———. 50 acres.
Tuggle, Benjamin. Va. Private. 11 Mar. 1840. 50 acres.
Tuggle, Benjamin. Va. Private. 11 Mar. 1840. 50 acres.
Tuggle, Henry. Va. Private. 3 Feb. 1784. 100 acres.
Tuggle, Henry. Va. Private. 21 Jan. 1805. 100 acres.
Tuggle, Thomas. Va. Private. 12 Mar. 1840. 50 acres.
Tuggle, Thomas. Va. Private. 12 Mar. 1840. 50 acres.
Tuggles, Joshua. Va. Private. 18 Dec. 1783. 100 acres.
Tuggles, Joshua. Va. Private. 2 Mar. 1846. 100 acres.
Tuggles, Joshua. Va. Private. 3 Oct. 1853. 100 acres.
Tulford, Edward. N.C. Private. 24 Dec. 1796. 640 acres.
Tull, Thomas. Pa. ———. 8 Jan. 1803. 200 acres.
Tulley, Abel. N.C. Private. 14 Feb. 1796. 640 acres to heirs.
Tulley, James. Pa. Private. 13 Oct. 1786. 200 acres.
Tully, John D. Md. Private. ———. 50 acres.
Tully, Samuel. N. Y. Private. 8 Jul. 1790. 600 acres.
Tully, William. Ga. Refugee. 27 Apr. 1784. 287 1/2 acres.
Tuman, Peter. N. Y. Private. 8 Jul. 1790. 600 acres.
Tumand, Peter. N.Y. ———. 13 Sep. 1790. 500 acres to heirs.
Tumbleson, Evin. Md. Private. ———. 50 acres.
Tune, William. Va. Sergeant. 6 Dec. 1783. 200 acres.
Tunison, Anthony. Pa. Sergeant. ———. 250 acres.
Tunison, Garrett. Va. Surgeon. 7 Jun. 1834. 6000 acres.
Tunison, Garrit. N. Y. Surgeon. 9 Jul. 1790. 1900 acres.
Tunnel, James. Va. Seaman. 9 Dec. 1833. 100 acres.
Tunnel, William. Va. Seaman. 9 Dec. 1833. 100 acres.
Tunnell, James. Va. Seaman. 9 Aug. 1841. 50 acres.
Tunnell, James. Va. Seaman. 9 Aug. 1841. 50 acres.
Tunnell, Joseph. Va. Seaman. 9 Dec. 1833. 100 acres.
Tunnell, Joseph. Va. Seaman. 9 Aug. 1841. 50 acres.
Tunnell, Joseph. Va. Seaman. 9 Aug. 1841. 50 acres.
Tunnell, William. Va. Quartermaster. 17 Sep. 1851. 856 acres.
Tunnell, William. Va. Quartermaster. 17 Sep. 1851. 285 acres.
Tunnell, William. Va. Quartermaster. 17 Sep. 1851. 285 acres.
Tunnell, William. Va. Quartermaster. 17 Sep. 1851. 713 acres.
Tunnell, William. Va. Quartermaster. 20 Dec. 1853. 427 acres.
Tunnell, William. Va. ———. 20 Oct. 1837. 100 acres.
Tunnis, Nehemiah. Ga. Sergeant. 15 Apr. 1784. 345 acres.
Tunstall, Edward. Va. Sergeant. 19 Dec. 1782. 200 acres.
Tunstall, Henry. Va. Sergeant. 24 Feb. 1784. 200 acres.
Tunstall, Thomas, Jr. Va. Sergeant Major. 15 Oct. 1783. 200 acres.
Tupman, John. Va. Master. 1 Apr. 1784. 2666 2/3 acres.
Turberville, George Lee. Va. Captain. 14 Dec. 1809. 4611 acres.
Turcot, Francis. N. Y. ———. ———. 500 acres.
Tureman, Garrett. Ga. ———. 23 Apr. 1784. 287 1/2 acres.
Tureman, George. Ga. ———. 22 Jul. 1784. 287 1/2 acres.
Tureman, John. Ga. ———. 23 Apr. 1784. 200 acres.
Tureman, Martin. Ga. ———. 22 Apr. 1784. 500 acres.
Turk, James. Va. Private. 24 Jun. 1783. 100 acres.
Turk, Robert. Va. Private. 24 Jun. 1783. 100 acres.
Turkentine, Manly. Pa. Private. ———. 200 acres.
Turknet, George. Ga. ———. 23 Apr. 1784. 287 1/2 acres.

Turknet, Henry. Ga. ———. 23 Apr. 1784. 287 1/2 acres.
Turley, James. Va. Private. 28 Nov. 1786. 100 acres.
Turley, John. Ga. Soldier. 2 Jan. 1786. ———.
Turley, Peter. Ga. Soldier. 15 Jul. 1785. ———.
Turlington, Jacob. Va. Private. 3 Nov. 1787. 100 acres.
Turnbull, Stephen. Va. Captain. 15 Mar. 1834. 4000 acres.
Turnbull, William. Pa. General. ———. 500 acres.
Turner, Abiel. Mass. ———. 9 Jun. 1829. 200 acres.
Turner, Abraham. Ga. Minute Man. 14 Feb. 1785. ———.
Turner, Absolam. N.C. Private. 30 Sep. 1785. 640 acres to heirs.
Turner, Adam. N.C. Private. 21 Aug. 1820. 640 acres.
Turner, Andrew. N.C. Private. 22 Dec. 1796. 640 acres to heirs.
Turner, Benaiah. N.C. Lieutenant. 12 Sep. 1789. 2560 acres.
Turner, Benjamin. N.C. Private. 9 Nov. 1784. 640 acres to Ezekiel Turner, heir.
Turner, Charles. Ga. Soldier. 27 Apr. 1784. 230 acres.
Turner, Daniel. N.C. Private. 24 Nov. 1796. 640 acres to heirs.
Turner, David. Ga. Captain Lieutenant. 19 Mar. 1784. 600 acres to heirs.
Turner, David. Va. Private. 2 Feb. 1819. 100 acres.
Turner, Dennis. Ga. Soldier. 24 — 1785. ———.
Turner, Eleazer. S.C. ———. 21 Jan. 1785. 200 acres.
Turner, Elisha. Mass. Private. 20 Feb. 1833. 200 acres to daughter Lydia Turner, wife of Samuel A. Turner.
Turner, Francis. Va. Private. 13 Sep. 1783. 100 acres.
Turner, George. Ga. Soldier. 27 Apr. 1784. 230 acres.
Turner, George. S.C. Major. 15 Oct. 1784. 400 acres.
Turner, George. Va. Private. 5 Mar. 1788. 100 acres.
Turner, George. Va. Private. 10 Mar. 1790. 100 acres.
Turner, Henry. Ga. Minute Man. 17 Jan. 1785. 287 1/2 acres.
Turner, Isham. Va. Private. 25 Nov. 1789. 100 acres.
Turner, Jacob. N.C. Captain. 7 May 1784. 3840 acres to James Turner, heir.
Turner, John. Ga. Minute Man. 22 Mar. 1785. 250 acres.
Turner, John. Ga. Refugee. 1785. 500 acres. ———.
Turner, John. Md. Private. ———. 50 acres.
Turner, John. Md. Private. ———. 50 acres.
Turner, John. Md. Sergeant. ———. 50 acres.
Turner, John. Md. Matross. ———. 50 acres.
Turner, John. Md. Private. ———. 50 acres. Of Morris Co.
Turner, John. N.C. Private. 9 Nov. 1784. 274 acres.
Turner, John. N.C. Quartermaster. 4 Dec. 1801. 2560 acres to heirs.
Turner, John. N.C. Private. 24 Jul. 1820. 640 acres to heirs.
Turner, John. Pa. ———. 3 Nov. 1786. 200 acres.
Turner, John. Va. Private. 4 Feb. 1784. 2666 2/3 acres.
Turner, John. Va. Sergeant. 31 May 1784. 200 acres.
Turner, John. Va. Private. 11 Dec. 1811. 200 acres.
Turner, Jonathan. Ga. Soldier. 5 Sep. 1785. ———.
Turner, Joseph. S.C. ———. 21 Jan. 1785. 200 acres.
Turner, Maltiah. N.C. Sergeant. 18 Aug. 1784. 1000 acres.
Turner, Peter. Ga. Soldier. 24 — 1785. ———.
Turner, Peter. N. Y. Private. 7 Jul. 1790. 600 acres.
Turner, Richard. Va. Private. 24 Sep. 1784. 200 acres.
Turner, Robert. N.C. Lieutenant. 10 Oct. 1820. 2560 acres to heirs.
Turner, Sampson. Ga. Refugee. ———. 500 acres.
Turner, Samson. N.C. Private. 14 Dec. 1796. ——— acres.
Turner, Simon. N.C. Private. 22 Dec. 1796. 640 acres to heirs.

Turner, Solomon. Ga. Refugee. 22 Mar. 1785. 250 acres.

Turner, Solomon. Md. Private. ———. 50 acres.

Turner, Thomas. Va. Private. 25 Nov. 1789. 100 acres.

Turner, Thomas, Jr. Ga. Soldier. 24 — 1785. ———.

Turner, Thomas, Sr. Ga. Soldier. 24 — 1785. ———.

Turner, Titus Jennings. N.C. Private. 1 Jul. 1825. 640 acres.

Turner, William. N.C. Private. 7 Jan. 1786. 640 acres to heirs.

Turner, William. Va. Private. 30 Jul. 1783. 100 acres.

Turner, William. Va. Private. 5 Mar. 1788. 100 acres.

Turner, William. Va. Private. 11 Jun. 1833. 100 acres.

Turney, Isaac. Conn. Sufferer. Fairfield. 20.3.5.

Turney, John. Conn. Sufferer. Fairfield. 526.12.2.

Turney, Stephen. Conn. Sufferer. Fairfield. 88.5.4.

Turnham, Thomas. Va. Private. 30 Jun. 1784. 100 acres.

Turpin, John. Va. Midshipman. 17 Sep. 1851. 592 2/3 acres.

Turpin, John. Va. Midshipman. 17 Sep. 1851. 592 2/3 acres.

Turpin, John. Va. Midshipman. 17 Sep. 1851. 592 2/3 acres.

Turpin, John. Va. Midshipman. 17 Sep. 1851. 888 2/3 acres.

Turpin, Obadiah. Va. Sergeant. 17 Apr. 1784. 200 acres.

Turpin, William. N.C. Private. 5 Sep. 1821. 640 acres.

Turvey, William. Va. Private. 5 Dec. 1783. 200 acres.

Tuthill, Azariah. N. Y. Lieutenant. 9 Jul. 1790. 1200 acres.

Tutson, Charles. N.C. Private. 12 Sep. 1785. 640 acres to heirs.

Tutt, Benjamin. Ga. ———. 21 Apr. 1784. 1000 acres.

Tutt, Charles. Va. Lieutenant. 17 Apr. 1783. 2666 2/3 acres.

Tutt, James. Ga. ———. 21 Apr. 1784. 500 acres.

Tutt, James. Va. Midshipman. 7 Dec. 1821. 2666 2/3 acres.

Tutt, Richard. S.C. ———. 1 May 1797. 188 acres.

Tutten, William. Md. Private. ———. 50 acres.

Tuttle, Abraham. Conn. Sufferer. New/East Haven. 4.4.0.

Tuttle, Abraham, Jr. Conn. Sufferer. New/East Haven. 27.2.6.

Tuttle, Daniel. Conn. Sufferer. New/East Haven. 13.2.2.

Tuttle, Hezekiah. Conn. Sufferer. New/East Haven. 54.3.3.

Tuttle, James. N.Y. ———. 13 Sep. 1790. 500 acres to heirs.

Tuttle, Joseph. Conn. Sufferer. New/East Haven. 93.3.6.

Tuttle, Richard. Conn. Sufferer. New/East Haven. 13.4.0.

Tuttle, Samuel. Me. Lieutenant. 8 Sep. 1838. 600 acres. Portland.

Tuttle, Samuel. Conn. Sufferer. New/East Haven. 270.19.6.

Tuttle, Stephen. Conn. Sufferer. New/East Haven. 0.17.3

Tuttle, Timothy. Conn. Sufferer. New/East Haven. 79.9.5.

Tweedle, John. Ga. Sergeant. 26 May 1784. 287 1/2 acres.

Twench, George. Md. Sergeant. ———. 50 acres.

Twig, Daniel. N.C. Private. 20 Sep. 1784. 274 acres.

Twigg, Daniel. N.C. Fifer. 8 Aug. 1821. 154 acres.

Twigg, Daniel. N.C. Musician. 19 Dec. 1825. 428 acres to heirs.

Twiggs, John. Ga. Brigadier General. 13 Apr. 1784. 1437 1/2 acres.

Twiss, Robert. Mass. Corporal. 26 Sep. 1833. 200 acres.

Twitty, George. Ga. ———. 27 Apr. 1784. 200 acres.

Tyack, Thomas. Md. Sergeant. ———. 50 acres.

Tyack, Thomas D. N.C. Fife Major. 21 Aug. 1820. 1000 acres.

Tyce, William. N.Y. ———. 13 Sep. 1790. 500 acres to heirs.

Tycowit, Francis. Md. Private. ———. 50 acres.

Tygert, Daniel. Va.-Ind. Private. 108 acres.

Tyler, Andrew. Me. Sergeant. 10 Jun. 1835. 200 acres. Frankfort.

Tyler, Bartlet. N.C. Private. 15 Dec. 1797. 640 acres to heirs.
Tyler, Daniel. Va. Private. 2 Jun. 1827. 100 acres.
Tyler, Henry. Va. Midshipman. 4 Jun. 1835. 2666 2/3 acres.
Tyler, John. Va. Lieutenant. 1 Jul. 1784. 2666 2/3 acres.
Tyler, Moses. N.C. Musician. 30 Nov. 1801. 428 acres.
Tyler, Owen. N.C. Private. 25 Oct. 1783. 640 acres.
Tyler, William. Va. Private. 14 Oct. 1783. 100 acres.
Tyler, William. Va. Private. 26 May 1785. 200 acres.
Tylor, Benjamin. Va. Private. 26 May 1785. 200 acres.
Tyner, Arthur. N.C. Private. 29 Apr. 1784. 274 acres.
Tyner, Arthur. N.C. Private. 11 May 1785. 640 acres to heirs.
Tyner, Arthur Pearce. N.C. Private. 19 Jan. 1786. 640 acres to heir Nicholas Tyner.
Tyner, Nicholas. N.C. Private. 29 Apr. 1784. 266 acres.
Tyner, Richard. Ga. ———. ———. 250 acres.
Tyon, Michael. N. Y. ———. ———. 500 acres.
Tyree, John. Va. Private. 30 Dec. 1784. 100 acres.
Tyree, William. Va. Private. 10 Apr. 1783. 100 acres.
Tyser, Cornelius. Va. Private. 18 Apr. 1783. 100 acres.
Tyson, Abraham. N.C. Private. 2 Sep. 1820. 640 acres to heirs.
Tyson, Gresham, Jr. N.C. Private. 8 Mar. 1796. 640 acres to heirs.
Tyson, Henry. N.C. Private. 28 Feb. 1814. 274 acres.
Ulmer, George. Me. ———. 17 Sep. 1835. 200 acres. Hope.
Ultz, George. Pa. Private. ———. 200 acres.
Underdue, Demcey. N.C. Private. 14 Oct. 1783. 640 acres.
Underdunk, Titus. N. Y. Private. 8 Jul. 1790. 500 acres.
Underhill, James. N.C. Private. 30 Sep. 1785. 274 acres.
Underhill, William. Va. Captain. 7 Dec. 1830. 1333 1/3 acres.
Underhill, William. Va. Captain. 7 Dec. 1830. 1333 1/3 acres.
Underhill, William. Va. Captain. 7 Dec. 1830. 2666 2/3 acres.
Underwood, Gideon. Va. Sergeant. 19 Mar. 1783. 200 acres.
Underwood, Howell. N.C. Private. 30 Sep. 1785. 640 acres to heirs.
Underwood, James. N.C. Private. 30 Sep. 1785. 640 acres to heirs.
Underwood, Richard. Ga. ———. 4 Oct. 1785. ———.
Underwood, Samuel. Ga. ———. 22 Apr. 1784. 287 1/2 acres.
Underwood, Shadrack. N.C. ———. 8 Mar. 1785. 640 acres to heirs.
Ungerman, Nicholas. Pa. Sergeant. 9 Jun. 1803. 250 acres to Peter and Elizabeth Smith, assignees.
Unkey, John. Pa. Private. 23 Nov. 1787. 200 acres to Ludwick Orbigust, assignee.
Upchurch, Charles. N.C. Private. 21 Nov. 1795. 228 acres.
Upright, Michael. N. Y. Private. 8 Jul. 1790. 600 acres.
Upshaw, James. Va. Captain. 14 Jun. 1784. 4000 acres.
Upshaw, James. Va Captain. 13 Mar. 1834. 4000 acres.
Upshaw, Thomas. Va. Captain. 15 Apr. 1783. 4000 acres.
Upson, Jesse. Conn. Sufferer. New/East Haven. 47.18.0.
Upton, Edward. Ga. ———. 27 Apr. 1784. 287 1/2 acres.
Upton, John. N.C. Private. 30 Sep. 1785. 640 acres.
Upton, Joseph. N.C. Private. 30 Sep. 1785. 640 acres to heirs.
Upton, Josiah. N.C. Private. 24 Jan. 1800. 274 acres to heirs.
Upton, Michael. Pa. Sergeant. 11 Oct. 1786. 250 acres.
Upton, Philip. Ga. ———. 27 Apr. 1784. 287 1/2 acres.
Upton, Willis. N.C. Private. 30 Sep. 1785. 640 acres.
Usher, William. Va. Private. 12 Jul. 1783. 100 acres.
Uthest, John. Alias Hans Jost Hess. N. Y. Private. 8 Jul. 1790. 600 acres.
Utter, Gilbert. N. Y. Private. 8 Jul. 1790. 500 acres.

Utter, John. N. Y. Matross. 8 Jul. 1790. 600 acres.
Utterback, Benjamin. Va. Private. 20 Nov. 1783. 100 acres.
Vacher, F. John. N. Y. Surgeon. 9 Jul. 1790. 1900 acres.
Vacon, Jesse. Ga. ———. 17 May 1784. ———.
Vaden, Braddock. Va. Private. 5 Nov. 1784. 200 acres.
Vaiden, John. Va. Corporal. 28 May 1783. 200 acres.
Valentine, Edward. Va. Captain. 15 Mar. 1784. 4000 acres.
Valentine, Isham. Va. Private. 20 Dec. 1784. 100 acres.
Valentine, John. Va. Private. 30 Dec. 1814. 100 acres.
Valentine, Joseph. Va. Private. 10 May 1784. 100 acres.
Valentine, Josiah. Va. Lieutenant. 24 Jun. 1830. 1333 1/3 acres.
Valentine, Josiah. Va. Lieutenant. 24 Jun. 1830. 1333 1/3 acres.
Valentine, Malachi. N.C. Private. 17 Dec. 1785. 640 acres heirs.
Valentine, Peter. N.C. Private. 28 Sep. 1785. 640 acres to heirs.
Valentine, Silas. N.C. Private. 30 Sep. 1785. 640 acres to heirs.
Valetine, Jacob. Va. Captain. 13 Mar. 1783. 4000 acres.
Valkenburgh, V. Francis. N. Y. Private. 8 Jul. 1790. 600 acres.
Vallance, William. N.Y. ———. 13 Sep. 1790. 500 acres to heirs.
Vallentine, Thomas. N.C. Private. 30 Sep. 1785. 640 acres to heirs.
Van Lear, William. Pa. Major. ———. 500 acres.
VanAmburg, Abram. N. Y. Private. 8 Jul. 1790. 600 acres.
VanAtta, John. N. Y. Private. 8 Jul. 1790. 600 acres.
VanAtter, Joseph. N. Y. Private. 8 Jul. 1790. 600 acres.
VanBlaricum, James. N. Y. Sergeant. 8 Jul. 1790. 600 acres.
VanBonscoten, Peter. N. Y. Lieutenant. 9 Jul. 1790. 1200 acres.
VanBunhagle, B. C. John. N. Y. Private. 8 Jul. 1790. 600 acres.
VanBunschoten, Elias. N. Y. Captain. 9 Jul. 1790. 1800 acres.
Vancampen, Moses. Pa. Lieutenant. 24 Sep. 1787. 200 acres.
Vancampen, Moses. Pa. Private. 24 Sep. 1887 [?sic]. 200 acres.
Vancap, Laurence. Va. Private. 14 Nov. 1796. 100 acres.
Vance, David. N.C. Private. 29 Sep. 1784. 228 acres.
Vance, Elijah. N.C. Private. 29 Sep. 1784. 228 acres.
Vance, Hanley. Va.-Ind. Private. 108 acres.
Vance, James. N.C. Private. 7 Dec. 1797. 640 acres to heirs.
Vance, John. N.C. Captain. 27 Nov. 1783. 3840 acres to John Vance, heir.
Vance, John. N.C. Lieutenant. 27 Nov. 1783. 2560 acres.
Vance, Joseph. Va. Private. 20 Jun. 1783. 100 acres.
Vance, Patrick. Ga. ———. 27 Apr. 1784. 287 1/2 acres.
Vance, Robert. Va. Captain. 17 Jun. 1783. 4000 acres.
Vance, Robert. Va. Captain. 31 Dec. 1806. 666 2/3 acres.
Vance, William. Me. ———. 9 Sep. 1835. 200 acres. Readfield.
Vance, William. N.C. Corporal. 6 Jan. 1784. 428 acres.
Vancort, John. Pa. Lieutenant. 2 Apr. 1787. 200 acres to Henry and Berry, executors.
VanCortland, Philip. N. Y. Colonel. 3 Jul. 1790. 3000 acres.
Vancourt, John. Pa. Lieutenant. 2 Apr. 1787. 200 acres.
VanCourt, John. Pa. Lieutenant. 2 Apr. 1787. 200 acres.
Vandeburgh, Henry. N. Y. Captain. 9 Jul. 1790. 1800 acres.
Vandemarkin, Cornelius. N. Y. Private. 8 Jul. 1790. 600 acres.
Vanderburgh, Bartholomew. N. Y. Ensign. 9 Jul. 1790. 1100 acres.
Vanderfield, William. N.C. Private. 30 Sep. 1785. 640 acres to heirs.
Vanderhest, Jesse. Ga. Minute Man. 3 Apr. 1785. ———.
VanderHeyden, Jacob. N. Y. ———. ———. 500 acres.
Vanderheyden, Nanning. N. Y. Lieutenant. 9 Jul. 1790. 1000 acres.
Vanderhorst, John. S.C. Major. 18 Jul. 1784. 400 acres.

Vandermarken, Gysbert. N.Y. ———. 13 Sep. 1790. 500 acres to heirs.
Vanderwerken, James. N. Y. Private. 8 Jul. 1790. 600 acres.
VanDeuson, Abram. N. Y. Corporal. 8 Jul. 1790. 600 acres.
Vandevour, John. N.Y. ———. 13 Sep. 1790. 500 acres to heirs.
Vandewall, Marks. Va. Lieutenant. 6 Sep. 1809. 222 acres.
Vandiford, Noah. N.C. Private. 12 Dec. 1806. 640 acres to heirs.
VanDubogart, Nicholas. N. Y. Corporal. 8 Jul. 1790. 600 acres.
VanDuerson, William. Conn. Sufferer. New/East Haven. 62.4.3.
Vanduvall, Markes. Va. Lieutenant. 13 Dec. 1782. 2666 2/3 acres.
VanDyck, Cornelius. N. Y. Lieutenant Colonel. 9 Jul. 1790. 2700 acres.
VanDyck, John. N. Y. Captain. 26 Sep. 1792. 1200 acres.
VanDyck, Peter. N. Y. Private. 8 Jul. 1790. 500 acres.
Vandyke, Charles. N.C. Private. 15 Feb. 1797. 640 acres.
VanEverin, Martin. N. Y. Private. 8 Jul. 1790. 600 acres.
VanGelder, Jacob. N.Y. ———. 13 Sep. 1790. 500 acres to heirs.
VanGilder, Matthew. N. Y. Private. 8 Jul. 1790. 600 ares.
VanHoosen, Garrett. N. Y. Private. 8 Jul. 1790. 600 acres.
Vanhorn, Isaac. Pa. Captain. 26 Jan. 1801. 500 acres.
VanHovenbargh, Rudolphus. N. Y. Lieutenant. 9 Jul. 1790. 1200 acres.
VanHuff, John. Mass. Private. 13 Jan. 1831. 200 acres.
VanHuysen, John. N.Y. ———. 20 Mar. 1793. 500 acres to heirs.
VanHuysen, John. N. Y. ———. 20 Mar. 1793. 500 acres.
VanIngen, Dirck. N.Y. Physician & Surgeon. 8 Oct. 1792. 2250 acres.
Vankelner, John. Pa. Private. 30 Mar. 1787. 200 acres.
Vankirk, John. Pa. Sergeant. 9 May 1787. 250 acres.
Vankleck, Henry. N. Y. Corporal. 8 Jul. 1790. 600 acres.
VanKleck, Peter. N.Y. Sergeant. 13 Sep. 1790. 500 acres to heirs.
VanKlief, Lawrence. N. Y. Private. 8 Jul. 1790. 600 acres.
Vanlooling, Joseph. Pa. Private. 6 Jul. 1787. 200 acres.
Vanmarter, William. Va. Private. 24 Oct. 1821. 100 acres.
Vanmeter, Isaac. Va.-Ind. Private. 108 acres.
Vanmeter, Jacob. Va.-Ind. Ensign. 2156 acres.
Vanmeter, Joseph. Va. Ensign. 3 Jun. 1783. 2666 2/3 acres.
Vann, Cader. Ga. Minute Man. ———. 287 1/2 acres.
Vann, Henry. Va. Private. 23 Jun. 1783. 200 acres.
Vann, James. Ga. ———. 24 May 1784. 287 1/2 acres.
Vann, John. Ga. Refugee. Sep. 1785. ———.
Vann, Peter. Ga. Refugee. Sep. 1785. ———.
Vann, Ralph. Ga. Soldier. 4 Feb. 1785. ———.
Vann, Thomas. Ga. ———. 27 Apr. 1784. 800 acres.
Vanness, Cornelius. N. Y. Private. 8 Jul. 1790. 600 acres.
Vanney, Vincent. N. Y. Private. 8 Jul. 1790. 600 acres.
VanNorman, Isaac. N. Y. Private. 8 Jul. 1790. 600 acres.
VanNorth, John. N. Y. Drummer. 8 Jul. 1790. 600 acres.
VanNote, Charles. N. Y. Private. 8 Jul. 1790. 500 acres.
VanOrden, Albert. N. Y. Private. 8 Jul. 1790. 600 acres.
VanOrsdall, Jacobus. N. Y. ———. ———. 200 acres to his children.
Vanoy, Andrew. N.C. Captain. 16 Aug. 1821. 3840 acres.
VanPlaten, Philip Frederick. S.C. Lieutenant. 2 May 1785. 200 acres to Ephraim Mitchell, administrator, in trust.
VanRennselaer, Nicholas. N. Y. Captain. 9 Jul. 1790. 1800 acres.
VanRensselaer, Jeremiah. N.Y. Lieutenant. 9 Jul. 1790. 1200 acres.
VanSchaick, Goose. N. Y. Colonel. 9 Jul. 1790. 3000 acres.
VanSice, John. N. Y. Private. 8 Jul. 1790. 600 acres.

VanSlyck, Martin. N. Y. Private. 8 Jul. 1790. 600 acres.
VanTassel, Cornelius. N.Y. Private. 13 Sep. 1790. 500 acres to heirs.
VanVechten, Tobias. N.Y. Lieutenant. 13 Sep. 1790. 1200 acres to heirs.
VanVorst, Jellis D. N. Y. ———. 13 Apr. 1792. 500 acres.
VanVost, Christian. N.Y. ———. 13 Sep. 1790. 500 acres to heirs.
VanWagenen, Teunis. N. Y. Lieutenant. 9 Jul. 1790. 1200 acres.
VanWort, Henry. New York. Lieutenant. 9 Jul. 1790. 1200 acres.
Vanzant, Isaac. Ga. ———. 17 Apr. 1784. 287 1/2 acres.
Vanzant, John. Md. Private. ———. 50 acres.
VanZile, Egbert. N. Y. Private. 13 Sep. 1790. 500 acres.
Vardon, Thomas. Pa. Private. ———. 200 acres to John Donnell, assignee.
Variel, Joseph. N. Y. Matross. 9 Jul. 1790. 500 acres.
Varkize, James. N.C. Lieutenant. 16 Aug. 1821. 2560 acres.
Varlow, John. Md. Private. ———. 50 acres.
Varlow, Stephen. Md. Private. ———. 50 acres.
Varner, Joseph. Va. Private. 5 Apr. 1831. 200 acres.
Varner, Philip. Pa. Private. 2 Nov. 1786. 200 acres.
Vasser, Daniel. Va. Sergeant. 24 Feb. 1784. 200 acres.
Vasser, Isham. Va. Corporal. 3 Feb. 1784. 200 acres.
Vastenous, Louis. N. Y. ———. ———. 500 acres.
Vaughan, Claiborne. Va. Surgeon's Mate. 20 Feb. 1784. 2666 2/3 acres.
Vaughan, Claiborne. Va. Surgeon. 31 Dec. 1851. 3333 1/3 acres.
Vaughan, Claiborne. Va. Surgeon's Mate. 23 May 1855. 1333 1/3 acres.
Vaughan, Claiborne. Va. Surgeon's Mate. 23 May 1855. 2666 2/3 acres.
Vaughan, Cornelius. Md. Private. ———. 50 acres.
Vaughan, Daniel. N.C. Private. 6 Dec. 1796. 640 acres to heirs.
Vaughan, James. Va. Mate. 19 May 1838. 1333 1/3 acres.
Vaughan, James. Va. Mate. 19 May 1838. 1333 1/3 acres.
Vaughan, John. Va.-Ind. Sergeant. 216 acres.
Vaughan, John. Md. Sergeant. ———. 50 acres.
Vaughan, John. Mass. Private. 19 Nov. 1832. 200 acres to heirs.
Vaughan, John. Va. Lieutenant. 19 Feb. 1784. 2666 2/3 acres.
Vaughan, Patrick. Va. Private. 30 Jun. 1784. 100 acres.
Vaughan, Richard. Va. Private. 5 Nov. 1783. 100 acres.
Vaughan, Sherwood. Va. Private. 10 Mar. 1786. 200 acres.
Vaughan, Thomas. Va. Private. 17 Jan. 1784. 100 acres.
Vaughan, West. N.C. Private. 28 Aug. 1820. 640 acres to heirs.
Vaughan, William. Md. Private. ———. 50 acres.
Vaughan, William. Va. Sergeant. 17 Sep. 1850. 100 acres.
Vaughan, William. Via. Sergeant. 17 Sep. 1850. 100 acres.
Vaughn, Abraham. N.C. Private. 19 May 1784. 640 acres.
Vaughn, Alexander. Ga. ———. 23 Apr. 1784. 200 acres.
Vaughn, James. N.C. Private. 20 Jan. 1785. 640 acres to heirs.
Vaughn, James. Va. Sergeant. 25 Apr. 1785. 200 acres.
Vaughn, Jesse. Ga. ———. 23 Apr. 1784. 200 acres.
Vaughn, Jesse. Va. Private. 13 Nov. 1810. 100 acres.
Vaughn, John. Va. Sergeant. 29 Oct. 1791. 200 acres.
Vaughn, Richard. N.C. ———. 21 May 1784. 640 acres to heir.
Vaughn, Thomas. Pa. Private. 26 Mar. 1813. 200 acres.
Vaulx, Daniel. Ga. ———. 27 Apr. 1784. 950 acres.
Vaun, Michael. Conn. Sufferer. New/East Haven. 3.13.10.
Vaun, ———. S.C. ———. 3 Aug. 1795. 200 acres to Martha Vaun.
Vause, William. Va. Captain. 25 Nov. 1784. 4000 acres.
Vause, William. Va. Captain. 13 Dec. 1833. 666 2/3 acres.

Vawter, Benjamin. Va. Private. 4 Jun. 1783. 100 acres.
Vawter, Benjamin. Va. Private. 9 Aug. 1799. 100 acres.
Vawter, Beverley. Va. Private. 1 Apr. 1785. 100 acres.
Vawter, William. Va. Lieutenant. 20 Jan. 1783. 2666 2/3 acres.
Veal, Solomon. Va. Sergeant. 29 Jun. 1783. 200 acres.
Veazy, Jacob. Ga. ———. 21 Apr. 1784. 287 1/2 acres.
Veazy, James. Md. ———. ———. 50 acres.
Veeder, Aaron. N.Y. ———. 13 Sep. 1790. 500 acres to heirs.
Velven, Robert. N.C. Fifer. 30 Sep. 1785. 1000 acres to heirs.
Venial, Jacob. Pa. Dragoon. 24 Nov. 1786. 200 acres.
Venice, John. N. Y. Private. 8 Jul. 1790. 600 acres.
Venshioner, George. Va.-Ind. Private. 108 acres.
Venters, Arthur. N.C. Private. 30 Sep. 1785. 640 acres to heirs.
Venters, William. N.C. Private. 30 Sep. 1785. 640 acres to heirs.
Ventress, John. N.C. Private. 9 Sep. 1785. 640 acres to heirs.
Ventris, Malachi. N.C. Private. 8 May 1826. 640 acres to heir Elizabeth Venters.
Venturet, Moses. Conn. Sufferer. New/East Haven. 31.8.0.
Venus, Patrick. N.C. Private. 30 Sep. 1785. 640 acres to heirs.
Vericule, Joseph. N. Y. ———. ———. 500 acres.
Verlie, Bernard. N. Y. ———. ———. 500 acres.
Verlie, Francis. N. Y. ———. ———. 500 acres.
Verlie, Michael. N. Y. ———. ———. 500 acres.
Vermillion, Benjamin. Ga. ———. 29 Apr. 1784. 200 acres.
Vermillion, Samuel. Md. Private. ———. 50 acres.
Vermilyea, John. N. Y. Matross. 9 Jul. 1790. 500 acres.
Verner, John. Pa. Private. 12 Apr. 1787. 200 acres.
Vernon, Frederick. Pa. Major. ———. 300 acres.
Vernon, Frederick. Pa. Major. ———. 300 acres.
Vernon, George. Md. Private. ———. 50 acres.
Vernon, Job. Pa. Captain. 28 Sep. 1787. 500 acres.
Vernon, Richard. Va. Private. 16 May 1834. 100 acres.
Vernon, Robert. N.C. Lieutenant. 12 May 1784. 1280 acres.
Vernon, Thomas. Pa. ———. 1 Apr. 1809. 300 acres in trust &c.
Vernon, Thomas. Va. Private. 12 Apr. 1784. 100 acres.
Vernoy, Joseph. Va. Private. 18 Mar. 1784. 200 acres.
Verrian, John. N. Y. Private. 6 Jul. 1790. 600 acres.
Verrier, James. N.C. Lieutenant. 21 Aug. 1820. 1494 acres.
Verrity, Gilbert. N. Y. Private. 8 Jul. 1790. 600 acres.
Verser, Joel. Va. Private. 25 Feb. 1784. 100 acres.
Vest, George. Va. Private. 27 Jul. 1784. 100 acres.
Via, Littleberry. Va. Private. 25 Jan. 1812. 100 acres.
Vick, Burwell. Ga. ———. 17 Apr. 1784. 200 acres.
Vick, Isaiah. N.C. Private. 15 Feb. 1797. 274 acres.
Vick, Thomas. Ga. ———. 17 Apr. 1784. 450 acres.
Vicker, Robert. Pa. Matross. ———. 200 acres.
Vickers, Edward. Md. Private. ———. 50 acres.
Vickers, Marmaduke. N.C. Private. 26 May 1784. 640 acres.
Vickers, Rieley. N.C. Private. 22 Dec. 1796. 228 acres.
Vickers, Solomon. Ga. Soldier. 17 May 1784. 230 acres to heirs.
Vickers, Thomas. Ga. ———. 27 Apr. 1784. 287 1/2 acres.
Vickers, William. Pa. Private. ———. 200 acres.
Vickers, William. Va. Private. 26 Jul. 1784. 100 acres.
Vickery, Henry. N.C. Private. 10 Aug. 1785. 640 acres to heir.

Vickery, John. N.C. Private. 20 Apr. 1784. 640 acres.
Vickins, William. Va. Private. 21 Jun. 1784. 200 acres.
Victoire, Foelix. N. Y. Lieutenant. ———. 1000 acres.
Victor, John. Va. Lieutenant. 19 Mar. 1834. 2666 2/3 acres.
Victorius, Frederick. Pa. Private. ———. 200 acres.
Vincent, John. Md. Private. ———. 50 acres.
Vincent, John. Va. Corporal. 5 Oct. 1789. 200 acres.
Vincent, Joseph. N. Y. Private. 8 Jul. 1790. 500 acres.
Vinegardner, John. Pa. Private. 19 Sep. 1787. 200 acres.
Vinette, John B. N. Y. ———. ———. 500 acres.
Viney, Thomas. N.C. Private. 10 Aug. 1785. 640 acres.
Vinson, Charterite. N.C. Private. 30 Sep. 1785. 640 acres to heirs.
Vinson, George. N.C. Private. 30 Sep. 1785. 640 acres to heirs.
Vinson, John. N.C. Private. 10 Aug. 1785. 640 acres to heirs.
Vinson, Moses. N.C. Private. 12 Mar. 1785. 640 acres to heirs.
Vinson, William. N.C. Private. 28 Sep. 1785. 640 acres to heirs.
Vinters, Daniel. N.C. ———. 25 Jun. 1785. 640 acres to heirs.
Vinters, Moses. N.C. Private. 21 Jan. 1818. 274 acres to heirs.
Violet, John. Va. Private. 23 Jun. 1783. 200 acres.
Virgil, Asa. Mass. Corporal. 1 Feb. 1833. 200 acres to heirs.
Viskers, John. Va. Private. 26 Apr. 1783. 200 acres.
Visor, Abraham. N.C. Private. 9 Dec. 1797. 640 acres to heirs.
Vize, Henry. N.C. Private. 8 Aug. 1821. 640 acres.
Vogan, John. Pa. ———. ———. 200 acres.
Voglusan, Armand. Va. Captain. 25 Nov. 1782. 4000 acres.
Vollentine, Daniel. N.C. Private. 9 Apr. 1788. 640 acres.
Volvoy, John. S.C. ———. 2 Jul. 1787. 200 acres.
VonHorn, John. N. Y. Private. 8 Jul. 1790. 600 acres.
Vosburgh, I. Peter. N. Y. Captain. 17 Aug. 1790. 1800 acres.
Vose, Benjamin. Conn. Sufferer. Groton. 6.8.6.
Voss, Joseph. N.C. Private. 19 May 1784. 640 acres.
Voules, Henry. Va. Adjutant. 28 May 1856. 1580 3/9 acres.
Voules, Henry. Va. Adjutant. 28 May 1856. 790 1/9 acres.
Vowell, William. N.C. Private. 21 Aug. 1820. 640 acres.
Vowles, Charles. Va. Lieutenant. 6 Mar. 1783. 2666 2/3 acres.
Vowles, Henry. Va. Captain Lieutenant. 3 Mar. 1783. 4000 acres.
Vowles, Henry. Va. Lieutenant & Adjutant. 21 Aug. 1798. 2666 2/3 acres.
Vowles, Henry. Va. Captain. 21 Aug. 1798. 666 2/3 acres.
Vowles, Henry. Va. Adjutant. 20 Oct. 1859. 790 acres.
Vowles, Henry. Va. Adjutant. 20 Oct. 1859. 395 acres.
Vowles, Walter. Va. Captain. 6 Mar. 1783. 4666 2/3 acres.
Vowles, Walter. Va Captain. 30 May 1856. 105 acres.
Vredenburgh, Peter. N. Y. Private. 6 Jul. 1790. 600 acres.
Vredenburgh, William. N. Y. Private. 8 Jul. 1790. 600 acres.
Vulva, Thomas. N.Y. ———. 13 Sep. 1790. 500 acres to heirs.
Waddle, Jacob. N.C. Sergeant. 5 Sep. 1821. 1000 acres.
Waddle, James. S.C. Soldier. 21 Jan. 1785. 200 acres.
Waddle, Nathaniel. N.C. ———. 20 Dec. 1800. 640 acres to assignee Frederick Deboe.
Waddle, William. N. Y. Private. 8 Jul. 1790. 500 acres.
Waddy, Samuel. Va. Sergeant. 18 — 1827. 200 acres.
Waddy, Shapleigh. Va. Midshipman. 30 Jun. 1784. 2666 2/3 acres.
Waddy, Thomas. Va. Private. 31 Dec. 1785. 200 acres.
Wade, Acra. Va. Private. 25 Feb. 1784. 200 acres.

Wade, Andrew. N.C. Private. 29 Nov. 1783. 228 acres.
Wade, Benjmain. Va. Private. 20 May 1823. 100 acres.
Wade, Daniel. N.C. Musician. 5 Sep. 1821. 1000 acres.
Wade, David. Va. Private. 1 Apr. 1783. 100 acres.
Wade, Edward. Md. Private. ———. 50 acres.
Wade, Edward. Va. Lieutenant. 14 Dec. 1837. 3330 2/3 acres.
Wade, Edward. Va. Lieutenant. 14 Dec. 1837. 150 acres.
Wade, Harrison. Va. Private. 20 May 1823. 100 acres.
Wade, Hezekiah. Ga. Captain. 19 Jul. 1784. 575 acres.
Wade, John. Ga. Refugee. 15 Apr. 1784. 287 1/2 acres.
Wade, John. Md. Private. ———. 50 acres.
Wade, Joseph J. N.C. Captain. 16 Aug. 1821. 3840 acres.
Wade, Moses. Va. Private. 12 Jun. 1783. 100 acres.
Wade, Nathaniel. Ga. Refugee. 17 Apr. 1784. 287 1/2 acres.
Wade, Nehemiah. Ga. Refugee. 17 Apr. 1784. 287 1/2 acres.
Wade, Robert. Ga. ———. 17 May 1784. ———.
Wade, Thomas. Pa. Private. ———. 200 acres.
Wade, William. Md. Matross. ———. 50 acres.
Wade, William. Pa. Private. 23 Oct. 1786. 200 acres.
Wadkins, William. N.C. ———. 13 Jun. 1785. 640 acres to heirs.
Wadsworth, William. N.C. Private. 3 Feb. 1785. 640 acres.
Wafield, George. Va. Private. 20 Jun. 1783. 100 acres.
Wagg, James. Me. ———. 5 Jun. 1835. 200 acres. Durham.
Waggerman, Emanuel. N. Y. Private. 7 Jul. 1790. 600 acres.
Waggoner, Andrew. Va. Major. 11 Jun. 1783. 6222 acres.
Waggoner, Andrew. Va. Major. 18 Nov. 1807. 592 1/2 acres.
Waggoner, Andrew. Va. Major. 18 Nov. 1807. 592 1/2 acres.
Waggoner, William. Va. Sergeant. 2 Oct. 1784. 200 acres.
Waggonman, George. N. Y. Private. 8 Jul. 1790. 600 acres.
Wagner, Geroge. Ga. ———. 17 May 1784. ———.
Wagner, Henry. Ga. ———. 17 May 1784. ———.
Wagner, James. Ga. ———. 15 Mar. 1784. 250 acres.
Wagner, William. Ga. ———. 14 Sep. 1784. 287 1/2 acres.
Wagnon, Thomas. Ga. Soldier. 20 Apr. 1784. 230 acres.
Wagnoner, John Peter. Ga. Lieutenant. 23 Sep. 1783. 400 acres.
Wagoner, Jacob. Pa. Private. 31 Aug. 1787. 200 acres.
Wagoner, James. N.C. ———. 15 Jun. 1785. 640 acres to heir.
Wagonman, John Michael. Ga. ———. 26 May 1784. 575 acres.
Waide, John. Va. Corporal. 23 Jul. 1824. 200 acres.
Wainright, George. Ga. ———. 23 Apr. 1784. 287 1/2 acres.
Wainwright, Obadiah. N.C. Private. 26 May 1784. 640 acres.
Waiscoat, David. Ga. ———. 15 Apr. 1784. 500 acres.
Waistcoat, Joshua. Me. ———. 4 May 1835. 200 acres to widow Deborah Waistcoat. Hartford.
Wait, William. Mass. Private. 5 Nov. 1832. 200 acres.
Waite, Asa. Mass. Corporal. 12 Jul. 1833. 200 acres to widow Rebecca Waite.
Wakaranthrow, James. N.Y. Captain. 29 Jan. 1791. 1800 acres. [an Indian].
Wakefield, William. N.C. Private. 24 Nov. 1803. 274 acres.
Wakeman, Andrew. Conn. Sufferer. Fairfield. 207.14.2.
Wakeman, Ebenezer. Conn. Sufferer. Fairfield. 68.12.1.
Wakeman, Jessup. Conn. Sufferer. Fairfield. 12.9.11.
Wakeman, Joseph. Conn. Sufferer. Fairfield. 167.3.8.
Wakeman, Joseph. Conn. Sufferer. Fairfield. 4.0.0.
Wakeman, Ruth. Conn. Sufferer. Fairfield. 22.8.1.

Wakeman, Thomas Hanford. Conn. Sufferer. Fairfield. 239.6.10.

Waker, Green. N.C. Private. 30 Sep. 1785. 640 acres to heirs.

Walch, David. Va. Matross. 23 Mar. 1790. 200 acres.

Walch, John. N. Y. Private. 8 Jul. 1790. 500 acres.

Walcott, Clement. Pa. Private. 25 Nov. 1786. 200 acres to Andrew Bemer, assignee.

Walden, Ambrose. Va. Lieutenant. 27 Jan./ 26 Feb. 1852. 666 2/3 acres.

Walden, Ambrose. Va. Lieutenant. 27 Jan./ 26 Feb. 1852. 666 2/3 acres.

Walden, Ambrose. Va. Lieutenant. 27 Jan./ 26 Feb. 1852. 666 2/3 acres.

Walden, Ambrose. Va. Lieutenant. 27 Jan./ 26 Feb. 1852. 666 2/3 acres.

Walden, Charles. Va. Private. 24 Nov. 1817. 200 acres.

Walden, David. N.C. Private. 5 Sep. 1821. 640 acres.

Walden, George. Va. Sergeant. 14 Apr. 1783. 200 acres.

Walden, George. Va. Private. 1 Aug. 1799. 100 acres.

Walden, John. Va. Corporal. 27 Jun. 1783. 200 acres.

Walden, Robert. Ga. ———. 17 Apr. 1784. 287 1/2 acres.

Walden, Spencer. Va. Private. 22 Jan. 1788. 100 acres.

Walden, Thomas. N.C. Private. 1 Dec. 1796. 640 acres.

Walden, Zachariah. Va. Private. 25 Feb. 1783. 100 acres.

Waldrop, Joseph. S.C. ———. 3 Sep. 1792. 200 acres.

Wale, George. Va. Private. 10 Feb. 1817. 100 acres.

Wale, William. Va. Private. 10 Feb. 1817. 100 acres.

Walen, Barney. Va.-Ind. Private. 108 acres. [Waters].

Wales, Samuel. Mass. Private. 12 Mar. 1834. 200 acres.

Wales, Timothy. N. Y. Private. 8 Jul. 1790. 500 acres.

Walker, Aaron. N.C. Private. 30 Sep. 1785. 640 acres.

Walker, Andrew. Pa. Captain. ———. 500 acres.

Walker, Benjamin. N.Y. Lieutenant Colonel. 2 Sep. 1790. 2700 acres.

Walker, David. Ga. Soldier. 21 Apr. 1784. 287 1/2 acres.

Walker, David. Va. Lieutenant. 20 May 1783. 2666 2/3 acres.

Walker, Edward. Ga. ———. 16 Jul. 1784. 287 1/2 acres.

Walker, Edward. N. Y. Private. 7 Jul. 1790. 600 acres.

Walker, Edward. Va. Private. 23 Jun. 1783. 200 acres.

Walker, Elisha. Ga. ———. 20 Feb. 1784. 250 acres.

Walker, George. Va. Matross. 17 Jan. 1833. 100 acres.

Walker, George. Va. ———. 19 Sep. 1833. 100 acres.

Walker, Henry. Pa. Private. 13 May 1789. 200 acres.

Walker, Henry. Va. Private. 15 Oct. 1783. 100 acres.

Walker, Isaac. Ga. ———. 20 Apr. 1784. 287 1/2 acres.

Walker, Jacob. Va. Captain. 13 Jun. 1783. 4000 acres.

Walker, James. Ga. Refugee. Sep. 1785. ———.

Walker, James. Va. Sailor. 30 Jun. 1784. 100 acres.

Walker, James. Va. Seaman. 8 Jun. 1833. 100 acres.

Walker, Jeremiah. Va. Private. 31 Oct. 1783. 100 acres.

Walker, Jeremiah. Va. Private. 3 Mar. 1784. 200 acres.

Walker, John. Ga. ———. 16 Jul. 1784. 287 1/2 acres.

Walker, John. Va.-Ind. Sergeant. 216 acres.

Walker, John. Me. Private. 22 Apr. 1835. 200 acres to widow Nancy Walker. Anson.

Walker, John. Md. Sergeant. ———. 50 acres.

Walker, John. Md. Private. ———. 50 acres.

Walker, John. N.Y. ———. 20 Jan. 1791. 500 acres to heirs.

Walker, John. N.C. Major. 25 Oct. 1783. 1709 acres.

Walker, John. N.C. Sergeant. 7 Jan. 1784. 357 acres.

Walker, John. Va. Private. 10 Oct. 1783. 200 acres.

Walker, John. Va. Private. 15 Oct. 1783. 100 acres.
Walker, John. Va. Private. 3 Nov. 1787. 100 acres.
Walker, John. Va. Private. 26 Nov. 1792. 200 acres.
Walker, John. Va. Ensign. 11 Sep. 1809. 1333 1/3 acres.
Walker, John. Va. Ensign. 11 Sep. 1809. 1333 1/3 acres.
Walker, John. Va. Sergeant. 11 Aug. 1834. 120 acres.
Walker, John. Va. Sergeant. 21 Jan. 1835. 80 acres.
Walker, Joseph. Ga. Soldier. 22 Apr. 1784. 287 1/2 acres.
Walker, Joseph. N.C. Captain. 11 Jan. 1822. 3840 acres to heirs.
Walker, Joseph. S.C. ———. 21 Jan. 1785. 200 acres.
Walker, Justus. N.Y. ———. 20 Jan. 1791. 500 acres to heirs.
Walker, Levin. Va. Lieutenant. 21 Jan. 1784. 2666 2/3 acres.
Walker, Levin. Va. Lieutenant. 30 Mar. 1784. 2666 2/3 acres.
Walker, Matthias. N. Y. Private. 8 Jul. 1790. 600 acres.
Walker, Moses. N.C. Private. 27 Nov. 1783. 228 acres.
Walker, Nehemiah. Va. Private. 9 Jun. 1831. 100 acres.
Walker, Richard. N.C. Private. 17 Feb. 1824. 640 acres.
Walker, Richard Shewell. N.C. Sergeant. 30 Sep. 1785. 1000 acres to heirs.
Walker, Robert. Ga. Soldier. 4 Apr. 1785. ———.
Walker, Robert. Md. Private. ———. 50 acres.
Walker, Samuel. N. Y. Private. 7 Jul. 1790. 600 acres.
Walker, Samuel. Pa. Private. 15 Jan. 1787. 200 acres.
Walker, Samuel. Va. Captain. 7 Apr. 1831. 4000 acres.
Walker, Saunders. Ga. Chaplain. 22 Apr. 1784. 747 1/2 acres.
Walker, Silvanus. Ga. ———. 22 Apr. 1784. 287 1/2 acres.
Walker, Thomas. Ga. Private. 5 Sep. 1785. 250 acres.
Walker, Thomas. Ga. Refugee. Sep. 1785. ———.
Walker, Thomas. Va.-Ind. Private. 108 acres.
Walker, Thomas. N.C. Wagon Master. 16 Aug. 1821. 1000 acres.
Walker, Thomas. Pa. Private. 4 Sep. 1787. 200 acres to Martha Walker, administratrix.
Walker, Thomas. Va. Private. 19 Jan. 1786. 100 acres.
Walker, Thomas. Va. Captain. 4 May 1833. 4000 acres.
Walker, Thomas. Va. Captain. 4 Apr. 1861. 1172 acres.
Walker, Walter. N.C. Private. 2 Feb. 1786. 640 acres.
Walker, William. Ga. Captain. 22 Apr. 1784. 575 acres.
Walker, William. Ga. Minute Man. 22 Apr. 1784. 287 1/2 acres.
Walker, William. N.C. Private. 28 May 1784. 640 acres.
Walker, William. N.C. Sergeant. 11 Jul. 1785. 1000 acres to heirs.
Walker, William. N.C. Sergeant. 30 Sep. 1785. 640 acres to heirs.
Walker, William. N.C. Private. 14 Dec. 1797. 640 acres to heirs.
Walker, William. N.C. Private. 21 Aug. 1820. 640 acres.
Walker, William. Pa. Private. 10 Mar. 1795. 200 acres to Clement Biddle, assignee.
Walker, William. S.C. ———. 7 Nov. 1791. 200 acres.
Walker, William. Va. Private. 23 Apr. 1783. 100 acres.
Walkins, Joseph. N.C. Private. 30 Sep. 1785. 640 acres to heirs.
Wall, Arthur. Ga. Soldier. 6 Sep. 1784. 287 1/2 acres.
Wall, Daniel. Ga. ———. 17 May 1784. ———.
Wall, David. Ga. Minute Man. 7 Apr. 1784. ———.
Wall, Edward. Md. ———. ———. 50 acres.
Wall, Francis. Ga. Minute Man. 21 Apr. 1784. 287 1/2 acres.
Wall, Gilbert. S.C. ———. 5 Nov. 1792. 200 acres to Richard Wall, heir at law.
Wall, James. N.C. Lieutenant. 21 Apr. 1784. 2560 acres.
Wall, Joel. N.C. Sergeant. 26 Aug. 1785. 1000 acres.

Wall, John. Ga. Minute Man. 21 Apr. 1784. 287 1/2 acres.
Wall, John. N.C. Private. 21 Jul. 1821. 640 acres to heirs.
Wall, Patrick. N.Y. ———. 13 Sep. 1790. 500 acres to heirs.
Wall, Sampson. Ga. ———. 21 Apr. 1784. 287 1/2 acres.
Wall, William. Va. Private. 23 Feb. 1831. 100 acres.
Wallace, Absalom. Ga. Refugee. 26 Feb. 1784. 500 acres.
Wallace, Absalom. N.C. Private. 30 Sep. 1785. 640 acres to heirs.
Wallace, Adam. Va. Captain. 22 Jun. 1784. 4000 acres.
Wallace, Adam. Va. Captain. 26 May 1838. 91 acres.
Wallace, Adam. Va. Captain. 26 May 1838. 91 acres.
Wallace, Adam. Va. Captain. 13 Dec. 1843. 111 acres.
Wallace, Adam. Va. Captain. 13 Dec. 1843. 50 5/11 acres.
Wallace, Adam. Va. Captain. 11 Oct. 1844. 30 3/11 acres.
Wallace, Adam. Va. Captain. 11 Oct. 1844. 10 1/11 acres.
Wallace, Andrew. Va. Captain. 23 Jun. 1784. 4000 acres.
Wallace, Andrew. Va. Captain. 26 May 1838. 177 1/4 acres.
Wallace, Andrew. Va. Captain. 26 May 1838. 177 1/4 acres.
Wallace, Andrew. Va. Captain. 13 Dec. 1843. 177 1/4 acres.
Wallace, Andrew. Va. Captain. 13 Dec. 1843. 80 1/2 acres.
Wallace, Andrew. Va. Captain. 11 Oct. 1844. 48 3/11 acres.
Wallace, Andrew. Va. Captain. 11 Oct. 1844. 16 1/11 acres.
Wallace, Brown. N.C. Private. 30 Sep. 1785. 640 acres to heirs.
Wallace, Charnel. Ga. ———. 3 Apr. 1786. 575 acres.
Wallace, David. Va. Lieutenant. 8 Feb. 1808. 2666 2/3 acres.
Wallace, Edward. Va. Private. 11 May 1784. 200 acres.
Wallace, Edward. Va. Private. 15 Apr. 1853. 200 acres.
Wallace, Edward. Va. Private. 30 Jun. 1786. 100 acres.
Wallace, Gustavus B. Va. Colonel. 2 Oct. 1807. 926 acres.
Wallace, Gustavus B. Va. Lieutenant Colonel. 25 Jan. 1783. 7000 acres.
Wallace, James. Ga. ———. ———. 287 1/2 acres.
Wallace, James. N.C. Lieutenant. 5 Aug. 1821. 2560 acres to heirs.
Wallace, James. Va. Surgeon. 26 May 1783. 6000 acres.
Wallace, James. Va. Private. 8 Aug. 1783. 100 acres.
Wallace, James. Va. Ensign. 23 Jun. 1784. 2666 2/3 acres.
Wallace, James. Va. Surgeon. 11 Sep. 1807. 1916 acres.
Wallace, John. Ga. ———. 21 Apr. 1784. 200 acres.
Wallace, John. N.C. Private. 15 Aug. 1820. 640 acres to heirs.
Wallace, John. Va. Private. 7 Jun. 1783. 100 acres.
Wallace, Joseph. Va. Private. 11 Jul. 1835. 100 acres.
Wallace, Matthew, Jr. N.C. Private. 17 Dec. 1796. 640 acres to heirs.
Wallace, Micajah. Ga. ———. 17 May 1784. ———.
Wallace, Nathaniel. Va. Private. 23 Jan. 1793. 200 acres.
Wallace, Thomas. N.C. Private. 1 Sep. 1785. 640 acres to heirs.
Wallace, Thomas. Va. Lieutenant. 22 Oct. 1790. 2666 2/3 acres.
Wallace, William. Ga. Soldier. 15 Apr. 1784. 287 1/2 acres.
Wallace, William. Ga. Soldier. 23 Apr. 1784. 287 1/2 acres.
Wallace, William. N. Y. Private. 3 Jul. 1790. 600 acres.
Wallace, William. Va. Sailor. 28 Feb. 1831. 100 acres.
Wallace, William B. Va. Lieutenant. 30 May 1783. 2666 2/3 acres.
Wallace, William B. Va. Lieutenant. 16 Nov. 1796. 889 acres.
Wallace, William B. Va. Lieutenant. 2 Oct. 1807. 74 acres.
Wallard, Jonathan. N.C. Private. 30 Sep. 1785. 640 acres.
Waller, Allen. Va. Ensign. 5 Feb. 1798. 2666 2/3 acres.
Waller, Allen. Va. Ensign. 22 Jan. 1822. 799 acres, 3 rods, and 24 poles.

Waller, Allen. Va. Ensign. 22 Jan. 1822. 977 acres, 2 rods, and 24 poles.
Waller, Allen. Va. Ensign. 22 Jan. 1822. 822 acres, 3 rods, and 22 poles.
Waller, Benjamin. Ga. Refugee. 15 Mar. 1784. 250 acres.
Waller, Daniel. Va. Private. 14 Jun. 1784. 100 acres.
Waller, Edward. Va. Major. 15 Apr. 1853. 2822 2/3 acres.
Waller, Edward. Va. Major. 10 Mar. 1785. 2500 acres.
Waller, Edward. Va. Major. 10 Mar. 1785. 2833 2/3 acres.
Waller, Edward. Va. Major. 10 Jul. 1857. 2833 2/3 acres.
Waller, Jacob. N.C. Private. 9 Dec. 1797. 640 acres.
Waller, Jeremiah. Ga. Minute Man. 10 Dec. 1784. ———.
Waller, John. Ga. Minute Man. Apr. 1785. ———.
Waller, John. Va. Sergeant. 13 Aug. 1784. 200 acres.
Waller, John. Va. Sergeant. 13 Jun. 1788. 200 acres.
Waller, Joshua. Ga. Private. ———. 250 acres.
Waller, Martin. N. Y. Corporal. 8 Jul. 1790. 600 acres.
Waller, Nathaniel. N.C. Private. 1 Jul. 1825. 640 acres.
Waller, Samuel. Ga. ———. 17 May 1784. ———.
Waller, William. Ga. ———. 15 Apr. 1784. 287 1/2 acres.
Waller, William. Va. Private. 26 Apr. 1783. 200 acres.
Waller, William. Va. Private. 20 Jun. 1783. 100 acres.
Waller, William. Va. Private. 20 Feb. 1784. 200 acres.
Wallerson, Robert. Va. Corporal. 16 Dec. 1783. 200 acres.
Wallicon, Daniel, Jr. Ga. Refugee. 21 Apr. 1784. 575 acres.
Wallis, Charles. Ga. Private. ———. 250 acres.
Wallis, George. N.C. Fife Major. 24 Nov. 1783. 857 acres.
Wallis, George. Va. Major. 28 Jun. 1784. 7110 2/3 acres.
Wallis, Moses. N.C. Private. 28 Aug. 1820. 640 acres to heirs.
Wallis, Thomas. Pa. Sergeant. 6 Apr. 1794. 200 acres to Francis Kirkpatrick, assignee.
Walliser, Christian. N. Y. Private. 8 Jul. 1790. 600 acres.
Walls, Lois. Conn. Sufferer. New/East Haven. 8.18.4.
Walls, Thomas. Va. Lieutenant. 20 Oct. 1830. 2666 2/3 acres.
Walsh, Benjamin. Ga. ———. 17 May 1784. ———.
Walsh, Edward. Ga. Major. 15 Apr. 1784. 690 acres.
Walsh, Patrick. Ga. Soldier. 4 Jun. 1784. ———.
Walsh, Robert. N.C. Private. 8 Jul. 1820. 640 acres to heirs.
Walsley, Charles. N.C. Private. 15 Feb. 1797. 274 acres.
Walsworth, Samuel. Conn. Sufferer. Groton. 10.11.6.
Walter, Christopher. Pa. Private. 28 Sep. 1787. 200 acres.
Walter, Edward. Md. Private. ———. 50 acres.
Walter, Jacob. N. Y. Private. 8 Jul. 1790. 600 acres.
Walter, John. Pa. Private. 31 Aug. 1789. 200 acres.
Walter, Joseph. Ga. ———. 30 Jul. 1784. 230 acres.
Walter, Thomas. Pa. Private. 19 Oct. 1786. 200 acres to Mary Ripley and Peter Ripley, heirs.
Walters, Isaac. Va. Boatswain. 26 Feb. 1831. 2666 2/3 acres.
Walters, John. N.C. Private. 22 Aug. 1820. 640 acres.
Walters, Richard C. Va. Captain Lieutenant. 11 Jan 1810. 555 1/2 acres.
Walters, Spencer. Va. ———. 28 Mar. 1837. 100 acres.
Walters, Walter. N.C. Private. 21 Aug. 1820. 640 acres.
Walthour, Andrew. Ga. Refugee. 21 Apr. 1784. 287 1/2 acres.
Waltman, Ludwig. Pa. Private. 23 Jan. 1787. 200 acres.
Waltman, Michael. Md. Private. ———. 50 acres.
Walton, Elijah. Va. Private. 12 Apr. 1784. 100 acres.
Walton, George. Ga. Commissary. 13 Apr. 1784. 575 acres.

Walton, George. Ga. ———. 1784. 750 acres.

Walton, George. Pa. Fifer. 20 Sep. 1787. 200 acres.

Walton, George, Jr. Ga. Lieutenant. 19 Mar. 1784. 400 acres to heirs.

Walton, Jesse. Ga. ———. 21 Apr. 1784. 460 acres to heirs.

Walton, Jesse. Ga. ———. 13 Apr. 1784. 250 acres.

Walton, John. Ga. ———. ———. 287 1/2 acres.

Walton, John. N. Y. Private. 8 Jul. 1790. 600 acres.

Walton, Josiah. Ga. ———. ———. 287 1/2 acres.

Walton, Michael. N.C. Private. 13 Sep. 1820. 274 acres.

Walton, Newel. Ga. Refugee. 13 Apr. 1784. 575 acres.

Walton, Robert. Ga. Refugee. 25 May 1784. 287 1/2 acres.

Walton, Thomas. Ga. ———. 20 Apr. 1784. 1000 acres.

Walton, Thomas. N.C. Sergeant. 5 Sep. 1821. 2560 acres.

Walton, Thomas, Jr. Ga. ———. ———. 287 1/2 acres.

Walton, Thomas, Sr. Ga. ———. ———. 287 1/2 acres.

Walton, Tilman. Va. Sergeant. 10 Mar. 1784. 200 acres.

Walton, William. Ga. ———. 17 May 1784. ———.

Walton, William. N.C. Captain. 22 Oct. 1783. 3840 acres.

Waltz, Michael. Pa. Private. 28 Nov. 1797. 200 acres.

Wambozie, Emanuel. Ga. ———. 17 May 1784. ———.

Wamsley, William. Va. Private. 7 May 1832. 200 acres.

Wandel, Adam. N. Y. Gunner. 9 Jul. 1790. 600 acres.

Wandell, Jacob. N. Y. Matross. 9 Jul. 1790. 500 acres.

Wandolph, Jacob. Pa. Private. 21 Oct. 1786. 200 acres.

Wane, Richard. Conn. Sufferer. Fairfield. 5.8.3.

Wann, John. Pa. ———. 9 Mar. 1795. 200 acres to John Nicholson.

Wanner, Michael. Pa. ———. 20 Oct. 1787. 200 acres to John Kline, assignee.

Waples, Samuel. Va. Lieutenant. 20 Mar. 1807. 2666 2/3 acres.

Warbuton, William. Va. Private. 5 Mar. 1833. 100 acres.

Ward, Abijah. N. Y. Private. 8 Jul. 1790. 500 acres.

Ward, Benjamin. Ga. Refugee. 25 May 1784. 287 1/2 acres.

Ward, Benjamin. Md. Sergeant. ———. 50 acres.

Ward, Benjamin. N.C. Private. 28 Sep. 1785. 640 acres to heirs.

Ward, Bryant. Ga. ———. 20 Apr. 1784. 287 1/2 acres.

Ward, Charles. Ga. ———. 25 May 1784. 287 1/2 acres.

Ward, Charles. N.C. Private. 2 Feb. 1786. 640 acres to heirs.

Ward, Daniel. S.C. Dolfirt. 5 Dec 1785. 200 acres to Frederick Ward, brother and heir at law.

Ward, David. N.C. Private. 15 Jul. 1785. 640 acres to heirs.

Ward, Drury. N.C. Private. 23 Oct. 1783. 274 acres.

Ward, Elijah. N.C. Private. 10 Dec. 1788. 640 acres to heirs.

Ward, Experience. Conn. Sufferer. Groton. 2.19.5.

Ward, Francis. N.C. Private. 15 Jul. 1785. 640 acres to heir.

Ward, Frederick. S.C. ———. 7 Nov. 1785. 200 acres.

Ward, George. Md. Private. ———. 50 acres.

Ward, George. Va. Private. 30 Aug. 1783. 100 acres.

Ward, Hopper. Va. Private. 7 Apr. 1838. 200 acres.

Ward, Hugh. Ga. Minute Man. 6 May 1785. ———.

Ward, Hugh. Va. Private. 5 Feb. 1785. 200 acres.

Ward, Isaac. N.C. Private. 30 Sep. 1785. 640 acres.

Ward, Jabez. Mass. Private. 9 Jul. 1833. 200 acres.

Ward, James. N.C. Private. 15 Jul. 1785. 640 acres to heir.

Ward, James. Va. Private. 18 Jun. 1833. 100 acres.

Ward, Job. N.C. Private. 20 Sep. 1821. 640 acres.

Ward, John. Ga. Minute Man. 20 Apr. 1784. 287 1/2 acres.
Ward, John. Md. ———. ———. 50 acres.
Ward, John. N. Y. Private. 8 Jul. 1790. 600 acres.
Ward, John. N.C. Private. 24 Oct. 1783. 640 acres.
Ward, John. N.C. Fifer. 22 Apr. 1785. 1000 acres.
Ward, John. Pa. Private. 28 Aug. 1787. 200 acres.
Ward, John. Pa. Lieutenant. 28 Aug. 1787. 200 acres.
Ward, John. Pa. Lieutenant. 28 Aug. 1787. 200 acres to William Turnbull, assignee.
Ward, John. Pa. Private. 12 Jan. 1786. 200 acres.
Ward, John. Pa. ———. ———. 200 acres.
Ward, John. Conn. Sufferer. New/East Haven. 25.7.6.
Ward, John. Conn. Sufferer. New London. 17.5.4.
Ward, John Peter. S.C. Lieutenant. 2 May 1785. 200 acres.
Ward, Laurence. Va. Private. 2 Jul. 1784. 100 acres.
Ward, Mary. Conn. Sufferer. New London. 28.0.0.
Ward, Michael. N.C. Private. 30 Sep. 1785. 640 acres to heirs.
Ward, Peter. Ga. Minute Man. 14 Jun. 1785. ———.
Ward, Peter. Md. ———. ———. 50 acres.
Ward, Peter. N.C. Private. 12 Sep. 1785. 640 acres to heirs.
Ward, Richard. N.C. Sergeant. 1 Aug. 1821. 1000 acres.
Ward, Richard. S.C. Soldier. 5 Dec. 1785. 200 acres to Frederick Ward, son and heir at law.
Ward, Robert. N. Y. Fifer. 8 Jul. 1790. 600 acres.
Ward, Samuel. Ga. ———. 20 Apr. 1784. 287 1/2 acres.
Ward, Solomon. N.C. Private. 10 Aug. 1785. 640 acres to heirs.
Ward, Thomas. N.C. Private. 7 Dec. 1819. 228 acres to heir William Ward.
Ward, Thomas. N.C. Private. 1 Aug. 1821. 640 acres.
Ward, Thomas. Va. Private. 20 Sep. 1797. 100 acres.
Ward, William. N.C. Private. 6 Sep. 1821. 640 acres.
Ward, William. Pa. Sergeant. ———. 250 acres.
Ward, William. S.C. Lieutenant. 21 Jan. 1785. 200 acres.
Ward, William. Va. Private. 16 Jan. 1786. 100 acres.
Ward, William. Conn. Sufferer. New/East Haven. 22.11.7.
Ward, Zadock. N. Y. Private. 8 Jul. 1790. 500 acres.
Warden, Thomas. Me. ———. 17 May 1835. 200 acres to widow Ednah Warden. Wells.
Wardman, Edward. Ga. Minute Man. 24 Aug. 1785. ———.
Wardman, Hugh. Ga. Minute Man. 24 Aug. 1785. ———.
Wardman, Isaac. Ga. Minute Man. 24 Aug. 1785. ———.
Wardman, Jacob. Ga. Minute Man. 5 May 1785. ———.
Wardwell, Joseph. Me. Ensign. 29 Apr. 1835. 200 acres. Rumford.
Ware, Francis. Md. Lieutenant. ———. 200 acres.
Ware, George. N.C. Private. 19 Jan. 1786. 274 acres.
Ware, Henry, Jr. Ga. ———. 15 Apr. 1784. 287 1/2 acres.
Ware, Henry, Sr. Ga. ———. 21 Apr. 1784. 400 acres.
Ware, James. Ga. Soldier. 21 Apr. 1784. 287 1/2 acres.
Ware, James. S.C. ———. 2 Oct. 1786. 200 acres.
Ware, John. Ga. Refugee. 15 Apr. 1784. 287 1/2 acres.
Ware, Moses. Ga. Soldier. 5 Sep. 1785. ———.
Ware, Moses. Va. Sergeant. 23 Jun. 1783. 400 acres.
Ware, Nicholas. Ga. ———. 15 Apr. 1784. 287 1/2 acres.
Ware, Robert. Ga. ———. 15 Apr. 1787. 287 1/2 acres.
Ware, Samuel. Va. Sergeant. 17 Jan. 1811. 200 acres.
Ware, Thomas. N.C. Private. 17 Dec. 1785. 640 acres to heirs.
Ware, William. Ga. ———. 15 Mar. 1784. 250 acres.

Ware, William. Va. Private. 12 Jul. 1783. 100 acres.
Warfield, Walter. Md. Surgeon. ———. 200 acres.
Warfield, Walter. Va. Surgeon. 19 May 1833. 6000 acres.
Warick, William. Va. Sergeant. 16 Jun. 1783. 200 acres.
Waring, Basil. Md. Lieutenant. ———. 200 acres.
Waring, Bray. Ga. Refugee. Sep. 1785. ———.
Waring, Isaac. Conn. Sufferer. Norwalk. 3.10.0.
Waring, Joseph. Conn. Sufferer. Norwalk. 14.18.1.
Waring, Nathan. Conn. Sufferer. Norwalk. 32.14.7.
Waring, Peter. Ga. Refugee. Sep. 1785. ———.
Waring, Thomas. Va. Captain. 8 May 1838. 500 acres.
Waring, Thomas. Va. Captain. 8 May 1838. 500 acres.
Waring, Thomas. Va. Captain. 8 May 1838. 500 acres.
Waring, Thomas. Va. Captain. 8 May 1838. 1312 1/2 acres.
Waring, Thomas. Va. Captain. 8 May 1838. 937 1/2 acres.
Waring, Thomas. Va. Captain. 19 Feb. 1842. 166 acres.
Waring, Thomas. Va. Captain. 19 Feb. 1842. 84 acres.
Warldon, Charles. N.C. Private. 30 Sep. 1785. 640 acres.
Warley, Felix. S.C. Major. 16 Jul. 1784. 400 acres.
Warley, George. S.C. Captain. 16 Jul. 1784. 300 acres.
Warley, Jospeh. S.C. Major. 15 Oct. 1784. 400 acres to Felix Warley, administrator, in trust for the heirs.
Warlick, Jeremiah. Pa. Sergeant. ———. 250 acres.
Warman, Thomas. Va. Captain. 22 May 1783. 2000 acres.
Warman, Thomas. Va. Captain. 22 May 1783. 1000 acres.
Warman, Thomas. Va. Captain. 22 May 1783. 1000 acres.
Warneck, Frederick. Va. Lieutenant Colonel. 9 Jun. 1783. 5000 acres.
Warneck, Frederick. Va. Lieutenant Colonel. 9 Jun. 1783. 200 acres.
Warneck, Frederick. Va. Lieutenant Colonel. 9 Jun. 1783. 200 acres.
Warneck, Frederick. Va. Lieutenant Colonel. 9 Jun. 1783. 200 acres.
Warneck, Frederick. Va. Lieutenant Colonel. 9 Jun. 1783. 200 acres.
Warneck, Frederick. Va. Lieutenant Colonel. 9 Jun. 1783. 200 acres.
Warner, Harden. N.C. Private. 13 Nov. 1795. 640 acres.
Warner, Jacob. Pa. Private. 15 Mar. 1786. 200 acres.
Warner, John. N.C. Private. 13 Nov. 1795. 320 acres.
Warner, John. Pa. Private. ———. 200 acres.
Warner, John. Va. Musician. 19 Jun. 1783. 200 acres.
Warner, John. Va. Musician. 19 Jun. 1783. 100 acres.
Warner, John. Va. Sergeant. 20 Aug. 1784. 200 acres.
Warner, John. Conn. Sufferer. New/East Haven. 4.2.6.
Warner, John Dieter. Pa. Ranger. 17 Aug. 1789. 200 acres.
Warner, Ludwick. Pa. Private. 31 Oct. 1786. 200 acres to Catherine Bush, devisee.
Warner, Martin. Pa. ———. ———. 200 acres to heirs.
Warner, Richard. N.C. Private. 13 Nov. 1795. 640 acres to heirs.
Warner, Thomas. N. Y. Matross. 9 Jul. 1790. 500 acres.
Warner, Thomas. N. Y. Lieutenant. 9 Jul. 1790. 1000 acres.
Warner, William. Pa. Sergeant. 14 May 1787. 250 acres to Stephen Loudon, assignee.
Warnock, John. S.C. ——— 4 Dec. 1786. 200 acres.
Warnock, Robert. Ga. ———. 17 May 1784. ———.
Warren, Drury. Va. Private. 19 Sep. 1786. 100 acres.
Warren, Edward. N.C. Private. 2 Aug. 1784. 228 acres.
Warren, Gabriel. Va. Private. 20 Nov. 1785 [?1784]. 100 acres.
Warren, Hezekiah. N.C. Private. 30 Sep. 1785. 640 acres to heirs.

Warren, James. Ga. ———. 15 Apr. 1784. 287 1/2 acres.
Warren, Jeremiah. Ga. Refugee. 17 May 1784. ———.
Warren, John. Va. Private. 1 Aug. 1783. 200 acres.
Warren, John. Va. Private. 31 Jan. 1792. 100 acres.
Warren, Matthew. N.C. Private. 4 Aug. 1821. 640 acres.
Warren, Nathaniel. Me. Soldier. 11 Sep. 1835. 200 acres to widow Margaret Warren. Hiram.
Warren, Pelatiah. Me. ———. 2 Jul. 1835. 200 acres. Monmouth.
Warren, Samuel. N.C. Private. 1 Sep. 1785. 640 acres to heirs.
Warren, Samuel. S.C. Captain. 5 Dec. 1785. 200 acres.
Warren, Thomas. N.C. Private. 26 Aug. 1785. 640 acres to heirs.
Warren, William. Mass. Private. 13 Jan 1831. 200 acres.
Warren, William. N. Y. Corporal. 8 Jul. 1790. 500 acres.
Warren, William. N.C. Private. 2 Aug. 1784. 228 acres.
Warren, Zebulon. N.C. ———. 3 Dec. 1797. 1000 acres to heirs.
Warrener, Robert. Va. Private. 16 Dec. 1809. 100 acres.
Warring, Benjamin. N. Y. Corporal. 8 Jul. 1790. 500 acres.
Warring, Henry. Va. Lieutenant. 29 Mar. 1785. 2666 2/3 acres.
Warrington, John. Va. Private. 15 Jan. 1808. 261 acres.
Warrington, Stephen. Va. Quartermaster. 31 Dec. 1851. 710 2/3 acres.
Warrington, Stephen. Va. Quartermaster. 31 Dec. 1851. 710 2/3 acres.
Warrington, Stephen. Va. Quartermaster. 31 Dec. 1851. 710 2/3 acres.
Warrington, Stephen. Va. Quartermaster. 13 Jun. 1853. 266 2/3 acres.
Warrington, Stephen. Va. Quartermaster. 14 Sep. 1854. 178 2/3 acres.
Warrington, Stephen. Va. Quartermaster. 11 Jan. 1855. 88 2/3 acres.
Warrior, Daniel. Md. Drummer. ———. 50 acres.
Warson, Rebecca. Conn. Sufferer. Norwalk. 4.8.3.
Warters, Abraham. Md. ———. ———. 50 acres.
Warton, Spencer. Va. Seaman. 9 Dec. 1833. 100 acres.
Warwick, Robert. N.C. Private. 22 Apr. 1785. 228 acres.
Warwick, Shadrach. N.C. Private. 9 Nov. 1784. 640 acres.
Warwick, Thomas. N.C. Private. 1 Aug. 1821. 640 acres.
Warwick, Wiott. N.C. Private. 9 Nov. 1784. 640 acres.
Wasgatt, Davis. Me. Sergeant. 3 Dec. 1835. 200 acres. Mount Desert.
Wash, Benjamin. Va. Private. 16 Feb. 1784. 100 acres.
Wash, Thomas. Va. Sergeant. 16 Feb. 1784. 200 acres.
Wash, William. Ga. ———. 16 Apr. 1784. 230 acres.
Washburn, Solomon. Mass. ———. 31 Jul. 1835. 200 acres to widow Hannah Washburn.
Washington, Dread. N.C. Private. 30 Sep. 1785. 640 acres to heirs.
Washington, Etheldred. N.C. Fifer. 20 Apr. 1784. 1000 acres to William Washington, heir.
Washington, George. Va. Lieutenant. 19 Feb. 1783. 2666 2/3 acres.
Washington, John. Va. Captain. 19 Mar. 1832. 2000 acres.
Washington, John. Va. Captain. 19 Mar. 1832. 666 2/3 acres.
Washington, John. Va. Captain. 10 Aug. 1832. 666 2/3 acres.
Washington, John. Va. Captain. 10 Aug. 1832. 666 2/3 acres.
Washington, John. Va. Captain. 26 Feb. 1838. 352 acres.
Washington, John. Va. Captain. 26 Feb. 1838. 175 1/3 acres.
Washington, John. Va. ———. 7 May 1838. 288 1/2 acres.
Washington, John. Va. ———. 7 May 1838. 288 1/2 acres.
Washington, William. N.C. Ensign. 25 Oct. 1783. 1096 acres.
Washington, William. N.C. Sergeant. 5 Sep. 1821. 1000 acres.
Washington, William. Va. Lieutenant Colonel. 17 Jul. 1783. 7000 acres.
Washington, William. Va. Colonel. 24 Jul. 1824. 231 1/2 acres.

Washington, William. Va. Colonel. 24 Jul. 1824. 231 1/2 acres.
Wasley, John. N.C. Private. 17 Dec. 1785. 274 acres.
Wasson, Esther. Conn. Sufferer. Norwalk. 5.0.8.
Wasson, John. Me. ———. 16 Jun. 1835. 200 acres. Brooksville.
Wasson, John. Conn. Sufferer. Fairfield. 161.5.10.
Wasson, Thomas. Me. ———. 16 Jun. 1835. 200 acres. Brooksville.
Wate [or Wyatt], Thomas. Md. Private. ———. 50 acres.
Wate, Willliam. Md. Surgeon's Mate. ———. 200 acres.
Waterbury, Ezra. Conn. Sufferer. Norwalk. 11.6.4.
Waterfield, John. Va. Private. 25 May 1785. 200 acres.
Waterfield, Meshack. Va. Private. 15 Sep. 1809. 100 acres.
Waterfield, Peter. Va. Private. 15 Dec. 1783. 100 acres.
Waterhouse, Joseph. Me. ———. 10 Aug. 1835. 200 acres. Standish.
Waterman, Henry. N.Y. ———. 20 Jan. 1791. 500 acres to heirs.
Waterman, Joseph. Me. ———. 7 May 1835. 200 acres. Knox.
Waterman, Malachi. Me. Private. 23 Oct. 1835. 200 acres to widow Mary Waterman. Baldwin.
Waters, Charles. Ga. ———. 22 Apr. 1784. 287 1/2 acres.
Waters, Isaac. N.C. Private. 8 Dec. 1796. 640 acres to heirs.
Waters, James. Ga. ———. 28 Jul. 1784. 287 1/2 acres.
Waters, James. Va. Sergeant. 1 Nov. 1783. 400 acres.
Waters, James. Va. Sailor. 19 Dec. 1783. 100 acres.
Waters, Jeremiah. N.C. Private. 26 May 1784. 640 acres.
Waters, John. Ga. ———. 21 Apr. 1784. 200 acres.
Waters, John. Md. ———. ———. 50 acres.
Waters, John. N.C. Private. 30 Nov. 1785. 640 acres to heirs.
Waters, John. N.C. Musician. 3 Dec. 1797. 1000 acres.
Waters, John. Va. Sergeant. 29 Jun. 1835. 160 acres.
Waters, John. Va. Sergeant. 29 Jun. 1835. 80 acres.
Waters, John. Va. Sergeant. 29 Jun. 1835. 80 acres.
Waters, John. Va. Sergeant. 29 Jun. 1835. 80 acres.
Waters, Rawley. Ga. Minute Man. 17 Jan. 1784. 287 1/2 acres.
Waters, Richard. Ga. ———. 21 Apr. 1784. 200 acres.
Waters, Richard. Md. Captain. ———. 200 acres.
Waters, Richard. Va. Captain Lieutenant. 5 Jul. 1783. 4000 acres.
Waters, Richard. Va. Captain Lieutenant. 7 Jan. 1784. 666 2/3 acres.
Waters, Robert. Conn. Sufferer. Norwalk. 11.15.4.
Waters, Robert. Conn. Sufferer. Norwalk. 6.0.0.
Waters, Solomon. N.C. Private. 19 May 1784. 640 acres.
Waters, Solomon. N.C. Drummer. 15 Feb. 1797. 360 acres balance.
Waters, Thomas. N.C. Private. 17 Dec. 1785. 640 acres to heirs.
Waters, Thomas. Va. Private. 18 Aug. 1783. 200 acres.
Waters, William. N.C. Lieutenant. 9 Nov. 1784. 2011 acres.
Waters, William. N.C. Private. 9 Apr. 1788. 640 acres to heirs.
Waters, William. Conn. Sufferer. Greenwich. 11.12.2.
Waters, York. Md. Private. ———. 50 acres.
Watherholt, Jacob. Va. Private. 5 Apr. 1784. 100 acres.
Watkins, Benjamin. N. Y. Private. 8 Jul. 1790. 600 acres.
Watkins, David. Va. Private. 20 Mar. 1789. 100 acres.
Watkins, Evan. N.C. Private. 7 Jan. 1786. 640 acres to heirs.
Watkins, Gassaway. Md. Lieutenant. ———. 200 acres.
Watkins, George. Va. Pilot. 31 Dec. 1851. 2666 2/3 acres.
Watkins, James. Va. Lieutenant. 19 Apr. 1831. 600 acres.
Watkins, James. Va. Lieutenant. 19 Apr. 1831. 600 acres.

Watkins, James. Va. Lieutenant. 19 Apr. 1831. 1000 acres.
Watkins, James. Va. Lieutenant. 13 Jul. 1832. 1800 acres.
Watkins, Jesse. Va. Private. 9 Jun. 1785. 100 acres.
Watkins, John. Ga. ———. 22 Apr 1784. 287 1/2 acres.
Watkins, John. Va. Sergeant. 12 Mar. 1784. 200 acres.
Watkins, John. Va. Captain. 20 Dec. 1839. 444 acres.
Watkins, John. Va. Captain. 20 Dec. 1839. 296 acres.
Watkins, John. Va. Captain. 20 Dec. 1839. 296 acres.
Watkins, John. Va. Captain. 18 Sep. 1875. 296 acres.
Watkins, John. Va. Captain. 20 Dec. 1839. 296 acres.
Watkins, John. Va. Captain. 24 Mar. 1845. 380 6/7 acres.
Watkins, John. Va. Captain. 24 Mar. 1845. 380 6/7 acres.
Watkins, John. Va. Captain. 24 Mar. 1845. 190 3/7 acres.
Watkins, John. Va. Captain. 24 Mar. 1845. 190 3/7 acres.
Watkins, John. Va. Captain. 24 Mar. 1845. 190 3/7 acres.
Watkins, John. Va. Captain. 24 Mar. 1845. 190 3/7 acres.
Watkins, John. Va. Captain. 24 Mar. 1845. 380 6/7 acres.
Watkins, John. Va. Captain. 24 Mar. 1845. 380 6/7 acres.
Watkins, John. Va. Captain. 24 Mar. 1845. 380 6/7 acres.
Watkins, Robert. Va. Sergeant. 2 Jul. 1784. 200 acres.
Watkins, Robert. Va. Ensign. 23 Jul. 1832. 888 8/9 acres.
Watkins, Robert. Va. Ensign. 23 Jul. 1832. 888 8/9 acres.
Watkins, Robert. Va. Ensign. 23 Jul. 1832. 888 8/9 acres.
Watkins, Robert. Va. Ensign. 24 Mar. 1834. 2666 2/3 acres.
Watkins, Robert. Va. Ensign. 29 Dec. 1851. 727 acres.
Watkins, Samuel. Va.-Ind. Private. 108 acres.
Watkins, Samuel. Va. Private. 17 Jul. 1784. 200 acres.
Watkins, Shadrack. N.C. Private. 10 Dec. 1821. 640 acres to heirs.
Watkins, Walton. N.C. Private. 2 Feb. 1786. 640 acres.
Watkins, William. Md. Drummer. ———. 50 acres.
Watkins, William. Va. Private. 1 May 1783. 200 acres.
Watkins, William. Va. Pilot. 28 Feb. 1841. 2666 2/3 acres.
Watkins, Zacheus. Mass. Private. 22 Jul. 1833. 200 acres.
Watkinson, James. Va. Private. 19 Nov. 1833. 100 acres.
Watkinson, Levin. Va. Private. 15 Jun. 1807. 100 acres.
Watkinson, William. Va. Private. 19 Nov. 1833. 100 acres.
Watlington, John. Va. Captain. 29 Mar. 1838. 666 2/3 acres.
Watlington, John. Va. Captain. 29 Mar. 1838. 1333 1/3 acres.
Watlington, John. Va. Captain. 13 Mar. 1841. 533 1/3 acres.
Watlington, John. Va. Captain. 13 Mar. 1841. 533 1/3 acres.
Watlington, John. Va. Captain. 13 Mar. 1841. 266 2/3 acres.
Watlington, John. Va. Captain. 20 Jun. 1840. 444 4/9 acres.
Watlington, John. Va. Captain. 20 Jun. 1840. 222 2/9 acres.
Watlington, John. Va. Captain. 6 Feb. 1854. 428 4/7 acres.
Watlington, John. Va. Captain. 6 Feb. 1854. 428 4/7 acres.
Watlington, John. Va. Captain. 6 Feb. 1854. 428 4/7 acres.
Watlington, John. Va. Captain. 6 Feb. 1854. 428 4/7 acres.
Watlington, John. Va. Captain. 6 Feb. 1854. 61 11/49 acres.
Watlington, John. Va. Captain. 6 Feb. 1854. 61 11/49 acres.
Watlington, John. Va. Captain. 6 Feb. 1854. 61 11/49 acres.
Watlington, John. Va. Captain. 6 Feb. 1854. 183 33/49 acres.
Watlington, John. Va. Captain. 6 Feb. 1854. 61 11/49 acres.
Watlington, John. Va. Captain. 6 Feb. 1854. 714 2/7 acres.
Watlington, John. Va. Captain. 1 Dec. 1854. 428 4/7 acres.

Watlington, John. Va. Captain. 1 Dec. 1854. 124 6/7 acres.
Watlington, John. Va. Captain. 29 Jan. 1855. 142 acres.
Watlington, John. Va. Captain. 29 Jan. 1855. 214 20/28 acres.
Watlington, John. Va. Captain. 29 Jan. 1855. 53 19/28 acres.
Watlington, John. Va. Captain. 29 Jan. 1855. 53 19/28 acres.
Watlington, John. Va. Captain. 29 Jan. 1855. 53 19/28 acres.
Watlington, John. Va. Captain. 29 Jan. 1855. 53 19/28 acres.
Watrous, John. Conn. Sufferer. Ridgefield. 3.12.0.
Watson, Benjamin. Ga. Private. ———. 250 acres.
Watson, Benjamin. Pa. ———. ———. 200 acres.
Watson, David. Va. Private. 2 May 1809. 200 acres.
Watson, Demcy. N.C. Private. 7 Dec. 1797. 640 acres to heirs.
Watson, Douglas. Ga. ———. 22 Apr. 1784. 450 acres.
Watson, George. Ga. ———. 15 Mar. 1784. 250 acres.
Watson, George. Md. Private. ———. 50 acres.
Watson, Jacob. Ga. Soldier. 1784. 287 1/2 acres.
Watson, Jacob. N.C. Private. 17 Dec. 1785. 640 acres.
Watson, James. Va. Private. 19 Jan. 1785. 100 acres.
Watson, James. Va. Private. 19 May 1823. 100 acres.
Watson, Johannes. Va. Captain. 3 May 1823. 5333 1/3 acres.
Watson, Johannes. Va. Captain. 3 May 1823. 5333 1/3 acres.
Watson, Johannes. Va. Captain. ———. 5333 1/3 acres.
Watson, John. Ga. Private. ———. 250 acres.
Watson, John. Pa. Sergeant. 21 Mar. 1787. 250 acres.
Watson, Joseph. N. Y. Private. 7 Jul. 1790. 600 acres.
Watson, Levi. N.Y. Drummer. 20 Jan. 1791. 500 acres to heirs.
Watson, Lewis. Ga. refugee. 17 Apr. 1784. 287 1/2 acres.
Watson, Lott. N.C. Private. 19 May 1784. 640 acres.
Watson, Micajah. N.C. Private. 20 May 1793. 365 acres.
Watson, Miles. N.C. Private. 18 Dec. 1804. 640 acres to heirs.
Watson, Peter. Ga. ———. 17 Apr. 1784. 287 1/2 acres.
Watson, Philip. N.C. Private. 15 Feb. 1797. 274 acres.
Watson, Robert. Ga. Soldier. 15 Jul. 1785. ———.
Watson, Thomas. Ga. ———. 14 Jul. 1784. 287 1/2 acres.
Watson, Thomas. Md. Private. ———. 50 acres.
Watson, Thomas W. Pa. Private. ———. 200 acres to Stephen Loudon, assignee.
Watson, Walter. Md. Private. ———. 50 acres.
Watson, William. Ga. ———. 22 Apr. 1784. 300 acres.
Watson, William. N.C. Private. 30 Sep. 1785. 640 acres to heirs.
Watson, William. Va. Corporal. 28 Apr. 1783. 400 acres.
Watson, Willis. Ga. Minute Man. 1784. 287 1/2 acres.
Watt, Joseph. Pa. ———. 16 Dec. 1808. 200 acres.
Watts, Abraham. N.C. Private. 17 Dec. 1796. 375 acres.
Watts, Andrew. N.C. Private. 22 Dec. 1796. 274 acres.
Watts, Andrew. N.C. Private. 9 Sep. 1820. 366 acres to heirs.
Watts, Francis. Pa. Private. 30 Sep. 1787. 200 acres.
Watts, Garrot. N.C. Sergeant. 17 Dec. 1785. 1000 acres to heirs.
Watts, George. Ga. ———. ———. 287 1/2 acres.
Watts, Gideon. Va. Private. 2 Dec. 1783. 200 acres.
Watts, Jacob. Ga. Minute Man. 17 May 1784. ———.
Watts, John. Ga. Soldier. 5 Sep. 1785. ———.
Watts, John. Va. Captain. 31 Oct. 1783. 4666 2/3 acres.
Watts, John. Va. Captain. 17 Aug. 1807. 277 acres.
Watts, Martin. Va. Private. 18 Mar. 1784. 200 acres.

Watts, Reuben. Va. Private. 24 Nov. 1784. 100 acres.
Watts, Samuel. Va. Corporal. 14 Aug. 1785. 200 acres.
Watts, Solomon. Md. ———. ———. 50 acres.
Watts, Thomas. Ga. ———. 21 Apr. 1784. 500 acres.
Watts, Thomas. N.C. Sergeant. 17 Dec. 1785. 1000 acres to heirs.
Watts, Thomas. S.C. ———. 6 Feb. 1797. 19 acres to James Timms, administrator, in trust for the heirs.
Watts, Thomas. S.C. ———. 6 Feb. 1797. 81 acres to James Timms, administrator, in trust for the heirs.
Watts, Thomas. S.C. ———. 6 Feb. 1797. 100 acres to James Timms, administrator, in trust for the heirs.
Watts, William. N.C. Private. 27 Dec. 1786. 640 acres to heirs.
Watts, William. Va. Private. 30 Jun. 1784. 100 acres.
Wattson, Everitt. N.C. Private. 30 Sep. 1785. 640 acres to heirs.
Waudin, John. Ga. Surgeon. 24 Jun. 1784. 920 acres.
Waugh, James. Va. Private. 18 Dec. 1798. 100 acres.
Waughmock, Jesse. N.C. Private. 30 Sep. 1785. 640 acres to heirs.
Wawman, Thomas. Va. Captain. 20 May 1823. 777 7/9 acres.
Way, Ebenezer. Conn. Sufferer. New London. 15.16.1.
Way, Edward. Ga. Refugee. 17 Jul. 1784. 287 1/2 acres.
Way, John. N. Y. Sergeant. 8 Jul. 1790. 500 acres.
Way, John. Conn. Sufferer. New London. 590.3.11.
Way, John, Jr. Ga. Refugee. 26 May 1784. 287 1/2 acres.
Way, John, Sr. Ga. Refugee. 1 Jun. 1784. 500 acres.
Way, Joseph. Ga. Refugee. 26 May 1784. 250 acres.
Way, Samuel. Pa. Private. ———. 200 acres.
Way, William, Ga. Soldier. 5 Jun. 1784. ———.
Way, William, Jr. Ga. Refugee. 22 Nov. 1784. 287 1/2 acres.
Wayland, Joshua. Va. Private. 3 Jun. 1784. 100 acres.
Wayne, Anthony. Pa. Brigadier General. 28 Aug. 1787. 500 acres.
Wayne, Anthony. Pa. Brigadier General. 28 Aug. 1787. 500 acres.
Wayne, Anthony. Pa. Brigadier General. 28 Aug. 1787. 500 acres to Francis Johnston, assignee.
Wayne, Benjamin. Va. Private. 20 Oct. 1784. 100 acres.
Weatherington, Jacob. N.C. Private. 30 Sep. 1785. 640 acres to heirs.
Weatherley, Isaac. N.C. Private. 30 Sep. 1785. 640 acres to heirs.
Weathers, Benjamin. N.C. Sergeant. 30 Sep. 1785. 1000 acres to heirs.
Weathers, Edward. Ga. ———. 17 May 1784. ———.
Weathers, Valentine. S.C. ———. 6 Feb. 1792. 133 acres.
Weatherspoon, William. N.C. Private. 10 Aug. 1785. 640 acres to heir.
Weaver, Adam. N. Y. Private. 8 Jul. 1790. 600 acres.
Weaver, Anthony. Md. Private. ———. 50 acres.
Weaver, Benjamin. N.C. Private. 14 Dec. 1797. 228 acres.
Weaver, David. N. Y. Private. 8 Jul. 1790. 600 acres.
Weaver, Elijah. Va. Seaman. 14 Aug. 1834. 100 acres.
Weaver, George. N. Y. Private. 8 Jul. 1790. 600 acres.
Weaver, Henry. Pa. Private. ———. 200 acres.
Weaver, Isaiah. N.C. Private. 19 Jan. 1786. 640 acres.
Weaver, Jacob. Pa. Captain. ———. 500 acres.
Weaver, John. N. Y. Private. 8 Jul. 1790. 600 acres.
Weaver, John. N.C. Private. 28 Jul. 1784. 640 acres.
Weaver, John. Pa. ———. ———. 200 acres to Benjamin Steele, assignee.
Weaver, John. Va. Private. 14 Apr. 1783. 200 acres.
Weaver, John. Va. Private. 4 Feb. 1784. 200 acres.
Weaver, Lewis. N.C. Corporal. 16 Aug. 1821. 1000 acres.

Weaver, Moses. N.C. Private. 22 Apr. 1785. 274 acres.
Weaver, Samuel. N.C. Private. 30 Sep. 1785. 640 acres to heirs.
Weaver, Thomas. S.C. Captain. 21 Jan. 1785. 300 acres.
Weaver, Travis. N.C. Private. 15 Dec. 1797. 640 acres to heirs.
Weaver, William. N.C. Private. 22 Apr. 1785. 640 acres to heirs.
Webb, Amos. N. Y. Drummer. 9 Jul. 1790. 600 acres.
Webb, Andrew. Pa. Private. 22 Jan. 1787. 200 acres.
Webb, Austin. Ga. ———. 19 Apr. 1784. 287 1/2 acres.
Webb, Banks. Md. Private. ———. 50 acres.
Webb, Charles. N.C. Private. 30 Sep. 1785. 640 acres.
Webb, David. Conn. Sufferer. Norwalk. 1.10.8.
Webb, Edmund. Me. ———. 3 Jul. 1835. 200 acres. Gorham.
Webb, Francis. Va. Midshipman. 31 Jul. 1834. 2666 2/3 acres.
Webb, Gideon. N. Y. Matross. 9 Jul. 1790. 600 acres.
Webb, Isaac. Va. Lieutenant. 13 Jan. 1784. 2666 2/3 acres.
Webb, James. Va. Sailor. 6 Aug. 1783. 100 acres.
Webb, Jeremiah. Conn. Sufferer. Norwalk. 7.5.0.
Webb, Jesse. Ga. Refugee. 19 Apr. 1784. 287 1/2 acres.
Webb, John. Ga. Soldier. 1784. 230 acres.
Webb, John. Ga. Refugee. 19 Apr. 1784. 287 1/2 acres.
Webb, John. N. Y. Corporal. 8 Jul. 1790. 600 acres.
Webb, John. N.C. Private. 9 Nov. 1784. 640 acres.
Webb, John. Va. Lieutenant Colonel. 24 Dec. 1782. 6000 acres.
Webb, John. Va. Lieutenant Colonel. 18 Mar. 1834. 404 1/2 acres.
Webb, John. Va. Lieutenant Colonel. 5 Jun. 1834. 808 1/3 acres.
Webb, Joseph. N.C. Private. 22 Oct. 1783. 640 acres to Giles Webb.
Webb, Joseph. Va. Sailor. 12 Aug. 1785. 100 acres.
Webb, Joshua. N.C. Private. 30 Sep. 1785. 640 acres.
Webb, Lewis. N.C. Private. 7 Jan. 1786. 640 acres to heirs.
Webb, Lewis. Va. Captain. 18 Mar. 1834. 4444 acres.
Webb, Lewis. Va. Captain. 22 Mar. 1858. 444 acres.
Webb, Nathaniel. Me. Private. 10 Jul. 1835. 200 acres to widow Lydia Webb. New Castle.
Webb, Richard. Va. Private. 20 Apr. 1783. 200 acres.
Webb, Robert. Va. Pilot. 26 Feb. 1831. 2666 2/3 acres.
Webb, Sandy. N.C. Private. 9 Dec. 1797. 640 acres to heirs.
Webb, Stephen. N.C. Private. 5 Dec. 1796. 274 acres.
Webb, Tapley. Va. Seaman. 6 Jul. 1850. 100 acres.
Webb, Thomas. Ga. ———. 15 Apr. 1784. 650 acres.
Webb, Thomas. Va. Private. 8 Sep. 1783. 100 acres.
Webb, William. Ga. Refugee. 19 Apr. 1784. 287 1/2 acres.
Webb, William. N. Y. Matross. 9 Jul. 1790. 600 acres.
Webb, William. Pa. Private. 25 Oct. 1786. 200 acres.
Webber, Daniel. Mass. Sergeant. 13 Feb. 1833. 200 acres.
Webber, George. Me. ———. 17 Apr. 1835. 200 acres. Richmond.
Webber, John. Me. Private. 26 May 1835. 200 acres to widow Eunice Stevens. Littlefield.
Webber, Jonathan. Me. ———. 22 Aug. 1835. 200 acres. Kennebunk.
Webber, Joseph. Me. ———. 7 Aug. 1836. 200 acres to widow Elizabeth Woodbury.
Webber, Philip. Va. Sergeant. 2 Jun. 1783. 200 acres.
Webley, John. Va. Sergeant. 9 Jun. 1813. 200 acres.
Webster, Abner. Ga. Minute Man. 15 Apr. 1784. 287 1/2 acres.
Webster, Benjamin. Ga. Private. 17 May 1784. 230 acres.
Webster, John. Ga. ———. ———. 287 1/2 acres.

Webster, John Beatman. Pa. Lieutenant. 29 Sep. 1787. 200 acres.
Webster, John Beatman. Pa. Lieutenant. 29 Sep. 1787. 200 acres.
Webster, Jonathan. Ga. ———. ———. 287 1/2 acres.
Webster, Joseph B. Pa. Cadet. 29 Sep. 1787. 250 acres.
Webster, Richard. N.C. Private. 13 Dec. 1787. 640 acres.
Webster, Richard. Va. Private. 22 Oct. 1787. 100 acres.
Webster, Samuel. Ga. Minute Man. 17 Apr. 1784. 287 1/2 acres.
Webster, Thomas. Ga. Drummer. 1784. 230 acres.
Webster, Thomas. Md. ———. ———. 50 acres.
Webster, William. Ga. ———. 17 Apr. 1784. 287 1/2 acres.
Webster, William. N.C. Private. 30 Aug. 1820. 640 acres to heirs.
Wedgbar, William. Va. Private. 31 Jul. 1783. 200 acres.
Wedge, Samuel. Md. Private. ———. 50 acres.
Wedge, William. Md. Private. ———. 50 acres.
Weed, Bartholomew. Conn. Sufferer. Ridgefield. 3.13.4.
Weed, Ezra. N. Y. Sergeant. 3 Jul. 1790. 600 acres.
Weeden, Jonathan. Md. Private. ———. 50 acres.
Weedon, Augustine. Va. Sergeant. 30 Jun. 1783. 200 acres.
Weedon, George. Va. Brigadier General. Jan. 1783. 10,000 acres.
Weedon, George. Va. Brigadier General. 2 Jan. 1783. 1666 2/3 acres.
Weedon, George. Va. Brigadier General. 26 Jul. 1806. 1666 2/3 acres.
Weekly, Samuel. N. Y. Matross. 9 Jul. 1790. 500 acres.
Weeks, Abigail. Conn. Sufferer. Norwalk. 3.10.0.
Weeks, Benjamin. N.C. Private. 9 Nov. 1784. 640 acres.
Weeks, Cornelius. N.C. Sergeant. 7 Mar. 1785. 429 acres.
Weeks, Jacob. N. Y. Private. 8 Jul. 1790. 600 acres.
Weeks, James. N. Y. Private. 8 Jul. 1790. 500 acres.
Weeks, John. Conn. Sufferer. Greenwich. 9.14.5.
Weeks, Levy. N.C. Sergeant. 9 Nov. 1784. 500 acres.
Weeks, Silas. N.C. ———. 3 Feb. 1785. 640 acres to heir.
Weeks, Sylvanus. N.C. Private. 11 May 1785. 640 acres to heirs.
Weeks, Theophilus. N.C. Private. 11 May 1785. 274 acres.
Weghan, Conradt. N. Y. Private. 8 Jul. 1790. 600 acres.
Weidel, Christian. Pa. Private. 18 Jan. 1803. 200 acres.
Weidman, John. Pa. Lieutenant. ———. 200 acres.
Weidman, John. Pa. Private. 8 Jun. 1787. 200 acres.
Weight, Gabriel. N.C. Private. 30 Sep. 1785. 640 acres.
Weisenfels, F. Charles. N.Y. Lieutenant. 9 Jul. 1790. 1200 cres.
Weisenfels, Frederick. N. Y. Lieutenant Colonel Com. 9 Jul. 1790. 3000 acres.
Weitzell, Jacob. Pa. Lieutenant. 25 Oct. 1786. 200 acres.
Weitzell, John. S.C. Surgeon. 16 Jul. 1784. 300 acres.
Welborn, Curtus, Jr. Ga. Minute Men. 22 Apr. 1784. 287 1/2 acres.
Welborn, David. Ga. Soldier. 24 May 1784. 287 1/2 acres.
Welborn, Edward. Ga. Soldier. 24 May 1784. 287 1/2 acres.
Welborn, Robert. N.C. Private. 2 Feb. 1786. 320 acres.
Welch, Basel. N.C. Private. 21 Aug. 1820. 228 acres.
Welch, Benjamin. Ga. ———. 22 Apr. 1784. 287 1/2 acres.
Welch, Benjamin. Va. Private. 11 Mar. 1784. 100 acres.
Welch, Caleb. Ga. ———. 17 May 1784. ———.
Welch, David. Md. Sergeant. ———. 50 acres.
Welch, Dominick. Va. Private. 18 Mar. 1784. 200 acres.
Welch, Dominque. Va.-Ind. Private. 108 acres.
Welch, Edward. Ga. ———. 17 May 1784. 690 acres.
Welch, Garret. Md. ———. ———. 50 acres.

Welch, Goodman. N.C. Private. 30 Sep. 1785. 640 acres to heirs.
Welch, Isaac. Va. Private. 1 Mar. 1784. 100 acres.
Welch, James. Md. Bombadier. ———. 50 acres.
Welch, James. Md. Matross. ———. 50 acres.
Welch, James. Md. ———. ———. 50 acres.
Welch, John. Md. Private. ———. 50 acres.
Welch, John. Md. Private. ———. 50 acres.
Welch, John. N. Y. Private. 8 Jul. 1790. 600 acres.
Welch, John. N. Y. Matross. 3 Jul. 1790. 600 acres.
Welch, John. N.C. Captain. 20 Sep. 1784. 1508 acres.
Welch, John. Va. Sergeant. 5 Feb. 1785. 200 acres.
Welch, John. Conn. Sufferer. New London. 46.10.0.
Welch, Jonathan. Va. Private. 23 Jun. 1783. 200 acres.
Welch, Joseph. N. Y. Private. 13 Sep. 1790. 600 acres.
Welch, Joshua. Ga. Sergeant. 17 May 1784. 28 1/2 to heirs.
Welch, Lang. Va. Private. 26 Apr. 1783. 200 acres.
Welch, Lemuel. Me. Private. 4 Nov. 1836. 200 acres to his guardian Thomas Estes.
Welch, Nathaniel. Va. Captain. 7 Dec. 1832. 888 2/3 acres.
Welch, Nathaniel. Va. Brigade Quartermaster. 15 Jan. 1850. 638 2/3 acres.
Welch, Nathaniel. Va. Brigade Quartermaster. 25 Apr. 1853. 319 1/3 acres.
Welch, Nathaniel. Va. Brigade Quartermaster. 30 Jul. 1853. 638 2/3 acres.
Welch, Nathaniel. Va. Brigade Quartermaster. 6 Jul. 1860. 4887 1/3 acres.
Welch, Nathaniel. Va. Captain. ———. 888 2/3 acres.
Welch, Nathaniel. Va. Captain. 11 Apr. 1783. 4000 acres.
Welch, Nathnaiel. Va. ———. 28 May 1850. 319 1/3 acres.
Welch, Nicholas. Ga. ———. 23 Apr. 1784. 287 1/2 acres.
Welch, Nicholas. Md. Private. ———. 50 acres.
Welch, Patrick. Va. Sergeant. 24 Jan. 1784. 200 acres.
Welch, Richard. N. Y. Private. 8 Jul. 1790. 600 acres.
Welch, Robert. Va. Private. 9[?] Aug. 1783. 200 acres.
Welch, Selvaster. Va. Private. 11 Mar. 1784. 100 acres.
Welch, Walter. Conn. Sufferer. New London. 59.19.0.
Welch, William. N.C. Corporal. 25 Oct. 1783. 1000 acres.
Welcher, Jordan. Ga. ———. ———. 287 1/2 acres.
Welcher, William. Ga. ———. 22 Apr. 1784. 287 1/2 acres.
Weld, Benjamin. Me. Commissary of Hospital Department. 25 May 1838. 600 acres. Brunswick.
Welday, George. Va. Corporal. 28 Apr. 1783. 400 acres.
Welden, Jeremiah. N. Y. Private. 8 Jul. 1790. 500 acres.
Weldin, Andrew. Ga. ———. 16 Apr. 1784. 287 1/2 acres.
Weldon, John. Ga. ———. 22 Apr. 1784. 287 1/2 acres.
Weldon, Robert. N.Y. ———. 20 Jan. 1791. 500 acres to heirs.
Weldy, William. Va. Private. 3 Jul. 1784. 200 acres.
Welker, Daniel. Pa. Private. 9 Jun. 1806. 200 acres.
Wellborn, Thomas. Ga. ———. 22 Apr. 1784. 287 1/2 acres.
Welles, Benjamin. N.C. Private. 17 Dec. 1785. 640 acres.
Wellford, Philip. Ga. ———. ———. 287 1/2 acres.
Wellington, Jonathan. Mass. Drum Major. 3 Jun. 1828. 200 acres.
Wellman, James. N.C. Private. 30 Sep. 1785. 640 acres to heirs.
Wells, Abigail. Ga. ———. 17 May 1784. ———.
Wells, Andrew. Ga. Refugee. 24 Aug. 1784. ———.
Wells, Benjamin, Jr. Ga. ———. 25 May 1784. 287 1/2 acres.
Wells, Benjamin, Sr. ———. Ga. 23 Apr. 1784. 575 acres.
Wells, Daniel. N.C. Private. 30 Sep. 1785. 640 acres to heirs.

Wells, Gideon. Conn. Sufferer. Fairfield. 29.8.8.
Wells, Humphrey. Ga. Surgeon. 28 Jul 1784. 1107 1/2 acres to heirs.
Wells, Humphrey. Md. Private. ———. 50 acres.
Wells, Jacob. Ga. Refugee. 4 May 1785. ———.
Wells, Jacob. N.C. Private. 12 Sep. 1785. 640 acres to heirs.
Wells, James. Me. Private. 7 Sep. 1838. 200 acres to widow Mary Wells. Rome.
Wells, James. Va. Private. 28 Nov. 1783. 100 acres.
Wells, Jeremiah. Ga. Refugee. 24 Aug. 1784. ———.
Wells, John. Ga. ———. 20 Apr. 1784. 287 1/2 acres.
Wells, John. Md. Private. ———. 50 acres.
Wells, John. N. Y. Private. 7 Jul. 1790. 600 acres.
Wells, John. N.C. Private. 22 Oct. 1783. 640 acres.
Wells, John. Va. Private. 5 Jan. 1811. 200 acres.
Wells, Jordan. Ga. ———. 28 Feb. 1784. 250 acres.
Wells, Joseph. Ga. Minute Man. 23 Apr. 1784. 287 1/2 acres.
Wells, Moses. Conn. Sufferer. New/East Haven. 256.7.4.
Wells, Nathaniel. Va. Private. 31 Mar. 1814. 200 acres.
Wells, Robert. Ga. Refugee. 24 Aug. 1784. ———.
Wells, Uriah. N.C. Private. 11 Feb. 1796. 640 acres to heirs.
Wells, William. Ga. ———. 20 Apr. 1784. 287 1/2 acres.
Wells, Zebulon. N.C. Private. 30 Sep. 1785. 640 acres.
Welsh, James. Pa. Private. 27 Aug. 1787. 200 acres.
Welsh, John. N. Y. ———. 16 Sep. 1801 [sic 1803]. 500 acres.
Welsh, John. Pa. Private. 22 Nov. 1786. 200 acres.
Welsh, John. Pa. Private. ———. 200 acres.
Welsh, John. Pa. Private. 3 Feb. 1807. 200 acres.
Welsh, Michael. Pa. Private. 24 Dec. 1789. 200 acres to Jesse Dewees, assignee.
Welsh, Noel. N.C. Private. 5 Dec. 1797. 640 acres to heirs.
Welsh, Philip. Md. Private. ———. 50 acres.
Welsh, Thomas. N.C. Private. 9 Sep. 1785. 640 acres to heirs.
Welsh, Thomas. Pa. Private. 31 Oct. 1787. 200 acres to William Powers, assignee.
Welsher, Jeremiah. Ga. ———. 15 Apr. 1784. 287 1/2 acres.
Welsher, John. Ga. ———. 25 May 1784. 287 1/2 acres.
Weltner, Ludowick. Md. Lieutenant Colonel. ———. 200 acres.
Welty, Michael. Pa. Private. 6 Dec. 1786. 200 acres.
Wenday, Absalom. N.C. Private. 13 Dec. 1796. 365 acres.
Wendell, H. Jacob. N. Y. Lieutenant. 9 Jul. 1790. 1200 acres.
Wendell, Jacob. N. Y. Sergeant. 8 Jul. 1790. 600 acres.
Wendell, John. N. Y. Private. 8 Jul. 1790. 600 acres.
Wendell, John. N. Y. Private. 8 Jul. 1790. 500 acres.
Wensett, James. N.C. Private. 30 Sep. 1785. 640 acres to heirs.
Wentworth, Edward. Conn. Sufferer. Norwalk. 80.13.1.
Wentworth, Jedediah. Mass. Corporal. 1 Feb. 1833. 200 acres.
Wentworth, Josiah. Conn. Sufferer. Norwalk. 151.16.0.
Wentworth, Lemuel. Me. Private. 4 Aug. 1835. 200 acres. Hope.
Wentworth, Paul. Me. Private. 10 May 1836. 200 acres to widow Mary Wentworth. Knox.
Werchers, Peter. Ga. ———. 17 May 1784. ———.
Wereat, John. Ga. Refugee. 24 May 1784. 287 1/2 acres.
Werton, Edward. N.C. Private. 30 Sep. 1785. 640 acres to heirs.
Wertz, George. Pa. Lieutenant. 27 Oct. 1786. 200 acres to Mary Wertz, widow.
Wescot, Samuel. Me. Soldier. 23 Jul. 1835. 200 acres to widow Nancy Wescot. Portland.
Wesley, Samuel. N.C. Private. 13 Sep. 1820. 640 acres.
Wessels, Hercules. N. Y. Corporal. 9 Jul. 1790. 600 acres.

Wessels, John. N. Y. Matross. 6 Jul. 1790. 600 acres.
Wessels, John. Va. Private. 19 Nov. 1833. 100 acres.
West, Alexander. Md. Private. ———. 50 acres.
West, Beriah. Va. Corporal. 4 Apr. 1786. 200 acres.
West, Charles. Va. Major. 16 Jun. 1784. 5333 1/3 acres.
West, Cyperan. N.C. Private. 20 Jan. 1785. 640 acres to heirs.
West, Francis. N.C. Private. 12 Mar. 1785. 640 acres to heirs.
West, Francis. N.C. Private. 17 Dec. 1785. 640 acres to heirs.
West, Isaac. Me. Soldier. 21 Sep. 1835. 200 acres. Jay.
West, James. Ga. ———. 15 Mar. 1784. 250 acres.
West, James. Md. Private. ———. 50 acres.
West, James. N.C. Private. 15 Feb. 1797. 228 acres.
West, John. Ga. ———. 17 Apr. 1784. 287 1/2 acres.
West, John. Md. Private. ———. 50 acres.
West, John. N. Y. Sergeant. 8 Jul. 1790. 600 acres.
West, John T. Md. Fifer. ———. 50 acres.
West, Joseph. N.C. Sergeant. 27 Jul. 1785. 357 acres.
West, Levi. N.C. Drummer. 18 Aug. 1784. 428 acres.
West, Levi. N.C. Musician. 5 Sep. 1821. 1000 acres.
West, Nathaniel. N.C. Private. 4 Aug. 1821. 640 acres.
West, Randolph. Va. Private. 14 Jun. 1784. 100 acres.
West, Randolph. Va. Private. 19 Jun. 1833. 100 acres.
West, Samuel. Ga. Major. 27 Sep. 1784. 862 1/2 acres.
West, Thomas. Pa. Private. ———. 200 acres.
West, Thomas. Va. Private. 10 Jun. 1784. 100 acres.
West, Thomas. Va. Captain. 31 Mar. 1807. 4000 acres.
West, Thomas. Va. Captain. 18 Dec. 1833. 5333 1/3 acres.
West, Thomas. Va. Captain. 17 Jun. 1834. 666 2/3 acres.
West, Thomas. Va. Captain. 17 Jun. 1834. 666 2/3 acres.
West, Thomas. Va. Captain. 17 Jun. 1834. 666 2/3 acres.
West, Thomas. Va. Captain. 17 Jun. 1834. 666 2/3 acres.
West, Thomas. Va. Captain. 17 Jun. 1834. 666 2/3 acres.
West, Thomas. Va. Captain. 17 Jun. 1834. 666 2/3 acres.
West, Thomas. Va. Captain. 17 Jun. 1834. 666 2/3 acres.
West, Thomas. Va. Captain. 17 Jun. 1834. 666 2/3 acres.
West, William. Ga. Refugee. 21 Apr. 1784. 287 1/2 acres.
West, William. Md. Private. ———. 50 acres.
West, William. N.C. Private. 26 Dec. 1821. 182 acres.
West, William. Va. Sailor. 13 Feb. 1784. 100 acres.
Westbrook, John. Ga. ———. 20 Apr. 1784. 287 1/2 acres.
Westbrook, John, Sr. Ga. ———. 20 Apr. 1784. 287 1/2 acres.
Westbrook, Stephen. Ga. Lieutenant. 20 Apr. 1784. 690 acres.
Westbrook, William. N.C. Private. 7 Dec. 1809. 274 acres.
Westcoat, David. Ga. ———. 17 May 1784. ———.
Westcott, Elizabeth. Conn. Sufferer. New London. 87.6.0.
Westcott, Wright. Va. Captain. 9 Apr. 1783. 4000 acres.
Westcott, Wright. Va. Captain. 15 Mar. 1834. 4000 acres.
Wester, Aquilla. N.C. Corporal. 11 Feb. 1796. 1000 acres to heirs.
Wester, William. Va. Sergeant. 6 Mar. 1784. 400 acres.
Westmoreland, Joseph. Va. Private. 23 Mar. 1784. 100 acres.
Westmorland, Jesse. Va. Private. 23 Mar. 1784. 100 acres.
Weston, Digges. Va. Private. 4 Jan. 1834. 200 acres.
Weston, Isaac. Va. Private. 17 Jun. 1789. 100 acres.
Weston, Joseph. Me. ———. 24 Jun. 1835. 200 acres. Otisfield.
Westwardhall, Francis. N.C. Private. 7 Dec. 1783. 640 acres.

Wetherall, John. Va. Private. 5 Jun. 1784. 100 acres.
Wetherick, George. N. Y. Private. 8 Jul. 1790. 600 acres.
Wetherick, Michael. N. Y. Private. 8 Jul. 1790. 600 acres.
Wetherington, Joseph. N.C. Private. 13 Nov. 1795. 274 acres.
Wethers, Valentine. S.C. ———. 7 May 1792. 62 acres.
Wetherstine, John. N. Y. Private. 8 Jul. 1790. 600 acres.
Wetmore, Noah, Rev. Conn. Sufferer. Danbury. 28.3.0.
Weymouth, Corbin. N.C. Private. 4 Mar. 1784. 365 acres.
Whaland, William. Md. Private. ———. 50 acres.
Whale, John. Va. Private. 26 Apr. 1783. 200 acres.
Whalen, Richard. N. Y. Private. 8 Jul. 1790. 600 acres.
Whalen, Walter. N. Y. Private. 8 Jul. 1790. 600 acres.
Whaley, Ezekiel. N.C. Fife Major. 4 Mar. 1784. 1000 acres.
Whaley, James. Va. Private. 14 Nov. 1814. 100 acres.
Whaley, John. Va. Private. 7 Sep. 1797. 200 acres.
Whaley, Zadock. Md. Private. ———. 50 acres.
Whalin, Joseph. Mass. ———. 9 Jul. 1834. 200 acres.
Whaling, James. Md. Gunner. ———. 50 acres.
Whaling, John. Va. Private. 13 Dec. 1784. 200 acres.
Wharry, Robert. Pa. Surgeon. 12 Feb. 1789. 300 acres.
Wharton, Jacob. N.C. Private. 12 Dec. 1806. 640 acres to heirs.
Wharton, James. N.C. Private. 26 Nov. 1796. 640 acres to heirs.
Wharton, John. Va. Boatswain. 30 Dec. 1851. 2000 acres.
Wharton, John. Va. Boatswain. 9 Apr. 1853. 666 2/3 acres.
Wharton, John. Va. Boatswain. 9 Mar. 1853. 1333 1/3 acres.
Wharton, John. Va. Boatswain. 9 Mar. 1853. 666 2/3 acres.
Wharton, Timothy. N.C. Private. 1 Dec. 1796. 640 acres to heirs.
Whatley, Aaron. Ga. ———. 17 May 1784. ———.
Whatley, Edmund. Ga. ———. 27 Sep. 1784. 287 1/2 acres.
Whatley, John. Ga. ———. 13 Apr. 1784. 287 1/2 acres.
Whatley, Michael, Sr. Ga. ———. 13 Apr. 1784. 287 1/2 acres.
Whatley, Orman. Ga. ———. 15 Mar. 1784. 250 acres.
Whatley, Richard. Ga. ———. 26 May 1784. 287 1/2 acres.
Whatley, Samuel. Ga. Refugee. 21 Apr. 1784. 287 1/2 acres.
Whatley, Thomas. Ga. ———. 17 May 1784. ———.
Whatley, Walton. Ga. Refugee. 17 May 1784. ———.
Whatley, Wharton. Ga. ———. 12 Jun. 1784. 287 1/2 acres.
Whatley, Willis. Ga. Soldier. 3 Oct. 1785. 230 acres.
Whatley, Wilson. Ga. Soldier. 3 Oct. 1785. 230 acres to heirs.
Whayne, Benjamin. Va. Private 12 Dec. 1833. 200 acres.
Whealer, Benjamin. N.C. Private. 30 Sep. 1785. 640 acres to heirs.
Whealer, John. Va. Private. 30 Dec. 1784. 100 acres.
Whealey, Isum. N.C. Sergeant. 30 Sep. 1785. 1000 acres to heirs.
Wheat, Hezekiah. Ga. Refugee. 29 Jul 1784. 287 1/2 acres.
Wheat, John. Ga. ———. ———. 250 acres.
Wheatley, Sylvester. Md. Private. ———. 50 acres.
Wheatley, William. Md. Private. ———. 50 acres.
Wheatley, William. Va. Private. 20 Jun. 1785. 200 acres.
Wheaton, Peter. Pa. Private. 18 Oct. 1787. 200 acres.
Wheeden, Job. Mass. Sergeant Major. 12 Sep. 1834. 200 acres to widow Elizabeth Wheeden.
Wheeler, Charles. Md. Private. ———. 50 acres.
Wheeler, David. N.C. Corporal. 26 May 1784. 1000 acres.
Wheeler, Edward. Mass. Private. 1 Mar. 1833. 200 acres.

Wheeler, Empery. N.C. ———. 29 Apr. 1784. 640 acres to Elizabeth Underwood & Mourning Wheeler, coheiresses.

Wheeler, Henry. N. Y. Private. 7 Jul. 1790. 600 acres.

Wheeler, Isaac. N. Y. Drummer. 8 Jul. 1790. 600 acres.

Wheeler, Isaac. N.C. ———. 10 Aug. 1785. 640 acres.

Wheeler, Isham. Ga. ———. 21 Apr. 1784. 287 1/2 acres.

Wheeler, James. Mass. Private. 9 Jul. 1834. 200 acres.

Wheeler, James. Va. Private. 30 Dec. 1784. 100 acres.

Wheeler, John. Md. ———. ———. 50 acres.

Wheeler, John. Mass. Private. 18 Oct. 1833. 200 acres.

Wheeler, John. N. Y. Private. 8 Jul. 1790. 600 acres.

Wheeler, Richard. Md. Corporal. ———. 50 acres.

Wheeler, Richard. N. Y. Private. 8 Jul. 1790. 600 acres.

Wheeler, Samuel. N. Y. Private. 8 Jul. 1790. 600 acres.

Wheeler, Samuel. N.C. Private. 10 Dec. 1788. 228 acres.

Wheeler, Thomas. Md. ———. ———. 50 acres.

Wheeler, Thomas. Mass. Mariner. 18 Apr. 1828. 200 acres.

Wheeler, Thomas. Pa. Private. 18 Oct. 1786. 200 acres.

Wheeler, Timothy. N. Y. Private. 13 Jul. 1790. 500 acres.

Wheeler, William. N. Y. Matross. 9 Jul. 1790. 500 acres.

Wheeler, Zephaniah. Ga. ———. 17 May 1784. ———.

Wheeley, John. Va. Private. 26 May 1783. 100 acres.

Wheller, John. Va. Private. 25 Apr. 1783. 200 acres.

Whelp, Anthony. New York. Captain. 9 Jul. 1790. 1800 acres.

Whelpley, Ebenezer. Conn. Sufferer. Greenwich. 1.8.8.

Whelpley, Elizabeth. Conn. Sufferer. Norwalk. 17.17.8.

Whelpley, Isaac. Conn. Sufferer. Greenwich. 21.8.0.

Whelpley, James. Conn. Sufferer. Norwalk. 4.5.4.

Wherley, Matthew. Va. Private. 19 Apr. 1784. 100 acres.

Whidbey, Richard. N.C. Lieutenant. 5 Sep. 1821. 2590 acres.

Whiggans, John. Ga. ———. 22 Apr. 1784. 287 1/2 acres.

Whiggins, William. Ga. ———. 27 Sep. 1784. 287 1/2 acres.

Whipple, Daniel. Pa. Ranger. 26 Jul. 1787. 200 acres.

Whipple, Nathan. N. Y. Private. 8 Jul. 1790. 500 acres.

Whirley, Peter. Va. Private. 30 Dec. 1784. 100 acres.

Whisler, Jacob. Pa. Private. 25 Oct. 1786. 200 acres.

Whistler, Sawney. Va. Private. 17 May 1784. 200 acres.

Whitaker, Burton. N.C. Private. 12 Dec. 1808. 640 acres to heirs.

Whitaker, James. N.C. Private. 9 Dec. 1797. 640 acres to heirs.

Whitaker, James. Va. Private. 30 Apr. 1783. 200 acres.

Whitaker, Jeremiah. Mass. Corporal. 15 Jan. 1834. 200 acres.

Whitaker, John. Ga. Captain. 17 May 1784. ———.

Whitaker, Joseph. N.C. Private. 30 Sep. 1785. 640 acres to heirs.

Whitaker, Josiah. N.C. Private. 30 Sep. 1785. 640 acres to heirs.

Whitaker, Neal. N.C. Private. 19 Jan. 1786. 640 acres.

Whitaker, Richard. S.C. ———. 4 Jul. 1785. 200 acres.

Whitaker, Samuel. Ga. ———. 20 Apr. 1784. 287 1/2 acres.

Whitaker, Silas. Mass. Private. 9 Jul. 1834. 200 acres.

Whitaker, Thomas. Va. Private. 5 Mar. 1785. 100 acres.

Whitaker, William. Va. Lieutenant. 13 Dec. 1783. 2666 2/3 acres.

Whitby, Thomas. Ga. ———. 19 Jul. 1784. 287 1/2 acres.

Whitcomb, John. Md. Private. ———. 50 acres.

Whitcomb, Motley. Md. Private. ———. 50 acres.

White, Abraham. Va. Private. 26 Jul. 1784. 100 acres.

White, Ambrose. Va. Private. 21 Dec. 1833. 200 acres.
White, Anthony W. Va. Lieutenant Colonel Commandant. 25 Jan. 1787. 6666 2/3 acres.
White, Benjamin. N.C. Private. 19 May 1784. 640 acres.
White, Benjamin. N.C. Private. 16 Sep. 1820. 640 acres to heirs.
White, Benjamin. Va. Private. 14 Dec. 1785. 100 acres.
White, Burrell. N.C. Private. 29 Oct. 1821. 640 acres to heirs.
White, Caleb. Va. Private. 23 Nov. 1795. 200 acres.
White, Daniel. N.C. Private. 25 Jul. 1784. 228 acres.
White, David. Md. Matross. ———. 50 acres.
White, Demsy. Ga. ———. 16 Jul. 1784. 287 1/2 acres.
White, Ebenezer, Rev. Conn. Sufferer. Danbury. 218.7.4.
White, Edward. Md. ———. ———. 50 acres.
White, Edward. Va. Private. 30 Sep. 1783. 100 acres.
White, Elijah. N.C. Private. 11 Feb. 1796. 640 acres to heirs.
White, Elisha. N.C. Private. 16 Aug. 1821. 640 acres.
White, Elisha. Va. Captain. 13 Apr. 1833. 4000 acres.
White, Ephraim. N. Y. Private. 8 Jul. 1790. 600 acres.
White, Ezekiel. N.C. Private. 22 Oct. 1783. 274 acres.
White, Ezekiel. N.C. Private. 6 Dec. 1797. 640 acres to heirs.
White, Francis. Pa. Lieutenant. 22 Nov. 1787. 200 acres.
White, Francis. Pa. Lieutenant. 22 Nov. 1787. 200 acres.
White, George. N.C. Private. 12 Mar. 1785. 640 acres to heirs.
White, George. Pa. Dragoon. 12 Jun. 1787. 200 acres.
White, George. Va. Private. 29 Mar. 1784. 100 acres.
White, Hains. N.C. Private. 23 May 1821. 640 acres.
White, Henry. N.C. Private. 20 Apr. 1784. 228 acres.
White, Jacob. N.C. Private. 27 Oct. 1783. 274 acres.
White, Jacob. N.C. Musician. 11 Feb. 1796. 1000 acres.
White, Jacob, Jr. N.C. Private. 27 Oct. 1783. 274 acres.
White, Jacobus. Va. Carpenter. 26 Feb. 1831. 2666 2/3 acres.
White, Jacobus. Va. Carpenter. 8 Nov. 1831. 1333 1/3 acres.
White, Jacobus. Va. Carpenter. 8 Nov. 1831. 1333 1/3 acres.
White, James. Ga. Soldier. 11 Sep. 1783. 200 acres.
White, James. Ga. Captain. 13 Sep. 1784. 575 acres.
White, James. Md. Private. ———. 50 acres.
White, James. N. Y. Sergeant. 8 Jul. 1790. 500 acres.
White, James. N.C. Private. 31 Mar. 1810. 640 acres to heirs.
White, James. S.C. ———. 4 Jul. 1791. 200 acres.
White, James. Va. Private. 2 Jun. 1783. 200 acres.
White, James. Va. Private 3 Jun. 1783. 100 acres.
White, James. Va. Private. 26 Apr. 1784. 100 acres.
White, James. Va. Private. 29 Jun. 1784. 100 acres.
White, James. Va. Corporal. 21 Nov. 1787. 400 acres.
White, Jedediah. Va. Private. 30 Dec. 1808. 100 acres.
White, Jesse. N.C. Private. 7 Jan. 1786. 640 acres to heirs.
White, Jesse. Va. Private. 6 Dec. 1785. 100 acres.
White, John. Ga. ———. ———. 230 acres.
White, John. Ga. ———. 22 Apr. 1784. 287 1/2 acres.
White, John. Ga. Colonel. 17 May 1784. 1150 acres to heirs.
White, John. N.Y. ———. 20 Jan. 1791. 500 acres to heirs.
White, John. N.C. Private. 22 Oct. 1783. 228 acres.
White, John. N.C. Sergeant. 20 Apr. 1784. 1000 acres to heirs.
White, John. N.C. Private. 9 Nov. 1784. 640 acres to heir.

White, John. N.C. Private. 22 Apr. 1809. 640 acres to heirs.
White, John. N.C. Private. 23 Dec. 1809. 640 acres to heirs.
White, John. Va. Lieutenant. 27 May 1783. 2666 2/3 acres.
White, John. Va. Lieutenant. 16 Dec. 1782. 2666 2/3 acres.
White, John. Va. Lieutenant. 13 Jan. 1784. 444 acres.
White, John. Va. Sailor. 7 May 1784. 100 acres.
White, John. Va. Lieutenant. 29 Apr. 1807. 333 1/3 acres.
White, John. Va. Private. 28 Feb. 1839. 100 acres.
White, John, Jr. Conn. Sufferer. New/East Haven. 23.18.3.
White, Jonathan. Md. Private. ———. 50 acres.
White, Jonathan. N. Y. Matross. 9 Jul. 1790. 500 acres.
White, Joseph. Ga. ———. 13 Sep. 1784. 287 1/2 acres.
White, Joseph. Md. Private. ———. 50 acres.
White, Joseph. N.C. Private. 5 Sep. 1821. 640 acres.
White, Joseph. Pa. Private. 5 Dec. 1804. 200 acres.
White, Joseph. Va. Private. 11 Dec. 1798. 100 acres.
White, Joseph. Va. Pilot. 7 May 1838. 1666 2/3 acres.
White, Joseph. Va. Pilot. 3 Feb. 1841. 1000 acres.
White, Joseph M. Conn. Sufferer. Danbury. 31.7.8.
White, Joseph, Sr. N.C. Private. 10 Sep. 1821. 640 acres to heirs.
White, Joshua. Me. ———. 30 Jun. 1835. 200 acres to widow Margaret White. Fairfield.
White, Layton. Va.-Ind. Private. 108 acres.
White, Malicha. N.C. Private. 29 Sep. 1784. 640 acres.
White, Matthew. N.C. Lieutenant. 4 Aug. 1821. 2560 acres.
White, Nicholas. Ga. ———. 1 Oct. 1784. 287 1/2 acres.
White, Paul. N.C. Private. 22 May 1820. 640 acres to heirs.
White, Peter. N. Y. Private. 8 Jul. 1790. 600 acres.
White, Randall. Va.-Ind. Private. 108 acres.
White, Randolph. Va. Private. 31 Oct. 1791. 100 acres.
White, Richard. Ga. ———. 17 May 1784. ———.
White, Richard. N.C. ———. 14 May 1784. 327 acres to Lieut. Col. John Armstrong, heir.
White, Richard. Va. Private. 25 Jun. 1783. 200 acres.
White, Robert. N.C. Private. 22 Sep. 1795. 640 acres to heirs.
White, Robert. Va. Captain. 5 Apr. 1783. 4000 acres.
White, Robert. Va. Private. 28 May 1784. 100 acres.
White, Robert. Va. Captain. 15 Nov. 1799. 1333 1/3 acres.
White, Robert. Va. Midshipman. 15 May 1838. 2666 2/3 acres.
White, Samuel. Ga. ———. 17 May 1784. ———.
White, Samuel. N.C. Private. 8 Dec. 1796. 640 acres.
White, Samuel. Conn. Sufferer. New/East Haven. 3.0.0.
White, Samuel B. Md. Private. ———. 50 acres.
White, Stephen. N.Y. ———. 20 Jan. 1791. 500 acres to heirs.
White, Stephen. N.C. Sergeant. 20 Apr. 1784. 1000 acres to heirs.
White, Tarpley. Va. Captain. 24 Dec. 1782. 4000 acres.
White, Tarpley. Va. Captain. 1 Jun. 1805. 333 1/3 acres.
White, Tarpley. Va. Captain. 1 Jun. 1805. 333 1/3 acres.
White, Thomas. Ga. Soldier. 26 May 1784. 287 1/2 acres.
White, Thomas. N.C. Trooper. 21 Oct. 1783. 228 acres.
White, Thomas. N.C. Captain. 22 Oct. 1783. 3840 acres to James White, heir.
White, Thomas. S.C. Lieutenant. 21 Jan. 1785. 300 acres.
White, Thomas. Va. Lieutenant. 30 Jan. 1784. 2666 2/3 acres.
White, Thomas. Va. Private. 4 Feb. 1784. 100 acres.
White, Walter. N.C. Private. 26 Aug. 1785. 640 acres to heirs.
White, William. Ga. ———. 20 Apr. 1784. 400 acres.

White, William. N.C. Private. 20 Apr. 1784. 640 acres.
White, William. N.C. ———. 29 Apr. 1784. 274 acres.
White, William. N.C. Sergeant. 23 Nov. 1790. 357 acres.
White, William. N.C. Private. 23 Nov. 1797. 640 acres to heirs.
White, William. N.C. Ensign. 13 Dec. 1804. 2560 acres to heirs.
White, William. Va. Lieutenant. 20 Jan. 1783. 2666 2/3 acres.
White, William. Va. Captain. 11 Mar. 1783. 4000 acres.
White, William. Va. Captain. 26 Jun. 1783. 4000 acres.
White, William. Va. Captain. 17 Feb. 1784. 666 2/3 acres.
White, William. Va. Private. 5 Apr. 1784. 100 acres.
White, William. Va. Private. 7 Apr. 1784. 100 acres.
White, William. Va. Private. 19 Jan. 1785. 100 acres.
White, William. Va. Captain. 5 Nov. 1808. 722 acres.
White, William. Va. Captain. 5 Nov. 1808. 722 acres.
White, William. Va. Surgeon's Mate. 26 Feb. 1831. 4000 acres.
White, William. Va. Captain. 25 Mar. 1840. 18 1/2 acres.
White, William. Va. Captain. 25 Mar. 1840. 18 1/2 acres.
White, William. Va. Captain. 25 Mar. 1840. 18 1/2 acres.
White, William. Va. Captain. 25 Mar. 1840. 18 1/2 acres.
White, William. Va. Captain. 25 Mar. 1840. 74 acres.
White, William. Va. Lieutenant. 20 Sep. 1850. 810 2/11 acres.
White, William. Va. Lieutenant. 22 Oct. 1850. 101 3/11 acres.
White, William. Va. Lieutenant. 6 Mar. 1851. 202 6/11 acres.
White, William. Va. Surgeon's Mate. 14 Sep. 1831. 1000 acres.
White, William. Va. Surgeon's Mate. 14 Sep. 1831. 1000 acres.
White, William. Va. Surgeon's Mate. 14 Sep. 1831. 2000 acres.
White, Wright. Conn. Sufferer. Fairfield. 46.8.0.
Whitear, Abigail. Conn. Sufferer. Fairfield. 111.13.11.
Whitecotton, James. Va.-Ind. Private. 108 acres.
Whitecox, John. N.C. Private. 11 Feb. 1796. 640 acres to heirs.
Whitehead, Jehiel. Conn. Sufferer. Fairfield. 6.16.2.
Whitehead, John. N. Y. Private. 8 Jul. 1790. 500 acres.
Whitehead, John. Conn. Sufferer. Fairfield. 17.8.0.
Whitehead, Matthew. N.C. Private. 9 Dec. 1805. 640 acres to heirs.
Whitehead, Robert. Va.-Ind. Private. 108 acres.
Whitehead, Thomas. N.C. Private. 17 Dec. 1785. 640 acres to heirs.
Whitehead, William. Va.-Ind. Private. 108 acres.
Whitehead, William. N. Y. Drummer. 8 Jul. 1790. 600 acres.
Whitehead, William. N.C. Private. 29 Apr. 1784. 228 acres.
Whitehead, William. N.C. Private. 13 Sep. 1820. 228 acres.
Whitehend, John. Va. Sailor. 31 Jan. 1784. 100 acres.
Whitehouse, Joel. N.C. Private. 17 Jul. 1784. 274 acres.
Whitehurst, Charles. N.C. Private. 17 Dec. 1804. 640 acres to heirs.
Whiteman, John. Pa. Private. 14 Sep. 1790. 200 acres.
Whitesides, John. Ga. ———. 21 Apr. 1784. 287 1/2 acres.
Whitfield, Edward. Va. Private. 27 Apr. 1784. 100 acres.
Whitfield, Haynes. Va. Sailor. 20 Nov. 1783. 100 acres.
Whitfield, Jesse. N.C. Private. 9 Nov. 1784. 640 acres to William Whitfield.
Whitfield, Jesse. N.C. Private. 9 Nov. 1784. 640 acres to William Whitfield, heir.
Whiting, Beverley. Va. Ensign. 10 Oct. 1806. 2666 2/3 acres.
Whiting, Ebenezer. Conn. Sufferer. Norwalk. 108.13.9.
Whiting, Francis. Va. Lieutenant. 19 Feb. 1783. 2666 2/3 acres.
Whiting, Francis. Va. Lieutenant. 21 Dec. 1807. 333 acres.

Whiting, Henry. Va. Captain. 31 Jan. 1784. 4000 acres.

Whiting, John. Conn. Sufferer. New/East Haven. 158.16.3.

Whitletors, Levi. Va. Private. 24 Nov. 1783. 100 acres.

Whitley, Arthur. N.C. Private. 24 Nov. 1796. 228 acres.

Whitley, Hance. N.C. Private. 2 Feb. 1786. 228 acres.

Whitley, Solomon. N.C. Private. 24 Dec. 1785. 640 acres.

Whitley, Thomas. N.C. Musician. 5 Sep. 1821. 1000 acres.

Whitley, William. Va.-Ind. Private. 108 acres.

Whitley, William. N.C. Private. 24 Nov. 1796. 640 acres to heirs.

Whitlock, James. Pa. Private. 29 Sep. 1787. 200 acres.

Whitlock, Robert. N.C. Private. 9 Nov. 1784. 640 acres.

Whitlock, William. N.C. Private. 17 Dec. 1785. 640 acres to heirs.

Whitlow, Benjamin. Pa. ———. 250 acres.

Whitlow, Francis. Va. Private. 19 Feb. 1783. 100 acres.

Whitlow, Michael. Va. Private. 28 Feb. 1784. 200 acres.

Whitlow, William. N.C. Private. 17 Dec. 1785. 640 acres to heirs.

Whitman, John. Ga. ———. 7 Jun. 1785. 230 acres.

Whitman, John. Pa. Private. ———. 200 acres.

Whitman, Solomon. Conn. Sufferer. Norwalk. 17.17.6.

Whitman, William. N.C. Private. 9 Sep. 1785. 640 acres to heirs.

Whitmer, Everhard. Pa. Sergeant. 20 May 1787. 250 acres.

Whitmill, Blount. N.C. Subaltern. 27 Nov. 1783. 824 acres.

Whitmill, Thomas Blount. N.C. ———. 17 May 1817. 1676 acres to heirs.

Whitmore, Amos. N. Y. Corporal. 9 Jul. 1790. 600 acres.

Whitmore, James. N. Y. Gunner. 7 Jul. 1790. 600 acres.

Whitmore, William. Va. Corporal. 1 May 1783. 400 acres.

Whitmore, William. Va. Private. 16 Dec. 1784. 100 acres.

Whitney, David. Conn. Sufferer. Norwalk. 0.12.0.

Whitney, Ebenezer. Mass. Private. 18 Oct. 1833. 200 acres.

Whitney, Eleazer. Mass. Private. 8 Nov. 1833. 200 acres.

Whitney, Isaac. Me. Private. 14 May 1835. 200 acres. Lisbon.

Whitney, James R. N.C. Private. 8 Dec. 1795. 640 acres.

Whitney, Jesse. Me. ———. 22 May 1835. 200 acres to widow Charity Whtney. Saco.

Whitney, Joseph. Conn. Sufferer. Norwalk. 182.11.2.

Whitney, Lois. Conn. Sufferer. Norwalk. 88.11.1 1/4.

Whitney, Peter. Conn. Sufferer. Fairfield. 7.9.0.

Whitney, Samuel, Jr. Conn. Sufferer. Fairfield. 26.10.2.

Whitney, Stephen. Conn. Sufferer. Norwalk. 19.5.0.

Whitney, Timothy. Conn. Sufferer. Norwalk. 0.17.6.

Whiton, Israel. Mass. Private. 7 Jan. 1834. 200 acres.

Whitsel, John. Ga. Surgeon. ———. 250 acres.

Whitsell, Jacob. Va. Private. 9 May 1785. 100 acres.

Whitsell, Philip. N.C. Drummer. 29 Apr. 1784. 1000 acres to heir.

Whitson, Anthony. Va. Private. 3 Jul. 1784. 100 acres.

Whitt, Isham. Va. Private. 9 Mar. 1809. 100 acres.

Whitt, Richard. Ga. Soldier. 24 Apr. 1784. ———.

Whitt, Robert. Va. Private. 29 Jun. 1835. 100 acres.

Whitt, Shadrach. Va. Private. 12 Dec. 1792. 200 acres.

Whittaker [or Whitton], William. Md. Private. ———. 50 acres.

Whitten, Austin. Ga. Minute Man. 26 May 1784. 287 1/2 acres.

Whitten, Daniel. Va. Private. 17 Jul. 1884. 100 acres.

Whitten, John. Me. ———. 16 Apr. 1835. 200 acres to widow Jane Whitten. Topsham.

Whittington, Bartholomew. S.C. ———. 3 Mar. 1788. 200 acres.

Whittington, Cornelius. Ga. ———. 22 Apr. 1784. 287 1/2 acres.
Whittington, Edward. S.C. ———. 4 Jul. 1791. 200 acres.
Whittington, Ephraim. S.C. ———. 5 Dec. 1791. 200 acres.
Whittington, Griff. S.C. ———. 2 Jul. 1792. 200 acres.
Whittington, Isaac. S.C. ———. 2 May 1791. 200 acres.
Whittington, Jarret. S.C. ———. 3 Oct. 1791. 188 acres.
Whittlesey, Chauncey, Rev. Conn. Sufferer. New/East Haven. 326.6.3.
Whittlesey, Newton. Conn. Sufferer. New/East Haven. 33.3.0.
Whittom, William. Md. Matross. ———. 50 acres.
Whitton, Isum. N.C. Private. 30 Sep. 1785. 640 acres to heirs.
Whitton, John. Ga. Minute Man. 14 Feb. 1785. ———.
Whitton, Philip. Ga. Minute Man. 22 Mar. 1785. 250 acres.
Whitton, Robert. Ga. ———. 17 May 1784. ———.
Whood, William. N.C. Private. 26 Nov. 1796. 640 acres to heirs.
Whorton, Lemuel. N.C. Private. 3 Aug. 1820. 274 acres to heirs.
Wicker, Willis. N.C. Sergeant. 3 Aug. 1820. 357 acres to heirs.
Wickham, Stephen. N. Y. Private. 8 Jul. 1790. 600 acres.
Wickle, John. Pa. Matross. ———. 200 acres.
Wickley, John. S.C. Captain. 21 Jan. 1785. 300 acres.
Wickliffe, Arenton. Va. Private. 9 Dec. 1833. 100 acres.
Wickliffe, Benjamin. Va. Private. 9 Dec. 1833 [7 Mar.1835]. 100 acres.
Wickliffe, Moses. Va. Private. 9 Dec. 1833 [7 Mar. 1835]. 100 acres.
Wickman, John. Ga. Minute Man. 22 Mar. 1785. 250 acres.
Widdows, Robert. Va. Private. 9 Aug. 1783. 100 acres.
Wideman, Adam. Ga. Refugee. 19 Jul. 1784. 287 1/2 acres.
Widows, Abraham. Pa. Private. 6 Apr. 1787. 200 acres.
Wiely, Richard. Md. Private. ———. 50 acres.
Wier, Andrew. Pa. Private. 16 Dec. 1802. 200 acres.
Wiery, Michael. Md. Fifer. ———. 50 acres.
Wietzell, John. Pa. Lieutenant. ———. 200 acres.
Wigans, Noah. Ga. ———. 17 May 1784. ———.
Wiggans, Willis. N.C. Sergeant. 22 Dec. 1796. 357 acres.
Wiggens, James. N.C. Private. 30 Sep. 1785. 640 acres.
Wiggens, Noah. N.C. Private. 10 Dec. 1788. 228 acres.
Wiggins, Arthur. N.C. Private. 15 Feb. 1797. 228 acres.
Wiggins, Charles. N.C. Private. 30 Sep. 1785. 640 acres.
Wiggins, Henry. N.C. Private. 4 Aug. 1821. 640 acres.
Wiggins, Jacob. N.C. Sergeant. 27 Jul. 1785. 1000 acres.
Wiggins, James. N.C. Private. 8 Dec. 1796. 640 acres to heirs.
Wiggins, Levi. N.C. Private. 20 Apr. 1784. 640 acres.
Wiggins, Malachi. N.C. Private. 27 Nov. 1819. 274 acres.
Wiggins, Matthew. N.C. Private. 29 Apr. 1784. 274 acres.
Wiggins, Thomas. N.C. Private. 9 Nov. 1784. 640 acres to Samuel Wiggins, heir.
Wiggins, Thomas. Pa. Sergeant. 5 Apr. 1787. 250 acres.
Wiggins, William, Jr. Ga. ———. 21 Apr. 1784. 287 1/2 acres.
Wiggins, William, Sr. Ga. ———. 21 Apr. 1784. 287 1/2 acres.
Wiggins, Willis. N.C. Private. 6 Dec. 1796. 228 acres.
Wiggle, Dempsey. N.C. Private. 29 Sep. 1785. 640 acres.
Wight, John. Me. ———. 24 Aug. 1835. 200 acres. Bluehill.
Wightman, Joseph. N.Y. ———. 20 Jan. 1791. 500 acres to heirs.
Wigley, Dempsey. N.C. Private. 30 Sep. 1785. 640 acres.
Wigley, Job. Va. Private. 3 Jul. 1784. 100 acres.
Wigley, Samuel. N.C. Private. 29 Sep. 1785. 640 acres to heirs.

Wigley, Thomas. N.C. Private. 30 Sep. 1785. 640 acres.
Wigton, John. Pa. Ranger. 24 Jul. 1787. 200 acres.
Wigton, John. Pa. Paymaster. 24 Jul. 1787. 200 acres.
Wilbert, Jacob. N. Y. Private. 8 Jul. 1790. 600 acres.
Wilborn, Cooper. Ga. Minute Man. 14 Jul. 1785. ———.
Wilburn, John. N.C. Private. 1 Sep. 1785. 640 acres to heirs.
Wilcocks, John. N.C. Private. 19 May 1784. 640 acres.
Wilcox, David. N.C. Private. 18 Jan. 1792. 274 acres.
Wilcox, Elias. N. Y. Sergeant. 9 Jul. 1790. 500 acres.
Wilcox, John. Me. Matross. 26 Sep. 1838. 200 acres. Monmouth.
Wilcox, John. N. Y. Sergeant. 8 Jul. 1790. 600 acres.
Wilcox, John. N.Y. Drummer. 20 Jan. 1791. 500 acres to heirs.
Wilder, Absalom. N.C. Private. 11 Feb. 1796. 640 acres to heirs.
Wilder, Dread. Ga. ———. 21 Apr. 1784. 287 1/2 acres.
Wilder, George. Ga. Minute Man. 24 Aug. 1785. ———.
Wilder, George. Va. Sailor. 13 Feb. 1784. 100 acres.
Wilder, James. Va. Sailor. 27 Jul. 1783. 100 acres.
Wilder, Malachi. Ga. ———. 16 Sep. 1784. 287 1/2 acres.
Wilder, Randol. N.C. Corporal. 30 Sep. 1785. 1000 acres to heirs.
Wilder, Sampson. Ga. ———. 22 Apr. 1784. 287 1/2 acres.
Wilder, Samuel. Ga. ———. 17 May 1784. ———.
Wilder, Shubal. Mass. ———. 22 Jul. 1833. 200 acres.
Wilder, William. Ga. ———. 22 Apr. 1784. 287 1/2 acres.
Wildes, Charles. Ga. ———. 17 May 1784. ———.
Wildie, Roger. N.C. Private. 28 Sep. 1785. 640 acres.
Wildman, Comfort. Conn. Sufferer. Danbury. 11.14.2.
Wildman, Daniel. Conn. Sufferer. Danbury. 31.19.7.
Wildman, Joseph. Conn. Sufferer. Danbury. 278.5.4.
Wildman, Thomas. Conn. Sufferer. Danbury. 3.11.4.
Wildman, Timothy. Conn. Sufferer. Danbury. 2.13.4.
Wiley, Edward. N. Y. Private. 8 Jul. 1790. 500 acres.
Wiley, Ephraim. Me. ———. 19 Aug. 1835. 200 acres. St. George.
Wiley, Samuel. Mass. ———. 27 May 1831. 200 acres.
Wiley, Stephen. N.C. Private. 17 Feb. 1824. 640 acres.
Wilhelm, Henry. Pa. ———. 17 Nov. 1796. 200 acres.
Wilhiby, Jesse. Va. Private. 19 Feb. 1784. 100 acres.
Wilhite, Richard. N.C. Private. 9 Dec. 1797. 640 acres to heirs.
Wilkelow, John. N. Y. Private. 8 Jul. 1790. 600 acres.
Wilkenson, James. N.C. Private. 23 Apr. 1785. 640 acres to heirs.
Wilkenson, John. Md. Sergeant. ———. 50 acres.
Wilkenson, William. Pa. ———. 9 May 1794. 200 acres.
Wilkerson, Barnabas. Va. Sergeant. 21 Nov. 1783. 200 acres.
Wilkerson, Benjamin. Va. Private. 30 Nov. 1784. 100 acres.
Wilkerson, David. Va. Private. 23 Feb. 1784. 200 acres.
Wilkerson, Drury. Va. Private. 27 Feb. 1784. 100 acres.
Wilkerson, Hammon. Ga. Soldier. 6 Dec. 1785. 230 acres.
Wilkerson, John. Md. Private. ———. 50 acres.
Wilkerson, John. N.C. Matross. 14 Oct. 1783. 640 acres.
Wilkerson, John. N.C. Private. 23 Apr. 1784. 640 acres.
Wilkerson, John. Va. Private. 15 Dec. 1785. 200 acres.
Wilkerson, Richard. N.C. Private. 7 Dec. 1797. 640 acres to heirs.
Wilkerson, Thomas. Va. Private. 21 Nov. 1783. 100 acres.
Wilkerson, Young. Va. Lieutenant. 15 Nov. 1822. 1333 1/3 acres.
Wilkerson, Young. Va. Lieutenant. 15 Nov. 1822. 1333 1/3 acres.

Wilkes, John. Pa. Matross. 10 Mar. 1787. 200 acres to Stephen Loudon, assignee.
Wilkes, Matthew. Conn. Sufferer. Danbury. 3.9.4.
Wilkeson, William. Md. Private. ———. 50 acres.
Wilkin, Benjamin. N.C. Private. 15 Jul. 1785. 640 acres to heirs.
Wilkin, Robert. Pa. Captain. ———. 500 acres.
Wilkins, Burrell. N.C. Private. 28 Sep. 1785. 640 acres to heirs.
Wilkins, Clement. Ga. ———. 17 May 1784. ———.
Wilkins, David. Ga. Private. 1784. 250 acres.
Wilkins, Edward. Me. Drum Major. 20 Oct. 1835. 200 acres to widow Bridget Wilkins. Exeter.
Wilkins, Elisha. N.C. Private. 15 Jul. 1785. 640 acres to heir.
Wilkins, Gabriel. Ga. Minute Man. 17 Apr. 1784. 287 1/2 acres.
Wilkins, George. N.C. Private. 12 Sep. 1785. 640 acres to heirs.
Wilkins, James. Va. Private. 13 May 1785. 200 acres.
Wilkins, John. Ga. Minute Man. 4 May 1785. 287 1/2 acres.
Wilkins, John. Pa. Surgeon. ———. 300 acres.
Wilkins, Jonas. N.C. Private. 15 Jul. 1785. 640 acres to heir.
Wilkins, Jordon. N.C. Private. 12 Sep. 1785. 640 acres to heirs.
Wilkins, Joseph. N.C. Private. 28 Sep. 1785. 640 acres.
Wilkins, Joshua. N.C. Private. 24 Jul. 1820. 640 acres to heirs.
Wilkins, Nathaniel. Va. Lieutenant. 19 May 1823. 2666 2/3 acres.
Wilkins, Nathaniel. Va. ———. 2 Jul. 1833. 66 2/3 acres.
Wilkins, Nathaniel. Va. ———. 2 Jul. 1833. 66 2/3 acres.
Wilkins, Nathaniel. Va. ———. 2 Jul. 1833. 66 2/3 acres.
Wilkins, Nathaniel. Va. ———. 2 Jul. 1833. 66 2/3 acres.
Wilkins, Nathaniel. Va. ———. 10 Jul. 1833. 111 acres.
Wilkins, Nathaniel. Va. ———. 10 Jul. 1833. 111 acres.
Wilkins, Nathaniel. Va. ———. 10 Jul. 1833. 111 acres.
Wilkins, Nathnaiel. Va. ———. 2 Jul. 1833. 66 2/3 acres.
Wilkins, Robert. Va. Private. 27 Dec. 1796. 200 acres.
Wilkins, Thomas. Va. Drummer. 1 Aug. 1783. 200 acres.
Wilkins, Thomas. Va. Private. 15 Jun. 1785. 200 acres.
Wilkins, William. Ga. ———. 17 Apr. 1784. 287 1/2 acres.
Wilkins, William. N.C. Private. 11 Feb. 1796. 640 acres to heirs.
Wilkinson, David. Mass. ———. 14 Jan. 1832. 200 acres to children Allan Wilkinson, Rocellana Hoag, and Catharine Marshall.
Wilkinson, John. Ga. Minute Men. 22 Apr. 1784. 287 1/2 acres.
Wilkinson, Reubin. N.C. Lieutenant. 29 Sep. 1784. 2560 acres.
Wilkinson, Robert. N. Y. Sergeant. 8 Jul. 1790. 600 acres.
Wilkinson, William. Ga. Soldier. 1 Jan. 1785. ———. Of Mecklenburg Co., Va.
Wilkinson, William. N.C. Private. 22 Apr. 1785. 274 acres.
Wilkinson, Young. Md. Lieutenant. ———. 200 acres.
Wilks, Burrell. Va. Sergeant. 21 Nov. 1783. 200 acres.
Wilks, Francis. N.C. Private. 28 May 1784. 228 acres.
Will, Conrad. Pa. Private. 25 Oct. 1786. 200 acres.
Willard, John. Va. Private. 18 Nov. 1830. 100 acres.
Willard, William. Pa. Private. 6 Apr. 1787. 200 acres.
Willcocks, David. N.C. Private. 3 Mar. 1784. 640 acres.
Wille, William. Conn. Sufferer. Danbury. 1.8.7 1/2.
Willet, Thomas. Pa. Private. 6 Apr. 1787. 200 acres.
Willett, Charles. Md. Private. ———. 50 acres.
Willett, Marinus. N. Y. Lieutenant Colonel Com. 9 Jul. 1790. 3000 acres.
Willett, Waitman. Va. Private. 9 Nov. 1868. 200 acres.
Willey, David. Mass. Private. 1 May 1832. 200 acres to heirs.

Willfred, Philip. Ga. Minute Man. 6 May 1785. ———.

William. N.C. Private. 22 Feb. 1785. 228 acres.

Williams, A. Henry. N. Y. Lieutenant. 9 Jul. 1790. 1200 acres.

Williams, Alexander. Va. Private. 21 Apr. 1784. 100 acres.

Williams, Arthur. N.C. Private. 24 Nov. 1796. 640 acres to heirs.

Williams, Benjamin. Md. Private. ———. 50 acres.

Williams, Benjamin. Md. Private. ———. 50 acres.

Williams, Benjamin. Md. Private. ———. 50 acres.

Williams, Benjamin. N.C. Captain. 6 Jan. 1784. 1828 acres.

Williams, Benjamin. N.C. Private. 8 Dec. 1796. 640 acres to heirs.

Williams, Benjamin. Va. Private. 9 Feb. 1822. 200 acres.

Williams, Burton. Ga. Minute Men. 15 Mar. 1784. 250 acres.

Williams, Carol. Ga. Private. 7 May 1784. 200 acres.

Williams, Charles. Ga. Lieutenant. 25 May 1784. 460 acres to heirs.

Williams, Charles. Ga. ———. 22 Apr. 1784. 287 1/2 acres.

Williams, Charles. Md. Private. ———. 50 acres.

Williams, Charles. N. Y. Private. 8 Jul. 1790. 600 acres.

Williams, Charles. N.C. Private. 18 Dec. 1807. 640 acres to heirs.

Williams, Charles. Va. Private. 2 Mar. 1784. 100 acres.

Williams, Charles. Va. Private. 12 Jan. 1842. 100 acres.

Williams, Christopher. Va. Private. 26 Apr. 1783. 200 acres.

Williams, Daniel. Va.-Ind. Private. 108 acres.

Williams, Daniel. Md. Private. ———. 50 acres.

Williams, Daniel. Mass. Private. 1 May 1832. 200 acres to heirs.

Williams, Daniel. N.C. Captain. 2 Dec. 1785. 2285 acres.

Williams, Daniel. Va. Private. 12 Jun. 1784. 100 acres.

Williams, Daniel. Va. Private. 22 Nov. 1787. 200 acres.

Williams, Daniel. Conn. Sufferer. Groton. 7.13.0.

Williams, David. Md. Private. ———. 50 acres.

Williams, David. N.C. Private. 12 Oct. 1795. 640 acres to heirs.

Williams, David. Va. Lieutenant. 18 Jun. 1783. 2666 2/3 acres.

Williams, David. Va. Lieutenant. 23 Sep. 1809. 1536 1/2 acres.

Williams, David. Va. Lieutenant. 23 Sep. 1809. 1536 1/2 acres.

Williams, David. Va. Ensign. 4 Jun. 1783. 2666 2/3 acres.

Williams, Dudley. N.C. Private. 26 May 1784. 640 acres.

Williams, Edward. Ga. Minute Man. 5 May 1785. 287 1/2 acres.

Williams, Edward. N.C. Private. 26 May 1784. 640 acres.

Williams, Eli. Ga. Soldier. ———. 20 Apr. 1785. ———.

Williams, Elias. Pa. Sergeant. 5 Apr. 1803. 250 acres to Joseph Asheton, assignee.

Williams, Elijah. Ga. ———. 17 May 1784. ———.

Williams, Elisha. N.C. Private. 9 Nov. 1783. 274 acres.

Williams, Elizabeth. Pa. ———. 14 May 1812. 200 acres.

Williams, Eunice. Conn. Sufferer. Groton. 15.19.0.

Williams, Francis. N.Y. ———. 20 Jan. 1791. 500 acres to heirs.

Williams, Francis. N.C. Private. 22 Oct. 1783. 640 acres.

Williams, Frederick. Ga. ———. 21 Apr. 1784. 287 1/2 acres.

Williams, Gabriel. Md. Sergeant. ———. 50 acres.

Williams, George. Ga. ———. 19 Apr. 1784. 862 1/2 acres.

Williams, George. Md. Sergeant. ———. 50 acres.

Williams, George. N.C. Private. 3 Feb. 1785. 228 acres.

Williams, George. Va. Private. 19 Jun. 1783. 200 acres.

Williams, Henry. Va. Private. 18 Aug. 1783. 100 acres.

Williams, Herbert. N.C. Non Commissioned Officer. 14 May 1784. 1000 acres to James Williams, heir.

Williams, Hickman. N.C. Private. 22 Dec. 1796. 228 acres.
Williams, Isaac. Ga. ———. 17 May 1784. ———.
Williams, Isaac. N. Y. Matross. 9 Jul. 1790. 500 acres.
Williams, Isaac. S.C. Soldier. 21 Jan. 1785. 200 acres.
Williams, Jacob. N.C. Private. 2 Feb. 1786. 274 acres.
Williams, James. Ga. ———. 15 Apr. 1784. 287 1/2 acres.
Williams, James. Md. Private. ———. 50 acres.
Williams, James. Md. ———. ———. 50 acres.
Williams, James. Mass. Sergeant. 13 Dec. 1833. 200 acres to heirs.
Williams, James. N.C. Private. 20 Mar. 1785. 274 acres.
Williams, James. N.C. Corporal. 10 Aug. 1785. 1000 acres to heirs.
Williams, James. N.C. Captain. 25 Nov. 1796. 3840 acres to heirs.
Williams, James. Va. Captain. 20 May 1783. 4666 2/3 acres.
Williams, James. Va. Private. 19 Mar. 1810. 100 acres.
Williams, James. Va. Captain. 2 Oct. 1807. 388 acres, 3 rods, and 13 poles.
Williams, James. Va. Private. 12 Mar. 1840. 100 acres.
Williams, Jarrett. Va. Lieutenant. 3 Mar. 1784. 2666 2/3 acres.
Williams, Jarrott. Va.-Ind. Lieutenant. 2156 acres.
Williams, Jarvis. Md. Private. ———. 50 acres.
Williams, Jeremiah. Md. Corporal. ———. 50 acres.
Williams, Jesse. N.C. Sergeant. 30 Sep. 1785. 1000 acres to heirs.
Williams, Jesse. N.C. Private. 12 Dec. 1785. 640 acres.
Williams, John. Ga. Minute Man. 15 Apr. 1784. 287 1/2 acres.
Williams, John. Ga. ———. 1784. 287 1/2 acres.
Williams, John. Va.-Ind. Captain. Dec. 1791. 3234 acres.
Williams, John. Va.-Ind. Sergeant. 216 acres.
Williams, John. Me. Private. 15 Jun. 1835. 200 acres. Wiscasset.
Williams, John. Md. Private. ———. 50 acres.
Williams, John. Md. Private. ———. 50 acres.
Williams, John. N. Y. Private. 8 Jul. 1790. 500 acres.
Williams, John. N. Y. Private. 8 Jul. 1790. 600 acres.
Williams, John. N.C. Sergeant. 20 Apr. 1784. 1144 acres.
Williams, John. N.C. Private. 29 Apr. 1784. 274 acres.
Williams, John. N.C. Private. 29 Sep. 1784. 640 acres to William Williams, heir.
Williams, John. N.C. Private. 24 Dec. 1785. 640 acres to heirs.
Williams, John. N.C. Private. 14 Jan. 1835. 457 acres.
Williams, John. Pa. Corporal. 25 Jul. 1787. 200 acres.
Williams, John. Pa. Fifer. 25 Aug. 1782. 200 acres.
Williams, John. Pa. Drummer. 22 Jun. 1797. 200 acres to Daniel Vanosten, assignee.
Williams, John. Pa. Drummer. 23 Dec. 1786. 200 acres.
Williams, John. S.C. ———. 21 Jan. 1785. 200 acres.
Williams, John. S.C. ———. 7 Jul. 1788. 200 acres.
Williams, John. Va. Captain. 3 Mar. 1783. 4000 acres.
Williams, John. Va. Private. 15 Apr. 1783. 200 acres.
Williams, John. Va. Sergeant. 19 Jun. 1783. 400 acres.
Williams, John. Va. Sergeant. 19 Jun. 1783. 200 acres.
Williams, John. Va. Sergeant. 23 Jun. 1783. 400 acres.
Williams, John. Va. Private. 4 Feb. 1784. 200 acres.
Williams, John. Va. Private. 18 Oct. 1784. 200 acres.
Williams, John. Va. Captain. 20 Dec. 1791. 4000 acres.
Williams, John. Va. Private. 20 Apr. 1813. 100 acres.
Williams, John. Va. Pilot. 25 May 1832. 2666 2/3 acres.
Williams, John. Conn. Sufferer. Fairfield. 116.0.9.

Williams, John Pugh. N.C. Captain. 17 Dec. 1785. 1371 acres.
Williams, John, Jr. Conn. Sufferer. Fairfield. 13.19.0.
Williams, Joseph. Ga. Minute Man. 20 Apr. 1784. 287 1/2 acres.
Williams, Joseph. N.C. Private. 22 Mar. 1785. 274 acres.
Williams, Joseph. N.C. Private. 10 Aug. 1785. 640 acres to heirs.
Williams, Joseph. Pa. Corporal. 29 Oct. 1787. 200 acres to Jonathan Hoye, assignee.
Williams, Joseph. S.C. ———. 4 Dec. 1786. 200 acres.
Williams, Joshua. Ga. ———. 25 May 1784. 287 1/2 acres.
Williams, Jotham. Conn. Sufferer. New/ East Haven. 2.19.9.
Williams, Jotham. Conn. Sufferer. New/ East Haven. 6.0.0.
Williams, Lemuel. Me. Lieutenant. 4 Mar. 1842. 600 acres to widow Anna Williams. Anson.
Williams, Lewis. Pa. Private. 30 Jul. 1787. 200 acres.
Williams, Lilburn. Md. Captain. ———. 200 acres.
Williams, Masson. N.C. Private. 22 Oct. 1783. 228 acres.
Williams, Moses. Va. Sailor. 30 Jun. 1784. 100 acres.
Williams, Nathan. Md. Captain. ———. 200 acres.
Williams, Nathan B. N.C. Lieutenant. 8 Mar. 1796. 2560 acres to heirs.
Williams, Nathaniel. Ga. Minute Man. 1784. 287 1/2 acres.
Williams, Nathaniel. Mass. Private. 6 Jul. 1832. 200 acres to assignee Jacob Decker.
Williams, Nathaniel. N.C. Lieutenant. 20 Oct. 1783. 2560 acres.
Williams, Nathaniel. N.C. Private. 2 Dec. 1785. 228 acres.
Williams, Nathaniel. Pa. Private. 24 Mar. 1787. 200 acres to Catherine Asterman, devisee.
Williams, Nehemiah. N.C. Private. 22 Dec. 1796. 228 acres.
Williams, Oliver. N.C. Private. 30 Sep. 1785. 640 acres to heirs.
Williams, Otho Holland. Md. Brigadier General. ———. 200 acres.
Williams, Peter. N.C. Sergeant. 2 Aug. 1784. 1000 acres.
Williams, Peter. N.C. Private. 12 Sep. 1785. 640 acres to heirs.
Williams, Peter. Conn. Sufferer. Groton. 27.7.6.
Williams, Philemon. Va. Private. 17 Apr. 1783. 200 acres.
Williams, Phillip. N.C. Private. 2 Feb. 1786. 640 acres.
Williams, Powell. Pa. Private. ———. 200 acres to widow.
Williams, Ralph. N.C. Captain. 22 Oct. 1783. 1142 acres.
Williams, Reubin. Va. Private. 19 Mar. 1810. 100 acres.
Williams, Rice. Va. Private. 17 Dec. 1783. 100 acres.
Williams, Richard. N. Y. Corporal. 9 Jul. 1790. 600 acres.
Williams, Robert. Ga. ———. 17 May 1784. ———.
Williams, Robert. N.Y. ———. 20 Jan. 1791. 500 acres to heirs.
Williams, Robert. N.C. Private. 9 Nov. 1783. 274 acres.
Williams, Robert. N.C. Private. 8 Dec. 1796. 640 acres.
Williams, Robert. N.C. Private. 5 Sep. 1821. 640 acres.
Williams, Robert. Va. Private. 29 Apr. 1807. 100 acres.
Williams, Samuel. Ga. Minute Man. 16 Sep. 1785. 287 1/2 acres.
Williams, Samuel. N.C. Private. 9 Nov. 1784. 640 acres.
Williams, Sion. N.C. Private. 15 Aug. 1820. 640 acres to heirs.
Williams, Solomon. N.C. Private. 9 Nov. 1784. 640 acres.
Williams, Theophilus. N.C. ———. 29 Apr. 1784. 640 acres to John Williams, heir.
Williams, Theophilus. N.C. Private. 30 Sep. 1785. 640 acres to heirs.
Williams, Theoplius. N.C. Ensign. 6 Dec. 1792. 1096 acres.
Williams, Thomas. Ga. Soldier. 22 Apr. 1784. 287 1/2 acres.
Williams, Thomas. Ga. ———. 6 Apr. 1785. 287 1/2 acres to heirs.
Williams, Thomas. Md. Drummer. ———. 50 acres.

Williams, Thomas. N. Y. Lieutenant. 9 Jul. 1790. 1200 acres.
Williams, Thomas. N.C. ———. 1 Mar. 1784. 640 acres to James Williams, heir.
Williams, Thomas. N.C. Private. 30 Sep. 1785. 640 acres to heirs.
Williams, Thomas. N.C. Private. 6 Sep. 1821. 640 acres to heirs.
Williams, Thomas. Va. Private. 1 Apr. 1783. 100 acres.
Williams, Thomas. Va. Private. 3 Jan. 1785. 100 acres.
Williams, Uriah. N. Y. Private. 8 Jul. 1790. 600 acres.
Williams, William. N.C. Captain. 18 Jun. 1785. 3840 acres.
Williams, William. N.C. Private. 10 Aug. 1785. 640 acres.
Williams, William. N.C. Captain. 30 Nov. 1785. 3840 acres.
Williams, William. N.C. Private. 18 Dec. 1793. 228 acres.
Williams, William. N.C. Private. 23 Nov. 1797. 228 acres.
Williams, William. Pa. ———. 13 May 1794. 200 acres to Jacob Majers, assignee.
Williams, William. Pa. Private. ———. 200 acres.
Williams, William. Pa. Private. 18 Oct. 1786. 200 acres.
Williams, William. Va. Private. 1 Apr. 1783. 100 acres.
Williams, William. Va. Private. 28 Jun. 1783. 200 acres.
Williams, William. Va. Private. 5 Aug. 1834. 66 1/3 acres.
Williams, William. Va. Private. 14 Mar. 1840. 133 1/3 acres.
Williams, William. Va. Private. 23 Dec. 1850. 133 1/3 acres.
Williams, Zacheriah. Md. ———. ———. 50 acres.
Williams, Zacheriah. N.C. Private. 30 Sep. 1785. 640 acres.
Williams, Zadock. N.C. Private. 29 Apr. 1784. 280 acres.
Williams, Zebedee. N.C. Private. 25 Nov. 1796. 274 acres.
Williams, Zebediah. Va. Private. 1 Apr. 1783. 100 acres.
Williamson, Benjamin. N.C. Sergeant. 30 Sep. 1785. 1000 acres to heirs.
Williamson, Charles. Ga. ———. 25 May 1784. 460 acres to heirs.
Williamson, Charles. N.C. Private. 9 Sep. 1820. 274 acres.
Williamson, George. N.C. Private. 17 Dec. 1785. 640 acres to heirs.
Williamson, Henry. N.C. Private. 10 Feb. 1800. 274 acres.
Williamson, Hugh. N.C. Surgeon. 2 Aug. 1784. 4800 acres.
Williamson, James. N. Y. Sergeant. 8 Jul. 1790. 600 acres.
Williamson, Job. N.C. Private. 30 Sep. 1785. 640 acres to heirs.
Williamson, John. N. Y. Private. 8 Jul. 1790. 500 acres.
Williamson, John. N.C. Private. 2 Nov. 1795. 640 acres to heirs.
Williamson, John. Pa. Private. 10 Mar. 1795. 200 acres to Clement Biddle, assignee.
Williamson, John. Va. Private. 23 Apr. 1798. 100 acres.
Williamson, Joseph. Va. Private. 19 Feb. 1798. 100 acres.
Williamson, Lawrence Lot. Va. Private. 26 Apr. 1783. 100 acres.
Williamson, Littleton. Ga. Soldier. 20 Apr. 1784. 230 acres.
Williamson, Micajah. Ga. Lieutenant Colonel. 28 Feb. 1784. 800 acres.
Williamson, Micajah, Jr. ———. Ga. 19 Apr. 1784. 287 1/2 acres.
Williamson, Peter. Ga. ———. 19 Apr. 1784. 600 acres.
Williamson, Robert. Ga. Refugee. 17 May 1784. ———.
Williamson, Robert. N.C. Private. 17 Feb. 1824. 640 acres.
Williamson, William. N.C. Private. 19 Nov. 1796. 228 acres.
Williard, Stephen. N.C. Private. 7 Jan. 1786. 640 acres to heirs.
Willie, Richard. Ga. Refugee. 20 Apr. 1784. 287 1/2 acres to heirs.
Willie, Robert. N.C. Private. 30 Sep. 1785. 640 acres.
Willie, William. Ga. Refugee. 20 Apr. 1784. 287 1/2 acres to heirs.
Williford, Joseph. N.C. Private. 22 Apr. 1785. 640 acres.
Williford, Lewis. N.C. Private. 4 Sep. 1820. 640 acres to heirs.

Willigan, David. N.Y. ———. 13 Sep. 1790. 500 acres to heirs.
Willing, James. Pa. Captain. 16 Oct. 1786. 500 acres.
Willing, John. Md. Private. ———. 50 acres.
Willing, John. Md. ———. ———. 50 acres.
Willis, Augustin. N.C. Sergeant. 17 Feb. 1824. 1000 acres.
Willis, Benjamin. N. Y. Private. 13 Sep. 1790. 600 acres.
Willis, Brittain. Ga. Minute Man. 15 Mar. 1784. 250 acres.
Willis, Daniel. Md. Drummer. ———. 50 acres.
Willis, George. N.C. Private. 24 Jul. 1821. 640 acres.
Willis, Henry. Va. Captain. 23 Jun. 1783. 4000 acres.
Willis, Henry. Va. Midshipman. 4 Jun. 1835. 2666 2/3 acres.
Willis, Isaiah. Ga. ———. 15 Apr. 1784. 287 1/2 acres.
Willis, Isham. Ga. ———. 17 May 1784. ———.
Willis, Jacob. N.C. Private. 30 Sep. 1785. 640 acres to heirs.
Willis, James. N.C. Private. 30 Sep. 1785. 640 acres to heirs.
Willis, James. Va. Sailor. 19 Sep. 1787. 100 acres.
Willis, John. Md. Private. ———. 50 acres.
Willis, John. Va. Major. 6 Jun. 1783. 6222 acres.
Willis, John. Conn. Sufferer. Greenwich. 47.18.11.
Willis, John W. Va. Major. 1 Aug. 1799. 888 5/6 acres.
Willis, John W. Va. Major. 11 Sep. 1807. 144 1/3 acres.
Willis, Joseph. Ga. Minute Man. 17 Jan. 1785. 287 1/2 acres.
Willis, Josiah. N.C. Private. 30 Sep. 1785. 640 acres to heirs.
Willis, Lewis. Ga. ———. 19 Apr. 1784. 1000 acres.
Willis, Meshack. Ga. ———. ———. 230 acres.
Willis, Richard. Ga. ———. 19 Apr. 1784. 1000 acres.
Willis, Robert. Ga. ———. 25 May 1784. 287 1/2 acres.
Willis, Solomon. N.C. Private. 12 Sep. 1785. 640 acres to heirs.
Willis, Taylor. N.C. Private. 17 Dec. 1785. 640 acres to heirs.
Willis, Thomas. Me. Corporal. 20 Aug. 1835. 200 acres to widow Joanna Willis. St. George.
Willis, William. Pa. Matross. 24 Feb. 1787. 200 acres.
Willis, William. Va. Private. 31 Jul. 1783. 200 acres.
Willis, William. Va. Sergeant. 21 Feb. 1787. 200 acres.
Willis, William. Va. Seaman. 15 Jul. 1834. 100 acres.
Willis, Willis. N.C. Private. 4 Sep. 1820. 640 acres to heirs.
Willis, Wilton. N.C. Private. 24 Dec. 1785. 640 acres.
Williston, Noah, Rev. Conn. Sufferer. New/East Haven. 27.0.0.
Willkinson, Thomas. Va. Private. 9 Oct. 1830. 100 acres.
Willmott, Frederick. Md. Private. ———. 50 acres.
Willoughby, Edline. Va. Private. 19 Aug. 1822. 100 acres.
Willoughby, Edwin. N.C. Private. 14 Dec. 1796. 640 acres.
Willoughby, James. N.C. Private. 3 Dec. 1796. 640 acres to heirs.
Willoughby, James. Va. Sergeant. 9 Jun. 1831. 200 acres.
Willoughby, John. N.C. Private. 26 Aug. 1785. 640 acres to heirs.
Willoughby, John. N.C. Private. 3 Dec. 1796. 640 acres.
Willoughby, Solomon. N.C. Private. 30 Sep. 1785. 640 acres to heirs.
Willoughby, William. Ga. Private. 17 May 1784. 230 acres.
Willoughby, William. Va. Private. 3 Feb. 1784. 100 acres.
Willoughby, William. Va. Private. 11 Jun. 1831. 200 acres.
Wills, Edward. Pa. Private. 31 Oct. 1786. 200 acres.
Wills, Edward. Va. Captain. 7 Nov. 1811. 500 acres.
Wills, Edward. Va. Captain. 7 Nov. 1811. 500 acres.
Wills, Edward. Va. Captain. 7 Nov. 1811. 500 acres.

Wills, Edward. Va. Captain. 7 Nov. 1811. 500 acres.
Wills, Edward. Va. Captain. 7 Nov. 1811. 500 acres.
Wills, Edward. Va. Captain. 7 Nov. 1811. 500 acres.
Wills, Edward. Va. Captain. 7 Nov. 1811. 500 acres.
Wills, Edward. Va. Captain. 7 Nov. 1811. 500 acres.
Wills, George. Va. Private. 29 Mar. 1788. 200 acres.
Wills, Jacob. Ga. ———. ———. 287 1/2 acres.
Wills, John. Ga. ———. 17 May 1784. ———.
Wills, John. N.Y. ———. 20 Jan. 1791. 500 acres to heirs.
Wills, John. Va. Private. 24 Apr. 1783. 200 acres.
Wills, Nathaniel. Va. Private. 2 Nov. 1792. 200 acres.
Wills, Richard. Pa. Private. 10 Sep. 1789. 200 acres.
Wills, Thomas. Va. Captain. 6 Mar. 1801. 400 acres.
Wills, Thomas. Va. Captain. 5 Mar. 1801. 1000 acres.
Wills, Thomas. Va. Captain. 5 Mar. 1802. 2600 acres.
Willson, Barney. Md. Private. ———. 50 acres.
Willson, Benjamin. Md. ———. ———. 50 acres.
Willson, David. Md. Private. ———. 50 acres.
Willson, George. Md. Private. ———. 50 acres.
Willson, James. Md. Private. ———. 50 acres.
Willson, James. Md. Private. ———. 50 acres.
Willson, John. Md. Private. ———. 50 acres.
Willson, Robert. N. Y. Ensign. 9 Jul. 1790. 1200 acres.
Willson, Samuel. Md. Sergeant. ———. 50 acres.
Willson, Samuel. N. Y. Private. 6 Jul. 1790. 500 acres.
Willson, Thomas. N. Y. Private. 8 Jul. 1790. 500 acres.
Willson, William. Md. Private. ———. 50 acres.
Willson, William. Md. Private. ———. 50 acres.
Willson, William. Md. Private. ———. 50 acres.
Willson, William. Md. ———. ———. 50 acres.
Wilmeten, Jeffrey. Conn. Sufferer. Greenwich. 9.12.6.
Wilmington, John. Va. Sergeant. 1 Mar. 1784. 200 acres.
Wilmot, Daniel. Conn. Sufferer. New/East Haven. 42.16.3.
Wilmot, Francis. Conn. Sufferer. Greenwich. 6.0.0.
Wilmot, Robert. Md. Lieutenant. ———. 200 acres.
Wilmot, Samuel. Conn. Sufferer. New/East Haven. 62.16.2.
Wilmot, Thomas. Conn. Sufferer. New/East Haven. 2.14.0.
Wilmot, William. Md. Captain. ———. 200 acres.
Wilmoth, Francis. N. Y. Private. 6 Jul. 1790. 500 acres.
Wilmott, John. N. Y. Private. 8 Jul. 1790. 600 acres.
Wilmott, Robert. Va. Lieutenant. 13 Mar. 1822. 1333 1/3 acres.
Wilmott, Robert. Va. Lieutenant. 13 Mar. 1822. 1333 1/3 acres.
Wilrich, Jacob. Pa. ———. 4 Oct. 1803. 200 acres.
Wilrich, Jacob. Pa. Private. 4 Dec. 1805. 200 acres to William Whitman, assignee.
Wilse, Jacob. N. Y. Corporal. 9 Jul. 1790. 500 acres.
Wilsey, William. N. Y. Private. 8 Jul. 1790. 600 acres.
Wilshance, William. Pa. Private. 26 Sep.1787. 200 acres.
Wilson, Abner. Conn. Sufferer. Ridgefield. 9.0.0.
Wilson, Abraham. N. Y. Private. 7 Jul. 1790. 600 acres.
Wilson, Alfred. N.C. Private. 24 Dec. 1796. 228 acres.
Wilson, Alvin. Va. Midshipman. 25 Jan. 1838. 1779 acres.
Wilson, Alvin. Va. Midshipman. 25 Jan. 1838. 887 2/3 acres.
Wilson, Andrew. Ga. ———. 17 May 1784. ———.

Wilson, Bazil. S.C. ———. 5 Sep. 1791. 200 acres.
Wilson, Charles. Me. ———. 11 Jun. 1835. 200 acres to widow Achsah Jordan. Raymond.
Wilson, David. Ga. Minute Man. 17 May 1784. ———.
Wilson, David. Va. Corporal. 23 Jul. 1824. 400 acres.
Wilson, Edward. Va.-Ind. Private. 108 acres.
Wilson, Edward. Me. Private. 16 Jul. 1835. 200 acres. Cumberland.
Wilson, Francis. N.C. Private. 8 Dec. 1796. 640 acres to heirs.
Wilson, George. N.C. Private. 7 Jan. 1786. 640 acres to heirs.
Wilson, George. N.C. Corporal. 23 Mar. 1813. 1000 acres to heirs.
Wilson, George. Va. Lieutenant Colonel. 26 May 1831. 375 acres.
Wilson, George. Va. Lieutenant Colonel. 26 May 1831. 375 acres.
Wilson, George. Va. Lieutenant Colonel. 26 May 1831. 375 acres.
Wilson, George. Va. Lieutenant Colonel. 26 May 1831. 375 acres.
Wilson, George. Va. Lieutenant Colonel. 26 May 1831. 375 acres.
Wilson, George. Va. Lieutenant Colonel. 26 May 1831. 375 acres.
Wilson, George. Va. Lieutenant Colonel. ———. 375 acres.
Wilson, George. Va. Lieutenant Colonel. ———. 375 acres.
Wilson, George. Va. Lieutenant Colonel. 6 Nov. 1832. 187 1/2 acres.
Wilson, George. Va. Lieutenant Colonel. 6 Nov. 1832. 187 1/2 acres.
Wilson, George. Va. Lieutenant Colonel. 6 Nov. 1832. 187 1/2 acres.
Wilson, George. Va. Lieutenant Colonel. 6 Nov. 1832. 187 1/2 acres.
Wilson, George. Va. Lieutenant Colonel. 21 Mar. 1833. 750 acres.
Wilson, George. Va. Colonel. 17 Apr. 1834. 750 acres.
Wilson, George. Va. Colonel. 26 Jul. 1833. 250 acres.
Wilson, George. Va. Colonel. 26 Jul. 1833. 125 acres.
Wilson, George. Va. Colonel. 17 Jun. 1834. 187 1/2 acres.
Wilson, George. Va. Colonel. 17 Jun. 1834. 562 1/2 acres.
Wilson, Henry. S.C. ———. 3 Oct. 1791. 76 acres.
Wilson, Henry. S.C. ———. 7 Dec. 1789. 30 acres.
Wilson, Henry. S.C. ———. 7 Dec. 1789. 32 acres.
Wilson, Henry. S.C. ———. 7 Dec. 1789. 10 acres.
Wilson, Henry. S.C. ———. 1 Feb. 1790. 76 acres.
Wilson, Henry. S.C. ———. 3 Sep. 1789. 52 acres.
Wilson, Henry. Va. Private. 5 Aug. 1793. 100 acres.
Wilson, Hugh. Ga. Minute Man. 26 May 1784. 287 1/2 acres.
Wilson, Isaac. Va. Sergeant. 27 Jun. 1783. 100 acres.
Wilson, James. Ga. Refugee. 23 Apr. 1784. 287 1/2 acres.
Wilson, James. N. Y. Private. 8 Jul. 1790. 500 acres.
Wilson, James. Pa. Captain. 29 Aug. 1787. 500 acres.
Wilson, James. Pa. Private. 5 Apr. 1787. 200 acres.
Wilson, James. Pa. Sergeant. 19 Oct. 1786. 250 acres to Catherine Wilson, widow.
Wilson, James. S.C. Captain. 21 Jan. 1785. 300 acres to Capt. Henry Moore in trust for the heirs.
Wilson, James. Va. Private. 24 Jun. 1783. 100 acres.
Wilson, James. Va. Sergeant. 26 Mar. 1784. 200 acres.
Wilson, James. Va. Private. 31 Jan. 1786. 100 acres.
Wilson, John. Ga. Captain. 23 Apr. 1784. 287 1/2 acres.
Wilson, John. Ga. Lieutenant. 23 Apr. 1784. 460 acres.
Wilson, John. N.C. Private. 1 Sep. 1785. 640 acres to heirs.
Wilson, John. N.C. Private. 7 Dec. 1797. 640 acres to heirs.
Wilson, John. N.C. Private. 21 Jul. 1820. 640 acres.
Wilson, John. Pa. Private. 30 Oct. 1787. 200 acres.
Wilson, John. Va. Private. 16 Dec. 1783. 100 acres.

Wilson, John. Va. Lieutenant. 1 Oct. 1787. 2666 2/3 acres.
Wilson, John. Va. Midshipman. 8 Nov. 1834. 2666 2/3 acres.
Wilson, John. Va. Lieutenant. 22 Jul. 1835. 666 acres.
Wilson, John. Va. Lieutenant. 22 Jul. 1835. 300 acres.
Wilson, John. Va. Lieutenant. 17 Sep. 1836. 366 acres.
Wilson, John. Va. Lieutenant. 17 Sep. 1836. 666 acres.
Wilson, John. Va. Lieutenant. 4 Jan. 1856. 666 2/3 acres.
Wilson, John. Va. Lieutenant. 17 Sep. 1836. 666 acres.
Wilson, John. Conn. Sufferer. Fairfield. 5.4.0.
Wilson, John Maddox. Va. Private. 1 Jul. 1784. 100 acres.
Wilson, Joseph. Va. Midshipman. 17 Mar. 1835. 100 acres.
Wilson, Joseph. Va. Midshipman. 24 Jul. 1835. 2566 2/3 acres.
Wilson, Mahlon. Va. Private. 23 Jan. 1810. 200 acres.
Wilson, Nathaniel. Conn. Sufferer. Fairfield. 10.17.6.
Wilson, Peter. Va. Private. 12 Apr. 1784. 100 acres.
Wilson, Robert. Ga. Minute Man. 26 May 1784. 287 1/2 acres.
Wilson, Robert. N.C. Surgeon. 4 May 1818. 4800 acres to heirs.
Wilson, Robert. Pa. Private. 9 Jul. 1787. 200 acres.
Wilson, Robert. S.C. ———. 7 Sepl 1795. 102 1/2 acres to James Timms, administrator.
Wilson, Robert. S.C. ———. 7 Feb. 1791. 200 acres.
Wilson, Robert. S.C. ———. 6 Feb. 1797. 5 1/2 acres.
Wilson, Robert. S.C. ———. 6 Feb. 1797. 2 acres.
Wilson, Robert. S.C. ———. 6 Feb. 1797. 8 acres.
Wilson, Robert. S.C. ———. 6 Feb. 1797. 40 acres.
Wilson, Samuel. Ga. Minute Man. 26 May 1784. 287 1/2 acres.
Wilson, Samuel. N.C. Private. 9 Nov. 1784. 640 acres to heirs.
Wilson, Stacey. Va. Sergeant. 27 Jun. 1783. 400 acres.
Wilson, Thomas. Va.-Ind. Lieutenant. 2156 acres.
Wilson, Thomas. N. Y. ———. 3 Dec. 1806. 500 acres.
Wilson, Thomas. Pa. Sergeant. 4 Aug. 1787. 250 acres.
Wilson, Thomas. Va. Lieutenant. 29 Oct. 1791. 2666 2/3 acres.
Wilson, Thomas. Conn. Sufferer. New/East Haven. 50.18.10.
Wilson, Whitfield. N.C. Sergeant. 22 Dec. 1796. 1000 acres to heirs.
Wilson, Whitfield. Va. Private. 15 Dec. 1785. 200 acres.
Wilson, William. N.C. Private. 22 Dec. 1796. 274 acres.
Wilson, William. Pa. Captain. ———. 500 acres.
Wilson, William. Pa. Private. 28 Aug. 1787. 200 acres.
Wilson, William. S.C. ———. 2 Oct. 1786. 100 acres.
Wilson, Willis. N.C. ———. 10 Aug. 1785. 640 acres to heirs.
Wilson, Willis. Va. Lieutenant. 15 Aug. 1782. 2666 2/3 acres.
Wilson, Willis. Va. Captain. 1 Apr. 1784. 5333 1/3 acres.
Wilson, Willis. Va. Lieutenant. 13 Dec. 1808. 333 1/3 acres.
Wilson, Willis. Va. Captain. 15 Mar. 1834. 943 8/9 acres.
Wilson, Willis. Va. Captain. 6 Jul. 1840. 156 acres.
Wilson, Willis. Va. Captain. 6 Jul. 1840. 312 2/9 acres.
Wilsy, Isaac. N. Y. Private. 8 Jul. 1790. 600 acres.
Wiltsie, John. N.Y. ———. 20 Jan. 1791. 500 acres to heirs.
Wimber, Thomas. Md. Private. ———. 50 acres.
Wimberly, Moses. N.C. Private. 12 Dec. 1796. 640 acres to heirs.
Wimbish, John. Va. Sergeant. 23 Mar. 1784. 200 acres.
Wimbro, Ebern. Va. Seaman. 5 Jun. 1833. 100 acres.
Wimer, Caspar. N.C. Private. 30 Sep. 1785. 640 acres to heirs.
Wimpie, Thomas. N.C. Private. 30 Sep. 1785. 640 acres to heirs.

Wimyre, Frederick. N. Y. Private. 8 Jul. 1790. 600 acres.

Winans, Silas. N. Y. ———. 14 Aug. 1807. 450 acres.

Winbern, Henry. N.C. Private. 22 Oct. 1783. 389 acres.

Winborn, John. N.C. Lieutenant. 22 Oct. 1783. 2560 acres to William Winborn, heir.

Winborn, John. N.C. Private. 30 Sep. 1785. 640 acres to heirs.

Winbright, William. N.C. Private. 28 Nov. 1795. 640 acres to heirs.

Winchell, Jedediah. Mass. Private. 5 Feb. 1833. 200 acres.

Winchester, George. Md. Lieutenant. ———. 200 acres.

Winchester, George. Va. Lieutenant. 21 Apr. 1820. 2666 2/3 acres.

Winchester, James. Md. Captain. ———. 200 acres.

Winchester, John B. Mass. Corporal. 3 Jun. 1828. 200 acres.

Windell, Jonathan. Md. Private. ———. 50 acres.

Winder, Jesse. Va. Sergeant. 2 Sep. 1783. 200 acres.

Winder, Levin. Md. Lieutenant Colonel. ———. 200 acres.

Windham, George. Md. Private. ———. 50 acres.

Windom, Thomas. Md. Sergeant. ———. 50 acres.

Window, Henry. Va. Private. 15 Jun. 1807. 100 acres.

Windsor, John. N. Y. Private. 8 Jul. 1790. 600 acres.

Wine, James. N.C. Private. 19 Jan. 1786. 640 acres.

Winford, Henry. N. Y. Fifer. 8 Jul. 1790. 500 acres.

Winfree, Jacob. Va. Captain. 30 May 1838. 2000 acres.

Winfree, Jacob. Va. Captain. 30 May 1838. 666 2/3 acres.

Winfree, Jacob. Va. Captain. 30 May 1838. 888 2/3 acres.

Winfree, Jacob. Va. Captain. 30 May 1838. 444 1/3 acres.

Winfree, John. Va. Sergeant. 14 Oct. 1811. 200 acres.

Winfrey, Jacob. Ga Captain. 1784. 690 acres to heirs.

Wingall, Martin. Va. Private. 10 Mar. 1784. 100 acres.

Wingart, Adam. Pa. Private. ———. 200 acres.

Wingate, Andrew. Md. Private. ———. 50 acres.

Wingate, Elias. Va. Private. 20 Dec. 1803. 100 acres.

Wingate, Elias. Va. Sergeant. 31 Mar. 1814. 400 acres.

Wingfield, Jacob. N.C. Private. 30 Sep. 1785. 640 acres to heirs.

Wink, John. Pa. Private. ———. 200 acres to Richard Leedom, assignee.

Winkfield, James. Va. Private. 28 Oct. 1799. 100 acres.

Winkfield, John. Ga. ———. 22 Apr. 1784. 800 acres.

Winkfield, John, Jr. Ga. ———. 22 Apr. 1784. 800 acres.

Winkler, Frederick. Pa. Private. 1 Mar. 1804. 200 acres to Robert Frazier, assignee.

Winkler, Frederick. Pa. Private. 9 Oct. 1786. 200 acres.

Winkler, Joseph. Pa. Private. 30 Sep. 1787. 200 acres.

Winkles, Josiah. N.C. Private. 30 Sep. 1785. 640 acres to heirs.

Winlock, Joseph. Va. Lieutenant. 31 Mar. 1783. 1333 1/3 acres.

Winlock, Joseph. Va. Lieutenant. 31 Mar. 1783. 1333 1/3 acres.

Winlock, Joseph. Va. Lieutenant. 11 Mar. 1800. 444 1/2 acres.

Winn, Benjamin. Ga. Private. 10 Dec. 1784. 250 acres.

Winn, Elisha. Va. Corporal. 5 Dec. 1809. 200 acres.

Winn, Harrison. Va. Private. 18 Dec. 1786. 200 acres.

Winn, James. Va. Corporal. 5 Dec. 1809. 200 acres.

Winn, John. Ga. Private. 10 Dec. 1784. 250 acres.

Winn, John. Pa. Sergeant. 27 Sep. 1787. 250 acres.

Winn, Joseph. Ga. Refugee. 5 Jun. 1784. ———.

Winn, Minor. S.C. ———. 2 May 1785. 200 acres.

Winn, Peter. Ga. Refugee. 5 Nov. 1784. ———.

Winn, Peter. N.Y. ———. 18 Mar. 1791. 500 acres to heirs.
Winn, Robert. Ga. ———. 20 Apr. 1784. 287 1/2 acres.
Winn, Samuel. Me. Lieutenant. 2 May 1838. 600 acres to widow Louis Winn. Kennebunk.
Winn, Webster. Pa. Private. 24 Mar. 1789. 200 acres.
Winningham, Abner. Ga. ———. 15 Mar. 1784. 250 acres.
Winningham, James. Ga. ———. 17 May 1784. ———.
Winningham, John. Ga. ———. 28 Feb. 1784. 250 acres.
Winningham, Thomas. Ga. ———. 22 Apr. 1784. 287 1/2 acres.
Winnot, Obediah. N.C. Private. 23 Apr. 1784. 640 acres.
Winoak, John. N.C. Private. 30 Sep. 1785. 640 acres to heirs.
Winphrey, John. Va. Private. 29 Aug. 1783. 100 acres.
Winshett, Samuel. Ga. ———. 21 Apr. 1784. 287 1/2 acres.
Winslow, John. Me. ———. 18 Jul. 1837. 200 acres to widow Mary Winslow. Minot.
Winsor, Peter. Mass. ———. 9 May 1828. 200 acres.
Winstead, Frederick. N.C. Lieutenant. 9 Dec. 1797. 392 acres.
Winstell, Thomas. N.C. Private. 12 Sep. 1785. 640 acres to heirs.
Winstoff, Matthew. Pa. Private. 27 Nov. 1788. 200 acres.
Winston, John. Va. Captain. 5 Mar. 1783. 4000 acres.
Winston, Robert. Va. Private. 2 Oct. 1792. 100 acres.
Winston, William. Va. Lieutenant. 27 Aug. 1783. 2666 2/3 acres.
Winston, William Bobby. Va. Private. 11 Jul. 1835. 100 acres.
Winstore, Benjamin. Va. Ensign. 26 Apr. 1783. 2666 2/3 acres.
Winter, George. Va. Private. 26 May 1783. 100 acres.
Winters, Frederick. Ga. ———. 22 Apr. 1784. 287 1/2 acres.
Winters, Patrick. Ga. ———. 17 May 1784. ———.
Winters, Stephen. Va. Private. 23 Jun. 1783. 200 acres.
Winters, Thomas. N. Y. Sergeant. 9 Jul. 1790. 600 acres.
Winters, Thomas. N.C. Private. 3 Feb. 1785. 640 acres.
Winters, Timothy. Pa. Private. 9 Oct. 1786. 200 acres.
Wirtz, George. Pa. ———. ———. 200 acres to heirs.
Wiscot, Samuel. Me. Soldier. 23 Jul. 1835. 200 acres to widow Nancy Wiscot. Portland.
Wisdom, John. N.C. Private. 17 Dec. 1785. 640 acres to heirs.
Wise, Abram. N.C. Private. 25 Jun. 1785. 274 acres.
Wise, Allice. Conn. Sufferer. New/East Haven. 9.6.0.
Wise, Edward. Va. Private. 14 Feb. 1834. 100 acres.
Wise, James. Ga. Private. Sep. 1785. 250 acres.
Wise, John. N.C. Private. 29 Sep. 1784. 274 acres.
Wise, John. N.C. Corporal. 24 Nov. 1797. 357 acres.
Wise, John. Pa. Private. 25 Jun. 1804. 200 acres.
Wise, John. Conn. Sufferer. New/East Haven. 31.15.0.
Wise, Joseph. Ga. 30 Jul. 1784. 287 1/2 acres.
Wise, Peter. Ga. Soldier. 5 Sep. 1785. ———.
Wise, Samuel. S.C. Major. 21 Jan. 1785. 400 acres.
Wise, Samuel. Va. Private. 13 Feb. 1784. 100 acres.
Wise, Sheridy. Ga. ———. ———. 287 1/2 acres.
Wise, William. Ga. Refugee. ———. 500 acres.
Wise, William. N. Y. Fifer. 9 Jul. 1790. 600 acres.
Wisemore, Abraham. Pa. Private. 28 Aug. 1787. 200 acres.
Wisener, John. Ga. Minute Man. 15 Apr. 1784. 287 1/2 acres.
Wiser, Michael. Md. Private. ———. 50 acres.
Wiser, Solomon. Pa. Private. ———. 200 acres.
Wisfenbagh, Henry. N. Y. Private. 8 Jul. 1790. 500 acres.

Wishart, Thomas. Va. Lieutenant. 28 Sep. 1810. 2666 2/3 acres.

Wishart, William. N.C. Private. 13 Jan. 1792. 640 acres to heirs.

Wistner, Samuel. N.C. Private. 3 Dec. 1796. 640 acres.

Witham, Caleb. Me. Private. 6 Jul. 1835. 200 acres to widow Lucretia Witham. Woolwich.

Witham, James. Me. Seaman. 9 Sep. 1835. 200 acres to widow Olive Witham. Kittery.

Withan, William. N.Y. ———. 20 Jan. 1791. 500 acres to heirs.

Withee, Uzziel. Me. ———. 30 Apr. 1835. 200 acres. Hartland.

Witherford, William. Va. Private. 12 Mar. 1840. 100 acres.

Witherham, John. Pa. Private. 12 Jan. 1787. 200 acres.

Witherington, Jesse. N.C. Private. 30 Sep. 1785. 640 acres to heirs.

Withers, James. Va. Lieutenant. 11 Apr. 1833. 2666 2/3 acres.

Withers, John. S.C. ———. 2 Mar. 1789. 200 acres.

Withers, William. Va. Lieutenant. 28 Nov. 1822. 2666 2/3 acres.

Withington, Peter. Pa. Captain. 29 Jun. 1789. 500 acres.

Withington, Robert. Me. ———. 30 Apr. 1835. 200 acres to widow Abigail Withington. Monument.

Witman, William. Pa. ———. 7 Feb. 1806. 200 acres.

Witman, William, Jr. Pa. ———. 9 Mar. 1807. 200 acres.

Witon [Whiting], Elijah. N.Y. Sergeant. 9 Jul. 1790. 600 acres.

Witt, Jesse. Va. Private. 19 Dec. 1807. 100 acres.

Witt, Robert. Va.-Ind. Private. 108 acres.

Wittington, Burrell. S.C. ———. 2 Jun. 1788. 200 acres.

Witty, John. N.C. Private. 21 Oct. 1783. 366 acres.

Witzell, Michael. N. Y. Lieutenant. 9 Jul. 1790. 1000 acres.

Woelpfer, John D. Pa. Captain. 2 Nov. 1786. 500 acres.

Wofler, John. Va. Private. 18 Dec. 1783. 100 acres.

Wolcott, Simon. Conn. Sufferer. New London. 1,083.9.1.

Wolf, Andrew. Va. Private. 5 Feb. 1785. 200 acres.

Wolf, Christopher. N.C. Private. 26 Aug. 1785. 640 acres to heirs.

Wolf, George. Va. Private. 19 Feb. 1784. 100 acres.

Wolf, John. Pa. Private. 17 Oct. 1786. 200 acres.

Wolfe, Anthony. Conn. Sufferer. New London. 4.14.0.

Wolfe, Lucretia. Conn. Sufferer. New London. 4.16.0.

Wolfenberger, Philip. Va. Private. 25 Dec. 1784. 200 acres.

Wolfgang, David. Pa. Private. 31 Jul. 1787. 200 acres.

Wollard, John. Va. Private. 9 Feb. 1784. 100 acres.

Womack, Ephraim. Va. Corporal. 16 Jan. 1784. 200 acres.

Womack, Jesse. Ga. ———. ———. 287 1/2 acres.

Womack, John. Ga. Soldier. 6 May 1785. ———.

Womack, Richard. Ga. Soldier. 19 Dec. 1785. 230 acres to heirs.

Womack, William. N.C. Quartermaster. 1 Aug. 1821. 1000 acres.

Womble, Demsey. N.C. Private. 24 Oct. 1783. 640 acres.

Womble, John. N.C. Private. Aug. 1787. 640 acres.

Womwell, Benjamin. N.C. Private. 27 Jul. 1785. 228 acres.

Woneycutt, Edward. Va. Lieutenant. 15 Apr. 1833. 4000 acres.

Woneycutt, Edward. Va. Lieutenant. 28 Jun. 1834. 1000 acres.

Woneycutt, Edward. Va. Lieutenant. 28 Jun. 1834. 3000 acres.

Wonks, John. N.C. Private. 16 Apr. 1821. 640 acres.

Wood, Abigail. Conn. Sufferer. Danbury. 18.7.4.

Wood, Abraham. Ga. ———. 2 May 1785. 287 1/2 acres.

Wood, Allen. Va. Pilot. 10 Apr. 1838. 1111 acres.

Wood, Allen. Va. Pilot. 10 Apr. 1838. 666 2/3 acres.

Wood, Allen. Va. Pilot. 10 Apr. 1838. 889 acres.

Wood, Archibald. N.C. Private. 21 Aug. 1795. 228 acres.

Wood, Benjamin. S.C. Soldier. 2 May 1785. 200 acres.
Wood, Benjamin. Va. Private. 14 Mar. 1789. 200 acres.
Wood, Benjamin. Conn. Sufferer. Danbury. 1.5.4.
Wood, Charles. N.C. Corporal. 20 Oct. 1783. 1000 acres.
Wood, Charles. N.C. Private. 6 Dec. 1783. 274 acres.
Wood, Christopher. Ga. ———. ———. 287 1/2 acres.
Wood, Christopher, Jr. Ga. ———. 2 May 1785. 287 1/2 acres.
Wood, Daniel. N. Y. Captain. 9 Jul. 1790. 1800 acres.
Wood, David. Conn. Sufferer. Danbury. 288.14.0.
Wood, Ebenezer. N. Y. Private. 13 Sep. 1790. 600 acres.
Wood, Edward. Ga. Captain. 20 Dec. 1783. 600 acres.
Wood, Edward. Va. Private. 12 Apr. 1783. 200 acres.
Wood, Edward. Va. Private. 3 Dec. 1785. 100 acres.
Wood, Elijah. Conn. Sufferer. Danbury. 2.7.0.
Wood, Erastarcus, Jr. Ga. ———. ———. ———.
Wood, Francis. S.C. ———. 5 Feb. 1787. 250 acres.
Wood, Gerrard. Md. Surgeon's Mate. ———. 200 acres.
Wood, Hannah. Conn. Sufferer. Danbury. 4.11.4.
Wood, Henry. Ga. Refugee. 20 Feb. 1784. 250 acres.
Wood, Hezekiah. Ga. ———. 19 Apr. 1784. 700 acres.
Wood, Holland. Mass. Private. 18 Oct. 1833. 200 acres.
Wood, Isaiah. N.C. Private. 30 Sep. 1785. 640 acres.
Wood, Isham. N.C. Private. 25 Jun. 1785. 274 acres.
Wood, Israel. Conn. Sufferer. Greenwich. 182.0.11.
Wood, James. Ga. Captain. 16 Mar. 1784. 400 acres.
Wood, James. Ga. Lieutenant. 25 May 1784. 460 acres.
Wood, James. Ga. Corporal. 29 Jan. 1784. 200 acres.
Wood, James. Va.-Ind. Private. 108 acres.
Wood, James. Md. Private. ———. 50 acres.
Wood, James. Md. Sergeant. ———. 50 acres.
Wood, James. N. Y. Private. 7 Jul. 1790. 600 acres.
Wood, James. Va. Colonel. 7 Apr. 1783. 1000 acres.
Wood, James. Va. Colonel. 7 Apr. 1783. 1000 acres.
Wood, James. Va. Colonel. 7 Apr. 1783. 4666 2/3 acres.
Wood, James. Va. Colonel. 22 Aug. 1783. 200 acres.
Wood, James. Va. Pilot. 18 Mar. 1840. 1666 2/3 acres.
Wood, James. Va. Pilot. 19 Jun. 1841. 200 acres.
Wood, James. Va. Pilot. 19 Jul. 1841. 100 acres.
Wood, James. Va. Pilot. 18 Jun. 1853. 700 acres.
Wood, James. Va. Pilot. 24 Jul. 1841. 100 acres.
Wood, James, Jr. Ga. ———. 17 Sep. 1784. 287 1/2 acres.
Wood, Jesse. N.Y. ———. 20 Jan. 1791. 500 acres to heirs.
Wood, Jesse. Va. Private. 26 Sep. 1783. 100 acres.
Wood, John. Ga. Paymaster with rank of Captain. 26 Oct. 1784. 690 acres.
Wood, John. Ga. Minute Man. 1784. 287 1/2 acres.
Wood, John. N. Y. Captain. 16 Jan. 1795. 2000 acres.
Wood, John. N.C. Private. 10 Nov. 1783. 360 acres.
Wood, John. N.C. Sergeant. 10 Aug. 1785. 1000 acres.
Wood, John. Va. Sergeant. 12 Dec. 1783. 200 acres.
Wood, John. Va. Private. 6 Mar. 1784. 100 acres.
Wood, John. Va. Private. 30 Jun. 1784. 100 acres.
Wood, John. Va. Private. 2 Nov. 1787. 100 acres.
Wood, John. Conn. Sufferer. Danbury. 262.15.11.
Wood, John L. Va. Private. 3 Nov. 1783. 100 acres.

Wood, Jonathan. Ga. ———. 21 Apr. 1784. 287 1/2 acres.
Wood, Jonathan. Ga. ———. 20 Feb. 1784. 250 acres.
Wood, Joseph. Ga. Acting Paymaster. 1 Jul. 1784. ———.
Wood, Joseph. N.C. Private. 22 Apr. 1785. 640 acres to heirs.
Wood, Joseph. Va. Private. 23 Jun. 1783. 200 acres.
Wood, Joshua. Ga. Refugee. 17 May 1784. 287 1/2 acres.
Wood, Josiah. Me. ———. 16 May 1835. 200 acres. Porter.
Wood, Matthew. N.C. Captain. 20 Apr. 1784. 1622 acres.
Wood, Nathan. Ga. ———. 17 May 1784. ———.
Wood, Nathaniel. Ga. ———. 22 Apr. 1784. 287 1/2 acres.
Wood, Nathaniel. N.C. Private. 30 Sep. 1785. 640 acres to heirs.
Wood, Nicholas. Va. Private. 22 Aug. 1783. 200 acres.
Wood, Philip. Va. Private. 28 Apr. 1783. 200 acres.
Wood, Preserve. Conn. Sufferer. Danbury. 3.9.4
Wood, Robert. Va. Private. 26 Apr. 1783. 200 acres.
Wood, Robertson. Md. Private. ———. 50 acres.
Wood, Samuel. N. Y. Private. 13 Sep. 1790. 600 acres.
Wood, Samuel. Pa. Private. 23 Oct. 1942. 200 acres.
Wood, Samuel. Pa. ———. 2 Oct. 1786. 200 acres.
Wood, Samuel. Va. Private. 26 Mar. 1819. 200 acres.
Wood, Samuel. Conn. Sufferer. Danbury. 1.5.4.
Wood, Solomon. N.C. Private. 26 Aug. 1785. 640 acres to heirs.
Wood, Thomas. Md. Private. ———. 50 acres.
Wood, Thomas. Md. Private. ———. 50 acres.
Wood, Thomas. Md. Private. ———. 50 acres.
Wood, Thomas. N.C. Private. 30 Sep. 1785. 640 acres to heirs.
Wood, Thomas. Va. Sergeant Major. 23 Jun. 1783. 400 acres.
Wood, Timothy. Va. Private. 22 Jan. 1812. 200 acres.
Wood, Titus. N.C. Private. 12 Sep. 1785. 640 acres to heirs.
Wood, William. S.C. Soldier. 21 Jan. 1785. 200 acres.
Wood, William. S.C. ———. 2 Oct. 1785. 200 acres.
Wood, William. Va. Pilot. 22 Mar. 1837. 1333 1/3 acres.
Wood, William. Va. Corporal. 22 Aug. 1783. 400 acres.
Wood, William. Va. Private. 7 Apr. 1787. 100 acres.
Wood, William. Va. Pilot. 24 Feb. 18—. 444 1/3 acres.
Wood, William. Va. Pilot. 24 Feb. 18—. 444 1/3 acres.
Wood, William. Va. Pilot. 24 Feb. 18—. 444 1/3 acres.
Woodard, Bennet. N.C. Private. 22 Dec. 1796. 640 acres to heirs.
Woodbridge, Christopher. Me. Captain. 8 Aug. 1838. 600 acres to widow Sarah Woodbridge. Hallowell.
Woodbridge, Christopher. Conn. Sufferer. Groton. 1.3.0.
Woodbury, Benjamin. Mass. Private. 26 Sep. 1833. 200 acres.
Woodbury, Israel. Mass. ———. 22 Jul. 1833. 200 acres.
Woodcock, John. Va. Private. 18 Apr. 1783. 100 acres.
Woodcock, Peter. N. Y. Private. 7 Jul. 1790. 600 acres.
Woodford, William. Va. Brigadier General. 15 Aug. 1783. 10,000 acres.
Woodford, William. Va. Brigadier General. 18 Mar. 1834. 1750 acres.
Woodford, William. Va. Brigadier General. 27 Mar. 1840. 666 1/2 acres.
Woodford, William. Va. Brigadier General. 27 Mar. 1840. 1333 acres.
Woodland, Rhody. Md. Private. ———. 50 acres.
Woodley, Thomas. N.C. Private. 12 Dec. 1785. 640 acres to heirs.
Woodliff, George. N.C. Private. 20 Sep. 1784. 640 acres to heirs.
Woodliff, Thomas. N.C. Private. 7 Dec. 1797. 640 acres to heirs.
Woodman, Edward. N.C. Private. 26 May 1784. 228 acres.

Woodman, John. Va. Private. 23 Jun. 1783. 200 acres.

Woodmore, Cornelius. N. Y. Private. 6 Jul. 1790. 600 acres.

Woodroff, Hardin. Va. Private. 25 Jan. 1813. 100 acres.

Woodrough, John. N.C. Private. 28 Sep. 1785. 640 acres to heirs.

Woodruff, Ephraim. N. Y. Lieutenant. 9 Jul. 1790. 1200 acres.

Woodruff, Hunlock. New York. Surgeon. 9 Jul. 1790. 1900 acres.

Woodruff, Joseph. Ga. Major. 13 Apr. 1784. 690 acres.

Woodruff, Samuel. N.Y. Surgeon's Mate. 14 Jun. 1793. 1500 acres.

Woodrum, Stephen. Va. Private. 20 Feb. 1797. 200 acres.

Woods, Alexander. Va. Private. 22 Mar. 1786. 233 2/3 acres.

Woods, Cornelius. Pa. Private. 3 Nov. 1786. 200 acres.

Woods, David. Md. ———. ———. 50 acres.

Woods, Demsy. Ga. ———. 21 Apr. 1784. 200 acres.

Woods, Hugh. Ga. Minute Man. 30 Apr. 1785. 575 acres.

Woods, James. Va. Colonel. 9 Jun. 1785. 1111 acres.

Woods, Joshua. Ga. Minute Man. 1784. 287 1/2 acres.

Woods, Middleton. Ga. ———. 17 May 1784. ———.

Woods, Richard. Ga. Refugee. 19 Apr. 1784. 287 1/2 acres.

Woods, Samuel. Pa. Sergeant. ———. 250 acres.

Woods, William. Ga. ———. 25 May 1784. 250 acres.

Woods, William. Va. Private. 23 Jun. 1783. 200 acres.

Woodson, Absalom. Va. Private. 3 Feb. 1784. 100 acres.

Woodson, Charles. Va. Sergeant Major. 15 Feb. 1834. 200 acres.

Woodson, Frederick. Va. Captain. 29 Apr. 1783. 4000 acres.

Woodson, Hughes. Va. Captain. 11 Sep. 1783. 4000 acres.

Woodson, Joseph. Va. Captain. 5 May 1809. 100 acres.

Woodson, Joseph. Va. Captain. 5 May 1809. 100 acres.

Woodson, Joseph. Va. Captain. 5 May 1809. 100 acres.

Woodson, Joseph. Va. Captain. 5 May 1809. 100 acres.

Woodson, Joseph. Va. Captain. 5 May 1809. 100 acres.

Woodson, Joseph. Va. Captain. 5 May 1809. 100 acres.

Woodson, Joseph. Va. Captain. 5 May 1809. 100 acres.

Woodson, Joseph. Va. Captain. 5 May 1809. 100 acres.

Woodson, Joseph. Va. Captain. 5 May 1809. 100 acres.

Woodson, Joseph. Va. Captain. 5 May 1809. 100 acres.

Woodson, Joseph. Va. Captain. 5 May 1809. 100 acres.

Woodson, Joseph. Va. Captain. 5 May 1809. 100 acres.

Woodson, Joseph. Va. Captain. 5 May 1809. 100 acres.

Woodson, Joseph. Va. Captain. 5 May 1809. 100 acres.

Woodson, Joseph. Va. Captain. 5 May 1809. 100 acres.

Woodson, Joseph. Va. Captain. 5 May 1809. 100 acres.

Woodson, Joseph. Va. Captain. 5 May 1809. 100 acres.

Woodson, Joseph. Va. Captain. 5 May 1809. 100 acres.

Woodson, Joseph. Va. Captain. 5 May 1809. 100 acres.

Woodson, Joseph. Va. Captain. 5 May 1809. 150 acres.

Woodson, Joseph. Va. Captain. 5 May 1809. 150 acres.

Woodson, Joseph. Va. Captain. 5 May 1809. 150 acres.

Woodson, Joseph. Va. Captain. 5 May 1809. 150 acres.

Woodson, Joseph. Va. Captain. 5 May 1809. 150 acres.

Woodson, Joseph. Va. Captain. 5 May 1809. 150 acres.

Woodson, Joseph. Va. Captain. 5 May 1809. 125 acres.

Woodson, Joseph. Va. Captain. 5 May 1809. 125 acres.

Woodson, Joseph. Va. Captain. 5 May 1809. 125 acres.

Woodson, Joseph. Va. Captain. 5 May 1809. 125 acres.
Woodson, Joseph. Va. Captain. 5 May 1809. 125 acres.
Woodson, Joseph. Va. Captain. 5 May 1809. 75 acres.
Woodson, Joseph. Va. Captain. 5 May 1809. 97 acres.
Woodson, Joseph. Va. Captain. 5 May 1809. 97 acres.
Woodson, Joseph. Va. Captain. 5 May 1809. 50 acres.
Woodson, Joseph. Va. Captain. 5 May 1809. 50 acres.
Woodson, Joseph. Va. Captain. 5 May 1809. 50 acres.
Woodson, Joseph. Va. Captain. 5 May 1809. 50 acres.
Woodson, Joseph. Va. Captain. 5 May 1809. 50 acres.
Woodson, Obediah. Va. Lieutenant. 24 Jul. 1824. 222acres.
Woodson, Obediah. Va. Lieutenant. 24 Jul. 1824. 222 acres.
Woodson, Obediah. Va. Lieutenant. 24 Jul. 1824. 222 acres.
Woodson, Obediah. Va. Lieutenant. 24 Jul. 1824. 222 acres.
Woodson, Obediah. Va. Lieutenant. 24 Jul. 1824. 222 acres.
Woodson, Obediah. Va. Lieutenant. 24 Jul. 1824. 222 acres.
Woodson, Obediah. Va. Lieutenant. 17 Dec. 1838. 222 acres.
Woodson, Obediah. Va. Lieutenant. 24 Jul. 1824. 222 acres.
Woodson, Obediah. Va. Lieutenant. 24 Jul. 1824. 222 acres.
Woodson, Obediah. Va. Lieutenant. 24 Jul. 1824. 222 acres.
Woodson, Obediah. Va. Lieutenant. 24 Jul. 1824. 222 acres.
Woodson, Obediah. Va. Lieutenant. 24 Jul. 1824. 222 acres.
Woodson, Obediah. Va. Lieutenant. 24 Jul. 1824. 222 acres.
Woodson, Robert. Va. Captain. 15 Mar. 1783. 4000 acres.
Woodson, Robert. Va. Captain. 15 Mar. 1783. 666 2/3 acres.
Woodson, Robert. Va. Captain. 8 Jan. 1809. 277 1/2 acres.
Woodson, Robert. Va. Captain. 8 Jan. 1809. 277 1/2 acres.
Woodson, Samuel. Va. Captain. 18 Dec. 1893. 500 2/3 acres.
Woodson, Samuel. Va. Captain. 18 Dec. 1893. 166 1/2 acres.
Woodson, Samuel. Va. Captain. 18 Dec. 1839. 166 1/2 acres.
Woodson, Samuel. Va. Captain. 18 Dec. 1839. 55 1/2 acres.
Woodson, Samuel. Va. ———. 14 Oct. 1852. 166 2/3 acres.
Woodson, Samuel. Va. ———. 14 Oct. 1852. 111 acres.
Woodson, Samuel. Va. ———. 14 Oct. 1852. 166 2/3 acres.
Woodson, Samuel. Va. Captain. 29 Dec. 1852. 250 acres.
Woodson, Samuel. Va. Captain. 29 Dec. 1852. 250 acres.
Woodson, Samuel. Va. Captain. 29 Dec. 1852. 166 2/3 acres.
Woodson, Samuel. Va. Captain. 25 Apr. 1853. 166 1/2 acres.
Woodson, Samuel. Va. Captain. 25 Apr. 1853. 55 1/2 acres.
Woodson, Samuel. Va. Captain. 31 May 1853. 500 acres.
Woodson, Samuel. Va. Captain. 31 May 1853. 166 2/3 acres.
Woodson, Samuel. Va. Captain. 31 May 1853. 166 2/3 acres.
Woodson, Samuel. Va. Captain. 31 May 1853. 55 1/2 acres.
Woodson, Samuel. Va. Captain. 2 Oct. 1860. 222 acres.
Woodson, Samuel. Va. Captain. 9 Aug. 1867. 666 2/3 acres.
Woodson, Samuel. Va. Captain. 22 Oct. 1852. 166 2/3 acres.
Woodson, Samuel. Va. Captain. 22 Oct. 1852. 166 2/3 acres.
Woodson, Samuel. Va. Captain. 13 Jan. 1853. 55 1/2 acres.
Woodson, Tarlton. Va. Major. 28 Oct. 1783. 5333 1/3 acres.
Woodson, Tarlton. Va. Major. 29 Dec. 1808. 1777 2/3 acres.
Woodson, William. Va. Lieutenant. 24 Jul. 1824 2666 2/3 acres.
Woodsworth, Thomas. Ga. ———. 25 May 1784. 287 1/2 acres.
Woodward, Caleb. N.C. Private. 4 Sep. 1820. 640 acres to heirs.
Woodward, Charles. Va. Private. 1 Apr 1783. 100 acres.

Woodward, David. N.C. Private. 15 Feb. 1797. 274 acres.
Woodward, George. N.C. Private. 30 Sep. 1785. 640 acres.
Woodward, James. Me. ———. 30 Apr. 1835. 200 acres to widow Ruth Woodward. Bowdoinham.
Woodward, John. N.C. Private. 4 Sep. 1820. 640 acres to heirs.
Woodward, John. Conn. Sufferer. New/East Haven. 838.17.3.
Woodward, John, Jr. Conn. Sufferer. New/East Haven. 740.19.11.
Woodward, Micajah. N.C. Private. 17 Dec. 1785. 640 acres to heirs.
Woodward, Peter. N. Y. Lieutenant. 9 Jul. 1790. 1200 acres.
Woodworth, Asa. Mass. Private. 6 Jul. 1832. 200 acres to heirs.
Woolard, Benjamin. N.C. Private. 28 Sep. 1785. 640 acres to heirs.
Wooldridge, Daniel. Va. Private. 18 Aug. 1797. 100 acres.
Wooldridge, Joseph. Va. Private. 26 Nov. 1791. 100 acres.
Woolfolk, Francis. Va. Sergeant. 27 Aug. 1783. 200 acres.
Woolfolk, William. Va. Sergeant. 29 Jan. 1784. 200 acres.
Woolfolk, William. Va. Cornet. 13 Nov. 1821. 1266 2/3 acres.
Woolfolk, William. Va. Cornet. 13 Nov. 1821. 600 acres.
Woolfolk, William. Va. Cornet. 13 Nov. 1821. 600 acres.
Woolford, Michael. Md. Private. ———. 50 acres.
Woolford, Solomon. Va. Private. 13 Mar. 1797. 100 acres.
Woolford, Thomas. Md. Colonel. ———. 200 acres.
Woolford, Thomas. Md. Colonel. ———. 200 acres.
Woolford, Thomas. Md. Private. ———. 50 acres.
Woolford, William. Md. Lieutenant. ———. 200 acres.
Woollard, Jesse. N.C. Private. 2 Aug. 1784. 228 acres.
Woolward, James. N.C. Private. 12 Sep. 1785. 640 acres to heirs.
Woosley, Aaron. Va. Private. 2 Mar. 1784. 200 acres.
Woosley, Moses. Va. Private. 7 Feb. 1784. 100 acres.
Woosley, Thomas. Va. Private. 2 Mar. 1784. 200 acres.
Wooster, Thomas. Conn. Sufferer. New/East Haven. 590.15.1.
Wooten, Christopher. N.C. Private. 7 Dec. 1783. 640 acres to Nathaniel Wooten, heir.
Wooten, Jesse. N.C. Private. 6 Feb. 1823. 640 acres.
Wooten, Thomas. N.C. Private. 12 Sep. 1785. 640 acres to heirs.
Wooton, Benjamin. Ga. ———. 17 May 1784. ———.
Wooton, James. Ga. ———. 21 Apr. 1784. 287 1/2 acres.
Wooton, James, Jr. Ga. ———. 21 Apr. 1784. 287 1/2 acres.
Wooton, Nathan. Ga. ———. 21 Apr. 1784. 287 1/2 acres.
Wooton, Richard B. Ga. ———. 17 May 1784. ———.
Wooton, Thomas. Ga. Lieutenant. 15 Mar. 1784. 240 acres.
Wooton, William. N.C. Private. 4 Sep. 1820. 640 acres to heirs.
Wootten, Thomas. Ga. ———. 15 Mar. 1784. 250 acres.
Wootten, Thomas. Va. Private. 23 Jan. 1784. 200 acres.
Work, William. Pa. Private. 8 Sep. 1787. 200 acres.
Worke, George. Pa. Private. ———. 200 acres.
Worley, James. N.C. Sergeant. 18 Dec. 1793. 1000 acres.
Worley, John. Pa. Private. 9 Nov. 1786. 200 acres to James Doran, assignee.
Worley, Mathew. Va. Private. 22 Mar. 1827. 200 acres.
Wornock, Jesse. Ga. ———. 22 Apr. 1784. 287 1/2 acres.
Wornock, Robert. Ga. ———. 17 May 1784. ———.
Worrell, George. Pa. Private. 13 May 1805. 200 acres.
Worrell, George. Pa. Private. 15 May 1805. 200 acres.
Worrell, Thomas. Pa. ———. 2 May 1785. 200 acres to Richard Leedom, assignee.
Worseley, John. N.C. Private. 11 Jul. 1785. 640 acres to heirs.

Worsham, Daniel. Va. Private. 7 May 1814. 200 acres.

Worsham, John. Va. Lieutenant. 27 Feb. 1784. 2666 2/3 acres.

Worsham, Joshua. Va. Private. 6 Dec. 1798. 200 acres.

Worsham, Richard. Va. Lieutenant. 18 Mar. 1783. 1000 acres.

Worsham, Richard. Va. Lieutenant. 18 Mar. 1783. 1666 2/3 acres.

Worsham, Richard. Va. Lieutenant. 19 Aug. 1820. 350 acres.

Worsham, Richard. Va. Lieutenant. 19 Aug. 1820. 353 1/2 acres.

Worsham, William. Va. Lieutenant. 23 Nov. 1784. 2666 2/3 acres.

Worsley, Bryan. N.C. Private. 29 Sep. 1784. 640 acres.

Worsley, Bryan. N.C. Private. 13 Nov. 1795. 365 acres to heirs.

Worsley, John. N.C. Private. 4 May 1785. 640 acres to heirs.

Worster, Thomas. Me. Private. 20 Nov. 1835. 200 acres to widow Susan Worster. Sanford.

Worth, William. Va. Sailor. 5 Jun. 1783. 100 acres.

Worthingon, Edward J. Va. ———. 21 Feb. 1834. 666 2/3 acres.

Worthington, Edward. Va.-Ind. Captain. 3234 acres.

Worthington, Edward. Va. Captain. 21 Jan. 1834. 666 2/3 acres.

Worthington, Edward. Va. Captain. 22 Aug. 1834. 666 2/3 acres.

Worthington, Edward. Va. Captain. 1 Nov. 1853. 666 2/3 acres.

Worthington, Edward. Va. ———. 27 Aug. 1835. 500 acres.

Worthington, Edward. Va. ———. 27 Aug. 1835. 666 1/3 acres.

Worthington, Edward. Va. ———. 27 Aug. 1835. 666 2/3 acres.

Wotton, William. N.C. Sergeant. 13 Sep. 1820. 1000 acres.

Wray, George. Va. Midshipman. 1 Mar. 1851. 100 acres.

Wren, Alexander. Va. Private. 21 Nov. 1783. 100 acres.

Wren, Joseph. Pa. Private. ———. 200 acres.

Wren, Nathan. Va. Ensign. 8 Nov. 1832. 2666 2/3 acres.

Wren, Robert. Va. Private. 27 Jan. 1786. 100 acres.

Wren, Travis. Va. Private. 24 Jul. 1784. 100 acres.

Wren, William. N.C. Private. 22 Dec. 1796. 274 acres.

Wren, William. N.C. Corporal. 14 Jul. 1820. 726 acres to heirs.

Wright, Abednego. Ga. Refugee. 17 Apr. 1784. 287 1/2 acres.

Wright, Abel. Va. Private. 15 Jun. 1807. 100 acres.

Wright, Abram. N.C. Sergeant. 31 Aug. 1795. 640 acres to heirs.

Wright, Absolom. Md. Private. ———. 50 acres.

Wright, Adam. N.C. Fifer. 14 May 1784. 1000 acres.

Wright, Arthur. Ga. ———. 17 May 1784. ———.

Wright, Barruck. N. Y. Private. 6 Jul. 1790. 600 acres.

Wright, Benjamin. N. Y. Private. 8 Jul. 1790. 600 acres.

Wright, Charles. Pa. Corporal. 3 Jan. 1787. 200 acres.

Wright, Cyprian. Mass. ———. 28 Feb. 1829. 200 acres to his children Jonathan Wright and Ara Wright.

Wright, David. N.C. Lieutenant. 15 Sep. 1820. 1036 acres to heirs.

Wright, Edmund. N.C. Private. 22 Apr. 1785. 228 acres.

Wright, Edward. Md. Private. ———. 50 acres.

Wright, Edward. N. Y. Private. 8 Jul. 1790. 600 acres.

Wright, Ezekiel. Ga. Soldier. 5 Jun. 1785. 230 acres.

Wright, George. Va. Private. 22 Aug. 1812. 200 acres.

Wright, Habakuk. Ga. Refugee. 17 Apr. 1784. 287 1/2 acres.

Wright, Henderson. Pa. Private. 2 Oct. 1786. 200 acres.

Wright, Henry. Ga. ———. 17 May 1784. ———.

Wright, Henry. Mass. ———. 22 Jul. 1833. 200 acres.

Wright, Isaiah. Ga. ———. 17 Apr. 1784. 287 1/2 acres.

Wright, Jacob. N. Y. Captain. 9 Jul. 1790. 1200 acres.

Wright, James. Ga. ———. 17 Apr. 1784. 287 1/2 acres.
Wright, James. N.C. Private. 17 Dec. 1785. 640 acres to heirs.
Wright, James. Va. Captain. 9 Mar. 1784. 4666 2/3 acres.
Wright, James. Va. Private. 5 Apr. 1784. 100 acres.
Wright, James. Va. Private. 14 Apr. 1803. 100 acres.
Wright, James. Va. Private. 22 Apr. 1820. 100 acres.
Wright, Jarrott. Va. Corporal. 20 Aug. 1787. 200 acres.
Wright, Jesse. Md. Private. ———. 50 acres.
Wright, John. Ga. ———. 17 Apr. 1784. 287 1/2 acres.
Wright, John. Md. Private. ———. 50 acres.
Wright, John. N. Y. Private. 8 Jul. 1790. 600 acres.
Wright, John. N.C. Private. 26 Aug. 1785. 640 acres to heirs.
Wright, John. Va. Private. 9 Dec. 1783. 100 acres.
Wright, John. Va. Sergeant. 19 Apr. 1806. 400 acres.
Wright, John. Va. Private. 8 Jul. 1808. 200 acres.
Wright, John. Va. Private. 21 Aug. 1809. 100 acres.
Wright, Joseph. Me. ———. 1835. 200 acres. Raymond.
Wright, Joseph Allen. Conn. Sufferer. Norwalk. 95.18.8.
Wright, Jotham. N. Y. Lieutenant. 13 Sep. 1790. 1200 acres.
Wright, Meshack. Ga. ———. 17 May 1784. ———.
Wright, Moses. Va. Private. 16 Apr. 1784. 100 acres.
Wright, Nathan. Md. Lieutenant. ———. 200 acres.
Wright, Owen. Ga. ———. 2 Jan. 1786. ———.
Wright, Patrick. Va. Captain. 9 Dec. 1782. 4000 acres.
Wright, Patrick. Va. Captain. 23 May 1835. 4000 acres.
Wright, Paul. Va. Private. 7 Feb. 1784. 100 acres.
Wright, Peter. N.C. Private. 12 Sep. 1785. 640 acres to heirs.
Wright, Prince Orange. N.C. Private. 2 Jan. 1810. 640 acres to heirs.
Wright, Richard. Va. Private. 16 Jun. 1783. 100 acres.
Wright, Robert. N. Y. Private. 7 Jul. 1790. 600 acres.
Wright, Robert. N.Y. Captain. 13 Sep. 1790. 1800 acres.
Wright, Robert. Va. Private. 10 Jun. 1783. 100 acres.
Wright, Sampson. N.C. Private. 5 Dec. 1796. 274 acres.
Wright, Samuel. Md. Private. ———. 50 acres.
Wright, Samuel. N. Y. Private. 8 Jul. 1790. 600 acres.
Wright, Shadrick. Ga. Captain. 26 May 1784. 690 acres to heirs.
Wright, Stephen. Ga. ———. 1784. 287 1/2 acres.
Wright, Stephen. N.C. Private. 13 Dec. 1796. 640 acres to heirs.
Wright, Thomas. N.C. Private. 13 Dec. 1796. 640 acres to heirs.
Wright, Thomas. N.C. Private. 22 Dec. 1796. 274 acres.
Wright, Thomas. Va. Private. 23 Jun. 1783. 100 acres.
Wright, Thomas. Va. Private. 16 Apr. 1785. 200 acres.
Wright, William. Ga. ———. 17 Apr. 1784. 287 1/2 acres.
Wright, William. N.C. Private. 12 Sep. 1785. 640 acres to heirs.
Write, Levi. N.C. Private. 24 Nov. 1796. 640 acres to heirs.
Wuins, William. N. Y. Private. 8 Jul. 1790. 500 acres.
Wyart, Benjamin. Va. Private. 20 May 1783. 200 acres.
Wyatt, Carey. Va. Captain Lieutenant. 6 Feb. 1783. 4000 acres.
Wyatt, Edward. Va. Private. 11 Mar. 1788. 100 acres.
Wyatt, Ephraim. N.C. Private. 30 Sep. 1785. 640 acres to heirs.
Wyatt, Francis. Va. Corporal. 16 Oct. 1847. 100 acres.
Wyatt, Francis. Va. Corporal. 16 Oct. 1847. 100 acres.
Wyatt, George. Va. Sergeant. 6 Mar. 1784. 200 acres.
Wyatt, James. N.C. ———. 8 Mar. 1785. 640 acres.

Wyatt, John. N. Y. Private. 8 Jul. 1790. 600 acres.
Wyatt, John. N.C. Sergeant. 21 Jan. 1818. 1000 acres to heirs.
Wyatt, John. Va. Private. 29 May 1783. 100 acres.
Wyatt, John. Va. Private. 20 May 1808. 100 acres.
Wyatt, Jonathan. N.C. Private. 30 Sep. 1785. 640 acres.
Wyatt, Pitman. Va. Private. 10 May 1784. 100 acres.
Wyatt, Thomas. Va. Private. 7 Jun. 1811. 200 acres.
Wyatt, William. Va. Private. 3 Jun. 1783. 100 acres.
Wybert, Frederick. N. Y. Private. 8 Jul. 1790. 500 acres.
Wyche, Batt. Ga. Refugee. 3 Apr. 1784. ———.
Wyche, George. Ga. ———. 30 Sep. 1784. ———.
Wyche, John. Ga. ———. 20 Apr. 1784. 500 acres.
Wyche, Samuel. Ga. ———. 17 May 1784. ———.
Wyer, Cornelius. Pa. Private. 15 Nov. 1786. 200 acres to Richard Leedom, assignee.
Wylie, George, Jr. Va. Sergeant Major. 7 Feb. 1783. 200 acres.
Wylie, Thomas. Pa. Chaplain. 19 Dec. ——. 500 acres.
Wyncoop, Abigail. Conn. Sufferer. Fairfield. 59.15.0.
Wyne, Benjamin. Va. Private. 4 Dec. 1783. 200 acres.
Wynkoop, Jacobus. N. Y. Captain. 9 Jul. 1790. 1500 acres.
Wynn, Knibb. N.C. Sergeant. 1 Aug. 1821. 1000 acres.
Wynn, William. N.C. Private. 1 Aug. 1821. 640 acres.
Wynne, Joshua. Ga. Refugee. 22 Apr. 1784. 575 acres.
Wynne, Samuel. Va. Private. 31 May 1821. 100 acres.
Wynnne, Jones. N.C. Private. 9 Nov. 1784. 457 acres.
Wyns, John. N.C. Private. 30 Sep. 1785. 640 acres to heirs.
Wyron, Stephen. N.C. Private. 9 Feb. 1796. 228 acres.
Wysham, John. Md. ———. ———. 50 acres.
Wyshover, Jacob. N. Y. Private. 8 Jul. 1790. 500 acres. Alias Waiskabor.
Yager, John. Va. Private. 26 Feb. 1785. 200 acres.
Yager, John. Va. Private. 9 May 1833. 200 acres.
Yager, Leonard. Pa. Private. ———. 200 acres.
Yancey, Absalum. Va. Private. 5 Oct. 1785. 100 acres.
Yancey, George. N.C. Private. 2 Feb. 1786. 640 acres.
Yancey, John. N.C. ———. 14 Jun. 1785. 640 acres to heir.
Yancey, John. Va. Regimental Quartermaster. 11 Dec. 1811. 2666 2/3 acres.
Yancey, John. Va. Regimental Quartermaster. 26 Nov. 1858. 2666 2/3 acres.
Yancey, Layton. Va. Captain. 25 Mar. 1813. 333 1/3 acres.
Yancey, Leighton. Va. Subaltern. 12 Apr. 1784. 2666 2/3 acres.
Yancey, Leighton. Va. Captain. 12 Jan. 1798. 1334 1/3 acres.
Yancey, Lewis. Va. Private. 5 Jun. 1784. 100 acres.
Yancey, Lewis. Va. Sergeant. 10 May 1822. 200 acres.
Yancey, Ludwell. Va. Private. 11 May 1784. 100 acres.
Yancey, Robert. Va. Captain. 20 Jan. 1783. 1000 acres.
Yancey, Robert. Va. Captain. 30 Jan. 1783. 3000 acres.
Yancey, Robert. Va. Captain. 31 May 1784. 666 2/3 acres.
Yancy, James. Va. Corporal. 14 Aug. 1785. 200 acres.
Yankerfield, John. Ga. ———. 17 Sep. 1784. 287 1/2 acres.
Yarborough, James. Ga. ———. 14 Sep. 1784. 287 1/2 acres.
Yarborough, Lewis. S.C. Soldier. 21 Jan. 1785. 200 acres.
Yarborough, Littleton. Ga. ———. 27 Apr. 1784. 287 1/2 acres.
Yarborough, Thomas. Ga. ———. 15 Apr. 1784. 287 1/2 acres.
Yarborough, William. Ga. Refugee. 14 Sep. 1784. 287 1/2 acres.
Yarborough, William. S.C. Soldier. 21 Jan. 1785. 200 acres.

Yarbrough, Charles. Va. Lieutenant. 8 Sep. 1783. 2666 2/3 acres.
Yarbrough, Charles. Va. Lieutenant. 14 May 1838. 287 acres.
Yarbrough, David. N.C. Private. 17 Sep. 1785. 640 acres to heirs.
Yarbrough, Edward. N.C. Captain. 23 Oct. 1783. 3840 acres.
Yarbrough, James. N.C. Private. 1 Oct. 1801. 640 acres to heirs.
Yarbrough, John. Va. Private. 11 Jun. 1821. 200 acres.
Yarbrough, Reuben. N.C. Sergeant. 22 Feb. 1800. 358 acres.
Yarby, Jonas. N.C. Private. 9 Dec. 1797. 640 acres to heirs.
Yarby, Joseph. N.C. Private. 22 Dec. 1796. 274 acres.
Yarkins, Benajah. N.C. Sergeant. 7 Jan. 1786. 1000 acres to heirs.
Yarrington, Oliver. Va. Private. 5 Jun. 1783. 100 acres.
Yarrington, William. N. Y. Private. 3 Jul. 1790. 600 acres.
Yates, Bartholomew. Va. Private. 18 Nov. 1795. 2666 2/3 acres.
Yates, George. Va. Surgeon's Mate. 8 Sep. 1787. 2000 acres.
Yates, George. Va. Surgeon's Mate. 8 Sep. 1787. 666 2/3 acres.
Yates, George. Va. Surgeon's Mate. 2 Aug. 1854. 190 10/21 acres.
Yates, George. Va. Surgeon's Mate. 2 Aug. 1854. 285 15/21 acres.
Yates, George. Va. Surgeon's Mate. 2 Aug. 1854. 142 37/42 acres.
Yates, George. Va. Surgeon's Mate. 2 Aug. 1854. 190 10/21 acres.
Yates, George. Va. Surgeon's Mate. 2 Aug. 1854. 190 10/21 acres.
Yates, George. Va. Surgeon's Mate. 2 Aug. 1854. 190 10/21 acres.
Yates, George. Va. Surgeon's Mate. 5 Mar. 1855. 142 3/4 acres.
Yates, Isaac. Va.-Ind. Private. 108 acres.
Yates, John. N.C. Private. 17 Oct. 1783. 640 acres.
Yates, John. Va. Lieutenant. 18 Jan. 1786. 2666 2/3 acres.
Yates, John. Va. Lieutenant. 5 Jul. 1834. 2666 2/3 acres.
Yates, Richard. Md. ———. ———. 50 acres.
Yates, William. N.C. Private. 5 Sep. 1821. 640 acres.
Yates, William. Va. Lieutenant Colonel. 9 Aug. 1817. 1000 acres.
Yates, William. Va. Lieutenant Colonel. 9 Aug. 1817. 500 acres.
Yates, William. Va. Lieutenant Colonel. 9 Aug. 1817. 330 acres.
Yates, William. Va. Lieutenant Colonel. 9 Aug. 1817. 170 acres.
Yates, William. Va. Lieutenant Colonel. 9 Apr. 1818. 200 acres.
Yates, William. Va. Lieutenant Colonel. 9 Apr. 1818. 160 acres.
Yates, William. Va. Lieutenant Colonel. 9 Apr. 1818. 640 acres.
Yates, William. Va. Lieutenant Colonel. 9 Apr. 1818. 500 acres.
Yates, William. Va. Lieutenant Colonel. 9 Apr. 1818. 100 acres.
Yates, William. Va. Lieutenant Colonel. 9 Apr. 1818. 100 acres.
Yates, William. Va. Lieutenant Colonel. 9 Apr. 1818. 100 acres.
Yates, William. Va. Lieutenant Colonel. 9 Apr. 1818. 100 acres.
Yates, William. Va. Lieutenant Colonel. 9 Apr. 1818. 100 acres.
Yates, William. Va. Lieutenant Colonel. 8 Jul. 1818. 100 acres.
Yates, William. Va. Lieutenant Colonel. 8 Jul. 1818. 100 acres.
Yates, William. Va. Lieutenant Colonel. 8 Jul. 1818. 100 acres.
Yates, William. Va. Lieutenant Colonel. 8 Jul. 1818. 133 acres.
Yates, William. Va. Lieutenant Colonel. 8 Jul. 1818. 133 acres.
Yates, William. Va. Lieutenant Colonel. 8 Jul. 1818. 133 acres.
Yates, William. Va. Lieutenant Colonel. 8 Jul. 1818. 433 2/3 acres.
Yates, William. Va. Lieutenant Colonel. 8 Jul. 1818. 433 2/3 acres.
Yates, William. Va. Lieutenant Colonel. 8 Jul. 1818. 433 2/3 acres.
Yates, William. Va. Lieutenant Colonel. 8 Jul. 1818. 433 2/3 acres.
Yeamans, Eleazer. N. Y. Private. 3 Jul. 1790. 600 acres.
Yearly, Isaiah. N.C. Private. 30 Sep. 1785. 640 acres to heirs.
Yearly, John. N.C. Private. 30 Sep. 1785. 640 acres to heirs.

Yearly, Samuel. Va. Sergeant. 12 Aug. 1785. 200 acres.
Yeast, Jacob. Md. Private. ———. 50 acres.
Yeates, Thomas. Md. ———. ———. 50 acres.
Yeatman, Charles. Va. Private. 29 Aug. 1812. 200 acres.
Yeger, Henry. Va. Private. 20 Feb. 1784. 100 acres.
Yeomans, Isaac. N. Y. Private. 24 Aug. 1790. 500 acres.
Yeomans, Jeremiah. N. Y. Private. 8 Jul. 1790. 600 acres.
Yeomans, Moses. N.Y. Lieutenant. 9 Jul. 1790. 1200 acres.
Yerington, Ezekial. Conn. Sufferer. Groton. 2.7.6.
Yerkse, John. N. Y. Bombardier. 9 Jul. 1790. 500 acres.
Yesterday, Charles. Ga. Soldier. 4 Oct. 1785. ———.
Yingling, F. John. N. Y. Private. 8 Jul. 1790. 600 acres.
Yoes, James. N.C. Private. 22 Dec. 1796. 274 acres.
Yoress, John. N. Y. Private. 8 Jul. 1790. 600 acres.
York, Henry. Conn. Sufferer. New/East Haven. 4.4.10.
York, James. Ga. Minute Man. 25 May 1784. 287 1/2 acres.
York, James. Ga. Refugee. 25 May 1784. 287 1/2 acres.
York, John. Ga. Refugee. 15 Mar. 1784. 250 acres.
York, William. Md. ———. ———. 50 acres.
York, William. N.C. Private. 9 Nov. 1784. 533 acres.
Yost, John. Pa. ———. 6 Apr. 1794. 200 acres to Daniel Steever, assignee.
Yost, Martin. Pa. Private. 30 Jan. 1787. 200 acres.
Young, Abraham. Me. ———. 20 May 1835. 200 acres to widow Rebecca Washburn. Paris.
Young, Anthony. Ga. Minute Man. 3 Sep. 1785. ———.
Young, Benjamin. N.C. Private. 12 Dec. 1796. 640 acres to heirs.
Young, Christian. Pa. ———. ———. 200 acres.
Young, Daniel. Ga. Lieutenant. 15 Mar. 1784. 250 acres.
Young, David. Md. Matross. ———. 50 acres.
Young, Duncan. Va. Private. 18 Jun. 1784. 200 acres.
Young, Edward. Ga. Minute Man. 27 Apr. 1784. 287 1/2 acres.
Young, Frederick. Va. Sergeant. 1 Apr. 1783. 200 acres.
Young, George. Pa. Private. 3 Nov. 1786. 200 acres.
Young, George. Va. Private. 22 Feb. 1799. 100 acres.
Young, Godfrey. Md. Private. ———. 50 acres.
Young, Guy. N.Y. Captain. 9 Jul. 1790. 1500 acres.
Young, Henry. Md. Private. ———. 50 acres.
Young, Henry. Pa. Private. 17 Apr. 1813. 200 acres.
Young, Henry. Va. Captain. 21 May 1783. 4000 acres.
Young, Henry. Va. Captain. 27 Feb. 1795. 666 2/3 acres.
Young, Henry. Va. Captain. 22 Jan. 1808. 500 acres.
Young, Henry. Va. Quartermaster General. 30 Dec. 1851. 6666 2/3 acres.
Young, Isaac. N.C. Private. 25 Nov. 1796. 640 acres to heirs.
Young, Isaac. N.C. Private. 13 Sep. 1820. 640 acres.
Young, Isham. Ga. Refugee. 27 Apr. 1784. 575 acres.
Young, Jacob. Md. Drummer. ———. 50 acres.
Young, Jacob. Pa. Private. ———. 200 acres.
Young, James. Ga. ———. ———. 287 1/2 acres.
Young, James. Me. Private. 30 May 1836. 200 acres to widow Abigail Elliott. Readfield.
Young, James. Me. ———. 1 Aug. 1835. 200 acres to widow Martha Young. Kennebunk.
Young, James. Conn. Sufferer. New London. 13.2.0.
Young, John. Me. Private. 26 Jan. 1836. 200 acres to widow Hannah (Banks) Young.

Young, John. Md. Corporal. ———. 50 acres.
Young, John. Md. Private. ———. 50 acres.
Young, John. N. Y. Private. 7 Jul. 1790. 600 acres.
Young, John. N.Y. Surgeon's Mate. 26 Sep. 1792. 1500 acres.
Young, John. N.C. Private. 20 Apr. 1784. 228 acres.
Young, John. N.C. Corporal. 14 Dec. 1797. 357 acres.
Young, John. Pa. Private. 15 Sep. 1837. 200 acres to William McCoy.
Young, John. Pa. Private. 24 May 1787. 200 acres to John Cummings, assingee.
Young, John. S.C. ———. 6 Jun. 1785. 200 acres.
Young, John. Va. Private. 23 Jun. 1783. 200 acres.
Young, John, Jr. Ga. Refugee. 27 Apr. 1784. 287 1/2 acres.
Young, John, Sr. Ga. Minute Man. 3 Sep. 1785. 287 1/2 acres.
Young, Joseph. N.Y. Physician & Surgeon. ———. 2250 acres.
Young, Joseph. Pa. Private. 27 Sep. 1787. 200 acres.
Young, Marcus. Pa. ———. ———. 200 acres to his widow.
Young, Marcus. Pa. Lieutenant. 25 Apr. 1787. 200 acres.
Young, Nathan. Va. Sergeant. 23 Jun. 1783. 200 acres.
Young, Nathaniel. Me. ———. 8 May 1835. 200 acres. Greenwood.
Young, Peter. Ga. Refugee. 21 Jul. 1784. ———.
Young, Robert. Pa. Private. 5 Apr. 1787. 200 acres.
Young, Robert. Va. Private. 5 Apr. 1784. 100 acres.
Young, Robert. Va. Lieutenant. 21 Mar. 1807. 3555 acres.
Young, Robert, Jr. N.C. Private. 14 Dec. 1796. 640 acres.
Young, Samuel. Md. Private. ———. 50 acres.
Young, Samuel. Va. Private. 3 Dec. 1783. 100 acres.
Young, Sion. N.C. Private. 10 Nov. 1783. 640 acres.
Young, Stephen. Va. Captain. 24 Dec. 1813. 1000 acres.
Young, Stephen. Va. Captain. 24 Dec. 1813. 1000 acres.
Young, Stephen. Va. Captain. 24 Dec. 1813. 1000 acres.
Young, Stephen. Va. Captain. 24 Dec. 1813. 1000 acres.
Young, Thomas. N.C. Private. 7 Dec. 1797. 228 acres.
Young, Thomas. Va. Captain. 21 Nov. 1787. 4000 acres.
Young, William. Ga. Lieutenant. 22 Mar. 1784. 287 1/2 acres.
Young, William. N.C. Private. 28 Sep. 1785. 640 acres to heirs.
Young, William. Va. Sergeant. 25 Feb. 1784. 200 acres.
Youngblood, Abraham. Ga. Soldier. 23 Apr. 1784. 287 1/2 acres.
Youngblood, Isaac. Ga. Soldier. 23 Apr. 1784. 287 1/2 acres.
Youngblood, James. Ga. Soldier. 20 Feb. 1784. 250 acres.
Youngblood, John, Sr. Ga. Refugee. 13 Sep. 1784. 287 1/2 acres.
Youngblood, Jonathan. Ga. ———. 28 Feb. 1784. 250 acres.
Youngblood, Peter. Ga. Refugee. 27 Apr. 1784. 575 acres.
Younger, Joshua. Va. Private. 16 Mar. 1822. 200 acres.
Youngs, Christopher. N. Y. Corporal. 8 Jul. 1790. 500 acres.
Youngs, Richard. Conn. Sufferer. Norwalk. 31.5.11.
Yours, William. Va. Corporal. 8 Mar. 1783. 200 acres.
Yowell, Samuel. Va. Private. 26 Nov. 1783. 100 acres.
Yowell, Thomas. Va. Private. 23 Dec. 1811. 100 acres.
Zachary, James. Ga. ———. 27 Apr. 1784. 287 1/2 acres.
Zachrias, John M. Pa. Ranger. 11 Jun. 1787. 200 acres.
Zanes, John. Pa. Private. 20 Oct. 1786. 200 acres to William Banquet, assignee.
Zarenisus, Christopher. N. Y. Private. 8 Jul. 1790. 600 acres.
Zarlett, Timothy. N.C. Private. 19 Jan. 1786. 640 acres.
Zarlett, Zacheriah. N.C. Private. 19 Jan. 1786. 640 acres.
Zeallott, Shadrach. N.C. Private. 7 Jan. 1786. 640 acres to heirs.

Zealot, Nelson. N.C. Sergeant. 7 Jan. 1786. 1000 acres to heirs.

Zealott, Jonathan. N.C. Private. 17 Dec. 1785. 274 acres.

Zealott, Joshua. N.C. Private. 7 Jan. 1786. 640 acres.

Zealott, William. N.C. Private. 17 Dec. 1785. 274 acres.

Zearlett, James. N.C. Private. 19 Jan. 1786. 640 acres.

Zeastor, Michael. N. Y. Private. 8 Jul. 1790. 600 acres.

Zeigler, David. Pa. Captain. 28 Feb. 1794. 500 acres.

Zellars, Michael. N. Y. Private. 8 Jul. 1790. 600 acres.

Zettler, Daniel. Ga. Refugee. 29 Jan. 1784. 500 acres.

Zettler, Matthew. Ga. Refugee. 5 Mar. 1784. 250 acres.

Zettler, Nathaniel. Ga. Refugee. 15 Mar. 1784. 250 acres.

Zill, John. Pa. ———. 1 Oct. 1787. 200 acres.

Zimmerman, William. Va. Sergeant. 9 Aug. 1783. 200 acres.

Zimmermon, John. Va. Private. 29 Jun. 1785. 100 acres.

Zinn, Jacob. Ga. Lieutenant. 27 Apr. 1787. 287 1/2 acres.

Zockledge, William. Va.-Ind. Private. 108 acres.

Zutson, John. N.C. Private. 30 Sep. 1785. 640 acres to heirs.

Index to Heirs, Representatives, and Other Assignees